Street by Stre

NEWCASTLE

SUNDERLAND

DURHAM, GATESHEAD, SOUTH SHIELDS, TYNEMOUTH

Blyth, Chester-le-Street, Cramlington, North Shields, Peterlee, Ponteland, Seaham, Stanley, Washington, Whitley Bay

Ist edition May 2001

Published by AA Publishing (a trading name of Automobile Association Developments Limited, whose registered office is Norfolk House, Priestley Road, Basingstoke, Hampshire, RG24 9NY. Registered number 1878835).

Mapping produced by the Cartographic Department of The Automobile Association.

A CIP Catalogue record for this book is available from the British Library.

Printed by G. Canale & C. S.P.A., Torino, Italy

The contents of this atlas are believed to be correct at the time of the latest revision. However, the publishers cannot be held responsible for loss occasioned to any person acting or refraining from action as a result of any material in this atlas, nor for any errors, omissions or changes in such material. The publishers would welcome information to correct any errors or omissions and to keep this atlas up to date. Please write to Publishing, The Automobile Association, Fanum House, Basing View, Basingstoke, Hampshire, RG21 4EA.

Ref: MD051

Key to map pages ii-iii

Key to map symbols iv-1

Enlarged scale pages 2-5

Street by Street 6-209

Index – towns & villages 210-211

Index – streets 212-264

Index – featured places 265-273

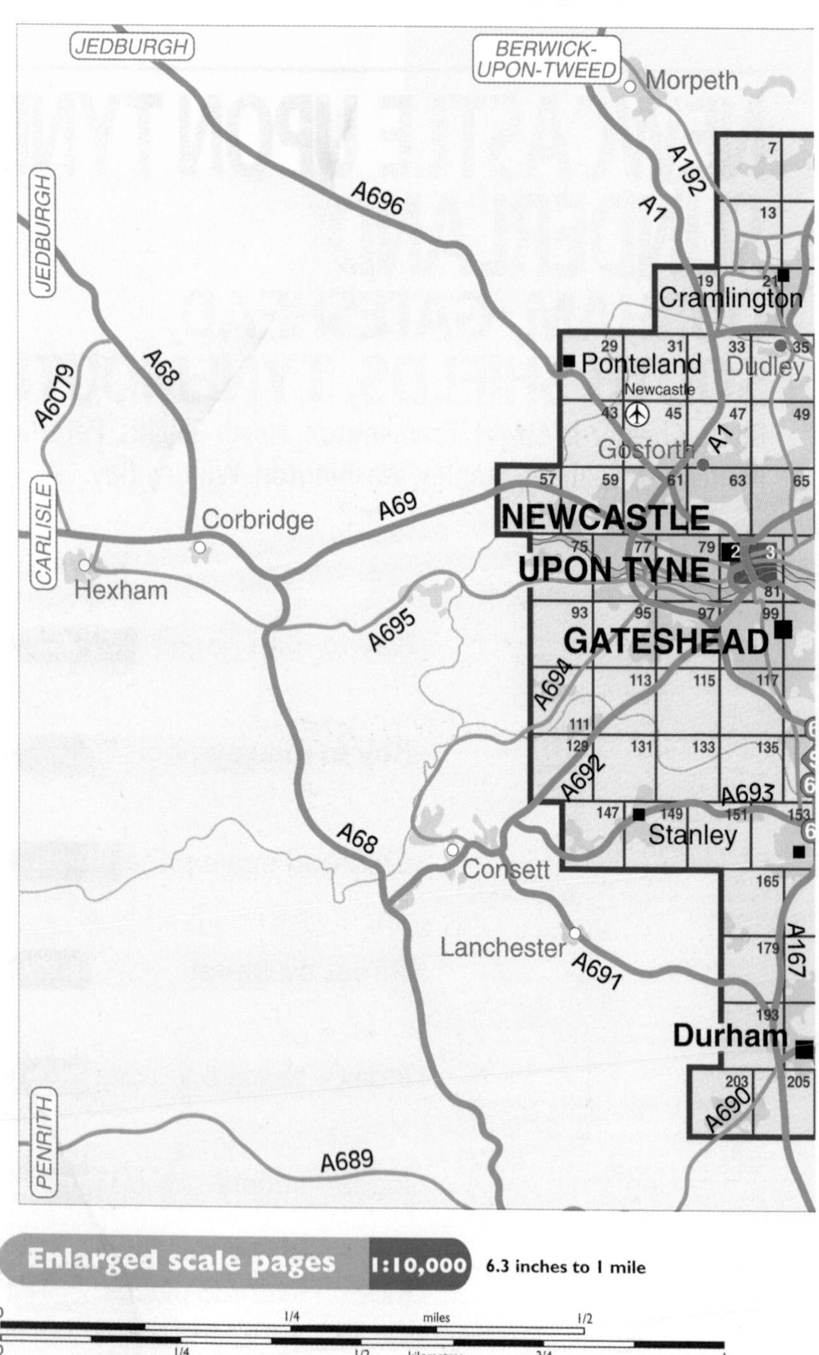

Enlarged scale pages 1:10,000 6.3 inches to 1 mile

0 1/4 miles 1/2

0 1/4 1/2 kilometres 3/4 1

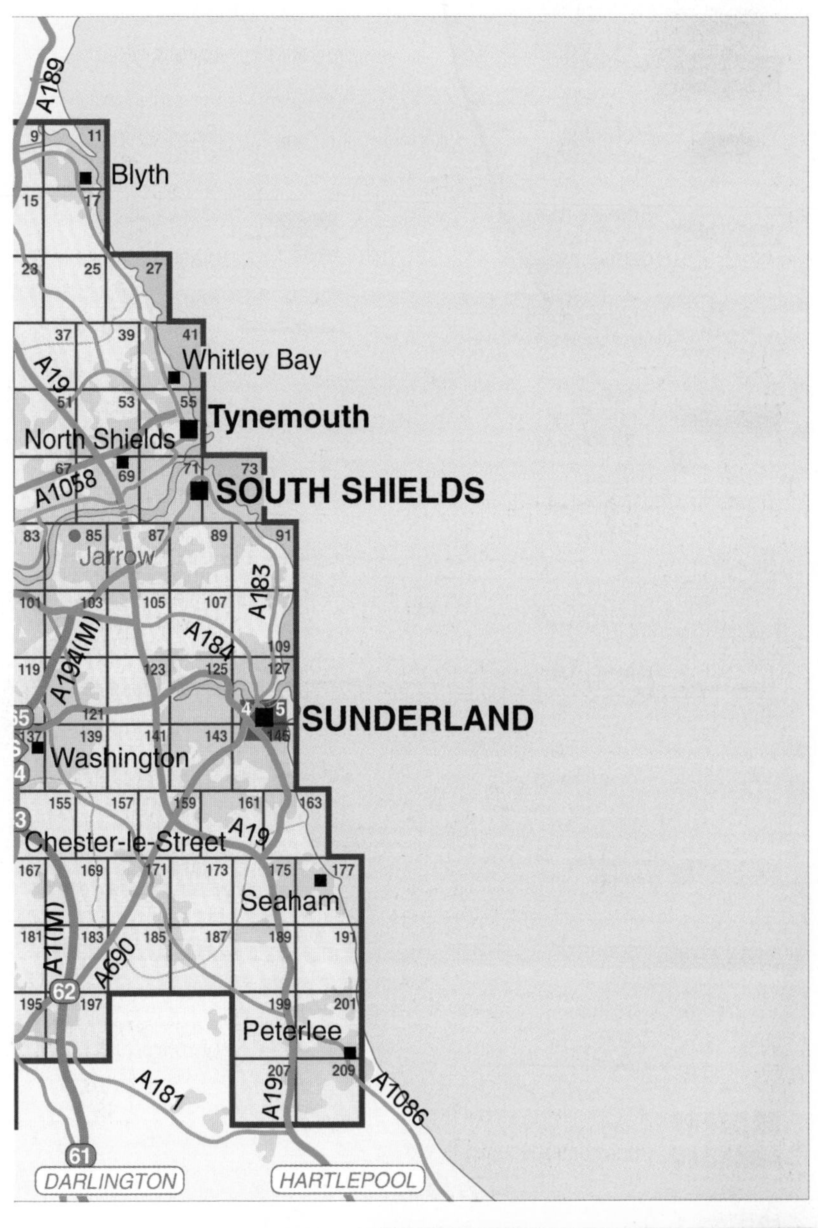

3.6 inches to 1 mile **Scale of main map pages 1:17,500**

0 1/2 miles 1

0 1/2 1 kilometres 1 1/2

Junction 9 Motorway & junction

Services Motorway service area

Primary road single/dual carriageway

Services Primary road service area

A road single/dual carriageway

B road single/dual carriageway

Other road single/dual carriageway

Restricted road

Private road

One way street

Pedestrian street

Track/ footpath

Road under construction

Road tunnel

P Parking

P+ Park & Ride

Bus/coach station

Railway & main railway station

Railway & minor railway station

Underground station

Light railway & station

Preserved private railway

LC Level crossing

Tramway

Ferry route

Airport runway

Boundaries- borough/ district

Mounds

93 Page continuation 1:17,500

7 Page continuation to enlarged scale 1:10,000

River/canal lake, pier

Aqueduct lock, weir

465 Winter Hill — Peak (with height in metres)

Beach

Coniferous woodland

Broadleaved woodland

Mixed woodland

Park

Cemetery

Built-up area

Featured building

City wall

A&E — Accident & Emergency hospital

Toilet

Toilet with disabled facilities

Petrol station

PH — Public house

PO — Post Office

Public library

Tourist Information Centre

Castle

Historic house/ building

Wakehurst Place NT — National Trust property

Museum/ art gallery

Church/chapel

Country park

Theatre/ performing arts

Cinema

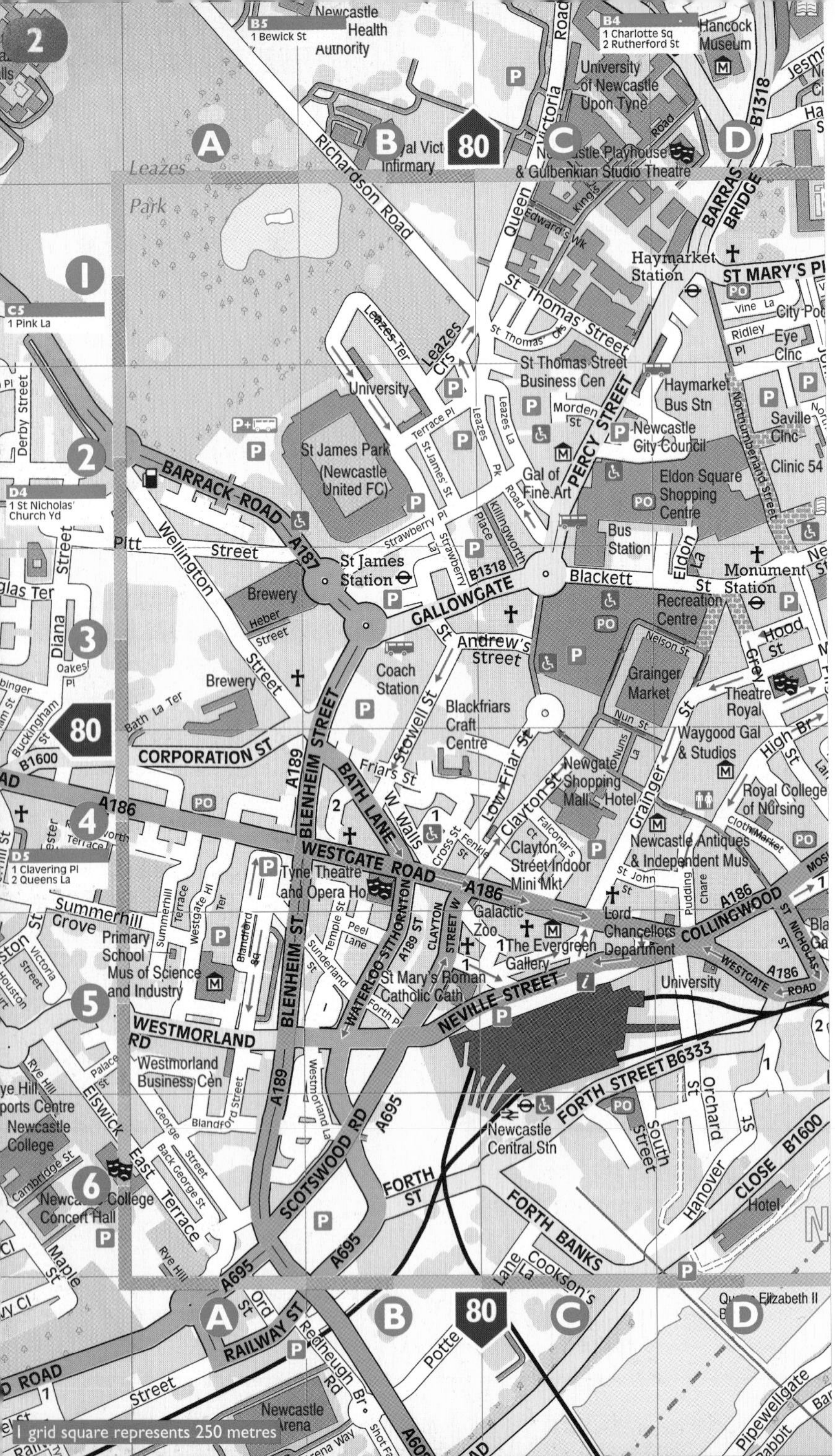
2
80
Newcastle Health Authority
B5
1 Bewick St
B4
1 Charlotte Sq
2 Rutherford St
Hancock Museum
University of Newcastle Upon Tyne
Royal Victoria Infirmary
Newcastle Playhouse & Gulbenkian Studio Theatre
Leazes Park
Richardson Road
Barras Bridge
Haymarket Station
St Mary's Pl
C5
1 Pink La
St Thomas' Street
St Thomas Street Business Cen
Haymarket Bus Stn
University
St James Park (Newcastle United FC)
Newcastle City Council
Gal of Fine Art
Eldon Square Shopping Centre
Percy Street
Northumberland Street
Barrack Road
D4
1 St Nicholas' Church Yd
Pitt Street
Wellington Street
St James Station
Gallowgate
Blackett St
Monument Station
Brewery
Coach Station
Recreation Centre
Grainger Market
Blackfriars Craft Centre
Theatre Royal
Waygood Gal & Studios
Corporation St
Blenheim Street
Bath Lane
Newgate Shopping Mall
Hotel
Royal College of Nursing
Clayton Street Indoor Mini Mkt
Newcastle Antiques & Independent Mus
D5
1 Clavering Pl
2 Queens La
Westgate Road
Tyne Theatre and Opera Ho
Galactic Zoo
The Evergreen Gallery
Lord Chancellors Department
Collingwood
Summerhill Grove
Primary School
Mus of Science and Industry
St Mary's Roman Catholic Cath
Neville Street
University
Westmorland Rd
Westmorland Business Cen
Forth Street B6333
Newcastle Central Stn
Rye Hill Sports Centre
Newcastle College
Newcastle College Concert Hall
Scotswood Rd
Forth St
Forth Banks
Close B1600
Hotel
Railway St
Newcastle Arena
Pipewellgate
1 grid square represents 250 metres

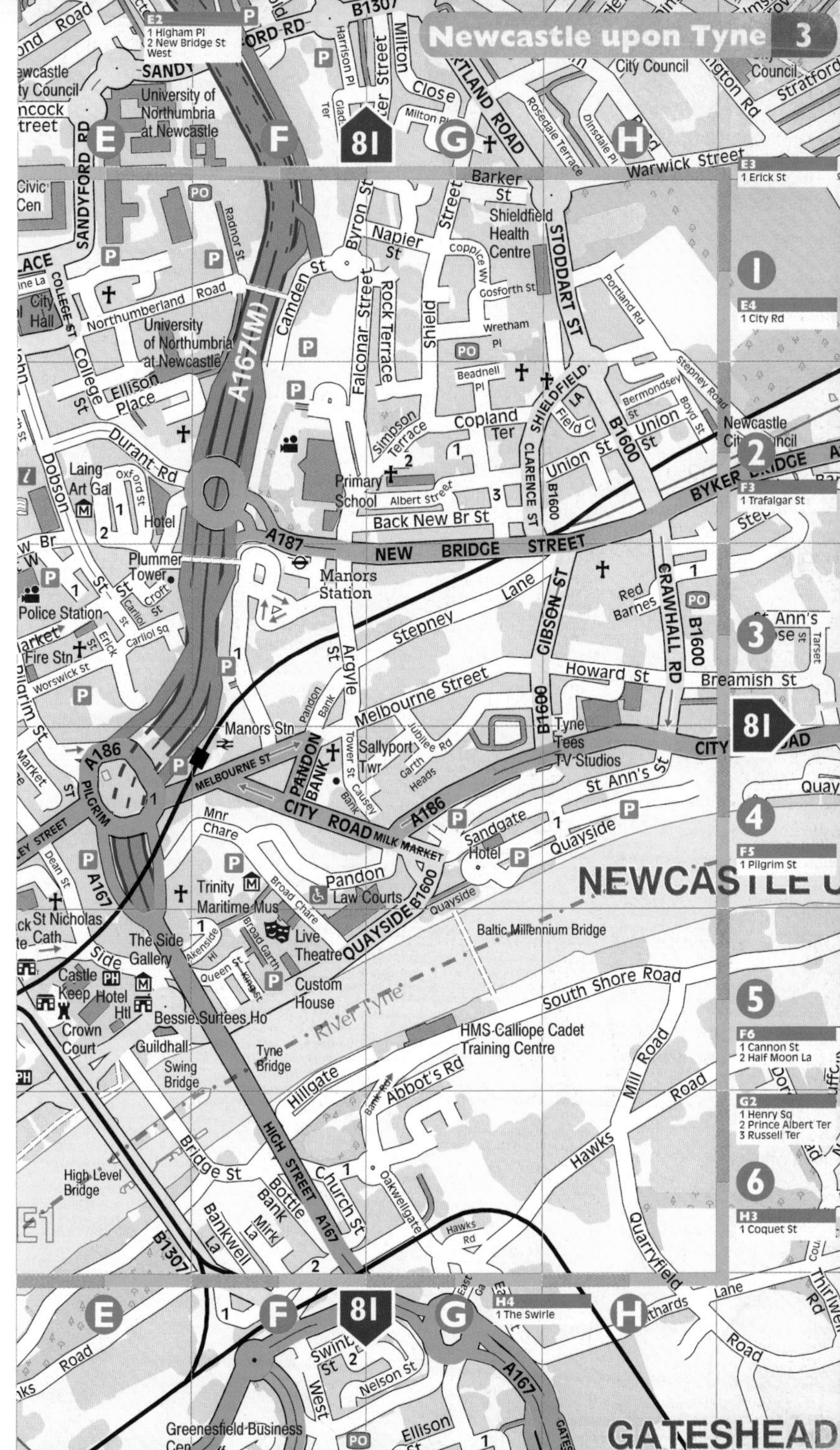
E2
1 Higham Pl
2 New Bridge St West
B1307
Harrison Pl
Milton Close
Milton Pl
City Council
Stratford
Newcastle City Council
Sandyford Rd
University of Northumbria at Newcastle
E
F
81
G
H
Rosedale Terrace
Dinsdale Pl
Warwick Street
E3
1 Erick St
Civic Cen
PO
Radnor St
Barker St
Byron St
Shieldfield Health Centre
Stoddart St
Napier St
Coppice Wy
Gosforth St
Portland Rd
Camden St
Falconar Street
Rock Terrace
Shield Street
City Hall
College St
Northumberland Road
University of Northumbria at Newcastle
A167(M)
Wretham Pl
E4
1 City Rd
Beadnell Pl
Shieldfield La
Stepney Road
Bermondsey St
Boyd St
Ellison Place
Simpson Terrace
Copland Ter
Field Cl
Union St
B1600
Clarence St
Newcastle City Council
2
Byker Bridge
Durant Rd
Laing Art Gal
Oxford St
Dobson St
Primary School
Albert Street
Back New Br St
F3
1 Trafalgar St
Hotel
A187
New Bridge Street
Plummer Tower
Manors Station
Gibson St
Crawhall Rd
Red Barnes
Croft St
Carliol St
Police Station
Carliol Sq
Stepney Lane
Argyle St
St Ann's Close
3
Tarset
Fire Stn
Erick St
Worswick St
Pilgrim St
Howard St
Breamish St
Melbourne Street
Pandon Bank
Jubilee Rd
Manors Stn
Tyne Tees TV Studios
City Road
A186
Melbourne St
Pandon Bank
Tower St
Sallyport Twr
Garth Heads
St Ann's St
Quays
Causey Bank
City Road
Milk Market
Mnr Chare
Sandgate Hotel
Quayside
4
Dean St
A167
Trinity Maritime Mus
Broad Chare
Pandon
Law Courts
F5
1 Pilgrim St
NEWCASTLE U
St Nicholas Cath
Quayside B1600
Quayside
Baltic Millennium Bridge
Live Theatre
Akenside Hl
Broad Garth
The Side Gallery
Side
Queen St
King St
Custom House
South Shore Road
Castle Keep
Hotel
Htl
5
River Tyne
Bessie Surtees Ho
HMS Calliope Cadet Training Centre
Crown Court
Guildhall
F6
1 Cannon St
2 Half Moon La
Mill Road
Swing Bridge
Tyne Bridge
Hillgate
Abbot's Rd
Bank Rd
Road
G2
1 Henry Sq
2 Prince Albert Ter
3 Russell Ter
Hawks Road
High Level Bridge
Bridge St
High Street A167
Church St
Oakwellgate
Bottle Bank
6
Bankwell La
Mirk La
Quarryfield
H3
1 Coquet St
E1
B1307
Hawks Rd
East
Lane
H4
1 The Swirle
Thirlwell Rd
Road
Swinburne St
Nelson St
West
A167
Greenesfield Business Cen
Ellison St
GATESHEAD

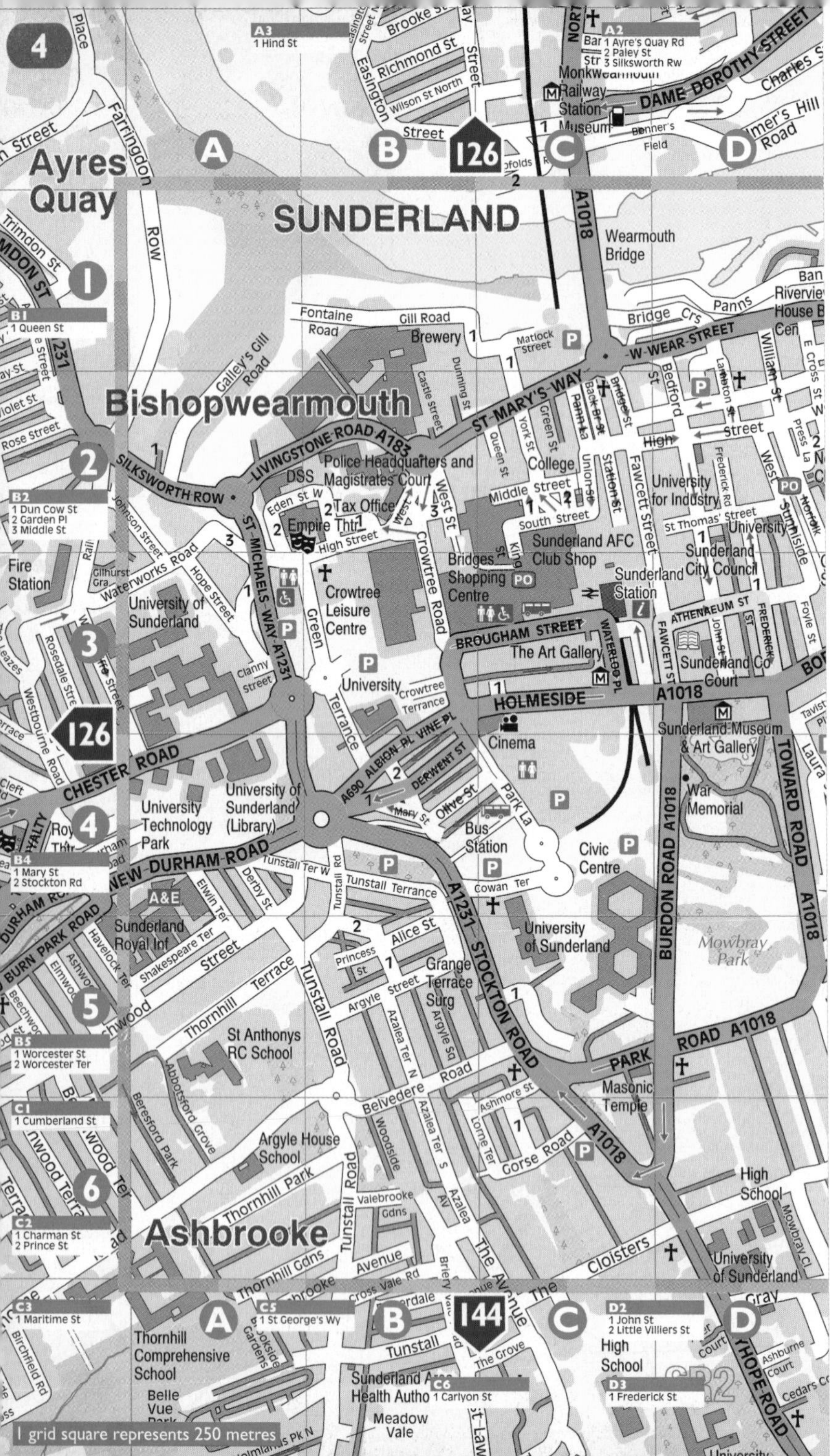

4
A3
1 Hind St
A2
1 Ayre's Quay Rd
2 Paley St
3 Silksworth Rw
Ayres Quay
SUNDERLAND
Bishopwearmouth
Ashbrooke
Monkwearmouth Railway Station Museum
DAME DOROTHY STREET
Charles St
Bonner's Field
Roker Baths Rd
Richmond St
Wilson St North
Easington Street
Brooke St
Farringdon Row
126
A
B
C
D
1
2
3
4
5
6
B1
1 Queen St
B2
1 Dun Cow St
2 Garden Pl
3 Middle St
B4
1 Mary St
2 Stockton Rd
B5
1 Worcester St
2 Worcester Ter
C1
1 Cumberland St
C2
1 Charman St
2 Prince St
C3
1 Maritime St
C5
1 St George's Wy
C6
1 Carlyon St
D2
1 John St
2 Little Villiers St
D3
1 Frederick St
A1018
Wearmouth Bridge
Riverview House
Panns Bank
Bridge Crs
W WEAR STREET
Fontaine Road
Gill Road
Brewery
Matlock Street
Galley's Gill Road
Dunning St
Castle Street
ST MARY'S WAY
LIVINGSTONE ROAD A183
SILKSWORTH ROW
Police Headquarters and Magistrates Court
DSS
Tax Office
Empire Thtr
High Street
Eden St W
West St
Crowtree Road
Crowtree Leisure Centre
Queen St
York St
Green St
College
Middle Street
South Street
Union St
Station St
Fawcett Street
Bedford St
Lambton St
High Street
William St
Frederick Rd
University for Industry
St Thomas' Street
University
Sunderland City Council
Sunniside
Norfolk
Bridges Shopping Centre
Sunderland AFC Club Shop
Sunderland Station
ATHENAEUM ST
BROUGHAM STREET
The Art Gallery
WATERLOO PL
HOLMESIDE
A1018
Sunderland Co Court
Sunderland Museum & Art Gallery
Fire Station
Waterworks Road
Hope Street
University of Sunderland
ST MICHAELS WAY A1231
Clanny Street
Green Terrace
University
Crowtree Terrace
Rosedale Street
Westbourne Road
CHESTER ROAD
A690 ALBION PL VINE PL
DERWENT ST
Olive St
Mary St
Park La
Cinema
Bus Station
University Technology Park
University of Sunderland (Library)
NEW DURHAM ROAD
Tunstall Ter W
Tunstall Rd
Tunstall Terrace
Cowan Ter
Civic Centre
War Memorial
TOWARD ROAD
BURDON ROAD A1018
Mowbray Park
A&E
Sunderland Royal Inf
Elwin Ter
Derby St
BURN PARK ROAD
Shakespeare Ter
Street
Thornhill Terrace
Tunstall Road
Princess St
Alice St
Grange Terrace Surg
A1231 STOCKTON ROAD
University of Sunderland
Argyle Street
Azalea Ter N
Argyle Sq
St Anthonys RC School
Belvedere Road
PARK ROAD A1018
Masonic Temple
Abbotsford Grove
Beresford Park
Argyle House School
Woodside
Ashmore St
Lorne Ter
Gorse Road
A1018
High School
Thornhill Park
Tunstall Road
Valebrooke Gdns
Azalea Ter S
Azalea Av
The Avenue
Cloisters
University of Sunderland
Mowbray Cl
Thornhill Gdns
Avenue
144
Cross Vale Rd
Tunstall
The Grove
Thornhill Comprehensive School
Belle Vue Park
Sunderland Area Health Autho
Meadow Vale
High School
Ashburne Court
Cedars Ct
THOPE ROAD
SR2
Birchfield Rd
Holmlands Pk N
1 grid square represents 250 metres

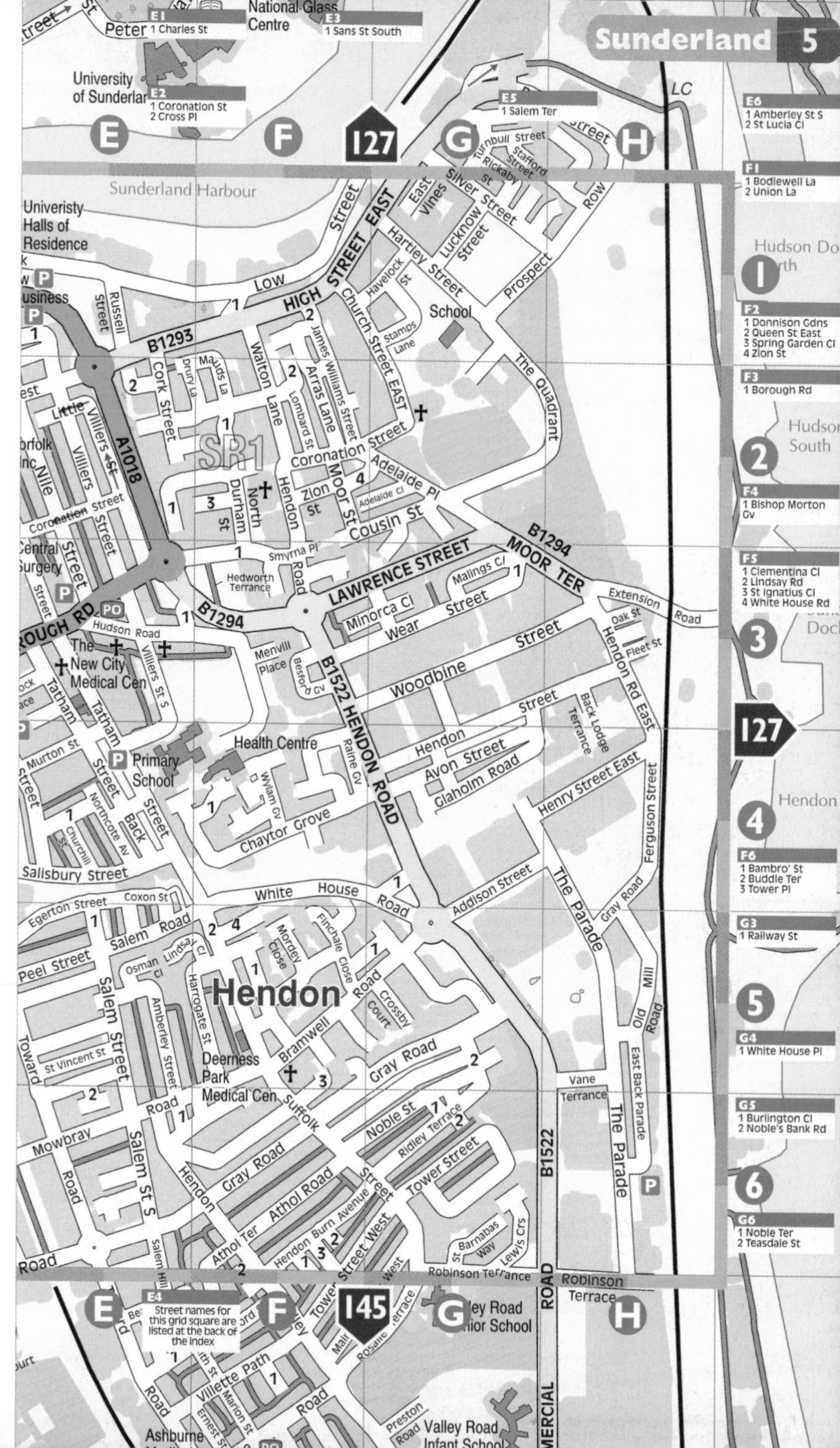
Sunderland 5
E1
1 Charles St
E2
1 Coronation St
2 Cross Pl
E3
1 Sans St South
E5
1 Salem Ter
E6
1 Amberley St S
2 St Lucia Cl
F1
1 Bodlewell La
2 Union La
F2
1 Donnison Gdns
2 Queen St East
3 Spring Garden Cl
4 Zion St
F3
1 Borough Rd
F4
1 Bishop Morton Gv
F5
1 Clementina Cl
2 Lindsay Rd
3 St Ignatius Cl
4 White House Rd
F6
1 Bambro' St
2 Buddle Ter
3 Tower Pl
G3
1 Railway St
G4
1 White House Pl
G5
1 Burlington Cl
2 Noble's Bank Rd
G6
1 Noble Ter
2 Teasdale St
E4
Street names for this grid square are listed at the back of the index
127
145
National Glass Centre
University of Sunderland
Sunderland Harbour
Univeristy Halls of Residence
Hudson Dock North
Hudson Dock South
Hendon
SR1
LC
Low Street
HIGH STREET EAST
B1293
A1018
B1294
MOOR TER
LAWRENCE STREET
B1522 HENDON ROAD
B1522
Church Street EAST
Coronation Street
Hartley Street
Prospect Row
The Quadrant
School
Health Centre
Primary School
The New City Medical Cen
Central Surgery
Deerness Park Medical Cen
Valley Road Infant School
Woodbine Street
Hendon Street
Avon Street
Glaholm Road
Henry Street East
Ferguson Street
Hendon Rd East
Extension Road
Addison Street
The Parade
Gray Road
Old Mill Road
East Back Parade
Vane Terrace
White House Road
Chaytor Grove
Salisbury Street
Salem Road
Salem Street
Salem St S
Peel Street
Mowbray Road
Suffolk Street
Athol Road
Tower Street
Tower Street West
Noble St
Ridley Terrace
Robinson Terrace
St Barnabas Way
Lewis Crs
Villette Path
Ashburne
Preston Road
Hendon Burn Avenue
Athol Ter
Bramwell Road
Crossby Court
Finchale Close
Mordey Close
Harrogate St
Amberley Street
St Vincent St
Osman Cl
Lindsay Cl
Egerton Street
Coxon St
Northcote Av
Churchill St
Murton St
Tatham Street
Villiers Street
Villiers St S
Hudson Road
Nile Street
Cork Street
Walton Lane
Arras Lane
Moor St
Zion St
Durham St
North Hendon Road
Smyrna Pl
Hedworth Terrace
Adelaide Pl
Adelaide Cl
Cousin St
Minorca Cl
Wear Street
Malings Cl
Menvill Place
Besford Gv
Raine Gv
Wylam Gv
Back Lodge Terrace
Oak St
Fleet St
Havelock St
Stamps Lane
Lucknow Street
Silver Street
East Vines
Turnbull Street
Stafford Street
Rickaby St
Russell Street
Drury La
Mauds La
James Williams Street
Lombard St
Marion St
Ernest St

C3
1 Chipchase Cl
2 Durham Cl
3 Netherdale
A
B
C
1
2
3
4
5
6
Burnt House
Ripley Cl
Ayton Ct
Knaresborough Cl
Skipton Cl
Dunstanburgh
Warwick Gv
Dover Close
Hylton Cl
Conway Cl
Netherton Lane
Blue House Farm
NETHERTON LANE
North Ridge
Meadowdale Crs
Link Av
Netherton Lane
Red House Farm
Cemetery
Westlea
B1331
North Farm
The Grange
Oakdale
South Farm
Hallwood Cl
Nedderton
HARTFORD ROAD
A192
Netherton Moor Farm
12
1 grid square represents 500 metres

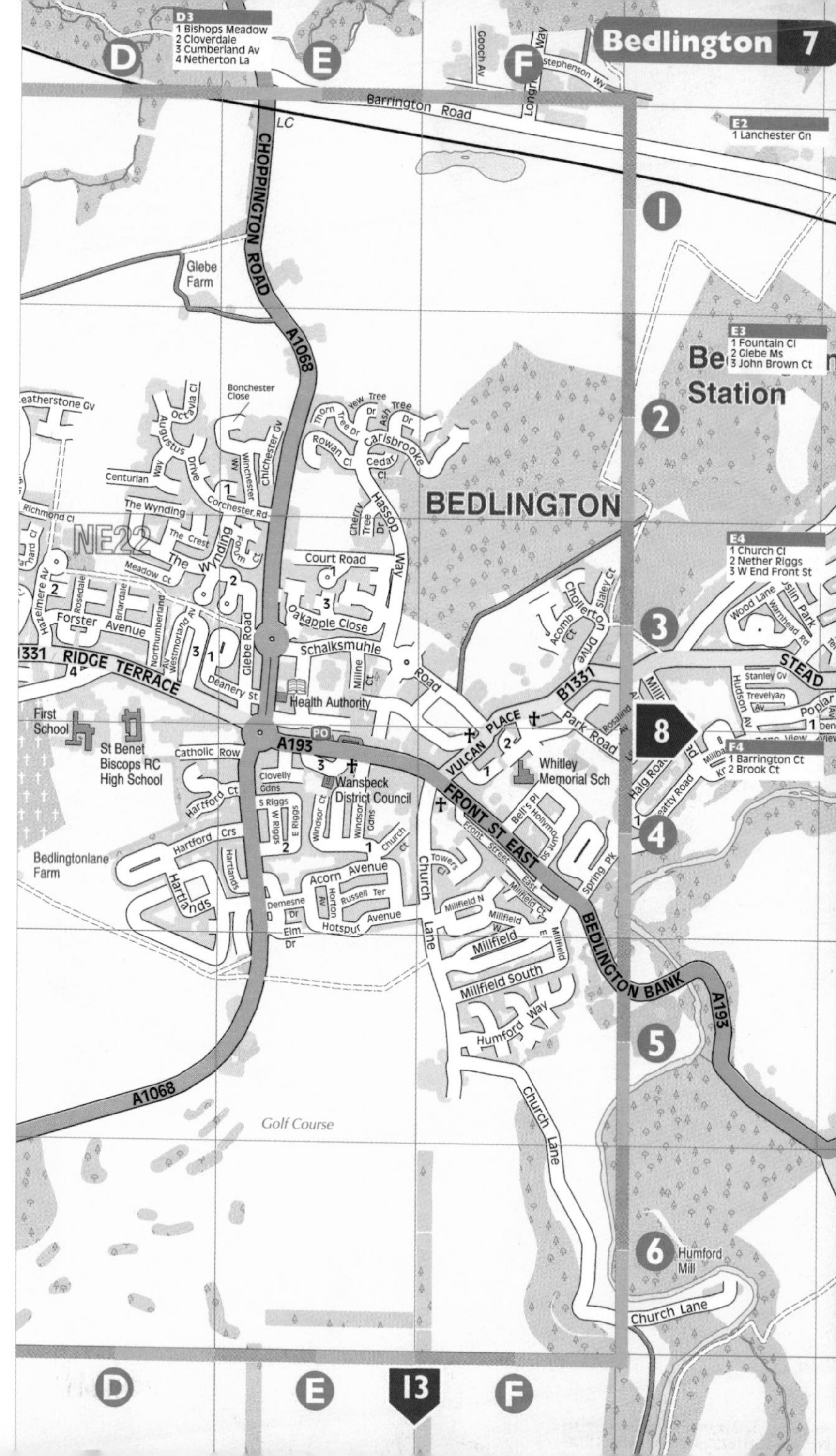
D3
1 Bishops Meadow
2 Cloverdale
3 Cumberland Av
4 Netherton La
E2
1 Lanchester Gn
E3
1 Fountain Cl
2 Glebe Ms
3 John Brown Ct
E4
1 Church Cl
2 Nether Riggs
3 W End Front St
F4
1 Barrington Ct
2 Brook Ct
BEDLINGTON
NE22
Barrington Road
CHOPPINGTON ROAD
A1068
Glebe Farm
RIDGE TERRACE
A193
FRONT ST EAST
BEDLINGTON BANK
VULCAN PLACE
B1331
Park Road
Schalksmuhle Road
Health Authority
Wansbeck District Council
Whitley Memorial Sch
First School
St Benet Biscops RC High School
Bedlingtonlane Farm
Golf Course
Church Lane
Humford Mill
Millfield South
Humford Way
Hassop Way
Court Road
Oakapple Close
Forster Avenue
Acorn Avenue
Hotspur Avenue
Hartford Crs
Hartlands
Catholic Row
Bedlington Station
STEAD
Haig Road
Beatty Road
Spring Pk
13

A
B
C
1
2
3
4
5
6
7
14
A3
1 Wanny Rd
A4
1 Cornwell Crs
B2
1 Lampton Ct
2 Lumley Ct
3 Waverley Av
B3
1 Clement Av
2 Edgewood Av
3 Trotter Gv
C1
1 Greenwood Av
2 Sleekburn Av
C2
1 Cherrytree Ct
2 Edward Rd
3 George Rd
4 Knox Cl
Bedlington Station
BEDLINGTON
Bedlington Station Co First Sch
The Gables Medical Group
Bedlington Community High School
Bedlington Stead County First School
Whitley Memorial Sch
Bebside Social Club House
Bebside Hall
Humford Mill
Wallington Close
Barrington Road
Station Road
Stead Lane
B1331
Palace Road
Front St East
Bedlington Bank
A193
Bebside Road
Bebside Furnace Road
Hathery Lane
Horton
Church Lane
Humford Way
1 grid square represents 500 metres

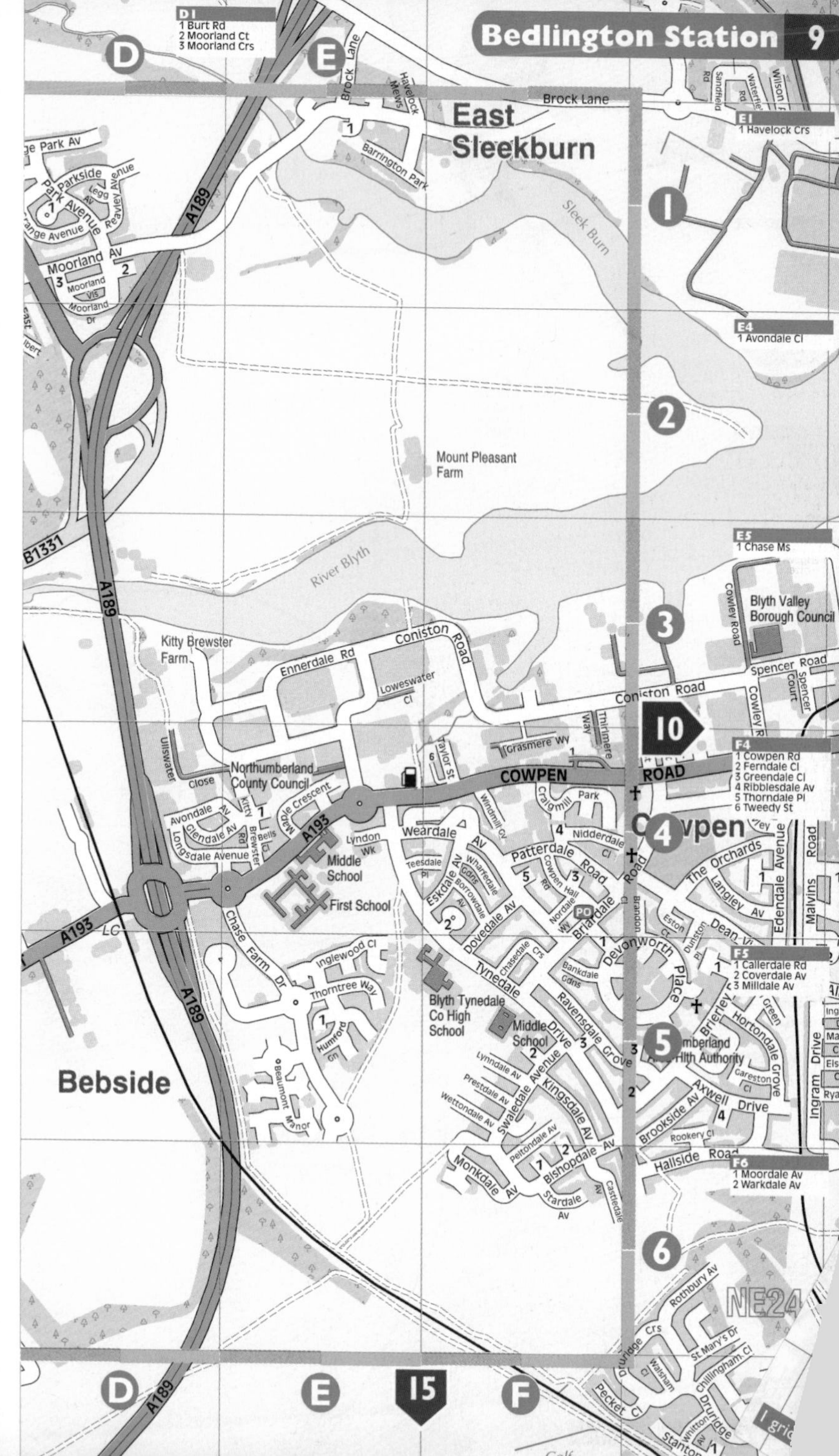
D1
1 Burt Rd
2 Moorland Ct
3 Moorland Crs
East Sleekburn
Brock Lane
Havelock Mews
Barrington Park
Park Avenue
Parkside
Reavley Avenue
Grange Avenue
Moorland Av
Moorland Vls
Moorland Dr
A189
B1331
Sleek Burn
E1
1 Havelock Crs
E4
1 Avondale Cl
Mount Pleasant Farm
River Blyth
E5
1 Chase Ms
Blyth Valley Borough Council
Cowley Road
Spencer Road
Spencer Court
Kitty Brewster Farm
Ennerdale Rd
Coniston Road
Loweswater Cl
Ullswater Close
Northumberland County Council
Grasmere Wy
Thirlmere Way
Taylor St
COWPEN ROAD
F4
1 Cowpen Rd
2 Ferndale Cl
3 Greendale Cl
4 Ribblesdale Av
5 Thorndale Pl
6 Tweedy St
Cowpen
Avondale Av
Glendale Av
Longsdale Avenue
Kitty Brewster Rd
Bells Cl
Maple Crescent
A193
Lyndon Wk
Middle School
First School
Weardale Av
Teesdale Pl
Eskdale Av
Wharfedale Gdns
Borrowdale Av
Patterdale Road
Cowpen Hall Rd
Nordale Wy
Briardale Road
Nidderdale Cl
Craigmill Park
Windmill Gv
The Orchards
Langley Av
Edendale Avenue
Malvins Road
Dean View
Eston Ct
Dunston Pl
Devonworth Place
Brandon Cl
Dovedale Av
Tynedale
Chasedale Crs
Bankdale Gdns
Ravensdale Grove
F5
1 Callerdale Rd
2 Coverdale Av
3 Milldale Av
Chase Farm Dr
Inglewood Cl
Thorntree Way
Humford Gn
Blyth Tynedale Co High School
Middle School
Drive
Brierley
Hortondale Grove
Green
Northumberland Area Hlth Authority
Gareston Cl
Ingram Drive
Bebside
Beaumont Manor
Lynndale Av
Prestdale Av
Wettondale Av
Swaledale Avenue
Kingsdale Av
Brookside Av
Axwell Drive
Rookery Cl
Hallside Road
Peltondale Av
Bishopdale Av
Monkdale Av
Stardale Av
Castledale Av
F6
1 Moordale Av
2 Warkdale Av
NE24
Rotnbury Av
Druridge Crs
Walsham Cl
St Mary's Dr
Chillingham Cl
Druridge
Pecket Cl
Whitton Av
Stanton
10
15
D
E
F
1
2
3
4
5
6

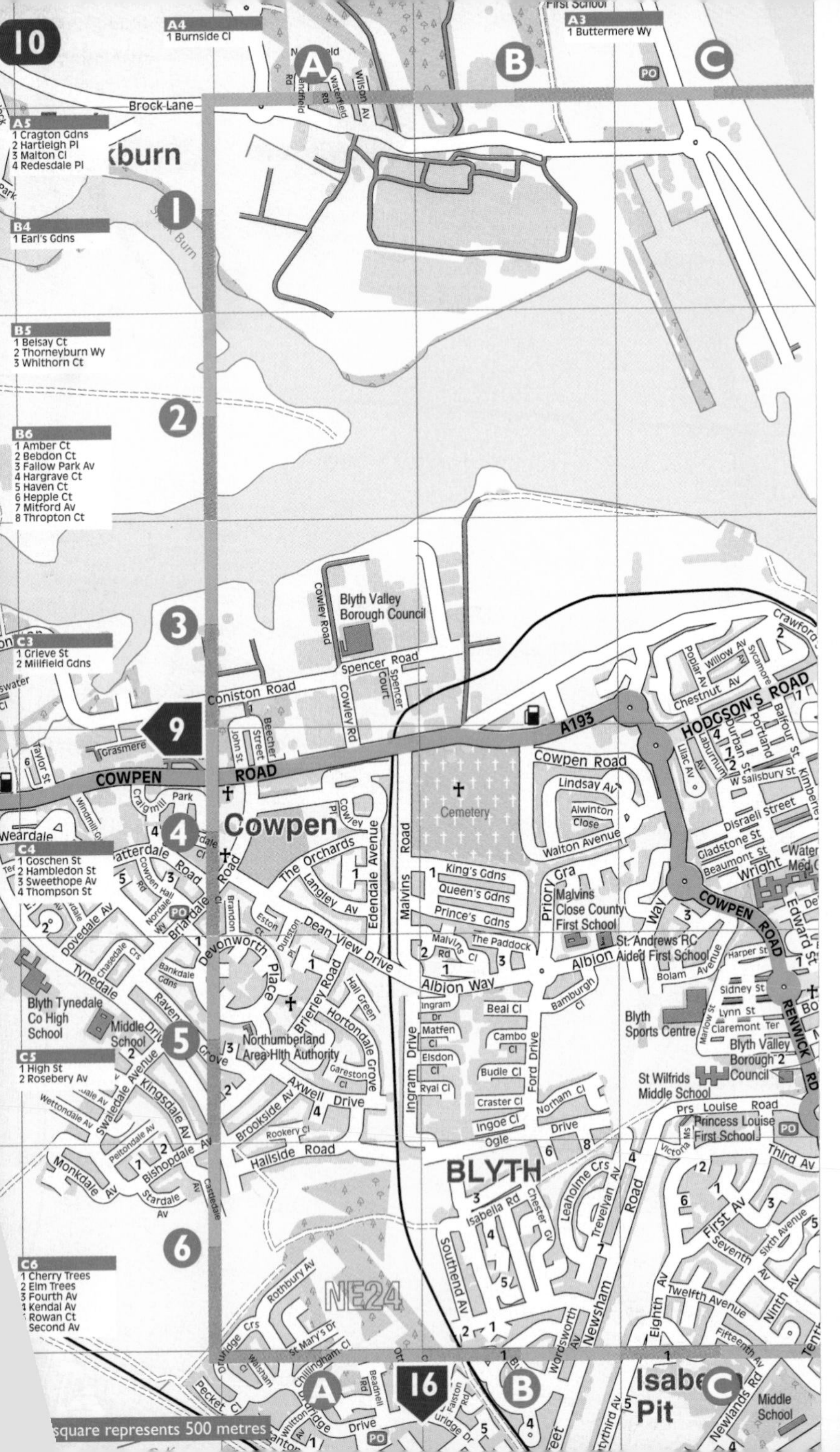
A4
1 Burnside Cl
A3
1 Buttermere Wy
First School
A
B
C
PO
Brock Lane
Wilson Av
Waterfield Rd
A5
1 Cragton Gdns
2 Hartleigh Pl
3 Malton Cl
4 Redesdale Pl
kburn
1
B4
1 Earl's Gdns
Burn
B5
1 Belsay Ct
2 Thorneyburn Wy
3 Whithorn Ct
2
B6
1 Amber Ct
2 Bebdon Ct
3 Fallow Park Av
4 Hargrave Ct
5 Haven Ct
6 Hepple Ct
7 Mitford Av
8 Thropton Ct
3
C3
1 Grieve St
2 Millfield Gdns
Cowley Road
Blyth Valley
Borough Council
Spencer Road
Spencer Court
Coniston Road
Cowley Rd
9
Grasmere
John St
Beecher Street
Taylor St
COWPEN
ROAD
A193
Crawford
Poplar Av
Willow Av
Sycamore
Chestnut Av
HODGSON'S ROAD
Balfour St
Durban St
Portland
Laburnum
Lilac Av
W Salisbury St
Kimberley
Cowpen Road
Lindsay Av
Alwinton Close
Cemetery
Walton Avenue
Disraeli Street
Gladstone St
Beaumont St
Wright
Park
Craigmill
Windmill
Weardale
4
Cowpen
Cowley Pl
Edendale Avenue
The Orchards
Langley Av
C4
1 Goschen St
2 Hambledon St
3 Sweethope Av
4 Thompson St
Patterdale Road
Cowpen Hall Rd
Nordale Wy
Briardale Road
Brandon
Eston Ct
Dunston Pl
Dean View Drive
Malvins Road
King's Gdns
Queen's Gdns
Prince's Gdns
Priory Gra
Malvins Close County First School
Way
COWPEN ROAD
Edward St
Dovedale Av
Chasedale Crs
Tynedale
Devonworth Place
Bankdale Gdns
Malvins Rd
Malvins Cl
The Paddock
St. Andrews RC Aided First School
Albion Way
Albion Way
Bolam Avenue
Harper St
Sidney St
Lynn St
Claremont Ter
RENWICK RD
Blyth Tynedale Co High School
Middle School
Raven
Drive
5
Grove
Brierley Road
Hall Green
Hortondale Grove
Northumberland Area Hlth Authority
Ingram Dr
Matfen Cl
Elsdon Cl
Ryal Cl
Beal Cl
Cambo Cl
Bamburgh Cl
Ford Drive
Budle Cl
Blyth Sports Centre
Marlow St
Blyth Valley Borough Council
St Wilfrids Middle School
C5
1 High St
2 Rosebery Av
Swaledale Avenue
Kingsdale Av
Wettondale Av
Gareston Cl
Axwell Drive
Brookside Av
Rookery Cl
Ingram Drive
Craster Cl
Ingoe Cl
Norham Cl
Drive
Ogle
Prs Louise Road
Princess Louise First School
Peltondale Av
Bishopdale Av
Monkdale Av
Stardale Av
Castledale
Hallside Road
BLYTH
Leaholme Crs
Trevelyan Av
Road
Victoria Ms
Third Av
First Av
Isabella Rd
Chester Gv
Southend Av
6
C6
1 Cherry Trees
2 Elm Trees
3 Fourth Av
4 Kendal Av
Rowan Ct
Second Av
Rothbury Av
NE24
Seventh Av
Sixth Avenue
Twelfth Avenue
Ninth Av
Fifteenth Av
Eighth Av
Newsham
Wordsworth Av
Drumridge Crs
Walsham Cl
St Mary's Dr
Chillingham Cl
Pecket Cl
A
16
B
Isabella Pit
C
Beadnell Rd
Falston Rd
Drive
Newlands Rd
Middle School
Tenth
square represents 500 metres

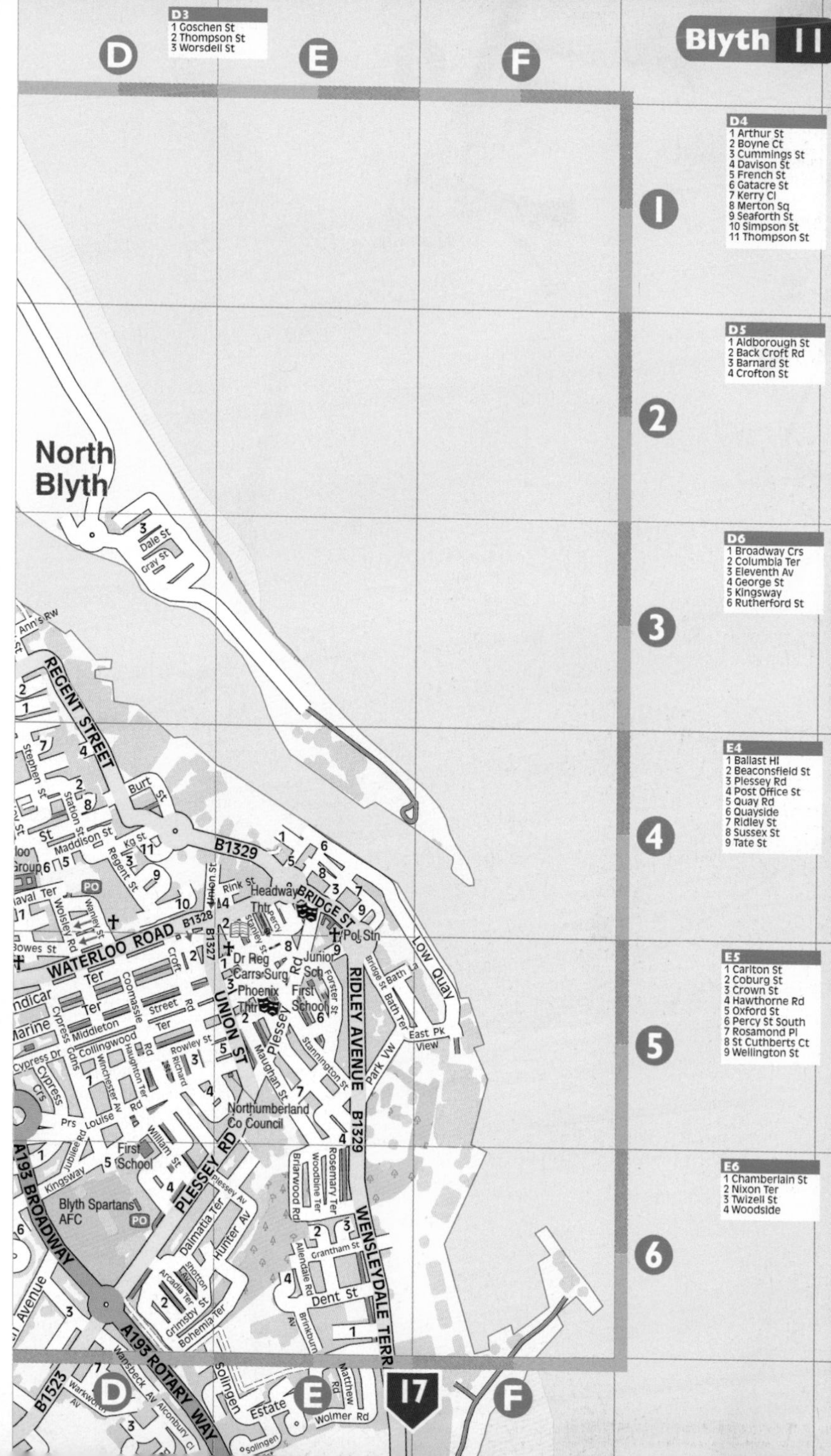
D3
1 Goschen St
2 Thompson St
3 Worsdell St
D
E
F
D4
1 Arthur St
2 Boyne Ct
3 Cummings St
4 Davison St
5 French St
6 Gatacre St
7 Kerry Cl
8 Merton Sq
9 Seaforth St
10 Simpson St
11 Thompson St
1
D5
1 Aldborough St
2 Back Croft Rd
3 Barnard St
4 Crofton St
2
North Blyth
Dale St
Gray St
D6
1 Broadway Crs
2 Columbia Ter
3 Eleventh Av
4 George St
5 Kingsway
6 Rutherford St
3
Regent Street
E4
1 Ballast Hl
2 Beaconsfield St
3 Plessey Rd
4 Post Office St
5 Quay Rd
6 Quayside
7 Ridley St
8 Sussex St
9 Tate St
4
Burt St
Maddison St
Station St
Stephen St
Kg St
Regent St
B1329
Rink St
Headway Thtr
Bridge St
Pol Stn
Waterloo Road
B1328
B1327
Union St
Wanley St
Wolsley Rd
Bowes St
Dr Reg Carrs Surg
Junior Sch
Phoenix Thtr
First School
Forster St
Ridley Avenue
Bath Ter
Low Quay
E5
1 Carlton St
2 Coburg St
3 Crown St
4 Hawthorne Rd
5 Oxford St
6 Percy St South
7 Rosamond Pl
8 St Cuthberts Ct
9 Wellington St
5
Coomassie
Middleton
Collingwood
Cypress Gdns
Cypress Dr
Cypress Crs
Winchester Av
Haughton Ter
Rowley St
Richard St
Maughan St
Stannington St
Park Vw
East Pk View
Northumberland Co Council
Louise
Jubilee Rd
Kingsway
First School
William St
Plessey Rd
Briarwood Rd
Woodbine Ter
Rosemary Ter
B1329
E6
1 Chamberlain St
2 Nixon Ter
3 Twizell St
4 Woodside
6
Blyth Spartans AFC
PO
A193 Broadway
Dalmatia Ter
Hunter Av
Plessey Av
Grantham St
Wensleydale Terr
Shotton Av
Arcadia Ter
Grimsby St
Bohemia Ter
Allendale Rd
Dent St
Brinkburn Av
A193 Rotary Way
B1523
Warkworth Av
Wansbeck Av
Alconbury Cl
Solingen
Estate
Matthew Rd
Wolmer Rd
17

A
6
B
C
HART
Netherton Moor Farm
A192
SHIELDS ROAD
Plessey Woods Country Park
Hartford Dr
Hartford Hall
East Moor
1
Hartford Bridge
2
HARTFORD BANK
3
A1068
Lane
Shotton
4
Nels
Nelson Road
5
Road
Baker
LANE
FISHER
Shotton Lane
Bolam Business Park
Lane
6
Bassington
Drive
Bassingt
A1068
elson
A
20
B
C
1 grid square represents 500 metres

F4
1 Colbury Cl
2 Denholm Av
3 Hanover Pl
4 Hartside Crs
F5
1 Carmel Gv
2 Castleton Cl
3 Cheadle Av
4 Ilford Av
5 Ingham Gv
6 Whitehill Rd
F6
1 Yardley Gv
2 Yeovil Cl
D
E
7
F
River Blyth
East Hartford
West Hartford Farm
Scott Street
Everard St
Wrightson St
Ormston Street
14
A192
A1171
Dearham Grove
Denby Cl
Delamere Crs
Daylesford Rd
Denshaw Cl
Kelsey Wy
Fairville
Fonteyn Pl
Fern Avenue
Horton Drive
Hauxley Drive
Hilton Cl
Cariby Way
Atley Way
Highstead Av
Brunton Way
Boulmer Av
Bondene Wy
Arlington Gv
Annfield Rd
Ashwood Cl
Horton Burn
Sheldon Gv
Sandford
Silkwood Cl
Sefton Ct
Crow Hall Road
Moorland Way
Colbourne Avenue
Windsor Ct
Halkirk Wy
Woburn Close
Prestbury Av
Glenfield Av
Pendleton Drive
Porlock Ct
Underwood Gv
Horton Drive
Ilford Avenue
Northburn County First School
Selby Close
Silverdale Road
Nelson Drive
South Nelson Road
South Nelson Rd
York Cl
Yarmouth Drive
Yelverton Court
Brockwell Clinic
Brockwell County Middle School
Tintagel Cl
Totnes Drive
Taunton Pl
Tiverton Pl
Torcross Way
Faversham Pl
Farnborough Cl
Frome Pl
Forres Pl
Newlyn Drive
Filton Cl
Filey Cl
Twyford Close
Bolam Business Park
Blagdon Crs
Nelson Avenue
Scott Avenue
Chichester Av
Lane
Ross Gv
Northumberland Co Council
Arcot Avenue
Burdon Av
Crow
Nelson Village
21
Reigate Sq
Rotherfield Cl
Ringwood Drive
First School
Needham Place
Ranmore Cl
Ryde Pl
Nayland Rd
Nairn Road
PO

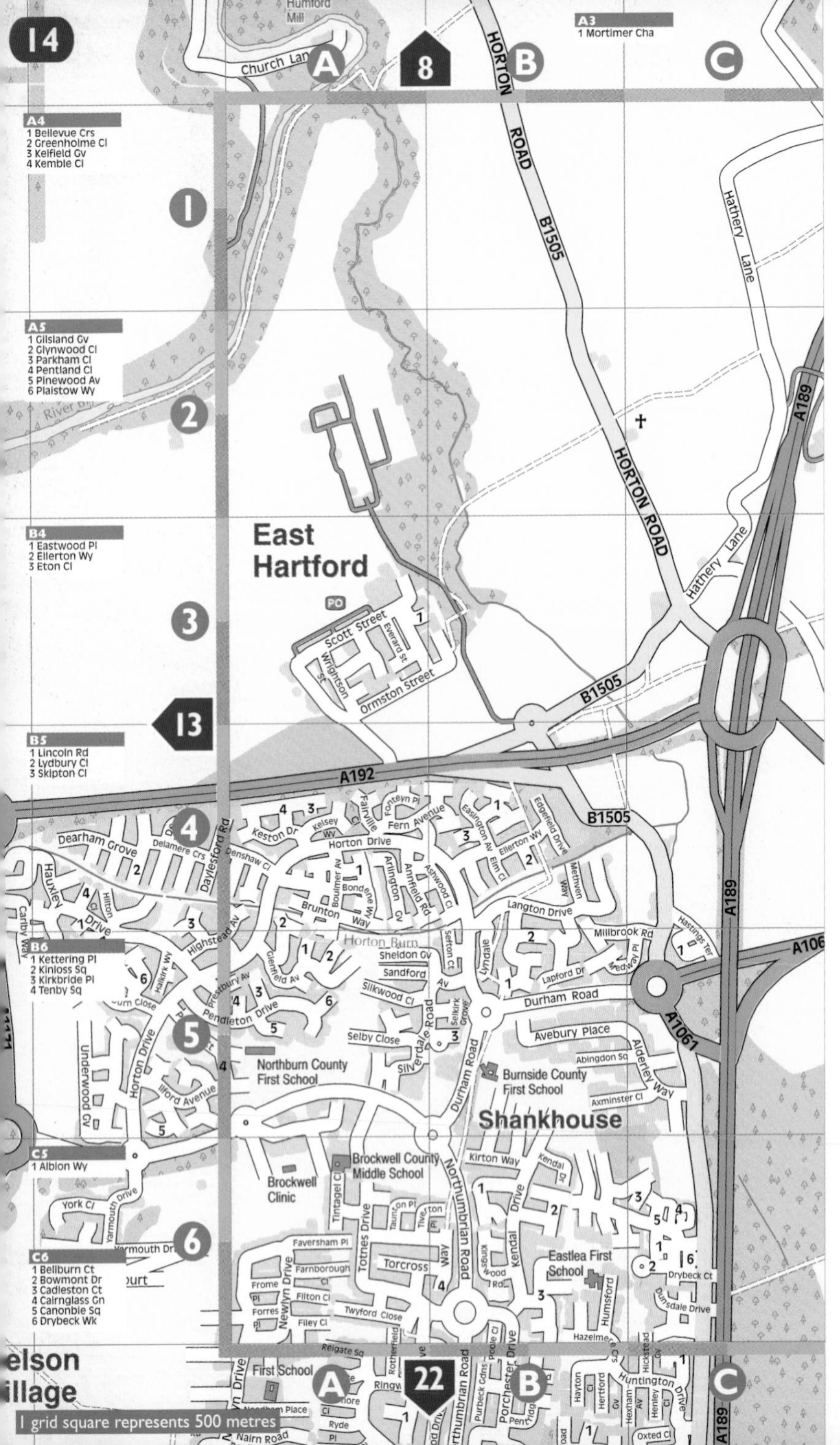
A3
1 Mortimer Cha
A4
1 Bellevue Crs
2 Greenholme Cl
3 Kelfield Gv
4 Kemble Cl
A5
1 Gilsland Gv
2 Glynwood Cl
3 Parkham Cl
4 Pentland Cl
5 Pinewood Av
6 Plaistow Wy
B4
1 Eastwood Pl
2 Ellerton Wy
3 Eton Cl
B5
1 Lincoln Rd
2 Lydbury Cl
3 Skipton Cl
B6
1 Kettering Pl
2 Kinloss Sq
3 Kirkbride Pl
4 Tenby Sq
C5
1 Albion Wy
C6
1 Bellburn Ct
2 Bowmont Dr
3 Cadleston Ct
4 Cairnglass Gn
5 Canonbie Sq
6 Drybeck Wk
East Hartford
Shankhouse
HORTON ROAD
B1505
A192
A189
A1061
Northburn County First School
Burnside County First School
Brockwell County Middle School
Brockwell Clinic
Eastlea First School
Church Lane
Hathery Lane
Durham Road
Northumbrian Road
Horton Drive
Scott Street
Ormston Street
1 grid square represents 500 metres

8
13
22

D
E
9
F
A189
Druridge Crs
St Mary's Dr
Chillingham Cl
Walsham Cl
Pecket Cl
Druridge Drive
Whitton Gv
Stanton Av
Beadnell Rd
Otterburn Gv
Cresswell Dr
PO
Golf Course
Kielder Close
Holystone Cl
Elliott St
Warwick
Winship
Blyth New Delaval County First School
PO
Delaval St
Beatrice Av
Plessey Road
Low Horton Farm
Park Dr
St Bedes Pl
Delaval Cresent
NEWCASTLE
New Delaval
The Oval
Laverock Hall Road
Cottingwood Gn
Cottingwood
16
A1061
A192
LAVEROCK HALL ROAD
Laverock Hall
Stickley Farm
A192
D
E
23
F
North Moor Farm
1
2
3
4
5
6

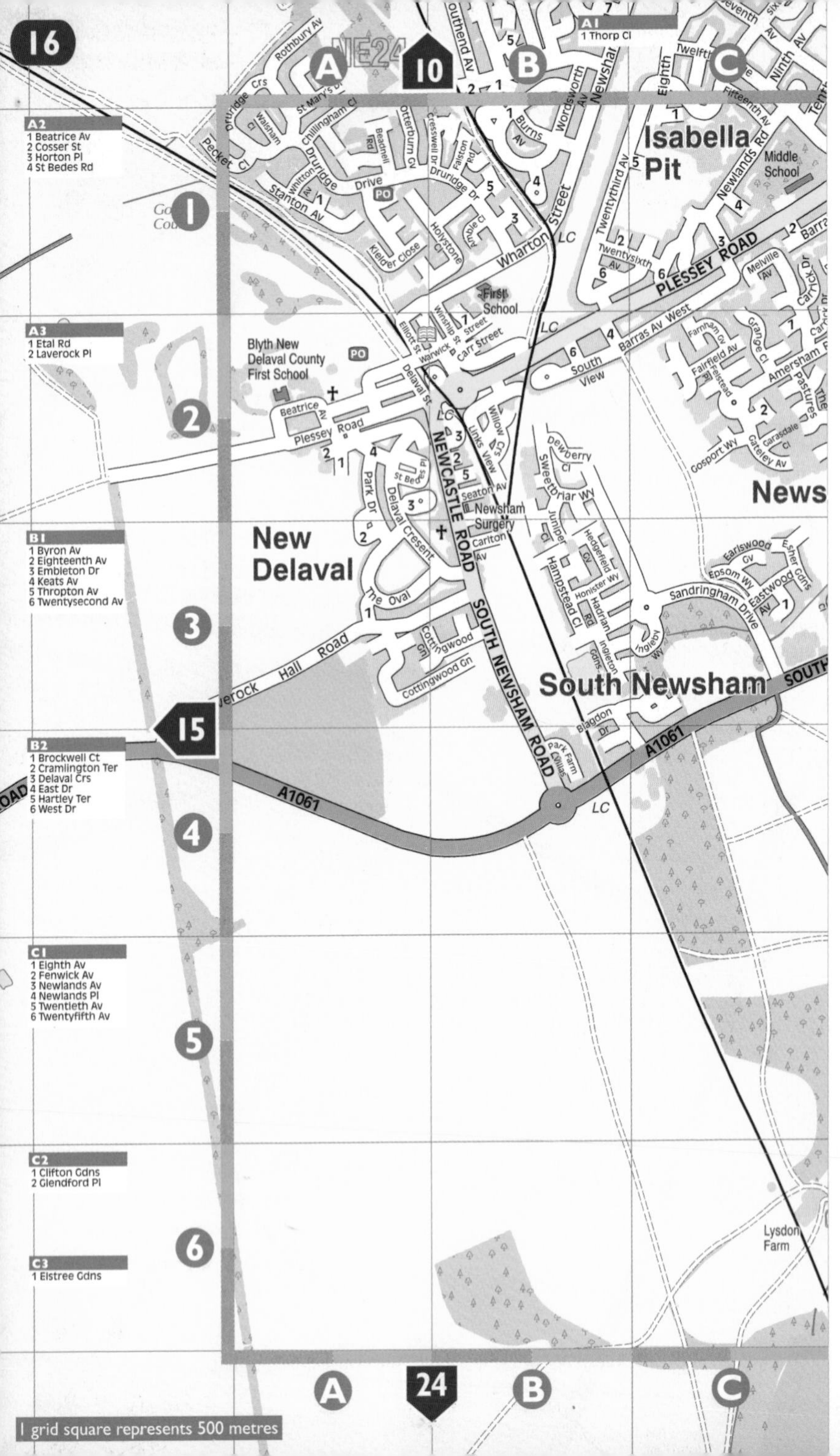
A2
1 Beatrice Av
2 Cosser St
3 Horton Pl
4 St Bedes Rd
A3
1 Etal Rd
2 Laverock Pl
B1
1 Byron Av
2 Eighteenth Av
3 Embleton Dr
4 Keats Av
5 Thropton Av
6 Twentysecond Av
B2
1 Brockwell Ct
2 Cramlington Ter
3 Delaval Crs
4 East Dr
5 Hartley Ter
6 West Dr
C1
1 Eighth Av
2 Fenwick Av
3 Newlands Av
4 Newlands Pl
5 Twentieth Av
6 Twentyfifth Av
C2
1 Clifton Gdns
2 Glendford Pl
C3
1 Elstree Gdns
A1
1 Thorp Cl
NE24
10
15
24
Isabella Pit
New Delaval
South Newsham
News
Blyth New Delaval County First School
Newsham Surgery
First School
Middle School
Lysdon Farm
PLESSEY ROAD
NEWCASTLE ROAD
SOUTH NEWSHAM ROAD
A1061
Wharton Street
Plessey Road
Laverock Hall Road
Sandringham Drive
1 grid square represents 500 metres

D1
1 Amberley Wy
2 Ashford Cl
3 Aylesford Sq
4 Bexhill Sq
5 Coquet Av
6 Guillemot Cl
7 Seafield Rd
D2
1 Dalston Pl
2 Downe Cl
3 Redshank Dr
South Beach
Link House
Beachway
LINKS ROAD
ROTARY WAY A193
A193 ROTARY WAY
B1329
B1523
NEWSHAM ROAD
Solingen Estate
Wolmer Rd
Cemetery
Gloucester Lodge Farm
Hartley Links
Seaton Sluice Middle School
Seaton Red House Farm
Conway Gr
Alston Grove
Dorking Close
Albatross Way
Kittiwake Close
Shearwater Way
Mallard Wy
Tern Cl
Fulmar Drive
Elder Close
Heron Close
Avocet Cl
Teal Avenue
Cormorant Wy
Petrel Wy
Sandpiper Cl
Kingfisher Wy
Osprey Dr
Plover Cl
Dunlin Dr
Curlew Way
Lapwing Cl
Deal Cl
Dunkeld Cl
Dunblane Dr
Amersham Rd
Grebe Cl
Guillemot Cl
Bromley Gdns
Banbury Way
Burnham Cl
Appledore Rd
Addington Dr
Alconbury Cl
Wansbeck Av
Warkworth Av
Grimsby St
Bohemia Ter
Arcadia Ter
Matthew Rd
LEYDALE TERRACE
ham
D E F
1 2 3 4 5 6
11
25

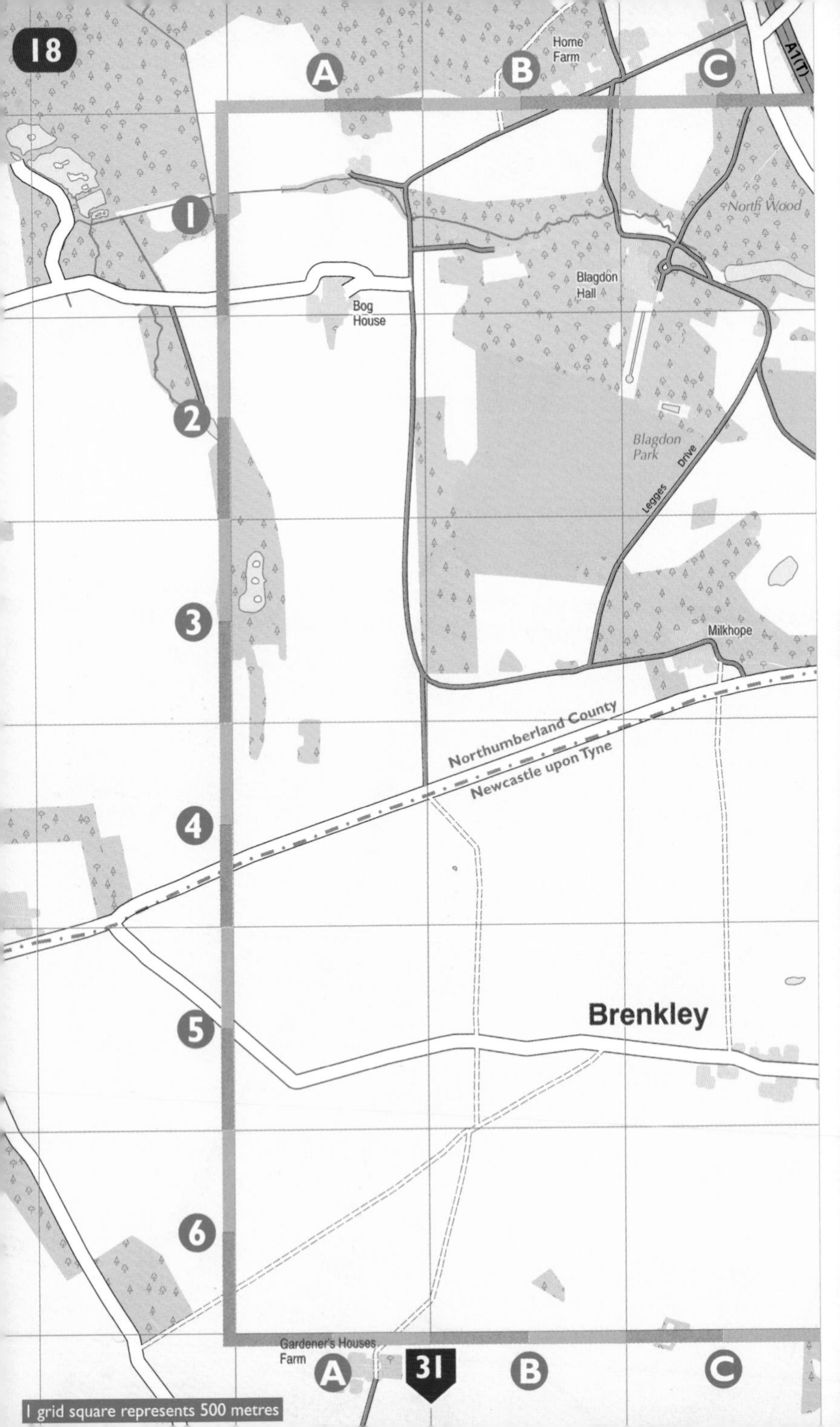

A
B
C
Home Farm
A1(T)
1
North Wood
Blagdon Hall
Bog House
2
Blagdon Park
Legges Drive
3
Milkhope
Northumberland County
Newcastle upon Tyne
4
5
Brenkley
6
Gardener's Houses Farm
31
1 grid square represents 500 metres

D
E
F
1
2
3
4
5
6
20
32
Plessey North Moor Farm
Moor Plantation
Fusilier Plantation
A1068
South Drive
Shotton Grange
A1(T)
Waterloo Plantation
Plessey South Moor Farm
Hoys Wood
FISHER LANE
Seven Mile House Farm
Hotel
B1318

A
12
B
C
A1068
Bassington
Drive
Bassingt
Nelson
A1172
Plessey North Moor
Farm
Moor
Plantation
A1068
Kielder Av
Beacon Lane
White Hall
Farm
19
Waterloo
Plantation
Plessey South
Moor Farm
A1068
FISHER LANE
Arcot Hall
Golf Course
Club House
Mile
Farm
A1(T)
Hotel
A19(T)
Sandy's Letch
A
33
B
C
1
2
3
4
5
6
1 grid square represents 500 metres

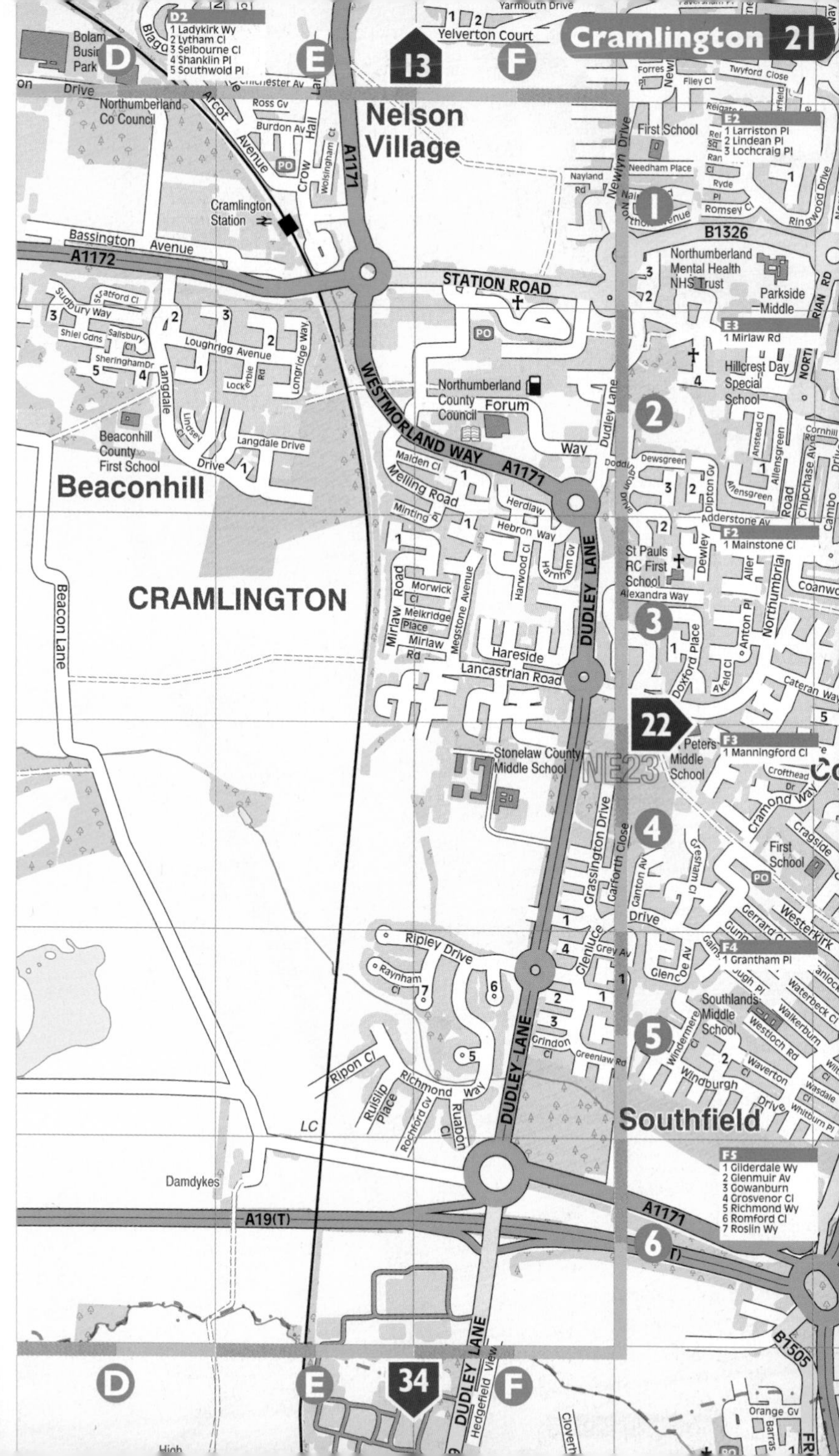
13
22
34
D2
1 Ladykirk Wy
2 Lytham Cl
3 Selbourne Cl
4 Shanklin Pl
5 Southwold Pl
E2
1 Larriston Pl
2 Lindean Pl
3 Lochcraig Pl
E3
1 Mirlaw Rd
F2
1 Mainstone Cl
F3
1 Manningford Cl
F4
1 Grantham Pl
F5
1 Gilderdale Wy
2 Glenmuir Av
3 Gowanburn
4 Grosvenor Cl
5 Richmond Wy
6 Romford Cl
7 Roslin Wy
Nelson Village
Beaconhill
CRAMLINGTON
Southfield
NE23
Cramlington Station
Northumberland Co Council
Northumberland County Council
Forum
Beaconhill County First School
Northumberland Mental Health NHS Trust
Parkside Middle
Hillcrest Day Special School
St Pauls RC First School
Stonelaw County Middle School
Southlands Middle School
First School
Bolam Business Park
Damdykes
Yelverton Court
Yarmouth Drive
STATION ROAD
WESTMORLAND WAY
DUDLEY LANE
Dudley Lane
Beacon Lane
Bassington Avenue
Arcot Avenue
Loughrigg Avenue
Langdale Drive
Lancastrian Road
Ripley Drive
Richmond Way
Alexandra Way
Cramond Way
Westerkirk
Windburgh Drive
Grassington Drive
Garforth Close
Newlyn Drive
A1171
A1172
A19(T)
B1326
B1505
LC

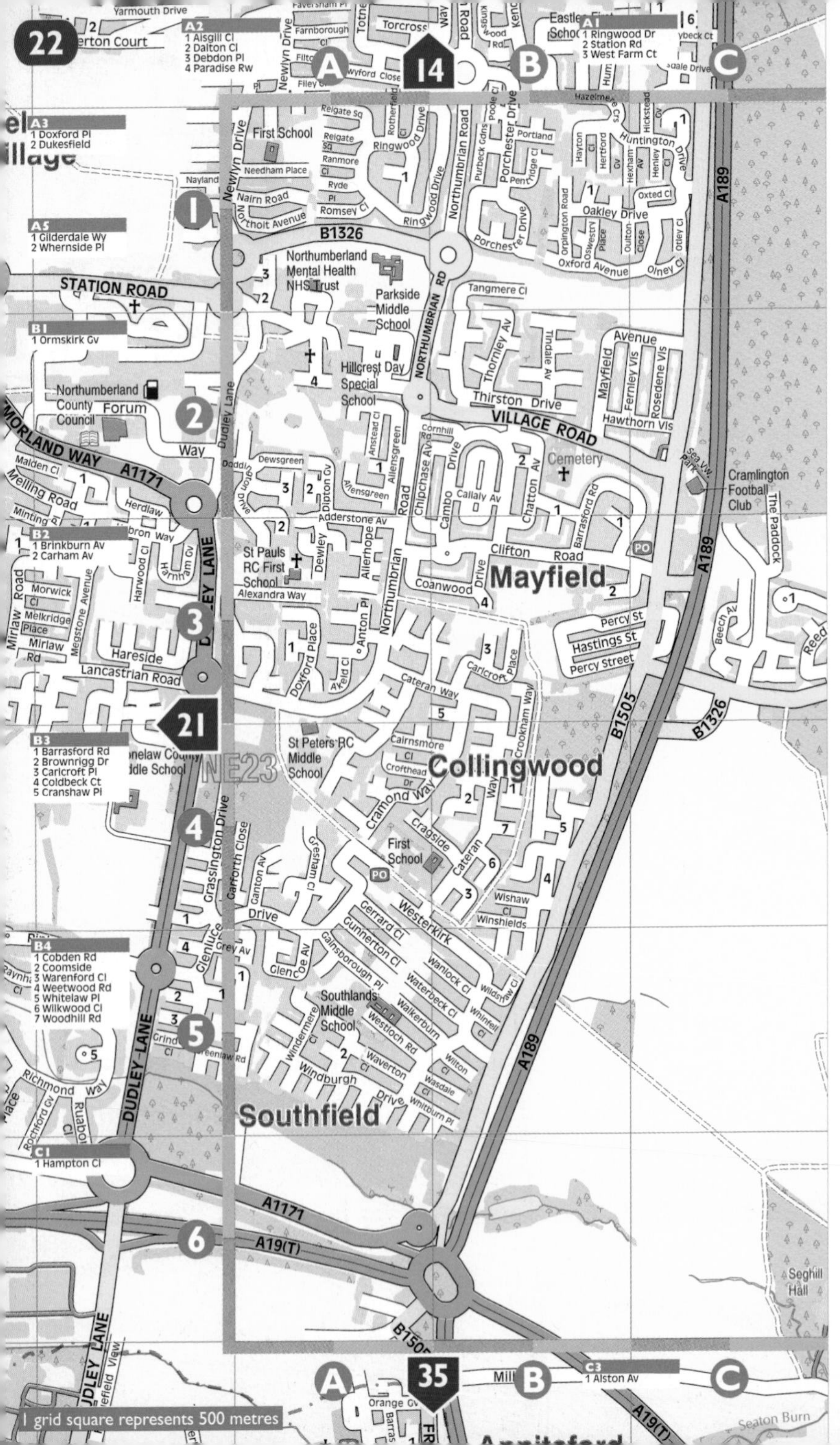

A2
1 Aisgill Cl
2 Dalton Cl
3 Debdon Pl
4 Paradise Rw
A1
1 Ringwood Dr
2 Station Rd
3 West Farm Ct
A3
1 Doxford Pl
2 Dukesfield
A5
1 Gilderdale Wy
2 Whernside Pl
B1
1 Ormskirk Gv
B2
1 Brinkburn Av
2 Carham Av
B3
1 Barrasford Rd
2 Brownrigg Dr
3 Carlcroft Pl
4 Coldbeck Ct
5 Cranshaw Pl
B4
1 Cobden Rd
2 Coomside
3 Warenford Cl
4 Weetwood Rd
5 Whitelaw Pl
6 Wilkwood Cl
7 Woodhill Rd
C1
1 Hampton Cl
C3
1 Alston Av
14
21
35
A
B
C
1
2
3
4
5
6
Yarmouth Drive
Newlyn Drive
Farnborough Cl
Torcross Way
Hazelmere Crs
Huntington Drive
First School
Reigate Sq
Ringwood Drive
Needham Place
Ranmore Cl
Ryde Pl
Nayland
Nairn Road
Romsey Cl
Northolt Avenue
Northumbrian Road
Purbeck Gdns
Porchester Drive
Portland
Pentridge Cl
Hayton Cl
Hertford Gv
Hexham Av
Henley Cl
Hickstead Gv
Oxted Cl
Oakley Drive
Orpington Road
Oswestry Place
Oulton Close
Otley Cl
Oxford Avenue
Olney Cl
A189
B1326
Northumberland Mental Health NHS Trust
STATION ROAD
Parkside Middle School
Tangmere Cl
Thornley Av
Tindale Av
Avenue
Mayfield
Fernley Vls
Rosedene Vls
Hillcrest Day Special School
NORTHUMBRIAN RD
Thirston Drive
VILLAGE ROAD
Hawthorn Vls
Northumberland County Council
Forum Way
Dudley Lane
MORLAND WAY
A1171
Malden Cl
Melling Road
Minting Pl
Herdlaw
Hebron Way
Dewsgreen
Doddington Drive
Dipton Gv
Allensgreen
Anstead Cl
Cornhill Rd
Chipchase Av
Cambo Drive
Callaly Av
Chatton Av
Cemetery
Barrasford Rd
Sea Vw. Park
Cramlington Football Club
The Paddock
Adderstone Av
Allerhope
Dewley
St Pauls RC First School
Harwood Cl
Harnham Gv
DUDLEY LANE
Morwick Cl
Melkridge Place
Megstone Avenue
Mirlaw Road
Mirlaw Rd
Alexandra Way
Clifton Road
Coanwood Drive
Mayfield
PO
Percy St
Hastings St
Percy Street
Beech Av
Reed
Hareside
Lancastrian Road
Doxford Place
Anton Pl
Akeld Cl
Carlcroft Place
Cateran Way
Crookham Way
B1505
St Peters RC Middle School
Cairnsmore Cl
Crofthead Dr
Collingwood
Stonelaw County Middle School
NE23
Cramond Way
Cragside
Grassington Drive
Garforth Close
Ganton Av
Gresham Cl
First School
Westerkirk
Wishaw Cl
Winshields
Drive
Gerrard Cl
Gunnerton Cl
Glenluce
Grey Av
Glencoe Av
Gainsborough Pl
Wanlock Cl
Wildshaw Cl
Waterbeck Cl
Whinfell Cl
Walkerburn
Southlands Middle School
Westloch Rd
Windermere Cl
Grindon Cl
Greenlaw Rd
Waverton Cl
Wilton Cl
Wasdale Cl
Windburgh Drive
Whitburn Pl
Richmond Way
Rochford Gv
Ruabon Cl
Southfield
DUDLEY LANE
A19(T)
Seghill Hall
B1505
Mill
Orange Gv
Barras
Seaton Burn
A19(T)
1 grid square represents 500 metres

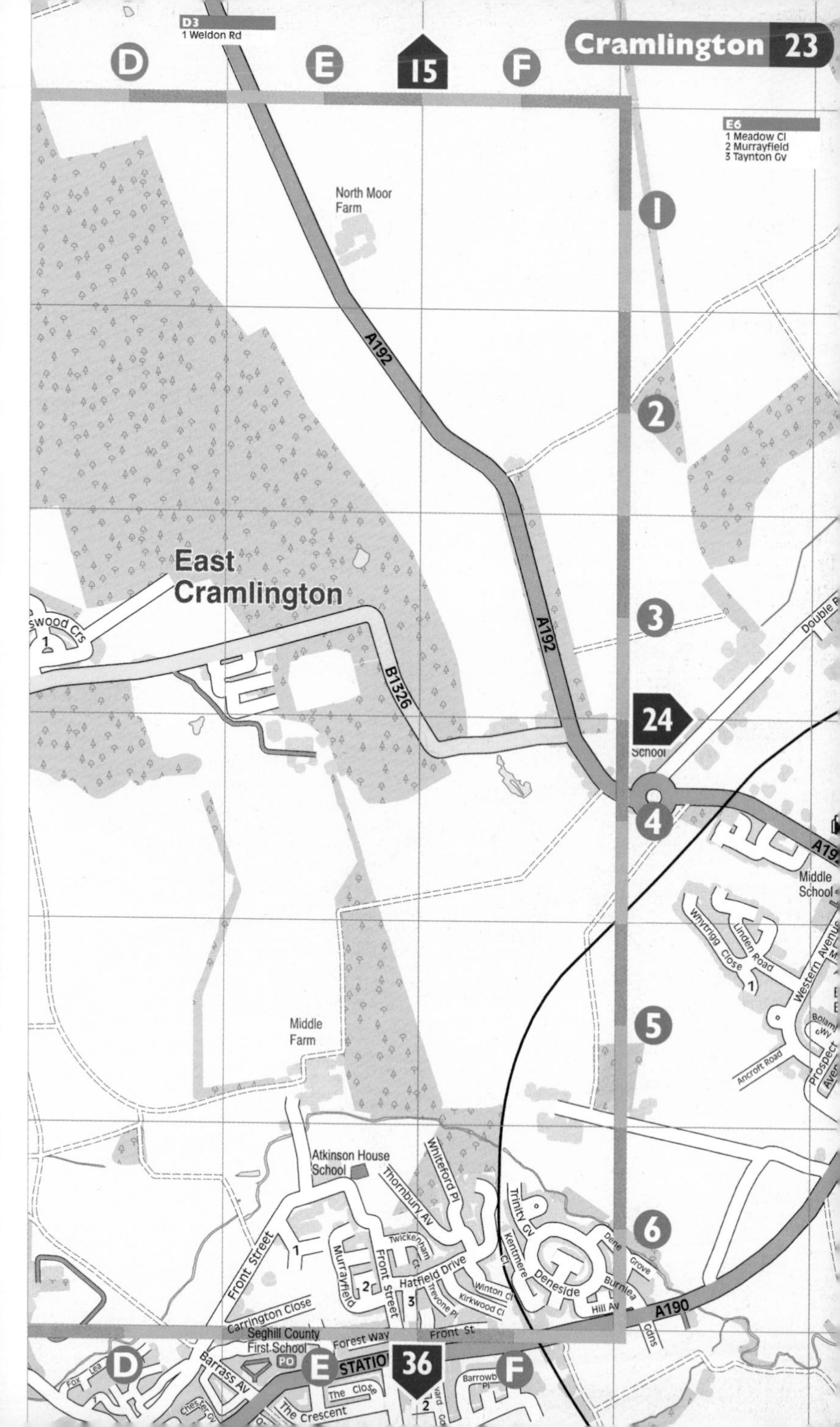
D3
1 Weldon Rd
D
E
15
F
E6
1 Meadow Cl
2 Murrayfield
3 Taynton Gv
1
2
3
4
5
6
24
36
North Moor Farm
A192
A192
East Cramlington
B1326
Middle Farm
Atkinson House School
School
Middle School
Whytrigg Close
Linden Road
Western Avenue
Ancroft Road
Prospect Ave
Double R
A19
Front Street
Thornbury Av
Whiteford Pl
Murrayfield
Front Street
Twickenham Ct
Hatfield Drive
Trevone Pl
Kirkwood Cl
Winton Cl
Trinity Gv
Kentmere Cl
Deneside
Dene Grove
Burnlea
Hill Av
Gdns
A190
Carrington Close
Seghill County First School
Forest Way
Front St
Barrass Av
Fox Lea
The Close
The Crescent
Barrowb Pl
Yard
STATIO

16
23
37
A5
1 St Stephen's Cl
B5
1 Astley Gdns
2 Rothley Gv
3 Starlight Crs
C2
1 Maple Ct
2 Wansbeck Gv
C5
1 Ambleside Cl
2 Kearsley Cl
3 Wallington Ct
C6
1 Vanborough Ct
SEATON
DELAVAL
A192
A190
ASTLEY ROAD
AVENUE ROAD
Double Row
Bristol
Street
Avon Court
Dorchester Ct
Chipchase Ct
Bradbury Ct
Hastings Gdns
Montrose Close
Melton Drive
Mountford Rd
Hastings Terrace
Alston Rd
Lysdon Av
Gloria Av
Seaburn View
Hester Av
Meadow View
Clinic
First School
Allenheads
Middle School
Doctors Surg
Blyth Valley Borough Council
Western Avenue
Linden Road
Whytrigg Close
Blyth St
Prospect Av
Mitford Av
Bolam Wy
Prospect Avenue
Glanton Av
Avenue Road
Ancroft Road
Astley Community High School
Greenlands Ct
Avenue Head Farm
Seaton Terrace
Hartley St
Sinclair Gdns
Viewpk
Park Road
Park View
Ridsdale Cl
Fontburn Road
Whitton Pl
Hallington Dr
Mindrum Wy
Elsdon Rd
Whitfield Rd
Bavington Road
Swinburn Road
Acomb Avenue
Avenue
Swarland Road
Staward Av
Kyloe Av
Paston Rd
Woodside Av
Denham Drive
Newburgh Av
Ashkirk Wy
Thornhill Cl
Melrose Av
Sandown Cl
Whiteford Pl
Thornbury Av
Twickenham Ct
Hatfield Drive
Trevone Pl
Winton Cl
Kirkwood Cl
Trinity Gv
Kentmere Cl
Deneside
Dene Grove
Burnlea
Hill Av
Gdns
Front St
ROAD
Barrowburn Pl
B1326
Farm
THE
1 grid square represents 500 metres

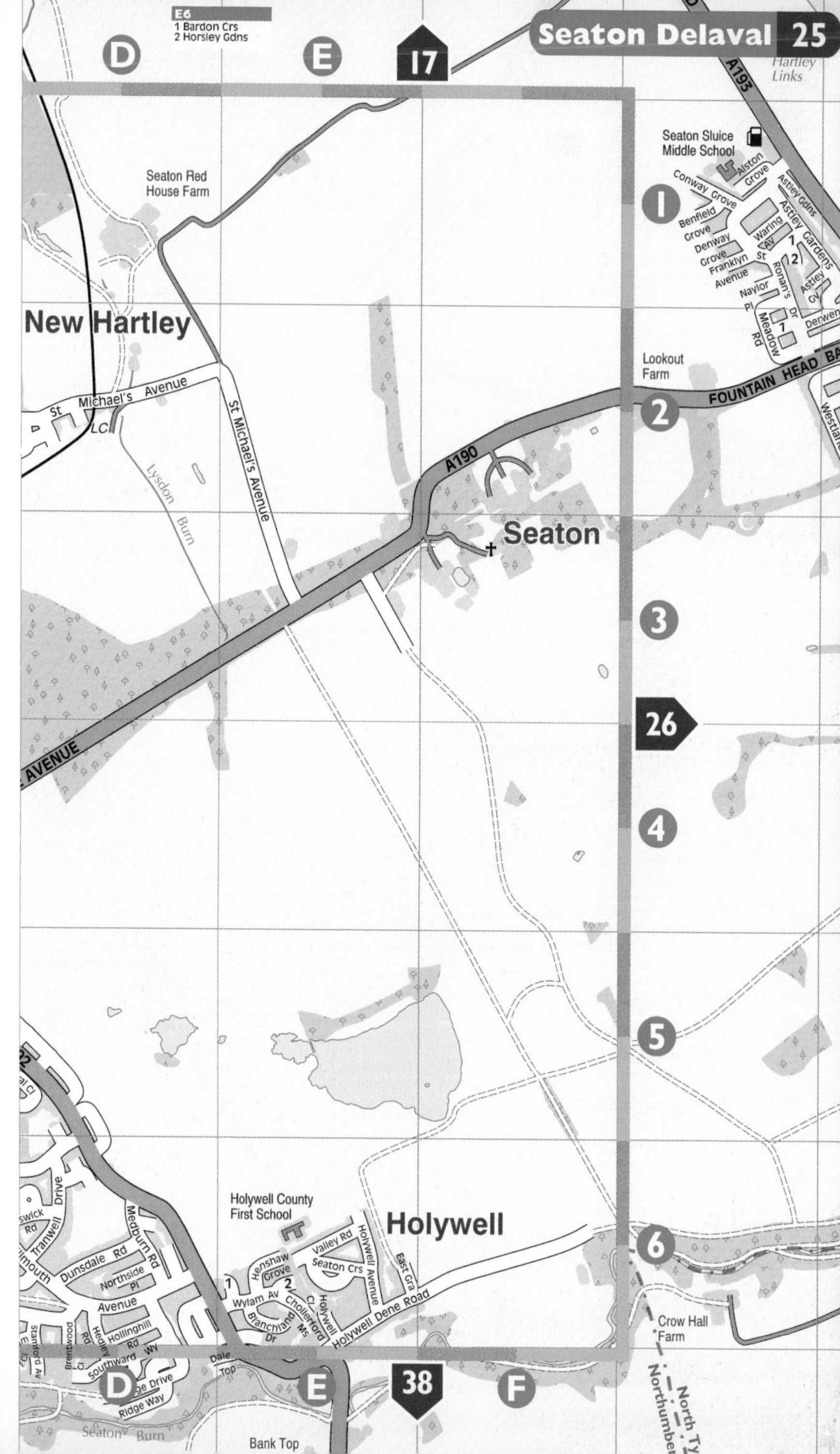
E6
1 Bardon Crs
2 Horsley Gdns
D
E
17
Hartley Links
A193
Seaton Sluice Middle School
Alston Grove
Conway Grove
Benfield Grove
Denway Grove
Franklyn Avenue
Waring Av
St Ronan's Dr
Astley Gdns
Astley Gardens
Astley Gv
Naylor Pl
Meadow Rd
Derwent
Seaton Red House Farm
New Hartley
St Michael's Avenue
LC
Lysdon Burn
Lookout Farm
FOUNTAIN HEAD BANK
Westlands
A190
Seaton
AVENUE
26
Holywell County First School
Holywell
Tranwell Drive
Medburn Rd
Dunsdale Rd
Northside Pl
Avenue
Hollinghill Rd
Southward Wy
Henshaw Grove
Valley Rd
Seaton Crs
Holywell Avenue
East Gra
Wylam Av
Blanchland Dr
Chollerford Ms
Holywell Cl
Holywell Dene Road
Crow Hall Farm
Dale Top
Ridge Drive
Ridge Way
Seaton Burn
Bank Top
38
F
North Ty
Northumbe

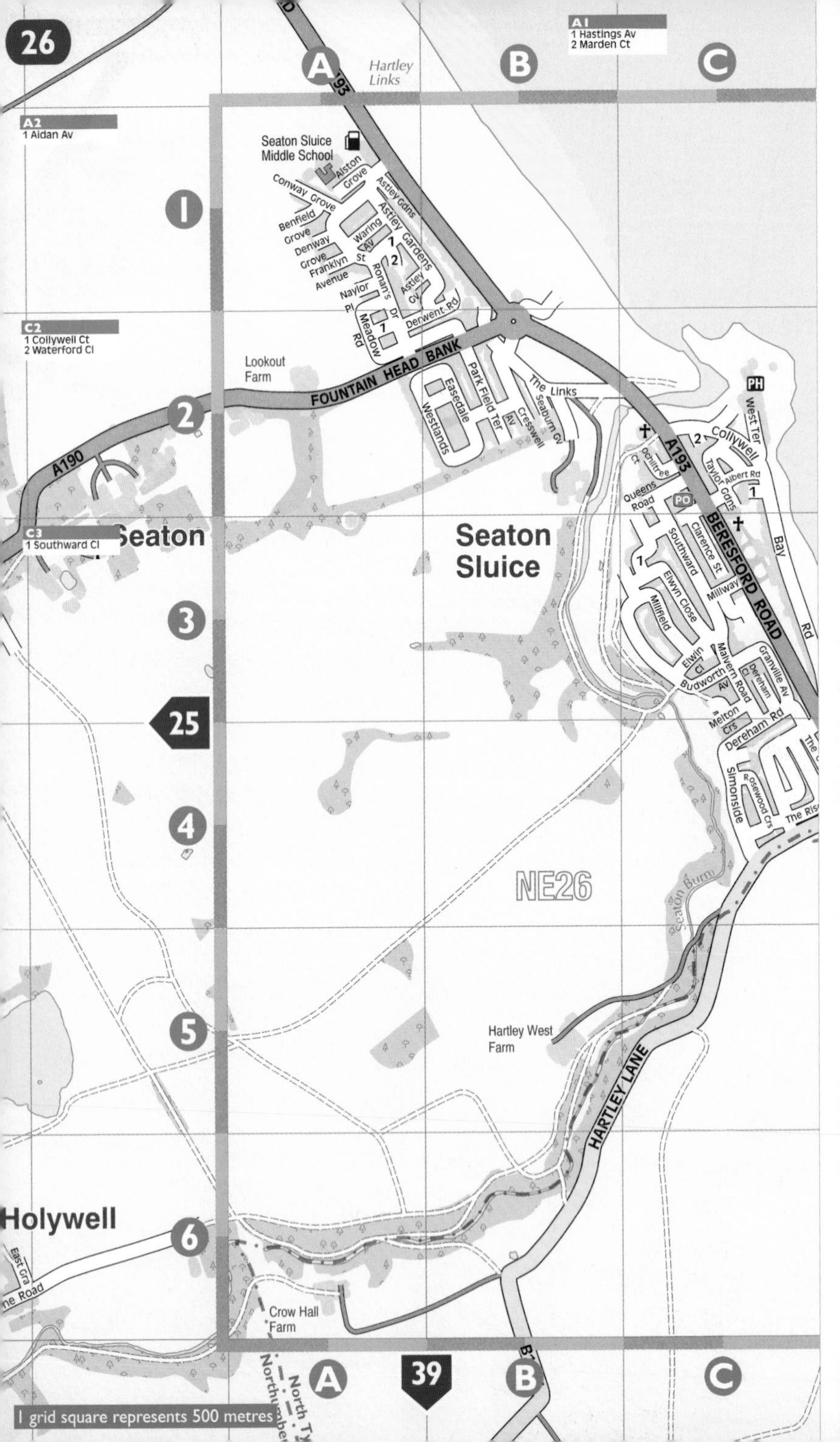
A1
1 Hastings Av
2 Marden Ct
A2
1 Aidan Av
C2
1 Collywell Ct
2 Waterford Cl
C3
1 Southward Cl
A
B
C
1
2
3
4
5
6
25
39
Hartley Links
A193
Seaton Sluice Middle School
Alston Grove
Conway Grove
Astley Gdns
Astley Gardens
Benfield Grove
Denway Grove
Waring Av
Franklyn St
Avenue
Naylor Pl
Ronan's Dr
Astley Gv
Derwent Rd
Meadow Rd
FOUNTAIN HEAD BANK
Lookout Farm
Easedale
Westlands
Park Field Ter
Cresswell Av
The Links
Seaburn Gv
A190
Seaton
Seaton Sluice
West Ter
Collywell
Ochiltree Ct
Taylor Gdns
Albert Rd
Queens Road
PO
PH
BERESFORD ROAD
Southward
Clarence St
Bay Rd
Millway
Elwyn Close
Millfield
Elwin Cl
Malvern Road
Budworth Av
Dereham Cl
Granville Av
Melton Crs
Dereham Rd
Simonside
Rosewood Crs
The Rise
NE26
Seaton Burn
Hartley West Farm
HARTLEY LANE
Holywell
East Gra
Road
Crow Hall Farm
North Ty
Northumbe

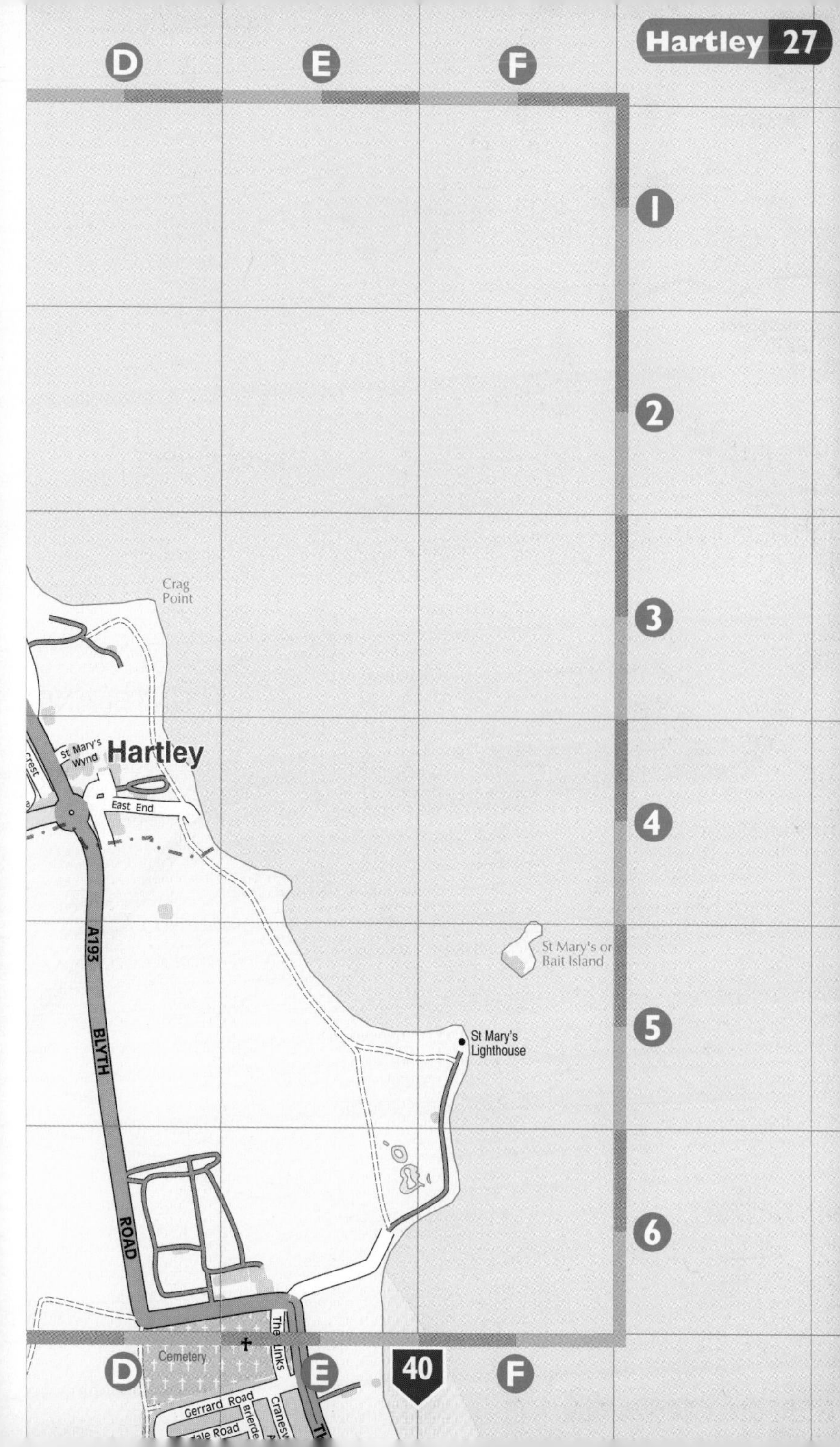
D
E
F
1
2
3
4
5
6
Crag Point
Hartley
St Mary's Wynd
East End
A193
BLYTH
ROAD
St Mary's or Bait Island
St Mary's Lighthouse
Cemetery
The Links
Gerrard Road
40

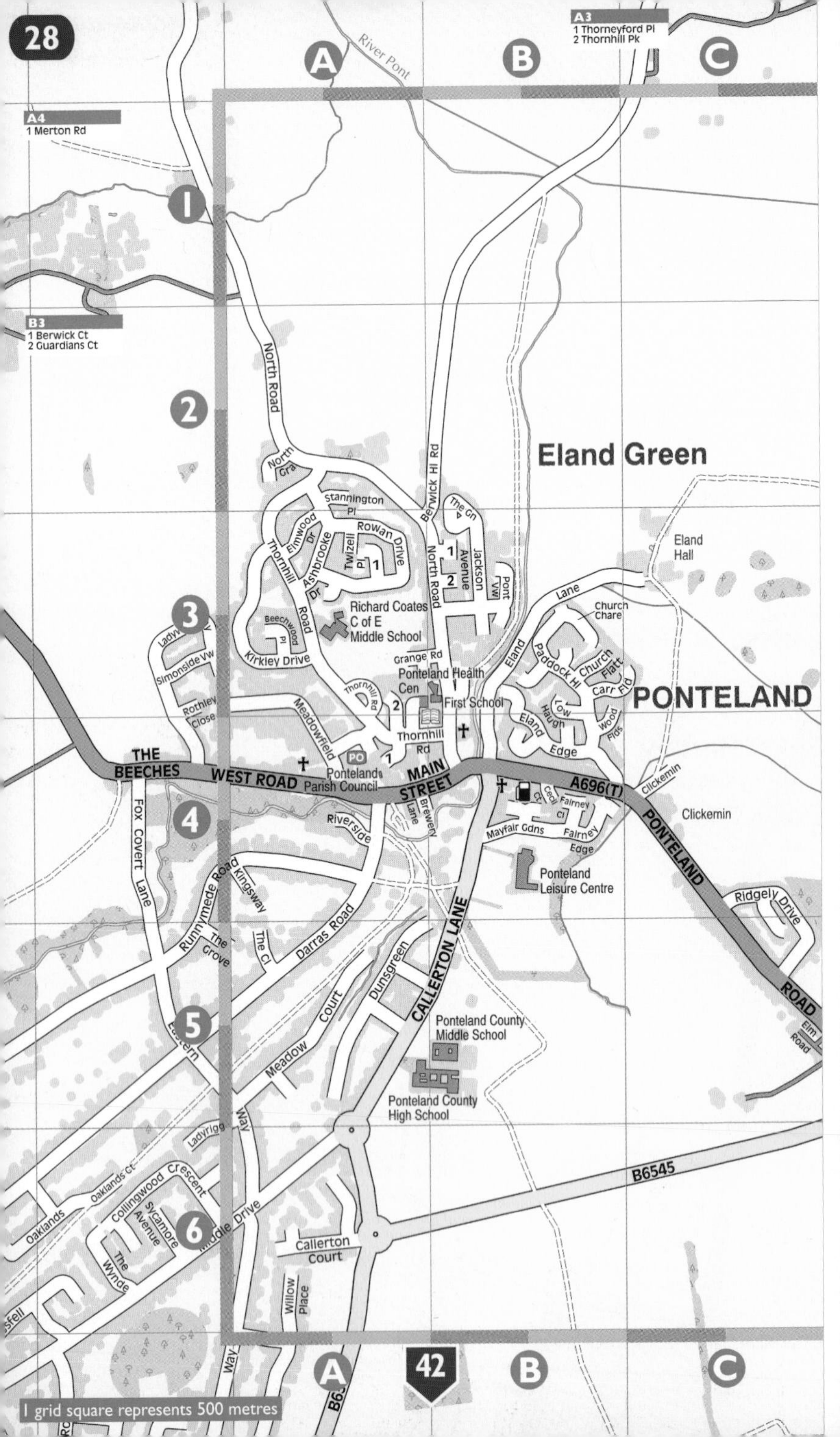
A3
1 Thorneyford Pl
2 Thornhill Pk
A4
1 Merton Rd
B3
1 Berwick Ct
2 Guardians Ct
River Pont
Eland Green
PONTELAND
Eland Hall
North Road
North Gra
Stannington Pl
Elmwood Dr
Rowan Drive
Twizell Pl
Ashbrooke Dr
Thornhill Road
Berwick Hl Rd
North Road
The Gn
Avenue
Jackson
Pont Vw
Lane
Church Chare
Richard Coates C of E Middle School
Beechwood Pl
Kirkley Drive
Simonside Vw
Rothley Close
Grange Rd
Ponteland Health Cen
First School
Thornhill Rd
Meadowfield
Eland
Paddock Hl
Church Flatt
Carr Fld
Low Haugh
Eland Edge
Wood Flds
Thornhill Rd
THE BEECHES
WEST ROAD
Ponteland Parish Council
MAIN STREET
A696(T)
Clickemin
Brewery Lane
Riverside
Cecil Ct
Fairney Cl
Mayfair Gdns
Fairney Edge
PONTELAND ROAD
Ponteland Leisure Centre
Fox Covert Lane
Runnymede Road
Kingsway
The Grove
The Cl
Darras Road
Dunsgreen
CALLERTON LANE
Ridgely Drive
Elm Road
Eastern Way
Meadow Court
Ponteland County Middle School
Ponteland County High School
Ladyrigg
Oaklands Ct
Oaklands
Collingwood Crescent
Sycamore Avenue
The Wynde
Middle Drive
B6545
Callerton Court
Willow Place
42
1 grid square represents 500 metres

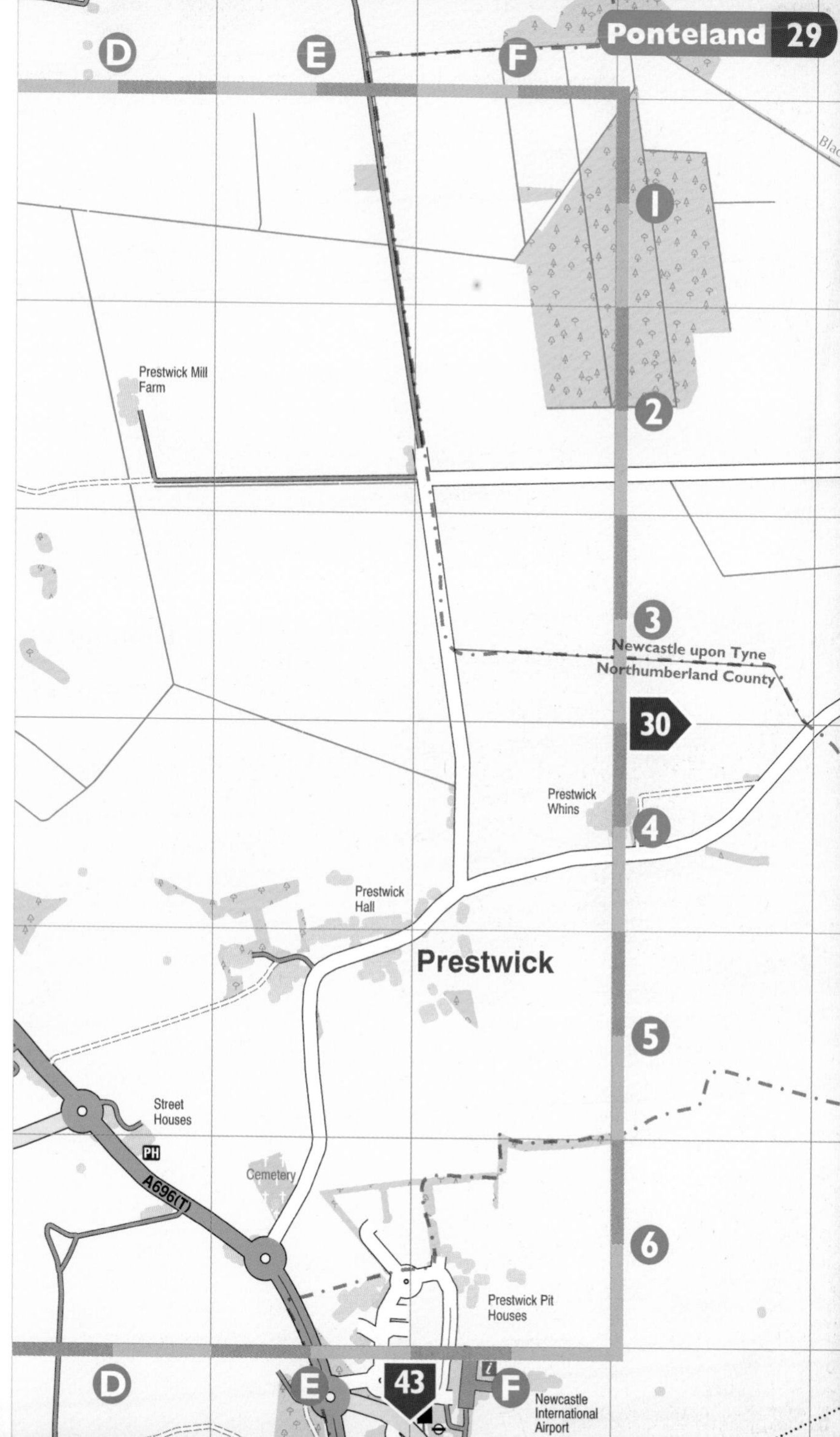
D
E
F
1
2
Prestwick Mill
Farm
3
Newcastle upon Tyne
Northumberland County
30
Prestwick
Whins
4
Prestwick
Hall
Prestwick
5
Street
Houses
PH
A696(T)
Cemetery
6
Prestwick Pit
Houses
D
E
43
F
Newcastle
International
Airport
Airport Station

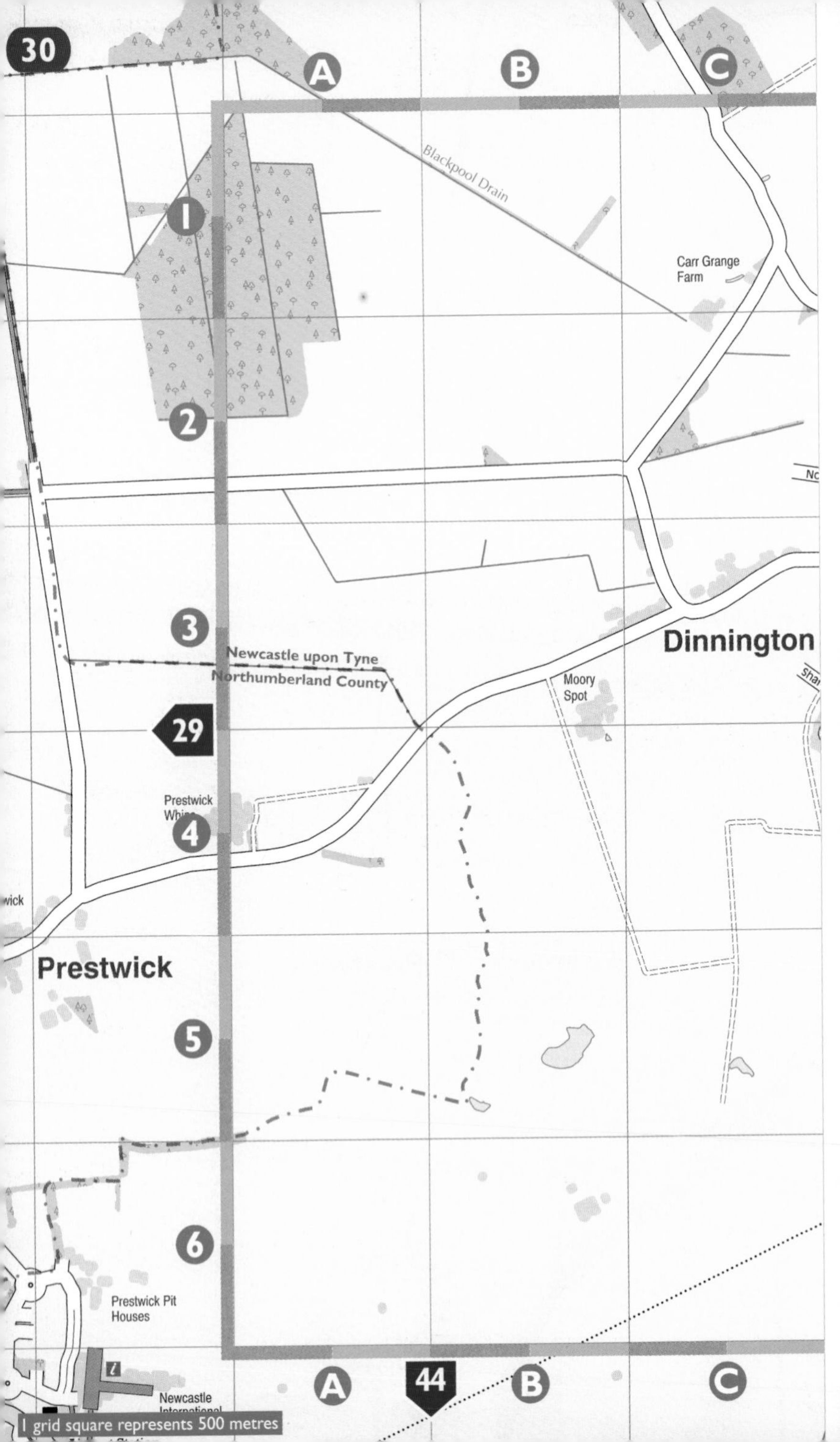

A
B
C
Blackpool Drain
1
Carr Grange
Farm
2
3
Newcastle upon Tyne
Northumberland County
Dinnington
Moory
Spot
29
Prestwick
4
Prestwick
5
6
Prestwick Pit
Houses
Newcastle
A
44
B
C
1 grid square represents 500 metres

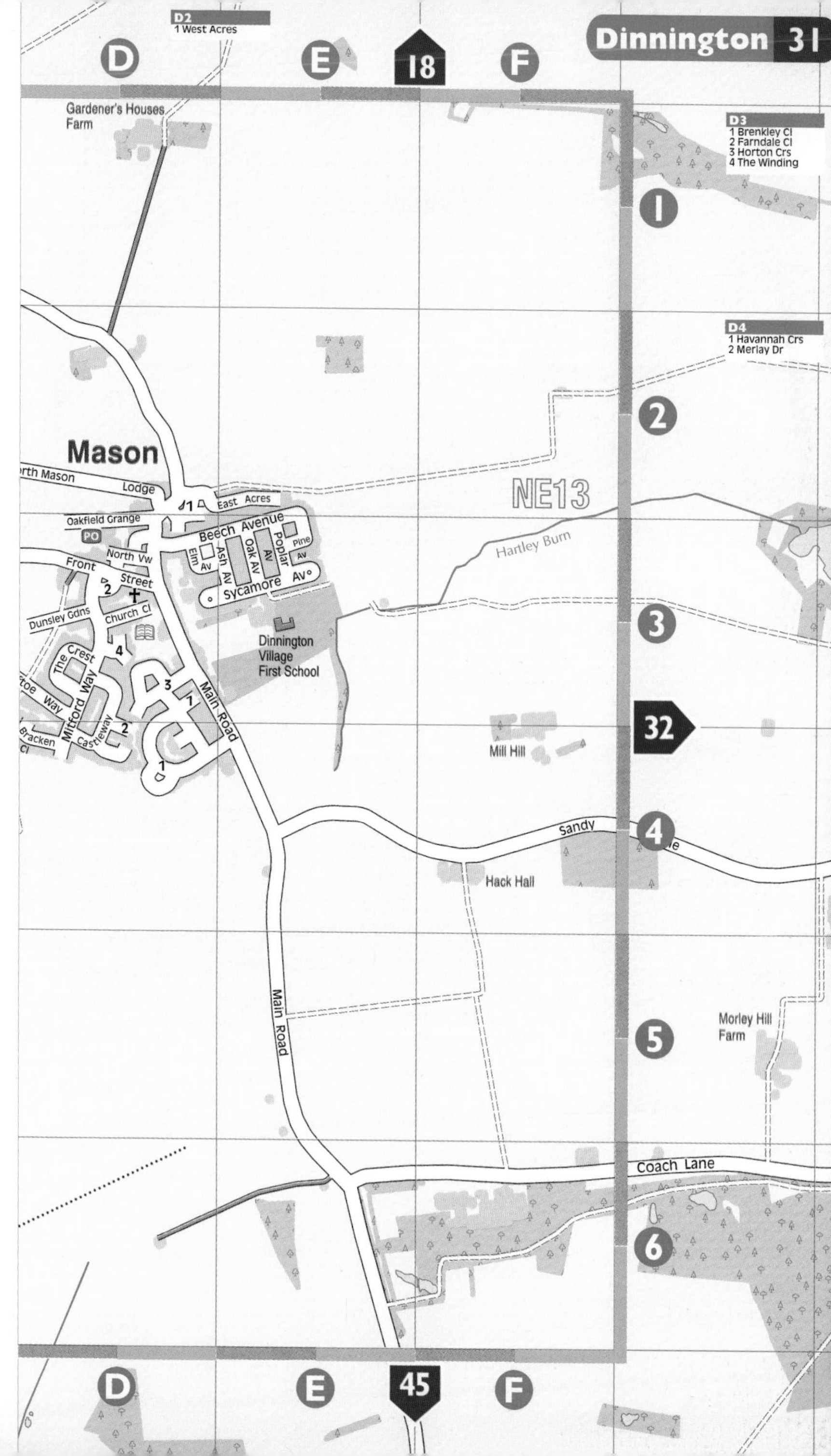
D2
1 West Acres
D3
1 Brenkley Cl
2 Farndale Cl
3 Horton Crs
4 The Winding
D4
1 Havannah Crs
2 Merlay Dr
D
E
18
F
Gardener's Houses Farm
Mason
North Mason Lodge
East Acres
Oakfield Grange
PO
Beech Avenue
Oak Av
Poplar Av
Pine Av
Elm Av
Ash Av
Sycamore Av
North Vw
Front Street
Dunsley Gdns
Church Cl
The Crest
Mitford Way
Castleway
Bracken Cl
Main Road
Dinnington Village First School
NE13
Hartley Burn
Mill Hill
32
Sandy Lane
Hack Hall
Morley Hill Farm
Coach Lane
1
2
3
4
5
6
D
E
45
F

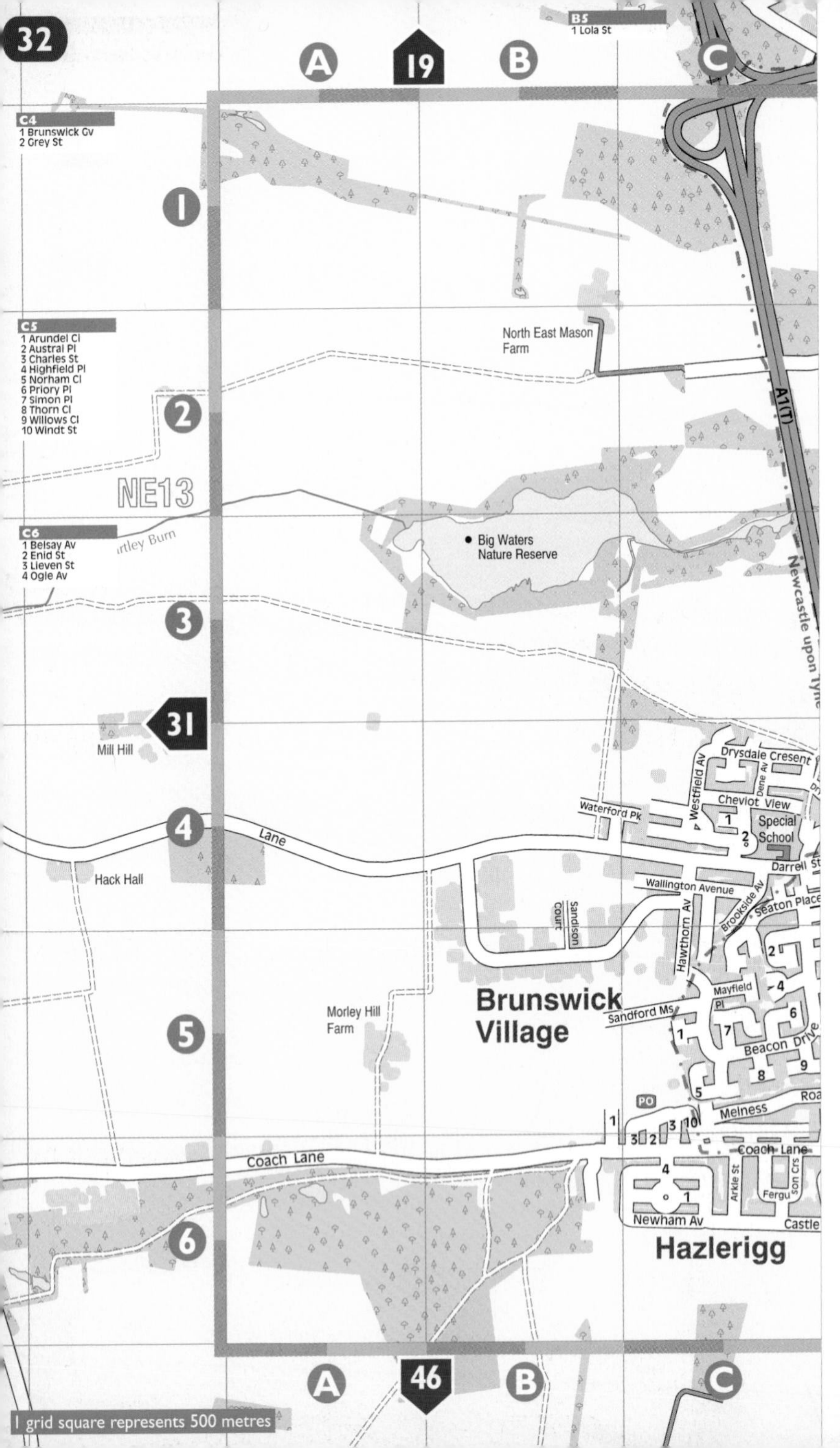
B5
1 Lola St
A
19
B
C
C4
1 Brunswick Gv
2 Grey St
C5
1 Arundel Cl
2 Austral Pl
3 Charles St
4 Highfield Pl
5 Norham Cl
6 Priory Pl
7 Simon Pl
8 Thorn Cl
9 Willows Cl
10 Windt St
C6
1 Belsay Av
2 Enid St
3 Lieven St
4 Ogle Av
NE13
North East Mason Farm
A1(T)
Big Waters Nature Reserve
Newcastle upon Tyne
31
Mill Hill
Drysdale Cresent
Westfield Av
Dene Av
Cheviot View
Waterford Pk
Special School
Lane
Hack Hall
Darrell St
Wallington Avenue
Sandison Court
Hawthorn Av
Brookside Av
Seaton Place
Brunswick Village
Mayfield Pl
Sandford Ms
Morley Hill Farm
Beacon Drive
PO
Melness
Road
Coach Lane
Coach Lane
Arkle St
Ferguson Crs
Newham Av
Castle
Hazlerigg
A
46
B
C
1 grid square represents 500 metres

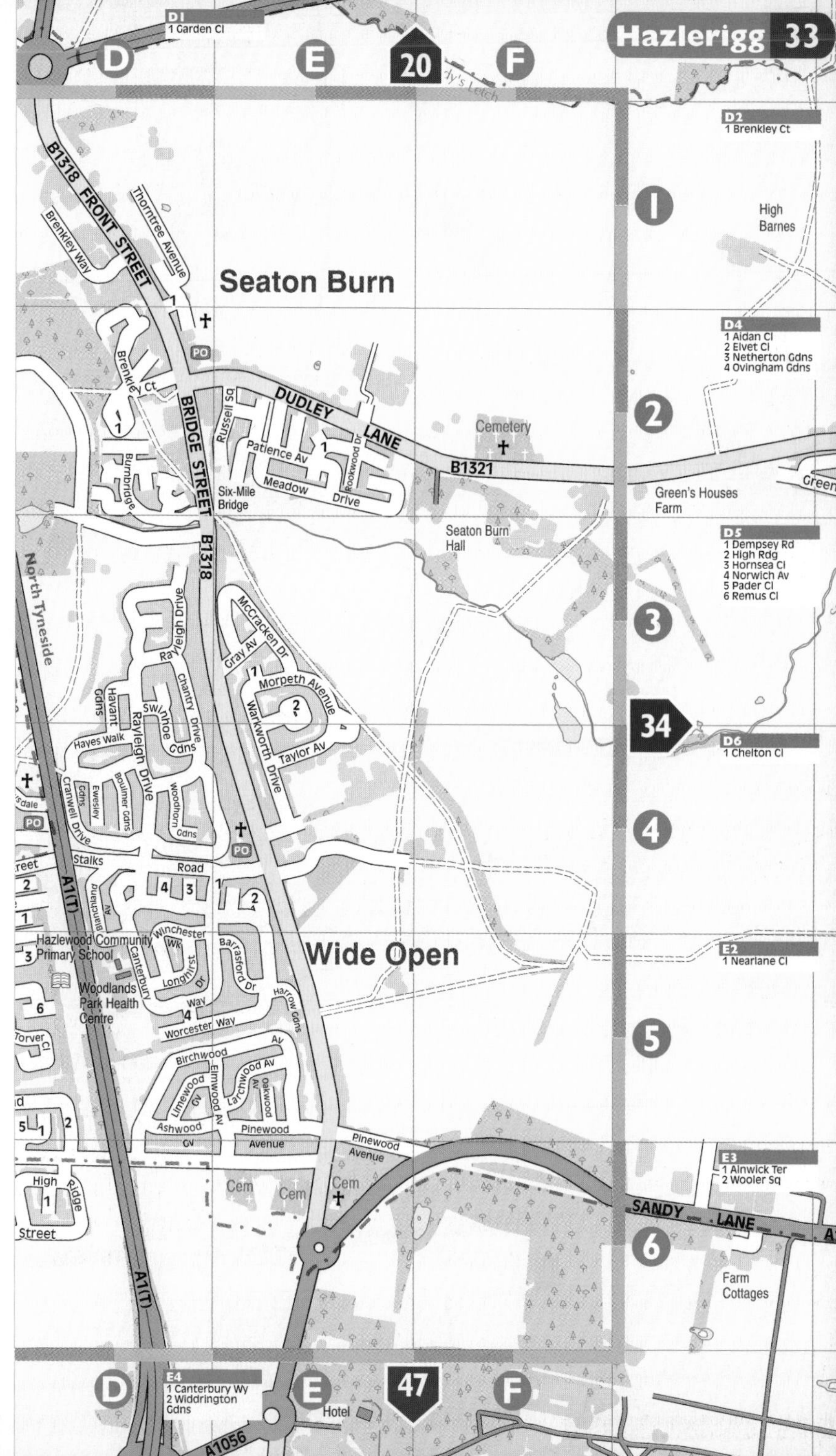
D1
1 Garden Cl
D
E
20
F
D2
1 Brenkley Ct
1
High
Barnes
B1318 FRONT STREET
Brenkley Way
Thorntree Avenue
Seaton Burn
D4
1 Aidan Cl
2 Elvet Cl
3 Netherton Gdns
4 Ovingham Gdns
PO
Brenkley Ct
BRIDGE STREET
Russell Sq
DUDLEY
LANE
Cemetery
2
Patience Av
Rookwood Dr
B1321
Burnbridge
Meadow
Drive
Six-Mile
Bridge
Green's Houses
Farm
Green
Seaton Burn
Hall
D5
1 Dempsey Rd
2 High Rdg
3 Hornsea Cl
4 Norwich Av
5 Pader Cl
6 Remus Cl
B1318
North Tyneside
Rayleigh Drive
McCracken Dr
3
Gray Av
Morpeth Avenue
Havant
Gdns
Chantry Drive
Swinhoe Gdns
Rayleigh Drive
Warkworth Drive
34
D6
1 Chelton Cl
Hayes Walk
Taylor Av
Cranwell Drive
Gdns
Ewesley
Boulmer Gdns
Woodhorn
Gdns
PO
4
PO
Stalks
Road
Street
A1(T)
Blanchland Av
Hazlewood Community
Primary School
Winchester
Wk
Canterbury
Barrasford Dr
Wide Open
E2
1 Nearlane Cl
Longhirst
Dr
Way
Woodlands
Park Health
Centre
Harrow Gdns
Torver Cl
Worcester Way
5
Birchwood
Av
Larchwood Av
Limewood
Gv
Elmwood Av
Oakwood Av
Ashwood
Gv
Pinewood
Avenue
Pinewood
Avenue
E3
1 Alnwick Ter
2 Wooler Sq
High
Ridge
Cem
Cem
Cem
SANDY
LANE
Street
6
A1(T)
Farm
Cottages
D
E4
1 Canterbury Wy
2 Widdrington
Gdns
E
47
F
Hotel
A1056

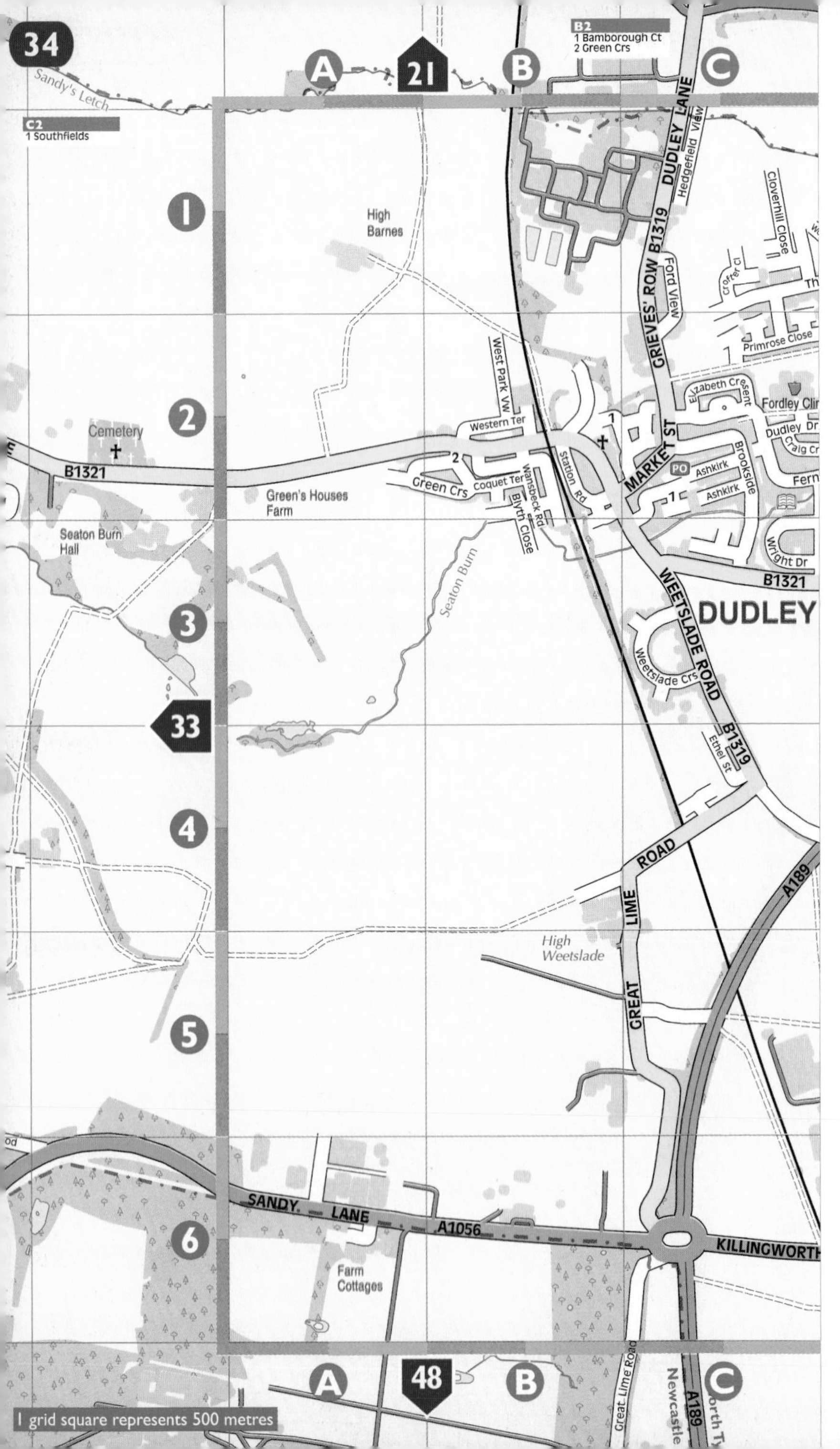
B2
1 Bamborough Ct
2 Green Crs
C2
1 Southfields
A
21
B
C
Sandy's Letch
DUDLEY LANE
Hedgefield View
Cloverhill Close
1
High
Barnes
B1319
GRIEVES' ROW
Ford View
Crofter Cl
Primrose Close
West Park Vw
2
Cemetery
Elizabeth Cresent
Fordley Clin
Western Ter
Dudley Dr
Craig Cr
B1321
2
MARKET ST
Station Rd
PO
Ashkirk
Brookside
Fern
Green Crs
Coquet Ter
Green's Houses
Farm
Wansbeck Rd
Blyth Close
1
Ashkirk
Seaton Burn
Hall
Seaton Burn
Wright Dr
B1321
WEETSLADE ROAD
DUDLEY
3
Weetslade Crs
33
B1319
Ethel St
4
ROAD
LIME
A189
High
Weetslade
GREAT
5
SANDY
LANE
A1056
6
KILLINGWORTH
Farm
Cottages
A
48
B
C
Great Lime Road
Newcastle
A189
1 grid square represents 500 metres

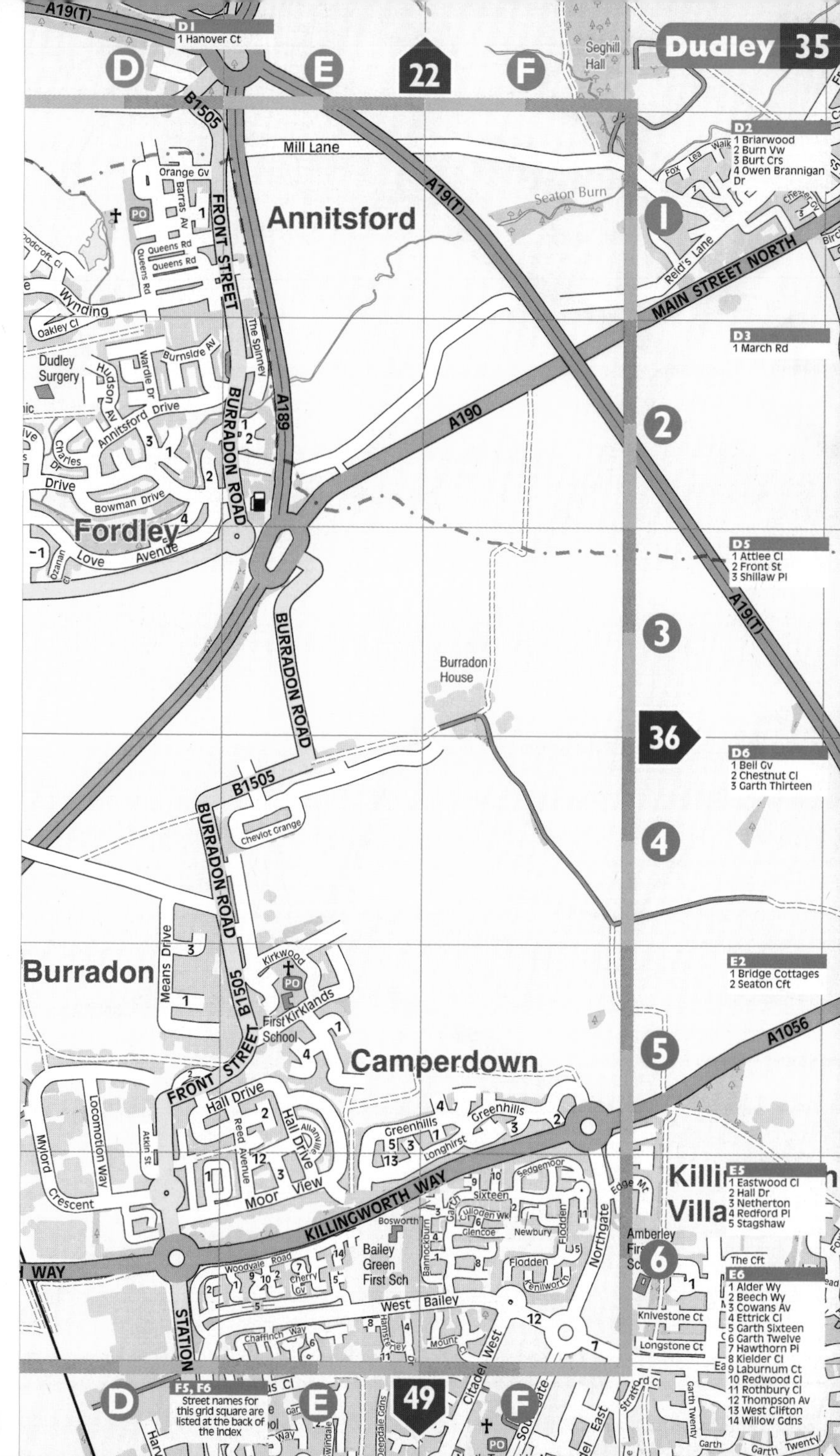
Dudley 35
22
36
49
D
E
F
1
2
3
4
5
6
A19(T)
D1
1 Hanover Ct
B1505
Mill Lane
Seghill Hall
Seaton Burn
Annitsford
Orange Gv
Barras Av
Queens Rd
FRONT STREET
BURRADON ROAD
A189
A190
The Spinney
Wynding
Oakley Cl
Dudley Surgery
Hudson Av
Wardle Dr
Burnside Av
Annitsford Drive
Charles Dr
Drive
Bowman Drive
Fordley
Love Avenue
Ozanan Cl
D2
1 Briarwood
2 Burn Vw
3 Burt Crs
4 Owen Brannigan Dr
Reid's Lane
MAIN STREET NORTH
D3
1 March Rd
D5
1 Attlee Cl
2 Front St
3 Shillaw Pl
Burradon House
D6
1 Bell Gv
2 Chestnut Cl
3 Garth Thirteen
Cheviot Grange
E2
1 Bridge Cottages
2 Seaton Cft
Burradon
Means Drive
Kirkwood
Kirklands
First School
Camperdown
A1056
Hall Drive
Reed Avenue
Allanville
Moor View
Locomotion Way
Mylord Crescent
Atkin St
Greenhills
Longhirst
KILLINGWORTH WAY
Sedgemoor
Sixteen
Culloden Wk
Glencoe
Newbury
Flodden
Northgate
Edge Mt
Bosworth
Bannockburn
Garth
Bailey Green First Sch
Woodvale Road
Cherry Gv
West Bailey
Kenilworth
Chaffinch Way
Hamsterley Dr
Mount Cl
West
Citadel
STATION
E5
1 Eastwood Cl
2 Hall Dr
3 Netherton
4 Redford Pl
5 Stagshaw
Amberley
The Cft
E6
1 Alder Wy
2 Beech Wy
3 Cowans Av
4 Ettrick Cl
5 Garth Sixteen
6 Garth Twelve
7 Hawthorn Pl
8 Kielder Cl
9 Laburnum Ct
10 Redwood Cl
11 Rothbury Cl
12 Thompson Av
13 West Clifton
14 Willow Gdns
Knivestone Ct
Longstone Ct
Garth Twenty
F5, F6
Street names for this grid square are listed at the back of the index
Deepdale Gdns
Swindale
Stratford Cl

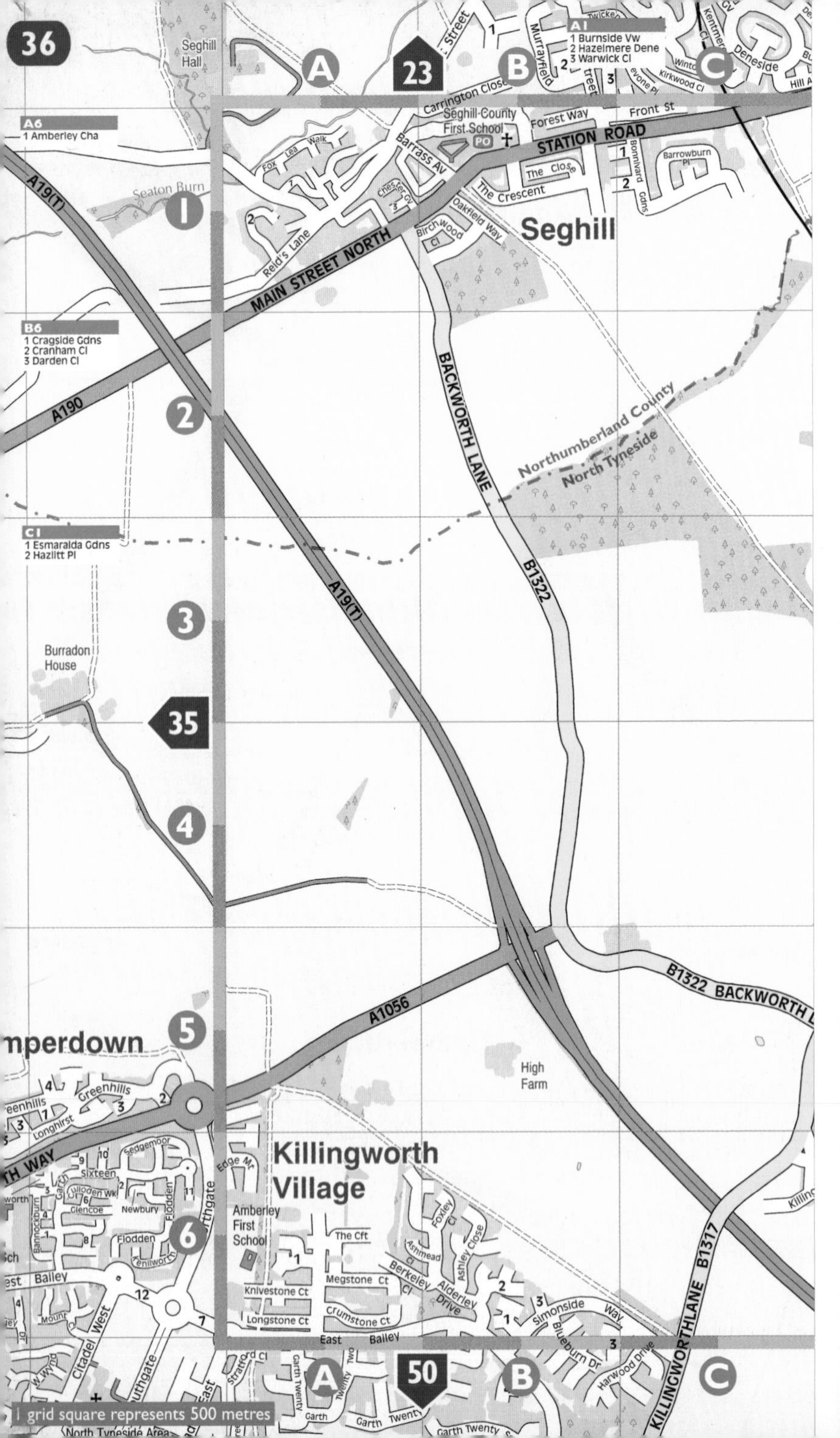

Seghill Hall
A
23
B
C
A1
1 Burnside Vw
2 Hazelmere Dene
3 Warwick Cl
A6
1 Amberley Cha
Seaton Burn
1
Carrington Close
Seghill County First School
Forest Way
Front St
STATION ROAD
Barrass Av
Fox Lea Walk
Reid's Lane
Chester Gv
The Close
The Crescent
Barrowburn Pl
Bonnivard Gdns
Oakfield Way
Birchwood Cl
Seghill
MAIN STREET NORTH
A19(T)
B6
1 Cragside Gdns
2 Cranham Cl
3 Darden Cl
A190
2
BACKWORTH LANE
Northumberland County
North Tyneside
C1
1 Esmaralda Gdns
2 Hazlitt Pl
B1322
3
Burradon House
35
4
B1322 BACKWORTH L
A1056
5
mperdown
High Farm
Greenhills
Longhirst
Killingworth Village
Sedgemoor
Sixteen
Culloden Wk
Glencoe
Newbury
Flodden
Kenilworth
Bannockburn
Amberley First School
The Cft
Megstone Ct
Knivestone Ct
Longstone Ct
Crumstone Ct
Foxley Cl
Ashmead Cl
Ashley Close
Berkeley Cl
Alderley Drive
Simonside Way
Bluebell Dr
Harwood Drive
KILLINGWORTH LANE B1317
East Bailey
Citadel West
6
50
A
B
C
1 grid square represents 500 metres
North Tyneside Area

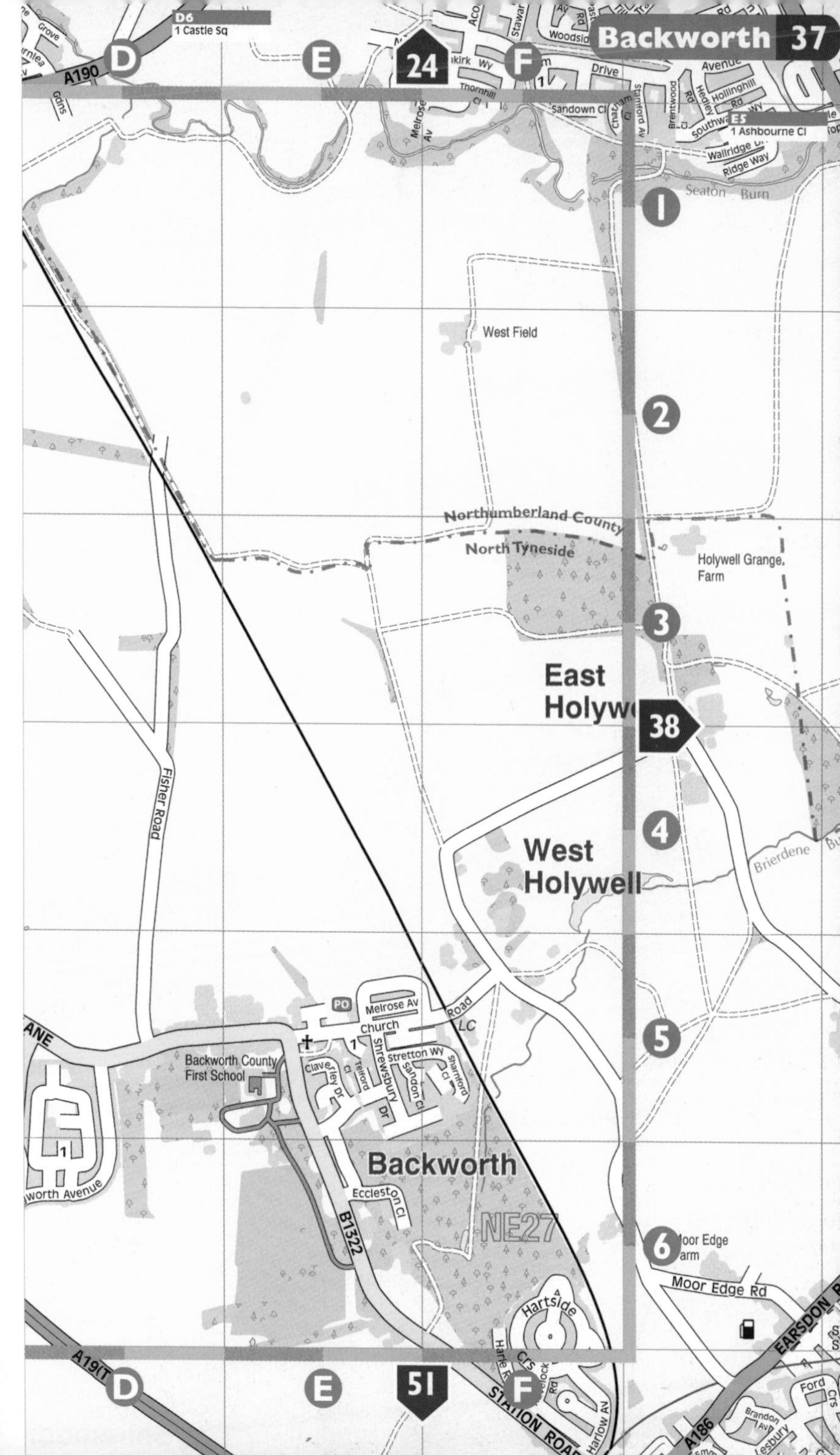

D6
1 Castle Sq
D
E
24
F
A190
Grove
Gdns
Thornhill Cl
Melrose Av
Drive
Avenue
Woodside
Sandown Cl
Chatham Cl
Stamford Av
Brentwood Cl
Hedley Rd
Hollinghill Rd
Southway
E5
1 Ashbourne Cl
Wallridge Dr
Ridge Way
Seaton Burn
1
West Field
2
Northumberland County
North Tyneside
Holywell Grange Farm
3
East Holywell
38
Fisher Road
4
West Holywell
Brierdene Burn
PO
Melrose Av
Church
Road
LC
5
Backworth County First School
Claverley Dr
Telford Cl
Shrewsbury Dr
Stretton Wy
Sandon Cl
Sharnford Cl
Backworth
Eccleston Cl
B1322
NE27
6
Moor Edge Farm
Moor Edge Rd
Hartside Crs
EARSDON RD
A19(T)
D
E
51
F
STATION ROAD
Harlow Av
A186
Ford Crs
Brandon Av
Lesbury

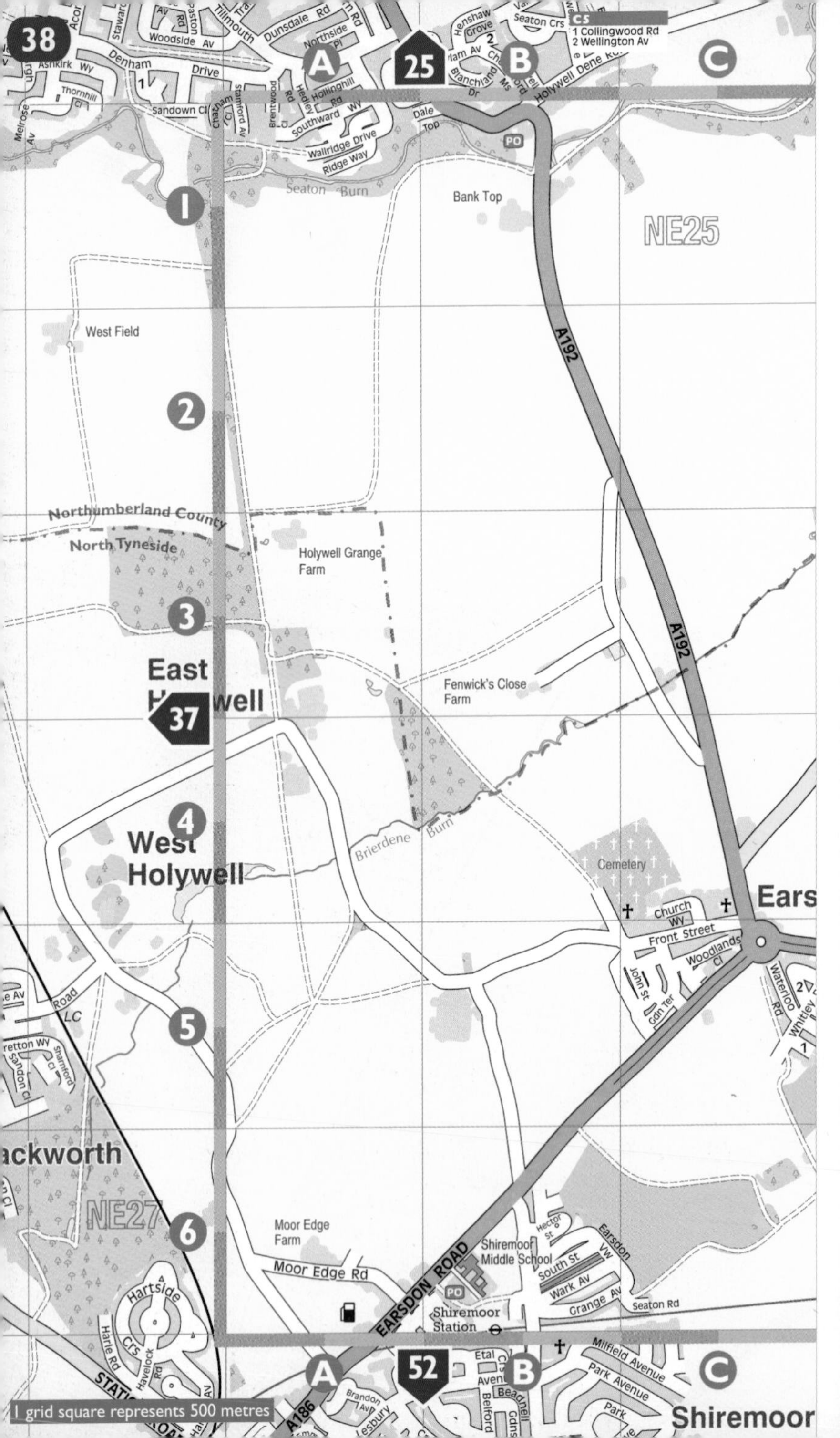

C5
1 Collingwood Rd
2 Wellington Av
25
A
B
C
Woodside Av
Denham Drive
Dunsdale Rd
Northside Pl
Hollinghill Rd
Southward Wy
Wallridge Drive
Ridge Way
Sandown Cl
Thornhill Cl
Ashkirk Wy
Stamford Av
Chatham Cl
Brentwood Cl
Hedley Rd
Henshaw Grove
Seaton Crs
Holywell Dene Rd
Blanchland Dr
Dale Top
PO
Seaton Burn
Bank Top
NE25
West Field
A192
Northumberland County
North Tyneside
Holywell Grange Farm
Fenwick's Close Farm
East Holywell
37
West Holywell
Brierdene Burn
Cemetery
Church Wy
Front Street
Woodlands Cl
John St
Gdn Ter
Waterloo Rd
Whitley
Road
LC
Sandon Cl
Shamford Cl
NE27
Hartside Crs
Harle Rd
Havelock Rd
Moor Edge Farm
Moor Edge Rd
EARSDON ROAD
Shiremoor Middle School
Hector St
Earsdon Vw
South St
Wark Av
Grange Av
Seaton Rd
Shiremoor Station
A186
52
Etal Crs
Beadnell Gdns
Belford
Brandon Av
Milfield Avenue
Park Avenue
Park
Shiremoor
1
2
3
4
5
6

D6
1 Harewood Crs
D
E
26
F
Crow Hall Farm
B1325
North Tyneside
Northumberland County
E4
1 Dovecote Cl
Gerrard Road
Garsdale Road
Westley Cl
Westley Av
Hastings
F5
1 Newsteads Cl
Brierdene Burn
Brier Dene Farm
1
2
Whitley Lodge First School
Glebe School
St Lucia Close
Woodburn Drive
Claremont Road
Claremont Surgery
Carolyn Wy
Carolyn Crs
Willoughby Drive
Cragside
Longridge Drive
Monkridge
Ross Wy
Rothley Wy
Beaumont Drive
Beaconsfield Cl
Darvall Cl
Dipton Rd
Dachet Rd
Chevington Gv
Earnshaw Way
Hillsden Rd
Haddington Rd
Huntly Rd
Gainsborough Cl
Gainsborough Road
Hertford Cl
Hascombe Cl
Cranleigh Pl
Craster Cl
3
40
HARTLEY LANE
Well Rdg Pk
Well Rdg Cl
Caseton Close
Westgate Cl
Red House
The Ridings
First School
The Chesters
Beaumont Park Surgery
Hepscott Dr
MONKSEATON DRIVE
Whitley Bay High School
4
Melbury
Ashbury Drive
Thornbury Dr
Cheldon Cl
Mill Dyke Cl
North Ridge
Berrishill Gv
Tollis Cl
Monkseaton
Alder Gv
Deneholm
Denebank
Ivanhoe
The Gn
Hermiston
Hazeldene
Hillfield
Uplands
Valehead
Valley Gardens
Langdale
Hartley Avenue
Holywell
Birkdale
Chathill Cl
Elford Cl
Meadowfield
Lytham
Muirfield
Fairways Drive
Newsteads
Turnberry
Rosemount Wy
Carnoustie Ct
Sandown
West Monkseaton Station
sdon
A192
Monkseaton Rd
Holly Av
Nelson Rd
Hesleyside Rd
Redheugh Rd
Tarset Rd
Greystead Rd
Burnbank Av
Warwick Rd
Haddon Cl
Haddon Gn
Wilton Drive
Wilton Gdns
EARSDON ROAD
Kielder Road
Kielder Houxty Rd
Ludlow Dr
Hatfield Gdns
Wentworth Gdns
Arundel Drive
Church Cl
Sandringham Drive
Marina Drive
Marina Dr
Drive
First School
Otterburn Avenue
Otterburn Av
Thorntree
Harewood Crs
PO
5
The Dene
Seaton Crs
Windsor Road
Ashbrooke
Relton Ter
Back La
The Fold
Percy Ter
Street
Pykerley Rd
Front
Elmwood Rd
Woodleigh Road
Beechwood Av
Brantwood Avenue
Belmont
Mitchell Av
Westfield Av
Oakland Avenue
Eastfield
Holmwood Av
Meadow Rd
Dale Rd
Cauldwell
Monkseaton Clinic
Middle School
Bygate Rd
St George's Crs
Beverley Pk
Vernon Drive
6
Crawford Avenue
Wembley Avenue
Paignton Avenue
Closefield Grove
Bromley Avenue
First School
Eastward Gn
Holm Gn
Middle Gn
Fairfield Gn
Fair Gn
Fairfield Drive
Abbey Cl
Grange Cl
Grange Park
Medical Cen
Melbourne Crs
Seatonville Crs
Springfield Gv
Lena Av
Roker
Churchill Avenue
D
E
53
F
West Monkseaton
Cauldwell Avenue
Drumoyne
Canberra Av
Langley Av
Townsville Av
Selwyn Av
Gardens
A192
SEATON
Oaktree Gdns
Cedartree

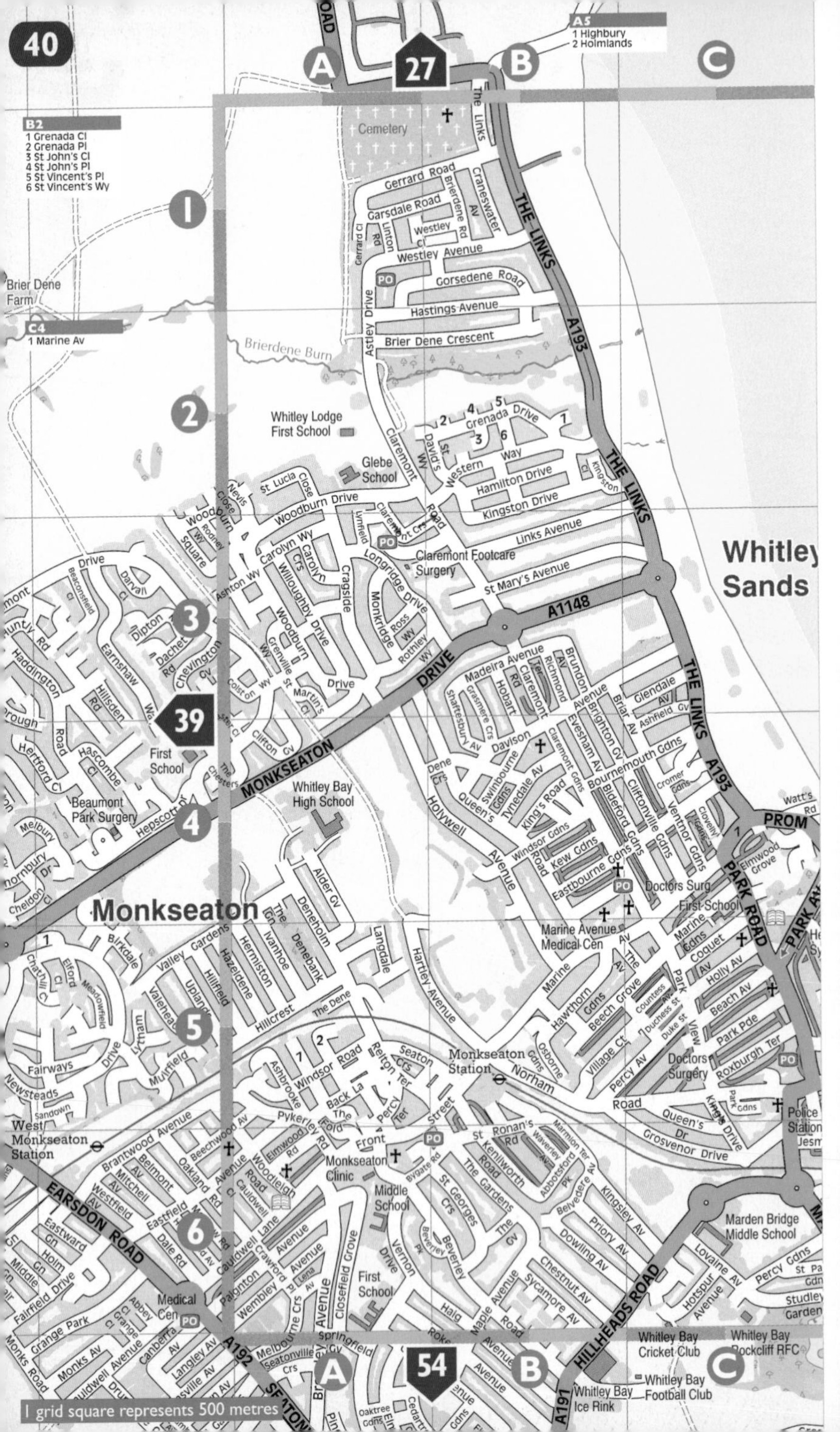
A5
1 Highbury
2 Holmlands
B2
1 Grenada Cl
2 Grenada Pl
3 St John's Cl
4 St John's Pl
5 St Vincent's Pl
6 St Vincent's Wy
C4
1 Marine Av
27
39
54
Whitley Sands
Monkseaton
Cemetery
Brier Dene Farm
Brierdene Burn
Whitley Lodge First School
Glebe School
Claremont Footcare Surgery
Whitley Bay High School
Beaumont Park Surgery
First School
Monkseaton Station
West Monkseaton Station
Monkseaton Clinic
Middle School
Marine Avenue Medical Cen
Doctors Surgery
Marden Bridge Middle School
Whitley Bay Cricket Club
Whitley Bay Rockcliff RFC
Whitley Bay Football Club
Whitley Bay Ice Rink
Medical Cen
Police Station
THE LINKS
A193
A1148
MONKSEATON DRIVE
EARSDON ROAD
A192
HILLHEADS ROAD
A191
PARK ROAD
PROM
1 grid square represents 500 metres

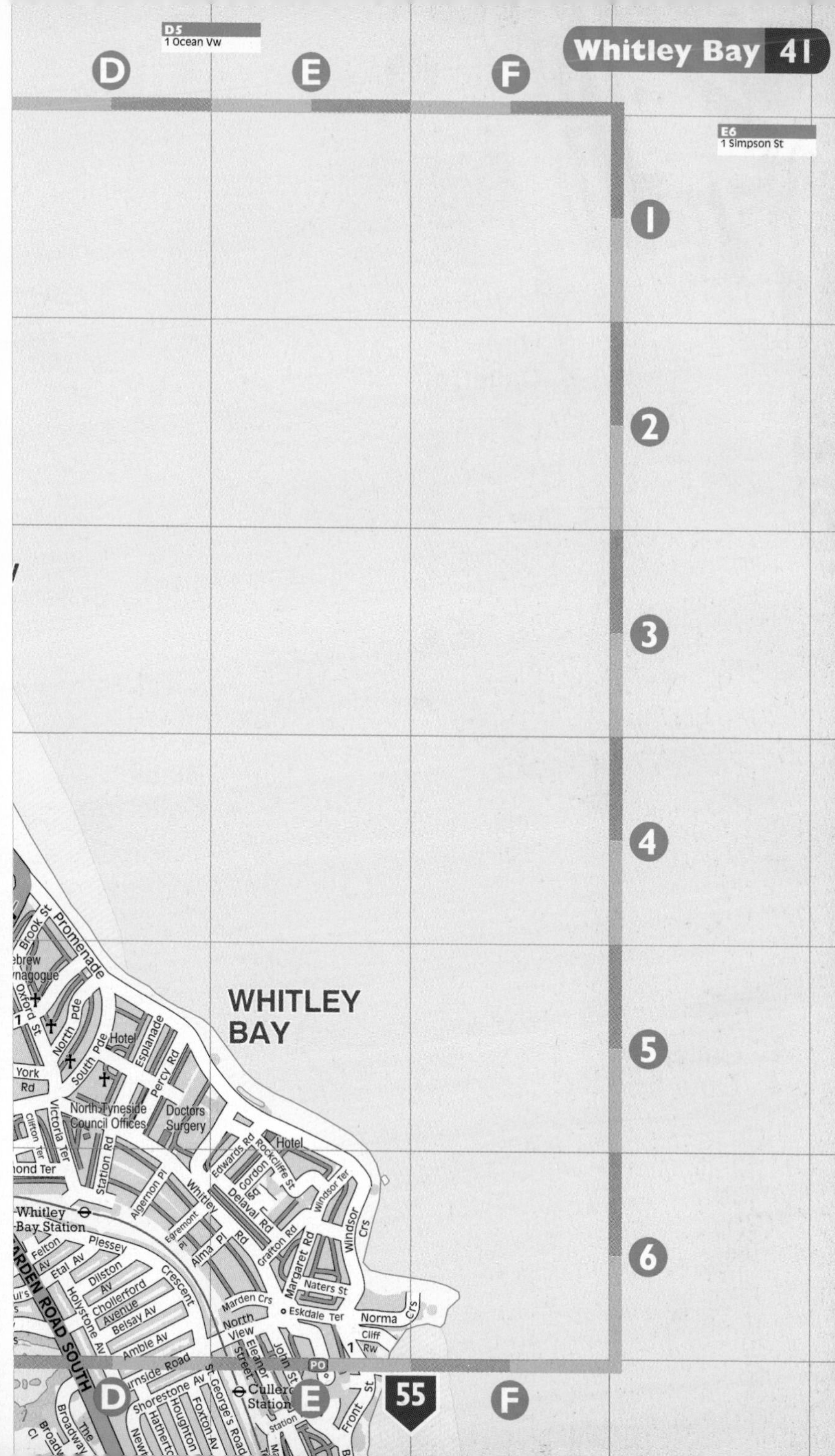
D5
1 Ocean Vw
E6
1 Simpson St
D
E
F
1
2
3
4
5
6
WHITLEY
BAY
Promenade
Brook St
Oxford St
North Pde
South Pde
Hotel
Esplanade
Percy Rd
York Rd
Victoria Ter
Clifton Ter
North Tyneside Council Offices
Doctors Surgery
Station Rd
Algernon Pl
Whitley Rd
Edwards Rd
Rockcliffe St
Gordon Sq
Hotel
Windsor Ter
Delaval Rd
Whitley Bay Station
Egremont Pl
Alma Pl
Grafton Rd
Margaret Rd
Windsor Crs
Felton Av
Plessey
Etal Av
Dilston Av
Chollerford Avenue
Crescent
Belsay Av
Holystone Av
Amble Av
Naters St
Marden Crs
Eskdale Ter
Norma Crs
Cliff Rw
North View
Eleanor Street
John St
PO
55
MARDEN ROAD SOUTH
Shorestone Av
St George's Road
Foxton Av
Houghton
Cullercoats Station
Front St
Broadway
The Broadway

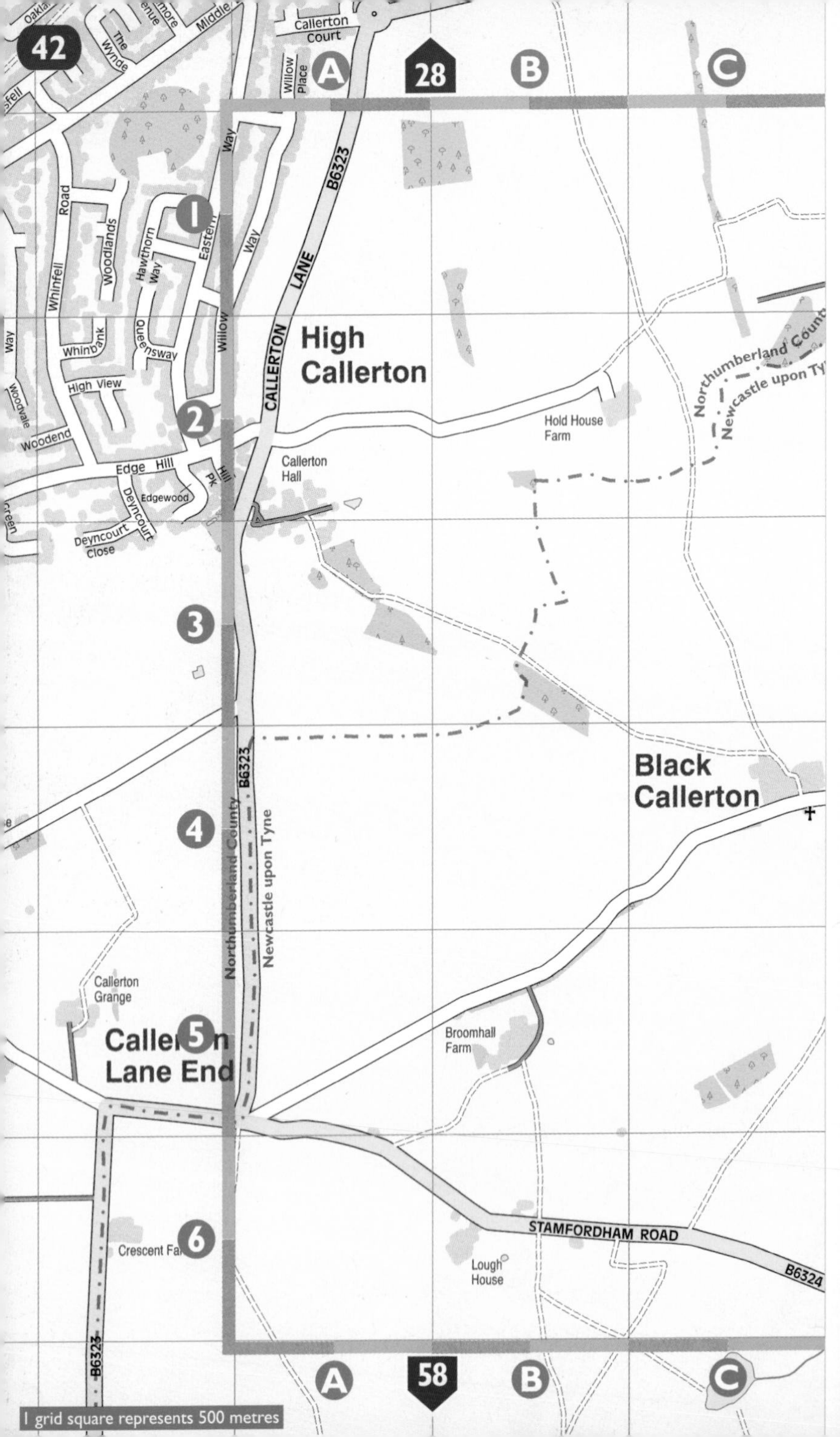

28
A
B
C
Callerton Court
Willow Place
Middle
The Wynde
Way
Road
Whinfell
Woodlands
Hawthorn Way
Eastern Way
Way
Willow Way
Queensway
Whinbank
High View
Woodvale
Woodend
Edge Hill
Hill Pk
Edgewood
Deyncourt
Deyncourt Close
B6323
CALLERTON LANE
High Callerton
Callerton Hall
Hold House Farm
Northumberland County
Newcastle upon Tyne
1
2
3
4
5
6
Black Callerton
B6323
Callerton Grange
Callerton Lane End
Broomhall Farm
Crescent Farm
Lough House
STAMFORDHAM ROAD
B6324
B6323
58
1 grid square represents 500 metres

D
E
29
Prestwick
Houses
Newcastle
International
Airport
Airport Station
I
B6918
A696(T)
Freightway
2
Woolsingt
Hall
Hotel
LC
Callerton
Park Station
Low
Luddick
3
B6918
44
Duke's
Meadow
The Ov
Grove
Hollywell
4
Woolsington
A696
5
Butterlaw
Callerton
6
Low
Newbiggin
Lowbiggin
Whorlton
Hall
D
E
59
F
Simon

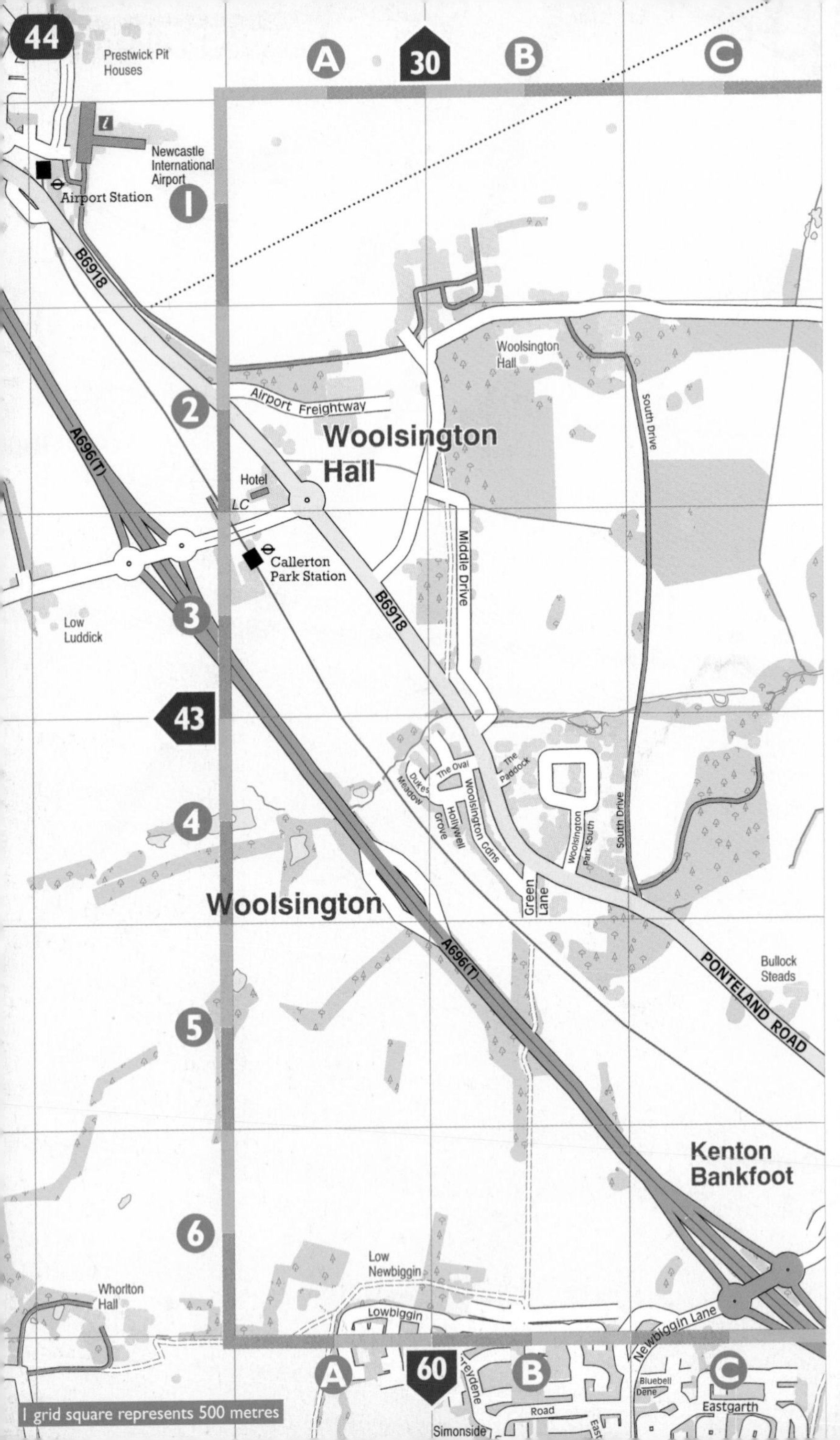

A
30
B
C
Prestwick Pit Houses
Newcastle International Airport
Airport Station
1
B6918
2
Airport Freightway
Woolsington Hall
Woolsington Hall
South Drive
Hotel
LC
Callerton Park Station
Middle Drive
B6918
A696(T)
Low Luddick
3
43
The Oval
The Paddock
Dukes Meadow
Woolsington Gdns
Hollywell Grove
Woolsington Park South
South Drive
4
Green Lane
Woolsington
A696(T)
PONTELAND ROAD
Bullock Steads
5
Kenton Bankfoot
6
Low Newbiggin
Whorlton Hall
Lowbiggin
Newbiggin Lane
A
60
B
C
Bluebell Dene
Eastgarth
Road
Simonside
1 grid square represents 500 metres

D5
1 Elstree Ct
D
E
31
F
D6
1 Honiton Ct
1
West Brunton
Farm
E4
1 Hersham Cl
Sunnyside
2
Brunton Lane
E5
1 Kirkham Av
3
46
E6
1 Belvedere Pkwy
2 Ilminster Ct
Ouse Burn
Brunton Bridge
Farm
4
Kingston
Launceston Cl
Huntingdon Cl
Hereford Ct
Park
Farn Ct
Road
Woodend Way
Chicheste Cl
Soulby Ct
Skelton Ct
Warcop
F4
1 Aberdeen Ct
2 Hersham Cl
Epsom Ct
Newcastle
Falcons Rugby
Football Club
Fawdon Lane
Hastings Av
Windsor Way
Lichfield Cl
Cranbrook Court
Hauxley
Cresswell
Fawdon
Brunton Rd
Brunton Road
Lancing Ct
Cranleigh Av
Windsor Way
Warwick Ct
5
Dorrington Road
Dykefield Avenue
Hersham Cl
Colnbrook Ct
Marlborough Ct
Amherst Road
Fawdon
Teddington Cl
Pinewood Cl
MAIN ROAD
Kingston
Park Station
Kingston Park
Primary School
Kingston
Park
F5
1 Faversham Ct
2 Hawkshead Ct
3 Lancaster Ct
4 Ousby Ct
5 Wraysbury Ct
LC
Station Road
The Crs
Bank Foot
Station
The Gables
PO
Witton Ct
Stuart Ct
Kingston Pk Av
Milverton Ct
Wilmington Cl
Velville Cl
Tudor Way
Petherton Ct
Belvedere
Retail Park
6
Linacre Cl
Warbeck Cl
Lydford Ct
Somerton Ct
Brunton Lane
Hillsview
Surgery
Rowan
Emden Rd
Thornbury Cl
PONTELAND ROAD
Redland Av
Carsdale Rd
A1(T)
Hillsview
A696(T)
Tudor Way
Sheen Ct
Dymock Ct
Urswick Ct
Beaminster Wy
Ebchester Ct
Beaminster Wy
Brodrick Cl
Saxondale Road
Apsley
Crs
Avenue
Kinross Drive
D
E
61
F
Fourstones
Quentin Av

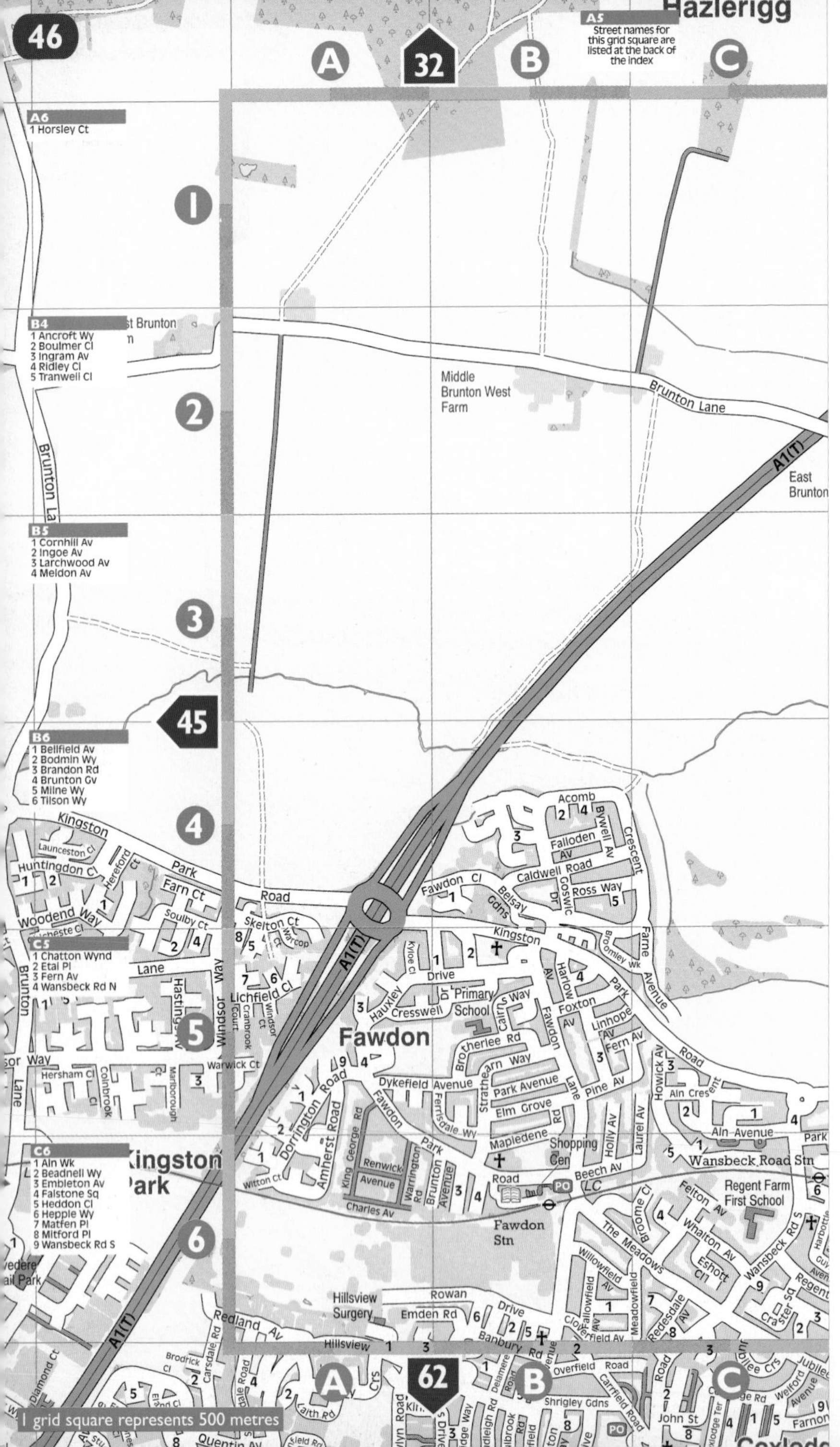
Hazlerigg
A5
Street names for this grid square are listed at the back of the index
A
32
B
C
A6
1 Horsley Ct
1
B4
1 Ancroft Wy
2 Boulmer Cl
3 Ingram Av
4 Ridley Cl
5 Tranwell Cl
Middle Brunton West Farm
Brunton Lane
2
Brunton La
A1(T)
East Brunton
B5
1 Cornhill Av
2 Ingoe Av
3 Larchwood Av
4 Meldon Av
3
45
B6
1 Bellfield Av
2 Bodmin Wy
3 Brandon Rd
4 Brunton Gv
5 Milne Wy
6 Tilson Wy
4
Kingston Park Road
Launceston Cl
Huntingdon Cl
Hereford Ct
Farn Ct
Woodend Way
Soulby Ct
Skelton Ct
Warcop Ct
C5
1 Chatton Wynd
2 Etal Pl
3 Fern Av
4 Wansbeck Rd N
Lane
Hastings
Windsor Way
Lichfield Cl
Court
Cranbrook
Windsor Ct
5
Hersham Cl
Colnbrook
Marlborough
Warwick Ct
Acomb
Falloden Av
Bywell Av
Crescent
Caldwell Road
Ross Way
Goswick Dr
Fawdon Cl
Belsay Gdns
Kingston
Bromley Wk
Farne Avenue
Kyloe Cl
Drive
Hauxley Dr
Cresswell
Primary School
Cairns Way
Harlow Av
Foxton Av
Park
Linhope Av
Fern Av
Fawdon
Brotherlee Rd
Strathearn Way
Dykefield Avenue
Ferrisdale Wy
Park Avenue
Elm Grove
Pine Av
Lane
Howick Av
Road
Aln Crescent
Aln Avenue
Wansbeck Road Stn
Dorrington Road
Amherst Road
King George Rd
Renwick Avenue
Warrington Rd
Brunton Avenue
Fawdon Park
Mapledene Rd
Shopping Cen
Holly Av
Laurel Av
Beech Av
Road
PO
LC
Witton Ct
Charles Av
Fawdon Stn
Regent Farm First School
Felton Av
Broome Cl
The Meadows
Whalton Av
Eshott Cl
Wansbeck Rd S
C6
1 Aln Wk
2 Beadnell Wy
3 Embleton Av
4 Falstone Sq
5 Heddon Cl
6 Hepple Wy
7 Matfen Pl
8 Mitford Pl
9 Wansbeck Rd S
Kingston Park
6
Hillsview Surgery
Rowan Drive
Emden Rd
Willowfield Av
Fallowfield Av
Meadowfield
Redesdale Av
Craster Sq
Regent
Redland Av
Carsdale Rd
Hillsview
Banbury Rd
Cloverfield Av
Jubilee Crs
Brodrick Cl
Diamond Ct
Overfield Road
Carrfield Road
Shrigley Gdns
John St
Welford Avenue
62
1 grid square represents 500 metres

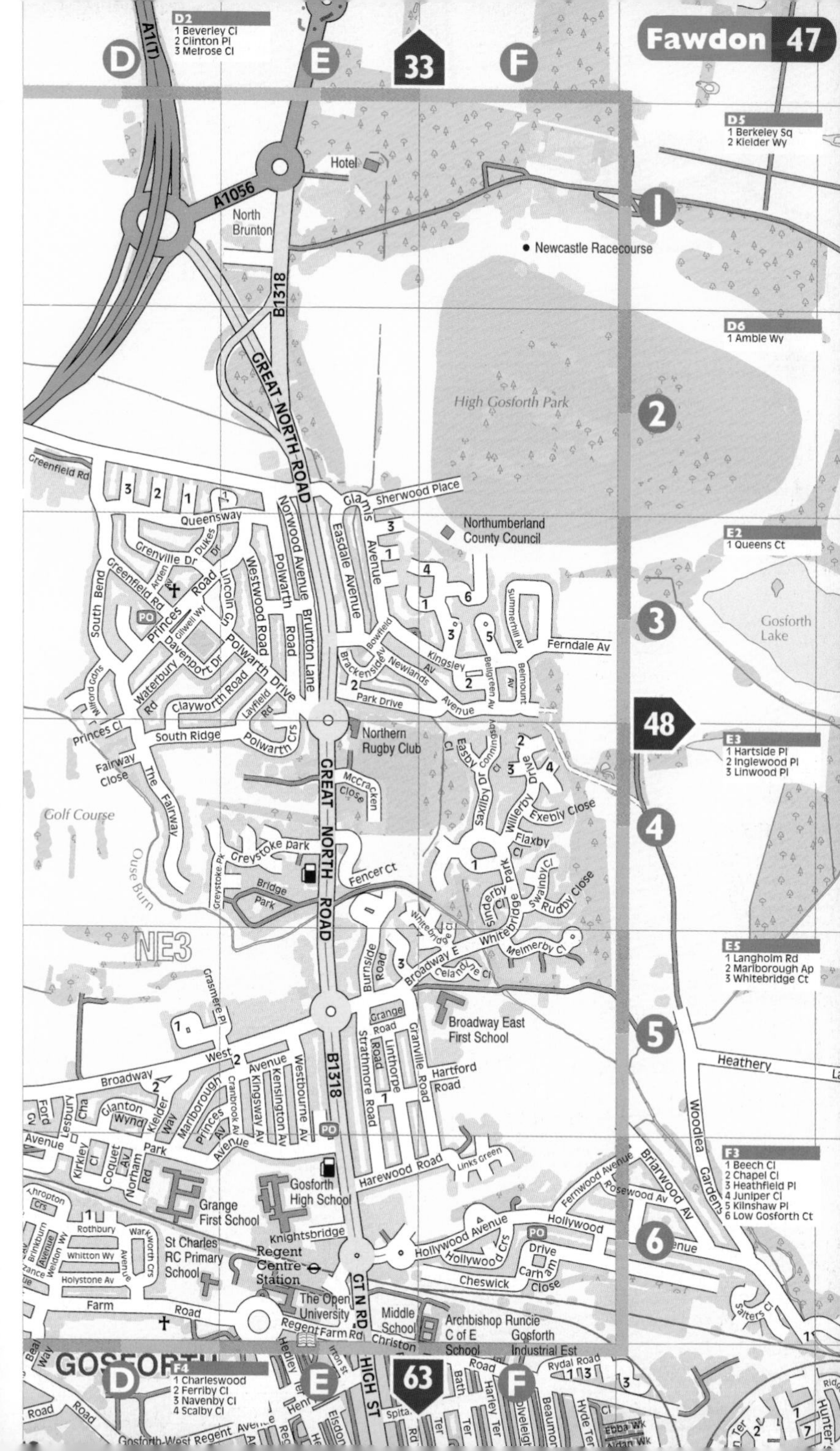
D2
1 Beverley Cl
2 Clinton Pl
3 Melrose Cl
D5
1 Berkeley Sq
2 Kielder Wy
D6
1 Amble Wy
E2
1 Queens Ct
E3
1 Hartside Pl
2 Inglewood Pl
3 Linwood Pl
E5
1 Langholm Rd
2 Marlborough Ap
3 Whitebridge Ct
F3
1 Beech Cl
2 Chapel Cl
3 Heathfield Pl
4 Juniper Cl
5 Kilnshaw Pl
6 Low Gosforth Ct
F4
1 Charleswood
2 Ferriby Cl
3 Navenby Cl
4 Scalby Cl
Hotel
North Brunton
Newcastle Racecourse
High Gosforth Park
Northumberland County Council
Gosforth Lake
Northern Rugby Club
Golf Course
Ouse Burn
NE3
Broadway East First School
Grange First School
Gosforth High School
St Charles RC Primary School
Regent Centre Station
The Open University
Middle School
Archbishop Runcie C of E School
Gosforth Industrial Est
GOSFORTH
A1(T)
A1056
B1318
GREAT NORTH ROAD
33
48
63

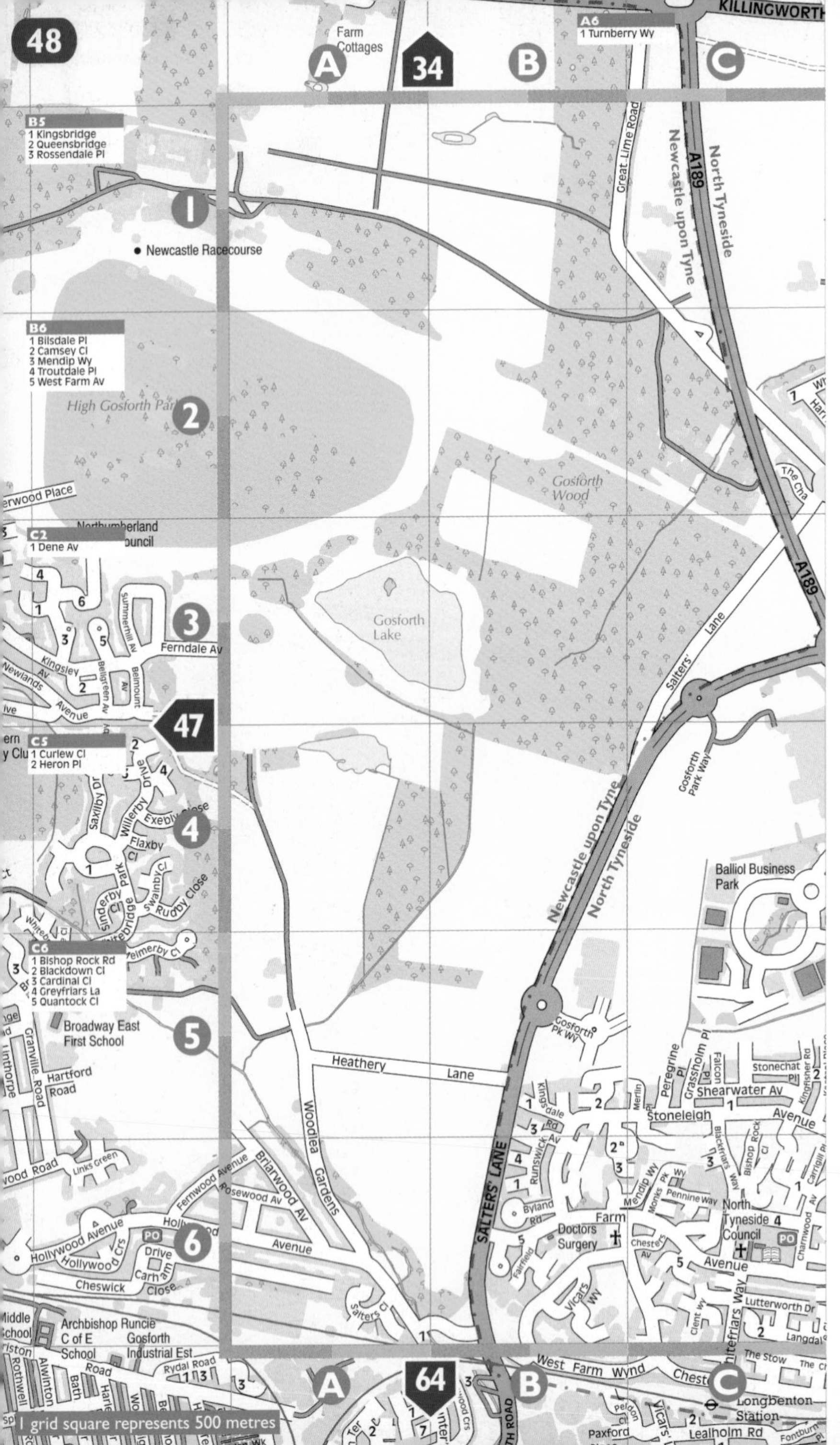
KILLINGWORTH
Farm Cottages
A
34
B
C
A6
1 Turnberry Wy
B5
1 Kingsbridge
2 Queensbridge
3 Rossendale Pl
Great Lime Road
Newcastle upon Tyne
North Tyneside
A189
1
Newcastle Racecourse
B6
1 Bilsdale Pl
2 Camsey Cl
3 Mendip Wy
4 Troutdale Pl
5 West Farm Av
High Gosforth Park
2
Gosforth Wood
The Cha
Northumberland
C2
1 Dene Av
Gosforth Lake
3
Summerhill Av
Ferndale Av
Kingsley Av
Bellgreen Av
Belmount Av
Newlands Avenue
Salters' Lane
47
C5
1 Curlew Cl
2 Heron Pl
Gosforth Park Way
Saxilby Dr
Willerby Drive
Exeby Close
4
Flaxby Cl
Swainby Cl
Rudby Close
Sinderby Cl
Whitebridge Park
Newcastle upon Tyne
North Tyneside
Balliol Business Park
C6
1 Bishop Rock Rd
2 Blackdown Cl
3 Cardinal Cl
4 Greyfriars La
5 Quantock Cl
Helmerby Cl
Broadway East First School
5
Granville Road
Hartford Road
Heathery Lane
Gosforth Pk Wy
Peregrine Pl
Grassholm Pl
Falcon Pl
Stonechat Pl
Kingfisher Rd
Shearwater Av
Merlin Pl
Kingsdale Rd
Stoneleigh Avenue
Woodlea Gardens
Runswick Av
Blackfriars Way
Bishop Rock Cl
Carrigill Pl
Links Green
Fernwood Avenue
Briarwood Av
Rosewood Av
Mendip Wy
Monks Pk Wy
Pennine Way
SALTERS' LANE
Byland Rd
Farm
North Tyneside Council
Charnwood Av
Hollywood Avenue
Hollywood Crs
Drive
6
Avenue
Doctors Surgery
Chester Av
Avenue
Fairfield
Carham Close
Cheswick
Vicars Wy
Whitefriars Way
Lutterworth Dr
Client Wy
Salters Cl
Langdale
Middle School
Archbishop Runcie C of E School
Gosforth Industrial Est
Road
Rydal Road
West Farm Wynd
The Stow
Chester
A
64
B
C
Longbenton Station
Alwinton
Bath
Rothwell
Peldon Cl
Vicars
Paxford
Lealholm Rd
Fontburn
TH ROAD
1 grid square represents 500 metres

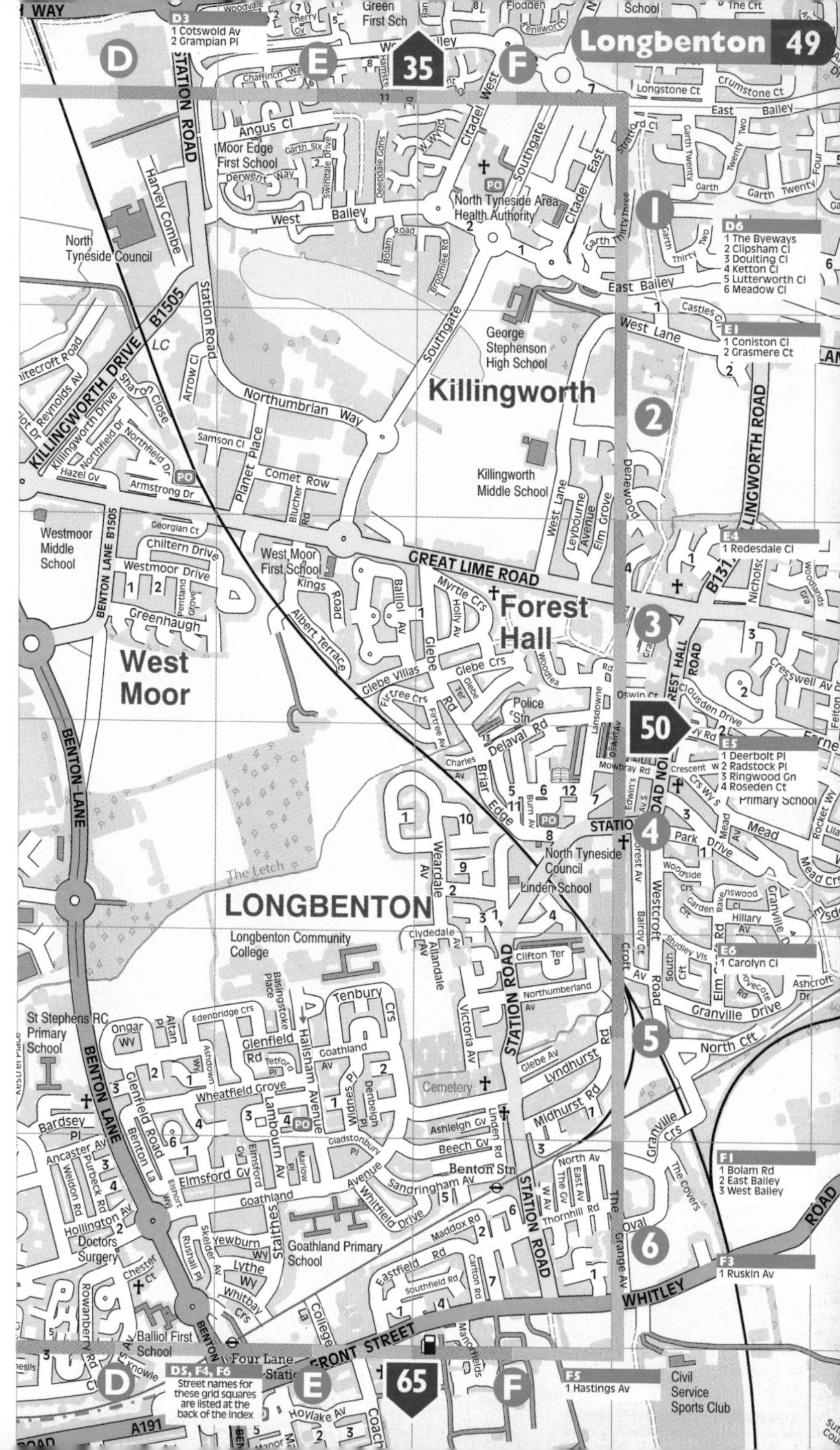
D
E
F
35
Green
First Sch
D3
1 Cotswold Av
2 Grampian Pl
STATION ROAD
Angus Cl
Moor Edge
First School
Derwent Way
West Balley
Citadel West
Southgate
PO
North Tyneside Area
Health Authority
Citadel East
Longstone Ct
Crumstone Ct
East Balley
Stratford Cl
Garth Twenty
Garth Twenty Four
Garth Thirty Three
D6
1 The Byeways
2 Clipsham Cl
3 Doulting Cl
4 Ketton Cl
5 Lutterworth Cl
6 Meadow Cl
Harvey Combe
North
Tyneside Council
Bolam Road
Broomlee Rd
East Balley
Castles Gn
West Lane
E1
1 Coniston Cl
2 Grasmere Ct
KILLINGWORTH DRIVE B1505
Station Road
Southgate
George
Stephenson
High School
Killingworth
Whitecroft Road
Reynolds Av
Killingworth Drive
Sharon Close
Arrow Cl
Northumbrian Way
KILLINGWORTH ROAD
Northfield Dr
Hazel Gv
Samson Cl
Planet Place
Comet Row
Killingworth
Middle School
Armstrong Dr
Blucher Rd
West Lane
Leybourne Avenue
Elm Grove
Denewood
E4
1 Redesdale Cl
Westmoor
Middle School
BENTON LANE B1505
Georgian Ct
Chiltern Drive
Westmoor Drive
Pentland Grove
West Moor
First School
Kings Road
GREAT LIME ROAD
Balliol Av
Myrtle Crs
Holly Av
Forest
Hall
B1317
Nicholson
Greenhaugh
Albert Terrace
Glebe Rd
Glebe Crs
FOREST HALL ROAD
Cresswell Av
West
Moor
Glebe Villas
Firtree Crs
Firtree Av
Woodlea
Oswin Ct
Clousden Drive
Police
Stn
Delaval Rd
Lansdowne Rd
50
E5
1 Deerbolt Pl
2 Radstock Pl
3 Ringwood Gn
4 Roseden Ct
BENTON LANE
Charles Av
Briar Edge
Mowbray Rd
Edwin's Av S
Crescent Way S
Primary School
Burn Av
PO
STATION
Park Drive
Mead Av
Mead Crs
Rocket Wy
Weardale Av
North Tyneside
Council
Linden School
Forest Av
Westcroft Road
Woodside Crs
Ravenswood Cl
Garden Cft
Hillary Av
Granville Dr
The Letch
LONGBENTON
Longbenton Community
College
Clydedale Av
Allandale Av
Clifton Ter
Balroy Ct
Studley Vls
South Cft
Elm Cft Rd
E6
1 Carolyn Cl
Ashcroft Dr
Croft Av
Basingstoke Place
Tenbury Crs
Northumberland Av
Granville Drive
St Stephens RC
Primary
School
Ongar Wy
Altan Pl
Edenbridge Crs
Glenfield Rd
Hailsham Avenue
Victoria Av
STATION ROAD
5
North Cft
Ashdown Wy
Tetford Rd
Goathland Av
Denbeigh Pl
Cemetery
Glebe Av
Lyndhurst Rd
Wheatfield Grove
Glenfield Road
Lambourn Av
Widnes Pl
Midhurst Rd
Granville Crs
Bardsey Pl
BENTON LANE
PO
Ashleigh Gv
Linden Rd
Ancaster Av
Purbeck Rd
Weldon Rd
Benton La
Elmsford Gv
Elmsford
Marlow
Gladstonbury Pl
Beech Gv
Benton Stn
North Av
East Av
The Gv
W Av
The Covers
F1
1 Bolam Rd
2 East Balley
3 West Balley
Hollington Av
Goathland
Avenue
Whitfield Drive
Sandringham Av
Thornhill Rd
Doctors
Surgery
Yewburn Wy
Staithes
Goathland Primary
School
Maddox Rd
Carlton Rd
STATION ROAD
The Grange Av
Oval
6
F3
1 Ruskin Av
Skelder Av
Rushall Pl
Lythe Wy
Chester Ct
Rowanberry Rd
Whitbay Crs
Eastfield Rd
Southfield Rd
WHITLEY ROAD
College
Balliol First
School
BENTON
FRONT STREET
Manorfields
Four Lane
Station
D5, F4, F6
Street names for
these grid squares
are listed at the
back of the index
65
F5
1 Hastings Av
Civil
Service
Sports Club
A191
Hoylake Av

36
A
B
C
A1
1 Green La
A2
1 East Stoneycroft
2 West Stoneycroft
A3
1 Clousden Gra
2 Earlington Ct
3 Errington Ter
4 Willowdene
A4
1 Ashwood Cl
2 Cedar Wy
3 East Forest Hall Rd
A5
1 Studley Vls
B1
1 Applewood
2 Downswood
3 Garleigh Cl
4 Garth Twenty Five
5 Garth Twenty Four
6 Goodwood
7 Greenwood
8 Hazelwood
9 Rosewood
C3
1 Roseberry Gra
C4
1 Humshaugh Cl
2 Margaret Dr
3 William Cl
Killingworth
Killingworth Moor
Palmersville
Benton
Forest Hall
NE12
North Tyneside Area Health Authority
Killingworth Middle School
East House Farm
Ivy Road Primary School
North Tyneside Council
Linden School
Police Sth
Cemetery
North Tyne Industrial Est
Bellway Industrial Est
Megabowl
East Benton Farm
Palmers Station
KILLINGWORTH LANE B1317
WEST LANE B1317
B1317 KILLINGWORTH ROAD
GREAT LIME ROAD
FOREST HALL ROAD
ROAD NORTH
STATION ROAD
WHITLEY ROAD
49
66
1 grid square represents 500 metres

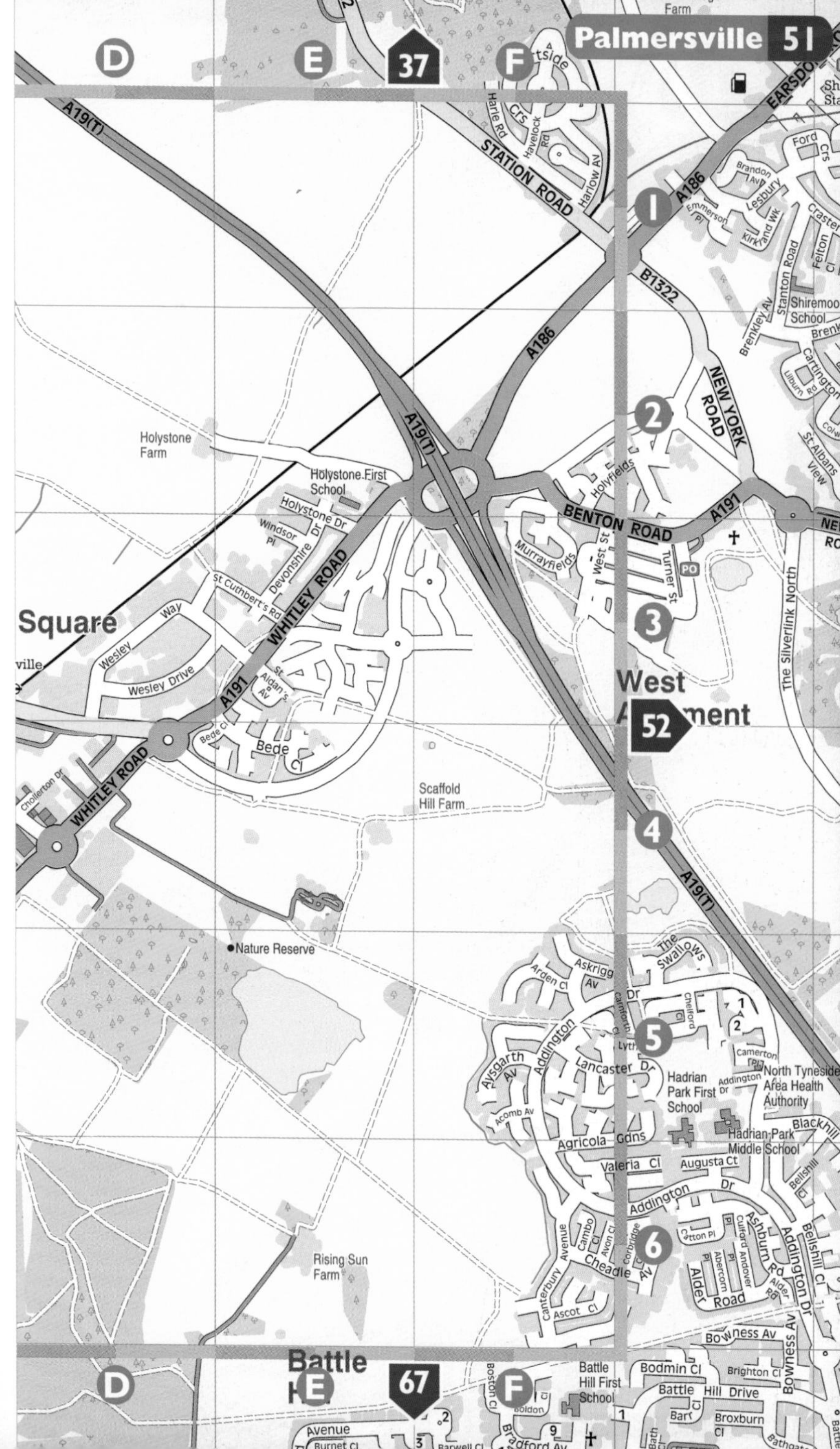
D
E
37
F
A19(T)
STATION ROAD
Harle Rd
Havelock Rd
Harlow Av
A186
B1322
NEW YORK ROAD
Emmerson Pl
Brandon Av
Lesbury
Kirkland Wk
Ford Crs
Craster
Felton Cl
Stanton Road
Shiremoor School
Brenkley Av
Cartington
Lilburn Rd
St Albans View
EARSDON
Farm
Holystone Farm
Holystone First School
Holystone Dr
Windsor Pl
Devonshire Dr
St Cuthbert's Rd
WHITLEY ROAD
Wesley Way
Wesley Drive
Square
A191
St Aidan's Av
Bede Cl
Bede Cl
Holyfields
BENTON ROAD
Murrayfields
West St
Turner St
PO
The Silverlink North
West Allotment
52
Scaffold Hill Farm
Chollerton Dr
Nature Reserve
The Swallows
Askrigg Av
Arden Cl
Carnforth Cl
Chelford
Addington
Aysgarth Av
Lancaster Dr
Lytham
Acomb Av
Hadrian Park First School
Camerton Pl
Addington Dr
North Tyneside Area Health Authority
Blackhill
Hadrian Park Middle School
Agricola Gdns
Valeria Cl
Augusta Ct
Bellshill Cl
Addington Dr
Cotton Pl
Clifford
Andover
Ashburn Rd
Alder Rd
Alder Road
Abercorn
Canterbury Avenue
Cambo Cl
Avon Cl
Corbridge Av
Cheadle Av
Ascot Cl
Bowness Av
Addington Dr
Bellshill Cl
Rising Sun Farm
Battle Hill
D
E
67
F
Boston Cl
Boldon
Battle Hill First School
Bodmin Cl
Brighton Cl
Battle Hill Drive
Barr Cl
Broxburn Cl
Bath Cl
Bathgate
Avenue
Burnet Cl
Barwell Cl
Bradford Av

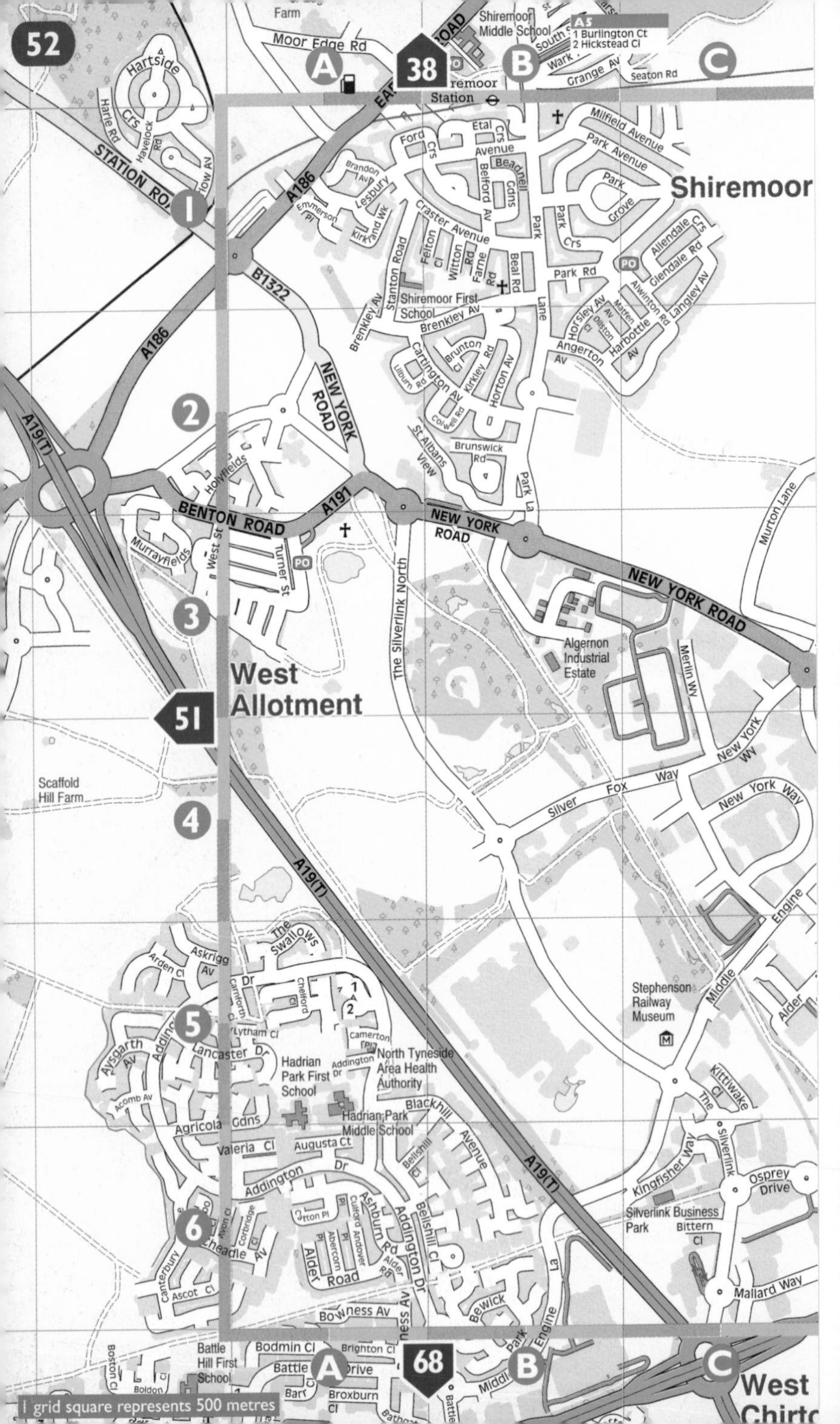

1 grid square represents 500 metres

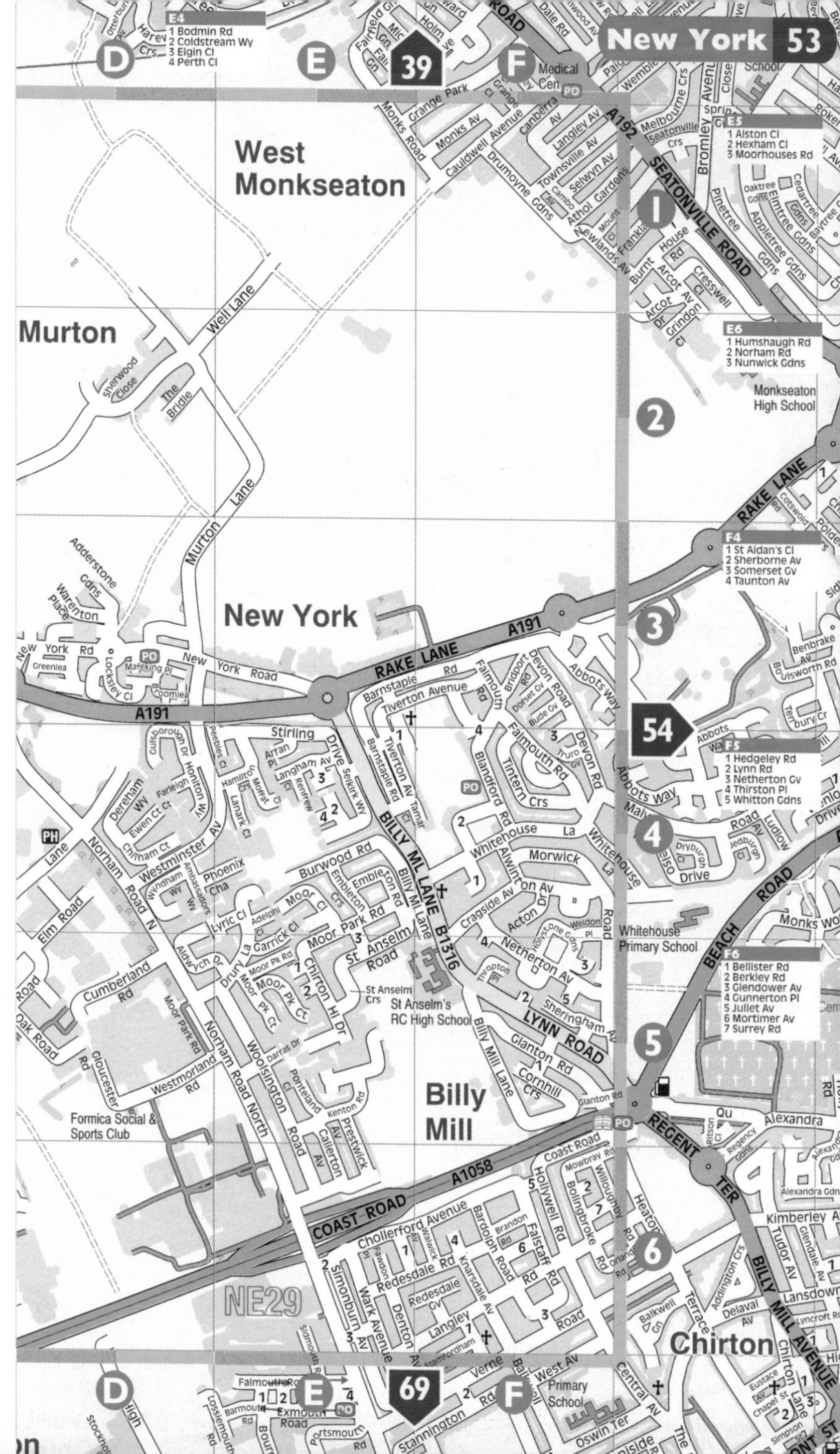
D
E
F
39
54
69
1
2
3
4
5
6
E4
1 Bodmin Rd
2 Coldstream Wy
3 Elgin Cl
4 Perth Cl
E5
1 Alston Cl
2 Hexham Cl
3 Moorhouses Rd
E6
1 Humshaugh Rd
2 Norham Rd
3 Nunwick Gdns
F4
1 St Aidan's Cl
2 Sherborne Av
3 Somerset Gv
4 Taunton Av
F5
1 Hedgeley Rd
2 Lynn Rd
3 Netherton Gv
4 Thirston Pl
5 Whitton Gdns
F6
1 Bellister Rd
2 Berkley Rd
3 Glendower Av
4 Gunnerton Pl
5 Juliet Av
6 Mortimer Av
7 Surrey Rd
West Monkseaton
Murton
New York
Billy Mill
Chirton
NE29
Medical Cen
PO
PH
Monkseaton High School
Whitehouse Primary School
St Anselm's RC High School
Formica Social & Sports Club
Primary School
A191
A192
A1058
B1316
RAKE LANE
SEATONVILLE ROAD
BEACH ROAD
COAST ROAD
LYNN ROAD
BILLY ML LANE
BILLY MILL AVENUE
REGENT TER
Grange Park
Monks Road
Monks Av
Cauldwell Avenue
Drumoyne Gdns
Canberra Av
Langley Av
Townsville Av
Selwyn Av
Athol Gardens
Newlands Av
Melbourne Crs
Seatonville Crs
Bromley Avenue
Pinetree Gdns
Appletree Gdns
Elmtree Gdns
Cedartree Gdns
Oaktree Gdns
Burnt House Rd
Arcot Av
Arcot Dr
Cresswell Cl
Grindon Cl
Well Lane
Sherwood Close
The Bridle
Murton Lane
Adderstone Gdns
Warenton Place
New York Rd
New York Road
Greenlea
Locksley Cl
Mafeking Pl
Broomlea
Barnstaple Rd
Tiverton Avenue
Tiverton Av
Falmouth Rd
Bridport Rd
Devon Road
Dorset Gv
Bude Gv
Abbots Way
Truro Gv
Blandford Rd
Tintern Crs
Whitehouse La
Morwick
Alwinton Av
Cragside Av
Acton Dr
Netherton Av
Sheringham Av
Glanton Rd
Cornhill Crs
Billy Mill Lane
Stirling Drive
Selkirk Wy
Arran Pl
Langham Av
Renfrew
Hamilton Crs
Moffat Cl
Lanark Cl
Peebles Cl
Gulsborough Dr
Honiton Wy
Dereham Wy
Farleigh
Ewen Ct
Chiltham Ct
Westminster Av
Wyndham Wy
Ambassadors Wy
Phoenix Cha
Lyric Cl
Adelphi
Moor Cl
Garrick Cl
Drury La
Aldwych Dr
Burwood Rd
Embleton Crs
Embleton Rd
Moor Park Rd
St Anselm Road
St Anselm Crs
Chirton Hl Dr
Moor Pk Ct
Moor Pk Rd
Norham Road N
Norham Road North
Elm Road
Oak Road
Cumberland Rd
Gloucester Rd
Westmorland Rd
Moor Park Rd
Woolsington Road
Darras Dr
Ponteland Cl
Kenton Rd
Callerton Av
Prestwick
Cholllerford Avenue
Bardolph Road
Brandon
Falstaff Rd
Hollywell Rd
Mowbray Rd
Bolingbroke Rd
Willoughby
Heaton
Orlando Rd
Redesdale Rd
Redesdale Gv
Knarsdale Av
Langley
Simonburn Av
Wark Avenue
Denton Av
Fawdon Pl
Warwick
Stamfordham
Verne
West Av
Central Av
Oswin Ter
Stannington
Falmouth Rd
Barmouth Rd
Exmouth Road
Portsmouth Rd
Lossiemouth Rd
Sidmouth Rd
Benbrake Av
Boulsworth Rd
Tenbury Cr
Drybrugh Cl
Jedburgh Cl
Ludlow
Kelso Drive
Monks Wood
Ritson Cl
Regency Gdns
Alexandra
Alexandra Gdns
Kimberley Av
Tudor Av
Glendale Av
Lansdowne
Lyncroft Rd
Addington Crs
Delaval Av
Balkwell Gn
Terrace
Eustace Av
Chapel St
Chirton Lane
Simpson St
Cotswold Rd
Polden
Glanton Rd
Coast Road

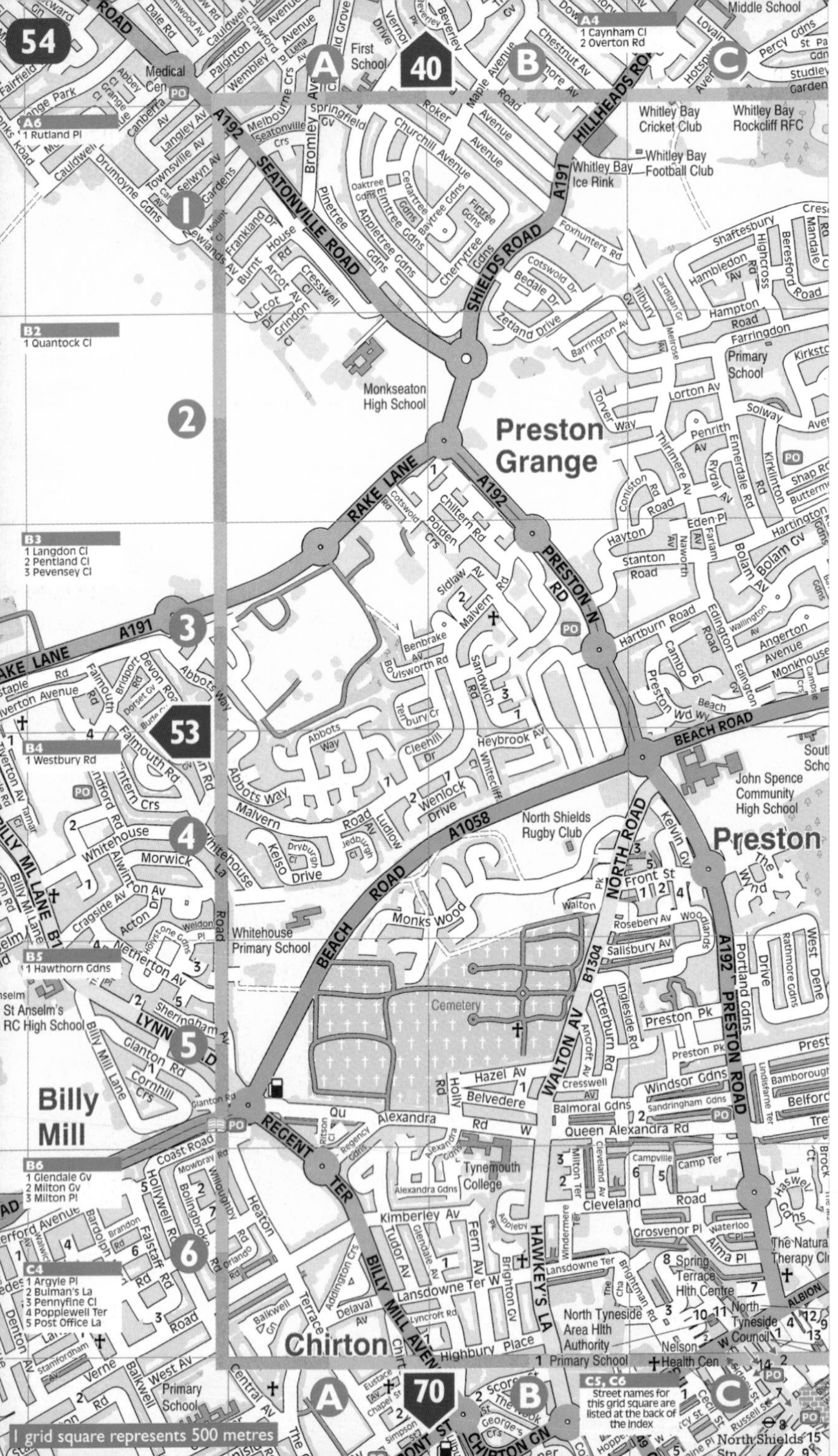

54
40
53
70
A
B
C
1
2
3
4
5
6
A4
1 Caynham Cl
2 Overton Rd
A6
1 Rutland Pl
B2
1 Quantock Cl
B3
1 Langdon Cl
2 Pentland Cl
3 Pevensey Cl
B4
1 Westbury Rd
B5
1 Hawthorn Gdns
B6
1 Glendale Gv
2 Milton Gv
3 Milton Pl
C4
1 Argyle Pl
2 Bulman's La
3 Pennyfine Cl
4 Popplewell Ter
5 Post Office La
C5, C6
Street names for this grid square are listed at the back of the index
Middle School
First School
Medical Cen
Whitley Bay Cricket Club
Whitley Bay Rockcliff RFC
Whitley Bay Football Club
Whitley Bay Ice Rink
Monkseaton High School
Preston Grange
Primary School
John Spence Community High School
Preston
North Shields Rugby Club
Whitehouse Primary School
St Anselm's RC High School
Cemetery
Tynemouth College
Billy Mill
Chirton
Spring Terrace Hlth Centre
North Tyneside Area Hlth Authority
North Tyneside Council
The Natural Therapy Cl
Health Cen
North Shields
SEATONVILLE ROAD
SHIELDS ROAD
HILLHEADS ROAD
RAKE LANE
PRESTON N RD
BEACH ROAD
NORTH ROAD
PRESTON ROAD
REGENT TER
BILLY MILL AVENUE
BILLY ML LANE
WALTON AV
HAWKEY'S LA
CHIRTON GN
A192
A191
A1058
B1304
Coast Road
Queen Alexandra Rd
Cleveland Road
Grosvenor Pl
Lansdowne Ter W
Highbury Place
Kimberley Av
Malvern Road
Wenlock Drive
Abbots Way
Whitehouse La
Whitehouse Road
Sheringham Av
Glanton Rd
Cornhill Crs
Hartburn Road
Stanton Road
Hayton Road
Coniston Rd
Farringdon Road
Hampton Road
Beresford Road
Shaftesbury Cres
Zetland Drive
Foxhunters Rd
Churchill Avenue
Roker Avenue
Appletree Gdns
Pinetree Gdns
Cresswell Cl
Front St
Rosebery Av
Salisbury Av
Preston Pk
Windsor Gdns
Balmoral Gdns
Hazel Av
Belvedere
Monks Wood
Kelso Drive
Acton Dr
Cragside Av
Netherton Av
Falmouth Rd
Caldwell
Drumoyne Gdns
Townsville Av
Newlands Av
1 grid square represents 500 metres

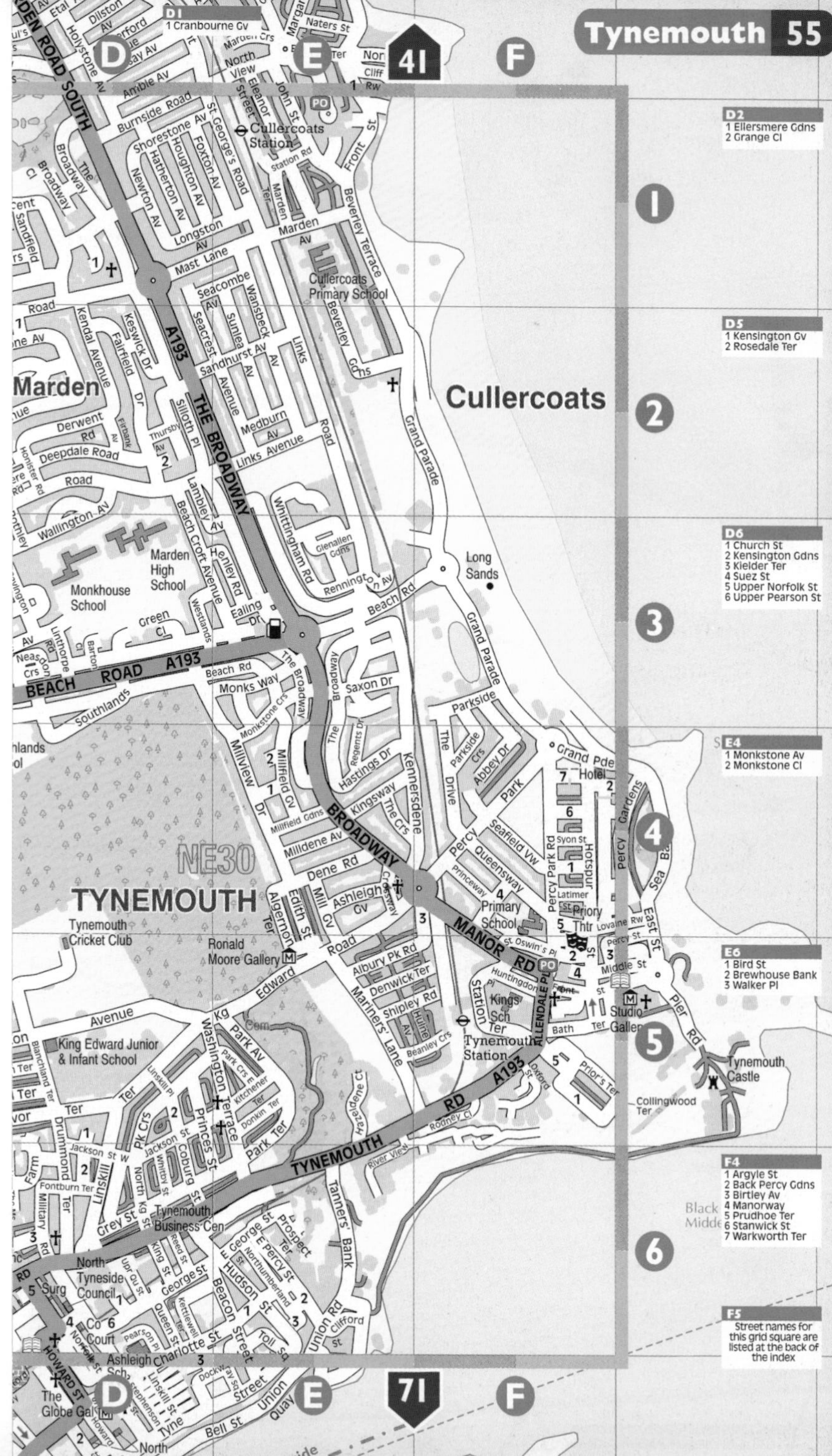

Tynemouth 55
D1
1 Cranbourne Gv
D2
1 Ellersmere Gdns
2 Grange Cl
D5
1 Kensington Gv
2 Rosedale Ter
D6
1 Church St
2 Kensington Gdns
3 Kielder Ter
4 Suez St
5 Upper Norfolk St
6 Upper Pearson St
E4
1 Monkstone Av
2 Monkstone Cl
E6
1 Bird St
2 Brewhouse Bank
3 Walker Pl
F4
1 Argyle St
2 Back Percy Gdns
3 Birtley Av
4 Manorway
5 Prudhoe Ter
6 Stanwick St
7 Warkworth Ter
F5
Street names for this grid square are listed at the back of the index
41
71
D
E
F
1
2
3
4
5
6
Cullercoats
Marden
TYNEMOUTH
NE30
Cullercoats Station
Cullercoats Primary School
Marden High School
Monkhouse School
Long Sands
Tynemouth Cricket Club
Ronald Moore Gallery
King Edward Junior & Infant School
Tynemouth Station
Tynemouth Castle
Tynemouth Business Cen
North Tyneside Council
The Globe Gal
Priory Thtr
Studio Gallery
Grand Pde Hotel
Primary School
Kings Sch
Collingwood Ter
THE BROADWAY
A193
BEACH ROAD
MANOR RD
TYNEMOUTH RD
BROADWAY
Grand Parade
Beverley Terrace
Mast Lane
Marden Av
Links Avenue
Whittingham Rd
Beach Rd
Hastings Dr
Saxon Dr
Kennersdene
Edward Road
Avenue
Washington Terrace
Princes St
Tanners' Bank
Mariners' Lane
Pier Rd
Percy Gardens
Seafield Vw
Queensway
Front St
Middle St
Hotspur St
Percy Park Rd
Allendale Pl
Huntingdon Pl
Prior's Ter
Howard St
Tyne St
Bell St
Union Quay
Union Rd
Clifford St
Toll Sq
Hudson St
Beacon Street
Charlotte St
Linskill St
Drummond Ter
Military Rd
Grey St
North Kg St
Coburg St
Jackson St
Park Av
Park Ter
Kitchener Ter
Donkin Ter
Rodney Cl
River View
Hazeldene Ct
Denwick Ter
Albury Pk Rd
Shipley Rd
Beanley Crs
Dene Rd
Milldene Av
Millfield Gv
Millview Dr
Algernon Ter
Edith St
Mill Gv
Ashleigh Gv
Kingsway
The Crs
The Drive
Parkside
Abbey Dr
Park
Princeway
Southlands
Monks Way
Green Cl
Ealing Dr
Beach Croft Avenue
Henley Rd
Westlands
Lambley Av
Wallington Av
Deepdale Road
Derwent Rd
Kendal Avenue
Keswick Dr
Fairfield Dr
Silloth Pl
Thursby Av
Seacrest Av
Seacombe Av
Wansbeck Av
Sandhurst Av
Medburn Av
Links Road
Burnside Road
Shorestone Av
Houghton Av
Foxton Av
Hatherton Av
Newton Av
Longston Av
St George's Road
Amble Av
Holystone Av
Dilston Av
Marden Crs
Naters St
North View
Eleanor Street
John St
Station Rd
Marden Ter
Front St
Cliff Rw
The Broadway
Broadway Cl
Sandfield
Linthorpe Rd
Barton Cl
Neasdon Crs
Renningt on Av
Glenallen Gdns
Beverley Gdns
George St
E George St
E Percy St
Prospect Ter
Northumberland
Queen St
King St
Reed St
Fontburn Ter
Co Court
Surg
Ashleigh Sch
Pearson Pl
Stephenson
Dockwray Sq
Kettlewell Ter
Black Middens

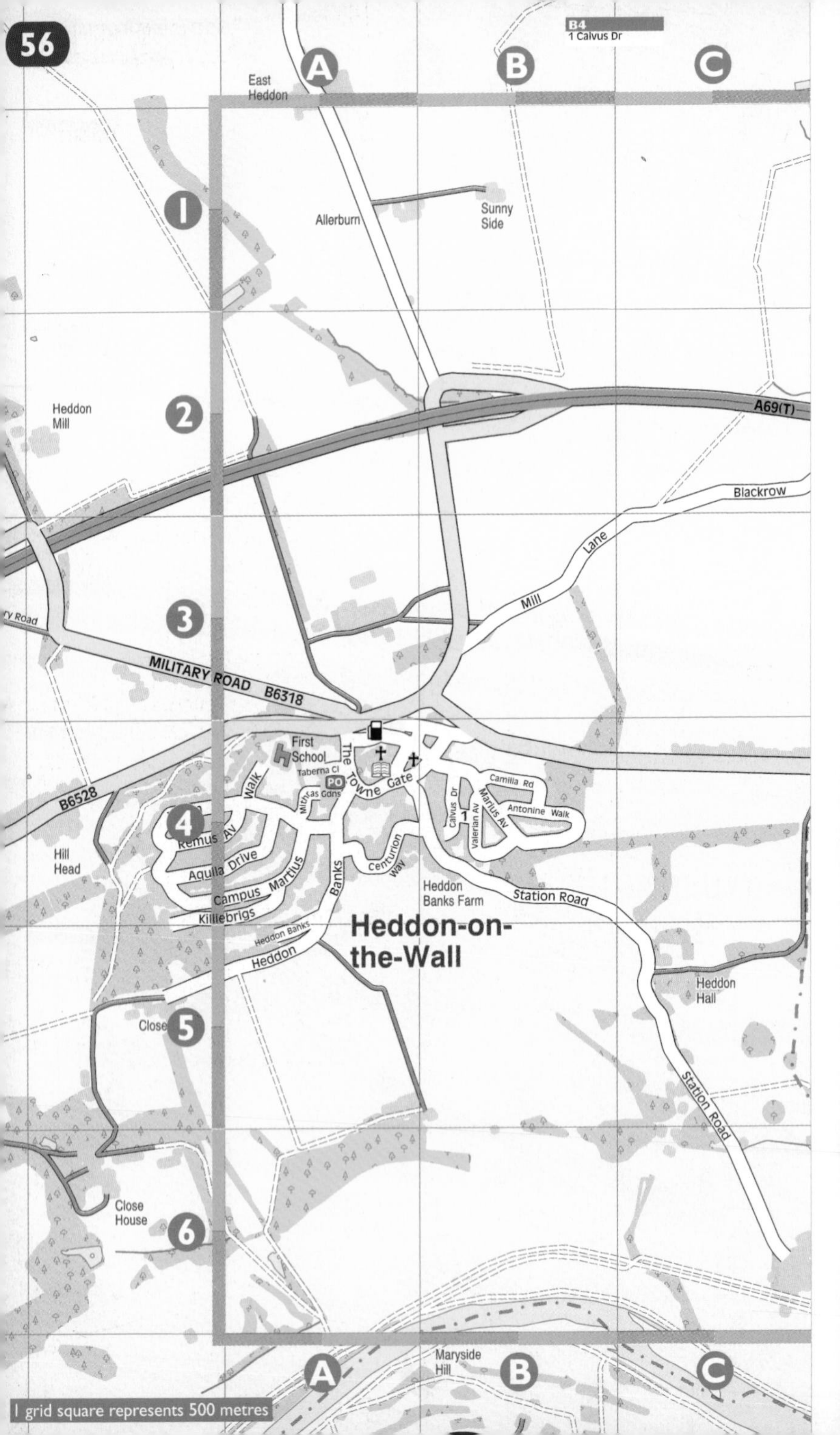
B4
1 Calvus Dr
A
B
C
East Heddon
1
Allerburn
Sunny Side
2
Heddon Mill
A69(T)
Blackrow
Lane
Mill
3
ry Road
MILITARY ROAD B6318
First School
The Towne Gate
Taberna Cl
PO
Mithras Gdns
Walk
Camilla Rd
Calvus Dr
Valerian Av
Marius Av
Antonine Walk
B6528
4
Remus Av
Aquila Drive
Campus Martius
Killebrigs
Banks
Centurion Way
Hill Head
Heddon Banks Farm
Station Road
Heddon-on-the-Wall
Heddon Banks
Heddon
Heddon Hall
Close
5
Station Road
Close House
6
Maryside Hill
A
B
C
1 grid square represents 500 metres

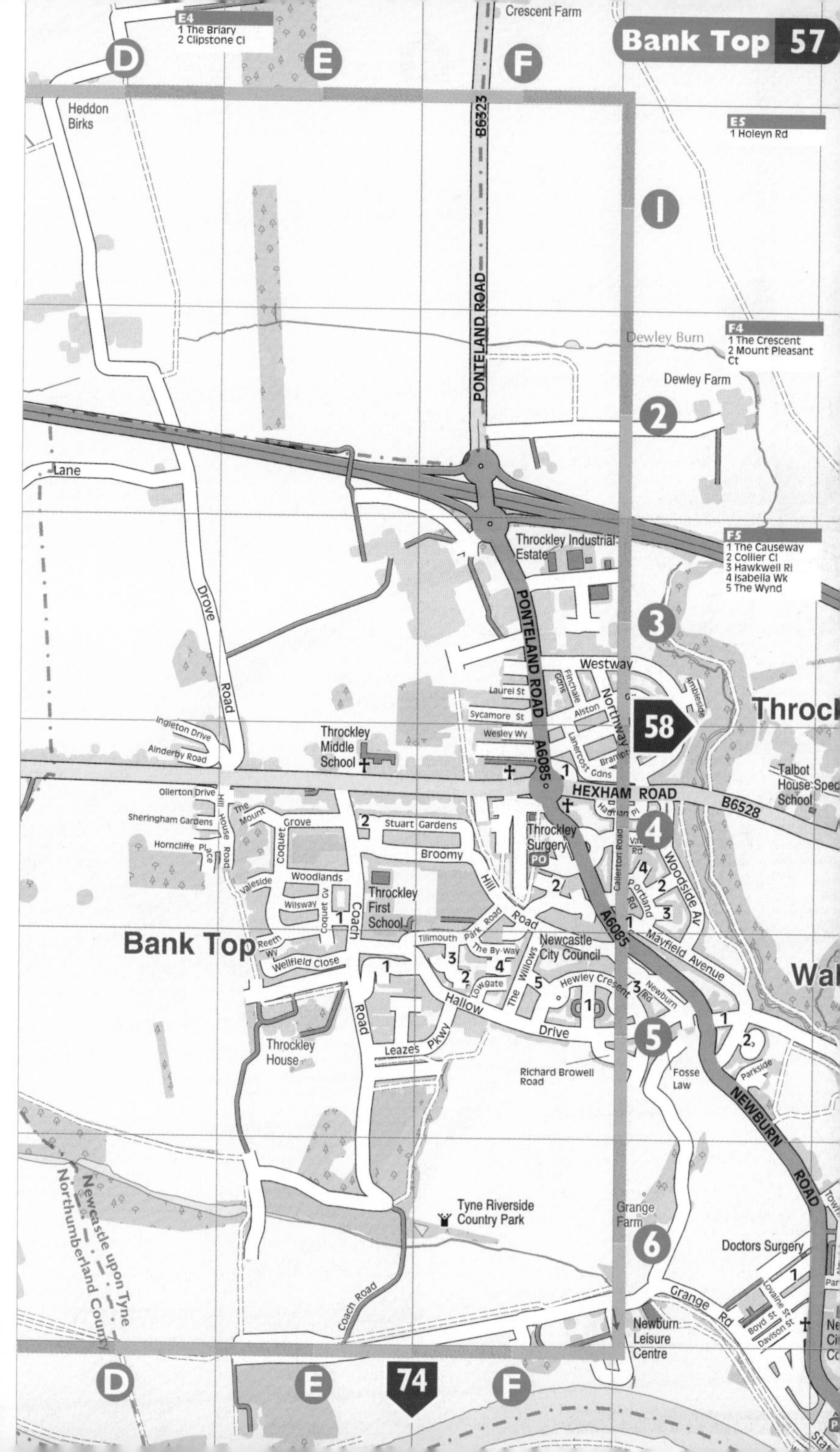
E4
1 The Briary
2 Clipstone Cl
D
E
F
Crescent Farm
E5
1 Holeyn Rd
Heddon Birks
B6323
PONTELAND ROAD
Dewley Burn
F4
1 The Crescent
2 Mount Pleasant Ct
Dewley Farm
Lane
Throckley Industrial Estate
F5
1 The Causeway
2 Collier Cl
3 Hawkwell Ri
4 Isabella Wk
5 The Wynd
Drove Road
Westway
Laurel St
Sycamore St
Wesley Wy
Finchale Gdns
Alston
Northway
Lanercost Gdns
Ambleside
58
Throc
Ingleton Drive
Ainderby Road
Throckley Middle School
A6085
HEXHAM ROAD
B6528
Talbot House Spec School
Ollerton Drive
Sheringham Gardens
Horncliffe Place
Hill House Road
The Mount
Coquet Grove
Stuart Gardens
Broomy Hill Road
Throckley Surgery
PO
Callerton Road
Woodside Av
Portland Rd
Valeside
Woodlands
Wilsway
Coquet Gv
Throckley First School
Coach Road
Tillimouth Park Road
The By-Way
Lowgate
The Willows
Newcastle City Council
Hewley Crescent
Newburn Rd
Mayfield Avenue
Wa
Bank Top
Reeth Wy
Wellfield Close
Hallow Drive
Leazes Pkwy
Throckley House
Richard Browell Road
Fosse Law
Parkside
NEWBURN ROAD
Newcastle upon Tyne
Northumberland County
Tyne Riverside Country Park
Grange Farm
Doctors Surgery
Coach Road
Grange Rd
Lovaine St
Boyd St
Davison St
Newburn Leisure Centre
74

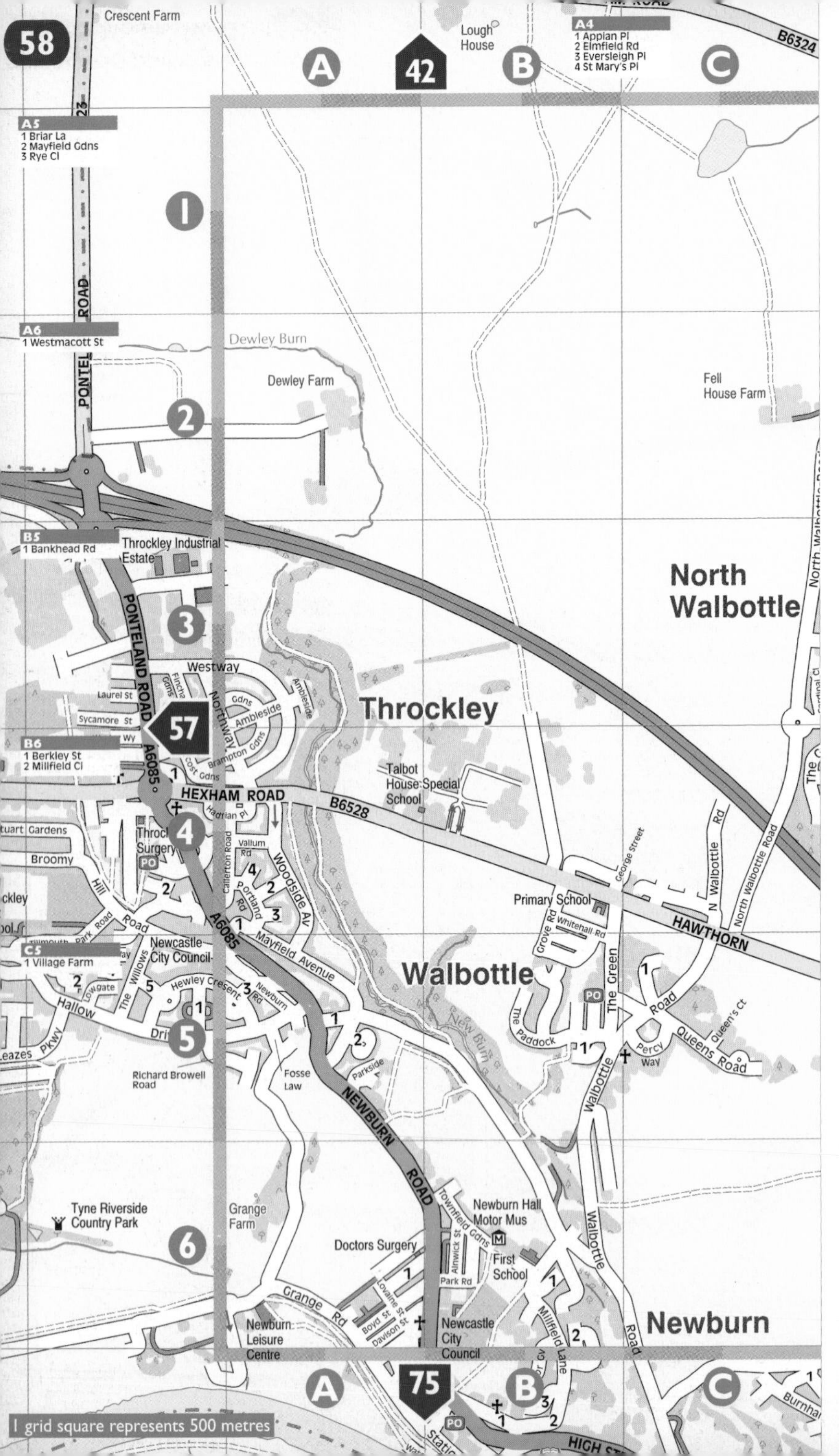
Crescent Farm
Lough House
A4
1 Appian Pl
2 Elmfield Rd
3 Eversleigh Pl
4 St Mary's Pl
B6324
A
42
B
C
A5
1 Briar La
2 Mayfield Gdns
3 Rye Cl
1
PONTELAND ROAD
A6
1 Westmacott St
Dewley Burn
Dewley Farm
Fell House Farm
2
B5
1 Bankhead Rd
Throckley Industrial Estate
North Walbottle
North Walbottle Road
3
PONTELAND ROAD
Westway
Laurel St
Sycamore St
Northway
Ambleside
Ambleside Gdns
Brampton Gdns
Throckley
57
B6
1 Berkley St
2 Millfield Cl
A6085
HEXHAM ROAD
B6528
Hadrian Pl
Talbot House Special School
4
Callerton Road
Vallum Rd
Portland Rd
Woodside Av
Broomy Hill Road
Stuart Gardens
Park Road
George Street
N Walbottle Rd
Primary School
Grove Rd
Whitehall Rd
HAWTHORN
C5
1 Village Farm
Newcastle City Council
A6085
Mayfield Avenue
Walbottle
The Green
The Willows
Hewley Crescent
Newburn Rd
Hallow Drive
Leazes Pkwy
5
Richard Browell Road
Fosse Law
Parkside
New Burn
The Paddock
Percy Way
Road
Queens Road
Queen's Ct
Walbottle
NEWBURN ROAD
Tyne Riverside Country Park
Grange Farm
6
Townfield Gdns
Newburn Hall Motor Mus
Doctors Surgery
Alnwick St
Park Rd
First School
Walbottle Road
Grange Rd
Lovaine St
Boyd St
Davison St
Newburn Leisure Centre
Newcastle City Council
Millfield Lane
Newburn
A
75
B
C
PO
HIGH ST
Burnhall
1 grid square represents 500 metres

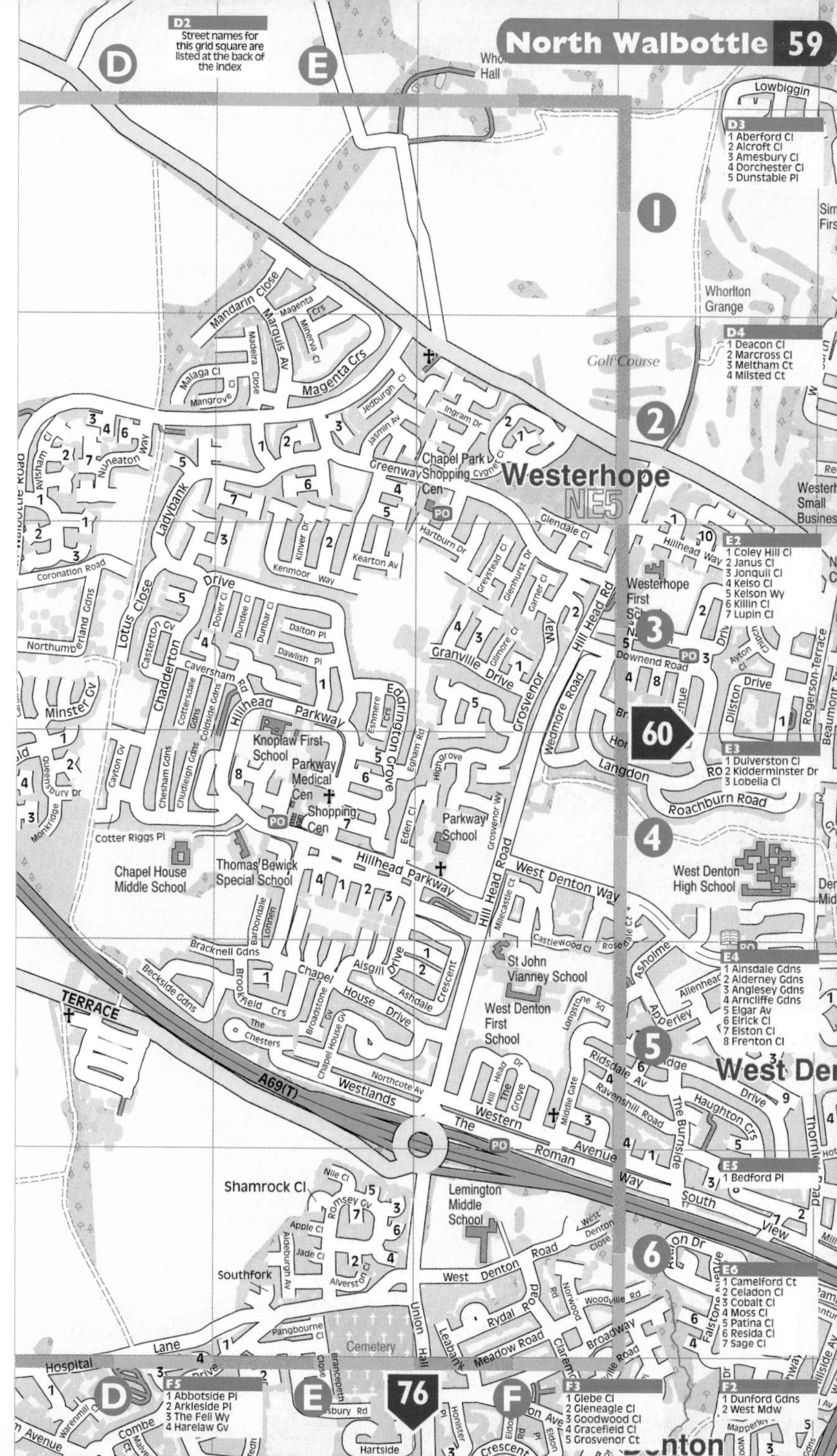
D2
Street names for this grid square are listed at the back of the index
D3
1 Aberford Cl
2 Alcroft Cl
3 Amesbury Cl
4 Dorchester Cl
5 Dunstable Pl
D4
1 Deacon Cl
2 Marcross Cl
3 Meltham Ct
4 Milsted Ct
E2
1 Coley Hill Cl
2 Janus Cl
3 Jonquil Cl
4 Kelso Cl
5 Kelson Wy
6 Killin Cl
7 Lupin Cl
E3
1 Dulverston Cl
2 Kidderminster Dr
3 Lobelia Cl
E4
1 Ainsdale Gdns
2 Alderney Gdns
3 Anglesey Gdns
4 Arncliffe Gdns
5 Elgar Av
6 Elrick Cl
7 Elston Cl
8 Frenton Cl
E5
1 Bedford Pl
E6
1 Camelford Ct
2 Celadon Cl
3 Cobalt Cl
4 Moss Cl
5 Patina Cl
6 Resida Cl
7 Sage Cl
F5
1 Abbotside Pl
2 Arkleside Pl
3 The Fell Wy
4 Harelaw Gv
F3
1 Glebe Cl
2 Gleneagle Cl
3 Goodwood Cl
4 Gracefield Cl
5 Grosvenor Ct
F2
1 Dunford Gdns
2 West Mdw
Westerhope
NE5
West Denton
Whorlton Grange
Golf Course
Chapel Park Shopping Cen
Knoplaw First School
Parkway Medical Cen
Shopping Cen
Parkway School
Chapel House Middle School
Thomas Bewick Special School
Westerhope First School
West Denton High School
St John Vianney School
West Denton First School
Lemington Middle School
Cemetery
Hillhead Parkway
Hill Head Road
West Denton Way
Chapel House Drive
Westlands
The Roman Avenue
A69(T)
West Denton Road
Union Hall
60
76

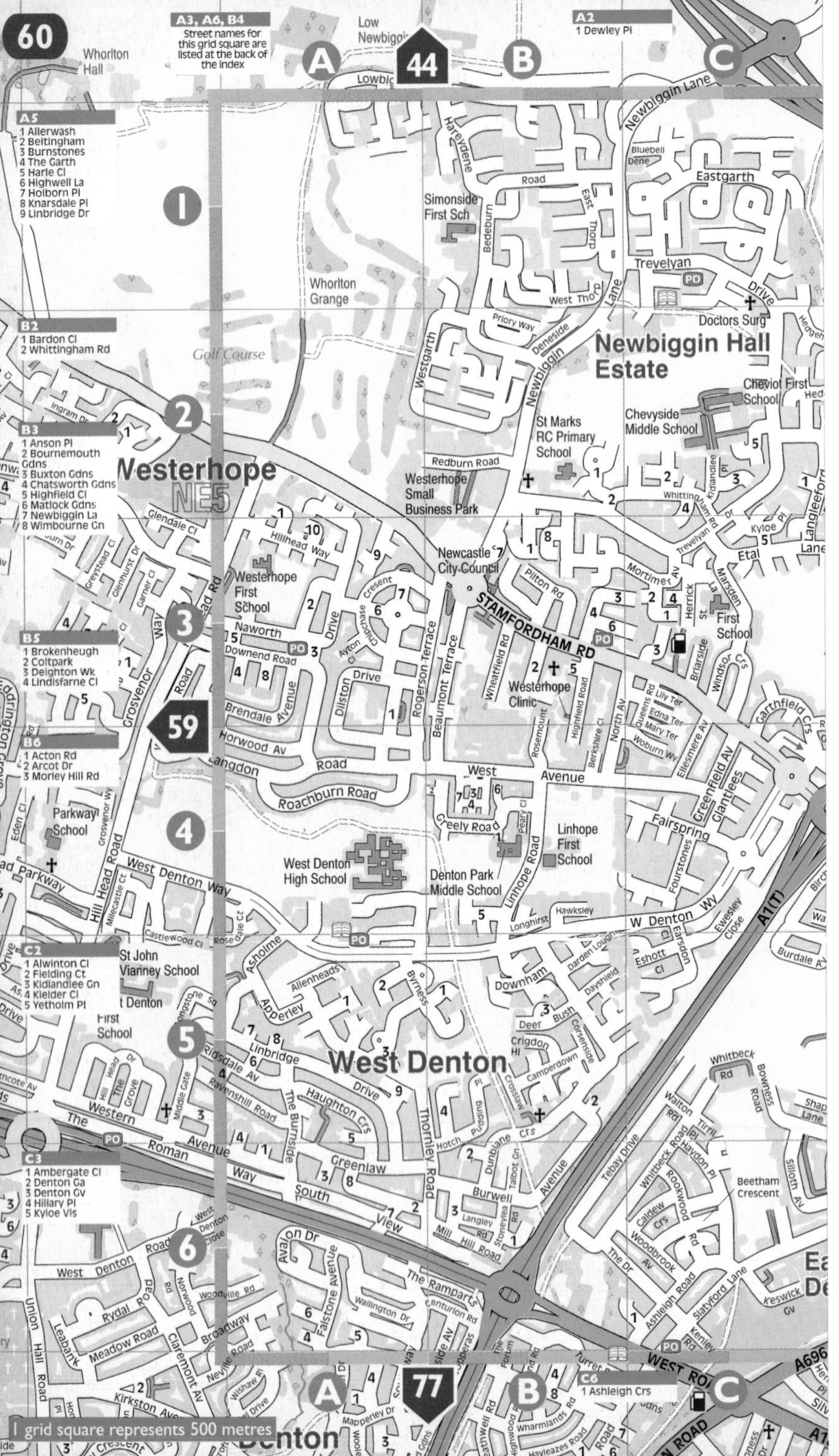
A3, A6, B4
Street names for this grid square are listed at the back of the index
A2
1 Dewley Pl
A5
1 Allerwash
2 Beltingham
3 Burnstones
4 The Garth
5 Harle Cl
6 Highwell La
7 Holborn Pl
8 Knarsdale Pl
9 Linbridge Dr
B2
1 Bardon Cl
2 Whittingham Rd
B3
1 Anson Pl
2 Bournemouth Gdns
3 Buxton Gdns
4 Chatsworth Gdns
5 Highfield Cl
6 Matlock Gdns
7 Newbiggin La
8 Wimbourne Gn
B5
1 Brokenheugh
2 Coltpark
3 Deighton Wk
4 Lindisfarne Cl
B6
1 Acton Rd
2 Arcot Dr
3 Morley Hill Rd
C2
1 Alwinton Cl
2 Fielding Ct
3 Kidlandlee Gn
4 Kielder Cl
5 Yetholm Pl
C3
1 Ambergate Cl
2 Denton Ga
3 Denton Gv
4 Hillary Pl
5 Kyloe Vls
C6
1 Ashleigh Crs
44
59
77
Whorlton Hall
Low Newbiggin
Whorlton Grange
Golf Course
Simonside First Sch
Newbiggin Hall Estate
Westerhope
NE5
Westerhope First School
Westerhope Small Business Park
Newcastle City Council
St Marks RC Primary School
Chevyside Middle School
Cheviot First School
Doctors Surg
Westerhope Clinic
First School
Parkway School
West Denton High School
Denton Park Middle School
Linhope First School
St John Vianney School
West Denton
Beetham Crescent
Stamfordham Rd
West Avenue
West Denton Way
W Denton Wy
The Western Avenue
West Road
A1(T)
A696
Denton
1 grid square represents 500 metres

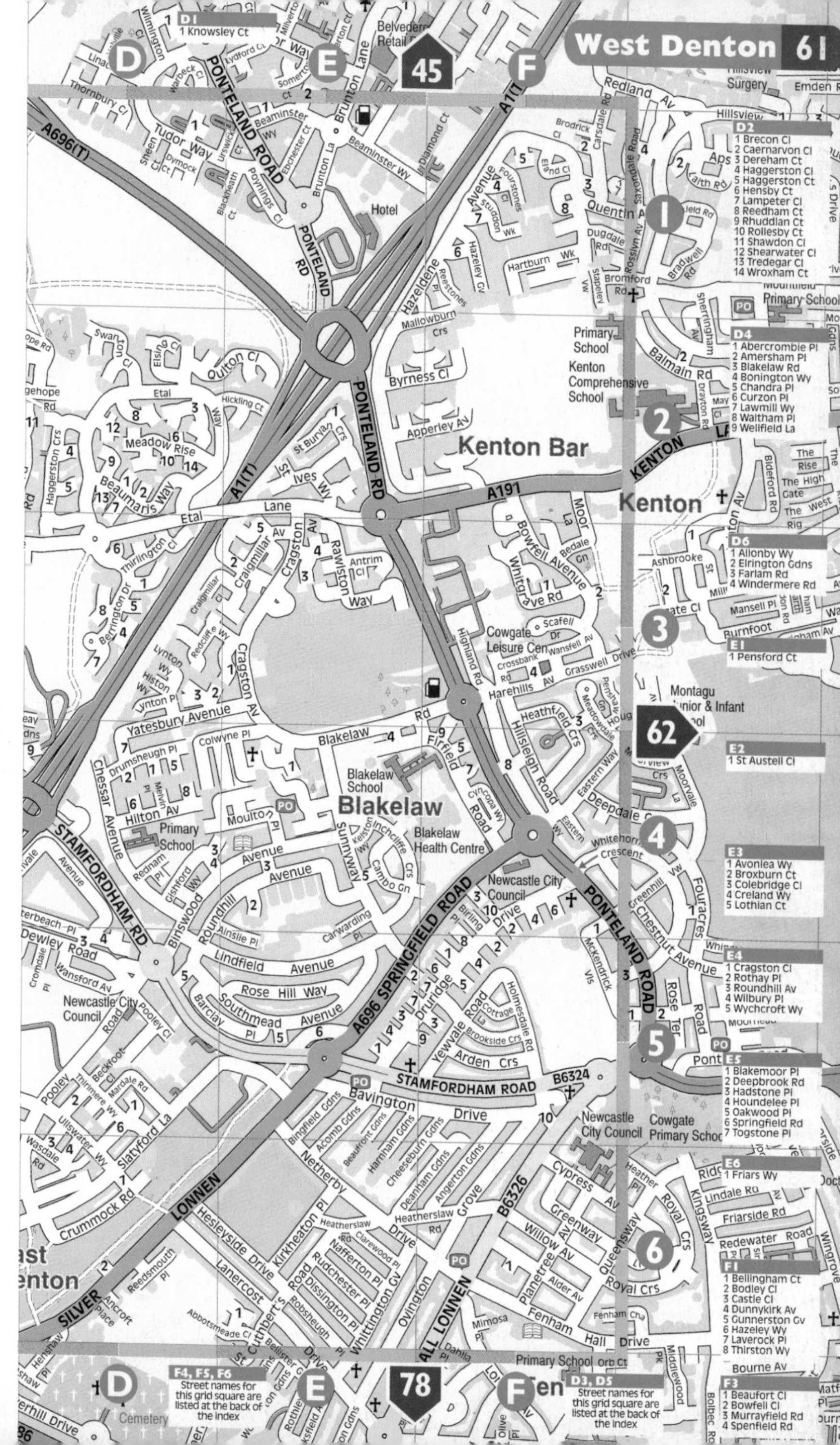
D1
1 Knowsley Ct
D2
1 Brecon Cl
2 Caernarvon Cl
3 Dereham Ct
4 Haggerston Cl
5 Haggerston Ct
6 Hensby Ct
7 Lampeter Cl
8 Reedham Ct
9 Rhuddlan Ct
10 Rollesby Ct
11 Shawdon Cl
12 Shearwater Cl
13 Tredegar Cl
14 Wroxham Ct
D4
1 Abercrombie Pl
2 Amersham Pl
3 Blakelaw Rd
4 Bonington Wy
5 Chandra Pl
6 Curzon Pl
7 Lawmill Wy
8 Waltham Pl
9 Wellfield La
D6
1 Allonby Wy
2 Elrington Gdns
3 Farlam Rd
4 Windermere Rd
E1
1 Pensford Ct
E2
1 St Austell Cl
E3
1 Avonlea Wy
2 Broxburn Ct
3 Colebridge Cl
4 Creland Wy
5 Lothian Ct
E4
1 Cragston Cl
2 Rothay Pl
3 Roundhill Av
4 Wilbury Pl
5 Wychcroft Wy
E5
1 Blakemoor Pl
2 Deepbrook Rd
3 Hadstone Pl
4 Houndelee Pl
5 Oakwood Pl
6 Springfield Rd
7 Togstone Pl
E6
1 Friars Wy
F1
1 Bellingham Ct
2 Bodley Cl
3 Castle Cl
4 Dunnykirk Av
5 Gunnerston Gv
6 Hazeley Wy
7 Laverock Pl
8 Thirston Wy
F3
1 Beaufort Cl
2 Bowfell Cl
3 Murrayfield Rd
4 Spenfield Rd
F4, F5, F6
Street names for this grid square are listed at the back of the index
D3, D5
Street names for this grid square are listed at the back of the index
45
62
78
D
E
F
1
2
3
4
5
6
Kenton Bar
Kenton
Blakelaw
PONTELAND ROAD
PONTELAND RD
A1(T)
A696(T)
A191
A696 SPRINGFIELD ROAD
STAMFORDHAM ROAD
STAMFORDHAM RD
B6324
B6326
SILVER LONNEN
KENTON LA
Belvedere Retail Pk
Hillsview Surgery
Hotel
Primary School
Kenton Comprehensive School
Cowgate Leisure Cen
Montagu Junior & Infant School
Blakelaw School
Blakelaw Health Centre
Newcastle City Council
Cowgate Primary School
Cemetery
Tudor Way
Beaminster Wy
Brunton Lane
Redland Av
Quentin Av
Hartburn Wk
Mallowburn Crs
Byrness Cl
Apperley Av
Balmain Rd
Etal Lane
Meadow Rise
Beaumaris Way
Quton Cl
Cragston Av
Rawlston Way
Bowfell Avenue
Whitgrave Rd
Yatesbury Avenue
Blakelaw Rd
Hillsleigh Road
Heathfield Crs
Harehills Av
Grasswell Drive
Deepdale Crs
Hilton Av
Chessar Avenue
Roundhill Avenue
Lindfield Avenue
Rose Hill Way
Southmead Avenue
Sunnyway
Chestnut Avenue
Fouracres
Whitehorn Crescent
Arden Crs
Bavington Drive
Netherby Drive
Heatherslaw Drive
Grove
Cypress Av
Greenway
Willow Av
Royal Crs
Kingsway
Queensway
Fenham Hall Drive
Friarside Rd
Redewater Road
Wingrove
Dewley Road
Crummock Rd
Slatyford La
Lanercost
Hesleyside Drive
Ovington
Whittington Gv
Bourne Av
Primary School
Drive

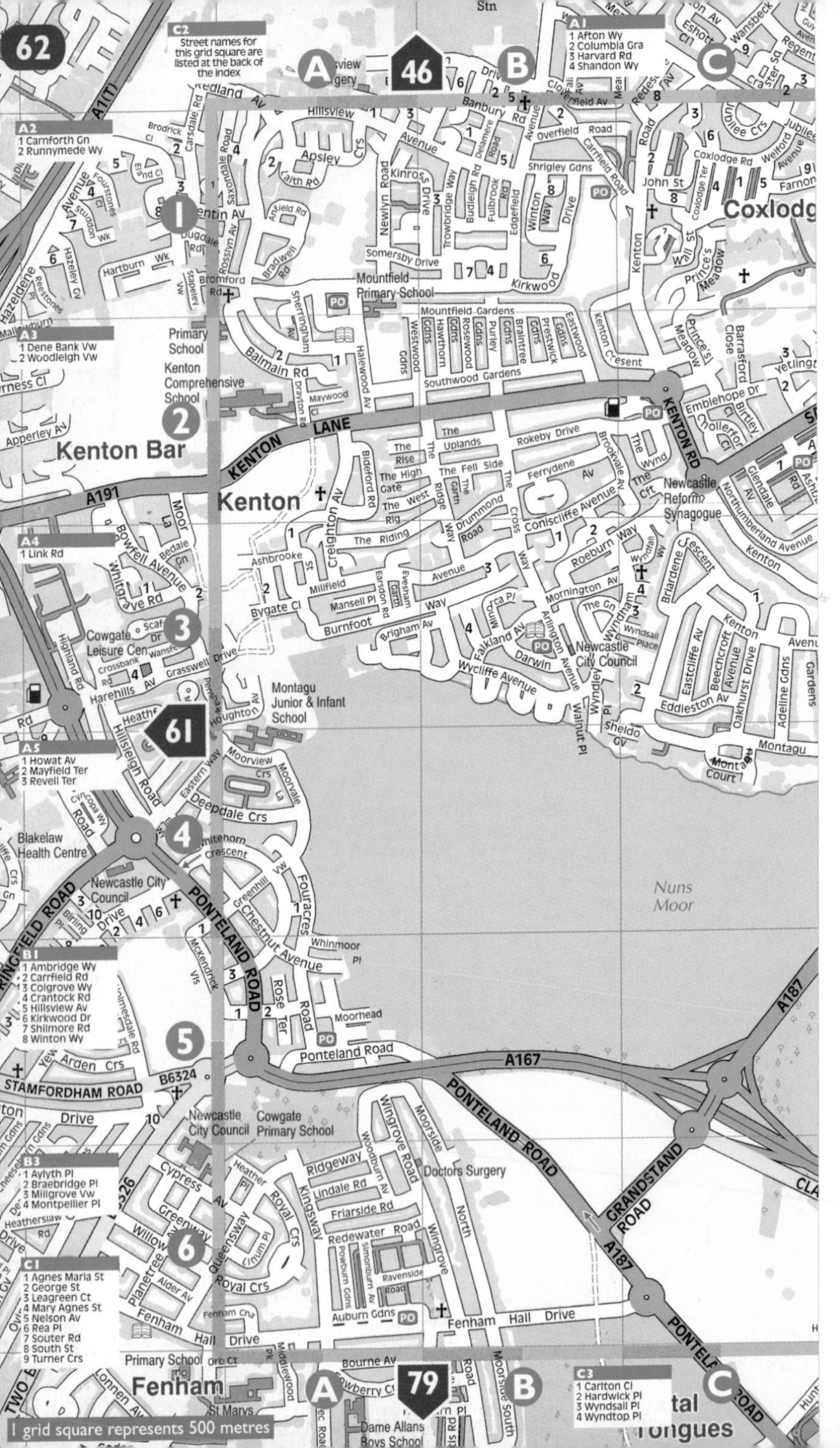
46
C2
Street names for this grid square are listed at the back of the index
A1
1 Afton Wy
2 Columbia Gra
3 Harvard Rd
4 Shandon Wy
A2
1 Carnforth Gn
2 Runnymede Wy
A3
1 Dene Bank Vw
2 Woodleigh Vw
A4
1 Link Rd
A5
1 Howat Av
2 Mayfield Ter
3 Revell Ter
B1
1 Ambridge Wy
2 Carrfield Rd
3 Colgrove Wy
4 Crantock Rd
5 Hillsview Av
6 Kirkwood Dr
7 Shilmore Rd
8 Winton Wy
B3
1 Aylyth Pl
2 Braebridge Pl
3 Millgrove Vw
4 Montpellier Pl
C1
1 Agnes Maria St
2 George St
3 Leagreen Ct
4 Mary Agnes St
5 Nelson Av
6 Rea Pl
7 Souter Rd
8 South St
9 Turner Crs
C3
1 Carlton Cl
2 Hardwick Pl
3 Wyndsail Pl
4 Wyndtop Pl
Kenton Bar
Kenton
Coxlodge
Fenham
Nuns Moor
KENTON LANE
KENTON RD
A191
A1(T)
A167
A187
B6324
PONTELAND ROAD
STAMFORDHAM ROAD
GRANDSTAND ROAD
Mountfield Primary School
Kenton Comprehensive School
Primary School
Cowgate Leisure Cen
Montagu Junior & Infant School
Newcastle Reform Synagogue
Newcastle City Council
Blakelaw Health Centre
Cowgate Primary School
Doctors Surgery
Dame Allans Boys School
61
79
1 grid square represents 500 metres

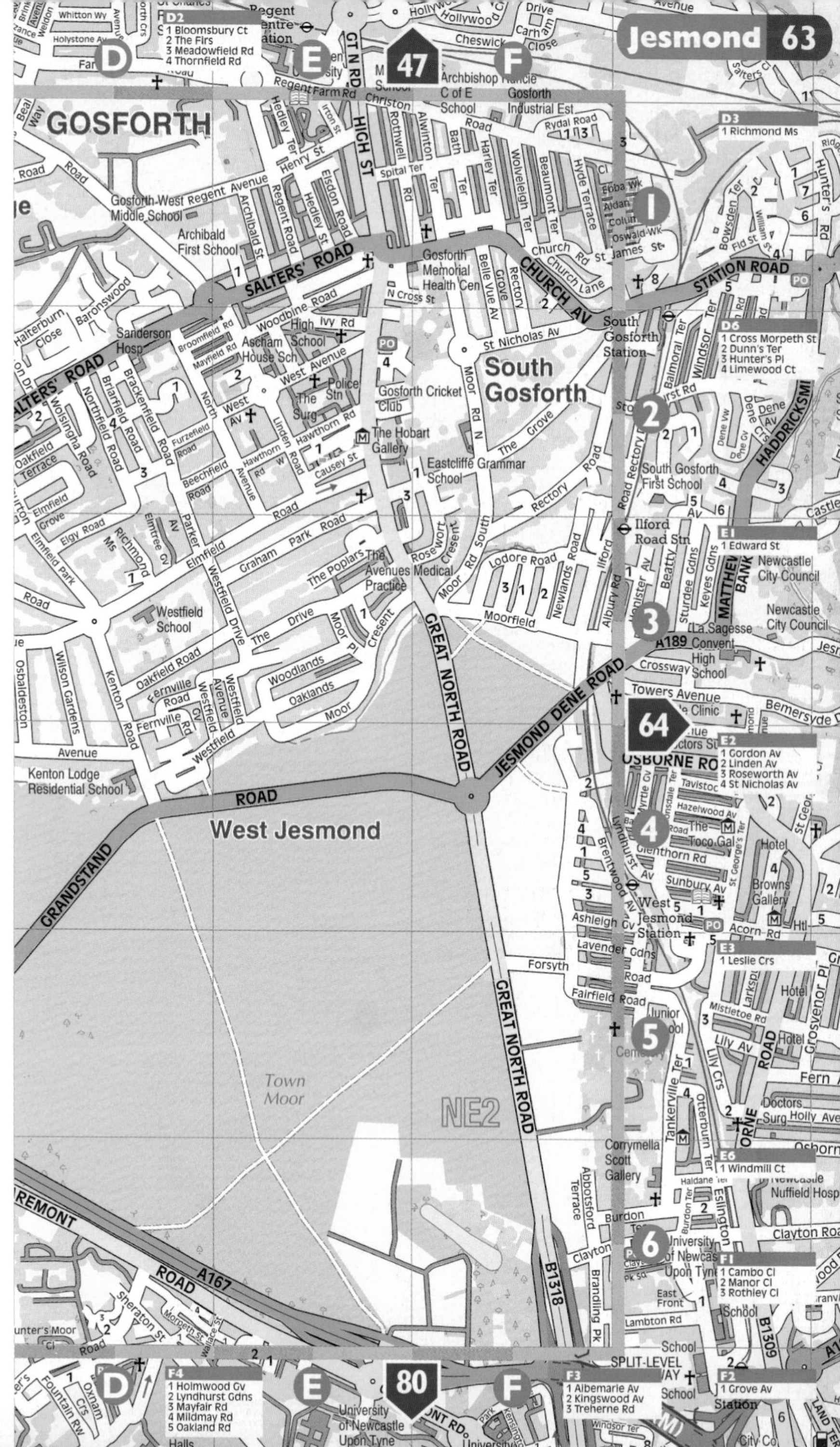

D2
1 Bloomsbury Ct
2 The Firs
3 Meadowfield Rd
4 Thornfield Rd
D3
1 Richmond Ms
D6
1 Cross Morpeth St
2 Dunn's Ter
3 Hunter's Pl
4 Limewood Ct
E1
1 Edward St
E2
1 Gordon Av
2 Linden Av
3 Roseworth Av
4 St Nicholas Av
E3
1 Leslie Crs
E6
1 Windmill Ct
F1
1 Cambo Cl
2 Manor Cl
3 Rothley Cl
F2
1 Grove Av
F3
1 Albemarle Av
2 Kingswood Av
3 Treherne Rd
F4
1 Holmwood Gv
2 Lyndhurst Gdns
3 Mayfair Rd
4 Mildmay Rd
5 Oakland Rd
47
64
80
GOSFORTH
South Gosforth
West Jesmond
Town Moor
NE2
SALTERS' ROAD
HIGH ST
GREAT NORTH ROAD
JESMOND DENE ROAD
CHURCH AV
STATION ROAD
GRANDSTAND ROAD
CLAREMONT ROAD
A167
A189
B1318
B1309
Gosforth West Middle School
Archibald First School
Sanderson Hosp
Ascham House Sch
High School
Gosforth Memorial Health Cen
Gosforth Cricket Club
The Hobart Gallery
Eastcliffe Grammar School
The Avenues Medical Practice
Westfield School
Kenton Lodge Residential School
Archbishop Runcie C of E School
Gosforth Industrial Est
South Gosforth Station
South Gosforth First School
Ilford Road Stn
Newcastle City Council
La Sagesse Convent High School
West Jesmond Station
Junior School
Cemetery
Corrymella Scott Gallery
Browns Gallery
Newcastle Nuffield Hospital
University of Newcastle Upon Tyne

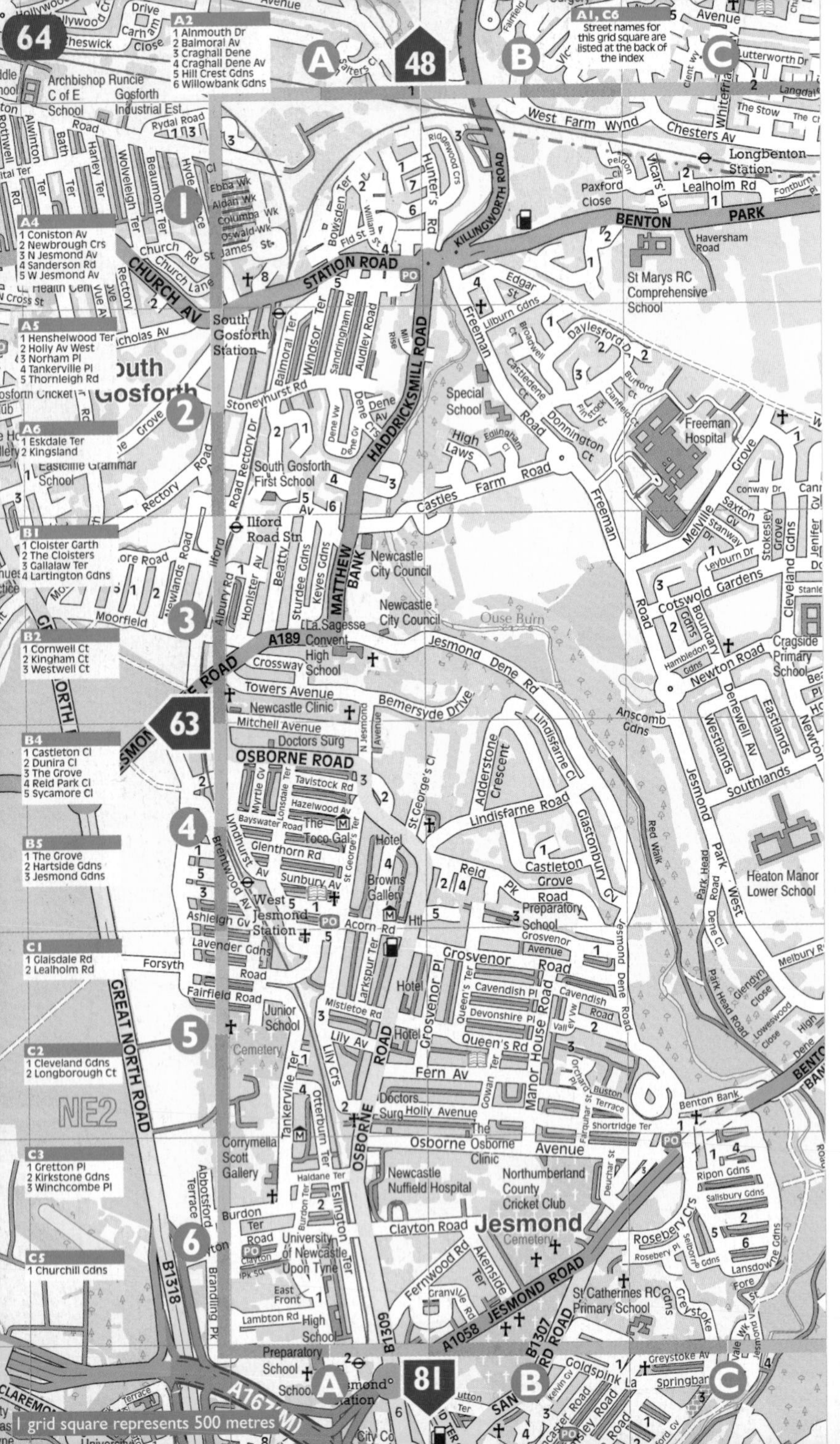
A2
1 Alnmouth Dr
2 Balmoral Av
3 Craghall Dene
4 Craghall Dene Av
5 Hill Crest Gdns
6 Willowbank Gdns
A1, C6
Street names for this grid square are listed at the back of the index
A
48
B
C
A4
1 Coniston Av
2 Newbrough Crs
3 N Jesmond Av
4 Sanderson Rd
5 W Jesmond Av
A5
1 Henshelwood Ter
2 Holly Av West
3 Norham Pl
4 Tankerville Pl
5 Thornleigh Rd
A6
1 Eskdale Ter
2 Kingsland
B1
1 Cloister Garth
2 The Cloisters
3 Gallalaw Ter
4 Lartington Gdns
B2
1 Cornwell Ct
2 Kingham Ct
3 Westwell Ct
B4
1 Castleton Cl
2 Dunira Cl
3 The Grove
4 Reid Park Cl
5 Sycamore Cl
B5
1 The Grove
2 Hartside Gdns
3 Jesmond Gdns
C1
1 Glaisdale Rd
2 Lealholm Rd
C2
1 Cleveland Gdns
2 Longborough Ct
C3
1 Gretton Pl
2 Kirkstone Gdns
3 Winchcombe Pl
C5
1 Churchill Gdns
Archbishop Runcie C of E School
Gosforth Industrial Est
West Farm Wynd
Chesters Av
Longbenton Station
Lealholm Rd
Paxford Close
BENTON PARK
KILLINGWORTH ROAD
STATION ROAD
CHURCH AV
South Gosforth Station
South Gosforth
St Marys RC Comprehensive School
HADDRICKSMILL ROAD
Special School
High Laws
Castles Farm Road
South Gosforth First School
Freeman Hospital
Freeman Road
Ilford Road Stn
MATTHEW BANK
Newcastle City Council
Ouse Burn
Cotswold Gardens
La Sagesse Convent High School
A189
Jesmond Dene Rd
Crossway
Towers Avenue
Newcastle Clinic
Bemersyde Drive
Mitchell Avenue
Doctors Surg
63
OSBORNE ROAD
Tavistock Rd
Hazelwood Av
Cragside Primary School
Newton Road
Lindisfarne Road
Adderstone Crescent
Glastonbury Gv
Jesmond Park West
Heaton Manor Lower School
The Toco Gal
Browns Gallery
West Jesmond Station
Acorn Rd
Castleton Grove
Reid Pk Road
Preparatory School
Grosvenor Road
Forsyth Road
Fairfield Road
Junior School
GREAT NORTH ROAD
Cemetery
NE2
Fern Av
Queen's Rd
Cavendish Pl
Devonshire Pl
Holly Avenue
Osborne Avenue
Benton Bank
Corrymella Scott Gallery
Newcastle Nuffield Hospital
Northumberland County Cricket Club
Jesmond
Clayton Road
University of Newcastle Upon Tyne
High School
Ripon Gdns
Salisbury Gdns
Rosebery Crs
Lansdowne Gdns
St Catherines RC Primary School
Greystoke Gdns
A1058 JESMOND ROAD
B1309
B1307
B1318
Brandling Pk
Preparatory School
Goldspink La
Greystoke Av
Springbank
81
A167(M)
1 grid square represents 500 metres

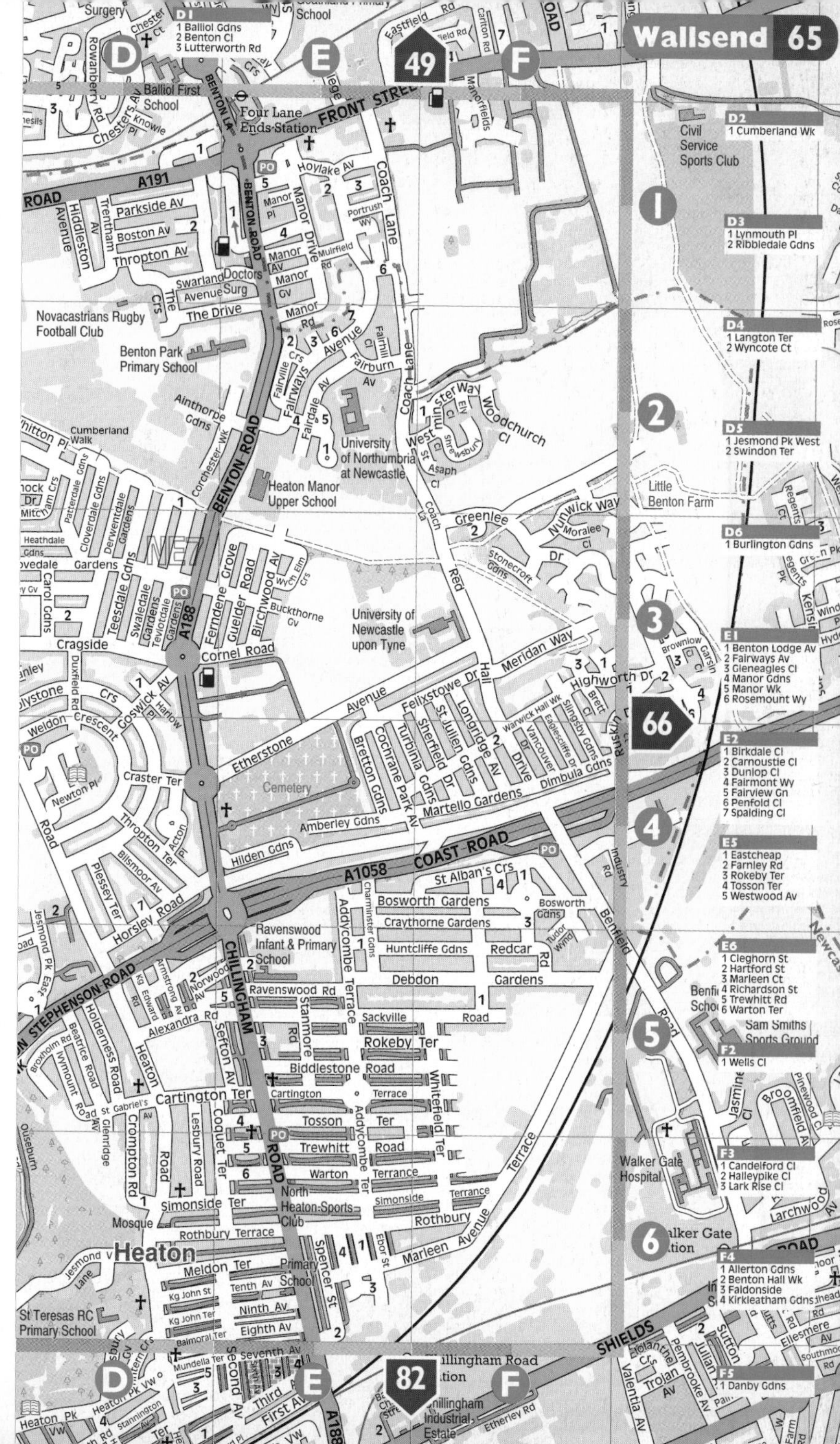
Wallsend 65
49
66
82
D1
1 Balliol Gdns
2 Benton Cl
3 Lutterworth Rd
D2
1 Cumberland Wk
D3
1 Lynmouth Pl
2 Ribbledale Gdns
D4
1 Langton Ter
2 Wyncote Ct
D5
1 Jesmond Pk West
2 Swindon Ter
D6
1 Burlington Gdns
E1
1 Benton Lodge Av
2 Fairways Av
3 Gleneagles Cl
4 Manor Gdns
5 Manor Wk
6 Rosemount Wy
E2
1 Birkdale Cl
2 Carnoustie Cl
3 Dunlop Cl
4 Fairmont Wy
5 Fairview Gn
6 Penfold Cl
7 Spalding Cl
E5
1 Eastcheap
2 Farnley Rd
3 Rokeby Ter
4 Tosson Ter
5 Westwood Av
E6
1 Cleghorn St
2 Hartford St
3 Marleen Ct
4 Richardson St
5 Trewhitt Rd
6 Warton Ter
F2
1 Wells Cl
F3
1 Candelford Cl
2 Halleypike Cl
3 Lark Rise Cl
F4
1 Allerton Gdns
2 Benton Hall Wk
3 Faldonside
4 Kirkleatham Gdns
F5
1 Danby Gdns
Civil Service Sports Club
Little Benton Farm
Four Lane Ends Station
Balliol First School
Novacastrians Rugby Football Club
Benton Park Primary School
University of Northumbria at Newcastle
Heaton Manor Upper School
University of Newcastle upon Tyne
Cemetery
Ravenswood Infant & Primary School
North Heaton Sports Club
Heaton
St Teresas RC Primary School
Walker Gate Hospital
Sam Smiths Sports Ground
Chillingham Industrial Estate
NE7
FRONT STREET
BENTON ROAD
A191
A188
A1058 COAST ROAD
STEPHENSON ROAD
CHILLINGHAM ROAD
SHIELDS
Coach Lane
Etherstone Avenue
Meridan Way
Benfield Road
Marleen Avenue
Newton Pl
Cragside
Debdon Gardens
Sackville Road
Rokeby Ter
Biddlestone Road
Cartington Ter
Tosson Ter
Trewhitt Road
Warton Terrace
Simonside Ter
Rothbury Terrace
Meldon Ter
Larchwood Av

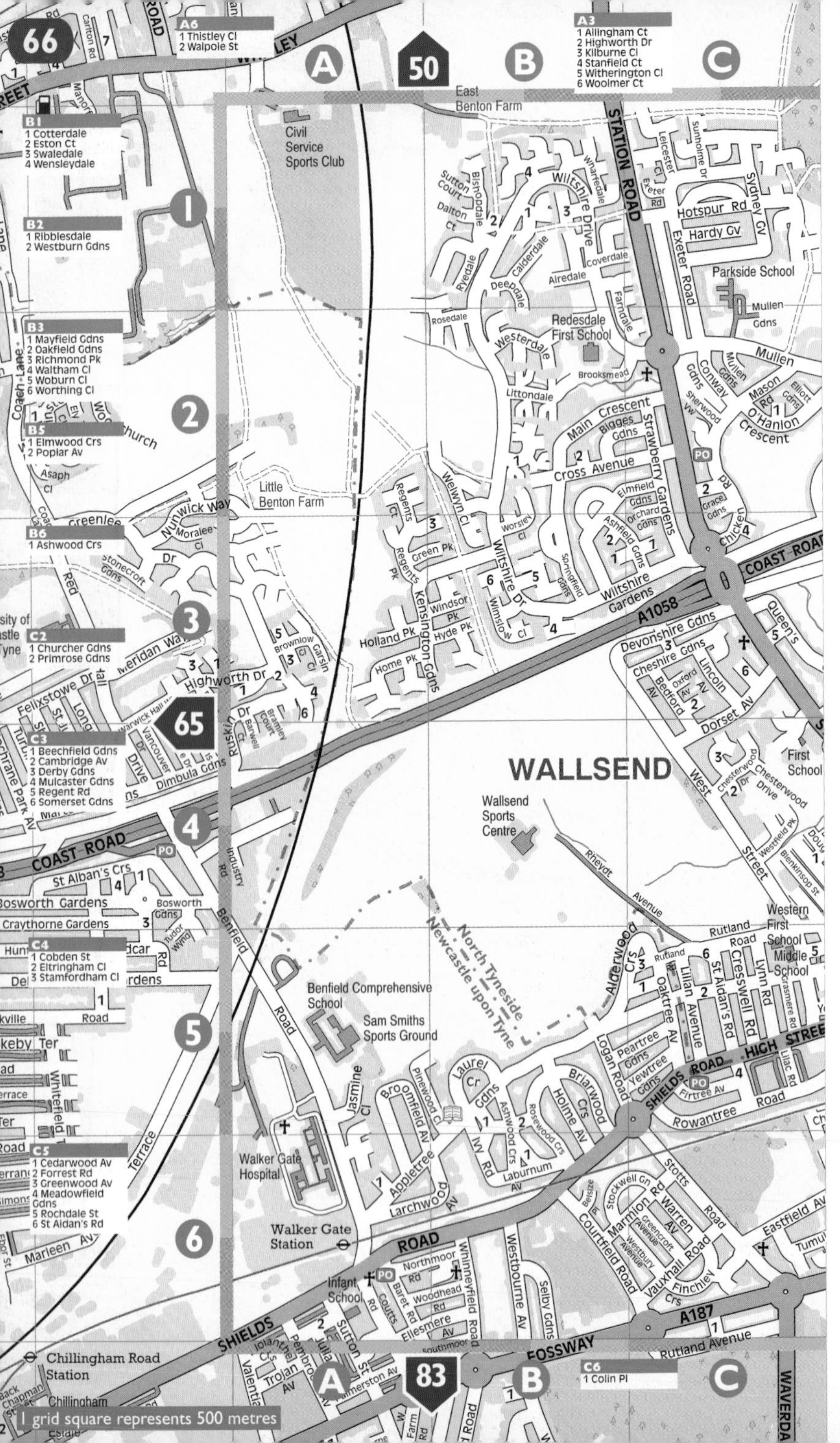
A6
1 Thistley Cl
2 Walpole St
A3
1 Allingham Ct
2 Highworth Dr
3 Kilburne Cl
4 Stanfield Ct
5 Witherington Cl
6 Woolmer Ct
B1
1 Cotterdale
2 Eston Ct
3 Swaledale
4 Wensleydale
B2
1 Ribblesdale
2 Westburn Gdns
B3
1 Mayfield Gdns
2 Oakfield Gdns
3 Richmond Pk
4 Waltham Cl
5 Woburn Cl
6 Worthing Cl
B5
1 Elmwood Crs
2 Poplar Av
B6
1 Ashwood Crs
C2
1 Churcher Gdns
2 Primrose Gdns
C3
1 Beechfield Gdns
2 Cambridge Av
3 Derby Gdns
4 Mulcaster Gdns
5 Regent Rd
6 Somerset Gdns
C4
1 Cobden St
2 Eltringham Cl
3 Stamfordham Cl
C5
1 Cedarwood Av
2 Forrest Rd
3 Greenwood Av
4 Meadowfield Gdns
5 Rochdale St
6 St Aidan's Rd
C6
1 Colin Pl
50
65
83
East Benton Farm
Civil Service Sports Club
Little Benton Farm
STATION ROAD
Wiltshire Drive
Hotspur Rd
Hardy Gv
Exeter Road
Sydney Gv
Parkside School
Redesdale First School
Mullen Gdns
Main Crescent
Cross Avenue
Strawberry Gardens
O'Hanlon Crescent
Wiltshire Gardens
COAST ROAD
A1058
Kensington Gdns
Holland Pk
Devonshire Gdns
Cheshire Gdns
Dorset Av
WALLSEND
Wallsend Sports Centre
First School
West Street
Chesterwood Drive
Rheydt Avenue
North Tyneside
Newcastle upon Tyne
Benfield Comprehensive School
Sam Smiths Sports Ground
Benfield Road
Industry Rd
Alderwood Crs
Rutland Road
Western First School
Middle School
Lilian Avenue
Cresswell Rd
Lynn Rd
HIGH STREET
SHIELDS ROAD
Firtree Av
Rowantree Road
Walker Gate Hospital
Walker Gate Station
Larchwood Av
Appletree
Laburnum Av
Holme Av
Briarwood Crs
Logan Road
Courtfield Road
Marmion Rd
Stotts Road
Vauxhall Road
Westbourne Av
Whinneyfield Road
Eastfield Av
Infant School
A187
FOSSWAY
Rutland Avenue
Chillingham Road Station
Highworth Dr
Ruskin Dr
Meridan Way
Felixstowe Dr
Nunwick Way
Greenlee Dr
Stonecroft Gdns
Dimbula Gdns
Vancouver Drive
St Alban's Crs
Bosworth Gardens
Craythorne Gardens
Coach Lane
Terrace
Marleen Av
SHIELDS ROAD
Trojan Av
Sutton St
WAVERDALE

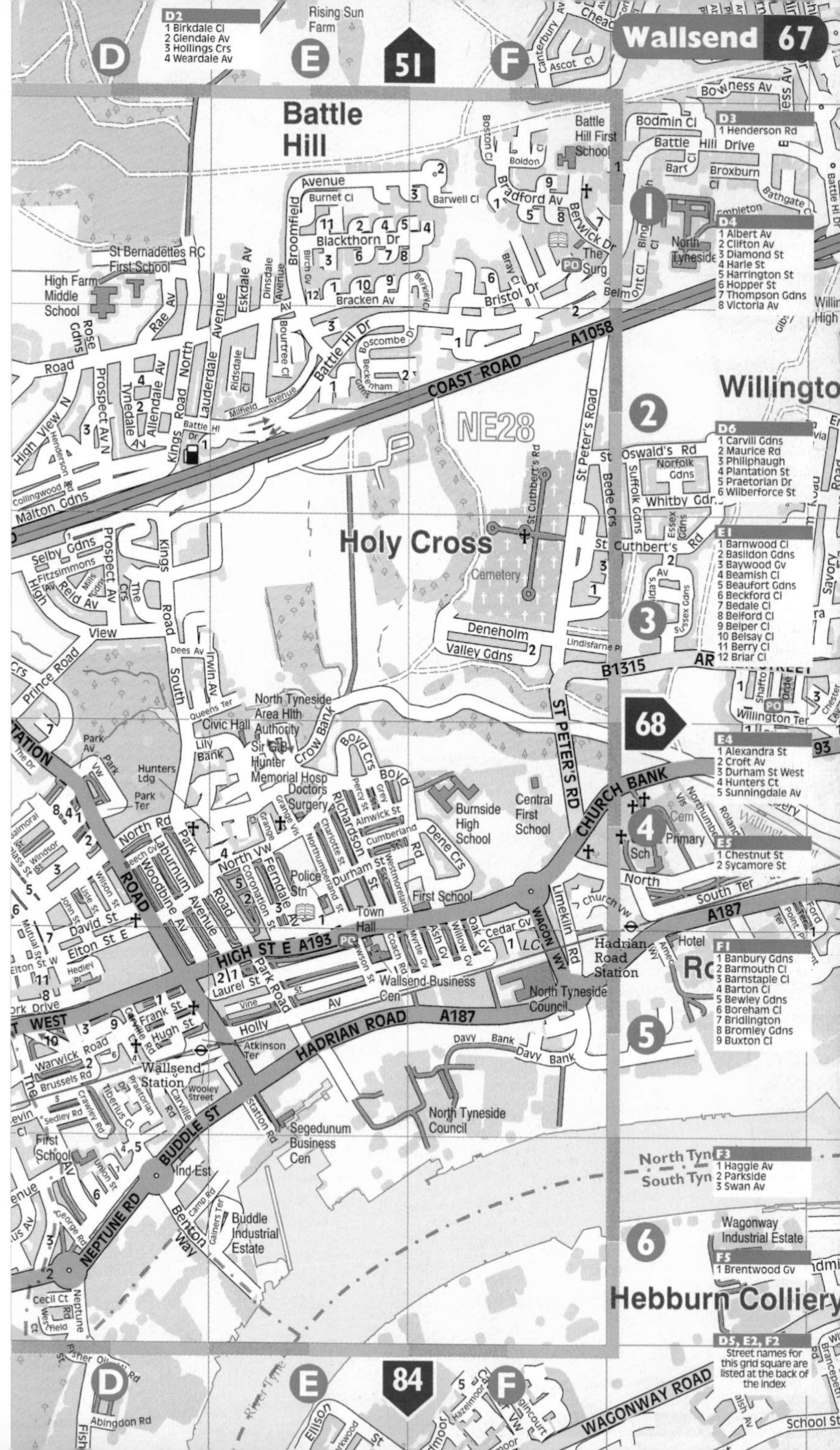
D2
1 Birkdale Cl
2 Glendale Av
3 Hollings Crs
4 Weardale Av
Rising Sun Farm
D
E
51
F
Battle Hill
Battle Hill First School
Bowness Av
Bodmin Cl
Battle Hill Drive
D3
1 Henderson Rd
Broxburn Cl
Bathgate
Embleton
D4
1 Albert Av
2 Clifton Av
3 Diamond St
4 Harle St
5 Harrington St
6 Hopper St
7 Thompson Gdns
8 Victoria Av
North Tyneside
Avenue
Burnet Cl
Barwell Cl
Bradford Av
Berwick Dr
Blackthorn Dr
Broomfield Avenue
Birch Gv
Bracken Av
Bristol Dr
Boscombe Dr
Battle Hl Dr
Beckenham Gdns
Bourtree Cl
Dinsdale Av
St Bernadettes RC First School
High Farm Middle School
Rose Gdns
Rae Av
Eskdale Av
Avenue
North Road
Lauderdale Avenue
Ridsdale Cl
Milfield Avenue
Allendale Av
Tynedale Av
Prospect Av N
High View N
Henderson Rd
Collingwood Rd
Malton Gdns
Kings Road
Battle Hl Dr
COAST ROAD
A1058
NE28
Willington
St Peter's Road
St Oswald's Rd
Norfolk Gdns
Suffolk Gdns
Whitby Gdns
Essex Gdns
Bede Crs
St Cuthbert's Rd
D6
1 Carvill Gdns
2 Maurice Rd
3 Philiphaugh
4 Plantation St
5 Praetorian Dr
6 Wilberforce St
E1
1 Barnwood Cl
2 Basildon Gdns
3 Baywood Gv
4 Beamish Cl
5 Beaufort Gdns
6 Beckford Cl
7 Bedale Cl
8 Belford Cl
9 Belper Cl
10 Belsay Cl
11 Berry Cl
12 Briar Cl
Holy Cross
Cemetery
Selby Gdns
Fitzsimmons Av
Mills Gdns
Reid Av
Prospect Av
The Crs
High View
Deneholm
Valley Gdns
Lindisfarne Pl
Sussex Gdns
B1315
Prince Road
Dees Av
Irwin Av
South
Queens Ter
North Tyneside Area Hlth Authority
Civic Hall
Lily Bank
Sir G B Hunter Memorial Hosp
Crow Bank
Boyd Crs
Boyd
ST PETER'S RD
68
Shafto
Orde
Willington Ter
E4
1 Alexandra St
2 Croft Av
3 Durham St West
4 Hunters Ct
5 Sunningdale Av
CHURCH BANK
Cem
Primary
Sch
E5
1 Chestnut St
2 Sycamore St
STATION
Park Av
Park Vw
Hunters Ldg
Park Ter
Doctors Surgery
Richardson St
Percy St
Grey St
Alnwick St
Cumberland
Burnside High School
Central First School
Dene Crs
North Rd
Laburnum
Park
Grange Vis
Beech Gv
Woodbine Av
Avenue
North Vw
Coronation St
Ferndale
Police Stn
Charlotte St
Northumberland St
Durham St
Westmoreland
First School
Town Hall
ROAD
Windsor
Wilson St
Lisle St
John St
David St
Elton St E
Elton St W
Mutual St
Hedley Pl
HIGH ST E A193
Park Road
Laurel St
Lawson St
Coach Rd
Ash Gv
Myrtle Gv
Willow Gv
Oak Gv
Cedar Gv
LC
WAGON WY
Limekiln Rd
Church Vw
Hadrian Road Station
North Tyneside Council
A187
South Ter
North
Hotel
F1
1 Banbury Gdns
2 Barmouth Cl
3 Barnstaple Cl
4 Barton Cl
5 Bewley Gdns
6 Boreham Cl
7 Bridlington
8 Bromley Gdns
9 Buxton Cl
Wallsend Business Cen
Vine
Holly Av
HADRIAN ROAD
A187
Davy Bank
York Drive
WEST
Frank St
Hugh St
Warwick Road
Brussels Rd
The
Atkinson Ter
Wallsend Station
Wooley Street
Carville Rd
Praetorian
Tiberius Cl
Crawley Rd
Sedley Rd
Station Rd
BUDDLE ST
Segedunum Business Cen
North Tyneside Council
First School
Union St
Ind Est
North Tyne
South Tyne
F3
1 Haggie Av
2 Parkside
3 Swan Av
NEPTUNE RD
Camp Rd
Gainers Ter
Benton Way
Buddle Industrial Estate
George Rd
Wagonway Industrial Estate
F5
1 Brentwood Gv
Hebburn Colliery
Cecil Ct
Neptune Rd
Westfield
D5, E2, F2
Street names for this grid square are listed at the back of the index
D
Abingdon Rd
E
River Tyne
84
Ellison St
F
Hazelmoor
WAGONWAY ROAD
School St
Brancepeth

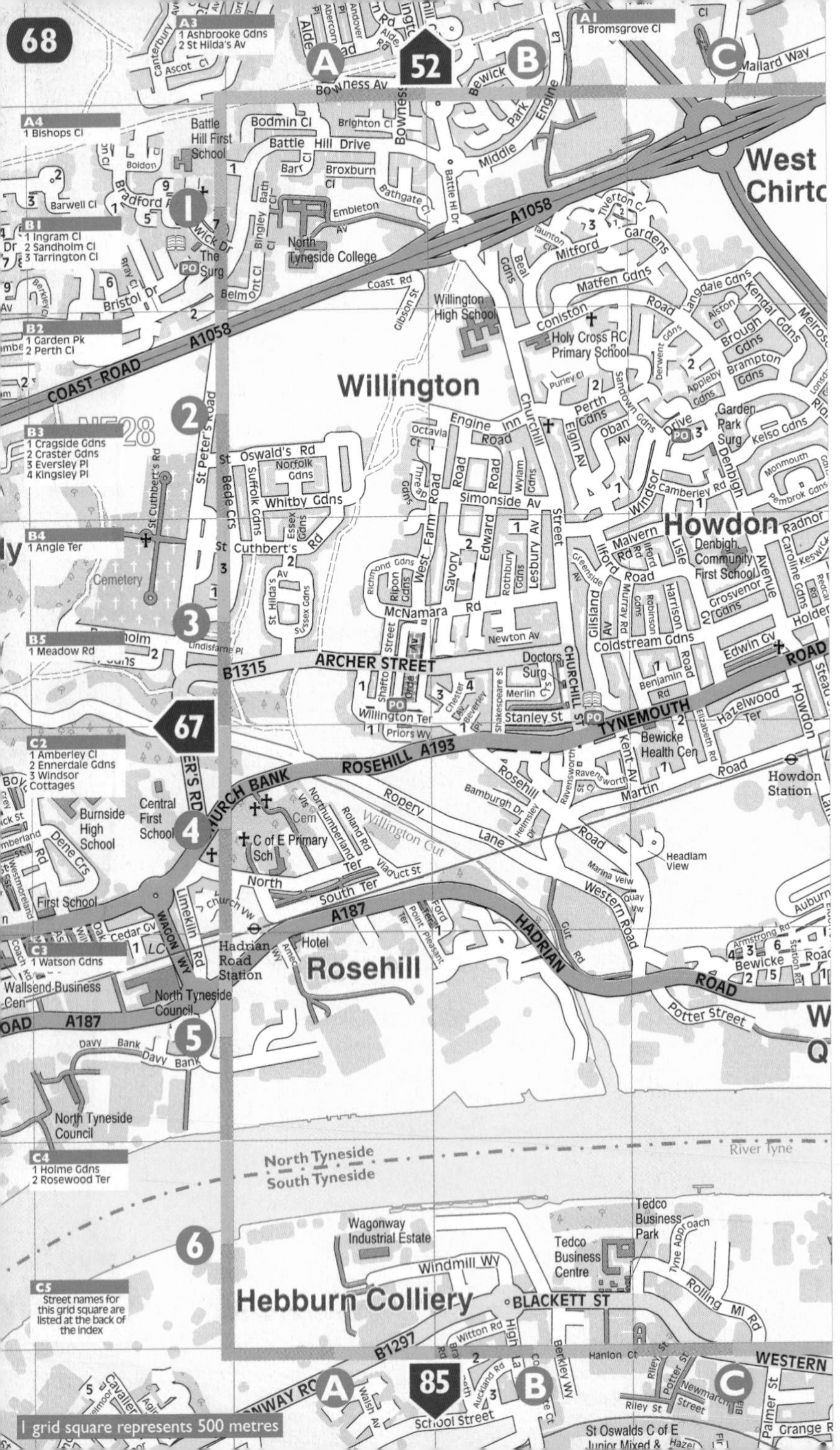
A3
1 Ashbrooke Gdns
2 St Hilda's Av
A1
1 Bromsgrove Cl
A
52
B
C
Mallard Way
Bowness Av
A4
1 Bishops Cl
Battle Hill First School
Bodmin Cl
Brighton Cl
Battle Hill Drive
Broxburn Cl
Bathgate Cl
Embleton Av
North Tyneside College
Middle Engine
Battle Hl Dr
West Chirto
A1058
B1
1 Ingram Cl
2 Sandholm Cl
3 Tarrington Cl
Bradford Av
Bristol Dr
The Surg
Belmont Cl
Bingley Cl
Tiverton Cl
Taunton Cl
Mitford Gardens
Beal Gdns
Matfen Gdns
Coast Rd
Gibson St
Willington High School
B2
1 Garden Pk
2 Perth Cl
COAST ROAD
A1058
Coniston Road
Holy Cross RC Primary School
Langdale Gdns
Kendal Gdns
Alston Cl
Brough Gdns
Derwent Gdns
Brampton Gdns
Appleby Gdns
Melrose
Willington
NE28
Churchill Street
Purley Cl
Perth Gdns
Sandown Gdns
Elgin Av
Oban Av
Drive
Garden Park Surg
Kelso Gdns
Denbigh
B3
1 Cragside Gdns
2 Craster Gdns
3 Eversley Pl
4 Kingsley Pl
St Cuthbert's Rd
St Peter's Road
St Oswald's Rd
Norfolk Gdns
Suffolk Gdns
Whitby Gdns
Essex Gdns
Octavia Ct
Engine Inn Road
Three Gdns
West Farm Road
Savory Road
Edward Road
Wylam Gdns
Simonside Av
Windsor
Camberley Rd
Monmouth
Pembrok Gdns
Howdon
Radnor
B4
1 Angle Ter
Cemetery
Bede Crs
St Cuthbert's Rd
St Hilda's Av
Sussex Gdns
Richmond Gdns
Ripon Gdns
Rothbury Gdns
Lesbury Av
Greenside Av
Ilford Road
Malvern Rd
Ilford Rd
Lisle
Denbigh Community First School
Avenue
Caroline Gdns
Keswick
McNamara Rd
Newton Av
Gilsland Av
Murray Rd
Robinson Gdns
Harrison Road
Grosvenor Gdns
Gv
Holder
B5
1 Meadow Rd
Lindisfarne Pl
B1315
ARCHER STREET
Shafto Street
Orde Av
Doctors Surg
Coldstream Gdns
Edwin Gv
ROAD
Benjamin Rd
Chester Av
Beverley Pl
Shakespeare St
Merlin Ct
Stanley St
CHURCHILL ST
TYNEMOUTH
Hazelwood Ter
Elizabeth Rd
Howdon
67
Willington Ter
Priors Wy
C2
1 Amberley Cl
2 Ennerdale Gdns
3 Windsor Cottages
ROSEHILL A193
CHURCH BANK
Rosehill
Ravensworth
Kent Av
Bewicke Health Cen
Martin Road
Howdon Station
Burnside High School
Central First School
Vis Cem
Northumberland Rd
Roland Rd
Ropery Lane
Willington Cut
Bamburgh Dr
Helmsley Dr
Road
Headlam View
C of E Primary Sch
Dene Crs
North Ter
South Ter
Viaduct St
Marina View
Quay Vw
Western Road
Church Vw
First School
Limekiln Rd
WAGON WY
A187
HADRIAN
Cedar Gv
Hadrian Road Station
Hotel
Rosehill
Gut Rd
Armstrong Rd
Bewicke
Station Rd
C3
1 Watson Gdns
Wallsend Business Cen
North Tyneside Council
ROAD
A187
Potter Street
5
Davy Bank
North Tyneside Council
C4
1 Holme Gdns
2 Rosewood Ter
North Tyneside
South Tyneside
River Tyne
6
Wagonway Industrial Estate
Tedco Business Park
Tedco Business Centre
Tyne Approach
Windmill Wy
C5
Street names for this grid square are listed at the back of the index
Hebburn Colliery
BLACKETT ST
Rolling Ml Rd
B1297
Witton Rd
High La
Berkley Wy
Hanlon Ct
WESTERN
85
Auckland Rd
Riley St
Potter St
Newmarch Street
Palmer St
Walsh Av
School Street
St Oswalds C of E Junior Mixed &
Grange R
1 grid square represents 500 metres

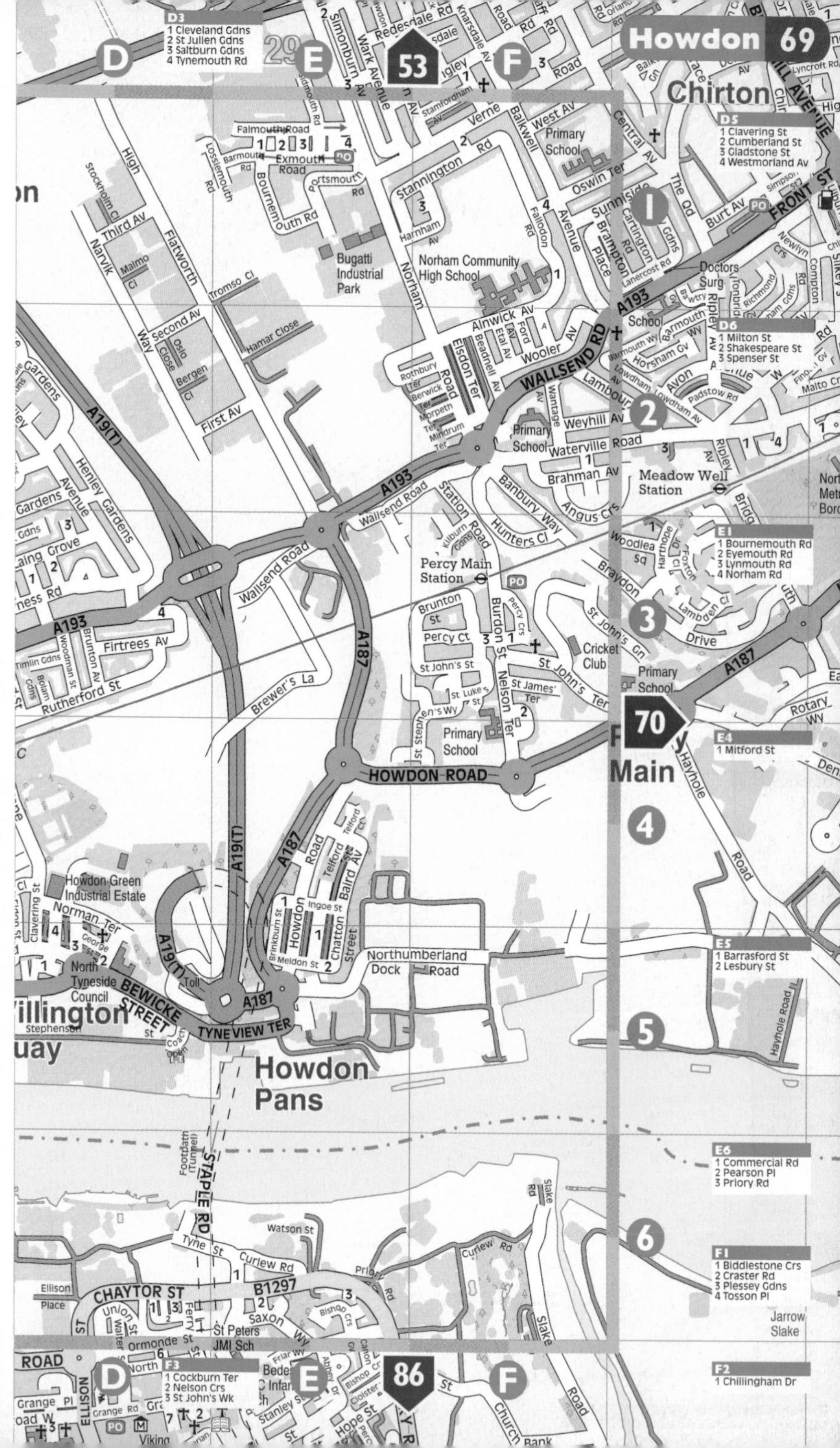

D3
1 Cleveland Gdns
2 St Jullen Gdns
3 Saltburn Gdns
4 Tynemouth Rd
D5
1 Clavering St
2 Cumberland St
3 Gladstone St
4 Westmorland Av
D6
1 Milton St
2 Shakespeare St
3 Spenser St
E1
1 Bournemouth Rd
2 Eyemouth Rd
3 Lynmouth Rd
4 Norham Rd
E4
1 Mitford St
E5
1 Barrasford St
2 Lesbury St
E6
1 Commercial Rd
2 Pearson Pl
3 Priory Rd
F1
1 Biddlestone Crs
2 Craster Rd
3 Plessey Gdns
4 Tosson Pl
F2
1 Chillingham Dr
F3
1 Cockburn Ter
2 Nelson Crs
3 St John's Wk
Chirton
Howdon Pans
Percy Main
Willington Quay
Meadow Well Station
Percy Main Station
Norham Community High School
Bugatti Industrial Park
Howdon Green Industrial Estate
North Tyneside Council
Cricket Club
Primary School
Jarrow Slake
A193
A187
A19(T)
WALLSEND RD
HOWDON ROAD
BEWICKE STREET
TYNE VIEW TER
CHAYTOR ST
B1297
STAPLE RD
FRONT ST
Northumberland Dock Road
Hayhole Road
53
70
86

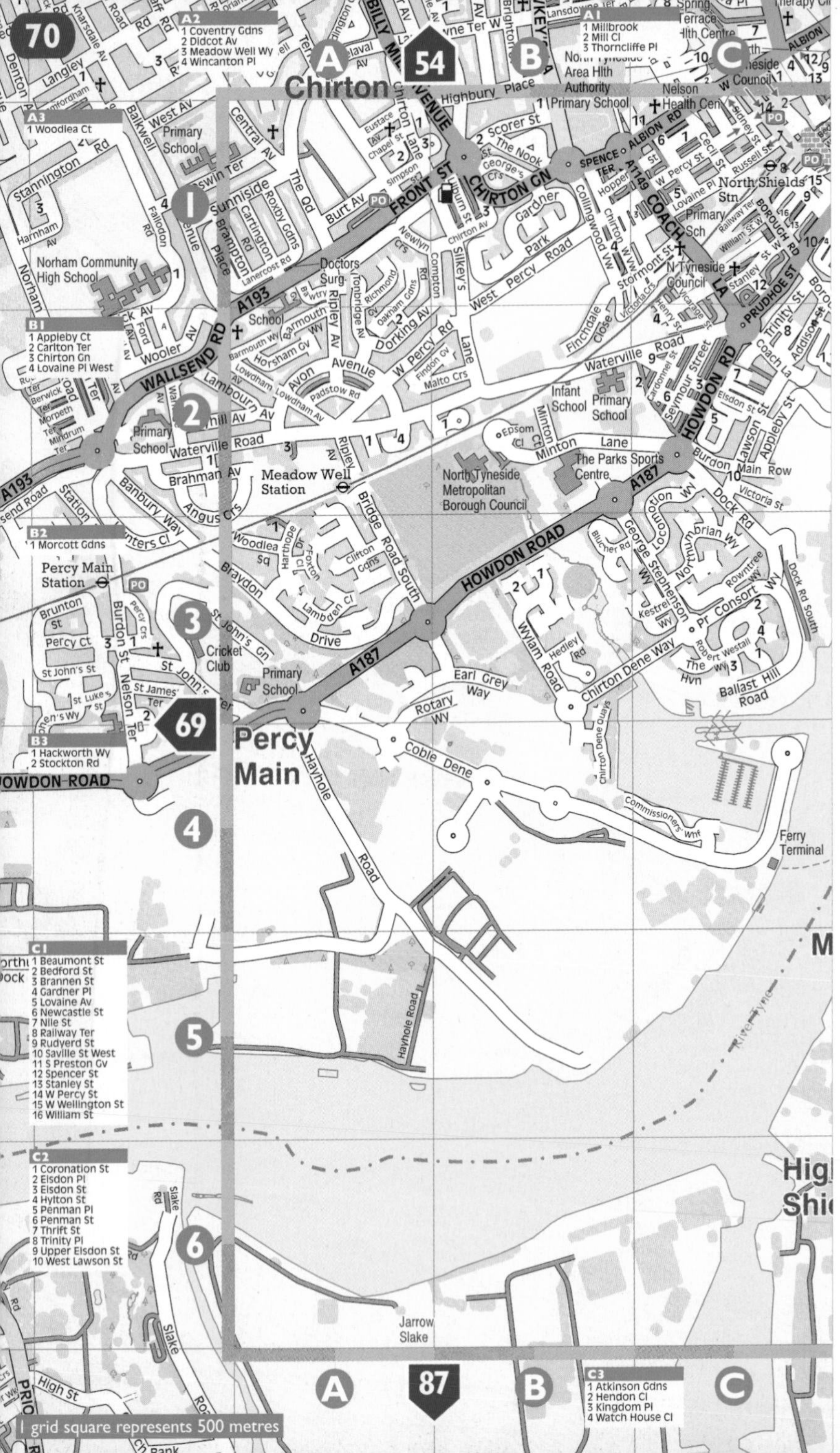
A2
1 Coventry Gdns
2 Didcot Av
3 Meadow Well Wy
4 Wincanton Pl
A1
1 Millbrook
2 Mill Cl
3 Thorncliffe Pl
A3
1 Woodlea Ct
B1
1 Appleby Ct
2 Carlton Ter
3 Chirton Gn
4 Lovaine Pl West
B2
1 Morcott Gdns
B3
1 Hackworth Wy
2 Stockton Rd
C1
1 Beaumont St
2 Bedford St
3 Brannen St
4 Gardner Pl
5 Lovaine Av
6 Newcastle St
7 Nile St
8 Railway Ter
9 Rudyerd St
10 Saville St West
11 S Preston Gv
12 Spencer St
13 Stanley St
14 W Percy St
15 W Wellington St
16 William St
C2
1 Coronation St
2 Elsdon Pl
3 Elsdon St
4 Hylton St
5 Penman Pl
6 Penman St
7 Thrift St
8 Trinity Pl
9 Upper Elsdon St
10 West Lawson St
C3
1 Atkinson Gdns
2 Hendon Cl
3 Kingdom Pl
4 Watch House Cl
A
B
C
1
2
3
4
5
6
54
69
87
Chirton
Percy Main
Billy Mill Avenue
Highbury Place
Front St
Chirton Gn
Albion Rd
Coach La
Howdon Rd
Howdon Road
Wallsend Rd
A193
A187
A1149
West Percy Road
Waterville Road
Avon Avenue
Minton Lane
Norham Community High School
North Tyneside Area Hlth Authority
Primary School
Nelson Health Cen
N Tyneside Council
North Shields Stn
Meadow Well Station
Percy Main Station
North Tyneside Metropolitan Borough Council
The Parks Sports Centre
Infant School
Doctors Surg
Cricket Club
Earl Grey Way
Rotary Wy
Coble Dene
Commissioners' Wharf
Chirton Dene Way
Chirton Dene Quays
Ballast Hill Road
Dock Rd South
George Stephenson Wy
Locomotion Wy
Bridge Road South
Hayhole Road
Ferry Terminal
River Tyne
Jarrow Slake
Slake Rd
High St
1 grid square represents 500 metres

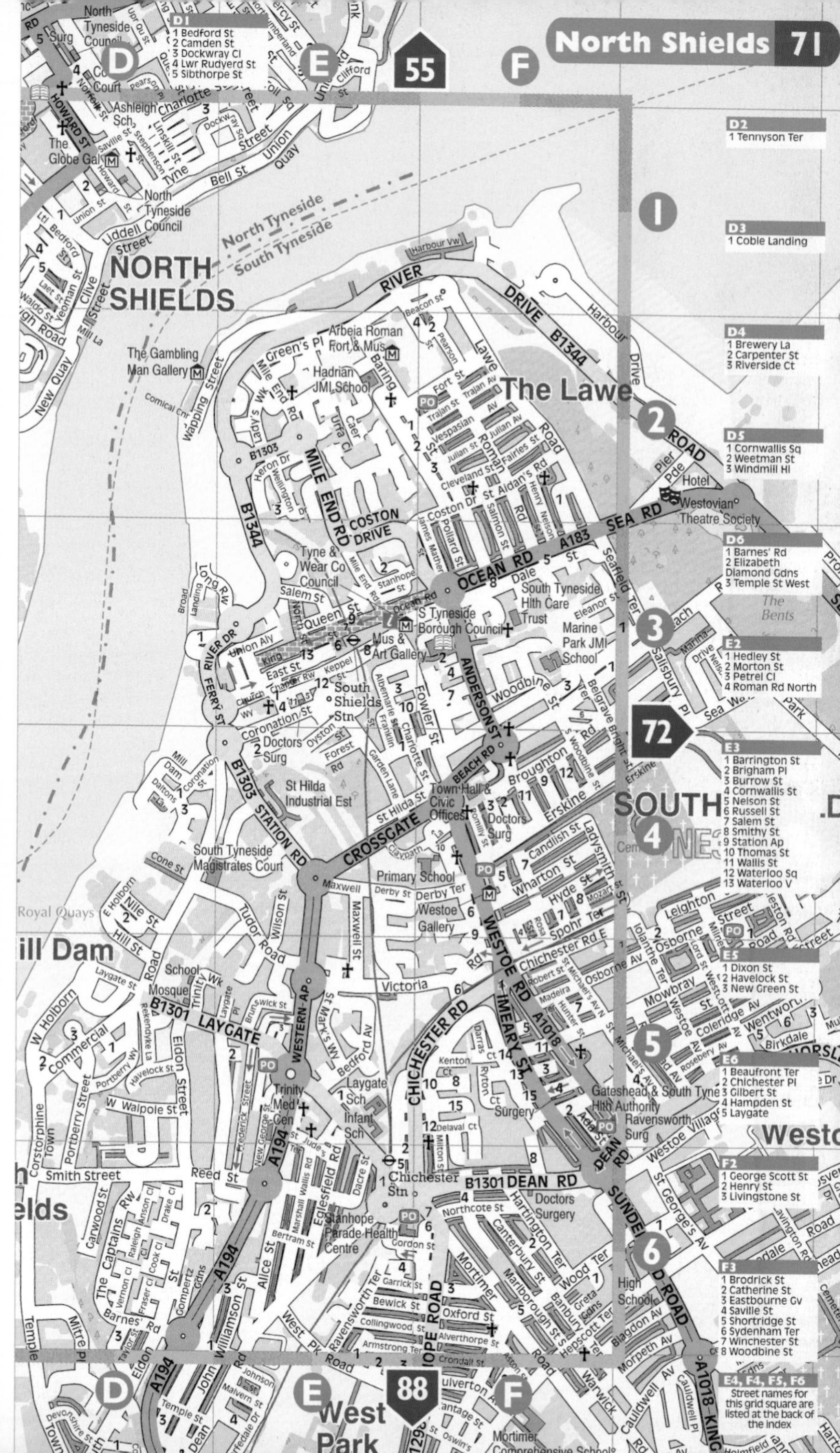
North Shields 71
55
72
88
D
E
F
D
E
F
2
3
4
5
6
D1
1 Bedford St
2 Camden St
3 Dockwray Cl
4 Lwr Rudyerd St
5 Sibthorpe St
D2
1 Tennyson Ter
D3
1 Coble Landing
D4
1 Brewery La
2 Carpenter St
3 Riverside Ct
D5
1 Cornwallis Sq
2 Weetman St
3 Windmill Hl
D6
1 Barnes' Rd
2 Elizabeth Diamond Gdns
3 Temple St West
E2
1 Hedley St
2 Morton St
3 Petrel Cl
4 Roman Rd North
E3
1 Barrington St
2 Brigham Pl
3 Burrow St
4 Cornwallis St
5 Nelson St
6 Russell St
7 Salem St
8 Smithy St
9 Station Ap
10 Thomas St
11 Wallis St
12 Waterloo Sq
13 Waterloo V
E5
1 Dixon St
2 Havelock St
3 New Green St
E6
1 Beaufront Ter
2 Chichester Pl
3 Gilbert St
4 Hampden St
5 Laygate
F2
1 George Scott St
2 Henry St
3 Livingstone St
F3
1 Brodrick St
2 Catherine St
3 Eastbourne Gv
4 Saville St
5 Shortridge St
6 Sydenham Ter
7 Winchester St
8 Woodbine St
E4, F4, F5, F6
Street names for this grid square are listed at the back of the index
NORTH SHIELDS
North Tyneside
South Tyneside
The Lawe
SOUTH
Westoe
West Park
Royal Quays
RIVER DRIVE B1344
OCEAN RD A183
SEA RD
MILE END RD
CROSSGATE
STATION RD
WESTOE RD
DEAN RD
LAYGATE
WESTERN AP
CHICHESTER RD
Arbeia Roman Fort & Mus
Hadrian JMI School
Tyne & Wear Co Council
S Tyneside Borough Council
Mus & Art Gallery
South Shields Stn
St Hilda Industrial Est
Town Hall & Civic Offices
South Tyneside Magistrates Court
South Tyneside Hlth Care Trust
Marine Park JMI School
Westovian Theatre Society
Chichester Stn
Stanhope Parade Health Centre
Gateshead & South Tyne Hlth Authority
Mortimer Comprehensive School
The Gambling Man Gallery
The Globe Gal
Westoe Gallery
Primary School
Doctors Surgery
High School

A3
1 Wouldhave Ct
A4
1 Aldwych St
2 Fitzpatrick Pl
A5
1 August Pl
2 Catherine Cookson Ct
3 Gleneagles
4 Ingham Gra
5 Sunningdale
6 Turnberry
A6
1 College Dr
B6
1 Eastfield Rd
2 North Vw
C5
1 Bideford Gdns
South Pier
Herd Sand
The Lawe
SEA ROAD
DRIVE B1344
Harbour Drive
Pier Pde
Hotel
Westovian Theatre Society
Amphitheatre
The Bents
Promenade
SOUTH SHIELDS
NE33
Cemetery
COAST ROAD A183
Westoe
Horsley Hill
South Tyneside College
Infant School
High School
Town Hall & Civic Offices
S Tyneside Borough Council
South Tyneside Hlth Care Trust
Gateshead & South Tyneside Hlth Authority
Ravensworth Surg
Doctors Surgery
Chichester Stn
B1301 DEAN RD
SUNDERLAND ROAD
HIGHFIELD ROAD
HORSLEY HL RD B1301
South Tyneside Area Hlth Authority
1 grid square represents 500 metres

71
89

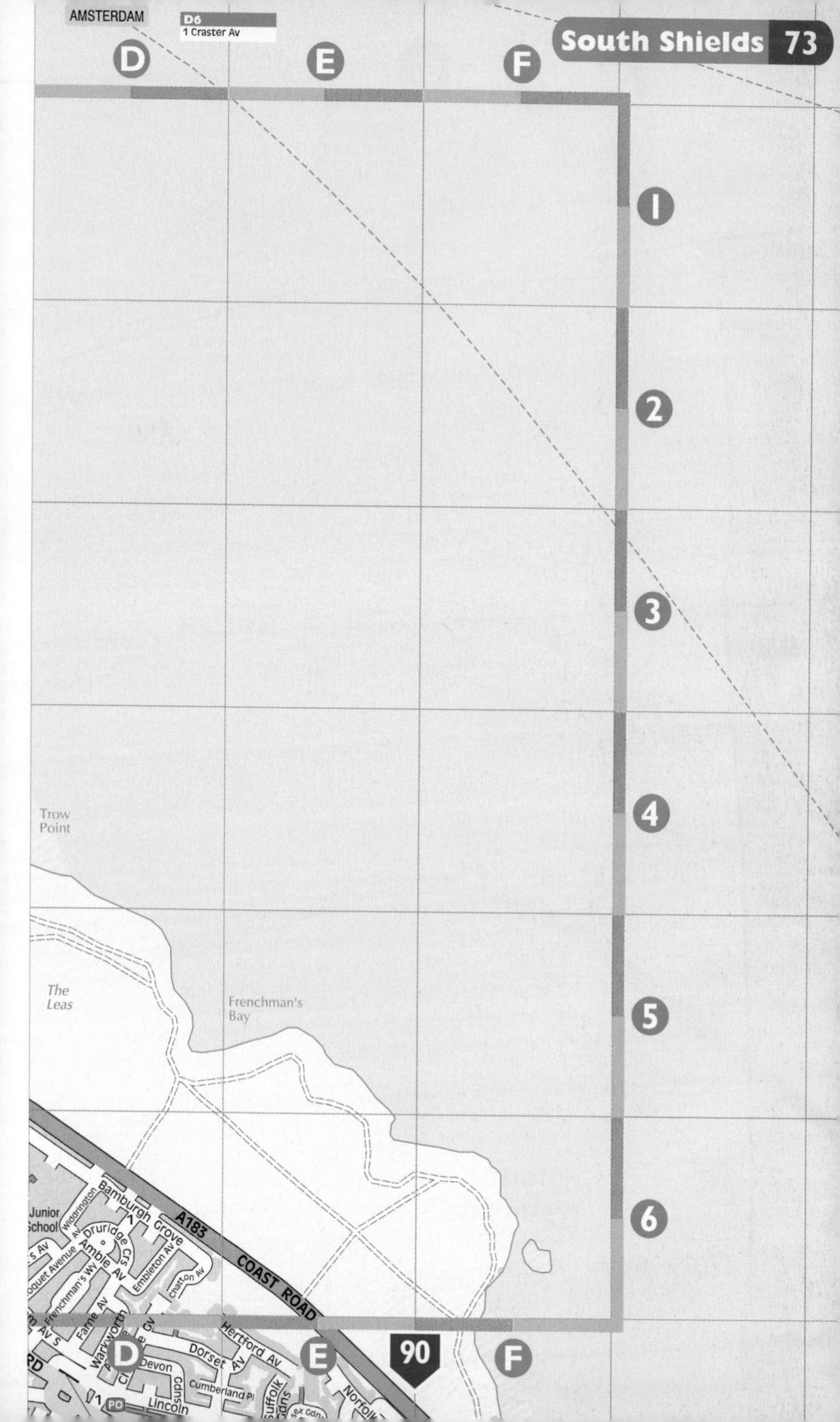
AMSTERDAM
D6
1 Craster Av
D
E
F
1
2
3
4
5
6
Trow Point
The Leas
Frenchman's Bay
Junior School
Bamburgh Grove
Widdrington
Druridge Crs
Amble Av
Embleton Av
Chatton Av
Frenchman's Wy
Farne Av
Warkworth
A183
COAST ROAD
Devon
Dorset Av
Hertford Av
Cumberland Pl
Lincoln
Suffolk
Norfolk
PO
90

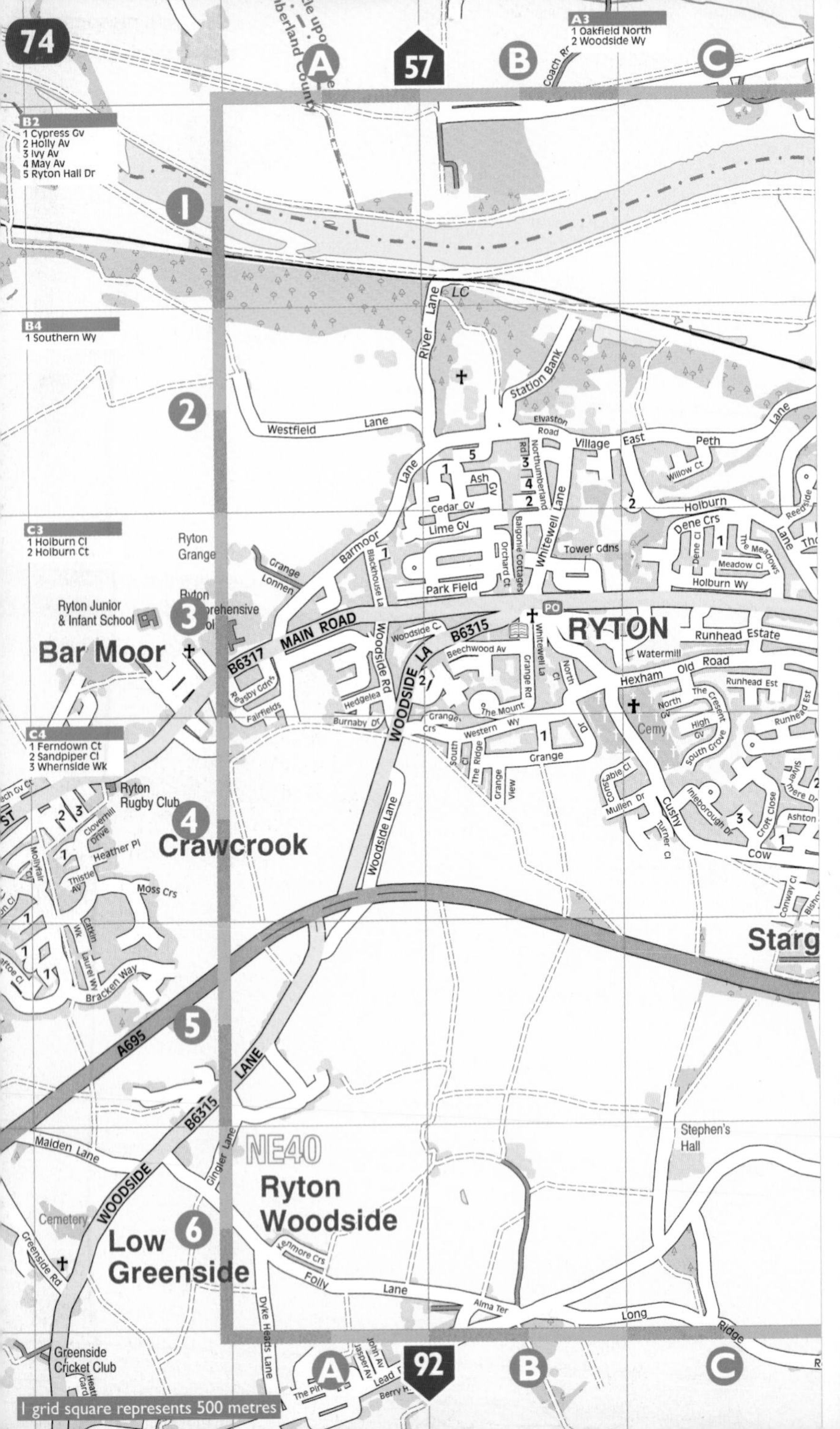
57
A3
1 Oakfield North
2 Woodside Wy
B2
1 Cypress Gv
2 Holly Av
3 Ivy Av
4 May Av
5 Ryton Hall Dr
B4
1 Southern Wy
C3
1 Holburn Cl
2 Holburn Ct
C4
1 Ferndown Ct
2 Sandpiper Cl
3 Whernside Wk
Coach Rd
River Lane
LC
Station Bank
Westfield Lane
Elvaston Road
Village East
Peth
Lane
Willow Ct
Holburn
Ash Gv
Cedar Gv
Lime Gv
Northumberland Rd
Whitewell Lane
Dene Crs
Dene Cl
The Meadows
Meadow Cl
Holburn Wy
Tower Gdns
Park Field
Orchard Ct
Balgonie Cottages
Barmoor Lane
Blackhouse La
Grange Lonnen
Ryton Grange
Ryton Comprehensive School
Ryton Junior & Infant School
Bar Moor
B6317
MAIN ROAD
B6315
Woodside Rd
Woodside Ct
WOODSIDE LA
Beechwood Av
Grange Rd
Whitewell La
North Cl
PO
RYTON
Runhead Estate
Watermill
Hexham Old Road
Runhead Est
The Cresent
North Gv
High Gv
South Grove
Cemy
Reasby Gdns
Fairfields
Hedgelea
Burnaby Dr
Grange Crs
The Mount
Western Wy
South Crs
The Ridge
Grange View
Grange Dr
Constable Cl
Mullen Dr
Cushy Cow
Turner Cl
Ingleborough Dr
Croft Close
Ashton
Conway Cl
Starg
Ryton Rugby Club
Crawcrook
Clovermill Drive
Heather Pl
Mollyfair
Thistle Av
Moss Crs
Catkin Wk
Laurel Wy
Bracken Way
Woodside Lane
A695
LANE
B6315
WOODSIDE
Maiden Lane
Gingler Lane
NE40
Ryton Woodside
Stephen's Hall
Cemetery
Greenside Rd
Low Greenside
Kenmore Crs
Folly Lane
Alma Ter
Long Ridge
Dyke Heads Lane
Greenside Cricket Club
John Av
Jasper Av
Lead
Berry
The Pit
92
1 grid square represents 500 metres

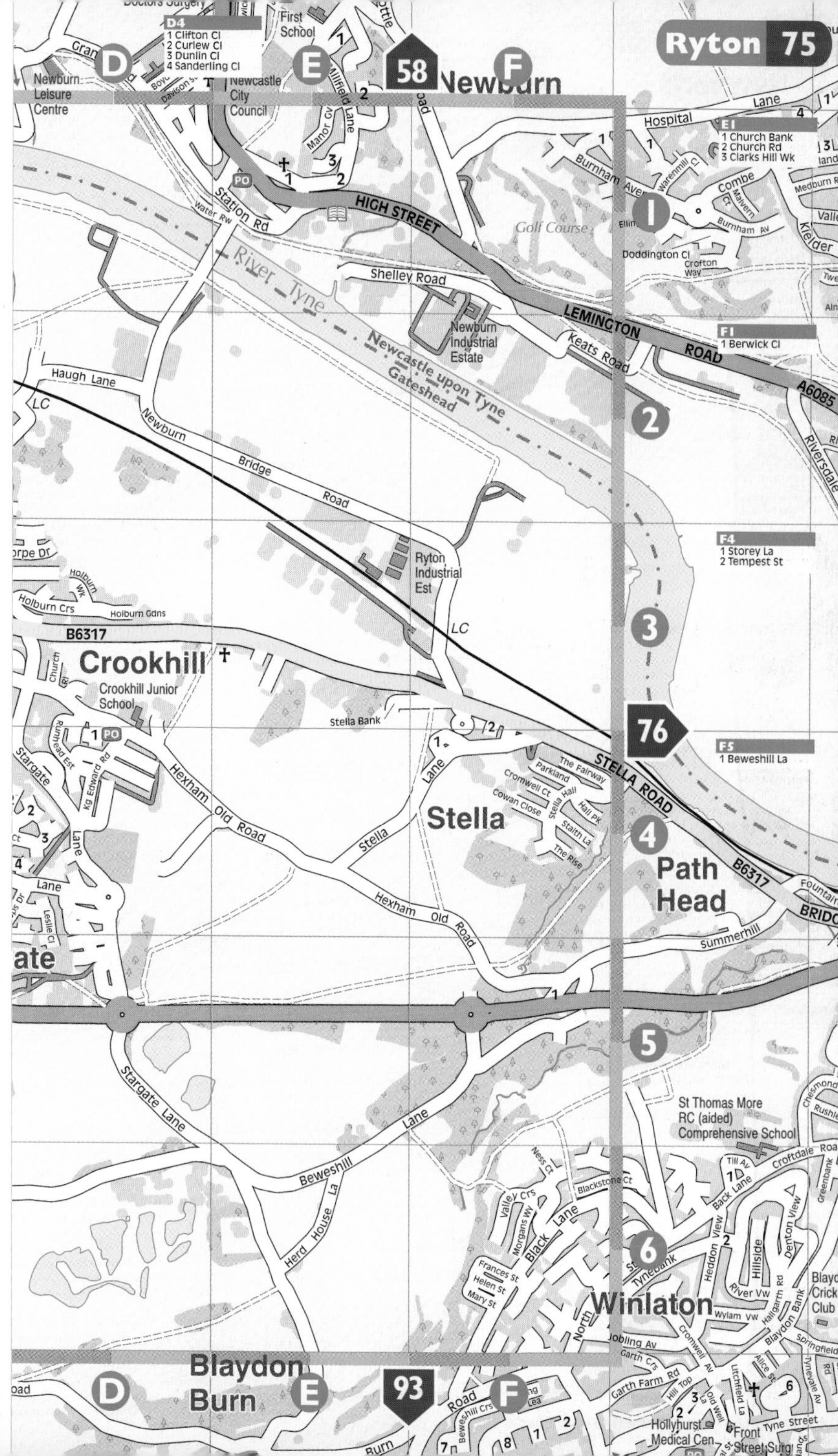
D4
1 Clifton Cl
2 Curlew Cl
3 Dunlin Cl
4 Sanderling Cl
E1
1 Church Bank
2 Church Rd
3 Clarks Hill Wk
F1
1 Berwick Cl
F4
1 Storey La
2 Tempest St
F5
1 Beweshill La
58
76
93
Newburn
Newburn Leisure Centre
Newcastle City Council
First School
Millfield Lane
Manor Gv
HIGH STREET
Station Rd
Water Rw
River Tyne
Newcastle upon Tyne
Gateshead
Shelley Road
Newburn Industrial Estate
LEMINGTON ROAD
A6085
Keats Road
Hospital Lane
Burnham Ave
Warenmill Cl
Combe
Malvern Ct
Burnham Av
Golf Course
Doddington Cl
Crofton Way
Medburn Rd
Kielder
Riversdale
Haugh Lane
Newburn Bridge Road
Ryton Industrial Est
LC
B6317
Crookhill
Crookhill Junior School
Holburn Crs
Holburn Gdns
Holburn Wk
Stella Bank
Stella Lane
Stella
STELLA ROAD
The Fairway
Parkland
Cromwell Ct
Cowan Close
Stella Hall
Hall Pk
Staith La
The Rise
Path Head
Fountain
Summerhill
Hexham Old Road
Stargate
Rumhead Est
Kg Edward Rd
Lane
Leslie Cl
Stargate Lane
Beweshill Lane
Herd House La
Ness Ct
Blackstone Ct
Valley Crs
Morgans Wy
Black Lane
Frances St
Helen St
Mary St
Winlaton
North
Tynebank
St Thomas More RC (aided) Comprehensive School
Till Av
Back Lane
Croftdale Road
Greenbank
Chesmond
Rushley
Heddon View
Hillside
Denton View
River Vw
Hallgarth Rd
Blaydon Bank
Wylam Vw
Blaydon Cricket Club
Jobling Av
Garth Crs
Garth Farm Rd
Hill Top
Cromwell Av
Old Well La
Litchfield La
Alice St
Tynevale Av
Springfield Rd
Tyne Street
Front Street
Hollyhurst Medical Cen
Blaydon Burn
Beweshill Crs
Road
Burn

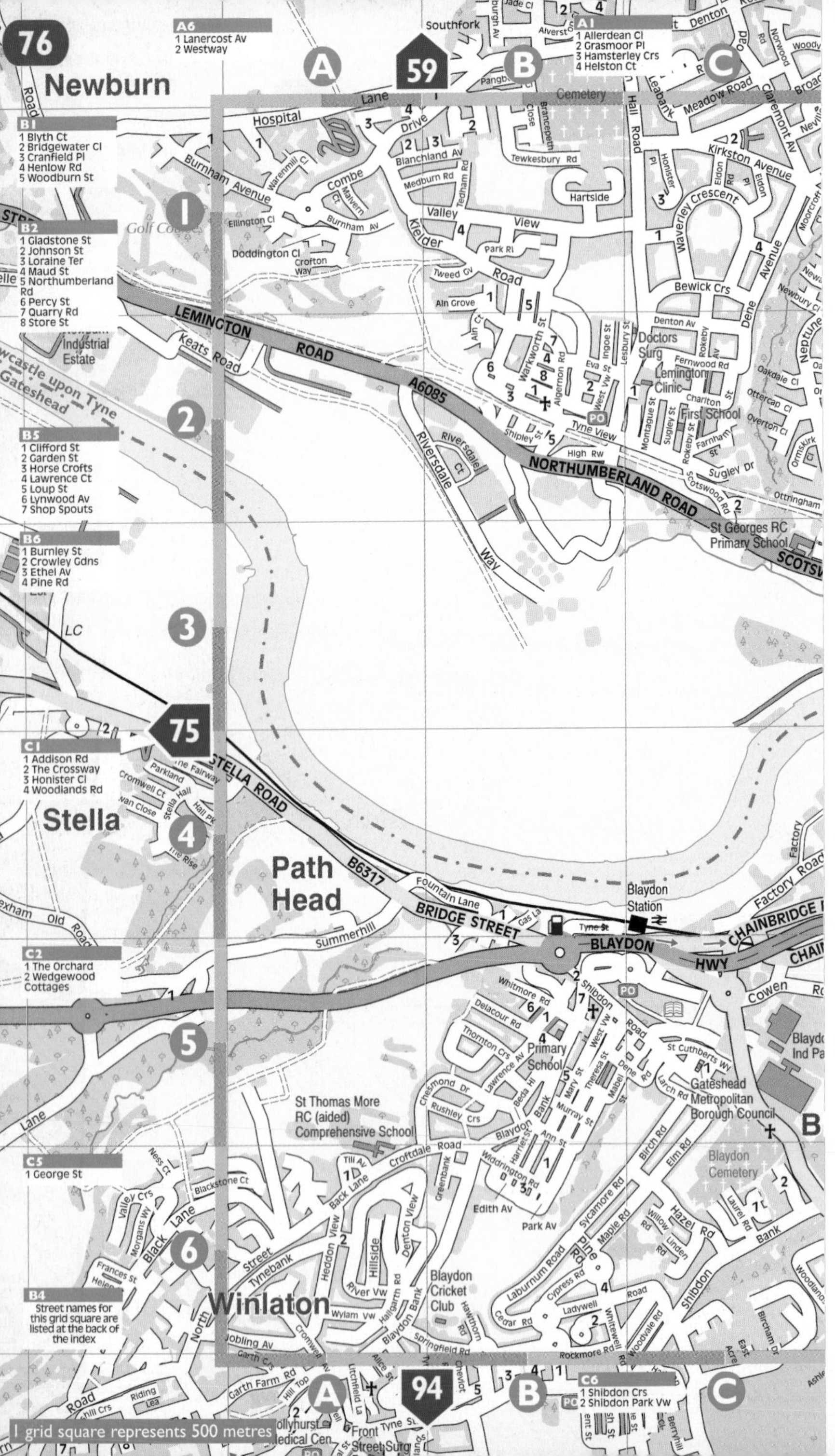

76
Newburn
A6
1 Lanercost Av
2 Westway
B1
1 Blyth Ct
2 Bridgewater Cl
3 Cranfield Pl
4 Henlow Rd
5 Woodburn St
B2
1 Gladstone St
2 Johnson St
3 Loraine Ter
4 Maud St
5 Northumberland Rd
6 Percy St
7 Quarry Rd
8 Store St
B5
1 Clifford St
2 Garden St
3 Horse Crofts
4 Lawrence Ct
5 Loup St
6 Lynwood Av
7 Shop Spouts
B6
1 Burnley St
2 Crowley Gdns
3 Ethel Av
4 Pine Rd
C1
1 Addison Rd
2 The Crossway
3 Honister Cl
4 Woodlands Rd
C2
1 The Orchard
2 Wedgewood Cottages
C5
1 George St
B4
Street names for this grid square are listed at the back of the index
A1
1 Allerdean Cl
2 Grasmoor Pl
3 Hamsterley Crs
4 Helston Ct
C6
1 Shibdon Crs
2 Shibdon Park Vw
59
75
94
A
B
C
1
2
3
4
5
6
Southfork
Cemetery
Hospital
Lane
Drive
Blanchland Av
Medburn Rd
Tedham Rd
Burnham Avenue
Warenmill Cl
Combe
Malvern
Burnham Av
Ellington Cl
Doddington Cl
Crofton Way
Golf Course
Valley
View
Kielder
Road
Park Rl
Tweed Gv
Aln Grove
Brancepeth Close
Tewkesbury Rd
Hartside
Hall Road
Leabank
Meadow Road
Claremont Av
Kirkston Avenue
Honister Pl
Waverley Crescent
Eldon
Bewick Crs
Dene Avenue
Denton Av
Doctors Surg
Lemington Clinic
Fernwood Rd
First School
Chariton
Ingoe St
Lesbury St
Eva St
West Vw
Warkworth St
Algernon Rd
Tyne View
High Rw
Shipley St
Montague St
Sugley St
Rokeby St
Farnham St
Sugley Dr
Oakdale Cl
Ottercap Cl
Overton Cl
Ottringham
Scotswood Rd
St Georges RC Primary School
LEMINGTON ROAD
A6085
Keats Road
Industrial Estate
Newcastle upon Tyne
Gateshead
Riversdale
Riversdale Ct
Riversdale Way
NORTHUMBERLAND ROAD
SCOTSW
LC
Stella
STELLA ROAD
The Fairway
Parkland
Cromwell Ct
Stella Hall
Hall Pk
The Rise
Path Head
B6317
Fountain Lane
BRIDGE STREET
Gas La
Tyne St
Blaydon Station
BLAYDON HWY
CHAINBRIDGE
Factory Road
Cowen Rd
Summerhill
Hexham Old Road
Whitmore Rd
Shibdon Road
Delacour Rd
Thornton Crs
Primary School
Lawrence Av
West Vw
Dene Rd
St Cuthberts Wy
Gateshead Metropolitan Borough Council
Larch Rd
Blaydon Cemetery
Laurel Rd
Bank
Chesmond Dr
Rushley Crs
Beda Hl
Blaydon Bank
Mary St
Theresa St
Mabel St
Murray St
Ann St
Harriet St
Widdrington Rd
Birch Rd
Elm Rd
Edith Av
Park Av
Sycamore Rd
Maple Rd
Willow Rd
Linden Rd
Hazel Rd
St Thomas More RC (aided) Comprehensive School
Croftdale Road
Till Av
Back Lane
Greenbank
Denton View
Heddon View
Hillside
River Vw
Hallgarth Rd
Blaydon Bank
Blaydon Cricket Club
Hawthorn Rd
Springfield Rd
Chevlot
Laburnum Road
Pine Rd
Cypress Rd
Ladywell
Whitewell Rd
Woodvale Rd
Cedar Rd
Rockmore Rd
Shibdon
Bircham Dr
East Acre
Ness Ct
Blackstone Ct
Valley Crs
Morgans Wy
Black Lane
Frances St
Street
Tynebank
Winlaton
Wylam Vw
Cromwell
North
Jobling Av
Garth Crs
Garth Farm Rd
Hill Top
Litchfield La
Alice St
Riding Lea
Front Street Surg
Tyne St
Berryhill
Lane
1 grid square represents 500 metres

D1
1 Carlton Gdns
2 Flexbury Gdns
3 Shelford Gdns
4 Styford Gdns
5 West Copperas
D2
1 Lintzford Gdns
2 Malton Cl
3 Maple Cl
4 Matfen Cl
5 Norfolk Wy
D3
1 St George's Pl
2 St George's Rd
3 St George's Ter
D6
1 Napier Wy
E1
1 Castlenook Pl
2 Copperas La
3 Hextol Gdns
4 Legion Gv
5 Legion Rd
6 Overdene
7 Rockcliffe Gdns
8 West Vallum
E2
1 Ravenburn Gdns
E3
1 Langham Rd
2 Parmontley St
F2
1 Inglemere Pl
2 Muscott Gv
F3
1 Sandmere Pl
F4
1 Lightwood Av
2 Pretoria St
60
78
95
Denton Burn
Lemington
Bell's Close
Benwell
Scotswood
Blaydon Haughs
BLAYDON
Broadwood Junior & Infant School
Doctors Surgery
St Bedes RC Primary School
Waverley First School
Benwell Hill Cricket Club
St Cuthberts RC Lower School
Delaval Primary School
Primary School
Adamsez West Industrial Estate
Blaydon Business Park
Blaydon Haugh Industrial Estate
Blaydon Business Centre
Derwenthaugh Industrial Est
Blaydon Swimming Pool
Gateshead Area Health Authority
WEST ROAD
DENTON ROAD
SCOTSWOOD ROAD
CHAIN BR ROAD
DERWENTHAUGH ROAD
RIVERSIDE WAY
SHIBDON ROAD
B6328 WHICKHAM VIEW
A1(T)
A69
A695
A6085
A696
A186
A1114
B6317
River Tyne

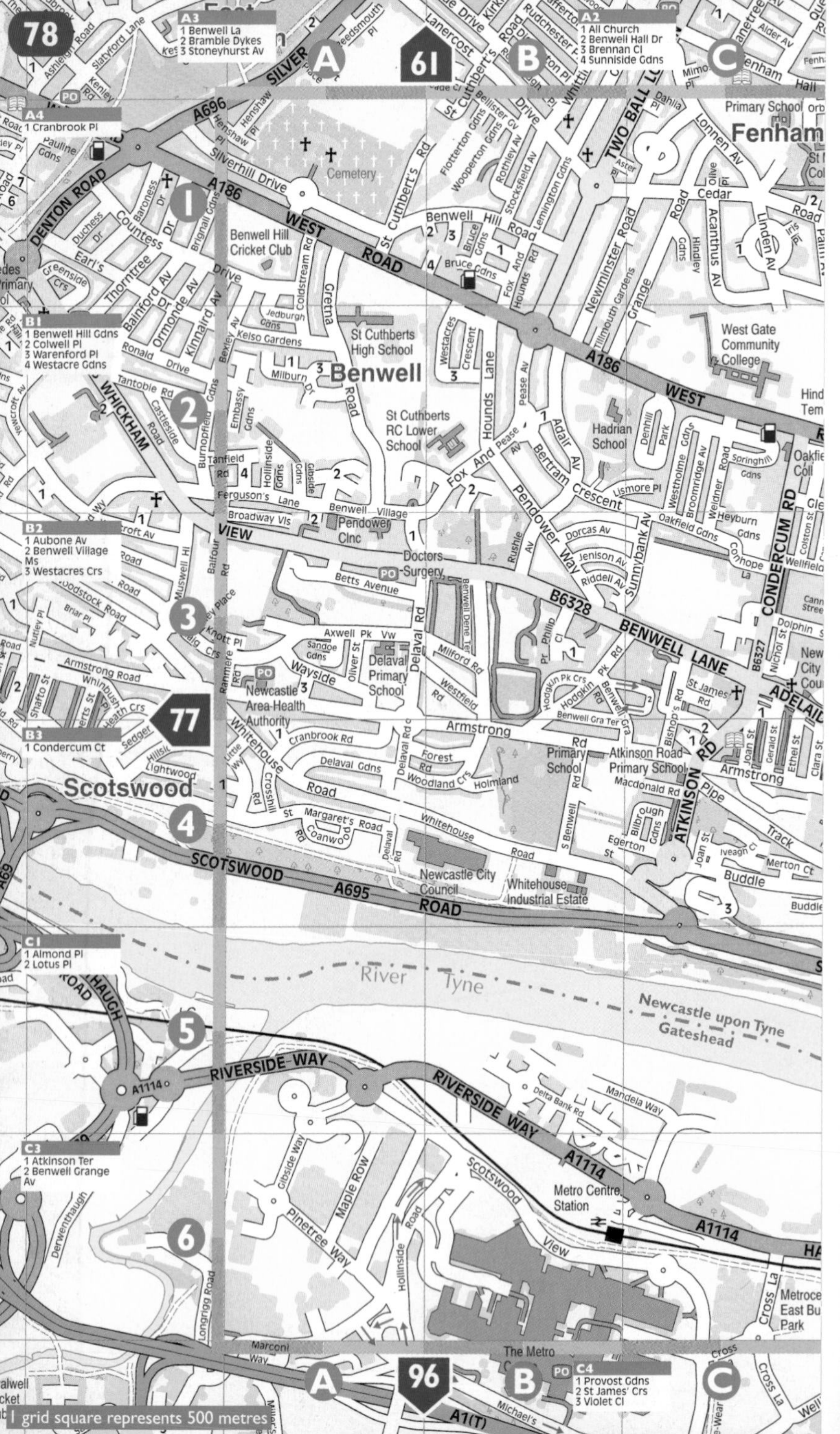

78
61
77
96
A
B
C
1
2
3
4
5
6
A3
1 Benwell La
2 Bramble Dykes
3 Stoneyhurst Av
A2
1 All Church
2 Benwell Hall Dr
3 Brennan Cl
4 Sunniside Gdns
A4
1 Cranbrook Pl
B1
1 Benwell Hill Gdns
2 Colwell Pl
3 Warenford Pl
4 Westacre Gdns
B2
1 Aubone Av
2 Benwell Village Ms
3 Westacres Crs
B3
1 Condercum Ct
C1
1 Almond Pl
2 Lotus Pl
C3
1 Atkinson Ter
2 Benwell Grange Av
C4
1 Provost Gdns
2 St James' Crs
3 Violet Cl
Fenham
Benwell
Scotswood
Cemetery
Benwell Hill Cricket Club
St Cuthberts High School
St Cuthberts RC Lower School
West Gate Community College
Hadrian School
Pendower Clnc
Doctors Surgery
Delaval Primary School
Newcastle Area Health Authority
Primary School
Atkinson Road Primary School
Newcastle City Council
Whitehouse Industrial Estate
Metro Centre Station
The Metro
Metrocentre East Business Park
River Tyne
Newcastle upon Tyne
Gateshead
A186 WEST ROAD
A696
DENTON ROAD
SILVERHILL DRIVE
TWO BALL LONNEN
WHICKHAM VIEW
B6328 BENWELL LANE
CONDERCUM RD
ATKINSON RD
A695 SCOTSWOOD ROAD
RIVERSIDE WAY
A1114
A1(T)
Armstrong Road
Whitehouse Road
Pendower Way
Fox And Hounds Lane
Hawthorn Road
Benwell Village
Betts Avenue
Delaval Rd
Pinetree Way
Maple Row
Gibside Way
Hollinside Road
Longrigg Road
Scotswood View
Mandela Way
Delta Bank Rd
1 grid square represents 500 metres

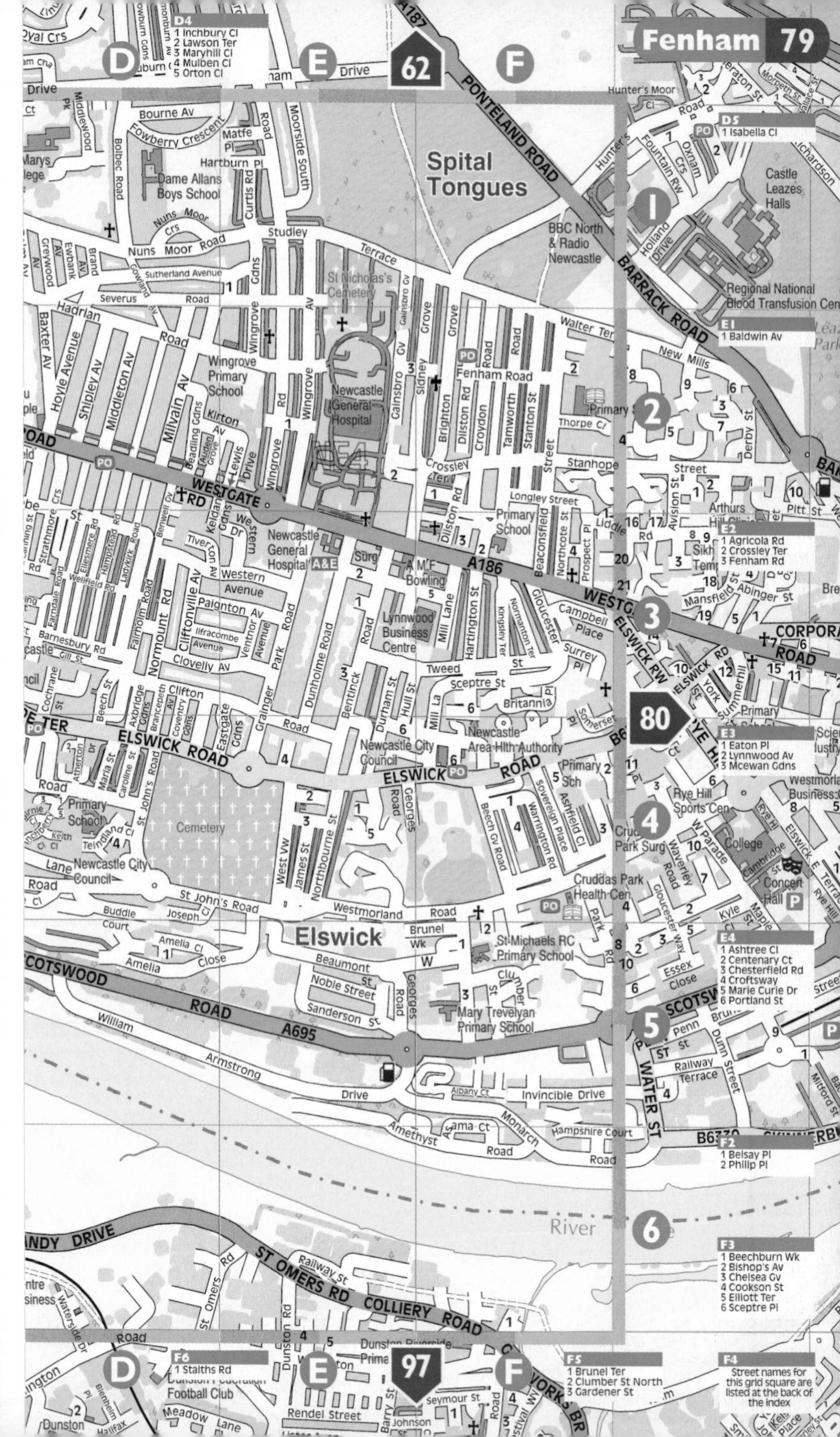
D4
1 Inchbury Cl
2 Lawson Ter
3 Maryhill Cl
4 Mulben Cl
5 Orton Cl
D5
1 Isabella Cl
E1
1 Baldwin Av
E2
1 Agricola Rd
2 Crossley Ter
3 Fenham Rd
E3
1 Eaton Pl
2 Lynnwood Av
3 Mcewan Gdns
E4
1 Ashtree Cl
2 Centenary Ct
3 Chesterfield Rd
4 Croftsway
5 Marie Curie Dr
6 Portland St
F2
1 Belsay Pl
2 Philip Pl
F3
1 Beechburn Wk
2 Bishop's Av
3 Chelsea Gv
4 Cookson St
5 Elliott Ter
6 Sceptre Pl
F6
1 Staiths Rd
F5
1 Brunel Ter
2 Clumber St North
3 Gardener St
F4
Street names for this grid square are listed at the back of the index
Spital Tongues
Elswick
PONTELAND ROAD
BARRACK ROAD
WESTGATE RD
ELSWICK ROAD
SCOTSWOOD ROAD
ST OMERS RD
COLLIERY ROAD
Newcastle General Hospital
Dame Allans Boys School
BBC North & Radio Newcastle
Regional National Blood Transfusion Cen
Castle Leazes Halls
Wingrove Primary School
St Nicholas's Cemetery
Lynnwood Business Centre
Newcastle City Council
Newcastle Area Hlth Authority
Rye Hill Sports Cen
College
Concert Hall
Cruddas Park Health Cen
St Michaels RC Primary School
Mary Trevelyan Primary School
Cemetery
River
62
80
97

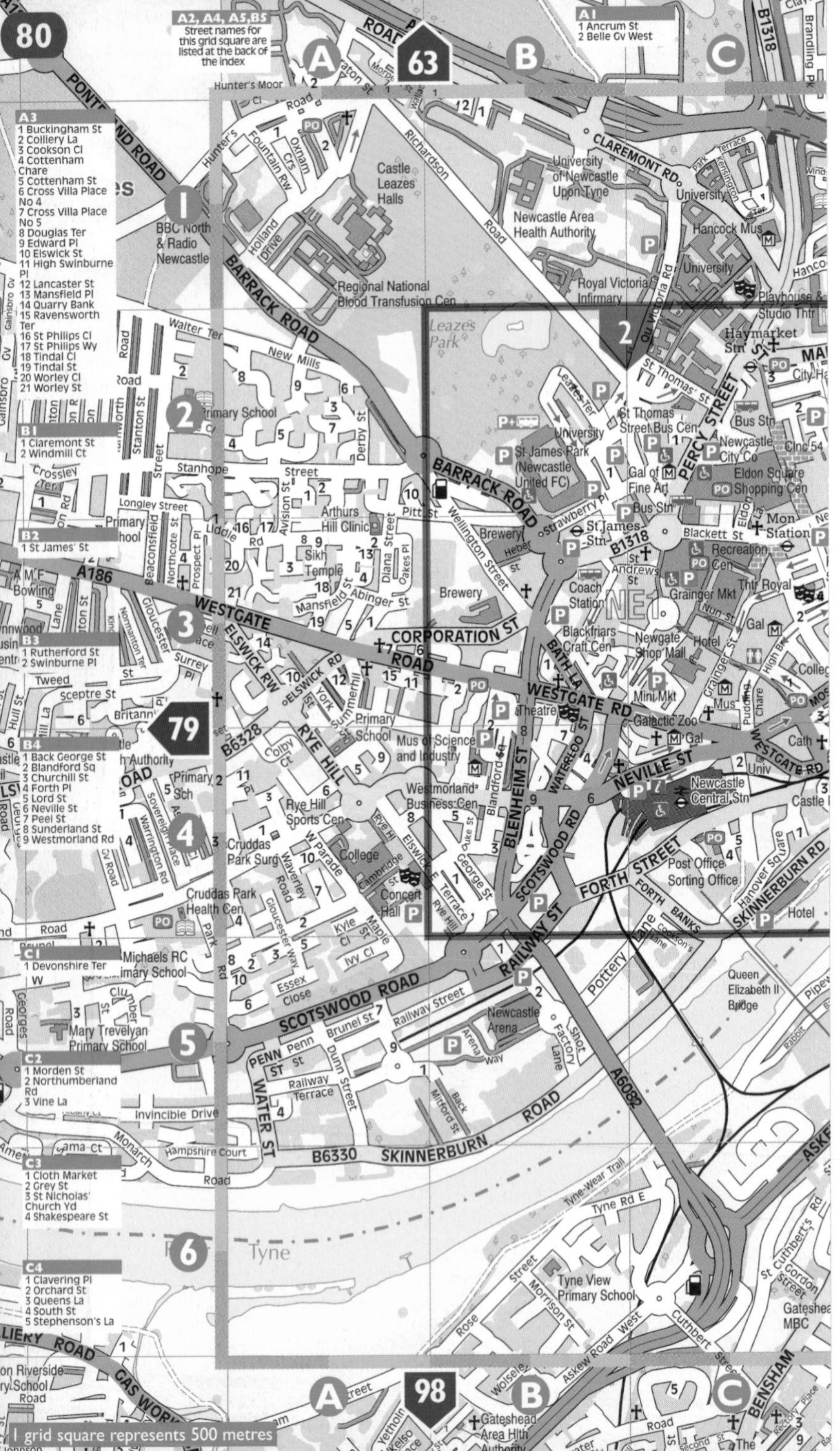
A2, A4, A5, B5
Street names for this grid square are listed at the back of the index
A1
1 Ancrum St
2 Belle Gv West
A3
1 Buckingham St
2 Colliery La
3 Cookson Cl
4 Cottenham Chare
5 Cottenham St
6 Cross Villa Place No 4
7 Cross Villa Place No 5
8 Douglas Ter
9 Edward Pl
10 Elswick St
11 High Swinburne Pl
12 Lancaster St
13 Mansfield Pl
14 Quarry Bank
15 Ravensworth Ter
16 St Philips Cl
17 St Philips Wy
18 Tindal Cl
19 Tindal St
20 Worley Cl
21 Worley St
B1
1 Claremont St
2 Windmill Ct
B2
1 St James' St
B3
1 Rutherford St
2 Swinburne Pl
B4
1 Back George St
2 Blandford Sq
3 Churchill St
4 Forth Pl
5 Lord St
6 Neville St
7 Peel St
8 Sunderland St
9 Westmorland Rd
C1
1 Devonshire Ter
C2
1 Morden St
2 Northumberland Rd
3 Vine La
C3
1 Cloth Market
2 Grey St
3 St Nicholas' Church Yd
4 Shakespeare St
C4
1 Clavering Pl
2 Orchard St
3 Queens La
4 South St
5 Stephenson's La
63
79
98
A
B
C
1
2
3
4
5
6
PONTELAND ROAD
BARRACK ROAD
CLAREMONT RD
Richardson Road
Castle Leazes Halls
University of Newcastle Upon Tyne
Newcastle Area Health Authority
Royal Victoria Infirmary
Regional National Blood Transfusion Cen
BBC North & Radio Newcastle
Hancock Mus
University
Playhouse & Studio Thtr
Haymarket Stn
Leazes Park
St Thomas' St
PERCY STREET
St James Park (Newcastle United FC)
Gal of Fine Art
Bus Stn
Newcastle City Co
Eldon Square Shopping Cen
St James Stn
Blackett St
Recreation Cen
Mon Station
Grainger Mkt
Thtr Royal
Coach Station
NE1
Blackfriars Craft Cen
Newgate Shop Mall
Hotel
Mini Mkt
WESTGATE RD
CORPORATION ST
WESTGATE ROAD
A186
Arthurs Hill Clinic
Sikh Temple
Brewery
Wellington Street
Primary School
Stanhope Street
Longley Street
ELSWICK RD
RYE HILL
Mus of Science and Industry
Westmorland Business Cen
Rye Hill Sports Cen
College
Concert Hall
BLENHEIM ST
SCOTSWOOD RD
NEVILLE ST
Newcastle Central Stn
Galactic Zoo
FORTH STREET
Post Office Sorting Office
SKINNERBURN RD
Cruddas Park Surg
Cruddas Park Health Cen
SCOTSWOOD ROAD
RAILWAY ST
Railway Street
Newcastle Arena
Queen Elizabeth II Bridge
PENN ST
WATER ST
Railway Terrace
Dunn Street
Invincible Drive
Hampshire Court
B6330 SKINNERBURN ROAD
A6082
Tyne
Tyne-Wear Trail
Tyne Rd E
Tyne View Primary School
Askew Road West
Gateshead MBC
BENSHAM
Gateshead Area Hlth Authority
Mary Trevelyan Primary School
Michaels RC Primary School
COLLIERY ROAD
GAS WORKS
1 grid square represents 500 metres

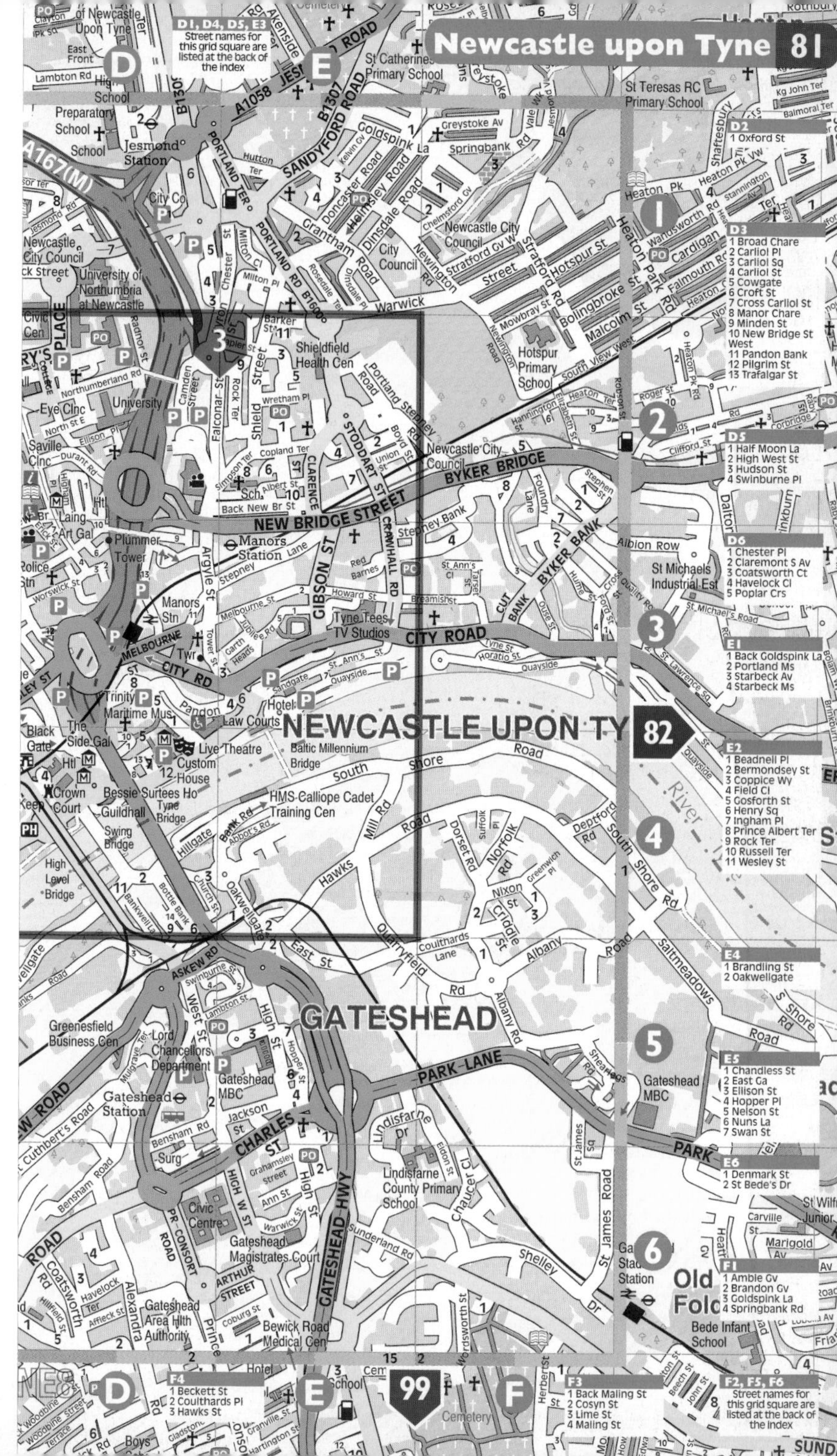
D1, D4, D5, E3
Street names for this grid square are listed at the back of the index
D2
1 Oxford St
D3
1 Broad Chare
2 Carliol Pl
3 Carliol Sq
4 Carliol St
5 Cowgate
6 Croft St
7 Cross Carliol St
8 Manor Chare
9 Minden St
10 New Bridge St West
11 Pandon Bank
12 Pilgrim St
13 Trafalgar St
D5
1 Half Moon La
2 High West St
3 Hudson St
4 Swinburne Pl
D6
1 Chester Pl
2 Claremont S Av
3 Coatsworth Ct
4 Havelock Cl
5 Poplar Crs
E1
1 Back Goldspink La
2 Portland Ms
3 Starbeck Av
4 Starbeck Ms
E2
1 Beadnell Pl
2 Bermondsey St
3 Coppice Wy
4 Field Cl
5 Gosforth St
6 Henry Sq
7 Ingham Pl
8 Prince Albert Ter
9 Rock Ter
10 Russell Ter
11 Wesley St
E4
1 Brandling St
2 Oakwellgate
E5
1 Chandless St
2 East Ga
3 Ellison St
4 Hopper Pl
5 Nelson St
6 Nuns La
7 Swan St
E6
1 Denmark St
2 St Bede's Dr
F1
1 Amble Gv
2 Brandon Gv
3 Goldspink La
4 Springbank Rd
F2, F5, F6
Street names for this grid square are listed at the back of the index
F3
1 Back Maling St
2 Cosyn St
3 Lime St
4 Maling St
F4
1 Beckett St
2 Coulthards Pl
3 Hawks St
NEWCASTLE UPON TY
82
GATESHEAD
99
A167(M)
A1058 JESMOND ROAD
SANDYFORD ROAD
B1307
PORTLAND TER
PORTLAND RD B1600
Jesmond Station
St Catherines Primary School
St Teresas RC Primary School
Heaton Pk
Heaton Park Rd
Newcastle City Council
City Council
University of Northumbria at Newcastle
Shieldfield Health Cen
Hotspur Primary School
NEW BRIDGE STREET
BYKER BRIDGE
BYKER BANK
CITY ROAD
CITY RD
MELBOURNE ST
Manors Station
Plummer Tower
Laing Art Gal
Tyne Tees TV Studios
St Michaels Industrial Est
Albion Row
Law Courts
Live Theatre
Custom House
Trinity Maritime Mus
Baltic Millennium Bridge
HMS Calliope Cadet Training Cen
Black Gate
The Side Gal
Crown Court
Bessie Surtees Ho
Guildhall
Tyne Bridge
Swing Bridge
High Level Bridge
South Shore Road
Hawks Road
Quarryfield Rd
Albany Rd
Saltmeadows Rd
Greenesfield Business Cen
Lord Chancellors Department
Gateshead MBC
Gateshead Station
PARK LANE
CHARLES ST
GATESHEAD HWY
HIGH W ST
PR CONSORT ROAD
ARTHUR STREET
Civic Centre
Gateshead Magistrates Court
Gateshead Area Hlth Authority
Bewick Road Medical Cen
Lindisfarne County Primary School
St James Road
Shelley Dr
Gateshead Stadium Station
Old Fold
Bede Infant School
Cemetery
Coatsworth Rd
Alexandra Rd
Bensham Road
St Cuthbert's Road
NEW ROAD
NE8

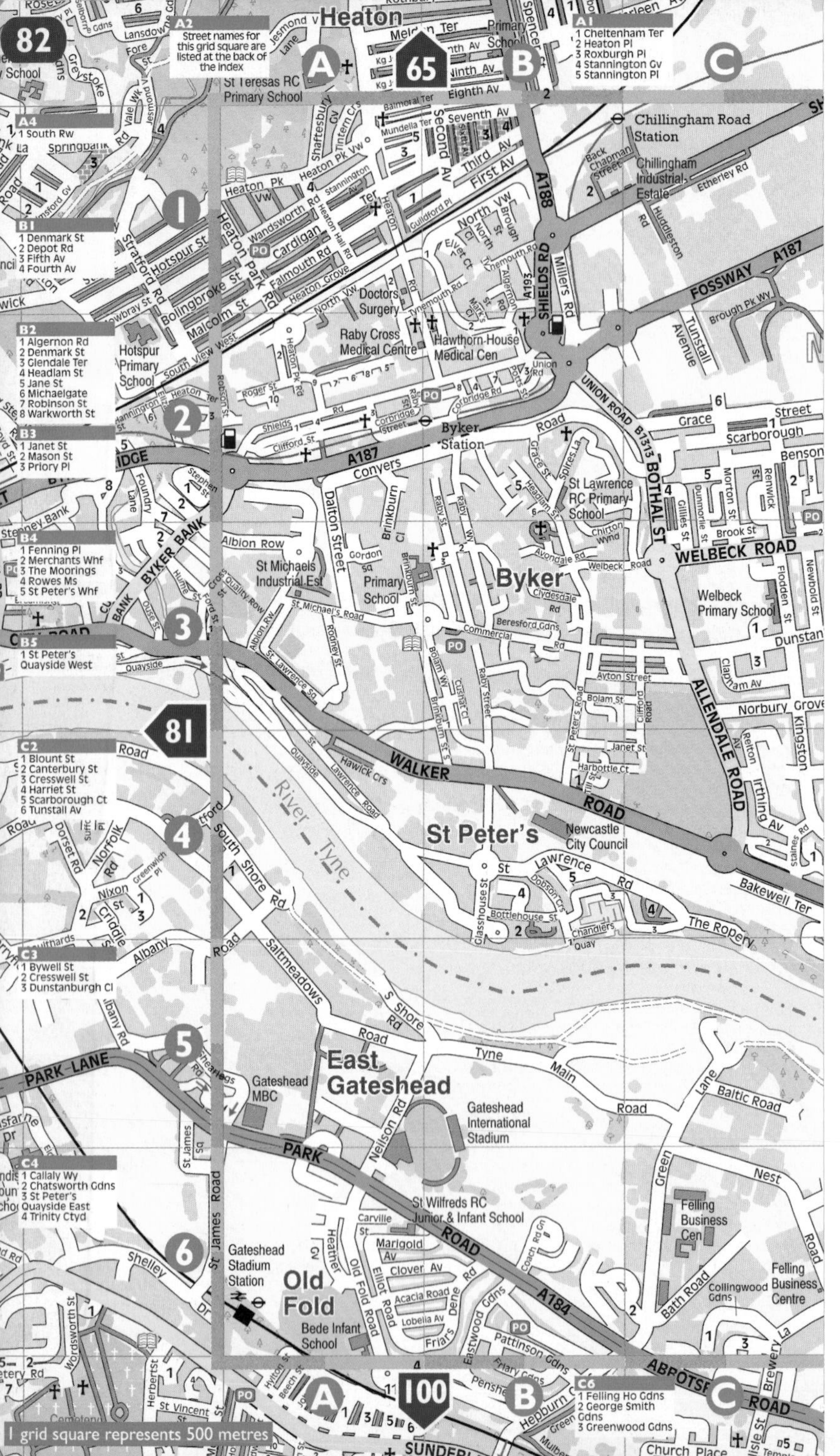
A2
Street names for this grid square are listed at the back of the index
A1
1 Cheltenham Ter
2 Heaton Pl
3 Roxburgh Pl
4 Stannington Gv
5 Stannington Pl
A4
1 South Rw
B1
1 Denmark St
2 Depot Rd
3 Fifth Av
4 Fourth Av
B2
1 Algernon Rd
2 Denmark St
3 Glendale Ter
4 Headlam St
5 Jane St
6 Michaelgate
7 Robinson St
8 Warkworth St
B3
1 Janet St
2 Mason St
3 Priory Pl
B4
1 Fenning Pl
2 Merchants Whf
3 The Moorings
4 Rowes Ms
5 St Peter's Whf
B5
1 St Peter's Quayside West
C2
1 Blount St
2 Canterbury St
3 Cresswell St
4 Harriet St
5 Scarborough Ct
6 Tunstall Av
C3
1 Bywell St
2 Cresswell St
3 Dunstanburgh Cl
C4
1 Callaly Wy
2 Chatsworth Gdns
3 St Peter's Quayside East
4 Trinity Ctyd
C6
1 Felling Ho Gdns
2 George Smith Gdns
3 Greenwood Gdns
Heaton
65
81
100
A
B
C
1
2
3
4
5
6
St Teresas RC Primary School
Chillingham Road Station
Chillingham Industrial Estate
Hotspur Primary School
Doctors Surgery
Raby Cross Medical Centre
Hawthorn House Medical Cen
Byker Station
St Lawrence RC Primary School
Byker
St Michaels Industrial Est
Primary School
Welbeck Primary School
St Peter's
Newcastle City Council
River Tyne
East Gateshead
Gateshead MBC
Gateshead International Stadium
St Wilfreds RC Junior & Infant School
Felling Business Cen
Felling Business Centre
Gateshead Stadium Station
Old Fold
Bede Infant School
FOSSWAY
A187
A188
SHIELDS RD
BOTHAL ST
WELBECK ROAD
WALKER ROAD
ALLENDALE ROAD
UNION ROAD B1313
BYKER BANK
PARK LANE
PARK ROAD
A184
ABBOTSFORD ROAD
Heaton Park Rd
Hotspur St
Stratford Rd
Bolingbroke St
Malcolm St
South View West
Heaton Grove
Falmouth Rd
Cardigan Ter
Wandsworth Rd
Heaton Pk Vw
Shaftesbury Gv
Tintern Cres
Seventh Av
Eighth Av
Ninth Av
Second Av
Third Av
First Av
Guildford Pl
North Vw
Millers Rd
Tynemouth Rd
Roger St
Corbridge Street
Shields Rd
Clifford St
Conyers Road
Dalton Street
Brinkburn Cl
Albion Row
St Michael's Road
Commercial Rd
Raby Street
Avondale Rd
Clydesdale Rd
Beresford Gdns
Ayton Street
Bolam St
Janet St
Harbottle Ct
Grace Street
Scarborough
Benson
Morton St
Brook St
Flodden St
Newbold St
Dunstan
Clapham Av
Norbury Grove
Kingston
Irthing Av
Bakewell Ter
The Ropery
Chandlers Quay
Bottlehouse St
Glasshouse St
St Lawrence Rd
Dobson Cres
Hawick Crs
St Lawrence Road
Quayside
South Shore Rd
Saltmeadows Road
S Shore Rd
Tyne Main Road
Baltic Road
Green Lane
Nest Road
Bath Road
Collingwood Gdns
Brewery La
Neilson Rd
Carville St
Marigold Av
Clover Av
Acacia Road
Lobelia Av
Old Fold Road
Elliot Road
Dene Rd
Friars
Coach Rd Gn
Eastwood Gdns
Pattinson Gdns
Friary Gdns
Hepburn Gdns
St James Road
St James Sq
Shelley Dr
Wordsworth St
Herbert St
St Vincent St
Sunderland
Church Place
Albany Road
Dorset Rd
Norfolk Rd
Nixon St
Criddle St
Foundry Lane
Stepney Bank
Quayside
Springbank Rd
Greystoke
Lansdowne
Jesmond Vale
Tunstall Avenue
Brough Pk Wy
Etherley Rd
Huddleston Rd
1 grid square represents 500 metres

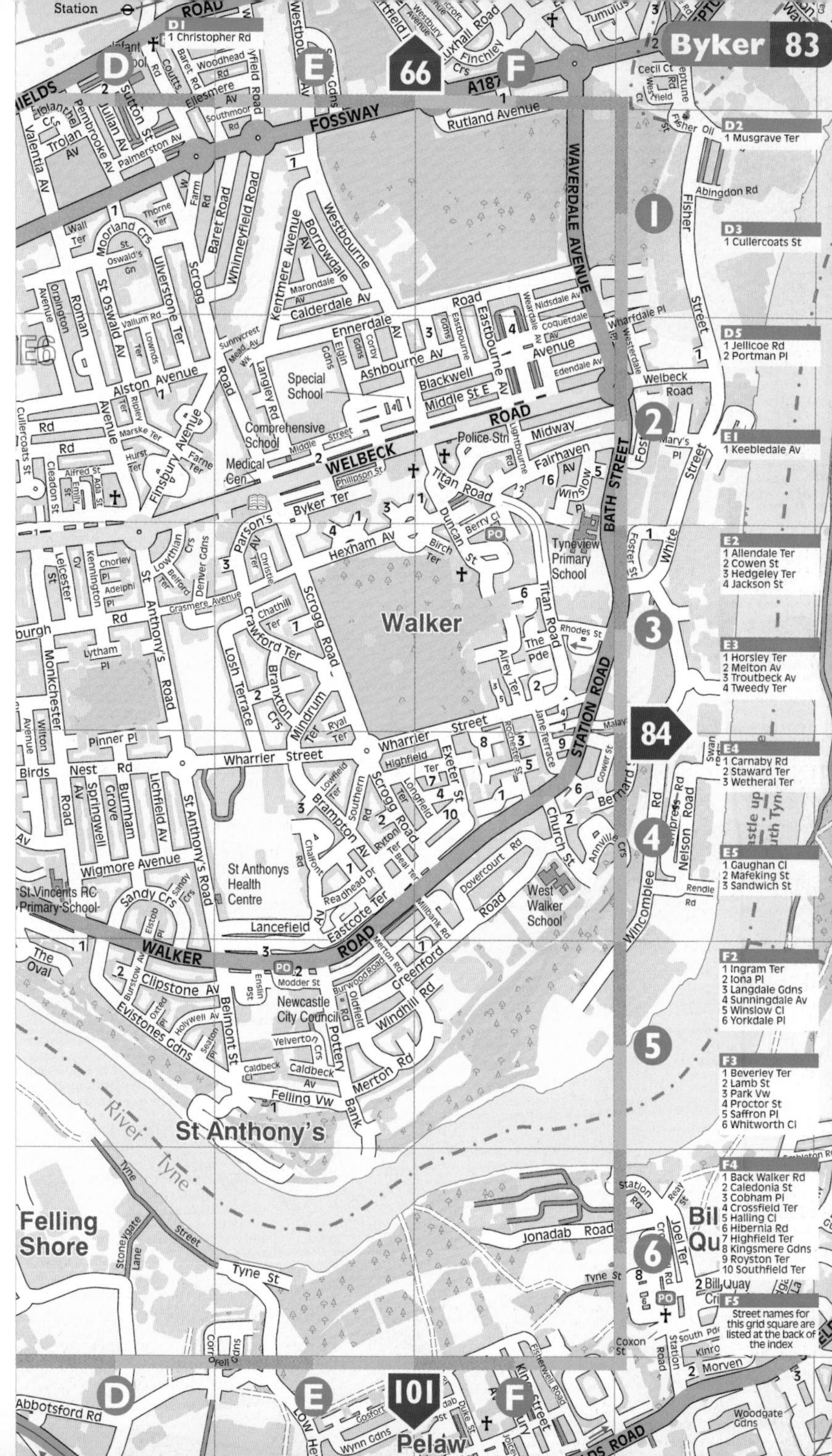

D1
1 Christopher Rd
D2
1 Musgrave Ter
D3
1 Cullercoats St
D5
1 Jellicoe Rd
2 Portman Pl
E1
1 Keebledale Av
E2
1 Allendale Ter
2 Cowen St
3 Hedgeley Ter
4 Jackson St
E3
1 Horsley Ter
2 Melton Av
3 Troutbeck Av
4 Tweedy Ter
E4
1 Carnaby Rd
2 Staward Ter
3 Wetheral Ter
E5
1 Gaughan Cl
2 Mafeking St
3 Sandwich St
F2
1 Ingram Ter
2 Iona Pl
3 Langdale Gdns
4 Sunningdale Av
5 Winslow Cl
6 Yorkdale Pl
F3
1 Beverley Ter
2 Lamb St
3 Park Vw
4 Proctor St
5 Saffron Pl
6 Whitworth Cl
F4
1 Back Walker Rd
2 Caledonia St
3 Cobham Pl
4 Crossfield Ter
5 Halling Cl
6 Hibernia Rd
7 Highfield Ter
8 Kingsmere Gdns
9 Royston Ter
10 Southfield Ter
F5
Street names for this grid square are listed at the back of the index
66
84
101
Walker
St Anthony's
Felling Shore
Pelaw
River Tyne
FOSSWAY
WELBECK ROAD
WALKER ROAD
WAVERDALE AVENUE
BATH STREET
STATION ROAD
A187
Special School
Comprehensive School
Medical Cen
Police Stn
Tyneview Primary School
St Anthonys Health Centre
St Vincents RC Primary School
West Walker School
Newcastle City Council
Wharrier Street
Fisher Street
Scrogg Road
St Anthony's Road
Jonadab Road
Tyne St
Abbotsford Rd

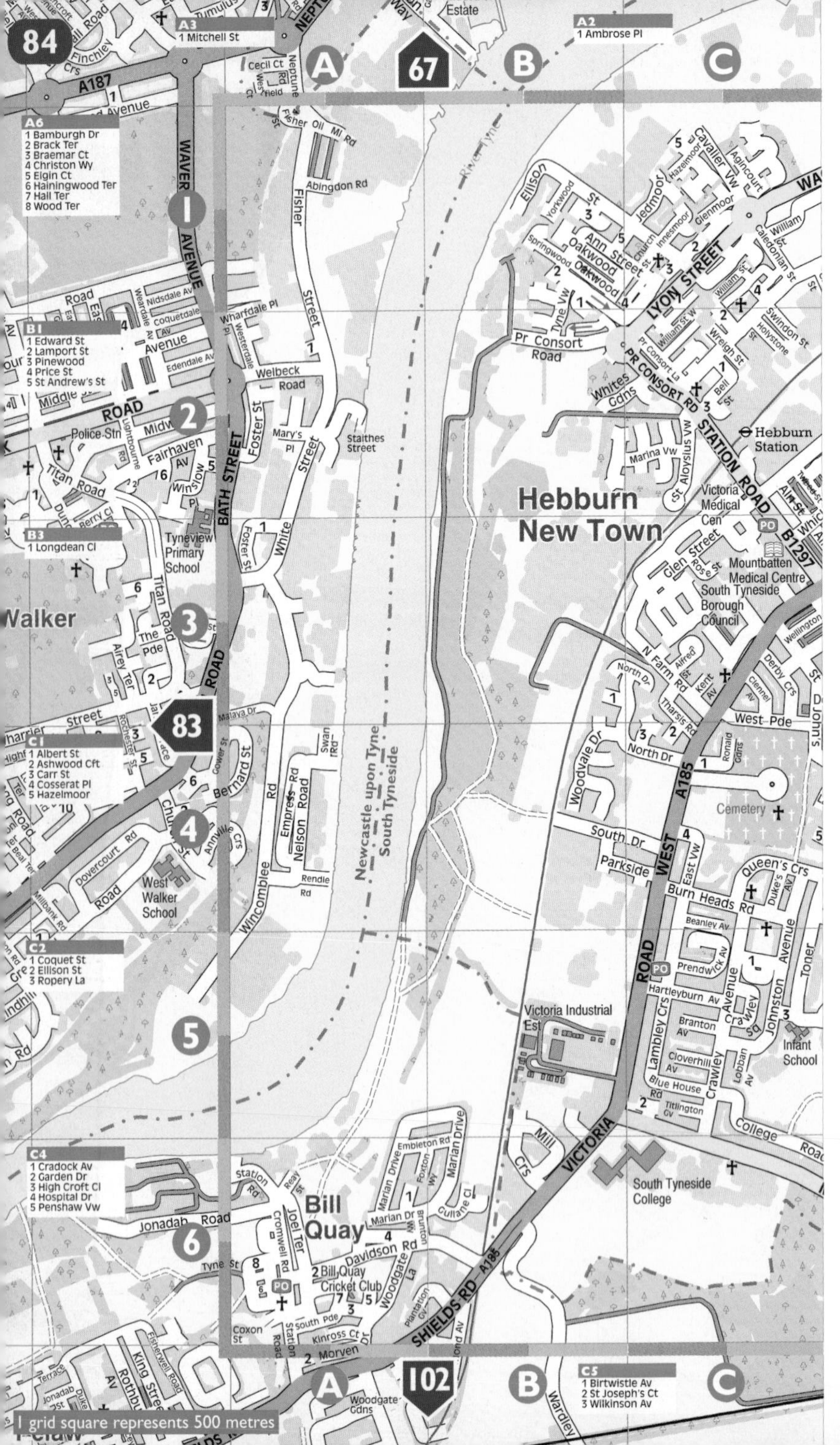
A3
1 Mitchell St
A2
1 Ambrose Pl
A6
1 Bamburgh Dr
2 Brack Ter
3 Braemar Ct
4 Christon Wy
5 Elgin Ct
6 Hainingwood Ter
7 Hall Ter
8 Wood Ter
B1
1 Edward St
2 Lamport St
3 Pinewood
4 Price St
5 St Andrew's St
B3
1 Longdean Cl
C1
1 Albert St
2 Ashwood Cft
3 Carr St
4 Cosserat Pl
5 Hazelmoor
C2
1 Coquet St
2 Ellison St
3 Ropery La
C4
1 Cradock Av
2 Garden Dr
3 High Croft Cl
4 Hospital Dr
5 Penshaw Vw
C5
1 Birtwistle Av
2 St Joseph's Ct
3 Wilkinson Av
67
83
102
Hebburn New Town
Walker
Bill Quay
Newcastle upon Tyne
South Tyneside
River Tyne
Hebburn Station
Victoria Medical Cen
Mountbatten Medical Centre
South Tyneside Borough Council
Tyneview Primary School
West Walker School
Victoria Industrial Est
South Tyneside College
Bill Quay Cricket Club
Infant School
Cemetery
Police Stn
BATH STREET
WAVERLEY AVENUE
LYON STREET
STATION ROAD
PR CONSORT RD
VICTORIA ROAD WEST
SHIELDS RD
A185
B1297
A187
1 grid square represents 500 metres

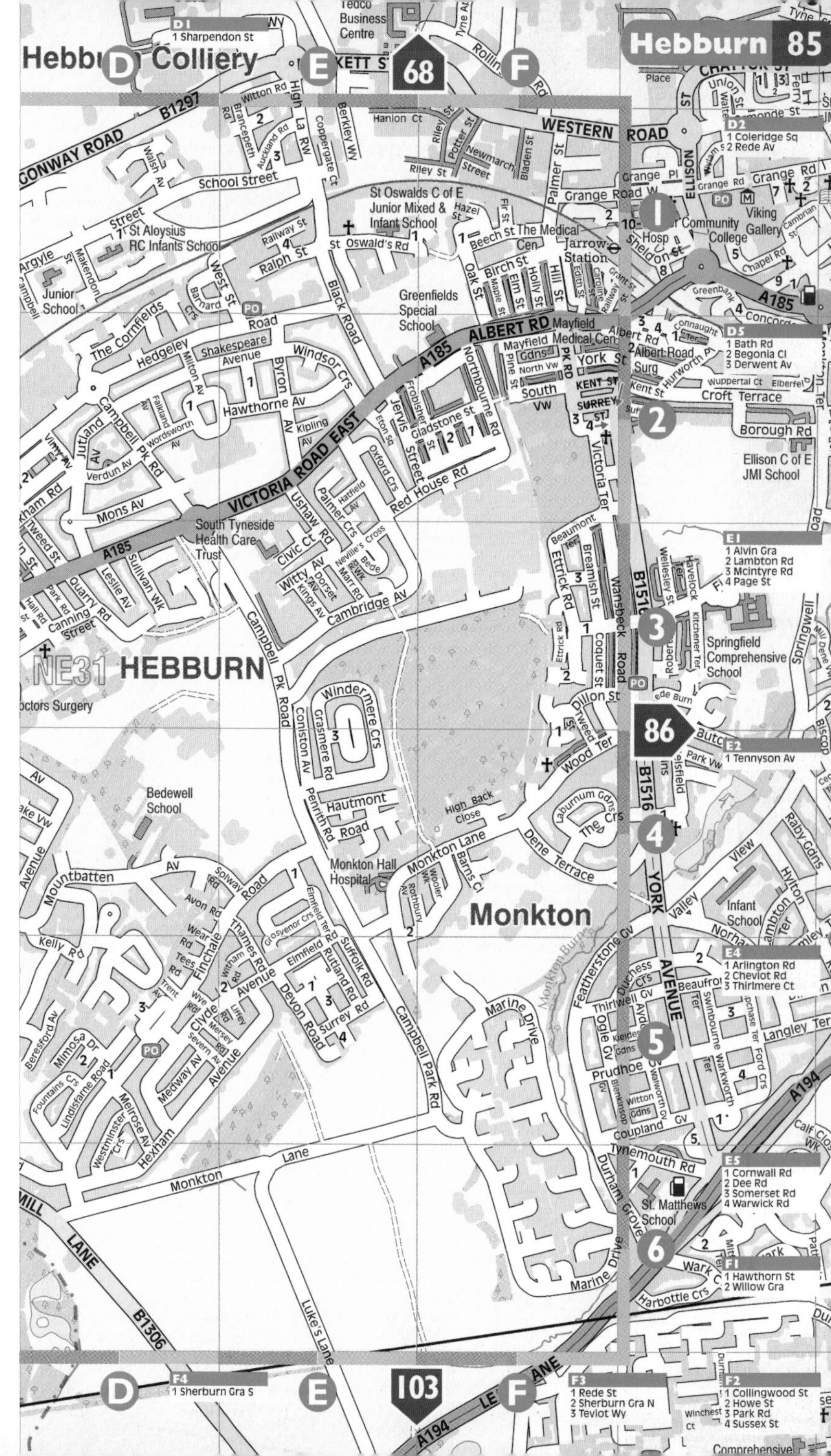
D1
1 Sharpendon St
D2
1 Coleridge Sq
2 Rede Av
D5
1 Bath Rd
2 Begonia Cl
3 Derwent Av
E1
1 Alvin Gra
2 Lambton Rd
3 Mcintyre Rd
4 Page St
E2
1 Tennyson Av
E4
1 Arlington Rd
2 Cheviot Rd
3 Thirlmere Ct
E5
1 Cornwall Rd
2 Dee Rd
3 Somerset Rd
4 Warwick Rd
F1
1 Hawthorn St
2 Willow Gra
F2
1 Collingwood St
2 Howe St
3 Park Rd
4 Sussex St
F3
1 Rede St
2 Sherburn Gra N
3 Teviot Wy
F4
1 Sherburn Gra S
68
86
103
Hebburn Colliery
Tedco Business Centre
NE31 HEBBURN
Monkton
B1297
CONWAY ROAD
WESTERN ROAD
School Street
St Oswalds C of E Junior Mixed & Infant School
St Aloysius RC Infants School
Junior School
Greenfields Special School
The Medical Cen
Jarrow Station
Community College
Viking Gallery
A185
ALBERT RD
VICTORIA ROAD EAST
South Tyneside Health Care Trust
Croft Terrace
Borough Rd
Ellison C of E JMI School
Springfield Comprehensive School
Wansbeck Road
B1516
Campbell Pk Road
Cambridge Av
Bedewell School
Monkton Hall Hospital
Monkton Lane
Dene Terrace
YORK AVENUE
Marine Drive
Campbell Park Rd
Durham Grove
St. Matthews School
Infant School
A194
B1306
MILL LANE
Luke's Lane
Doctors Surgery

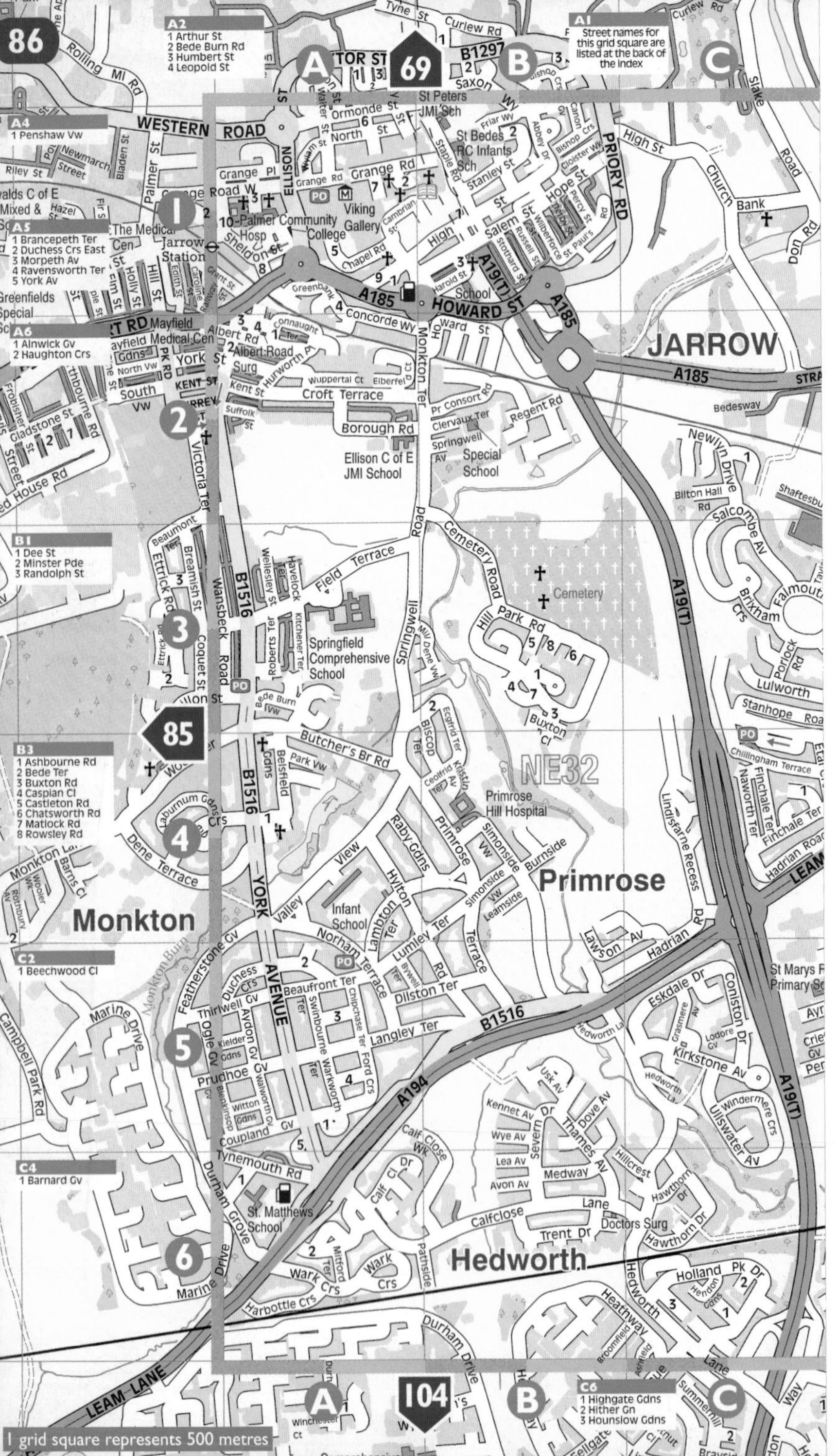

86
A2
1 Arthur St
2 Bede Burn Rd
3 Humbert St
4 Leopold St
69
A1
Street names for this grid square are listed at the back of the index
A4
1 Penshaw Vw
A5
1 Brancepeth Ter
2 Duchess Crs East
3 Morpeth Av
4 Ravensworth Ter
5 York Av
A6
1 Alnwick Gv
2 Haughton Crs
B1
1 Dee St
2 Minster Pde
3 Randolph St
B3
1 Ashbourne Rd
2 Bede Ter
3 Buxton Rd
4 Caspian Cl
5 Castleton Rd
6 Chatsworth Rd
7 Matlock Rd
8 Rowsley Rd
C2
1 Beechwood Cl
C4
1 Barnard Gv
C6
1 Highgate Gdns
2 Hither Gn
3 Hounslow Gdns
85
104
A
B
C
1
2
3
4
5
6
JARROW
Monkton
Primrose
Hedworth
NE32
Tyne St
Curlew Rd
B1297
Saxon Wy
Rolling Mill Rd
WESTERN ROAD
Ormonde St
North St
St Peters JMI Sch
St Bedes RC Infants Sch
Friar Wy
Abbey Dr
Bishop Crs
Cloister Wk
Canon Gv
PRIORY RD
High St
Church Bank
Slake Road
Don Rd
Newmarch Street
Riley St
Bladen St
Palmer St
Grange Pl
Grange Rd
Grange Road W
ELLISON ST
Walter St
Wylam St
Viking Gallery
Palmer Community College
Hosp
The Medical Cen
Jarrow Station
Sheldon St
Chapel Rd
Cambrian St
Stanley St
Staple Rd
Hope St
Salem St
Percy St
Russell St
Wilberforce St
St Paul's Rd
Stothard St
Harold St
School
A19(T)
A185
HOWARD ST
Greenbank
Concorde Wy
Ward St
Monkton Ter
Elm St
Holly St
Hill St
Edith St
Grant St
Caroline St
Railway St
Greenfields Special Sch
Mayfield Medical Cen
Albert Rd
Albert Road Surg
Connaught Ter
Hurworth Pl
Kent St
Wuppertal Ct
Elberfeld Ct
Croft Terrace
York St
North Vw
South Vw
PK RD
KENT ST
SURREY
Suffolk St
Borough Rd
Ellison C of E JMI School
Pr Consort Rd
Clervaux Ter
Springwell Av
Regent Rd
Special School
Bedesway
Newlyn Drive
Bilton Hall Rd
Shaftesbury
Salcombe Av
Brixham Crs
Falmouth
Porlock Rd
Lulworth
Stanhope Road
Chillingham Terrace
Naworth Ter
Finchale Ter
Hadrian Road
LEAM
Gladstone St
Frobisher
Jarvis Street
Red House Rd
Victoria Ter
Beaumont Ter
Breamish St
Ettrick Rd
Coquet St
Wansbeck Road
B1516
Field Terrace
Wellesley St
Havelock Ter
Kitchener Ter
Roberts Ter
Springfield Comprehensive School
Springwell Road
Mill Dene Vw
Cemetery Road
Cemetery
Hill Park Rd
Buxton Cl
Bede Burn Vw
Butcher's Br Rd
Park Vw
Belsfield Gdns
Biscop Ter
Ecgfrid Ter
Ceolfrid Ter
Kristin Av
Primrose Hill Hospital
Lindisfarne Recess
Laburnum Gdns
Dene Terrace
Monkton Lane
Barns Cl
Wooler Wk
Rothbury Av
YORK AVENUE
Valley View
Raby Gdns
Hylton
Primrose
Simonside Vw
Burnside
Leamside
Lambton Ter
Lumley Ter
Infant School
Norham Terrace
Lawson Av
Hadrian Rd
St Marys RC Primary Sch
Featherstone Gv
Duchess Crs
Thirlwell Gv
Aydon Gv
Beaufront Ter
Chipchase Ter
Swinburne Ter
Bywell Ter
Dilston Ter
Langley Ter
Ford Crs
Warkworth Ter
Kielder Gdns
Ogle Gv
Prudhoe Gv
Witton Gdns
Walworth Gv
Blenkinsop Gv
Coupland Gv
Tynemouth Rd
St. Matthews School
Marine Drive
Campbell Park Rd
Monkton Burn
Durham Grove
A194
Eskdale Dr
Coniston Dr
Grasmere Av
Lodore Gv
Kirkstone Av
Windermere Crs
Ullswater Av
Hedworth La
Usk Av
Kennet Av
Severn Dr
Thames Av
Dove Av
Wye Av
Lea Av
Avon Av
Medway
Hillcrest
Hawthorn Dr
Calf Close Wk
Calf Cl Dr
Calfclose Lane
Trent Dr
Doctors Surg
Mitford Ter
Wark Crs
Patnside
Harbottle Crs
Holland Pk Dr
Hendon Gdns
Heathway
Hedworth Lane
Broomfield
Durham Drive
LEAM LANE
Winchester Ct
Comprehensive
Summerhill
Fellgate
Brayside
Way
1 grid square represents 500 metres

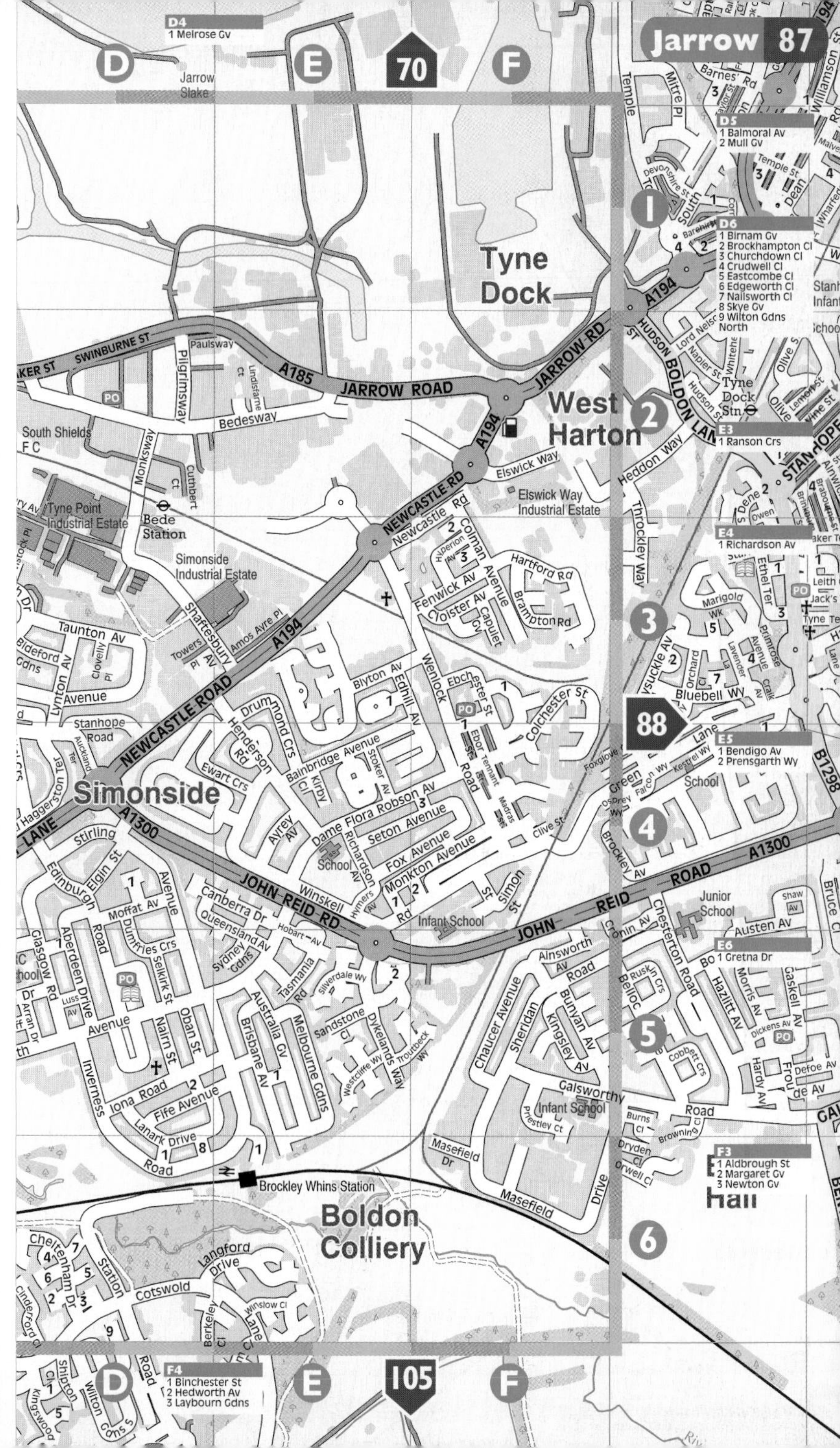
D4
1 Melrose Gv
Jarrow Slake
70
D5
1 Balmoral Av
2 Mull Gv
D6
1 Birnam Gv
2 Brockhampton Cl
3 Churchdown Cl
4 Crudwell Cl
5 Eastcombe Cl
6 Edgeworth Cl
7 Nailsworth Cl
8 Skye Gv
9 Wilton Gdns North
Tyne Dock
West Harton
SWINBURNE ST
JARROW ROAD
A185
A194
JARROW RD
Paulsway
Pilgrimsway
Lindisfarne Ct
Bedesway
Monksway
Cuthbert Ct
South Shields F C
Tyne Point Industrial Estate
Bede Station
Simonside Industrial Estate
Elswick Way
Elswick Way Industrial Estate
NEWCASTLE RD
Newcastle Rd
Heddon Way
Throckley Way
HUDSON ST
BOLDON LANE
Tyne Dock Stn
E3
1 Ranson Crs
E4
1 Richardson Av
Colman Avenue
Hartford Rd
Brampton Rd
Fenwick Av
Cloister Av
Capulet Gv
Hyperion Av
Marigold Wk
Orchard Cl
Primrose
Bluebell Wy
Ethel Ter
88
E5
1 Bendigo Av
2 Prensgarth Wy
B1298
Taunton Av
Bideford Gdns
Clovelly Pl
Lynton Av
Avenue
Shaftesbury Av
Towers Pl
Amos Ayre Pl
NEWCASTLE ROAD
Stanhope Road
Auckland Ter
Blyton Av
Edhill Av
Wenlock Road
Ebchester St
Colchester St
Drummond Crs
Henderson Rd
Ewart Crs
Bainbridge Avenue
Kirby Cl
Stoker Av
Ebor St
Tennant St
Madras St
Clive St
Foxglove
Green Lane
Kestrel Wy
Falcon Wy
Osprey Wy
School
Simonside
A1300
Stirling
Dame Flora Robson Av
Seton Avenue
Ayrey Av
Richardson Av
Fox Avenue
Monkton Avenue
Simon St
Brockley Av
JOHN REID ROAD
Junior School
Shaw Av
Austen Av
E6
1 Gretna Dr
Edinburgh Road
Elgin St
Moffat Av
Dumfries Crs
Selkirk St
Canberra Dr
Queensland Av
Hobart Av
Sydney Gdns
Winskell
JOHN REID RD
Hymers Av
Infant School
Ainsworth Av
Road
Chesterton Road
Hazlitt Av
Morris Av
Gaskell Av
Glasgow Rd
Aberdeen Drive
Luss Av
Arran Dr
Avenue
Oban St
Nairn St
Tasmania Rd
Australia Gv
Brisbane Av
Melbourne Gdns
Silverdale Wy
Sandstone Cl
Dykelands Way
Westcliffe Wy
Troutbeck Wy
Chaucer Avenue
Sheridan
Bunyan Av
Kingsley Av
Belloc
Ruskin Crs
Cobbett Crs
Dickens Av
Hardy Av
Froude Av
Defoe Av
Inverness
Iona Road
Fife Avenue
Lanark Drive
Road
Galsworthy Road
Infant School
Prestley Ct
Burns Cl
Browning Cl
Dryden Cl
Orwell Cl
F3
1 Aldbrough St
2 Margaret Gv
3 Newton Gv
Masefield Dr
Masefield Drive
Brockley Whins Station
Boldon Colliery
Cheltenham Dr
Station
Langford Drive
Cotswold
Winslow Cl
Berkeley Cl
Lane
Cinderford Cl
F4
1 Binchester St
2 Hedworth Av
3 Laybourn Gdns
105
Shipton
Wilton Gdns S
Road
Kingswood

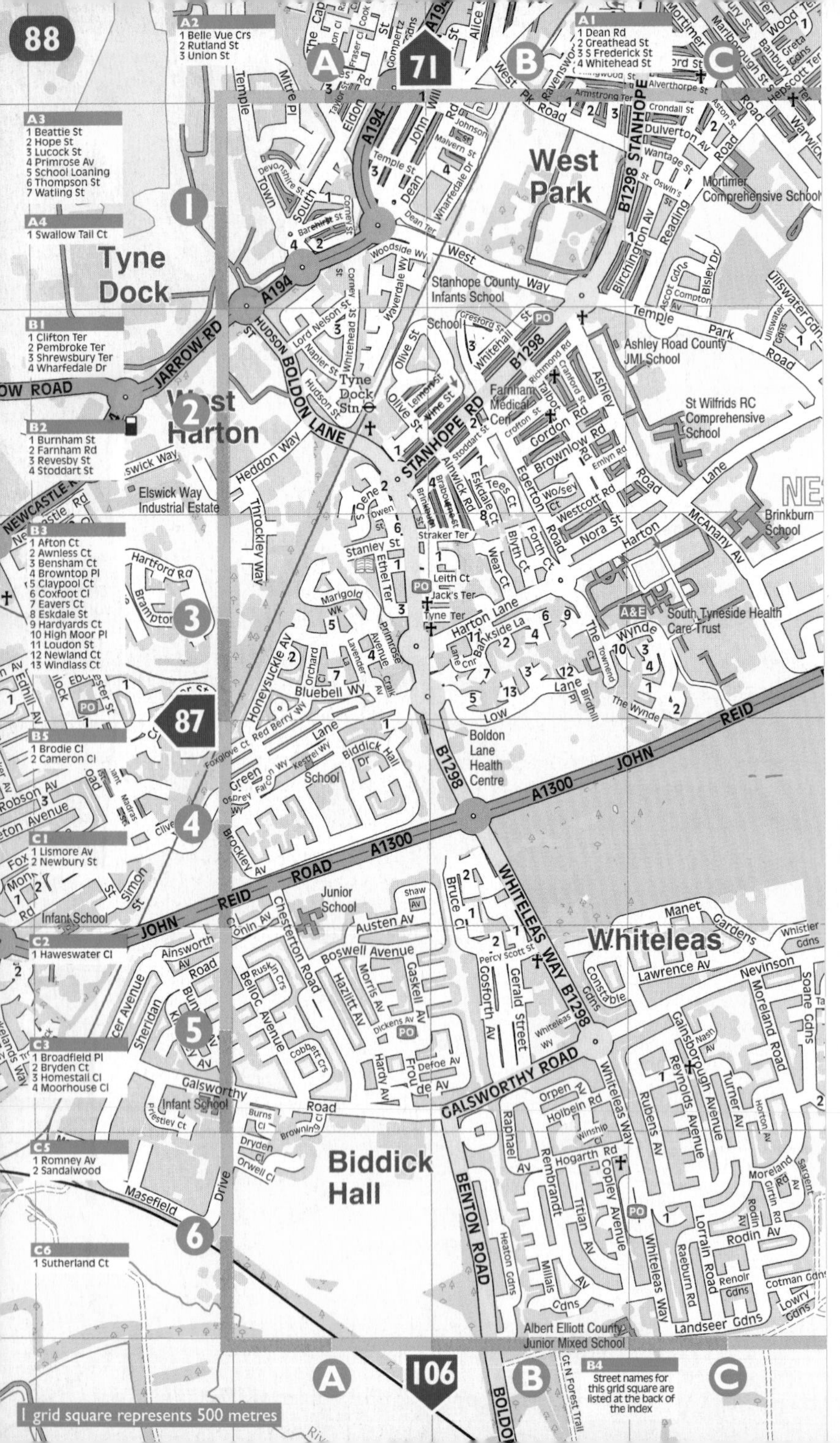
88
A2
1 Belle Vue Crs
2 Rutland St
3 Union St
A1
1 Dean Rd
2 Greathead St
3 S Frederick St
4 Whitehead St
A3
1 Beattie St
2 Hope St
3 Lucock St
4 Primrose Av
5 School Loaning
6 Thompson St
7 Watling St
A4
1 Swallow Tail Ct
B1
1 Clifton Ter
2 Pembroke Ter
3 Shrewsbury Ter
4 Wharfedale Dr
B2
1 Burnham St
2 Farnham Rd
3 Revesby St
4 Stoddart St
B3
1 Afton Ct
2 Awnless Ct
3 Bensham Ct
4 Browntop Pl
5 Claypool Ct
6 Coxfoot Cl
7 Eavers Ct
8 Eskdale St
9 Hardyards Ct
10 High Moor Pl
11 Loudon St
12 Newland Ct
13 Windlass Ct
B5
1 Brodie Cl
2 Cameron Cl
C1
1 Lismore Av
2 Newbury St
C2
1 Haweswater Cl
C3
1 Broadfield Pl
2 Bryden Ct
3 Homestall Cl
4 Moorhouse Cl
C5
1 Romney Av
2 Sandalwood
C6
1 Sutherland Ct
B4
Street names for this grid square are listed at the back of the index
71
87
106
Tyne Dock
West Harton
West Park
Whiteleas
Biddick Hall
A194
JARROW RD
HUDSON ST
BOLDON LANE
STANHOPE RD
B1298
A1300
JOHN REID ROAD
WHITELEAS WAY
GALSWORTHY ROAD
BENTON ROAD
Tyne Dock Stn
Stanhope County Infants School
Ashley Road County JMI School
St Wilfrids RC Comprehensive School
Mortimer Comprehensive School
Brinkburn School
South Tyneside Health Care Trust
Boldon Lane Health Centre
Elswick Way Industrial Estate
Junior School
Infant School
Albert Elliott County Junior Mixed School
1 grid square represents 500 metres

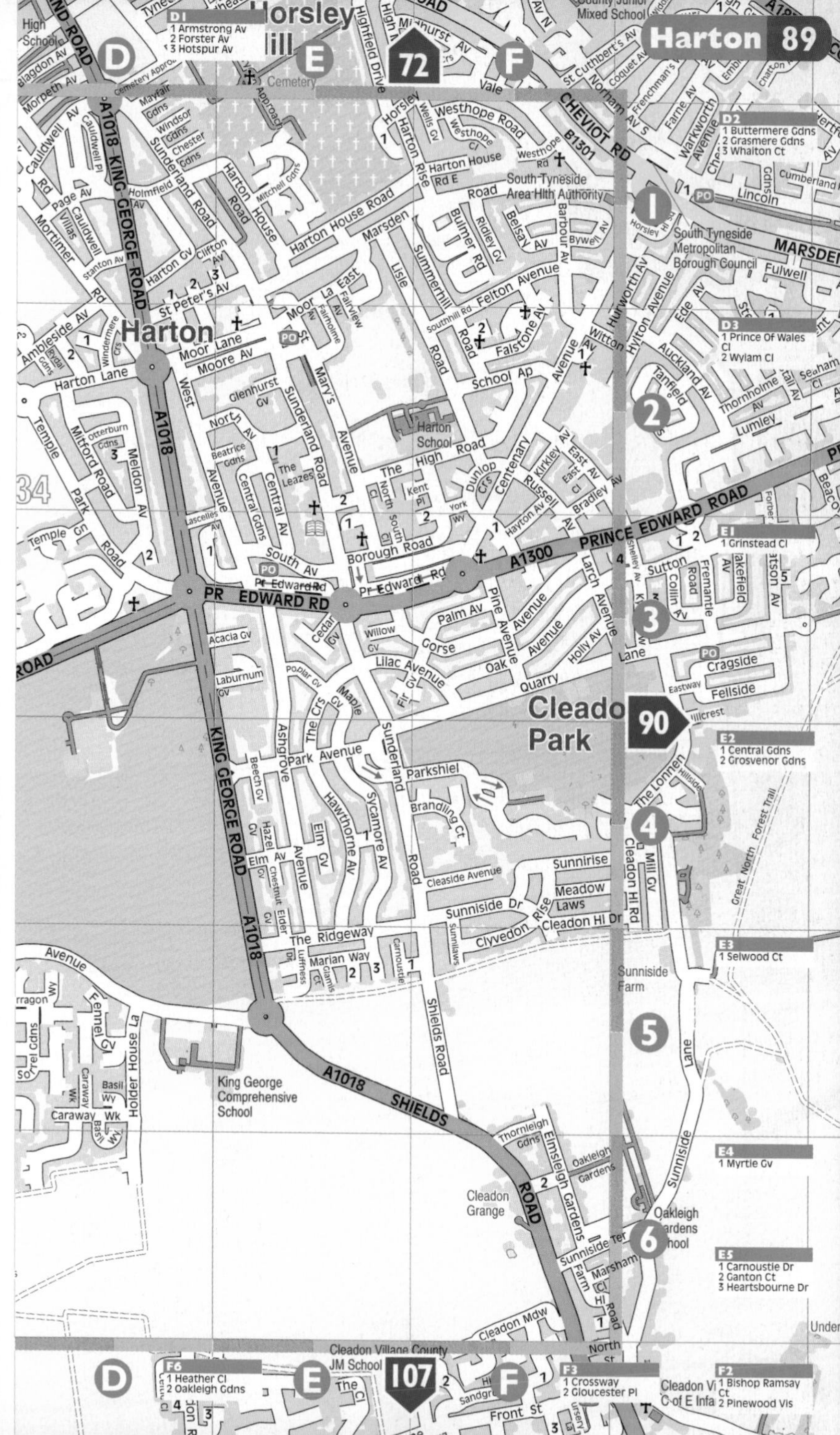

Horsley Hill
D
E
F
72
D1
1 Armstrong Av
2 Forster Av
3 Hotspur Av
High School
Cemetery
Mixed School
Cemetery Approach
Mayfair Gdns
Windsor Gdns
Chester Gdns
Morpeth Av
Blagdon Av
Cauldwell Av
Cauldwell Pl
Cauldwell Villas
A1018 KING GEORGE ROAD
Sunderland Road
Harton House Road
Harton Road
Mitchell Gdns
Highfield Drive
Horsley Hill Road
Wells Gv
Westhope Road
Westhope Cl
Westhope Rd
Harton House Rd E
Harton Rise
Vale
Norham Av S
St Cuthbert's Av
Coquet Av
Frenchman's Wy
Farne Av
Warkworth Avenue
CHEVIOT RD
B1301
South Tyneside Area Hlth Authority
South Tyneside Metropolitan Borough Council
MARSDEN
Fulwell
Lincoln Gdns
Cumberland Pl
D2
1 Buttermere Gdns
2 Grasmere Gdns
3 Whalton Ct
1
2
3
4
5
6
PO
Page Av
Mortimer Rd
Holmfield Av
Stanton Av
Harton Gv
Clifton Av
St Peter's Av
Ambleside Av
Rydal Gdns
Windermere Crs
Harton
Harton Lane
Moor Lane
Moore Av
Moor La East
Fairholme Av
Fairview Av
St Mary's Avenue
Marsden Road
Lisle Road
Summerhill
Bulmer Rd
Ridley Gv
Belsay Av
Barbour Av
Bywell Av
Felton Avenue
Southhill Rd
Falstone Av
School Ap
Witton Avenue
Hurworth Av
Hylton Avenue
Ede Av
Auckland Av
Tanfield
Thornholme Av
Lumley
Seaham
D3
1 Prince Of Wales Cl
2 Wylam Cl
Temple Park Road
Mitford Road
Otterburn Gdns
Meldon Av
A1018
West Avenue
Glenhurst Gv
North Av
Beatrice Gdns
Central Gdns
Central Av
The Leazes
Harton School
The High Road
North Cl
South Cl
Kent Pl
York Wy
Dunlop Crs
Centenary Avenue
Russell Av
Kirkley Av
East Av
East Cl
Bradley Av
Hayton Av
PRINCE EDWARD ROAD
A1300
Temple Gn
Lascelles Av
South Av
Borough Road
Pr Edward Rd
PR EDWARD RD
ROAD
E1
1 Grinstead Cl
Shelley Av
Sutton
Collin Av
Fremantle Road
Wakefield Av
Watson Av
Palm Av
Pine Avenue
Larch Avenue
Cedar Gv
Willow Gv
Gorse
Lilac Avenue
Oak Avenue
Holly Av
Quarry Lane
Cragside
Fellside
Eastway
Acacia Gv
Laburnum Gv
Poplar Gv
The Crs
Maple Gv
Fir Gv
Cleadon Park
90
Hillcrest
E2
1 Central Gdns
2 Grosvenor Gdns
KING GEORGE ROAD
Beech Gv
Ashgrove
Park Avenue
Sunderland Road
Parkshiel
Brandling Ct
The Lonnen
Hillside
Great North Forest Trail
Hazel Gv
Elm Av
Elm Gv
Hawthorne Av
Sycamore Av
Chestnut Gv
Elder Gv
Avenue
Cleaside Avenue
Sunnirise
Meadow Laws
Sunniside Dr
Rise
Cleadon Hl Dr
Cleadon Hl Rd
Mill Gv
Clyvedon Rise
Sunnilaws
The Ridgeway
Luffness Dr
Marian Way
Glamis Ct
Carnoustie
E3
1 Selwood Ct
Sunniside Farm
Lane
Avenue
Fennel Gv
Sorrel Gdns
Caraway Wk
Basil Wy
Holder House La
King George Comprehensive School
A1018 SHIELDS ROAD
Shields Road
Sunniside
Thornleigh Gdns
Elmsleigh Gardens
Oakleigh Gardens
E4
1 Myrtle Gv
Cleadon Grange
Oakleigh Gardens School
Sunniside Ter
Marsham Cl
Farm Hl Road
E5
1 Carnoustie Dr
2 Ganton Ct
3 Heartsbourne Dr
Cleadon Mdw
North St
Cleadon Village County JM School
107
F6
1 Heather Cl
2 Oakleigh Gdns
F3
1 Crossway
2 Gloucester Pl
F2
1 Bishop Ramsay Ct
2 Pinewood Vis
The Cl
Front St
Cleadon Vi C of E Infa

90
73
89
108
A
B
C
1
2
3
4
5
6
A1
1 Horsley Hill Sq
A2
1 Charles Baker Wk
A3
1 Ashridge Cl
2 Carden Av
3 Flaunden Cl
4 Shilton Cl
5 Watson Pl
B1
1 Hampshire Wy
2 Redwell Ct
B2
1 White Horse Vw
C2
1 Quarry La
COAST ROAD
A183
CHEVIOT RD
B1301
MARSDEN LANE
PRINCE EDWARD ROAD EAST
PRINCE EDWARD ROAD
A1300
REDWELL
Marsden
Marsden Hall
Cleadon Hills Farm
Sunniside Farm
Cleadon Grange
Oakleigh Gardens School
Undercliff
South Tyneside Metropolitan Borough Council
South Tyneside Area Hlth Authority
County Junior Mixed School
Harton School
Great North Forest Trail
SHIELDS ROAD
Sunniside Lane
Cragside
Fellside
Hillcrest
Eastway
The Lonnen
Cleadon Hl Rd
Cleadon Hl Dr
Sunnirise
Meadow Laws
Sunniside Dr
Cleaside Avenue
Parkshiel
Brandling Ct
Sunderland Road
Shields Road
Quarry Lane
Larch Avenue
Pine Avenue
Palm Av
Oak Avenue
Holly Av
Gorse
Lilac Avenue
Watson Av
Wakefield Av
Fremantle Road
Collin Av
Kyffin Vw
Sutton
Lumley Avenue
Thornholme Av
Tunstall Av
Seaham Cl
Steward Crescent
Walworth Av
Fulwell Avenue
Chirton Av
Tanfield Gdns
Auckland Av
Ede Av
Hylton Avenue
Hurworth Av
Lincoln Road
Dorset Av
Hertford Av
Devon Gdns
Cumberland Pl
Suffolk Gdns
Norfolk Road
Westmorland Rd
Grotto Rd
Grotto Gdns
Fallow Rd
Lizard Lane
Beaconside
Valley
Lakeside
Cliffside
Quarry Lane
Thornleigh Gdns
Elmsleigh Gdns
Oakleigh Gardens
Sunniside Ter
Marsham Cl
Farm Hl Road
Cleadon Mdw
Sandgrove
High
North St
Cleadon Village C of E Infant School
PO
1 grid square represents 500 metres

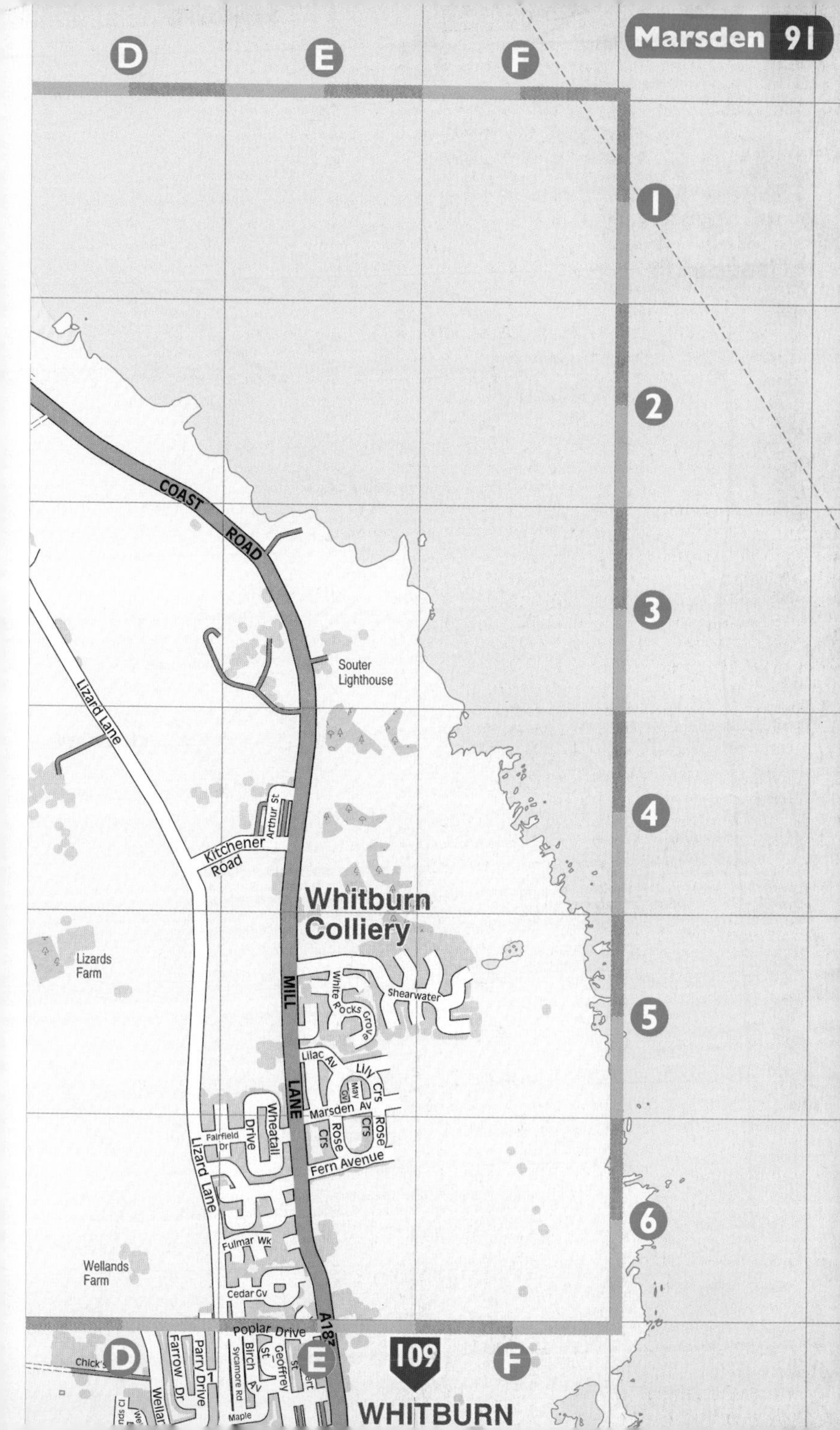
D
E
F
1
2
3
4
5
6
COAST ROAD
Souter Lighthouse
Lizard Lane
Arthur St
Kitchener Road
Whitburn Colliery
Lizards Farm
MILL LANE
White Rocks Grove
Shearwater
Lilac Av
Lily Crs
May Gv
Marsden Av
Rose Crs
Wheatall Drive
Fairfield Dr
Fern Avenue
Fulmar Wk
Wellands Farm
Cedar Gv
Poplar Drive
A183
Chick's
Farrow Dr
Parry Drive
Sycamore Rd
Birch Av
Geoffrey St
Maple
109
WHITBURN

92
Low Greenside
A
B
C
74
A1
1 The Oaks
Kenmore Crs
Lane
Alma Ter
Long Ridge
B4
1 Barlow Crs
Heathfield Gardens
Dyke Heads Lane
John Av
Jasper Av
Lead Road
Berry Hill
The Pines
Lead
Burnhills Gdns
PO
Whiteley Cl
Greenside
1
Burnhills Lane
2
Reeley Mires Farm
SPEN LANE
3
Ricklees Farm
Barlow Burn
Barlow
Barlow Lane
4
B6315 ROGUES LANE
Barlow Fell Road
Ashtree Lane
5
Pawston Road
COLLINGDON RD
Collingdon Gn
PO
6
High Spen Court
Ashfield Ct
Spen Lane
Spen Banks
Sherburn Tower Farm
Spen Burn
Fell View
A
110
B
C
1 grid square represents 500 metres
Hookergate
Spen Burn

E2
1 Farndale Cl
2 Waverley Cl
D
E
75
F
Winlaton
Blaydon
Burn
Burn
Road
Barlow Lane
Knobbyends Lane
West
Lane
Norman's Riding
Farm
Garesfield Lane
Thornley Lane
Scotland
Head
Church Street
Mill Lane
94
Winlaton
Low
Thornley
Thornley
Bank
Hollinhill
Lane
A694
HAUGH ROAD
River Derwent
Hollin Hill
Rowlands Gill
D
E
111
F
F1
1 Birchgate Cl
2 Brockwell Cl
3 The Close
4 Daryl Cl
5 Greenwell Cl
6 Herd Cl
7 Milner Crs
8 Owlet Cl
9 Waterloo St
F2
1 Barlowfield Cl
2 Brandon Cl
3 Burnthouse Cl
4 Cresswell Cl
5 Lyndhurst Cl
6 Stampley Cl
7 Whinney Cl
8 Woodburn Cl
NE21
West Lane Junior
& Infant School
Hollyhurst
Medical Cen
The
Clinc
1
2
3
4
5
6

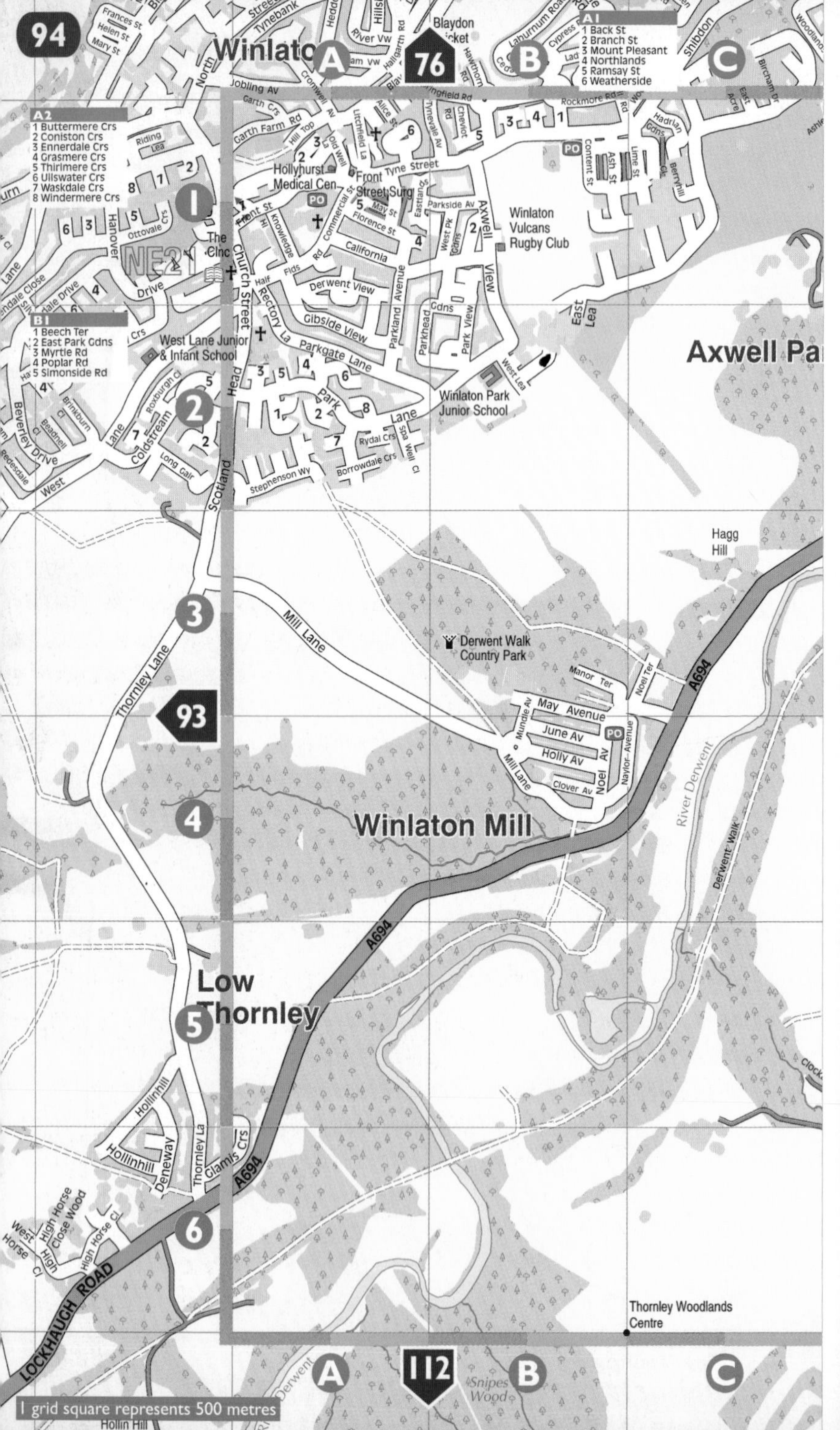
Winlaton
A
B
C
76
Blaydon
A1
1 Back St
2 Branch St
3 Mount Pleasant
4 Northlands
5 Ramsay St
6 Weatherside
A2
1 Buttermere Crs
2 Coniston Crs
3 Ennerdale Crs
4 Grasmere Crs
5 Thirlmere Crs
6 Ullswater Crs
7 Waskdale Crs
8 Windermere Crs
B1
1 Beech Ter
2 East Park Gdns
3 Myrtle Rd
4 Poplar Rd
5 Simonside Rd
1
2
3
4
5
6
NE21
Hollyhurst Medical Cen
Front Street Surg
Winlaton Vulcans Rugby Club
West Lane Junior & Infant School
Winlaton Park Junior School
Axwell Park
Hagg Hill
Derwent Walk Country Park
Winlaton Mill
Low Thornley
93
A694
River Derwent
Derwent Walk
Thornley Woodlands Centre
LOCKHAUGH ROAD
112
Snipes Wood
Hollin Hill
Mill Lane
Thornley Lane
Scotland Head
Church Street
Garth Farm Rd
Tyne Street
California
Derwent View
Gibside View
Parkgate Lane
Park Lane
Parkland Avenue
Axwell View
East Lea
May Avenue
June Av
Holly Av
Clover Av
Noel Av
Manor Ter
Hollinhill
Deneway
Glamis Crs
Stephenson Wy
Borrowdale Crs
Rydal Crs
Beverley Drive
Hanover Drive
1 grid square represents 500 metres

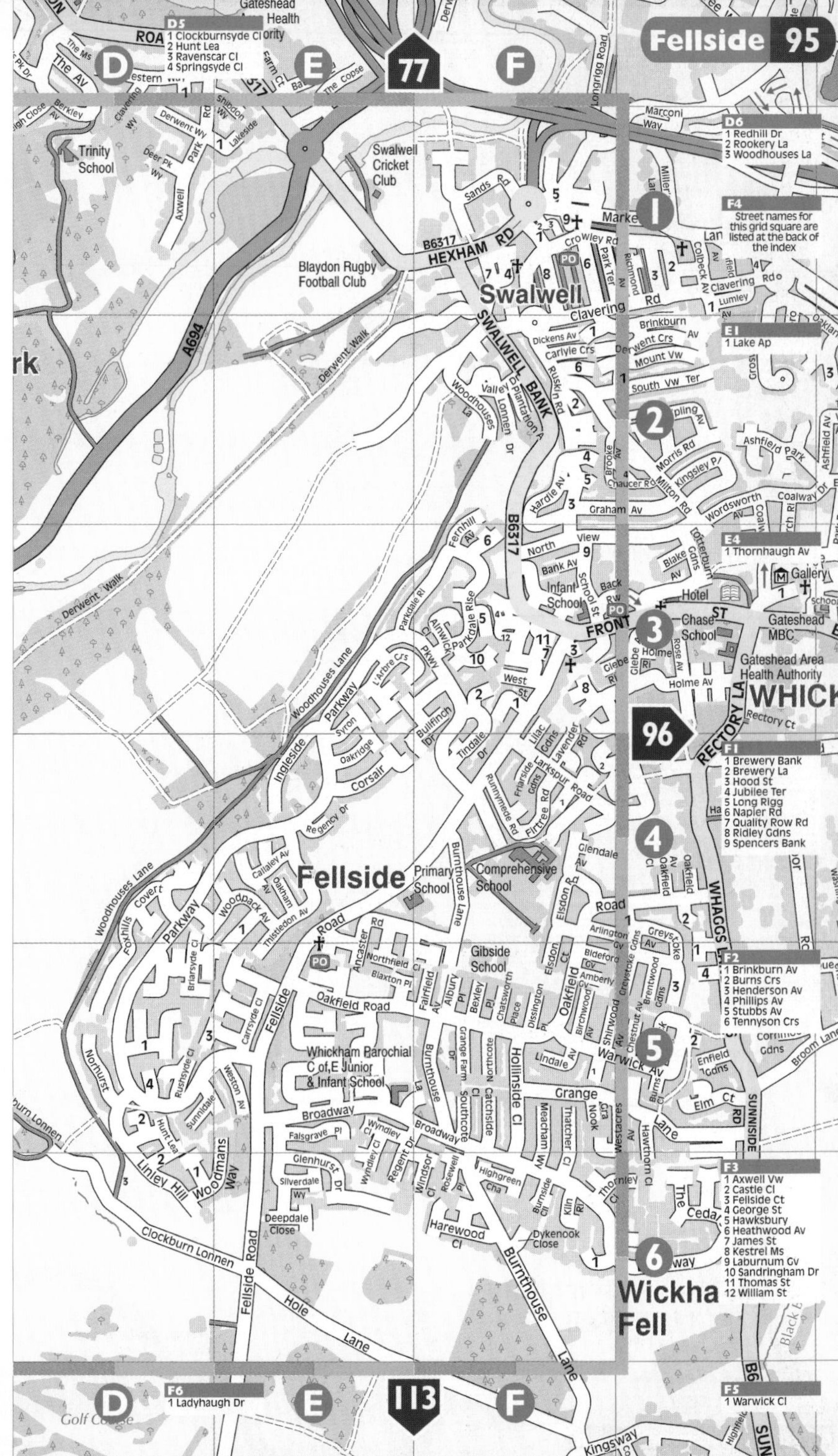
D5
1 Clockburnsyde Cl
2 Hunt Lea
3 Ravenscar Cl
4 Springsyde Cl
D6
1 Redhill Dr
2 Rookery La
3 Woodhouses La
F4
Street names for this grid square are listed at the back of the index
E1
1 Lake Ap
E4
1 Thornhaugh Av
F1
1 Brewery Bank
2 Brewery La
3 Hood St
4 Jubilee Ter
5 Long Rigg
6 Napier Rd
7 Quality Row Rd
8 Ridley Gdns
9 Spencers Bank
F2
1 Brinkburn Av
2 Burns Crs
3 Henderson Av
4 Phillips Av
5 Stubbs Av
6 Tennyson Crs
F3
1 Axwell Vw
2 Castle Cl
3 Fellside Ct
4 George St
5 Hawksbury
6 Heathwood Av
7 James St
8 Kestrel Ms
9 Laburnum Gv
10 Sandringham Dr
11 Thomas St
12 William St
F6
1 Ladyhaugh Dr
F5
1 Warwick Cl
D
E
F
77
96
113
1
2
3
4
5
6
Swalwell
Fellside
Wickham Fell
WHICK
Trinity School
Swalwell Cricket Club
Blaydon Rugby Football Club
Infant School
Chase School
Gateshead MBC
Gateshead Area Health Authority
Primary School
Comprehensive School
Gibside School
Whickham Parochial C of E Junior & Infant School
Gallery
Hotel
Golf Course
A694
B6317
HEXHAM RD
SWALWELL BANK
FRONT ST
RECTORY LA
WHAGGS LA
SUNNISIDE RD
Derwent Walk
Woodhouses Lane
Fellside Road
Burnthouse Lane
Clockburn Lonnen
Hole Lane
Oakfield Road
Broadway
Parkway
Warwick Av
Grange Lane
Kingsway
Broom Lane
Longrigg Road
Linley Hill
Woodmans Way
Northurst

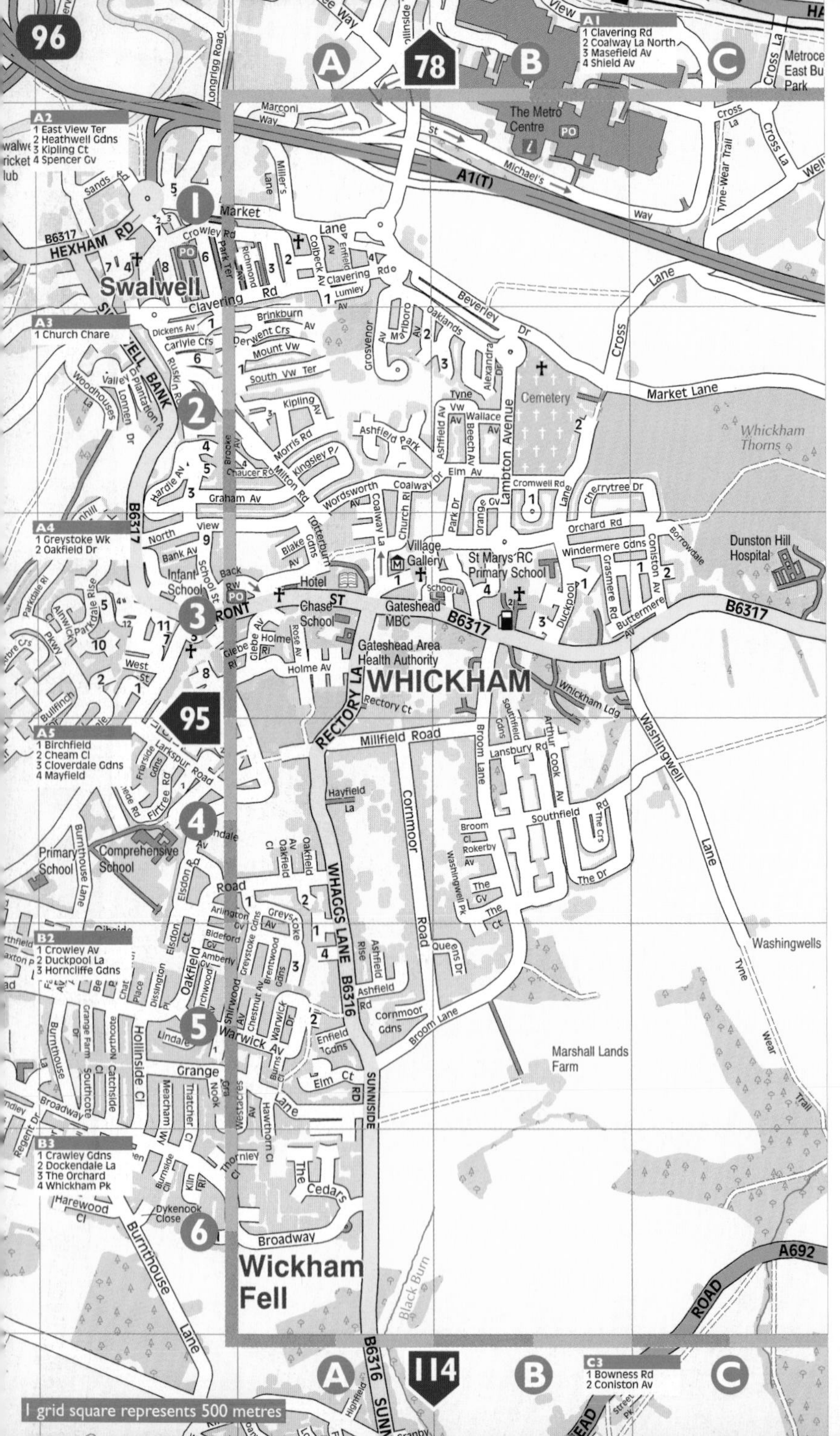

A
78
B
C
A1
1 Clavering Rd
2 Coalway La North
3 Masefield Av
4 Shield Av
Metrocentre East Business Park
A2
1 East View Ter
2 Heathwell Gdns
3 Kipling Ct
4 Spencer Gv
Marconi Way
The Metro Centre
PO
A1(T)
St Michael's Way
Cross La
Tyne-Wear Trail
Millers Lane
Longrigg Road
Sands Rd
HEXHAM RD
B6317
Market Lane
Crowley Rd
Park Ter
Richmond
Colbeck Av
Enfield Av
Clavering Rd
Lumley Av
Swalwell
Clavering Rd
Beverley Dr
Cross Lane
A3
1 Church Chare
Dickens Av
Brinkburn Av
Carlyle Crs
Derwent Crs
Mount Vw
South Vw Ter
Grosvenor Av
Marlboro Av
Oaklands
Alexandra Dr
Cemetery
Market Lane
Whickham Thorns
Woodhouses La
Valley Dr
Plantation Av
Lonnen Dr
Ruskin Rd
Kipling Av
Morris Rd
Kingsley Pl
Ashfield Park
Tyne Vw
Ashfield Av
Beech Av
Wallace Av
Lambton Avenue
Chaucer Rd
Milton Rd
Hardie Av
Graham Av
Wordsworth Av
Coalway Dr
Elm Av
Cromwell Rd
Cherrytree Dr
Lane
B6317
A4
1 Greystoke Wk
2 Oakfield Dr
North View
Bank Av
Infant School
School St
Back Rw
Blake Gdns
Lotterburn
Coalway La
Church Ri
Park Dr
Orange Gv
Village Gallery
St Marys RC Primary School
Orchard Rd
Windermere Gdns
Coniston Av
Borrowdale
Dunston Hill Hospital
Grasmere Rd
Buttermere Av
Duckpool
Hotel
PO
FRONT ST
Chase School
Gateshead MBC
School La
B6317
Parkdale Ri
Parkdale Rise
Alnwick Cl
Pkwy
West St
Glebe Rl
Glebe Av
Holme Rl
Rose Av
Holme Av
Gateshead Area Health Authority
WHICKHAM
Whickham Ldg
Bullfinch
95
RECTORY LA
Rectory Ct
Southfield Gdns
Arthur Cook Av
Washingwell
A5
1 Birchfield
2 Cheam Cl
3 Cloverdale Gdns
4 Mayfield
Friarside Gdns
Larkspur Road
Firtree Rd
Millfield Road
Broom Lane
Lansbury Rd
Hayfield La
Cornmoor Road
Southfield Rd
The Crs
Burnthouse Lane
Primary School
Comprehensive School
Elsdon Rd
Oakfield Cl
Oakfield
Broom Cl
Rokerby Av
Washingwell Pk
The Gv
The Ct
The Dr
Lane
Road
Arlington Gv
Greystoke Gdns
Greystoke Av
Bideford Gv
Amberly
WHAGGS LANE B6316
Ashfield Rise
Queens Dr
Washingwells
B2
1 Crowley Av
2 Duckpool La
3 Horncliffe Gdns
Elsdon Ct
Dissington Pl
Oakfield
Shirwood
Chestnut Av
Brentwood Gdns
Ashfield Rd
Cornmoor Gdns
Broom Lane
Tyne Wear Trail
Burnthouse La
Grange Farm Dr
Northcote
Hollinside Cl
Lindale
Warwick Av
Warwick Dr
Enfield Gdns
Marshall Lands Farm
Grange
Nook
Westacres
Burns Cl
Elm Ct
SUNNISIDE RD
Southcote
Catchside Cl
Broadway
Meacham Wy
Thatcher Cl
Lane
Hawthorn Cl
B3
1 Crawley Gdns
2 Dockendale La
3 The Orchard
4 Whickham Pk
Burnside Cl
Kiln Ri
Thornley Cl
The Cedars
Harewood Cl
Dykenook Close
Broadway
Burnthouse Lane
Wickham Fell
Black Burn
A692
ROAD
B6316
A
114
B
C
C3
1 Bowness Rd
2 Coniston Av
1 grid square represents 500 metres

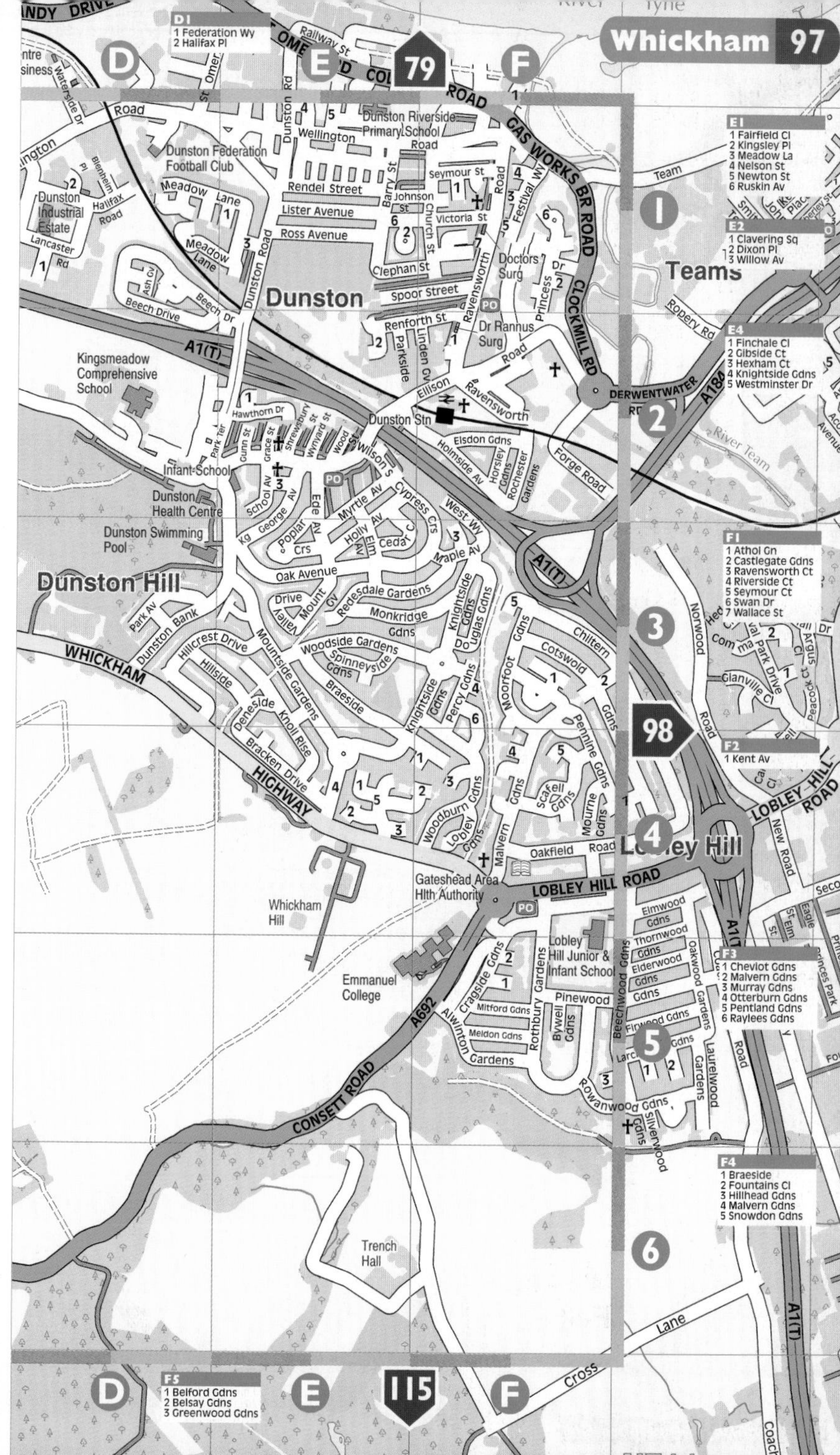
D1
1 Federation Wy
2 Halifax Pl
D
E
79
F
E1
1 Fairfield Cl
2 Kingsley Pl
3 Meadow La
4 Nelson St
5 Newton St
6 Ruskin Av
E2
1 Clavering Sq
2 Dixon Pl
3 Willow Av
E4
1 Finchale Cl
2 Gibside Ct
3 Hexham Ct
4 Knightside Gdns
5 Westminster Dr
F1
1 Athol Gn
2 Castlegate Gdns
3 Ravensworth Ct
4 Riverside Ct
5 Seymour Ct
6 Swan Dr
7 Wallace St
F2
1 Kent Av
F3
1 Cheviot Gdns
2 Malvern Gdns
3 Murray Gdns
4 Otterburn Gdns
5 Pentland Gdns
6 Raylees Gdns
F4
1 Braeside
2 Fountains Cl
3 Hillhead Gdns
4 Malvern Gdns
5 Snowdon Gdns
F5
1 Belford Gdns
2 Belsay Gdns
3 Greenwood Gdns
115
Dunston
Dunston Hill
Teams
Lobley Hill
Dunston Riverside Primary School
Dunston Federation Football Club
Dunston Industrial Estate
Kingsmeadow Comprehensive School
Infant School
Dunston Health Centre
Dunston Swimming Pool
Dunston Stn
Doctors Surg
Dr Rannus Surg
Gateshead Area Hlth Authority
Lobley Hill Junior & Infant School
Emmanuel College
Whickham Hill
Trench Hall
WHICKHAM HIGHWAY
CONSETT ROAD
A692
A1(T)
A184
LOBLEY HILL ROAD
GAS WORKS BR ROAD
CLOCKMILL RD
DERWENTWATER RD
River Team
River Tyne
Rendel Street
Lister Avenue
Ross Avenue
Spoor Street
Clephan St
Oak Avenue
Redesdale Gardens
Monkridge Gdns
Woodside Gardens
Hillcrest Drive
Mountside Gardens
Beech Drive
Meadow Lane
Dunston Road
Forge Road
Norwood Road
Oakfield Road
Cross Lane

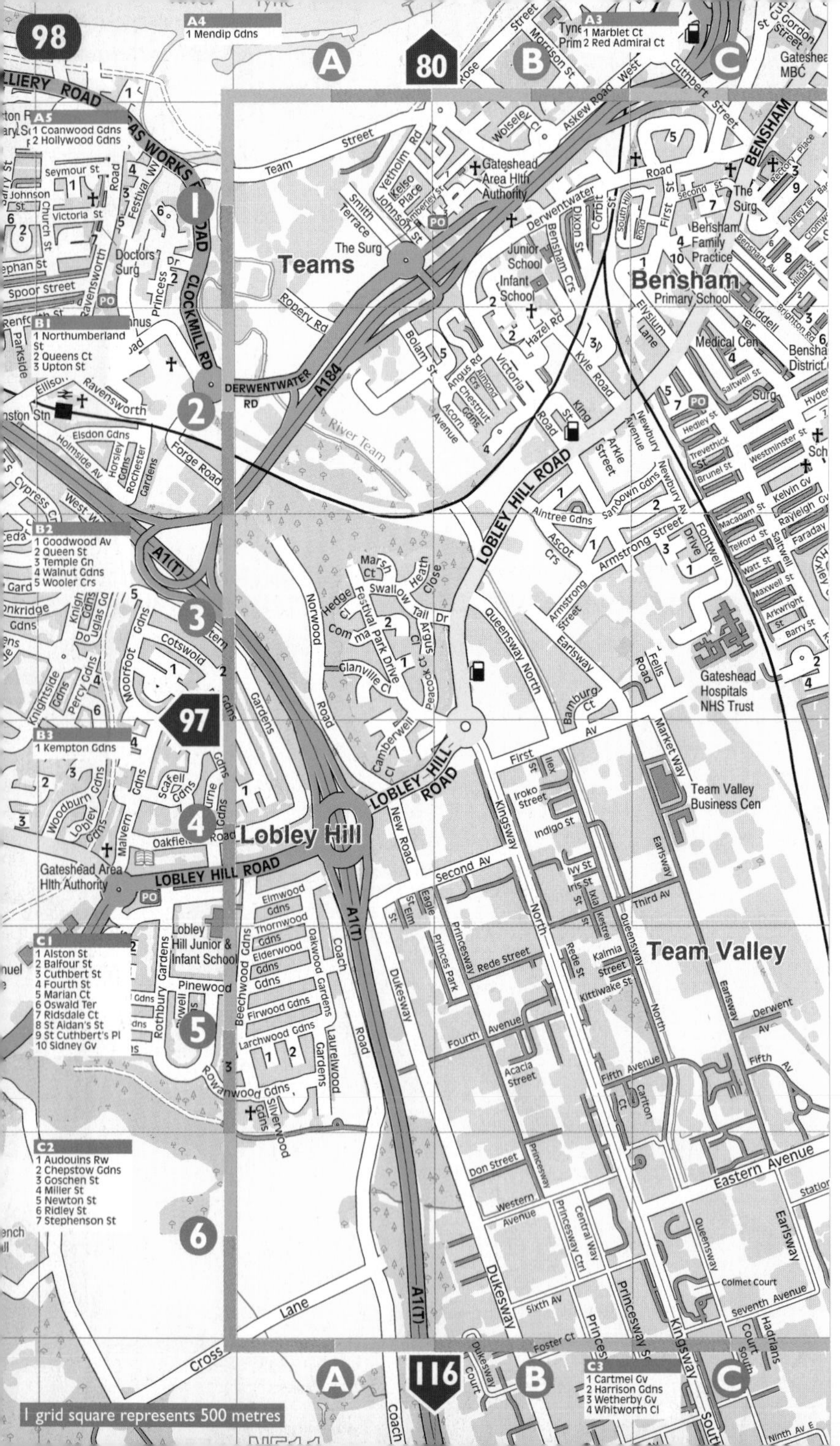
A4
1 Mendip Gdns
A
80
B
A3
1 Marblet Ct
2 Red Admiral Ct
C
A5
1 Coanwood Gdns
2 Hollywood Gdns
B1
1 Northumberland St
2 Queens Ct
3 Upton St
B2
1 Goodwood Av
2 Queen St
3 Temple Gn
4 Walnut Gdns
5 Wooler Crs
B3
1 Kempton Gdns
C1
1 Alston St
2 Balfour St
3 Cuthbert St
4 Fourth St
5 Marian Ct
6 Oswald Ter
7 Ridsdale Ct
8 St Aidan's St
9 St Cuthbert's Pl
10 Sidney Gv
C2
1 Audouins Rw
2 Chepstow Gdns
3 Goschen St
4 Miller St
5 Newton St
6 Ridley St
7 Stephenson St
C3
1 Cartmel Gv
2 Harrison Gdns
3 Wetherby Gv
4 Whitworth Cl
Teams
Bensham
Lobley Hill
Team Valley
97
116
A
B
C
1
2
3
4
5
6
Colliery Road
Gas Works Road
Clockmill Rd
Derwentwater Rd
A184
A1(T)
Lobley Hill Road
Team Street
Askew Road West
Bensham Road
Kingsway North
Queensway North
Earlsway
Dukesway
Princesway
Eastern Avenue
Western Avenue
Team Valley Business Cen
Gateshead Hospitals NHS Trust
Gateshead Area Hlth Authority
Bensham Family Practice
Bensham Primary School
Lobley Hill Junior & Infant School
River Team
Cross Lane
Coach Road
1 grid square represents 500 metres

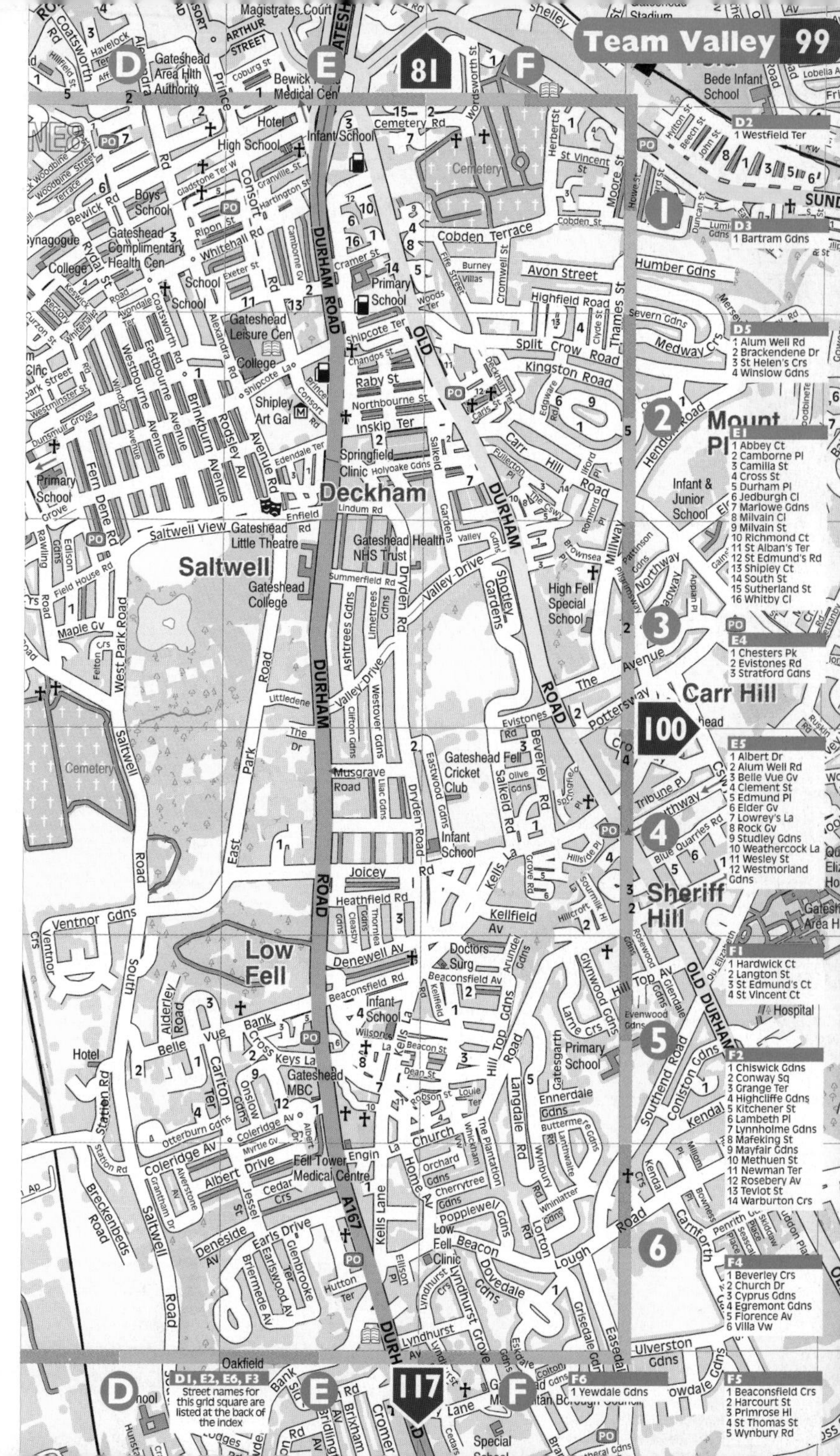
D2
1 Westfield Ter
D3
1 Bartram Gdns
D5
1 Alum Well Rd
2 Brackendene Dr
3 St Helen's Crs
4 Winslow Gdns
E1
1 Abbey Ct
2 Camborne Pl
3 Camilla St
4 Cross St
5 Durham Pl
6 Jedburgh Cl
7 Marlowe Gdns
8 Milvain Cl
9 Milvain St
10 Richmond Ct
11 St Alban's Ter
12 St Edmund's Rd
13 Shipley Ct
14 South St
15 Sutherland St
16 Whitby Cl
E4
1 Chesters Pk
2 Evistones Rd
3 Stratford Gdns
E5
1 Albert Dr
2 Alum Well Rd
3 Belle Vue Gv
4 Clement St
5 Edmund Pl
6 Elder Gv
7 Lowrey's La
8 Rock Gv
9 Studley Gdns
10 Weathercock La
11 Wesley St
12 Westmorland Gdns
F1
1 Hardwick Ct
2 Langton St
3 St Edmund's Ct
4 St Vincent Ct
F2
1 Chiswick Gdns
2 Conway Sq
3 Grange Ter
4 Highcliffe Gdns
5 Kitchener St
6 Lambeth Pl
7 Lynnholme Gdns
8 Mafeking St
9 Mayfair Gdns
10 Methuen St
11 Newman Ter
12 Rosebery Av
13 Teviot St
14 Warburton Crs
F4
1 Beverley Crs
2 Church Dr
3 Cyprus Gdns
4 Egremont Gdns
5 Florence Av
6 Villa Vw
F6
1 Yewdale Gdns
F5
1 Beaconsfield Crs
2 Harcourt St
3 Primrose Hl
4 St Thomas St
5 Wynbury Rd
D1, E2, E6, F3
Street names for this grid square are listed at the back of the index
81
100
117
Deckham
Saltwell
Low Fell
Carr Hill
Sheriff Hill
Mount Pl
Durham Road
Old Durham Road
Gateshead Leisure Cen
Shipley Art Gal
Gateshead Little Theatre
Gateshead College
Gateshead Health NHS Trust
High Fell Special School
Gateshead Fell Cricket Club
Gateshead MBC
Fell Tower Medical Centre
Low Fell Beacon Clinic
Magistrates Court
Bewick Medical Cen
Cemetery

A2
1 Bayswater Rd
2 Ettrick Gdns
3 Fielding Pl
4 Landseer Gdns
5 Leyton Pl
6 Trent Gdns
A1
Street names for this grid square are listed at the back of the index
A3
1 Atholl Gdns
2 Hadrian Pl
3 Morland Gdns
A4
1 Centurion Wy
2 Church La
3 Egremont Dr
4 Fosse Ter
5 Hewson Pl
6 Watling Pl
7 Woolerton Dr
A5
1 Coniston Pl
B1
1 Asher St
B2
1 Brearley Wy
2 Ellerbeck Cl
3 Flexbury Gdns
4 Millfield Gdns
5 Tarlton Crs
6 Warkworth Gdns
7 Windsor Gdns
8 Woodlands Ter
B3
1 Blackburn Gn
2 Greenbourne Gdns
3 Heatherwell Gn
4 Windy Ridge Vls
B4
1 Furrowfield
2 Lanercost Gdns
3 Woodvale Gdns
C1
1 Brandling La
2 Brandling Pl
3 Field St
4 Helmsdale Av
5 Noble St
6 Providence Pl
7 Quarry Rw
C2
1 Croudace Rw
2 Davidson St
3 Elliott Dr
4 Holly Park Vw
5 Park Rw
6 Stainton Dr
7 Thompson Pl
8 Werhale Gn
C3
1 Belgrave Ter
2 Oval Park Vw
3 Picherwell
4 Wentworth Cl
C4
1 College Cl
C5
1 Campion Gdns
82
99
118
Old Fold
Felling Business Centre
Abbotsford Road
Sunderland Road
Felling Stn
FELLING
Mount Pleasant
Carr Hill
Sheriff Hill
Windy Nook
Whitehills
Beacon Lough
Queen Elizabeth Hospital
Gateshead Area Hlth Authority
A&E
High Fell Special School
Windy Nook Primary School
Larkspur Primary School
St Edmunds RC Comprehensive School
St Albans Medical Group
St Oswalds Clinic
Gateshead Metropolitan Borough Council
Gateshead MBC
Old Durham Road
Split Crow Road
Kingston Road
Albion Street
Whitehill Drive
Rectory Road East
Coltsfoot Gdns
Sundew Rd
Harebell Road
Moss Side
1 grid square represents 500 metres

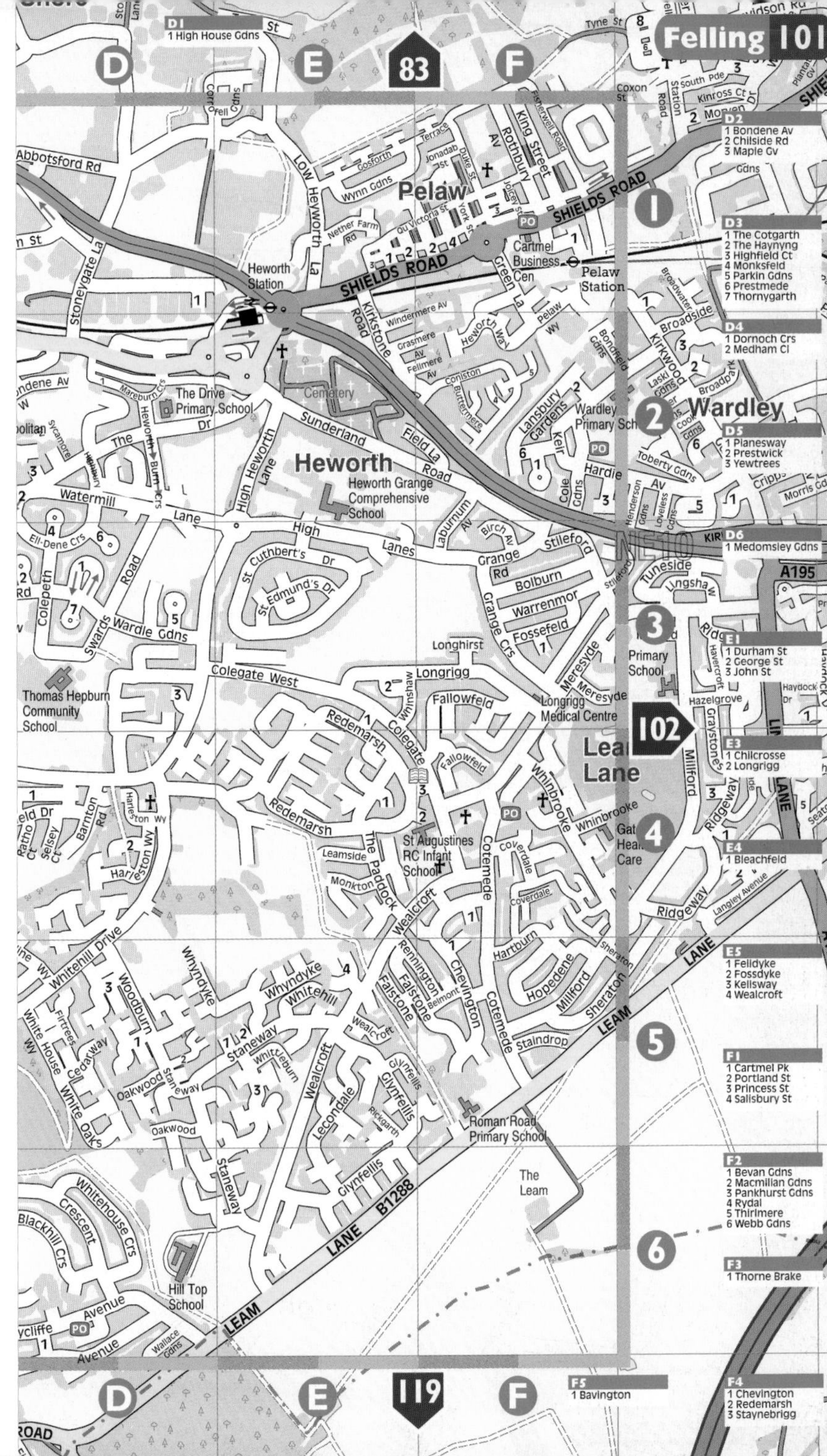
D1
1 High House Gdns
D2
1 Bondene Av
2 Chilside Rd
3 Maple Gv
D3
1 The Cotgarth
2 The Haynyng
3 Highfield Ct
4 Monksfeld
5 Parkin Gdns
6 Prestmede
7 Thornygarth
D4
1 Dornoch Crs
2 Medham Cl
D5
1 Planesway
2 Prestwick
3 Yewtrees
D6
1 Medomsley Gdns
E1
1 Durham St
2 George St
3 John St
E3
1 Chilcrosse
2 Longrigg
E4
1 Bleachfeld
E5
1 Felldyke
2 Fossdyke
3 Kellsway
4 Wealcroft
F1
1 Cartmel Pk
2 Portland St
3 Princess St
4 Salisbury St
F2
1 Bevan Gdns
2 Macmillan Gdns
3 Pankhurst Gdns
4 Rydal
5 Thirlmere
6 Webb Gdns
F3
1 Thorne Brake
F4
1 Chevington
2 Redemarsh
3 Staynebrigg
F5
1 Bavington
83
102
119
Pelaw
Heworth
Wardley
Leam Lane
Shields Road
Abbotsford Rd
Low Heyworth La
Heworth Station
Pelaw Station
Cartmel Business Cen
The Drive Primary School
Cemetery
Heworth Grange Comprehensive School
Sunderland Road
Field La
Watermill Lane
High Lanes
High Heworth Lane
Wardley Primary Sch
Thomas Hepburn Community School
Colegate West
Colegate
Redemarsh
Longrigg Medical Centre
St Augustines RC Infant School
Roman Road Primary School
The Leam
Hill Top School
Whitehill Drive
Leam Lane B1288
A195
Primary School
Stileford
Grange Rd
Grange Crs
Ridgeway
Millford
Cotemede
Staneway
Wealcroft
Whyndyke
Whitehill
Oakwood
White Oaks
Whitehouse Crs
Crescent
Blackhill Crs
Avenue

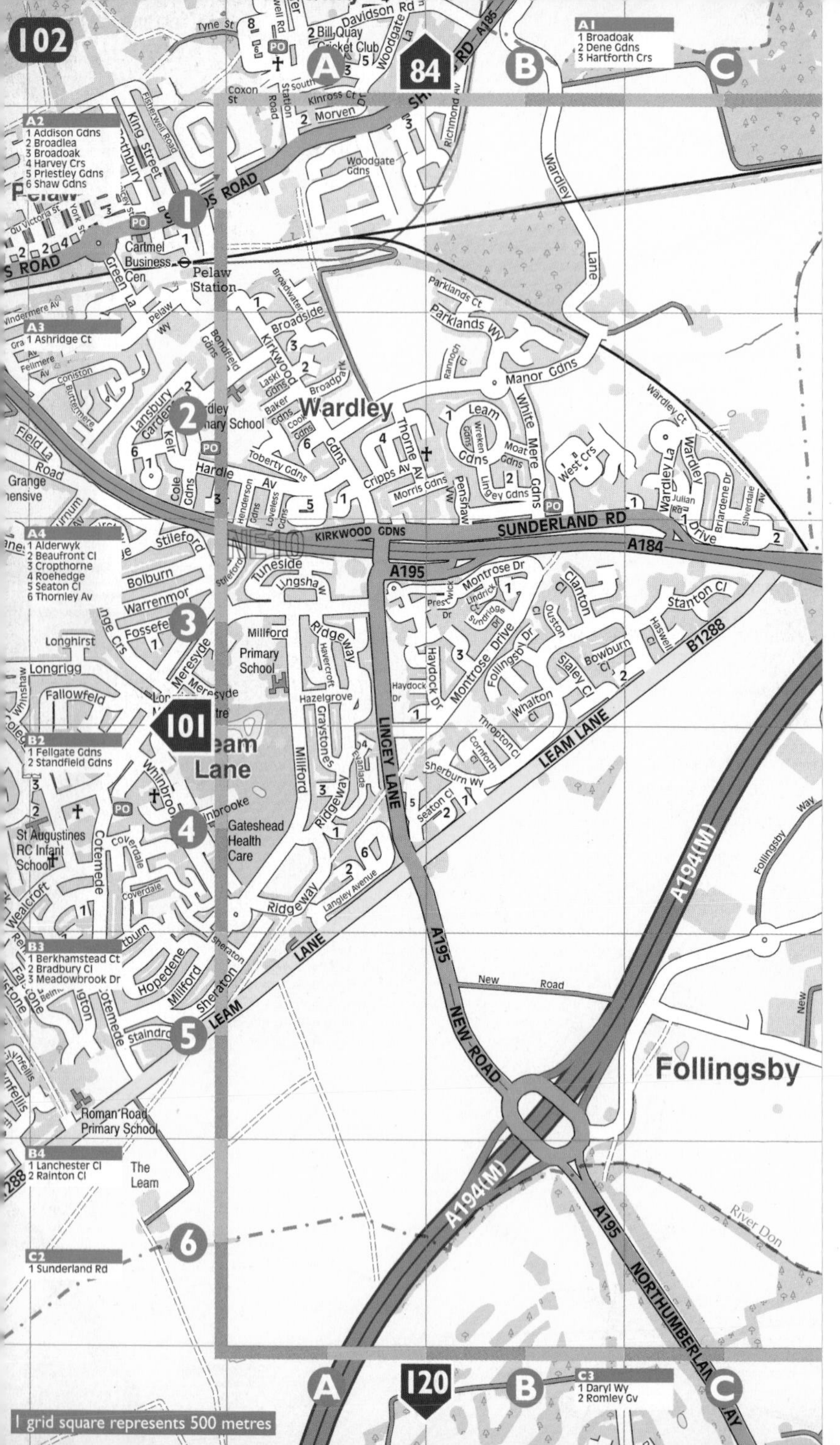
A1
1 Broadoak
2 Dene Gdns
3 Hartforth Crs
A2
1 Addison Gdns
2 Broadlea
3 Broadoak
4 Harvey Crs
5 Priestley Gdns
6 Shaw Gdns
A3
1 Ashridge Ct
A4
1 Alderwyk
2 Beaufront Cl
3 Cropthorne
4 Roehedge
5 Seaton Cl
6 Thornley Av
B2
1 Fellgate Gdns
2 Standfield Gdns
B3
1 Berkhamstead Ct
2 Bradbury Cl
3 Meadowbrook Dr
B4
1 Lanchester Cl
2 Rainton Cl
C2
1 Sunderland Rd
C3
1 Daryl Wy
2 Romley Gv
Wardley
Leam Lane
Follingsby
Pelaw Station
Cartmel Business Cen
Millford Primary School
Gateshead Health Care
St Augustines RC Infant School
Roman Road Primary School
The Leam
SUNDERLAND RD
A184
A195
A194(M)
LINGEY LANE
NEW ROAD
LEAM LANE
B1288
River Don
84
101
120
1 grid square represents 500 metres

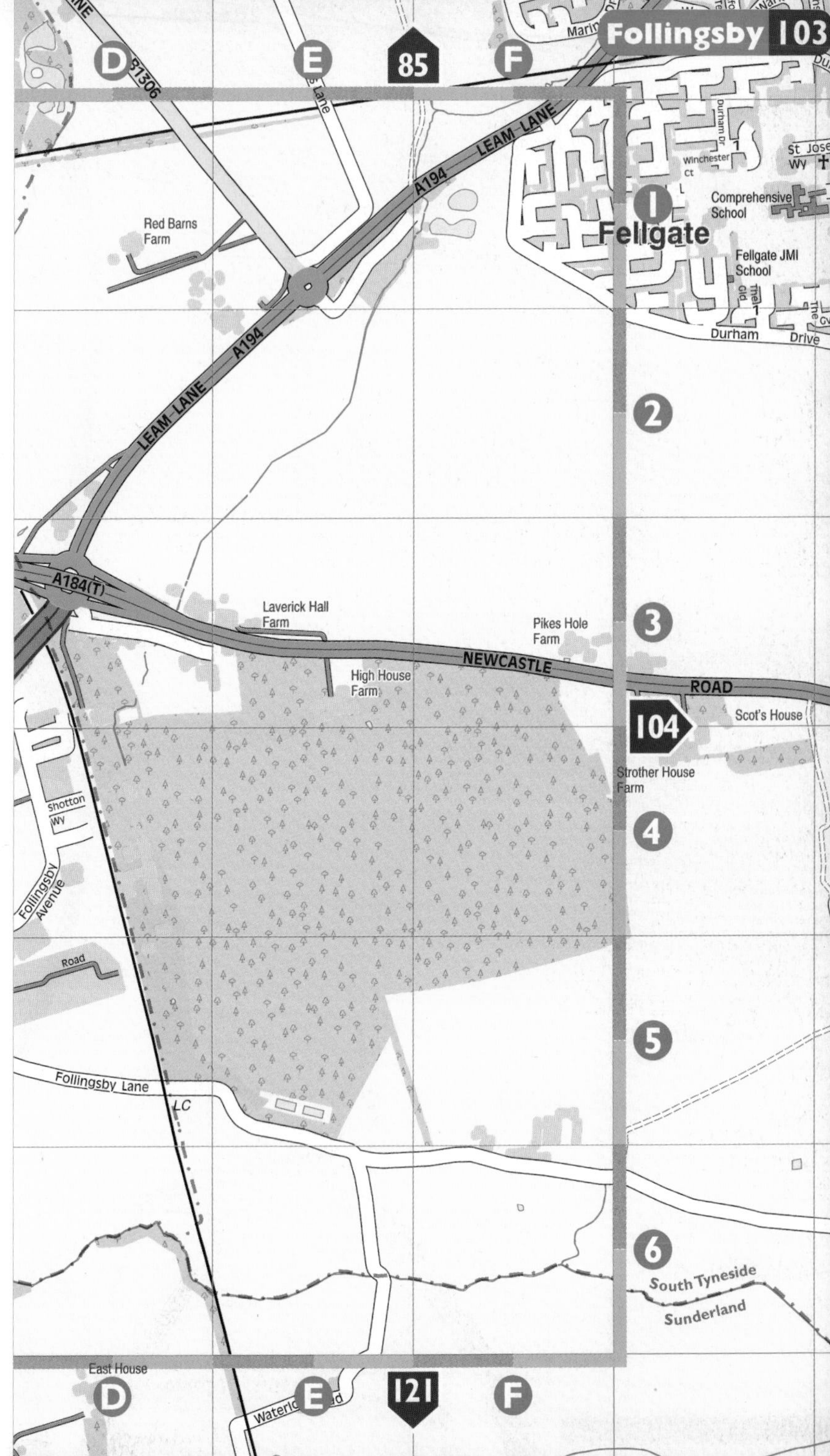
D
E
85
F
B1306
Lane
LEAM LANE
A194
Red Barns Farm
Durham Dr
Winchester Ct
St Jose Wy
1
Comprehensive School
Fellgate
Fellgate JMI School
The Old
The Gv
Durham Drive
2
LEAM LANE
A194
A184(T)
Laverick Hall Farm
Pikes Hole Farm
3
NEWCASTLE
ROAD
High House Farm
104
Scot's House
Strother House Farm
Shotton Wy
Follingsby Avenue
4
Road
5
Follingsby Lane
LC
6
South Tyneside
Sunderland
East House
D
E
121
F
Waterloo Road

Hedworth
A1
1 Don Dixon Dr
A2
1 The Bower
C1
1 Badminton Cl
2 Fieldway
86
103
122
Marine Dr
Wark Crs
Harbottle Crs
Holland Pk Dr
Hendon Gdns
LEAM LANE
A194
Durham Dr
Winchester Ct
St Joseph's Wy
Comprehensive School
Fellgate
Fellgate JMI School
The Gld
The Gv
Limecroft
Durham Drive
Heathway
Broomfield
Ashfield
Avenue
Fellgate
Lane
Summerhill
Chestnut Cl
Linkway
Brayside
Firbanks
Westlands
Southlands
Moorlands
Fieldway
A19(T)
Abingdon Way
Hedworth
Abingdon
Brooklands Way
Pike Farm
NEWCASTLE ROAD
Scot's House
A184(T)
West House Farm
Strother House Farm
West Pastures
South Tyneside
Sunderland
Downhill Lane
Hylton Grove Farm
1 grid square represents 500 metres

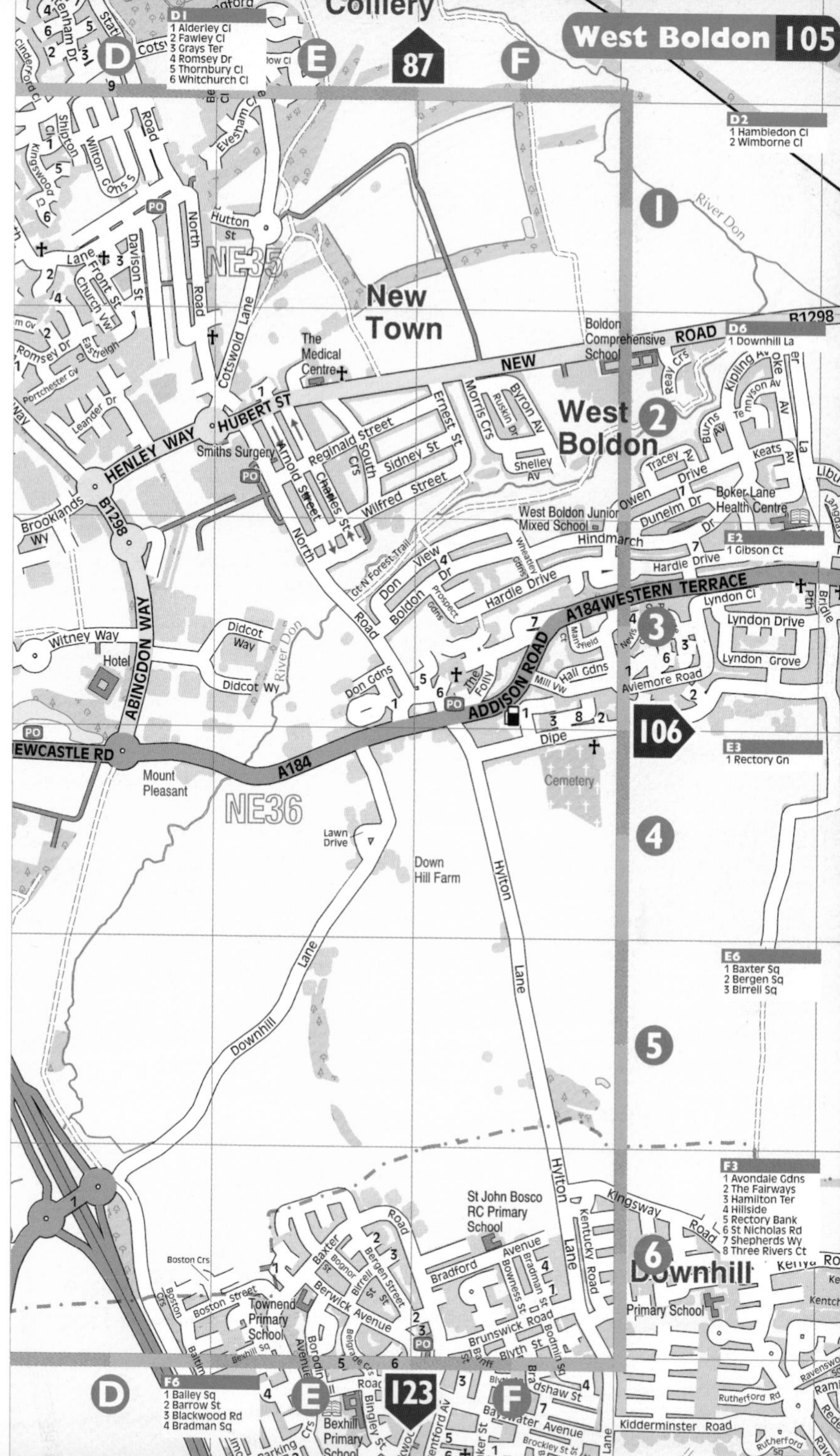
D1
1 Alderley Cl
2 Fawley Cl
3 Grays Ter
4 Romsey Dr
5 Thornbury Cl
6 Whitchurch Cl
87
D2
1 Hambledon Cl
2 Wimborne Cl
D6
1 Downhill La
E2
1 Gibson Ct
E3
1 Rectory Gn
E6
1 Baxter Sq
2 Bergen Sq
3 Birrell Sq
F3
1 Avondale Gdns
2 The Fairways
3 Hamilton Ter
4 Hillside
5 Rectory Bank
6 St Nicholas Rd
7 Shepherds Wy
8 Three Rivers Ct
F6
1 Bailey Sq
2 Barrow St
3 Blackwood Rd
4 Bradman Sq
106
123
New Town
West Boldon
Downhill
NE35
NE36
River Don
Mount Pleasant
Down Hill Farm
Cemetery
Boldon Comprehensive School
The Medical Centre
Smiths Surgery
West Boldon Junior Mixed School
Boker Lane Health Centre
St John Bosco RC Primary School
Townend Primary School
Bexhill Primary School
Primary School
Hotel
HENLEY WAY
HUBERT ST
NEW ROAD
B1298
A184 WESTERN TERRACE
ADDISON ROAD
NEWCASTLE RD
A184
ABINGDON WAY
Hylton Lane
Downhill Lane
Kingsway Road
Kentucky Road
Kidderminster Road

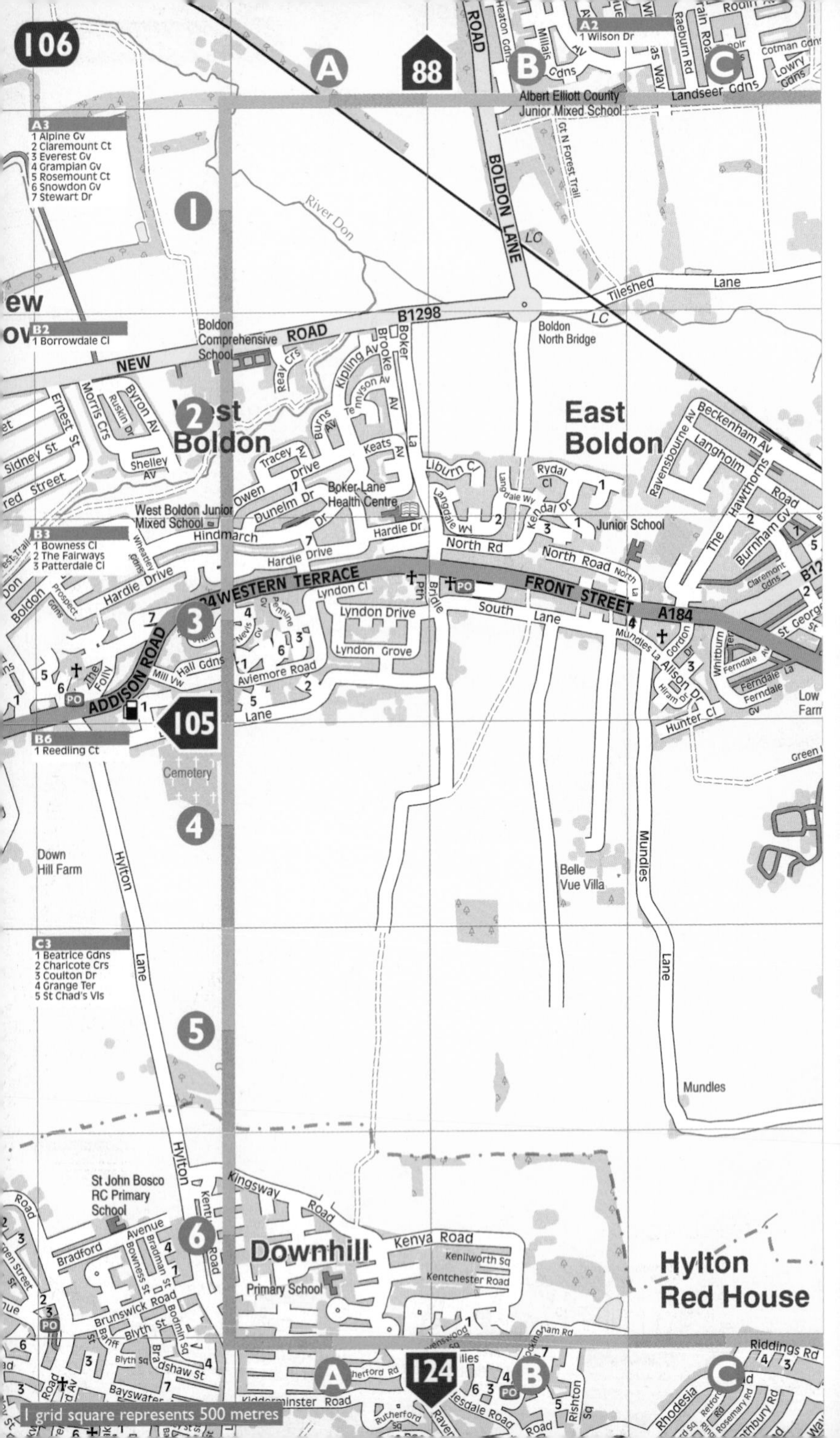
A3
1 Alpine Gv
2 Claremount Ct
3 Everest Gv
4 Grampian Gv
5 Rosemount Ct
6 Snowdon Gv
7 Stewart Dr
A2
1 Wilson Dr
B2
1 Borrowdale Cl
B3
1 Bowness Cl
2 The Fairways
3 Patterdale Cl
B6
1 Reedling Ct
C3
1 Beatrice Gdns
2 Charlcote Crs
3 Coulton Dr
4 Grange Ter
5 St Chad's Vls
88
105
124
West Boldon
East Boldon
Downhill
Hylton Red House
Albert Elliott County Junior Mixed School
Boldon Comprehensive School
West Boldon Junior Mixed School
Boker Lane Health Centre
Junior School
St John Bosco RC Primary School
Primary School
Boldon North Bridge
Cemetery
Down Hill Farm
Belle Vue Villa
Mundles
Low Farm
River Don
BOLDON LANE
NEW ROAD
B1298
Tileshed Lane
FRONT STREET
A184
WESTERN TERRACE
ADDISON ROAD
North Road
North Rd
South Lane
Mundles Lane
Hylton Lane
Kingsway Road
Kenya Road
Kenilworth Sq
Kentchester Road
Bradford Avenue
Brunswick Road
Blyth St
Bayswater
Kidderminster Road
Rhodesia
Riddings Rd
The Hawthorns
Beckenham Av
Ravensbourne Av
Langholm
Burnham Gv
Whitburn Ter
Ferndale La
Hunter Cl
Alison Dr
Gordon Dr
Lyndon Drive
Lyndon Grove
Lyndon Cl
Aviemore Road
Hall Gdns
Mill Vw
The Folly
Hindmarch Dr
Hardie Drive
Hardie Dr
Dunelm Dr
Owen Drive
Tracey Av
Keats Av
Burns Av
Kipling Av
Tennyson Av
Brooke Av
Boker La
Reay Crs
Byron Av
Ruskin Dr
Shelley Av
Morris Crs
Ernest St
Sidney St
Liburn Cl
Langdale Wy
Kendal Dr
Rydal Cl
Landseer Gdns
Raeburn Rd
Millais Gdns
Heaton Gdns
Cotman Gdns
Lowry Gdns
Gt N Forest Trail
Bridle Pth
Green La
1 grid square represents 500 metres

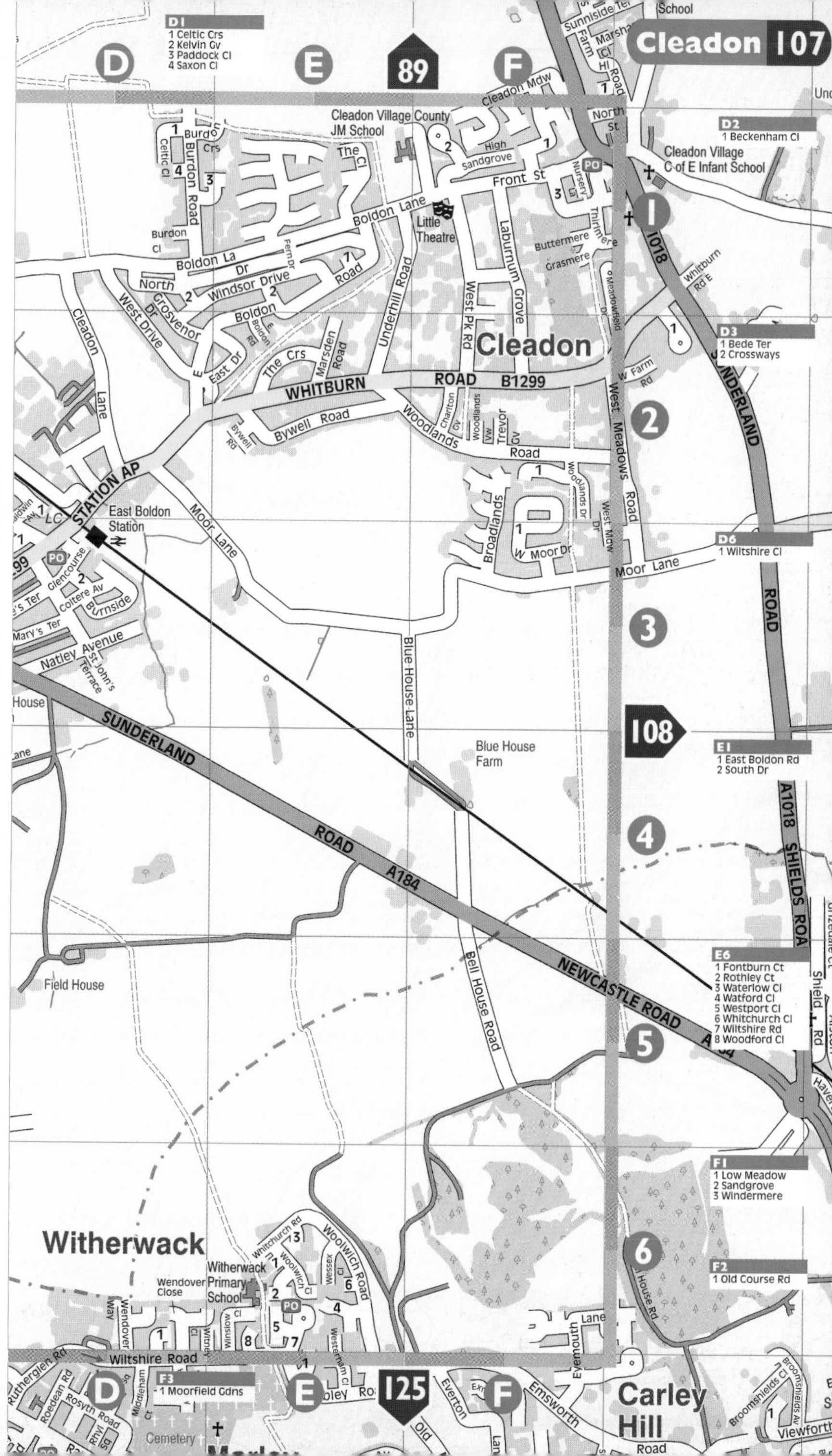
D1
1 Celtic Crs
2 Kelvin Gv
3 Paddock Cl
4 Saxon Cl
D
E
89
F
D2
1 Beckenham Cl
D3
1 Bede Ter
2 Crossways
D6
1 Wiltshire Cl
E1
1 East Boldon Rd
2 South Dr
E6
1 Fontburn Ct
2 Rothley Ct
3 Waterlow Cl
4 Watford Cl
5 Westport Cl
6 Whitchurch Cl
7 Wiltshire Rd
8 Woodford Cl
F1
1 Low Meadow
2 Sandgrove
3 Windermere
F2
1 Old Course Rd
F3
1 Moorfield Gdns
108
125
1
2
3
4
5
6
Cleadon
Witherwack
Carley Hill
Cleadon Village County JM School
Cleadon Village C of E Infant School
Little Theatre
East Boldon Station
Blue House Farm
Field House
Witherwack Primary School
Cemetery
School
Sunniside Ter
Marsham Cl
Farm Hl Road
Cleadon Mdw
North St
High Sandgrove
Front St
Boldon Lane
Boldon La
The Cl
Burdon Crs
Burdon Road
Celtic Cl
Burdon Cl
North Dr
Windsor Drive
Fern Dr
Road
Grosvenor Dr
West Drive
Boldon Dr
East Dr
The Crs
Marsden Road
Underhill Road
West Pk Rd
Laburnum Grove
Nursery La
Buttermere
Thirlmere
Grasmere
Meadowfield Dr
Whitburn Rd E
Cleadon Lane
WHITBURN ROAD B1299
W Farm Rd
West Meadows Road
SUNDERLAND ROAD
A1018
Bywell Road
Bywell Rd
Woodlands Road
Charlton Gv
Woodlands Vw
Trevor Gv
Woodlands Dr
West Mdw Dr
Broadlands
W Moor Dr
Moor Lane
STATION AP
Glencourse
Coltere Av
Burnside
Mary's Ter
Natley Avenue
St John's Terrace
House
Lane
Blue House Lane
SUNDERLAND ROAD A184
NEWCASTLE ROAD
Bell House Road
A1018 SHIELDS ROAD
Grizedale Ct
Shield Rd
Alston
Haversham
Whitchurch Rd
Woolwich Road
Woolwich Cl
Wessex Cl
Wendover Close
Wendover Way
Winslow Cl
Witney
Westernam Cl
Wiltshire Road
Evemouth
Lane
House Rd
Ruthergien Rd
Roedean Rd
Rosyth Road
Middleham Ct
Everton
Emsworth
Broomshields Cl
Broomshields Av
Viewforth
Road

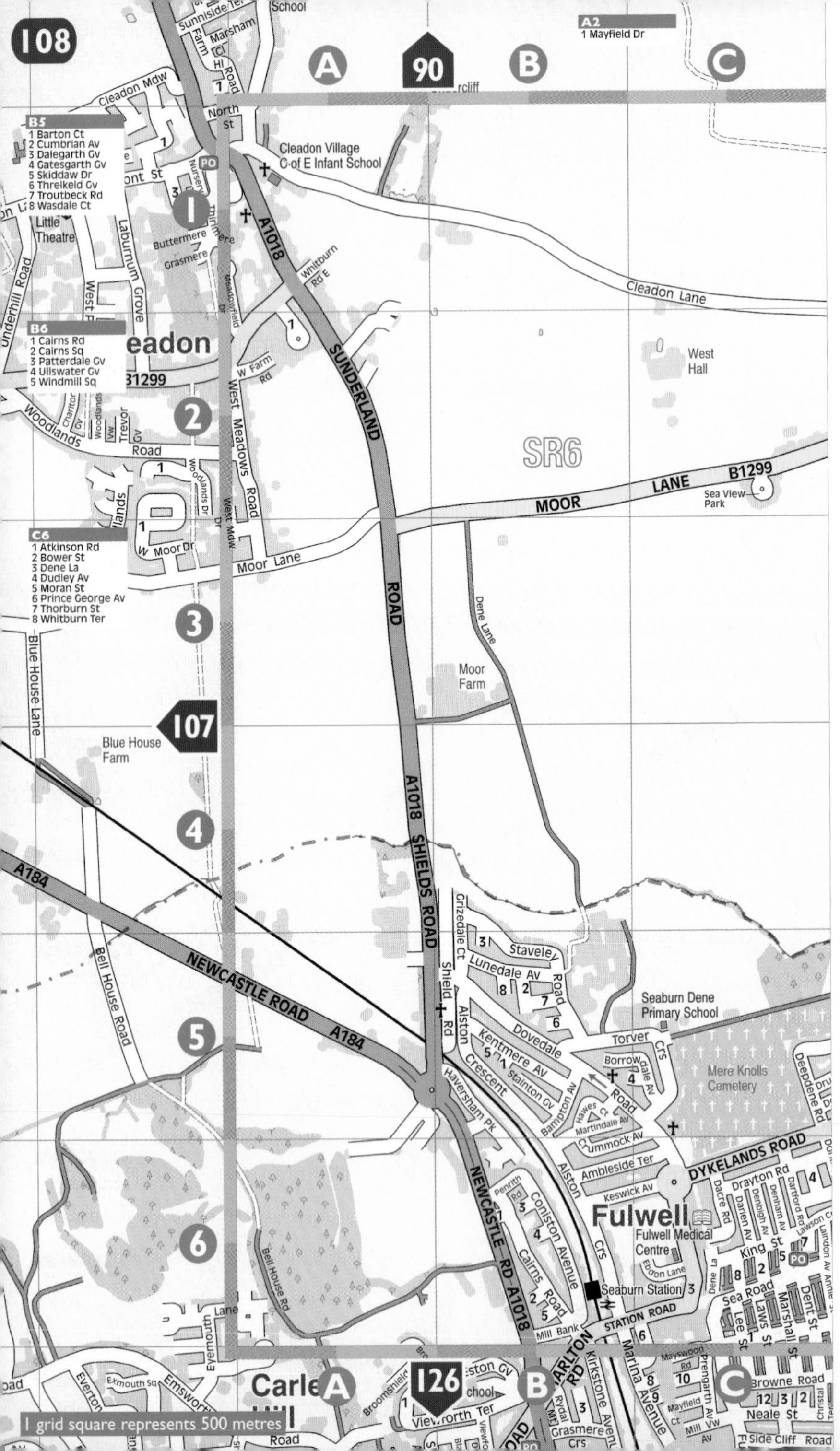

A
90
B
C
A2
1 Mayfield Dr
B5
1 Barton Ct
2 Cumbrian Av
3 Dalegarth Gv
4 Gatesgarth Gv
5 Skiddaw Dr
6 Threlkeld Gv
7 Troutbeck Rd
8 Wasdale Ct
B6
1 Cairns Rd
2 Cairns Sq
3 Patterdale Gv
4 Ullswater Gv
5 Windmill Sq
C6
1 Atkinson Rd
2 Bower St
3 Dene La
4 Dudley Av
5 Moran St
6 Prince George Av
7 Thorburn St
8 Whitburn Ter
School
Sunniside Ter
Farm
Marsham Cl
Hl
Road
Cleadon Mdw
North St
Cleadon Village C of E Infant School
PO
Front St
Nursery
Little Theatre
Laburnum Grove
Buttermere
Grasmere
Thirlmere
Underhill Road
West
Meadowfield Dr
A1018
Whitburn Rd E
Cleadon Lane
eadon
B1299
W Farm Rd
SUNDERLAND
West Hall
Woodlands
Trevor Gv
Road
West Meadows Road
Woodlands Dr
SR6
MOOR LANE B1299
Sea View Park
West Mdw Dr
W Moor Dr
Moor Lane
ROAD
Dene Lane
Moor Farm
Blue House Lane
107
Blue House Farm
A1018 SHIELDS ROAD
A184
Bell House Road
NEWCASTLE ROAD
A184
Grizedale Ct
Staveley Road
Lunedale Av
Shield Rd
Alston Crescent
Dovedale
Kentmere Av
Stainton Gv
Seaburn Dene Primary School
Torver Crs
Borrowdale Av
Road
Mere Knolls Cemetery
Deepdene Rd
Haversham Pk
Bampton Av
Hawes Ct
Martindale Av
Crummock Av
Ambleside Ter
Keswick Av
DYKELANDS ROAD
Drayton Rd
Dacre Rd
Darien Av
Denbigh Av
Denham Av
Dartford Rd
Lawson Ct
NEWCASTLE RD A1018
Penrith Rd
Coniston Avenue
Cairns Road
Alston Crs
Fulwell
Fulwell Medical Centre
King St
Eddon Lane
Dene La
Sea Road
Laws St
Marshall St
Dent St
Lee St
Seaburn Station
STATION ROAD
Bell House Rd
Lane
Eyemouth Lane
Mill Bank
CARLTON RD
Kirkstone Avenue
Marina Avenue
Mayswood Rd
Prengarth Av
Mayfield Ct
Mill Vw
Browne Road
Neale St
Side Cliff Road
Exmouth Sq
Emsworth
Everton
Carle
Hill
126
Broomshield
Eston Gv
School
Viewforth Ter
Rydal Mt
Grasmere Crs
Road
1 grid square represents 500 metres

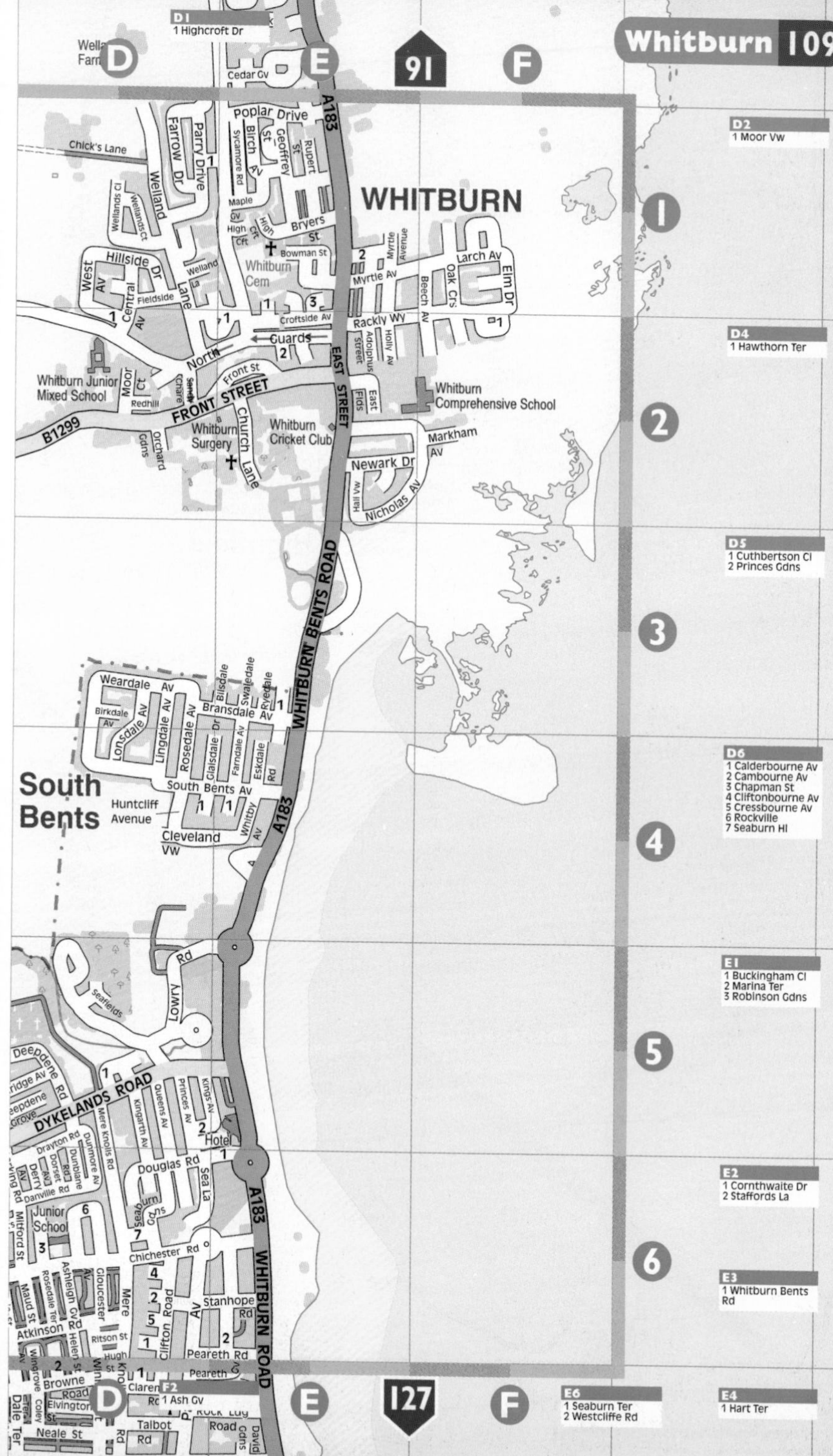
D1
1 Highcroft Dr
D
E
91
F
Welland Farm
Cedar Gv
Poplar Drive
A183
Farrow Dr
Parry Drive
Geoffrey St
Birch Av
Sycamore Rd
Rupert St
Chick's Lane
Welland
Wellands Cl
Wellands Ct
Maple Gv
High Cft
Bryers St
WHITBURN
Bowman St
Whitburn Cem
Myrtle Av
Myrtle Avenue
Larch Av
Oak Crs
Beech Av
Elm Dr
Hillside Dr
West Av
Central Av
Fieldside
Lane
Croftside Av
Rackly Wy
Adolphus Street
Holly Av
Guards
North
Front St
EAST STREET
Whitburn Junior Mixed School
Moor Ct
Sandy Chare
Redhill
FRONT STREET
B1299
Orchard Gdns
Whitburn Surgery
Church Lane
Whitburn Cricket Club
East Flds
Whitburn Comprehensive School
Markham Av
Newark Dr
Hall Vw
Nicholas Av
WHITBURN BENTS ROAD
Weardale Av
Bilsdale
Swaledale
Ryedale
Bransdale Av
Birkdale Av
Lonsdale Av
Lingdale Av
Rosedale Av
Glaisdale Dr
Farndale Av
Eskdale Rd
South Bents Av
South Bents
Huntcliff Avenue
Whitby Av
Cleveland Vw
Lowry Rd
Seafields
Deepdene Rd
Deepdene Grove
DYKELANDS ROAD
Mere Knolls Rd
Kingarth Av
Queens Av
Princes Av
Kings Av
Hotel
Drayton Rd
Dunmore Av
Dunblane Rd
Dorset Av
Derry Av
Danville Rd
Douglas Rd
Sea La
Seaburn Gdns
Junior School
Mitford St
Chichester Rd
Ashleigh Gv
Rosedale Ter
Gloucester Av
Mere Av
Maud St
Clifton Road
Stanhope Rd
Atkinson Rd
Helen St
Ritson St
Hugh St
Peareth Rd
Peareth Gv
Browne Road
Wingrove Av
Elvington St
Coley Ter
Dale Ter
Neale St
Talbot Rd
Road
David Gdns
WHITBURN ROAD
F2
1 Ash Gv
127
D2
1 Moor Vw
1
D4
1 Hawthorn Ter
2
D5
1 Cuthbertson Cl
2 Princes Gdns
3
D6
1 Calderbourne Av
2 Cambourne Av
3 Chapman St
4 Cliftonbourne Av
5 Cressbourne Av
6 Rockville
7 Seaburn Hl
4
E1
1 Buckingham Cl
2 Marina Ter
3 Robinson Gdns
5
E2
1 Cornthwaite Dr
2 Staffords La
6
E3
1 Whitburn Bents Rd
E6
1 Seaburn Ter
2 Westcliffe Rd
E4
1 Hart Ter

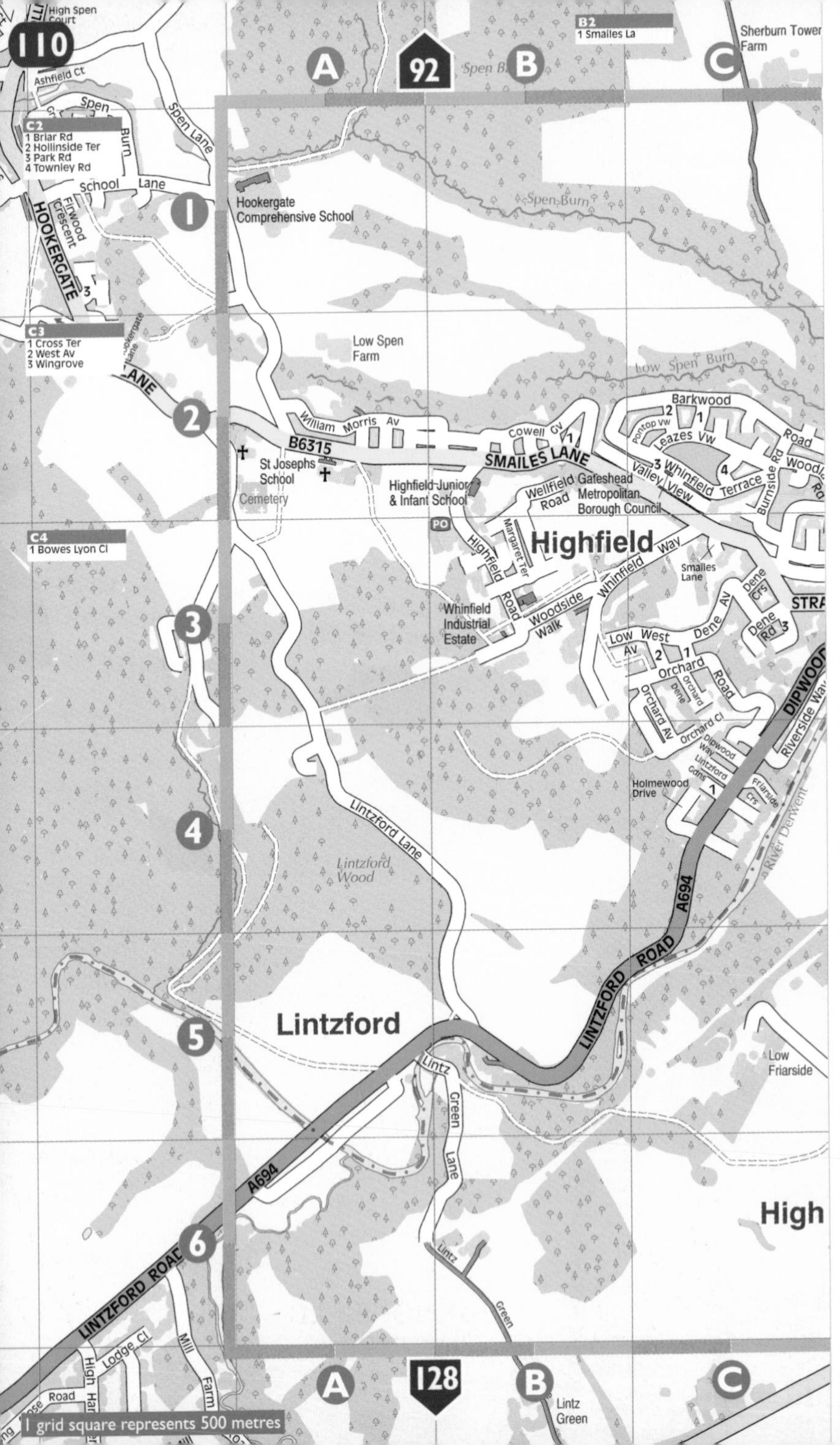
110
92
128
A
B
C
1
2
3
4
5
6
High Spen Court
Ashfield Ct
Spen Burn
Spen Lane
School Lane
HOOKERGATE
Firwood Crescent
C2
1 Briar Rd
2 Hollinside Ter
3 Park Rd
4 Townley Rd
C3
1 Cross Ter
2 West Av
3 Wingrove
C4
1 Bowes Lyon Cl
B2
1 Smailes La
Sherburn Tower Farm
Spen Burn
Hookergate Comprehensive School
Low Spen Farm
Low Spen Burn
Barkwood
Road
William Morris Av
B6315
SMAILES LANE
Cowell Gv
Pontop Vw
Leazes Vw
Whinfield Terrace
Valley View
Burnside Rd
St Josephs School
Cemetery
Highfield Junior & Infant School
Wellfield Road
Gateshead Metropolitan Borough Council
Highfield
Highfield Road
Margaret Ter
Whinfield Way
Smailes Lane
Woodside Walk
Whinfield Industrial Estate
Low West Av
Dene Av
Dene Crs
Dene Rd
Orchard Road
Orchard Av
Orchard Cl
Dipwood Way
Lintzford Gdns
Holmewood Drive
Friarside Crs
Riverside Way
DIPWOOD
River Derwent
Lintzford Lane
Lintzford Wood
A694
LINTZFORD ROAD
Lintzford
Lintz Green Lane
Low Friarside
High
Lintz Green
LINTZFORD ROAD
A694
Lodge Cl
High Ham
Mill Farm
Road
Lintz Green
1 grid square represents 500 metres

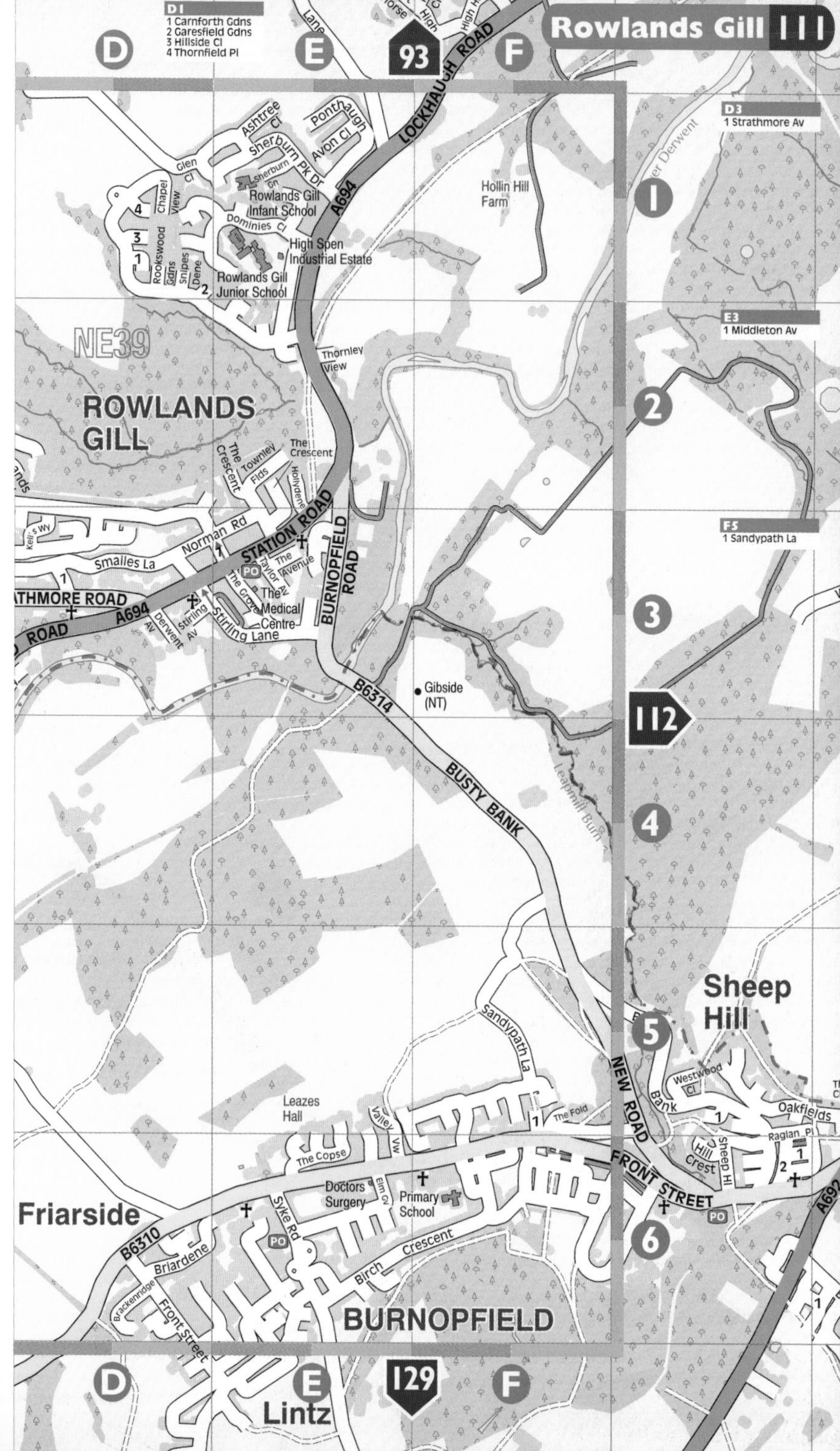

D1
1 Carnforth Gdns
2 Garesfield Gdns
3 Hillside Cl
4 Thornfield Pl
D3
1 Strathmore Av
E3
1 Middleton Av
F5
1 Sandypath La
93
112
129
ROWLANDS GILL
NE39
LOCKHAUGH ROAD
A694
STATION ROAD
BURNOPFIELD ROAD
B6314
BUSTY BANK
Hollin Hill Farm
Rowlands Gill Infant School
Rowlands Gill Junior School
High Spen Industrial Estate
Thornley View
The Crescent
Townley Flds
Hollydene
Norman Rd
Smailes La
The Avenue
Taylor Av
The Grove
The Medical Centre
Stirling Lane
Derwent Av
Stirling Av
Gibside (NT)
Leapmill Burn
Sheep Hill
NEW ROAD
FRONT STREET
Westwood Cl
Oakfields
Raglan Pl
Hill Crest
Sheep Hl
A692
Sandypath La
The Fold
Leazes Hall
Valley Vw
The Copse
Doctors Surgery
Elm Gv
Primary School
Syke Rd
Birch Crescent
Briardene
Brackenridge
Front Street
B6310
Friarside
BURNOPFIELD
Lintz

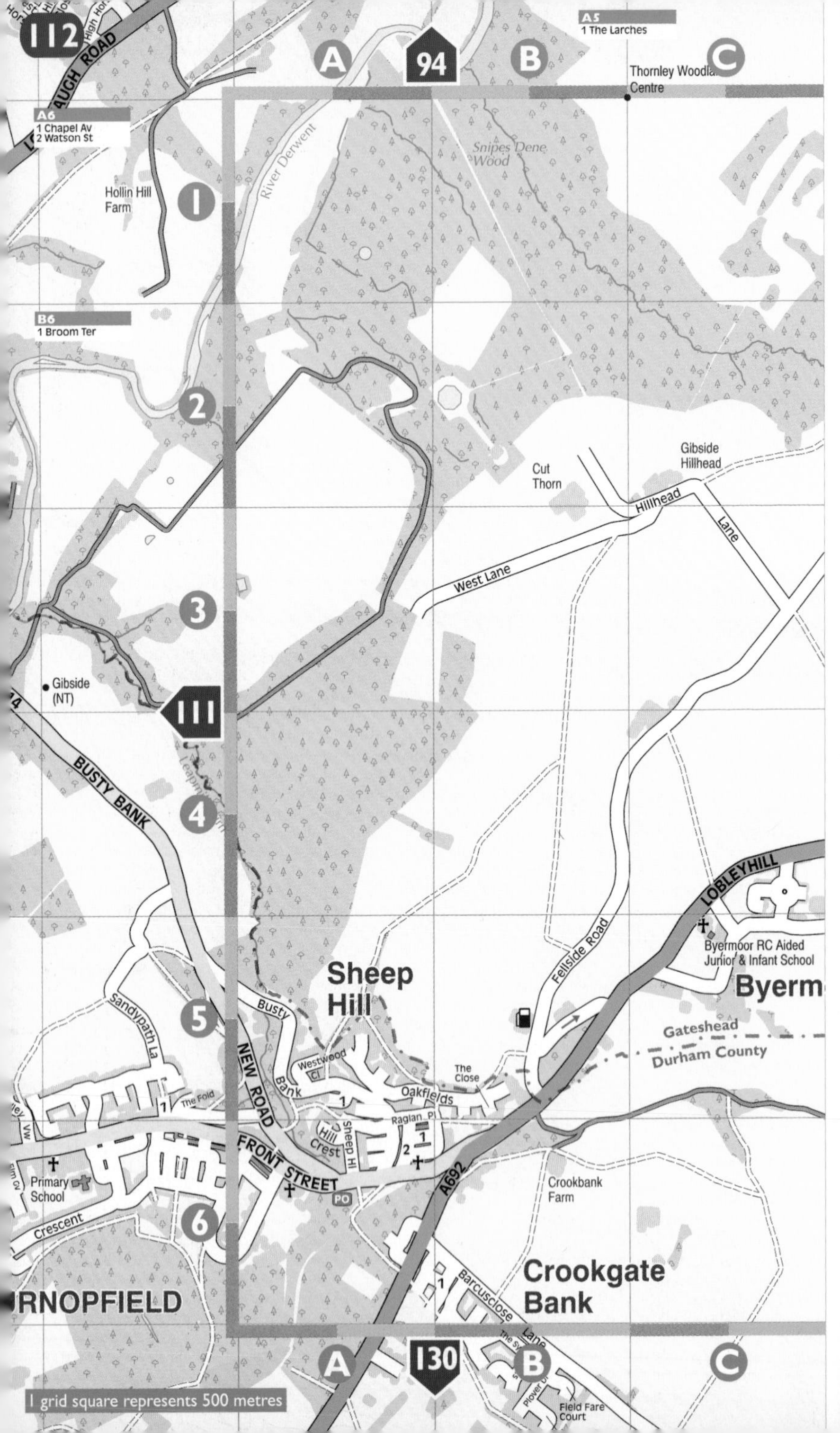
94
A
B
C
A5
1 The Larches
Thornley Woodla
Centre
A6
1 Chapel Av
2 Watson St
High Ho
ROAD
Hollin Hill
Farm
River Derwent
Snipes Dene
Wood
1
B6
1 Broom Ter
2
Cut
Thorn
Gibside
Hillhead
Hillhead
Lane
West Lane
3
Gibside
(NT)
111
BUSTY BANK
4
LOBLEYHILL
Fellside Road
Byermoor RC Aided
Junior & Infant School
Sheep
Hill
Byerm
Sandypath La
5
Busty
Bank
Westwood
Cl
NEW ROAD
The
Close
Oakfields
Gateshead
Durham County
The Fold
Raglan Pl
Hill
Crest
Sheep Hl
FRONT STREET
PO
A692
Primary
School
Crookbank
Farm
Crescent
6
Barcusclose
Lane
Crookgate
Bank
RNOPFIELD
A
130
B
C
Plover
Field Fare
Court
1 grid square represents 500 metres

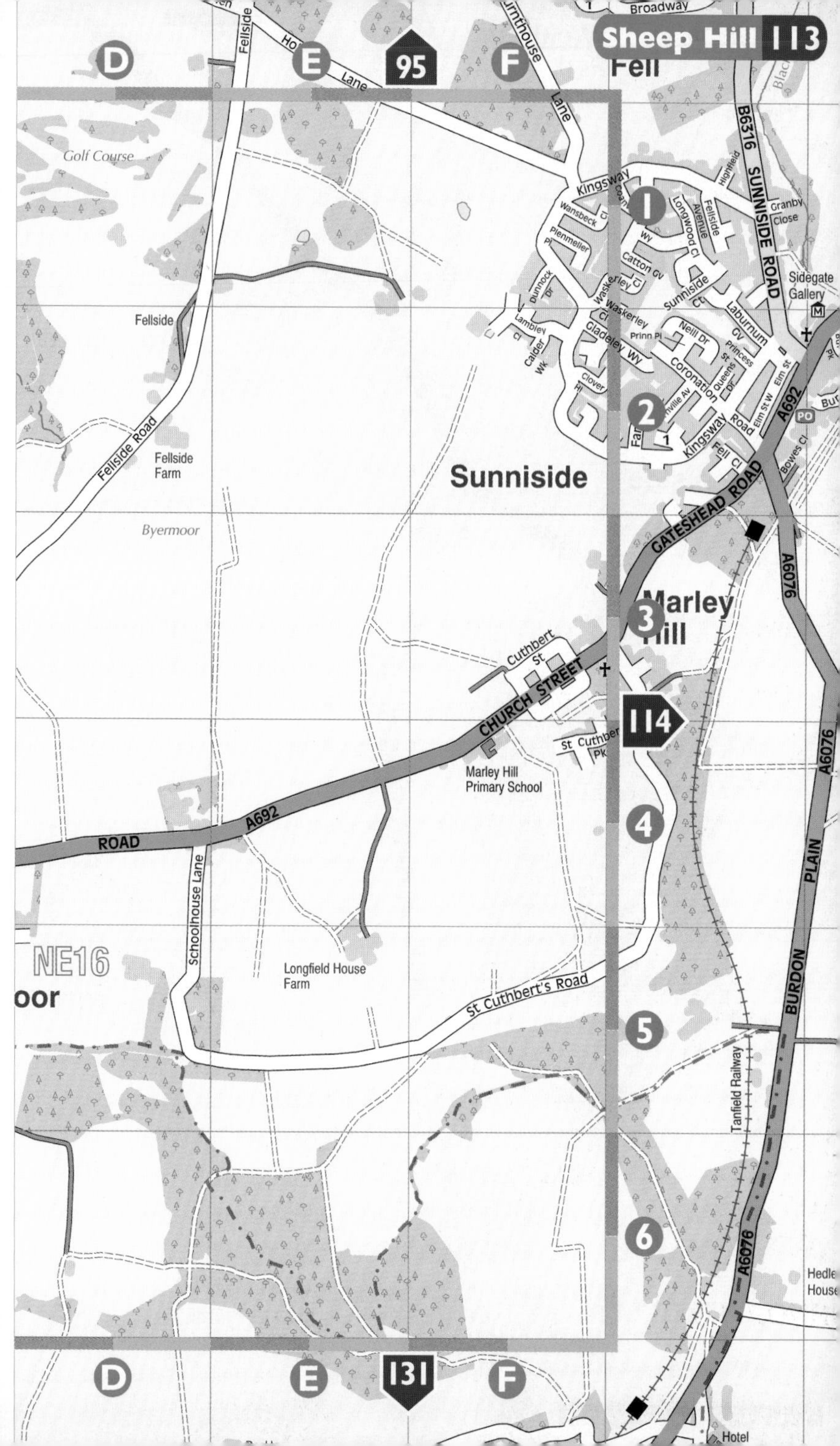
Broadway
Fellside
Lane
Burnthouse Lane
Fell
95
D
E
F
Golf Course
B6316 SUNNISIDE ROAD
Kingsway
Highfield
Wansbeck Cl
Plenmeller Pl
Longwood Cl
Avenue
Fellside
Granby Close
Catton Gv
Sunniside Ct
Laburnum Gv
Sidegate Gallery
Dunnock Dr
Waskerley Cl
Waskerley Cl
Lambley Cl
Gladeley Wy
Prinn Pl
Neill Dr
Calder Wk
Coronation
Princess St
Queens Dr
Elm St
Elm St W
Clover Hl
Kingsway
Road
A692
PO
Fell Cl
Bowes Cl
Fellside
Fellside Road
Fellside Farm
Sunniside
Byermoor
GATESHEAD ROAD
A6076
Marley Hill
Cuthbert St
CHURCH STREET
114
St Cuthbert Pk
Marley Hill Primary School
A692
ROAD
A6076
PLAIN
BURDON
Schoolhouse Lane
NE16
oor
Longfield House Farm
St Cuthbert's Road
Tanfield Railway
A6076
Hedley House
131
D
E
F
Hotel
1
2
3
4
5
6

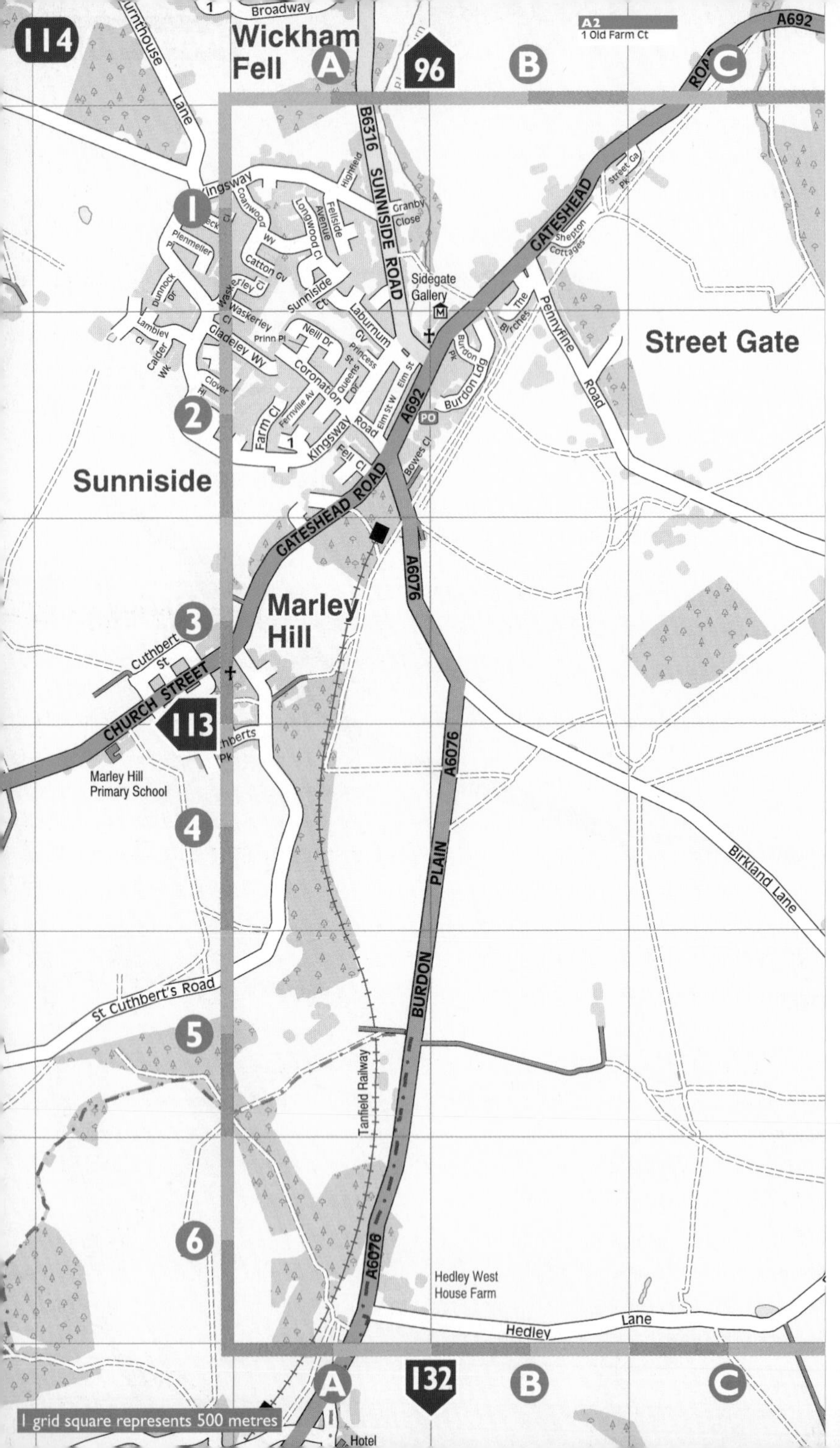

Wickham Fell
Broadway
A
96
B
C
A2
1 Old Farm Ct
A692
Kingsway
Lane
B6316 SUNNISIDE ROAD
Highfield
Coanwood Wy
Longwood Cl
Avenue
Fellside
Granby Close
Plenmeller Pl
Catton Gv
Dunnock Dr
Waskerley Cl
Waskerley
Sunniside Ct
Laburnum Gv
Sidegate Gallery
GATESHEAD
Street Ga Pk
Shepton Cottages
The Birches
Pennyfine Road
Street Gate
Lambley Cl
Calder Wk
Gladeley Wy
Prinn Pl
Neill Dr
Coronation
Princess St
Queens Dr
Elm St
Elm St W
Burdon Pk
Burdon Ldg
Clover Hl
Farm Cl
Fernville Av
Kingsway
Road
A692
PO
Fell Cl
Bowes Cl
Sunniside
GATESHEAD ROAD
A6076
Marley Hill
Cuthbert St
CHURCH STREET
113
Cuthberts Pk
Marley Hill Primary School
A6076
BURDON PLAIN
Birkland Lane
St Cuthbert's Road
Tanfield Railway
A6076
Hedley West House Farm
Hedley Lane
132
Hotel
1 grid square represents 500 metres

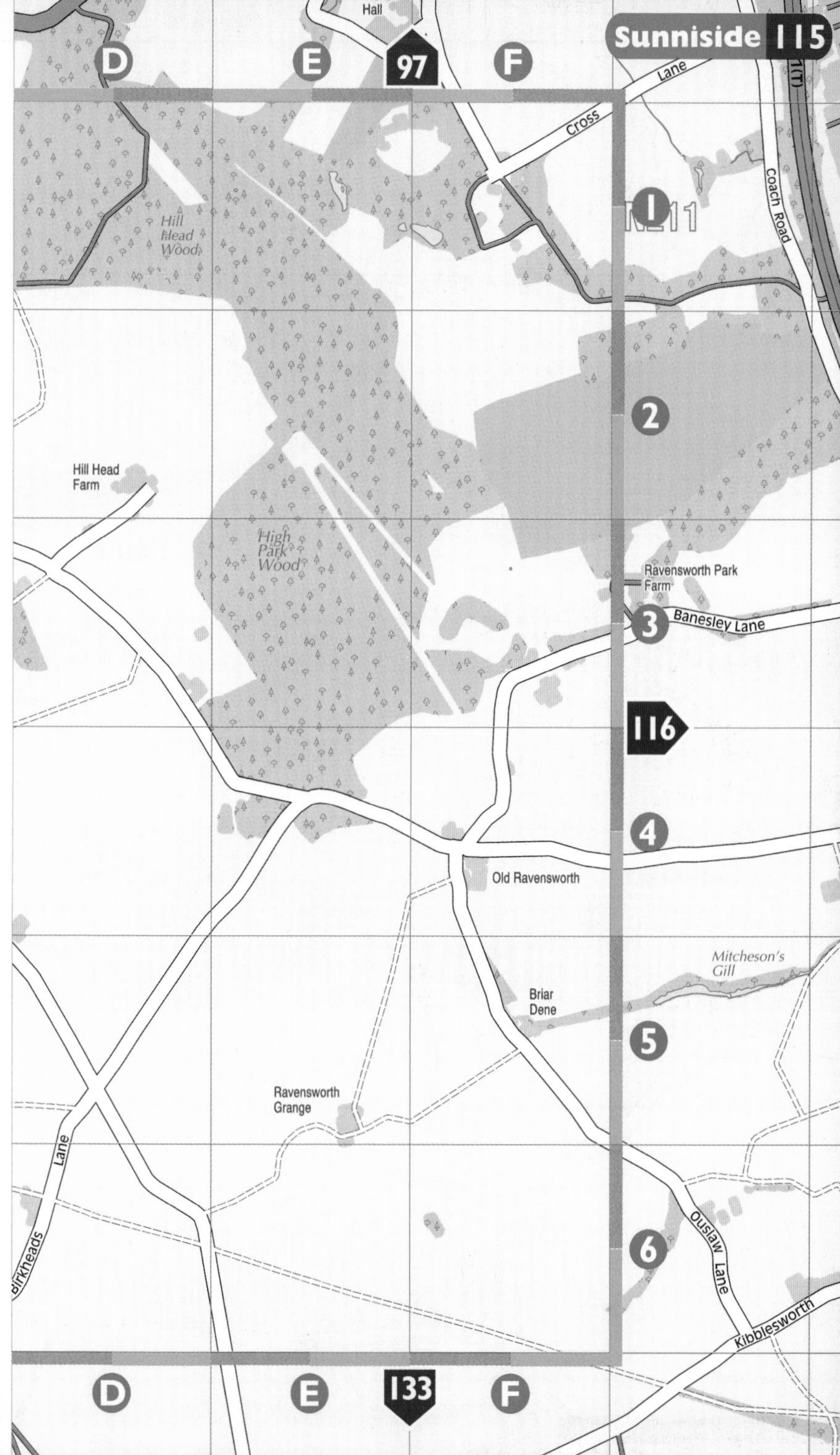
Hall
D
E
97
F
Lane
Cross
Coach Road
1
NE11
Hill
Head
Wood
2
Hill Head
Farm
High
Park
Wood
Ravensworth Park
Farm
3
Banesley Lane
116
4
Old Ravensworth
Mitcheson's
Gill
Briar
Dene
5
Ravensworth
Grange
Lane
Birkheads
6
Ouslaw Lane
Kibblesworth
D
E
133
F

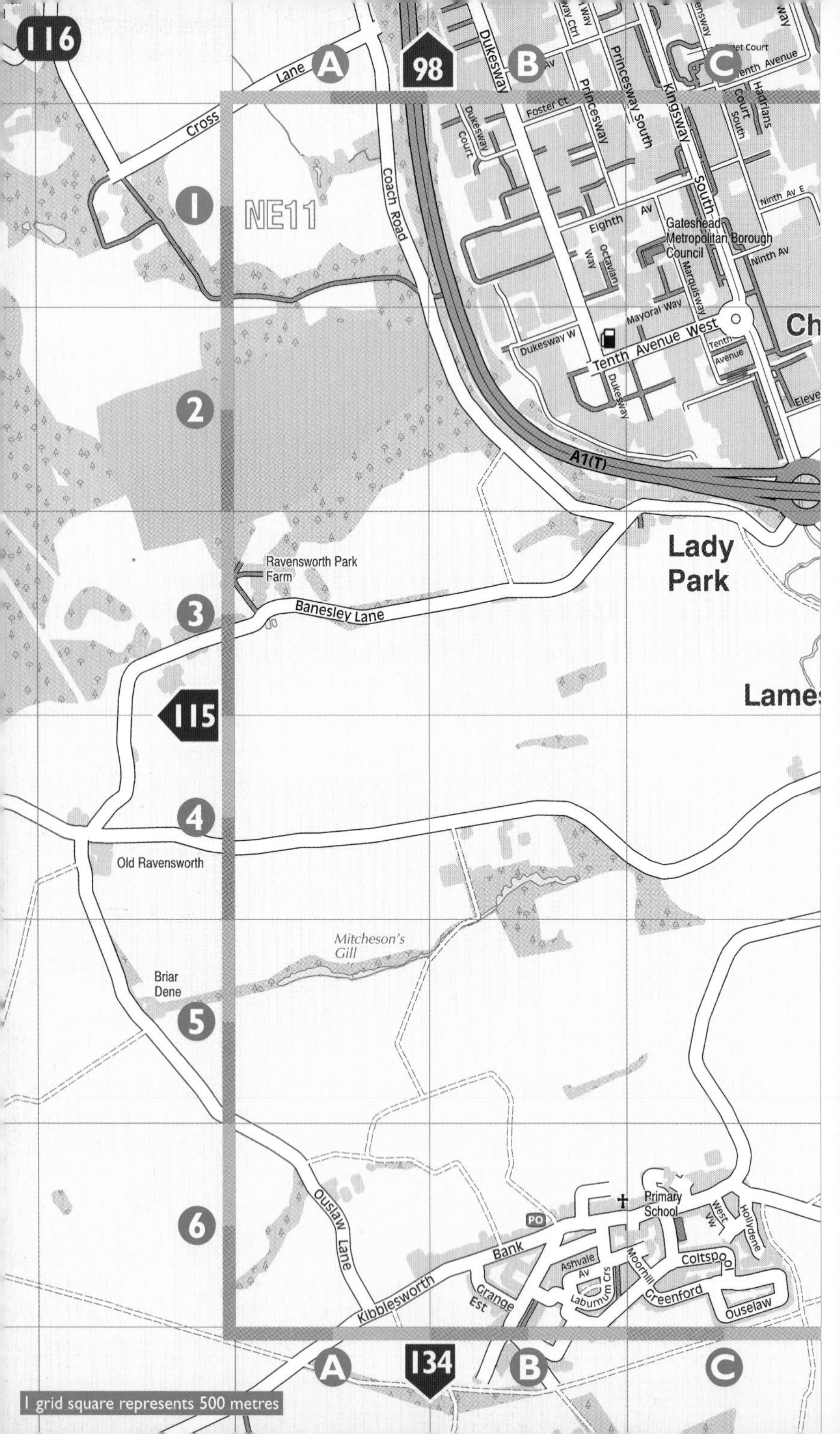
A
B
C
98
Lane
Cross
Dukesway
Princesway
Princesway South
Kingsway
Kingsway South
Foster Ct
Dukesway Court
Hadrians Court South
Ninth Av E
Ninth Av
Eighth Av
Octavian Way
Gateshead Metropolitan Borough Council
Marquisway
Mayoral Way
Dukesway W
Tenth Avenue West
Tenth Avenue
Ch
NE11
Coach Road
A1(T)
Lady Park
Ravensworth Park Farm
Banesley Lane
Lames
115
Old Ravensworth
Mitcheson's Gill
Briar Dene
Ouslaw Lane
Kibblesworth Bank
Grange Est
Ashvale Av
Laburnum Crs
Moorhill
Greenford
Coltspool
Ouselaw
Primary School
West Vw
Hollydene
PO
134
1
2
3
4
5
6
1 grid square represents 500 metres

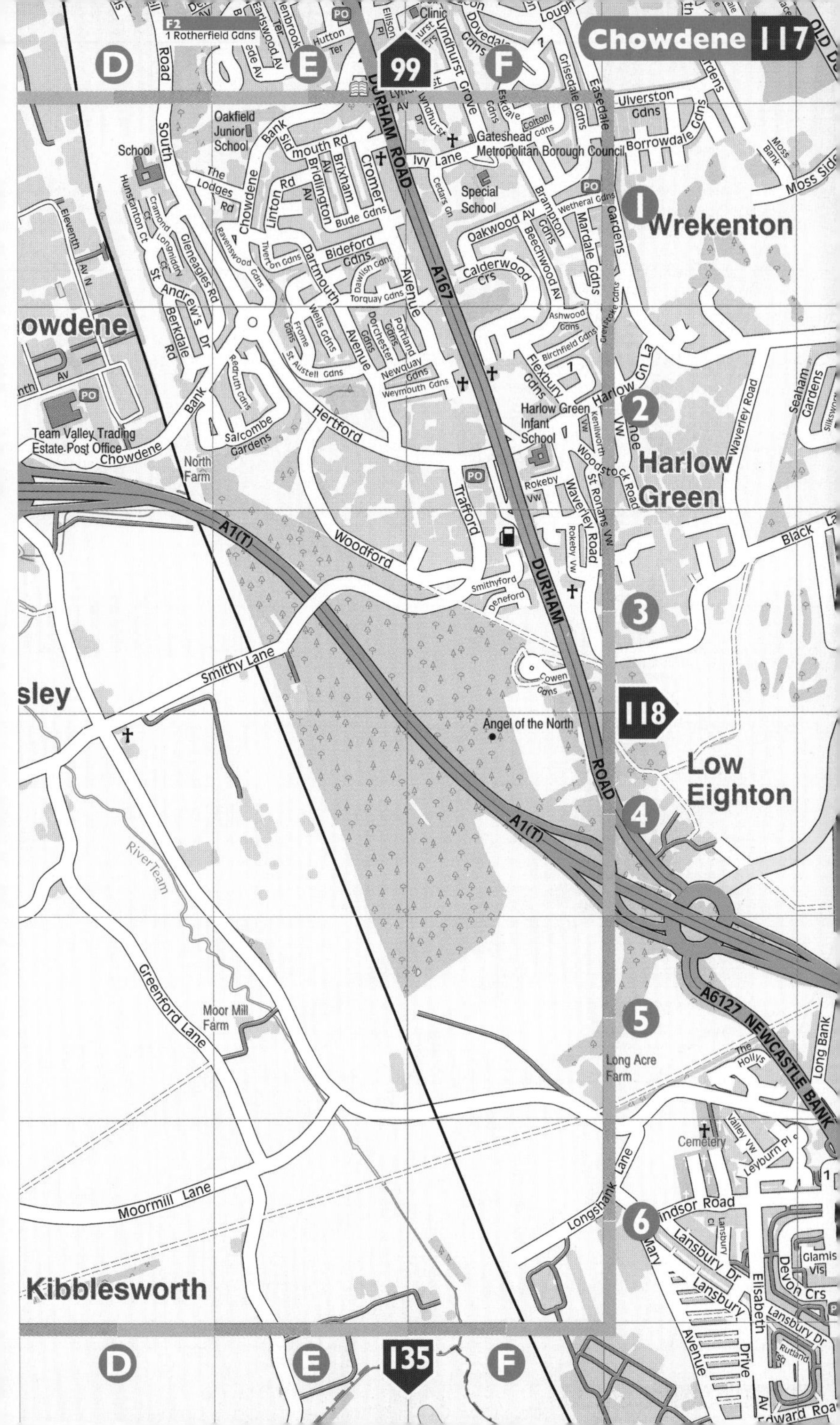
F2
1 Rotherfield Gdns
D
E
F
99
Wrekenton
Harlow Green
Low Eighton
Kibblesworth
118
135
Oakfield Junior School
School
Special School
Gateshead Metropolitan Borough Council
Harlow Green Infant School
Team Valley Trading Estate Post Office
North Farm
Angel of the North
Moor Mill Farm
Long Acre Farm
Cemetery
DURHAM ROAD
A167
A1(T)
A6127 NEWCASTLE BANK
Smithy Lane
Greenford Lane
Moormill Lane
Longshank Lane
Chowdene Bank
Woodford
Hertford
Trafford
Ivy Lane
Waverley Road
Black La
River Team
Lansbury Dr
Windsor Road
Elisabeth Drive
Long Bank
Clinic
PO
1
2
3
4
5
6

118
100
117
136
A
B
C
1
2
3
4
5
6
Beacon Lough
B2
1 Springwell Av
St Edmunds RC Comprehensive School
B6
1 Newcastle Rd
C1
1 Brandon Gdns
2 Marsden Gv
C2
1 Cypress Rd
Gateshead Metropolitan Borough Council
Wrekenton
Harlow Green
Low Eighton
BIRTLEY
NE9
DURHAM ROAD
OLD DURHAM ROAD
A167
B1296
LONG BANK
A1(T)
A6127 NEWCASTLE BANK
Ulverston Gdns
Borrowdale Gdns
Moss Side
Moss Bank
Torver Place
Newby
Easedale
Dovedale Gdns
Grisedale Gdns
Eskdale
Colton Gdns
Lyndhurst Av
Ivy Lane
Cedars Gn
Cromer Gdns
Special School
Oakwood Av
Beechwood Av
Calderwood Crs
Mardale Gdns
Gardens
Ashwood Gdns
Birchfield Gdns
Greystoke Gdns
Flexbury Gdns
Harlow Gn La
Ivanhoe Vw
Kenilworth
Woodstock Road
St Ronans Vw
Waverley Road
Rokeby Vw
Harlow Green Infant School
Trafford
Smithyford
Deneford
Newquay Gdns
Weymouth Gdns
Dorchester Gdns
Cowen
Angel of the North
Hamsterley Crs
Beamish Gdns
Plawsworth Gdns
Easington Av
Shincliffe Gdns
Burnmoor Gdns
Rugby Gdns
Boldon Gdns
Infant & Junior School
Wrekenton Health Centre
Doctors Surgery
Infant School
Wingate Gdns
Ryhope Gdns
Lanchester
Whitburn Gdns
SPRINGWELL R
Seaburn Gdns
Seaham Gardens
Silksworth Gdns
Stanley Gdns
Wynyard Gdns
Wrekenton Row
Tanfield Rd
Hazelwood Cl
Tanfield Place
Galloping Green Road
Dyke
Ravensworth Av
Rockcliffe Way
Jubilee Av
Springfield Av
Black Lane
Larch Cl
Sandy Lane
Thomas St
Dunkirk Farm
Long Acre Farm
The Hollys
Long Bank
Northdene
Dene Ct
Birtley East Primary School
Malone Gdns
Cemetery
Valley Vw
Leyburn Pl
Windsor Road
Lansbury Cl
Lansbury Dr
Lansbury
Mary Av
Elisabeth Drive
Glamis Vls
Devon Crs
Selkirk Crs
Garside Avenue
Wilson Av
Edward Road
Longshank Lane
DURHAM RO
PO
1 grid square represents 500 metres

F6
1 Highheath
School
D
E
101
F
LEAM
Wallace Gdns
Avenue
ROAD
I
B1288
Somerford
Fairhaven
Highbury Cl
Highbury Av
Eighton Banks
Oakwood Close
Uplands Way
Heugh
Windsor Road
Highworth Dr
Aldsworth Cl
Charlbury Cl
Highworth Dr
Road
Bowes Rly
Fell Road
PO
Springwell Village Primary School
Peareth
Hall
Milton Pl
Shelley Av
Stoney Lane
Springwell
Beech Grove
Stafford Villas
Sycamore Gv
Mount House
Broom Ct
Mount Road
Mount Lane
B1288
A194(M)
Sunderland
Gateshead
B1288
A194(M)
WASHINGTON HWY
A1231
Junction 65
A1(T)
Road
Donkin
Cragside
Lambert Rd
University of Sunderland
Armstrong Rd
Whitworth Rd
Blackfell Road
Doddfell Cl
Baugh Cl
Herdinghill
1
Swarth Cl
Craggyknowe
Westernmoor
Penyghent Wy
Thirlmoor
Mickle Cl
Road
Shunner Cl
Emblehope
Knoulberry
Blackfell
Pipershaw
Blackfell
Knoulberry
Chevlot Cl
Stridingedge
Blackfell Primary School
PO
Road
Rushyrig
Bink Moss
Phoenix Rd
Brockwell Rd
Hutton Cl
SUNDER
137
D
E
F
Crowther
Road
Hotel
2
Stone Cellar Road
6
Gleneagles Dr
Nairn Cl
The Farthings
Peareth Hall Rd
Doncrest Rd
Farm Cl
High Cft
Donridge
Special School
3
Donwell
Donvale Rd
Donvale Road
Wellburn Rd
120
St Andrews Av
Bristol Av
Oxford Av
Cambridge Av
Well Bank Road
Raydale Av
Garsdale Av
4
St Andrews Av
Durham Av
Wharfedale Av
Blue House Lane
Rosse Cl
Saddleback
Parsons Rd
HAVANNAH ROAD
Albany
5
A1290
Moorside
Infants School
Brandy La
Mardale
Ravenstone
PO
Moorway
Lingmell
Grizedale
Rosegill
Thorngill
6
Moorway
Dalegarth
A182
SUNDERLAND HWY
Bamburgh Cl

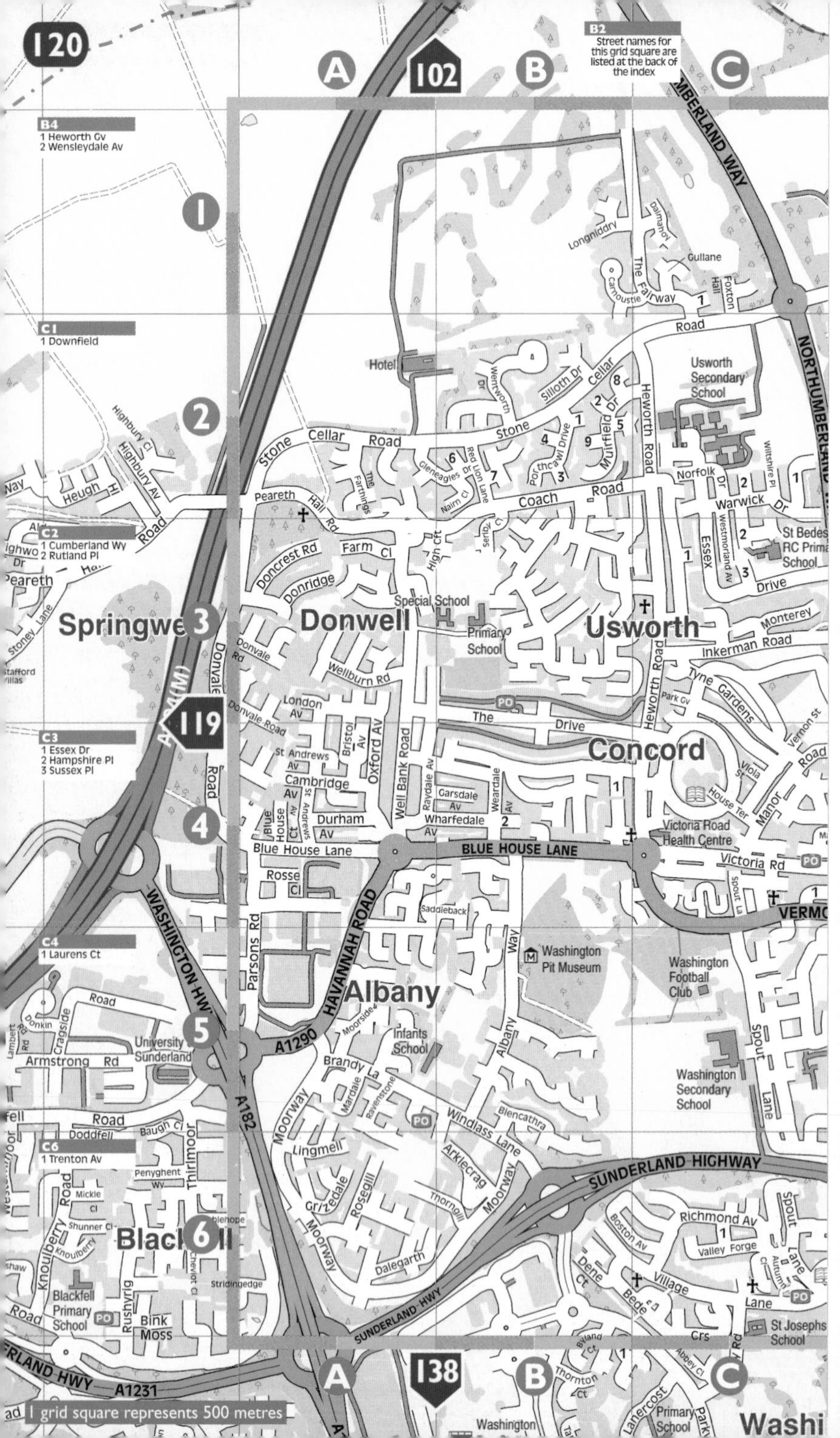
A
102
B
C
B2
Street names for this grid square are listed at the back of the index
B4
1 Heworth Gv
2 Wensleydale Av
C1
1 Downfield
C2
1 Cumberland Wy
2 Rutland Pl
C3
1 Essex Dr
2 Hampshire Pl
3 Sussex Pl
C4
1 Laurens Ct
C6
1 Trenton Av
1
2
3
4
5
6
119
138
Springwell
Donwell
Usworth
Concord
Albany
Blackfell
Stone Cellar Road
Coach Road
Blue House Lane
BLUE HOUSE LANE
HAVANNAH ROAD
A1290
A182
WASHINGTON HWY
SUNDERLAND HIGHWAY
SUNDERLAND HWY
NORTHUMBERLAND WAY
A1231
Hotel
Special School
Primary School
Usworth Secondary School
St Bedes RC Primary School
Washington Pit Museum
Washington Football Club
Washington Secondary School
Infants School
Victoria Road Health Centre
University of Sunderland
Blackfell Primary School
St Josephs School
Primary School
Washington
1 grid square represents 500 metres

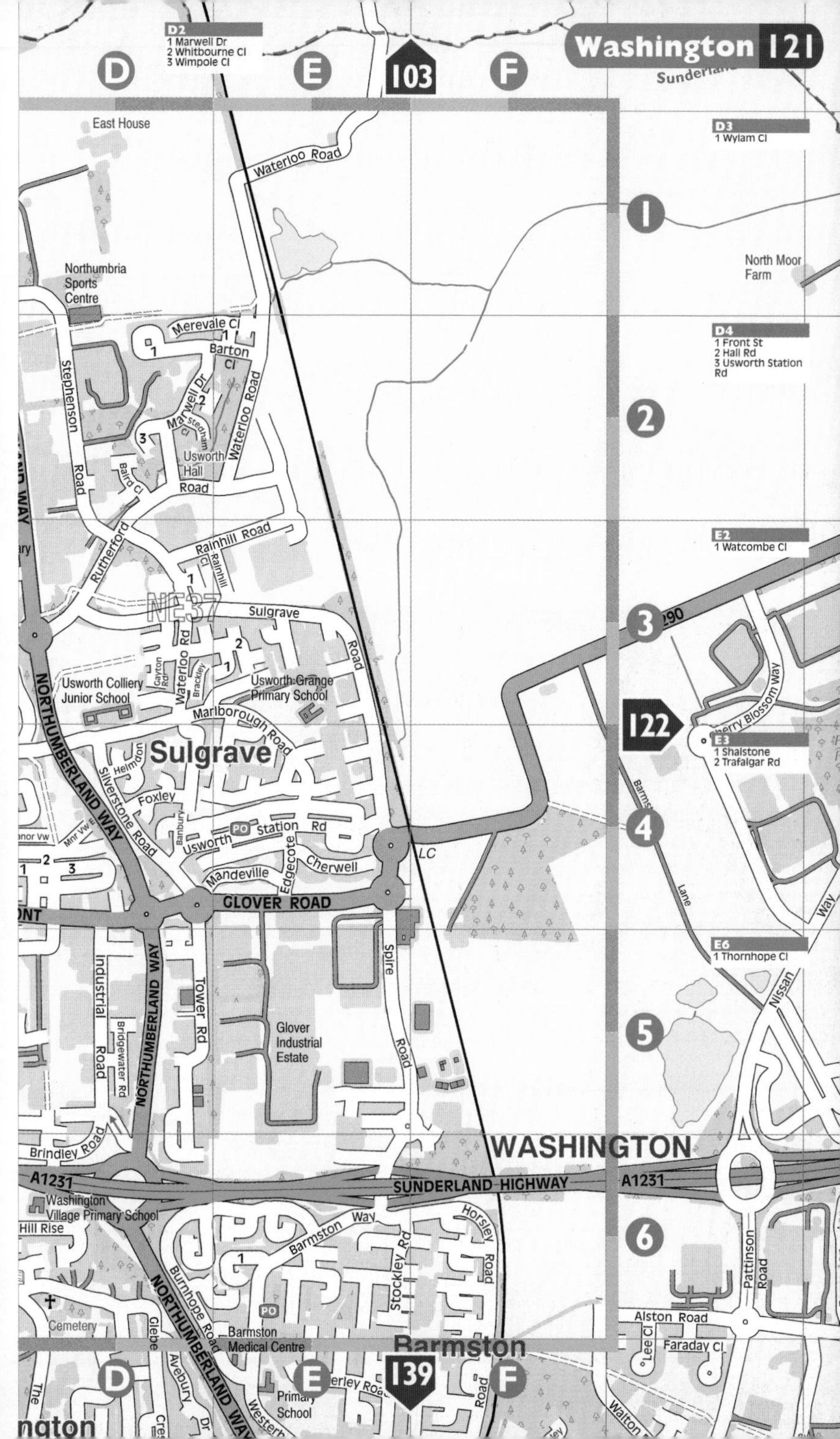
D2
1 Marwell Dr
2 Whitbourne Cl
3 Wimpole Cl
D
E
F
103
Sunderland
D3
1 Wylam Cl
East House
Waterloo Road
North Moor Farm
Northumbria Sports Centre
Merevale Cl
Barton Cl
D4
1 Front St
2 Hall Rd
3 Usworth Station Rd
Stephenson Road
Marwell Dr
Usworth Hall
Waterloo Road
Baird Cl
Road
Rainhill Road
Rutherford
Rainhill
E2
1 Watcombe Cl
NE37
Sulgrave Road
A1290
Usworth Colliery Junior School
Gayton Rd
Waterloo Rd
Brackley
Usworth Grange Primary School
Marlborough Road
122
Cherry Blossom Way
E3
1 Shalstone
2 Trafalgar Rd
Sulgrave
Helmdon
Silverstone Road
Foxley
Banbury
Usworth Station Rd
Mnr Vw E
Manor Vw
Edgecote
Cherwell
Mandeville
LC
NORTHUMBERLAND WAY
GLOVER ROAD
Barmston Lane
Way
E6
1 Thornhope Cl
Nissan
Industrial Road
Bridgewater Rd
NORTHUMBERLAND WAY
Tower Rd
Glover Industrial Estate
Spire Road
WASHINGTON
Brindley Road
A1231
SUNDERLAND HIGHWAY
A1231
Washington Village Primary School
Hill Rise
Horsley Road
Barmston Way
Burnhope Road
NORTHUMBERLAND WAY
Stockley Rd
Pattinson Road
Cemetery
Barmston Medical Centre
Glebe
Alston Road
Lee Cl
Faraday Cl
Barmston
139
Avebury Dr
The
Primary School
Road
Walton
Cres

122
South Tyneside
Sunderland
A
104
B
Downhill
Lane
C
Hylton Grove Farm
A1290
1
North Moor Farm
North East Aircraft Museum
2
West Moor Farm
3
A1290
Cherry Blossom Way
121
Peepy Plantation
Nissan Way
Barmston Lane
4
LC
Nissan Way
Spire Road
5
Barmston Lane
SUNDERLAND HIGHWAY
WASHINGTON
SUNDERLAND HIGHWAY
A1231
Barmston La
Horsley Road
Low Barmston Farm
6
Stockley Rd
Pattinson Road
Barmston Lane
Alston Road
Barmston
Lee Cl
Faraday Cl
A
140
B
C
Wildfowl and
1 grid square represents 500 metres

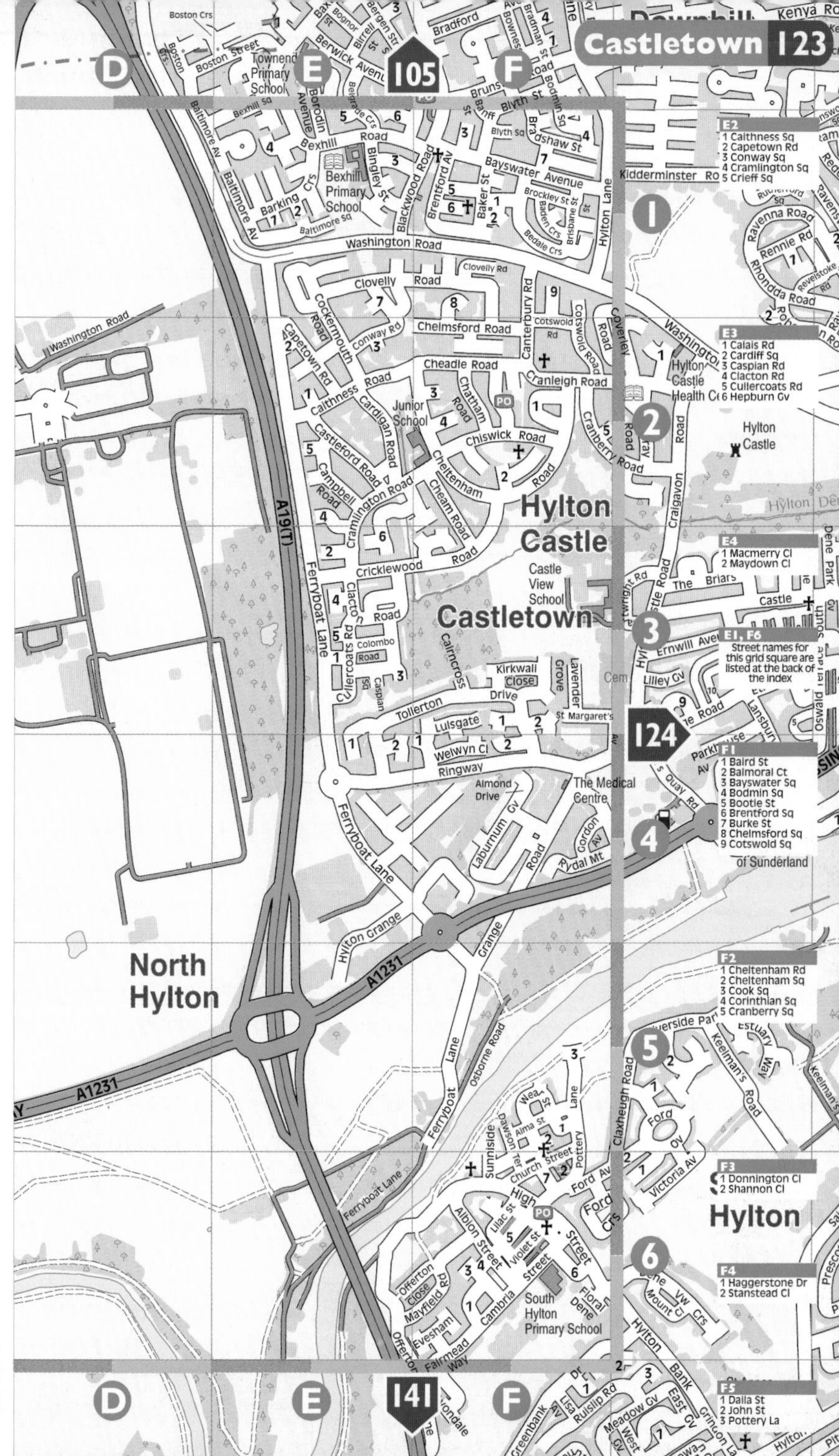
105
D
E
F
Townend Primary School
Bexhill Primary School
Washington Road
Clovelly Road
Chelmsford Road
Cheadle Road
Cranleigh Road
Caithness Road
Junior School
Chiswick Road
Cheltenham
Cramlington Road
Cricklewood Road
Hylton Castle
Castle View School
Castletown
Ferryboat Lane
Tollerton Drive
Ringway
The Medical Centre
Hylton Castle Health Ce
Hylton Castle
Hylton Dene
Kidderminster Ro
Bayswater Avenue
Hylton Lane
A19(T)
A1231
Hylton Grange
North Hylton
Osborne Road
Claxheugh Road
Church Street
High Street
South Hylton Primary School
Hylton
124
141
1
2
3
4
5
6
E2
1 Caithness Sq
2 Capetown Rd
3 Conway Sq
4 Cramlington Sq
5 Crieff Sq
E3
1 Calais Rd
2 Cardiff Sq
3 Caspian Rd
4 Clacton Rd
5 Cullercoats Rd
6 Hepburn Gv
E4
1 Macmerry Cl
2 Maydown Cl
E1, F6
Street names for this grid square are listed at the back of the index
F1
1 Baird St
2 Balmoral Ct
3 Bayswater Sq
4 Bodmin Sq
5 Bootle St
6 Brentford Sq
7 Burke St
8 Chelmsford Sq
9 Cotswold Sq
F2
1 Cheltenham Rd
2 Cheltenham Sq
3 Cook Sq
4 Corinthian Sq
5 Cranberry Sq
F3
1 Donnington Cl
2 Shannon Cl
F4
1 Haggerstone Dr
2 Stanstead Cl
F5
1 Dalla St
2 John St
3 Pottery La

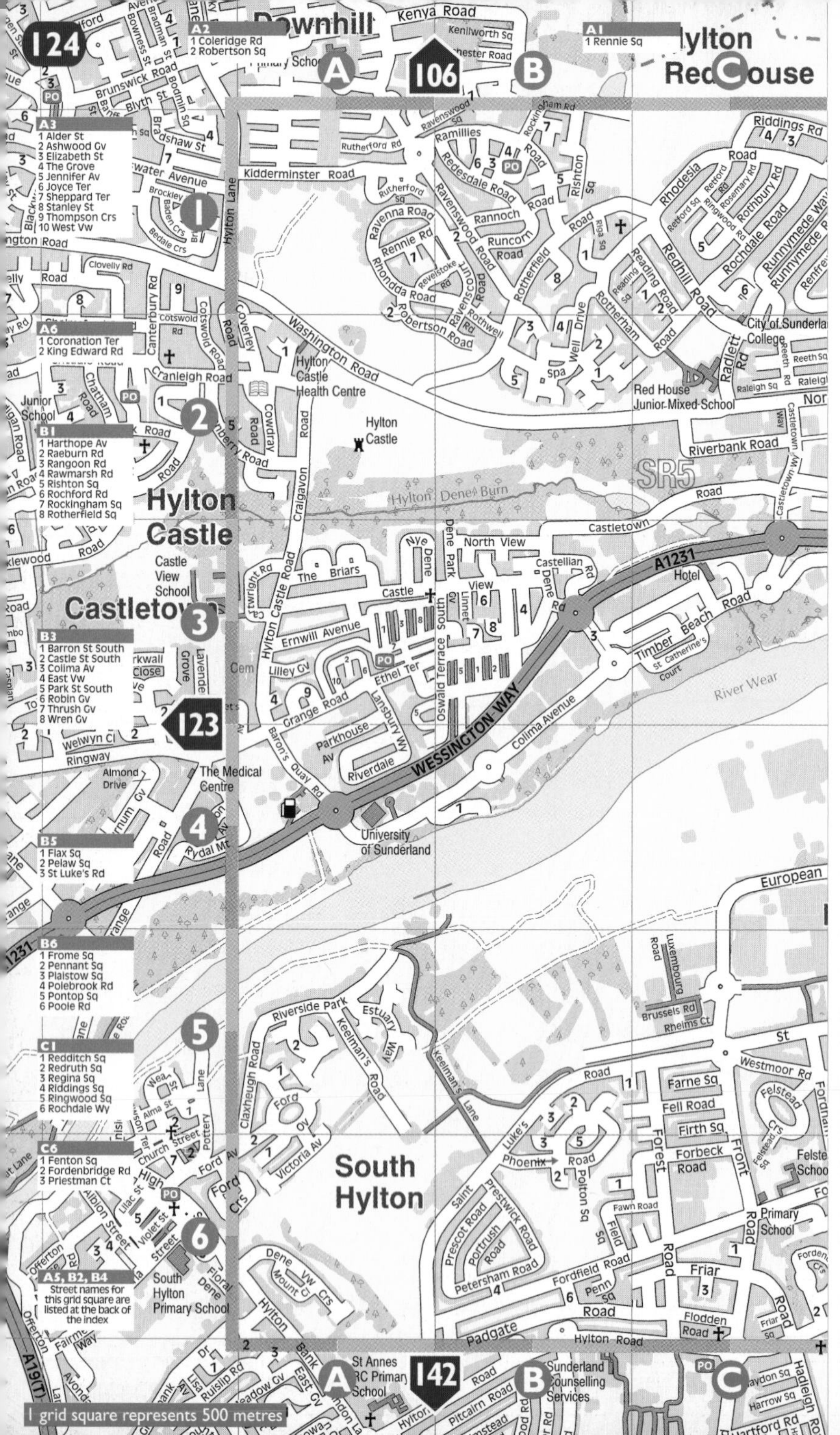

124
A2
1 Coleridge Rd
2 Robertson Sq
Downhill
Kenya Road
Kenilworth Sq
106
A
B
C
A1
1 Rennie Sq
Hylton
Red House
A3
1 Alder St
2 Ashwood Gv
3 Elizabeth St
4 The Grove
5 Jennifer Av
6 Joyce Ter
7 Sheppard Ter
8 Stanley St
9 Thompson Crs
10 West Vw
Brunswick Road
Blyth St
Bradshaw St
Avenue
Hylton Lane
Kidderminster Road
Rutherford Rd
Ramillies
Redesdale Road
Rockingham Road
Rishton Sq
Riddings Rd
Rhodesia Road
Rannoch
Runcorn Road
Ravenna Road
Rennie Rd
Rhondda Road
Robertson Road
Ravenswood Road
Ravenscourt
Rothwell Rd
Rotherfield Road
Well Drive
Spa
Rotherham Road
Reading Road
Redhill Road
Rochdale Road
Rothbury Rd
Runnymede Way
Runnymede Road
Radlett Rd
City of Sunderland College
Reeth Rd
Reeth Sq
Raleigh Sq
Raleigh
Red House Junior Mixed School
Riverbank Road
SR5
Castletown Way
Clovelly Rd
Canterbury Rd
Cotswold Rd
Cranleigh Road
A6
1 Coronation Ter
2 King Edward Rd
Chatham Road
Junior School
B1
1 Harthope Av
2 Raeburn Rd
3 Rangoon Rd
4 Rawmarsh Rd
5 Rishton Sq
6 Rochford Rd
7 Rockingham Sq
8 Rotherfield Sq
Coverley Road
Cowdray Road
Washington Road
Hylton Castle Health Centre
Hylton Castle
Hylton Dene Burn
Craigavon Road
Hylton Castle
Castle View School
Castletown
B3
1 Barron St South
2 Castle St South
3 Colima Av
4 East Vw
5 Park St South
6 Robin Gv
7 Thrush Gv
8 Wren Gv
Lavender Grove
Cem
123
Hylton Castle Road
The Briars
Castle View
Ernwill Avenue
Lilley Gv
Grange Road
Ethel Ter
Lansbury Way
Parkhouse Av
Riverdale
Dene Park
Nye Dene
North View
Castellian Rd
Dene Rd
Castletown Road
A1231
Hotel
Timber Beach Road
St Catherine's Court
River Wear
Oswald Terrace South
WESSINGTON WAY
Colima Avenue
Baron's Quay Rd
Welwyn Cl
Ringway
Almond Drive
The Medical Centre
Rydal Mt
University of Sunderland
B5
1 Flax Sq
2 Pelaw Sq
3 St Luke's Rd
B6
1 Frome Sq
2 Pennant Sq
3 Plaistow Sq
4 Polebrook Rd
5 Pontop Sq
6 Poole Rd
European
Luxembourg Road
Brussels Rd
Rheims Ct
St
Westmoor Rd
Riverside Park
Estuary Way
Keelman's Road
Keelman's Lane
C1
1 Redditch Sq
2 Redruth Sq
3 Regina Sq
4 Riddings Sq
5 Ringwood Sq
6 Rochdale Wy
Claxheugh Road
Ford Ov
Victoria Av
Ford Av
Ford Crs
Pottery Lane
Church Street
C6
1 Fenton Sq
2 Fordenbridge Rd
3 Priestman Ct
South Hylton
Luke's Road
Phoenix Road
Polton Sq
Saint Luke's
Farne Sq
Fell Road
Firth Sq
Forbeck Road
Forest Road
Front Road
Felstead Crs
Felstead School
Primary School
Fawn Road
Field Sq
Prescot Road
Prestwick Road
Portrush Road
Petersham Road
Fordfield Road
Penn Sq
Friar Sq
Friar Road
Flodden Road
Padgate Road
Hylton Road
Albion Street
Lilac St
Violet St
High Street
Offerton Rd
Offerton
A5, B2, B4
Street names for this grid square are listed at the back of the index
South Hylton Primary School
Dene Vw Crs
Mount Ct
Hylton Bank
East Gv
St Annes RC Primary School
142
Sunderland Counselling Services
Pitcairn Road
Harrow Sq
Hadleigh Rd
A19(T)
Ruislip Rd
1 grid square represents 500 metres

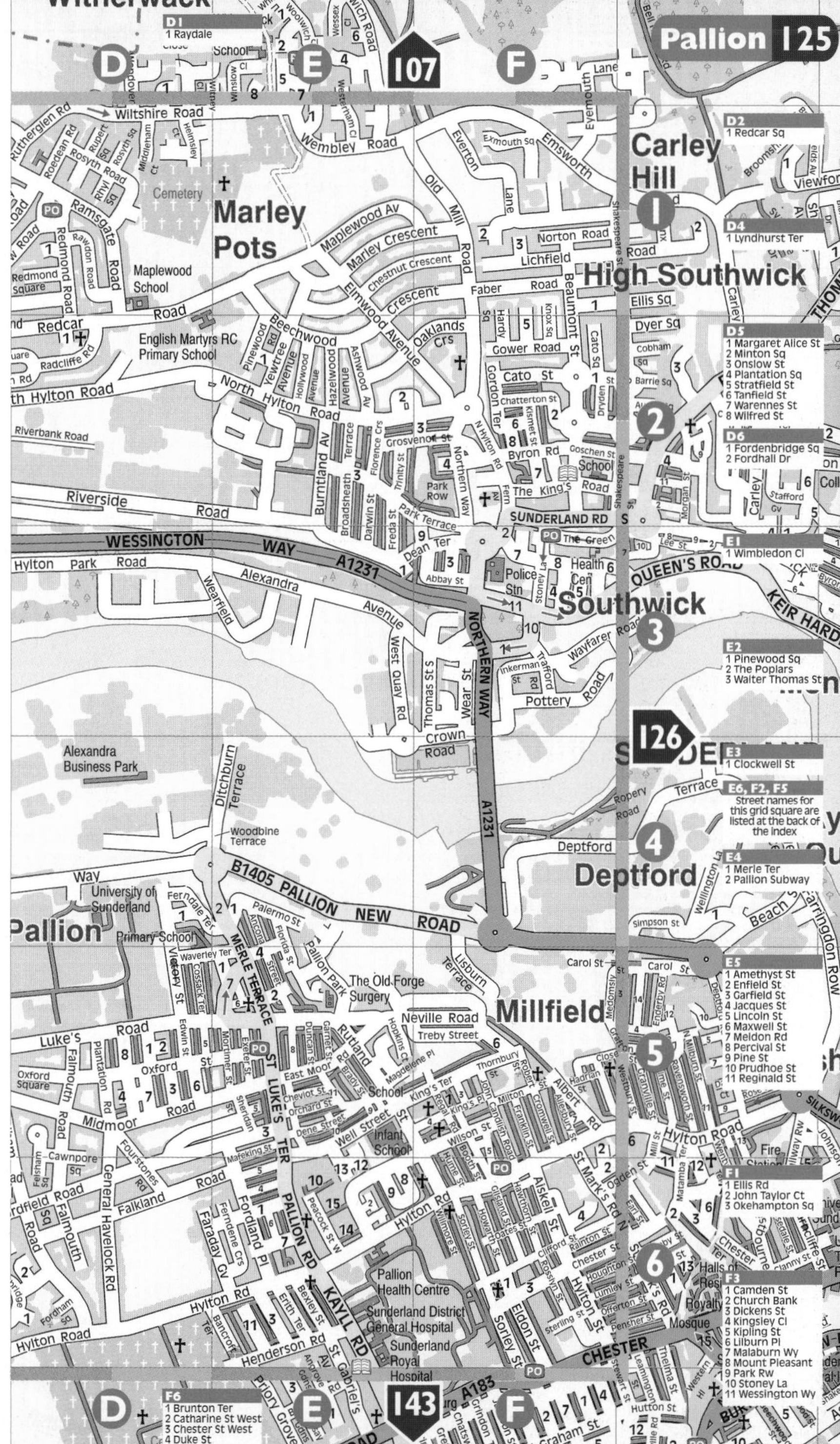
107
126
143
Witherwack
Carley Hill
Marley Pots
High Southwick
Southwick
Deptford
Pallion
Millfield
Cemetery
Maplewood School
English Martyrs RC Primary School
Alexandra Business Park
University of Sunderland
Primary School
The Old Forge Surgery
Police Stn
Health Cen
Infant School
Pallion Health Centre
Sunderland District General Hospital
Sunderland Royal Hospital
WESSINGTON WAY A1231
NORTHERN WAY
B1405 PALLION NEW ROAD
QUEEN'S ROAD
SUNDERLAND RD
Wembley Road
Wiltshire Road
North Hylton Road
Riverside Road
Hylton Park Road
Alexandra Avenue
Hylton Road
Chester Road
Kayll Rd
Pallion Rd
St Luke's Ter
Merle Terrace
Ditchburn Terrace
Woodbine Terrace
D1
1 Raydale
D2
1 Redcar Sq
D4
1 Lyndhurst Ter
D5
1 Margaret Alice St
2 Minton Sq
3 Onslow St
4 Plantation Sq
5 Stratfield St
6 Tanfield St
7 Warennes St
8 Wilfred St
D6
1 Fordenbridge Sq
2 Fordhall Dr
E1
1 Wimbledon Cl
E2
1 Pinewood Sq
2 The Poplars
3 Walter Thomas St
E3
1 Clockwell St
E6, F2, F5
Street names for this grid square are listed at the back of the index
E4
1 Merle Ter
2 Pallion Subway
E5
1 Amethyst St
2 Enfield St
3 Garfield St
4 Jacques St
5 Lincoln St
6 Maxwell St
7 Meldon Rd
8 Percival St
9 Pine St
10 Prudhoe St
11 Reginald St
F1
1 Ellis Rd
2 John Taylor Ct
3 Okehampton Sq
F3
1 Camden St
2 Church Bank
3 Dickens St
4 Kingsley Cl
5 Kipling St
6 Lilburn Pl
7 Malaburn Wy
8 Mount Pleasant
9 Park Rw
10 Stoney La
11 Wessington Wy
F6
1 Brunton Ter
2 Catharine St West
3 Chester St West
4 Duke St

126
A2, A4, A6, C1
Street names for this grid square are listed at the back of the index
108
A1
1 Burnhope Dr
2 Clarendon Sq
A3
1 Attwood Gv
2 Close St
3 Lee St
4 Maypole Cl
5 Pemberton Cl
6 Queen's Rd
7 South Ter
8 Suddick St
9 Usher St
10 Vedra St
A5
1 Alliance Pl
2 Alliance St
3 Cirencester St
4 Dryborough St
5 Hyacinth Ct
6 Hylton Rd
7 Jasmine Ct
8 Lansdowne St
9 Marguerite Ct
10 Marigold Ct
11 Millburn St
12 North Ravensworth St
13 Queensberry St
14 St Cuthbert's Ter
B1
1 Bywell Av
2 Elizabeth St
3 Honister Dr
4 Joannah St
B2
1 Boundary St
2 Edith St
3 Newbridge Av
4 Northwood Ct
B3
1 Chilton St
2 Crozier St
3 Empress St
4 Finsbury St
5 Hood Cl
6 North St
7 Ross St
B4
1 Easington St N
2 Stadium Wy
B5
1 Dun Cow St
2 Dunning St
3 Eden St West
4 Galley's Gill Rd
5 Garden Pl
6 Middle St
7 Paley St
8 Queen St
B6
1 Clanny St
2 Crowtree Rd
3 Crowtree Ter
4 Elwin Ter
5 Green Ter
6 Hope St
7 Mary St
8 St Michaels Wy
9 Silksworth Rw
10 Stockton Rd
11 Tunstall Rd
12 Tunstall Ter W
C2
1 Burscough Crs
2 Edgeworth Crs
3 Fairlands East
4 Leeds St
5 Moreland St
6 Wearmouth Av
C3, C4, C5, C6
Street names for this grid square are listed at the back of the index
Carley Hill
High Southwick
Southwick
Monkwearmouth
SUNDERLAND
Ayres Quay
Deptford
Millfield
Bishopwearmouth
125
144
Sunderland Football Club
Monkwearmouth Hospital
Sunderland Retail Park
Sunderland Bowling Cen
Wearmouth Bridge
University Halls of Residence
Police Headquarters and Magistrates Court
Empire Theatre
Sunderland Stn
Sunderland Mus & Art Gallery
War Memorial
University of Sunderland
University (Library)
Sunderland Royal Inf
Mowbray Park
St Anthonys RC School
THOMPSON ROAD
NEWCASTLE ROAD
QUEEN'S ROAD
KEIR HARDIE WAY
TRIMDON ST
CHESTER ROAD
NEW DURHAM RD
STOCKTON RD
NORTH BR ST
DAME DOROTHY ST
HOLMESIDE
BOROUGH RD
TOWARD ROAD
PARK ROAD
STATION ROAD
CHARLTON RD
SUNDERLAND RD
1 grid square represents 500 metres

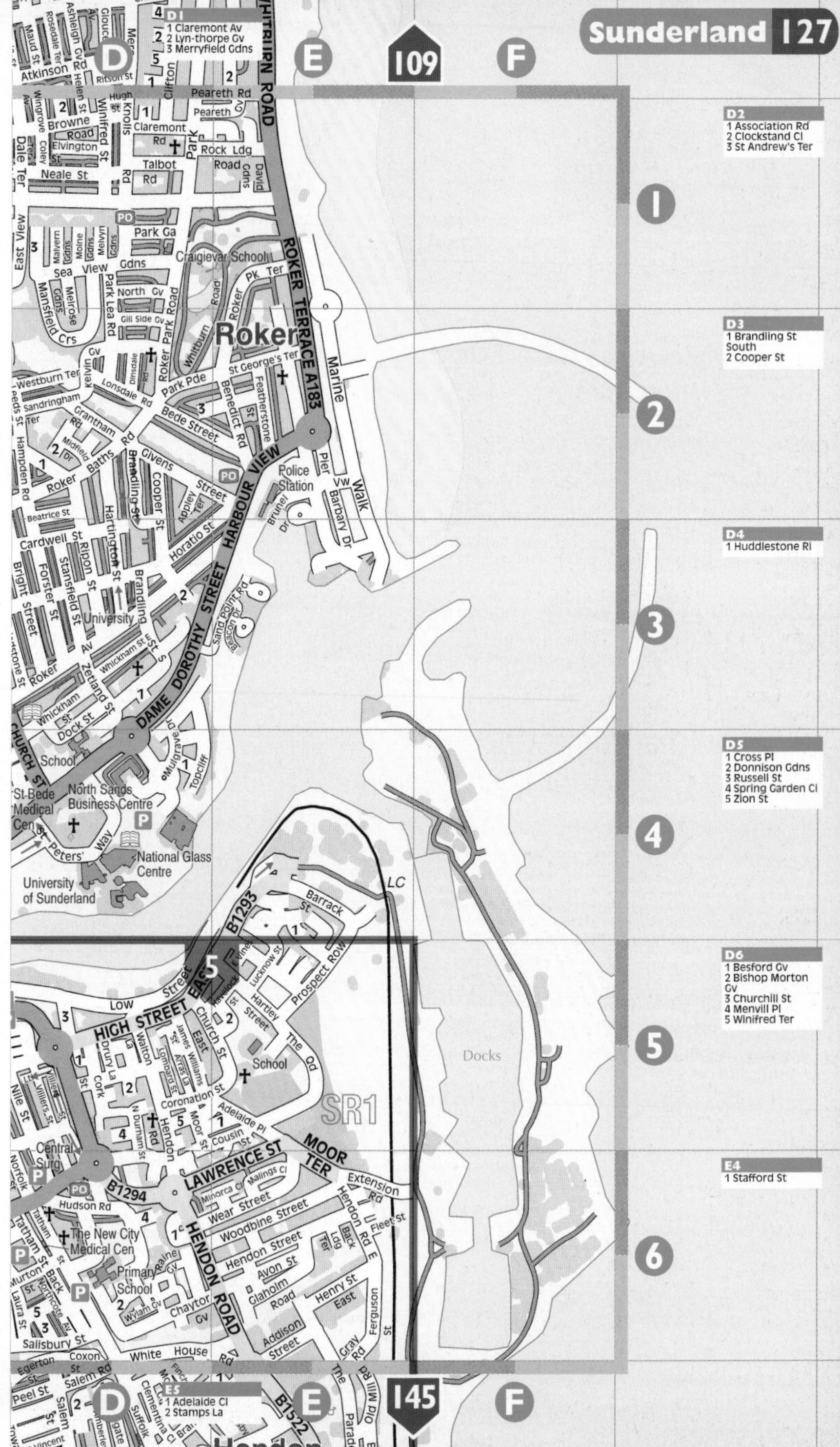

D2
1 Association Rd
2 Clockstand Cl
3 St Andrew's Ter

D3
1 Brandling St South
2 Cooper St

D4
1 Huddlestone Ri

D5
1 Cross Pl
2 Donnison Gdns
3 Russell St
4 Spring Garden Cl
5 Zion St

D6
1 Besford Gv
2 Bishop Morton Gv
3 Churchill St
4 Menvill Pl
5 Winifred Ter

E4
1 Stafford St

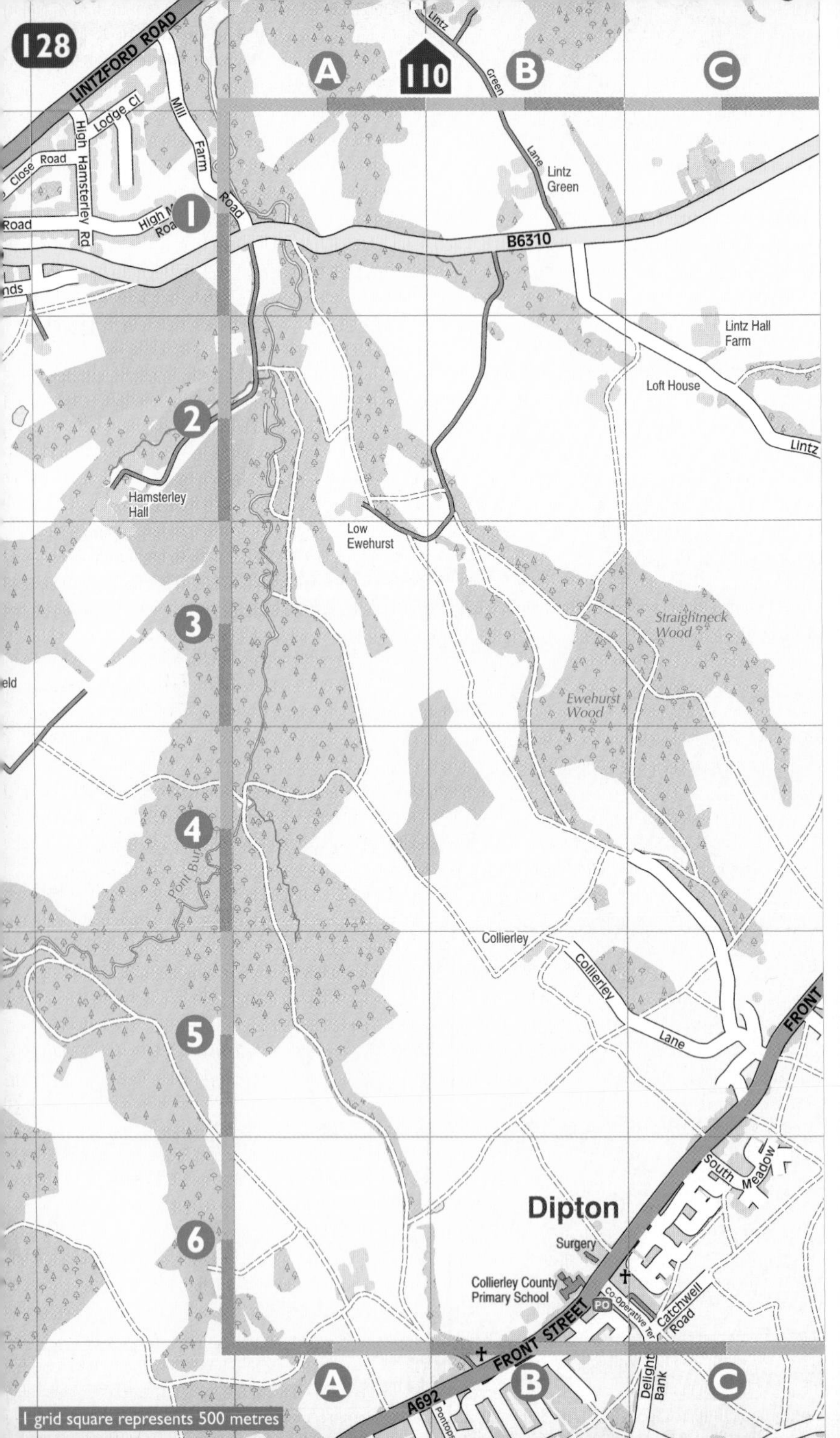

128
110
A
B
C
LINTZFORD ROAD
Lodge Cl
High Hamsterley Rd
Mill Farm Road
Close Road
Road
High Mill Road
1
2
3
4
5
6
Lintz Green Lane
Lintz Green
B6310
Lintz Hall Farm
Loft House
Lintz
Hamsterley Hall
Low Ewehurst
Straightneck Wood
Ewehurst Wood
Pont Burn
Collierley
Collierley Lane
FRONT
South Meadow
Dipton
Surgery
Collierley County Primary School
PO
Co-Operative Ter
Catchwell Road
FRONT STREET
A692
Delight Bank
1 grid square represents 500 metres

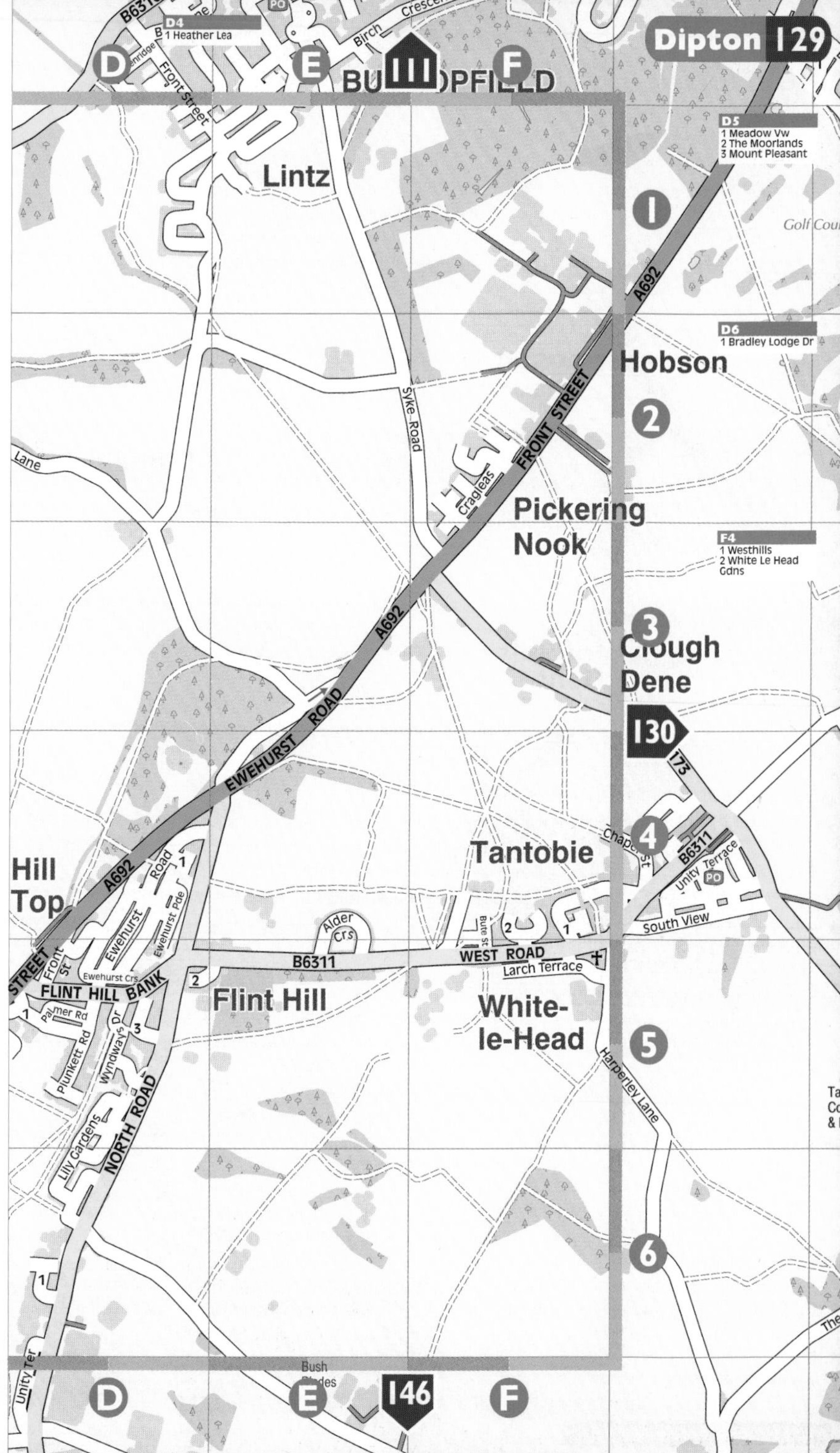

D4
1 Heather Lea
D5
1 Meadow Vw
2 The Moorlands
3 Mount Pleasant
D6
1 Bradley Lodge Dr
F4
1 Westhills
2 White Le Head Gdns
BURNOPFIELD
111
Lintz
Hobson
Pickering Nook
Clough Dene
130
Tantobie
Hill Top
Flint Hill
White-le-Head
146
Bush Blades
A692
FRONT STREET
EWEHURST ROAD
Syke Road
Cragleas
Front Street
Birch Crescent
B6310
Lane
B6311
WEST ROAD
Larch Terrace
Alder Crs
Bute St
Chapel St
Unity Terrace
South View
Harperley Lane
FLINT HILL BANK
NORTH ROAD
Ewehurst Crs
Ewehurst Pde
Ewehurst Road
Front St
Palmer Rd
Plunkett Rd
Wyndways Dr
Lily Gardens
Unity Ter
Golf Cour
PO
173
D
E
F
1
2
3
4
5
6

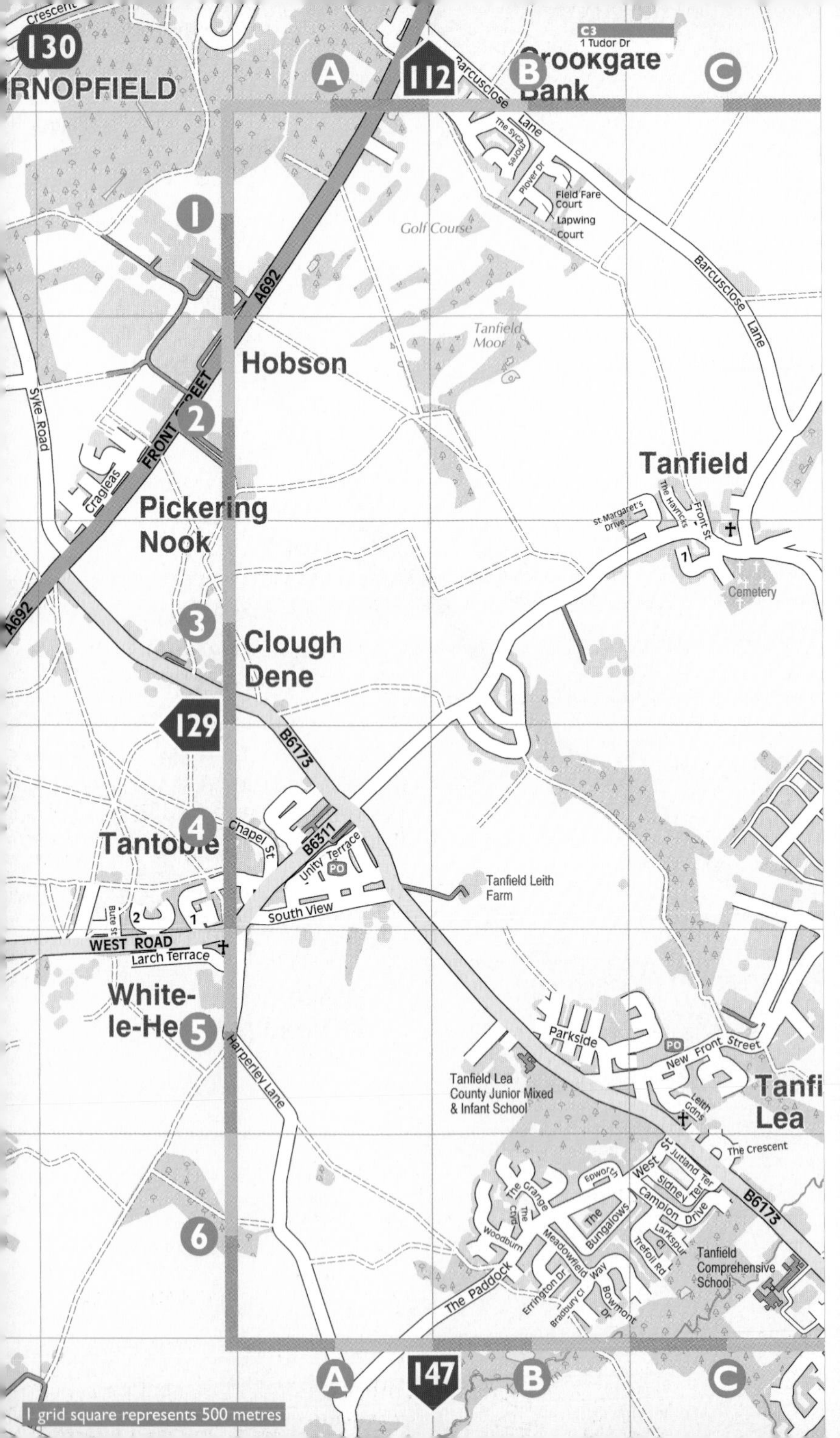
130
RNOPFIELD
A
112
B
C
C3
1 Tudor Dr
Crookgate Bank
Barcusclose Lane
The Sycamores
Plover Dr
Field Fare Court
Lapwing Court
Golf Course
1
A692
Hobson
Tanfield Moor
FRONT STREET
2
Syke Road
Cragleas
Tanfield
The Hayricks
Front St
St Margaret's Drive
Cemetery
Pickering Nook
3
Clough Dene
129
B6173
4
Chapel St
Tantobie
B6311
Unity Terrace
PO
Tanfield Leith Farm
Bute St
South View
WEST ROAD
Larch Terrace
White-le-Head
5
Harperley Lane
Parkside
PO
New Front Street
Tanfield Lea County Junior Mixed & Infant School
Tanfield Lea
Leith Gdns
The Crescent
West St
Jutland Ter
Sidney Ter
Epworth
The Grange
The Crest
Campion Drive
The Bungalows
B6173
Woodburn
Meadowfield Way
Larkspur Cl
Trefoil Rd
Tanfield Comprehensive School
6
The Paddock
Errington Dr
Bradbury Cl
Bowmont Dr
A
147
B
C
1 grid square represents 500 metres

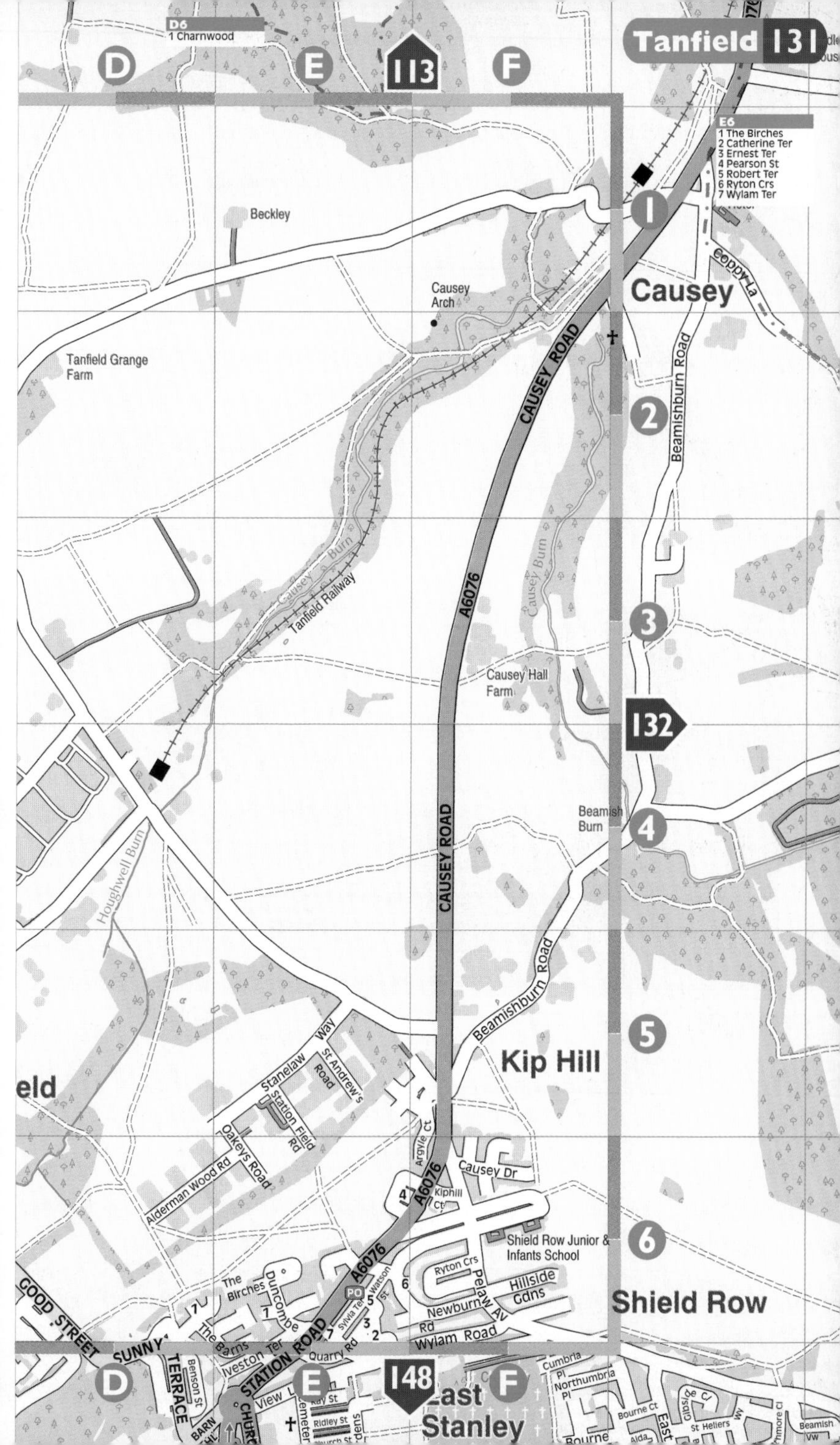

Tanfield 131
D6
1 Charnwood
D
E
113
F
E6
1 The Birches
2 Catherine Ter
3 Ernest Ter
4 Pearson St
5 Robert Ter
6 Ryton Crs
7 Wylam Ter
Beckley
Causey
Coppy La
Causey Arch
Tanfield Grange Farm
CAUSEY ROAD
Beamishburn Road
1
2
3
4
5
6
Causey Burn
Tanfield Railway
A6076
Causey Hall Farm
132
Beamish Burn
Houghwell Burn
Kip Hill
Stanelaw Way
St Andrew's Road
Station Field Rd
Oakeys Road
Alderman Wood Rd
eld
Argyle Ct
Causey Dr
Kiphill Ct
Shield Row Junior & Infants School
Ryton Crs
Pelaw Av
Hillside Gdns
Newburn Rd
Wylam Road
Shield Row
The Birches
Duncombe
Watson St
Sylvia Ter
GOOD STREET
SUNNY TERRACE
The Barns
Ilveston Ter
STATION ROAD
Quarry Rd
PO
Benson St
148
East Stanley
Cumbria Pl
Northumbria Pl
Bourne Ct
Gibside Cl
St Helliers Wy
Ridley St
Kay St
Beamish Vw

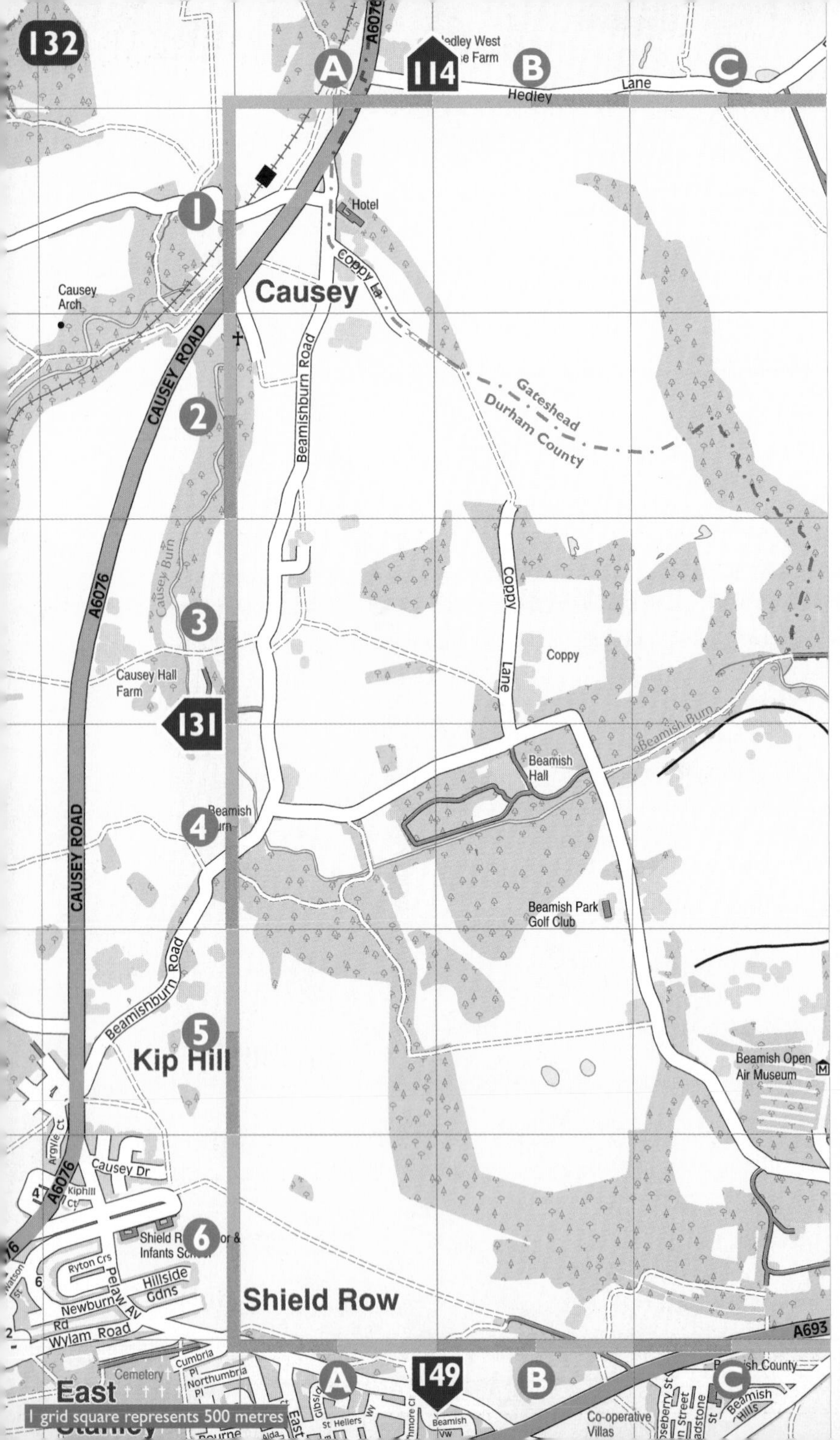
132
114
A
B
C
Hedley West
Farm
Hedley
Lane
Hotel
Coppy La
Causey
Causey Arch
CAUSEY ROAD
A6076
Beamishburn Road
Gateshead
Durham County
Causey Burn
Coppy Lane
Coppy
Causey Hall
Farm
131
Beamish-Burn
Beamish
Hall
Beamish
Burn
Beamish Park
Golf Club
Kip Hill
Beamish Open
Air Museum
Argyle Ct
Causey Dr
Kiphill
Ct
Shield Row Junior &
Infants School
Ryton Crs
Pelaw Av
Hillside
Gdns
Newburn
Rd
Wylam Road
Watson
St
Shield Row
A693
149
Cemetery
Cumbria
Pl
Northumbria
Pl
East
Stanley
Gibside
St Hellers
Wy
East
Beamish
Vw
Beamish County
Co-operative
Villas
Roseberry St
Gladstone
St
Beamish
Hills
1
2
3
4
5
6
1 grid square represents 500 metres

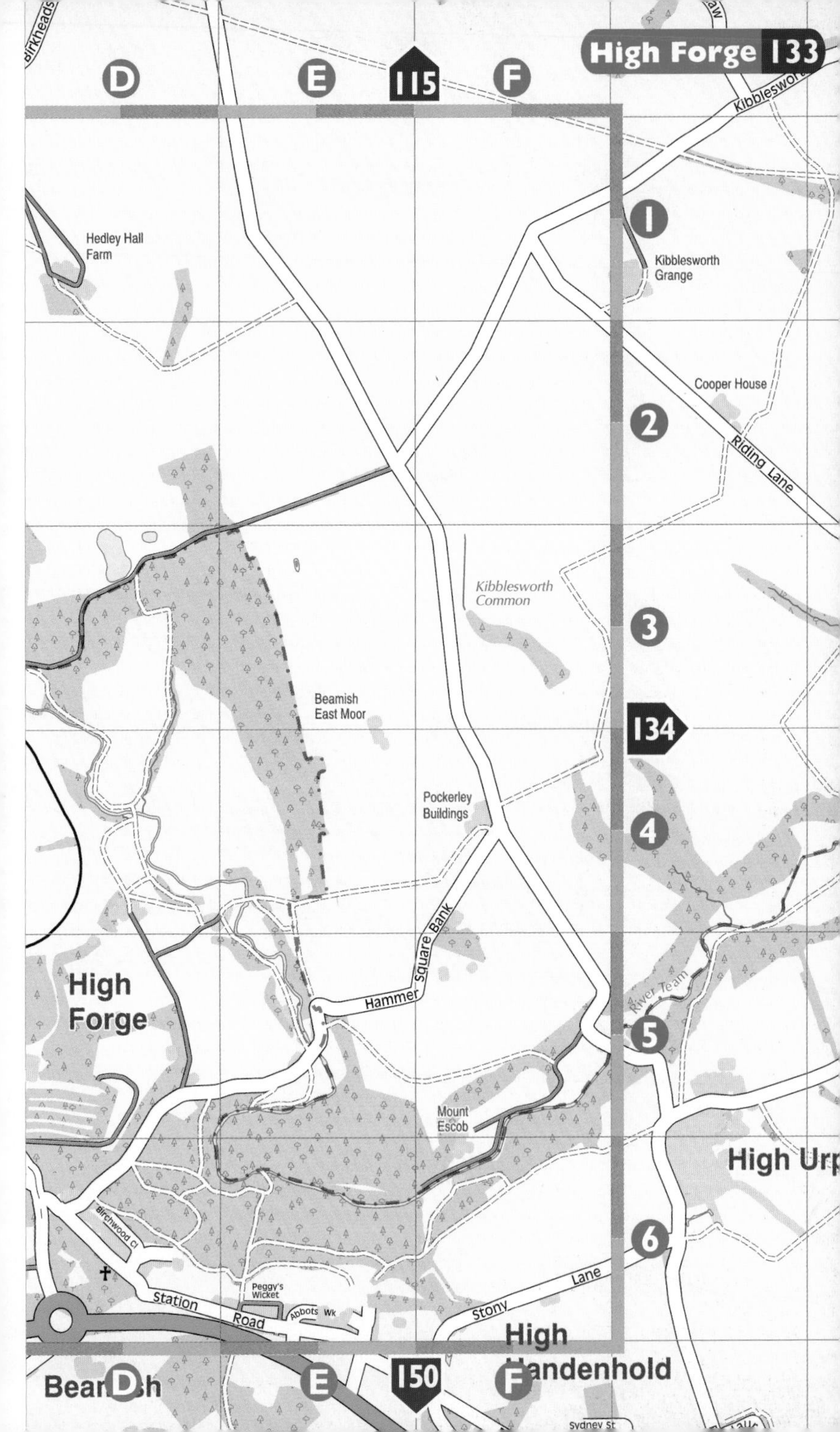

D
E
115
F
Birkheads
Kibblesworth
Hedley Hall
Farm
1
Kibblesworth
Grange
Cooper House
2
Riding Lane
Kibblesworth
Common
3
Beamish
East Moor
134
Pockerley
Buildings
4
Square Bank
Hammer
River Team
5
High
Forge
Mount
Escob
High Urp
Birchwood Cl
6
Lane
Stony
Peggy's
Wicket
Station
Road
Abbots Wk
High
Handenhold
Beamish
D
E
150
F
Sydney St

116
A
B
C
Kibblesworth Grange
Cooper House
Riding Lane
Riding Farm
Kibblesworth Common
133
Pockerley Buildings
Mill La
Abbotside
Walden Cl
Leyburn Cl
Square Bank
River Team
Mount Escob
High Urpeth
Stony Lane
High Handenhold
New
151
Bank
Ashvale Av
Laburnum Crs
Grange Est
Moorhill
Greenford
Coltspool
Ouselaw
Fairfield
1
2
3
4
5
6
1 grid square represents 500 metres

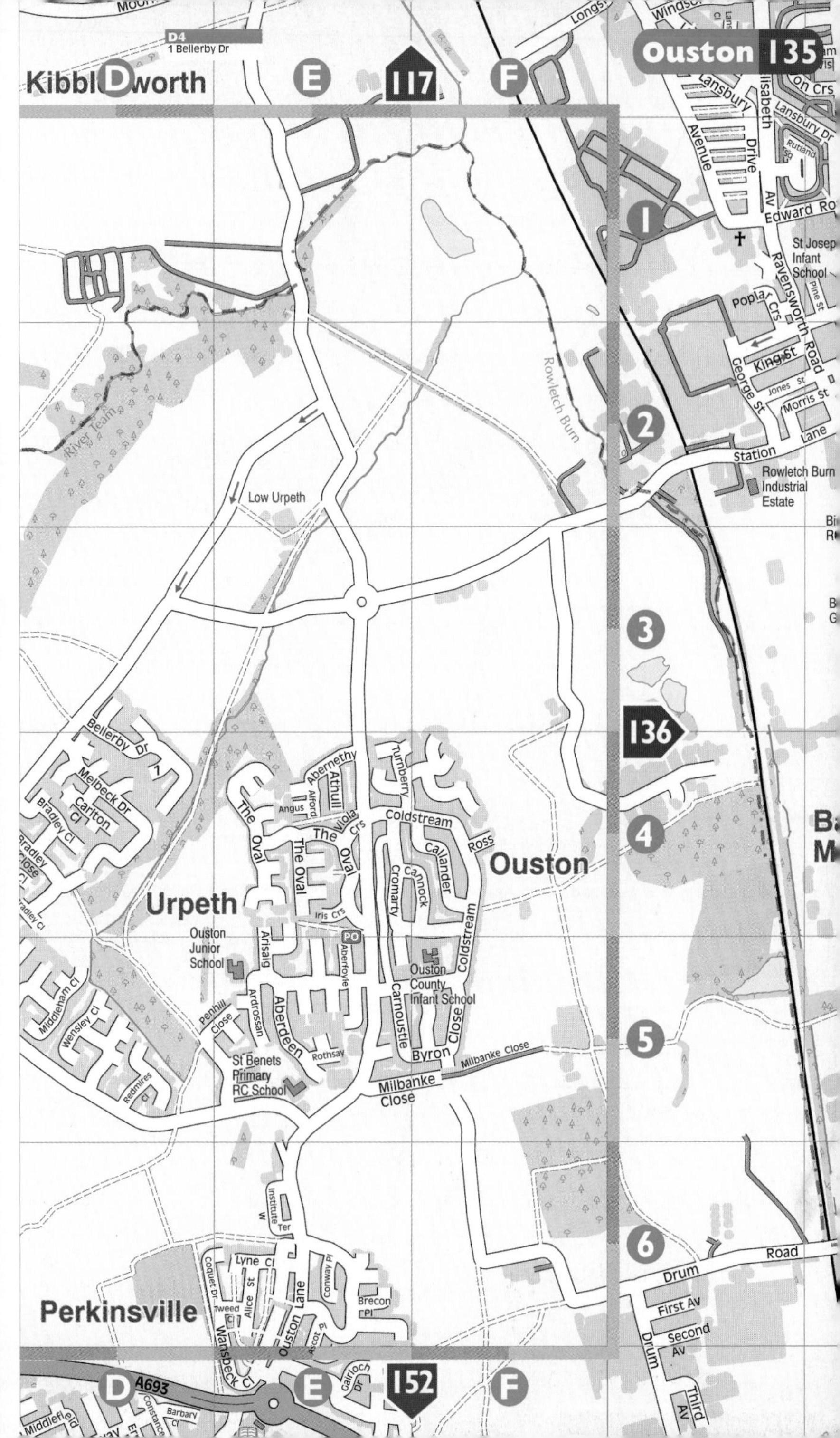

Ouston 135
D4
1 Bellerby Dr
Kibblesworth
117
152
136
Low Urpeth
River Team
Rowletch Burn
Urpeth
Ouston
Perkinsville
Lansbury
Avenue
Elisabeth Drive
Lansbury Dr
Rutland
Edward Rd
Av
St Joseph Infant School
Ravensworth Road
Poplar Crs
King St
George St
Jones St
Morris St
Station Lane
Rowletch Burn Industrial Estate
Bellerby Dr
Melbeck Dr
Carlton Cl
Bradley Cl
Bradley Close
Abernethy
Athull
Alford
Angus
Turnberry
Coldstream
Viola Crs
The Oval
Callander
Ross
Cannock
Cromarty
Iris Crs
Arisaig
Aberfoyle
Ouston Junior School
Ouston County Infant School
Ardrossan
Aberdeen
Carnoustie
Close
Penhill Close
St Benets Primary RC School
Rothsay
Byron
Milbanke Close
Middleham Cl
Wensley Cl
Redmires
Institute Ter
Lyne Cl
Coquet Dr
Alice St
Conway Pl
Brecon Pl
Tweed Cl
Ouston Lane
Ascot Pl
Wansbeck Cl
Gairloch Dr
A693
Constance
Barbary Cl
Middlefield
Drum Road
Drum
First Av
Second Av
Third Av
D
E
F
1
2
3
4
5
6

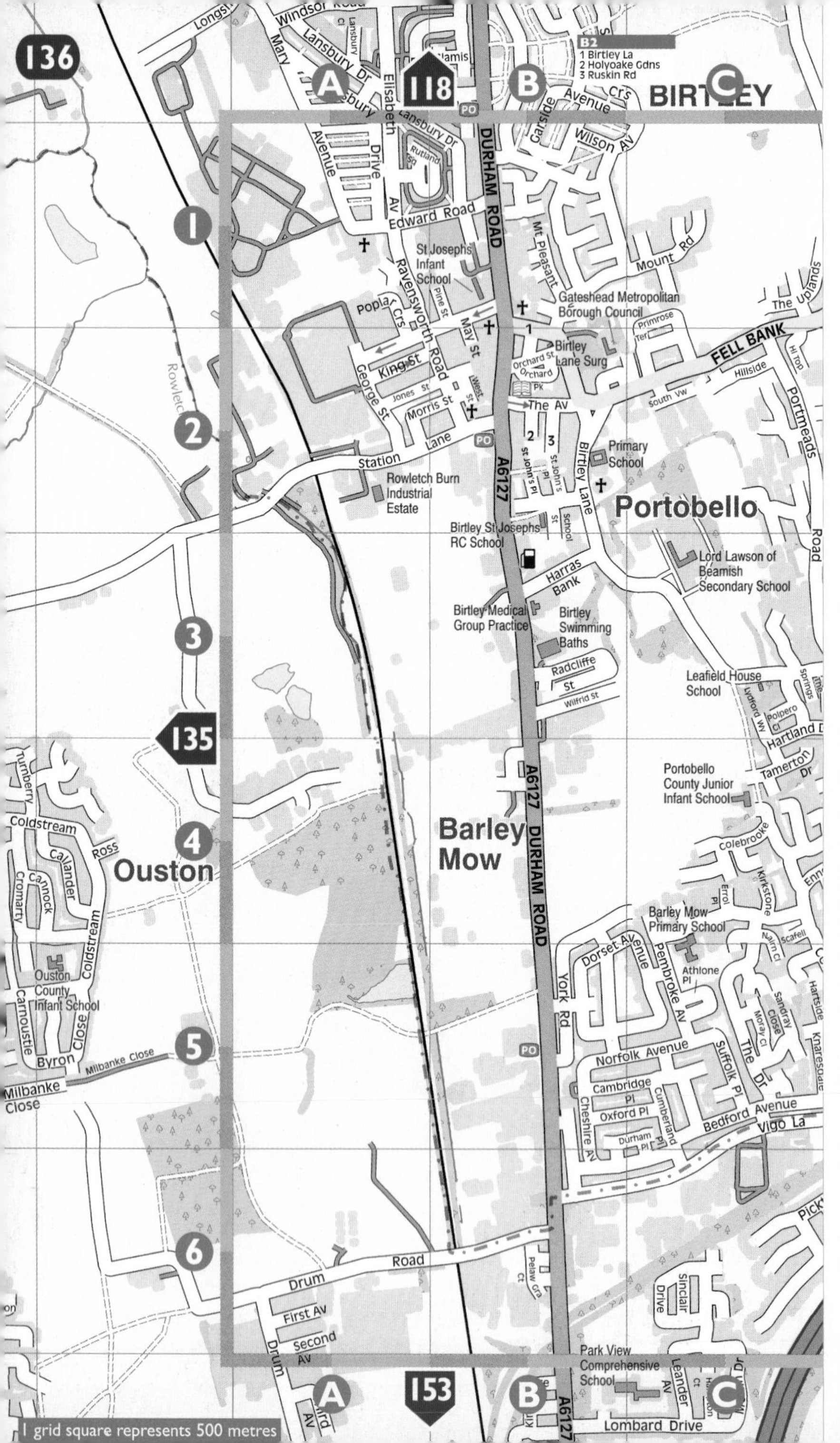

136
118
135
153
A
B
C
1
2
3
4
5
6
B2
1 Birtley La
2 Holyoake Gdns
3 Ruskin Rd
BIRTLEY
Portobello
Barley Mow
Ouston
DURHAM ROAD
A6127
Windsor Road
Lansbury Dr
Ellisabeth Drive
Mary Avenue
Garside Avenue
Wilson AV
Edward Road
St Josephs Infant School
Ravensworth Road
Mount Rd
Mt Pleasant
Gateshead Metropolitan Borough Council
The Uplands
Primrose Ter
FELL BANK
Hillside
Hi Top
Portmeads Road
Poplar Crs
King St
George St
Jones St
Morris St
May St
West St
Orchard St
Orchard
Birtley Lane Surg
South Vw
The Av
Station Lane
Rowletch Burn Industrial Estate
Primary School
Birtley Lane
St John's Pl
St John's
School St
Birtley St Josephs RC School
Harras Bank
Lord Lawson of Beamish Secondary School
Birtley Medical Group Practice
Birtley Swimming Baths
Radcliffe St
Wilfrid St
Leafield House School
Lydford Wy
Polpero Cl
Hartland Dr
Tamerton Dr
Portobello County Junior Infant School
Colebrooke
Kirkstone
Errol Pl
Barley Mow Primary School
Dorset Avenue
Pembroke Av
Athlone Pl
Nairn Cl
Scafell
Hartside
Sandray Close
Moray Cl
The Dr
Knaresdale
York Rd
Norfolk Avenue
Suffolk Pl
Cambridge Pl
Oxford Pl
Cheshire Av
Cumberland Pl
Durham Pl
Bedford Avenue
Vigo La
Turnberry
Coldstream
Callander
Ross
Cannock
Cromarty
Ouston County Infant School
Carnoustie
Close
Byron
Milbanke Close
Drum Road
First Av
Second Av
Drum
Pelaw Gra Ct
Sinclair Drive
Park View Comprehensive School
Leander Av
Lombard Drive
PO
Pk
1 grid square represents 500 metres

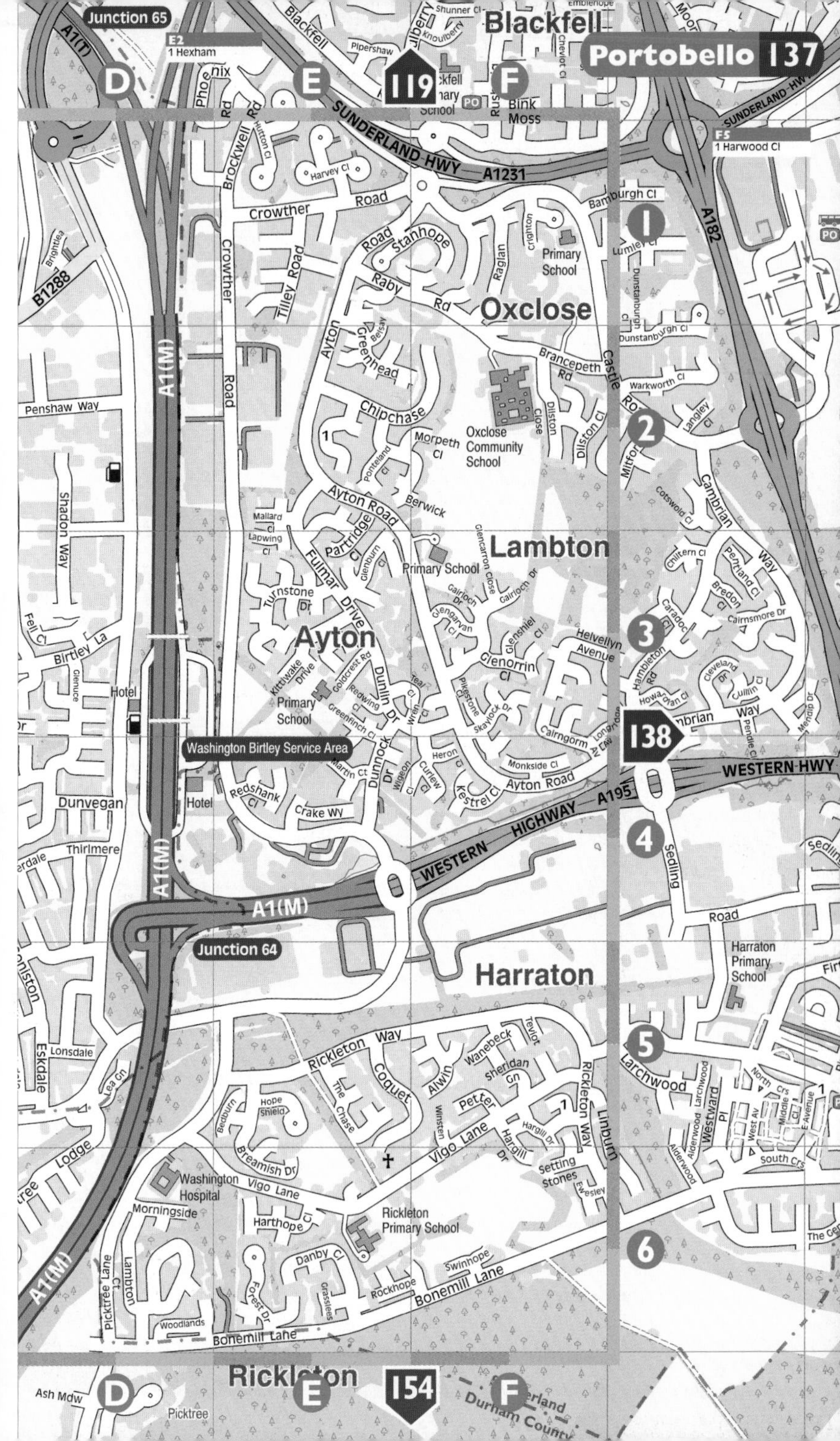
Junction 65
Blackfell
Oxclose
Lambton
Ayton
Harraton
Rickleton
Washington Birtley Service Area
Junction 64
Oxclose Community School
Primary School
Washington Hospital
Rickleton Primary School
Harraton Primary School
Hotel
SUNDERLAND HWY
A1231
WESTERN HIGHWAY
A195
WESTERN HWY
A1(M)
A182
B1288
E2
1 Hexham
F5
1 Harwood Cl
119
138
154
Bonemill Lane
Vigo Lane
Rickleton Way
Ayton Road
Crowther Road
Sedling Road
Cambrian Way
Durham County

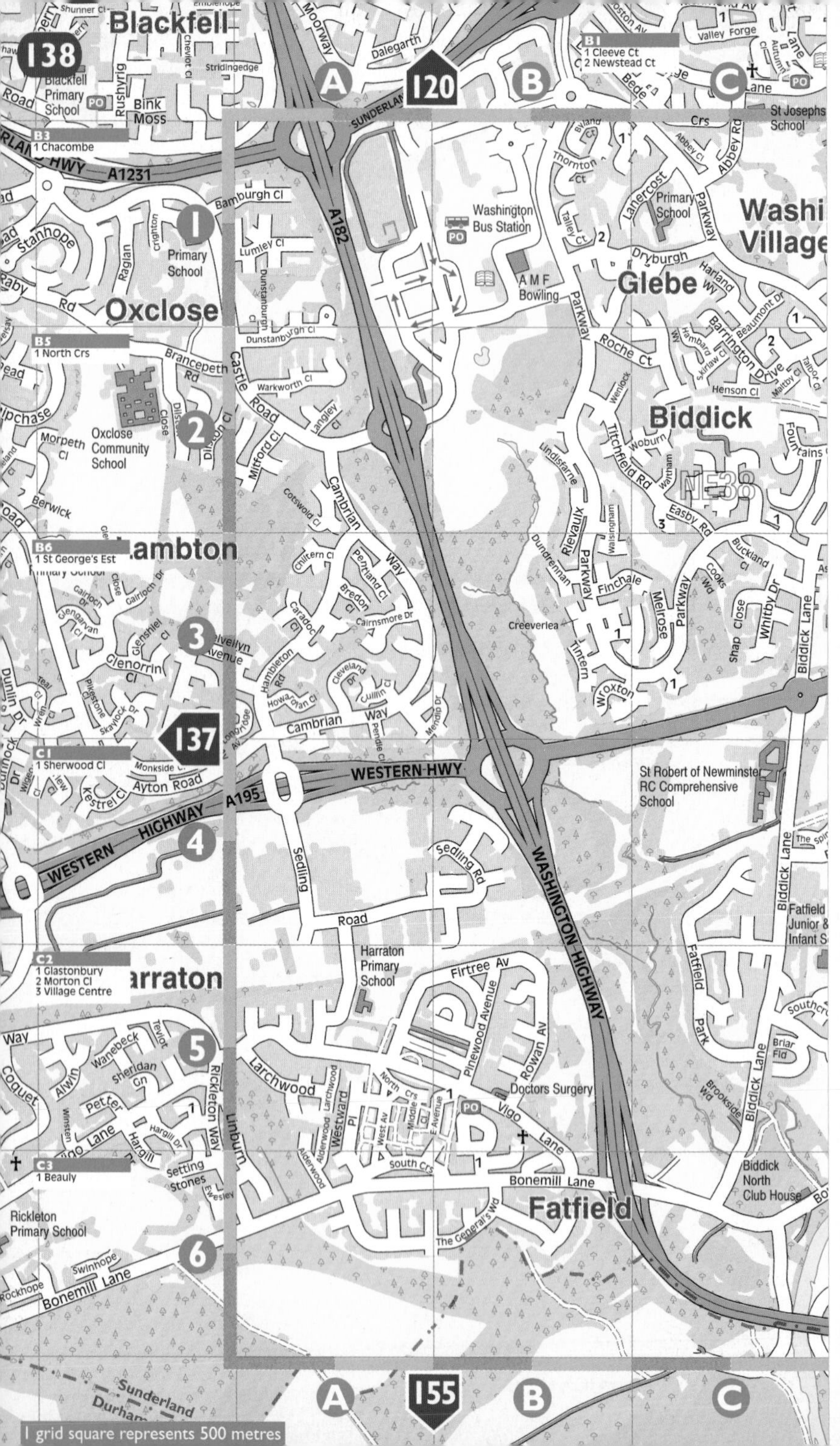

138
Blackfell
Blackfell Primary School
Bink Moss
Rushyrig
Cheviot Cl
Stridingedge
Dalegarth
Moorway
A
120
B
C
B1
1 Cleeve Ct
2 Newstead Ct
Valley Forge
St Josephs School
B3
1 Chacombe
A1231
Bamburgh Cl
1
Primary School
Oxclose
Stanhope
Raglan
Crighton
Lumley Cl
A182
Washington Bus Station
A M F Bowling
Washington Village
Glebe
Lanercost
Primary School
Abbey Rd
Parkway
Thornton Ct
Talley Ct
Dryburgh
Harland Wy
Beaumont Dr
Barrington Drive
Roche Ct
B5
1 North Crs
Brancepeth Rd
Castle Road
Dunstanburgh Cl
Warkworth Cl
Langley Cl
Mitford Cl
2
Oxclose Community School
Morpeth Cl
Dilston Cl
Berwick
Cambrian Way
Cotswold Cl
Biddick
Henson Cl
Titchfield Rd
Woburn
Waltham
Lindisfarne
Rievaulx
Walsingham
Easby Rd
NE38
Fountains
B6
1 St George's Est
Lambton
Primary School
Gairloch Dr
Glengarvan Cl
Glenshiel Cl
Glenorrin Cl
3
Helvellyn Avenue
Chiltern Cl
Pentland Cl
Bredon Cl
Caradoc Cl
Cairnsmore Dr
Hambleton Rd
Howardian Cl
Cleveland Dr
Cuillin Cl
Dundrennan
Parkway
Finchale
Melrose
Creeverlea
Tintern
Wroxton
Buckland Cl
Cooks Wd
Whitby Dr
Snap Close
Biddick Lane
Dunlin Dr
Wren Cl
Teal Cl
Pikestone Cl
Skaylock Dr
137
Longridge Av
Pendle Cl
Mendip Dr
C1
1 Sherwood Cl
Monkside Cl
Ayton Road
Kestrel Cl
A195
WESTERN HWY
WESTERN HIGHWAY
4
St Robert of Newminster RC Comprehensive School
Sedling Road
Sedling Rd
WASHINGTON HIGHWAY
The Spinney
Fatfield Junior & Infant School
C2
1 Glastonbury
2 Morton Cl
3 Village Centre
Harraton
Harraton Primary School
Firtree Av
Pinewood Avenue
Rowan Av
Fatfield Park
Southcroft
Briar Fld
5
Wanebeck
Teviot
Sheridan Gn
Alwin
Coquet
Petter
Winsten
Hargill
Hargill Dr
Vigo Lane
Rickleton Way
Linburn
Larchwood
Westward Pl
West Av
North Crs
Middle Cl
E Avenue
Doctors Surgery
Brookside Wd
C3
1 Beauly
Setting Stones
Eyesley
Alderwood
South Crs
Bonemill Lane
Fatfield
Biddick North Club House
Rickleton Primary School
The General's Wd
6
Swinhope
Rockhope
Bonemill Lane
Sunderland
Durham
155
1 grid square represents 500 metres

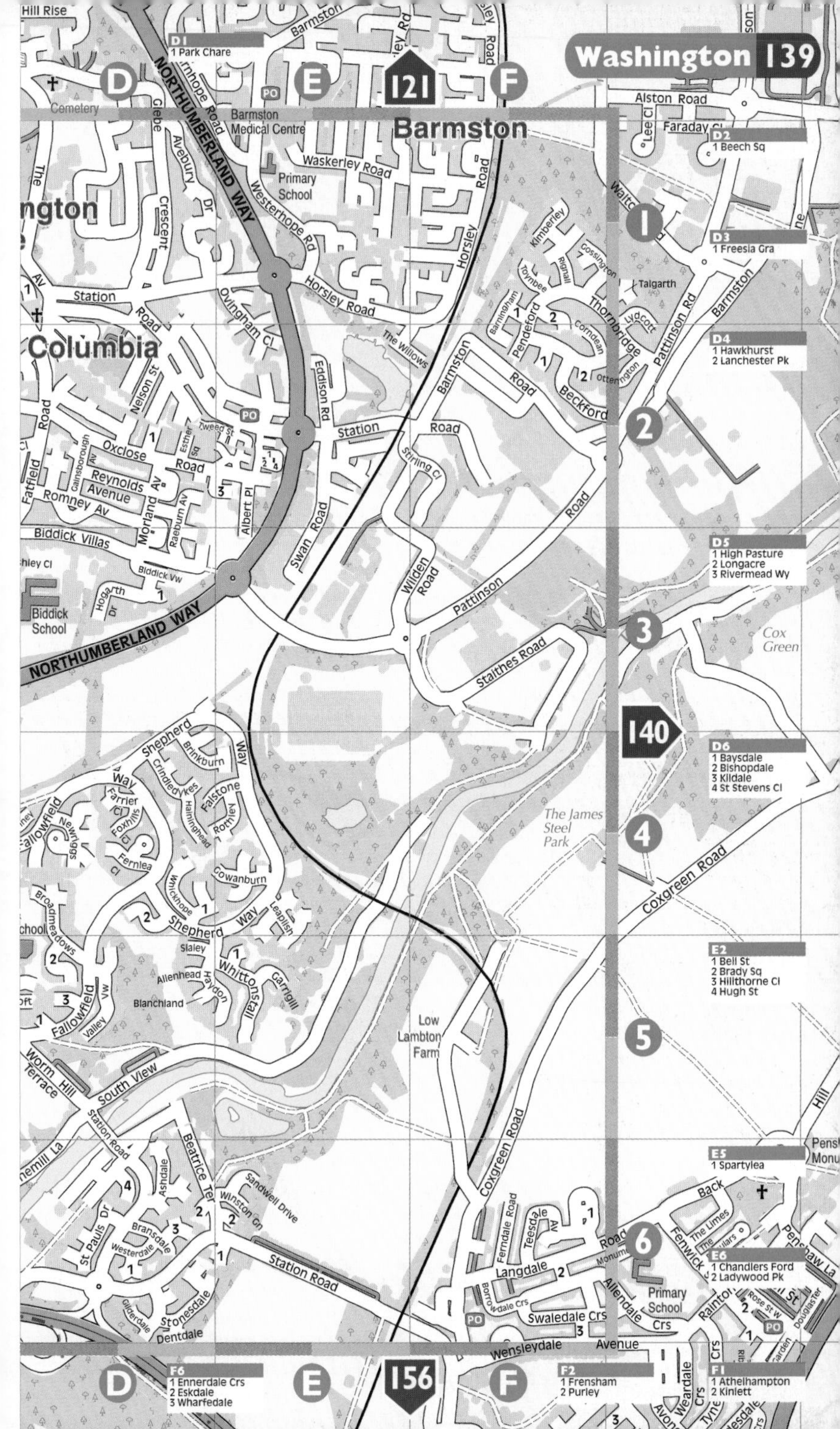

Washington 139
121
140
156
D
E
F
1
2
3
4
5
6
Barmston
Columbia
Cox Green
The James Steel Park
Low Lambton Farm
Barmston Medical Centre
Primary School
Biddick School
Cemetery
NORTHUMBERLAND WAY
Westerhope Rd
Horsley Road
Waskerley Road
Station Road
Pattinson Road
Barmston Road
Staithes Road
Wilden Road
Swan Road
Eddison Rd
Stirling Cl
The Willows
Thornbridge
Beckford
Pendeford
Coxgreen Road
Shepherd Way
Fallowfield
Station Road
South View
Worm Hill Terrace
Beatrice Ter
Sandwell Drive
Winston Gn
Swaledale Crs
Wensleydale Avenue
Allendale Crs
Langdale
Teesdale Av
Ferndale Road
Alston Road
Faraday Cl
Oxclose Road
Reynolds Avenue
Romney Av
Biddick Villas
Nelson St
Morland Av
Albert Pl
Crescent
Avebury Dr
Ovingham Cl
D1
1 Park Chare
D2
1 Beech Sq
D3
1 Freesia Gra
D4
1 Hawkhurst
2 Lanchester Pk
D5
1 High Pasture
2 Longacre
3 Rivermead Wy
D6
1 Baysdale
2 Bishopdale
3 Kildale
4 St Stevens Cl
E2
1 Bell St
2 Brady Sq
3 Hillthorne Cl
4 Hugh St
E5
1 Spartylea
E6
1 Chandlers Ford
2 Ladywood Pk
F6
1 Ennerdale Crs
2 Eskdale
3 Wharfedale
F2
1 Frensham
2 Purley
F1
1 Athelhampton
2 Kinlett

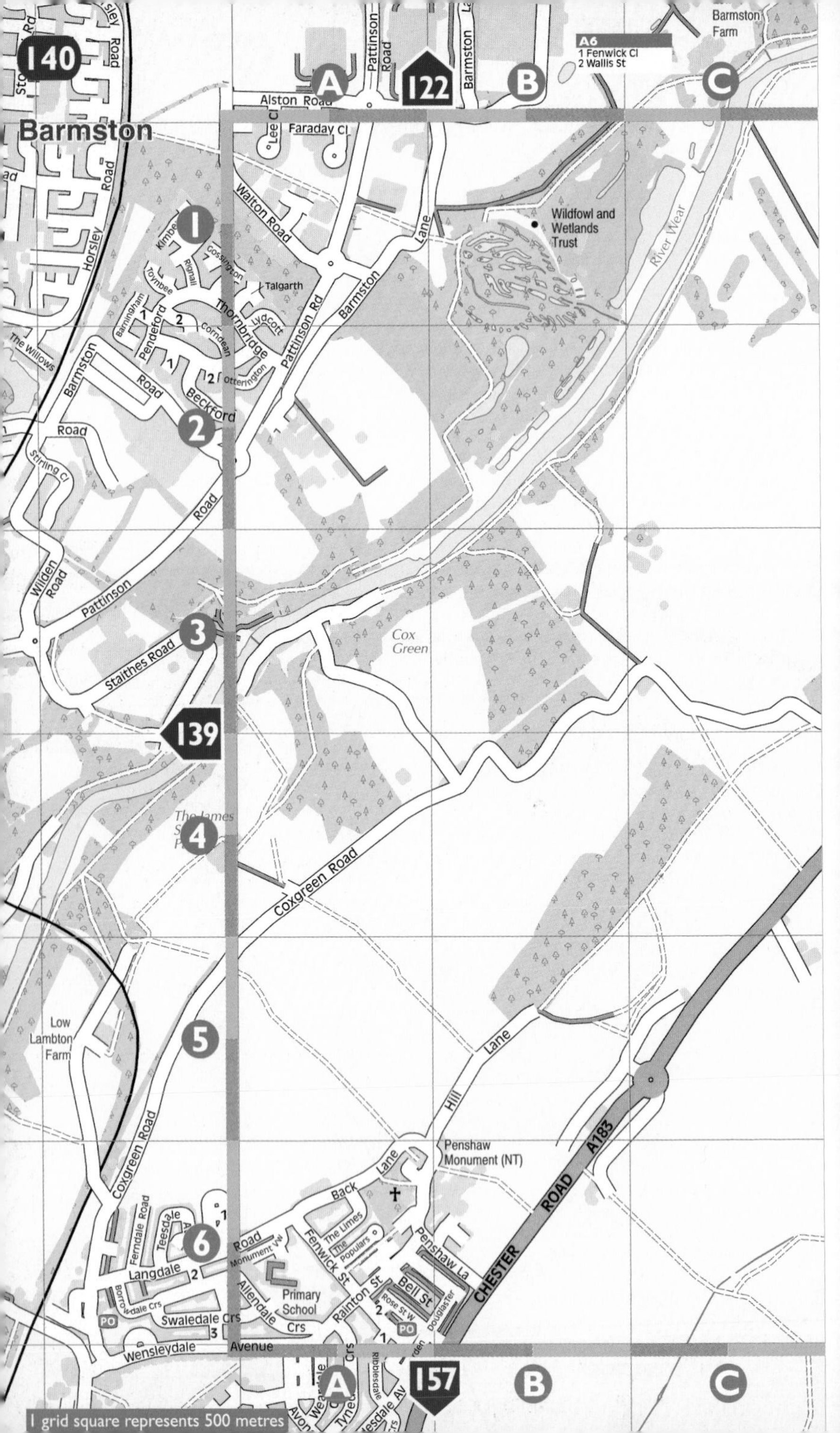
140
122
139
157
A
B
C
A6
1 Fenwick Cl
2 Wallis St
Barmston Farm
Barmston
Alston Road
Pattinson Road
Barmston Lane
Lee Cl
Faraday Cl
Horsley Road
Walton Road
Wildfowl and Wetlands Trust
River Wear
Kimber
Gossington
Rignall
Toynbee
Talgarth
Thornbridge
Barningham
Pendeford
Comdean
Lydcott
The Willows
Barmston Road
Otterington
Pattinson Rd
Beckford
Road
Stirling Cl
Wilden Road
Pattinson Road
Staithes Road
Cox Green
The James
Coxgreen Road
Low Lambton Farm
Hill Lane
Penshaw Monument (NT)
A183
CHESTER ROAD
Back Lane
Ferndale Road
Teesdale
Monument Vw
The Limes
The Populars
Fenwick St
Penshaw La
Langdale
Borrowdale Crs
Primary School
Allendale Crs
Rainton St
Bell St
Rose St W
Douglaster
PO
Swaledale Crs
Wensleydale Avenue
Ribblesdale
1 grid square represents 500 metres

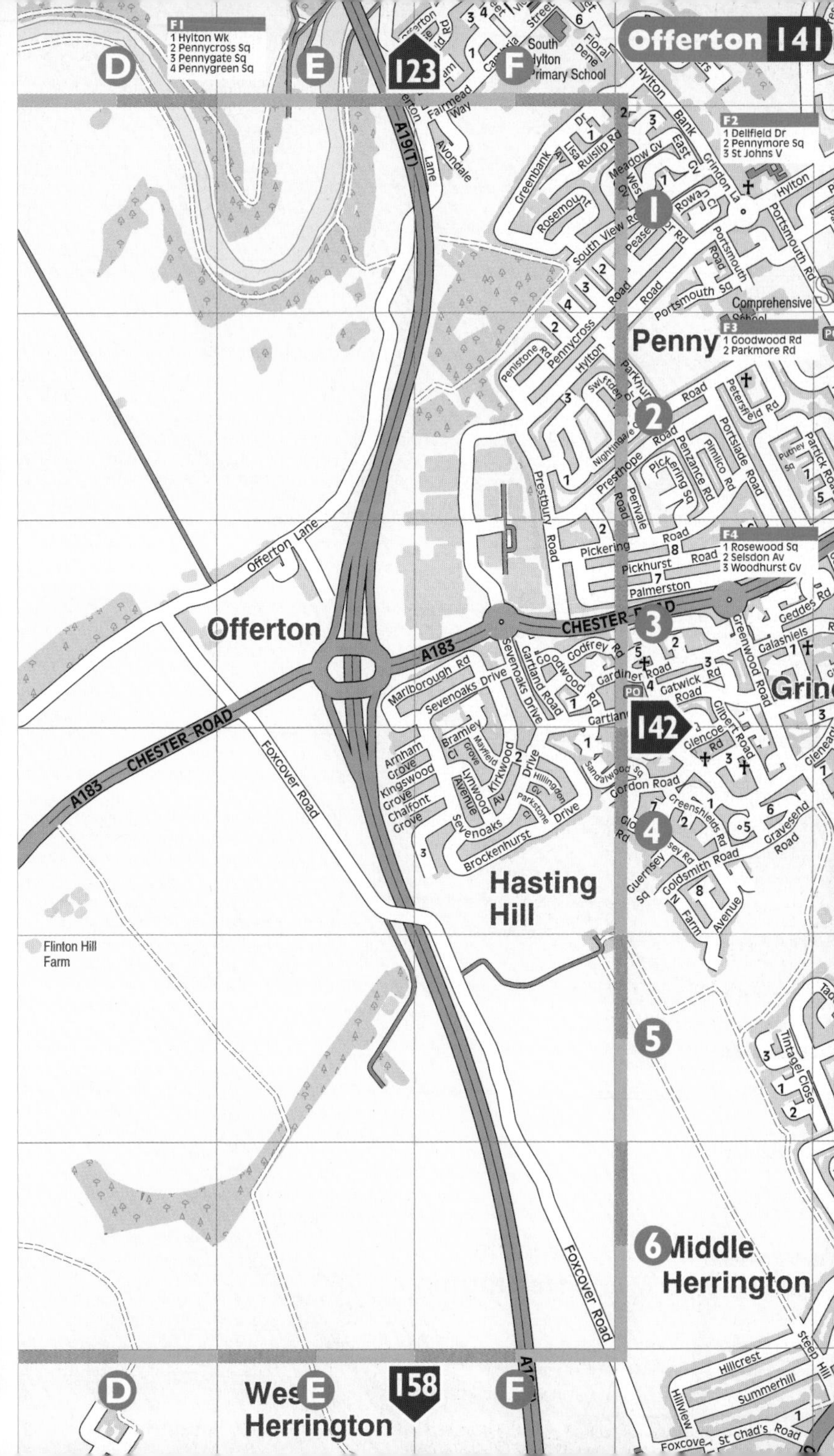
F1
1 Hylton Wk
2 Pennycross Sq
3 Pennygate Sq
4 Pennygreen Sq
D
E
123
F
South Hylton Primary School
F2
1 Dellfield Dr
2 Pennymore Sq
3 St Johns V
F3
1 Goodwood Rd
2 Parkmore Rd
F4
1 Rosewood Sq
2 Selsdon Av
3 Woodhurst Gv
A19(T)
Offerton Lane
Offerton
CHESTER ROAD
A183
Foxcover Road
Penny
Comprehensive School
Portsmouth Rd
Portsmouth Sq
Grindon La
Hylton Bank
South View Rd
Pennycross Rd
Penistone Rd
Prestbury Road
Presthope Road
Pickering Road
Pickhurst Road
Palmerston
Greenwood Road
Galashiels
Geddes Rd
Grinc
Gatwick Road
Gilbert Road
Glencoe Rd
Gardiner Road
Gartland Road
Godfrey Rd
Goodwood Rd
Sevenoaks Drive
Marlborough Rd
Bramley Cl
Mayfield Grove
Lynwood Avenue
Kirkwood Av
Hillingdon Gv
Parkstone Cl
Brockenhurst Drive
Arnham Grove
Kingswood Grove
Chalfont Grove
Gordon Road
Greenshields Rd
Gravesend Road
Goldsmith Road
Guernsey Sq
N Farm Avenue
Hasting Hill
142
Flinton Hill Farm
Tintagel Close
5
6
Middle Herrington
Hillcrest
Summerhill
Hillview
Steep Hill
St Chad's Road
Foxcover
West Herrington
158

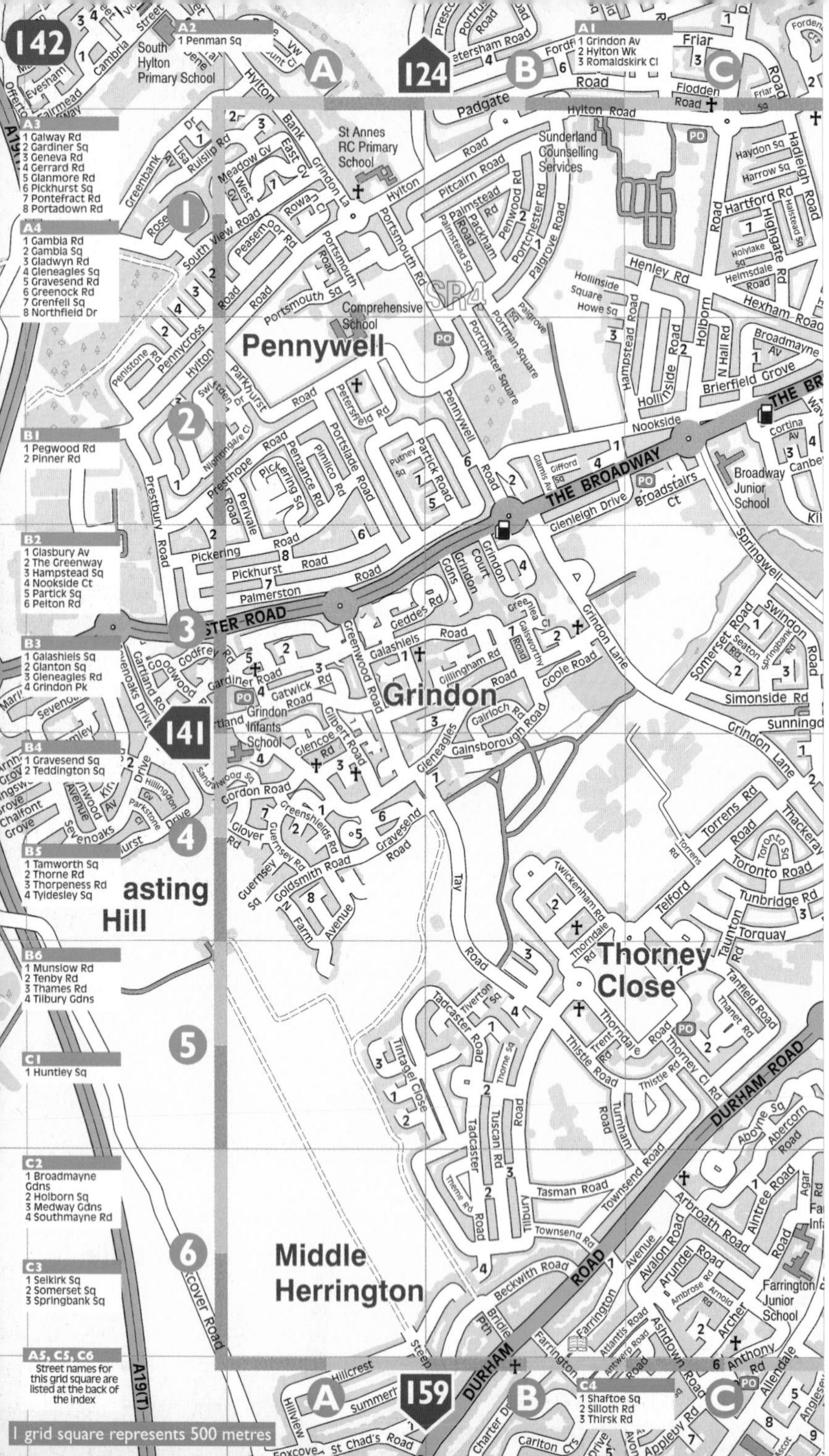
142
124
141
159
A
B
C
1
2
3
4
5
6
A1
1 Grindon Av
2 Hylton Wk
3 Romaldskirk Cl
A2
1 Penman Sq
A3
1 Galway Rd
2 Gardiner Sq
3 Geneva Rd
4 Gerrard Rd
5 Glanmore Rd
6 Pickhurst Sq
7 Pontefract Rd
8 Portadown Rd
A4
1 Gambia Rd
2 Gambia Sq
3 Gladwyn Rd
4 Gleneagles Sq
5 Gravesend Rd
6 Greenock Rd
7 Grenfell Sq
8 Northfield Dr
B1
1 Pegwood Rd
2 Pinner Rd
B2
1 Glasbury Av
2 The Greenway
3 Hampstead Sq
4 Nookside Ct
5 Partick Sq
6 Pelton Rd
B3
1 Galashiels Sq
2 Glanton Sq
3 Gleneagles Rd
4 Grindon Pk
B4
1 Gravesend Sq
2 Teddington Sq
B5
1 Tamworth Sq
2 Thorne Rd
3 Thorpeness Rd
4 Tyldesley Sq
B6
1 Munslow Rd
2 Tenby Rd
3 Thames Rd
4 Tilbury Gdns
C1
1 Huntley Sq
C2
1 Broadmayne Gdns
2 Holborn Sq
3 Medway Gdns
4 Southmayne Rd
C3
1 Selkirk Sq
2 Somerset Sq
3 Springbank Sq
C4
1 Shaftoe Sq
2 Silloth Rd
3 Thirsk Rd
A5, C5, C6
Street names for this grid square are listed at the back of the index
1 grid square represents 500 metres
Pennywell
Grindon
Thorney Close
Middle Herrington
asting Hill
SR4
South Hylton Primary School
St Annes RC Primary School
Sunderland Counselling Services
Comprehensive School
Grindon Infants School
Broadway Junior School
Farrington Junior School
THE BROADWAY
DURHAM ROAD
Hylton Road
Hylton Bank
Padgate Road
Pitcairn Road
Portsmouth Rd
Pennywell Road
Grindon Lane
Springwell
Hollinside Square
Henley Rd
Hexham Road
Brierfield Grove
Nookside
Glenleigh Drive
Broadstairs Ct
Pickering Road
Pickhurst Road
Palmerston Road
Prestbury Road
Presthope Road
Portslade Road
Penzance Rd
Pimlico Rd
Partick Road
Petersfield Rd
Parkhurst Road
Galashiels Road
Geddes Rd
Greenwood Road
Gillingham Rd
Goole Road
Gainsborough Road
Gleneagles Road
Gordon Road
Goldsmith Road
Gravesend Road
Farm Avenue
Tay Road
Torrens Road
Toronto Road
Tunbridge Rd
Torquay
Telford Rd
Taunton Rd
Tanfield Road
Thorndale Road
Thistle Road
Turnham Road
Tuscan Rd
Tadcaster Road
Tintagel Close
Tasman Road
Townsend Road
Tilbury Road
Beckwith Road
Arbroath Road
Avalon Road
Arundel Road
Ashdown Road
Aintree Road
Farrington
Hillcrest
Summerhill
Foxcove
St Chad's Road
Charter Dr
Carlton Crs
Somerset Road
Swindon Road
Simonside Rd
Sunningdale
Thackeray
Friar Road
Flodden Road
Hadleigh Road
Highgate Rd
Hartford Rd
Ruislip Rd
South View Road
Pennycross Road
Peasemoor Rd
Penistone Rd
Garthland Rd
Godfrey Rd
Gardiner Road
Gatwick Rd
Gilbert Road
Glencoe Rd
Sevenoaks
Chalfont Grove
A19(T)
Foxcover Road

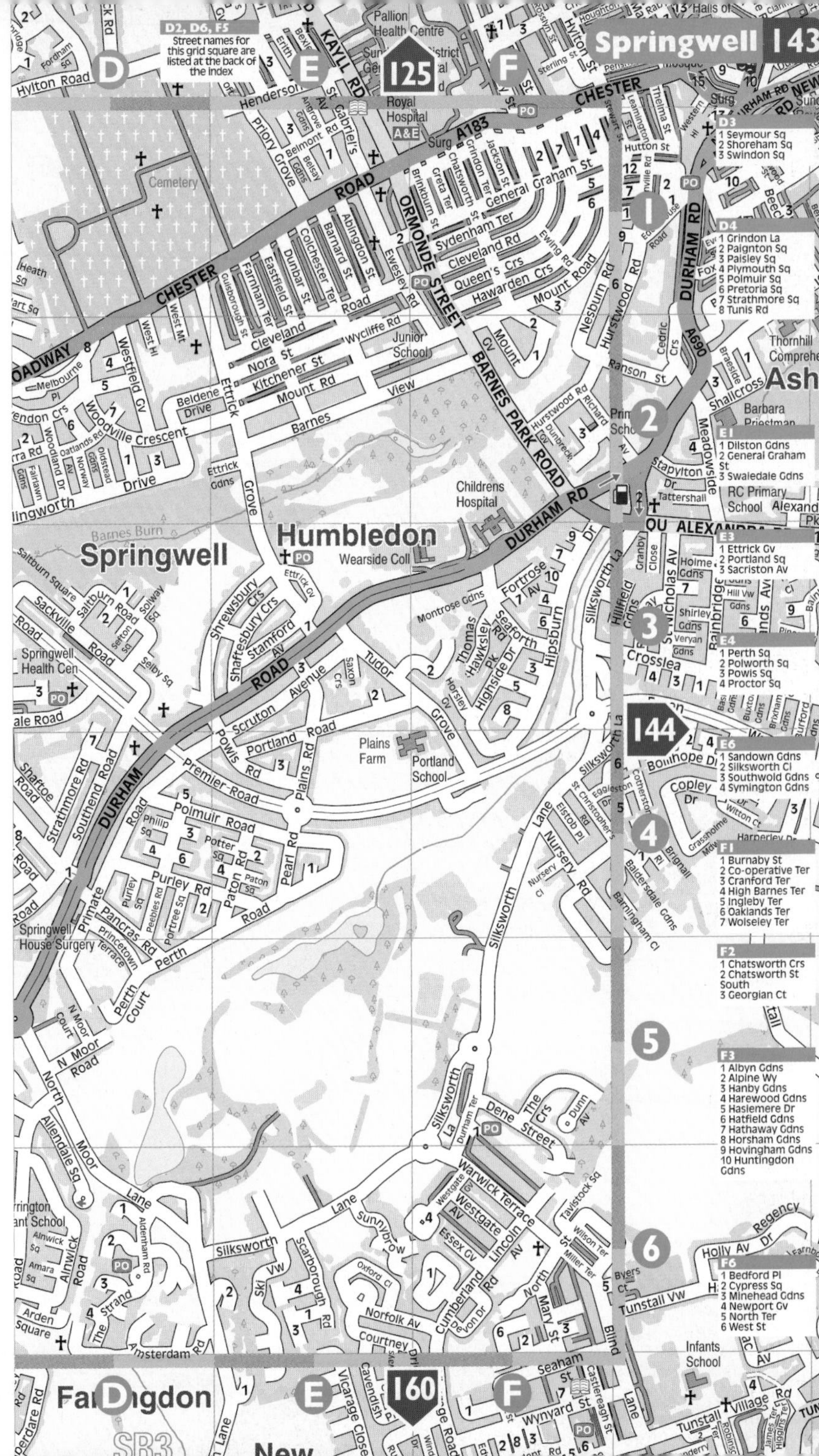
D2, D6, F5
Street names for this grid square are listed at the back of the index
125
144
160
D3
1 Seymour Sq
2 Shoreham Sq
3 Swindon Sq
D4
1 Grindon La
2 Paignton Sq
3 Paisley Sq
4 Plymouth Sq
5 Polmuir Sq
6 Pretoria Sq
7 Strathmore Sq
8 Tunis Rd
E1
1 Dilston Gdns
2 General Graham St
3 Swaledale Gdns
E3
1 Ettrick Gv
2 Portland Sq
3 Sacriston Av
E4
1 Perth Sq
2 Polworth Sq
3 Powis Sq
4 Proctor Sq
E6
1 Sandown Gdns
2 Silksworth Cl
3 Southwold Gdns
4 Symington Gdns
F1
1 Burnaby St
2 Co-operative Ter
3 Cranford Ter
4 High Barnes Ter
5 Ingleby Ter
6 Oaklands Ter
7 Wolseley Ter
F2
1 Chatsworth Crs
2 Chatsworth St South
3 Georgian Ct
F3
1 Albyn Gdns
2 Alpine Wy
3 Hanby Gdns
4 Harewood Gdns
5 Haslemere Dr
6 Hatfield Gdns
7 Hathaway Gdns
8 Horsham Gdns
9 Hovingham Gdns
10 Huntingdon Gdns
F6
1 Bedford Pl
2 Cypress Sq
3 Minehead Gdns
4 Newport Gv
5 North Ter
6 West St
Springwell
Humbledon
Farringdon
Cemetery
Royal Hospital
Pallion Health Centre
Childrens Hospital
Wearside Coll
Plains Farm
Portland School
Junior School
Thornhill Comprehensive
Barbara Priestman
RC Primary School
Springwell Health Cen
Springwell House Surgery
Infants School
Chester Road
Durham Road
Barnes Park Road
Ormonde Street
Silksworth Lane
North Moor Road
Hylton Road
Kayll Rd
A183
A690
SR3

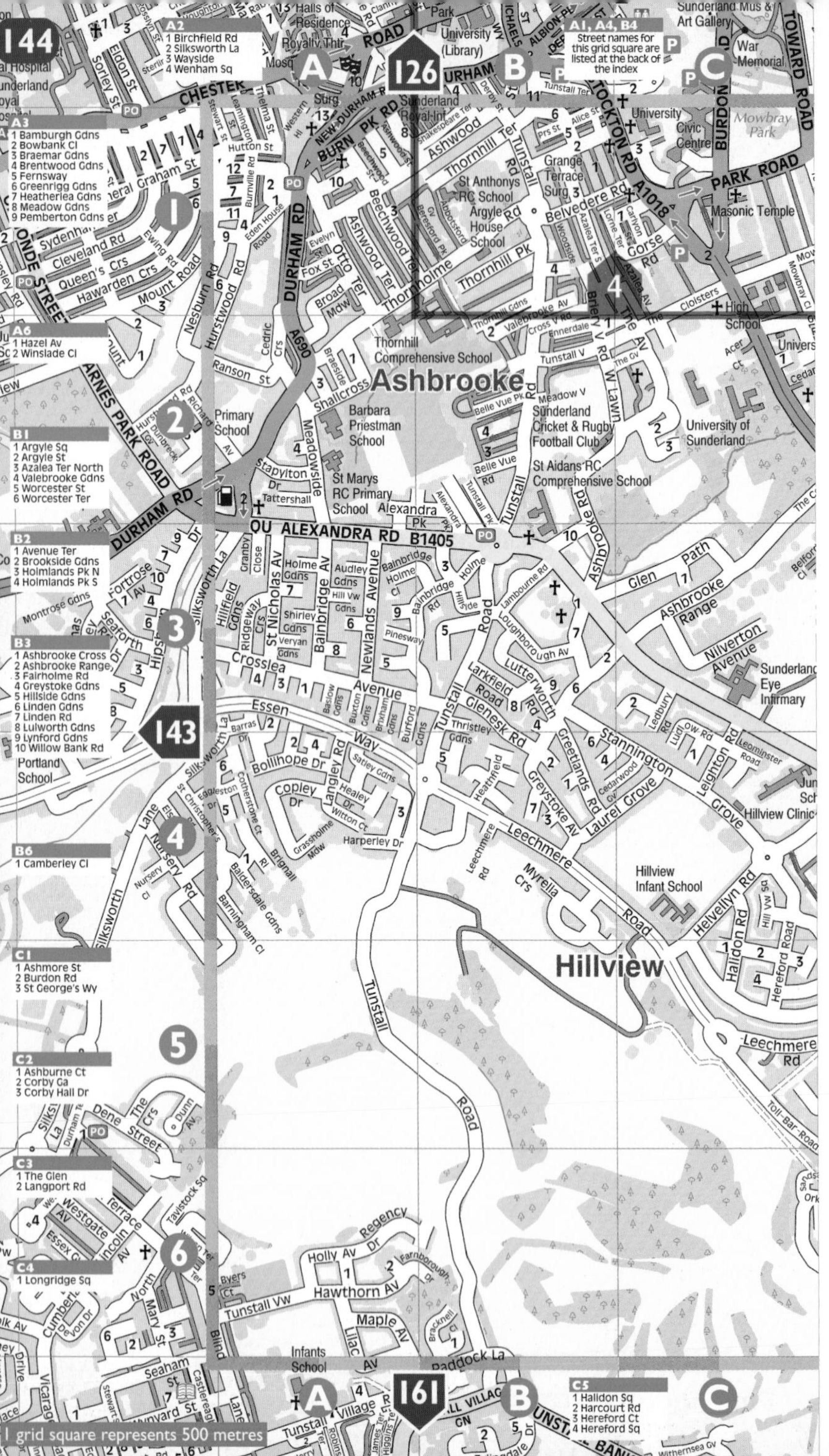
A2
1 Birchfield Rd
2 Silksworth La
3 Wayside
4 Wenham Sq
A1, A4, B4
Street names for this grid square are listed at the back of the index
A3
1 Bamburgh Gdns
2 Bowbank Cl
3 Braemar Gdns
4 Brentwood Gdns
5 Fernsway
6 Greenrigg Gdns
7 Heatherlea Gdns
8 Meadow Gdns
9 Pemberton Gdns
A6
1 Hazel Av
2 Winslade Cl
B1
1 Argyle Sq
2 Argyle St
3 Azalea Ter North
4 Valebrooke Gdns
5 Worcester St
6 Worcester Ter
B2
1 Avenue Ter
2 Brookside Gdns
3 Holmlands Pk N
4 Holmlands Pk S
B3
1 Ashbrooke Cross
2 Ashbrooke Range
3 Fairholme Rd
4 Greystoke Gdns
5 Hillside Gdns
6 Linden Gdns
7 Linden Rd
8 Lulworth Gdns
9 Lynford Gdns
10 Willow Bank Rd
B6
1 Camberley Cl
C1
1 Ashmore St
2 Burdon Rd
3 St George's Wy
C2
1 Ashburne Ct
2 Corby Ga
3 Corby Hall Dr
C3
1 The Glen
2 Langport Rd
C4
1 Longridge Sq
C5
1 Halldon Sq
2 Harcourt Rd
3 Hereford Ct
4 Hereford Sq
126
143
161
Ashbrooke
Hillview
Sunderland Royal Hospital
Sunderland Mus & Art Gallery
War Memorial
University (Library)
Sunderland Royal Inf
Mowbray Park
University
Civic Centre
Masonic Temple
St Anthonys RC School
Argyle House School
Grange Terrace Surg
Thornhill Comprehensive School
Barbara Priestman School
St Marys RC Primary School
Primary School
Sunderland Cricket & Rugby Football Club
St Aidans RC Comprehensive School
University of Sunderland
Sunderland Eye Infirmary
Hillview Clinic
Hillview Infant School
Portland School
Infants School
High School
CHESTER ROAD
DURHAM ROAD
DURHAM RD
A690
BURN PK RD
NEW DURHAM RD
STOCKTON RD A1018
PARK ROAD
TOWARD ROAD
BURDON RD
QU ALEXANDRA RD B1405
BARNES PARK ROAD
Tunstall Rd
Ashwood
Thornhill Ter
Thornhill Pk
Thornholme
Belvedere Rd
Gorse Rd
Cloisters
Ashbrooke Rd
Glen Path
Ashbrooke Range
Nilverton Avenue
Stannington Grove
Leighton Rd
Laurel Grove
Leechmere Road
Leechmere Rd
Toll-Bar-Road
Helvellyn Rd
Halidon Rd
Hereford Road
Essen Way
Crosslea Avenue
Bollihope Dr
Copley Dr
Tunstall Road
Hawthorn Av
Holly Av
Regency Dr
Tunstall Vw
Maple Av
Paddock La
Tunstall Village
Westgate
Dene Street
Tavistock Sq
Silksworth Lane
Nursery Rd
Hurstwood Rd
Nesburn Rd
Ranson St
Meadowside
Stapylton Dr
Mount Road
Hawarden Crs
Queen's Crs
Cleveland Rd
Sydenham
1 grid square represents 500 metres

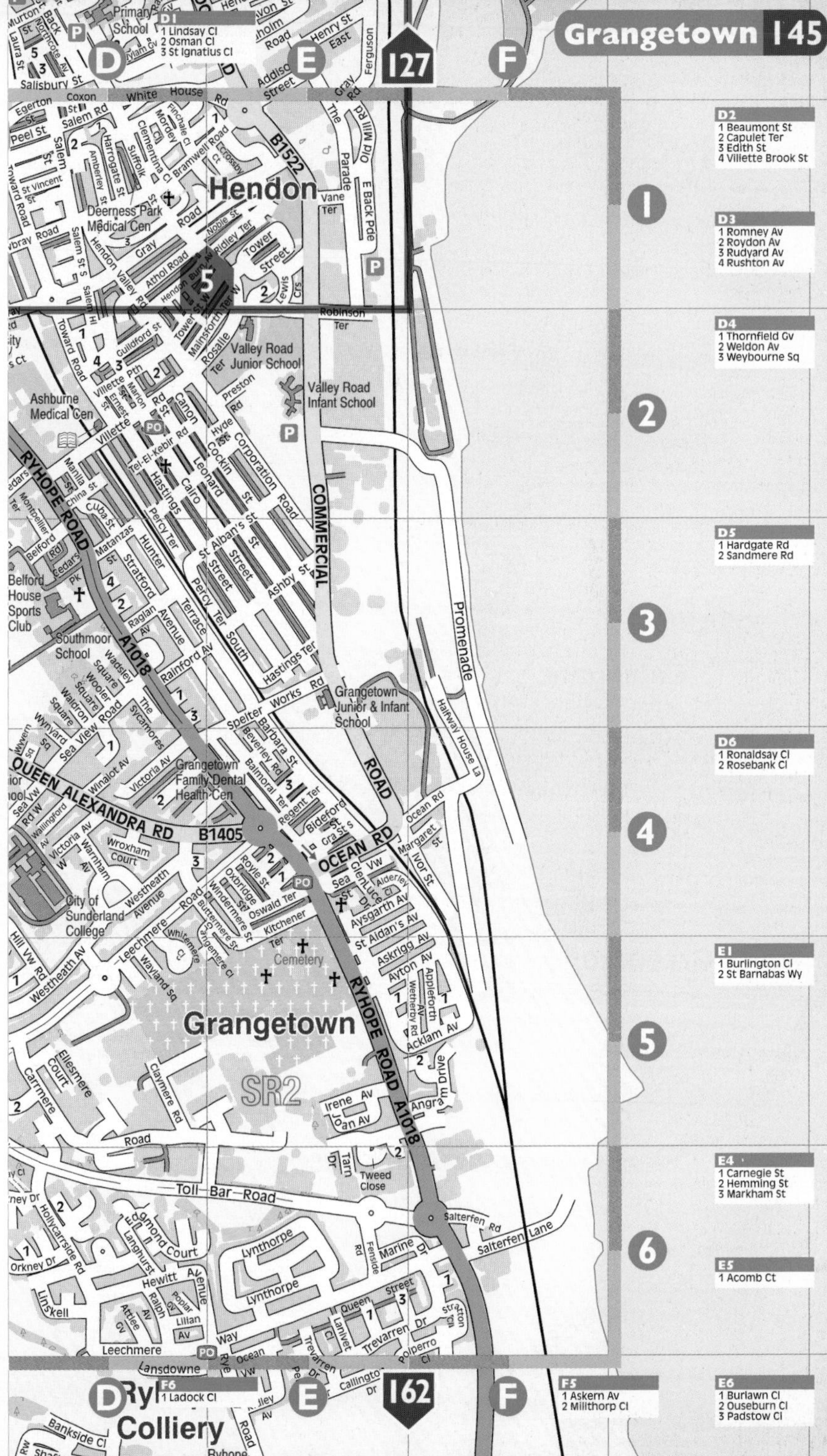
127
162
D
E
F
1
2
3
4
5
6
D1
1 Lindsay Cl
2 Osman Cl
3 St Ignatius Cl
D2
1 Beaumont St
2 Capulet Ter
3 Edith St
4 Villette Brook St
D3
1 Romney Av
2 Roydon Av
3 Rudyard Av
4 Rushton Av
D4
1 Thornfield Gv
2 Weldon Av
3 Weybourne Sq
D5
1 Hardgate Rd
2 Sandmere Rd
D6
1 Ronaldsay Cl
2 Rosebank Cl
E1
1 Burlington Cl
2 St Barnabas Wy
E4
1 Carnegie St
2 Hemming St
3 Markham St
E5
1 Acomb Ct
E6
1 Burlawn Cl
2 Ouseburn Cl
3 Padstow Cl
F5
1 Askern Av
2 Millthorp Cl
F6
1 Ladock Cl
Hendon
Grangetown
SR2
Ryhope Colliery
Primary School
Deerness Park Medical Cen
Valley Road Junior School
Valley Road Infant School
Ashburne Medical Cen
Belford House Sports Club
Southmoor School
Grangetown Junior & Infant School
Grangetown Family Dental Health Cen
City of Sunderland College
Cemetery
Promenade
RYHOPE ROAD
A1018
COMMERCIAL ROAD
QUEEN ALEXANDRA RD
B1405
B1522
OCEAN RD
Toll Bar Road
Salterfen Rd
Salterfen Lane
White House Rd
Coxon St
Robinson Ter
Spelter Works Rd
Halfway House La
Corporation Road
Villette Rd
Salisbury St
Toward Road
Hendon Valley Rd
Gray Road
Athol Road
Tower Street
Ocean Rd
Ivor St
Margaret St
Westheath Avenue
Leechmere Rd
Lansdowne
Ryhope

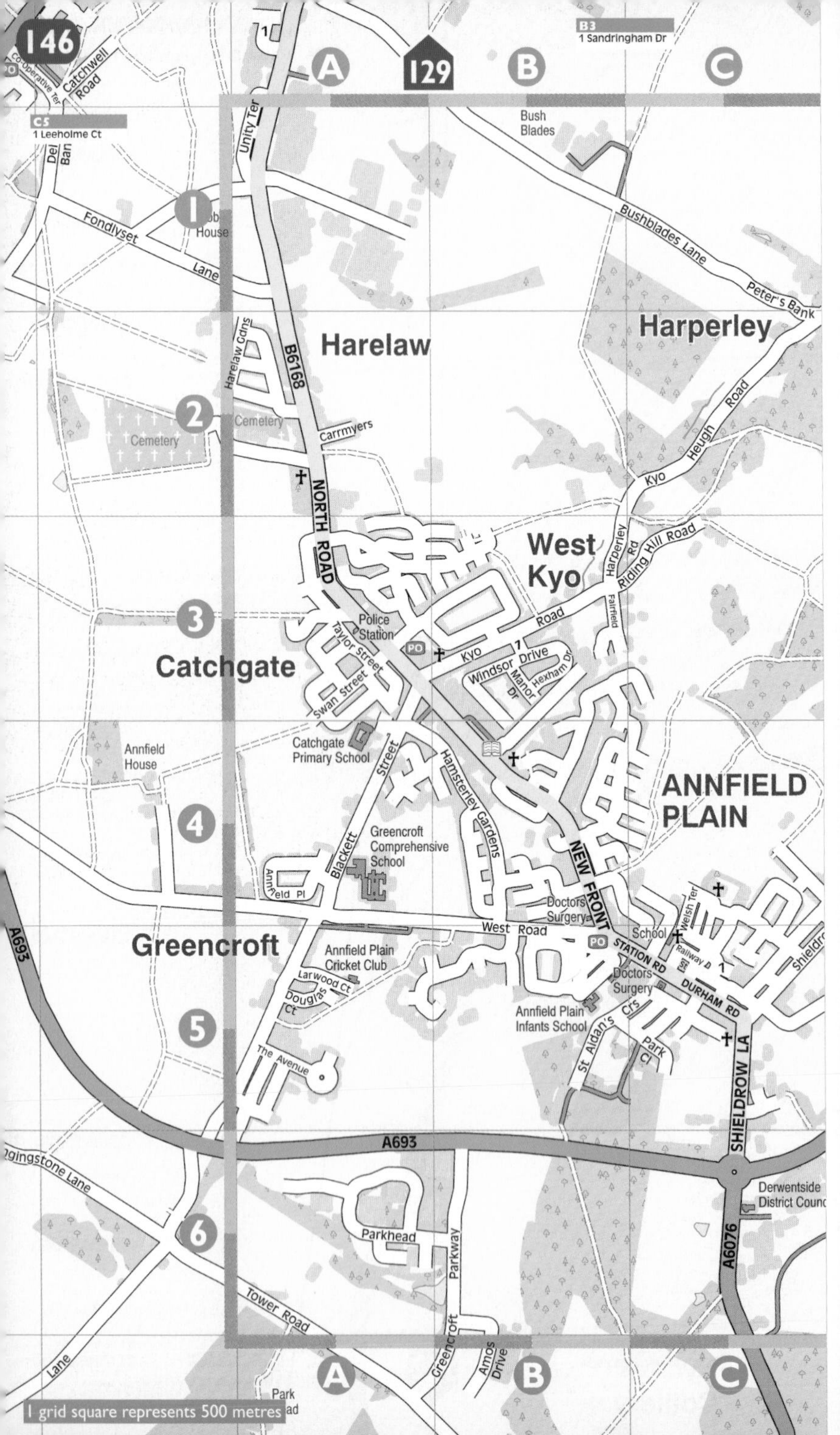
129
A
B
C
1
2
3
4
5
6
B3
1 Sandringham Dr
C5
1 Leeholme Ct
Co-operative Ter
Catchwell Road
Unity Ter
Bush Blades
Bushblades Lane
Peter's Bank
Harperley
Harelaw
Fondlyset Lane
House
Harelaw Gdns
B6168
Cemetery
Cemetery
Carrmyers
Heugh Road
Kyo
NORTH ROAD
West Kyo
Harperley Rd
Riding Hill Road
Fairfield
Police Station
Taylor Street
PO
Kyo Road
Windsor Drive
Manor Dr
Hexham Dr
Catchgate
Swan Street
Catchgate Primary School
Annfield House
Street
Hamsterley Gardens
ANNFIELD PLAIN
Greencroft Comprehensive School
Blackett
Annfield Pl
NEW FRONT
Doctors Surgery
West Road
Greencroft
Annfield Plain Cricket Club
School
Welsh Ter
STATION RD
Railway
DURHAM RD
Doctors Surgery
Larwood Ct
Douglas Ct
Annfield Plain Infants School
St Aidan's Crs
Park Cl
SHIELDROW LA
The Avenue
A693
A693
Tower Road
Parkhead
Parkway
Derwentside District Counc
A6076
Greencroft
Amos Drive
Lane
Park
I grid square represents 500 metres

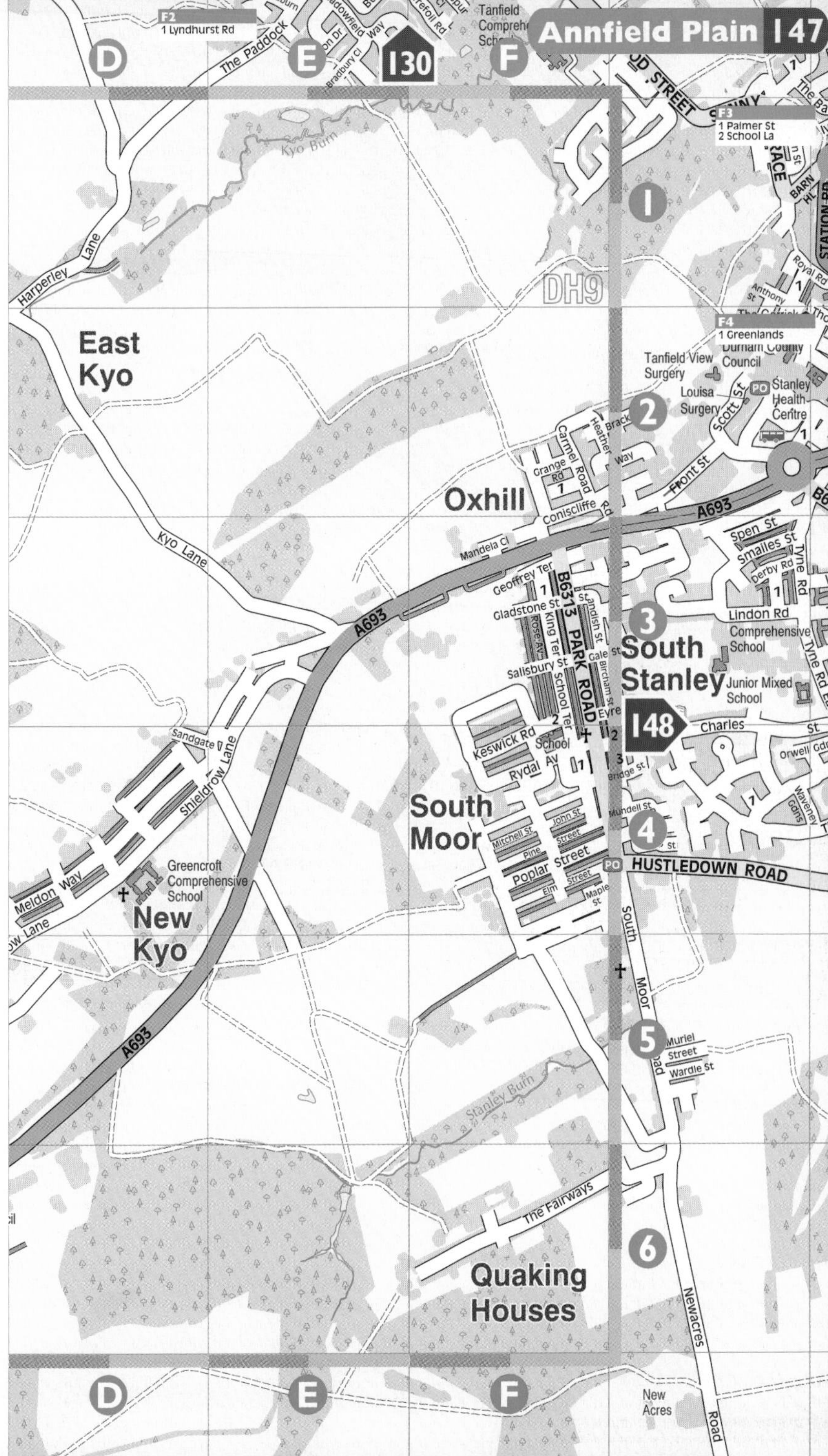

F2
1 Lyndhurst Rd
The Paddock
Bradbury Cl
130
Tanfield Comprehensive School
D
E
F
F3
1 Palmer St
2 School La
STATION RD
BARN HL
Royal Rd
Anthony St
Kyo Burn
1
DH9
Harperley Lane
East Kyo
F4
1 Greenlands
Tanfield View Surgery
Durham County Council
Louisa Surgery
Scott St
PO
Stanley Health Centre
2
Heather Way
Carmel Road
Grange Rd
Front St
Oxhill
Conscliffe Rd
A693
B6532
Kyo Lane
Mandela Cl
Spen St
Smailes St
Derby Rd
Tyne Rd
Geoffrey Ter
B6313
Gladstone St
Rose Av
King Ter
PARK ROAD
Standish St
3
Lindon Rd
Comprehensive School
South Stanley
Junior Mixed School
Tyne Rd East
Salisbury St
School Ter
Gale St
Bircham St
Eyre
148
Charles St
Orwell Gdns
Keswick Rd
School
Rydal Av
Bridge St
Sandgate
Shieldrow Lane
Mundell St
4
John St
Street
South Moor
Mitchell St
Pine
Poplar Street
HUSTLEDOWN ROAD
Elm Street
Maple St
Waveney Gdns
Meldon Way
Greencroft Comprehensive School
New Kyo
South Moor Road
5
Muriel Street
Wardle St
Stanley Burn
The Fairways
6
Quaking Houses
Newacres Road
New Acres

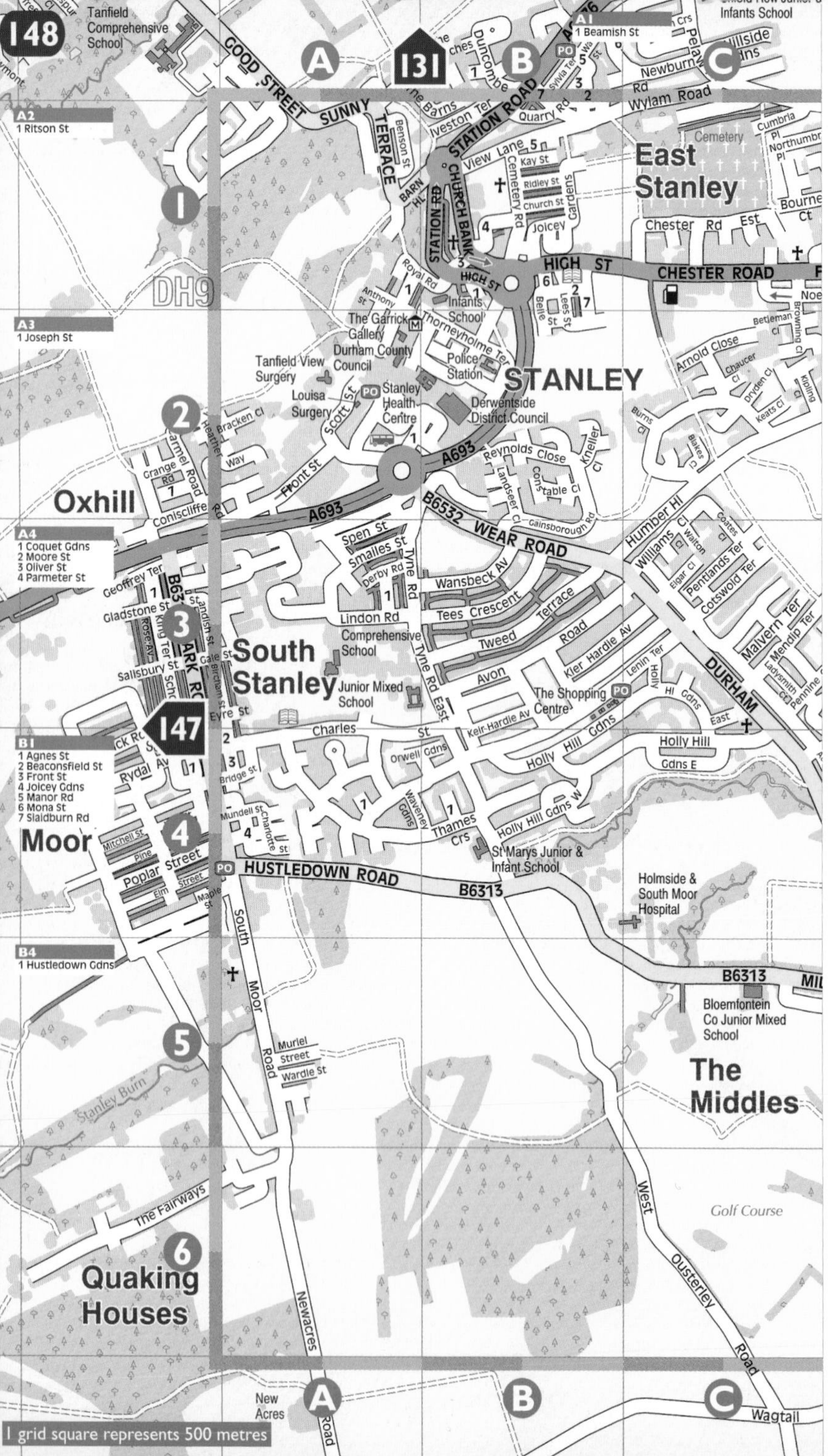

148
Tanfield Comprehensive School
A
131
B
C
A1
1 Beamish St
Infants School
Hillside Gdns
Newburn Rd
Wylam Road
Duncombe
STATION ROAD
GOOD STREET
SUNNY TERRACE
Benson St
Weston Ter
Quarry Rd
Sylvia Ter
A2
1 Ritson St
East Stanley
Cemetery
Cumbria Pl
Northumbria Pl
Bourne Ct
View Lane
Kay St
Ridley St
Church St
Cemetery Rd
Gardens
Joicey
Chester Rd
Est
STATION RD
CHURCH BANK
BARN HL
1
I
DH9
HIGH ST
CHESTER ROAD
Royal Rd
Anthony St
Infants School
Belle St
Lees St
Noel
Betjeman Cl
Browning Cl
A3
1 Joseph St
The Garrick Gallery
Durham County Council
Thorneyholme Ter
Police Station
STANLEY
Arnold Close
Chaucer Cl
Dryden Cl
Keats Cl
Kipling
Tanfield View Surgery
Louisa Surgery
Scott St
Stanley Health Centre
Derwentside District Council
Burns Cl
Blakes Cl
2
Heather Way
Bracken Cl
Carmel Road
Grange Rd
Oxhill
Coniscliffe Rd
Front St
A693
Reynolds Close
Kneller Cl
Landseer Cl
Constable Cl
Gainsborough Rd
Humber Hl
Williams Cl
Walton Cl
Elgar Cl
Coates Cl
Pentlands Ter
Cotswold Ter
A4
1 Coquet Gdns
2 Moore St
3 Oliver St
4 Parmeter St
B6532 WEAR ROAD
Spen St
Smailes St
Derby Rd
Tyne Rd
Wansbeck Av
Tees Crescent
Terrace
Tweed
Road
Kier Hardie Av
Lenin Ter
Holly Hl
Gdns
Malvern Ter
Mendip Ter
Ladysmith Cl
Pennine
Geoffrey Ter
Gladstone St
King Ter
Rose Av
Standish St
3
Salisbury St
Gale St
Bircham St
South Stanley
Lindon Rd
Comprehensive School
Junior Mixed School
Tyne Rd East
Avon
The Shopping Centre
DURHAM
East
147
Eyre St
Charles St
Keir-Hardie Av
Holly Hill Gdns
Holly Hill
Gdns E
B1
1 Agnes St
2 Beaconsfield St
3 Front St
4 Joicey Gdns
5 Manor Rd
6 Mona St
7 Slaidburn Rd
Rydal Av
Bridge St
Orwell Gdns
Waveney Gdns
Thames Crs
Holly Hill Gdns W
Moor
Mitchell St
Pine
Poplar Street
Elm Street
Maple St
4
Mundell St
Charlotte St
HUSTLEDOWN ROAD
B6313
St Marys Junior & Infant School
Holmside & South Moor Hospital
B4
1 Hustledown Gdns
South Moor Road
Muriel Street
Wardle St
5
Stanley Burn
B6313
Bloemfontein Co Junior Mixed School
The Middles
West Ousterley Road
Golf Course
The Fairways
6
Quaking Houses
Newacres Road
New Acres
Wagtail
1 grid square represents 500 metres

Stanley 149
D1
1 St Aubyn's Wy
Shiel D ow
E
132
F
A693
Beamish County School
Beamish
D3
1 Pankhurst Pl
Bourne Ct
East St
Gibside Cl
St Hellers Wy
Strathmore Cl
Beamish Vw
Alda Cl
Broom Cl
Co-operative Villas
Roseberry St
John Street
Gladstone St
Beamish Hills
HILL TOP
FRONT ST
PO
Ruskin Cl
Masefield Cl
Thorntree Ter
Acton Dene
Milton Cl
Aberfoyle Ct
Spencer Cl
Ballater Cl
Colville Ct
Kinross Dr
Brentwood Ct
Gullane Cl
Harwick Ct
Hawick Ct
Elgin Gv
Girvan Cl
Forres Court
Burnside JMI School
Eden Hill Farm
Fonteyn Nightingale
Potter Pl
Bronte Pl
Twizell Lane
150
Twizell Hall
Stanley Wood
Stanley Burn
ROAD
B6532
Woodside Gardens
Twizell Burn
ROAD
PO
Oak Terrace
Dr Dhuny's Surgery
Hazel Ter
Palm Ter
Beech Ter
CRAGHEAD
Front St
B6313
Thomas St
Thomas St
John St
EDWARD ST
Wagtail Lane
Wylam St
Railway St
Ousterley
Craghead
Ousterley Ter
Wagtail Ter
LOWERY
Lane
D
E
F
White House Farm
Humbleburn
1
2
3
4
5
6

150
133
149
A
B
C
1
2
3
4
5
6
Station Road
Peggy's Wicket
Stone Lane
High Handen
A693
Beamish County School
Beamish
Roseberry St
John Street
Gladstone St
Beamish Hills
-operative
las
New Road
Sydney S
Arthur
West Pelton
Edenfield
Green's Bank
PO
Summerfield
Plantation View
County Junior Middle & Infant School
Orchard Cl
Eden Hill Farm
Twizell Lane
Gran
Villa
Stone Row
West street
Albert St
Queen St
Pine St
Twizell Hall
Newbridge Banks
Twizell Burn
BLUEHOUSE BANK
LANE
CRAGHEAD
B6313
Thomas St
John St
White Hall Farm
Craghead
LOWERY LANE
Lane
Humbleburn
White House Fa
1 grid square represents 500 metres

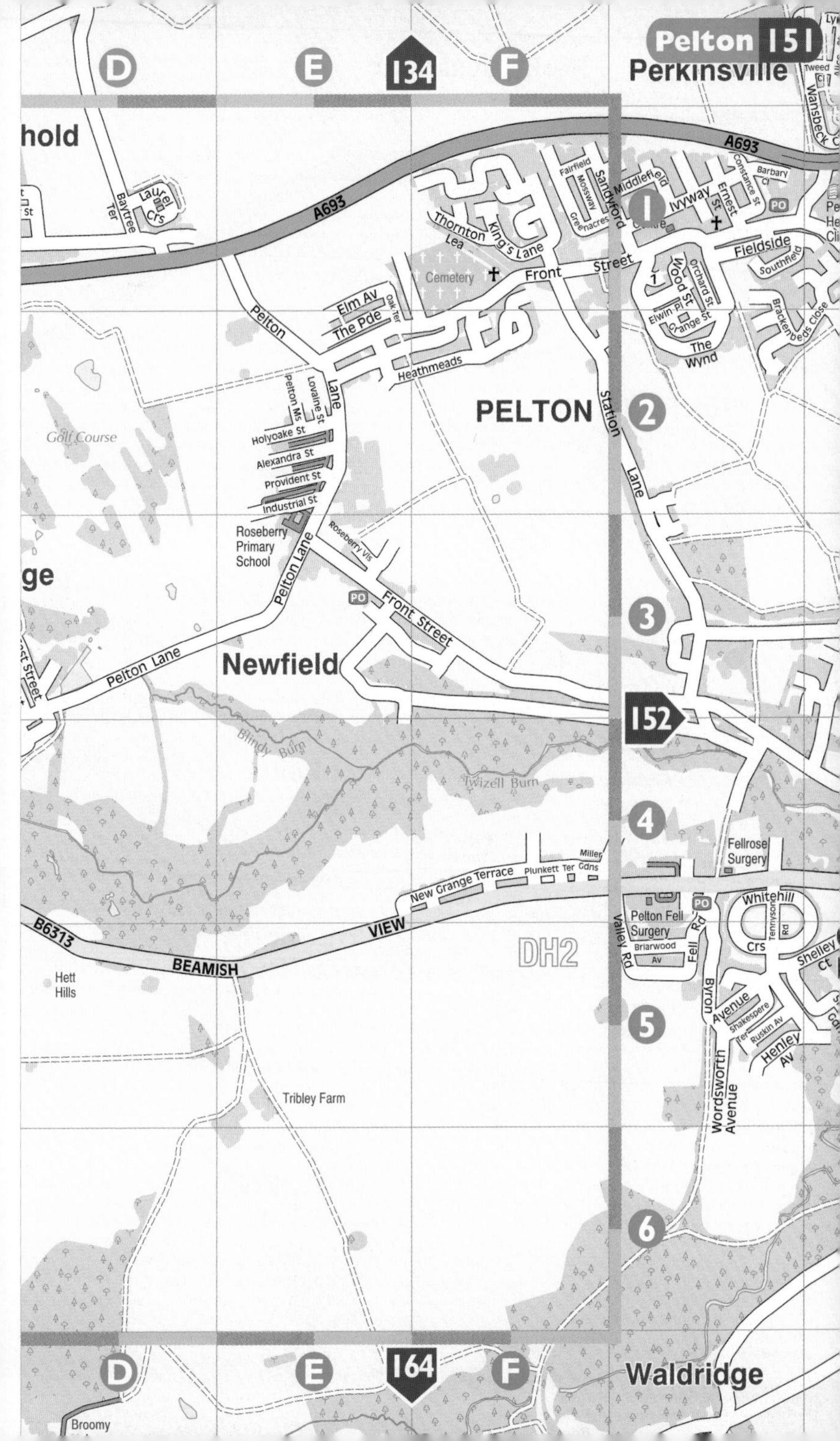

D
E
134
F
Perkinsville
hold
A693
Laurel Crs
Baytree Ter
Fairfield
Mossway
Sandyford
Middlefield
Greenacres
Ivyway
Ernest St
Constance St
Barbary Cl
PO
Thornton Lea
King's Lane
Centre
Fieldside
Southfield
Cemetery
Front Street
Wood St
Orchard St
Elwin Pl
Grange St
The Wynd
Brackenbeds Close
Elm Av
Oak Ter
The Pde
Pelton Lane
Heathmeads
Pelton Ms
Lovaine St
PELTON
Station Lane
Golf Course
Holyoake St
Alexandra St
Provident St
Industrial St
Roseberry Primary School
Roseberry Vls
ge
PO
Front Street
Pelton Lane
Newfield
152
Blindy Burn
Twizell Burn
Fellrose Surgery
Miller Gdns
Plunkett Ter
New Grange Terrace
Whitehill Crs
Tennyson Rd
B6313
VIEW
BEAMISH
Pelton Fell Surgery
Briarwood Av
Valley Rd
Fell Rd
DH2
Shelley Ct
Hett Hills
Byron Avenue
Shakespere Ter
Ruskin Av
Henley Av
Wordsworth Avenue
Tribley Farm
D
E
164
F
Waldridge
Broomy

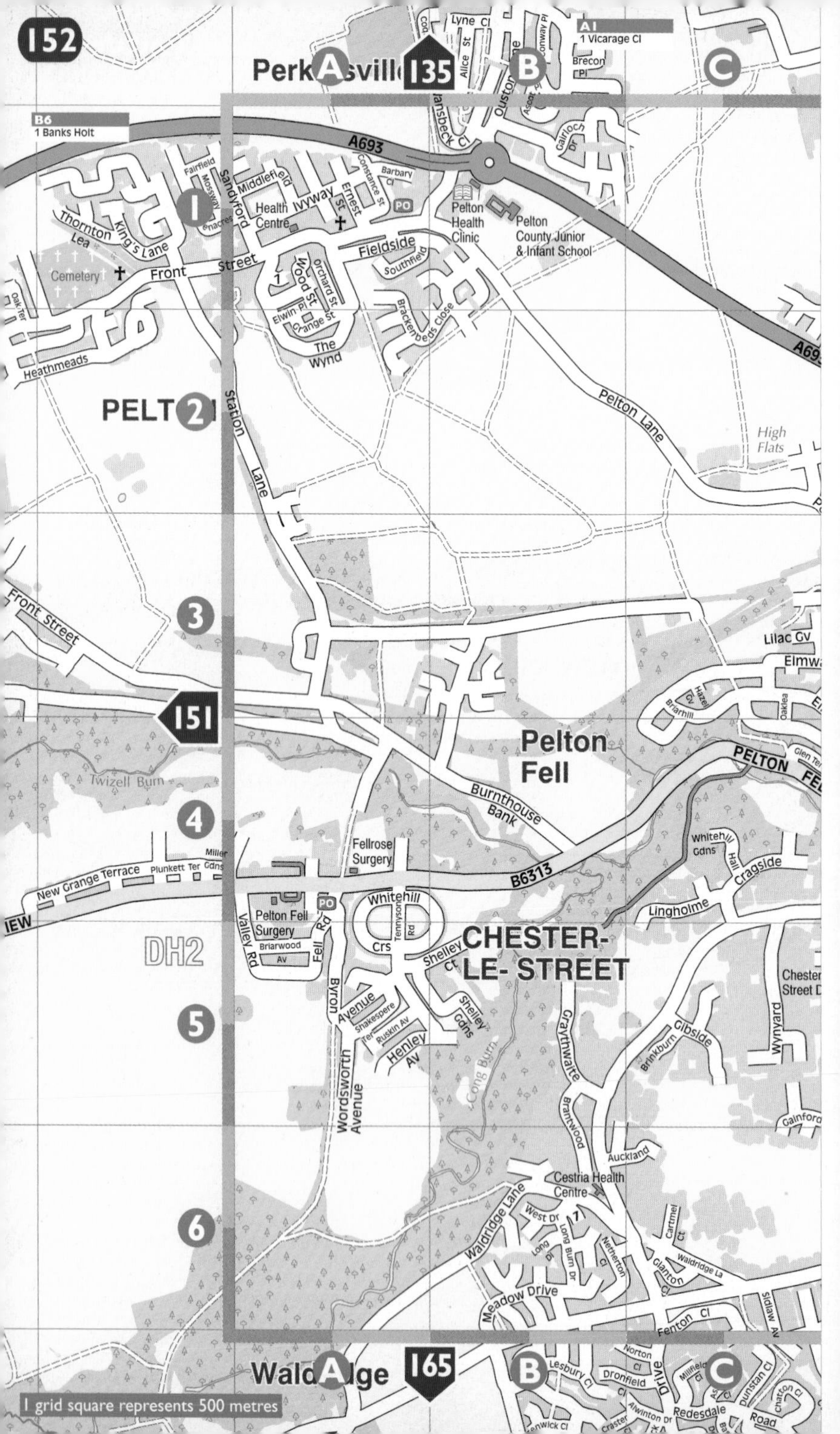

Perkinsville
135
A1
1 Vicarage Cl
B6
1 Banks Holt
A693
Pelton Health Clinic
Pelton County Junior & Infant School
Health Centre
Cemetery
PELTON
Station Lane
Pelton Lane
High Flats
Front Street
151
Twizell Burn
Pelton Fell
Burnthouse Bank
PELTON FELL
Fellrose Surgery
Pelton Fell Surgery
B6313
New Grange Terrace
CHESTER-LE-STREET
DH2
Whitehill Crs
Wordsworth Avenue
Cong Burn
Cestria Health Centre
Waldridge Lane
Meadow Drive
Waldridge
165
1 grid square represents 500 metres

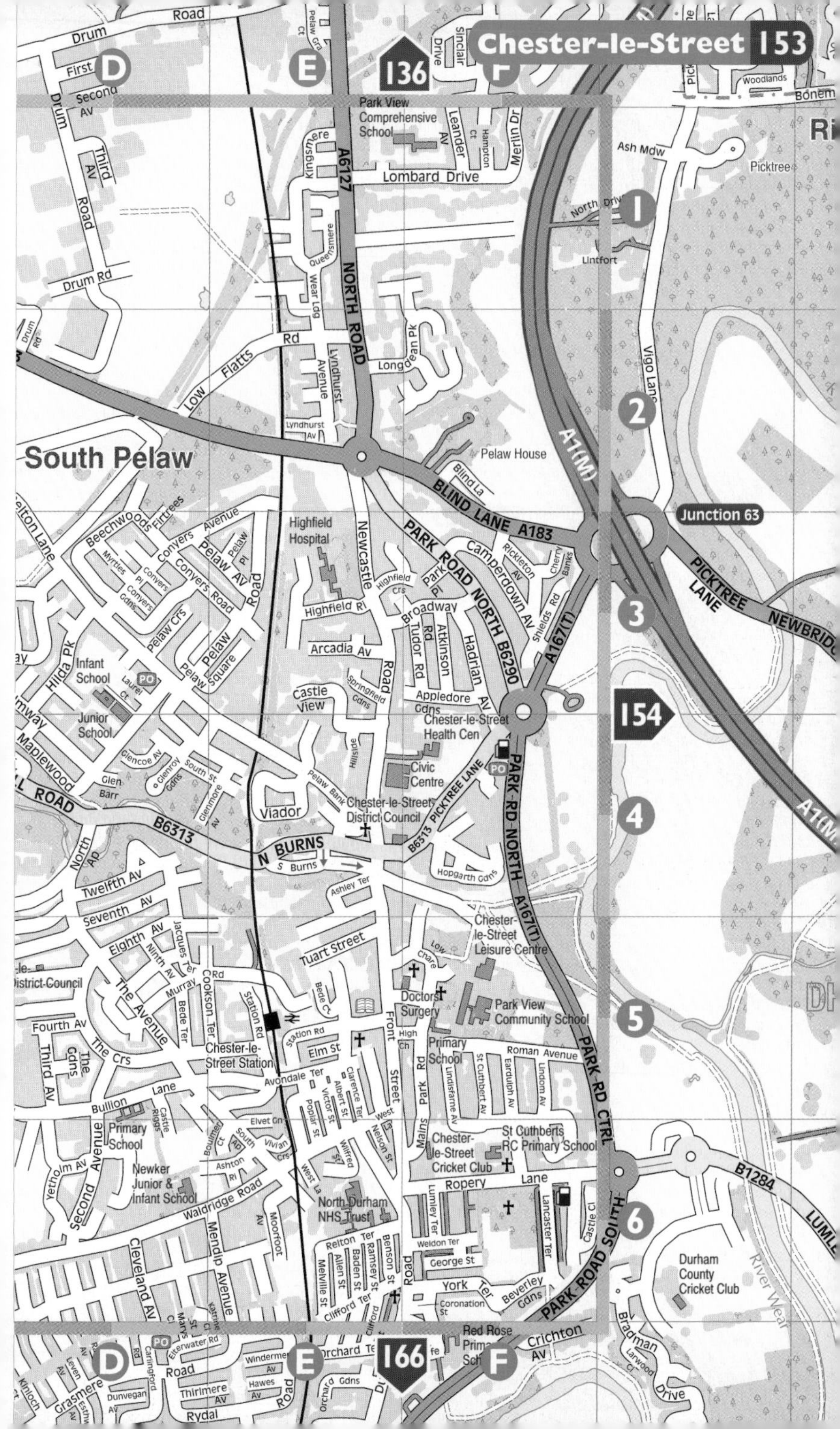

South Pelaw
Junction 63
A1(M)
NORTH ROAD
A6127
BLIND LANE A183
PARK ROAD NORTH B6290
PICKTREE LANE
B6313
N BURNS
PARK RD NORTH A167(T)
PARK RD CTRL
PARK ROAD SOUTH
B1284
Highfield Hospital
Park View Comprehensive School
Pelaw House
Chester-le-Street Health Cen
Civic Centre
Chester-le-Street District Council
Chester-le-Street Leisure Centre
Park View Community School
Chester-le-Street Station
Chester-le-Street Cricket Club
St Cuthberts RC Primary School
North Durham NHS Trust
Newker Junior & Infant School
Durham County Cricket Club
River Wear
Picktree
Lintfort
136
154
166

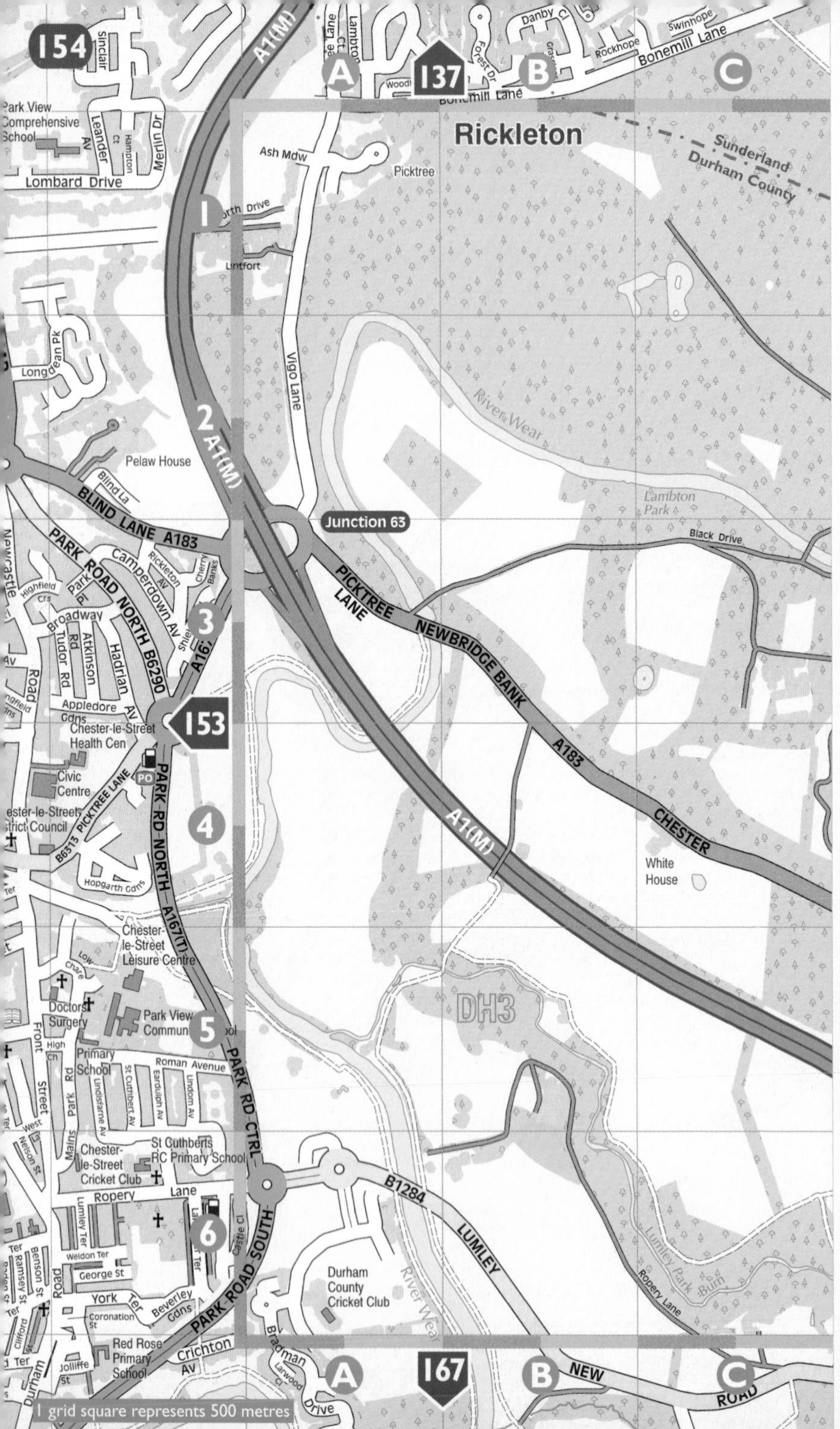

154
137
A
B
C
Rickleton
Sunderland
Durham County
Park View Comprehensive School
Lombard Drive
Pelaw House
Picktree
Ash Mdw
Lintfort
Vigo Lane
River Wear
Lambton Park
Black Drive
Junction 63
A1(M)
BLIND LANE A183
PARK ROAD NORTH B6290
PICKTREE LANE
NEWBRIDGE BANK
A183
CHESTER
White House
153
Chester-le-Street Health Cen
Civic Centre
B6313 PICKTREE LANE
PARK RD NORTH A167(T)
Chester-le-Street Leisure Centre
Doctors Surgery
Park View Community School
Primary School
Roman Avenue
PARK RD CTRL
Chester-le-Street Cricket Club
St Cuthberts RC Primary School
Ropery Lane
B1284
LUMLEY
PARK ROAD SOUTH
Durham County Cricket Club
DH3
Lumley Park Burn
Ropery Lane
Red Rose Primary School
Crichton Av
167
NEW ROAD
1
2
3
4
5
6
1 grid square represents 500 metres

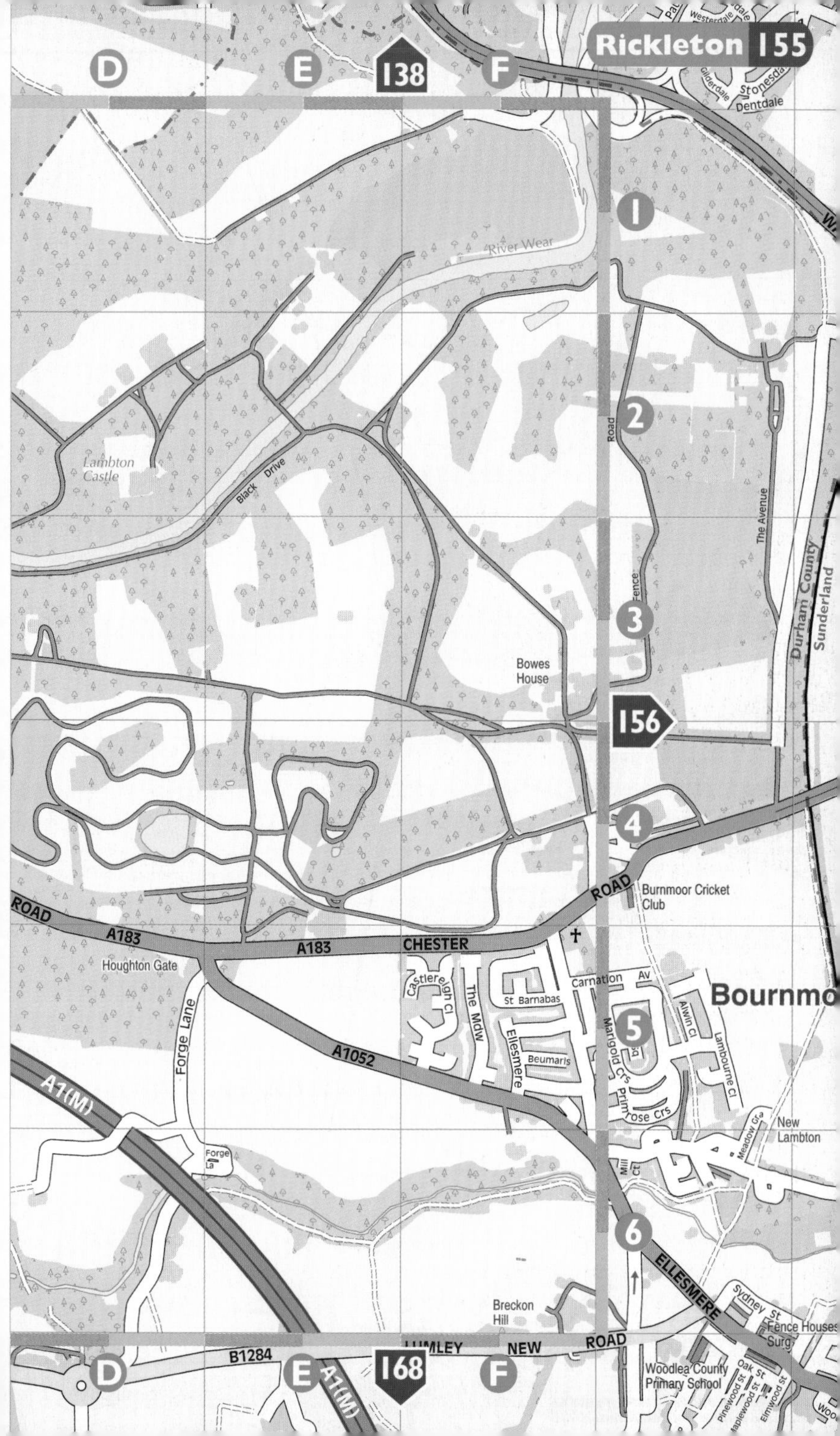

D
E
138
F
Westerdale
Gilderdale
Stonesdale
Dentdale
1
River Wear
Lambton Castle
Black Drive
Road
2
The Avenue
Durham County
Sunderland
Fence
3
Bowes House
156
4
ROAD
Burnmoor Cricket Club
ROAD
A183
A183
CHESTER
Houghton Gate
Castlereagh Cl
The Mdw
St Barnabas
Carnation Av
Bournmo
Forge Lane
Ellesmere
Marigold Crs
5
Alwin Cl
Lambourne Cl
A1052
Beumaris
Primrose Crs
A1(M)
New Lambton
Meadow Gra
Forge La
Mill Ct
6
ELLESMERE
Breckon Hill
Sydney St
Fence Houses Surg
B1284
LUMLEY
NEW
ROAD
D
E
A1(M)
168
F
Woodlea County Primary School
Oak St
Pinewood St
Maplewood St
Elmwood St

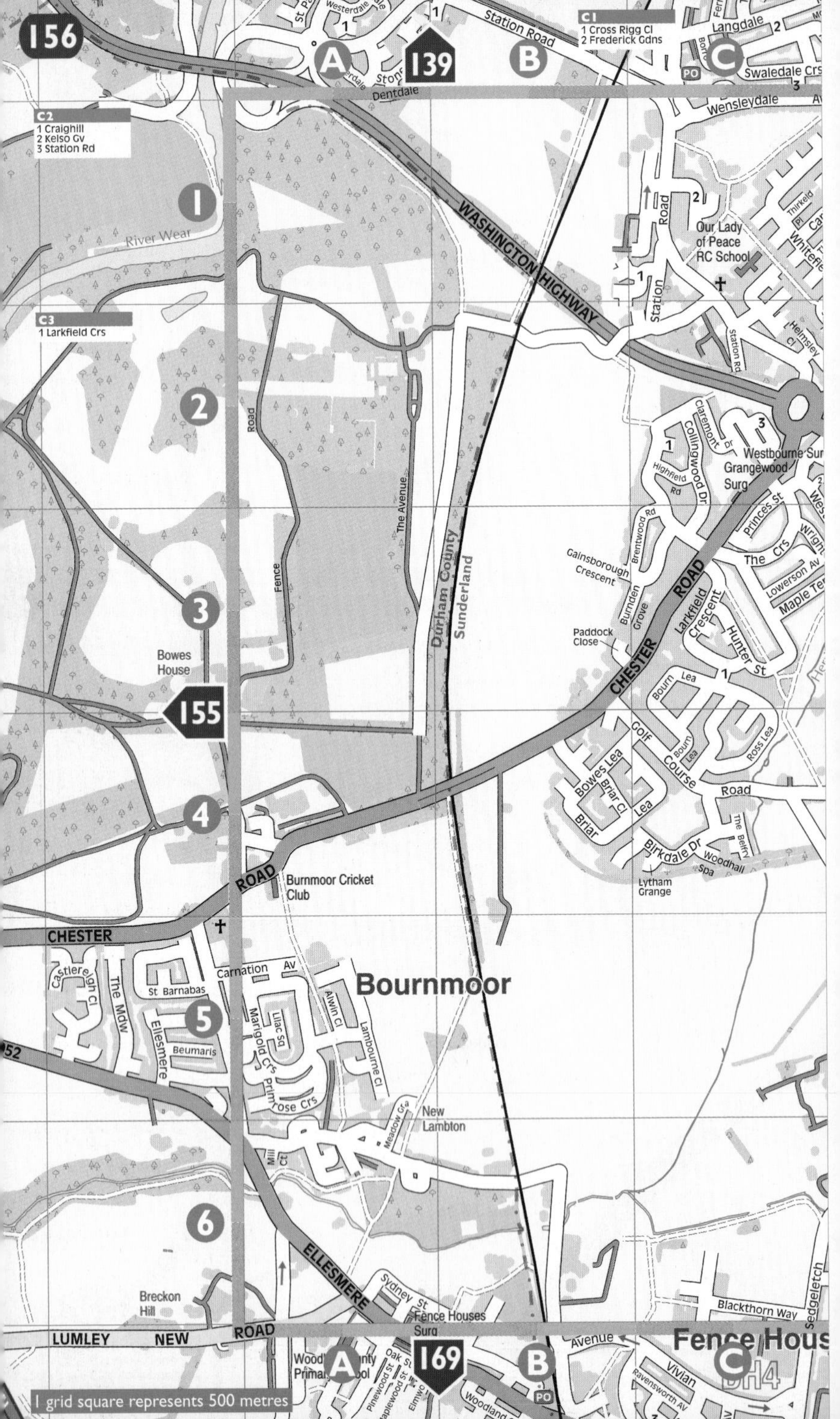

A
B
C
139
Station Road
C1
1 Cross Rigg Cl
2 Frederick Gdns
Langdale
Swaledale Crs
Wensleydale
Dentdale
C2
1 Craighill
2 Kelso Gv
3 Station Rd
River Wear
WASHINGTON HIGHWAY
Our Lady of Peace RC School
Station Road
C3
1 Larkfield Crs
Road
The Avenue
Fence
Durham County
Sunderland
Claremont Dr
Collingwood Dr
Highfield Rd
Westbourne Surg
Grangewood Surg
Princes St
The Crs
Brentwood Rd
Gainsborough Crescent
Burnden Grove
CHESTER ROAD
Larkfield Crescent
Hunter St
Lowerson Av
Maple Ter
Paddock Close
Bowes House
155
Bourn Lea
Golf Course Road
Ross Lea
Bowes Lea
Briar Cl
Briar Lea
Birkdale Dr
Woodhall Spa
The Belfry
Lytham Grange
Burnmoor Cricket Club
CHESTER
Castlereigh Cl
The Mdw
St Barnabas
Carnation Av
Alwin Cl
Lambourne Cl
Bournmoor
Ellesmere
Beumaris
Marigold Crs
Lilac Sq
Primrose Crs
New Lambton
Meadow Gra
Mill Ct
ELLESMERE
Breckon Hill
Sydney St
Fence Houses Surg
Blackthorn Way
Sedgeletch
LUMLEY NEW ROAD
Avenue
Fence Hous
169
Vivian
Ravensworth Av
Oak St
Pinewood St
Maplewood St
Woodland
PO
DH4
1 grid square represents 500 metres

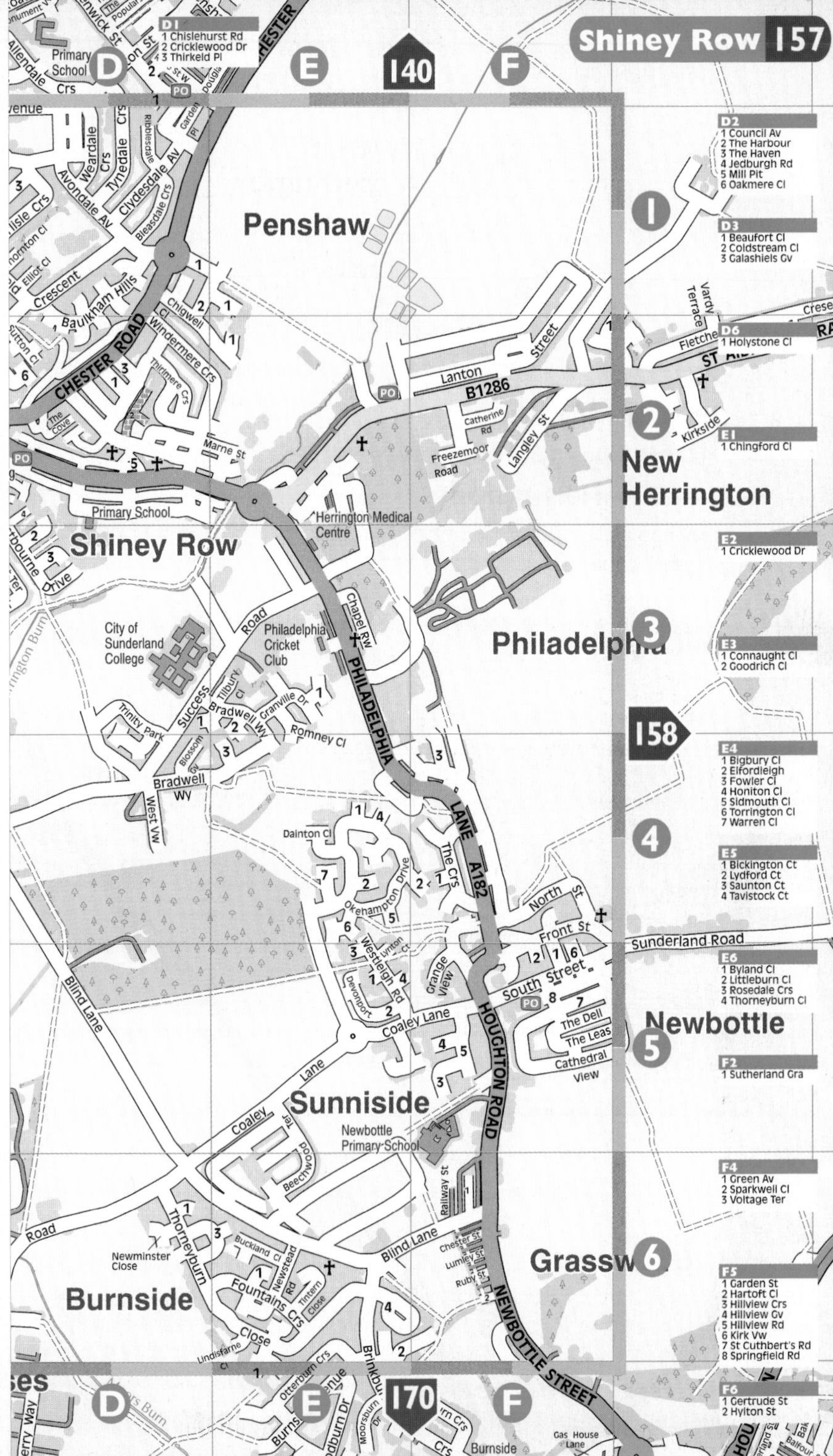
D1
1 Chislehurst Rd
2 Cricklewood Dr
3 Thirkeld Pl
D2
1 Council Av
2 The Harbour
3 The Haven
4 Jedburgh Rd
5 Mill Pit
6 Oakmere Cl
D3
1 Beaufort Cl
2 Coldstream Cl
3 Galashiels Gv
D6
1 Holystone Cl
E1
1 Chingford Cl
E2
1 Cricklewood Dr
E3
1 Connaught Cl
2 Goodrich Cl
E4
1 Bigbury Cl
2 Elfordleigh
3 Fowler Cl
4 Honiton Cl
5 Sidmouth Cl
6 Torrington Cl
7 Warren Cl
E5
1 Bickington Ct
2 Lydford Ct
3 Saunton Ct
4 Tavistock Ct
E6
1 Byland Cl
2 Littleburn Cl
3 Rosedale Crs
4 Thorneyburn Cl
F2
1 Sutherland Gra
F4
1 Green Av
2 Sparkwell Cl
3 Voltage Ter
F5
1 Garden St
2 Hartoft Cl
3 Hillview Crs
4 Hillview Gv
5 Hillview Rd
6 Kirk Vw
7 St Cuthbert's Rd
8 Springfield Rd
F6
1 Gertrude St
2 Hylton St
140
158
170
Penshaw
Shiney Row
New Herrington
Philadelphia
Newbottle
Sunniside
Burnside
Grasswell
CHESTER ROAD
B1286
PHILADELPHIA LANE
A182
HOUGHTON ROAD
NEWBOTTLE STREET
Lanton Street
Catherine Rd
Freezemoor Road
Langley St
Kirkside
Fletcher Terrace
Vardy Terrace
Herrington Medical Centre
Chapel Rw
Philadelphia Cricket Club
City of Sunderland College
Success Road
Trinity Park
Tilbury Cl
Bradwell Wy
Granville Dr
Romney Cl
Blossom
West Vw
Dainton Cl
Okehampton Drive
Lynton Ct
Westleigh Rd
Devonport
Grange View
The Crs
North St
Front St
Sunderland Road
South Street
The Dell
The Leas
Cathedral View
Coaley Lane
Blind Lane
Newbottle Primary School
Beechwood
Railway St
Chester St
Lumley St
Ruby St
Thorneyburn
Newminster Close
Buckland Cl
Newstead Rd
Fountains Crs
Tintern Close
Lindisfarne Cl
Otterburn Crs
Moorsburn Dr
Gas House Lane
Marne St
Primary School
Crescent
Baulkham Hills
Chigwell Cl
Windermere Crs
Thirlmere Crs
Avondale Av
Weardale Crs
Tynedale Crs
Clydesdale Av
Bleasdale Crs
Ribblesdale
Garden Pl
Allendale Crs
Elliot Cl
The Cove
Westbourne Drive
Sutton Cl
Road

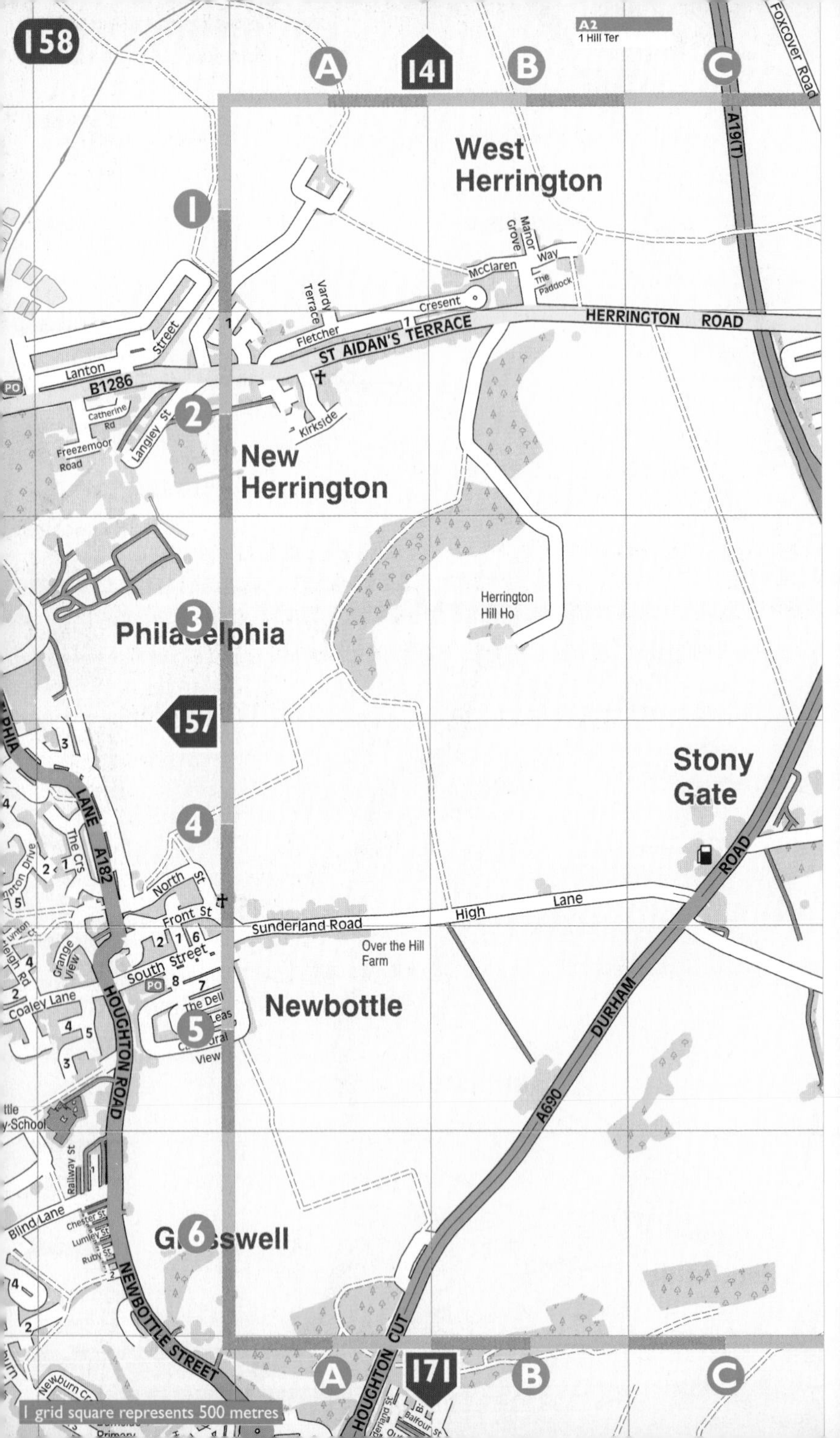

A2
1 Hill Ter
A
141
B
C
Foxcover Road
A19(T)
West Herrington
Manor Grove
Way
McClaren
The Paddock
Vardy Terrace
Cresent
Fletcher
ST AIDAN'S TERRACE
HERRINGTON ROAD
Lanton
Street
B1286
PO
Catherine Rd
Langley St
Kirkside
Freezemoor Road
New Herrington
Herrington Hill Ho
Philadelphia
157
Stony Gate
LANE
A182
The Crs
North St
Front St
Sunderland Road
High
Lane
ROAD
Over the Hill Farm
South Street
PO
The Dell
Leas
Cathedral View
Newbottle
Coaley Lane
Grange View
HOUGHTON ROAD
DURHAM
A690
Railway St
Blind Lane
Chester St
Lumley St
Ruby St
Grasswell
NEWBOTTLE STREET
HOUGHTON CUT
171
Newburn Cr
Balfour St

Middle Herrington
D1
1 St Chad's Crs
142
E1
1 Algiers Rd
2 Berkeley Cl
3 Lambton Ct
4 Lulworth Ct
5 Lumley Ct
Farri
SR3
E2
1 Braemar Gdns
East Herrington
E3
1 Grayling Ct
160
F1
1 Aldershot Rd
2 Aldershot Sq
3 Aldwych Rd
4 Allendale Rd
5 Anglesey Sq
6 Anthony Rd
7 Appleby Sq
8 Ashford Rd
9 Ashwell Rd
10 Aston Sq
11 Conway Gdns
F2
1 Maidstone Cl
2 Marbury Cl
3 Matfen Dr
4 Melsonby Cl
5 Merrington Cl
6 Merrion Cl
F3
1 Maplebeck Cl
2 Maxton Cl
3 Midsomer Cl
4 Milsted Cl
5 Minskip Cl
6 Montford Cl
Durham Road
A690
B1286
City Way
A19(T)
Silksworth Road
Doxford Pk Way
East Herrington Primary School
Farringdon School
Benedict Biscop C of E School
Low Haining
Haining
Warden Law North Farm
Hangmans Lane
Salter's
Silksworth Lane
172
D
E
F
1
2
3
4
5
6

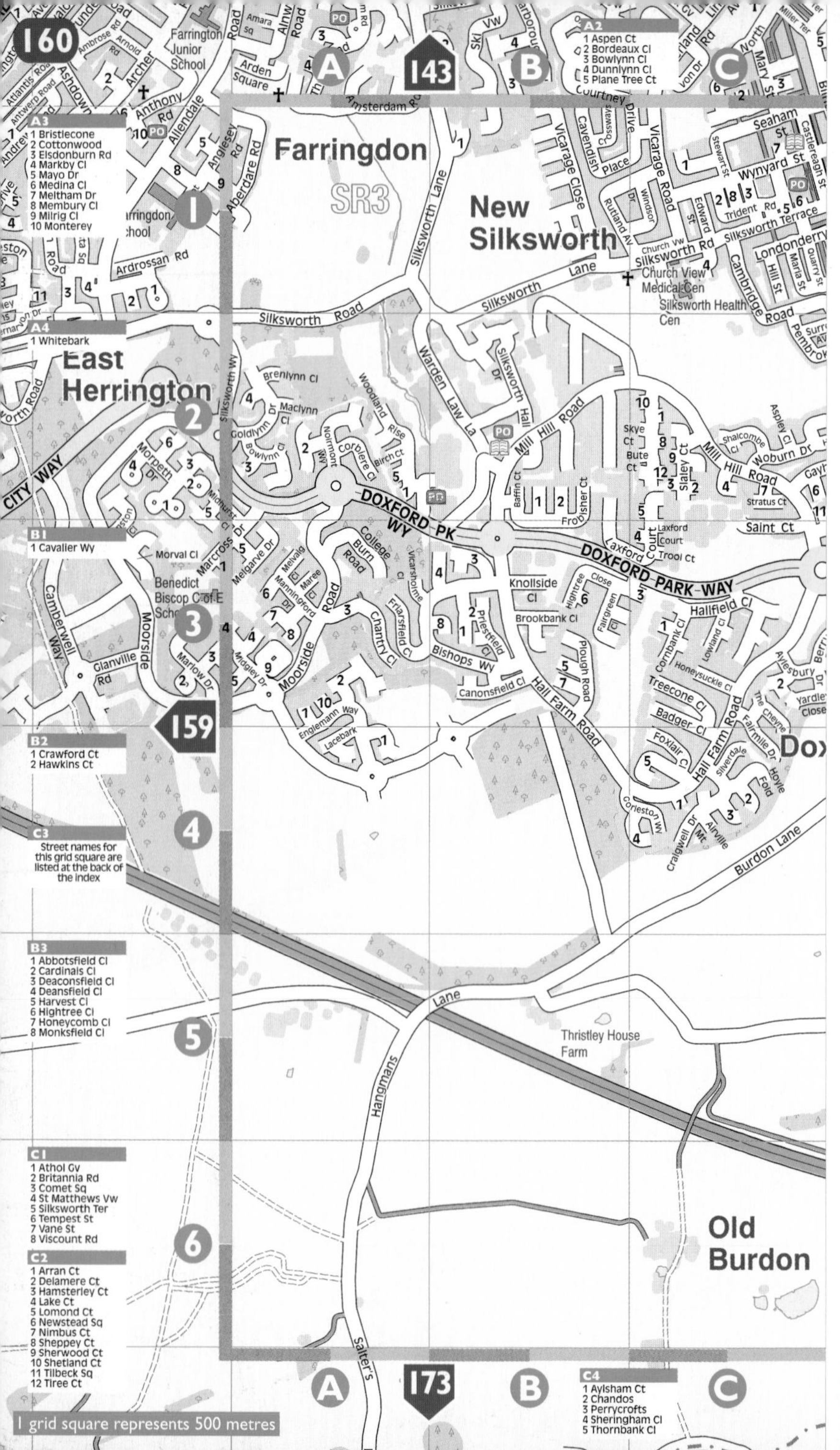
143
A
B
C
A2
1 Aspen Ct
2 Bordeaux Cl
3 Bowlynn Cl
4 Dunnlynn Cl
5 Plane Tree Ct
A3
1 Bristlecone
2 Cottonwood
3 Elsdonburn Rd
4 Markby Cl
5 Mayo Dr
6 Medina Cl
7 Meltham Dr
8 Membury Cl
9 Milrig Cl
10 Monterey
A4
1 Whitebark
B1
1 Cavalier Wy
B2
1 Crawford Ct
2 Hawkins Ct
C3
Street names for this grid square are listed at the back of the index
B3
1 Abbotsfield Cl
2 Cardinals Cl
3 Deaconsfield Cl
4 Deansfield Cl
5 Harvest Cl
6 Hightree Cl
7 Honeycomb Cl
8 Monksfield Cl
C1
1 Athol Gv
2 Britannia Rd
3 Comet Sq
4 St Matthews Vw
5 Silksworth Ter
6 Tempest St
7 Vane St
8 Viscount Rd
C2
1 Arran Ct
2 Delamere Ct
3 Hamsterley Ct
4 Lake Ct
5 Lomond Ct
6 Newstead Sq
7 Nimbus Ct
8 Sheppey Ct
9 Sherwood Ct
10 Shetland Ct
11 Tilbeck Sq
12 Tiree Ct
C4
1 Aylsham Ct
2 Chandos
3 Perrycrofts
4 Sheringham Cl
5 Thornbank Cl
Farringdon
SR3
New Silksworth
East Herrington
Old Burdon
Farrington Junior School
Benedict Biscop C of E School
Church View Medical Cen
Silksworth Health Cen
Thristley House Farm
Amsterdam Rd
Silksworth Lane
Silksworth Road
Silksworth Rd
Silksworth Terrace
Aberdare Rd
Anglesey Rd
Allendale
Anthony Rd
Archer
Ardrossan Rd
Arden Square
City Way
Silksworth Wy
Brenlynn Cl
Maclynn Cl
Goldlynn Dr
Bowlynn Cl
Woodland Rise
Warden Law La
Silksworth Hall Dr
Mill Hill Road
Doxford Pk Wy
Doxford Park Way
Moorside Road
Camberwell Way
Glanville Rd
Marlow Dr
Marcross Dr
Melgarve Dr
Morval Cl
Morpeth Dr
College Burn Road
Chantry Cl
Friarsfield Cl
Vicarsholme Cl
Bishops Wy
Priestfield Cl
Canonsfield Cl
Knollside Cl
Brookbank Cl
Plough Road
Hall Farm Road
Hightree Close
Fairgreen Cl
Laxford Court
Trool Ct
Hallfield Cl
Cornbank Cl
Lowland Cl
Honeysuckle Cl
Treecone Cl
Badger Cl
Foxlair Cl
Burdon Lane
Hangmans Lane
Salter's Lane
Englemann Way
Lacebark
Frobisher Ct
Baffin Ct
Skye Ct
Bute Ct
Slaley Ct
Woburn Dr
Shalcombe Cl
Saint Ct
Stratus Ct
Aylesbury Dr
Yardley Close
The Cheyne
Fairmile Dr
Hoyle Fold
Silverdale
Corleston Wy
Craigwell Dr
Airville Mt
Vicarage Close
Vicarage Road
Cavendish Place
Courtney Drive
Rutland Av
Windsor Dr
Edward St
Trident Rd
Wynyard St
Seaham St
Stewart St
Castlereagh St
Londonderry
Cambridge Road
Hill St
Maria St
Quarry St
Church Vw
North Moor
Mary St
Miller Ter
Aspley Cl
159
173
Dox
1 grid square represents 500 metres

D1
1 Ainthorpe Cl
2 Fairways
3 Quarry Rd
4 Tunstall Vls
144
D2
1 Closeburn Sq
2 Danby Cl
3 Drybeck Sq
4 Monkswood Sq
D3
1 Leyfield Cl
E1
1 Boulby Cl
2 Hawsker Cl
3 Hilltop Gdns
4 Houlskye Cl
5 Levisham Cl
E2
1 Rodney Cl
F1
1 Runnymede
162
174
Tunstall
Doxford Park
Burdon
Tunstall Vw
Hawthorn
Infants School
Paddock La
Tunstall Village Rd
TUNSTALL VILLAGE GN
TUNSTALL BANK
Fylingdale Dr
Runswick Cl
Lidcombe Cl
Coathland Dr
Coathland Cl
Withernsea Gv
Ryemount Rd
Runcorn
Richmond
Ravensworth
Rushford
Ramillies
Rachel Cl
Rowell Cl
Ridgeway
Rothbury
Robinson Ter
James Ter
Higgins Ter
Londonderry Ter
Dorset La
Park Avenue
Aline St
Lord St
Robert St
Burdon Gv
Norman Av
Myrtle Gv
Davison Av
Orr Av
Quarry Rd
BURDON ROAD
B1286
Ruswarp Dr
Nettles Lane
Burdon Lane
Tunstall Lodge Farm
Lodgeside Meadow
Burdon Road
East Farm
Burn Hall Farm
Pacific Hall Farm
A19(T)
A1018
Sunderland
Durham County
Bankside Cl
Brick Rw
Western Hl
Ryhope Health Centre
RYHOPE STREET
Cheviot La
Back Ryhope St
Blyton Avenue
Stewart Av
Bevan Avenue
Smith Gv
Burdon Lane
Esdale
Leechmere
Lillian Av
Infant School

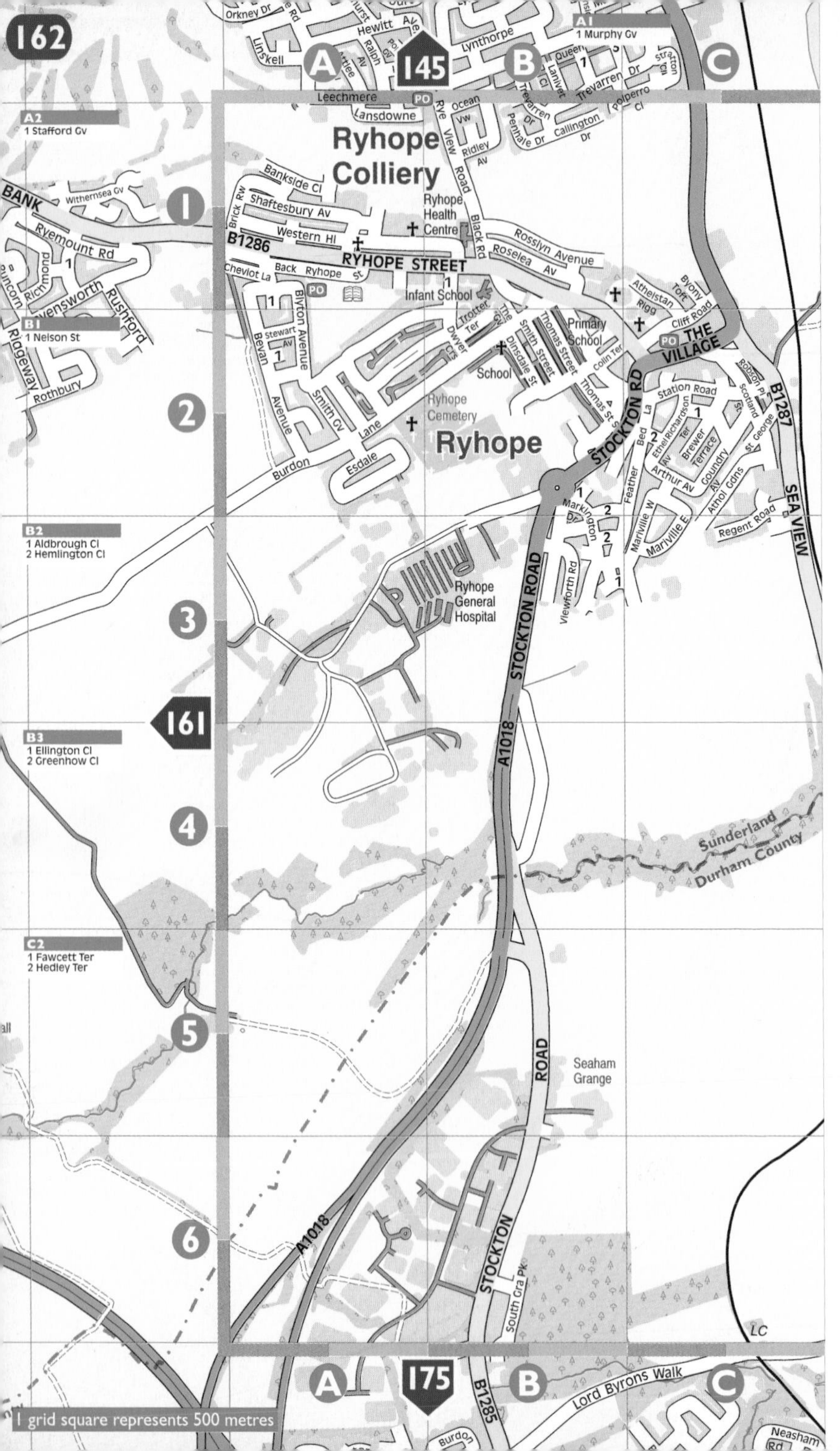
145
A
B
C
A1
1 Murphy Gv
A2
1 Stafford Gv
B1
1 Nelson St
B2
1 Aldbrough Cl
2 Hemlington Cl
B3
1 Ellington Cl
2 Greenhow Cl
C2
1 Fawcett Ter
2 Hedley Ter
Ryhope
Colliery
Ryhope
Ryhope Health Centre
Infant School
Primary School
School
Ryhope Cemetery
Ryhope General Hospital
Seaham Grange
RYHOPE STREET
B1286
STOCKTON ROAD
STOCKTON RD
A1018
THE VILLAGE
B1287
SEA VIEW
B1285
Sunderland
Durham County
Lord Byrons Walk
161
175
1
2
3
4
5
6
LC
1 grid square represents 500 metres

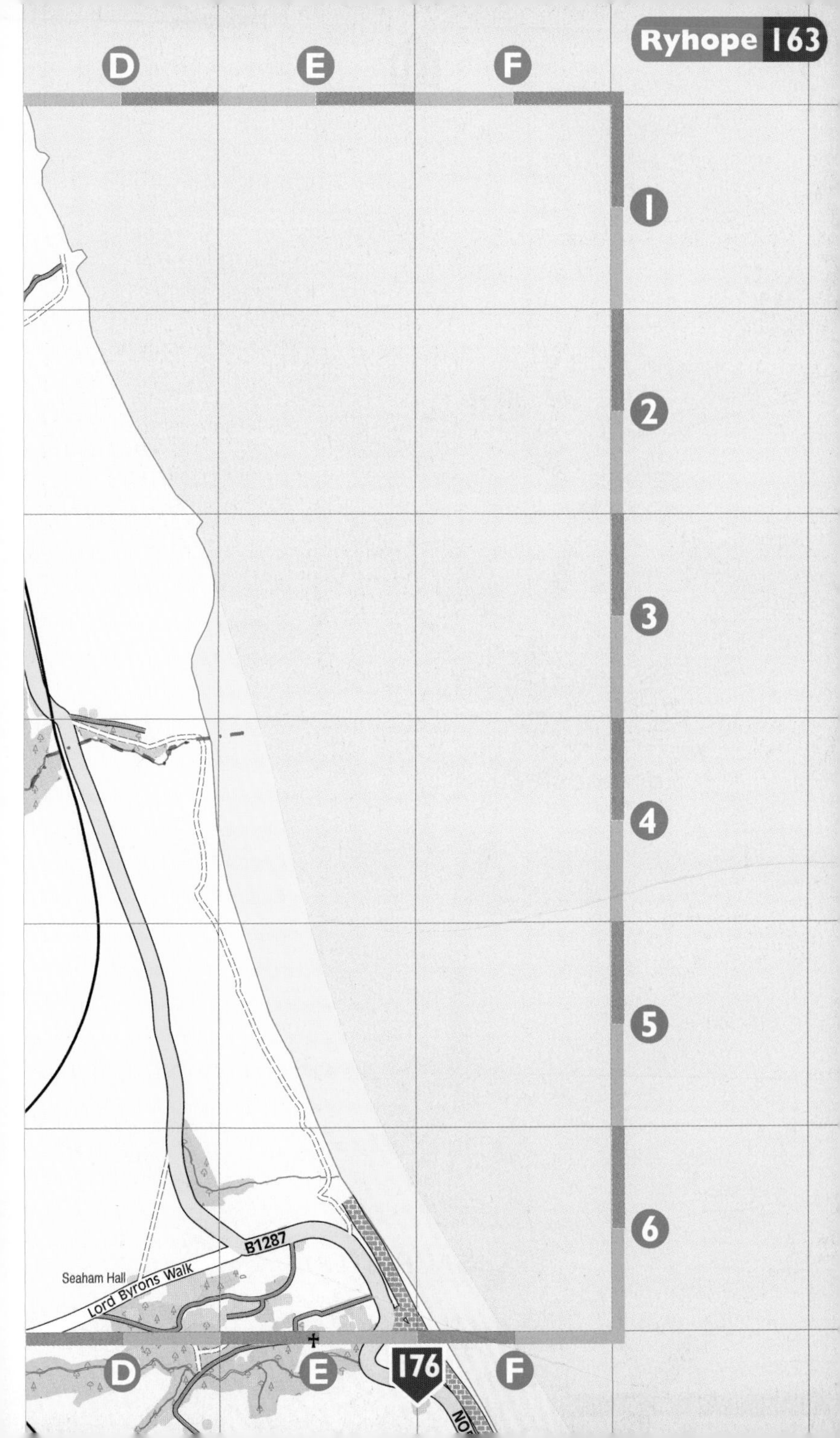
D
E
F
1
2
3
4
5
6
B1287
Seaham Hall
Lord Byrons Walk
D
E
F
176

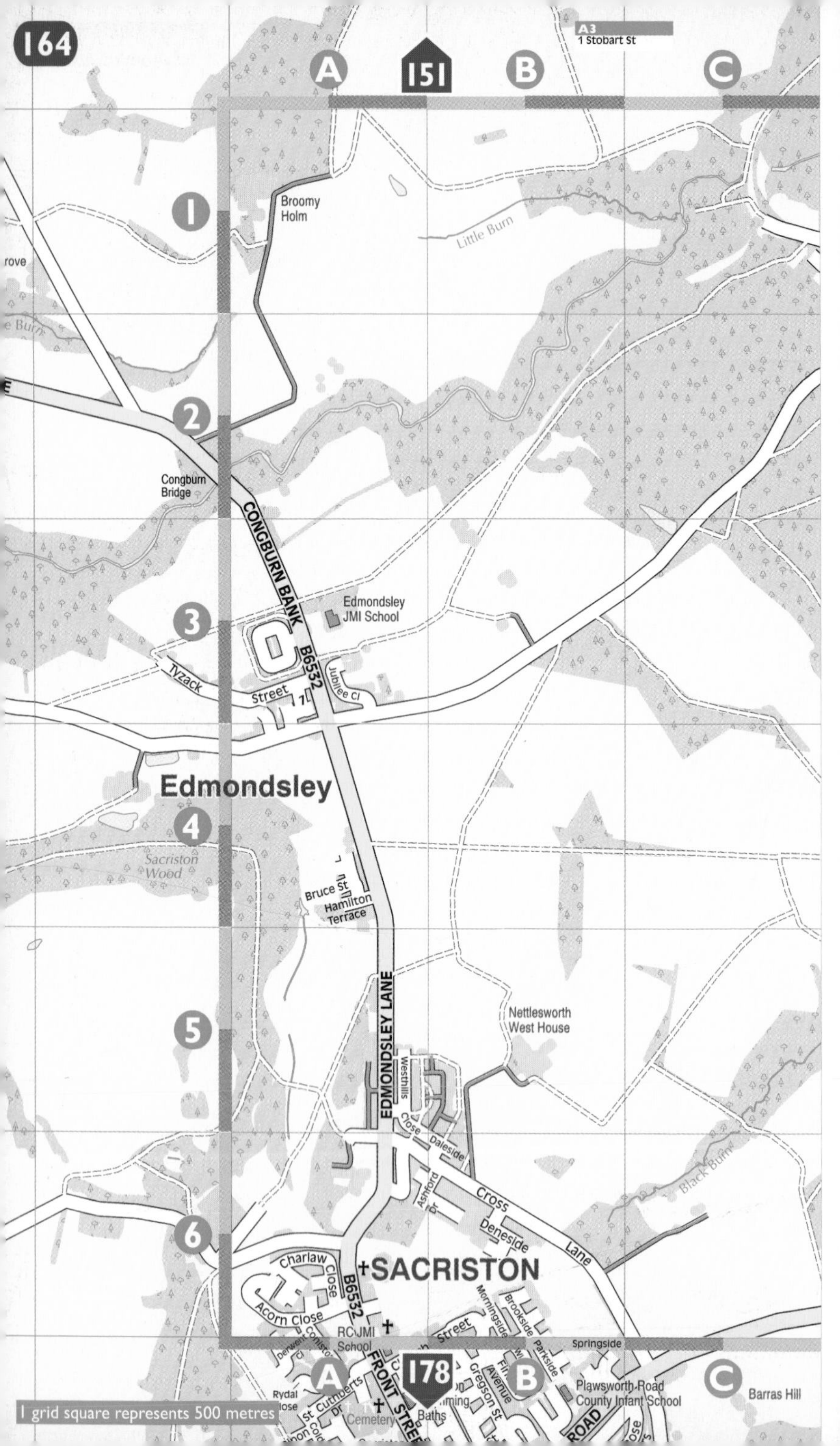
A3
1 Stobart St
A
151
B
C
1
2
3
4
5
6
Broomy Holm
Little Burn
rove
Congburn Bridge
CONGBURN BANK
B6532
Edmondsley JMI School
Tyzack Street
Jubilee Cl
Edmondsley
Sacriston Wood
Bruce St
Hamilton Terrace
EDMONDSLEY LANE
Nettlesworth West House
Westhills
Close
Daleside
Ashford Dr
Cross Lane
Deneside
Black Burn
SACRISTON
Charlaw Close
Acorn Close
RC JMI School
Morningside
Brookside
Parkside
Street
Springside
178
Gregson St
Avenue
Plawsworth Road County Infant School
Barras Hill
ROAD
Baths
Cemetery
St Cuthberts Dr
Rydal
FRONT STREET
1 grid square represents 500 metres

F2
1 Chillingham Dr
D
E
152
F
Waldridge
Olive St
Waldridge Lane
Fenton Cl
Norton Cl
Lesbury Cl
Dronfield Cl
Millfield Cl
Ashkirk Cl
Dunstan Cl
Chatton Cl
Alnwinton Dr
Redesdale Road
Fenwick Cl
Falstone Dr
Craster Cl
Alnwick Cl
Warkworth Drive
Rothbury Dr
Barford
Ingram Cl
Flodden Cl
Powburn Cl
Embleton Drive
Chillingham Drive
Hauxley Dr
Lilburn Cl
Denwick Close
Cheviot Vw
Warkworth Drive
Bewick Cl
Hawkhill Cl
Close
Prendwick
South Burn
Kinloch Ct
Grasmere
Leven Av
Rannoch Av
Esthwaite Av
Dunvegan Av
Carlingford Rd
Elterwater Rd
Marys St
Katrine Cl
PO
Road
Thirlmere Av
Rydal
Lomond Pl
Ullswater Rd
The Hermitage
1
2
A167(T)
The Dene
The Oval
Waldridge Fell Country Park
Chester Moor
3
The Crs
Waldridge Lane
Union Lane
The Gallery
166
Beaney Lane
4
5
Darley Court
Ugly Lane
Nettlesworth
Nettlesworth Primary School
Plawsworth
6
PARK VIEW
B6312
A167(T)
Hillmeads
Tanmeads
Mill Lane
Mill House
B6312
Tan Hills
Hawthorn
D
E
179
F
Sycamore Rd
Briar Cl

166
153
165
180
A
B
C
1
2
3
4
5
6
Chester Moor
Plawsworth
A167(T)
PARK ROAD
Waldridge La
Cleveland Av
Sidlaw Av
Fenton Cl
Norton Cl
Dronfield Cl
Drive
Warkworth
Redesdale
Road
Alnwick
Alwinton Dr
Craster
Ingram Cl
Chillingham Drive
Denwick Close
Cheviot Vw
Warkworth Drive
Bewick Cl
Hawkhill Cl
Prendwick Close
Lilburn Cl
Hauxley Dr
Powburn Cl
South Burn
Kinloch Ct
Grasmere
Leven Av
Ramoch
Esthwaite
Ullswater Rd
Lomond Pl
Dunvegan Av
Carlingford Rd
Elterwater Rd
Road
Windermere Av
Thirlmere Av
Hawes Av
Rydal
Road
Caragh Rd
Sheelin Av
Carrowmore Road
The Hermitage
Relton Ter
Allen St
Baden St
Ramsey St
Benson St
Clifford Ter
Clifford St
Orchard Ter
Orchard Gdns
Durham
Road
Weldon Ter
George St
York
Coronation St
Beverley Gdns
Jolliffe St
Red Rose Primary School
Crichton Av
A167(T)
The Dene
Holmhill
Lane
The Oval
The Crs
Waldridge Lane
Union Lane
The Gallery
Beaney Lane
Holmhill Lane
Wheatleywell Lane
Darley Court
Southhill Hall
B6312
A167(T)
Mill Lane
Mill House
Mill Lane
Cedar Avenue
Oak Cresce
1 grid square represents 500 metres

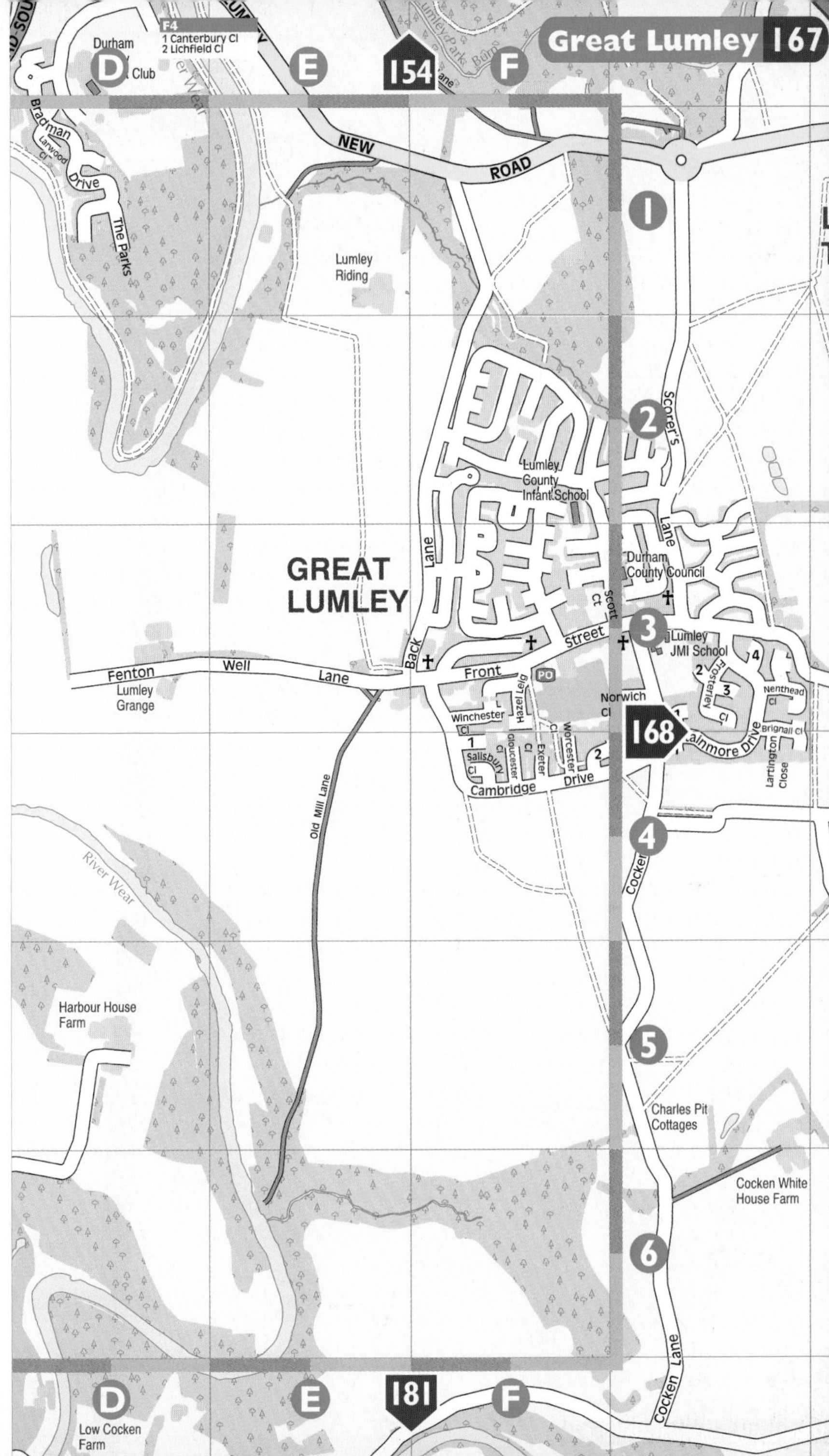

F4
1 Canterbury Cl
2 Lichfield Cl
Durham
Club
D
E
154
F
NEW
ROAD
Bradman
Larwood Cl
Drive
The Parks
Lumley Riding
1
2
Scorer's
Lane
Lumley County Infant School
Durham County Council
GREAT LUMLEY
Back
Lane
Scott
Ct
Street
Front
Fenton
Well
Lane
Lumley Grange
3
Lumley JMI School
Frosterley
Nenthead Cl
Norwich Cl
Winchester Cl
Hazel Leig
Salisbury Cl
Gloucester Cl
Exeter Cl
Worcester Cl
Cambridge
Drive
168
Rainmore Drive
Brignall Cl
Lartington Close
Old Mill Lane
River Wear
4
Cocken
Harbour House Farm
5
Charles Pit Cottages
Cocken White House Farm
6
Cocken Lane
181
Low Cocken Farm

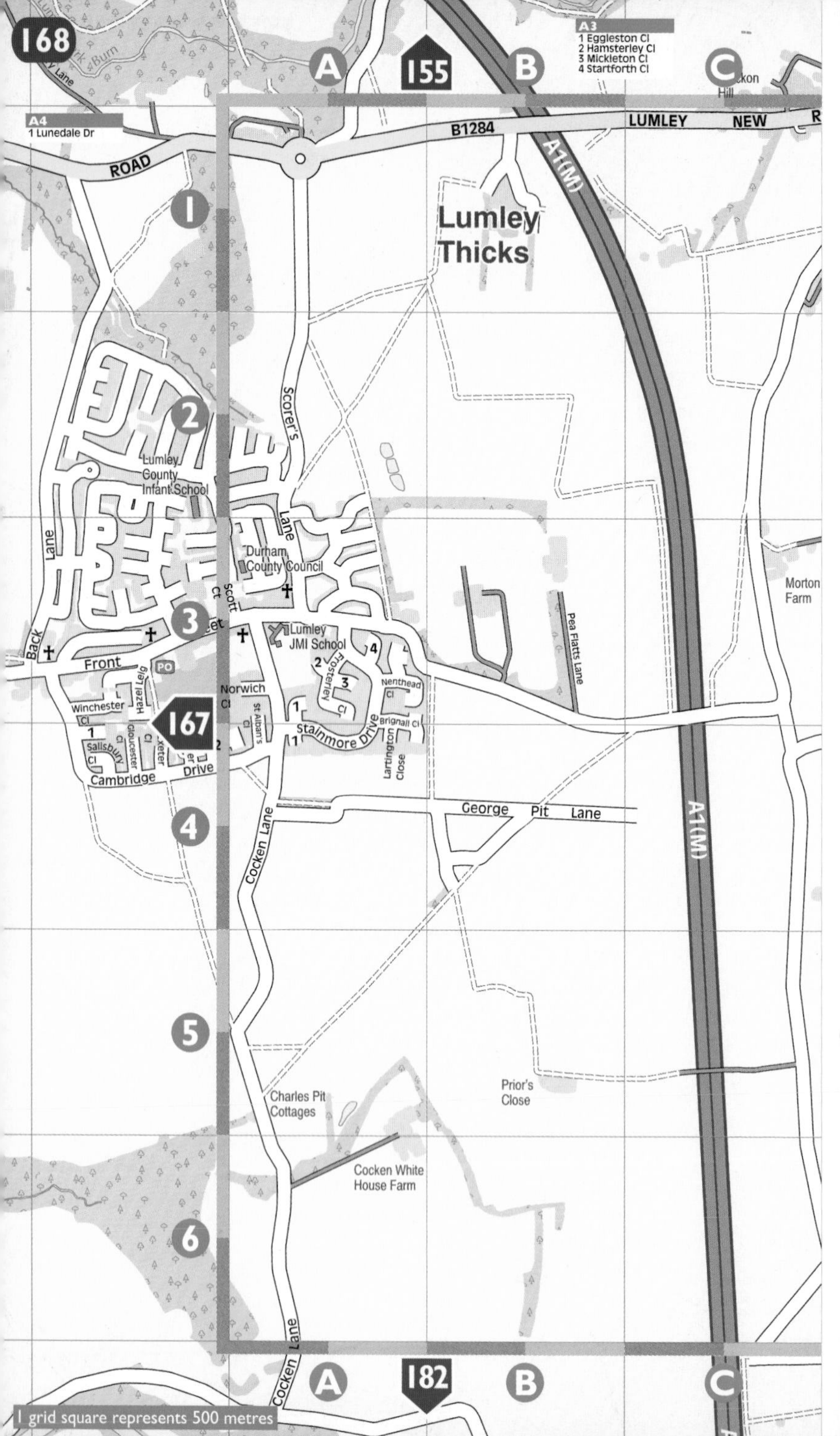
A3
1 Eggleston Cl
2 Hamsterley Cl
3 Mickleton Cl
4 Startforth Cl
A4
1 Lunedale Dr
155
182
167
A
B
C
1
2
3
4
5
6
B1284
LUMLEY
NEW
ROAD
A1(M)
Lumley Thicks
Scorer's Lane
Lumley County Infant School
Durham County Council
Scott Ct
Back Lane
Front
PO
Lumley JMI School
Frosterley Cl
Nenthead Cl
Norwich Cl
St Alban's
Winchester Cl
Hazel Leig
Salisbury Cl
Gloucester Cl
Exeter
Cambridge
Drive
Stainmore Drive
Brignall Cl
Lartington Close
Pea Flatts Lane
Morton Farm
George Pit Lane
Cocken Lane
Charles Pit Cottages
Prior's Close
Cocken White House Farm
1 grid square represents 500 metres

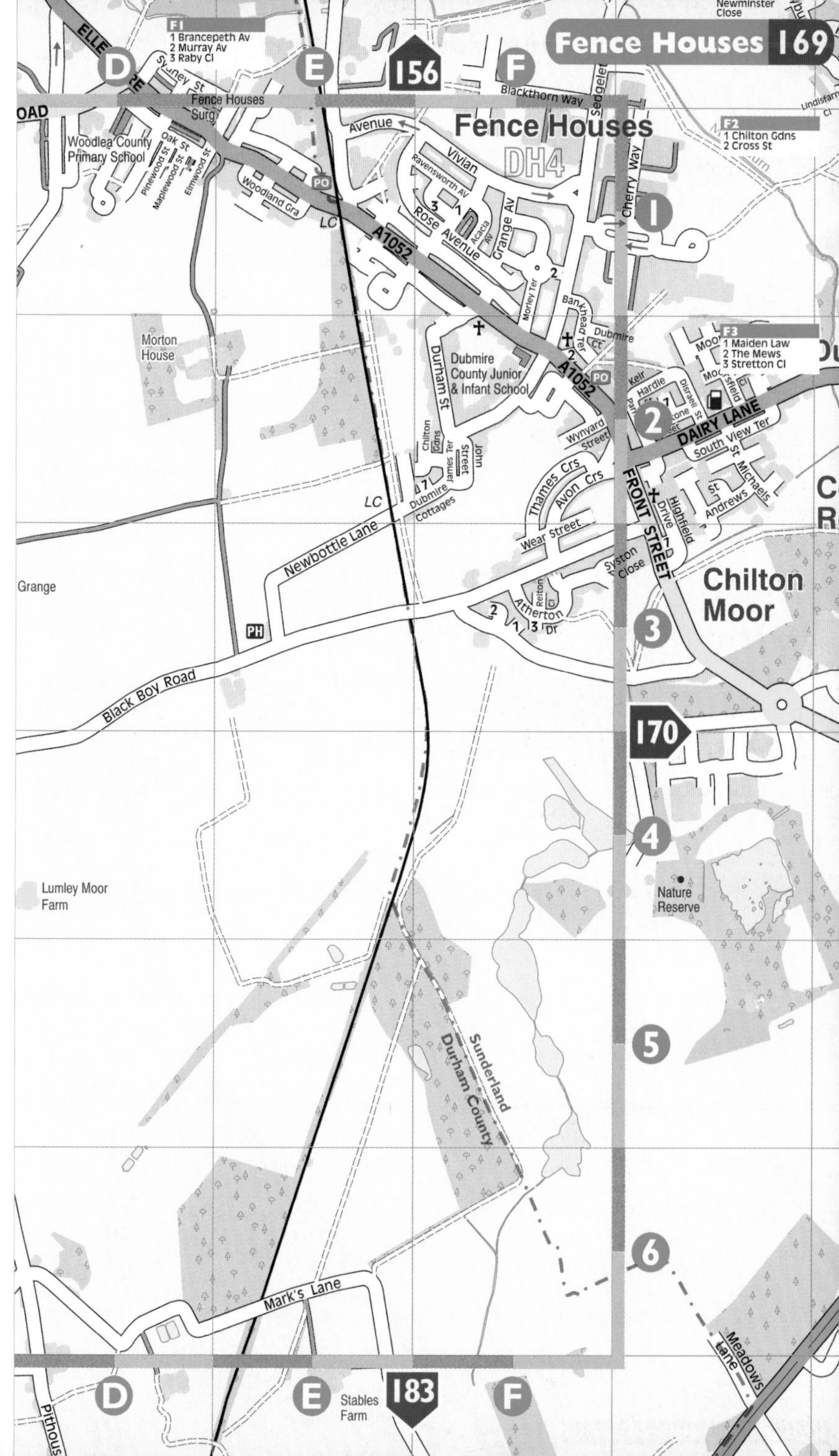
Fence Houses
DH4
Chilton Moor
F1
1 Brancepeth Av
2 Murray Av
3 Raby Cl
F2
1 Chilton Gdns
2 Cross St
F3
1 Maiden Law
2 The Mews
3 Stretton Cl
156
170
183
Newminster Close
Blackthorn Way
Sedgeletch
Cherry Way
Avenue
Vivian
Ravensworth Av
Rose Avenue
Acacia Av
Grange Av
Morley Ter
Bankhead Ter
Dubmire Ct
A1052
Sydney St
Fence Houses Surg
Woodlea County Primary School
Oak St
Pinewood St
Maplewood St
Elmwood St
Woodland Gra
PO
LC
Morton House
Durham St
Dubmire County Junior & Infant School
Chilton Gdns
James Ter
John Street
Dubmire Cottages
Wynyard Street
Thames Crs
Avon Crs
Wear Street
FRONT STREET
Highfield Drive
DAIRY LANE
South View Ter
St Michaels
St Andrews
Hardie
Disraeli St
Moorsfield
Keir
Syston Close
Relton Cl
Atherton Dr
Newbottle Lane
Grange
PH
Black Boy Road
Lumley Moor Farm
Nature Reserve
Sunderland
Durham County
Mark's Lane
Meadows Lane
Stables Farm
Pithouse
Lindisfarne Cl
D
E
F
1
2
3
4
5
6

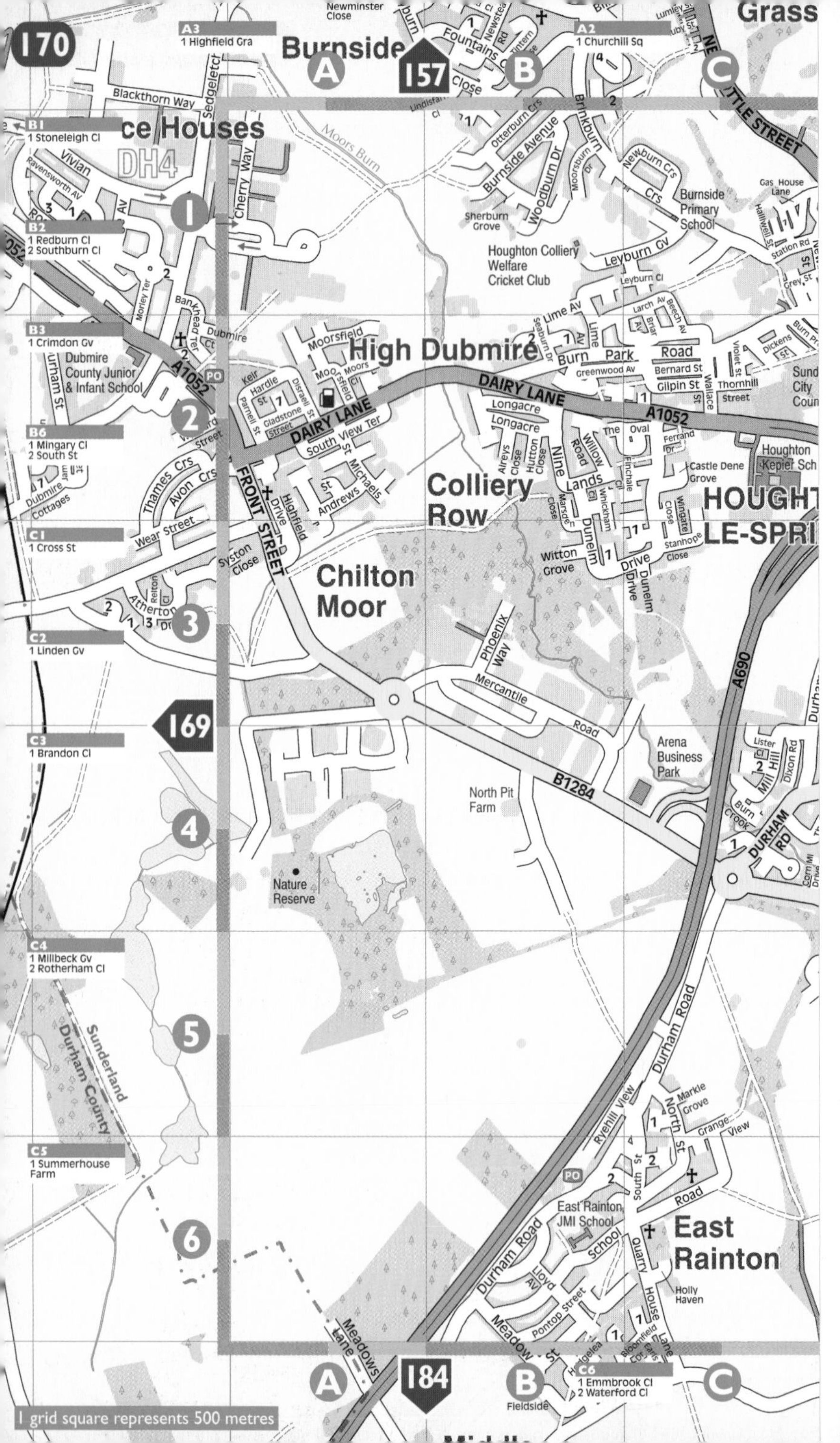

170
A3
1 Highfield Gra
Burnside
157
A2
1 Churchill Sq
Grass
Newminster Close
Fountains
Close
Tintern
Newstead Rd
NEWCASTLE STREET
B1
1 Stoneleigh Cl
Fence Houses
DH4
Vivian
Ravensworth Av
Blackthorn Way
Sedgeletch
Cherry Way
Moors Burn
Lindisfarne Cl
Otterburn Crs
Burnside Avenue
Woodburn Dr
Brinkburn
Moorsburn Dr
Newburn Crs
Burnside Primary School
Gas House Lane
Halliwell St
Station Rd
Grey St
B2
1 Redburn Cl
2 Southburn Cl
A1052
Sherburn Grove
Houghton Colliery Welfare Cricket Club
Leyburn Gv
Leyburn Cl
Morley Ter
Bankhead Ter
Dubmire Ct
B3
1 Crimdon Gv
Durham St
Dubmire County Junior & Infant School
PO
Moorsfield
High Dubmire
Lime Av
Seaburn Dr
Lime Av
Larch Av
Briar Av
Beech Av
Burn Park Road
Greenwood Av
Bernard St
Gilpin St
Wallace St
Violet St
Thornhill Street
Dickens St
Burn Prom
Sunderland City Council
Keir
Hardie St
Parnell St
Gladstone Street
Disraeli St
Moorsfield Moors Cl
DAIRY LANE
South View Ter
Longacre
Longacre
The Oval
Ferrand Dr
Houghton Kepier School
B6
1 Mingary Cl
2 South St
Dubmire Cottages
Thames Crs
Avon Crs
FRONT STREET
Highfield Drive
St Andrews
St Michaels
Colliery Row
Alreys Close
Hutton Close
Nine Lands
Willow Road
Finchale Cl
Whickham Cl
Marsden Close
Castle Dene Grove
HOUGHTON-LE-SPRING
C1
1 Cross St
Wear Street
Syston Close
Chilton Moor
Witton Grove
Dunelm Drive
Dunelm Drive
Wingate Close
Stanhope Close
Relton Cl
Atherton Dr
C2
1 Linden Gv
Phoenix Way
Mercantile Road
A690
169
C3
1 Brandon Cl
Arena Business Park
Lister Cl
Mill Hill
Dixon Rd
Burn Crook
DURHAM RD
B1284
North Pit Farm
Nature Reserve
C4
1 Millbeck Gv
2 Rotherham Cl
Sunderland
Durham County
Durham Road
Markle Grove
North St
Grange View
Ryehill View
C5
1 Summerhouse Farm
South St
Road
East Rainton JMI School
School
Durham Road
Quarry House Lane
East Rainton
Lloyd Av
Pontop Street
Holly Haven
Meadows Lane
Meadow St
Hedgelea
Bloomfield Dr
Earls Dr
184
C6
1 Emmbrook Cl
2 Waterford Cl
Fieldside
1 grid square represents 500 metres

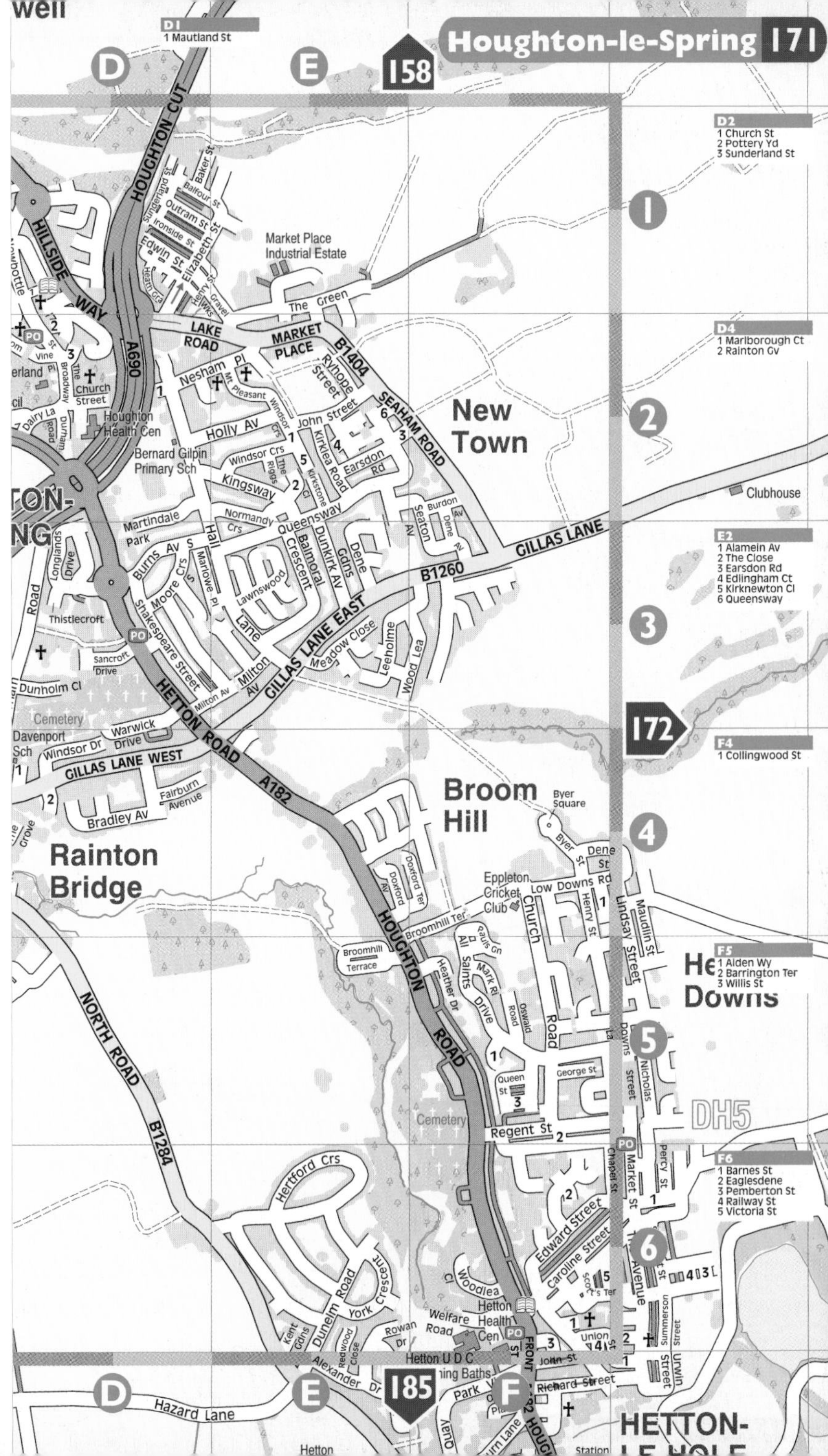
D1
1 Mautland St
D2
1 Church St
2 Pottery Yd
3 Sunderland St
D4
1 Marlborough Ct
2 Rainton Gv
E2
1 Alamein Av
2 The Close
3 Earsdon Rd
4 Edlingham Ct
5 Kirknewton Cl
6 Queensway
F4
1 Collingwood St
F5
1 Aiden Wy
2 Barrington Ter
3 Willis St
F6
1 Barnes St
2 Eaglesdene
3 Pemberton St
4 Railway St
5 Victoria St
158
172
185
New Town
Broom Hill
Rainton Bridge
DH5
HETTON-

A6
1 Eppleton Rw
2 Stephenson Cl
3 Victory St East
4 Victory St West
159
171
186
New Town
SEAHAM ROAD
Burdon Av
Seaton Av
Dene Av
GILLAS LANE
B1260
B1404
Clubhouse
Golf Course
Warden Law
Leeholme
Wood Lea
Broom Hill
Byer Square
Dene St
Low Downs Rd
Eppleton Cricket Club
Doxford Ter
Doxford Av
Broomhill Ter
HOUGHTON ROAD
All Saints Drive
Mark Rd
Heather Dr
Oswald Road
Church Road
Henry St
Lindsay Street
Maudlin St
Hetton Downs
Downs La
Nicholas Street
George St
Queen St
Cemetery
Regent St
DH5
PO
Chapel St
Market St
Percy St
Edward Street
S Market St
The Avenue
Summerson Street
Woodlea Cl
Hetton Health Cen
Welfare Road
Rowan Dr
Union St
Hetton U D C Swimming Baths
FRONT ST
A182
John St
Richard Street
Park View
Office Place
Alder Cl
Urwin Street
Downs Pit Lane
Great Eppleton
HETTON-LE-HOLE
Station
1 grid square represents 500 metres

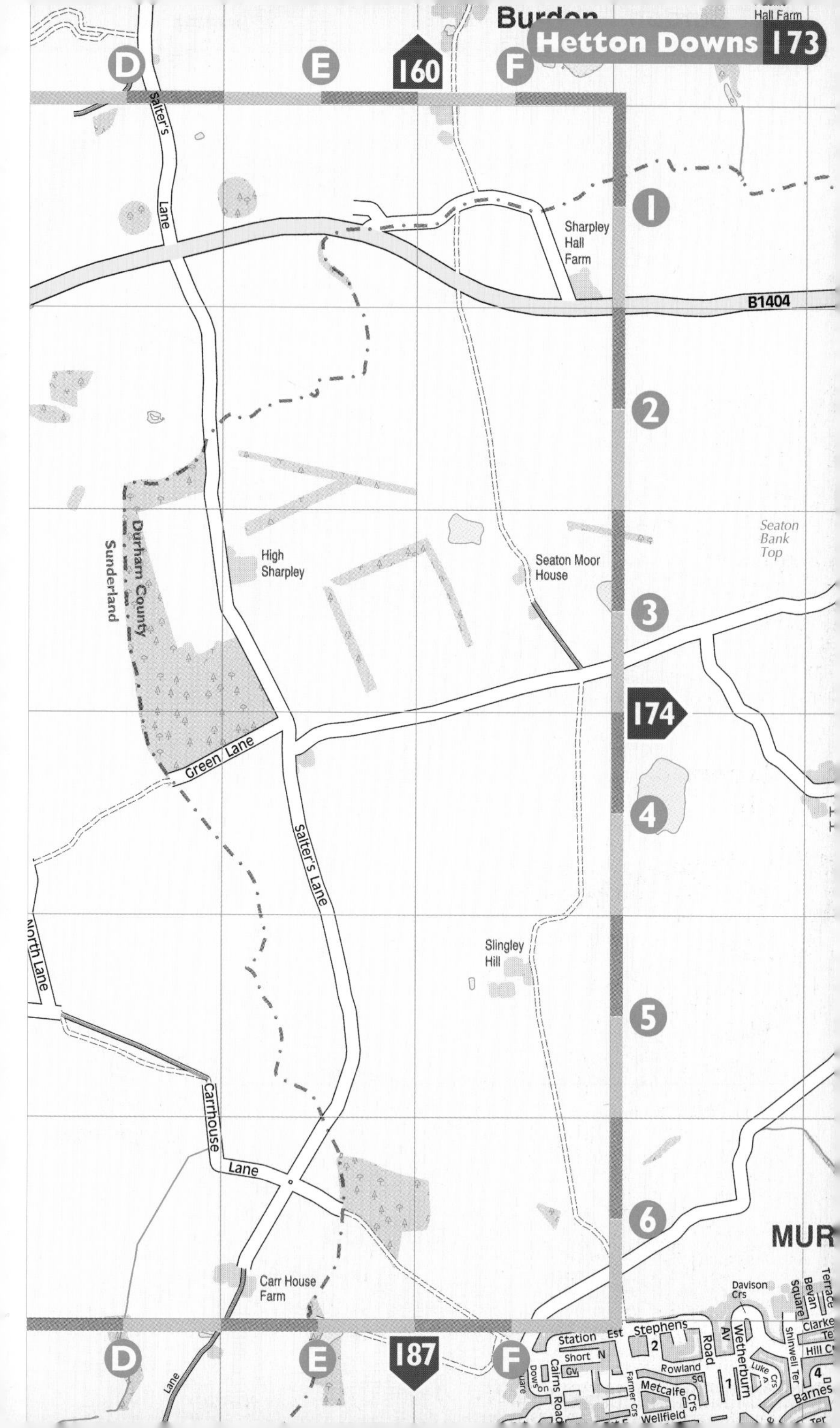
Burdon
Hall Farm
D
E
160
F
Salter's Lane
1
Sharpley Hall Farm
B1404
2
Seaton Bank Top
Durham County
Sunderland
High Sharpley
Seaton Moor House
3
174
Green Lane
4
Salter's Lane
North Lane
Slingley Hill
5
Carrhouse Lane
6
MUR
Carr House Farm
D
E
187
F
Lane
Station Est
Short
Gv
Cairns Road
Stephens Road
Av
Rowland Sq
Farmer Crs
Metcalfe Crs
Wellfield
Davison Crs
Wetherburn
Luke Crs
Bevan Square
Shinwell Ter
Terrace
Clarke
Hill Cr
Barnes
1
2
4

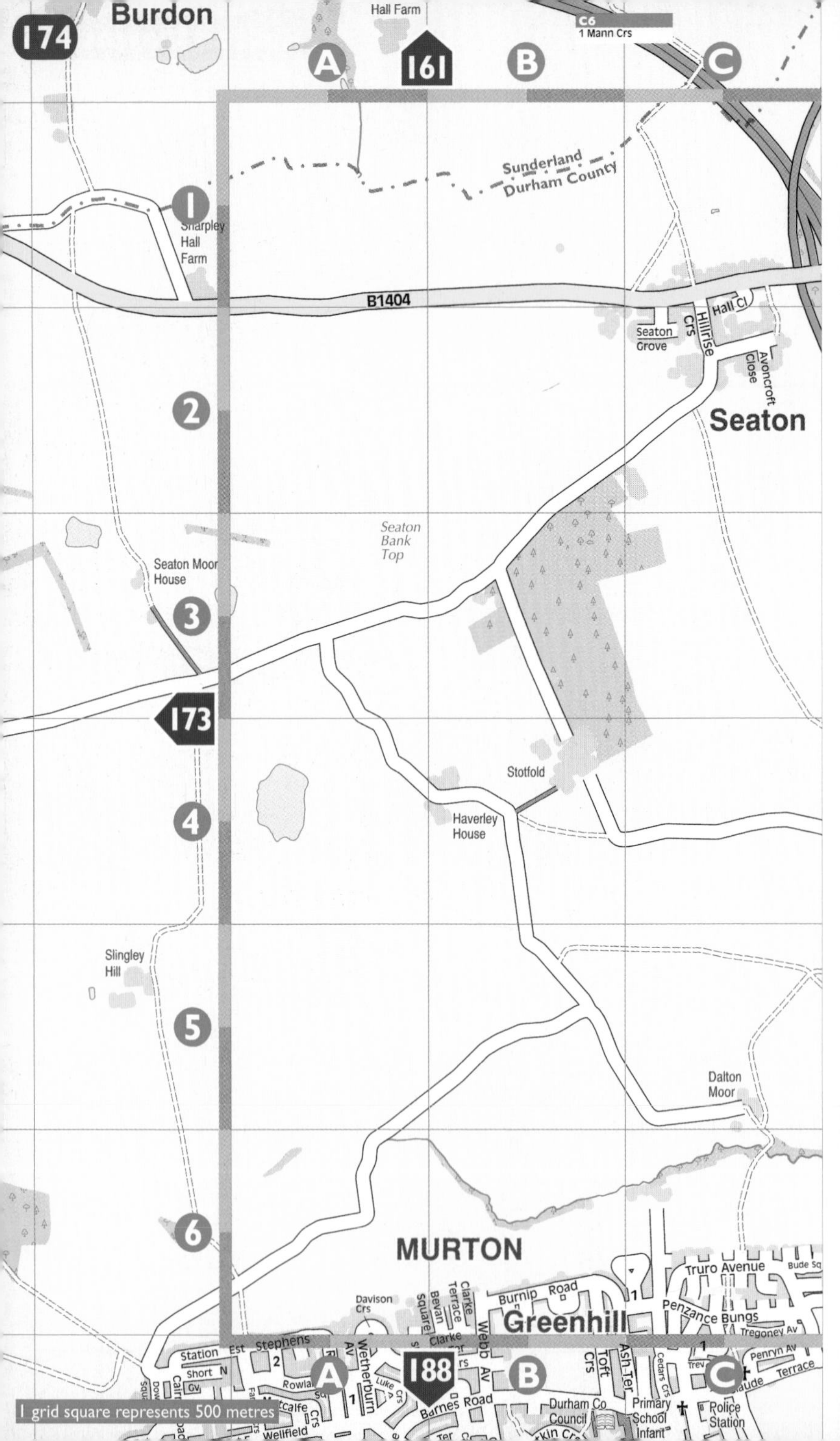

Burdon
Hall Farm
161
C6
1 Mann Crs
A
B
C
Sunderland
Durham County
1
Sharpley
Hall
Farm
B1404
Hall Cl
Crs
Hillrise
Seaton
Grove
Avoncroft
Close
2
Seaton
Seaton
Bank
Top
Seaton Moor
House
3
173
4
Stotfold
Haverley
House
Slingley
Hill
5
Dalton
Moor
6
MURTON
Truro Avenue
Bude Sq
Burnip Road
Davison
Crs
Square
Bevan
Terrace
Clarke
Terrace
Greenhill
Penzance Bungs
Tregoney Av
Station
Est
Stephens
Short
Gv
Wetherburn
Av
Clarke
Webb
Av
Crs
Toft
Ash Ter
Cedars Crs
Penryn Av
Claude
Terrace
188
Luke
Crs
Barnes Road
Durham Co
Council
Primary
School
Infant
Police
Station
Wellfield
1 grid square represents 500 metres

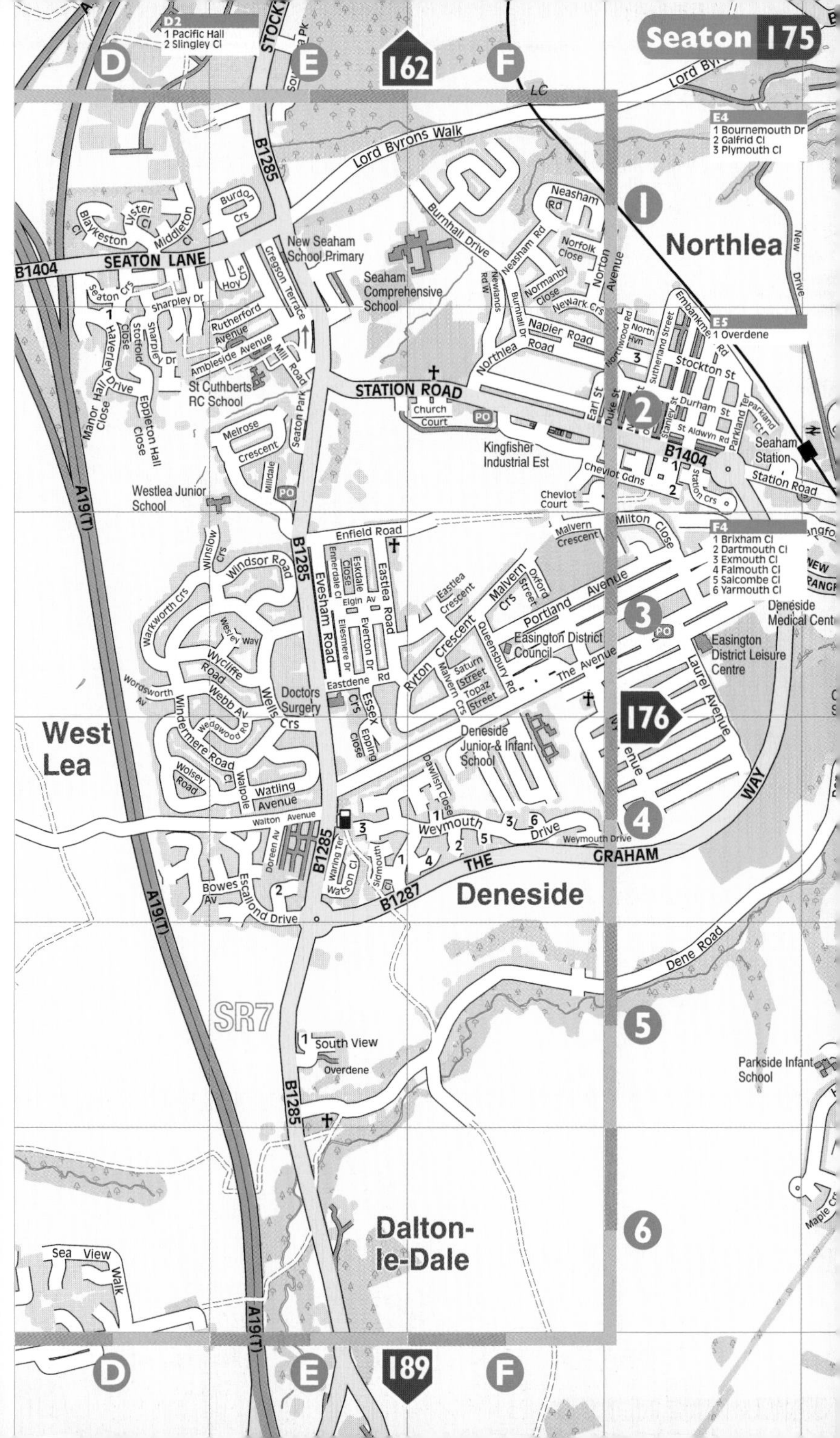
D2
1 Pacific Hall
2 Slingley Cl
E4
1 Bournemouth Dr
2 Galfrid Cl
3 Plymouth Cl
E5
1 Overdene
F4
1 Brixham Cl
2 Dartmouth Cl
3 Exmouth Cl
4 Falmouth Cl
5 Salcombe Cl
6 Yarmouth Cl
162
176
189
Northlea
Deneside
West Lea
Dalton-le-Dale
SR7
Seaham Comprehensive School
New Seaham School Primary
St Cuthberts RC School
Westlea Junior School
Kingfisher Industrial Est
Seaham Station
Easington District Council
Easington District Leisure Centre
Deneside Junior & Infant School
Doctors Surgery
Parkside Infant School
SEATON LANE
STATION ROAD
Lord Byrons Walk
THE GRAHAM WAY
Dene Road
Walton Avenue
Weymouth Drive
The Avenue
Portland Avenue
Station Road
A19(T)
B1285
B1404
B1287

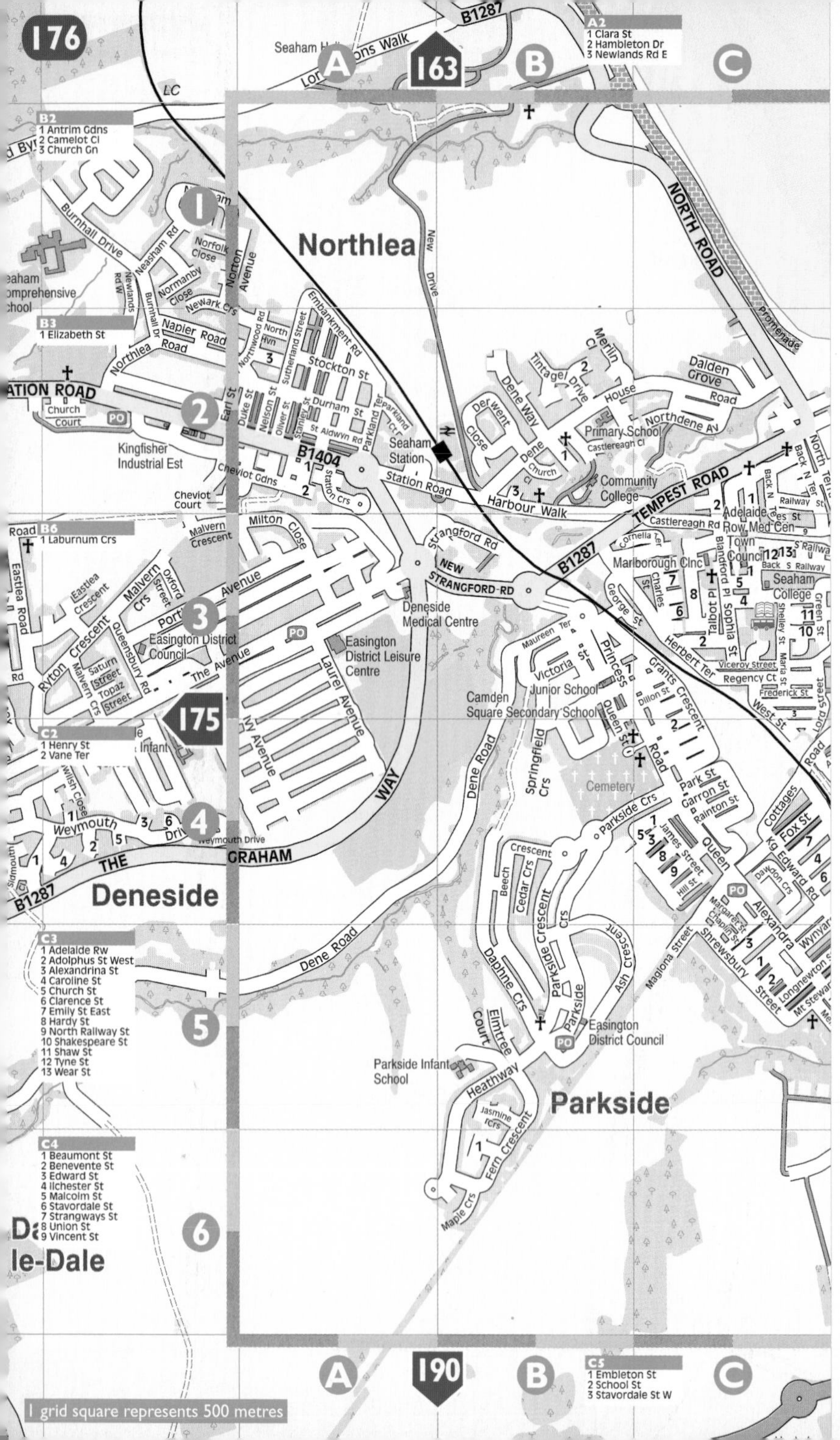

176
163
175
190
A
B
C
1
2
3
4
5
6
A2
1 Clara St
2 Hambleton Dr
3 Newlands Rd E
B2
1 Antrim Gdns
2 Camelot Cl
3 Church Gn
B3
1 Elizabeth St
B6
1 Laburnum Crs
C2
1 Henry St
2 Vane Ter
C3
1 Adelaide Rw
2 Adolphus St West
3 Alexandrina St
4 Caroline St
5 Church St
6 Clarence St
7 Emily St East
8 Hardy St
9 North Railway St
10 Shakespeare St
11 Shaw St
12 Tyne St
13 Wear St
C4
1 Beaumont St
2 Benevente St
3 Edward St
4 Ilchester St
5 Malcolm St
6 Stavordale St
7 Strangways St
8 Union St
9 Vincent St
C5
1 Embleton St
2 School St
3 Stavordale St W
Northlea
Deneside
Parkside
Seaham Station
Kingfisher Industrial Est
Easington District Council
Easington District Leisure Centre
Deneside Medical Centre
Camden Square Secondary School
Junior School
Community College
Primary School
Seaham College
Town Council
Row Med Cen
Cemetery
Parkside Infant School
Seaham Comprehensive School
NORTH ROAD
TEMPEST ROAD
STATION ROAD
NEW STRANGFORD RD
THE GRAHAM WAY
B1287
B1404
Promenade
I grid square represents 500 metres

D3
1 Aline St
2 Mary St
3 South Ter
D
E
F
D4
1 Robert St
2 Ropery Wk
1
D5
1 Londonderry St
2 Seaham St
2
Police Station
SEAHAM
PO
South Crs
3
Foundry Road
Primary School
2
1
Bottle Works Rd
Robert Sq
Albert St
Alfred St
Stewart St
Candlish Ter
Gas Works Road
3
4
Embankment
Hill Crs
Road
Dawdon
5
Edith Street
LC
Nose's Point
6
A182
D
E
F

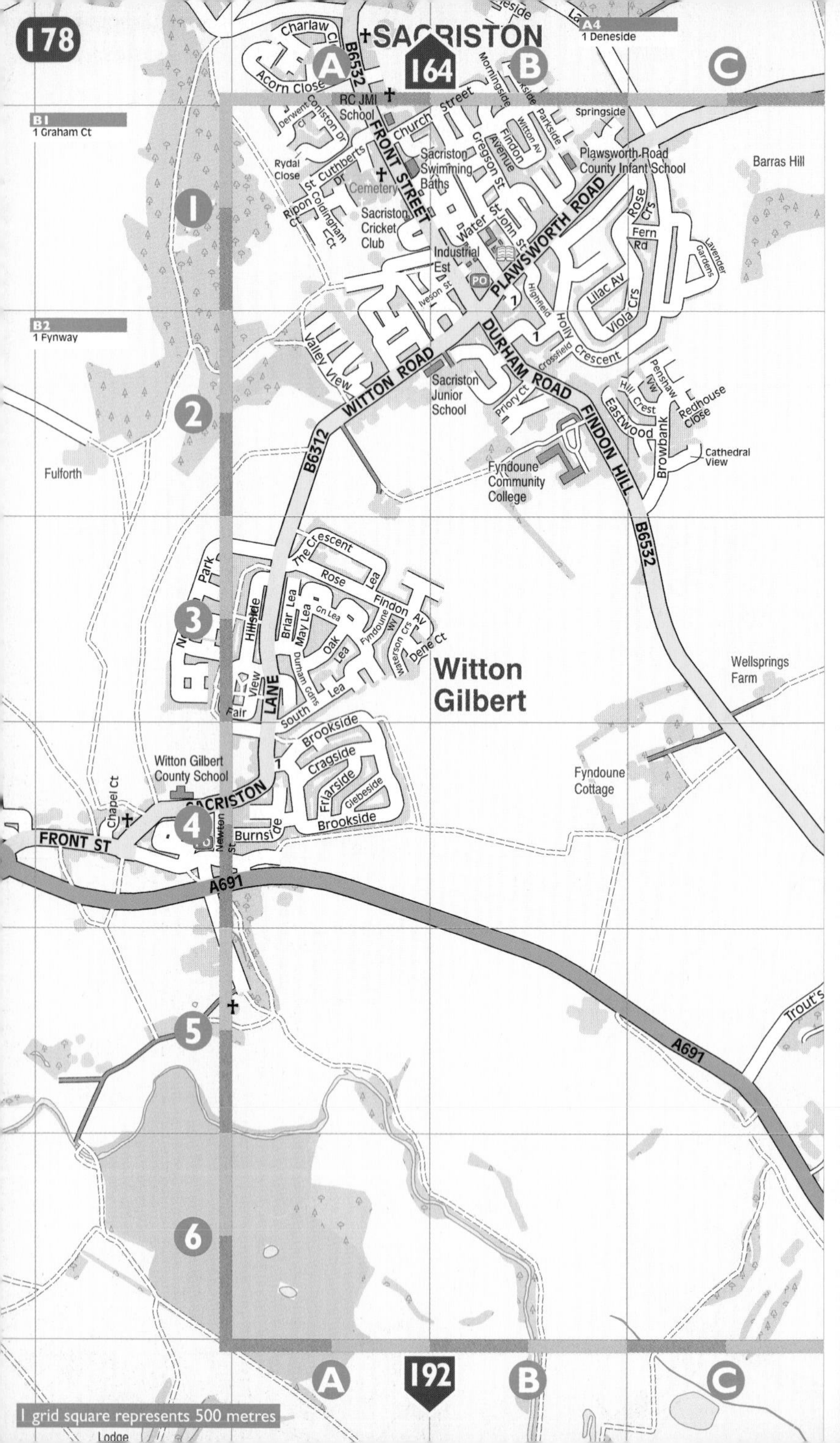
SACRISTON
164
A
B
C
A4
1 Deneside
B1
1 Graham Ct
B2
1 Fynway
Charlaw Cl
Acorn Close
B6532
RC JMI School
Derwent Cl
Coniston Dr
Church Street
FRONT STREET
Rydal Close
St Cuthberts Dr
Sacriston Swimming Baths
Cemetery
Ripon Ct
Coldingham Ct
Sacriston Cricket Club
Morningside
Parkside
Witton Av
Findon Avenue
Gregson St
Water St
St John St
Industrial Est
Iveson St
PO
PLAWSWORTH ROAD
Springside
Plawsworth Road County Infant School
Barras Hill
Rose Crs
Fern Rd
Lavender Gardens
Lilac Av
Viola Crs
Highfield
Holly Crescent
Crossfield
DURHAM ROAD
Valley View
WITTON ROAD
Sacriston Junior School
Priory Ct
Penshaw Vw
Hill Crest
Redhouse Close
Eastwood
Browbank
Cathedral View
FINDON HILL
Fyndoune Community College
B6312
Fulforth
B6532
The Crescent
Park
Rose Lea
Findon Av
Hillside
Briar Lea
May Lea
Gn Lea
Fyndoune Wy
Waterson Crs
Dene Ct
Oak Lea
Durham Gdns
Witton Gilbert
Wellsprings Farm
Fair View
LANE
South
Brookside
Cragside
Friarside
Glebeside
Witton Gilbert County School
Chapel Ct
SACRISTON
FRONT ST
Newton St
Burnside
Fyndoune Cottage
A691
Trout's
1
2
3
4
5
6
192
I grid square represents 500 metres
Lodge

F1
1 Church Vw
F5
1 Littlebridge Ct
F6
1 Aldhome Ct
Tan Hills
Kimblesworth
Hawthorn Close
Sycamore Rd
Briar Cl
Elm Crescent
Cedar Avenue
Oak Crescent
Mill House
Kimblesworth Grange
Potter House
Potterhouse Lane
Imex Business Centre
Smithfield
Abbey Road
The Orchard
Woodbine Rd
Folly Ter
Anvil Ct
Bishops Way
Hartside View
The Avenue
Hudspeth Crs
Mere Dr
Pity Me
Front Street
Beaumont Cl
Augustine Cl
Bridgemere Drive
Hatfield Cl
Alexandra Cl
Hartside Farm
Trouts Lane School
Durham County N H S Trust
Earls House Hospital
Sniperley Hall
Framwellgate Moor Comprehensive School
Chastleton Surgery
Lund Av
Gray Av
South Ter
Newton Drive
Aykley Rd
Ashleigh Av
Kirby Av
Durham Co Council
Finchale
Beech Road
Flambard Rd
Priory Rd
Caterhouse Rd
Bracken Field Rd
Frankland
A167(T)
B6312
B6532
A691
165
180
193
1
2
3
4
5
6
D
E
F

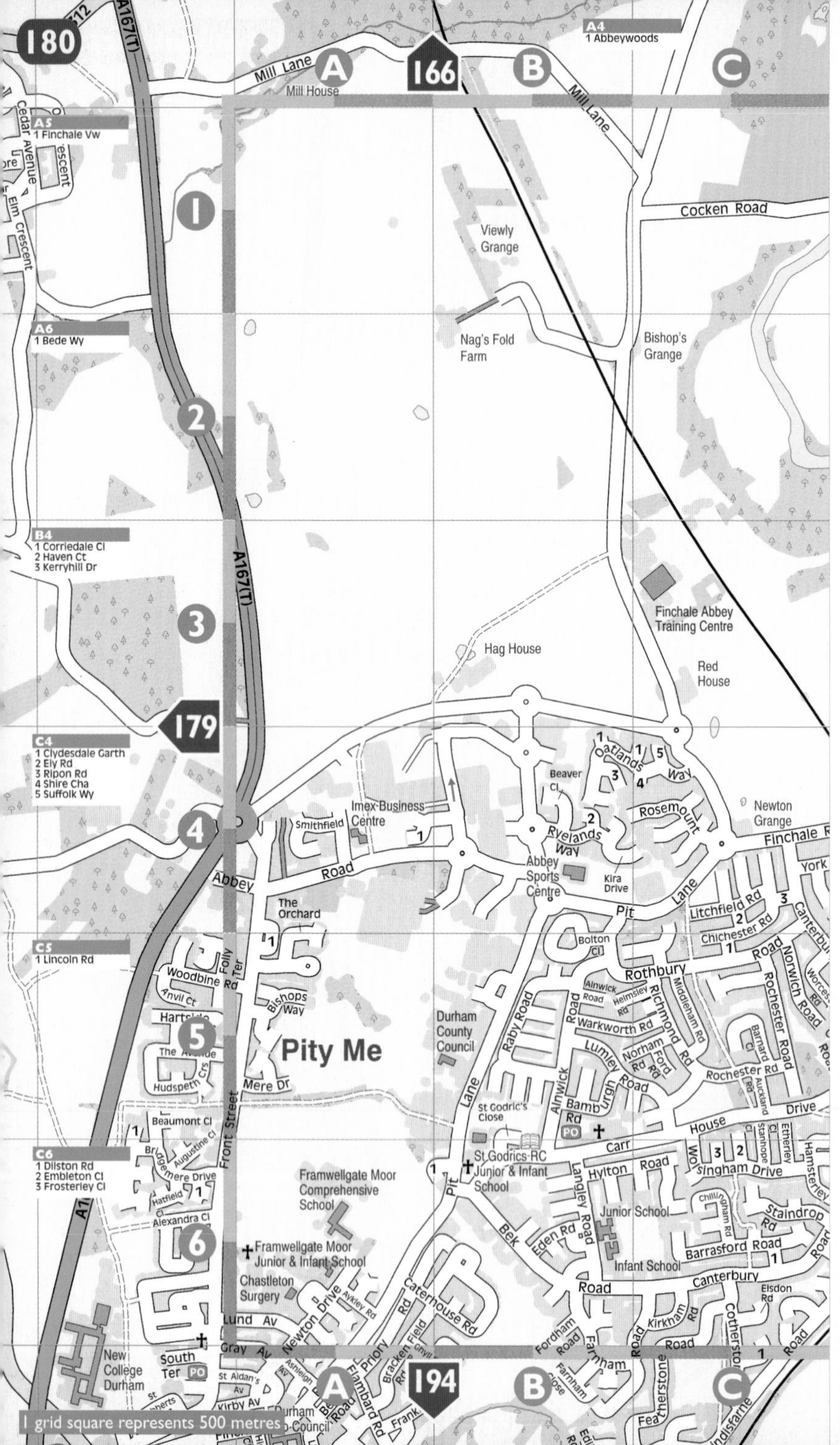

1 grid square represents 500 metres

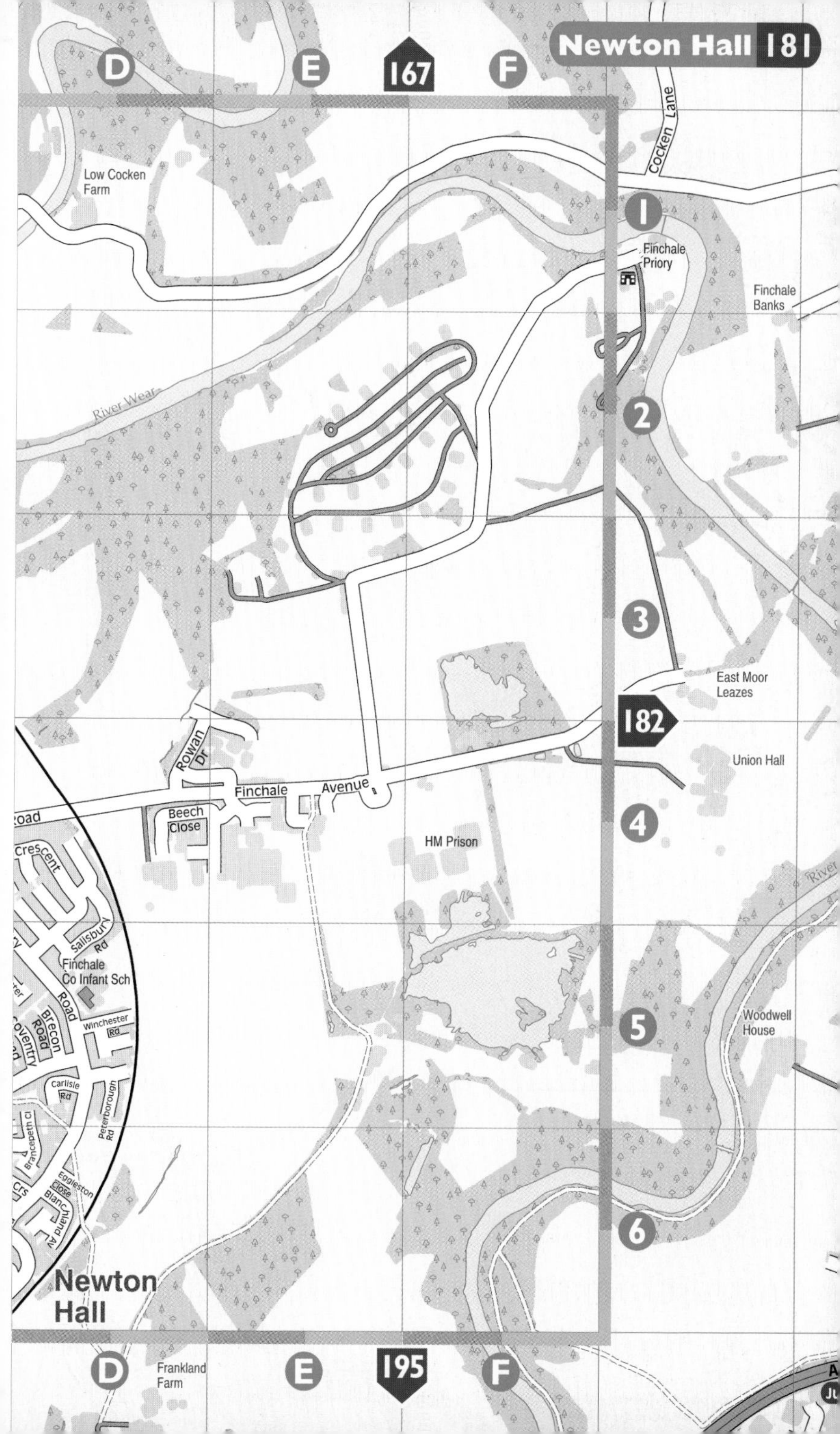
D
E
167
F
Cocken Lane
Low Cocken Farm
1
Finchale Priory
Finchale Banks
River Wear
2
3
East Moor Leazes
182
Union Hall
Rowan Dr
Finchale Avenue
Road
Beech Close
4
HM Prison
Crescent
Salisbury Rd
Finchale Co Infant Sch
Road
Brecon Road
Coventry
Winchester Rd
5
Woodwell House
Carlisle Rd
Peterborough Rd
Brancepeth Cl
Eggleston Close
Blanchland Av
Crs
6
Newton Hall
D
Frankland Farm
E
195
F

A
168
B
C
Cocken Lane
Finchale Priory
Finchale Banks
Cocken Road
Cocken Roa
Broom House
A1(M)
1
2
3
4
5
6
East Moor Leazes
181
Union Hall
Raintonpark Wood
HM Prison
River Wear
Woodwell House
Low Grange
A690
196
Junction 62
Falls Way
Dene
Kinley Road
Filby Dr.
Romney Dr
1 grid square represents 500 metres

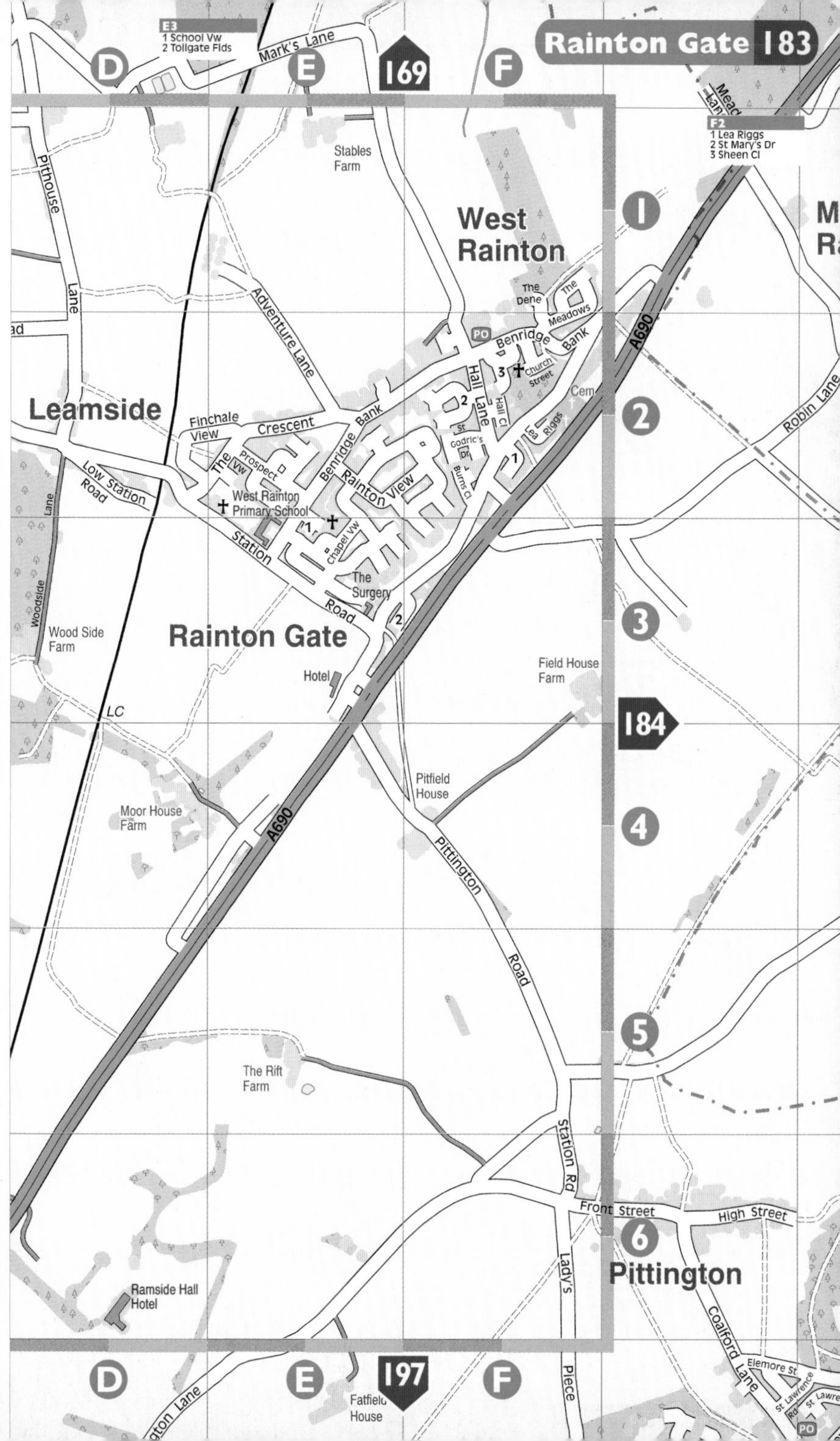
E3
1 School Vw
2 Tollgate Flds
Mark's Lane
169
D
E
F
F2
1 Lea Riggs
2 St Mary's Dr
3 Sheen Cl
Stables Farm
West Rainton
Pithouse Lane
Adventure Lane
The Dene
The Meadows
PO
Benridge Bank
Church Street
Hall Lane
Hall Cl
Lea Riggs
Cem
A690
Robin Lane
Leamside
Finchale View
Crescent
Benridge Bank
St Godric's Dr
Burns Cl
The Vw
Prospect
Rainton View
Low Station Road
West Rainton Primary School
Chapel Vw
Station Road
The Surgery
Woodside Lane
Wood Side Farm
Rainton Gate
Hotel
Field House Farm
LC
184
Pitfield House
Moor House Farm
Pittington Road
The Rift Farm
Station Rd
Front Street
High Street
Lady's Piece
Pittington
Ramside Hall Hotel
Coalford Lane
Elemore St
St Lawrence Rd
197
Fatfield House
1
2
3
4
5
6

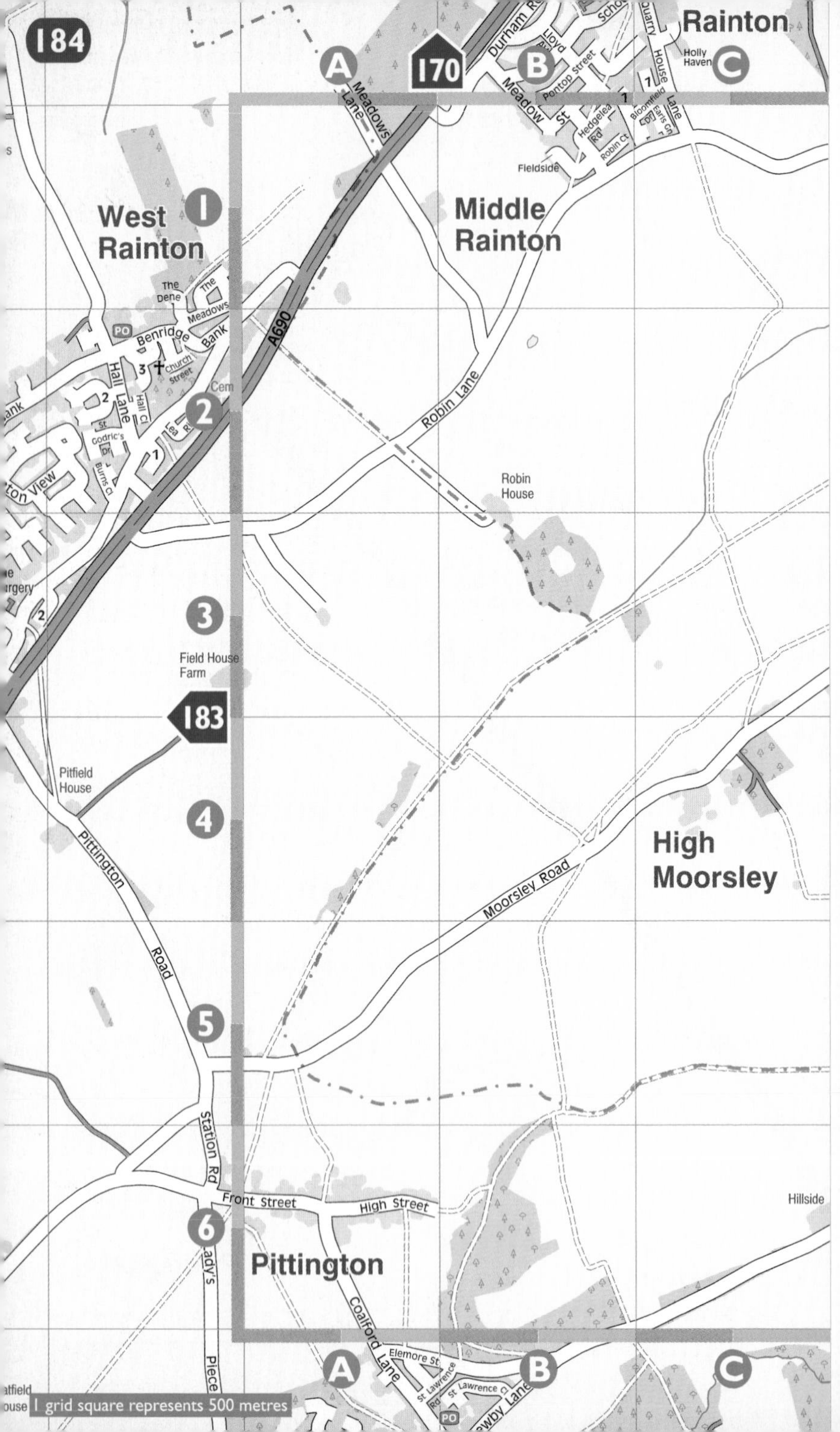

1 grid square represents 500 metres

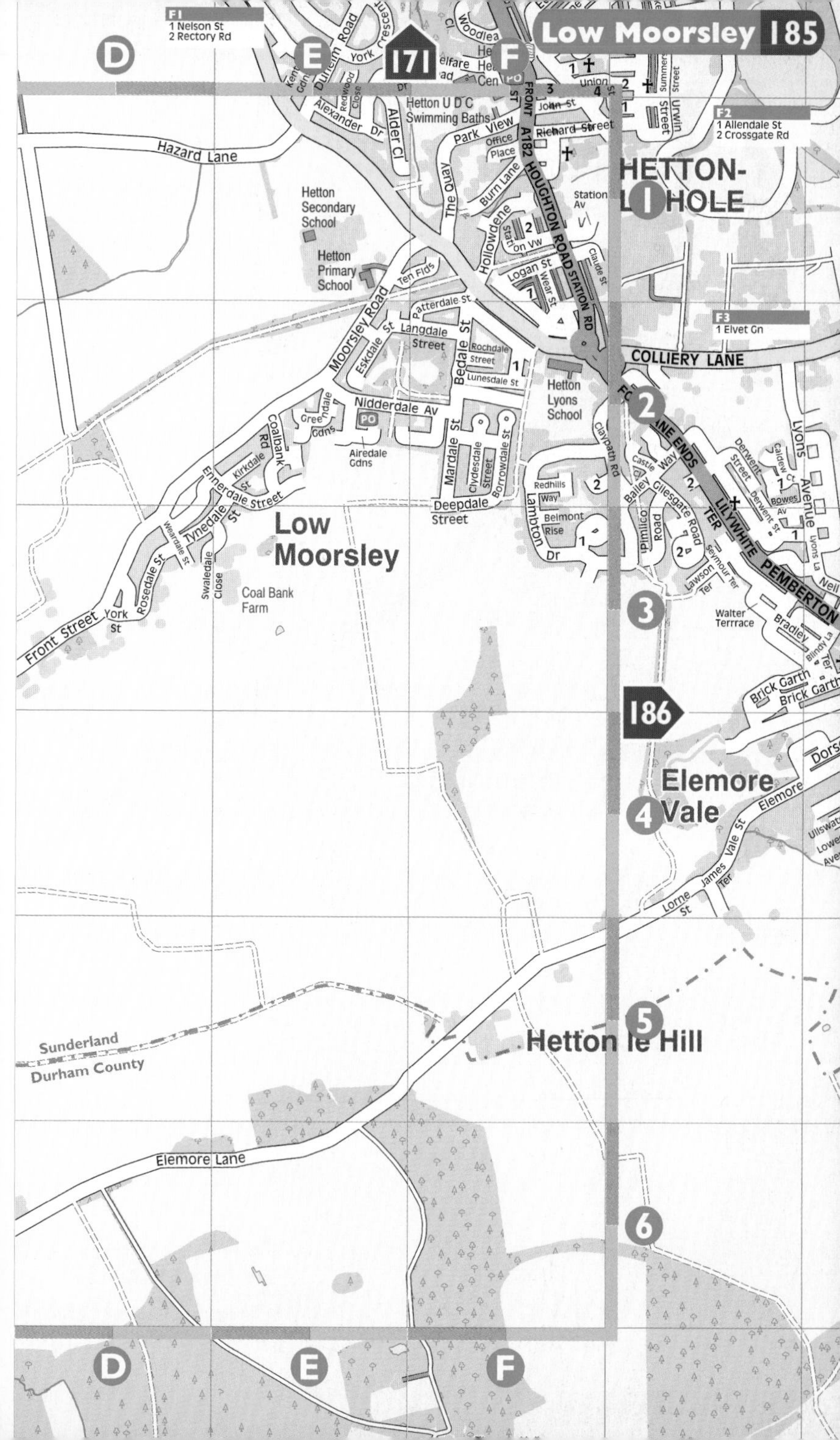
F1
1 Nelson St
2 Rectory Rd
F2
1 Allendale St
2 Crossgate Rd
F3
1 Elvet Gn
171
186
HETTON-LE-HOLE
Low Moorsley
Elemore Vale
Hetton le Hill
Hazard Lane
Hetton Secondary School
Hetton Primary School
Hetton U D C Swimming Baths
Hetton Lyons School
Coal Bank Farm
COLLIERY LANE
A182 HOUGHTON ROAD
STATION RD
FRONT ST
Moorsley Road
Front Street
Elemore Lane
Sunderland
Durham County
Alexander Dr
Alder Cl
Park View
The Quay
Burn Lane
Hollowdene
Office Place
Richard Street
John St
Union St
Logan St
Wear St
Claude St
Station Av
Ten Flds
Patterdale St
Eskdale St
Langdale Street
Bedale St
Rochdale Street
Lunesdale St
Nidderdale Av
Airedale Gdns
Coalbank Rd
Kirkdale St
Ennerdale Street
Tynedale St
Weardale St
Rosedale St
York St
Swaledale Close
Mardale St
Clydesdale Street
Borrowdale St
Deepdale Street
Redhills Way
Belmont Rise
Lambton Dr
Claypath Rd
Castle Way
Bailey
Pimlico Road
Gilesgate Road
LILYWHITE TER
PEMBERTON
Seymour Ter
Lawson Ter
Walter Terrrace
Bradley
Blindy La
Derwent Street
Derwent St
Caldew Ct
Bowes Av
Lyons Avenue
Lyons La
Brick Garth
Elemore Vale
James Ter
Lorne St
Durham Road
York Crescent
Redwood Close
Woodlea
PO

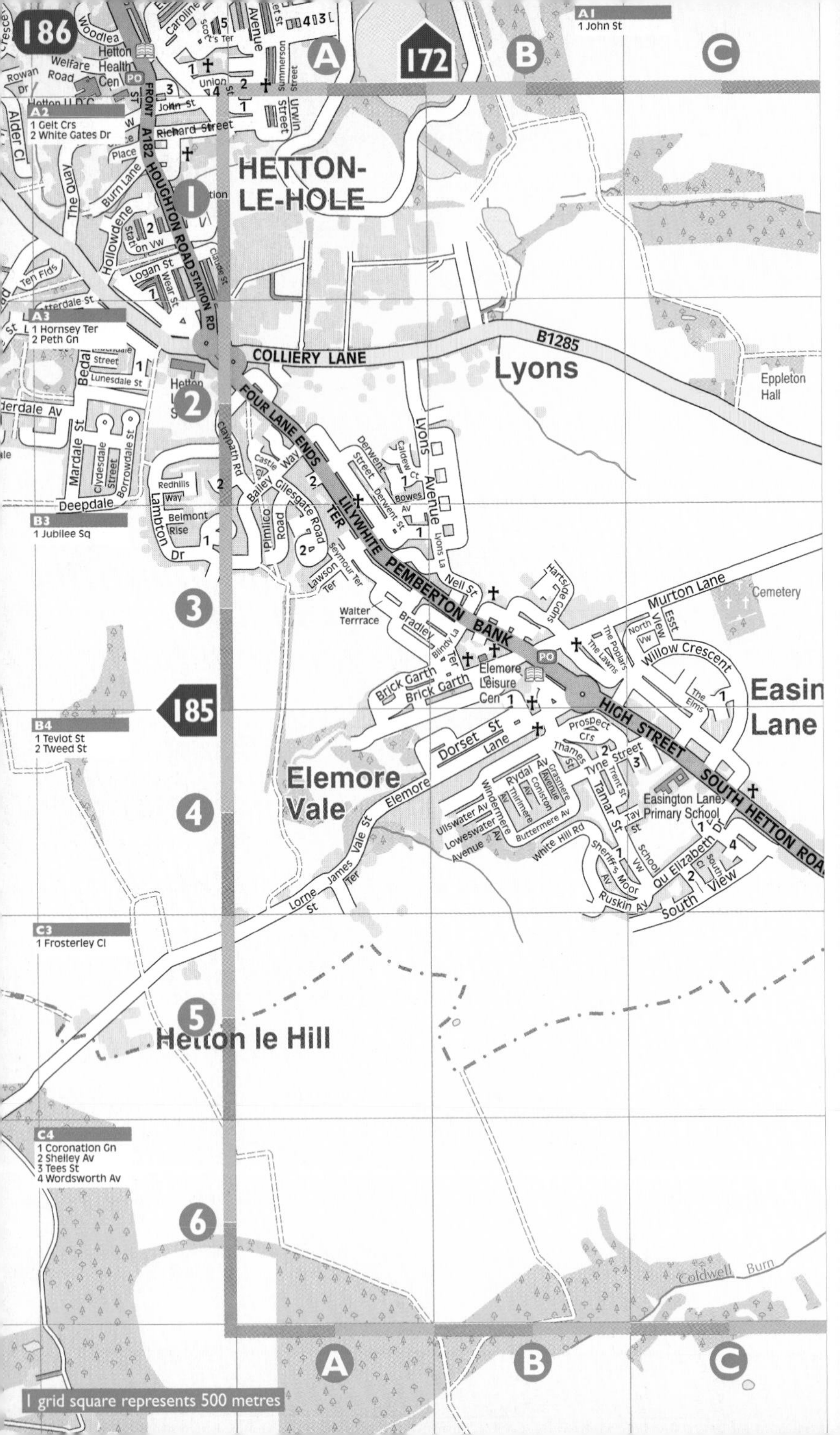

186
172
185
A
B
C
1
2
3
4
5
6
A1
1 John St
A2
1 Gelt Crs
2 White Gates Dr
A3
1 Hornsey Ter
2 Peth Gn
B3
1 Jubilee Sq
B4
1 Teviot St
2 Tweed St
C3
1 Frosterley Cl
C4
1 Coronation Gn
2 Shelley Av
3 Tees St
4 Wordsworth Av
HETTON-
LE-HOLE
Lyons
Eppleton
Hall
Cemetery
Easin
Lane
Elemore
Vale
Hetton le Hill
COLLIERY LANE
B1285
FOUR LANE ENDS
LILYWHITE TER
PEMBERTON BANK
HIGH STREET
SOUTH HETTON ROA
A182 HOUGHTON ROAD
FRONT ST
STATION RD
Murton Lane
Willow Crescent
Easington Lane Primary School
Elemore Leisure Cen
Walter Terrrace
Coldwell Burn
1 grid square represents 500 metres

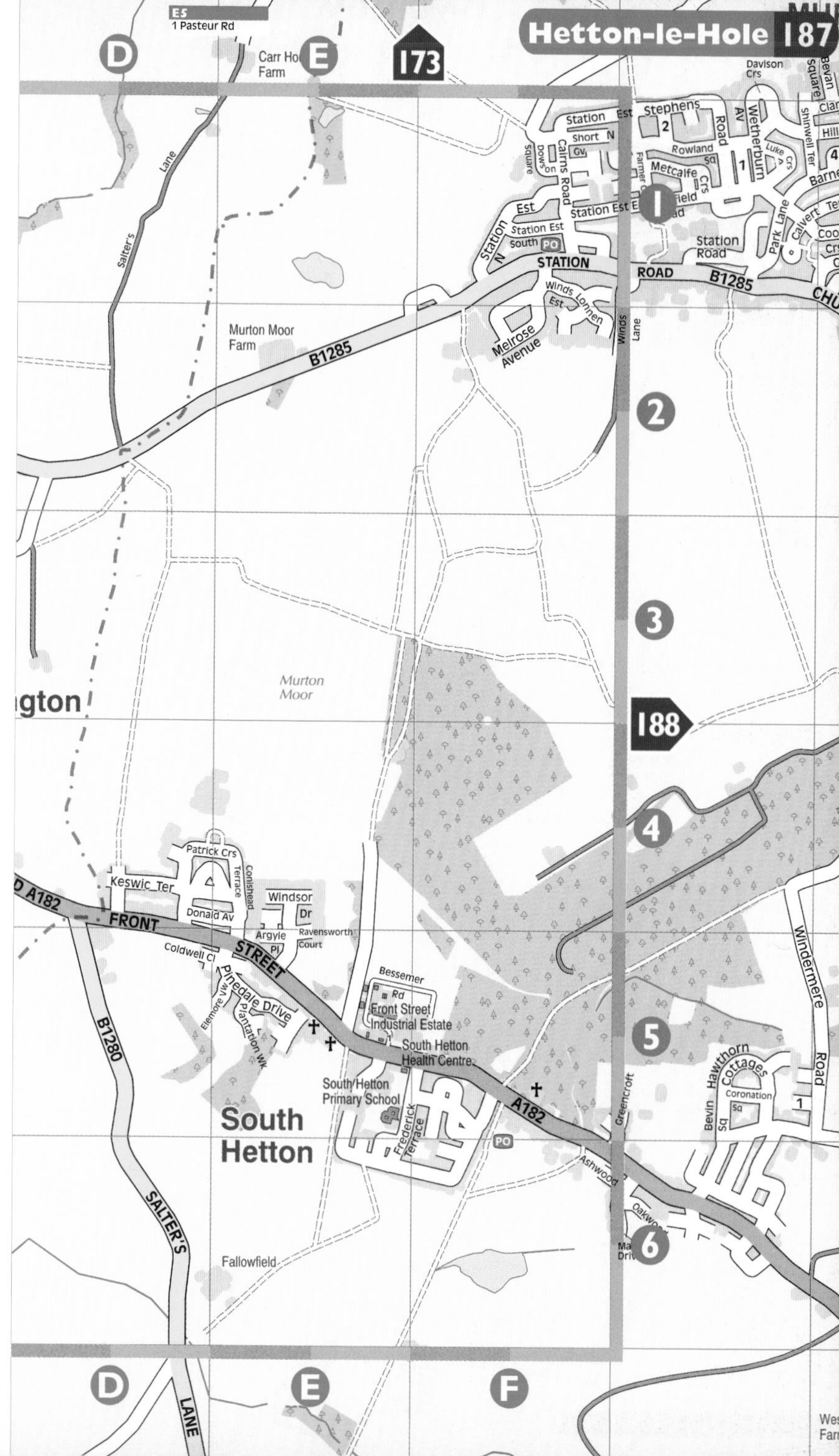
E5
1 Pasteur Rd
D
E
F
173
188
Carr House Farm
Murton Moor Farm
Murton Moor
B1285
Salter's Lane
STATION ROAD B1285
Station Est
Stephens
Short N
Gv
Dows on Square
Cairns Road
Rowland Sq
Metcalfe Crs
Wetherburn Av
Road
Luke Crs
Davison Crs
Bevan Square
Shinwell Ter
Clark
Hill
Barne
Station Est
Station Est South
PO
Station N
Station Road
Park Lane
Calvert Ter
Coo
Crs
Winds Lonnen Est
Melrose Avenue
Winds Lane
CHU
A182
FRONT STREET
Patrick Crs
Conishead Terrace
Keswic Ter
Windsor Dr
Donald Av
Argyle Pl
Ravensworth Court
Coldwell Cl
Pinedale Drive
Elemore Vw
Plantation Wk
Bessemer Rd
Front Street Industrial Estate
South Hetton Health Centre
South Hetton Primary School
Frederick Terrace
South Hetton
B1280
SALTER'S LANE
Fallowfield
Greencroft
Ashwood
Oakwood
Ma Dri
Windermere Road
Hawthorn Cottages
Coronation Sq
Bevin Sq
Wes Farm
1
2
3
4
5
6

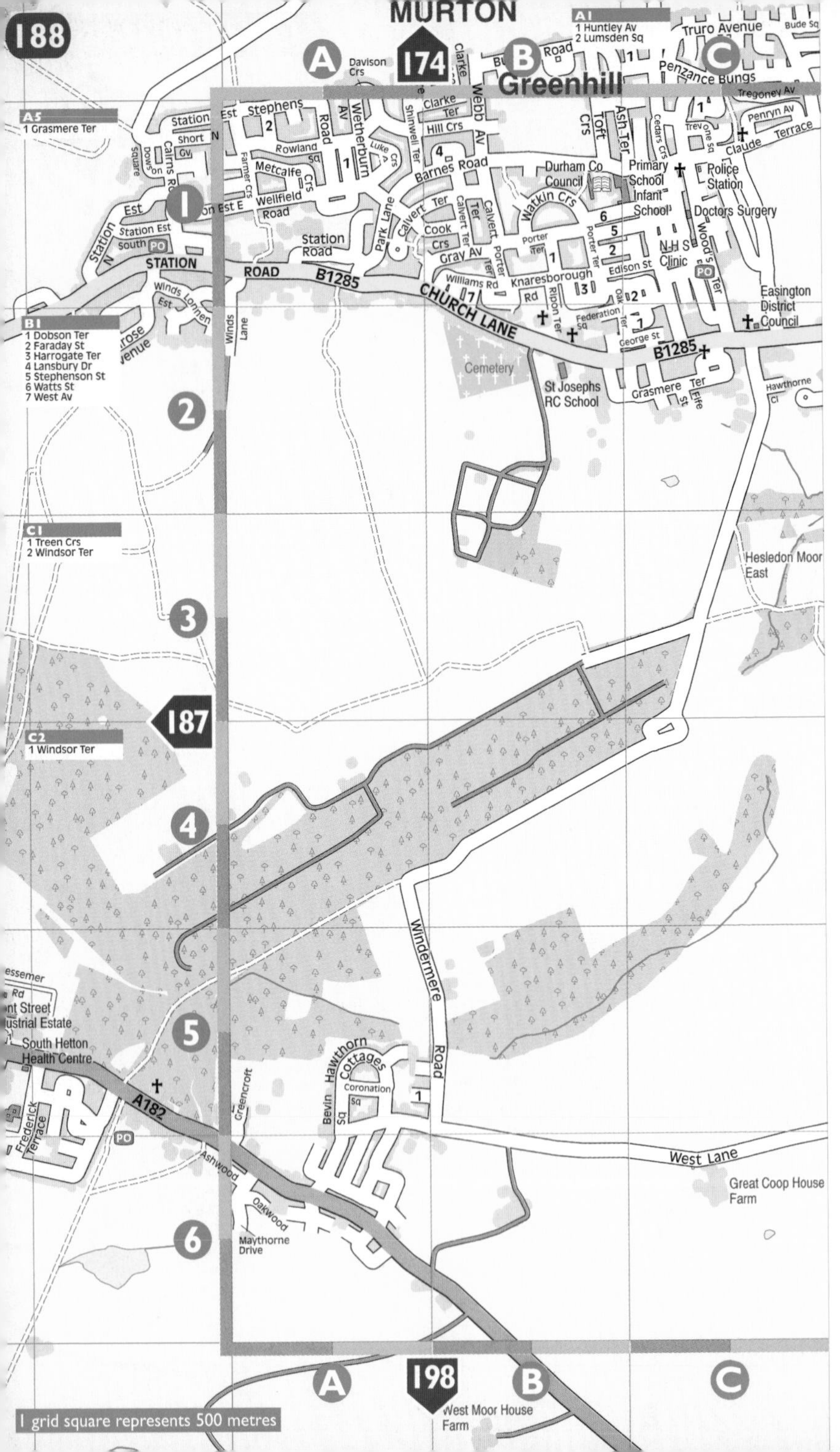
MURTON
174
Greenhill
A1
1 Huntley Av
2 Lumsden Sq
A5
1 Grasmere Ter
B1
1 Dobson Ter
2 Faraday St
3 Harrogate Ter
4 Lansbury Dr
5 Stephenson St
6 Watts St
7 West Av
C1
1 Treen Crs
2 Windsor Ter
C2
1 Windsor Ter
Davison Crs
Truro Avenue
Bude Sq
Penzance Bungs
Tregoney Av
Penryn Av
Claude Terrace
Station Est
Stephens
Wetherburn Av
Clarke Ter
Webb Av
Hill Crs
Rowland Sq
Metcalfe Crs
Wellfield Road
Barnes Road
Durham Co Council
Primary School
Infant School
Police Station
Doctors Surgery
Watkin Crs
Station Road
Park Lane
Calvert Ter
Cook Crs
Gray Av
Porter Ter
Knaresborough Rd
Ripon Ter
Edison St
N H S Clinic
PO
Easington District Council
STATION ROAD
B1285
CHURCH LANE
Williams Rd
Federation Sq
Oak Ter
George St
Winds Lane
Winds Lonnen Est
Cemetery
St Josephs RC School
Grasmere Ter
Fife St
Hawthorne Cl
Hesledon Moor East
187
Windermere Road
South Hetton Health Centre
A182
Frederick Terrace
PO
Greencroft
Ashwood
Oakwood
Maythorne Drive
Hawthorn Cottages
Coronation Sq
Bevin Sq
West Lane
Great Coop House Farm
198
West Moor House Farm
A
B
C
1
2
3
4
5
6
1 grid square represents 500 metres

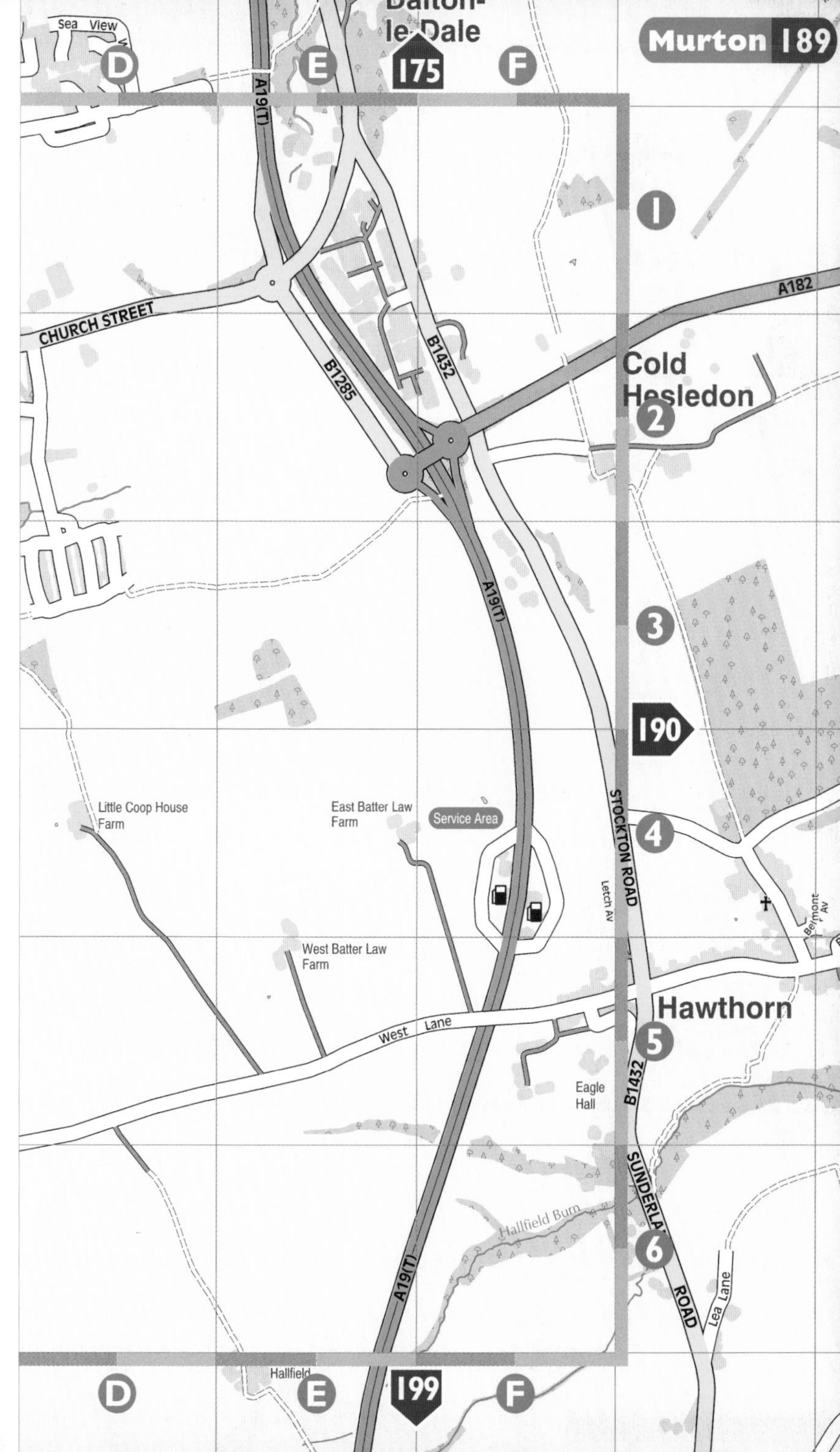
Sea View
D
E
F
Dalton-le-Dale
175
A19(T)
CHURCH STREET
B1285
B1432
A182
Cold Hesledon
1
2
3
4
5
6
190
Little Coop House Farm
East Batter Law Farm
Service Area
West Batter Law Farm
STOCKTON ROAD
Letch Av
Belmont Av
Hawthorn
West Lane
Eagle Hall
B1432
SUNDERLAND ROAD
Hallfield Burn
Lea Lane
Hallfield
199

190

A
176
B
C
1
2
3
4
5
6
189
200
A182
B1432
A19(T)
Cold
Hesledon
Hesledon
East House
Service Area
STOCKTON ROAD
Letch Av
Belmont Av
Barn Hollows
Hawthorn
West Lane
Eagle
Hall
B1432
SUNDERLAND
ROAD
Hawthorn Burn
Thorpe Lea West
Hallfield Burn
Lea Lane
Petwell Lane
1 grid square represents 500 metres

D
E
177
F
A182
1
2
Kinley Hill
Chourdon Point
3
Hawthorn Hive
Hawthorn Burn
4
Beacon Point
Shippersea Bay
5
6
White Lea
Dene Av
East
West Av
D
E
201
F
The Crs
EASINGTON

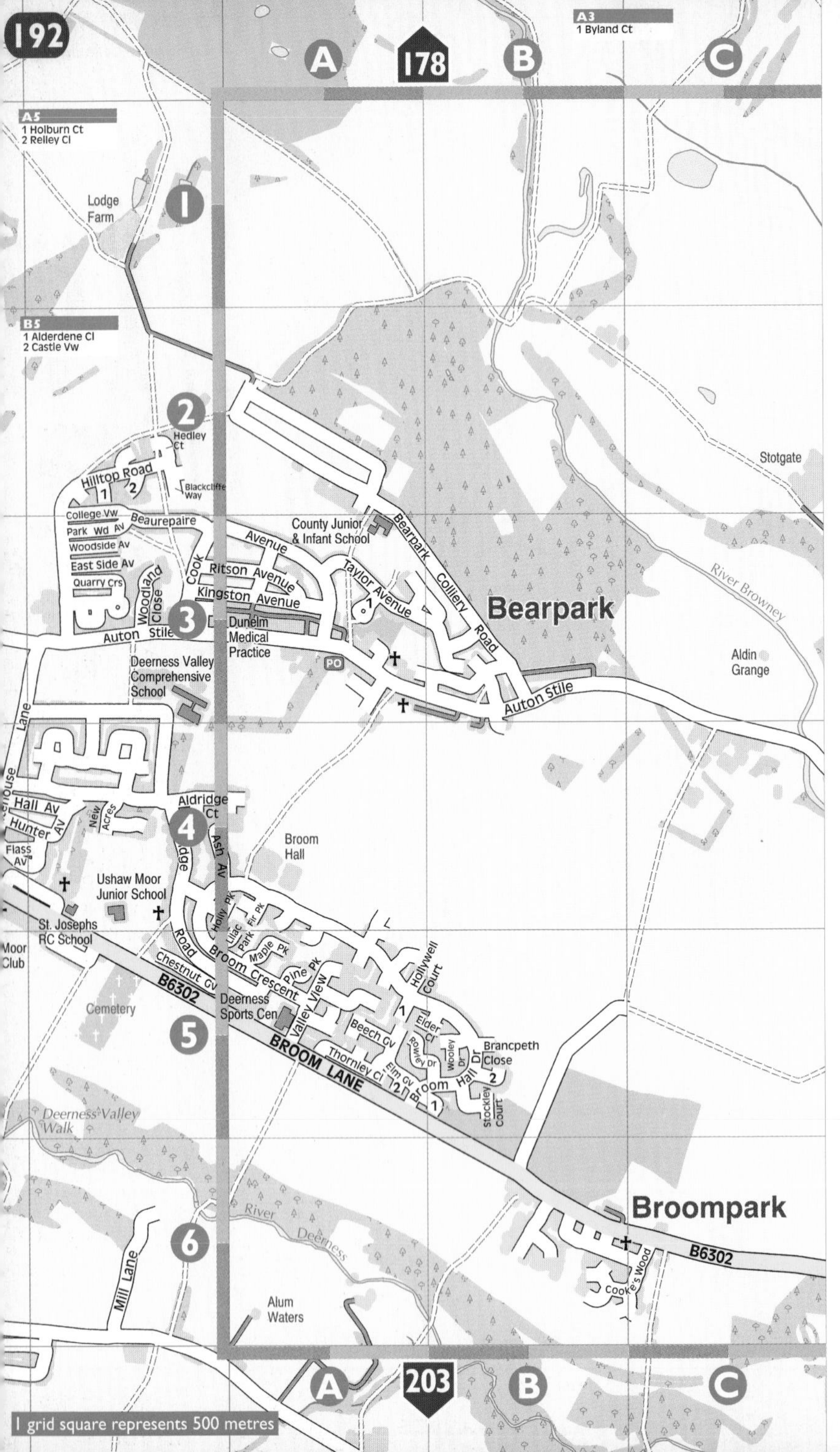
A3
1 Byland Ct
178
A5
1 Holburn Ct
2 Relley Cl
Lodge Farm
B5
1 Alderdene Cl
2 Castle Vw
Hedley Ct
Hilltop Road
Blackcliffe Way
College Vw
Beaurepaire
Park Wd Av
Woodside Av
East Side Av
Quarry Crs
Woodland Close
Cook
Ritson Avenue
Kingston Avenue
Avenue
County Junior & Infant School
Taylor Avenue
Bearpark Colliery Road
Bearpark
Stotgate
River Browney
Aldin Grange
Auton Stile
Dunelm Medical Practice
PO
Deerness Valley Comprehensive School
Lane
Hall Av
Hunter Av
Flass Av
New Acres
Aldridge Ct
Ash Av
Broom Hall
Ushaw Moor Junior School
St. Josephs RC School
Moor Club
Holly Pk
Lilac Park
Fir Pk
Maple Pk
Pine Pk
Hollywell Court
Road
Broom Crescent
Chestnut Gv
B6302
Cemetery
Deerness Sports Cen
Valley View
Beech Gv
Elder Cl
Rowley Dr
Wooley Dr
Brancpeth Close
Broom Hall Dr
Thornley Cl
Elm Gv
Stockley Court
BROOM LANE
Deerness Valley Walk
River Deerness
Broompark
Cooke's Wood
Mill Lane
Alum Waters
203
1 grid square represents 500 metres

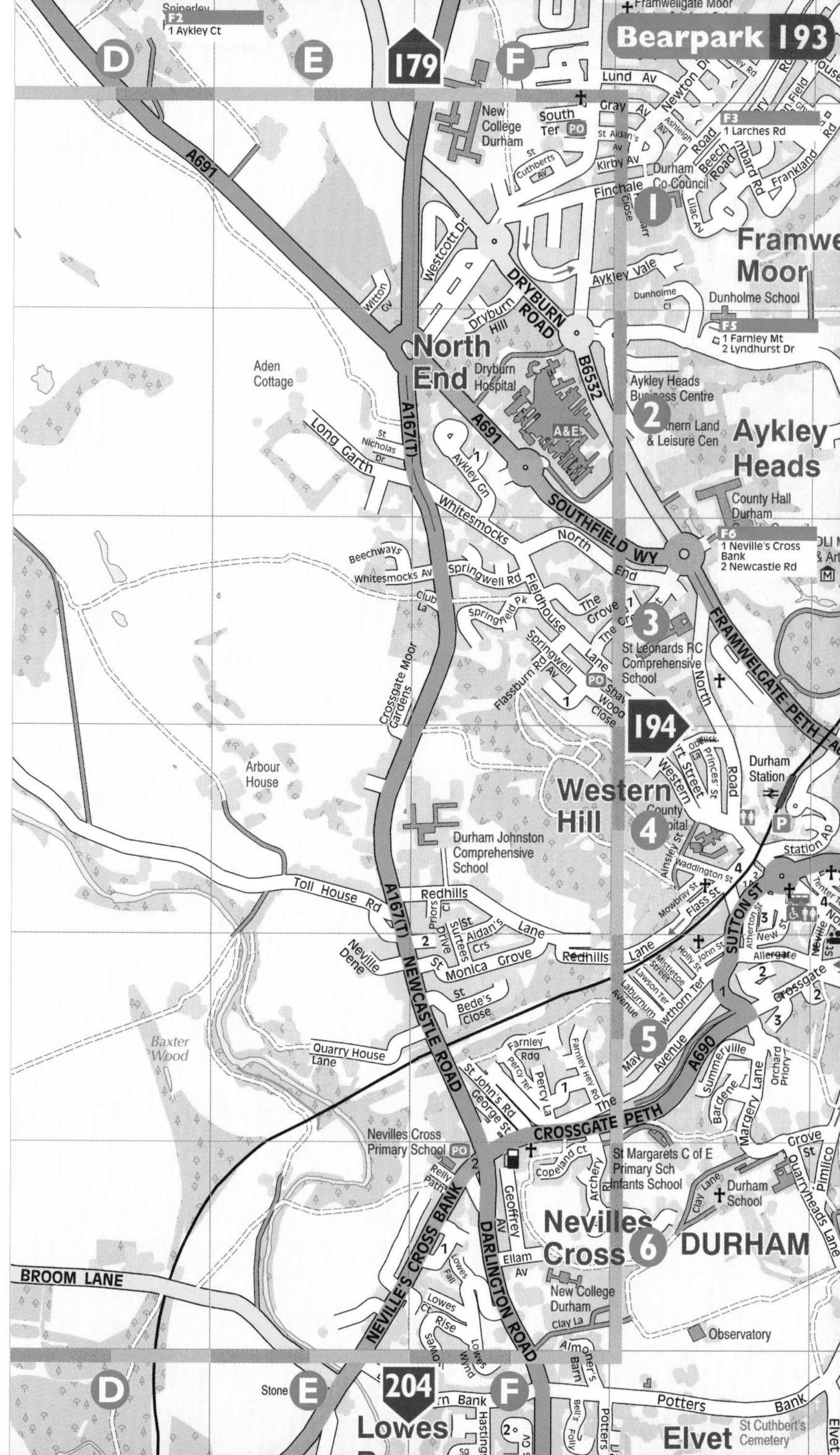
179
194
204
D
E
F
1
2
3
4
5
6
F2
1 Aykley Ct
F3
1 Larches Rd
F5
1 Farnley Mt
2 Lyndhurst Dr
F6
1 Neville's Cross Bank
2 Newcastle Rd
North End
Framwelgate Moor
Aykley Heads
Western Hill
Nevilles Cross
DURHAM
Elvet
Lowes
A691
A167(T)
B6532
A690
DRYBURN ROAD
SOUTHFIELD WY
FRAMWELGATE PETH
NEWCASTLE ROAD
CROSSGATE PETH
NEVILLE'S CROSS BANK
DARLINGTON ROAD
BROOM LANE
New College Durham
Durham Co Council
Dunholme School
Dryburn Hospital
Aykley Heads Business Centre
County Hall Durham
St Leonards RC Comprehensive School
Durham Station
Durham Johnston Comprehensive School
Nevilles Cross Primary School
St Margarets C of E Primary Sch Infants School
Durham School
Observatory
St Cuthbert's Cemetery
Aden Cottage
Arbour House
Baxter Wood
Toll House Rd
Quarry House Lane
Long Garth
Whitesmocks
North End
Springwell Rd
Fieldhouse Lane
Redhills Lane
Monica Grove
Potters Bank
Station Ap
Sutton St
Crossgate
Allergate
Margery Lane
Summerville
Aykley Vale
Westcott Dr
Lund Av
Beech Road
Frankland

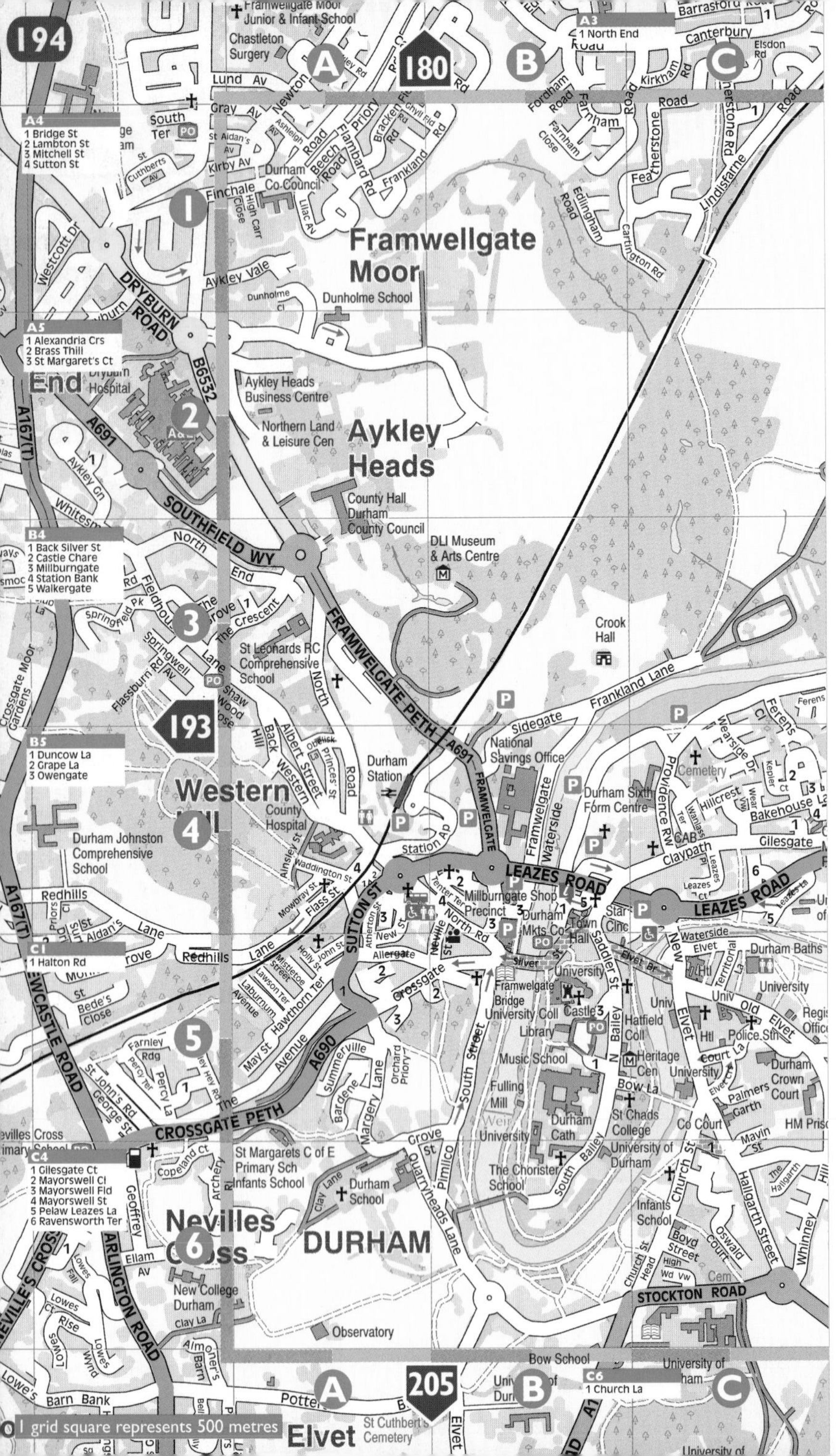

180
A
B
C
Framwellgate Moor Junior & Infant School
Chastleton Surgery
Lund Av
Gray Av
Newton
Ashleigh Av
Road
Beech Road
Flambard Rd
Priory
Bracken Fld
Chyll Fld Rd
Frankland Rd
A3
1 North End
Barrasford Road
Canterbury
Elsdon Rd
Fordham Road
Farnham Road
Farnham Close
Kirkham Rd
Featherstone Rd
Lindisfarne Road
Edlingham Road
Cartington Rd
A4
1 Bridge St
2 Lambton St
3 Mitchell St
4 Sutton St
South Ter
PO
St Aidan's Av
Kirby Av
Cuthberts Av
Durham Co Council
Finchale
High Carr Close
Lilac Av
1
Framwellgate Moor
Westcott Dr
Aykley Vale
DRYBURN ROAD
Dunholme Cl
Dunholme School
A5
1 Alexandria Crs
2 Brass Thill
3 St Margaret's Ct
End
Dryburn Hospital
B6532
2
Aykley Heads Business Centre
Northern Land & Leisure Cen
Aykley Heads
A167(T)
A691
Aykley Gn
Whitesmocks
SOUTHFIELD WY
County Hall Durham County Council
DLI Museum & Arts Centre
B4
1 Back Silver St
2 Castle Chare
3 Millburngate
4 Station Bank
5 Walkergate
North End
Fieldhouse
Springfield Pk
3
The Grove
The Crescent
Springwell Av
Flassburn Rd
Lane
FRAMWELGATE PETH
St Leonards RC Comprehensive School
North Road
Crook Hall
Frankland Lane
PO
Shaw Wood Close
193
Crossgate Moor Gardens
B5
1 Duncow La
2 Grape La
3 Owengate
Western Hill
4
Hill
Back Western
Albert Street
Obelisk La
Princes' St
Durham Station
County Hospital
Sidegate
National Savings Office
Framwellgate Waterside
Durham Sixth Form Centre
Providence Rw
Wearside Dr
Ferens Cl
Cemetery
Kepler Ct
Hillcrest
Bakehouse La
Gilesgate
Claypath
CAB
Leazes Pl
A691 FRAMWELGATE
Durham Johnston Comprehensive School
Station Ap
Ainsley St
Waddington St
Mowbray St
Flass St
SUTTON ST
Atherton St
New St
Tenter Ter
North Rd
LEAZES ROAD
Millburngate Shop Precinct
Durham Mkts Co
Town Hall
Star Cinc
Waterside
Elvet
Durham Baths
Redhills
Priors Cl
St Aidan's
Lane
Redhills Lane
C1
1 Halton Rd
John St
Holly St
Mistletoe Street
Lawson Ter
Laburnum Avenue
Allergate
Crossgate
Silver St
Framwelgate Bridge
University Coll
University
Castle
Library
Saddler St
Elvet Br
New Elvet
Territorial La
Old Elvet
University
Police Stn
Regis Office
Bede's Close
5
Farnley Rdg
Percy Ter
Percy La
Hawthorn Ter
May St
Avenue
A690
Summerville
Bardene
Margery Lane
Orchard Priory
South Street
Music School
N Bailey
Hatfield Coll
Heritage Cen
Court La
Durham Crown Court
Fulling Mill
Bow La
St Chads College
University of Durham
Palmers Garth
Co Court
Mavin St
HM Prison
NEWCASTLE ROAD
St John's Rd
George St
CROSSGATE PETH
Nevilles Cross Primary School
Durham Cath
Weir
South Bailey
The Chorister School
C4
1 Gilesgate Ct
2 Mayorswell Cl
3 Mayorswell Fld
4 Mayorswell St
5 Pelaw Leazes La
6 Ravensworth Ter
Copeland Ct
Archery Ri
St Margarets C of E Primary Sch Infants School
Grove St
Pimlico
Quarryheads Lane
Clay Lane
Durham School
Church St
Infants School
Boyd Street
Oswald Court
Hallgarth Street
Whinney Hill
Nevilles Cross
6
Geoffrey Av
DURHAM
Ellam Av
New College Durham
NEVILLE'S CROSS
ARLINGTON ROAD
Lowes Fall
Lowes Rise
Lowes Wynd
Clay La
Observatory
Almoner's Barn
Church St Head
High Wd Vw
Cem
STOCKTON ROAD
Bow School
C6
1 Church La
University of Durham
Lowe's Barn Bank
Potters Bank
205
Elvet
St Cuthbert's Cemetery
A1
1 grid square represents 500 metres

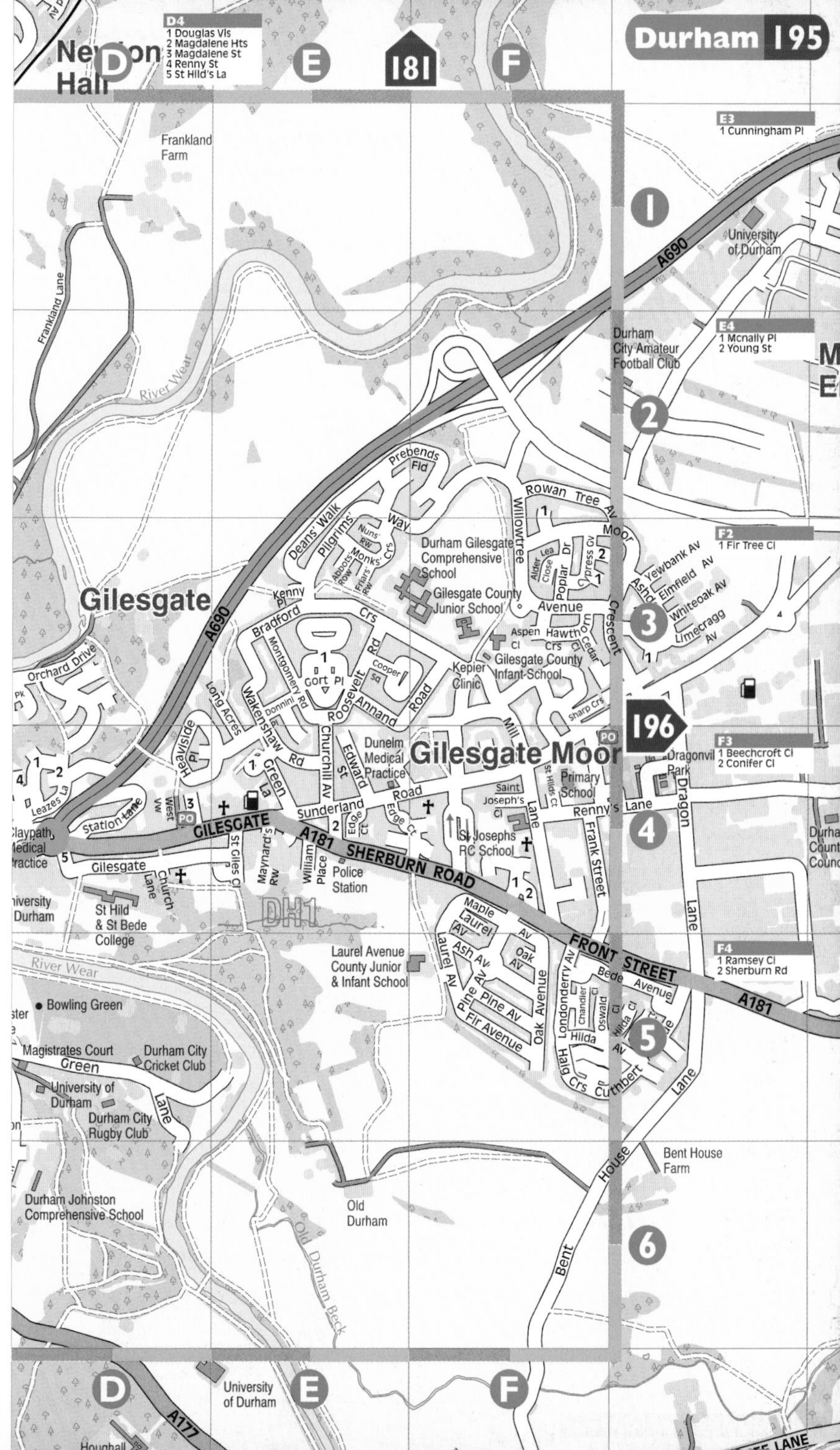

D4
1 Douglas Vls
2 Magdalene Hts
3 Magdalene St
4 Renny St
5 St Hild's La
181
E3
1 Cunningham Pl
E4
1 Mcnally Pl
2 Young St
F2
1 Fir Tree Cl
F3
1 Beechcroft Cl
2 Conifer Cl
F4
1 Ramsey Cl
2 Sherburn Rd
196
Newton Hall
Frankland Farm
Frankland Lane
River Wear
A690
University of Durham
Durham City Amateur Football Club
Gilesgate
Gilesgate Moor
Durham Gilesgate Comprehensive School
Gilesgate County Junior School
Gilesgate County Infant School
Kepier Clinic
Dunelm Medical Practice
St Josephs RC School
Primary School
Dragonville Park
Claypath Medical Practice
St Hild & St Bede College
Police Station
DH1
Laurel Avenue County Junior & Infant School
A181 SHERBURN ROAD
FRONT STREET
GILESGATE
Bowling Green
Magistrates Court
Durham City Cricket Club
Durham City Rugby Club
Durham Johnston Comprehensive School
Old Durham
Old Durham Beck
Bent House Farm
Bent House Lane
University of Durham
A177
Houghall

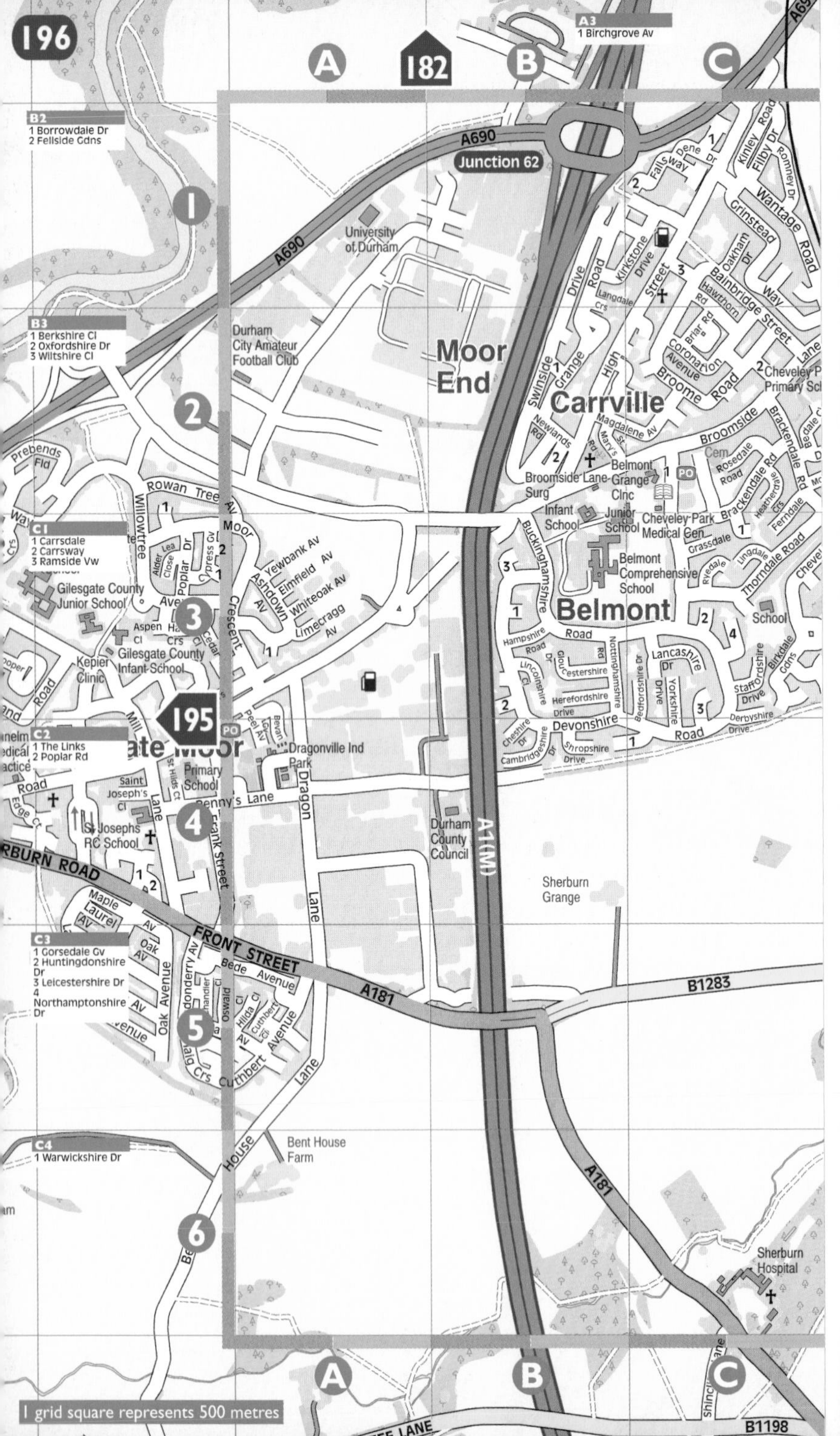

182
A
B
C
A3
1 Birchgrove Av
B2
1 Borrowdale Dr
2 Fellside Gdns
B3
1 Berkshire Cl
2 Oxfordshire Dr
3 Wiltshire Cl
C1
1 Carrsdale
2 Carrsway
3 Ramside Vw
C2
1 The Links
2 Poplar Rd
C3
1 Gorsedale Gv
2 Huntingdonshire Dr
3 Leicestershire Dr
4 Northamptonshire Dr
C4
1 Warwickshire Dr
A690
Junction 62
University of Durham
Durham City Amateur Football Club
Moor End
Carrville
Belmont
Broomside Lane Surg
Belmont Grange Clnc
Infant School
Junior School
Cheveley Park Medical Cen
Belmont Comprehensive School
Cheveley Park Primary Sch
School
Gilesgate County Junior School
Gilesgate County Infant School
Kepier Clinic
195
Dragonville Ind Park
Primary School
St Josephs RC School
Durham County Council
A1(M)
Sherburn Grange
FRONT STREET
A181
B1283
Bent House Farm
Sherburn Hospital
B1198
1 grid square represents 500 metres

D2
1 Borrowdale Cl
2 Ennerdale Cl
3 Patterdale Cl
183
E4
1 Harrison Garth
2 Liddle Av
3 Park House Cl
E5
1 Blair Cl
2 Crawford Cl
F5
1 Hallgarth Vls
2 Peart Cl
Pittington Lane
Fatfield House
Lady's Piece Lane
Priors Grange
Hallgarth
Broomside House
Coalford Beck
Cookshold Lane
Scardale Way
Ullerdale Cl
Drive
Coniston Close
Brookdale
Dowsey Rd
Whitegates Road
Lady Anne Rd
Coalford Rd
Usher Av
Cummings Avenue
Forster Av
Gray Avenue
Beech Road
Kidd Avenue
Sports Centre
Stanley Close
Liddle Av
Hallgarth Street
King St
George St
Mitford Dr
Whalton Cl
Meldon Av
Sherburn
FRONT STREET
B1283
Railway Close
Smith Cl
St Mary's Drive
Cem
Church Wynd
St Cuthberts Wy
Talisman Close
The Crescent
Hope St
Mill Lane
Chapel Ct
Sherburnhouse Beck
Mill Lane
Hallgarth
Rams Hotel

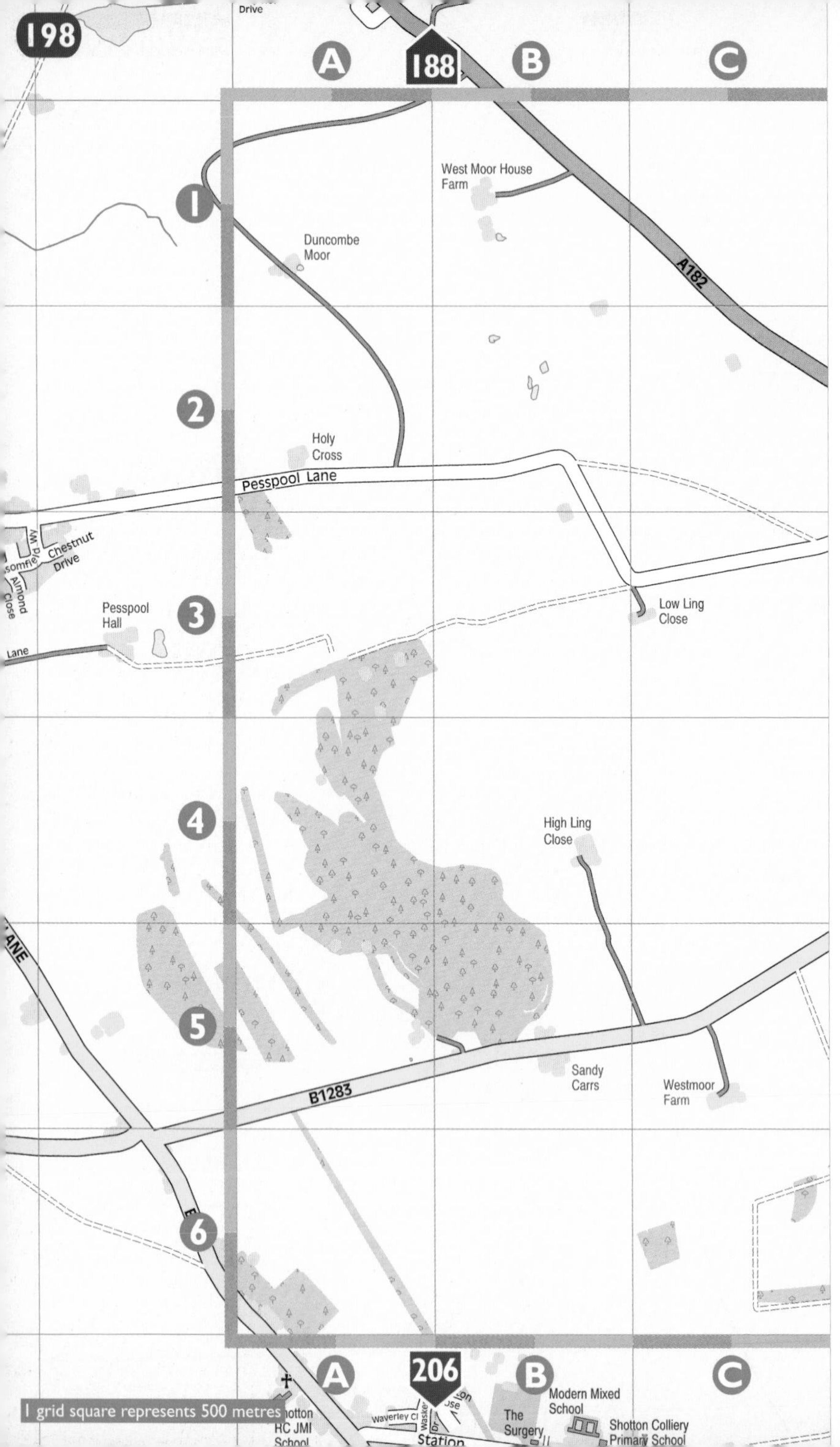

Drive
A
188
B
C
1
2
3
4
5
6
West Moor House
Farm
Duncombe
Moor
A182
Holy
Cross
Pesspool Lane
Chestnut
Drive
Almond
Close
Pesspool
Hall
Lane
Low Ling
Close
High Ling
Close
LANE
B1283
Sandy
Carrs
Westmoor
Farm
A
206
B
C
Modern Mixed
School
The
Surgery
Shotton Colliery
Primary School
Waverley Cl
Station
1 grid square represents 500 metres

F3
1 St Mary's Cl
2 St Thomas Cl
3 Westcliff Cl
D
E
F
189
207
200
1
2
3
4
5
6
Hallfield
EASINGTON
A19(T)
B1432
HALL WALKS
ROSEMARY LANE
Pesspool Lane
The Grove
Glen Dene School
The Spinney
Cadwell Lane
PO
Easington District Council
Sunderland Rd
Low Row
School
Halfield Drive
Clappersgate
South Side
Rymers Close
Durham Lane
Tudor Grange
Cemetery
Stockton Road
Easington Comprehensive School
Nursery Gdns
THORPE ROAD
Sea Vw
Gra Av
A1086
Durham Lane
B1283 DURHAM LANE
Moor House Farm
Andrew's
Kitching Road
Hackworth Road
Easington District Council
Mill Hill
Lowhills Road
Garside Grove
Liddle Cl
Nottingham Place
Buckingham Road
Rigg
Acre Rigg Junior & Infant School
Layburn Place
Chester Pl
Acre
Warwick Pl
Gloucester Place
Cottingham Close
Davy Drive
Pease Road
Lister Road
Mill Hill
COOK
Drive
Way

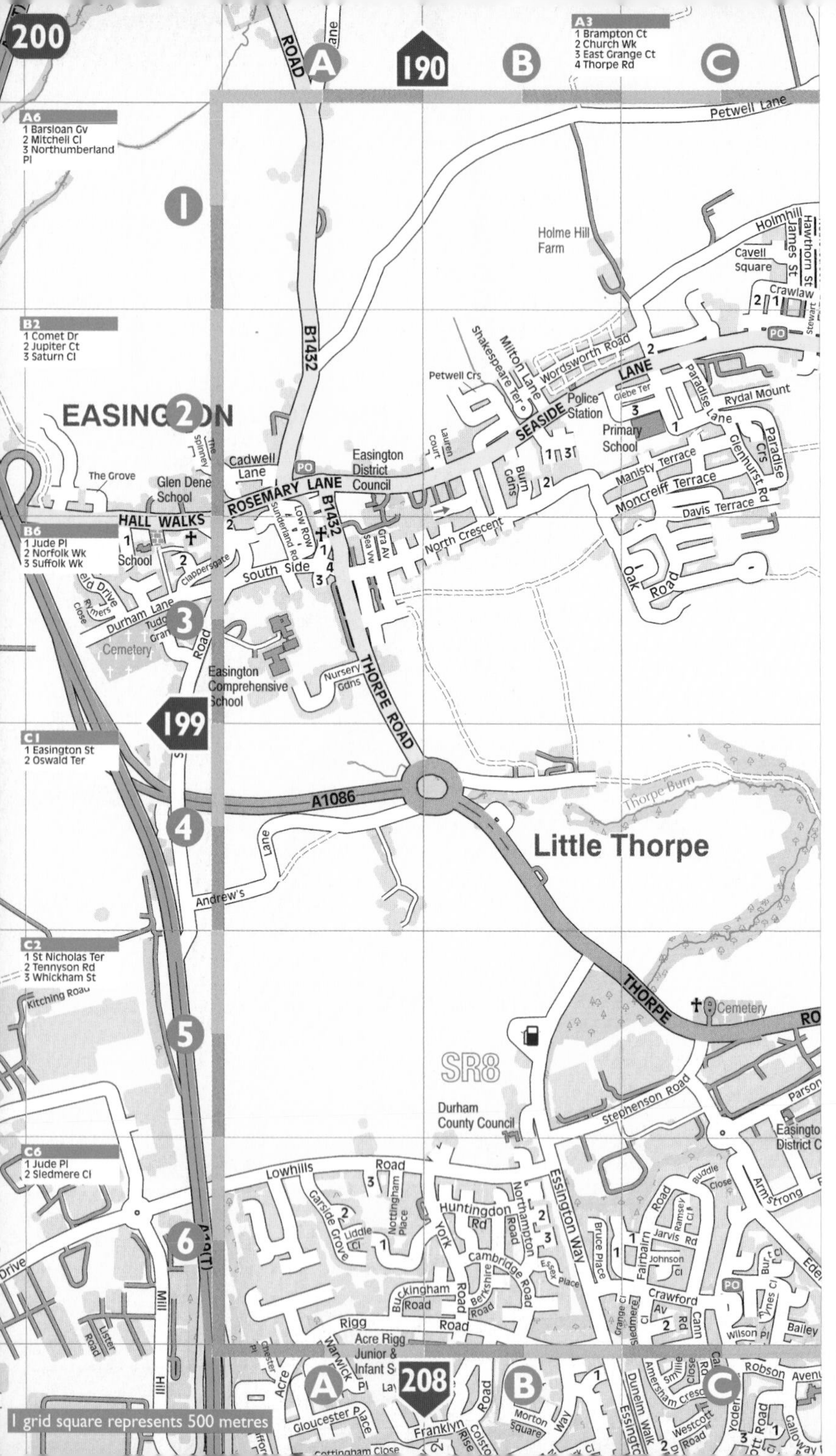
A
190
B
C
A3
1 Brampton Ct
2 Church Wk
3 East Grange Ct
4 Thorpe Rd
A6
1 Barsloan Gv
2 Mitchell Cl
3 Northumberland Pl
B2
1 Comet Dr
2 Jupiter Ct
3 Saturn Cl
B6
1 Jude Pl
2 Norfolk Wk
3 Suffolk Wk
C1
1 Easington St
2 Oswald Ter
C2
1 St Nicholas Ter
2 Tennyson Rd
3 Whickham St
C6
1 Jude Pl
2 Sledmere Cl
Petwell Lane
Holme Hill Farm
Holmhill
Cavell Square
James St
Hawthorn St
Crawlaw
Stewart
B1432
EASINGTON
Petwell Crs
Milton Lane
Shakespeare Ter
Wordsworth Road
SEASIDE LANE
Glebe Ter
Paradise Lane
Rydal Mount
Police Station
Primary School
Paradise Crs
Glenhurst Rd
Manisty Terrace
Moncreiff Terrace
Davis Terrace
Oak Road
The Spinney
Cadwell Lane
The Grove
Glen Dene School
HALL WALKS
ROSEMARY LANE
Easington District Council
Lauren Court
Burn Gdns
Sunderland Rd
Low Row
Gra Av
Sea Vw
North Crescent
School
Clappersgate
South Side
Durham Lane
Rymers Close
Tudor Grange
Cemetery
Road
Easington Comprehensive School
Nursery Gdns
THORPE ROAD
199
A1086
Thorpe Burn
Lane
Little Thorpe
Andrew's
Kitching Road
THORPE ROAD
Cemetery
SR8
Durham County Council
Stephenson Road
Parson
Easington District C
Lowhills Road
Carside Grove
Liddle Cl
Nottingham Place
Huntingdon Rd
York Road
Northampton Road
Essington Way
Bruce Place
Fairbairn Road
Ramsey Cl
Jarvis Rd
Buddle Close
Armstrong
Johnson Cl
Cambridge Road
Essex Place
Berkshire Road
Buckingham Road
Crawford Av
Rd
Cann
Grange Cl
Sledmere Cl
Wilson Pl
Burt Cl
Tynes Cl
Bailey
Eden
Rigg Road
Acre Rigg Junior & Infant S
Drive
Mill Hill
Lister Road
A19(T)
Chester Pl
Acre
Warwick Pl
208
Robson Avenue
Smillie Close
Amersham Cresc
Westcott Road
Dunelm Walk
Gloucester Place
Franklyn Rise
Coniston
Morton Square
Way
Yoden
Scott Road
Galloway
Cottingham Close
1 grid square represents 500 metres

EASINGTON
COLLIERY
Horden
D2
1 Vincent St
White Lea
191
209
D
E
F
1
2
3
4
5
6
Dene Av
East View
Raby Av
West Av
The Crs
Lane
Cem
John Street
Thomas St
Thorpe St
Memorial Avenue
Tower St
Abbot Street
Ashton St
Office Street
School Street
Welfare Close
B1283
PO
Bede Street
STATION ROAD
Paradise
Horden Burn
Horden Point
SUNDERLAND ROAD
Maritime Crs
A1086
Wilkinson Rd
Webb Sq
Thorpe Road
Horden & Easington RC Primary School
Kilburn Drive
Timber Rd
Beaumont Crs
Bruce
Kirkup Road
Moutter Cl
Naisbitt Av
Faraday Road
Yoden Crs
Belford St
Alnwick St
Morpeth St
Rothbury Av
Newcastle Av
Sunderland Av
Northumberland St
Durham Av
Blackhills Road
Thompson St
Sea Vw Gdns
Durham County Council
Park
Yoden
Rise
Lane
Eden Hall Infant School
Doctors Surg
First Street
Third
Nelson
Claxton St
Park La
Eden Street
SUNDERLAND R

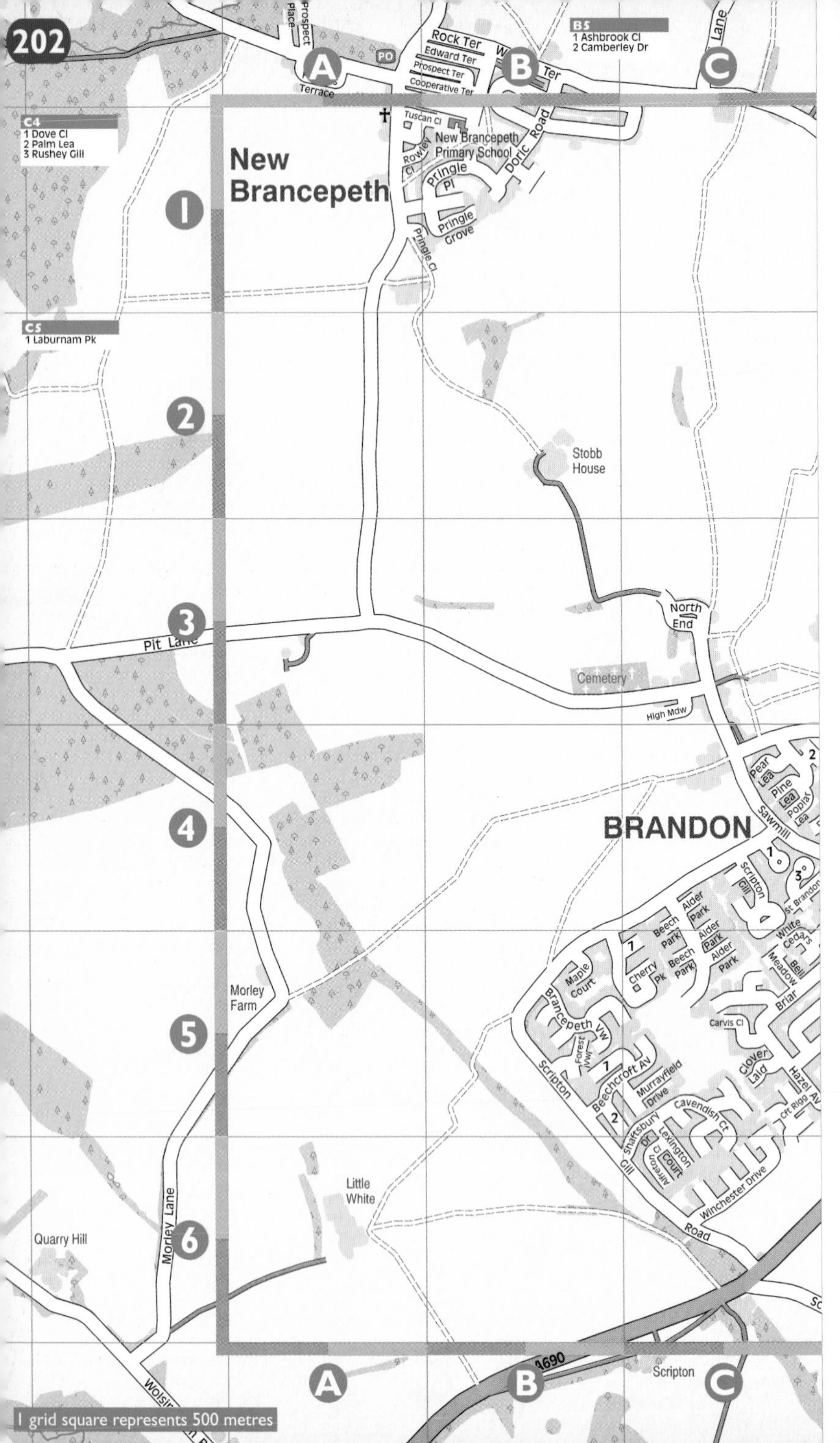
B5
1 Ashbrook Cl
2 Camberley Dr
C4
1 Dove Cl
2 Palm Lea
3 Rushey Gill
C5
1 Laburnam Pk
Prospect Place
Rock Ter
Edward Ter
Prospect Ter
Cooperative Ter
Terrace
PO
Tuscan Cl
New Brancepeth
New Brancepeth Primary School
Doric Road
Rowley Cl
Pringle Pl
Pringle Grove
Pringle Cl
Stobb House
North End
Pit Lane
Cemetery
High Mdw
BRANDON
Pear Lea
Pine Lea
Poplar Lea
Sawmill
Scripton Gill
Alder Park
Beech Park
Cherry Pk
Maple Court
Brancepeth Vw
Forest Vw
Beechcroft Av
Murrayfield Drive
Carvis Cl
Clover Laid
Hazel Av
Cavendish Ct
Shaftsbury Dr
Lexington Court
Alfreton Cl
Winchester Drive
Scripton Gill Road
Cedars
Meadow
Briar
Bell
White
Morley Farm
Little White
Quarry Hill
Morley Lane
Wolsingham Rd
A690
Scripton
1 grid square represents 500 metres

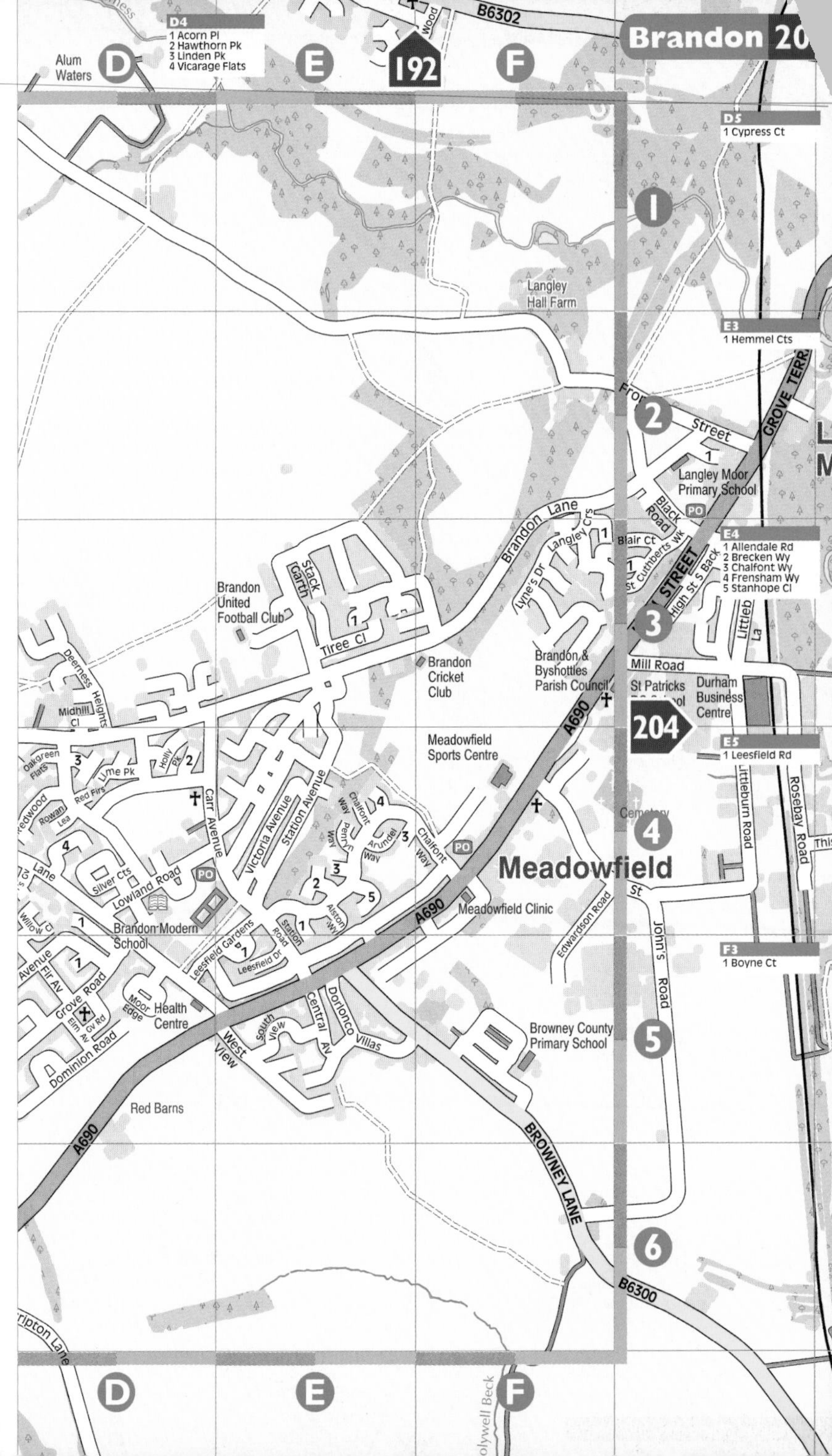
D4
1 Acorn Pl
2 Hawthorn Pk
3 Linden Pk
4 Vicarage Flats
D5
1 Cypress Ct
E3
1 Hemmel Cts
E4
1 Allendale Rd
2 Brecken Wy
3 Chalfont Wy
4 Frensham Wy
5 Stanhope Cl
E5
1 Leesfield Rd
F3
1 Boyne Ct
192
204
Alum Waters
B6302
Langley Hall Farm
Brandon Lane
Front Street
Black Road
Grove Terr
Langley Moor Primary School
Brandon United Football Club
Stack Garth
Tiree Cl
Brandon Cricket Club
Brandon & Byshottles Parish Council
Blair Ct
St Cuthberts Wk
Mill Road
St Patricks
Durham Business Centre
Meadowfield Sports Centre
Deerness Heights
Midhill Cl
Oakgreen Flats
Lime Pk
Holly Pk
Red Firs
Redwood
Rowan Lea
Carr Avenue
Victoria Avenue
Station Avenue
Chalfont Way
Penryn Way
Arundel Way
Meadowfield
Cemetery
Littleburn Road
Rosebay Road
Silver Cts
Lowland Road
Brandon Modern School
Meadowfield Clinic
Edwardson Road
St John's Road
Leesfield Gardens
Leesfield Dr
Station Road
Alston Wk
A690
Fir Av
Grove Road
Elm Av
Gv Rd
Moor Edge
Health Centre
Dominion Road
West View
South View
Central Av
Dorlonco Villas
Browney County Primary School
Red Barns
Browney Lane
B6300
Holywell Beck

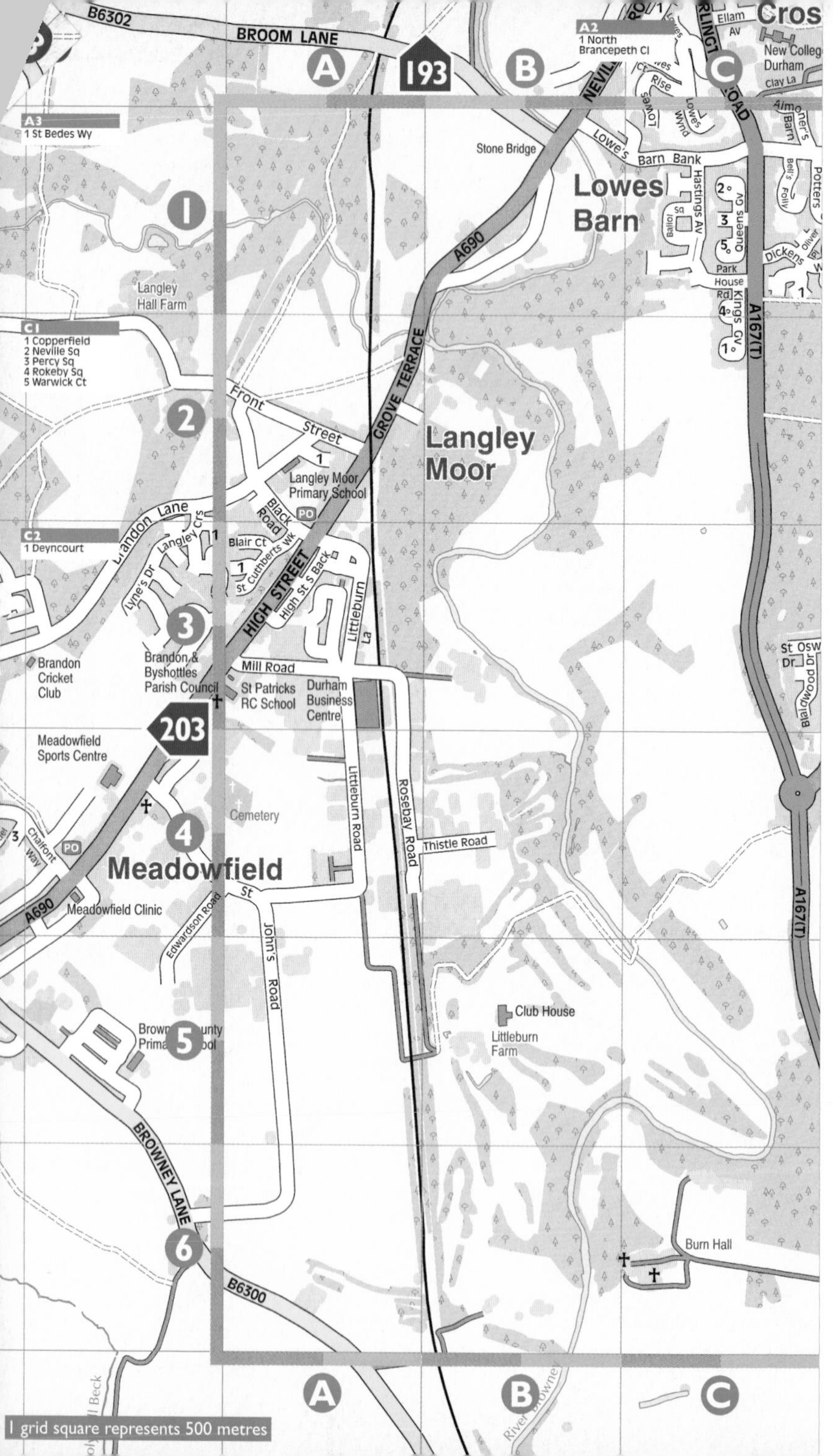

B6302
BROOM LANE
A
193
B
C
A2
1 North
Brancepeth Cl
Ellam Av
New College
Durham
Clay La
Aimoner's Barn
A3
1 St Bedes Wy
Stone Bridge
Lowe's Barn Bank
Lowes
Barn
Hastings Av
Queens Gv
Balliol Sq
Bell's Folly
Potters
Dickens
Oliver
Park House Rd
Kings Gv
A167(T)
A690
1
Langley
Hall Farm
C1
1 Copperfield
2 Neville Sq
3 Percy Sq
4 Rokeby Sq
5 Warwick Ct
GROVE TERRACE
Front Street
2
Langley
Moor
Langley Moor
Primary School
Black Road
PO
Brandon Lane
Langley Crs
Blair Ct
St Cuthberts Wk
C2
1 Deyncourt
Lyne's Dr
HIGH STREET
High St S Back
Littleburn La
3
St Osw Dr
Blackwood Dr
Brandon
Cricket
Club
Brandon &
Byshottles
Parish Council
Mill Road
St Patricks
RC School
Durham
Business
Centre
203
Meadowfield
Sports Centre
Littleburn Road
Rosebay Road
Cemetery
Chalfont Way
PO
4
Thistle Road
Meadowfield
St
Meadowfield Clinic
Edwardson Road
John's Road
Club House
Littleburn
Farm
5
BROWNEY LANE
6
Burn Hall
B6300
River Browney
Beck
1 grid square represents 500 metres

D1
1 Pickwick Cl
D
E
F
194
Observatory
Bow School
University of Durham
Potters Bank
Elvet Hill
St Cuthbert's Cemetery
Elvet Hill Road
SOUTH ROAD A177
Trevelyan College
Grey College
St Aidans College
University of Durham
Houghall College
A177
Nickleby Chare
Millhill Lane
Van Mildert College
Hollingside Lane
Botanic Gardens
Club House
Golf Course
SOUTH MONEY SLACK A177
Cemetery
Durham High School
Cedar Dr
SOUTH ROAD
Farm Road
Farewell Hall
High Houghall
Low Butterby
River Wear
Low Burnhall
Croxdale Wood House
1
2
3
4
5
6

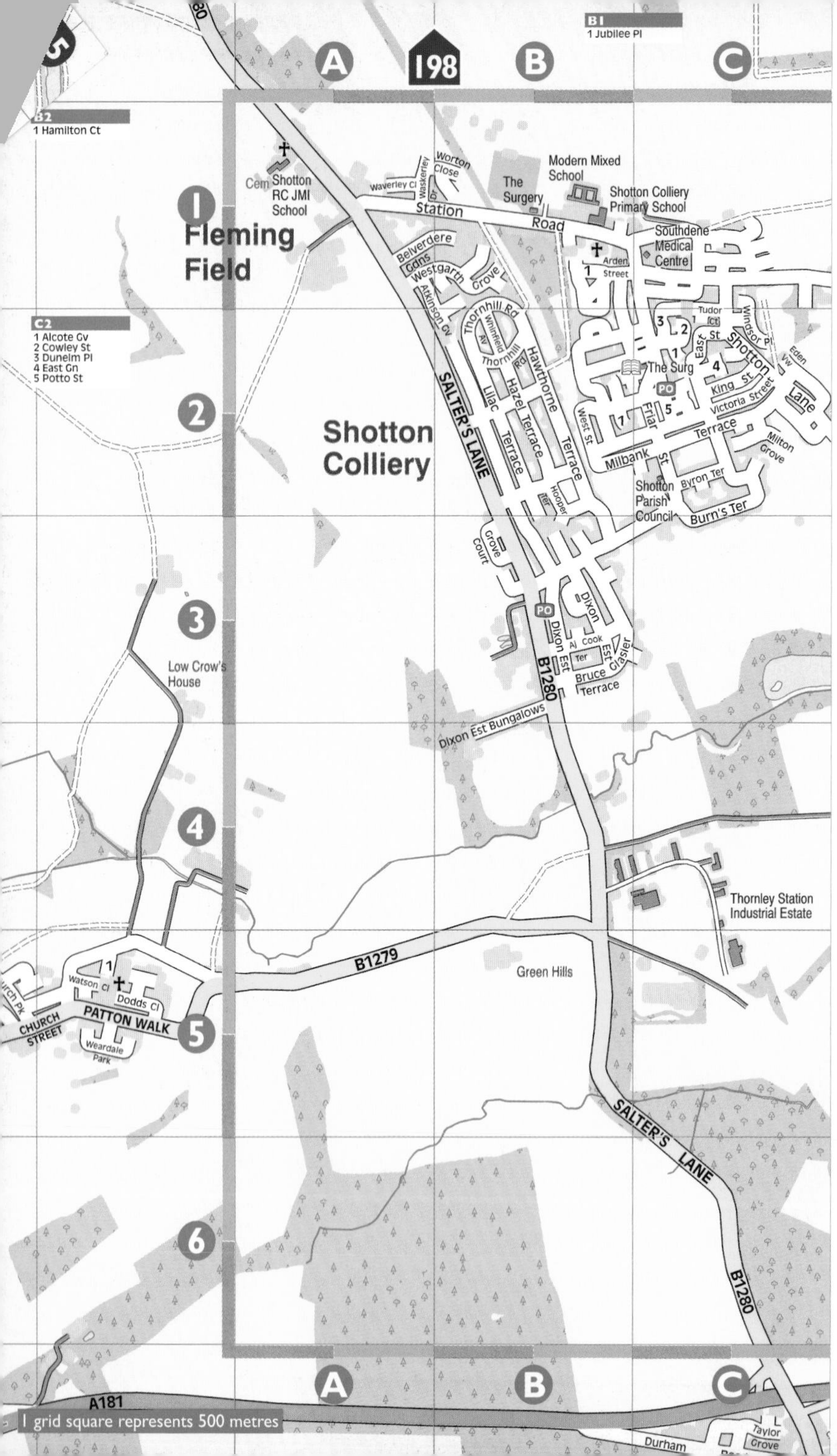

198
A
B
C
B1
1 Jubilee Pl
B2
1 Hamilton Ct
C2
1 Alcote Gv
2 Cowley St
3 Dunelm Pl
4 East Gn
5 Potto St
1
2
3
4
5
6
Fleming Field
Shotton Colliery
Cem
Shotton RC JMI School
Waverley Cl
Waskerley
Worton Close
The Surgery
Modern Mixed School
Shotton Colliery Primary School
Station Road
Southdene Medical Centre
Belverdere Gdns
Westgarth Grove
Arden Street
Atkinson Gv
Thornhill Rd
Whitfield Av
Thornhill Rd
Hawthorne Terrace
Lilac Terrace
Hazel Terrace
SALTER'S LANE
Tudor Ct
Windsor Pl
East St
Shotton Lane
Eden Vw
The Surg
PO
King St
Victoria Street
Friar St
West St
Terrace
Milbank
Milton Grove
Shotton Parish Council
Byron Ter
Burn's Ter
Hooper Ter
Grove Court
Dixon
Dixon Est
Aj Cook Ter
Est
Glasier
Bruce Terrace
B1280
Low Crow's House
Dixon Est Bungalows
Thornley Station Industrial Estate
B1279
Green Hills
Watson Cl
Dodds Cl
PATTON WALK
CHURCH STREET
Weardale Park
SALTER'S LANE
B1280
A181
Durham
Taylor Grove
1 grid square represents 500 metres

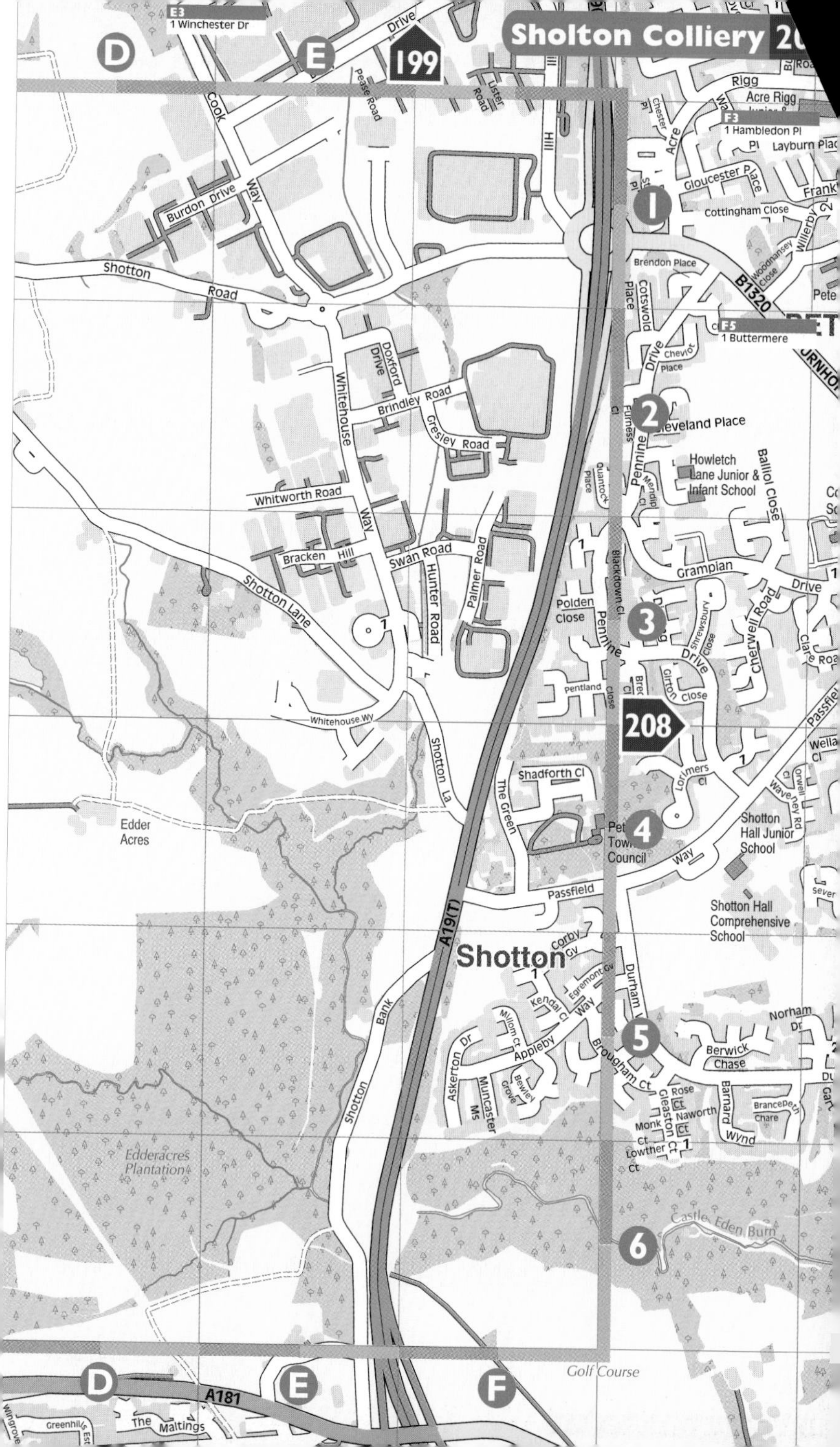

E3
1 Winchester Dr
D
E
199
Drive
Pease Road
Lister Road
Hill
Cook
Way
Burdon Drive
Shotton
Road
Whitehouse
Doxford Drive
Brindley Road
Gresley Road
Whitworth Road
Way
Bracken Hill
Swan Road
Hunter Road
Palmer Road
Shotton Lane
Whitehouse Wy
Shotton La
Edder Acres
The Green
Shadforth Cl
Passfield
A19(T)
Shotton
Corby Gv
Egremont Gv
Kendal Cl
Appleby
Way
Millom Ct
Askerton Dr
Muncaster Ms
Bewley Grove
Shotton Bank
Edderacres Plantation
Golf Course
D
E
F
A181
Wingrove
Greenhills Est
The Maltings
Rigg
Acre Rigg
F3
1 Hambleden Pl
Layburn Place
Chester Pl
Acre
Gloucester Place
Frank
Cottingham Close
Willerby
Woodnansey Close
Brendon Place
B1320
Pete
Cotswold Place
F5
1 Buttermere
Drive
Cheviot Place
2
Cleveland Place
Furness Cl
Pennine
Mendip Cl
Howletch Lane Junior & Infant School
Balliol Close
Quantock Place
Blackdown Cl
Grampian
Drive
Polden Close
3
Pennine
Shrewsbury Close
Cherwell Road
Clare Road
Drive
Girton Close
Pentland Close
208
Lorimers Cl
Passfield
Wella Cl
Orwell Cl
Waveney Rd
4
Peterlee Town Council
Way
Shotton Hall Junior School
Shotton Hall Comprehensive School
Durham Way
5
Norham Dr
Berwick Chase
Brougham Ct
Gleaston Ct
Rose Ct
Naworth Ct
Barnard Wynd
Brancepeth Chare
Monk Ct
Lowther Ct
6
Castle Eden Burn
I

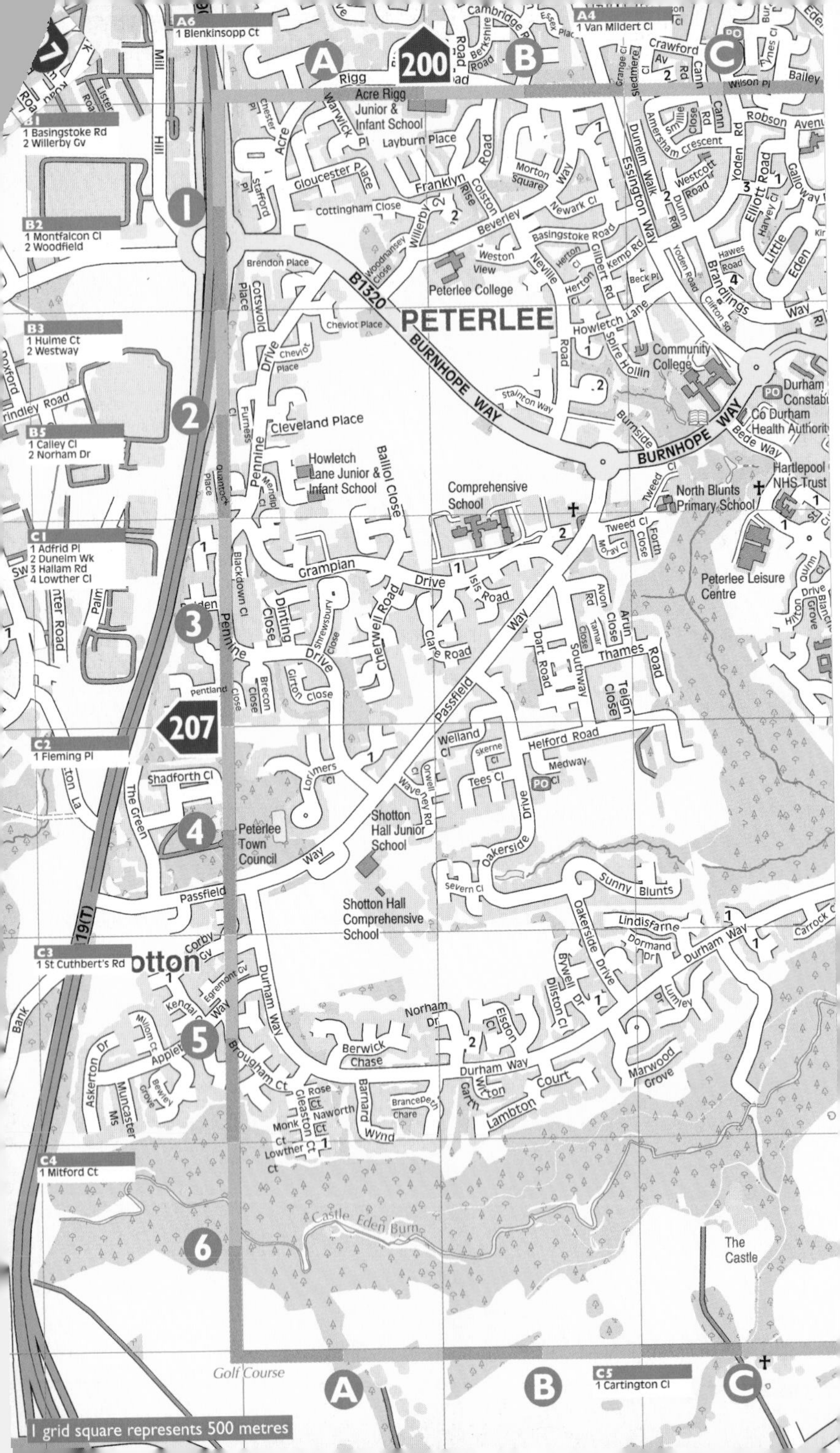

200
207
A
B
C
1
2
3
4
5
6
A6
1 Blenkinsopp Ct
A4
1 Van Mildert Cl
B1
1 Basingstoke Rd
2 Willerby Gv
B2
1 Montfalcon Cl
2 Woodfield
B3
1 Hulme Ct
2 Westway
B5
1 Calley Cl
2 Norham Dr
C1
1 Adfrid Pl
2 Dunelm Wk
3 Hallam Rd
4 Lowther Cl
C2
1 Fleming Pl
C3
1 St Cuthbert's Rd
C4
1 Mitford Ct
C5
1 Cartington Cl
PETERLEE
B1320
BURNHOPE WAY
Acre Rigg Junior & Infant School
Layburn Place
Gloucester Place
Franklyn Rise
Colston Road
Cottingham Close
Beverley
Morton Square
Newark Cl
Essington Way
Dunelm Walk
Amersham Crescent
Westcott Road
Yoden Rd
Elliott Road
Galloway
Little Eden
Brandlings Way
Robson Avenue
Crawford Av
Cambridge Road
Berkshire Road
Wilson Pl
Bailey
Basingstoke Road
Peterlee College
Weston View
Neville Road
Gilbert Rd
Kemp Rd
Beck Pl
Howletch Lane
Spire Hollin
Community College
Brendon Place
Cotswold Place
Cheviot Place
Pennine Drive
Cleveland Place
Howletch Lane Junior & Infant School
Balliol Close
Comprehensive School
Stainton Way
Burnside
Durham Constabulary
Co Durham Health Authority
Bede Way
Hartlepool NHS Trust
North Blunts Primary School
Peterlee Leisure Centre
Tweed Cl
Grampian Drive
Isis Road
Dinting Close
Shrewsbury Close
Cherwell Road
Clare Road
Passfield Way
Dart Road
Southway
Avon Close
Arun Road
Thames Road
Teign Close
Blackdown Cl
Girton Close
Pentland Close
Brecon Close
Welland Cl
Skerne Cl
Tees Cl
Helford Road
Medway Cl
Lorimers Cl
Shotton Hall Junior School
Shotton Hall Comprehensive School
Shadforth Cl
The Green
Peterlee Town Council
Passfield Way
Oakerside Drive
Severn Cl
Sunny Blunts
Lindisfarne
Dormand Dr
Durham Way
Carrock Ct
Bywell Dr
Dilston Cl
Lumley
Marwood Grove
Norham Dr
Elsdon Cl
Berwick Chase
Durham Way
Lambton Court
Wharton Garth
Brancepeth Chare
Barnard Wynd
Rose Ct
Naworth Ct
Gleaston Ct
Monk Ct
Lowther Ct
Brougham Ct
Durham Way
Corby Gv
Egremont Gv
Kendal
Appleby Way
Askerton Dr
Millom Ct
Muncaster Ms
Bewley Grove
Bank
19(T)
Castle Eden Burn
The Castle
Golf Course
1 grid square represents 500 metres

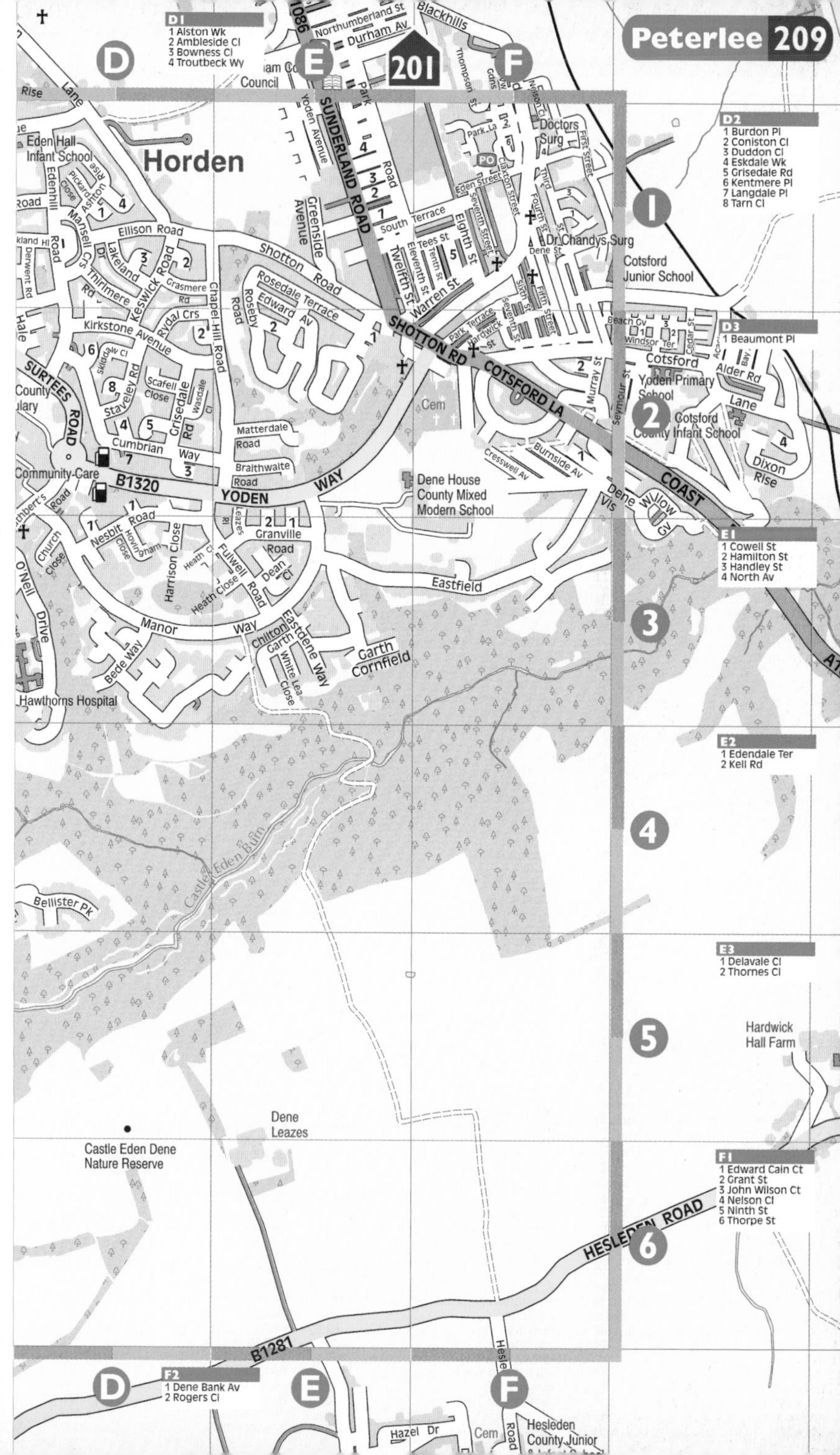

D1
1 Alston Wk
2 Ambleside Cl
3 Bowness Cl
4 Troutbeck Wy
D2
1 Burdon Pl
2 Coniston Cl
3 Duddon Cl
4 Eskdale Wk
5 Grisedale Rd
6 Kentmere Pl
7 Langdale Pl
8 Tarn Cl
D3
1 Beaumont Pl
E1
1 Cowell St
2 Hamilton St
3 Handley St
4 North Av
E2
1 Edendale Ter
2 Kell Rd
E3
1 Delavale Cl
2 Thornes Cl
F1
1 Edward Cain Ct
2 Grant St
3 John Wilson Ct
4 Nelson Cl
5 Ninth St
6 Thorpe St
F2
1 Dene Bank Av
2 Rogers Cl
201
Horden
Eden Hall Infant School
Sunderland Road
Shotton Rd
Cotsford La
Coast
Yoden Way
B1320
Surtees Road
Cumbrian Way
Kirkstone Avenue
Ellison Road
Chapel Hill Road
Shotton Road
Rosedale Terrace
Manor Way
Eastfield
Dene House County Mixed Modern School
Cotsford Junior School
Yoden Primary School
Cotsford County Infant School
Doctors Surg
Dr Chandys Surg
Community Care
Hawthorns Hospital
Castle Eden Burn
Bellister Pk
Dene Leazes
Castle Eden Dene Nature Reserve
Hesleden Road
B1281
Hardwick Hall Farm
Hazel Dr
Hesleden County Junior
Cem
Garth Cornfield
Granville Road
Fulwell Road
Harrison Close
Nesbit Road
Church Close
O'Neill Drive
Bede Way
Chilton Garth
Eastdene Way
White Lea Close
Dixon Rise
Alder Rd
Dene Vis
Burnside Av
Cresswell Av
Murray St
Seymour St
Warren St
South Terrace
Eden Street
Northumberland St
Durham Av
Blackhills
Yoden Avenue
Greenside Avenue
Keswick Road
Lakeland Dr
Thirlmere Rd
Rydal Crs
Grasmere Rd
Staveley Rd
Scafell Close
Grisedale Rd
Matterdale Road
Braithwaite Road
Council

Albany 120 A5
Annfield Plain 146 C4
Annitsford 35 E1
Axwell Park 94 C2
Aykley Heads 194 A2
Ayres Quay 126 A4
Ayton 137 E3
Backworth 37 E6
Bank Top 57 D5
Barley Mow 136 B4
Barlow 92 C4
Barmston 139 E1
Battle Hill 67 E1
Beaconhill 21 D2
Beacon Lough 100 B6
Beamish 150 A1
Bearpark 192 B3
Bebside 9 D5
Bedlington 7 F2
Bedlington Station 8 A2
Bell's Close 77 D2
Belmont 196 B3
Bensham 98 C1
Benton Square 50 C3
Benwell 78 A2
Biddick 138 C2
Biddick Hall 88 A6
Bill Quay 84 A6
Billy Mill 53 F5
Birtley 118 C6
Bishopwearmouth 126 A5
Black Callerton 42 C4
Blackfell 119 F6
Blakelaw 61 E4
Blaydon 76 C5
Blaydon Burn 93 D1
Blaydon Haughs 77 D4
Blyth 10 B6
Boldon Colliery 87 E6
Bournmoor 156 A5
Brandon 202 B4
Brenkley 18 B5
Broom Hill 171 F4
Broompark 192 C6
Brunswick Village 32 B5
Burdon 161 D5
Burnopfield 111 E6
Burnside 157 D6
Burradon 35 D5
Byermoor 112 C5
Byker 82 B3
Callerton 43 D6
Camperdown 35 E5
Carley Hill 126 A1
Carr Hill 100 A3
Carrville 196 B2
Castletown 123 F3
Causey 132 A1
Chester-le-Street 152 B5
Chester Moor 165 F3
Chilton Moor 170 A3
Chirton 54 A6
Chowdene 117 D2
Cleadon 107 F2
Cleadon Park 89 F3
Clough Dene 130 A3
Cold Hesledon 190 A2
Colliery Row 170 B2
Collingwood 22 A4
Columbia 139 D2
Concord 120 B4
Cowpen 10 A4
Coxlodge 62 C1
Craghead 149 F6
Cramlington 21 D3
Crookgate Bank 112 B6
Crookhill 75 D3
Cullercoats 55 F2
Dalton-le-Dale 175 E6
Dawdon 177 D5
Deckham 99 E2
Deneside 175 F4
Denton Burn 77 D1
Deptford 125 F4
Dinnington 30 C3
Dipton 128 B6
Donwell 120 A3
Downhill 106 A6
Doxford Park 160 C4
Dudley 34 C3
Dunston 97 E1
Dunston Hill 97 D3
Durham 194 A6
Earsdon 38 C4
Easington 199 F2
Easington Colliery 201 E1
Easington Lane 186 C3
East Boldon 106 B2
East Cramlington 23 D3
East Denton 60 C6
East Gateshead 82 A5
East Hartford 14 A3
East Herrington 159 F2
East Holywell 37 F3
East Kyo 147 D2
East Rainton 170 C6
East Sleekburn 9 F1
East Stanley 148 C1
Eighton Banks 118 C2
Eland Green 28 B2
Elemore Vale 186 A4
Elswick 79 E5
Elvet Hill 205 D1
Farringdon 160 A1
Fatfield 138 B6
Fawdon 46 A5
Fellgate 103 F1
Felling 100 B2
Felling Shore 83 D6
Fellside 95 E4
Fence Houses 169 F1
Fenham 78 C1
Flint Hill 129 E5
Follingsby 102 C5
Fordley 35 D3
Forest Hall 49 F3
Framwellgate Moor 194 A1
Fulwell 108 B6
Gateshead 81 E5
Gilesgate 195 D3
Gilesgate Moor 195 E4
Glebe 138 B1
Gosforth 63 D1
Grangetown 145 D5
Grange Villa 150 C3
Grasswell 157 F6
Great Eppleton 172 C5
Great Lumley 167 E3
Greenhill 174 B6
Grindon 142 A3
Hallgarth 197 F2
Harelaw 146 A2
Harlow Green 118 A2
Harperley 146 C2
Harraton 137 F5
Hartley 27 D4
Harton 89 D2
Hasting Hill 141 F4
Hawthorn 190 A5
Hazlerigg 32 C6
Heaton 65 D6
Hebburn 85 D3
Hebburn Colliery 68 A6
Hebburn New Town 84 B2
Heddon-on-the-Wall 56 A5
Hedworth 86 B6
Hendon 5 F5
Hetton Downs 172 A5
Hetton-le-Hill 185 F5
Hetton-le-Hole 186 A1
Heworth 101 E2
High Callerton 42 A2
High Dubmire 170 A2
Highfield 110 B3
High Forge 133 D5
High Friarside 110 C6
High Handenhold 150 C1
High Moorsley 184 C4
High Shields 70 C6
High Southwick 125 F1
High Urpeth 134 A6
Hill Top 129 D4
Hillview 144 B5
Hobson 130 A2
Holy Cross 67 E3
Holywell 25 E6
Horden 209 D1
Horsley Hill 72 B6
Houghton-le-Spring 170 C2
Howdon 68 C3
Howdon Pans 69 E5
Humbledon 143 E3
Hylton Castle 123 F2
Hylton Red House 106 C6
Isabella Pit 16 C1
Jarrow 86 C2
Jesmond 64 B6
Kenton 61 F2
Kenton Bankfoot 44 C6
Kenton Bar 61 F2
Kibblesworth 117 D6
Killingworth 49 F2
Killingworth Moor 50 C2
Killingworth Village 36 A6
Kimblesworth 179 D1
Kingston Park 45 F6
Kip Hill 131 F5
Lady Park 116 C3
Lambton 137 F3
Lamesley 116 C3
Langley Moor 204 B2
The Lawe 71 F2
Leam Lane 101 F4
Leamside 183 D2
Lemington 77 D2
Lintz 129 E1
Lintzford 110 A5
Little Thorpe 200 B4
Lobley Hill 98 A4
Longbenton 49 E4
Low Eighton 118 A4
Lowes Barn 204 B1
Low Fell 99 E5
Low Moorsley 185 E3
Low Thornley 93 F5
Lumley Thicks 168 B1
Lyons 186 B2
Marden 54 C2
Marley Hill 114 A3
Marley Pots 125 E1
Marsden 90 B3
Mason 31 D2
Mayfield 22 B3
Meadowfield 203 F4
Middle Herrington 142 A6
Middle Rainton 184 B1
The Middles 148 C5
Mill Dam 70 C5
Millfield 125 F5
Monkseaton 39 F4
Monkton 85 F4
Monkwearmouth 126 A3
Moor End 196 B2
Mount Pleasant 100 A2
Murton 53 D2
Murton 174 A6
Nedderton 6 A4
Nelson Village 21 E1
Nettlesworth 165 D6
Nevilles Cross 193 F6
Newbiggin Hall Estate 60 B2
Newbottle 158 A5
New Brancepeth 202 A1
Newburn 58 C6
Newcastle upon Tyne 3 H4
New Delaval 16 A3
Newfield 151 E3
New Hartley 25 D2
New Herrington 158 A2
New Kyo 147 D4
Newsham 15 F1
Newsham 16 B1
New Silksworth 160 B1
Newton Hall 181 D6
New Town 105 E1
New Town 171 F2
New York 53 E3
North Blyth 11 D2
North End 193 E2
North Hylton 123 D5
Northlea 176 A1
North Shields 71 D1
North Walbottle 58 C3
Offerton 141 D3
Old Burdon 160 C6
Old Fold 82 A6
Ouston 135 F4
Oxclose 137 F1
Oxhill 147 F2
Pallion 124 C4
Palmersville 50 C3
Parkside 176 B5
Path Head 76 A4
Pelaw 101 E1
Pelton 151 F2
Pelton Fell 152 B4
Pennywell 142 A2
Penshaw 157 E1
Percy Main 70 A4
Perkinsville 135 D6
Peterlee 208 A2
Philadelphia 157 F3

Pickering Nook 129 F2
Pittington 184 A6
Pity Me 180 A5
Plawsworth 165 F6
Ponteland 28 C3
Portobello 136 B2
Preston 54 C4
Preston Grange 54 B2
Prestwick 29 F5
Primrose 86 B4
Quaking Houses 147 F6
Rainton Bridge 171 D4
Rainton Gate 183 D3
Rickleton 154 B1
Roker 127 E2
Rosehill 68 A5
Rowlands Gill 111 D2
Ryhope 162 B2
Ryhope Colliery 162 A1
Ryton 74 B3
Ryton Woodside 74 A6
Sacriston 164 A6
St Anthony's 83 D5
St Peter's 82 B4
Saltwell 99 D3
Scotswood 77 F4
Seaham 177 D3
Seaton 25 F3
Seaton 174 C2
Seaton Burn 33 E1
Seaton Delaval 24 B4
Seaton Sluice 26 B3
Seghill 36 B1
Shankhouse 14 B5
Sheep Hill 112 A5
Sherburn 197 F5
Sheriff Hill 100 A4
Shield Row 132 A6
Shiney Row 157 D3
Shiremoor 52 C1
Shotton 207 F5
Shotton Colliery 206 A2
Simonside 87 D4
South Beach 17 F2
South Bents 109 D4
Southfield 22 A5
South Gosforth 63 F2
South Hetton 187 E5
South Hylton 124 A6
South Moor 147 F4
South Newsham 16 B3
South Pelaw 153 D2
South Shields 71 F4
South Stanley 148 A3
Southwick 125 F3
Spital Tongues 79 F1
Springwell 119 F3
Springwell 143 D3
Stanley 148 B2
Stargate 74 C5
Stella 75 F4
Stony Gate 158 C4
Street Gate 114 C2
Sulgrave 121 D4
Sunderland 4 A1
Sunderland 125 F4
Sunniside 113 F2
Sunniside 157 E5
Swalwell 95 F1
Tanfield 130 C2
Tanfield Lea 130 C5
Tan Hills 165 E6
Tantobie 129 F4
Teams 98 A1
Team Valley 98 C5
Thorney Close 142 B5
Throckley 58 A3
Tunstall 161 E1
Tyne Dock 87 F1
Tynemouth 55 D4
Urpeth 135 D4
Usworth 120 B3
Walbottle 58 A5
Waldridge 165 D1
Walker 83 E3
Wallsend 66 B4
Wardley 102 A2
Washington 121 F6
Washington Village 138 C1
West Allotment 52 A3
West Boldon 105 F2
West Chirton 68 C1
West Denton 60 A5
Westerhope 59 F2
Western Hill 193 F4
West Harton 87 F2
West Herrington 158 B1
West Holywell 37 F4
West Jesmond 63 D4
West Kyo 146 B3
Westlea 6 C4
West Lea 175 D4
West Monkseaton 53 E1
West Moor 49 D3
Westoe 72 A5
West Park 88 B1
West Pelton 150 B1
West Rainton 183 F1
Whickham 96 A3
Whitburn 109 E1
Whitburn Colliery 91 E4
Whitehills 100 C5
Whiteleas 88 B5
White-le-Head 129 F5
Whitley Bay 41 E5
Whitley Sands 40 C3
Wickham Fell 96 A6
Wide Open 33 E5
Willington 68 A2
Willington Quay 68 C5
Windy Nook 100 C4
Winlaton 75 F6
Winlaton Mill 94 A4
Witherwack 107 D6
Witton Gilbert 178 B3
Woolsington 43 F4
Woolsington Hall 44 A2
Wrekenton 118 A1

USING THE STREET INDEX

Street names are listed alphabetically. Each street name is followed by its postal town or area locality, the Postcode District, the page number, and the reference to the square in which the name is found.

Example: **Abbey Ct** *GATE* NE8 **99** E1 1

Some entries are followed by a number in a blue box. This number indicates the location of the street within the referenced grid square. The full street name is listed at the side of the map page.

GENERAL ABBREVIATIONS

ACC ACCESS
ALY ALLEY
AP APPROACH
AR ARCADE
ASS ASSOCIATION
AV AVENUE
BCH BEACH
BLDS BUILDINGS
BND BEND
BNK BANK
BR BRIDGE
BRK BROOK
BTM BOTTOM
BUS BUSINESS
BVD BOULEVARD
BY BYPASS
CATH CATHEDRAL
CEM CEMETERY
CEN CENTRE
CFT CROFT
CH CHURCH
CHA CHASE
CHYD CHURCHYARD
CIR CIRCLE
CIRC CIRCUS
CL CLOSE
CLFS CLIFFS
CMP CAMP
CNR CORNER
CO COUNTY
COLL COLLEGE
COM COMMON
COMM COMMISSION
CON CONVENT
COT COTTAGE
COTS COTTAGES
CP CAPE
CPS COPSE
CR CREEK
CREM CREMATORIUM
CRS CRESCENT
CSWY CAUSEWAY
CT COURT
CTRL CENTRAL
CTS COURTS
CTYD COURTYARD
CUTT CUTTINGS
CV COVE
CYN CANYON
DEPT DEPARTMENT
DL DALE
DM DAM
DR DRIVE
DRO DROVE
DRY DRIVEWAY
DWGS DWELLINGS
E EAST
EMB EMBANKMENT
EMBY EMBASSY
ESP ESPLANADE
EST ESTATE
EX EXCHANGE
EXPY EXPRESSWAY
EXT EXTENSION
F/O FLYOVER
FC FOOTBALL CLUB
FK FORK
FLD FIELD
FLDS FIELDS
FLS FALLS
FLS FLATS
FM FARM
FT FORT
FWY FREEWAY
FY FERRY
GA GATE
GAL GALLERY
GDN GARDEN
GDNS GARDENS
GLD GLADE
GLN GLEN
GN GREEN
GND GROUND
GRA GRANGE
GRG GARAGE
GT GREAT
GTWY GATEWAY
GV GROVE
HGR HIGHER
HL HILL
HLS HILLS
HO HOUSE
HOL HOLLOW
HOSP HOSPITAL
HRB HARBOUR
HTH HEATH
HTS HEIGHTS
HVN HAVEN
HWY HIGHWAY

IMP	IMPERIAL
IN	INLET
IND EST	INDUSTRIAL ESTATE
INF	INFIRMARY
INFO	INFORMATION
INT	INTERCHANGE
IS	ISLAND
JCT	JUNCTION
JTY	JETTY
KG	KING
KNL	KNOLL
L	LAKE
LA	LANE
LDG	LODGE
LGT	LIGHT
LK	LOCK
LKS	LAKES
LNDG	LANDING
LTL	LITTLE
LWR	LOWER
MAG	MAGISTRATE
MAN	MANSIONS
MD	MEAD
MDW	MEADOWS
MEM	MEMORIAL
MKT	MARKET
MKTS	MARKETS
ML	MALL
ML	MILL
MNR	MANOR
MS	MEWS
MSN	MISSION
MT	MOUNT
MTN	MOUNTAIN
MTS	MOUNTAINS
MUS	MUSEUM
MWY	MOTORWAY
N	NORTH
NE	NORTH EAST
NW	NORTH WEST
O/P	OVERPASS
OFF	OFFICE
ORCH	ORCHARD
OV	OVAL
PAL	PALACE
PAS	PASSAGE
PAV	PAVILION
PDE	PARADE
PH	PUBLIC HOUSE
PK	PARK
PKWY	PARKWAY
PL	PLACE
PLN	PLAIN
PLNS	PLAINS
PLZ	PLAZA
POL	POLICE STATION
PR	PRINCE
PREC	PRECINCT
PREP	PREPARATORY
PRIM	PRIMARY
PROM	PROMENADE
PRS	PRINCESS
PRT	PORT
PT	POINT
PTH	PATH
PZ	PIAZZA
QD	QUADRANT
QU	QUEEN
QY	QUAY
R	RIVER
RBT	ROUNDABOUT
RD	ROAD
RDG	RIDGE
REP	REPUBLIC
RES	RESERVOIR
RFC	RUGBY FOOTBALL CLUB
RI	RISE
RP	RAMP
RW	ROW
S	SOUTH
SCH	SCHOOL
SE	SOUTH EAST
SER	SERVICE AREA
SH	SHORE
SHOP	SHOPPING
SKWY	SKYWAY
SMT	SUMMIT
SOC	SOCIETY
SP	SPUR
SPR	SPRING
SQ	SQUARE
ST	STREET
STN	STATION
STR	STREAM
STRD	STRAND
SW	SOUTH WEST
TDG	TRADING
TER	TERRACE
THWY	THROUGHWAY
TNL	TUNNEL
TOLL	TOLLWAY
TPK	TURNPIKE
TR	TRACK
TRL	TRAIL
TWR	TOWER
U/P	UNDERPASS
UNI	UNIVERSITY
UPR	UPPER
V	VALE
VA	VALLEY
VIAD	VIADUCT
VIL	VILLA
VIS	VISTA
VLG	VILLAGE
VLS	VILLAS
VW	VIEW
W	WEST
WD	WOOD
WHF	WHARF
WK	WALK
WKS	WALKS
WLS	WELLS
WY	WAY
YD	YARD
YHA	YOUTH HOSTEL

POSTCODE TOWNS AND AREA ABBREVIATIONS

ASHBK/HED/RY	Ashbrooke/Hedon/Ryhope
BDLGTN	Bedlington
BDN/LAN/SAC	Brandon/Lanchester/Sacriston
BLAY	Blaydon
BLYTH	Blyth
BOL	Boldon
BOLCOL	Boldon Colliery
BW/LEM/TK/HW	Benwell/Lemington/Throckley/Heddon-on-the-Wall
BYK/HTN/WLK	Byker/Heaton/Walker
CLDN/WHIT/ROK	Cleadon/Whitburn/Roker
CLS/BIR/GTL	Chester-le-Street/Birtley/Great Lumley
CLSW/PEL	Chester-le-Street west/Pelton
CNUT	Central Newcastle upon Tyne
CRAM	Cramlington
DHAM	Durham
DIN/WO	Dinnington/Wide Open
DUN/TMV	Dunston/Team Valley
ELS/FEN	Elswick/Fenham
FELL	Felling
GATE	Gateshead
GOS/KPK	Gosforth/Kingston Park
HAR/WTLS	Harton/Whiteleas
HEBB	Hebburn
HLH	Hetton-le-Hole
HLS	Houghton-le-Spring
JES	Jesmond
JRW	Jarrow
LGB/HTN	Longbenton/Heaton
LGB/KIL	Longbenton/Killingworth
LWF/SPW/WRK	LowFell / Springwell/Wrekenton
MLFD/PNYW	Millfield/Pennywell
MONK	Monkseaton
NSHW	North Shields west
PLEE/EAS	Peterlee/Easington
PONT/DH	Ponteland/Darras Hall
RDHAMSE	Rural Durham south & east
RHTLP	Rural Hartlepool
ROWG	Rowlands Gill
RYTON	Ryton
SEA/MUR	Seaham/Murton
SMOOR	Shiremoor
SSH	South Shields
STKFD/GP	Stakeford/Guide Post
STLY/ANP	Stanley/Annfield Plain
SUND	Sunderland
SUNDSW	Sunderland southwest
SWCK/CAS	Southwick/Castletown
TYNE/NSHE	Tynemouth/North Shields east
WASHN	Washington north
WASHS	Washington south
WBAY	Whitley Bay
WD/WHPE/BLK	West Denton/Westerhope/Blakelaw
WICK/BNPF	Wickham/Burnopfield
WLSD/HOW	Wallsend/Howdon

Abb - Act

Index - streets

A

Abbay St *SWCK/CAS* SR5 … **125** F3
Abbey Cl *MONK* NE25 … **39** F6
WASHS NE38 … **138** C1
Abbey Ct *GATE* NE8 … **99** E1
Abbey Dr *JRW* NE32 … **86** B1
TYNE/NSHE NE30 … **55** F4
WD/WHPE/BLK NE5 … **59** D2
Abbey Rd *DHAM* DH1 … **179** F4
WASHS NE38 … **138** C1
Abbeywoods *DHAM* DH1 … **180** A4
Abbotsfield Cl *SUNDSW* SR3 … **160** B3
Abbotsford Gv *ASHBK/HED/RY* SR2 … **4** A5
Abbotsford Pk *MONK* NE25 … **40** B6
Abbotsford Rd *FELL* NE10 … **100** C1
Abbotsford Ter *JES* NE2 … **63** F6
Abbotside Cl *CLSW/PEL* DH2 … **134** C4
Abbotside Pl
WD/WHPE/BLK NE5 … **59** F5
Abbotsmeade Cl
WD/WHPE/BLK NE5 … **61** D6
Abbot's Rd *GATE* NE8 … **3** G6
Abbots' Rw *DHAM* DH1 … **195** E3
Abbot St *PLEE/EAS* SR8 … **201** E1
Abbots Wk *STLY/ANP* DH9 … **133** E6
Abbots Wy *NSHW* NE29 … **53** F3
Abbs St *SWCK/CAS* SR5 … **126** C3
Abercorn Pl *WLSD/HOW* NE28 … **52** A6
Abercorn Rd
BW/LEM/TK/HW NE15 … **77** F3
SUNDSW SR3 … **142** C5
Abercrombie Pl
WD/WHPE/BLK NE5 … **61** D4
Aberdare Rd *SUNDSW* SR3 … **159** F1
Aberdeen *CLSW/PEL* DH2 … **135** E5
Aberdeen Ct *DIN/WO* NE13 … **45** F4
Aberdeen Dr *JRW* NE32 … **87** D4
Aberford Cl *WD/WHPE/BLK* NE5 … **59** D3
Aberfoyle *CLSW/PEL* DH2 … **135** E5
Aberfoyle Ct *STLY/ANP* DH9 … **149** D2
Abernethy *CLSW/PEL* DH2 … **135** E4
Abingdon Rd *BYK/HTN/WLK* NE6 … **84** A1
Abingdon Sq *CRAM* NE23 … **14** B5
Abingdon St *MLFD/PNYW* SR4 … **143** E1
Abingdon Wy *BOL* NE36 … **105** D3
BOLCOL NE35 … **104** C1
Abinger St *ELS/FEN* NE4 … **80** A3
Aboyne Sq *SUNDSW* SR3 … **142** C5
Acacia Av *HLS* DH4 … **169** F1
Acacia Gv *HAR/WTLS* NE34 … **89** D3
Acacia Rd *FELL* NE10 … **82** A6
Acacia St *DUN/TMV* NE11 … **98** B5
Acanthus Av *ELS/FEN* NE4 … **78** C1
Acer Ct *ASHBK/HED/RY* SR2 … **144** C2
Acklam Av *ASHBK/HED/RY* SR2 … **145** E5
Acomb Av *MONK* NE25 … **24** C6
WLSD/HOW NE28 … **51** F5
Acomb Ct *ASHBK/HED/RY* SR2 … **145** E5
BDLGTN NE22 … **7** F3
Acomb Crs *GOS/KPK* NE3 … **46** B4
Acomb Gdns *WD/WHPE/BLK* NE5 … **61** E6
Acorn Av *BDLGTN* NE22 … **7** E4
GATE NE8 … **98** B2
Acorn Cl *BDN/LAN/SAC* DH7 … **164** A6
Acorn Pl *BDN/LAN/SAC* DH7 … **203** D4
Acorn Rd *JES* NE2 … **64** A4
Acre Rigg Rd *PLEE/EAS* SR8 … **208** A1
Acton Dene *STLY/ANP* DH9 … **149** E2
Acton Dr *NSHW* NE29 … **53** F4

Acton Pl LGB/HTN NE7 65 D4
Acton Rd WD/WHPE/BLK NE5 60 B6 1
Adair Av BW/LEM/TK/HW NE15 78 B2
Ada St BYK/HTN/WLK NE6 83 D2
SSH NE33 71 F5
Adderstone Av CRAM NE23 22 A3
Adderstone Crs JES NE2 64 B4
Adderstone Gdns NSHW NE29 53 D3
Addington Crs NSHW NE29 54 A6
Addington Dr BLYTH NE24 17 D1
WLSD/HOW NE28 51 F5
Addison Ct WLSD/HOW NE28 68 C5 1
Addison Gdns FELL NE10 102 A2 1
Addison Rd BOL NE36 105 F3
BW/LEM/TK/HW NE15 76 C1 1
Addison St ASHBK/HED/RY SR2 5 G5
NSHW NE29 70 C2
Addycombe Ter
BYK/HTN/WLK NE6 65 E5
Adelaide Cl SUND SR1 5 F2
Adelaide Pl SUND SR1 5 G2
Adelaide Rw SEA/MUR SR7 176 C3 1
Adelaide Ter ELS/FEN NE4 78 C3
Adeline Gdns GOS/KPK NE3 62 C4
Adelphi Cl NSHW NE29 53 E4
Adelphi Pl BYK/HTN/WLK NE6 83 D3
Adfrid Pl PLEE/EAS SR8 208 C1 1
Admiral Wy SUNDSW SR3 159 E3
Adolphus St CLDN/WHIT/ROK SR6 109 E2
Adolphus St West
SEA/MUR SR7 176 C3 2
Adventure La HLS DH4 183 E1
Affleck St GATE NE8 81 D6
Afton Ct HAR/WTLS NE34 88 B3 1
Afton Wy GOS/KPK NE3 62 A1 1
Agar Rd SUNDSW SR3 142 C6
Agincourt HEBB NE31 84 C1
LGB/KIL NE12 35 F6 1
Agnes Maria St GOS/KPK NE3 62 C1 1
Agnes St STLY/ANP DH9 148 B1 1
Agricola Gdns WLSD/HOW NE28 51 F6
Agricola Rd ELS/FEN NE4 79 E2 1
Aidan Av WBAY NE26 26 A2 1
Aidan Cl DIN/WO NE13 33 D4 1
STLY/ANP DH9 149 D1
Aidan Wk GOS/KPK NE3 63 F1
Aiden Wy HLH DH5 171 F5 1
Ailesbury St MLFD/PNYW SR4 125 F5
Ainderby Rd BW/LEM/TK/HW NE15 57 D4
Ainsdale Gdns
WD/WHPE/BLK NE5 59 E4 1
Ainsley St DHAM DH1 194 A4
Ainslie Pl WD/WHPE/BLK NE5 61 D5
Ainsworth Av HAR/WTLS NE34 87 F5
Ainthorpe Cl SUNDSW SR3 161 D1 1
Ainthorpe Gdns LGB/HTN NE7 65 D2
Aintree Gdns GATE NE8 98 B2
Aintree Rd SUNDSW SR3 142 C6
Airedale WLSD/HOW NE28 66 B1
Airedale Gdns HLH DH5 185 E2
Aireys Cl HLS DH4 170 B2
Airey Ter BYK/HTN/WLK NE6 83 F3
GATE NE8 98 C1
Airport Freightway DIN/WO NE13 44 A2
Airville Mt SUNDSW SR3 160 C4
Aisgill Cl CRAM NE23 22 A2 1
Aisgill Dr WD/WHPE/BLK NE5 59 E5
Aiskell St MLFD/PNYW SR4 125 F6
Aj Cook Ter RDHAMSE DH6 206 B3
Akeld Cl CRAM NE23 22 A3
Akenside Hl CNUT NE1 3 E5
Akenside Ter JES NE2 64 B6
Alamein Av HLH DH5 171 E2 1
Alansway Gdns SSH NE33 71 F6 1
Albany Av LGB/KIL NE12 49 F4 1
Albany Ct ELS/FEN NE4 79 F5
Albany Rd GATE NE8 81 F5
Albany St East SSH NE33 71 F6 2
Albany St West SSH NE33 71 F6 3
Albany Wy WASHN NE37 120 B5
Albatross Wy BLYTH NE24 17 D3
Albemarle Av JES NE2 63 F3 1
Albemarle St SSH NE33 71 E3
Albert Av WLSD/HOW NE28 67 D4 1
Albert Dr LWF/SPW/WRK NE9 99 E5 1
Albert Pl LWF/SPW/WRK NE9 99 E6 1
WASHS NE38 139 E3
Albert Rd BDLGTN NE22 8 C2
JRW NE32 86 A1 1
MLFD/PNYW SR4 125 F5
WBAY NE26 26 C2
Albert St CLS/BIR/GTL DH3 153 E5
CLSW/PEL DH2 150 C3
DHAM DH1 194 A3
HEBB NE31 84 C1 1
JES NE2 3 G2
SEA/MUR SR7 176 C4
Albert Ter LGB/KIL NE12 49 E3
Albion Pl SUND SR1 4 B4
Albion Rd TYNE/NSHE NE30 54 C6
Albion Rd West NSHW NE29 70 C1
Albion Rw BYK/HTN/WLK NE6 82 A2 1
Albion St FELL NE10 100 C4
MLFD/PNYW SR4 123 F6
Albion Ter NSHW NE29 54 C6 1
Albion Wy BLYTH NE24 10 B5
CRAM NE23 14 C5 1
Albury Park Rd TYNE/NSHE NE30 55 E5
Albury Pl WICK/BNPF NE16 95 F5
Albury Rd JES NE2 63 F3
Albyn Gdns SUNDSW SR3 143 F3 1
Alconbury Cl BLYTH NE24 17 D1
Alcote Gv RDHAMSE DH6 206 C2 1
Alcroft Cl WD/WHPE/BLK NE5 59 D3 2
Aldborough St BLYTH NE24 11 D5 1
Aldbrough Cl
ASHBK/HED/RY SR2 162 B2 1
Aldbrough St HAR/WTLS NE34 87 F3 1
Aldeburgh Av
BW/LEM/TK/HW NE15 59 E6
Aldenham Rd SUNDSW SR3 143 D6
Alder Av ELS/FEN NE4 61 F6
Alder Cl HLH DH5 185 E1
Alder Crs STLY/ANP DH9 129 E4
Alderdene Cl
BDN/LAN/SAC DH7 192 B5 1
Alder Gv MONK NE25 40 A4
Alder Lea Cl DHAM DH1 195 F3
Alderley Cl ASHBK/HED/RY SR2 145 E4
BOLCOL NE35 105 D1 1
Alderley Dr LGB/KIL NE12 36 B6
Alderley Rd LWF/SPW/WRK NE9 99 D5
Alderley Wy CRAM NE23 14 C5
Alderman Wood Rd
STLY/ANP DH9 131 D6
Alderney Gdns
WD/WHPE/BLK NE5 59 E4 2
Alder Pk BDN/LAN/SAC DH7 202 C5
Alder Rd NSHW NE29 52 C5
WLSD/HOW NE28 52 A6
Aldershot Rd SUNDSW SR3 159 F1 1
Aldershot Sq SUNDSW SR3 159 F1 2
Alder St SWCK/CAS SR5 124 A3 1
Alder Wy LGB/KIL NE12 35 E6 1
Alderwood WASHS NE38 138 A6
Alderwood Crs BYK/HTN/WLK NE6 66 B5
Alderwyk FELL NE10 102 A4 1
Aldhome Ct DHAM DH1 179 F6 1
Aldsworth Cl LWF/SPW/WRK NE9 119 E3
Aldwick Rd BW/LEM/TK/HW NE15 77 E2
Aldwych Dr NSHW NE29 53 D5
Aldwych Rd SUNDSW SR3 159 F1 3
Aldwych Sq SUNDSW SR3 159 F2
Aldwych St SSH NE33 72 A4 1
Alexander Dr HLH DH5 185 E1
Alexander Ter
CLDN/WHIT/ROK SR6 126 C1 1
Alexandra Av SWCK/CAS SR5 125 E3
Alexandra Cl DHAM DH1 179 F6
Alexandra Dr WICK/BNPF NE16 96 B2
Alexandra Gdns NSHW NE29 54 A6
Alexandra Pk ASHBK/HED/RY SR2 144 B2
SUNDSW SR3 144 A2
Alexandra Rd BYK/HTN/WLK NE6 65 D5
GATE NE8 99 D2
Alexandra St CLSW/PEL DH2 151 E2
WLSD/HOW NE28 67 E4 1
Alexandra Wy CRAM NE23 22 A3
Alexandria Crs DHAM DH1 194 A5 1
Alexandrina St SEA/MUR SR7 176 C3 3
Alford CLSW/PEL DH2 135 E4
Alfred Av BDLGTN NE22 8 A3
Alfred St BYK/HTN/WLK NE6 83 D2
HEBB NE31 84 C3
SEA/MUR SR7 177 D4
Alfreton Cl BDN/LAN/SAC DH7 202 C6
Algernon LGB/KIL NE12 35 F5 1
Algernon Pl WBAY NE26 41 D6
Algernon Rd BW/LEM/TK/HW NE15 76 B2
BYK/HTN/WLK NE6 82 B2 1
Algernon Ter TYNE/NSHE NE30 55 E4
Algiers Rd SUNDSW SR3 159 E1 1
Alice St ASHBK/HED/RY SR2 4 B5
BLAY NE21 94 A1
CLSW/PEL DH2 135 E6
SSH NE33 71 E6
Aline St SEA/MUR SR7 177 D3 1
SUNDSW SR3 161 D1
Alison Dr BOL NE36 106 C3
Allandale Av LGB/KIL NE12 49 F5
Allanville LGB/KIL NE12 35 E6
All Church BW/LEM/TK/HW NE15 78 A2 1
Allendale Av WLSD/HOW NE28 67 D2
Allendale Crs HLS DH4 139 F6
SMOOR NE27 52 C1
Allendale Dr HAR/WTLS NE34 72 C6
Allendale Pl TYNE/NSHE NE30 55 F5
Allendale Rd BDN/LAN/SAC DH7 203 E4 1
BLYTH NE24 11 E6
BYK/HTN/WLK NE6 82 C3
SUNDSW SR3 159 F1 4
Allendale Sq SUNDSW SR3 143 D5
Allendale St HLH DH5 185 F2 1
Allendale Ter BYK/HTN/WLK NE6 83 E2 1
Allenhead WASHS NE38 139 D5
Allenheads MONK NE25 24 B4
WD/WHPE/BLK NE5 60 A5
Allensgreen CRAM NE23 22 A2
Allen St CLS/BIR/GTL DH3 153 E6
Allerdean Cl
BW/LEM/TK/HW NE15 76 A1 1
Allergate DHAM DH1 194 A5
Allerhope CRAM NE23 22 A3
Allerton Gdns
BYK/HTN/WLK NE6 65 F4 1
Allerwash WD/WHPE/BLK NE5 60 A5 1
Allhusen Ter GATE NE8 100 A1 1
Alliance Pl MLFD/PNYW SR4 126 A5 1
Alliance St MLFD/PNYW SR4 126 A5 2
Allingham Ct LGB/HTN NE7 66 A3 1
Alloa Rd SUNDSW SR3 142 C6 1
Allonby Wy WD/WHPE/BLK NE5 61 D6 1
All Saints Dr HLH DH5 171 F4
Alma Pl NSHW NE29 54 C6
WBAY NE26 41 D6
Alma St MLFD/PNYW SR4 123 F5
Alma Ter RYTON NE40 74 B6
Almond Crs GATE NE8 98 B2
Almond Dr SWCK/CAS SR5 123 F4
Almond Pl ELS/FEN NE4 78 C1 1
Almoner's Barn DHAM DH1 193 F6
Aln Av GOS/KPK NE3 46 C6
Aln Ct BW/LEM/TK/HW NE15 76 B2
Aln Crs GOS/KPK NE3 46 C5
Aln Gv BW/LEM/TK/HW NE15 76 B1
Alnham Ct GOS/KPK NE3 46 A5 1
Alnmouth Av NSHW NE29 69 F2
Alnmouth Dr GOS/KPK NE3 64 A2 1
Aln St HEBB NE31 84 C2
Aln Wk GOS/KPK NE3 46 C6 1
Alnwick Av NSHW NE29 69 F2
Alnwick Cl CLSW/PEL DH2 165 F1
WICK/BNPF NE16 95 F3
Alnwick Gv JRW NE32 86 A6 1
Alnwick Rd DHAM DH1 180 B5
HAR/WTLS NE34 88 B2
SUNDSW SR3 143 D6
Alnwick Sq SUNDSW SR3 143 D6
Alnwick St BW/LEM/TK/HW NE15 58 B6
PLEE/EAS SR8 201 E5
WLSD/HOW NE28 67 E4
Alnwick Ter DIN/WO NE13 33 E3 1
Alpine Gv BOL NE36 106 A3 1
Alpine Wy SUNDSW SR3 143 F3 2
Alresford LGB/KIL NE12 35 F6 2
Alston Av BYK/HTN/WLK NE6 83 D2
CRAM NE23 22 C3 1
Alston Cl NSHW NE29 53 E5 1
WLSD/HOW NE28 68 C2
Alston Crs CLDN/WHIT/ROK SR6 108 B6
Alston Gdns BW/LEM/TK/HW NE15 57 F3
Alston Gv WBAY NE26 26 A1
Alston Rd MONK NE25 24 C2
WASHS NE38 122 A6
Alston St GATE NE8 98 C1 1
Alston Wk PLEE/EAS SR8 209 D1 1
Alston Wy BDN/LAN/SAC DH7 203 E4
Altan Pl LGB/KIL NE12 49 D5
Alum Well Rd
LWF/SPW/WRK NE9 99 D5 1
LWF/SPW/WRK NE9 99 E5 2
Alverston Cl BW/LEM/TK/HW NE15 59 E6
Alverstone Av LWF/SPW/WRK NE9 99 D6
Alverthorpe St SSH NE33 71 F6
Alvin Gra JRW NE32 85 E1 1
Alwin WASHS NE38 137 F5
Alwin Cl HLS DH4 156 A5
Alwinton Av NSHW NE29 53 F4
Alwinton Cl BLYTH NE24 10 B4
WD/WHPE/BLK NE5 60 C2 1
Alwinton Dr CLSW/PEL DH2 165 F1
Alwinton Gdns DUN/TMV NE11 97 F5
Alwinton Rd SMOOR NE27 52 C1
Alwinton Ter GOS/KPK NE3 63 F1
Amara Sq SUNDSW SR3 143 D6
Ambassadors Wy NSHW NE29 53 D4
Amber Ct BLYTH NE24 10 B6 1
Ambergate Cl
WD/WHPE/BLK NE5 60 C3 1
Amberley Cha LGB/KIL NE12 36 A6 1
Amberley Cl WLSD/HOW NE28 68 C2 1
Amberley Gdns LGB/HTN NE7 65 E4
Amberley St ASHBK/HED/RY SR2 5 E5
GATE NE8 98 A1
Amberley St South
ASHBK/HED/RY SR2 5 E6 1
Amberley Wy BLYTH NE24 17 D1 1
Amberly Gv WICK/BNPF NE16 95 F5
Amble Av HAR/WTLS NE34 73 D6
MONK NE25 55 D1
Amble Cl BLYTH NE24 16 B1
Amble Gv JES NE2 81 F1 1
Amble Pl LGB/KIL NE12 50 B3
Ambleside BW/LEM/TK/HW NE15 58 A3
Ambleside Av HAR/WTLS NE34 89 D2
SEA/MUR SR7 175 D2
Ambleside Cl MONK NE25 24 C5 1
PLEE/EAS SR8 209 D1 2
Ambleside Ter
CLDN/WHIT/ROK SR6 108 B6
Amble Wy GOS/KPK NE3 47 D6 1
Ambridge Wy GOS/KPK NE3 62 B1 1
Ambrose Pl BYK/HTN/WLK NE6 84 A2 1
Ambrose Rd SUNDSW SR3 142 C6

Amec Wy WLSD/HOW NE28 68 A5
Amelia Cl ELS/FEN NE4 79 D5
Amelia Gdns SUNDSW SR3 159 D1
Amersham Crs PLEE/EAS SR8 208 C1
Amersham Pl
WD/WHPE/BLK NE5 61 D4 2
Amersham Rd BLYTH NE24 16 C2
Amesbury Cl
WD/WHPE/BLK NE5 59 D3 3
Amethyst Rd ELS/FEN NE4 79 E6
Amethyst St MLFD/PNYW SR4 125 E5 1
Amherst Rd GOS/KPK NE3 46 A6
Amos Ayre Pl HAR/WTLS NE34 87 E3
Amsterdam Rd SUNDSW SR3 143 D6
Amy St SWCK/CAS SR5 126 A2 1
Ancaster Av LGB/KIL NE12 49 D6
Ancaster Rd WICK/BNPF NE16 95 E5
Ancona St MLFD/PNYW SR4 125 E4
Ancroft Av NSHW NE29 54 B5
Ancroft Pl WD/WHPE/BLK NE5 61 D6
Ancroft Rd MONK NE25 24 A5
Ancroft Wy GOS/KPK NE3 46 B4 1
Ancrum St JES NE2 80 A1 1
Anderson St SSH NE33 71 F3
Andover Pl WLSD/HOW NE28 52 A6
Andrew Rd SUNDSW SR3 159 E1
Andrew's La PLEE/EAS SR8 199 F4
Anfield Rd GOS/KPK NE3 62 A1
Angerton Av SMOOR NE27 52 B2
TYNE/NSHE NE30 54 C3
Angerton Gdns
WD/WHPE/BLK NE5 61 F6
Anglesey Gdns
WD/WHPE/BLK NE5 59 E4 3
Anglesey Rd SUNDSW SR3 159 F1
Anglesey Sq SUNDSW SR3 159 F1 5
Angle Ter WLSD/HOW NE28 68 B4 1
Angram Dr ASHBK/HED/RY SR2 145 F5
Angrove Gdns MLFD/PNYW SR4 125 E6
Angus CLSW/PEL DH2 135 E4
Angus Cl LGB/KIL NE12 49 E1
Angus Crs NSHW NE29 69 F2
Angus Rd GATE NE8 98 B2
Annand Rd DHAM DH1 195 E3
Anne Dr LGB/KIL NE12 50 C4
Annfield Pl STLY/ANP DH9 146 A4
Annfield Rd CRAM NE23 14 A4
Annie St CLDN/WHIT/ROK SR6 108 C6
Annitsford Dr CRAM NE23 35 D2
Ann's Rw BLYTH NE24 11 D3
Ann St BLAY NE21 76 B5
GATE NE8 81 E6
HEBB NE31 84 B1
Annville Crs BYK/HTN/WLK NE6 83 F4
Anscomb Gdns LGB/HTN NE7 64 B3
Anson Cl SSH NE33 71 D6
Anson Pl WD/WHPE/BLK NE5 60 B3 1
Anstead Cl CRAM NE23 22 A2
Anthony Rd SUNDSW SR3 159 F1 6
Anthony St STLY/ANP DH9 148 A1
Antonine Wk
BW/LEM/TK/HW NE15 56 B4
Anton Pl CRAM NE23 22 A3
Antrim Cl WD/WHPE/BLK NE5 61 E3
Antrim Gdns SEA/MUR SR7 176 B2 1
Antwerp Rd SUNDSW SR3 159 E1
Anvil Ct DHAM DH1 179 F5
Apperley WD/WHPE/BLK NE5 60 A5
Apperley Av GOS/KPK NE3 61 E2
Appian Pl BW/LEM/TK/HW NE15 58 A4 1
LWF/SPW/WRK NE9 100 A3
Appleby Ct NSHW NE29 70 B1 1
Appleby Gdns WLSD/HOW NE28 68 C2
Appleby Pk NSHW NE29 54 B6
Appleby Rd SUNDSW SR3 159 F1
Appleby Sq SUNDSW SR3 159 F1 7
Appleby St NSHW NE29 70 C2
Appleby Wy PLEE/EAS SR8 207 F5
Apple Cl BW/LEM/TK/HW NE15 59 E6
Appledore Gdns CLS/BIR/GTL DH3 153 F3
Appledore Rd BLYTH NE24 17 D1
Appleforth Av
ASHBK/HED/RY SR2 145 F5
Appletree Gdns BYK/HTN/WLK NE6 66 A6
MONK NE25 54 A1
Applewood LGB/KIL NE12 50 B1 1
Appley Ter CLDN/WHIT/ROK SR6 127 D3
Apsley Crs GOS/KPK NE3 62 A1
Arbroath Rd SUNDSW SR3 142 C6
Arcadia Av CLS/BIR/GTL DH3 153 E3
Arcadia Ter BLYTH NE24 11 D6
Archbold Ter JES NE2 81 D1 1
Archer Rd SUNDSW SR3 142 C6
Archer Sq SUNDSW SR3 142 C6 2
Archer St WLSD/HOW NE28 68 A3
Archery Ri DHAM DH1 193 F6
Archibald St GOS/KPK NE3 63 E1
Arcot Av CRAM NE23 13 D6
MONK NE25 54 A1
Arcot Dr MONK NE25 54 A2
WD/WHPE/BLK NE5 60 B6 2
Arden Av GOS/KPK NE3 47 D3
Arden Cl WLSD/HOW NE28 51 F5
Arden Crs WD/WHPE/BLK NE5 61 F5
Arden Sq SUNDSW SR3 143 D6
Arden St RDHAMSE DH6 206 B1
Ardrossan CLSW/PEL DH2 135 E5
Ardrossan Rd SUNDSW SR3 159 F1
Arena Wy ELS/FEN NE4 80 B5
Argus Cl DUN/TMV NE11 98 A3
Argyle Ct STLY/ANP DH9 131 F6
Argyle Pl NSHW NE29 54 C4 1
RDHAMSE DH6 187 E5
Argyle Sq ASHBK/HED/RY SR2 4 B5
Argyle St ASHBK/HED/RY SR2 4 B5
CNUT NE1 3 F3
HEBB NE31 85 D1
TYNE/NSHE NE30 55 F4 1
Arisaig CLSW/PEL DH2 135 E4
Arklecrag WASHN NE37 120 B6
Arkleside Pl WD/WHPE/BLK NE5 59 F5 2
Arkle St DIN/WO NE13 32 C6
GATE NE8 98 B2
Arkwright St GATE NE8 98 C3
Arlington Av GOS/KPK NE3 62 B3
Arlington Gv CRAM NE23 14 A4
WICK/BNPF NE16 95 F4
Arlington Rd HEBB NE31 85 E4 1
Arlington St MLFD/PNYW SR4 125 E6 1
Armstrong Av BYK/HTN/WLK NE6 65 D5
HAR/WTLS NE34 89 D1 1
Armstrong Dr LGB/KIL NE12 49 D2
Armstrong Rd
BW/LEM/TK/HW NE15 77 E3
ELS/FEN NE4 78 C4
PLEE/EAS SR8 200 C6
WASHN NE37 119 E5
WLSD/HOW NE28 68 C5
Armstrong St DUN/TMV NE11 98 B3
GATE NE8 98 B3
Armstrong Ter SSH NE33 71 E6
Arncliffe Av MLFD/PNYW SR4 143 D2 1
Arncliffe Gdns
WD/WHPE/BLK NE5 59 E4 4
Arnham Gv MLFD/PNYW SR4 141 E4
Arnold Cl STLY/ANP DH9 148 C2
Arnold Rd SUNDSW SR3 142 C6
Arnold St BOLCOL NE35 105 E2
Arran Ct SUNDSW SR3 160 C2 1
Arran Dr JRW NE32 87 D5
Arran Pl NSHW NE29 53 E4
Arras La SUND SR1 5 F2
Arrow Cl LGB/KIL NE12 49 D2
Arthur Av ASHBK/HED/RY SR2 162 C2
Arthur Cook Av WICK/BNPF NE16 96 B3
Arthur St BLYTH NE24 11 D4 1
CLDN/WHIT/ROK SR6 91 E4
GATE NE8 81 D6
JRW NE32 86 A2 1
STLY/ANP DH9 150 C1
Arun Cl PLEE/EAS SR8 208 B3
Arundel Cl BDLGTN NE22 8 B1
DIN/WO NE13 32 C5 1
Arundel Dr BW/LEM/TK/HW NE15 77 D1
MONK NE25 39 D6
Arundel Gdns LWF/SPW/WRK NE9 99 F5
SUNDSW SR3 159 E1
Arundel Rd SUNDSW SR3 142 C6
Arundel Wy BDN/LAN/SAC DH7 203 E4
Asama Ct ELS/FEN NE4 79 F6
Ascot Cl WLSD/HOW NE28 51 F6
Ascot Ct SUNDSW SR3 159 F1
Ascot Crs GATE NE8 98 B3
Ascot Gdns HAR/WTLS NE34 88 C2
Ascot Pl CLSW/PEL DH2 152 B1
Ash Av DHAM DH1 195 F5
DIN/WO NE13 31 D3
Ashberry Gv CLDN/WHIT/ROK SR6 126 C3
Ashbourne Av BYK/HTN/WLK NE6 83 E2
Ashbourne Cl SMOOR NE27 37 E5 1
Ashbourne Rd JRW NE32 86 B3 1
Ashbrook Cl BDN/LAN/SAC DH7 202 B5 1
Ashbrooke MONK NE25 40 A5
Ashbrooke Cross
ASHBK/HED/RY SR2 144 B3 1
Ashbrooke Dr PONT/DH NE20 28 A3
Ashbrooke Gdns
WLSD/HOW NE28 68 A3 1
Ashbrooke Range
ASHBK/HED/RY SR2 144 B3 2
Ashbrooke Rd
ASHBK/HED/RY SR2 144 B3
Ashbrooke St WD/WHPE/BLK NE5 62 A3
Ashburne Ct
ASHBK/HED/RY SR2 144 C2 1
Ashburn Rd WLSD/HOW NE28 52 A6
Ashburton Rd GOS/KPK NE3 62 C2
Ashbury MONK NE25 39 E4
Ashby St ASHBK/HED/RY SR2 145 E3
Ash Crs SEA/MUR SR7 176 B5
Ashcroft Dr LGB/KIL NE12 50 A5
Ashdale HLS DH4 139 D6
Ashdale Crs WD/WHPE/BLK NE5 59 E5
Ashdown Av DHAM DH1 196 A3
Ashdown Cl LGB/KIL NE12 49 D5 1
Ashdown Rd SUNDSW SR3 142 C6
Ashdown Wy LGB/KIL NE12 49 D5
Asher St GATE NE8 100 B1 1
Ashfield JRW NE32 104 C1
Ashfield Av WICK/BNPF NE16 96 B2
Ashfield Cl ELS/FEN NE4 79 F4
Ashfield Gdns WLSD/HOW NE28 66 B3
Ashfield Gv NSHW NE29 54 C6 2
WBAY NE26 40 C4
Ashfield Pk WICK/BNPF NE16 96 A2
Ashfield Ri WICK/BNPF NE16 96 A5
Ashfield Rd GOS/KPK NE3 62 C2
WICK/BNPF NE16 96 A5
Ashford Cl BLYTH NE24 17 D1 2
Ashford Dr BDN/LAN/SAC DH7 164 A6
Ashford Gv WD/WHPE/BLK NE5 59 D2 2
Ashford Rd SUNDSW SR3 159 F1 8
Ash Gv CLDN/WHIT/ROK SR6 109 F2 1
DUN/TMV NE11 97 D1
RYTON NE40 74 B2
WLSD/HOW NE28 67 F4
Ashgrove Av HAR/WTLS NE34 89 E4
Ashkirk CRAM NE23 34 C2
Ashkirk Cl CLSW/PEL DH2 165 F1
Ashkirk Wy MONK NE25 24 C6
Ashleigh Av DHAM DH1 194 A1
Ashleigh Cl BLAY NE21 94 C1
Ashleigh Crs WD/WHPE/BLK NE5 60 C6 1
Ashleigh Gv CLDN/WHIT/ROK SR6 109 D6
JES NE2 63 F4
LGB/KIL NE12 49 F5
TYNE/NSHE NE30 55 E4
Ashleigh Rd WD/WHPE/BLK NE5 60 C6
Ashley Cl LGB/KIL NE12 36 B6
WASHS NE38 138 C3
Ashley Rd HAR/WTLS NE34 88 B2
Ashley Ter CLS/BIR/GTL DH3 153 E4
Ashmead Cl LGB/KIL NE12 36 A6
Ash Mdw CLS/BIR/GTL DH3 154 A1
Ashmore St ASHBK/HED/RY SR2 4 C6
Asholme WD/WHPE/BLK NE5 60 A5
Ashridge Cl HAR/WTLS NE34 90 A3 1
Ashridge Ct FELL NE10 102 A3 1
Ash St BLAY NE21 94 B1
Ash Ter SEA/MUR SR7 188 B1
Ashton Ct RYTON NE40 74 C4
Ashton Ri CLSW/PEL DH2 153 E6
PLEE/EAS SR8 209 D1
Ashton St PLEE/EAS SR8 201 E2
Ashton Wy SUNDSW SR3 159 E2
WBAY NE26 39 F3
Ashtree Cl ELS/FEN NE4 79 E4 1
ROWG NE39 111 E1
Ash Tree Dr BDLGTN NE22 7 E2
Ashtree La BLAY NE21 92 B5
Ashvale Av DUN/TMV NE11 116 B6
Ashwell Rd SUNDSW SR3 159 F1 9
Ashwood RDHAMSE DH6 187 F6
Ashwood Av SWCK/CAS SR5 125 E2
Ashwood Cl CRAM NE23 14 A4
LGB/KIL NE12 50 A4 1
Ashwood Crs BYK/HTN/WLK NE6 66 B6 1
Ashwood Cft HEBB NE31 84 C1 2
Ashwood Gdns
LWF/SPW/WRK NE9 117 F2
Ashwood Gv DIN/WO NE13 33 D5
SWCK/CAS SR5 124 A3 2
Ashwood St ASHBK/HED/RY SR2 144 A1
Ashwood Ter ASHBK/HED/RY SR2 144 A1
Askern Av ASHBK/HED/RY SR2 145 F5 1
Askerton Dr PLEE/EAS SR8 207 F5
Askew Rd GATE NE8 80 C6
Askew Rd West GATE NE8 98 B1
Askrigg Av ASHBK/HED/RY SR2 145 E5
WLSD/HOW NE28 51 F5
Aspen Cl DHAM DH1 195 F3
Aspen Ct SUNDSW SR3 160 A2 1
Aspley Cl SUNDSW SR3 160 C2
Association Rd
CLDN/WHIT/ROK SR6 127 D2 1
Aster Pl ELS/FEN NE4 78 B1
Astley Dr WBAY NE26 40 A2
Astley Gdns MONK NE25 24 B5 1
WBAY NE26 26 A1
Astley Gv WBAY NE26 26 A1
Astley Rd MONK NE25 24 B4
Aston Sq SUNDSW SR3 159 F1 10
Aston St SSH NE33 88 C1
Athelhampton WASHS NE38 139 F1 1
Athelstan Rigg
ASHBK/HED/RY SR2 162 C1
Athenaeum St SUND SR1 4 D3
Atherton Dr ELS/FEN NE4 79 D4
HLS DH4 169 F3
Atherton St DHAM DH1 194 A5
Athlone Pl CLS/BIR/GTL DH3 136 C5
Athol Gdns ASHBK/HED/RY SR2 162 C2
MONK NE25 53 F1
Athol Gn DUN/TMV NE11 97 F1 1
Athol Gv SUNDSW SR3 160 C1 1
Atholl Gdns LWF/SPW/WRK NE9 100 A3 1
Athol Rd ASHBK/HED/RY SR2 5 F6
Athol Ter ASHBK/HED/RY SR2 5 F6
Athull CLSW/PEL DH2 135 E4
Atkinson Gdns NSHW NE29 70 C3 1
Atkinson Gv RDHAMSE DH6 206 A1
Atkinson Rd
CLDN/WHIT/ROK SR6 108 C6 1
CLS/BIR/GTL DH3 153 F3
ELS/FEN NE4 78 C4

Atkinson St WLSD/HOW NE28 67 D5 1
Atkinson Ter ELS/FEN NE4 78 C3 1
WLSD/HOW NE28 67 D5
Atkin St LGB/KIL NE12 35 D5
Atlantis Rd SUNDSW SR3 142 B6
Atley Wy CRAM NE23 13 D4
Attlee Cl CRAM NE23 35 D5 1
Attlee Gv ASHBK/HED/RY SR2 145 D6
Attwood Gv SWCK/CAS SR5 126 A3 1
Aubone Av
BW/LEM/TK/HW NE15 78 B2 1
Auburn Cl WLSD/HOW NE28 68 C4
Auburn Gdns ELS/FEN NE4 62 A6
Auckland CLSW/PEL DH2 152 B6
Auckland Av HAR/WTLS NE34 90 A2
Auckland Rd DHAM DH1 180 C5
HEBB NE31 85 E1
Auckland Ter JRW NE32 87 D4
Auden Gv ELS/FEN NE4 79 D2
Audley Gdns SUNDSW SR3 144 A3
Audley Rd GOS/KPK NE3 64 A2
Audouins Rw GATE NE8 98 C2 1
Augusta Ct WLSD/HOW NE28 52 A6
Augusta Sq SUNDSW SR3 159 F1
Augustine Cl DHAM DH1 179 F6
August Pl SSH NE33 72 A5 1
Augustus Dr BDLGTN NE22 7 D2
Austen Av HAR/WTLS NE34 88 A5
Austen Pl STLY/ANP DH9 148 C4
Austin Sq SWCK/CAS SR5 126 A2
Australia Gv HAR/WTLS NE34 87 E5
Austral Pl DIN/WO NE13 32 C5 2
Autumn Cl WASHS NE38 120 C6
Avalon Dr BW/LEM/TK/HW NE15 60 A6
Avalon Rd SUNDSW SR3 142 C6
Avebury Dr WASHS NE38 139 D1
Avebury Pl CRAM NE23 14 B5
Avenue Rd GATE NE8 99 E2
MONK NE25 24 B6
Avenue Ter ASHBK/HED/RY SR2 144 B2 1
The Avenue ASHBK/HED/RY SR2 4 B6
BLAY NE21 77 D6
CLS/BIR/GTL DH3 136 B2
CLS/BIR/GTL DH3 156 A3
CLSW/PEL DH2 153 D5
DHAM DH1 179 F5
DHAM DH1 193 F5
HLH DH5 172 A6
LWF/SPW/WRK NE9 99 F3
MONK NE25 24 C4
ROWG NE39 111 E3
SEA/MUR SR7 175 F3
STLY/ANP DH9 146 A5
WASHS NE38 139 D1
WBAY NE26 40 B5
WLSD/HOW NE28 67 D5
Avenue Vivian HLS DH4 169 E1
Aviemore Rd BOL NE36 106 A3
Avision St ELS/FEN NE4 80 A3
Avison Pl ELS/FEN NE4 80 A2 1
Avocet Cl BLYTH NE24 17 D3
Avolon Pl ELS/FEN NE4 80 A2 2
Avon Av JRW NE32 86 B6
NSHW NE29 70 A2
Avon Cl ROWG NE39 111 E1
WLSD/HOW NE28 51 F6
Avon Ct MONK NE25 24 C3
Avon Crs HLS DH4 169 F2
Avoncroft Cl SEA/MUR SR7 174 C2
Avondale MLFD/PNYW SR4 141 F1
Avondale Av BLYTH NE24 9 D4
HLS DH4 157 D1
LGB/KIL NE12 49 F4 2
Avondale Cl BLYTH NE24 9 E4 1
Avondale Gdns BOL NE36 105 F3 1
Avondale Rd BYK/HTN/WLK NE6 82 B3
Avondale Ter CLSW/PEL DH2 153 E5
GATE NE8 99 D2
Avonlea Wy WD/WHPE/BLK NE5 61 E3 1
Avonmouth Rd SUNDSW SR3 159 E1
Avonmouth Sq SUNDSW SR3 159 F1
Avon Rd HEBB NE31 85 D4
PLEE/EAS SR8 208 B3
STLY/ANP DH9 148 B3
Avon St GATE NE8 99 F1
SUND SR1 5 G4
Awnless Ct HAR/WTLS NE34 88 B3 2
Axbridge Gdns ELS/FEN NE4 79 D4
Axminster Cl CRAM NE23 14 B5
Axwell Dr BLYTH NE24 10 A5
Axwell Park Rd BLAY NE21 95 D1
Axwell Park Vw
BW/LEM/TK/HW NE15 78 A3
Axwell Vw BLAY NE21 94 B1
WICK/BNPF NE16 95 F3 1
Aycliffe Av LWF/SPW/WRK NE9 100 C6
Aycliffe Crs LWF/SPW/WRK NE9 100 C6
Aydon Gv JRW NE32 86 A5
Aykley Ct DHAM DH1 193 F2 1
Aykley Gn DHAM DH1 193 F2
Aykley Rd DHAM DH1 180 A6
Aykley V DHAM DH1 193 F1
Aylesbury Dr SUNDSW SR3 160 C3
Aylesbury Pl LGB/KIL NE12 49 D5 2
Aylesford Sq BLYTH NE24 17 D1 3
Aylsham Cl WD/WHPE/BLK NE5 59 D2
Aylsham Ct SUNDSW SR3 160 C4 1
Aylyth Pl GOS/KPK NE3 62 B3 1
Ayr Dr JRW NE32 86 C5
Ayre's Quay Rd SUND SR1 4 A2 1
Ayre's Ter NSHW NE29 54 C6 3
Ayrey Av HAR/WTLS NE34 87 E4
Aysgarth Av ASHBK/HED/RY SR2 145 E4
WLSD/HOW NE28 51 F5
Ayton Av ASHBK/HED/RY SR2 145 E5
Ayton Cl WD/WHPE/BLK NE5 60 A3
Ayton Ct BDLGTN NE22 6 C2
Ayton Rd WASHS NE38 137 E2
Ayton St BYK/HTN/WLK NE6 82 B3
Azalea Av ASHBK/HED/RY SR2 4 B6
Azalea Ter North
ASHBK/HED/RY SR2 4 B5
Azalea Ter South
ASHBK/HED/RY SR2 4 B6

B

Back Bridge St SUND SR1 4 C2
Back Chapman St
BYK/HTN/WLK NE6 82 B1
Back Croft Rd BLYTH NE24 11 D5 2
Back George St ELS/FEN NE4 2 A6
Back Goldspink La JES NE2 81 E1 1
Back Heaton Park Rd
BYK/HTN/WLK NE6 82 A2 2
Back La BLAY NE21 76 A6
CLS/BIR/GTL DH3 167 F3
HLS DH4 140 A6
MONK NE25 40 A5
Back Lodge Ter SUND SR1 5 H3
Back Maling St
BYK/HTN/WLK NE6 81 F3 1
Back Mitford St ELS/FEN NE4 80 A5 1
Back New Bridge St CNUT NE1 3 G2
Back North Bridge St
SWCK/CAS SR5 126 C4
Back North Railway St
SEA/MUR SR7 176 C2
Back North Ter SEA/MUR SR7 176 C2
Back Percy Gdns
TYNE/NSHE NE30 55 F4 2
Back Rw WICK/BNPF NE16 95 F3
Back Ryhope St
ASHBK/HED/RY SR2 162 A1
Back Silver St DHAM DH1 194 B4 1
Back South Railway St
SEA/MUR SR7 176 C3
Back Stephen St
BYK/HTN/WLK NE6 81 F2 1
Back St BLAY NE21 94 A1 1
Back Walker Rd
BYK/HTN/WLK NE6 83 F4 1
Back Western Hl DHAM DH1 194 A3
Back Woodbine St GATE NE8 98 C1
Backworth La CRAM NE23 36 B2
Baden Crs SWCK/CAS SR5 123 F1
Baden Powell St
LWF/SPW/WRK NE9 99 F3 1
Baden St CLS/BIR/GTL DH3 153 E6
Badger Cl SUNDSW SR3 160 C3
Badminton Cl BOLCOL NE35 104 C1 1
Baffin Ct SUNDSW SR3 160 B2
Baildon Cl WLSD/HOW NE28 67 E2 1
Bailey Ri PLEE/EAS SR8 200 C6
Bailey Sq SWCK/CAS SR5 105 F6 1
Bailey Wy HLH DH5 186 A2
Bainbridge Av HAR/WTLS NE34 87 E4
SUNDSW SR3 144 A3
Bainbridge Holme Cl
SUNDSW SR3 144 A3
Bainbridge Holme Rd
SUNDSW SR3 144 B3
Bainbridge St DHAM DH1 196 C1
Bainford Av BW/LEM/TK/HW NE15 77 F2
Baird Av WLSD/HOW NE28 69 E4
Baird Cl WASHN NE37 121 D2
Baird St SWCK/CAS SR5 123 F1 1
Bakehouse La DHAM DH1 194 C4
Baker Gdns FELL NE10 102 A2
Baker Rd CRAM NE23 12 C5
Baker St HLH DH5 171 D1
SWCK/CAS SR5 123 F1
Bakewell Ter BYK/HTN/WLK NE6 82 C4
Baldersdale Gdns SUNDSW SR3 144 A4
Baldwin Av BOL NE36 106 C3
ELS/FEN NE4 79 E1 1
Balfour Rd BW/LEM/TK/HW NE15 77 F3
Balfour St BLYTH NE24 10 C3
GATE NE8 98 C1 2
HLH DH5 171 D1
Balgonie Cottages RYTON NE40 74 B3
Baliol Sq DHAM DH1 204 C1
Balkwell Av NSHW NE29 69 F1
Balkwell Gn NSHW NE29 54 A6
Ballast Hl BLYTH NE24 11 E4 1
Ballast Hill Rd NSHW NE29 70 C3
Ballater Cl STLY/ANP DH9 149 D2
Balliol Av LGB/KIL NE12 49 E3
Balliol Cl PLEE/EAS SR8 208 A2
Balliol Gdns LGB/HTN NE7 65 D1 1
Balmain Rd GOS/KPK NE3 62 A2
Balmoral Av GOS/KPK NE3 64 A2 2
JRW NE32 87 D5 1
Balmoral Cl BDLGTN NE22 8 B2
Balmoral Ct SWCK/CAS SR5 123 F1 2
Balmoral Crs HLH DH5 171 E3
Balmoral Dr FELL NE10 100 B2
Balmoral Gdns NSHW NE29 54 B5
Balmoral St WLSD/HOW NE28 67 D4
Balmoral Ter ASHBK/HED/RY SR2 145 E4
BYK/HTN/WLK NE6 82 A1
GOS/KPK NE3 64 A2
SUNDSW SR3 159 E1
Balmoral Wy FELL NE10 100 B3
Balroy Ct LGB/KIL NE12 50 A4
Baltic Millennium Br CNUT NE1 3 G5
Baltic Rd FELL NE10 82 C5
Baltimore Av SWCK/CAS SR5 105 D6
Baltimore Sq SWCK/CAS SR5 123 E1
Bamborough Ct CRAM NE23 34 B2 1
Bamborough Ter TYNE/NSHE NE30 54 C5
Bambro' St ASHBK/HED/RY SR2 5 F6 1
Bamburgh Av SSH NE33 72 B5
Bamburgh Cl BLYTH NE24 10 B5
WASHS NE38 137 F1
Bamburgh Ct DUN/TMV NE11 98 B4
Bamburgh Dr FELL NE10 84 A6 1
WLSD/HOW NE28 68 B4
Bamburgh Gdns SUNDSW SR3 144 A3 1
Bamburgh Gv HAR/WTLS NE34 73 D6
Bamburgh Rd DHAM DH1 180 B5
LGB/KIL NE12 50 B4
WD/WHPE/BLK NE5 60 A3 1
Bampton Av CLDN/WHIT/ROK SR6 108 B5
Banbury WASHN NE37 121 D4
Banbury Gdns WLSD/HOW NE28 67 F1 1
Banbury Rd GOS/KPK NE3 46 B6
Banbury Ter SSH NE33 71 F6
Banbury Wy BLYTH NE24 16 C1
NSHW NE29 69 F2
Bancroft Ter MLFD/PNYW SR4 125 E6
Banesley La DUN/TMV NE11 116 A3
Banff St SWCK/CAS SR5 105 F6
Bank Av WICK/BNPF NE16 95 F3
Bankdale Gdns BLYTH NE24 9 F5
Bankhead Rd
BW/LEM/TK/HW NE15 58 B5 1
Bankhead Ter HLS DH4 169 F1
Bank Rd GATE NE8 3 G6
Banks Holt CLSW/PEL DH2 152 B6 1
Bankside Cl ASHBK/HED/RY SR2 162 A1
Bankside La HAR/WTLS NE34 88 B3
Bankside Rd BW/LEM/TK/HW NE15 77 E3
Bankwell La GATE NE8 3 F6
Bannister Dr LGB/KIL NE12 50 B4
Bannockburn LGB/KIL NE12 35 F6 3
Barbara St ASHBK/HED/RY SR2 145 E3
Barbary Cl CLSW/PEL DH2 152 A1
Barbary Dr CLDN/WHIT/ROK SR6 127 E2
Barbondale Lonnen
WD/WHPE/BLK NE5 59 E5
Barbour Av HAR/WTLS NE34 89 F1
Barclay Pl WD/WHPE/BLK NE5 61 D5
Barclay St SWCK/CAS SR5 126 C4 1
Barcusclose La WICK/BNPF NE16 112 B6
Bardolph Rd NSHW NE29 53 F6
Bardon Cl WD/WHPE/BLK NE5 60 B2 1
Bardon Crs MONK NE25 25 E6 1
Bardsey Pl LGB/KIL NE12 49 D6
Barehirst St SSH NE33 88 A1
Barents Cl WD/WHPE/BLK NE5 60 B4 1
Baret Rd BYK/HTN/WLK NE6 66 A6
Barford Dr CLSW/PEL DH2 165 F1
Baring St SSH NE33 71 E2
Barker St JES NE2 3 G1
Barking Crs SWCK/CAS SR5 123 E1
Barking Sq SWCK/CAS SR5 123 E1 1
Barkwood Rd ROWG NE39 110 C2
Barlow Crs BLAY NE21 92 B4 1
Barlow Fell Rd BLAY NE21 92 B5
Barlowfield Cl BLAY NE21 93 F2 1
Barlow La BLAY NE21 92 C4
Barmoor La RYTON NE40 74 A3
Barmouth Cl WLSD/HOW NE28 67 F1 2
Barmouth Rd NSHW NE29 69 E1
Barmouth Wy NSHW NE29 69 F2
Barmston La WASHN NE37 122 B6
WASHS NE38 140 A1
Barmston Rd WASHS NE38 139 F2
Barmston Wy WASHS NE38 121 E6
Barnard Cl BDLGTN NE22 6 C3
DHAM DH1 180 C5
Barnard Crs HEBB NE31 85 D1
Barnard Gv JRW NE32 86 C4 1
Barnard St BLYTH NE24 11 D5 3
MLFD/PNYW SR4 143 E1
Barnard Wynd PLEE/EAS SR8 208 A5
Barnesbury Rd ELS/FEN NE4 79 D3
Barnes Park Rd MLFD/PNYW SR4 143 F2
Barnes Rd SEA/MUR SR7 188 A1
SSH NE33 71 D6 1
Barnes St HLH DH5 171 F6 1
Barnes Vw MLFD/PNYW SR4 143 E2

Barn Hl *STLY/ANP* DH9 **148** A1
Barn Hollows *SEA/MUR* SR7 **190** B5
Barningham *WASHS* NE38 **139** F2
Barningham Cl *SUNDSW* SR3 **144** A4
Barns Cl *JRW* NE32 **85** F4
Barnstaple Cl *WLSD/HOW* NE28 **67** F1 3
Barnstaple Rd *NSHW* NE29 **53** E4
The Barns *STLY/ANP* DH9 **131** D6
Barnton Rd *FELL* NE10 **101** D4
Barnwood Cl *WLSD/HOW* NE28 **67** E1 1
Baroness Dr *BW/LEM/TK/HW* NE15 **77** F1
Baron's Quay Rd *SWCK/CAS* SR5 **124** A4
Baronswood *GOS/KPK* NE3 **63** D2
Barrack Rd *ELS/FEN* NE4 **80** A1
Barrack St *SUND* SR1 **127** E4
Barras Av *BLYTH* NE24 **16** C1
CRAM NE23 **35** D1
Barras Av West *BLYTH* NE24 **16** B2
Barras Br *CNUT* NE1 **2** D1
Barras Dr *SUNDSW* SR3 **144** A4
Barrasford Cl *GOS/KPK* NE3 **62** C2
Barrasford Dr *DIN/WO* NE13 **33** E5
Barrasford Rd *CRAM* NE23 **22** B3 1
DHAM DH1 **180** C6
Barrasford St *WLSD/HOW* NE28 **69** E5 1
Barrass Av *CRAM* NE23 **36** A1
Barr Cl *WLSD/HOW* NE28 **68** A1
Barrie Sq *SWCK/CAS* SR5 **126** A2
Barrington Av *TYNE/NSHE* NE30 **54** B2
Barrington Ct *BDLGTN* NE22 **7** F4 1
Barrington Dr *WASHS* NE38 **138** C1
Barrington Pk *BDLGTN* NE22 **9** E1
Barrington Rd *BDLGTN* NE22 **8** B1
STKFD/GP NE62 **7** E1
Barrington St *SSH* NE33 **71** E3 1
Barrington Ter *HLH* DH5 **171** F5 2
Barron St South *SWCK/CAS* SR5 **124** B3 1
Barrowburn Pl *CRAM* NE23 **36** C1
Barrow St *SWCK/CAS* SR5 **105** F6 2
Barry St *DUN/TMV* NE11 **97** E1
GATE NE8 **98** C3
Barsloan Gv *PLEE/EAS* SR8 **200** A6 1
Barton Cl *TYNE/NSHE* NE30 **55** D3
WASHN NE37 **121** D2
WLSD/HOW NE28 **67** F1 4
Barton Ct *CLDN/WHIT/ROK* SR6 **108** B5 1
Bartram Gdns *GATE* NE8 **99** D3 1
Bartram St *SWCK/CAS* SR5 **126** B1
Barwell Cl *WLSD/HOW* NE28 **67** F1
Barwell Ct *LGB/HTN* NE7 **66** A3
Basildon Gdns *WLSD/HOW* NE28 **67** E1 2
Basil Wy *HAR/WTLS* NE34 **89** D5
Basingstoke Pl *LGB/KIL* NE12 **49** E5
Basingstoke Rd *PLEE/EAS* SR8 **208** B1 1
Baslow Gdns *SUNDSW* SR3 **144** A3
Bassington Av *CRAM* NE23 **21** D1
Bassington Cl *ELS/FEN* NE4 **80** A2 3
Bassington Dr *CRAM* NE23 **12** C6
Bassington La *CRAM* NE23 **12** C6
Bates La *BLAY* NE21 **77** E6
Bath Cl *WLSD/HOW* NE28 **68** A1
Bathgate Cl *WLSD/HOW* NE28 **68** A1
Bathgate Sq *SWCK/CAS* SR5 **123** E1 2
Bath La *BLYTH* NE24 **11** E5
CNUT NE1 **2** B4
Bath Rd *FELL* NE10 **82** C6
HEBB NE31 **85** D5 1
Bath St *BYK/HTN/WLK* NE6 **83** F3
Bath Ter *BLYTH* NE24 **11** E5
GOS/KPK NE3 **63** F1
TYNE/NSHE NE30 **55** F5
Batley St *SWCK/CAS* SR5 **123** E1 3
Battle Hill Dr *WLSD/HOW* NE28 **67** D2
WLSD/HOW NE28 **68** B1
Baugh Cl *WASHN* NE37 **119** F6
Baulkham Hills *HLS* DH4 **157** D2
Bavington *FELL* NE10 **101** F5 1
Bavington Dr *WD/WHPE/BLK* NE5 **61** E5
Bavington Gdns *TYNE/NSHE* NE30 **54** C3
Bavington Rd *MONK* NE25 **24** C5
Bawtry Gv *NSHW* NE29 **70** A1
Baxter Av *ELS/FEN* NE4 **79** D2
Baxter Rd *SWCK/CAS* SR5 **105** E6
Baxter Sq *SWCK/CAS* SR5 **105** E6 1
Baybridge Rd
WD/WHPE/BLK NE5 **60** A3 2
Baysdale *HLS* DH4 **139** D6 1
Bayswater Av *SWCK/CAS* SR5 **123** F1
Bayswater Rd *GATE* NE8 **100** A2 1
JES NE2 **64** A4
Bayswater Sq *SWCK/CAS* SR5 **123** F1 3
Baytree Gdns *MONK* NE25 **54** A1
Baytree Ter *STLY/ANP* DH9 **151** D1
Baywood Gv *WLSD/HOW* NE28 **67** E1 3
Beach Av *WBAY* NE26 **40** C5
Beach Croft Av *TYNE/NSHE* NE30 **55** D2
Beachcross Rd
MLFD/PNYW SR4 **144** A1 1
Beach Gv *PLEE/EAS* SR8 **209** F2
Beach Rd *NSHW* NE29 **54** A5
SSH NE33 **71** F4
TYNE/NSHE NE30 **54** C4
Beach St *MLFD/PNYW* SR4 **126** A4
Beachville St *MLFD/PNYW* SR4 **144** A1 2
Beachway *BLYTH* NE24 **17** E2
Beach Wy *TYNE/NSHE* NE30 **54** C3
Beacon Dr *CLDN/WHIT/ROK* SR6 **127** E3
DIN/WO NE13 **32** C5
Beacon Gld *HAR/WTLS* NE34 **90** B2
Beacon La *CRAM* NE23 **20** C2
Beacon Lough Rd
LWF/SPW/WRK NE9 **99** F6
Beaconsfield Av
LWF/SPW/WRK NE9 **99** F5
Beaconsfield Cl *MONK* NE25 **39** F3
Beaconsfield Crs
LWF/SPW/WRK NE9 **99** F5 1
Beaconsfield Rd
LWF/SPW/WRK NE9 **99** E5
Beaconsfield St *BLYTH* NE24 **11** E4 2
ELS/FEN NE4 **79** F3
STLY/ANP DH9 **148** B1 2
Beaconside *HAR/WTLS* NE34 **90** B2
Beacon St *LWF/SPW/WRK* NE9 **99** E5
SSH NE33 **71** E2
TYNE/NSHE NE30 **55** D6
Beadling Gdns *ELS/FEN* NE4 **79** D2
Beadnell Av *NSHW* NE29 **69** F2
Beadnell Cl *BLAY* NE21 **93** F2
Beadnell Gdns *SMOOR* NE27 **52** B1
Beadnell Pl *JES* NE2 **3** G2
Beadnell Rd *BLYTH* NE24 **16** A1
Beadnell Wy *GOS/KPK* NE3 **46** C6 2
Beal Cl *BLYTH* NE24 **10** B5
Beal Dr *LGB/KIL* NE12 **50** B4
Beal Gdns *WLSD/HOW* NE28 **68** B1
Beal Rd *SMOOR* NE27 **52** B1
Beal Ter *BYK/HTN/WLK* NE6 **83** E4
Beal Wy *GOS/KPK* NE3 **63** D1
Beaminster Wy *GOS/KPK* NE3 **61** E1
WD/WHPE/BLK NE5 **61** E1
Beamishburn Rd *STLY/ANP* DH9 **131** F5
Beamish Cl *WLSD/HOW* NE28 **67** E1 4
Beamish Gdns
LWF/SPW/WRK NE9 **100** C6
Beamish Hills *STLY/ANP* DH9 **149** F1
Beamish St *STLY/ANP* DH9 **148** A1 1
Beamish Vw *CLSW/PEL* DH2 **151** D5
STLY/ANP DH9 **149** D1
Beaney La *CLSW/PEL* DH2 **165** E4
Beanley Av *HEBB* NE31 **84** C4
Beanley Crs *TYNE/NSHE* NE30 **55** E5
Beanley Pl *LGB/HTN* NE7 **64** C3
Bearpark Colliery Rd
BDN/LAN/SAC DH7 **192** A3
Beatrice Av *BLYTH* NE24 **16** A2 1
Beatrice Gdns *BOL* NE36 **106** C3 1
HAR/WTLS NE34 **89** D2
Beatrice St *CLDN/WHIT/ROK* SR6 **127** D3
Beatrice Ter *HLS* DH4 **139** D5
Beattie St *HAR/WTLS* NE34 **88** A3 1
Beatty Av *JES* NE2 **64** A3
Beatty Rd *BDLGTN* NE22 **8** A4
Beaufort Cl *HLS* DH4 **157** D3 1
WD/WHPE/BLK NE5 **61** F3 1
Beaufort Gdns *WLSD/HOW* NE28 **67** E1 5
Beaufront Cl *FELL* NE10 **102** A4 2
Beaufront Gdns *GATE* NE8 **100** A1 2
WD/WHPE/BLK NE5 **61** E6
Beaufront Ter *JRW* NE32 **86** A5
SSH NE33 **71** E6 1
Beauly *WASHS* NE38 **138** C3 1
Beaumaris Gdns *SUNDSW* SR3 **159** E1
Beaumaris Wy *WD/WHPE/BLK* NE5 **61** D2
Beaumont Cl *DHAM* DH1 **179** F5
Beaumont Crs *PLEE/EAS* SR8 **201** D5
Beaumont Dr *MONK* NE25 **39** E3
WASHS NE38 **138** C2
Beaumont Mnr *BLYTH* NE24 **9** E5
Beaumont Pl *PLEE/EAS* SR8 **209** D3 1
Beaumont St
ASHBK/HED/RY SR2 **145** D2 1
BLYTH NE24 **10** C4
ELS/FEN NE4 **79** E5
NSHW NE29 **70** C1 1
SEA/MUR SR7 **176** C4 1
SWCK/CAS SR5 **125** F1
Beaumont Ter *GOS/KPK* NE3 **63** F1
JRW NE32 **85** F3
WD/WHPE/BLK NE5 **60** B4
Beaver Cl *DHAM* DH1 **180** B4
Bebdon Ct *BLYTH* NE24 **10** B6 2
Bebside Furnace Rd *BLYTH* NE24 **8** C4
Bebside Rd *BLYTH* NE24 **8** B5
Beckenham Av *BOL* NE36 **106** C2
Beckenham Cl *BOL* NE36 **107** D2 1
Beckenham Gdns
WLSD/HOW NE28 **67** E2
Beckett St *GATE* NE8 **81** F4 1
Beckfoot Cl *WD/WHPE/BLK* NE5 **61** D5
Beckford *WASHS* NE38 **139** F2
Beckford Cl *WLSD/HOW* NE28 **67** E1 6
Beck Pl *PLEE/EAS* SR8 **208** C1
Beckside Gdns *WD/WHPE/BLK* NE5 **59** D5
Beckwith Rd *SUNDSW* SR3 **142** B6
Beda Hl *BLAY* NE21 **76** B5
Bedale Cl *DHAM* DH1 **196** C2
WLSD/HOW NE28 **67** E1 7
Bedale Crs *SWCK/CAS* SR5 **123** F1
Bedale Dr *MONK* NE25 **54** B1
Bedale Gn *WD/WHPE/BLK* NE5 **61** F3
Bedale St *HLH* DH5 **185** F2
Bedburn *WASHS* NE38 **137** E5
Bede Av *DHAM* DH1 **195** F5
Bede Burn Rd *JRW* NE32 **86** A2 2
Bedeburn Rd *WD/WHPE/BLK* NE5 **60** B1
Bede Burn Vw *JRW* NE32 **86** A3
Bede Cl *LGB/KIL* NE12 **51** D4
Bede Ct *CLS/BIR/GTL* DH3 **153** E5
GATE NE8 **81** F6 1
Bede Crs *WASHS* NE38 **120** B6
WLSD/HOW NE28 **67** F2
Bede St *CLDN/WHIT/ROK* SR6 **127** D2
PLEE/EAS SR8 **201** E2
Bedesway *JRW* NE32 **86** C2
Bede Ter *BOL* NE36 **107** D3 1
CLSW/PEL DH2 **153** D5
JRW NE32 **86** B3 2
Bede Wk *HEBB* NE31 **85** E3
Bede Wy *DHAM* DH1 **180** A6 1
PLEE/EAS SR8 **208** C2
Bedford Av *CLS/BIR/GTL* DH3 **136** C5
SSH NE33 **71** E5
WLSD/HOW NE28 **66** C3
Bedford Pl *SUNDSW* SR3 **143** F6 1
WD/WHPE/BLK NE5 **59** E5 1
Bedfordshire Dr *DHAM* DH1 **196** C4
Bedford St *NSHW* NE29 **70** C1 2
NSHW NE29 **71** D1 1
SUND SR1 **4** D1
Bedford Wy *NSHW* NE29 **70** C1
Bedlington Bank *BDLGTN* NE22 **7** F4
Beech Av *CLDN/WHIT/ROK* SR6 **109** F1
CRAM NE23 **22** C3
DIN/WO NE13 **31** D3
GOS/KPK NE3 **46** B6
HLS DH4 **170** C1
WICK/BNPF NE16 **96** B2
Beechburn Wk *ELS/FEN* NE4 **79** F3 1
Beech Cl *DHAM* DH1 **181** D4
GOS/KPK NE3 **47** F3 1
Beech Crs *SEA/MUR* SR7 **176** B4
Beechcroft Av *BDN/LAN/SAC* DH7 **202** B5
GOS/KPK NE3 **62** C3
Beechcroft Cl *DHAM* DH1 **195** F3 1
Beech Dr *DUN/TMV* NE11 **97** D1
Beecher St *BLYTH* NE24 **10** A3
Beechfield Gdns
WLSD/HOW NE28 **66** C3 1
Beechfield Rd *GOS/KPK* NE3 **63** D2
Beech Gv *BDN/LAN/SAC* DH7 **192** A5
HAR/WTLS NE34 **89** E4
LGB/KIL NE12 **49** F6
LWF/SPW/WRK NE9 **119** E3
WBAY NE26 **40** B5
WLSD/HOW NE28 **67** D4
Beech Grove Rd *ELS/FEN* NE4 **79** F4
Beech Pk *BDN/LAN/SAC* DH7 **202** C5
Beech Rd *DHAM* DH1 **194** A1
RDHAMSE DH6 **197** E4
Beech Sq *WASHS* NE38 **139** D2 1
Beech St *ELS/FEN* NE4 **79** D4
GATE NE8 **100** A1
JRW NE32 **85** F1
Beech Ter *BLAY* NE21 **94** B1 1
STLY/ANP DH9 **149** D5
Beech Wy *LGB/KIL* NE12 **35** E6 2
Beechways *DHAM* DH1 **193** E3
Beechwood Av
LWF/SPW/WRK NE9 **117** F1
MONK NE25 **39** F6
RYTON NE40 **74** B3
Beechwood Cl *JRW* NE32 **86** C2 1
Beechwood Crs *SWCK/CAS* SR5 **125** E2
Beechwood Gdns *DUN/TMV* NE11 **98** A5
Beechwood Pl *PONT/DH* NE20 **28** A3
Beechwoods *CLSW/PEL* DH2 **153** D3
Beechwood St
ASHBK/HED/RY SR2 **144** A1
Beechwood Ter
ASHBK/HED/RY SR2 **144** A1
HLS DH4 **157** E6
Beeston Av *SWCK/CAS* SR5 **123** E1 4
Beetham Crs *WD/WHPE/BLK* NE5 **60** C6
Beethoven St *SSH* NE33 **71** F4 1
Begonia Cl *HEBB* NE31 **85** D5 2
Bek Rd *DHAM* DH1 **180** B6
Beldene Dr *MLFD/PNYW* SR4 **143** D2
Belford Av *SMOOR* NE27 **52** B1
Belford Cl *ASHBK/HED/RY* SR2 **144** C3
WLSD/HOW NE28 **67** E1 8
Belford Gdns *DUN/TMV* NE11 **97** F5 1
Belford Rd *ASHBK/HED/RY* SR2 **145** D3
Belford St *PLEE/EAS* SR8 **201** E6
Belford Ter *BYK/HTN/WLK* NE6 **83** D3
TYNE/NSHE NE30 **54** C5
The Belfry *HLS* DH4 **156** C4
Belgrade Crs *SWCK/CAS* SR5 **105** E6
Belgrade Sq *SWCK/CAS* SR5 **123** E1 5
Belgrave Crs *BLYTH* NE24 **11** E5
Belgrave Pde *ELS/FEN* NE4 **80** A4 1
Belgrave Ter *FELL* NE10 **100** C3 1
SSH NE33 **71** F3
Bellburn Ct *CRAM* NE23 **14** C6 1
Belle Gv West *JES* NE2 **80** A1 2

Bellerby Dr CLSW/PEL DH2 135 D4 1
Belle St STLY/ANP DH9 148 B1
Belle Vue Av GOS/KPK NE3 63 F1
Belle Vue Bank LWF/SPW/WRK NE9 99 D5
Bellevue Crs CRAM NE23 14 A4 1
Belle Vue Crs SSH NE33 88 A2 1
Belle Vue Gv LWF/SPW/WRK NE9 99 E5 3
Belle Vue Pk ASHBK/HED/RY SR2 144 B2
Belle Vue Rd ASHBK/HED/RY SR2 144 B2
Bellfield Av GOS/KPK NE3 46 B6 1
Bellgreen Av GOS/KPK NE3 47 F3
Bell Gv LGB/KIL NE12 35 D6 1
Bell House Rd SWCK/CAS SR5 107 F5
Bellingham Cl WLSD/HOW NE28 67 F2 1
Bellingham Ct GOS/KPK NE3 61 F1 1
Bellingham Dr LGB/KIL NE12 50 B5
Bellister Gv WD/WHPE/BLK NE5 61 E6
Bellister Pk PLEE/EAS SR8 209 D4
Bellister Rd NSHW NE29 53 F6 1
Bell Meadow BDN/LAN/SAC DH7 202 C5
Belloc Av HAR/WTLS NE34 88 A5
Bells Cl BLYTH NE24 9 E4
BW/LEM/TK/HW NE15 77 D3
Bell's Folly DHAM DH1 204 C1
Bellshill Cl WLSD/HOW NE28 52 A6
Bell's Pl BDLGTN NE22 7 F4
Bell St HEBB NE31 84 C2
HLS DH4 140 A6
MLFD/PNYW SR4 125 E6 2
TYNE/NSHE NE30 71 D1
WASHS NE38 139 E2 1
Belmont FELL NE10 101 F5
Belmont Av MONK NE25 39 F6
SEA/MUR SR7 190 A4
Belmont Cl WLSD/HOW NE28 67 F1
Belmont Ri HLH DH5 185 F3
Belmont Rd MLFD/PNYW SR4 143 E1
Belmont St BYK/HTN/WLK NE6 83 E5
Belmount Av GOS/KPK NE3 47 F3
Belper Cl WLSD/HOW NE28 67 E1 9
Belsay WASHS NE38 137 E2
Belsay Av DIN/WO NE13 32 C6 1
HAR/WTLS NE34 89 F1
MONK NE25 41 D6
Belsay Cl WLSD/HOW NE28 67 E1 10
Belsay Ct BLYTH NE24 10 B5 1
Belsay Gdns DUN/TMV NE11 97 F5 2
GOS/KPK NE3 46 B4
MLFD/PNYW SR4 143 E1
Belsay Pl ELS/FEN NE4 79 F2 1
Belsfield Gdns JRW NE32 86 A4
Belsize Pl BYK/HTN/WLK NE6 66 B6
Beltingham WD/WHPE/BLK NE5 60 A5 2
Belvedere NSHW NE29 54 B5
Belvedere Av MONK NE25 40 B6
Belvedere Gdns LGB/KIL NE12 49 F6 1
Belvedere Pkwy GOS/KPK NE3 45 E6 1
Belvedere Rd ASHBK/HED/RY SR2 4 B6
Belverdere Gdns RDHAMSE DH6 206 A1
Bemersyde Dr JES NE2 64 A3
Benbrake Av NSHW NE29 54 A3
Bendigo Av HAR/WTLS NE34 87 E5 1
Benedict Rd CLDN/WHIT/ROK SR6 127 E2
Benevente St SEA/MUR SR7 176 C4 2
Benfield Gv WBAY NE26 26 A1
Benfield Rd BYK/HTN/WLK NE6 65 F4
Benjamin Rd WLSD/HOW NE28 68 C3
Benridge Bank HLS DH4 183 E2
Bensham Av GATE NE8 98 C1
Bensham Ct HAR/WTLS NE34 88 B3 3
Bensham Crs GATE NE8 98 B1
Bensham Rd GATE NE8 81 D6
Benson Rd BYK/HTN/WLK NE6 82 C2
Benson St CLS/BIR/GTL DH3 153 E6
STLY/ANP DH9 148 A1
Bent House La DHAM DH1 195 F6
Bentinck Rd ELS/FEN NE4 79 E4
Benton Bank BYK/HTN/WLK NE6 64 C5
JES NE2 64 C5
Benton Cl LGB/HTN NE7 65 D1 2
Benton Hall Wk LGB/HTN NE7 65 F4 2
Benton La LGB/KIL NE12 49 D5
Benton Lodge Av LGB/HTN NE7 65 E1 1
Benton Park Rd LGB/HTN NE7 64 B1
Benton Rd HAR/WTLS NE34 88 B6
LGB/HTN NE7 65 E1
SMOOR NE27 51 F2
Benton Wy WLSD/HOW NE28 67 D5 2
Bents Park Rd SSH NE33 72 A3
Benwell Dene Ter
BW/LEM/TK/HW NE15 78 B3
Benwell Grange Av
BW/LEM/TK/HW NE15 78 C3 2
Benwell Grange Rd
BW/LEM/TK/HW NE15 78 B3
Benwell Grange Ter
BW/LEM/TK/HW NE15 78 B3
Benwell Gv ELS/FEN NE4 79 D3
Benwell Hall Dr
BW/LEM/TK/HW NE15 78 A2 2
Benwell Hill Gdns
WD/WHPE/BLK NE5 78 B1 1
Benwell Hill Rd
WD/WHPE/BLK NE5 78 A1
Benwell La
BW/LEM/TK/HW NE15 78 A3 1
Benwell Village
BW/LEM/TK/HW NE15 78 A2
Benwell Village Ms
BW/LEM/TK/HW NE15 78 B2 2
Beresford Av HEBB NE31 85 D5
Beresford Gdns BYK/HTN/WLK NE6 82 B3
Beresford Pk ASHBK/HED/RY SR2 4 A5
ASHBK/HED/RY SR2 144 A1 3
Beresford Rd TYNE/NSHE NE30 54 C1
WBAY NE26 26 C3
Bergen Cl NSHW NE29 69 D2
Bergen Sq SWCK/CAS SR5 105 E6 2
Bergen St SWCK/CAS SR5 105 E6
Berkdale Rd LWF/SPW/WRK NE9 117 D2
Berkeley Cl BOLCOL NE35 105 D1
LGB/KIL NE12 36 A6
SUNDSW SR3 159 E1 2
Berkeley Sq GOS/KPK NE3 47 D5 1
Berkely St SSH NE33 71 F4 2
Berkhamstead Ct FELL NE10 102 B3 1
Berkley Av BLAY NE21 77 D6
Berkley Cl WLSD/HOW NE28 67 F1
Berkley Rd NSHW NE29 53 F6 2
Berkley St BW/LEM/TK/HW NE15 58 B6 1
Berkley Wy HEBB NE31 68 B6
Berkshire Cl DHAM DH1 196 B3 1
WD/WHPE/BLK NE5 60 B4
Berkshire Rd PLEE/EAS SR8 200 B6
Bermondsey St JES NE2 3 H2
Bernard St BYK/HTN/WLK NE6 83 F4
HLS DH4 170 C2
Berrington Dr WD/WHPE/BLK NE5 61 D3
Berrishill Gv MONK NE25 39 E4
Berry Cl BYK/HTN/WLK NE6 83 F3
WLSD/HOW NE28 67 E1 11
Berryfield Cl SUNDSW SR3 160 C3
Berry Hl RYTON NE40 92 A1
Berryhill Cl BLAY NE21 94 C1
Bertram Crs BW/LEM/TK/HW NE15 78 B2
Bertram St SSH NE33 71 E6
Berwick WASHS NE38 137 E2
Berwick Av SWCK/CAS SR5 105 E6
Berwick Cha PLEE/EAS SR8 208 A5
Berwick Cl
BW/LEM/TK/HW NE15 75 F1 1
Berwick Ct PONT/DH NE20 28 B3 1
Berwick Dr WLSD/HOW NE28 67 F1
Berwick Hill Rd PONT/DH NE20 28 B3
Berwick Sq SWCK/CAS SR5 123 E1 6
Berwick Ter NSHW NE29 69 F2
Besford Gv SUND SR1 5 F3
Betjeman Cl STLY/ANP DH9 148 C2
Betts Av BW/LEM/TK/HW NE15 78 A3
Beumaris HLS DH4 155 F5
Bevan Av ASHBK/HED/RY SR2 162 A2
Bevan Gdns FELL NE10 101 F2 1
Bevan Gv DHAM DH1 196 A3
Bevan Sq SEA/MUR SR7 174 B6
Beverley Cl GOS/KPK NE3 47 D2 1
Beverley Crs LWF/SPW/WRK NE9 99 F4 1
Beverley Dr BLAY NE21 93 E2
WICK/BNPF NE16 96 B1
Beverley Gdns CLS/BIR/GTL DH3 153 F6
TYNE/NSHE NE30 55 E1
Beverley Pk MONK NE25 40 A6
Beverley Pl WLSD/HOW NE28 68 B4
Beverley Rd ASHBK/HED/RY SR2 145 E4
LWF/SPW/WRK NE9 99 F4
MONK NE25 40 B6
Beverley Ter BYK/HTN/WLK NE6 83 F3 1
TYNE/NSHE NE30 55 E1
Beverley Wy PLEE/EAS SR8 208 B1
Bevin Sq RDHAMSE DH6 188 A5
Beweshill Crs BLAY NE21 93 F1
Beweshill La BLAY NE21 75 F5 1
Bewick Cl CLSW/PEL DH2 165 F2
Bewick Crs BW/LEM/TK/HW NE15 76 C1
Bewicke Rd WLSD/HOW NE28 68 C5
Bewicke St WLSD/HOW NE28 69 D5
Bewick Pk WLSD/HOW NE28 52 B6
Bewick Rd GATE NE8 99 D1
Bewick St CNUT NE1 2 B5 1
SSH NE33 71 E6
Bewley Gdns WLSD/HOW NE28 67 F1 8
Bewley Gv PLEE/EAS SR8 207 F5
Bexhill Rd SWCK/CAS SR5 123 E1
Bexhill Sq BLYTH NE24 17 D1 4
SWCK/CAS SR5 123 E1
Bexley Av BW/LEM/TK/HW NE15 77 F2
Bexley Pl WICK/BNPF NE16 95 F5
Bexley St MLFD/PNYW SR4 125 E6
Bickington Ct HLS DH4 157 E5 1
Biddick Hall Dr HAR/WTLS NE34 88 A4
Biddick La WASHS NE38 138 C3
Biddick Vw WASHS NE38 139 D3
Biddick Vls WASHS NE38 139 D3
Biddlestone Crs NSHW NE29 69 F1 1
Biddlestone Rd BYK/HTN/WLK NE6 65 E5
Bideford Gdns HAR/WTLS NE34 72 C5 1
JRW NE32 86 C3
LWF/SPW/WRK NE9 117 E1
WBAY NE26 40 B4
Bideford Gv WICK/BNPF NE16 95 F5
Bideford Rd GOS/KPK NE3 62 A2
Bideford St ASHBK/HED/RY SR2 145 E4
Bigbury Cl HLS DH4 157 E4 1
Bigges Gdns WLSD/HOW NE28 66 B2
Bilbrough Gdns ELS/FEN NE4 78 C4
Billy Mill Av NSHW NE29 54 A6
Billy Mill La NSHW NE29 53 F5
Bilsdale CLDN/WHIT/ROK SR6 109 E3
Bilsdale Pl LGB/KIL NE12 48 B6 1
Bilsmoor Av LGB/HTN NE7 65 D4
Bilton Hall Rd JRW NE32 86 C2
Binchester St HAR/WTLS NE34 87 F4 1
Bingfield Gdns WD/WHPE/BLK NE5 61 E6
Bingley Cl WLSD/HOW NE28 68 A1
Bingley St SWCK/CAS SR5 123 E1
Bink Moss WASHN NE37 119 F6
Binswood Av WD/WHPE/BLK NE5 61 D5
Bircham Dr BLAY NE21 76 C6
Bircham St STLY/ANP DH9 147 F3
Birch Av CLDN/WHIT/ROK SR6 109 E1
FELL NE10 101 F3
Birch Ct SUNDSW SR3 160 A2
Birch Crs WICK/BNPF NE16 111 E6
The Birches STLY/ANP DH9 131 E6 1
WICK/BNPF NE16 114 B1
Birchfield WICK/BNPF NE16 96 A5 1
Birchfield Gdns
BW/LEM/TK/HW NE15 77 D1
LWF/SPW/WRK NE9 117 F2
Birchfield Rd
ASHBK/HED/RY SR2 144 A2 1
Birchgate Cl BLAY NE21 93 F1 1
Birch Gv WLSD/HOW NE28 67 E1
Birchgrove Av DHAM DH1 196 A3 1
Birchington Av SSH NE33 88 B1
Birch Rd BLAY NE21 76 C6
Birch St JRW NE32 85 F1
Birch Ter BYK/HTN/WLK NE6 83 F3
Birchvale Av WD/WHPE/BLK NE5 60 C4
Birchwood Av DIN/WO NE13 33 D5
LGB/HTN NE7 65 E3
WICK/BNPF NE16 95 F5
Birchwood Cl CRAM NE23 36 A1
STLY/ANP DH9 133 D6
Birdhill Pl HAR/WTLS NE34 88 B3
Birds Nest Rd BYK/HTN/WLK NE6 83 D4
Bird St TYNE/NSHE NE30 55 E6 1
Birkdale MONK NE25 39 F5
SSH NE33 72 A5
Birkdale Av CLDN/WHIT/ROK SR6 109 D3
Birkdale Cl LGB/HTN NE7 65 E2 1
WLSD/HOW NE28 67 D2 1
Birkdale Dr HLS DH4 156 C4
Birkdale Gdns DHAM DH1 196 C3
Birkheads La DUN/TMV NE11 115 D6
Birkland La WICK/BNPF NE16 114 C4
Birling Pl WD/WHPE/BLK NE5 61 F4
Birnam Gv JRW NE32 87 D6 1
Birnie Cl ELS/FEN NE4 79 D4
Birrell Sq SWCK/CAS SR5 105 E6 3
Birrell St SWCK/CAS SR5 105 E6
Birtley Av TYNE/NSHE NE30 55 F4 3
Birtley Cl GOS/KPK NE3 62 C2
Birtley La CLS/BIR/GTL DH3 136 B2 1
Birtwistle Av HEBB NE31 84 C5 1
Biscop Ter JRW NE32 86 A3
Bishop Crs JRW NE32 69 E6
Bishopdale HLS DH4 139 D6 2
WLSD/HOW NE28 66 B1
Bishopdale Av BLYTH NE24 9 F6
Bishop Morton Gv SUND SR1 5 F4 1
Bishop Ramsay Ct
HAR/WTLS NE34 89 F2 1
Bishop Rock Cl LGB/KIL NE12 48 C6
Bishop Rock Rd LGB/KIL NE12 48 C6 1
Bishop's Av ELS/FEN NE4 79 F3 2
Bishops Cl WLSD/HOW NE28 68 A4 1
Bishops Dr RYTON NE40 74 C5
Bishops Meadow BDLGTN NE22 7 D3 1
Bishop's Rd ELS/FEN NE4 78 C4
Bishops Wy DHAM DH1 180 A5
SUNDSW SR3 160 B3
Bisley Dr HAR/WTLS NE34 88 C1
Bittern Cl WLSD/HOW NE28 52 C6
Black Boy Rd HLS DH4 169 D3
Blackburn Gn FELL NE10 100 B3 1
Blackdown Cl LGB/KIL NE12 48 C6 2
PLEE/EAS SR8 208 A3
Black Dr CLS/BIR/GTL DH3 154 C3
CLS/BIR/GTL DH3 155 E2
Blackett St CNUT NE1 2 C3
HEBB NE31 68 B6
STLY/ANP DH9 146 A4
Blackfell Rd WASHN NE37 119 E5
Blackfriars Wy LGB/KIL NE12 48 C5
Blackheath Cl WASHN NE37 120 B2 1
Blackheath Ct WD/WHPE/BLK NE5 61 D1
Blackhill Av WLSD/HOW NE28 52 A5
Blackhill Crs LWF/SPW/WRK NE9 100 C6
Blackhills Rd PLEE/EAS SR8 201 F6
Blackhouse La RYTON NE40 74 A3
Black La BLAY NE21 75 F6
LWF/SPW/WRK NE9 118 A3
Black Rd ASHBK/HED/RY SR2 162 B1
BDN/LAN/SAC DH7 204 A2

HEBB NE31 85 E1
Blackrow La *BW/LEM/TK/HW* NE15 56 C2
Blackstone Ct *BLAY* NE21 75 F6
Blackthorn Dr *WLSD/HOW* NE28 67 E1
Blackthorn Pl *ELS/FEN* NE4 80 A5 2
Blackthorn Wy *HLS* DH4 156 C6
Blackwell Av *BYK/HTN/WLK* NE6 83 F2
Blackwood Rd *SWCK/CAS* SR5 105 F6 3
Bladen St *JRW* NE32 85 F1
Blagdon Av *HAR/WTLS* NE34 72 A6
Blagdon Ct *BDLGTN* NE22 8 B2
Blagdon Crs *CRAM* NE23 13 D6
Blagdon Dr *BLYTH* NE24 16 B4
Blaidwood Dr *DHAM* DH1 204 C3
Blair Cl *RDHAMSE* DH6 197 E5 1
Blair Ct *BDN/LAN/SAC* DH7 204 A3
Blake Av *WICK/BNPF* NE16 96 A3
Blakelaw Rd *WD/WHPE/BLK* NE5 61 D4 3
Blakemoor Pl
WD/WHPE/BLK NE5 61 E5 1
Blakes Cl *STLY/ANP* DH9 148 C2
Blanche Gv *PLEE/EAS* SR8 208 C3
Blanchland *WASHS* NE38 139 D5
Blanchland Av
BW/LEM/TK/HW NE15 76 A1
DHAM DH1 181 D6
DIN/WO NE13 33 D4
Blanchland Cl *WLSD/HOW* NE28 67 F2 2
Blanchland Dr *MONK* NE25 25 E6
SWCK/CAS SR5 126 B1
Blanchland Ter *TYNE/NSHE* NE30 55 D5
Blandford Pl *SEA/MUR* SR7 176 C3
Blandford Rd *NSHW* NE29 53 F4
Blandford Sq *CNUT* NE1 2 A5
Blandford St *CNUT* NE1 2 A6
Blaxton Pl *WICK/BNPF* NE16 95 E5
Blaydon Bank *BLAY* NE21 76 A6
Blaydon Hwy *BLAY* NE21 76 B5
Blaykeston Cl *SEA/MUR* SR7 175 D1
Bleachfeld *FELL* NE10 101 E4 1
Bleasdale Crs *HLS* DH4 157 D1
Blencathra *WASHN* NE37 120 B5
Blenheim *LGB/KIL* NE12 35 F6 4
Blenheim Dr *BDLGTN* NE22 8 B1
Blenheim Pl *DUN/TMV* NE11 97 D1
Blenheim St *CNUT* NE1 2 A5
Blenkinsop Gv *JRW* NE32 85 F5
Blenkinsopp Ct *PLEE/EAS* SR8 208 A6 1
Blenkinsopp St *WLSD/HOW* NE28 66 C4
Blind La *CLS/BIR/GTL* DH3 153 F2
HLS DH4 157 D5
SUNDSW SR3 143 F6
Blindy La *HLH* DH5 186 B3
Bloomfield Dr *HLH* DH5 184 C1
Bloomsbury Ct *GOS/KPK* NE3 63 D2 1
Blossom Gv *HLS* DH4 157 D4
Blount St *BYK/HTN/WLK* NE6 82 C2 1
Blucher Rd *LGB/KIL* NE12 49 E3
NSHW NE29 70 B3
Bluebell Dene *WD/WHPE/BLK* NE5 60 C1
Bluebell Wy *HAR/WTLS* NE34 88 A3
Blueburn Dr *LGB/KIL* NE12 36 B6
Bluehouse Bank *STLY/ANP* DH9 150 B5
Blue House Ct *WASHN* NE37 120 A4
Blue House La
CLDN/WHIT/ROK SR6 107 E3
WASHN NE37 120 A4
Blue House Rd *HEBB* NE31 84 C5
Blue Quarries Rd
LWF/SPW/WRK NE9 100 A4
Blyth Cl *CRAM* NE23 34 B2
Blyth Ct *BW/LEM/TK/HW* NE15 76 B1 1
HAR/WTLS NE34 88 B3
Blyth Rd *WBAY* NE26 27 D5
Blyth Sq *SWCK/CAS* SR5 123 F1
Blyth St *MONK* NE25 24 B4
SWCK/CAS SR5 123 F1
Blyton Av *ASHBK/HED/RY* SR2 162 A1
HAR/WTLS NE34 87 E3
Bodlewell La *SUND* SR1 5 F1 1
Bodley Cl *GOS/KPK* NE3 61 F1 2
Bodmin Cl *WLSD/HOW* NE28 68 A1
Bodmin Rd *NSHW* NE29 53 E4 1
Bodmin Sq *SWCK/CAS* SR5 123 F1 4
Bodmin Wy *GOS/KPK* NE3 46 B6 2
Bognor St *SWCK/CAS* SR5 105 E6
Bohemia Ter *BLYTH* NE24 11 D6
Boker La *BOL* NE36 106 A2
Bolam Av *BLYTH* NE24 10 C5
TYNE/NSHE NE30 54 C3
Bolam Gdns *WLSD/HOW* NE28 69 D3
Bolam Gv *TYNE/NSHE* NE30 54 C3
Bolam Rd *LGB/KIL* NE12 49 F1 1
Bolam St *BYK/HTN/WLK* NE6 82 B3
GATE NE8 98 A2
Bolam Wy *BYK/HTN/WLK* NE6 82 B3
MONK NE25 24 B5
Bolbec Rd *ELS/FEN* NE4 79 D1
Bolburn *FELL* NE10 101 F3
Boldon Cl *WLSD/HOW* NE28 67 F1
Boldon Dr *BOL* NE36 105 E3
Boldon Gdns *LWF/SPW/WRK* NE9 118 B1
Boldon La *CLDN/WHIT/ROK* SR6 107 D1
HAR/WTLS NE34 88 B4
Boldon North Br *BOL* NE36 106 B2
Bolingbroke Rd *NSHW* NE29 53 F6
Bolingbroke St *BYK/HTN/WLK* NE6 81 F2
SSH NE33 71 F4 3
Bollihope Dr *SUNDSW* SR3 144 A4
Bolton Cl *DHAM* DH1 180 B5
Bonchester Cl *BDLGTN* NE22 7 E2
Bond Cl *SWCK/CAS* SR5 126 B3
Bondene Av *FELL* NE10 101 D2 1
Bondene Av West *FELL* NE10 100 C2
Bondene Wy *CRAM* NE23 14 A4
Bondfield Gdns *FELL* NE10 101 F2
Bondicarr Pl *WD/WHPE/BLK* NE5 61 F5 1
Bondicar Ter *BLYTH* NE24 10 C5
Bonemill La *CLS/BIR/GTL* DH3 137 D6
WASHS NE38 138 B6
Bonington Wy
WD/WHPE/BLK NE5 61 D4 4
Bonner's Fld *SWCK/CAS* SR5 126 C4
Bonnivard Gdns *CRAM* NE23 36 C1
Booth St *FELL* NE10 100 C2
MLFD/PNYW SR4 125 F5
Bootle St *SWCK/CAS* SR5 123 F1 5
Bordeaux Cl *SUNDSW* SR3 160 A2 2
Border Rd *WLSD/HOW* NE28 67 D5 3
Boreham Cl *WLSD/HOW* NE28 67 F1 6
Borodin Av *SWCK/CAS* SR5 105 E6
Borough Rd *HAR/WTLS* NE34 89 E3
JRW NE32 86 A2
NSHW NE29 70 C1
SUND SR1 4 D3
SUND SR1 5 F3 1
Borrowdale *WICK/BNPF* NE16 96 C3
Borrowdale Av *BLYTH* NE24 9 F4
BYK/HTN/WLK NE6 83 E1
CLDN/WHIT/ROK SR6 108 B5
Borrowdale Cl *BOL* NE36 106 B2 1
DHAM DH1 197 D2 1
Borrowdale Crs *BLAY* NE21 94 A2
HLS DH4 139 F6
Borrowdale Dr *DHAM* DH1 196 B2 1
Borrowdale Gdns
LWF/SPW/WRK NE9 118 A1
Borrowdale St *HLH* DH5 185 F2
Boscombe Dr *WLSD/HOW* NE28 67 E2 2
Boston Av *LGB/HTN* NE7 65 D1
WASHS NE38 120 B6
Boston Cl *WLSD/HOW* NE28 67 F1
Boston Crs *BOL* NE36 105 D6
SWCK/CAS SR5 105 D6
Boston St *SWCK/CAS* SR5 105 D6
Boswell Av *HAR/WTLS* NE34 88 A5
Bosworth *LGB/KIL* NE12 35 F6
Bosworth Gdns *BYK/HTN/WLK* NE6 65 E4
Bothal St *BYK/HTN/WLK* NE6 82 C2
Bottle Bank *GATE* NE8 3 F6
Bottlehouse St *BYK/HTN/WLK* NE6 82 B4
Bottle Works Rd *SEA/MUR* SR7 177 D3
Boulby Cl *SUNDSW* SR3 161 E1 1
Boulmer Av *CRAM* NE23 14 A4
Boulmer Cl *GOS/KPK* NE3 46 B4 2
Boulmer Ct *CLSW/PEL* DH2 153 E6
Boulmer Gdns *DIN/WO* NE13 33 D4
Boulsworth Rd *NSHW* NE29 54 A3
Boundary Gdns *LGB/HTN* NE7 64 C3
Boundary St *SWCK/CAS* SR5 126 B2 1
Bourne Av *ELS/FEN* NE4 79 D1
Bourne Ct *STLY/ANP* DH9 148 C1
Bournemouth Dr *SEA/MUR* SR7 175 E4 1
Bournemouth Gdns *WBAY* NE26 40 B4
WD/WHPE/BLK NE5 60 B3 2
Bournemouth Rd *NSHW* NE29 69 E1 1
Bourn Lea *HLS* DH4 156 C3
Bourtree Cl *WLSD/HOW* NE28 67 E2
Bowbank Cl *SUNDSW* SR3 144 A3 2
Bowburn Av *SWCK/CAS* SR5 124 B2 1
Bowburn Cl *FELL* NE10 102 B3
Bower St *CLDN/WHIT/ROK* SR6 108 C6 2
The Bower *JRW* NE32 104 A2 1
Bowes Av *SEA/MUR* SR7 175 D4
Bowes Cl *WICK/BNPF* NE16 114 A2
Bowes Lea *HLS* DH4 156 B4
Bowes Lyon Cl *ROWG* NE39 110 C4 1
Bowes St *BLYTH* NE24 10 C5
GOS/KPK NE3 64 A1 1
Bowfell Av *WD/WHPE/BLK* NE5 61 F3
Bowfell Cl *WD/WHPE/BLK* NE5 61 F3 2
Bowfield Av *GOS/KPK* NE3 47 E3
Bow La *DHAM* DH1 194 B5
Bowlynn Cl *SUNDSW* SR3 160 A2 3
Bowman Dr *CRAM* NE23 35 D2
Bowman St *CLDN/WHIT/ROK* SR6 109 E1
Bowmont Dr *CRAM* NE23 14 C6 2
STLY/ANP DH9 130 B6
Bowness Av *WLSD/HOW* NE28 52 A6
Bowness Cl *BOL* NE36 106 B3 1
PLEE/EAS SR8 209 D1 3
Bowness Pl *LWF/SPW/WRK* NE9 100 A6
Bowness Rd *WD/WHPE/BLK* NE5 60 C5
WICK/BNPF NE16 96 C3 1
Bowness St *SWCK/CAS* SR5 105 F6
Bowsden Ct *GOS/KPK* NE3 64 A1 2
Bowsden Ter *GOS/KPK* NE3 64 A1
Boyd Crs *WLSD/HOW* NE28 67 E4
Boyd Rd *WLSD/HOW* NE28 67 E4
Boyd St *BW/LEM/TK/HW* NE15 58 A6
DHAM DH1 194 C6
JES NE2 3 H2
Boyne Ct *BDN/LAN/SAC* DH7 203 F3 1
BLYTH NE24 11 D4 2
Brabourne St *HAR/WTLS* NE34 88 B2
Bracken Av *WLSD/HOW* NE28 67 E1
Brackenbeds Cl *CLSW/PEL* DH2 152 A1
Bracken Cl *DIN/WO* NE13 30 C4
STLY/ANP DH9 147 F2
Brackendale Rd *DHAM* DH1 196 C3
Brackendene Dr
LWF/SPW/WRK NE9 99 D5 2
Bracken Dr *DUN/TMV* NE11 97 E4
Bracken Field Rd *DHAM* DH1 194 A1
Brackenfield Rd *GOS/KPK* NE3 63 D2
Bracken Hl *PLEE/EAS* SR8 207 E3
Brackenridge *WICK/BNPF* NE16 111 D6
Brackenside *GOS/KPK* NE3 47 E3
Brackenwood Gv
ASHBK/HED/RY SR2 144 B4 1
Brackley *WASHN* NE37 121 D3
Bracknell Cl *SUNDSW* SR3 144 B6
Bracknell Gdns
WD/WHPE/BLK NE5 59 D5
Brack Ter *FELL* NE10 84 A6 2
Bradbury Cl *FELL* NE10 102 B3 2
STLY/ANP DH9 130 B6
Bradbury Ct *MONK* NE25 24 C2
Bradford Av *SWCK/CAS* SR5 105 F6
WLSD/HOW NE28 67 F1
Bradford Crs *DHAM* DH1 195 E3
Bradley Av *HAR/WTLS* NE34 89 F3
HLH DH5 171 D4
Bradley Cl *CLSW/PEL* DH2 134 C4
Bradley Lodge Dr
STLY/ANP DH9 129 D6 1
Bradley Ter *HLH* DH5 186 A3
Bradman Dr *CLS/BIR/GTL* DH3 154 A6
Bradman Sq *SWCK/CAS* SR5 105 F6 4
Bradman St *SWCK/CAS* SR5 105 F6
Bradshaw St *SWCK/CAS* SR5 123 F1
Bradwell Rd *GOS/KPK* NE3 62 A1
Bradwell Wy *HLS* DH4 157 D4
Brady Sq *WASHS* NE38 139 E2 2
Brady St *MLFD/PNYW* SR4 125 E5
Braebridge Pl *GOS/KPK* NE3 62 B3 2
Braemar Ct *FELL* NE10 84 A6 3
Braemar Dr *HAR/WTLS* NE34 72 C6
Braemar Gdns *SUNDSW* SR3 144 A3 3
SUNDSW SR3 159 E2 1
Braeside *ASHBK/HED/RY* SR2 144 A2
DUN/TMV NE11 97 F4 1
Brahman Av *NSHW* NE29 69 F2
Braintree Gdns *GOS/KPK* NE3 62 B2
Braithwaite Rd *PLEE/EAS* SR8 209 E2
Bramble Dykes
BW/LEM/TK/HW NE15 78 A3 2
Bramley Cl *MLFD/PNYW* SR4 141 F4
Bramley Ct *LGB/HTN* NE7 66 A3
Brampton Av *BYK/HTN/WLK* NE6 83 E4
Brampton Ct *PLEE/EAS* SR8 200 A3 1
Brampton Gdns
BW/LEM/TK/HW NE15 57 F4
LWF/SPW/WRK NE9 117 F1
WLSD/HOW NE28 68 C2
Brampton Pl *NSHW* NE29 69 F1
Brampton Rd *HAR/WTLS* NE34 87 F3
Bramwell Rd *ASHBK/HED/RY* SR2 5 F5
Brancepeth Av *ELS/FEN* NE4 79 D4
HLS DH4 169 F1 1
Brancepeth Chare *PLEE/EAS* SR8 208 A5
Brancepeth Cl
BW/LEM/TK/HW NE15 59 E6
DHAM DH1 181 D6
Brancepeth Rd *HEBB* NE31 68 B6
WASHS NE38 137 F2
Brancepeth Ter *JRW* NE32 86 A5 1
Brancepeth Vw
BDN/LAN/SAC DH7 202 B5
Branch St *BLAY* NE21 94 A1 2
Brancpeth Cl *BDN/LAN/SAC* DH7 192 B5
Brand Av *ELS/FEN* NE4 79 D1
Brandling Ct *HAR/WTLS* NE34 89 E4
Brandling La *FELL* NE10 100 C1 1
Brandling Pk *JES* NE2 63 F6
Brandling Pl *FELL* NE10 100 C1 2
Brandling St *CLDN/WHIT/ROK* SR6 127 D2
Brandling St South
CLDN/WHIT/ROK SR6 127 D3 1
Brandlings Wy *PLEE/EAS* SR8 208 C1
Brandon Av *SMOOR* NE27 52 A1
Brandon Cl *BLAY* NE21 93 F2 2
BLYTH NE24 10 A4
HLS DH4 170 C3 1
Brandon Gdns
LWF/SPW/WRK NE9 118 C1 1
Brandon Gv *JES* NE2 81 F1 2
Brandon La *BDN/LAN/SAC* DH7 203 F3
Brandon Rd *GOS/KPK* NE3 46 B6 3
NSHW NE29 53 F6
Brandy La *WASHN* NE37 120 A5
Brannen St *NSHW* NE29 70 C1 3
Bransdale *HLS* DH4 139 D6
Bransdale Av
CLDN/WHIT/ROK SR6 109 D3

Branston St SWCK/CAS SR5 126 A2
Branton Av HEBB NE31 84 C5
Brantwood CLSW/PEL DH2 152 B5
Brantwood Av MONK NE25 39 F6
Branxton Crs BYK/HTN/WLK NE6 83 E3
Brass Thill DHAM DH1 194 A5 2
Bray Cl WLSD/HOW NE28 67 F1
Braydon Dr NSHW NE29 69 F3
Brayside JRW NE32 104 C1
Breamish Dr WASHS NE38 137 E6
Breamish St CNUT NE1 3 H3
JRW NE32 85 F3
Brearley Wy FELL NE10 100 B2 1
Breckenbeds Rd
LWF/SPW/WRK NE9 99 D6
Brecken Wy BDN/LAN/SAC DH7 203 E4 2
Brecon Cl PLEE/EAS SR8 208 A3
WD/WHPE/BLK NE5 61 D2 1
Brecon Pl CLSW/PEL DH2 135 E6
Brecon Rd DHAM DH1 181 D5
Bredon Cl WASHS NE38 138 A3
Brendale Av WD/WHPE/BLK NE5 59 F3
Brendon Pl PLEE/EAS SR8 208 A1
Brenkley Av SMOOR NE27 52 A2
Brenkley Cl DIN/WO NE13 31 D3 1
Brenkley Ct DIN/WO NE13 33 D2 1
Brenkley Wy DIN/WO NE13 33 D1
Brenlynn Cl SUNDSW SR3 160 A2
Brennan Cl
BW/LEM/TK/HW NE15 78 A2 3
Brentford Av SWCK/CAS SR5 123 F1
Brentford Sq SWCK/CAS SR5 123 F1 6
Brentwood Av JES NE2 63 F4
Brentwood Cl MONK NE25 38 A1
Brentwood Ct STLY/ANP DH9 149 E2
Brentwood Gdns SUNDSW SR3 144 A3 4
WICK/BNPF NE16 96 A5
Brentwood Gv WLSD/HOW NE28 67 F5 1
Brentwood Rd HLS DH4 156 C3
Brettanby Rd FELL NE10 100 B3
Brett Cl LGB/HTN NE7 65 F3
Bretton Gdns LGB/HTN NE7 65 E4
Brewer's La NSHW NE29 69 E3
Brewer Ter ASHBK/HED/RY SR2 162 C2
Brewery Bank WICK/BNPF NE16 95 F1 1
Brewery La FELL NE10 100 C1
PONT/DH NE20 28 A4
SSH NE33 71 D4 1
WICK/BNPF NE16 95 F1 2
Brewhouse Bank
TYNE/NSHE NE30 55 E6 2
Briar Av BDN/LAN/SAC DH7 202 C5
HLS DH4 170 C2
WBAY NE26 40 B3
Briar Cl CLSW/PEL DH2 179 E1
HLS DH4 156 B4
WLSD/HOW NE28 67 E1 12
Briardale BDLGTN NE22 7 D3
Briardale Rd BLYTH NE24 9 F5
Briardene DHAM DH1 194 A5
WICK/BNPF NE16 111 D6
Briardene Cl SUNDSW SR3 159 E2
Briardene Crs GOS/KPK NE3 62 C3
Briardene Dr FELL NE10 102 C3
Briar Edge LGB/KIL NE12 49 F4
Briar Fld WASHS NE38 138 C5
Briarfield Rd GOS/KPK NE3 63 D2
Briarhill CLSW/PEL DH2 152 C3
Briar La BW/LEM/TK/HW NE15 58 A5 1
Briar Lea BDN/LAN/SAC DH7 178 A3
HLS DH4 156 B4
Briar Pl BW/LEM/TK/HW NE15 77 F3
Briar Rd DHAM DH1 196 C2
ROWG NE39 110 C2 1
Briarside WD/WHPE/BLK NE5 60 C3
The Briars SWCK/CAS SR5 124 A3
Briarsyde Cl WICK/BNPF NE16 95 D5
Briarwood CRAM NE23 35 D2 1
Briarwood Av CLSW/PEL DH2 152 A5
GOS/KPK NE3 48 A6
Briarwood Crs BYK/HTN/WLK NE6 66 B5
Briarwood Rd BLYTH NE24 11 E6
The Briary BW/LEM/TK/HW NE15 57 E4 1
Brick Garth HLH DH5 186 A3
Brick Rw ASHBK/HED/RY SR2 162 A1
Bridge Cottages CRAM NE23 35 E2 1
Bridge Crs SUND SR1 4 C1
Bridgemere Dr DHAM DH1 179 F6
Bridge Pk GOS/KPK NE3 47 E4
Bridge Rd South NSHW NE29 70 A2
Bridge St BLAY NE21 76 A4
BLYTH NE24 11 E5
DHAM DH1 194 A4 1
DIN/WO NE13 33 D2
GATE NE8 3 E6
STLY/ANP DH9 147 F4
SUND SR1 4 C2
Bridgewater Cl
BW/LEM/TK/HW NE15 76 B1 2
WLSD/HOW NE28 67 E2 3
Bridgewater Rd WASHN NE37 121 D5
Bridle Pth BOL NE36 106 B3
SUNDSW SR3 142 B6
The Bridle SMOOR NE27 53 D2
Bridlington WLSD/HOW NE28 67 F1 2
Bridlington Av
LWF/SPW/WRK NE9 117 E1
Bridport Rd NSHW NE29 53 F3
Brier Dene Crs WBAY NE26 40 A2
Brierdene Rd WBAY NE26 40 B1
Brierfield Gv MLFD/PNYW SR4 142 C2
Brierley Rd BLYTH NE24 10 A5
Briermede Av LWF/SPW/WRK NE9 99 E6
Brieryside WD/WHPE/BLK NE5 61 F4 1
Briery Vale Rd ASHBK/HED/RY SR2 4 B6
Brigham Av GOS/KPK NE3 62 A3
Brigham Pl SSH NE33 71 E3 2
Brightlea CLS/BIR/GTL DH3 137 D1
Brightman Rd NSHW NE29 54 B6
Brighton Cl WLSD/HOW NE28 68 A1
Brighton Gv ELS/FEN NE4 79 F2
NSHW NE29 54 B6
WBAY NE26 40 B3
Brighton Rd GATE NE8 98 C2
Bright St CLDN/WHIT/ROK SR6 127 D3
SSH NE33 71 F3
Brignall Cl CLS/BIR/GTL DH3 168 A4
Brignall Gdns
BW/LEM/TK/HW NE15 77 F1
Brignall Ri SUNDSW SR3 144 A4 1
Brindley Rd PLEE/EAS SR8 207 E2
WASHN NE37 121 D6
Brinkburn CLSW/PEL DH2 152 C5
WASHS NE38 139 D4
Brinkburn Av BLYTH NE24 11 E6
CRAM NE23 22 B2 1
GATE NE8 99 D2
GOS/KPK NE3 47 D6
WICK/BNPF NE16 95 F2 1
Brinkburn Cl BLAY NE21 93 F2
BYK/HTN/WLK NE6 82 A3
Brinkburn Crs HLS DH4 157 E6
Brinkburn St BYK/HTN/WLK NE6 82 A2 3
HAR/WTLS NE34 88 A2
MLFD/PNYW SR4 143 F1
WLSD/HOW NE28 69 E5
Brinkburn St South
BYK/HTN/WLK NE6 82 B3
Brisbane Av HAR/WTLS NE34 87 E5
Brisbane St SWCK/CAS SR5 123 F1
Bristlecone SUNDSW SR3 160 A3 1
Bristol Av WASHN NE37 120 A4
Bristol Dr WLSD/HOW NE28 67 F1
Bristol St MONK NE25 24 B3
Bristol Ter ELS/FEN NE4 79 F4 1
Britannia Pl ELS/FEN NE4 79 F3
Britannia Rd SUNDSW SR3 160 C1 2
Brixham Av LWF/SPW/WRK NE9 117 E1
Brixham Cl SEA/MUR SR7 175 F4 1
Brixham Crs JRW NE32 86 C3
Brixham Gdns SUNDSW SR3 144 A4
Broad Chare CNUT NE1 3 F4
Broadfield Pl HAR/WTLS NE34 88 C3 1
Broad Garth CNUT NE1 3 F5
Broad Landing SSH NE33 71 D3
Broadlands CLDN/WHIT/ROK SR6 107 F3
Broadlea FELL NE10 102 A2 2
Broadmayne Av MLFD/PNYW SR4 142 C2
Broadmayne Gdns
MLFD/PNYW SR4 142 C2 1
Broad Mdw ASHBK/HED/RY SR2 144 A1
Broadmeadows SUNDSW SR3 159 D2
WASHS NE38 139 D4
Broadmead Wy
BW/LEM/TK/HW NE15 77 F3
Broadoak FELL NE10 102 A2 3
FELL NE10 102 A1 1
Broadpark FELL NE10 102 A2
Broadsheath Ter SWCK/CAS SR5 125 E3
Broadside FELL NE10 102 A2
Broadstairs Ct MLFD/PNYW SR4 142 C2
Broadstone Gv
WD/WHPE/BLK NE5 59 E5
Broadwater FELL NE10 102 A1
Broadway BLYTH NE24 11 D6
BW/LEM/TK/HW NE15 59 F6
CLS/BIR/GTL DH3 153 F3
LWF/SPW/WRK NE9 100 A3
TYNE/NSHE NE30 55 E4
WICK/BNPF NE16 95 E5
Broadway Cl MONK NE25 55 D1
Broadway Crs BLYTH NE24 11 D6 1
Broadway East GOS/KPK NE3 47 E5
The Broadway HLS DH4 171 D2
MLFD/PNYW SR4 142 B2
TYNE/NSHE NE30 55 D1
Broadway Vls
BW/LEM/TK/HW NE15 78 A3
Broadway West GOS/KPK NE3 47 D5
Broadwell Ct GOS/KPK NE3 64 B2
Broadwood Rd
BW/LEM/TK/HW NE15 77 E1
Brockenhurst Dr
MLFD/PNYW SR4 141 F4
Brock Farm Ct TYNE/NSHE NE30 54 C6
Brockhampton Cl BOLCOL NE35 87 D6 2
Brock La BDLGTN NE22 9 E1
Brockley Av HAR/WTLS NE34 87 F4
Brockley St SWCK/CAS SR5 123 F1
Brockwell Cl BLAY NE21 93 F1 2
Brockwell Ct BLYTH NE24 16 B2 1
Brockwell Rd WASHS NE38 137 E1
Brodie Cl HAR/WTLS NE34 88 B5 1
Brodrick Cl GOS/KPK NE3 61 F1
Brodrick St SSH NE33 71 F3 1
Brokenheugh
WD/WHPE/BLK NE5 60 B5 1
Bromford Rd GOS/KPK NE3 61 F1
Bromley Av MONK NE25 54 A1
Bromley Gdns BLYTH NE24 17 D1
WLSD/HOW NE28 67 F1 3
Bromsgrove Cl WLSD/HOW NE28 68 A1 1
Bronte Pl STLY/ANP DH9 149 D4
Bronte St GATE NE8 100 A1 3
Brookbank Cl SUNDSW SR3 160 B3
Brook Ct BDLGTN NE22 7 F4 2
Brookdale DHAM DH1 197 D3
Brooke Av BOLCOL NE35 106 A2
WICK/BNPF NE16 95 F2
Brooke St SWCK/CAS SR5 126 B4
Brookfield Crs WD/WHPE/BLK NE5 59 E5
Brookland Dr LGB/KIL NE12 50 A1
Brookland Rd MLFD/PNYW SR4 125 E6 3
Brooklands Wy BOLCOL NE35 104 C2
Brookside BDN/LAN/SAC DH7 164 B6
BDN/LAN/SAC DH7 178 A4
CRAM NE23 34 C2
Brookside Av BLYTH NE24 10 A5
DIN/WO NE13 32 C5
Brookside Crs WD/WHPE/BLK NE5 61 F5
Brookside Gdns
ASHBK/HED/RY SR2 144 B2 2
Brookside Wd WASHS NE38 138 C5
Brooksmead WLSD/HOW NE28 66 B2
Brook St BYK/HTN/WLK NE6 82 C3
WBAY NE26 41 D5
Brookvale Av GOS/KPK NE3 62 B2
Broom Cl STLY/ANP DH9 149 D1
WICK/BNPF NE16 96 B4
Broom Ct LWF/SPW/WRK NE9 119 E3
Broome Cl GOS/KPK NE3 46 C6
Broome Rd DHAM DH1 196 C2
Broomfield JRW NE32 104 B1
Broomfield Av BYK/HTN/WLK NE6 66 A5
WLSD/HOW NE28 67 E1
Broomfield Rd GOS/KPK NE3 63 D2
Broom Hall Dr BDN/LAN/SAC DH7 192 A5
Broomhill Gdns
WD/WHPE/BLK NE5 61 F5 2
Broomhill Ter HLH DH5 171 E5
Broom La BDN/LAN/SAC DH7 192 A5
WICK/BNPF NE16 96 A5
Broomlea NSHW NE29 53 D3
Broomlee Rd LGB/KIL NE12 49 F1
Broomley Wk GOS/KPK NE3 46 B5
Broomridge Av
BW/LEM/TK/HW NE15 78 C3
Broomshields Av SWCK/CAS SR5 126 A1
Broomshields Cl SWCK/CAS SR5 126 A1
Broomside La DHAM DH1 196 C2
Broom Ter WICK/BNPF NE16 112 B6 1
Broomy Hill Rd
BW/LEM/TK/HW NE15 57 F4
Brotherlee Rd GOS/KPK NE3 46 B5
Brougham Ct PLEE/EAS SR8 207 F5
Brougham St SUND SR1 4 B3
Brough Gdns WLSD/HOW NE28 68 C2
Brough Park Wy
BYK/HTN/WLK NE6 82 C2
Brough St BYK/HTN/WLK NE6 82 B1
Broughton Rd SSH NE33 71 F4
Browbank BDN/LAN/SAC DH7 178 C2
Browne Rd CLDN/WHIT/ROK SR6 126 C1
Browney La BDN/LAN/SAC DH7 203 F5
Browning Cl HAR/WTLS NE34 88 A6
STLY/ANP DH9 148 C1
Brownlow Cl LGB/HTN NE7 66 A3
Brownlow Rd HAR/WTLS NE34 88 B2
Brownrigg Dr CRAM NE23 22 B3 2
Brownsea Pl LWF/SPW/WRK NE9 99 F3
Browntop Pl HAR/WTLS NE34 88 B3 4
Broxburn Cl WLSD/HOW NE28 68 A1
Broxburn Ct WD/WHPE/BLK NE5 61 E3 2
Broxholm Rd BYK/HTN/WLK NE6 65 D5
Bruce Cl HAR/WTLS NE34 88 B4
WD/WHPE/BLK NE5 60 B4 2
Bruce Gdns WD/WHPE/BLK NE5 78 B1
Bruce Glasier Ter RDHAMSE DH6 206 B3
Bruce Kirkup Rd PLEE/EAS SR8 201 D6
Bruce Pl PLEE/EAS SR8 200 B6
Bruce St BDN/LAN/SAC DH7 164 A4
Brundon Av WBAY NE26 40 B3
Brunel Dr CLDN/WHIT/ROK SR6 127 E3
Brunel St ELS/FEN NE4 80 A5
GATE NE8 98 C2
Brunel Ter ELS/FEN NE4 79 F5 1
Brunel Wk ELS/FEN NE4 79 E5
Brunswick Gv DIN/WO NE13 32 C4 1
Brunswick Rd SMOOR NE27 52 B2
SWCK/CAS SR5 105 F6
Brunswick St SSH NE33 71 E5
Brunton Av GOS/KPK NE3 46 B6
WLSD/HOW NE28 69 D3
Brunton Cl SMOOR NE27 52 B2
Brunton Gv GOS/KPK NE3 46 B6 4

Brunton La *DIN/WO* NE13 .... 45 F2
DIN/WO NE13 .... 46 C2
GOS/KPK NE3 .... 45 E5
GOS/KPK NE3 .... 47 E3
GOS/KPK NE3 .... 61 E1
Brunton Rd *DIN/WO* NE13 .... 45 D5
Brunton St *NSHW* NE29 .... 69 F3
Brunton Ter *MLFD/PNYW* SR4 ...... 125 F6 1
Brunton Wy *CRAM* NE23 .... 14 A4
FELL NE10 .... 84 A6
Brussels Rd *MLFD/PNYW* SR4 .... 124 C5
WLSD/HOW NE28 .... 67 D5
Bryden Ct *HAR/WTLS* NE34 .... 88 C3 2
Bryers St *CLDN/WHIT/ROK* SR6 .... 109 E1
Buckingham *SUNDSW* SR3 .... 143 D6 1
Buckingham Cl
CLDN/WHIT/ROK SR6 .... 109 E1 1
Buckingham Rd *PLEE/EAS* SR8 .... 200 A6
Buckinghamshire Rd *DHAM* DH1 .... 196 B3
Buckingham St *ELS/FEN* NE4 .... 80 A3 1
Buckland Cl *HLS* DH4 .... 157 E6
WASHS NE38 .... 138 C3
Buckthorne Gv *LGB/HTN* NE7 .... 65 E3
Buddle Cl *ELS/FEN* NE4 .... 78 C4
PLEE/EAS SR8 .... 200 C6
Buddle Ct *ELS/FEN* NE4 .... 79 D4
Buddle Rd *ELS/FEN* NE4 .... 78 C4
Buddle St *WLSD/HOW* NE28 .... 67 D6
Buddle Ter *ASHBK/HED/RY* SR2 ...... 5 F6 2
Bude Gdns *LWF/SPW/WRK* NE9 ...... 117 E1
Bude Gv *NSHW* NE29 .... 53 F3
Bude Sq *SEA/MUR* SR7 .... 174 C6
Budle Cl *BLYTH* NE24 .... 10 B5
Budleigh Rd *GOS/KPK* NE3 .... 62 B1
Budworth Av *WBAY* NE26 .... 26 C3
Bullfinch Dr *WICK/BNPF* NE16 .... 95 F4
Bullion La *CLSW/PEL* DH2 .... 153 D5
Bulman's La *NSHW* NE29 .... 54 C4 2
Bulmer Rd *HAR/WTLS* NE34 .... 89 F1
The Bungalows *STLY/ANP* DH9 .... 130 B6
Bunyan Av *HAR/WTLS* NE34 .... 87 F5
Burdale Av *WD/WHPE/BLK* NE5 .... 60 C5
Burdon Av *CRAM* NE23 .... 21 E1
HLH DH5 .... 171 F2
Burdon Cl *CLDN/WHIT/ROK* SR6 ...... 107 D1
Burdon Crs *CLDN/WHIT/ROK* SR6 ...... 107 D1
SEA/MUR SR7 .... 175 E1
Burdon Dr *PLEE/EAS* SR8 .... 207 D1
Burdon Gv *SUNDSW* SR3 .... 161 D1
Burdon La *ASHBK/HED/RY* SR2 .... 162 A2
SUNDSW SR3 .... 160 C4
Burdon Ldg *WICK/BNPF* NE16 .... 114 B2
Burdon Main Rw *NSHW* NE29 .... 70 C2
Burdon Pk *WICK/BNPF* NE16 .... 114 B2
Burdon Pl *PLEE/EAS* SR8 .... 209 D2 1
Burdon Pln *WICK/BNPF* NE16 .... 114 A5
Burdon Rd *ASHBK/HED/RY* SR2 .... 4 D5
CLDN/WHIT/ROK SR6 .... 107 D1
SUNDSW SR3 .... 161 D3
Burdon St *NSHW* NE29 .... 69 F3
Burdon Ter *JES* NE2 .... 63 F6
Burford Ct *LGB/HTN* NE7 .... 64 C2
Burford Gdns *SUNDSW* SR3 .... 144 A4
Burghley Rd *FELL* NE10 .... 100 B4
Burke St *SWCK/CAS* SR5 .... 123 F1 7
Burlawn Cl *ASHBK/HED/RY* SR2 .. 145 E6 1
Burleigh St *SSH* NE33 .... 71 F4 4
Burlington Cl *ASHBK/HED/RY* SR2 .. 5 G5 1
Burlington Ct *WLSD/HOW* NE28 .... 52 A5 1
Burlington Gdns
BYK/HTN/WLK NE6 .... 65 D6 1
Burnaby Dr *RYTON* NE40 .... 74 A4
Burnaby St *MLFD/PNYW* SR4 ...... 143 F1 1
Burn Av *LGB/KIL* NE12 .... 49 F4
Burnbank Av *MONK* NE25 .... 39 D5
Burnbridge *DIN/WO* NE13 .... 33 D2
Burn Crook *HLH* DH5 .... 170 C4
Burnden Gv *HLS* DH4 .... 156 B3
Burnet Cl *WLSD/HOW* NE28 .... 67 E1
Burney Vls *GATE* NE8 .... 99 F1
Burnfoot Wy *GOS/KPK* NE3 .... 62 A3
Burn Gdns *PLEE/EAS* SR8 .... 200 B2
Burnhall Dr *SEA/MUR* SR7 .... 175 F1
Burnham Av *BW/LEM/TK/HW* NE15 .. 75 F1
Burnham Cl *BLYTH* NE24 .... 17 D1
Burnham Gv *BOL* NE36 .... 106 C3
BYK/HTN/WLK NE6 .... 83 D4
Burnham St *HAR/WTLS* NE34 .... 88 B2 1
Burn Heads Rd *HEBB* NE31 .... 84 C4
Burnhills La *RYTON* NE40 .... 92 A2
Burnhope Dr *SWCK/CAS* SR5 .... 126 A1 1
Burnhope Rd *WASHS* NE38 .... 121 D6
Burnhope Wy *PLEE/EAS* SR8 .... 208 A2
Burnip Rd *SEA/MUR* SR7 .... 174 B6
Burn La *HLH* DH5 .... 185 F1
Burnlea Gdns *CRAM* NE23 .... 23 F6
Burnley St *BLAY* NE21 .... 76 B6 1
Burnmoor Gdns
LWF/SPW/WRK NE9 .... 118 C1
Burnopfield Gdns
BW/LEM/TK/HW NE15 .... 77 F2
Burnopfield Rd *ROWG* NE39 .... 111 E3
Burn Park Rd *ASHBK/HED/RY* SR2 .. 144 A1
HLS DH4 .... 170 B2
Burn Prom *HLS* DH4 .... 170 C2
Burn Rd *BLAY* NE21 .... 93 E1
Burns Av *BLYTH* NE24 .... 16 B1
BOLCOL NE35 .... 106 A2
Burns Av South *HLH* DH5 .... 171 D3
Burns Cl *HAR/WTLS* NE34 .... 88 A5
HLS DH4 .... 183 F2
STLY/ANP DH9 .... 148 C2
WICK/BNPF NE16 .... 96 A5
Burns Crs *WICK/BNPF* NE16 .... 95 F2 2
Burnside *BDLGTN* NE22 .... 8 C1
BDN/LAN/SAC DH7 .... 178 A4
BOL NE36 .... 107 D3
JRW NE32 .... 86 B4
PLEE/EAS SR8 .... 208 B2
Burnside Av *CRAM* NE23 .... 35 D2
HLS DH4 .... 170 B1
PLEE/EAS SR8 .... 209 F2
Burnside Cl *BLYTH* NE24 .... 10 A4 1
WICK/BNPF NE16 .... 95 F6
Burnside Rd *GOS/KPK* NE3 .... 47 E5
ROWG NE39 .... 110 C3
TYNE/NSHE NE30 .... 55 D1
The Burnside *WD/WHPE/BLK* NE5 .... 60 A5
Burnside Vw *CRAM* NE23 .... 36 A1 1
Burns St *JRW* NE32 .... 86 A1 2
Burn's Ter *RDHAMSE* DH6 .... 206 C3
Burnstones *WD/WHPE/BLK* NE5 .. 60 A5 3
Burnthouse Bank *CLSW/PEL* DH2 .. 152 B4
Burnthouse Cl *BLAY* NE21 .... 93 F2 3
Burnthouse La *WICK/BNPF* NE16 ...... 95 F6
Burnt House Rd *MONK* NE25 .... 54 A1
Burntland Av *SWCK/CAS* SR5 .... 125 E2
Burn Vw *CRAM* NE23 .... 35 D2 2
Burnville Rd *MLFD/PNYW* SR4 .... 144 A1
Burnville Rd South
MLFD/PNYW SR4 .... 144 A1 4
Burradon Rd *CRAM* NE23 .... 35 D4
Burrow St *SSH* NE33 .... 71 E3 3
Burscough Crs
CLDN/WHIT/ROK SR6 .... 126 C2 1
Burstow Av *BYK/HTN/WLK* NE6 .... 83 D5
Burt Av *NSHW* NE29 .... 70 A1
Burt Cl *PLEE/EAS* SR8 .... 200 C6
Burt Crs *CRAM* NE23 .... 35 D2 3
Burt Rd *BDLGTN* NE22 .... 9 D1 1
Burt St *BLYTH* NE24 .... 11 D4
Burwell Av *WD/WHPE/BLK* NE5 .... 60 B6
Burwood Cl *BYK/HTN/WLK* NE6 .... 83 F5 1
Burwood Rd *BYK/HTN/WLK* NE6 ...... 83 E5
NSHW NE29 .... 53 E4
Bushblades La *STLY/ANP* DH9 .... 146 B1
Buston Ter *JES* NE2 .... 64 B5
Busty Bank *WICK/BNPF* NE16 .... 111 F4
Butcher's Bridge Rd *JRW* NE32 .... 86 A4
Bute Ct *SUNDSW* SR3 .... 160 B2
Buteland Rd *BW/LEM/TK/HW* NE15 .. 77 E1
Bute St *STLY/ANP* DH9 .... 129 F4
Butsfield Gdns *SUNDSW* SR3 .... 144 A4 2
Buttermere *CLDN/WHIT/ROK* SR6 .. 107 F1
FELL NE10 .... 101 F2
PLEE/EAS SR8 .... 207 F5 1
Buttermere Av *HLH* DH5 .... 186 B4
WICK/BNPF NE16 .... 96 B3
Buttermere Cl
WD/WHPE/BLK NE5 .... 61 D5 1
Buttermere Crs *BLAY* NE21 .... 94 A2 1
Buttermere Gdns
HAR/WTLS NE34 .... 89 D2 1
LWF/SPW/WRK NE9 .... 99 F5
Buttermere Rd *TYNE/NSHE* NE30 ...... 54 C2
Buttermere St
ASHBK/HED/RY SR2 .... 145 D4
Buttermere Wy *BLYTH* NE24 .... 10 A3 1
Buxton Cl *JRW* NE32 .... 86 B3
WLSD/HOW NE28 .... 67 F1 9
Buxton Gdns *SUNDSW* SR3 .... 144 A3
WD/WHPE/BLK NE5 .... 60 B3 3
Buxton Rd *JRW* NE32 .... 86 B3 3
Byers Ct *SUNDSW* SR3 .... 144 A6
Byer Sq *HLH* DH5 .... 171 F4
Byer St *HLH* DH5 .... 171 F4
The Byeways *LGB/KIL* NE12 .... 49 D6 1
Bygate Cl *WD/WHPE/BLK* NE5 .... 62 A3
Bygate Rd *MONK* NE25 .... 40 A6
Byker Bank *BYK/HTN/WLK* NE6 .... 81 F3
Byker Br *CNUT* NE1 .... 3 H2
Byker Buildings
BYK/HTN/WLK NE6 .... 81 F2 2
Byker Ter *BYK/HTN/WLK* NE6 .... 83 E2
Byland Cl *HLS* DH4 .... 157 E6 1
Byland Ct *BDN/LAN/SAC* DH7 .... 192 A3 1
WASHS NE38 .... 138 B1
Byland Rd *LGB/KIL* NE12 .... 48 B6
Byony Toft *ASHBK/HED/RY* SR2 ...... 162 C1
Byrness *WD/WHPE/BLK* NE5 .... 60 A5
Byrness Cl *GOS/KPK* NE3 .... 61 E2
Byron Av *BLYTH* NE24 .... 16 B1 1
BOLCOL NE35 .... 105 F2
CLSW/PEL DH2 .... 152 A5
HEBB NE31 .... 85 E2
Byron Cl *CLSW/PEL* DH2 .... 135 F5
Byron Rd *SWCK/CAS* SR5 .... 125 F2
Byron St *JES* NE2 .... 3 F1
SWCK/CAS SR5 .... 126 A3
Byron Ter *RDHAMSE* DH6 .... 206 C2
The By-way *BW/LEM/TK/HW* NE15 .. 57 F5
Bywell Av *BW/LEM/TK/HW* NE15 ...... 77 D1
GOS/KPK NE3 .... 46 B4
HAR/WTLS NE34 .... 89 F1
SWCK/CAS SR5 .... 126 B1 1
Bywell Dr *PLEE/EAS* SR8 .... 208 B5
Bywell Gdns *DUN/TMV* NE11 .... 97 F5
LWF/SPW/WRK NE9 .... 100 A4
Bywell Rd *CLDN/WHIT/ROK* SR6 ...... 107 E2
Bywell St *BYK/HTN/WLK* NE6 .... 82 C3 1
Bywell Ter *JRW* NE32 .... 86 A5

C

Cadleston Ct *CRAM* NE23 .... 14 C6 3
Cadwell La *PLEE/EAS* SR8 .... 200 A2
Caernarvon Cl
WD/WHPE/BLK NE5 .... 61 D2 2
Caernarvon Dr *SUNDSW* SR3 .... 159 E2
Caer Urfa Cl *SSH* NE33 .... 71 E2
Cairncross *SWCK/CAS* SR5 .... 123 F3
Cairnglass Gn *CRAM* NE23 .... 14 C6 4
Cairngorm Av *WASHS* NE38 .... 137 F3
Cairnsmore Cl *CRAM* NE23 .... 22 A4
Cairnsmore Dr *WASHS* NE38 .... 138 A3
Cairns Rd *SEA/MUR* SR7 .... 187 F1
SWCK/CAS SR5 .... 108 B6 1
Cairns Sq *SWCK/CAS* SR5 .... 108 B6 2
Cairns Wy *GOS/KPK* NE3 .... 46 B5
Cairo St *ASHBK/HED/RY* SR2 .... 145 D2
Caithness Rd *SWCK/CAS* SR5 .... 123 E2
Caithness Sq *SWCK/CAS* SR5 .... 123 E2 1
Calais Rd *SWCK/CAS* SR5 .... 123 E3 1
Caldbeck Av *BYK/HTN/WLK* NE6 .... 83 E5
Caldbeck Cl *BYK/HTN/WLK* NE6 .... 83 E5
Calderbourne Av
CLDN/WHIT/ROK SR6 .... 109 D6 1
Calderdale *WLSD/HOW* NE28 .... 66 B1
Calderdale Av *BYK/HTN/WLK* NE6 .... 83 E2
Calder Wk *WICK/BNPF* NE16 .... 113 F2
Calderwood Crs
LWF/SPW/WRK NE9 .... 117 F1
Caldew Ct *HLH* DH5 .... 186 A2
Caldew Crs *WD/WHPE/BLK* NE5 .... 60 C6
Caldwell Rd *GOS/KPK* NE3 .... 46 B4
Caledonian St *HEBB* NE31 .... 84 C1
Caledonia St *BYK/HTN/WLK* NE6 .. 83 F4 2
Calf Close Dr *JRW* NE32 .... 86 A6
Calfclose La *JRW* NE32 .... 86 B6
Calf Close Wk *JRW* NE32 .... 86 A5
California *BLAY* NE21 .... 94 A1
Callaley Av *WICK/BNPF* NE16 .... 95 E4
Callaly Av *CRAM* NE23 .... 22 B2
Callaly Wy *BYK/HTN/WLK* NE6 ...... 82 C4 1
Callander *CLSW/PEL* DH2 .... 135 F4
Callerdale Rd *BLYTH* NE24 .... 9 F5 1
Callerton *LGB/KIL* NE12 .... 35 F5 2
Callerton Av *NSHW* NE29 .... 53 E5
Callerton Ct *PONT/DH* NE20 .... 28 A6
Callerton La *PONT/DH* NE20 .... 28 A5
WD/WHPE/BLK NE5 .... 42 A4
Callerton Rd *BW/LEM/TK/HW* NE15 .. 58 A4
Callerton Vw
WD/WHPE/BLK NE5 .... 59 D2 3
Calley Cl *PLEE/EAS* SR8 .... 208 B5 1
Callington Dr *ASHBK/HED/RY* SR2 .. 162 B1
Calvert Ter *SEA/MUR* SR7 .... 188 A1
Calvus Dr *BW/LEM/TK/HW* NE15 .. 56 B4 1
Camberley Cl *SUNDSW* SR3 .... 144 B6 1
Camberley Dr
BDN/LAN/SAC DH7 .... 202 B5 2
Camberley Rd *WLSD/HOW* NE28 ...... 68 C2
Camberwell Cl *DUN/TMV* NE11 .... 98 A4
Camberwell Wy *SUNDSW* SR3 .... 159 F3
Cambo Av *BDLGTN* NE22 .... 8 B3
MONK NE25 .... 53 F1
Cambo Cl *BLYTH* NE24 .... 10 B5
GOS/KPK NE3 .... 63 F1 1
WLSD/HOW NE28 .... 51 F6
Cambo Dr *CRAM* NE23 .... 22 B3
Cambo Gn *WD/WHPE/BLK* NE5 .... 61 E4
Cambo Pl *TYNE/NSHE* NE30 .... 54 C3
Camborne Gv *GATE* NE8 .... 99 E1
Camborne Pl *GATE* NE8 .... 99 E1 2
Cambourne Av
CLDN/WHIT/ROK SR6 .... 109 D6 2
Cambria Gn *MLFD/PNYW* SR4 ...... 123 F6 1
Cambrian St *JRW* NE32 .... 86 A1
Cambrian Wy *WASHS* NE38 .... 138 A2
Cambria St *MLFD/PNYW* SR4 .... 123 F6
Cambridge Av *HEBB* NE31 .... 85 E3
LGB/KIL NE12 .... 49 F4 3
WASHN NE37 .... 120 A4
WLSD/HOW NE28 .... 66 C3 2
Cambridge Dr *CLS/BIR/GTL* DH3 ...... 167 F4
Cambridge Pl *CLS/BIR/GTL* DH3 ...... 136 B5
Cambridge Rd *PLEE/EAS* SR8 .... 200 B6
SUNDSW SR3 .... 160 C1
Cambridgeshire Dr *DHAM* DH1 .... 196 B4
Cambridge St *ELS/FEN* NE4 .... 80 A4 2
Camden St *JES* NE2 .... 3 F1
SWCK/CAS SR5 .... 125 F3 1
TYNE/NSHE NE30 .... 71 D1 2

Camelford Ct
BW/LEM/TK/HW NE15 59 E6 1
Camelot Cl *SEA/MUR* SR7 176 B2 2
Cameron Cl *HAR/WTLS* NE34 88 B5 2
Camerton Pl *WLSD/HOW* NE28 52 A5
Camilla Rd *BW/LEM/TK/HW* NE15 56 B4
Camilla St *GATE* NE8 99 E1 3
Campbell Park Rd *HEBB* NE31 85 D2
Campbell Pl *ELS/FEN* NE4 79 F3
Campbell Rd *SWCK/CAS* SR5 123 E2
Campbell St *HEBB* NE31 84 C1
Camperdown *WD/WHPE/BLK* NE5 60 B5
Camperdown Av
CLS/BIR/GTL DH3 153 F3
Campion Dr *STLY/ANP* DH9 130 C6
Campion Gdns *FELL* NE10 100 C5 1
Camp Rd *WLSD/HOW* NE28 67 D6
Campsie Crs *TYNE/NSHE* NE30 54 C3
Camp Ter *NSHW* NE29 54 C6
Campville *NSHW* NE29 54 C6
Camsey Cl *LGB/KIL* NE12 48 B6 2
Canberra Av *MONK* NE25 53 F1
Canberra Dr *HAR/WTLS* NE34 87 D4
Canberra Rd *MLFD/PNYW* SR4 142 C2
Candelford Cl *LGB/HTN* NE7 65 F3 1
Candlish St *SSH* NE33 71 F4
Candlish Ter *SEA/MUR* SR7 177 D4
Canning St *ELS/FEN* NE4 78 C3
HEBB NE31 85 D3
Cannock *CLSW/PEL* DH2 135 E4
LGB/KIL NE12 35 F6 5
Cannock Dr *LGB/HTN* NE7 64 C2
Cannon St *GATE* NE8 3 F6 1
Cann Rd *PLEE/EAS* SR8 200 C6
Canonbie Sq *CRAM* NE23 14 C6 5
Canon Cockin St
ASHBK/HED/RY SR2 145 D2
Canon Gv *JRW* NE32 86 B1
Canonsfield Cl *SUNDSW* SR3 160 B3
Canterbury Av *WLSD/HOW* NE28 51 F6
Canterbury Cl *CLS/BIR/GTL* DH3 167 F4 1
Canterbury Rd *DHAM* DH1 180 C4
SWCK/CAS SR5 123 F2
Canterbury St
BYK/HTN/WLK NE6 82 C2 2
SSH NE33 71 F6
Canterbury Wy *DIN/WO* NE13 33 E4 1
Capetown Rd *SWCK/CAS* SR5 123 E2 2
The Captains Rw *SSH* NE33 71 D6
Capulet Gv *HAR/WTLS* NE34 87 F3
Capulet Ter *ASHBK/HED/RY* SR2 145 D2 2
Caradoc Cl *WASHS* NE38 138 A3
Caragh Rd *CLSW/PEL* DH2 166 B1
Caraway Wk *HAR/WTLS* NE34 89 D5
Carden Av *HAR/WTLS* NE34 90 A3 2
Cardiff Sq *SWCK/CAS* SR5 123 E3 2
Cardigan Gv *MONK* NE25 54 C1
Cardigan Rd *SWCK/CAS* SR5 123 E2
Cardigan Ter *BYK/HTN/WLK* NE6 82 A1
Cardinal Cl *LGB/KIL* NE12 48 C6 3
WD/WHPE/BLK NE5 59 D3
Cardinals Cl *SUNDSW* SR3 160 B3 2
Cardonnel St *NSHW* NE29 70 C2
Cardwell St *CLDN/WHIT/ROK* SR6 127 D3
Careen Crs *SUNDSW* SR3 159 D1
Carham Av *CRAM* NE23 22 B2 2
Carham Cl *GOS/KPK* NE3 47 F6
Carisbrooke *BDLGTN* NE22 7 E2
Caris St *GATE* NE8 99 F2
Carlby Wy *CRAM* NE23 13 E4
Carlcroft Pl *CRAM* NE23 22 B3 3
Carley Hill Rd *SWCK/CAS* SR5 126 A1
Carley Rd *SWCK/CAS* SR5 126 A2
Carlingford Rd *CLSW/PEL* DH2 166 A1
Carliol Sq *CNUT* NE1 3 E3
Carliol St *CNUT* NE1 3 E3
Carlisle Crs *HLS* DH4 156 C1
Carlisle Rd *DHAM* DH1 181 D5
Carlisle St *FELL* NE10 100 C1
Carlton Av *BLYTH* NE24 16 B3
Carlton Cl *CLSW/PEL* DH2 135 D4
GOS/KPK NE3 62 C3 1
Carlton Ct *DUN/TMV* NE11 98 C5
Carlton Crs *SUNDSW* SR3 159 E1
Carlton Gdns
BW/LEM/TK/HW NE15 77 D1 1
Carlton Rd *LGB/KIL* NE12 49 F6
Carlton St *BLYTH* NE24 11 E5 1
Carlton Ter *LWF/SPW/WRK* NE9 99 D5
NSHW NE29 70 B1 2
Carlyle Ct *WLSD/HOW* NE28 68 C5 2
Carlyle Crs *WICK/BNPF* NE16 95 F2
Carlyle St *WLSD/HOW* NE28 68 C5 3
Carlyon St *ASHBK/HED/RY* SR2 4 C6 1
Carmel Gv *CRAM* NE23 13 F5 1
Carmel Rd *STLY/ANP* DH9 147 F2
Carnaby Rd *BYK/HTN/WLK* NE6 83 E4 1
Carnation Av *HLS* DH4 155 F5
Carnegie Cl *HAR/WTLS* NE34 88 B4 1
Carnegie St *ASHBK/HED/RY* SR2 145 E4 1
Carnforth Cl *WLSD/HOW* NE28 51 F5
Carnforth Gdns
LWF/SPW/WRK NE9 100 A6
ROWG NE39 111 D1 1
Carnforth Gn *GOS/KPK* NE3 62 A2 1
Carnoustie *CLSW/PEL* DH2 135 E5
HAR/WTLS NE34 89 E5
WASHN NE37 120 B1
Carnoustie Cl *LGB/HTN* NE7 65 E2 2
Carnoustie Ct *MONK* NE25 39 E5
Carnoustie Dr *HAR/WTLS* NE34 89 E5 1
Carol Gdns *LGB/HTN* NE7 65 D3
Caroline Gdns *WLSD/HOW* NE28 68 C3
Caroline St *ELS/FEN* NE4 79 D4
HLH DH5 171 F6
JRW NE32 85 F1
SEA/MUR SR7 176 C3 4
Carol St *MLFD/PNYW* SR4 125 F5
Carolyn Cl *LGB/KIL* NE12 49 E6 1
Carolyn Crs *WBAY* NE26 40 A3
Carolyn Wy *WBAY* NE26 40 A3
Carpenter St *SSH* NE33 71 D4 2
Carr Av *BDN/LAN/SAC* DH7 203 D4
Carr Fld *PONT/DH* NE20 28 B3
Carrfield Rd *GOS/KPK* NE3 62 B1 2
Carr Hill Rd *LWF/SPW/WRK* NE9 99 F2
Carr House Dr *DHAM* DH1 180 B6
Carrhouse La *HLH* DH5 173 D5
Carrick Dr *BLYTH* NE24 16 C2
Carrigill Pl *LGB/KIL* NE12 48 C6
Carrington Cl *CRAM* NE23 36 B1
Carrmere Rd *ASHBK/HED/RY* SR2 145 D5
Carrmyers *STLY/ANP* DH9 146 A2
Carrock Cl *PLEE/EAS* SR8 208 C5
Carrowmore Rd *CLSW/PEL* DH2 166 B1
Carrsdale *DHAM* DH1 196 C1 1
Carr St *BLYTH* NE24 16 B2
HEBB NE31 84 C1 3
Carrsway *DHAM* DH1 196 C1 2
Carrsyde Cl *WICK/BNPF* NE16 95 E5
Carsdale Rd *GOS/KPK* NE3 61 F1
Cartington Av *SMOOR* NE27 52 A2
Cartington Cl *PLEE/EAS* SR8 208 C5 1
Cartington Ct *GOS/KPK* NE3 46 A5 2
Cartington Rd *DHAM* DH1 194 B1
NSHW NE29 70 A1
Cartington Ter *BYK/HTN/WLK* NE6 65 E5
Cartmel Ct *CLSW/PEL* DH2 152 C6
Cartmel Gv *GATE* NE8 98 C3 1
Cartmel Pk *FELL* NE10 101 F1 1
Cartwright Rd *SWCK/CAS* SR5 124 A3
Carville Rd *WLSD/HOW* NE28 67 D5
Carville St *FELL* NE10 82 A6
Carvill Gdns *WLSD/HOW* NE28 67 D6 1
Carvis Cl *BDN/LAN/SAC* DH7 202 C5
Carwarding Pl *WD/WHPE/BLK* NE5 61 E5
Caseton Cl *MONK* NE25 39 E4
Caspian Cl *JRW* NE32 86 B3 4
Caspian Rd *SWCK/CAS* SR5 123 E3 3
Caspian Sq *SWCK/CAS* SR5 123 E3
Castellian Rd *SWCK/CAS* SR5 124 B3
Casterton Gv *WD/WHPE/BLK* NE5 59 D3
Castle Chare *DHAM* DH1 194 B4 2
Castle Cl *CLS/BIR/GTL* DH3 153 F6
GOS/KPK NE3 61 F1 3
HLH DH5 186 A2
WICK/BNPF NE16 95 F3 2
Castledale Av *BLYTH* NE24 9 F6
Castledene Ct *GOS/KPK* NE3 64 B2
Castle Dene Gv *HLS* DH4 170 C2
Castleford Rd *SWCK/CAS* SR5 123 E2
Castlegate Gdns *GATE* NE8 97 F1 2
Castlenook Pl
BW/LEM/TK/HW NE15 77 E1 1
Castlereagh Cl *SEA/MUR* SR7 176 B2
Castlereagh Rd *SEA/MUR* SR7 176 C3
Castlereagh St *SUNDSW* SR3 160 C1
Castlereigh Cl *HLS* DH4 155 F5
Castle Riggs *CLSW/PEL* DH2 153 D5
Castle Rd *WASHS* NE38 137 F2
Castles Farm Rd *LGB/HTN* NE7 64 A2
Castles Gn *LGB/KIL* NE12 50 A1
Castleside Rd
BW/LEM/TK/HW NE15 77 F2
Castle Sq *SMOOR* NE27 37 D6 1
Castle St *DIN/WO* NE13 32 C6
SUND SR1 4 B2
Castle St South *SWCK/CAS* SR5 124 B3 2
Castleton Cl *CRAM* NE23 13 F5 2
JES NE2 64 B4 1
Castleton Gv *JES* NE2 64 B4
Castleton Rd *JRW* NE32 86 B3 3
Castletown Rd *SWCK/CAS* SR5 124 B3
Castletown Wy *SWCK/CAS* SR5 124 C2
Castle Vw *BDN/LAN/SAC* DH7 192 B5 2
CLS/BIR/GTL DH3 153 E3
SWCK/CAS SR5 124 A3
Castleway *DIN/WO* NE13 31 D4
Castlewood Cl *WD/WHPE/BLK* NE5 59 F4
Catchside Cl *WICK/BNPF* NE16 95 F5
Catchwell Rd *STLY/ANP* DH9 128 C6
Cateran Wy *CRAM* NE23 22 B4
Caterhouse Rd *DHAM* DH1 180 A6
Catharine St West
MLFD/PNYW SR4 125 F6 2
Cathedral Vw *BDN/LAN/SAC* DH7 178 C2
HLS DH4 157 F5
Catherine Cookson Ct *SSH* NE33 72 A5 2
Catherine Rd *HLS* DH4 157 F2
Catherine St *SSH* NE33 71 F3 2
Catherine Ter *STLY/ANP* DH9 131 E6 2
Catholic Rw *BDLGTN* NE22 7 D4
Cato Sq *SWCK/CAS* SR5 125 F2
Cato St *SWCK/CAS* SR5 125 F2 1
Catton Gv *WICK/BNPF* NE16 114 A1
Catton Pl *WLSD/HOW* NE28 52 A6
Cauldwell Av *HAR/WTLS* NE34 89 D1
MONK NE25 53 F1
Cauldwell Cl *MONK* NE25 40 A6
Cauldwell La *MONK* NE25 39 F6
Cauldwell Pl *HAR/WTLS* NE34 89 D1
Cauldwell Vls *HAR/WTLS* NE34 89 D1
Causeway *CLDN/WHIT/ROK* SR6 126 C4 2
LWF/SPW/WRK NE9 100 A4
The Causeway
BW/LEM/TK/HW NE15 57 F5 1
LWF/SPW/WRK NE9 99 F2
Causey Bank *CNUT* NE1 3 F4
Causey Dr *STLY/ANP* DH9 131 F6
Causey Rd *STLY/ANP* DH9 131 F4
Causey St *GOS/KPK* NE3 63 E2
Cavalier Vw *HEBB* NE31 84 C1
Cavalier Wy *SUNDSW* SR3 160 B1 1
Cavell Sq *PLEE/EAS* SR8 200 C1
Cavendish Ct *BDN/LAN/SAC* DH7 202 C5
Cavendish Pl *JES* NE2 64 B5
SUNDSW SR3 160 B1
Cavendish Rd *JES* NE2 64 B5
Caversham Rd *WD/WHPE/BLK* NE5 59 D3
Cawnpore Sq *MLFD/PNYW* SR4 125 D6
Caynham Cl *NSHW* NE29 54 A4 1
Cayton Gv *WD/WHPE/BLK* NE5 59 D4
Cecil Ct *PONT/DH* NE20 28 B4
WLSD/HOW NE28 67 D6
Cecil St *NSHW* NE29 70 C1
Cedar Av *CLSW/PEL* DH2 165 E6
Cedar Cl *BDLGTN* NE22 7 E2
DHAM DH1 195 F3
Cedar Crs *DUN/TMV* NE11 97 E3
LWF/SPW/WRK NE9 99 E6
SEA/MUR SR7 176 B4
Cedar Dr *DHAM* DH1 205 D3
Cedar Gv *CLDN/WHIT/ROK* SR6 91 E6
HAR/WTLS NE34 89 E3
RYTON NE40 74 B3
WLSD/HOW NE28 67 F5
Cedar Rd *BLAY* NE21 76 B6
ELS/FEN NE4 78 C1
Cedars Ct *ASHBK/HED/RY* SR2 144 C2
Cedars Crs *SEA/MUR* SR7 188 C1
Cedars Gn *LWF/SPW/WRK* NE9 117 F1
Cedars Pk *ASHBK/HED/RY* SR2 145 D3
The Cedars *ASHBK/HED/RY* SR2 144 C2
WICK/BNPF NE16 96 A6
Cedartree Gdns *MONK* NE25 54 A1
Cedarway *FELL* NE10 101 D5
Cedar Wy *LGB/KIL* NE12 50 A4 2
Cedarwood Av
BYK/HTN/WLK NE6 66 C5 1
Cedarwood Gv
ASHBK/HED/RY SR2 144 B4
Cedric Crs *ASHBK/HED/RY* SR2 144 A2
Celadon Cl
BW/LEM/TK/HW NE15 59 E6 2
Celandine Cl *GOS/KPK* NE3 47 F5
Celandine Wy *FELL* NE10 100 C4
Celtic Cl *CLDN/WHIT/ROK* SR6 107 D1
Celtic Crs *CLDN/WHIT/ROK* SR6 107 D1 1
Cemetery Ap *HAR/WTLS* NE34 72 A6
Cemetery Rd *GATE* NE8 99 E1
JRW NE32 86 B3
STLY/ANP DH9 148 B1
Centenary Av *HAR/WTLS* NE34 89 F2
Centenary Ct *ELS/FEN* NE4 79 E4 2
Central Av *BDN/LAN/SAC* DH7 203 E5
CLDN/WHIT/ROK SR6 109 D2
HAR/WTLS NE34 89 E2
NSHW NE29 70 A1
Central Gdns *HAR/WTLS* NE34 89 E2 1
Centurian Wy *BDLGTN* NE22 7 D2
Centurion Rd
BW/LEM/TK/HW NE15 60 A6
Centurion Wy
BW/LEM/TK/HW NE15 56 A4
LWF/SPW/WRK NE9 100 A4 1
Ceolfrid Ter *JRW* NE32 86 B4
Chacombe *WASHS* NE38 138 B3 1
Chadderton Dr
WD/WHPE/BLK NE5 59 D3
Chadwick St *WLSD/HOW* NE28 67 D5 4
Chaffinch Wy *LGB/KIL* NE12 35 E6
Chainbridge Rd *BLAY* NE21 76 C5
Chain Bridge Rd *BLAY* NE21 77 E5
Chalfont Gv *MLFD/PNYW* SR4 141 E4
Chalfont Rd *BYK/HTN/WLK* NE6 83 E4
Chalfont Wy *BDN/LAN/SAC* DH7 203 E4 3
Chalford Rd *SWCK/CAS* SR5 126 A2
Chamberlain St *BLYTH* NE24 11 E6 1
Chandler Cl *DHAM* DH1 195 F5
Chandlers Ford *HLS* DH4 139 E6 1
Chandlers Quay
BYK/HTN/WLK NE6 82 B4
Chandless St *GATE* NE8 81 E5 1
Chandos *SUNDSW* SR3 160 C4 2
Chandos St *GATE* NE8 99 E2

Chandra Pl WD/WHPE/BLK NE5 61 D4 5
Chantry Cl SUNDSW SR3 160 A3
Chantry Dr DIN/WO NE13 33 D3
Chapel Av WICK/BNPF NE16 112 A6 1
Chapel Cl GOS/KPK NE3 47 F3 2
Chapel Ct RDHAMSE DH6 197 F5
Chapel Hill Rd PLEE/EAS SR8 209 D1
Chapel House Dr
WD/WHPE/BLK NE5 59 E5
Chapel House Gv
BW/LEM/TK/HW NE15 59 E5
Chapel Rd JRW NE32 86 A1
Chapel Rw HLS DH4 157 E3
Chapel St HLH DH5 171 F6
NSHW NE29 70 A1
STLY/ANP DH9 129 F4
Chapel Vw HLS DH4 183 E3
ROWG NE39 111 D1
Chaplin St SEA/MUR SR7 176 C4
Chapman St
CLDN/WHIT/ROK SR6 109 D6 5
Chapter Rw SSH NE33 71 E3
Charlaw Cl BDN/LAN/SAC DH7 164 A6
Charlbury Cl LWF/SPW/WRK NE9 119 E3
Charlcote Crs BOL NE36 106 C3 2
Charles Av GOS/KPK NE3 46 A6
LGB/KIL NE12 49 F4
Charles Baker Wk
HAR/WTLS NE34 90 A2 1
Charles Dr CRAM NE23 35 D2
Charles St BOLCOL NE35 105 E2
CLDN/WHIT/ROK SR6 126 C4
DIN/WO NE13 32 C5 5
GATE NE8 81 E6
SEA/MUR SR7 176 C3
STLY/ANP DH9 148 A4
SUND SR1 5 E1 1
Charleswood GOS/KPK NE3 47 F4 1
Charlotte Cl ELS/FEN NE4 80 A5 5
Charlotte Sq CNUT NE1 2 B4 1
Charlotte St SSH NE33 71 E3
STLY/ANP DH9 148 A4
TYNE/NSHE NE30 71 D1
WLSD/HOW NE28 67 E4
Charlton Gv CLDN/WHIT/ROK SR6 107 F2
Charlton Rd SWCK/CAS SR5 126 B1
Charlton St BW/LEM/TK/HW NE15 76 C2
Charman St SUND SR1 4 C2 1
Charminster Gdns
BYK/HTN/WLK NE6 65 E4
Charnwood STLY/ANP DH9 131 D6 1
Charnwood Av LGB/KIL NE12 48 C6
Charter Dr SUNDSW SR3 159 E1
Chasedale Crs BLYTH NE24 9 F5
Chase Farm Dr BLYTH NE24 9 E4
Chase Ms BLYTH NE24 9 E5 1
The Chase LGB/KIL NE12 48 C2
NSHW NE29 54 B6
WASHS NE38 137 E5
Chatham Cl MONK NE25 37 F1
Chatham Rd SWCK/CAS SR5 123 F2
Chathill Cl MONK NE25 39 E5
Chathill Ter BYK/HTN/WLK NE6 83 E3
Chatsworth Crs
MLFD/PNYW SR4 143 F2 1
Chatsworth Gdns
BYK/HTN/WLK NE6 82 C4 2
WD/WHPE/BLK NE5 60 B3 4
Chatsworth Pl WICK/BNPF NE16 95 F5
Chatsworth Rd JRW NE32 86 B3 6
Chatsworth St MLFD/PNYW SR4 143 F1
Chatsworth St South
MLFD/PNYW SR4 143 F2 2
Chatterton St SWCK/CAS SR5 125 F2
Chatton Av CRAM NE23 22 B3
HAR/WTLS NE34 73 D6
Chatton Cl CLSW/PEL DH2 165 F1
Chatton St WLSD/HOW NE28 69 E5
Chatton Wynd GOS/KPK NE3 46 C5 1
Chaucer Av HAR/WTLS NE34 87 F5
Chaucer Cl GATE NE8 81 F6
STLY/ANP DH9 148 C2
Chaucer Rd WICK/BNPF NE16 95 F2
Chaytor Gv SUND SR1 5 F4
Chaytor St JRW NE32 69 D6
Cheadle Av CRAM NE23 13 F5 5
WLSD/HOW NE28 51 F6
Cheadle Rd SWCK/CAS SR5 123 F2
Cheam Cl WICK/BNPF NE16 96 A5 2
Cheam Rd SWCK/CAS SR5 123 F2
Cheeseburn Gdns
WD/WHPE/BLK NE5 61 E6
Cheldon Cl MONK NE25 39 E4
Chelford Cl WLSD/HOW NE28 52 A5
Chelmsford Gv JES NE2 81 F1
Chelmsford Rd SWCK/CAS SR5 123 F2
Chelmsford Sq SWCK/CAS SR5 123 F1 8
Chelsea Gdns GATE NE8 100 A2
Chelsea Gv ELS/FEN NE4 79 F3 5
Cheltenham Dr BOLCOL NE35 87 D6
Cheltenham Rd SWCK/CAS SR5 123 F2 1
Cheltenham Sq SWCK/CAS SR5 123 F2 2
Cheltenham Ter
BYK/HTN/WLK NE6 82 A1 1
Chelton Cl DIN/WO NE13 33 D6 1
Chepstow Gdns GATE NE8 98 C2 2
Chepstow Rd
BW/LEM/TK/HW NE15 77 E2
Chepstow St MLFD/PNYW SR4 126 A6 1
Cherry Banks CLS/BIR/GTL DH3 153 F3
Cherry Blossom Wy WASHN NE37 122 A4
Cherry Gv LGB/KIL NE12 35 E6
Cherry Pk BDN/LAN/SAC DH7 202 C5
Cherrytree Cl LGB/KIL NE12 50 B2
Cherrytree Ct BDLGTN NE22 8 C2 1
Cherry Tree Dr BDLGTN NE22 7 E3
Cherrytree Dr WICK/BNPF NE16 96 B2
Cherrytree Gdns
LWF/SPW/WRK NE9 99 F6
MONK NE25 54 B1
Cherry Trees BLYTH NE24 10 C6 1
Cherry Wy HLS DH4 170 A1
Cherwell WASHN NE37 121 E4
Cherwell Rd PLEE/EAS SR8 208 A3
Chesham Gdns WD/WHPE/BLK NE5 59 D4
Cheshire Av CLS/BIR/GTL DH3 136 B5
Cheshire Dr DHAM DH1 196 B4
Cheshire Gdns WLSD/HOW NE28 66 C3
Cheshire Gv HAR/WTLS NE34 90 A1
The Chesils LGB/KIL NE12 64 C1
Chesmond Dr BLAY NE21 76 A5
Chessar Av WD/WHPE/BLK NE5 61 D4
Chester Av WLSD/HOW NE28 68 B3
Chester Ct LGB/KIL NE12 49 D6
Chesterfield Rd ELS/FEN NE4 79 E4 5
Chester Gdns HAR/WTLS NE34 89 D1
Chester Gv BLYTH NE24 10 B6
CRAM NE23 36 A1
Chester Pl GATE NE8 81 D6 1
PLEE/EAS SR8 200 A6
Chester Rd CLS/BIR/GTL DH3 154 C4
HLS DH4 155 F5
MLFD/PNYW SR4 141 D4
MLFD/PNYW SR4 143 D1
STLY/ANP DH9 148 C1
Chester Road Est STLY/ANP DH9 148 C1
Chesters Av LGB/KIL NE12 48 C6
Chesters Pk LWF/SPW/WRK NE9 99 E4 1
The Chesters MONK NE25 39 F4
WD/WHPE/BLK NE5 59 E5
Chester St HLS DH4 157 F6
JES NE2 81 E1
MLFD/PNYW SR4 125 F6
Chester St East
MLFD/PNYW SR4 126 A6 2
Chester St West
MLFD/PNYW SR4 125 F6 5
Chester Ter SUND SR1 126 A6
Chester Ter North
MLFD/PNYW SR4 126 A6 5
Chesterton Rd HAR/WTLS NE34 88 A4
Chesterwood Dr WLSD/HOW NE28 66 C4
Chestnut Av BLYTH NE24 10 C3
MONK NE25 40 B6
WD/WHPE/BLK NE5 62 A4
WICK/BNPF NE16 96 A5
Chestnut Cl JRW NE32 104 C1
LGB/KIL NE12 35 D6 2
Chestnut Crs SWCK/CAS SR5 125 E1
Chestnut Gdns GATE NE8 98 B2
Chestnut Gv HAR/WTLS NE34 89 E4
Chestnut St WLSD/HOW NE28 67 E5 1
Cheswick Dr GOS/KPK NE3 47 F6
Cheveley Wk DHAM DH1 196 C3
Chevin Cl BYK/HTN/WLK NE6 66 C5
Chevington FELL NE10 101 F4 1
Chevington Gdns
WD/WHPE/BLK NE5 61 F5 5
Chevington Gv MONK NE25 39 F3
Cheviot Cl WASHN NE37 119 F6
Cheviot Ct SEA/MUR SR7 175 F2
Cheviot Gdns DUN/TMV NE11 97 F3 1
SEA/MUR SR7 175 F2
Cheviot Gra CRAM NE23 35 E4
Cheviot La ASHBK/HED/RY SR2 161 F1
Cheviot Pl PLEE/EAS SR8 208 A2
Cheviot Rd BLAY NE21 94 B1
HAR/WTLS NE34 72 C6
JRW NE32 85 E4 2
Cheviot St MLFD/PNYW SR4 125 E5
Cheviot Vw CLSW/PEL DH2 165 F2
DIN/WO NE13 32 C4
The Cheyne SUNDSW SR3 160 C3
Chichester Av CRAM NE23 13 E6
Chichester Cl GOS/KPK NE3 45 E5
Chichester Gv BDLGTN NE22 7 E2
Chichester Pl SSH NE33 71 E6 2
Chichester Rd
CLDN/WHIT/ROK SR6 109 D6
DHAM DH1 180 C5
SSH NE33 71 F5 1
Chichester Rd East SSH NE33 71 F5
Chicken Rd WLSD/HOW NE28 66 C3
Chick's La CLDN/WHIT/ROK SR6 109 D1
Chigwell Cl HLS DH4 157 D1
Chilcrosse FELL NE10 101 E3 1
Chilham Ct NSHW NE29 53 D4
Chillingham Cl BLYTH NE24 16 A1
Chillingham Dr CLSW/PEL DH2 165 F2 1
NSHW NE29 69 F2 1
Chillingham Rd BYK/HTN/WLK NE6 65 E5
DHAM DH1 180 C6
Chillingham Ter JRW NE32 86 C4
Chilside Rd FELL NE10 101 D2 2
Chiltern Cl WASHS NE38 138 A3
Chiltern Dr LGB/KIL NE12 49 D3
Chiltern Gdns DUN/TMV NE11 97 F3
Chiltern Rd NSHW NE29 54 B2
Chilton Gdns HLS DH4 169 F2 1
Chilton Garth PLEE/EAS SR8 209 E3
Chilton St SWCK/CAS SR5 126 B3 1
China St ASHBK/HED/RY SR2 145 D2
Chingford Cl HLS DH4 157 E1 1
Chipchase WASHS NE38 137 E2
Chipchase Av CRAM NE23 22 A3
Chipchase Cl BDLGTN NE22 6 C3 1
Chipchase Ct MONK NE25 24 B2
Chipchase Crs WD/WHPE/BLK NE5 60 A3
Chipchase Ter JRW NE32 86 A5
Chirton Av HAR/WTLS NE34 90 B2
NSHW NE29 70 B1
Chirton Dene Quays NSHW NE29 70 B4
Chirton Dene Wy NSHW NE29 70 B3
Chirton Gn NSHW NE29 70 B1 5
Chirton Gv HAR/WTLS NE34 90 B2
Chirton Hill Dr NSHW NE29 53 E5
Chirton La NSHW NE29 54 A6
Chirton West Vw NSHW NE29 70 B1
Chirton Wynd BYK/HTN/WLK NE6 82 B3
Chislehurst Rd HLS DH4 157 D1 1
Chiswick Gdns GATE NE8 99 F2 1
Chiswick Rd MONK NE25 24 C6
SWCK/CAS SR5 123 F2
Chollerford Av MONK NE25 41 D6
NSHW NE29 53 E6
Chollerford Cl GOS/KPK NE3 62 C2
Chollerford Ms MONK NE25 25 E6
Chollerton Dr BDLGTN NE22 7 F3
LGB/KIL NE12 50 C5
Choppington Rd STKFD/GP NE62 7 E1
Chorley Pl BYK/HTN/WLK NE6 83 D3
Chowdene Bank DUN/TMV NE11 117 D2
LWF/SPW/WRK NE9 117 E1
Christal Ter CLDN/WHIT/ROK SR6 126 C1
Christie Ter BYK/HTN/WLK NE6 83 E3
Christon Cl GOS/KPK NE3 64 A1 5
Christon Rd GOS/KPK NE3 63 E1
Christon Wy FELL NE10 84 A6 4
Christopher Rd
BYK/HTN/WLK NE6 83 D1 1
Chudleigh Gdns
WD/WHPE/BLK NE5 59 D4
Church Av GOS/KPK NE3 63 F1
Church Bank
BW/LEM/TK/HW NE15 75 E1 1
JRW NE32 86 C1
STLY/ANP DH9 148 B1
SWCK/CAS SR5 125 F3 2
WLSD/HOW NE28 67 F4
Church Chare PONT/DH NE20 28 B3
WICK/BNPF NE16 96 A3 1
Church Cl BDLGTN NE22 7 E4 1
DIN/WO NE13 31 D3
MONK NE25 39 E6
PLEE/EAS SR8 209 D3
SEA/MUR SR7 176 B2
Church Ct BDLGTN NE22 7 E4
SEA/MUR SR7 175 F2
Churchdown Cl BOLCOL NE35 87 D6 5
Church Dr LWF/SPW/WRK NE9 99 F4 2
Churcher Gdns WLSD/HOW NE28 66 C2 1
Church Flatt PONT/DH NE20 28 B3
Church Gn SEA/MUR SR7 176 B2 5
Churchill Av DHAM DH1 195 E4
MONK NE25 54 A1
SWCK/CAS SR5 125 F2 2
Churchill Gdns JES NE2 64 C5 1
Churchill Sq HLS DH4 170 A2 1
Churchill St SUND SR1 5 E4
WLSD/HOW NE28 68 B2
Church La BDLGTN NE22 7 F4
CLDN/WHIT/ROK SR6 109 E2
DHAM DH1 194 C6 1
GOS/KPK NE3 63 F1
LWF/SPW/WRK NE9 100 A4 2
SEA/MUR SR7 188 A1
Church Pl FELL NE10 100 C1
Church Ri RYTON NE40 75 D3
WICK/BNPF NE16 96 A3
Church Rd
BW/LEM/TK/HW NE15 75 E1 2
GOS/KPK NE3 63 F1
HLH DH5 171 F4
LWF/SPW/WRK NE9 99 E6
SMOOR NE27 37 E5
Church St BDN/LAN/SAC DH7 178 A1
BLAY NE21 93 F1
BYK/HTN/WLK NE6 83 F4
DHAM DH1 194 C6
DUN/TMV NE11 97 F1
GATE NE8 3 F6
HEBB NE31 84 C1
HLH DH5 171 D2 1
HLS DH4 171 D2
HLS DH4 183 F2

MLFD/PNYW SR4 123 F6
SEA/MUR SR7 176 C3 5
SEA/MUR SR7 188 C2
STLY/ANP DH9 148 B1
SWCK/CAS SR5 126 A2 2
TYNE/NSHE NE30 55 D6 1
WICK/BNPF NE16 113 F4
Church St East *SUND* SR1 5 F1
Church Street Head *DHAM* DH1 194 B6
Church St North
CLDN/WHIT/ROK SR6 126 C3
Church Vw *BOLCOL* NE35 105 D1
CLSW/PEL DH2 179 F1 1
SUNDSW SR3 160 C1
WLSD/HOW NE28 67 F4
Church Wk *PLEE/EAS* SR8 200 A3 2
Church Wy *MONK* NE25 38 C4
NSHW NE29 54 C6 4
SSH NE33 71 E3
Church Wynd *RDHAMSE* DH6 197 E5
Cinderford Cl *BOLCOL* NE35 86 C6
Cirencester St *MLFD/PNYW* SR4 126 A5 3
Citadel East *LGB/KIL* NE12 49 F1
Citadel West *LGB/KIL* NE12 49 F1
City Rd *CNUT* NE1 3 E4 1
City Wy *SUNDSW* SR3 159 E2
Civic Ct *HEBB* NE31 85 E3
Clacton Rd *SWCK/CAS* SR5 123 E3 4
Clanfield Ct *LGB/HTN* NE7 64 B2
Clanny St *SUND* SR1 4 A3
Clanton Cl *FELL* NE10 102 B3
Clapham Av *BYK/HTN/WLK* NE6 82 C3
Clappersgate *PLEE/EAS* SR8 199 F3
Clara St *ELS/FEN* NE4 78 C4
SEA/MUR SR7 176 A2 1
Claremont Av
BW/LEM/TK/HW NE15 59 F6
CLDN/WHIT/ROK SR6 127 D1 1
Claremont Crs *WBAY* NE26 40 A2
Claremont Dr *HLS* DH4 156 C2
Claremont Gdns *BOL* NE36 106 C3
WBAY NE26 40 B4
Claremont Rd
CLDN/WHIT/ROK SR6 127 D1
JES NE2 62 C6
WBAY NE26 40 A2
Claremont South Av *GATE* NE8 81 D6 2
Claremont St *GATE* NE8 99 D1 1
JES NE2 80 B1 1
Claremont Ter *BLYTH* NE24 10 C5
Claremount Ct *BOL* NE36 106 A3 2
Clarence St *JES* NE2 3 G2
SEA/MUR SR7 176 C3 6
SWCK/CAS SR5 125 F2 3
WBAY NE26 26 C3
Clarence Ter *CLS/BIR/GTL* DH3 153 E5
Clarendon Sq *SWCK/CAS* SR5 126 A1 2
Clare Rd *PLEE/EAS* SR8 208 A3
Clarewood Av *HAR/WTLS* NE34 72 C6
Clarewood Pl *WD/WHPE/BLK* NE5 61 E6
Clarke Ter *FELL* NE10 100 B2
SEA/MUR SR7 174 B6
Clarks Hill Wk
BW/LEM/TK/HW NE15 75 E1 3
Clasper St *ELS/FEN* NE4 80 A5 4
Claude St *HLH* DH5 185 F1
Claude Ter *SEA/MUR* SR7 188 C1
Claverdon St
WD/WHPE/BLK NE5 59 D2 4
Clavering Pl *CNUT* NE1 2 D5 1
Clavering Rd *WICK/BNPF* NE16 96 A1 1
Clavering Sq *DUN/TMV* NE11 97 E2 1
Clavering St *WLSD/HOW* NE28 69 D5 1
Clavering Wy *BLAY* NE21 95 D1
Claverley Dr *SMOOR* NE27 37 E5
Claxheugh Rd *MLFD/PNYW* SR4 124 A5 1
Claxton St *PLEE/EAS* SR8 209 F1
Clay La *DHAM* DH1 193 F6
Claymere Rd *ASHBK/HED/RY* SR2 145 D5
Claypath *DHAM* DH1 194 C4
Claypath La *SSH* NE33 71 E4
Claypath Rd *HLH* DH5 185 F2
Claypath St *BYK/HTN/WLK* NE6 81 F2 3
Claypool Ct *HAR/WTLS* NE34 88 B3 5
Clayton Park Sq *JES* NE2 64 A6
Clayton Rd *JES* NE2 63 F6
Clayton St *BDLGTN* NE22 8 C2
CNUT NE1 2 C4
JRW NE32 86 A1 3
Clayton St West *CNUT* NE1 2 B5
Clayworth Rd *GOS/KPK* NE3 47 D3
Cleadon Hill Dr *HAR/WTLS* NE34 89 F5
Cleadon Hill Rd *HAR/WTLS* NE34 90 A4
Cleadon La *BOL* NE36 107 D2
CLDN/WHIT/ROK SR6 108 B1
Cleadon Mdw
CLDN/WHIT/ROK SR6 107 F1
Cleadon St *BYK/HTN/WLK* NE6 83 D2
Cleasby Gdns *LWF/SPW/WRK* NE9 99 E4
Cleaside Av *HAR/WTLS* NE34 89 F4
Cleehill Dr *NSHW* NE29 54 A4
Cleeve Ct *WASHS* NE38 138 B1 1
Cleghorn St *BYK/HTN/WLK* NE6 65 E6 1
Clement Av *BDLGTN* NE22 8 B3 1
Clementina Cl *ASHBK/HED/RY* SR2 5 F5 1
Clement St *LWF/SPW/WRK* NE9 99 E5 4
Clennel Av *HEBB* NE31 84 C3
Clent Wy *LGB/KIL* NE12 48 C6
Clephan St *DUN/TMV* NE11 97 E1
Clervaux Ter *JRW* NE32 86 B2
Cleveland Av *CLSW/PEL* DH2 153 D6
NSHW NE29 54 B5
Cleveland Crs *NSHW* NE29 54 C6 5
Cleveland Dr *WASHS* NE38 138 A3
Cleveland Gdns *LGB/HTN* NE7 64 C2 1
WLSD/HOW NE28 69 D3 1
Cleveland Pl *PLEE/EAS* SR8 208 A2
Cleveland Rd *MLFD/PNYW* SR4 143 E2
Cleveland St *SSH* NE33 71 F2
Cleveland Ter *NSHW* NE29 54 C6 6
Cleveland Vw
CLDN/WHIT/ROK SR6 109 D4
Clickemin *PONT/DH* NE20 28 C4
Clifford Rd *BYK/HTN/WLK* NE6 82 C3
Clifford St *BLAY* NE21 76 B5 1
BYK/HTN/WLK NE6 82 A2
CLS/BIR/GTL DH3 166 B1
MLFD/PNYW SR4 125 F6
TYNE/NSHE NE30 55 E6
Clifford Ter *CLS/BIR/GTL* DH3 166 B1
Cliff Rd *ASHBK/HED/RY* SR2 162 C2
Cliff Rw *WBAY* NE26 41 E6
Cliffside *HAR/WTLS* NE34 90 B2
Clifton Av *HAR/WTLS* NE34 89 D1
WLSD/HOW NE28 67 D4 2
Cliftonbourne Av
CLDN/WHIT/ROK SR6 109 D6 4
Clifton Cl *RYTON* NE40 75 D4 1
Clifton Gdns *BLYTH* NE24 16 C2 1
LWF/SPW/WRK NE9 99 E3
NSHW NE29 70 A3
Clifton Gv *MONK* NE25 40 A4
Clifton Rd *CLDN/WHIT/ROK* SR6 127 D1
CRAM NE23 22 B3
ELS/FEN NE4 79 D3
Clifton Sq *PLEE/EAS* SR8 208 C1
Clifton Ter *LGB/KIL* NE12 49 F5
SSH NE33 88 B1 1
WBAY NE26 41 D5
Cliftonville Av *ELS/FEN* NE4 79 D3
Cliftonville Gdns *WBAY* NE26 40 C4
Clinton Pl *GOS/KPK* NE3 47 D2 2
Clipsham Cl *LGB/KIL* NE12 49 D6 2
Clipstone Av *BYK/HTN/WLK* NE6 83 D5
Clipstone Cl
BW/LEM/TK/HW NE15 57 E4 2
Clive St *HAR/WTLS* NE34 87 F4
NSHW NE29 71 D1
Clockburn Lonnen
WICK/BNPF NE16 94 C5
Clockburnsyde Cl
WICK/BNPF NE16 95 D5 1
Clockmill Rd *GATE* NE8 97 F1
Clockstand Cl
CLDN/WHIT/ROK SR6 127 D2 2
Clockwell St *SWCK/CAS* SR5 125 E3 1
Cloister Av *HAR/WTLS* NE34 87 F3
Cloister Garth *LGB/HTN* NE7 64 B1 1
The Cloisters *ASHBK/HED/RY* SR2 144 C2
LGB/HTN NE7 64 B1 2
Cloister Wk *JRW* NE32 86 B1
Close *CNUT* NE1 2 D6
Closeburn Sq *SUNDSW* SR3 161 D2 1
Closefield Gv *MONK* NE25 40 A6
Close St *MLFD/PNYW* SR4 125 F5
SWCK/CAS SR5 126 A3 2
The Close *BLAY* NE21 93 F1 3
CLDN/WHIT/ROK SR6 107 E1
CRAM NE23 36 B1
HLH DH5 171 E2 2
PONT/DH NE20 28 A5
WD/WHPE/BLK NE5 60 A6 1
WICK/BNPF NE16 112 B5
Cloth Market *CNUT* NE1 2 D4
Clousden Dr *LGB/KIL* NE12 50 A3
Clousden Gra *LGB/KIL* NE12 50 A3 1
Clovelly Av *ELS/FEN* NE4 79 D3
Clovelly Gdns *BDLGTN* NE22 7 E4
WBAY NE26 40 C4
Clovelly Pl *JRW* NE32 87 D3
Clovelly Rd *SWCK/CAS* SR5 123 E1
Clover Av *BLAY* NE21 94 B4
FELL NE10 82 A6
Cloverdale *BDLGTN* NE22 7 D3 2
Cloverdale Gdns *LGB/HTN* NE7 65 D3
WICK/BNPF NE16 96 A5 3
Cloverfield Av *GOS/KPK* NE3 46 B6
Clover Hl *WICK/BNPF* NE16 113 F2
Cloverhill Av *HEBB* NE31 84 C5
Cloverhill Cl *CRAM* NE23 34 C1
Clover Laid *BDN/LAN/SAC* DH7 202 C5
Club La *DHAM* DH1 193 F3
Clumber St *ELS/FEN* NE4 79 F5
Clumber St North *ELS/FEN* NE4 79 F5 2
Clyde Av *HEBB* NE31 85 D5
Clydedale Av *LGB/KIL* NE12 49 E5
Clydesdale Av *HLS* DH4 157 D1
Clydesdale Garth *DHAM* DH1 180 C4 1
Clydesdale Rd *BYK/HTN/WLK* NE6 82 B3
Clydesdale St *HLH* DH5 185 F2
Clyde St *GATE* NE8 99 F2
Clyvedon Ri *HAR/WTLS* NE34 89 F5
Coach La *DIN/WO* NE13 32 A6
LGB/HTN NE7 65 E1
NSHW NE29 70 C1
Coach Open *WLSD/HOW* NE28 69 D5
Coach Rd *BW/LEM/TK/HW* NE15 57 E4
DUN/TMV NE11 98 A5
WASHN NE37 120 B2
WLSD/HOW NE28 67 E5
Coach Road Gn *FELL* NE10 82 B6
Coalbank Rd *HLH* DH5 185 E2
Coaley La *HLS* DH4 157 E5
Coalford La *RDHAMSE* DH6 184 A6
Coalford Rd *RDHAMSE* DH6 197 E4
Coalway Dr *WICK/BNPF* NE16 96 A2
Coalway La *WICK/BNPF* NE16 96 A2
Coalway La North
WICK/BNPF NE16 96 A1 2
Coanwood Dr *CRAM* NE23 22 A3
Coanwood Gdns *DUN/TMV* NE11 98 A5 1
Coanwood Rd
BW/LEM/TK/HW NE15 78 A4
Coanwood Wy *WICK/BNPF* NE16 114 A1
Coast Rd *BYK/HTN/WLK* NE6 65 E4
HAR/WTLS NE34 90 C1
NSHW NE29 53 F6
SSH NE33 72 B5
WLSD/HOW NE28 67 F2
Coates Cl *STLY/ANP* DH9 148 C2
Coatsworth Ct *GATE* NE8 81 D6 3
Coatsworth Rd *GATE* NE8 81 D6
Cobalt Cl *BW/LEM/TK/HW* NE15 59 E6 3
Cobbett Crs *HAR/WTLS* NE34 88 A5
Cobden Rd *CRAM* NE23 22 B4 1
Cobden St *GATE* NE8 99 F1
WLSD/HOW NE28 66 C4 1
Cobden Ter *GATE* NE8 99 F1
Cobham Pl *BYK/HTN/WLK* NE6 83 F4 3
Cobham Sq *SWCK/CAS* SR5 126 A2
Coble Dene *NSHW* NE29 70 A4
Coble Landing *SSH* NE33 71 D3 1
Coburg St *BLYTH* NE24 11 E5 2
GATE NE8 81 E6
TYNE/NSHE NE30 55 D6
Cochrane Park Av *LGB/HTN* NE7 65 E4
Cochrane St *ELS/FEN* NE4 79 D3
Cochran St *BLAY* NE21 76 B4 1
Cockburn Ter *NSHW* NE29 69 F3 1
Cocken La *CLS/BIR/GTL* DH3 168 A4
DHAM DH1 182 A1
Cocken Rd *CLS/BIR/GTL* DH3 180 C1
DHAM DH1 182 B1
Cockermouth Rd *SWCK/CAS* SR5 123 E1
Colbeck Av *WICK/BNPF* NE16 96 A1
Colbourne Av *CRAM* NE23 13 D5
Colbury Cl *CRAM* NE23 13 F4 1
Colby Ct *ELS/FEN* NE4 80 A4
Colchester St *HAR/WTLS* NE34 87 F4
Colchester Ter *MLFD/PNYW* SR4 143 E1
Coldbeck Ct *CRAM* NE23 22 B3 4
Coldingham Ct *BDN/LAN/SAC* DH7 178 A1
Coldingham Gdns
WD/WHPE/BLK NE5 61 F4 2
Coldside Gdns *WD/WHPE/BLK* NE5 59 D4
Coldstream *CLSW/PEL* DH2 135 E4
Coldstream Av *SWCK/CAS* SR5 126 A2 3
Coldstream Cl *HLS* DH4 157 D3 2
Coldstream Dr *BLAY* NE21 93 F2
Coldstream Gdns *WLSD/HOW* NE28 68 B3
Coldstream Rd
BW/LEM/TK/HW NE15 78 A2
Coldstream Wy *NSHW* NE29 53 E4 2
Coldwell Cl *RDHAMSE* DH6 187 D5
Coldwell La *FELL* NE10 100 B3
Coldwell Park Av *FELL* NE10 100 B3
Coldwell Park Dr *FELL* NE10 100 B3
Coldwell St *FELL* NE10 100 C2
Colebridge Cl
WD/WHPE/BLK NE5 61 E3 3
Colebrooke *CLS/BIR/GTL* DH3 136 C4
Cole Gdns *FELL* NE10 101 F2
Colegate *FELL* NE10 101 E3
Colegate West *FELL* NE10 101 D3
Colepeth *FELL* NE10 101 D3
Coleridge Av *LWF/SPW/WRK* NE9 99 D6
SSH NE33 72 A5
Coleridge Rd *SWCK/CAS* SR5 124 A2 1
Coleridge Sq *HEBB* NE31 85 D2 1
Coley Hill Cl *WD/WHPE/BLK* NE5 59 E2 1
Coley Ter *CLDN/WHIT/ROK* SR6 127 D1
Colgrove Wy *GOS/KPK* NE3 62 B1 3
Colima Av *SWCK/CAS* SR5 124 B3 3
Colin Pl *BYK/HTN/WLK* NE6 66 C6 1
Colin Ter *ASHBK/HED/RY* SR2 162 B2
College Burn Rd *SUNDSW* SR3 160 A3
College Cl *FELL* NE10 100 C4 1
College Dr *SSH* NE33 72 A6 1
College La *LGB/HTN* NE7 49 E6
College Rd *HEBB* NE31 84 C5
College St *CNUT* NE1 3 E1
Collier Cl *BW/LEM/TK/HW* NE15 57 F5 2
Collierley La *STLY/ANP* DH9 128 B5
Colliery La *ELS/FEN* NE4 80 A3 2
HLH DH5 186 A2

Colliery Rd DUN/TMV NE11 79 E6
Collin Av HAR/WTLS NE34 90 A3
Collingwood Av WLSD/HOW NE28 67 D2
Collingwood Dr HLS DH4 156 C2
Collingwood Gdns FELL NE10 82 C6
Collingwood Rd MONK NE25 38 C5 1
Collingwood St CNUT NE1 2 D5
HEBB NE31 85 F2 1
HLH DH5 171 F4 1
SSH NE33 71 E6
SWCK/CAS SR5 126 A2 4
Collingwood Ter BLYTH NE24 11 D5
Collingwood Vw NSHW NE29 70 B1
Collywell Bay Rd WBAY NE26 26 C2
Collywell Ct WBAY NE26 26 C2 1
Colman Av HAR/WTLS NE34 87 F3
Colnbrook Cl GOS/KPK NE3 45 F5
Colombo Rd SWCK/CAS SR5 123 E3
Colston Ri PLEE/EAS SR8 208 B1
Colston St ELS/FEN NE4 78 C3
Colston Wy MONK NE25 39 F3
Coltere Av BOL NE36 107 D3
Colton Gdns LWF/SPW/WRK NE9 117 F1
Coltpark WD/WHPE/BLK NE5 60 B5 2
Coltsfoot Gdns FELL NE10 100 B5
Coltspool DUN/TMV NE11 116 C6
Columba St SWCK/CAS SR5 126 A2 5
Columba Wk GOS/KPK NE3 63 F1
Columbia Gra GOS/KPK NE3 62 A1 2
Columbia Ter BLYTH NE24 11 D6 2
Colville Ct STLY/ANP DH9 149 D2
Colwell Pl WD/WHPE/BLK NE5 78 B1 2
Colwell Rd SMOOR NE27 52 B2
Colwyne Pl WD/WHPE/BLK NE5 61 D4
Combe Dr BW/LEM/TK/HW NE15 76 A1
Comet Dr PLEE/EAS SR8 200 B2 1
Comet Rw LGB/KIL NE12 49 E2
Comet Sq SUNDSW SR3 160 C1 3
Comical Cnr SSH NE33 71 D2
Comma Ct DUN/TMV NE11 98 A3
Commercial Rd
ASHBK/HED/RY SR2 145 E2
BYK/HTN/WLK NE6 82 B3
GOS/KPK NE3 64 A1 4
JRW NE32 69 E6 1
SSH NE33 71 D5
Commercial St BLAY NE21 94 A1
Commissioners' Whf NSHW NE29 70 B4
Compton Av HAR/WTLS NE34 88 C1
Compton Rd NSHW NE29 70 B1
Concorde Wy JRW NE32 86 A2
Condercum Ct
BW/LEM/TK/HW NE15 78 B3 1
Condercum Rd ELS/FEN NE4 78 C3
Cone St SSH NE33 71 D4
Congburn Bank
BDN/LAN/SAC DH7 164 A2
Conhope La BW/LEM/TK/HW NE15 78 C3
Conifer Cl DHAM DH1 195 F3 2
Coniscliffe Av GOS/KPK NE3 62 B3
Coniscliffe Rd STLY/ANP DH9 147 F3
Conishead Ter RDHAMSE DH6 187 E4
Coniston CLS/BIR/GTL DH3 136 C5
FELL NE10 101 F2
Coniston Av HEBB NE31 85 E3
HLH DH5 186 B4
JES NE2 64 A4 1
SWCK/CAS SR5 108 B6
WICK/BNPF NE16 96 C3 2
Coniston Cl DHAM DH1 197 D2
LGB/KIL NE12 49 E1 1
PLEE/EAS SR8 209 D2 2
Coniston Crs BLAY NE21 94 A2 2
Coniston Dr BDN/LAN/SAC DH7 164 A6
JRW NE32 86 C5
Coniston Gdns
LWF/SPW/WRK NE9 100 A5
Coniston Pl LWF/SPW/WRK NE9 100 A5 1
Coniston Rd BLYTH NE24 9 E3
TYNE/NSHE NE30 54 B2
WLSD/HOW NE28 68 B2
Connaught Cl HLS DH4 157 E3 1
Connaught Ter JRW NE32 86 A2
Conningsby Cl GOS/KPK NE3 47 F4
Consett Rd DUN/TMV NE11 97 E5
Constable Cl RYTON NE40 74 B4
STLY/ANP DH9 148 B2
Constable Gdns HAR/WTLS NE34 88 B5
Constance St CLSW/PEL DH2 152 A1
Content St BLAY NE21 94 B1
Conway Cl BDLGTN NE22 6 C3
RYTON NE40 74 C5
Conway Dr LGB/HTN NE7 64 C2
Conway Gdns SUNDSW SR3 159 F1 11
WLSD/HOW NE28 66 C2
Conway Gv WBAY NE26 26 A1
Conway Pl CLSW/PEL DH2 135 E6
Conway Rd SWCK/CAS SR5 123 E2
Conway Sq LWF/SPW/WRK NE9 99 F2 2
SWCK/CAS SR5 123 E2 3
Conyers Av CLSW/PEL DH2 153 D3
Conyers Gdns CLSW/PEL DH2 153 D3
Conyers Pl CLSW/PEL DH2 153 D3
Conyers Rd BYK/HTN/WLK NE6 82 B2
CLSW/PEL DH2 153 D3
Cook Cl SSH NE33 71 D6
Cook Crs SEA/MUR SR7 188 A1
Cooke's Wd BDN/LAN/SAC DH7 192 B6
Cook Gdns FELL NE10 102 A2
Cookson Cl ELS/FEN NE4 80 A3 3
Cookson's La CNUT NE1 2 C6
Cookson St ELS/FEN NE4 79 F3 4
Cookson Ter CLSW/PEL DH2 153 D5
Cook Sq SWCK/CAS SR5 123 F2 3
Cooks Wd WASHS NE38 138 C3
Cook Wy PLEE/EAS SR8 207 D1
Coomassie Rd BLYTH NE24 11 D5
Coomside CRAM NE23 22 B4 2
Co-operative Ter
MLFD/PNYW SR4 143 F1 2
STLY/ANP DH9 128 B6
Cooper Sq DHAM DH1 195 E3
Cooper St CLDN/WHIT/ROK SR6 127 D3 2
Copeland Ct DHAM DH1 193 F6
Copland Ter JES NE2 3 G2
Copley Av HAR/WTLS NE34 88 B6
Copley Dr SUNDSW SR3 144 A4
Copperas La
BW/LEM/TK/HW NE15 77 E1 2
Copperfield DHAM DH1 204 C1 1
Coppergate Ct HEBB NE31 85 E1
Coppice Wy JES NE2 3 G1
Coppy La STLY/ANP DH9 132 B3
WICK/BNPF NE16 132 A1
The Copse BLAY NE21 77 E6
WICK/BNPF NE16 111 E6
Coquet WASHS NE38 137 E5
Coquet Av BLYTH NE24 17 D1 5
GOS/KPK NE3 47 D6
HAR/WTLS NE34 72 C6
WBAY NE26 40 C5
Coquetdale Av BYK/HTN/WLK NE6 83 F2
Coquet Dr CLSW/PEL DH2 135 D6
Coquet Gdns STLY/ANP DH9 148 A4 1
Coquet Gv BW/LEM/TK/HW NE15 57 E5
Coquet St CNUT NE1 3 H3 1
CNUT NE1 81 F2 4
HEBB NE31 84 C2 1
JRW NE32 85 F3
Coquet Ter BYK/HTN/WLK NE6 65 D5
CRAM NE23 34 B2
Corbiere Cl SUNDSW SR3 160 A2
Corbitt St GATE NE8 98 B1
Corbridge Cl WLSD/HOW NE28 52 A6
Corbridge Rd BYK/HTN/WLK NE6 82 B2
Corbridge St BYK/HTN/WLK NE6 82 A2
Corby Gdns BYK/HTN/WLK NE6 83 E2
Corby Ga ASHBK/HED/RY SR2 144 C2 2
Corby Gv PLEE/EAS SR8 207 F5
Corby Hall Dr
ASHBK/HED/RY SR2 144 C2 3
Corchester Rd BDLGTN NE22 7 D2
Corchester Wk LGB/HTN NE7 65 D2
Corinthian Sq SWCK/CAS SR5 123 F2 4
Cork St SUND SR1 5 E2
Cormorant Cl BLYTH NE24 17 E2
Cornbank Cl SUNDSW SR3 160 C3
Corndean WASHS NE38 139 F2
Cornelia Ter SEA/MUR SR7 176 B3
Cornel Rd LGB/HTN NE7 65 D3
Corney St SSH NE33 88 A1
The Cornfields HEBB NE31 85 D2
Cornforth Cl FELL NE10 102 B4
Cornhill Av GOS/KPK NE3 46 B5 1
Cornhill Crs NSHW NE29 53 F5
Cornhill Rd CRAM NE23 22 A2
SWCK/CAS SR5 126 A2 6
Corn Mill Dr HLH DH5 170 C4
Cornmoor Gdns WICK/BNPF NE16 96 A5
Cornmoor Rd WICK/BNPF NE16 96 A4
Cornthwaite Dr
CLDN/WHIT/ROK SR6 109 E2 1
Cornwallis Sq SSH NE33 71 D5 1
Cornwallis St SSH NE33 71 E3 4
Cornwall Rd HEBB NE31 85 E5 1
Cornwell Ct LGB/HTN NE7 64 B2 1
Cornwell Crs BDLGTN NE22 8 A4 1
Coronation Av DHAM DH1 196 C2
Coronation Gn HLH DH5 186 C4 1
Coronation Rd WD/WHPE/BLK NE5 59 D3
WICK/BNPF NE16 114 A2
Coronation Sq RDHAMSE DH6 188 A5
Coronation St CLS/BIR/GTL DH3 153 F6
NSHW NE29 70 C2 1
SUND SR1 5 E2 1
WLSD/HOW NE28 67 E4
Coronation Ter
MLFD/PNYW SR4 124 A6 1
Corporation Rd
ASHBK/HED/RY SR2 145 E2
Corporation St ELS/FEN NE4 2 A4
Corriedale Cl DHAM DH1 180 B4 1
Corrofell Gdns FELL NE10 83 D6
Corry Ct MLFD/PNYW SR4 143 D2 2
Corsair WICK/BNPF NE16 95 E4
Corsenside WD/WHPE/BLK NE5 60 B5
Corstorphine Town SSH NE33 71 D6
Cortina Av MLFD/PNYW SR4 142 C2
Cossack Ter MLFD/PNYW SR4 125 D5
Cosserat Pl HEBB NE31 84 C1 4
Cosser St BLYTH NE24 16 A2 2
Coston Dr SSH NE33 71 E3
Cosyn St BYK/HTN/WLK NE6 81 F3 2
Cotehill Rd WD/WHPE/BLK NE5 61 D5 2
Cotemede FELL NE10 101 F5
The Cotgarth FELL NE10 101 D3 1
Cotherstone Ct SUNDSW SR3 144 A4
Cotherstone Rd DHAM DH1 180 C6
Cotman Gdns HAR/WTLS NE34 88 C6
Cotsford La PLEE/EAS SR8 209 F2
Cotswold Av LGB/KIL NE12 49 D3 1
Cotswold Cl WASHS NE38 138 A2
Cotswold Dr MONK NE25 54 B1
Cotswold Gdns DUN/TMV NE11 97 F3
LGB/HTN NE7 64 C3
Cotswold La BOLCOL NE35 87 D6
Cotswold Pl PLEE/EAS SR8 208 A1
Cotswold Rd NSHW NE29 54 A2
SWCK/CAS SR5 123 F2
Cotswold Sq SWCK/CAS SR5 123 F1 9
Cotswold Ter STLY/ANP DH9 148 C3
Cottage La WD/WHPE/BLK NE5 61 F5
Cottages Rd SEA/MUR SR7 176 C4
Cottenham Chare ELS/FEN NE4 80 A3 4
Cottenham St ELS/FEN NE4 80 A3 5
Cotterdale WLSD/HOW NE28 66 B1 1
Cotter Riggs Pl
WD/WHPE/BLK NE5 59 D4
Cottersdale Gdns
WD/WHPE/BLK NE5 59 D3
Cottingham Cl PLEE/EAS SR8 208 A1
Cottingwood Gn BLYTH NE24 16 A3
Cottonwood SUNDSW SR3 160 A3 2
Coulthards La GATE NE8 81 F5
Coulthards Pl GATE NE8 81 F4 2
Coulton Dr BOL NE36 106 C3 3
Council Av HLS DH4 157 D2 1
Counden Rd WD/WHPE/BLK NE5 60 A3 3
Countess Av WBAY NE26 40 C5
Countess Dr BW/LEM/TK/HW NE15 77 F1
Coupland Gv JRW NE32 85 F5
Courtfield Rd BYK/HTN/WLK NE6 66 B6
Court La DHAM DH1 194 C5
Courtney Dr SUNDSW SR3 143 E6
Court Rd BDLGTN NE22 7 E3
The Court WICK/BNPF NE16 96 B4
The Courtyard STLY/ANP DH9 130 B6
Cousin St SUND SR1 5 F2
Coutts Rd BYK/HTN/WLK NE6 66 A6
Coventry Gdns ELS/FEN NE4 79 D4
NSHW NE29 70 A2 1
Coventry Rd DHAM DH1 180 C5
Coverdale FELL NE10 101 F4
WLSD/HOW NE28 66 B1
Coverdale Av BLYTH NE24 9 F5 2
Coverley Rd SWCK/CAS SR5 123 F1
The Covers LGB/KIL NE12 50 A6
The Cove HLS DH4 157 D2
Cowan Cl BLAY NE21 75 F4
Cowans Av LGB/KIL NE12 35 E6 3
Cowan Ter ASHBK/HED/RY SR2 4 B4
Cowdray Rd SWCK/CAS SR5 124 A2
Cowell Gv ROWG NE39 110 B2
Cowell St PLEE/EAS SR8 209 E1 1
Cowen Gdns LWF/SPW/WRK NE9 117 F3
Cowen Rd BLAY NE21 76 C5
Cowen St BYK/HTN/WLK NE6 83 E2 2
Cowley Pl BLYTH NE24 10 A4
Cowley Rd BLYTH NE24 10 A3
Cowley St RDHAMSE DH6 206 C2 2
Cowpen Hall Rd BLYTH NE24 9 F4
Cowpen Rd BLYTH NE24 9 F4 1
Coxfoot Cl HAR/WTLS NE34 88 B3 6
Coxgreen Rd HLS DH4 139 F6
Coxlodge Rd GOS/KPK NE3 62 C1
Coxlodge Ter GOS/KPK NE3 62 C1
Coxon St ASHBK/HED/RY SR2 5 E4
FELL NE10 84 A6
Cradock Av HEBB NE31 84 C4 1
Craggyknowe WASHN NE37 119 E6
Craghall Dene GOS/KPK NE3 64 A2 3
Craghall Dene Av JES NE2 64 A2 4
Craghead La STLY/ANP DH9 150 A5
Cragleas WICK/BNPF NE16 129 F2
Cragside BDN/LAN/SAC DH7 178 A4
CLSW/PEL DH2 152 C4
CRAM NE23 22 A4
HAR/WTLS NE34 90 A3
LGB/HTN NE7 65 D3
WBAY NE26 40 A3
Cragside Av NSHW NE29 53 F4
Cragside Gdns DUN/TMV NE11 97 F5
LGB/KIL NE12 36 B6 1
WLSD/HOW NE28 68 B3 1
Cragside Rd WASHN NE37 119 F5
Cragston Av WD/WHPE/BLK NE5 61 E3
Cragston Cl WD/WHPE/BLK NE5 61 E4 1
Cragton Gdns BLYTH NE24 10 A5 1
Craigavon Rd SWCK/CAS SR5 124 A3
Craig Crs CRAM NE23 34 C2
Craighill HLS DH4 156 C2 1
Craigmillar Av WD/WHPE/BLK NE5 61 E3
Craigmillar Cl WD/WHPE/BLK NE5 61 D3
Craigmill Pk BLYTH NE24 9 F4
Craigshaw Rd SWCK/CAS SR5 123 E1 7

Craigwell Dr *SUNDSW* SR3 160 C4
Craik Av *HAR/WTLS* NE34 88 A3
Crake Wy *WASHS* NE38 137 E4
Cramer St *GATE* NE8 99 E1
Cramlington Rd *SWCK/CAS* SR5 123 E3
Cramlington Sq *SWCK/CAS* SR5 123 E2 4
Cramlington Ter *BLYTH* NE24 16 B2 2
Cramond Ct *LWF/SPW/WRK* NE9 117 D1
Cramond Wy *CRAM* NE23 22 A4
Cranberry Rd *SWCK/CAS* SR5 123 F2
Cranberry Sq *SWCK/CAS* SR5 123 F2 5
Cranborne *SUNDSW* SR3 159 E2
Cranbourne Gv
TYNE/NSHE NE30 55 D1 1
Cranbrook Av *GOS/KPK* NE3 47 E5
Cranbrook Ct *GOS/KPK* NE3 46 A5
Cranbrook Pl
BW/LEM/TK/HW NE15 78 A4 1
Cranbrook Rd
BW/LEM/TK/HW NE15 78 A4
Craneswater Av *WBAY* NE26 40 B1
Cranfield Pl
BW/LEM/TK/HW NE15 76 B1 3
Cranford St *HAR/WTLS* NE34 88 B2
Cranford Ter *MLFD/PNYW* SR4 143 F1 3
Cranham Cl *LGB/KIL* NE12 36 B6 2
Cranleigh Av *DIN/WO* NE13 45 D5
Cranleigh Pl *MONK* NE25 39 F3
Cranleigh Rd *SWCK/CAS* SR5 123 F2
Cranshaw Pl *CRAM* NE23 22 B3 5
Crantock Rd *GOS/KPK* NE3 62 B1 4
Cranwell Dr *DIN/WO* NE13 33 D4
Craster Av *HAR/WTLS* NE34 73 D6 1
LGB/KIL NE12 50 B3
SMOOR NE27 52 A1
Craster Cl *BLYTH* NE24 10 B5
CLSW/PEL DH2 165 E1
MONK NE25 39 F4
Craster Gdns *WLSD/HOW* NE28 68 B3 2
Craster Rd *NSHW* NE29 69 F1 2
Craster Sq *GOS/KPK* NE3 46 C6
Craster Ter *LGB/HTN* NE7 65 D4
Crawford Av *PLEE/EAS* SR8 200 C6
Crawford Cl *RDHAMSE* DH6 197 E5 2
Crawford Ct *SUNDSW* SR3 160 B2 1
Crawford Pl *MONK* NE25 40 A6
Crawford St *BLYTH* NE24 10 C3
Crawford Ter *BYK/HTN/WLK* NE6 83 E3
Crawhall Rd *CNUT* NE1 3 H3
Crawlaw Rd *PLEE/EAS* SR8 200 C1
Crawley Av *HEBB* NE31 84 C5
Crawley Gdns *WICK/BNPF* NE16 96 B3 1
Crawley Rd *WLSD/HOW* NE28 67 D5
Crawley Sq *HEBB* NE31 84 C5
Craythorne Gdns
BYK/HTN/WLK NE6 65 E4
Creeverlea *WASHS* NE38 138 B3
Creighton Av *GOS/KPK* NE3 62 A3
Creland Wy *WD/WHPE/BLK* NE5 61 E3 4
The Crescent *BDN/LAN/SAC* DH7 178 A3
BW/LEM/TK/HW NE15 57 F4 1
CLDN/WHIT/ROK SR6 107 E2
CLSW/PEL DH2 153 D5
CLSW/PEL DH2 165 F3
CRAM NE23 36 B1
DHAM DH1 193 F3
DIN/WO NE13 45 D6
HAR/WTLS NE34 89 E4
HLS DH4 156 C3
HLS DH4 157 F4
HLS DH4 183 E2
JRW NE32 85 F4
LGB/HTN NE7 65 D1
PLEE/EAS SR8 201 D1
RDHAMSE DH6 197 E5
ROWG NE39 111 E2
RYTON NE40 74 C3
STLY/ANP DH9 130 C6
SUNDSW SR3 143 F5
TYNE/NSHE NE30 55 E4
WICK/BNPF NE16 96 B4
WLSD/HOW NE28 67 D3
Crescent Wy North *LGB/KIL* NE12 50 A4
Crescent Wy South *LGB/KIL* NE12 50 A4
Cressbourne Av
CLDN/WHIT/ROK SR6 109 D6 5
Cresswell Av *LGB/KIL* NE12 50 A3
NSHW NE29 54 B5
PLEE/EAS SR8 209 F2
WBAY NE26 26 B2
Cresswell Cl *BLAY* NE21 93 F2 4
MONK NE25 54 A1
Cresswell Dr *BLYTH* NE24 16 A1
GOS/KPK NE3 46 A5
Cresswell Rd *WLSD/HOW* NE28 66 C5
Cresswell St *BYK/HTN/WLK* NE6 82 C2 3
BYK/HTN/WLK NE6 82 C3 2
The Crest *BDLGTN* NE22 7 D3
DIN/WO NE13 31 D3
WBAY NE26 26 C4
Crichton Av *CLS/BIR/GTL* DH3 166 C1
Cricklewood Dr *HLS* DH4 157 E2 1
HLS DH4 157 D1 2
Cricklewood Rd *SWCK/CAS* SR5 123 E3
Criddle St *GATE* NE8 81 F4
Crieff Gv *JRW* NE32 86 C5
Crieff Sq *SWCK/CAS* SR5 123 E2 5
Crigdon Hl *WD/WHPE/BLK* NE5 60 B5
Crighton *WASHS* NE38 137 F1
Crimdon Gv *HLS* DH4 170 B3 1
Crindledykes *WASHS* NE38 139 D4
Cripps Av *FELL* NE10 102 A2
Croft Av *LGB/KIL* NE12 50 A5
WLSD/HOW NE28 67 E4 2
Croft Cl *RYTON* NE40 74 C4
Croftdale Rd *BLAY* NE21 76 A6
Crofter Cl *CRAM* NE23 34 C1
Crofthead Dr *CRAM* NE23 22 A4
Crofton St *BLYTH* NE24 11 D5 4
HAR/WTLS NE34 88 B2
Crofton Wy *BW/LEM/TK/HW* NE15 76 A1
Croft Rigg *BDN/LAN/SAC* DH7 202 C5
Croft Rd *BLYTH* NE24 11 D5
Croftside Av *CLDN/WHIT/ROK* SR6 109 E2
Croft St *CNUT* NE1 3 E3
Croftsway *ELS/FEN* NE4 79 E4 4
Croft Ter *JRW* NE32 86 A2
The Croft *GOS/KPK* NE3 62 C2
LGB/KIL NE12 36 A6
Cromarty *CLSW/PEL* DH2 135 E4
Cromarty St *CLDN/WHIT/ROK* SR6 126 C2
Cromdale Pl *WD/WHPE/BLK* NE5 61 D5
Cromer Av *LWF/SPW/WRK* NE9 117 E1
Cromer Gdns *WBAY* NE26 40 C4
Crompton Rd *BYK/HTN/WLK* NE6 65 D5
Cromwell Av *BLAY* NE21 76 A6
Cromwell Ct *BLAY* NE21 75 F4
Cromwell Rd *FELL* NE10 84 A6
WICK/BNPF NE16 96 B2
Cromwell St *GATE* NE8 99 F1
MLFD/PNYW SR4 125 F5
Cromwell Ter *GATE* NE8 98 C1
Crondall St *SSH* NE33 88 C1
Cronin Av *HAR/WTLS* NE34 87 F4
Crookham Wy *CRAM* NE23 22 B4
Cropthorne *FELL* NE10 102 A4 3
Cross Av *WLSD/HOW* NE28 66 B2
Crossbank Rd *WD/WHPE/BLK* NE5 61 F3
Crossbrook Rd
WD/WHPE/BLK NE5 61 F4 3
Crossby Ct *ASHBK/HED/RY* SR2 5 G5
Crossfield *BDN/LAN/SAC* DH7 178 B2
Crossfield Pk *FELL* NE10 100 B4
Crossfield Ter *BYK/HTN/WLK* NE6 83 F4 4
Crossgate *DHAM* DH1 194 A5
SSH NE33 71 E4
Crossgate Moor Gdns *DHAM* DH1 193 E4
Crossgate Peth *DHAM* DH1 193 F5
Crossgate Rd *HLH* DH5 185 F2 2
Crosshill Rd *BW/LEM/TK/HW* NE15 78 A4
Cross Keys La *LWF/SPW/WRK* NE9 99 E5
Cross La *BDN/LAN/SAC* DH7 164 B6
DUN/TMV NE11 78 C6
DUN/TMV NE11 115 F1
WICK/BNPF NE16 96 B2
Crosslaw *WD/WHPE/BLK* NE5 60 B5
Crosslea Av *SUNDSW* SR3 144 A3
Crossley Ter *ELS/FEN* NE4 79 E2 2
LGB/KIL NE12 50 B3
Cross Morpeth St *JES* NE2 63 D6 1
Cross Pde *ELS/FEN* NE4 80 A4 3
Cross Pl *SUND* SR1 5 E2 2
Cross Rigg Cl *HLS* DH4 156 C1 1
Cross Rw *GATE* NE8 100 A1
Cross St *BYK/HTN/WLK* NE6 81 F3
CNUT NE1 2 B4
GATE NE8 99 E1 4
HLS DH4 169 F2 2
HLS DH4 170 C1 1
Cross Ter *ROWG* NE39 110 C3 1
Cross Vale Rd *ASHBK/HED/RY* SR2 144 B2
Cross Villa Place No 4
ELS/FEN NE4 80 A3 6
Cross Villa Place No 5
ELS/FEN NE4 80 A3 7
Crossway *HAR/WTLS* NE34 89 F3 1
JES NE2 64 A3
LWF/SPW/WRK NE9 99 F4
TYNE/NSHE NE30 55 E4
Crossways *BOL* NE36 107 D3 2
SUNDSW SR3 160 B1
The Crossway
BW/LEM/TK/HW NE15 76 C1 2
The Cross Wy *GOS/KPK* NE3 62 B2
Croudace Rw *FELL* NE10 100 C2 1
Crow Bank *WLSD/HOW* NE28 67 E4
Crow Hall La *CRAM* NE23 21 E1
Crowhall La *FELL* NE10 100 C2
Crow Hall Rd *CRAM* NE23 13 E5
Crow La *SUNDSW* SR3 159 D1
Crowley Av *WICK/BNPF* NE16 96 B2 1
Crowley Gdns *BLAY* NE21 76 B6 2
Crowley Rd *WICK/BNPF* NE16 95 F1
Crown Rd *SWCK/CAS* SR5 125 F4
Crown St *BLYTH* NE24 11 E5 3
Crowther Rd *WASHS* NE38 137 E1
Crowtree Rd *SUND* SR1 4 B2
Crowtree Ter *SUND* SR1 4 B3
Croydon Rd *ELS/FEN* NE4 79 F2
Crozier St *SWCK/CAS* SR5 126 B3 2
Crudwell Cl *BOLCOL* NE35 87 D6 4
Crummock Av
CLDN/WHIT/ROK SR6 108 B6
Crummock Rd *WD/WHPE/BLK* NE5 61 D6
Crumstone Ct *LGB/KIL* NE12 36 A6
Cuba St *ASHBK/HED/RY* SR2 145 D2
Cuillin Cl *WASHS* NE38 138 A3
Culford Pl *WLSD/HOW* NE28 52 A6
Cullercoats Rd *SWCK/CAS* SR5 123 E3 5
Cullercoats St
BYK/HTN/WLK NE6 83 D3 1
Culloden Wk *LGB/KIL* NE12 35 F6 6
Cumberland Av *BDLGTN* NE22 7 D3 3
Cumberland Pl *CLS/BIR/GTL* DH3 136 C5
HAR/WTLS NE34 90 A1
Cumberland Rd *NSHW* NE29 53 D5
SUNDSW SR3 143 F6
Cumberland St *SUND* SR1 4 C1 1
WLSD/HOW NE28 67 E4
WLSD/HOW NE28 69 D5 2
Cumberland Wk *LGB/HTN* NE7 65 D2 1
Cumberland Wy *WASHN* NE37 120 C2 1
Cumbrian Av
CLDN/WHIT/ROK SR6 108 B5 2
Cumbrian Wy *PLEE/EAS* SR8 209 D2
Cumbria Pl *STLY/ANP* DH9 148 C1
Cummings Av *RDHAMSE* DH6 197 E4
Cummings St *BLYTH* NE24 11 D4 3
Cunningham Pl *DHAM* DH1 195 E3 1
Curlew Cl *LGB/KIL* NE12 48 C5 1
RYTON NE40 75 D4 2
WASHS NE38 137 F4
Curlew Rd *JRW* NE32 69 E6
Curlew Wy *BLYTH* NE24 17 D2
Curtis Rd *ELS/FEN* NE4 79 E1
Curzon Pl *WD/WHPE/BLK* NE5 61 D4 6
Curzon Rd West
WLSD/HOW NE28 67 D5 5
Curzon St *GATE* NE8 98 C2
Cushat Cl *BYK/HTN/WLK* NE6 82 B3
Cushy Cow La *RYTON* NE40 74 C4
Cut Bank *CNUT* NE1 81 F3
Cuthbert Av *DHAM* DH1 195 F5
Cuthbert Cl *DHAM* DH1 196 A5
Cuthbert Ct *JRW* NE32 87 D2
Cuthbertson Cl
CLDN/WHIT/ROK SR6 109 D5 1
Cuthbert St *GATE* NE8 98 C1 3
WICK/BNPF NE16 113 F3
Cygnet Cl *WD/WHPE/BLK* NE5 59 F2
Cyncopa Wy *WD/WHPE/BLK* NE5 61 F4
Cypress Av *ELS/FEN* NE4 61 F6
Cypress Ct *BDN/LAN/SAC* DH7 203 D5 1
Cypress Crs *BLYTH* NE24 11 D5
DUN/TMV NE11 97 E2
Cypress Dr *BLYTH* NE24 11 D5
Cypress Gdns *BLYTH* NE24 11 D5
Cypress Gv *DHAM* DH1 195 F3
RYTON NE40 74 B2 1
Cypress Rd *BLAY* NE21 76 B6
LWF/SPW/WRK NE9 118 C2 1
Cypress Sq *SUNDSW* SR3 143 F6 2
Cyprus Gdns *LWF/SPW/WRK* NE9 99 F4 3

D

Dachet Rd *MONK* NE25 39 F3
Dacre Rd *CLDN/WHIT/ROK* SR6 108 C6
Dacre St *SSH* NE33 71 E6
Dahlia Ct *MLFD/PNYW* SR4 126 A5
Dahlia Pl *ELS/FEN* NE4 61 F6
Dainton Cl *HLS* DH4 157 E4
Dairy La *HLS* DH4 170 C2
Dalden Gv *SEA/MUR* SR7 176 C2
Dalegarth *WASHN* NE37 120 A6
Dalegarth Gv
CLDN/WHIT/ROK SR6 108 B5 3
Dale Rd *MONK* NE25 39 F6
Daleside *BDN/LAN/SAC* DH7 164 B6
Dale St *BLYTH* NE24 11 D3
SSH NE33 71 F3
Dale Ter *CLDN/WHIT/ROK* SR6 127 D1
Dale Top *MONK* NE25 38 A1
Dalla St *MLFD/PNYW* SR4 123 F5 1
Dalmahoy *WASHN* NE37 120 C1
Dalmatia Ter *BLYTH* NE24 11 D6
Dalston Pl *BLYTH* NE24 17 D2 1
Dalton Cl *CRAM* NE23 22 A2 2
Dalton Ct *WLSD/HOW* NE28 66 B1
Dalton Pl *WD/WHPE/BLK* NE5 59 E3
Daltons La *SSH* NE33 71 D4
Dalton St *BYK/HTN/WLK* NE6 82 A2 4
Dame Dorothy St
CLDN/WHIT/ROK SR6 126 C4
Dame Flora Robson Av
HAR/WTLS NE34 87 E4
Danby Cl *SUNDSW* SR3 161 D2 2
WASHS NE38 137 E6
Danby Gdns *BYK/HTN/WLK* NE6 65 F5 1
Danville Rd *CLDN/WHIT/ROK* SR6 109 D6
Daphne Crs *SEA/MUR* SR7 176 B5
Darden Cl *LGB/KIL* NE12 36 B6 3
Darden Lough *WD/WHPE/BLK* NE5 60 B5

Darien Av CLDN/WHIT/ROK SR6 ...... 108 C6
Darley Ct CLSW/PEL DH2 ...... 165 F5
Darley Pl BW/LEM/TK/HW NE15 ...... 77 F3
Darlington Rd DHAM DH1 ...... 193 F6
Darras Ct SSH NE33 ...... 71 F5
Darras Dr NSHW NE29 ...... 53 E5
Darrell St DIN/WO NE13 ...... 32 C4
Dartford Rd CLDN/WHIT/ROK SR6 .. 108 C6
SSH NE33 ...... 72 B4
Dartmouth Av
LWF/SPW/WRK NE9 ...... 117 E1
Dartmouth Cl SEA/MUR SR7 ...... 175 F4 2
Dart Rd PLEE/EAS SR8 ...... 208 B3
Darvall Cl MONK NE25 ...... 39 F3
Darwin Crs GOS/KPK NE3 ...... 62 B3
Darwin St SWCK/CAS SR5 ...... 125 E3
Daryl Cl BLAY NE21 ...... 93 F1 4
Daryl Wy FELL NE10 ...... 102 C3 1
Davenport Dr GOS/KPK NE3 ...... 47 D3
David Gdns CLDN/WHIT/ROK SR6 .... 127 E1
Davidson Rd FELL NE10 ...... 84 A6
Davidson St FELL NE10 ...... 100 C2 2
David St WLSD/HOW NE28 ...... 67 D5
Davison Av SUNDSW SR3 ...... 161 D1
WBAY NE26 ...... 40 B4
Davison Crs SEA/MUR SR7 ...... 174 A6
Davison St BLYTH NE24 ...... 11 D4 4
BOLCOL NE35 ...... 105 D1
BW/LEM/TK/HW NE15 ...... 58 A6
Davis Ter PLEE/EAS SR8 ...... 200 C3
Davy Bank WLSD/HOW NE28 ...... 67 F5
Davy Dr PLEE/EAS SR8 ...... 199 E6
Dawdon Crs SEA/MUR SR7 ...... 176 C4
Dawlish Cl SEA/MUR SR7 ...... 175 F4
Dawlish Gdns LWF/SPW/WRK NE9 .. 117 E1
Dawlish Pl WD/WHPE/BLK NE5 ...... 59 E3
Dawson Ter MLFD/PNYW SR4 ...... 123 F5
Daylesford Dr LGB/HTN NE7 ...... 64 B2
Daylesford Rd CRAM NE23 ...... 13 F4
Dayshield WD/WHPE/BLK NE5 ...... 60 B5
Deacon Cl WD/WHPE/BLK NE5 ...... 59 D4 1
Deaconsfield Cl SUNDSW SR3 ...... 160 B3 3
Deal Cl BLYTH NE24 ...... 17 D2
Dean Cl PLEE/EAS SR8 ...... 209 E3
Deanery St BDLGTN NE22 ...... 7 D3
Deanham Gdns
WD/WHPE/BLK NE5 ...... 61 E6
Dean Rd SSH NE33 ...... 88 A1 1
Deansfield Cl SUNDSW SR3 ...... 160 B3 4
Dean St CNUT NE1 ...... 3 E4
LWF/SPW/WRK NE9 ...... 99 E5
Deans' Wk DHAM DH1 ...... 195 E3
Dean Ter SSH NE33 ...... 88 A1
SWCK/CAS SR5 ...... 125 E3
Dean View Dr BLYTH NE24 ...... 10 A4
Dearham Gv CRAM NE23 ...... 13 F4
Debdon Gdns BYK/HTN/WLK NE6 ...... 65 E5
Debdon Pl CRAM NE23 ...... 22 A2 3
Deckham Ter GATE NE8 ...... 99 F2
Deepbrook Rd
WD/WHPE/BLK NE5 ...... 61 E5 2
Deepdale WLSD/HOW NE28 ...... 66 B1
Deepdale Cl WICK/BNPF NE16 ...... 95 E6
Deepdale Crs WD/WHPE/BLK NE5 .... 61 F4
Deepdale Gdns LGB/KIL NE12 ...... 49 E1
Deepdale Rd TYNE/NSHE NE30 ...... 55 D2
Deepdale St HLH DH5 ...... 185 F3
Deepdene Gv
CLDN/WHIT/ROK SR6 ...... 108 C5
Deepdene Rd
CLDN/WHIT/ROK SR6 ...... 108 C5
Deerbolt Pl LGB/KIL NE12 ...... 49 E5 1
Deer Bush WD/WHPE/BLK NE5 ...... 60 B5
Deerness Hts BDN/LAN/SAC DH7 .... 203 D3
Dee Rd HEBB NE31 ...... 85 E5 2
Deer Park Wy BLAY NE21 ...... 95 D1
Dees Av WLSD/HOW NE28 ...... 67 D3
Dee St JRW NE32 ...... 86 B1 1
Defender Ct SWCK/CAS SR5 ...... 124 B4 1
Defoe Av HAR/WTLS NE34 ...... 88 A5
Deighton Wk
WD/WHPE/BLK NE5 ...... 60 B5 3
Delacour Rd BLAY NE21 ...... 76 B5
Delamere Ct SUNDSW SR3 ...... 160 C2 2
Delamere Crs CRAM NE23 ...... 13 F4
Delamere Rd GOS/KPK NE3 ...... 62 B1
Delaval Av NSHW NE29 ...... 54 A6
Delaval Ct BDLGTN NE22 ...... 8 B2
SSH NE33 ...... 71 F5
Delaval Crs BLYTH NE24 ...... 16 B2 3
Delavale Cl PLEE/EAS SR8 ...... 209 E3 1
Delaval Gdns
BW/LEM/TK/HW NE15 ...... 78 A4
Delaval Rd BW/LEM/TK/HW NE15 .... 78 A4
LGB/KIL NE12 ...... 49 F4
WBAY NE26 ...... 41 E6
Delaval St BLYTH NE24 ...... 16 A2
Delaval Ter BLYTH NE24 ...... 10 C4
GOS/KPK NE3 ...... 62 C2 1
Dellfield Dr MLFD/PNYW SR4 ...... 141 F2 1
The Dell HLS DH4 ...... 157 F5
Delta Bank Rd DUN/TMV NE11 ...... 78 B5
Demesne Dr BDLGTN NE22 ...... 7 E4
Dempsey Rd DIN/WO NE13 ...... 33 D5 1
Denbeigh Pl LGB/KIL NE12 ...... 49 E5
Denbigh Av CLDN/WHIT/ROK SR6 .... 108 C6
WLSD/HOW NE28 ...... 68 C2
Denby Cl CRAM NE23 ...... 13 F4
Dene Av BW/LEM/TK/HW NE15 ...... 76 C2
DIN/WO NE13 ...... 32 C4
GOS/KPK NE3 ...... 64 A2
HLH DH5 ...... 171 F2
LGB/KIL NE12 ...... 48 C2 1
PLEE/EAS SR8 ...... 201 D1
ROWG NE39 ...... 110 C3
Denebank MONK NE25 ...... 40 A5
Dene Bank Av PLEE/EAS SR8 ...... 209 F2 1
Dene Bank Vw GOS/KPK NE3 ...... 62 A3 1
Dene Cl LGB/HTN NE7 ...... 64 C4
RYTON NE40 ...... 74 C3
Dene Ct BDN/LAN/SAC DH7 ...... 178 A3
CLS/BIR/GTL DH3 ...... 118 B6
WASHS NE38 ...... 120 B6
Dene Crs GOS/KPK NE3 ...... 64 A2
ROWG NE39 ...... 110 C3
RYTON NE40 ...... 74 C3
WBAY NE26 ...... 40 B4
WLSD/HOW NE28 ...... 67 F4
Dene Dr DHAM DH1 ...... 196 C1
Deneford LWF/SPW/WRK NE9 ...... 117 F3
Dene Gdns FELL NE10 ...... 102 A1 2
HLH DH5 ...... 171 E3
Dene Gv CRAM NE23 ...... 23 F6
GOS/KPK NE3 ...... 64 A2
Deneholm MONK NE25 ...... 40 A4
WLSD/HOW NE28 ...... 67 F3
Dene House Rd SEA/MUR SR7 ...... 176 B2
Dene La CLDN/WHIT/ROK SR6 ...... 108 C6 3
Dene Pk SWCK/CAS SR5 ...... 124 B2
Dene Rd BLAY NE21 ...... 76 B5
ROWG NE39 ...... 110 C3
SEA/MUR SR7 ...... 176 A5
SWCK/CAS SR5 ...... 124 B3
TYNE/NSHE NE30 ...... 55 E4
Deneside BDN/LAN/SAC DH7 ...... 164 B6
BDN/LAN/SAC DH7 ...... 178 A4 1
CRAM NE23 ...... 23 F6
DUN/TMV NE11 ...... 97 E4
WD/WHPE/BLK NE5 ...... 60 B2
Deneside Av LWF/SPW/WRK NE9 ...... 99 D6
Dene St HLH DH5 ...... 171 F4
MLFD/PNYW SR4 ...... 125 E5
PLEE/EAS SR8 ...... 209 F1
SUNDSW SR3 ...... 143 F5
Dene Ter JRW NE32 ...... 85 F4
The Dene CLSW/PEL DH2 ...... 166 A2
HLS DH4 ...... 183 F1
MONK NE25 ...... 40 A5
Dene Vw BDLGTN NE22 ...... 8 B3
GOS/KPK NE3 ...... 64 A2
Dene View Crs MLFD/PNYW SR4 .... 124 A6
Dene Vw East BDLGTN NE22 ...... 8 B4
Dene Vw West BDLGTN NE22 ...... 8 A4
Dene Vls PLEE/EAS SR8 ...... 209 F2
Deneway ROWG NE39 ...... 93 F6
Dene Wy SEA/MUR SR7 ...... 176 B2
Denewell Av LGB/HTN NE7 ...... 64 C3
LWF/SPW/WRK NE9 ...... 99 E5
Denewood LGB/KIL NE12 ...... 50 A2
Denham Av CLDN/WHIT/ROK SR6 .... 108 C6
Denham Dr MONK NE25 ...... 24 C6
Denham Gv BLAY NE21 ...... 93 E2
Denhill Pk BW/LEM/TK/HW NE15 ...... 78 C2
Denholm Av CRAM NE23 ...... 13 F4 2
Denmark St BYK/HTN/WLK NE6 .... 82 B1 1
BYK/HTN/WLK NE6 ...... 82 B2 2
GATE NE8 ...... 81 E6 1
Denshaw Cl CRAM NE23 ...... 13 F4
Dentdale HLS DH4 ...... 156 A1
Denton Av BW/LEM/TK/HW NE15 .... 76 C2
NSHW NE29 ...... 53 E6
Denton Ga WD/WHPE/BLK NE5 .... 60 C3 2
Denton Gv WD/WHPE/BLK NE5 .... 60 C3 3
Denton Rd BW/LEM/TK/HW NE15 .... 77 E3
Denton Vw BLAY NE21 ...... 76 A6
Dent St BLYTH NE24 ...... 11 E6
CLDN/WHIT/ROK SR6 ...... 108 C6
Denver Gdns BYK/HTN/WLK NE6 ...... 83 D3
Denway Gv WBAY NE26 ...... 26 A1
Denwick Cl CLSW/PEL DH2 ...... 165 F2
Denwick Ter TYNE/NSHE NE30 ...... 55 E5
Depot Rd BYK/HTN/WLK NE6 ...... 82 B1 2
Deptford Rd GATE NE8 ...... 81 F4
MLFD/PNYW SR4 ...... 126 A5
Deptford Ter MLFD/PNYW SR4 ...... 125 F4
Derby Crs HEBB NE31 ...... 84 C3
Derby Gdns WLSD/HOW NE28 ...... 66 C3 3
Derby Rd STLY/ANP DH9 ...... 148 A3
Derbyshire Dr DHAM DH1 ...... 196 C4
Derby St ASHBK/HED/RY SR2 ...... 4 A4
ELS/FEN NE4 ...... 80 A2
JRW NE32 ...... 86 B1
SSH NE33 ...... 71 E4
Derby Ter SSH NE33 ...... 71 F4
Dereham Cl WBAY NE26 ...... 26 C3
Dereham Ct WD/WHPE/BLK NE5 .. 61 D2 3
Dereham Rd WBAY NE26 ...... 26 C4
Dereham Wy NSHW NE29 ...... 53 D4
Derry Av CLDN/WHIT/ROK SR6 ...... 109 D6
Derwent Av DUN/TMV NE11 ...... 98 C5
HEBB NE31 ...... 85 D5 3
ROWG NE39 ...... 111 D3
Derwent Cl BDN/LAN/SAC DH7 ...... 178 A1
SEA/MUR SR7 ...... 176 B2
Derwent Crs WICK/BNPF NE16 ...... 95 F2
Derwentdale Gdns LGB/HTN NE7 ...... 65 D3
Derwent Gdns WLSD/HOW NE28 ...... 68 C2
Derwenthaugh Rd BLAY NE21 ...... 77 F6
Derwent Rd PLEE/EAS SR8 ...... 209 D1
TYNE/NSHE NE30 ...... 55 D2
WBAY NE26 ...... 26 A2
Derwent St HLH DH5 ...... 186 A2
SUND SR1 ...... 4 B4
Derwent Vw BLAY NE21 ...... 94 A1
Derwent Wk WICK/BNPF NE16 ...... 94 C4
Derwentwater Rd GATE NE8 ...... 98 B1
Derwent Wy BLAY NE21 ...... 95 D1
LGB/KIL NE12 ...... 49 E1
Deuchar St JES NE2 ...... 64 B6
Devon Crs CLS/BIR/GTL DH3 ...... 118 A6
Devon Dr SUNDSW SR3 ...... 143 F6
Devon Gdns HAR/WTLS NE34 ...... 90 A1
Devonport HLS DH4 ...... 157 E5
Devon Rd HEBB NE31 ...... 85 E5
NSHW NE29 ...... 53 F4
Devonshire Dr LGB/KIL NE12 ...... 51 D3
SMOOR NE27 ...... 51 E3
Devonshire Gdns WLSD/HOW NE28 .. 66 B3
Devonshire Pl JES NE2 ...... 64 B5
Devonshire Rd DHAM DH1 ...... 196 B4
Devonshire St SSH NE33 ...... 88 A1
SWCK/CAS SR5 ...... 126 B3
Devonshire Ter JES NE2 ...... 80 C1 1
Devonworth Pl BLYTH NE24 ...... 9 F5
Dewberry Cl BLYTH NE24 ...... 16 B2
Dewley CRAM NE23 ...... 22 A3
Dewley Pl WD/WHPE/BLK NE5 ...... 60 A2 1
Dewley Rd WD/WHPE/BLK NE5 ...... 60 C5
Dewsgreen CRAM NE23 ...... 22 A2
Dexter Wy FELL NE10 ...... 100 B2
Deyncourt DHAM DH1 ...... 204 C2 1
Diamond Ct GOS/KPK NE3 ...... 61 E1
Diamond St WLSD/HOW NE28 ...... 67 D4 3
Diana St ELS/FEN NE4 ...... 80 A3
Dickens Av HAR/WTLS NE34 ...... 88 A5
WICK/BNPF NE16 ...... 95 F2
Dickens St HLS DH4 ...... 170 C2
SWCK/CAS SR5 ...... 125 F3 3
Dickens Wynd DHAM DH1 ...... 204 C1
Didcot Av NSHW NE29 ...... 70 A2 2
Didcot Wy BOL NE36 ...... 105 E3
BOLCOL NE35 ...... 105 E3
Dillon St JRW NE32 ...... 85 F3
SEA/MUR SR7 ...... 176 C3
Dilston Av MONK NE25 ...... 41 D6
Dilston Cl PLEE/EAS SR8 ...... 208 B5
SMOOR NE27 ...... 52 B2
WASHS NE38 ...... 137 F2
Dilston Dr WD/WHPE/BLK NE5 ...... 60 A3
Dilston Gdns MLFD/PNYW SR4 .... 143 E1 1
Dilston Rd DHAM DH1 ...... 180 C6 1
ELS/FEN NE4 ...... 79 F2
Dilston Ter JRW NE32 ...... 86 A5
Dimbula Gdns LGB/HTN NE7 ...... 65 F4
Dinsdale Av WLSD/HOW NE28 ...... 67 E1
Dinsdale Dr DHAM DH1 ...... 196 C2
Dinsdale Pl JES NE2 ...... 81 E1
Dinsdale Rd CLDN/WHIT/ROK SR6 .. 127 D2
JES NE2 ...... 81 E1
Dinsdale St ASHBK/HED/RY SR2 ...... 162 B2
Dinting Cl PLEE/EAS SR8 ...... 208 A3
Dipe La BOL NE36 ...... 105 F4
Dipton Gdns SUNDSW SR3 ...... 144 A4 3
Dipton Gv CRAM NE23 ...... 22 A2
Dipton Rd MONK NE25 ...... 39 F3
Dipwood Rd ROWG NE39 ...... 110 C3
Dipwood Wy ROWG NE39 ...... 110 C4
Disraeli St BLYTH NE24 ...... 10 C4
HLS DH4 ...... 170 A2
Dissington Pl WD/WHPE/BLK NE5 .... 61 E6
WICK/BNPF NE16 ...... 95 F5
Ditchburn Ter MLFD/PNYW SR4 ...... 125 E4
Dixon Est RDHAMSE DH6 ...... 206 B3
Dixon Estate Bungalows
RDHAMSE DH6 ...... 206 B4
Dixon Pl DUN/TMV NE11 ...... 97 E2 2
Dixon Rd HLH DH5 ...... 170 C4
Dixon's Sq CLDN/WHIT/ROK SR6 .. 126 C3 2
Dixon St GATE NE8 ...... 98 B1
SSH NE33 ...... 71 E5 1
Dobson Cl ELS/FEN NE4 ...... 80 A5 5
Dobson Crs BYK/HTN/WLK NE6 ...... 82 B4
Dobson Ter SEA/MUR SR7 ...... 188 B1 1
Dockendale La WICK/BNPF NE16 .. 96 B3 2
Dock Rd NSHW NE29 ...... 70 C2
Dock Rd South NSHW NE29 ...... 70 C3
Dock St CLDN/WHIT/ROK SR6 ...... 127 D4
Dockwray Cl TYNE/NSHE NE30 ...... 71 D1 3
Dockwray Sq TYNE/NSHE NE30 ...... 71 D1
Doddfell Cl WASHN NE37 ...... 119 F6
Doddington Cl
BW/LEM/TK/HW NE15 ...... 76 A1
Doddington Dr CRAM NE23 ...... 21 F2
Dolphin St ELS/FEN NE4 ...... 78 C3
Dominies Cl ROWG NE39 ...... 111 E1

Dominion Rd *BDN/LAN/SAC* DH7 203 D5
Donald Av *RDHAMSE* DH6 187 D4
Donald St *GOS/KPK* NE3 64 A1 5
Doncaster Rd *JES* NE2 81 E1
Doncrest Rd *WASHN* NE37 120 A3
Don Dixon Dr *JRW* NE32 104 A1 1
Don Gdns *BOL* NE36 105 E3
Donkin Rd *WASHN* NE37 119 E5
Donkin Ter *TYNE/NSHE* NE30 55 E5
Donnington Cl *SWCK/CAS* SR5 123 F3 1
Donnington Ct *GOS/KPK* NE3 64 B2
Donnini Pl *DHAM* DH1 195 E3
Donnison Gdns *SUND* SR1 5 F2 1
Donridge *WASHN* NE37 120 A3
Don Rd *JRW* NE32 86 C1
Don St *DUN/TMV* NE11 98 B6
Donvale Rd *WASHN* NE37 119 F3
Don Vw *BOL* NE36 105 E3
Dorcas Av *BW/LEM/TK/HW* NE15 78 B3
Dorchester Cl
WD/WHPE/BLK NE5 59 D3 4
Dorchester Ct *MONK* NE25 24 B2
Dorchester Gdns
LWF/SPW/WRK NE9 117 E2
Doreen Av *SEA/MUR* SR7 175 E4
Doric Rd *BDN/LAN/SAC* DH7 202 B1
Dorking Av *NSHW* NE29 70 A2
Dorking Cl *BLYTH* NE24 17 D2
Dorking Rd *CLDN/WHIT/ROK* SR6 108 C6
Dorlonco Vls *BDN/LAN/SAC* DH7 203 E5
Dormand Dr *PLEE/EAS* SR8 208 B5
Dornoch Crs *FELL* NE10 101 D4 1
Dorrington Rd *GOS/KPK* NE3 46 A6
Dorset Av *CLDN/WHIT/ROK* SR6 109 D6
CLS/BIR/GTL DH3 136 B5
HAR/WTLS NE34 90 A1
HEBB NE31 85 E3
WLSD/HOW NE28 66 C4
Dorset Gv *NSHW* NE29 53 F3
Dorset La *SUNDSW* SR3 161 D1
Dorset Rd *BW/LEM/TK/HW* NE15 77 E2
GATE NE8 81 F4
Dorset St *HLH* DH5 186 B4
Double Rw *MONK* NE25 24 A3
Douglas Cl *HAR/WTLS* NE34 88 B4 2
Douglas Ct *STLY/ANP* DH9 146 A5
Douglas Gdns *DUN/TMV* NE11 97 F3
Douglas Rd *CLDN/WHIT/ROK* SR6 109 D6
Douglass St *WLSD/HOW* NE28 66 C4
Douglas St *WLSD/HOW* NE28 68 C5 4
Douglas Ter *ELS/FEN* NE4 80 A3 8
HLS DH4 140 A6
Douglas Vls *DHAM* DH1 195 D4 1
Doulting Cl *LGB/KIL* NE12 49 D6 3
Dove Av *JRW* NE32 86 B5
Dove Cl *BDN/LAN/SAC* DH7 202 C4 1
Dovecote Cl *MONK* NE25 39 E4 1
Dovecote Rd *LGB/KIL* NE12 50 A5
Dovedale Av *BLYTH* NE24 9 F5
Dovedale Gdns *LGB/HTN* NE7 64 C3
LWF/SPW/WRK NE9 99 F6
Dovedale Rd *CLDN/WHIT/ROK* SR6 108 B5
Dover Cl *BDLGTN* NE22 6 C3
WD/WHPE/BLK NE5 59 E3
Dovercourt Rd *BYK/HTN/WLK* NE6 83 F4
Dowling Av *MONK* NE25 40 B6
Downe Cl *BLYTH* NE24 17 D2 2
Downend Rd *WD/WHPE/BLK* NE5 60 A3
Downfield *WASHN* NE37 120 C1 1
Downham *WD/WHPE/BLK* NE5 60 B5
Downhill La *BOL* NE36 105 D6 1
WASHN NE37 104 C6
Downs La *HLH* DH5 172 A5
Downs Pit La *HLH* DH5 172 C5
Downswood *LGB/KIL* NE12 50 B1 2
Dowsey Rd *RDHAMSE* DH6 197 E4
Dowson Sq *SEA/MUR* SR7 187 F1
Doxford Av *HLH* DH5 171 E4
Doxford Dr *PLEE/EAS* SR8 207 E2
Doxford Gdns
WD/WHPE/BLK NE5 61 F5 4
Doxford Park Wy *SUNDSW* SR3 160 A2
Doxford Pl *CRAM* NE23 22 A3 1
Doxford Ter *HLH* DH5 171 E4
Dragon La *DHAM* DH1 196 A4
Drake Cl *SSH* NE33 71 D6
Drayton Rd *CLDN/WHIT/ROK* SR6 108 C6
GOS/KPK NE3 62 A2
The Drive *CLS/BIR/GTL* DH3 136 C5
FELL NE10 101 D2
GOS/KPK NE3 63 E3
LGB/HTN NE7 65 D2
LWF/SPW/WRK NE9 99 E4
TYNE/NSHE NE30 55 F3
WASHN NE37 120 B3
WD/WHPE/BLK NE5 60 B6
WICK/BNPF NE16 96 B4
WLSD/HOW NE28 67 D4
Dronfield Cl *CLSW/PEL* DH2 165 E1
Drove Rd *BW/LEM/TK/HW* NE15 57 E3
Drummond Crs *HAR/WTLS* NE34 87 E3
Drummond Rd *GOS/KPK* NE3 62 B3
Drummond Ter *TYNE/NSHE* NE30 55 D5
Drumoyne Cl *SUNDSW* SR3 159 D2
Drumoyne Gdns *MONK* NE25 53 F1
Drum Rd *CLSW/PEL* DH2 153 D1
Drumsheugh Pl
WD/WHPE/BLK NE5 61 D4
Druridge Av *CLDN/WHIT/ROK* SR6 108 C5
Druridge Crs *BLYTH* NE24 16 A1
HAR/WTLS NE34 73 D6
Druridge Dr *BLYTH* NE24 16 A1
WD/WHPE/BLK NE5 61 F5
Drury La *NSHW* NE29 53 E5
SUND SR1 5 E2
Drybeck Ct *CRAM* NE23 14 C6
Drybeck Sq *SUNDSW* SR3 161 D2 3
Drybeck Wk *CRAM* NE23 14 C6 6
Dryborough St
MLFD/PNYW SR4 126 A5 4
Dryburgh *WASHS* NE38 138 B1
Dryburgh Cl *NSHW* NE29 54 A4
Dryburn Hl *DHAM* DH1 193 F2
Dryburn Rd *DHAM* DH1 193 F1
Dryden Cl *HAR/WTLS* NE34 88 A6
STLY/ANP DH9 148 C2
Dryden Rd *LWF/SPW/WRK* NE9 99 E3
Dryden St *SWCK/CAS* SR5 125 F2
Drysdale Ct *DIN/WO* NE13 32 C4
Drysdale Crs *DIN/WO* NE13 32 C4
Dubmire Cottages *HLS* DH4 169 E2
Dubmire Ct *HLS* DH4 169 F2
Duchess Crs *JRW* NE32 86 A5
Duchess Crs East *JRW* NE32 86 A5 2
Duchess Dr *BW/LEM/TK/HW* NE15 77 F1
Duchess St *WBAY* NE26 40 C5
Duckpool La *WICK/BNPF* NE16 96 B2 2
Duddon Cl *PLEE/EAS* SR8 209 D2 3
Duddon Pl *LWF/SPW/WRK* NE9 100 A6
Dudley Av *CLDN/WHIT/ROK* SR6 108 C6 4
Dudley Dr *CRAM* NE23 34 C2
Dudley Gdns *SUNDSW* SR3 159 E2
Dudley La *CRAM* NE23 21 F3
DIN/WO NE13 33 E2
Dugdale Rd *GOS/KPK* NE3 61 F1
Duke's Av *HEBB* NE31 84 C4
Dukes Dr *GOS/KPK* NE3 47 D3
Dukesfield *CRAM* NE23 22 A3 2
Dukes Meadow *DIN/WO* NE13 44 A4
Duke St *FELL* NE10 101 F1
MLFD/PNYW SR4 125 F6 4
SEA/MUR SR7 176 A2
WBAY NE26 40 C5
Duke St North
CLDN/WHIT/ROK SR6 126 C2
Dukesway *DUN/TMV* NE11 98 A5
Dulverston Cl
WD/WHPE/BLK NE5 59 E3 1
Dulverton Av *SSH* NE33 88 C1
Dumfries Crs *JRW* NE32 87 D4
Dunbar Cl *WD/WHPE/BLK* NE5 59 E3
Dunbar St *MLFD/PNYW* SR4 143 E1
Dunblane Crs *WD/WHPE/BLK* NE5 60 B6
Dunblane Dr *BLYTH* NE24 17 D2
Dunblane Rd
CLDN/WHIT/ROK SR6 109 D5
Dunbreck Gv *MLFD/PNYW* SR4 143 F2
Duncan St *BYK/HTN/WLK* NE6 83 F2
GATE NE8 100 A1
MLFD/PNYW SR4 125 E5
Duncombe Crs *STLY/ANP* DH9 131 E6
Duncow La *DHAM* DH1 194 B5 1
Dun Cow St *SUND* SR1 4 B2 1
Dundas St *CLDN/WHIT/ROK* SR6 126 C4 3
Dundas Wy *FELL* NE10 100 B2
Dundee Cl *WD/WHPE/BLK* NE5 59 E3
Dundrennan *WASHS* NE38 138 B3
Dunelm Dr *BOL* NE36 106 A3
HLS DH4 170 B2
Dunelm Pl *RDHAMSE* DH6 206 C2 3
Dunelm Rd *HLH* DH5 171 E6
Dunelm St *SSH* NE33 71 F4 5
Dunelm Wk *PLEE/EAS* SR8 208 C1 2
Dunford Gdns
WD/WHPE/BLK NE5 59 F2 1
Dunholm Cl *HLH* DH5 171 D3
Dunholme Cl *DHAM* DH1 194 A1
Dunholme Rd *ELS/FEN* NE4 79 E3
Dunira Cl *JES* NE2 64 B4 2
Dunkeld Cl *BLYTH* NE24 17 D2
Dunkirk Av *HLH* DH5 171 E3
Dunlin Cl *RYTON* NE40 75 D4 3
Dunlin Dr *BLYTH* NE24 17 D2
WASHS NE38 137 E3
Dunlop Cl *LGB/HTN* NE7 65 E2 3
Dunlop Crs *HAR/WTLS* NE34 89 F2
Dunmoor Cl *GOS/KPK* NE3 62 C2 2
Dunmore Av *CLDN/WHIT/ROK* SR6 109 D5
Dunmorlie St *BYK/HTN/WLK* NE6 82 C2
Dunn Av *SUNDSW* SR3 143 F5
Dunning St *SUND* SR1 4 B1
Dunnlynn Cl *SUNDSW* SR3 160 A2 4
Dunnock Dr *WASHS* NE38 137 E4
WICK/BNPF NE16 113 F1
Dunn Rd *PLEE/EAS* SR8 208 C1
Dunn's Ter *JES* NE2 63 D6 2
Dunn St *ELS/FEN* NE4 80 A5
Dunnykirk Av *GOS/KPK* NE3 61 F1 4
Dunsdale Dr *CRAM* NE23 14 C6
Dunsdale Rd *MONK* NE25 25 D6
Dunsgreen *PONT/DH* NE20 28 A5
Dunsley Gdns *DIN/WO* NE13 31 D3
Dunsmuir Gv *GATE* NE8 99 D2
Dunstable Pl
WD/WHPE/BLK NE5 59 D3 5
Dunstanburgh *BDLGTN* NE22 6 C3
Dunstanburgh Cl *BDLGTN* NE22 6 C3
BYK/HTN/WLK NE6 82 C3 3
WASHS NE38 138 A2
Dunstanburgh Rd
BYK/HTN/WLK NE6 82 C3
Dunstan Cl *CLSW/PEL* DH2 165 F1
Dunston Bank *DUN/TMV* NE11 97 D3
Dunston Pl *BLYTH* NE24 10 A5
Dunston Rd *DUN/TMV* NE11 97 E1
Dunvegan *CLS/BIR/GTL* DH3 137 D4
Dunvegan Av *CLSW/PEL* DH2 166 A1
Durant Rd *CNUT* NE1 3 E2
Durban St *BLYTH* NE24 10 C3
Durham Av *PLEE/EAS* SR8 201 E6
WASHN NE37 120 A4
Durham Cl *BDLGTN* NE22 6 C3 2
Durham Dr *BOLCOL* NE35 104 A2
JRW NE32 86 A6
Durham Gdns *BDN/LAN/SAC* DH7 178 A3
Durham Gv *JRW* NE32 85 F6
Durham La *PLEE/EAS* SR8 199 F3
RDHAMSE DH6 198 A5
Durham Pl *CLS/BIR/GTL* DH3 136 B5
GATE NE8 99 E1 5
Durham Rd *ASHBK/HED/RY* SR2 126 A6
BDN/LAN/SAC DH7 178 B2
CLS/BIR/GTL DH3 136 B1
CLS/BIR/GTL DH3 166 B1
CRAM NE23 14 B5
GATE NE8 99 E1
HLH DH5 158 B5
HLS DH4 171 D2
LWF/SPW/WRK NE9 99 E6
LWF/SPW/WRK NE9 117 F3
STLY/ANP DH9 146 C5
SUNDSW SR3 143 F3
Durham St *ELS/FEN* NE4 79 E4
FELL NE10 101 E1 1
HLS DH4 169 F2
SEA/MUR SR7 176 A2
WLSD/HOW NE28 67 E4
Durham St West
WLSD/HOW NE28 67 E4 3
Durham Ter *SUNDSW* SR3 143 F5
Durham Wy *PLEE/EAS* SR8 208 A5
Duxfield Rd *LGB/HTN* NE7 65 D3
Dwyer Crs *ASHBK/HED/RY* SR2 162 B2
Dyer Sq *SWCK/CAS* SR5 126 A2
Dykefield Av *GOS/KPK* NE3 46 A5
Dyke Heads La *RYTON* NE40 74 A6
Dykelands Rd
CLDN/WHIT/ROK SR6 108 C6
Dykelands Wy *HAR/WTLS* NE34 87 E5
Dykenook Cl *WICK/BNPF* NE16 95 F6
Dykes Wy *FELL* NE10 100 C5
Dymock Ct *WD/WHPE/BLK* NE5 61 D1

E

Eaglescliffe Dr *LGB/HTN* NE7 65 F3
Eaglesdene *HLH* DH5 171 F6 2
Eagle St *DUN/TMV* NE11 98 A4
Ealing Dr *TYNE/NSHE* NE30 55 E3
Eardulph Av *CLS/BIR/GTL* DH3 153 F5
Earl Grey Wy *NSHW* NE29 70 B3
Earlington Ct *LGB/KIL* NE12 50 A3 2
Earl's Dr *BW/LEM/TK/HW* NE15 77 F1
LWF/SPW/WRK NE9 99 E6
Earl's Gdns *BLYTH* NE24 10 B4 1
Earls Gn *HLH* DH5 184 C1
Earl St *MLFD/PNYW* SR4 126 A6
SEA/MUR SR7 175 F2
Earlsway *DUN/TMV* NE11 98 B3
Earlswood Av *LWF/SPW/WRK* NE9 99 E6
Earlswood Gv *BLYTH* NE24 16 C3
Earnshaw Wy *MONK* NE25 39 F3
Earsdon Cl *WD/WHPE/BLK* NE5 60 C4
Earsdon Rd *GOS/KPK* NE3 62 A3
HLH DH5 171 E2 3
MONK NE25 39 F6
SMOOR NE27 52 A1
Earsdon Vw *SMOOR* NE27 38 B6
Easby Cl *GOS/KPK* NE3 47 F4
Easby Rd *WASHS* NE38 138 C2
Easdale Av *GOS/KPK* NE3 47 E3
Easedale *WBAY* NE26 26 B2
Easedale Gdns *LWF/SPW/WRK* NE9 99 F6
Easington Av *CRAM* NE23 14 B4
LWF/SPW/WRK NE9 118 B1
Easington St *PLEE/EAS* SR8 200 C1 1
SWCK/CAS SR5 126 B4
Easington St North
SWCK/CAS SR5 126 B4 1
East Acre *BLAY* NE21 76 C6
East Acres *DIN/WO* NE13 31 D2
East Av *HAR/WTLS* NE34 89 F2
LGB/KIL NE12 49 F6

WASHS NE38 138 B5
East Back Pde ASHBK/HED/RY SR2 5 H5
East Bailey LGB/KIL NE12 35 F6 7
LGB/KIL NE12 49 F1 2
East Boldon Rd
CLDN/WHIT/ROK SR6 107 E1 1
Eastbourne Av BYK/HTN/WLK NE6 83 F1
GATE NE8 99 D2
Eastbourne Gdns
BYK/HTN/WLK NE6 83 F1
WBAY NE26 40 B4
Eastbourne Gv SSH NE33 71 F3 3
Eastcheap BYK/HTN/WLK NE6 65 E5 1
East Cleft Rd
ASHBK/HED/RY SR2 126 A6 4
Eastcliffe Av GOS/KPK NE3 62 C3
East Cl HAR/WTLS NE34 89 F2
Eastcombe Cl BOLCOL NE35 87 D6 5
Eastcote Ter BYK/HTN/WLK NE6 83 E5
East Crs BDLGTN NE22 8 C2
East Cross St SUND SR1 4 D1
Eastdene Rd SEA/MUR SR7 175 E3
Eastdene Wy PLEE/EAS SR8 209 E3
East Dr BLYTH NE24 16 B2 4
CLDN/WHIT/ROK SR6 107 D2
East End WBAY NE26 27 D4
Eastern Av DUN/TMV NE11 98 C6
Eastern Wy WD/WHPE/BLK NE5 61 F4
Eastfield PLEE/EAS SR8 209 F3
Eastfield Av BYK/HTN/WLK NE6 66 C6
MONK NE25 39 F6
Eastfield Rd HAR/WTLS NE34 72 B6 1
LGB/KIL NE12 49 E6
East Flds CLDN/WHIT/ROK SR6 109 E2
Eastfield St MLFD/PNYW SR4 143 E1
Eastfield Ter LGB/KIL NE12 49 F6 2
East Forest Hall Rd LGB/KIL NE12 50 A4 3
East Front JES NE2 64 A6
Eastgarth WD/WHPE/BLK NE5 60 C1
East Ga GATE NE8 81 E5 2
Eastgate Gdns ELS/FEN NE4 79 E4
East George Potts St SSH NE33 71 F5 2
East George St TYNE/NSHE NE30 55 E6
East Gra MONK NE25 25 E6
SWCK/CAS SR5 126 B1
East Grange Ct PLEE/EAS SR8 200 A3 3
East Gn RDHAMSE DH6 206 C2 4
East Gv MLFD/PNYW SR4 142 A1
East Hill Rd GATE NE8 100 A1
East Holborn SSH NE33 71 D4
Eastlands BLAY NE21 94 A1
LGB/HTN NE7 64 C3
East Lea BLAY NE21 94 B2
Eastlea Crs SEA/MUR SR7 175 F3
Eastlea Rd SEA/MUR SR7 175 E3
Eastleigh Cl BOLCOL NE35 105 D2
East Moffett St SSH NE33 71 F5 3
East Moor Rd MLFD/PNYW SR4 125 E5
East Park Gdns BLAY NE21 94 B1 2
East Park Rd LWF/SPW/WRK NE9 99 E4
East Park Vw BLYTH NE24 11 E5
East Percy St TYNE/NSHE NE30 55 E6
East Riggs BDLGTN NE22 7 E4
East Stevenson St SSH NE33 71 F5 4
East Stoneycroft LGB/KIL NE12 50 A2 1
East St CLDN/WHIT/ROK SR6 109 E2
CLSW/PEL DH2 150 C3
GATE NE8 81 E5
RDHAMSE DH6 206 C2
SSH NE33 71 E3
STLY/ANP DH9 149 D5
East Thorp WD/WHPE/BLK NE5 60 B1
East Vw CLDN/WHIT/ROK SR6 127 D1
HEBB NE31 84 C4
PLEE/EAS SR8 191 D6
SWCK/CAS SR5 124 B3 4
East View Ter WICK/BNPF NE16 96 A2 1
East Vines SUND SR1 5 G1
Eastward Gn MONK NE25 39 F6
Eastway HAR/WTLS NE34 90 A3
Eastwood BDN/LAN/SAC DH7 178 B2
Eastwood Av BLYTH NE24 16 C3
Eastwood Cl CRAM NE23 35 E5 1
Eastwood Gdns FELL NE10 100 B1
GOS/KPK NE3 62 B2
LWF/SPW/WRK NE9 99 F4
Eastwood Pl CRAM NE23 14 B4 1
Eaton Pl ELS/FEN NE4 79 E3 1
Eavers Ct HAR/WTLS NE34 88 B3 7
Ebba Wk GOS/KPK NE3 63 F1
Ebchester Ct GOS/KPK NE3 61 E1
Ebchester St HAR/WTLS NE34 87 F3
Ebdon La CLDN/WHIT/ROK SR6 108 C6
Ebor St BYK/HTN/WLK NE6 65 E6
HAR/WTLS NE34 87 F4
Eccleston Cl SMOOR NE27 37 E6
Eccleston Rd SSH NE33 72 A4
Ecgfrid Ter JRW NE32 86 B3
Eddison Rd WASHS NE38 139 E2
Eddleston Av GOS/KPK NE3 62 C3
Eddrington Gv WD/WHPE/BLK NE5 59 E3
Ede Av DUN/TMV NE11 97 E2
HAR/WTLS NE34 90 A2
Edenbridge Crs LGB/KIL NE12 49 D5
Eden Cl WD/WHPE/BLK NE5 59 E4
Edendale Av BLYTH NE24 10 A4
BYK/HTN/WLK NE6 83 F2
Edendale Ter GATE NE8 99 E2
PLEE/EAS SR8 209 E2 1
Edenfield STLY/ANP DH9 150 C1
Edenhill Rd PLEE/EAS SR8 209 D1
Eden House Rd MLFD/PNYW SR4 144 A1
Eden La PLEE/EAS SR8 200 C6
Eden Pl TYNE/NSHE NE30 54 C3
Eden Rd DHAM DH1 180 B6
Eden St PLEE/EAS SR8 209 F1
WLSD/HOW NE28 67 D5 6
Eden St West CLS/BIR/GTL DH3 168 B2
SUND SR1 4 A2
Eden Vw RDHAMSE DH6 206 C2
Edgar St GOS/KPK NE3 64 B1
Edgecote WASHN NE37 121 E4
Edge Ct DHAM DH1 195 E4
Edgefield Av GOS/KPK NE3 62 B1
Edgefield Dr CRAM NE23 14 B4
Edge Mt LGB/KIL NE12 35 F6
Edgewood Av BDLGTN NE22 8 B3 2
Edgeworth Cl BOLCOL NE35 87 D6 6
Edgeworth Crs
CLDN/WHIT/ROK SR6 126 C2 2
Edgmond Ct ASHBK/HED/RY SR2 145 D6
Edgware Rd GATE NE8 99 F2
Edhill Av HAR/WTLS NE34 87 E3
Edinburgh Rd JRW NE32 87 D4
Edington Gv TYNE/NSHE NE30 54 C3
Edington Rd TYNE/NSHE NE30 54 C3
Edison Gdns GATE NE8 99 D3
Edison St SEA/MUR SR7 188 B1
Edith Av BLAY NE21 76 B6
Edith St ASHBK/HED/RY SR2 145 D2 3
JRW NE32 85 F1
SEA/MUR SR7 177 D5
SWCK/CAS SR5 126 B2 2
TYNE/NSHE NE30 55 E4
Edlingham Cl GOS/KPK NE3 64 B2
Edlingham Ct HLH DH5 171 E2 4
Edlingham Rd DHAM DH1 194 B1
Edmondsley La
BDN/LAN/SAC DH7 164 A5
Edmund Pl LWF/SPW/WRK NE9 99 E5 5
Edna Ter WD/WHPE/BLK NE5 60 C3
Edward Av PLEE/EAS SR8 209 E1
Edward Burdis St
SWCK/CAS SR5 126 A2 7
Edward Cain Ct PLEE/EAS SR8 209 F1 1
Edward Pl ELS/FEN NE4 80 A3 9
Edward Rd BDLGTN NE22 8 C2 2
CLS/BIR/GTL DH3 136 A1
WLSD/HOW NE28 68 B3
Edwardson Rd BDN/LAN/SAC DH7 203 F5
Edwards Rd WBAY NE26 41 E6
Edward St BLYTH NE24 10 C4
DHAM DH1 195 E4
GOS/KPK NE3 63 E1 1
HEBB NE31 84 B1 1
HLH DH5 171 F6
SEA/MUR SR7 176 C4 3
STLY/ANP DH9 149 E6
SUNDSW SR3 160 C1
Edward's Wk CNUT NE1 2 C1
Edwin Gv WLSD/HOW NE28 68 C3
Edwins Av LGB/KIL NE12 50 A4
Edwin's Av South LGB/KIL NE12 50 A4
Edwin St BYK/HTN/WLK NE6 82 A2 5
HLH DH5 171 D1
MLFD/PNYW SR4 125 D5
Egerton Rd HAR/WTLS NE34 88 B2
Egerton St ASHBK/HED/RY SR2 5 E5
BW/LEM/TK/HW NE15 78 B4
Eggleston Cl CLS/BIR/GTL DH3 168 A3 1
DHAM DH1 181 D6
Eggleston Dr SUNDSW SR3 143 F4
Egham Rd WD/WHPE/BLK NE5 59 E4
Eglesfield Rd SSH NE33 71 E6
Eglinton St SWCK/CAS SR5 126 B3
Eglinton St North SWCK/CAS SR5 126 B3
Egremont Dr
LWF/SPW/WRK NE9 100 A4 3
Egremont Gdns
LWF/SPW/WRK NE9 99 F4 4
Egremont Gv PLEE/EAS SR8 207 F5
Egremont Pl WBAY NE26 41 D6
Eider Cl BLYTH NE24 17 D3
Eighteenth Av BLYTH NE24 16 B1 2
Eighth Av BLYTH NE24 16 C1 1
BYK/HTN/WLK NE6 65 E6
CLSW/PEL DH2 153 D5
Eighth St PLEE/EAS SR8 209 F1
Eighton Ter LWF/SPW/WRK NE9 118 C1
Eishort Wy LGB/KIL NE12 49 D6
Eland Cl GOS/KPK NE3 61 F1
Eland Edge PONT/DH NE20 28 B4
Eland La PONT/DH NE20 28 B3
Elberfield Ct JRW NE32 86 A2
Elder Cl BDN/LAN/SAC DH7 192 A5
Elder Gv HAR/WTLS NE34 89 E4
LWF/SPW/WRK NE9 99 E5 6
Elderwood Gdns DUN/TMV NE11 98 A5
Eldon La CNUT NE1 2 D3
Eldon Pl BW/LEM/TK/HW NE15 76 C1
Eldon Rd BW/LEM/TK/HW NE15 76 C1
Eldon St GATE NE8 81 F5
MLFD/PNYW SR4 125 F6
SSH NE33 71 D5
WLSD/HOW NE28 68 C4
Eleanor St SSH NE33 71 F3
TYNE/NSHE NE30 41 E6
Elemore La HLH DH5 186 A4
RDHAMSE DH6 185 D6
Elemore Vw RDHAMSE DH6 187 D5
Elenbel Av BDLGTN NE22 8 B3
Eleventh Av BLYTH NE24 11 D6 3
Eleventh St PLEE/EAS SR8 209 E1
Elford Cl MONK NE25 39 F5
Elfordleigh HLS DH4 157 E4 2
Elgar Av WD/WHPE/BLK NE5 59 E4 5
Elgar Cl STLY/ANP DH9 148 C3
Elgin Av SEA/MUR SR7 175 E3
WLSD/HOW NE28 68 B2
Elgin Cl NSHW NE29 53 E4 3
Elgin Ct FELL NE10 84 A6 5
Elgin Gdns BYK/HTN/WLK NE6 83 E2
Elgin Gv STLY/ANP DH9 149 D2
Elgin Rd LWF/SPW/WRK NE9 100 A2
Elgin St JRW NE32 87 D4
Elgy Rd GOS/KPK NE3 63 D3
Elisabeth Av CLS/BIR/GTL DH3 118 A6
Elizabeth Ct LGB/KIL NE12 50 C4
Elizabeth Crs CRAM NE23 34 C2
Elizabeth Diamond Gdns
SSH NE33 71 D6 2
Elizabeth Dr LGB/KIL NE12 50 C4
Elizabeth Rd WLSD/HOW NE28 68 C3
Elizabeth St BYK/HTN/WLK NE6 81 F2
HLH DH5 171 D1
SEA/MUR SR7 176 B3 1
SSH NE33 71 F4 6
SWCK/CAS SR5 124 A3 3
SWCK/CAS SR5 126 B1 2
Ellam Av DHAM DH1 193 F6
Ell-dene Crs FELL NE10 101 D3
Ellerbeck Cl FELL NE10 100 B2 2
Ellersmere Gdns
TYNE/NSHE NE30 55 D2 1
Ellerton Wy CRAM NE23 14 B4 2
FELL NE10 100 B2
Ellesmere HLS DH4 155 F5
Ellesmere Av BYK/HTN/WLK NE6 83 D1
WD/WHPE/BLK NE5 60 C4
Ellesmere Ct ASHBK/HED/RY SR2 145 D5
Ellesmere Dr SEA/MUR SR7 175 E3
Ellesmere Rd ELS/FEN NE4 79 D3
Ellington Cl ASHBK/HED/RY SR2 162 B3 1
BW/LEM/TK/HW NE15 76 A1
Elliot Cl HLS DH4 157 D1
Elliot Rd FELL NE10 100 A1 4
Elliott Dr FELL NE10 100 C2 3
Elliott Gdns WLSD/HOW NE28 66 C2
Elliott Rd PLEE/EAS SR8 208 C1
Elliott St BLYTH NE24 16 A2
Elliott Ter ELS/FEN NE4 79 F3 5
Ellison Pl CNUT NE1 3 E2
JRW NE32 69 D6
LWF/SPW/WRK NE9 99 E6
Ellison Rd DUN/TMV NE11 97 F2
PLEE/EAS SR8 209 D1
Ellison St GATE NE8 81 E5 3
HEBB NE31 84 C2 2
JRW NE32 86 A1 4
Ellis Rd SWCK/CAS SR5 125 F1 1
Ellis Sq SWCK/CAS SR5 126 A1
Elm Av BDN/LAN/SAC DH7 203 D5
CLSW/PEL DH2 151 E2
DIN/WO NE13 31 D3
DUN/TMV NE11 97 E3
HAR/WTLS NE34 89 E4
WICK/BNPF NE16 96 B2
Elm Cl CRAM NE23 14 B4
Elm Ct WICK/BNPF NE16 96 A5
Elm Crs CLSW/PEL DH2 179 E1
Elm Croft Rd LGB/KIL NE12 50 A5
Elm Dr BDLGTN NE22 7 E5
CLDN/WHIT/ROK SR6 109 F1
Elmfield Av DHAM DH1 196 A3
Elmfield Cl SUNDSW SR3 159 D2
Elmfield Gdns WLSD/HOW NE28 66 B2
Elmfield Gv GOS/KPK NE3 63 D3
Elmfield Pk GOS/KPK NE3 63 D3
Elmfield Rd
BW/LEM/TK/HW NE15 58 A4 2
GOS/KPK NE3 63 D3
HEBB NE31 85 E5
Elmfield Ter HEBB NE31 85 E4
Elm Gv BDN/LAN/SAC DH7 192 A5
GOS/KPK NE3 46 B5
HAR/WTLS NE34 89 E4
LGB/KIL NE12 49 F3
WICK/BNPF NE16 111 E6
Elm Rd BLAY NE21 76 C6
NSHW NE29 53 D5
PONT/DH NE20 28 C5
Elmsford Gv LGB/KIL NE12 49 E6
Elmsleigh Gdns
CLDN/WHIT/ROK SR6 89 F5
The Elms HLH DH5 186 C3

Elm St CLS/BIR/GTL DH3 153 E5
DUN/TMV NE11 98 A4
JRW NE32 85 F1
STLY/ANP DH9 147 F4
WICK/BNPF NE16 114 A2
Elm St West WICK/BNPF NE16 114 A2
Elmtree Ct SEA/MUR SR7 176 B5
Elmtree Gdns MONK NE25 54 A1
Elmtree Gv GOS/KPK NE3 63 D2
Elm Trees BLYTH NE24 10 C6 2
Elmway CLSW/PEL DH2 152 C3
Elmwood Av DIN/WO NE13 33 D5
SWCK/CAS SR5 125 E1
Elmwood Crs BYK/HTN/WLK NE6 66 B5 1
Elmwood Dr PONT/DH NE20 28 A3
Elmwood Gdns DUN/TMV NE11 98 A4
Elmwood Gv WBAY NE26 40 C4
Elmwood Rd MONK NE25 40 A6
Elmwood St
ASHBK/HED/RY SR2 144 A1 5
HLS DH4 169 D1
Elrick Cl WD/WHPE/BLK NE5 59 E4 6
Elrington Gdns
WD/WHPE/BLK NE5 61 D6 2
Elsdon Av MONK NE25 24 C5
Elsdonburn Rd SUNDSW SR3 160 A3 3
Elsdon Cl BLYTH NE24 10 B5
PLEE/EAS SR8 208 B5
Elsdon Ct WICK/BNPF NE16 95 F5
Elsdon Dr LGB/KIL NE12 50 B4
Elsdon Gdns DUN/TMV NE11 97 F2
Elsdon Pl NSHW NE29 70 C2 2
Elsdon Rd DHAM DH1 180 C6
GOS/KPK NE3 63 E1
WICK/BNPF NE16 95 F4
Elsdon St NSHW NE29 70 C2 3
Elsdon Ter NSHW NE29 69 F2
Elsing Cl WD/WHPE/BLK NE5 61 D2
Elstob Pl BYK/HTN/WLK NE6 83 D4
SUNDSW SR3 143 F4
Elston Cl WD/WHPE/BLK NE5 59 E4 7
Elstree Ct DIN/WO NE13 45 D5 1
Elstree Gdns BLYTH NE24 16 C3 1
Elswick East Ter ELS/FEN NE4 80 A4
Elswick Rd ELS/FEN NE4 79 E4
Elswick Rw ELS/FEN NE4 79 F3
Elswick St ELS/FEN NE4 80 A3 10
Elswick Wy HAR/WTLS NE34 87 F2
Elterwater Rd CLSW/PEL DH2 166 A1
Elton St East WLSD/HOW NE28 67 D5
Elton St West WLSD/HOW NE28 66 C5
Eltringham Cl WLSD/HOW NE28 66 C4 2
Elvaston Rd RYTON NE40 74 B2
Elvet Br DHAM DH1 194 B5
Elvet Cl DIN/WO NE13 33 D4 2
Elvet Ct BYK/HTN/WLK NE6 82 B1
Elvet Crs DHAM DH1 194 C5
Elvet Gn CLSW/PEL DH2 153 E6
HLH DH5 185 F3 1
Elvet Hill Rd DHAM DH1 205 E1
Elvington St CLDN/WHIT/ROK SR6 127 D1
Elwin Cl WBAY NE26 26 C3
Elwin Pl CLSW/PEL DH2 152 A2
Elwin Ter ASHBK/HED/RY SR2 4 A4
Elwyn Cl WBAY NE26 26 C3
Ely Cl LGB/KIL NE12 65 F2
Ely Rd DHAM DH1 180 C4 2
Elysium La GATE NE8 98 C1
Ely St GATE NE8 99 D1 2
Embankment Rd SEA/MUR SR7 176 A1
SEA/MUR SR7 177 D4
Embassy Gdns I
BW/LEM/TK/HW NE15 78 A2
Emblehope WASHN NE37 119 F6
Emblehope Dr GOS/KPK NE3 62 C2
Embleton Av GOS/KPK NE3 46 C6 3
HAR/WTLS NE34 73 D6
WLSD/HOW NE28 68 A1
Embleton Cl DHAM DH1 180 C6 2
Embleton Crs NSHW NE29 53 E4
Embleton Dr BLYTH NE24 16 B1 3
Embleton Gdns
WD/WHPE/BLK NE5 61 F5 3
Embleton Rd FELL NE10 84 A6
NSHW NE29 53 E4
Embleton St SEA/MUR SR7 176 C5 1
Emden Rd GOS/KPK NE3 46 A6
Emily St BYK/HTN/WLK NE6 83 D2
GATE NE8 100 A1 5
Emily St East SEA/MUR SR7 176 C3 7
Emlyn Rd HAR/WTLS NE34 88 B2
Emmbrook Cl HLH DH5 170 C6 1
Emmerson Pl SMOOR NE27 52 A1
Empress Rd BYK/HTN/WLK NE6 84 A4
Empress St SWCK/CAS SR5 126 B3 3
Emsworth Rd SWCK/CAS SR5 125 F1
Enderby Rd MLFD/PNYW SR4 126 A5
Enfield Av WICK/BNPF NE16 96 A1
Enfield Gdns WICK/BNPF NE16 96 A5
Enfield Rd LWF/SPW/WRK NE9 99 E3
SEA/MUR SR7 175 E3
Enfield St MLFD/PNYW SR4 125 E5 2
Engine Inn Rd WLSD/HOW NE28 68 B2
Engine La LWF/SPW/WRK NE9 99 E6
Englemann Wy SUNDSW SR3 160 A4
Enid Av CLDN/WHIT/ROK SR6 126 C1
Enid St DIN/WO NE13 32 C6 2
Ennerdale ASHBK/HED/RY SR2 144 B2
CLS/BIR/GTL DH3 136 C4
Ennerdale Cl DHAM DH1 197 D2 2
SEA/MUR SR7 175 E3
Ennerdale Crs BLAY NE21 94 A2 3
HLS DH4 139 F6 1
Ennerdale Gdns
LWF/SPW/WRK NE9 99 F5
WLSD/HOW NE28 68 C2 2
Ennerdale Rd BLYTH NE24 9 E3
BYK/HTN/WLK NE6 83 E2
TYNE/NSHE NE30 54 C2
Ennerdale St HLH DH5 185 D2
Enslin St BYK/HTN/WLK NE6 83 E5
Epping Cl SEA/MUR SR7 175 E4
Eppleton Hall Cl SEA/MUR SR7 175 D2
Eppleton Rw HLH DH5 172 A6 1
Epsom Cl NSHW NE29 70 B2
Epsom Ct GOS/KPK NE3 45 E5
Epsom Wy BLYTH NE24 16 C3
Epworth STLY/ANP DH9 130 B6
Equitable St WLSD/HOW NE28 67 D5 7
Erick St CNUT NE1 3 E3 1
Erith Ter MLFD/PNYW SR4 125 E6
Ernest St ASHBK/HED/RY SR2 145 D2
BOLCOL NE35 105 F2
CLSW/PEL DH2 152 A1
Ernest Ter STLY/ANP DH9 131 E6 3
Ernwill Av SWCK/CAS SR5 124 A3
Errington Dr STLY/ANP DH9 130 B6
Errington Ter LGB/KIL NE12 50 A3 3
Errol Pl CLS/BIR/GTL DH3 136 C4
Erskine Rd SSH NE33 71 F4
Erskine Wy SSH NE33 72 A4
Escallond Dr SEA/MUR SR7 175 E4
Esdale ASHBK/HED/RY SR2 162 A2
Esher Gdns BLYTH NE24 16 C3
Eshmere Crs WD/WHPE/BLK NE5 59 E4
Eshott Cl GOS/KPK NE3 46 C6
WD/WHPE/BLK NE5 60 C5
Eskdale CLS/BIR/GTL DH3 137 D5
HLS DH4 139 F6 2
Eskdale Av BLYTH NE24 9 F4
WLSD/HOW NE28 67 E2
Eskdale Cl SEA/MUR SR7 175 E3
Eskdale Ct HAR/WTLS NE34 88 B2
Eskdale Dr JRW NE32 86 C5
Eskdale Gdns LWF/SPW/WRK NE9 99 F6
Eskdale Rd CLDN/WHIT/ROK SR6 109 E4
Eskdale St HAR/WTLS NE34 88 B3 8
HLH DH5 185 E2
Eskdale Ter JES NE2 64 A6 1
WBAY NE26 41 E6
Eskdale Wk PLEE/EAS SR8 209 D2 4
Esk St LWF/SPW/WRK NE9 100 A3
Eslington Rd JES NE2 81 D1 2
Eslington Ter JES NE2 64 A6
Esmaralda Gdns CRAM NE23 36 C1 1
Esplanade WBAY NE26 41 D5
Espley Cl LGB/KIL NE12 50 C4
Espley Ct GOS/KPK NE3 46 A5 3
Essen Wy SUNDSW SR3 144 A3
Essex Cl ELS/FEN NE4 80 A5
Essex Crs SEA/MUR SR7 175 E3
Essex Dr WASHN NE37 120 C3 1
Essex Gdns HAR/WTLS NE34 90 B1
WLSD/HOW NE28 68 A3
Essex Gv SUNDSW SR3 143 F6
Essex Pl PLEE/EAS SR8 200 B6
Essington Wy PLEE/EAS SR8 200 B6
Esst Vw HLH DH5 186 C3
Esther Sq WASHS NE38 139 D2
Esthwaite Av CLSW/PEL DH2 166 A1
Eston Ct BLYTH NE24 10 A4
WLSD/HOW NE28 66 B1 2
Eston Gv SWCK/CAS SR5 126 B1
Estuary Wy MLFD/PNYW SR4 124 A5
Etal Av MONK NE25 41 D6
NSHW NE29 69 F2
Etal Crs JRW NE32 86 C4
SMOOR NE27 52 B1
Etal La WD/WHPE/BLK NE5 60 C3
Etal Pl GOS/KPK NE3 46 C5 2
Etal Rd BLYTH NE24 16 A3 1
Etal Wy WD/WHPE/BLK NE5 61 D2
Ethel Av ASHBK/HED/RY SR2 162 C2
BLAY NE21 76 B6 3
Ethel St CRAM NE23 34 C4
ELS/FEN NE4 78 C4
Ethel Ter HAR/WTLS NE34 88 A3
SWCK/CAS SR5 124 A3
Etherley Cl DHAM DH1 180 C5
Etherley Rd BYK/HTN/WLK NE6 82 C1
Etherstone Av LGB/HTN NE7 65 E4
Eton Cl CRAM NE23 14 B4 3
Eton Sq HEBB NE31 85 E2
Ettrick Cl LGB/KIL NE12 35 E6 4
Ettrick Gdns GATE NE8 100 A2 2
MLFD/PNYW SR4 143 D2
Ettrick Gv MLFD/PNYW SR4 143 E2
SUNDSW SR3 143 E3 1
Ettrick Rd JRW NE32 85 F3
European Wy MLFD/PNYW SR4 124 C4
Euryalus Ct SSH NE33 72 B5
Eustace Av NSHW NE29 70 A1
Evanlade FELL NE10 102 A4
Eva St BW/LEM/TK/HW NE15 76 B2
Evelyn St ASHBK/HED/RY SR2 144 A1
Evenwood Gdns
LWF/SPW/WRK NE9 100 A5
Everard St CRAM NE23 14 A3
Everest Gv BOL NE36 106 A3 3
Eversleigh Pl
BW/LEM/TK/HW NE15 58 A4 3
Eversley Pl WLSD/HOW NE28 68 B3 3
Everton Dr SEA/MUR SR7 175 E3
Everton La SWCK/CAS SR5 125 F1
Evesham MLFD/PNYW SR4 123 F6
Evesham Av WBAY NE26 40 B4
Evesham Cl BOLCOL NE35 105 E1
Evesham Garth GOS/KPK NE3 62 A3
Evesham Rd SEA/MUR SR7 175 E3
Evistones Gdns BYK/HTN/WLK NE6 83 D5
Evistones Rd
LWF/SPW/WRK NE9 99 E4 2
Ewart Crs HAR/WTLS NE34 87 D4
Ewbank Av ELS/FEN NE4 79 D1
Ewehurst Crs STLY/ANP DH9 129 D5
Ewehurst Pde STLY/ANP DH9 129 D5
Ewehurst Rd STLY/ANP DH9 129 D5
WICK/BNPF NE16 129 E4
Ewen Ct NSHW NE29 53 D4
Ewesley WASHS NE38 137 F6
Ewesley Cl WD/WHPE/BLK NE5 60 C4
Ewesley Gdns DIN/WO NE13 33 D4
Ewesley Rd MLFD/PNYW SR4 143 E1
Ewing Rd MLFD/PNYW SR4 144 A1 6
Exebly Cl GOS/KPK NE3 47 F4
Exeter Cl CLS/BIR/GTL DH3 167 F4
Exeter Rd WLSD/HOW NE28 66 C1
Exeter St BYK/HTN/WLK NE6 83 F4
GATE NE8 99 D1
MLFD/PNYW SR4 125 E5
Exmouth Cl SEA/MUR SR7 175 F4 3
Exmouth Rd NSHW NE29 69 E1
Exmouth Sq SWCK/CAS SR5 125 F1
Extension Rd SUND SR1 5 H3
Eyemouth La SWCK/CAS SR5 125 F1
Eyemouth Rd NSHW NE29 69 E1 2
Eyre St STLY/ANP DH9 147 F3

F

Faber Rd SWCK/CAS SR5 125 F1
Factory Rd BLAY NE21 76 C4
Fairbairn Rd PLEE/EAS SR8 200 C6
Fairburn Av HLH DH5 171 D4
LGB/HTN NE7 65 E2
Fairdale Av LGB/HTN NE7 65 E2
Fairfield CLSW/PEL DH2 151 F1
LGB/KIL NE12 48 B6
STLY/ANP DH9 146 B3
Fairfield Av BLYTH NE24 16 C2
WICK/BNPF NE16 95 F5
Fairfield Cl DUN/TMV NE11 97 E1 1
Fairfield Dr CLDN/WHIT/ROK SR6 91 D6
MONK NE25 39 E6
TYNE/NSHE NE30 55 D2
Fairfield Gn MONK NE25 39 E6
Fairfield Rd JES NE2 63 F5
Fairfields RYTON NE40 74 A4
Fair Gn MONK NE25 39 E6
Fairgreen Cl SUNDSW SR3 160 C3 1
Fairhaven LWF/SPW/WRK NE9 119 E2
Fairhaven Av BYK/HTN/WLK NE6 83 F2
Fairhill Cl LGB/HTN NE7 65 E2
Fairholme Av HAR/WTLS NE34 89 E2
Fairholme Rd SUNDSW SR3 144 B3 3
Fairholm Rd ELS/FEN NE4 79 D3
Fairlands East
CLDN/WHIT/ROK SR6 126 C2 3
Fairlands West SWCK/CAS SR5 126 C2
Fairlawn Gdns MLFD/PNYW SR4 143 D2
Fairles St SSH NE33 71 F2
Fairmead Wy MLFD/PNYW SR4 141 F1
Fairmile Dr SUNDSW SR3 160 C3
Fairmont Wy LGB/HTN NE7 65 E2 4
Fairney Cl PONT/DH NE20 28 B4
Fairney Edge PONT/DH NE20 28 B4
Fairspring WD/WHPE/BLK NE5 60 C4
Fairview Av HAR/WTLS NE34 89 E1
Fairview Gn LGB/HTN NE7 65 E2 5
Fairville Cl CRAM NE23 14 A4
Fairville Crs LGB/HTN NE7 65 E2
Fairway Cl GOS/KPK NE3 47 D4
Fairways MONK NE25 39 E5
SUNDSW SR3 161 D1 2
Fairways Av LGB/HTN NE7 65 E1 2
The Fairways BOL NE36 105 F3 2
BOL NE36 106 B3 2
STLY/ANP DH9 147 F6
The Fairway BLAY NE21 75 F4
GOS/KPK NE3 47 D4
WASHN NE37 120 C1
Falconar's Ct CNUT NE1 2 C4
Falconar St JES NE2 3 F2

Falcon Pl LGB/KIL NE12 48 C5
Falcon Wy HAR/WTLS NE34 88 A4
Faldonside BYK/HTN/WLK NE6 65 F4 3
Falkirk LGB/KIL NE12 35 F6 8
Falkland Av GOS/KPK NE3 62 B3
HEBB NE31 85 D2
Falkland Rd MLFD/PNYW SR4 125 D6
Falla Park Crs FELL NE10 100 B2
Falla Park Rd FELL NE10 100 B2
Falloden Av GOS/KPK NE3 46 B4
Fallodon Gdns
WD/WHPE/BLK NE5 61 F4 4
Fallodon Rd NSHW NE29 69 F1
Fallowfeld FELL NE10 101 F3
Fallowfield WASHS NE38 139 D5
Fallowfield Av GOS/KPK NE3 46 B6
Fallowfield Wy WASHS NE38 138 C4
Fallow Park Av BLYTH NE24 10 B6 3
Fallow Rd HAR/WTLS NE34 90 C2
Fallsway DHAM DH1 196 C1
Falmouth Cl SEA/MUR SR7 175 F4 4
Falmouth Dr JRW NE32 86 C3
Falmouth Rd BYK/HTN/WLK NE6 82 A1
MLFD/PNYW SR4 125 D5
NSHW NE29 53 F3
NSHW NE29 69 E1
Falmouth Sq MLFD/PNYW SR4 125 D6
Falsgrave Pl WICK/BNPF NE16 95 E5
Falstaff Rd NSHW NE29 53 F6
Falstone FELL NE10 101 E5
WASHS NE38 139 D4
Falstone Av BW/LEM/TK/HW NE15 60 A6
HAR/WTLS NE34 89 F2
Falstone Cl LGB/KIL NE12 50 C4
Falstone Dr CLSW/PEL DH2 165 E1
Falstone Sq GOS/KPK NE3 46 C6 4
Falston Rd BLYTH NE24 16 B1
Faraday Cl WASHS NE38 140 A1
Faraday Gv GATE NE8 98 C3
MLFD/PNYW SR4 125 D6
Faraday Rd PLEE/EAS SR8 201 D5
Faraday St SEA/MUR SR7 188 B1 2
Fareham Gv BOLCOL NE35 104 C2
Farlam Av TYNE/NSHE NE30 54 C3
Farlam Rd WD/WHPE/BLK NE5 61 D6 3
Farleigh Ct NSHW NE29 53 D4
Farm Cl WASHN NE37 120 A3
WICK/BNPF NE16 114 A2
Farm Ct BLAY NE21 77 E6
Farmer Crs SEA/MUR SR7 188 A1
Farm Hill Rd CLDN/WHIT/ROK SR6 89 F6
Farm Rd DHAM DH1 205 F3
Farm St SWCK/CAS SR5 126 A3
Farnborough Cl CRAM NE23 14 A6
Farnborough Dr SUNDSW SR3 144 A6
Farn Ct DIN/WO NE13 45 F4
Farndale WLSD/HOW NE28 66 B1
Farndale Av CLDN/WHIT/ROK SR6 109 E4
Farndale Cl BLAY NE21 93 E2 1
DIN/WO NE13 31 D3 2
Farndale Rd ELS/FEN NE4 79 D3
Farne Av GOS/KPK NE3 46 C4
HAR/WTLS NE34 90 A1
Farne Rd LGB/KIL NE12 50 A4
SMOOR NE27 52 B1
Farne Sq MLFD/PNYW SR4 124 C5
Farne Ter BYK/HTN/WLK NE6 83 D2
Farnham Cl DHAM DH1 194 B1
Farnham Gv BLYTH NE24 16 C2
Farnham Rd DHAM DH1 180 B6
HAR/WTLS NE34 88 B2 2
Farnham St BW/LEM/TK/HW NE15 76 C2
Farnham Ter MLFD/PNYW SR4 143 E1
Farnley Hey Rd DHAM DH1 193 F5
Farnley Mt DHAM DH1 193 F5 1
Farnley Rdg DHAM DH1 193 F5
Farnley Rd BYK/HTN/WLK NE6 65 E5 2
Farnon Rd GOS/KPK NE3 62 C1
Farquhar St JES NE2 64 B6
Farrier Cl WASHS NE38 139 D4
Farringdon Rd TYNE/NSHE NE30 54 C2
Farringdon Rw MLFD/PNYW SR4 126 A4
Farrington Av SUNDSW SR3 142 B6
Farrow Dr CLDN/WHIT/ROK SR6 109 D1
The Farthings WASHN NE37 120 A2
Fatfield Pk WASHS NE38 138 C5
Fatfield Rd WASHS NE38 139 D2
Faversham Ct GOS/KPK NE3 45 F5 1
Faversham Pl CRAM NE23 14 A6
Fawcett St SUND SR1 4 C2
Fawcett Ter
ASHBK/HED/RY SR2 162 C2 1
Fawdon Cl GOS/KPK NE3 46 A4
Fawdon La GOS/KPK NE3 45 F5
Fawdon Park Rd GOS/KPK NE3 46 A5 4
Fawdon Pl NSHW NE29 53 E6
Fawley Cl BOLCOL NE35 105 D1 2
Fawn Rd MLFD/PNYW SR4 124 B6
Feather Bed La
ASHBK/HED/RY SR2 162 C2
Featherstone Gv BDLGTN NE22 6 C2
JRW NE32 85 F5
Featherstone Rd DHAM DH1 194 C1
Featherstone St
CLDN/WHIT/ROK SR6 127 E2
Federation Sq SEA/MUR SR7 188 B2
Federation Wy DUN/TMV NE11 97 D1 1
Feetham Av LGB/KIL NE12 50 B4
Felixstowe Dr LGB/HTN NE7 65 E3
Fell Bank CLS/BIR/GTL DH3 136 C2
Fell Cl CLS/BIR/GTL DH3 137 D3
WICK/BNPF NE16 114 A2
Felldyke FELL NE10 101 E5 1
Fellgate Av JRW NE32 104 B1
Fellgate Gdns FELL NE10 102 B2 1
Felling House Gdns FELL NE10 82 C6 1
Felling Vw BYK/HTN/WLK NE6 83 E5
Fellmere Av FELL NE10 101 E2
Fell Rd CLSW/PEL DH2 152 A5
LWF/SPW/WRK NE9 119 E3
MLFD/PNYW SR4 124 C5
Fellside HAR/WTLS NE34 90 A3
Fellside Av WICK/BNPF NE16 114 A1
Fellside Ct WICK/BNPF NE16 95 F3 3
Fellside Gdns DHAM DH1 196 B2 2
Fellside Rd WICK/BNPF NE16 95 E5
WICK/BNPF NE16 112 B5
The Fell Side GOS/KPK NE3 62 B2
Fells Rd DUN/TMV NE11 98 C3
The Fell Wy WD/WHPE/BLK NE5 59 F5 3
Felsham Sq MLFD/PNYW SR4 125 D6
Felstead Crs MLFD/PNYW SR4 124 C5
Felstead Pl BLYTH NE24 16 C2
Felstead Sq MLFD/PNYW SR4 124 C6
Felton Av GOS/KPK NE3 46 C6
HAR/WTLS NE34 89 F2
MONK NE25 41 D6
Felton Cl SMOOR NE27 52 B1
Felton Crs GATE NE8 99 D3
Felton Dr LGB/KIL NE12 50 B3
Fencer Ct GOS/KPK NE3 47 E4
Fence Rd CLS/BIR/GTL DH3 156 A2
Fenham Cha ELS/FEN NE4 61 F6
Fenham Hall Dr ELS/FEN NE4 61 F6
Fenham Rd ELS/FEN NE4 79 E2 3
Fenkle St CNUT NE1 2 B4
Fennel Gv HAR/WTLS NE34 89 D5
Fenning Pl BYK/HTN/WLK NE6 82 B4 1
Fenside Rd ASHBK/HED/RY SR2 145 E6
Fenton Cl CLSW/PEL DH2 165 F1
Fenton Sq MLFD/PNYW SR4 124 C6 1
Fenton Well La CLS/BIR/GTL DH3 167 D3
Fenwick Av BLYTH NE24 16 C1 2
HAR/WTLS NE34 87 F3
Fenwick Cl CLSW/PEL DH2 165 E1
HLS DH4 140 A6 1
Fenwick St HLS DH4 140 A6
Ferens Cl DHAM DH1 194 C3
Ferens Pk DHAM DH1 194 C3
Ferguson Crs DIN/WO NE13 32 C6
Ferguson's La
BW/LEM/TK/HW NE15 77 F2
Ferguson St ASHBK/HED/RY SR2 5 H4
Fern Av CLDN/WHIT/ROK SR6 91 E6
CRAM NE23 14 A4
GOS/KPK NE3 46 C5 3
JES NE2 64 A5
NSHW NE29 54 B6
SWCK/CAS SR5 125 F2
Fern Crs SEA/MUR SR7 176 B6
Ferndale DHAM DH1 196 C3
Ferndale Av BOL NE36 106 C3
GOS/KPK NE3 47 F3
WLSD/HOW NE28 67 E4
Ferndale Cl BLYTH NE24 9 F4 2
Ferndale Gv BOL NE36 106 C3
Ferndale La BOL NE36 106 C3
Ferndale Rd HLS DH4 139 F6
Ferndale Ter MLFD/PNYW SR4 125 D4
Ferndene Crs MLFD/PNYW SR4 125 E6
Ferndene Gv LGB/HTN NE7 65 D3
Fern Dene Rd GATE NE8 99 D2
Ferndown Ct RYTON NE40 74 C4 1
Fern Dr CLDN/WHIT/ROK SR6 107 E1
CRAM NE23 34 C2
Fernhill Av WICK/BNPF NE16 95 F3
Fernlea Cl WASHS NE38 139 D4
Fernley Vls CRAM NE23 22 C2
Fern Rd BDN/LAN/SAC DH7 178 C1
Fern St MLFD/PNYW SR4 126 A5
Fernsway SUNDSW SR3 144 A3 5
Fernville Av WICK/BNPF NE16 114 A2
Fernville Rd GOS/KPK NE3 63 D4
Fernville St MLFD/PNYW SR4 144 A1 7
Fernwood Av GOS/KPK NE3 47 F6
Fernwood Cl SUNDSW SR3 160 C3 2
Fernwood Rd
BW/LEM/TK/HW NE15 76 C2
JES NE2 64 A6
Ferrand Dr HLS DH4 170 C2
Ferriby Cl GOS/KPK NE3 47 F4 2
Ferrisdale Wy GOS/KPK NE3 46 B5
Ferryboat La SWCK/CAS SR5 123 E4
Ferrydene Av GOS/KPK NE3 62 B2
Ferry St JRW NE32 69 D6
SSH NE33 71 D3
Festival Park Dr DUN/TMV NE11 98 A3
Festival Wy DUN/TMV NE11 97 F1
Field Cl JES NE2 3 H2
Field Fare Ct WICK/BNPF NE16 130 B1
Fieldhouse La DHAM DH1 193 F3
Field House Rd GATE NE8 99 D3
Fielding Ct WD/WHPE/BLK NE5 60 C2 2
Fielding Pl LWF/SPW/WRK NE9 100 A2 3
Field La FELL NE10 101 E2
Fieldside CLDN/WHIT/ROK SR6 109 D1
CLSW/PEL DH2 152 A1
HLH DH5 184 B1
Field Sq MLFD/PNYW SR4 124 B6
Field St FELL NE10 100 C1 3
GOS/KPK NE3 64 A1
Field Ter JRW NE32 86 A3
Fieldway BOLCOL NE35 104 B2
JRW NE32 104 C1 2
Fife Av JRW NE32 87 D5
Fife St GATE NE8 99 F1
SEA/MUR SR7 188 C2
Fifteenth Av BLYTH NE24 10 C6
Fifth Av BYK/HTN/WLK NE6 82 B1 3
DUN/TMV NE11 98 C5
Fifth St PLEE/EAS SR8 209 F1
Filby Dr DHAM DH1 196 C1
Filey Cl CRAM NE23 14 A6
Filton Cl CRAM NE23 14 A6
Finchale WASHS NE38 138 B3
Finchale Av DHAM DH1 181 E4
Finchale Cl ASHBK/HED/RY SR2 5 F5
DUN/TMV NE11 97 E4 1
HLS DH4 170 C2
Finchale Gdns
BW/LEM/TK/HW NE15 57 F3
Finchale Rd DHAM DH1 180 C4
HEBB NE31 85 D5
Finchale Ter JRW NE32 86 C4
Finchale Vw DHAM DH1 180 A5 1
HLS DH4 183 D2
Finchdale Cl NSHW NE29 70 B2
Finchley Crs BYK/HTN/WLK NE6 66 C6
Findon Av BDN/LAN/SAC DH7 178 A3
Findon Gv NSHW NE29 70 A2
Findon Hl BDN/LAN/SAC DH7 178 B2
Finsbury Av BYK/HTN/WLK NE6 83 D2
Finsbury St SWCK/CAS SR5 126 B3 4
Finsmere Av WD/WHPE/BLK NE5 61 D5 3
Finsmere Pl WD/WHPE/BLK NE5 61 D5 4
Finstock Ct LGB/HTN NE7 64 B2
Fir Av BDN/LAN/SAC DH7 203 D5
DHAM DH1 195 F5
Firbank Av TYNE/NSHE NE30 55 D2
Firbanks JRW NE32 104 C1
Firfield Rd WD/WHPE/BLK NE5 61 F4
Fir Gv HAR/WTLS NE34 89 E3
Fir Pk BDN/LAN/SAC DH7 192 A4
First Av BLYTH NE24 10 C6
BYK/HTN/WLK NE6 82 B1
CLSW/PEL DH2 136 A6
DUN/TMV NE11 98 B4
NSHW NE29 69 D2
The Firs GOS/KPK NE3 63 D2 2
Fir St JRW NE32 85 F1
First St GATE NE8 98 C1
PLEE/EAS SR8 209 F1
Firth Sq MLFD/PNYW SR4 124 C6
Firtree Av BYK/HTN/WLK NE6 66 C5
LGB/KIL NE12 49 F3
WASHS NE38 138 B5
Fir Tree Cl DHAM DH1 195 F2 1
Firtree Crs LGB/KIL NE12 49 E3
Firtree Gdns MONK NE25 54 B1
Firtree Rd WICK/BNPF NE16 95 F4
Firtrees CLSW/PEL DH2 153 D3
FELL NE10 101 D5
Firtrees Av WLSD/HOW NE28 69 D3
Firwood Gdns DUN/TMV NE11 98 A5
Fisher La CRAM NE23 12 B6
DIN/WO NE13 20 A5
Fisher Rd SMOOR NE27 37 D4
Fisher St BYK/HTN/WLK NE6 84 A1
WLSD/HOW NE28 84 A1
Fisherwell Rd FELL NE10 83 F6
Fitzpatrick Pl SSH NE33 72 A4 2
Fitzsimmons Av WLSD/HOW NE28 67 D3
Flambard Rd DHAM DH1 194 A1
Flassburn Rd DHAM DH1 193 F3
Flass St DHAM DH1 194 A4
Flaunden Cl HAR/WTLS NE34 90 A3 3
Flaxby Cl GOS/KPK NE3 47 F4
Flax Sq MLFD/PNYW SR4 124 B5 1
Fleet St SUND SR1 5 H3
Fleming Gdns FELL NE10 100 B3
Fleming Pl PLEE/EAS SR8 208 C2 1
Fletcher Crs HLS DH4 158 A2
Flexbury Gdns
BW/LEM/TK/HW NE15 77 D1 2
FELL NE10 100 B2 3
LWF/SPW/WRK NE9 117 F2
Flint Hill Bank STLY/ANP DH9 129 D5
Flodden LGB/KIL NE12 35 F6
Flodden Cl CLSW/PEL DH2 165 E1
Flodden Rd MLFD/PNYW SR4 124 C6
Flodden St BYK/HTN/WLK NE6 82 C3
Floral Dene MLFD/PNYW SR4 123 F6
Flora St BYK/HTN/WLK NE6 82 A2 6
Florence Av LWF/SPW/WRK NE9 99 F4 5
Florence Crs SWCK/CAS SR5 125 E2

Florence St BLAY NE21 .... 94 A1
Florida St MLFD/PNYW SR4 .... 125 E4
Flotterton Gdns
WD/WHPE/BLK NE5 .... 78 B1
The Fold MONK NE25 .... 40 A5
WICK/BNPF NE16 .... 111 F5
Folldon Av
CLDN/WHIT/ROK SR6 .... 126 C1 2
Follingsby Av FELL NE10 .... 103 D4
Follingsby Dr FELL NE10 .... 102 B3
Follingsby La FELL NE10 .... 103 D5
Follingsby Wy FELL NE10 .... 102 C4
Folly La RYTON NE40 .... 74 A6
Folly Ter DHAM DH1 .... 179 F5
The Folly BOL NE36 .... 105 F3
Fontaine Rd SUND SR1 .... 4 A1
Fontburn Ct SWCK/CAS SR5 .... 107 E6 1
Fontburn Pl LGB/HTN NE7 .... 64 C1
Fontburn Rd MONK NE25 .... 24 C5
Fontburn Ter TYNE/NSHE NE30 .... 55 D6
Fonteyn Pl CRAM NE23 .... 14 A4
STLY/ANP DH9 .... 149 D3
Fontwell Dr GATE NE8 .... 98 C3
Forbeck Rd MLFD/PNYW SR4 .... 124 C6
Forber Av HAR/WTLS NE34 .... 90 A2
Ford Av MLFD/PNYW SR4 .... 123 F6
NSHW NE29 .... 69 F2
Ford Crs JRW NE32 .... 86 A5
MLFD/PNYW SR4 .... 123 F6
SMOOR NE27 .... 52 A1
Ford Dr BLYTH NE24 .... 10 B5
Fordenbridge Crs
MLFD/PNYW SR4 .... 124 C6
Fordenbridge Rd
MLFD/PNYW SR4 .... 124 C6 2
Fordenbridge Sq
MLFD/PNYW SR4 .... 125 D6 1
Fordfield Rd MLFD/PNYW SR4 .... 124 B6
Ford Gv GOS/KPK NE3 .... 47 D5
Fordhall Dr MLFD/PNYW SR4 .... 125 D6 2
Fordham Rd DHAM DH1 .... 194 B1
MLFD/PNYW SR4 .... 124 C5
Fordham Sq MLFD/PNYW SR4 .... 125 D6
Fordland Pl MLFD/PNYW SR4 .... 125 E6
Ford Ov MLFD/PNYW SR4 .... 124 A5
Ford Rd DHAM DH1 .... 180 C5
Ford St BYK/HTN/WLK NE6 .... 81 F3
GATE NE8 .... 100 A1 6
Ford Ter WLSD/HOW NE28 .... 68 A4
Ford Vw CRAM NE23 .... 34 C1
Forest Av LGB/KIL NE12 .... 50 A4
Forest Dr WASHS NE38 .... 137 E6
Forest Hall Rd LGB/KIL NE12 .... 50 A3
Fore St JES NE2 .... 64 C6
Forest Rd BW/LEM/TK/HW NE15 .... 78 A4
MLFD/PNYW SR4 .... 124 C5
SSH NE33 .... 71 E4
Forest Vw BDN/LAN/SAC DH7 .... 202 B5
Forest Wy CRAM NE23 .... 36 B1
Forfar St SWCK/CAS SR5 .... 126 C2
Forge La CLS/BIR/GTL DH3 .... 155 D5
Forge Rd DUN/TMV NE11 .... 97 F2
Forres Ct STLY/ANP DH9 .... 149 D2
Forres Pl CRAM NE23 .... 14 A6
Forrest Rd WLSD/HOW NE28 .... 66 C5 2
Forster Av BDLGTN NE22 .... 7 D3
HAR/WTLS NE34 .... 89 D1 2
RDHAMSE DH6 .... 197 E4
Forster St BLYTH NE24 .... 11 E5
CLDN/WHIT/ROK SR6 .... 127 D3
Forsyth Rd JES NE2 .... 63 F5
Forth Banks CNUT NE1 .... 2 C6
Forth Cl PLEE/EAS SR8 .... 208 C3
Forth Ct HAR/WTLS NE34 .... 88 B3
Forth Pl CNUT NE1 .... 2 B5
Forth St CNUT NE1 .... 2 B6
Fortrose Av SUNDSW SR3 .... 143 F3
Fort St SSH NE33 .... 71 F2
Forum Ct BDLGTN NE22 .... 7 E3
The Forum BW/LEM/TK/HW NE15 .... 77 E1
Forum Wy CRAM NE23 .... 21 F2
Fossdyke FELL NE10 .... 101 E5 2
Fossefeld FELL NE10 .... 101 F3
Fosse Law BW/LEM/TK/HW NE15 .... 58 A5
Fosse Ter LWF/SPW/WRK NE9 .... 100 A4 4
Fossway BYK/HTN/WLK NE6 .... 66 C6
Foster St BYK/HTN/WLK NE6 .... 84 A3
Foundry La BYK/HTN/WLK NE6 .... 81 F2
JES NE2 .... 81 F2 5
Foundry Rd SEA/MUR SR7 .... 177 D3
Fountain Cl BDLGTN NE22 .... 7 E3 1
Fountain Gv HAR/WTLS NE34 .... 72 B6
Fountain Head Bank WBAY NE26 .... 26 A2
Fountain La BLAY NE21 .... 76 A4
Fountain Rw JES NE2 .... 80 A1
Fountains Cl DUN/TMV NE11 .... 97 F4 2
WASHS NE38 .... 138 C2
Fountains Crs HEBB NE31 .... 85 D5
HLS DH4 .... 157 E6
Fouracres Rd WD/WHPE/BLK NE5 .... 62 A4
Four Lane Ends HLH DH5 .... 186 A2
Fourstones WD/WHPE/BLK NE5 .... 60 C4
Fourstones Cl GOS/KPK NE3 .... 61 F1
Fourstones Rd MLFD/PNYW SR4 .... 125 D5
Fourth Av BLYTH NE24 .... 10 C6 3
BYK/HTN/WLK NE6 .... 82 B1 4
CLSW/PEL DH2 .... 153 D5
DUN/TMV NE11 .... 98 B5
Fourth St GATE NE8 .... 98 C1 4
PLEE/EAS SR8 .... 209 F1
Fowberry Crs ELS/FEN NE4 .... 79 D1
Fowberry Rd
BW/LEM/TK/HW NE15 .... 77 E4
Fowler Cl HLS DH4 .... 157 E4 3
Fowler St SSH NE33 .... 71 E3
Fox & Hounds La
BW/LEM/TK/HW NE15 .... 78 B2
Fox & Hounds Rd
WD/WHPE/BLK NE5 .... 78 B1
Fox Av HAR/WTLS NE34 .... 87 E4
Foxcover La SUNDSW SR3 .... 159 D1
Foxcover Rd MLFD/PNYW SR4 .... 141 E4
Foxglove Ct HAR/WTLS NE34 .... 87 F4
Foxhills Cl WASHS NE38 .... 139 D4
Foxhills Covert WICK/BNPF NE16 .... 95 D5
Foxhunters Rd MONK NE25 .... 54 B1
Foxlair Cl SUNDSW SR3 .... 160 C4
Fox Lea Wk CRAM NE23 .... 36 A1
Foxley WASHN NE37 .... 121 D4
Foxley Cl LGB/KIL NE12 .... 36 B6
Fox St ASHBK/HED/RY SR2 .... 144 A1
SEA/MUR SR7 .... 176 C4
Foxton Av GOS/KPK NE3 .... 46 B5
TYNE/NSHE NE30 .... 55 D1
Foxton Cl NSHW NE29 .... 70 A3
Foxton Hall WASHN NE37 .... 120 C1
Foxton Wy FELL NE10 .... 84 A6
Foyle St SUND SR1 .... 4 D3
Framwelgate DHAM DH1 .... 194 B4
Framwelgate Br DHAM DH1 .... 194 B5
Framwelgate Peth DHAM DH1 .... 194 A3
Framwelgate Waterside
DHAM DH1 .... 194 B4
Frances St BLAY NE21 .... 75 F6
Francis St CLDN/WHIT/ROK SR6 .... 126 C2
Frankham St
WD/WHPE/BLK NE5 .... 60 B4 3
Frankland Dr MONK NE25 .... 54 A1
Frankland La DHAM DH1 .... 194 B3
Frankland Rd DHAM DH1 .... 194 A1
Franklin St MLFD/PNYW SR4 .... 125 F5
SSH NE33 .... 71 E3
Franklyn Av WBAY NE26 .... 26 A1
Franklyn Rd PLEE/EAS SR8 .... 208 A1
Frank Pl NSHW NE29 .... 54 C6 7
Frank St DHAM DH1 .... 195 F4
SWCK/CAS SR5 .... 126 A2 8
WLSD/HOW NE28 .... 67 D5
Fraser Cl SSH NE33 .... 71 D6
Freda St SWCK/CAS SR5 .... 125 E3
Frederick Gdns HLS DH4 .... 156 C1 2
Frederick Rd SUND SR1 .... 4 D2
Frederick St MLFD/PNYW SR4 .... 123 F6 2
SEA/MUR SR7 .... 176 C3
SSH NE33 .... 71 E6
SUND SR1 .... 4 D3 1
Frederick Ter RDHAMSE DH6 .... 187 E6
Freeman Rd GOS/KPK NE3 .... 64 B2
LGB/HTN NE7 .... 64 B2
Freesia Gra WASHS NE38 .... 139 D3 1
Freezemoor Rd HLS DH4 .... 157 F2
Fremantle Rd HAR/WTLS NE34 .... 90 A3
Frenchman's Wy HAR/WTLS NE34 .... 90 A1
French St BLYTH NE24 .... 11 D4 5
Frensham WASHS NE38 .... 139 F2 1
Frensham Wy
BDN/LAN/SAC DH7 .... 203 E4 4
Frenton Cl WD/WHPE/BLK NE5 .... 59 E4 8
Friarage Av
CLDN/WHIT/ROK SR6 .... 126 C1 5
Friar Rd MLFD/PNYW SR4 .... 124 C6
Friars Dene Rd FELL NE10 .... 82 B6
Friarsfield Cl SUNDSW SR3 .... 160 A3
Friarside BDN/LAN/SAC DH7 .... 178 A4
Friarside Crs ROWG NE39 .... 110 C4
Friarside Gdns WICK/BNPF NE16 .... 95 F4
Friarside Rd ELS/FEN NE4 .... 62 A6
Friar Sq MLFD/PNYW SR4 .... 124 C6
Friars' Rw DHAM DH1 .... 195 E3
Friars St CNUT NE1 .... 2 B4
Friar St RDHAMSE DH6 .... 206 C2
Friars Wy WD/WHPE/BLK NE5 .... 61 E6 1
Friar Wy JRW NE32 .... 86 B1
Friary Gdns FELL NE10 .... 100 B1
Frobisher Ct SUNDSW SR3 .... 160 B3
Frobisher St HEBB NE31 .... 85 E2
Frome Gdns LWF/SPW/WRK NE9 .... 117 E2
Frome Pl CRAM NE23 .... 14 A6
Frome Sq MLFD/PNYW SR4 .... 124 B6 1
Front Rd MLFD/PNYW SR4 .... 124 C6
Front St BDN/LAN/SAC DH7 .... 178 A1
BDN/LAN/SAC DH7 .... 204 A2
BLAY NE21 .... 94 A1
BLYTH NE24 .... 8 C5
BOL NE36 .... 106 B3
BOLCOL NE35 .... 105 D1
CLDN/WHIT/ROK SR6 .... 107 F1
CLDN/WHIT/ROK SR6 .... 109 E2
CLS/BIR/GTL DH3 .... 153 E5
CLS/BIR/GTL DH3 .... 167 F3
CLSW/PEL DH2 .... 151 F1
CRAM NE23 .... 23 E6
CRAM NE23 .... 35 D1
CRAM NE23 .... 36 C1
DHAM DH1 .... 179 F6
DHAM DH1 .... 195 F5
DIN/WO NE13 .... 31 D3
DIN/WO NE13 .... 33 D1
HLH DH5 .... 171 F6
HLH DH5 .... 185 D3
HLS DH4 .... 157 F5
HLS DH4 .... 169 F2
LGB/HTN NE7 .... 65 E1
LGB/KIL NE12 .... 35 D5 2
MONK NE25 .... 38 C5
MONK NE25 .... 40 A6
NSHW NE29 .... 54 B4
NSHW NE29 .... 70 A1
RDHAMSE DH6 .... 183 F6
RDHAMSE DH6 .... 187 D4
RDHAMSE DH6 .... 197 F5
STLY/ANP DH9 .... 129 D5
STLY/ANP DH9 .... 130 C2
STLY/ANP DH9 .... 130 A4
STLY/ANP DH9 .... 148 A2
STLY/ANP DH9 .... 148 B1 3
STLY/ANP DH9 .... 148 C1
STLY/ANP DH9 .... 149 E5
TYNE/NSHE NE30 .... 55 F5
TYNE/NSHE NE30 .... 55 E1
WASHN NE37 .... 121 D4 1
WICK/BNPF NE16 .... 95 F3
WICK/BNPF NE16 .... 111 D6
WICK/BNPF NE16 .... 111 F6
WICK/BNPF NE16 .... 129 F2
Front St East BDLGTN NE22 .... 7 F4
Frosterley Cl CLS/BIR/GTL DH3 .... 168 A3
DHAM DH1 .... 180 C6 3
HLH DH5 .... 186 C3 1
Frosterley Gdns SUNDSW SR3 .... 144 A4 4
Frosterley Pl ELS/FEN NE4 .... 80 A2 4
Froude Av HAR/WTLS NE34 .... 88 A5
Fuchsia Pl WD/WHPE/BLK NE5 .... 61 F4 5
Fulbrook Rd GOS/KPK NE3 .... 62 B1
Fullerton Pl LWF/SPW/WRK NE9 .... 99 F2
Fulmar Dr BLYTH NE24 .... 17 D2
WASHS NE38 .... 137 E3
Fulmar Wk CLDN/WHIT/ROK SR6 .... 91 E6
Fulwell Av HAR/WTLS NE34 .... 90 A1
Fulwell Gn WD/WHPE/BLK NE5 .... 61 D5 5
Fulwell Rd
CLDN/WHIT/ROK SR6 .... 126 C3 3
PLEE/EAS SR8 .... 209 E3
Furnace Bank BDLGTN NE22 .... 8 C3
Furness Cl PLEE/EAS SR8 .... 208 A2
Furrowfield FELL NE10 .... 100 B4 1
Furzefield Rd GOS/KPK NE3 .... 63 D2
Fylingdale Dr SUNDSW SR3 .... 161 E1
Fyndoune Wy BDN/LAN/SAC DH7 .... 178 A3
Fynes Cl PLEE/EAS SR8 .... 200 C6
Fynway BDN/LAN/SAC DH7 .... 178 B2 1

G

The Gables DIN/WO NE13 .... 45 D6
Gainers Ter WLSD/HOW NE28 .... 67 E6
Gainford CLSW/PEL DH2 .... 152 C5
Gainsborough Av HAR/WTLS NE34 .... 88 C5
WASHS NE38 .... 139 D2
Gainsborough Cl MONK NE25 .... 39 E3
Gainsborough Crs HLS DH4 .... 156 B3
LWF/SPW/WRK NE9 .... 100 A3
Gainsborough Pl CRAM NE23 .... 22 A5
Gainsborough Rd
MLFD/PNYW SR4 .... 142 B4
STLY/ANP DH9 .... 148 B3
Gainsbro Gv ELS/FEN NE4 .... 79 E2
Gairloch Dr CLSW/PEL DH2 .... 152 B1
WASHS NE38 .... 137 F3
Gairloch Rd MLFD/PNYW SR4 .... 142 B3
Galashiels Gv HLS DH4 .... 157 D3 3
Galashiels Rd MLFD/PNYW SR4 .... 142 A3
Galashiels Sq MLFD/PNYW SR4 .... 142 B3 1
Gale St STLY/ANP DH9 .... 147 F3
Galfrid Cl SEA/MUR SR7 .... 175 E4 2
Gallalaw Ter GOS/KPK NE3 .... 64 B1 3
Galley's Gill Rd SUND SR1 .... 4 A2
Galloping Green Rd
LWF/SPW/WRK NE9 .... 118 C2
Galloway Rd PLEE/EAS SR8 .... 208 C1
Gallowgate CNUT NE1 .... 2 B3
Galsworthy Rd HAR/WTLS NE34 .... 87 F5
MLFD/PNYW SR4 .... 142 B3
Galway Rd MLFD/PNYW SR4 .... 142 A3 1
Gambia Rd MLFD/PNYW SR4 .... 142 A4 1
Gambia Sq MLFD/PNYW SR4 .... 142 A4 2
Ganton Av CRAM NE23 .... 22 A4
Ganton Cl WASHN NE37 .... 120 B2 2
Ganton Ct HAR/WTLS NE34 .... 89 E5 2
Garasdale Cl BLYTH NE24 .... 16 C2
Garden Cl DIN/WO NE13 .... 33 D1 1
Garden Cft LGB/KIL NE12 .... 50 A4
Garden Dr HEBB NE31 .... 84 C4 2

Gardener St ELS/FEN NE4 79 F5 3
Garden La SSH NE33 71 E4
Garden Pk WLSD/HOW NE28 68 B2 1
Garden Pl HLS DH4 157 D1
SUND SR1 4 B2 2
The Gardens CLSW/PEL DH2 153 D5
MONK NE25 40 B6
Garden St BLAY NE21 76 B5 2
HLS DH4 157 F5 1
Garden Ter MONK NE25 38 C5
Gardiner Rd MLFD/PNYW SR4 141 F3
Gardiner Sq MLFD/PNYW SR4 142 A3 2
Gardner Pk NSHW NE29 70 B1
Gardner Pl NSHW NE29 70 C1 4
Garesfield Gdns ROWG NE39 111 D1 2
Garesfield La BLAY NE21 93 E3
Gareston Cl BLYTH NE24 10 A5
Garfield St MLFD/PNYW SR4 125 E5 3
Garforth Cl CRAM NE23 21 F4
Garleigh Cl LGB/KIL NE12 50 B1 3
Garner Cl WD/WHPE/BLK NE5 59 F3
Garnet St MLFD/PNYW SR4 125 E5
Garrick Cl NSHW NE29 53 E5
Garrick St SSH NE33 71 E6
Garrigill WASHS NE38 139 E5
Garron St SEA/MUR SR7 176 C4
Garsdale Av WASHN NE37 120 A4
Garsdale Rd WBAY NE26 40 A1
Garside Av CLS/BIR/GTL DH3 136 B1
Garside Gv PLEE/EAS SR8 200 A6
Garsin Cl LGB/HTN NE7 66 A3
Garth Cornfield PLEE/EAS SR8 209 E3
Garth Crs BLAY NE21 94 A1
HAR/WTLS NE34 72 C5
Garth Farm Rd BLAY NE21 94 A1
Garthfield Crs WD/WHPE/BLK NE5 60 C4
Garth Heads CNUT NE1 3 G4
Garth Six LGB/KIL NE12 49 E1
Garth Sixteen LGB/KIL NE12 35 E6 5
The Garth GOS/KPK NE3 62 B2
WD/WHPE/BLK NE5 60 A5 4
Garth Thirteen LGB/KIL NE12 35 D6 3
Garth Thirty Three LGB/KIL NE12 49 F1
Garth Thirty Two LGB/KIL NE12 50 A1
Garth Twelve LGB/KIL NE12 35 E6 6
Garth Twenty LGB/KIL NE12 50 A1
Garth Twenty Five LGB/KIL NE12 50 B1 4
Garth Twenty Four
LGB/KIL NE12 50 B1 5
Garth Twenty Seven LGB/KIL NE12 50 B1
Garth Twenty Two LGB/KIL NE12 50 A1
Gartland Rd MLFD/PNYW SR4 141 F3
Garvey Vls LWF/SPW/WRK NE9 100 B4
Garwood St SSH NE33 71 D6
Gas House La HLS DH4 170 C1
Gaskell Av HAR/WTLS NE34 88 A5
Gas La BLAY NE21 76 B4
Gas Works Bridge Rd
DUN/TMV NE11 97 F1
Gas Works Rd SEA/MUR SR7 177 D4
Gatacre St BLYTH NE24 11 D4 6
Gateley Av BLYTH NE24 16 C2
Gatesgarth LWF/SPW/WRK NE9 99 F5
Gatesgarth Gv
CLDN/WHIT/ROK SR6 108 B5 4
Gateshead Hwy GATE NE8 81 E6
Gateshead Rd WICK/BNPF NE16 114 B1
Gatwick Rd MLFD/PNYW SR4 142 A3
Gaughan Cl BYK/HTN/WLK NE6 83 E5 1
Gayhurst Crs SUNDSW SR3 160 C2
Gayton Rd WASHN NE37 121 D3
Geddes Rd MLFD/PNYW SR4 142 A3
Gelt Crs HLH DH5 186 A2 1
General Graham St
MLFD/PNYW SR4 143 E1 2
General Havelock Rd
MLFD/PNYW SR4 125 D6
The General's Wd WASHS NE38 138 B6
Geneva Rd MLFD/PNYW SR4 142 A3 3
Genister Pl ELS/FEN NE4 61 F6 1
Geoffrey Av DHAM DH1 193 F6
Geoffrey St CLDN/WHIT/ROK SR6 109 E1
Geoffrey Ter STLY/ANP DH9 147 F3
George Pit La CLS/BIR/GTL DH3 168 B4
George Rd BDLGTN NE22 8 C2 3
WLSD/HOW NE28 67 D6
George Scott St SSH NE33 71 F2 1
George Smith Gdns FELL NE10 82 C6 2
Georges Rd ELS/FEN NE4 79 E5
George Stephenson Wy
NSHW NE29 70 B3
George St ASHBK/HED/RY SR2 162 C2
BLAY NE21 76 C5 1
BLYTH NE24 11 D6 4
CLS/BIR/GTL DH3 136 A2
CLS/BIR/GTL DH3 153 F6
DHAM DH1 193 F5
ELS/FEN NE4 2 A6
FELL NE10 101 E1 2
GOS/KPK NE3 62 C1 2
HLH DH5 171 F5
RDHAMSE DH6 197 E5
SEA/MUR SR7 176 B3
SEA/MUR SR7 188 B2
TYNE/NSHE NE30 55 D6
WD/WHPE/BLK NE5 58 B4
WICK/BNPF NE16 95 F3 4
WLSD/HOW NE28 69 D5
George St North
CLDN/WHIT/ROK SR6 126 C4 4
Georgian Ct LGB/KIL NE12 49 D3
MLFD/PNYW SR4 143 F2 3
Gerald St ELS/FEN NE4 78 C4
HAR/WTLS NE34 88 B5
Gerrard Cl CRAM NE23 22 A4
WBAY NE26 40 A1
Gerrard Rd MLFD/PNYW SR4 142 A3 4
WBAY NE26 40 A1
Gertrude St HLS DH4 157 F6 1
Ghyll Field Rd DHAM DH1 194 A1
Gibside CLSW/PEL DH2 152 C5
Gibside Cl STLY/ANP DH9 149 D1
Gibside Ct DUN/TMV NE11 97 E4 2
Gibside Gdns
BW/LEM/TK/HW NE15 78 A2
Gibside Vw BLAY NE21 94 A2
Gibside Wy WICK/BNPF NE16 78 A6
Gibson Ct BOLCOL NE35 105 E2 1
Gibson St CNUT NE1 3 H3
WLSD/HOW NE28 68 A2
Gifford Sq MLFD/PNYW SR4 142 B2
Gilbert Rd MLFD/PNYW SR4 142 A3
PLEE/EAS SR8 208 B1
Gilbert St SSH NE33 71 E6 3
Gilderdale HLS DH4 139 D6
Gilderdale Wy CRAM NE23 21 F5 1
CRAM NE23 22 A5 1
Gilesgate DHAM DH1 194 C4
Gilesgate Ct DHAM DH1 194 C4 1
Gilesgate Rd HLH DH5 186 A2
Gilhurst Gra SUND SR1 126 A6 5
Gillas La HLH DH5 171 F3
Gillas La East HLH DH5 171 E3
Gillas La West HLH DH5 171 D4
Gillies St BYK/HTN/WLK NE6 82 C2
Gillingham Rd MLFD/PNYW SR4 142 B3
Gill Rd SUND SR1 4 B1
Gill Side Gv CLDN/WHIT/ROK SR6 127 D2
Gill St ELS/FEN NE4 79 D3
Gilmore Cl WD/WHPE/BLK NE5 59 F3
Gilpin St HLS DH4 170 C2
Gilsland Av WLSD/HOW NE28 68 B3
Gilsland Gv CRAM NE23 14 A5 1
Gilsland St MLFD/PNYW SR4 125 F5 1
Gilwell Wy GOS/KPK NE3 47 D3
Girtin Rd HAR/WTLS NE34 88 C6
Girton Cl PLEE/EAS SR8 208 A3
Girvan Cl STLY/ANP DH9 149 D2
Gishford Wy WD/WHPE/BLK NE5 61 D4
Givens St CLDN/WHIT/ROK SR6 127 D2
Gladeley Wy WICK/BNPF NE16 113 F2
The Glade JRW NE32 104 A1
WD/WHPE/BLK NE5 58 C4
Gladstonbury Pl LGB/KIL NE12 49 E6
Gladstone Pl JES NE2 81 D1 3
Gladstone St BLYTH NE24 10 C4
BW/LEM/TK/HW NE15 76 B2 1
CLDN/WHIT/ROK SR6 126 C3
HEBB NE31 85 E2
HLS DH4 170 A2
STLY/ANP DH9 147 F3
STLY/ANP DH9 149 F1
WLSD/HOW NE28 69 D5 3
Gladstone Ter JES NE2 81 D1 4
Gladstone Ter West GATE NE8 99 D1
Gladwyn Rd MLFD/PNYW SR4 142 A4 3
Glaholm Rd ASHBK/HED/RY SR2 5 G4
Glaisdale Dr CLDN/WHIT/ROK SR6 109 D4
Glaisdale Rd LGB/HTN NE7 64 C1 1
Glamis Av GOS/KPK NE3 47 E2
MLFD/PNYW SR4 142 B2
Glamis Ct HAR/WTLS NE34 89 E5
Glamis Crs ROWG NE39 93 F6
Glamis Vls CLS/BIR/GTL DH3 118 B6
Glanmore Rd MLFD/PNYW SR4 142 A3 5
Glantlees WD/WHPE/BLK NE5 60 C4
Glanton Av MONK NE25 24 B5
Glanton Cl CLSW/PEL DH2 152 C6
Glanton Rd NSHW NE29 53 F5
Glanton Sq MLFD/PNYW SR4 142 B3 2
Glanton Wynd GOS/KPK NE3 47 D5
Glanville Cl DUN/TMV NE11 98 A3
Glanville Rd SUNDSW SR3 159 F3
Glasbury Av MLFD/PNYW SR4 142 B2 1
Glasgow Rd JRW NE32 87 D5
Glasshouse St BYK/HTN/WLK NE6 82 B5
Glastonbury WASHS NE38 138 C2 1
Glastonbury Gv JES NE2 64 B4
Gleaston Ct PLEE/EAS SR8 208 A5
Glebe Av LGB/KIL NE12 49 F5
WICK/BNPF NE16 96 A3
Glebe Cl WD/WHPE/BLK NE5 59 F3 1
Glebe Crs LGB/KIL NE12 49 F3
WASHS NE38 121 D6
Glebe Ms BDLGTN NE22 7 E3 2
Glebe Ri WICK/BNPF NE16 95 F3
Glebe Rd BDLGTN NE22 7 E3
LGB/KIL NE12 49 F3
Glebeside BDN/LAN/SAC DH7 178 A4
Glebe St ELS/FEN NE4 78 C2
Glebe Ter LGB/KIL NE12 49 F3
PLEE/EAS SR8 200 B2
Glebe Vls LGB/KIL NE12 49 E3
Glenallen Gdns TYNE/NSHE NE30 55 E3
Glen Barr CLSW/PEL DH2 153 D4
Glenbrooke Ter
LWF/SPW/WRK NE9 99 E6
Glenburn Cl WASHS NE38 137 E3
Glencarron Cl WASHS NE38 137 F2
Glen Cl ROWG NE39 111 D1
Glencoe LGB/KIL NE12 35 F6
Glencoe Av CLSW/PEL DH2 153 D4
CRAM NE23 22 A5
Glencoe Rd MLFD/PNYW SR4 142 A4
Glencourse BOL NE36 107 D3
Glendale Av BLYTH NE24 9 D4
GOS/KPK NE3 62 C2
NSHW NE29 54 A6
WBAY NE26 40 C3
WICK/BNPF NE16 95 F4
WLSD/HOW NE28 67 D2 2
Glendale Cl BLAY NE21 93 E2
SUNDSW SR3 159 E2
WD/WHPE/BLK NE5 59 F2
Glendale Gdns
LWF/SPW/WRK NE9 100 A5
Glendale Gv NSHW NE29 54 B6 1
Glendale Rd SMOOR NE27 52 C1
Glendale Ter BYK/HTN/WLK NE6 82 B2 3
Glendford Pl BLYTH NE24 16 C2 2
Glendower Av NSHW NE29 53 F6 3
Glendyn Cl LGB/HTN NE7 64 C5
Gleneagle Cl WD/WHPE/BLK NE5 59 F3 2
Gleneagles SSH NE33 72 A5 3
Gleneagles Cl LGB/HTN NE7 65 E1 3
Gleneagles Dr WASHN NE37 120 A2
Gleneagles Rd
LWF/SPW/WRK NE9 117 D1
MLFD/PNYW SR4 142 B3 3
Gleneagles Sq MLFD/PNYW SR4 142 A4 4
Glenesk Gdns
ASHBK/HED/RY SR2 144 B4 2
Glenesk Rd ASHBK/HED/RY SR2 144 B3
Glenfield Av CRAM NE23 14 A5
Glenfield Rd LGB/KIL NE12 49 E5
Glengarvan Cl WASHS NE38 137 F3
Glenhurst Dr WD/WHPE/BLK NE5 59 F3
WICK/BNPF NE16 95 E6
Glenhurst Gv HAR/WTLS NE34 89 E2
Glenhurst Rd PLEE/EAS SR8 200 C2
Glenleigh Dr MLFD/PNYW SR4 142 B3
Glen Luce Dr ASHBK/HED/RY SR2 145 E4
Glenluce Dr CRAM NE23 21 F5
Glenmoor HEBB NE31 84 C1
Glenmore Av CLSW/PEL DH2 153 D4
Glenmuir Av CRAM NE23 21 F5 2
Glenorrin Cl WASHS NE38 137 F3
Glen Pth ASHBK/HED/RY SR2 144 C3
Glenridge Av BYK/HTN/WLK NE6 65 D5
Glenroy Gdns CLSW/PEL DH2 153 D4
Glenshiel Cl WASHS NE38 137 F3
Glen St HEBB NE31 84 C3
Glen Ter CLSW/PEL DH2 152 C4
The Glen ASHBK/HED/RY SR2 144 C3 1
Glenthorn Rd JES NE2 64 A4
Glenuce CLS/BIR/GTL DH3 137 D3
Gloria Av MONK NE25 24 C2
Gloucester Av
CLDN/WHIT/ROK SR6 109 D6
Gloucester Cl CLS/BIR/GTL DH3 167 F4
Gloucester Pl HAR/WTLS NE34 89 F3 2
PLEE/EAS SR8 208 A1
Gloucester Rd ELS/FEN NE4 79 F3
NSHW NE29 53 D5
Gloucestershire Dr DHAM DH1 196 B3
Gloucester Ter ELS/FEN NE4 79 F4 2
Gloucester Wy ELS/FEN NE4 80 A4
Glover Rd MLFD/PNYW SR4 142 A4
WASHN NE37 121 E4
Glynfellis FELL NE10 101 E6
Glynwood Cl CRAM NE23 14 A5 2
Glynwood Gdns
LWF/SPW/WRK NE9 99 F5
Goathland Av LGB/KIL NE12 49 E5
Goathland Cl SUNDSW SR3 161 E1
Goathland Dr SUNDSW SR3 161 D1
Godfrey Rd MLFD/PNYW SR4 141 F3
Goldcrest Rd WASHS NE38 137 E3
Goldlynn Dr SUNDSW SR3 159 F2
Goldsmith Rd MLFD/PNYW SR4 142 A4
Goldspink La JES NE2 81 F1 3
Golf Course Rd HLS DH4 156 B4
Gompertz Gdns SSH NE33 71 D6
Goodrich Cl HLS DH4 157 E3 2
Good St STLY/ANP DH9 131 D6
Goodwood LGB/KIL NE12 50 B1 6
Goodwood Av GATE NE8 98 B2 1
Goodwood Cl
WD/WHPE/BLK NE5 59 F3 3
Goodwood Rd
MLFD/PNYW SR4 141 F3 1
Goole Rd MLFD/PNYW SR4 142 B3
Gordon Av GOS/KPK NE3 63 E2 1
SWCK/CAS SR5 123 F4
Gordon Dr BOL NE36 106 C3

Gordon Rd *HAR/WTLS* NE34 88 B2
MLFD/PNYW SR4 141 F4
Gordon Sq *BYK/HTN/WLK* NE6 82 A3
WBAY NE26 41 E6
Gordon St *GATE* NE8 80 C6
SSH NE33 71 E6
Gordon Ter *SWCK/CAS* SR5 125 F2
Gorleston Wy *SUNDSW* SR3 160 B4
Gorse Av *HAR/WTLS* NE34 89 F3
Gorsedale Gv *DHAM* DH1 196 C3 1
Gorsedene Rd *WBAY* NE26 40 B1
Gorse Rd *ASHBK/HED/RY* SR2 4 C6
Gort Pl *DHAM* DH1 195 E3
Goschen St *BLYTH* NE24 10 C4 1
BLYTH NE24 11 D3 1
GATE NE8 98 C2 3
SWCK/CAS SR5 125 F2
Gosforth Av *HAR/WTLS* NE34 88 B5
Gosforth Park Wy *LGB/KIL* NE12 48 B5
Gosforth St *JES* NE2 3 G1
Gosforth Ter *FELL* NE10 101 E1
Gosport Wy *BLYTH* NE24 16 C2
Gossington *WASHS* NE38 139 F1
Goswick Av *LGB/HTN* NE7 65 D4
Goswick Dr *GOS/KPK* NE3 46 B4
Goundry Av *ASHBK/HED/RY* SR2 162 C2
Gowanburn *CRAM* NE23 21 F5 3
WASHS NE38 139 D4
Gowan Ter *JES* NE2 64 B5
Gower Rd *SWCK/CAS* SR5 125 F2
Gower St *BYK/HTN/WLK* NE6 83 F4
Gower Wk *FELL* NE10 100 B2
Gowland Av *ELS/FEN* NE4 79 D1
Gracefield Cl *WD/WHPE/BLK* NE5 59 F3 4
Grace Gdns *WLSD/HOW* NE28 66 C2
Grace St *BYK/HTN/WLK* NE6 82 B2
DUN/TMV NE11 97 E2
Grafton Rd *WBAY* NE26 41 E6
Grafton St *BYK/HTN/WLK* NE6 82 A2 7
MLFD/PNYW SR4 125 F5
Graham Av *WICK/BNPF* NE16 95 F2
Graham Ct *BDN/LAN/SAC* DH7 178 B1 1
Graham Park Rd *GOS/KPK* NE3 63 E3
Grahamsley St *GATE* NE8 81 E6
Graham St *SSH* NE33 71 F4 7
The Graham Wy *SEA/MUR* SR7 175 F4
Grainger Park Rd *ELS/FEN* NE4 79 E4
Grainger St *CNUT* NE1 2 C4
Grampian Dr *PLEE/EAS* SR8 208 A3
Grampian Gv *BOL* NE36 106 A3 4
Grampian Pl *LGB/KIL* NE12 49 D3 2
Granby Cl *SUNDSW* SR3 144 A3
WICK/BNPF NE16 114 A1
Grand Pde *TYNE/NSHE* NE30 55 F4
Grandstand Rd *JES* NE2 62 B6
Grange Av *BDLGTN* NE22 8 C1
HLS DH4 169 F1
LGB/KIL NE12 50 A6
PLEE/EAS SR8 200 A3
SMOOR NE27 38 B6
Grange Cl *BLYTH* NE24 16 C2
MONK NE25 39 F6
PLEE/EAS SR8 200 B6
TYNE/NSHE NE30 55 D2 2
WLSD/HOW NE28 67 E4
Grange Crs *FELL* NE10 101 F3
RYTON NE40 74 B4
Grange Dr *RYTON* NE40 74 B4
Grange Est *DUN/TMV* NE11 116 B6
Grange Farm Dr *WICK/BNPF* NE16 95 F5
Grange La *WICK/BNPF* NE16 95 F5
Grange Lonnen *RYTON* NE40 74 A3
Grangemere Cl
ASHBK/HED/RY SR2 145 E4
Grange Nook *WICK/BNPF* NE16 95 F5
Grange Pk *MONK* NE25 53 E1
Grange Park Av *BDLGTN* NE22 8 C1
SWCK/CAS SR5 126 B1
Grange Pl *JRW* NE32 86 A1
Grange Rd *BW/LEM/TK/HW* NE15 58 A6
DHAM DH1 196 B2
ELS/FEN NE4 78 C2
FELL NE10 101 F3
GOS/KPK NE3 47 E5
JRW NE32 86 A1
PONT/DH NE20 28 A3
RYTON NE40 74 B3
STLY/ANP DH9 147 F2
SWCK/CAS SR5 123 F5
Grange Rd West *JRW* NE32 85 F1
Grange St *CLSW/PEL* DH2 152 A2
Grange St South
ASHBK/HED/RY SR2 145 E4
Grange Ter *BOL* NE36 106 C3 4
LWF/SPW/WRK NE9 99 F2 3
SWCK/CAS SR5 126 A2
The Grange *STLY/ANP* DH9 130 B6
Grange Vw *HLH* DH5 170 C5
HLS DH4 157 F5
RYTON NE40 74 B4
SWCK/CAS SR5 126 B1
Grange Vls *WLSD/HOW* NE28 67 E4
Grantham Dr *LWF/SPW/WRK* NE9 99 D6
Grantham Pl *CRAM* NE23 21 F4 1
Grantham Rd
CLDN/WHIT/ROK SR6 127 D2
JES NE2 81 E1
Grantham St *BLYTH* NE24 11 E6
Grants Crs *SEA/MUR* SR7 176 C3
Grant St *JRW* NE32 85 F1
PLEE/EAS SR8 209 F1 2
Granville Av *LGB/KIL* NE12 50 A3
WBAY NE26 26 C3
Granville Crs *LGB/KIL* NE12 50 A6
Granville Dr *HLS* DH4 157 E3
LGB/KIL NE12 50 A4
WD/WHPE/BLK NE5 59 F3
Granville Gdns *JES* NE2 64 C6 1
Granville Rd *GOS/KPK* NE3 47 E5
JES NE2 64 A6
PLEE/EAS SR8 209 E3
Granville St *GATE* NE8 99 E1
MLFD/PNYW SR4 126 A5
Grape La *DHAM* DH1 194 B5 2
Grasmere *CLDN/WHIT/ROK* SR6 107 F1
Grasmere Av *BYK/HTN/WLK* NE6 83 D3
FELL NE10 101 E2
HLH DH5 186 B4
JRW NE32 86 C5
Grasmere Ct *LGB/KIL* NE12 49 E1 2
Grasmere Crs *BLAY* NE21 94 A2 4
SWCK/CAS SR5 126 B1
WBAY NE26 40 B3
Grasmere Gdns *HAR/WTLS* NE34 89 D2 2
Grasmere Pl *GOS/KPK* NE3 47 D5
Grasmere Rd *CLSW/PEL* DH2 166 A1
HEBB NE31 85 E3
PLEE/EAS SR8 209 D1
WICK/BNPF NE16 96 B3
WLSD/HOW NE28 66 C5
Grasmere St *GATE* NE8 99 D1 3
Grasmere St West *GATE* NE8 99 D1 4
Grasmere Ter *RDHAMSE* DH6 188 A5 1
SEA/MUR SR7 188 C2
Grasmoor Pl
BW/LEM/TK/HW NE15 76 A1 2
Grassdale *DHAM* DH1 196 C3
Grassholme Mdw *SUNDSW* SR3 144 A4
Grassholm Pl *LGB/KIL* NE12 48 C5
Grassington Dr *CRAM* NE23 21 F4
Grasslees *WASHS* NE38 137 E6
Grasswell Dr *WD/WHPE/BLK* NE5 61 F3
Gravel Wks *HLH* DH5 171 D1
Gravesend Rd *MLFD/PNYW* SR4 142 A4 5
Gravesend Sq *MLFD/PNYW* SR4 142 B4 1
Gray Av *DHAM* DH1 193 F1
DIN/WO NE13 33 E3
RDHAMSE DH6 197 E4
SEA/MUR SR7 188 B1
Grayling Ct *SUNDSW* SR3 159 E3 1
Gray Rd *ASHBK/HED/RY* SR2 5 H5
Grays Ter *BOLCOL* NE35 105 D1 3
Graystones *FELL* NE10 102 A3
Gray St *BLYTH* NE24 11 D3
Graythwaite *CLSW/PEL* DH2 152 B5
Greathead St *SSH* NE33 88 A1 2
Great Lime Rd *DIN/WO* NE13 34 C5
LGB/KIL NE12 48 B1
Great North Forest Trail
HAR/WTLS NE34 90 C1
Great North Rd *GOS/KPK* NE3 47 E5
JES NE2 63 F6
Grebe Cl *BLYTH* NE24 17 D1
Greely Rd *WD/WHPE/BLK* NE5 60 B4
Greenacres *CLSW/PEL* DH2 151 F1
Green Av *HLS* DH4 157 F4 1
Greenbank *BLAY* NE21 76 B6
JRW NE32 86 A1
Greenbank Dr *MLFD/PNYW* SR4 141 F1
Greenbourne Gdns *FELL* NE10 100 B3 2
Green Cl *TYNE/NSHE* NE30 55 D3
Green Crs *CRAM* NE23 34 B2 2
Greencroft *RDHAMSE* DH6 188 A5
Greencroft Av *BYK/HTN/WLK* NE6 66 C6
Greendale Cl *BLYTH* NE24 9 F4 3
Greendale Gdns *HLH* DH5 185 E2
Greenfield Av *WD/WHPE/BLK* NE5 60 C4
Greenfield Rd *DIN/WO* NE13 47 D2
GOS/KPK NE3 47 D3
Greenfinch Cl *WASHS* NE38 137 E3
Greenford *DUN/TMV* NE11 116 C6
Greenford La *DUN/TMV* NE11 117 D5
Greenford Rd *BYK/HTN/WLK* NE6 83 E5
Greenhaugh *LGB/KIL* NE12 49 D3
Greenhead *WASHS* NE38 137 E2
Greenhills *LGB/KIL* NE12 35 F5
Greenhill Vw *WD/WHPE/BLK* NE5 62 A4
Green Hill Wk *HAR/WTLS* NE34 90 B2
Greenholme Cl *CRAM* NE23 14 A4 2
Greenhow Cl
ASHBK/HED/RY SR2 162 B3 2
Greenlands *STLY/ANP* DH9 147 F4 1
Greenlands Ct *MONK* NE25 24 C4
Green La *BOL* NE36 106 C4
DHAM DH1 195 E4
DIN/WO NE13 44 B4
FELL NE10 82 C6
HAR/WTLS NE34 88 A4
LGB/KIL NE12 50 A1 1
SEA/MUR SR7 173 D4
Greenlaw *WD/WHPE/BLK* NE5 60 A6
Greenlaw Rd *CRAM* NE23 21 F5
Green Lea *BDN/LAN/SAC* DH7 178 A3
Greenlea *NSHW* NE29 53 D3
Greenlea Cl *MLFD/PNYW* SR4 142 B3
Greenlee Dr *LGB/HTN* NE7 65 F3
Greenock Rd *MLFD/PNYW* SR4 142 A4 6
Green Pk *WLSD/HOW* NE28 66 A3
Greenrigg Gdns *SUNDSW* SR3 144 A3 6
Green's Bank *STLY/ANP* DH9 150 C1
Greenshields Rd *MLFD/PNYW* SR4 142 A4
Greenside Av *PLEE/EAS* SR8 209 E1
WLSD/HOW NE28 68 B3
Greenside Crs
BW/LEM/TK/HW NE15 77 F1
Green's Pl *SSH* NE33 71 E2
Green St *SEA/MUR* SR7 176 C3
SUND SR1 4 C2
Green Ter *SUND* SR1 4 B3
The Green *BW/LEM/TK/HW* NE15 58 B5
GOS/KPK NE3 62 B3
HLH DH5 171 E1
MONK NE25 40 A4
PLEE/EAS SR8 207 F4
PONT/DH NE20 28 B2
SWCK/CAS SR5 125 F3
Greenway *ELS/FEN* NE4 61 F6
WD/WHPE/BLK NE5 59 E2
The Greenway
MLFD/PNYW SR4 142 B2 2
Greenwell Cl *BLAY* NE21 93 F1 5
Greenwich Pl *GATE* NE8 81 F4
Greenwood *LGB/KIL* NE12 50 B1 7
Greenwood Av *BDLGTN* NE22 8 C1 1
BYK/HTN/WLK NE6 66 C5 3
HLS DH4 170 B2
Greenwood Gdns
DUN/TMV NE11 97 F5 3
FELL NE10 82 C6 3
Greenwood Rd *MLFD/PNYW* SR4 142 A3
Greetlands Rd
ASHBK/HED/RY SR2 144 B3
Gregson St *BDN/LAN/SAC* DH7 178 B1
Gregson Ter *SEA/MUR* SR7 175 E1
Grenada Cl *WBAY* NE26 40 B2 1
Grenada Dr *WBAY* NE26 40 B2
Grenada Pl *WBAY* NE26 40 B2 2
Grenfell Sq *MLFD/PNYW* SR4 142 A4 7
Grenville Dr *GOS/KPK* NE3 47 D3
Grenville Wy *WBAY* NE26 40 A3
Gresford St *SSH* NE33 88 B2
Gresham Cl *CRAM* NE23 22 A4
Gresley Rd *PLEE/EAS* SR8 207 F2
Greta Gdns *SSH* NE33 71 F6
Greta Ter *MLFD/PNYW* SR4 143 F1
Gretna Dr *HAR/WTLS* NE34 87 E6 1
Gretna Rd *BW/LEM/TK/HW* NE15 78 A1
Gretton Pl *LGB/HTN* NE7 64 C3 1
Grey Av *CRAM* NE23 21 F5
Greybourne Gdns
ASHBK/HED/RY SR2 144 B4 3
Greyfriars La *LGB/KIL* NE12 48 C6 4
Greystead Cl *WD/WHPE/BLK* NE5 59 F3
Greystead Rd *MONK* NE25 39 D5
Greystoke Av *ASHBK/HED/RY* SR2 144 B4
JES NE2 81 F1
WICK/BNPF NE16 96 A4
Greystoke Gdns
ASHBK/HED/RY SR2 144 B3 4
JES NE2 64 C6
LWF/SPW/WRK NE9 118 A2
WICK/BNPF NE16 96 A5
Greystoke Pk *GOS/KPK* NE3 47 E4
Greystoke Wk *WICK/BNPF* NE16 96 A4 1
Grey St *CNUT* NE1 2 D3
DIN/WO NE13 32 C4 2
HLS DH4 170 C1
TYNE/NSHE NE30 55 D6
WLSD/HOW NE28 67 E4
Greywood Av *ELS/FEN* NE4 79 D1
Grieves' Rw *CRAM* NE23 34 C2
Grieve St *BLYTH* NE24 10 C3 1
Grimsby St *BLYTH* NE24 11 D6
Grindon Av *MLFD/PNYW* SR4 142 A1 1
Grindon Cl *CRAM* NE23 21 F5
MONK NE25 54 A2
Grindon Ct *MLFD/PNYW* SR4 142 B3
Grindon Gdns *MLFD/PNYW* SR4 142 B3
Grindon La *MLFD/PNYW* SR4 142 A1
SUNDSW SR3 143 D4 1
Grindon Pk *MLFD/PNYW* SR4 142 B3 4
Grindon Ter *MLFD/PNYW* SR4 143 F1
Grinstead Cl *HAR/WTLS* NE34 89 E1 1
Grinstead Wy *DHAM* DH1 196 C1
Grisedale Gdns *LWF/SPW/WRK* NE9 99 F6
Grisedale Rd *PLEE/EAS* SR8 209 D2 5
Grizedale *WASHN* NE37 120 A6
Grizedale Ct *CLDN/WHIT/ROK* SR6 108 B4
Grosvenor Av *JES* NE2 64 B5
WICK/BNPF NE16 96 A2
Grosvenor Cl *CRAM* NE23 21 F5 4
Grosvenor Ct
WD/WHPE/BLK NE5 59 F3 5
Grosvenor Crs *HEBB* NE31 85 E5

Grosvenor Dr
CLDN/WHIT/ROK SR6 107 D1
HAR/WTLS NE34 72 B6
MONK NE25 40 C6
Grosvenor Gdns HAR/WTLS NE34 89 E2 2
JES NE2 64 C6 2
WLSD/HOW NE28 68 C3
Grosvenor Pl JES NE2 64 B5
NSHW NE29 54 C6
Grosvenor Rd HAR/WTLS NE34 72 A6
JES NE2 64 B5
Grosvenor St SWCK/CAS SR5 125 E2
Grosvenor Wy WD/WHPE/BLK NE5 59 F4
Grotto Gdns HAR/WTLS NE34 90 C2
Grotto Rd HAR/WTLS NE34 90 C2
Grove Av GOS/KPK NE3 63 F2 1
Grove Ct RDHAMSE DH6 206 B3
Grove Rd BDN/LAN/SAC DH7 203 D5
BW/LEM/TK/HW NE15 58 C5
LWF/SPW/WRK NE9 99 F4
Grove St DHAM DH1 194 A6
Grove Ter BDN/LAN/SAC DH7 204 A2
The Grove ASHBK/HED/RY SR2 144 C2
ASHBK/HED/RY SR2 162 B1
DHAM DH1 193 F3
GOS/KPK NE3 63 F2
HLH DH5 171 D4
JES NE2 64 B4 3
JES NE2 64 B5 1
JRW NE32 104 A1
LGB/KIL NE12 49 F6
MONK NE25 40 B6
PLEE/EAS SR8 199 F2
ROWG NE39 111 E3
SWCK/CAS SR5 124 A3 4
WD/WHPE/BLK NE5 59 F5
WICK/BNPF NE16 96 B4
Guardians Ct PONT/DH NE20 28 B3 2
Guelder Rd LGB/HTN NE7 65 E3
Guernsey Rd MLFD/PNYW SR4 142 A4
Guernsey Sq MLFD/PNYW SR4 142 A4
Guildford Pl BYK/HTN/WLK NE6 82 A1
Guildford St ASHBK/HED/RY SR2 145 D2
Guillemot Cl BLYTH NE24 17 D1 6
Guisborough Dr NSHW NE29 53 D4
Guisborough St MLFD/PNYW SR4 143 E1
Gullane WASHN NE37 120 C1
Gullane Cl FELL NE10 84 B6
STLY/ANP DH9 149 D2
Gunnerston Gv GOS/KPK NE3 61 F1 5
Gunnerton Cl CRAM NE23 22 A4
Gunnerton Pl NSHW NE29 53 F6 4
Gunn St DUN/TMV NE11 97 E2
Gut Rd WLSD/HOW NE28 68 B4
Guyzance Av GOS/KPK NE3 46 C6

H

Hackworth Rd PLEE/EAS SR8 199 E5
Hackworth Wy NSHW NE29 70 B3 1
Haddington Rd MONK NE25 39 E3
Haddon Cl MONK NE25 39 D5
Haddon Gn MONK NE25 39 D5
Haddricksmill Rd GOS/KPK NE3 64 A2
Hadleigh Rd MLFD/PNYW SR4 142 C1
Hadrian Av CLS/BIR/GTL DH3 153 F3
Hadrian Gdns BLAY NE21 94 C1
Hadrian Pl BW/LEM/TK/HW NE15 57 F4
LWF/SPW/WRK NE9 100 A3 2
Hadrian Rd BLYTH NE24 16 B3
ELS/FEN NE4 79 D2
JRW NE32 86 C5
WLSD/HOW NE28 67 E5
Hadrians Ct DUN/TMV NE11 98 C6
Hadrian St MLFD/PNYW SR4 125 F5
Hadstone Pl WD/WHPE/BLK NE5 61 E5 3
Haggerston Cl
WD/WHPE/BLK NE5 61 D2 4
Haggerston Ct
WD/WHPE/BLK NE5 61 D2 5
Haggerston Crs
WD/WHPE/BLK NE5 61 D2
Haggerstone Dr SWCK/CAS SR5 123 F4 1
Haggerston Ter JRW NE32 87 D4
Haggie Av WLSD/HOW NE28 67 F3 1
Haig Av MONK NE25 40 B6
Haig Crs BW/LEM/TK/HW NE15 77 F3
DHAM DH1 195 F5
Haig Rd BDLGTN NE22 8 A4
Hailsham Av LGB/KIL NE12 49 E5
Haininghead WASHS NE38 139 D4
Hainingwood Ter FELL NE10 84 A6 6
Haldane Ter JES NE2 64 A6
Hale Ri PLEE/EAS SR8 208 C2
Halewood Av GOS/KPK NE3 62 A2
Half Fields Rd BLAY NE21 94 A1
Half Moon La GATE NE8 3 F6 2
GATE NE8 81 D5 1
Halfway House La
ASHBK/HED/RY SR2 145 F3
Halidon Rd ASHBK/HED/RY SR2 144 C5
Halidon Sq ASHBK/HED/RY SR2 144 C5 1
Halifax Pl DUN/TMV NE11 97 D1 2
Halifax Rd DUN/TMV NE11 97 D1
Halkirk Wy CRAM NE23 13 F5
Hallam Rd PLEE/EAS SR8 208 C1 3
Hall Cl HLS DH4 183 F2
SEA/MUR SR7 174 C2
Hall Dr LGB/KIL NE12 35 E5 2
Halleypike Cl LGB/HTN NE7 65 F3 2
Hall Farm Rd SUNDSW SR3 160 B3
Hallfield Cl SUNDSW SR3 160 C3
Hallfield Dr PLEE/EAS SR8 199 F3
Hall Gdns BOL NE36 105 F3
FELL NE10 100 C3
Hallgarth Rd BLAY NE21 76 A6
Hallgarth St DHAM DH1 194 C6
RDHAMSE DH6 197 E4
The Hallgarth DHAM DH1 194 C6
Hallgarth Vls RDHAMSE DH6 197 F5 1
Hall Gn BLYTH NE24 10 A5
Halling Cl BYK/HTN/WLK NE6 83 F4 5
Hallington Dr MONK NE25 24 C5
Halliwell St HLS DH4 170 C1
Hall La HLH DH5 171 D3
HLS DH4 183 F2
Hallow Dr BW/LEM/TK/HW NE15 57 F5
Hall Pk BLAY NE21 75 F4
Hall Rd HEBB NE31 85 D3
WASHN NE37 121 D4 2
Hallside Rd BLYTH NE24 10 A6
Hall Ter FELL NE10 84 A6 7
Hall Vw CLDN/WHIT/ROK SR6 109 E2
Hall Wks PLEE/EAS SR8 199 F3
Halstead Sq MLFD/PNYW SR4 142 C1
Halterburn Cl GOS/KPK NE3 63 D2
Halton Rd DHAM DH1 194 C1 1
Hamar Cl NSHW NE29 69 E2
Hambard Wy WASHS NE38 138 C2
Hambledon Av TYNE/NSHE NE30 54 C1
Hambledon Cl BOLCOL NE35 105 D2 1
Hambledon Gdns LGB/HTN NE7 64 C3
Hambledon Pl PLEE/EAS SR8 207 F3 1
Hambledon St BLYTH NE24 10 C4 2
Hambleton Dr SEA/MUR SR7 176 A2 2
Hambleton Rd WASHS NE38 138 A3
Hamilton Ct RDHAMSE DH6 206 B2 1
Hamilton Crs ELS/FEN NE4 80 A2 5
NSHW NE29 53 E4
Hamilton Dr WBAY NE26 40 B2
Hamilton St PLEE/EAS SR8 209 E1 2
Hamilton Ter BDN/LAN/SAC DH7 164 A4
BOL NE36 105 F3 3
Hammer Square Bank
STLY/ANP DH9 133 E5
Hampden Rd
CLDN/WHIT/ROK SR6 127 D2
Hampden St SSH NE33 71 E6 4
Hampshire Ct ELS/FEN NE4 79 F6
Hampshire Pl WASHN NE37 120 C3 2
Hampshire Rd DHAM DH1 196 B3
Hampshire Wy HAR/WTLS NE34 90 B1 1
Hampstead Cl BLYTH NE24 16 B3
Hampstead Rd ELS/FEN NE4 79 D3
MLFD/PNYW SR4 142 C2
Hampstead Sq
MLFD/PNYW SR4 142 B2 3
Hampton Cl CRAM NE23 22 C1 1
Hampton Ct CLS/BIR/GTL DH3 153 F1
Hampton Dr FELL NE10 100 B2
Hampton Rd TYNE/NSHE NE30 54 C2
Hamsterley Cl CLS/BIR/GTL DH3 168 A3 2
Hamsterley Ct SUNDSW SR3 160 C2 3
Hamsterley Crs
BW/LEM/TK/HW NE15 76 A1 3
DHAM DH1 180 C6
LWF/SPW/WRK NE9 118 B1
Hamsterley Dr LGB/KIL NE12 35 E6
Hamsterley Gdns STLY/ANP DH9 146 B4
Hanby Gdns SUNDSW SR3 143 F3 3
Hancock St CNUT NE1 80 C1
Handel St MLFD/PNYW SR4 125 F5 2
SSH NE33 71 F4 8
Handley St PLEE/EAS SR8 209 E1 3
Handy Dr DUN/TMV NE11 78 C6
Hangmans La HLH DH5 160 A5
Hanlon Ct JRW NE32 85 E1
Hannington Pl
BYK/HTN/WLK NE6 81 F2 6
Hannington St BYK/HTN/WLK NE6 81 F2
Hanover Ct CRAM NE23 35 D1 1
Hanover Dr BLAY NE21 93 F1
Hanover Pl CRAM NE23 13 F4 3
MLFD/PNYW SR4 126 A4
Hanover St CNUT NE1 2 D6
Harbottle Av GOS/KPK NE3 46 C6
SMOOR NE27 52 B2
Harbottle Ct BYK/HTN/WLK NE6 82 B4
Harbottle Crs JRW NE32 86 A6
Harbour Dr SSH NE33 71 F1
The Harbour HLS DH4 157 D2 2
Harbour Vw CLDN/WHIT/ROK SR6 127 E3
SSH NE33 71 E1
Harbour Wk SEA/MUR SR7 176 B2
Harcourt Rd
ASHBK/HED/RY SR2 144 C5 2
Harcourt St LWF/SPW/WRK NE9 99 F5 2
Hardgate Rd
ASHBK/HED/RY SR2 145 D5 1
Hardie Av WICK/BNPF NE16 95 F2
Hardie Dr BOL NE36 105 F3
Hardwick Ct GATE NE8 99 F1 1
Hardwick Pl GOS/KPK NE3 62 C3 2
Hardwick St PLEE/EAS SR8 209 F2
Hardyards Ct HAR/WTLS NE34 88 B3 9
Hardy Av HAR/WTLS NE34 88 A5
Hardy Gv WLSD/HOW NE28 66 C1
Hardy Sq SWCK/CAS SR5 125 F1
Hardy St SEA/MUR SR7 176 C3 8
Harebell Rd LWF/SPW/WRK NE9 100 B6
Harehills Av WD/WHPE/BLK NE5 61 F3
Harelaw Gv WD/WHPE/BLK NE5 59 F5 4
Hareside CRAM NE23 21 F3
Harewood Cl WICK/BNPF NE16 95 F6
Harewood Crs MONK NE25 39 D6 1
Harewood Dr BDLGTN NE22 8 B2
Harewood Gdns SUNDSW SR3 143 F3 4
Harewood Rd GOS/KPK NE3 47 E6
Hareydene WD/WHPE/BLK NE5 60 B1
Hargill Dr WASHS NE38 137 F5
Hargrave Ct BLYTH NE24 10 B6 4
Harland Wy WASHS NE38 138 C1
Harle Cl WD/WHPE/BLK NE5 60 A5 5
Harle Rd SMOOR NE27 37 F6
Harleston Wy FELL NE10 101 D4
Harle St WLSD/HOW NE28 67 D4 4
Harley Ter GOS/KPK NE3 63 F1
Harlow Av GOS/KPK NE3 46 B5
SMOOR NE27 51 F1
Harlow Green La
LWF/SPW/WRK NE9 117 F2
Harlow Pl LGB/HTN NE7 65 D3
Harlow St MLFD/PNYW SR4 126 A6 6
Harnham Av NSHW NE29 69 E1
Harnham Gdns
WD/WHPE/BLK NE5 61 E6
Harnham Gv CRAM NE23 21 F3
Harold St JRW NE32 86 B1
Harperley Dr SUNDSW SR3 144 A4
Harperley La STLY/ANP DH9 129 F5
Harperley Rd STLY/ANP DH9 146 B3
Harper St BLYTH NE24 10 C5
Harras Bank CLS/BIR/GTL DH3 136 B3
Harriet St BLAY NE21 76 B6
BYK/HTN/WLK NE6 82 C2 4
Harrington St WLSD/HOW NE28 67 D4 5
Harriot Dr LGB/KIL NE12 48 C2
Harrison Cl PLEE/EAS SR8 209 D3
Harrison Gdns GATE NE8 98 C3 2
Harrison Garth RDHAMSE DH6 197 E4 1
Harrison Pl JES NE2 81 D1 5
Harrison Rd WLSD/HOW NE28 68 C3
Harrogate St ASHBK/HED/RY SR2 5 E5
Harrogate Ter SEA/MUR SR7 188 B1 3
Harrow Gdns DIN/WO NE13 33 E5
Harrow Sq MLFD/PNYW SR4 142 C1
Hartburn FELL NE10 101 F5
Hartburn Dr WD/WHPE/BLK NE5 59 F3
Hartburn Pl ELS/FEN NE4 79 D1
Hartburn Rd TYNE/NSHE NE30 54 B3
Hartburn Wk GOS/KPK NE3 61 F1
Hartford Bank CRAM NE23 12 B2
Hartford Br BDLGTN NE22 12 B2
Hartford Ct BDLGTN NE22 7 D4
Hartford Crs BDLGTN NE22 7 D4
Hartford Dr BDLGTN NE22 12 B1
Hartford Rd BDLGTN NE22 6 C6
GOS/KPK NE3 47 F5
HAR/WTLS NE34 87 F3
MLFD/PNYW SR4 142 C1
Hartford St BYK/HTN/WLK NE6 65 E6 2
Hartforth Crs FELL NE10 102 A1 3
Harthope Av SWCK/CAS SR5 124 B1 1
Harthope Cl WASHS NE38 137 E6
Harthope Dr NSHW NE29 70 A3
Hartington Rd TYNE/NSHE NE30 54 C3
Hartington St
CLDN/WHIT/ROK SR6 127 D2
ELS/FEN NE4 79 F3
GATE NE8 99 E1
Hartington Ter SSH NE33 71 F6
Hartland Dr CLS/BIR/GTL DH3 136 C4
Hartlands BDLGTN NE22 7 D4
Hartleigh Pl BLYTH NE24 10 A5 2
Hartley Av WBAY NE26 40 A5
Hartleyburn Av HEBB NE31 84 C5
Hartley La MONK NE25 39 D4
Hartley St MONK NE25 24 B5
SUND SR1 5 G1
Hartley Ter BLYTH NE24 16 B2 5
Hartoft Cl HLS DH4 157 F5 2
Harton Gv HAR/WTLS NE34 89 D1
Harton House Rd HAR/WTLS NE34 89 E1
Harton House Rd East
HAR/WTLS NE34 89 F1
Harton La HAR/WTLS NE34 88 B3
Harton Ri HAR/WTLS NE34 89 E1
Hartside BW/LEM/TK/HW NE15 76 B1
CLS/BIR/GTL DH3 136 C5
Hartside Crs BLAY NE21 93 E2
CRAM NE23 13 F4 4
SMOOR NE27 37 F6

Hartside Gdns *HLH* DH5 **186** B3
JES NE2 **64** B5 2
Hartside Pl *GOS/KPK* NE3 **47** E3 1
Hartside Vw *DHAM* DH1 **179** F5
Hart Sq *MLFD/PNYW* SR4 **142** C1
Hart Ter *CLDN/WHIT/ROK* SR6 **109** E4 1
Harvard Rd *GOS/KPK* NE3 **62** A1 3
Harvest Cl *SUNDSW* SR3 **160** B3 5
Harvey Cl *PLEE/EAS* SR8 **208** C1
WASHS NE38 **137** E1
Harvey Combe *LGB/KIL* NE12 **49** D1
Harvey Crs *FELL* NE10 **102** A2 4
Harwick Ct *STLY/ANP* DH9 **149** E2
Harwood Cl *CRAM* NE23 **21** F3
WASHS NE38 **137** F5 1
Harwood Dr *LGB/KIL* NE12 **50** B1
Hascombe Cl *MONK* NE25 **39** F4
Haslemere Dr *SUNDSW* SR3 **143** F3 5
Hassop Wy *BDLGTN* NE22 **7** E2
Hastings Av *DHAM* DH1 **204** C1
GOS/KPK NE3 **45** F5
LGB/KIL NE12 **49** F5 1
WBAY NE26 **26** A1 1
Hastings Ct *BDLGTN* NE22 **8** B2
Hastings Dr *TYNE/NSHE* NE30 **55** E4
Hastings Gdns *MONK* NE25 **24** C2
Hastings St *ASHBK/HED/RY* SR2 **145** D2
CRAM NE23 **22** B3
Hastings Ter *ASHBK/HED/RY* SR2 **145** E3
CRAM NE23 **14** C4
MONK NE25 **24** C1
Haswell Cl *FELL* NE10 **102** C3
Haswell Gdns *TYNE/NSHE* NE30 **54** C6
Hatfield Av *HEBB* NE31 **85** E2
Hatfield Cl *DHAM* DH1 **179** F6
Hatfield Dr *CRAM* NE23 **23** E6
Hatfield Gdns *MONK* NE25 **39** D6
SUNDSW SR3 **143** F3 6
Hathaway Gdns *SUNDSW* SR3 **143** F3 7
Hatherton Av *TYNE/NSHE* NE30 **55** D1
Hathery La *BLYTH* NE24 **14** C3
Haugh La *RYTON* NE40 **75** D2
Haughton Crs *JRW* NE32 **86** A6 2
WD/WHPE/BLK NE5 **60** A5
Haughton Ter *BLYTH* NE24 **11** D5
Hautmont Rd *HEBB* NE31 **85** E4
Hauxley *LGB/KIL* NE12 **35** F5 3
Hauxley Dr *CLSW/PEL* DH2 **165** E2
CRAM NE23 **13** F4
GOS/KPK NE3 **46** A5
Hauxley Gdns
WD/WHPE/BLK NE5 **61** F4 6
Havanna *LGB/KIL* NE12 **35** F5 4
Havannah Crs *DIN/WO* NE13 **31** D4 1
Havannah Rd *WASHN* NE37 **120** A5
Havant Gdns *DIN/WO* NE13 **33** D3
Havelock Cl *GATE* NE8 **81** D6 4
Havelock Crs *BDLGTN* NE22 **9** E1 1
Havelock Rd *SMOOR* NE27 **51** F1
Havelock St *SSH* NE33 **71** E5 2
SUND SR1 **5** F1
Havelock Ter
ASHBK/HED/RY SR2 **144** A1 8
GATE NE8 **81** D6
JRW NE32 **86** A3
Haven Ct *BLYTH* NE24 **10** B6 5
DHAM DH1 **180** B4 2
The Haven *HLS* DH4 **157** D2 3
NSHW NE29 **70** C3
Havercroft *FELL* NE10 **102** A3
Haverley Dr *SEA/MUR* SR7 **175** D2
Haversham Pk *SWCK/CAS* SR5 **108** B5
Haversham Rd *LGB/HTN* NE7 **64** C1
Hawarden Crs *MLFD/PNYW* SR4 **143** F1
Hawes Av *CLSW/PEL* DH2 **166** B1
Hawes Ct *CLDN/WHIT/ROK* SR6 **108** B5
Hawes Rd *PLEE/EAS* SR8 **208** C1
Haweswater Cl *HAR/WTLS* NE34 **88** C2 1
Hawick Ct *STLY/ANP* DH9 **149** D2
Hawick Crs *BYK/HTN/WLK* NE6 **82** A4
Hawkey's La *NSHW* NE29 **54** B6
Hawkhill Cl *CLSW/PEL* DH2 **165** F2
Hawkhurst *WASHS* NE38 **139** D4 1
Hawkins Ct *SUNDSW* SR3 **160** B2 2
Hawksbury *WICK/BNPF* NE16 **95** F3 5
Hawkshead Ct *DIN/WO* NE13 **45** F5 2
Hawkshead Pl
LWF/SPW/WRK NE9 **100** A5
Hawksley *WD/WHPE/BLK* NE5 **60** B4
Hawks Rd *GATE* NE8 **3** H6
Hawks St *GATE* NE8 **81** F4 5
Hawkwell Ri
BW/LEM/TK/HW NE15 **57** F5 3
Hawsker Cl *SUNDSW* SR3 **161** E1 2
Hawthorn Av *DIN/WO* NE13 **32** C5
SUNDSW SR3 **144** A6
Hawthorn Cl *CLSW/PEL* DH2 **179** E1
WICK/BNPF NE16 **96** A6
Hawthorn Cottages
RDHAMSE DH6 **188** A5
Hawthorn Crs *DHAM* DH1 **195** F3
Hawthorn Dr *DUN/TMV* NE11 **97** E2
JRW NE32 **86** C6
Hawthorne Av *HAR/WTLS* NE34 **89** E4
HEBB NE31 **85** E2
Hawthorne Cl *SEA/MUR* SR7 **188** C2
Hawthorne Rd *BLYTH* NE24 **11** E5 4
Hawthorne Ter *RDHAMSE* DH6 **206** B2
Hawthorn Gdns *GOS/KPK* NE3 **62** B2
NSHW NE29 **54** B5 1
WBAY NE26 **40** B5
Hawthorn Pk
BDN/LAN/SAC DH7 **203** D4 2
Hawthorn Pl *ELS/FEN* NE4 **80** A4 4
LGB/KIL NE12 **35** E6 7
Hawthorn Rd *BLAY* NE21 **76** B6
DHAM DH1 **196** C1
GOS/KPK NE3 **63** E2
Hawthorn Rd West *GOS/KPK* NE3 **63** E2
The Hawthorns *BOL* NE36 **106** C3
Hawthorn St *JRW* NE32 **85** F1 1
MLFD/PNYW SR4 **125** F6
PLEE/EAS SR8 **200** C1
Hawthorn Ter
CLDN/WHIT/ROK SR6 **109** D4 1
DHAM DH1 **194** A5
ELS/FEN NE4 **79** F4 3
WD/WHPE/BLK NE5 **58** C4
Hawthorn Vls *CRAM* NE23 **22** B2
Haydock Dr *FELL* NE10 **102** A3
Haydon *WASHS* NE38 **139** D5
Haydon Pl *WD/WHPE/BLK* NE5 **60** C6
Haydon Sq *MLFD/PNYW* SR4 **142** C1
Hayes Wk *DIN/WO* NE13 **33** D4
Hayfield La *WICK/BNPF* NE16 **96** A4
Hayhole Rd *NSHW* NE29 **70** A4
Hayleazes Rd
BW/LEM/TK/HW NE15 **77** E1
The Haynyng *FELL* NE10 **101** D3 2
The Hayricks *STLY/ANP* DH9 **130** C2
Hay St *SWCK/CAS* SR5 **126** B4
Hayton Av *HAR/WTLS* NE34 **89** F3
Hayton Cl *CRAM* NE23 **22** B1
Hayton Rd *TYNE/NSHE* NE30 **54** B3
Hazard La *HLH* DH5 **185** D1
Hazel Av *BDN/LAN/SAC* DH7 **202** C5
NSHW NE29 **54** B5
SUNDSW SR3 **144** A6 1
Hazeldene *MONK* NE25 **39** F5
Hazeldene Av *GOS/KPK* NE3 **61** E2
Hazeldene Ct *TYNE/NSHE* NE30 **55** E5
Hazeley Gv *GOS/KPK* NE3 **61** F1
Hazeley Wy *GOS/KPK* NE3 **61** F1 6
Hazel Gv *CLSW/PEL* DH2 **152** C3
Hazelgrove *FELL* NE10 **102** A3
Hazel Gv *HAR/WTLS* NE34 **89** E4
LGB/KIL NE12 **49** D2
Hazel Leigh *CLS/BIR/GTL* DH3 **167** F3
Hazelmere Av *BDLGTN* NE22 **7** D3
Hazelmere Crs *CRAM* NE23 **14** B6
Hazelmere Dene *CRAM* NE23 **36** A1 2
Hazelmoor *HEBB* NE31 **84** C1 5
Hazel Rd *BLAY* NE21 **76** C6
GATE NE8 **98** B2
Hazel St *JRW* NE32 **85** F1
Hazel Ter *RDHAMSE* DH6 **206** B2
STLY/ANP DH9 **149** D5
Hazelwood *LGB/KIL* NE12 **50** B1 8
Hazelwood Av *JES* NE2 **64** A4
SWCK/CAS SR5 **125** E2
Hazelwood Cl *LWF/SPW/WRK* NE9 **118** C2
Hazelwood Ter *WLSD/HOW* NE28 **68** C4
Hazledene Ter *MLFD/PNYW* SR4 **125** E6 4
Hazlitt Av *HAR/WTLS* NE34 **88** A5
Hazlitt Pl *CRAM* NE23 **36** C1 2
Headlam St *BYK/HTN/WLK* NE6 **82** B2 4
Headlam Vw *WLSD/HOW* NE28 **68** C4
Healey Dr *SUNDSW* SR3 **144** A4
Heartsbourne Dr
HAR/WTLS NE34 **89** E5 3
Heath Cl *DUN/TMV* NE11 **98** A3
PLEE/EAS SR8 **209** D3
Heath Crs *BW/LEM/TK/HW* NE15 **77** F4
Heathdale Gdns *LGB/HTN* NE7 **65** D3
Heather Cl *CLDN/WHIT/ROK* SR6 **89** F6 1
Heatherdale Crs *DHAM* DH1 **196** C3
Heather Dr *HLH* DH5 **171** F5
Heather Gv *FELL* NE10 **82** A6
Heather Lea *STLY/ANP* DH9 **129** D4 1
Heatherlea Gdns *SUNDSW* SR3 **144** A3 7
Heather Pl *ELS/FEN* NE4 **62** A6
Heatherslaw Rd
WD/WHPE/BLK NE5 **61** E6
Heather Wy *STLY/ANP* DH9 **147** F2
Heatherwell Gn *FELL* NE10 **100** B3 3
Heathery La *GOS/KPK* NE3 **48** A5
Heathfield *ASHBK/HED/RY* SR2 **144** B4
Heathfield Crs *WD/WHPE/BLK* NE5 **61** F3
Heathfield Pl *GOS/KPK* NE3 **47** F3 3
Heathfield Rd *LWF/SPW/WRK* NE9 **99** E4
Heath Gra *HLH* DH5 **171** D1
Heathmeads *CLSW/PEL* DH2 **151** E2
Heath Sq *MLFD/PNYW* SR4 **143** D1
Heathway *JRW* NE32 **86** B6
SEA/MUR SR7 **176** B5
Heathwell Gdns
WICK/BNPF NE16 **96** A2 2
Heathwell Rd
BW/LEM/TK/HW NE15 **77** E1
Heathwood Av *WICK/BNPF* NE16 **95** F3 6
Heaton Gdns *HAR/WTLS* NE34 **88** B6
Heaton Gv *BYK/HTN/WLK* NE6 **82** A1
Heaton Hall Rd *BYK/HTN/WLK* NE6 **82** A1
Heaton Park Rd
BYK/HTN/WLK NE6 **81** F1
Heaton Park Vw
BYK/HTN/WLK NE6 **82** A1
Heaton Pl *BYK/HTN/WLK* NE6 **82** A1 2
Heaton Rd *BYK/HTN/WLK* NE6 **65** D5
Heaton Ter *BYK/HTN/WLK* NE6 **81** F2
NSHW NE29 **54** A6
Heaviside Pl *DHAM* DH1 **195** D4
Heber St *ELS/FEN* NE4 **2** A3
Hebron Wy *CRAM* NE23 **21** F3
Hector St *SMOOR* NE27 **38** B6
Heddon Banks
BW/LEM/TK/HW NE15 **56** A5
Heddon Cl *GOS/KPK* NE3 **46** C6 5
Heddon Vw *BLAY* NE21 **76** A6
Heddon Wy *HAR/WTLS* NE34 **88** A2
Hedge Cl *DUN/TMV* NE11 **98** A3
Hedgefield Gv *BLYTH* NE24 **16** B3
Hedgefield Vw *CRAM* NE23 **34** C1
Hedgehope Rd
WD/WHPE/BLK NE5 **60** C2
Hedgelea *RYTON* NE40 **74** A3
Hedgelea Rd *HLH* DH5 **184** B1
Hedgeley Rd *HEBB* NE31 **85** D2
NSHW NE29 **53** F5 1
WD/WHPE/BLK NE5 **60** A6 2
Hedgeley Ter *BYK/HTN/WLK* NE6 **83** E2 3
Hedley La *WICK/BNPF* NE16 **114** B6
Hedley Pl *WLSD/HOW* NE28 **67** D5 8
Hedley Rd *MONK* NE25 **25** D6
NSHW NE29 **70** B3
Hedley St *GATE* NE8 **98** C2
GOS/KPK NE3 **63** E1
SSH NE33 **71** E2 1
Hedley Ter *ASHBK/HED/RY* SR2 **162** C2 2
GOS/KPK NE3 **47** E6
Hedworth Av *HAR/WTLS* NE34 **87** F4 2
Hedworth La *BOLCOL* NE35 **104** C1
JRW NE32 **86** C6
Hedworth Ter *SUND* SR1 **5** F3
Heighley St *BW/LEM/TK/HW* NE15 **77** E3
Helen St *BLAY* NE21 **75** F6
CLDN/WHIT/ROK SR6 **109** D6
Helford Rd *PLEE/EAS* SR8 **208** B4
Helmdon *WASHN* NE37 **121** D4
Helmsdale Av *FELL* NE10 **100** C1 4
Helmsdale Rd *MLFD/PNYW* SR4 **142** C1
Helmsley Cl *HLS* DH4 **156** C2
Helmsley Ct *SWCK/CAS* SR5 **125** D1
Helmsley Dr *WLSD/HOW* NE28 **68** B4
Helmsley Rd *DHAM* DH1 **180** B5
JES NE2 **81** E1
Helston Ct
BW/LEM/TK/HW NE15 **76** A1 4
Helvellyn Av *WASHS* NE38 **137** F3
Helvellyn Rd *ASHBK/HED/RY* SR2 **144** C4
Hemlington Cl
ASHBK/HED/RY SR2 **162** B2 2
Hemmel Cts *BDN/LAN/SAC* DH7 **203** E3 1
Hemming St
ASHBK/HED/RY SR2 **145** E4 2
Hemsley Rd *HAR/WTLS* NE34 **72** B5
Henderson Av *WICK/BNPF* NE16 **95** F2 3
Henderson Gdns *FELL* NE10 **102** A3
Henderson Rd *HAR/WTLS* NE34 **87** E3
MLFD/PNYW SR4 **143** E1
WLSD/HOW NE28 **67** D3 1
Hendersyde Cl
WD/WHPE/BLK NE5 **61** D3 1
Hendon Burn Av
ASHBK/HED/RY SR2 **5** F6
Hendon Cl *NSHW* NE29 **70** C3 2
Hendon Gdns *JRW* NE32 **86** C6
Hendon Rd *LWF/SPW/WRK* NE9 **100** A2
SUND SR1 **5** F2
Hendon Rd East *SUND* SR1 **5** H3
Hendon St *SUND* SR1 **5** G4
Hendon Valley Rd
ASHBK/HED/RY SR2 **5** E6
Henley Av *CLSW/PEL* DH2 **152** A5
Henley Cl *CRAM* NE23 **22** C1
Henley Gdns *WLSD/HOW* NE28 **69** D2
Henley Rd *MLFD/PNYW* SR4 **142** C1
TYNE/NSHE NE30 **55** D3
Henley Wy *BOLCOL* NE35 **105** D2
Henlow Rd
BW/LEM/TK/HW NE15 **76** B1 4
Henry Nelson St *SSH* NE33 **71** F2
Henry Sq *JES* NE2 **3** G2 1
Henry St *GOS/KPK* NE3 **63** E1
HLH DH5 **171** F4
HLH DH5 **171** D1
NSHW NE29 **70** C1
SEA/MUR SR7 **176** C2 1
SSH NE33 **71** F2 2
Henry St East *ASHBK/HED/RY* SR2 **5** G4
Hensby Ct *WD/WHPE/BLK* NE5 **61** D2 6
Henshaw Gv *MONK* NE25 **25** E6
Henshaw Pl *WD/WHPE/BLK* NE5 **77** F1
Henshelwood Ter *JES* NE2 **64** A5 1
Henson Cl *WASHS* NE38 **138** C2

Hepburn Gdns FELL NE10 100 B1
Hepburn Gv SWCK/CAS SR5 123 E3 6
Hepple Ct BLYTH NE24 10 B6 6
Hepple Wy GOS/KPK NE3 46 C6 6
Hepscott Dr MONK NE25 39 F4
Hepscott Ter HAR/WTLS NE34 88 C1
Herbert St GATE NE8 99 F1
Herbert Ter SEA/MUR SR7 176 C3
Herd Cl BLAY NE21 93 F1 6
Herd House La BLAY NE21 75 E6
Herdinghill WASHN NE37 119 E6
Herdlaw CRAM NE23 21 F2
Hereford Ct
ASHBK/HED/RY SR2 144 C5 3
DIN/WO NE13 45 F4
Hereford Rd ASHBK/HED/RY SR2 144 C5
Herefordshire Dr DHAM DH1 196 B3
Hereford Sq
ASHBK/HED/RY SR2 144 C5 4
Hermiston MONK NE25 40 A5
Heron Cl BLYTH NE24 17 D3
WASHS NE38 137 F4
Heron Dr SSH NE33 71 E2
Heron Pl LGB/KIL NE12 48 C5 2
Herrick St WD/WHPE/BLK NE5 60 C3
Herring Gull Cl BLYTH NE24 17 D3
Herrington Rd HLS DH4 158 B2
SUNDSW SR3 159 D1
Hersham Cl DIN/WO NE13 45 F4 2
DIN/WO NE13 45 E4 1
GOS/KPK NE3 45 F5
Hertford LWF/SPW/WRK NE9 117 E2
Hertford Av HAR/WTLS NE34 90 A1
Hertford Cl MONK NE25 39 E4
Hertford Crs HLH DH5 171 E6
Hertford Gv CRAM NE23 22 B1
Herton Cl PLEE/EAS SR8 208 B1
Hesket Ct GOS/KPK NE3 46 A5 5
Hesleden Rd RHTLP TS27 209 F6
Hesleyside Dr WD/WHPE/BLK NE5 61 D6
Hesleyside Rd MONK NE25 39 D5
Hester Av MONK NE25 24 C2
Hetton Rd HLH DH5 171 D3
Heugh Hl LWF/SPW/WRK NE9 119 F2
Hewitson Ter FELL NE10 100 B3
Hewitt Av ASHBK/HED/RY SR2 145 D6
Hewley Crs BW/LEM/TK/HW NE15 57 F5
Heworth Burn Crs FELL NE10 101 D2
Heworth Gv WASHN NE37 120 B4 1
Heworth Rd WASHN NE37 120 C2
Heworth Wy FELL NE10 101 F2
Hewson Pl LWF/SPW/WRK NE9 100 A4 5
Hexham WASHS NE38 137 E2 1
Hexham Av BYK/HTN/WLK NE6 83 E3
CRAM NE23 22 C1
HEBB NE31 85 D6
Hexham Cl NSHW NE29 53 E5 2
Hexham Ct DUN/TMV NE11 97 E4 3
Hexham Dr STLY/ANP DH9 146 B3
Hexham Old Rd RYTON NE40 74 B3
Hexham Rd BW/LEM/TK/HW NE15 57 F4
MLFD/PNYW SR4 142 C1
WICK/BNPF NE16 95 F1
Hextol Gdns
BW/LEM/TK/HW NE15 77 E1 3
Heybrook Av NSHW NE29 54 B4
Heyburn Gdns
BW/LEM/TK/HW NE15 78 C3
Hibernian Rd JRW NE32 86 A1 5
Hibernia Rd BYK/HTN/WLK NE6 83 F4 6
Hickling Ct WD/WHPE/BLK NE5 61 D2
Hickstead Cl WLSD/HOW NE28 52 A5 2
Hickstead Gv CRAM NE23 22 C1
Hiddleston Av LGB/HTN NE7 65 D1
Higgins Ter SUNDSW SR3 161 D1
Higham Pl CNUT NE1 3 E2 1
High Back Cl JRW NE32 85 F4
High Barnes Ter
MLFD/PNYW SR4 143 F1 4
High Br CNUT NE1 2 D4
Highbury FELL NE10 101 D2
MONK NE25 40 A5 1
Highbury Av LWF/SPW/WRK NE9 119 F2
Highbury Cl LWF/SPW/WRK NE9 119 F2
Highbury Pl NSHW NE29 70 B1
High Carr Cl DHAM DH1 194 A1
High Chare CLS/BIR/GTL DH3 153 E5
Highcliffe Gdns GATE NE8 99 F2 4
High Cft CLDN/WHIT/ROK SR6 109 E1
WASHN NE37 120 A3
High Croft Cl HEBB NE31 84 C4 3
Highcroft Dr
CLDN/WHIT/ROK SR6 109 D1 1
Highcross Rd TYNE/NSHE NE30 54 C1
High Dene LGB/HTN NE7 64 C5
Highfield BDN/LAN/SAC DH7 178 B1
WICK/BNPF NE16 114 A1
Highfield Cl WD/WHPE/BLK NE5 60 B3 5
Highfield Ct FELL NE10 101 D3 3
Highfield Crs CLS/BIR/GTL DH3 153 E3
Highfield Dr HAR/WTLS NE34 72 B6
HLS DH4 170 A2
Highfield Gra HLS DH4 170 A3 1
Highfield Pl DIN/WO NE13 32 C5 4
Highfield Ri CLS/BIR/GTL DH3 153 E3
Highfield Rd GATE NE8 99 F1
HAR/WTLS NE34 72 B6
HLS DH4 156 C2
ROWG NE39 110 B3
WD/WHPE/BLK NE5 60 B4
Highfield Ter BYK/HTN/WLK NE6 83 F4 7
High Flatworth NSHW NE29 69 D1
Highgate Gdns JRW NE32 86 C6 1
Highgate Rd MLFD/PNYW SR4 142 C1
The High Ga GOS/KPK NE3 62 A2
Highgreen Cha WICK/BNPF NE16 95 F6
High Gv RYTON NE40 74 C4
Highgrove WD/WHPE/BLK NE5 59 F4
Highheath WASHN NE37 119 F6 1
High Heworth La FELL NE10 101 E2
High Horse Cl ROWG NE39 93 F6
High Horse Close Wd ROWG NE39 93 F6
High House Gdns FELL NE10 101 D1 1
Highland Rd WD/WHPE/BLK NE5 61 F3
High La HLS DH4 158 B4
High Lane Rw HEBB NE31 68 B6
High La FELL NE10 101 E3
High Laws GOS/KPK NE3 64 B2
High Level Br CNUT NE1 3 E5
High Meadow HAR/WTLS NE34 72 B6
High Mdw BDN/LAN/SAC DH7 202 C3
High Moor Pl HAR/WTLS NE34 88 B3 10
High Pasture WASHS NE38 139 D5 1
High Rdg DIN/WO NE13 33 D5 2
The High Rd HAR/WTLS NE34 89 E2
High Rw BW/LEM/TK/HW NE15 76 B2
High Sandgrove
CLDN/WHIT/ROK SR6 107 F1
Highside Dr SUNDSW SR3 143 F3
Highstead Av CRAM NE23 13 F5
High St BDN/LAN/SAC DH7 204 A3
BLYTH NE24 10 C5 1
BW/LEM/TK/HW NE15 75 E1
DHAM DH1 196 B2
FELL NE10 100 C2
GATE NE8 3 F6
GOS/KPK NE3 63 E1
HLH DH5 186 B3
JRW NE32 86 B1
MLFD/PNYW SR4 123 F6
RDHAMSE DH6 184 A6
STLY/ANP DH9 148 B1
High St East SUND SR1 5 F1
WLSD/HOW NE28 67 E5
High Street South Back
BDN/LAN/SAC DH7 204 A3
High St West BYK/HTN/WLK NE6 66 C5
SUND SR1 4 C2
High Swinburne Pl
ELS/FEN NE4 80 A3 11
Hightree Cl SUNDSW SR3 160 B3 6
SUNDSW SR3 160 C3 3
High Vw WLSD/HOW NE28 67 D3
High Vw North WLSD/HOW NE28 67 D2
Highwell La WD/WHPE/BLK NE5 60 A5 6
High West St GATE NE8 81 D5 2
Highwood Rd
BW/LEM/TK/HW NE15 77 E1
High Wood Vw DHAM DH1 194 C6
Highworth Dr LGB/HTN NE7 66 A3 2
LWF/SPW/WRK NE9 119 E2
Hilda Av DHAM DH1 195 F5
Hilda Cl DHAM DH1 196 A5
Hilda Pk CLSW/PEL DH2 153 D3
Hilda St CLDN/WHIT/ROK SR6 126 C1 4
GATE NE8 98 C1
Hilden Gdns LGB/HTN NE7 65 E4
Hillary Av LGB/KIL NE12 50 A4
Hillary Pl WD/WHPE/BLK NE5 60 C3 4
Hill Av CRAM NE23 23 F6
Hill Crs SEA/MUR SR7 177 D5
SEA/MUR SR7 188 B1
Hill Crest BDN/LAN/SAC DH7 178 B2
WICK/BNPF NE16 112 A6
Hillcrest DHAM DH1 194 C4
HAR/WTLS NE34 90 A4
JRW NE32 86 B6
MONK NE25 40 A5
SUNDSW SR3 159 D1
Hillcrest Dr DUN/TMV NE11 97 D3
Hill Crest Gdns JES NE2 64 A2 5
Hillcroft LWF/SPW/WRK NE9 99 F4
Hill Dyke LWF/SPW/WRK NE9 118 B2
Hillfield MONK NE25 39 F5
Hillfield Gdns SUNDSW SR3 144 A3
Hillfield St GATE NE8 81 D6
Hillgate GATE NE8 3 F6
Hill Head Dr WD/WHPE/BLK NE5 59 F5
Hillhead Gdns DUN/TMV NE11 97 F4 3
Hillhead La WICK/BNPF NE16 112 C3
Hillhead Pkwy WD/WHPE/BLK NE5 59 E4
Hill Head Rd WD/WHPE/BLK NE5 59 F4
Hillheads Rd MONK NE25 54 B1
Hillhead Wy WD/WHPE/BLK NE5 60 A3
Hill House Rd
BW/LEM/TK/HW NE15 57 D4
Hillingdon Gv MLFD/PNYW SR4 141 F4
Hill La HLS DH4 140 B5
Hillmeads CLSW/PEL DH2 165 E6
Hill Park Rd JRW NE32 86 B3
Hill Ri WASHS NE38 121 D6
Hillrise Crs SEA/MUR SR7 174 C2
Hillsden Rd MONK NE25 39 F3
Hillside BDN/LAN/SAC DH7 178 A3
BLAY NE21 76 A6
BOL NE36 105 F3 4
CLS/BIR/GTL DH3 136 C2
CLS/BIR/GTL DH3 153 E4
DUN/TMV NE11 97 D3
HAR/WTLS NE34 90 A4
SUNDSW SR3 144 B3
Hillside Av BW/LEM/TK/HW NE15 77 E1
Hillside Cl ROWG NE39 111 D1 3
Hillside Crs BW/LEM/TK/HW NE15 77 F4
Hillside Dr CLDN/WHIT/ROK SR6 109 D1
Hillside Gdns STLY/ANP DH9 131 F6
SUNDSW SR3 144 B3 5
Hillside Pl LWF/SPW/WRK NE9 99 F4
Hillside Wy HLS DH4 171 D1
Hillsleigh Rd WD/WHPE/BLK NE5 61 F3
Hill St JRW NE32 85 F1
SEA/MUR SR7 176 C4
SSH NE33 71 D5
SUNDSW SR3 160 C1
Hillsview Av GOS/KPK NE3 62 B1 5
Hill Ter HLS DH4 158 A2 1
Hillthorne Cl WASHS NE38 139 E2 3
Hill Top BLAY NE21 94 A1
CLS/BIR/GTL DH3 136 C2
STLY/ANP DH9 149 D1
Hill Top Av LWF/SPW/WRK NE9 99 F5
Hill Top Gdns LWF/SPW/WRK NE9 99 F5
Hilltop Gdns SUNDSW SR3 161 E1 3
Hillview SUNDSW SR3 159 D1
Hillview Crs HLS DH4 157 F5 3
Hill View Gdns SUNDSW SR3 144 A3
Hillview Gv HLS DH4 157 F5 4
Hill View Rd ASHBK/HED/RY SR2 145 D4
Hillview Rd HLS DH4 157 F5 5
Hill View Sq ASHBK/HED/RY SR2 144 C4
Hilton Av WD/WHPE/BLK NE5 61 D4
Hilton Cl CRAM NE23 13 F4
Hilton Dr PLEE/EAS SR8 208 C3
Hindley Gdns ELS/FEN NE4 78 C1
Hindmarch Dr BOL NE36 105 F3
Hind St SUND SR1 4 A3 1
Hinkley Cl SUNDSW SR3 160 C2
Hipsburn Dr SUNDSW SR3 143 F3
Hiram Dr BOL NE36 106 C3
Histon Wy WD/WHPE/BLK NE5 61 D3
Hither Gn JRW NE32 86 C6 2
Hobart WBAY NE26 40 B3
Hobart Av HAR/WTLS NE34 87 E4
Hodgkin Park Crs
BW/LEM/TK/HW NE15 78 B3
Hodgkin Park Rd
BW/LEM/TK/HW NE15 78 B3
Hodgson's Rd BLYTH NE24 10 C4
Hodkin Gdns LWF/SPW/WRK NE9 100 A4
Hogarth Dr WASHS NE38 139 D3
Hogarth Rd HAR/WTLS NE34 88 B6
Holbein Rd HAR/WTLS NE34 88 B5
Holborn Pl WD/WHPE/BLK NE5 60 A5 7
Holborn Rd MLFD/PNYW SR4 142 C2
Holborn Sq MLFD/PNYW SR4 142 C2 2
Holburn Cl RYTON NE40 74 C3 1
Holburn Ct BDN/LAN/SAC DH7 192 A5 1
RYTON NE40 74 C3 2
Holburn Crs RYTON NE40 75 D3
Holburn Gdns RYTON NE40 75 D3
Holburn La RYTON NE40 74 C3
Holburn Wk RYTON NE40 75 D3
Holburn Wy RYTON NE40 74 C3
Holden Pl WD/WHPE/BLK NE5 61 F4 7
Holder House La HAR/WTLS NE34 89 D5
Holderness Rd BYK/HTN/WLK NE6 65 D5
WLSD/HOW NE28 68 C3
Hole La WICK/BNPF NE16 95 E6
Holeyn Rd BW/LEM/TK/HW NE15 57 E5 1
Holland Dr JES NE2 80 A1
Holland Pk WLSD/HOW NE28 66 A3
Holland Park Dr JRW NE32 86 C6
Hollinghill Rd MONK NE25 25 D6
Hollings Crs WLSD/HOW NE28 67 D2 3
Hollingside La DHAM DH1 205 E2
Hollington Av LGB/KIL NE12 49 D6
Hollinhill ROWG NE39 93 F6
Hollinhill La ROWG NE39 93 E6
Hollinside Cl WICK/BNPF NE16 95 F5
Hollinside Gdns
BW/LEM/TK/HW NE15 78 A2
Hollinside Rd MLFD/PNYW SR4 142 C2
WICK/BNPF NE16 78 A6
Hollinside Sq MLFD/PNYW SR4 142 B1
Hollinside Ter ROWG NE39 110 C2 2
Hollowdene HLH DH5 185 F1
Holly Av BLAY NE21 94 B4
CLDN/WHIT/ROK SR6 109 E2
DUN/TMV NE11 97 E3
GOS/KPK NE3 46 B6
HAR/WTLS NE34 89 F3
HLH DH5 171 D2
JES NE2 64 A5
LGB/KIL NE12 49 F3
MONK NE25 39 D5

RYTON NE40 74 B2 2
SUNDSW SR3 144 A6
WBAY NE26 40 C5
WLSD/HOW NE28 67 E5
Holly Av West JES NE2 64 A5 2
Hollybush Rd FELL NE10 100 B2
Hollycarrside Rd
ASHBK/HED/RY SR2 145 D6
Holly Crs BDN/LAN/SAC DH7 178 B2
Hollydene DUN/TMV NE11 116 C6
ROWG NE39 111 E2
Holly Hvn HLH DH5 170 C6
Holly Hl FELL NE10 100 C2
Holly Hill Gdns STLY/ANP DH9 148 B4
Holly Hill Gdns East
STLY/ANP DH9 148 C4
Holly Hill Gdns West
STLY/ANP DH9 148 B4
Hollymount Sq BDLGTN NE22 7 F4
Holly Pk BDN/LAN/SAC DH7 203 D4
Holly Park Vw FELL NE10 100 C2 4
Holly Rd NSHW NE29 54 B5
The Hollys CLS/BIR/GTL DH3 118 A5
Holly St DHAM DH1 194 A5
JRW NE32 85 F1
Hollywell Ct BDN/LAN/SAC DH7 192 A5
Hollywell Gv DIN/WO NE13 44 B4
Hollywell Rd NSHW NE29 53 F6
Hollywood Av GOS/KPK NE3 47 E6
SWCK/CAS SR5 125 E2
Hollywood Crs GOS/KPK NE3 47 F6
Hollywood Gdns DUN/TMV NE11 98 A5 2
Holme Av BYK/HTN/WLK NE6 66 B5
WICK/BNPF NE16 96 A3
Holme Gdns SUNDSW SR3 144 A3
WLSD/HOW NE28 68 C4 1
Holme Ri WICK/BNPF NE16 96 A3
Holmesdale Rd
WD/WHPE/BLK NE5 61 F5
Holmeside SUND SR1 4 C3
Holmewood Dr ROWG NE39 110 C4
Holmfield Av HAR/WTLS NE34 89 D1
Holm Gn MONK NE25 39 F6
Holmhill La CLS/BIR/GTL DH3 166 B3
PLEE/EAS SR8 200 C1
Holmland BW/LEM/TK/HW NE15 78 B4
Holmlands MONK NE25 40 A5 2
Holmlands Pk North
ASHBK/HED/RY SR2 144 B2 3
Holmlands Pk South
ASHBK/HED/RY SR2 144 B2 4
Holmside Av DUN/TMV NE11 97 F2
Holmwood Av MONK NE25 39 F6
Holmwood Gv JES NE2 63 F4 1
Holyfields SMOOR NE27 51 F2
Holylake Sq MLFD/PNYW SR4 142 C1
Holyoake Gdns
CLS/BIR/GTL DH3 136 B2 2
LWF/SPW/WRK NE9 99 E2
Holyoake St CLSW/PEL DH2 151 E2
Holystone Av GOS/KPK NE3 47 D6
MONK NE25 41 D6
Holystone Cl BLYTH NE24 16 B1
HLS DH4 157 D6 1
Holystone Crs LGB/HTN NE7 64 C3
Holystone Dr SMOOR NE27 51 E2
Holystone Gdns NSHW NE29 53 F5
Holystone St HEBB NE31 84 C2
Holywell Av BYK/HTN/WLK NE6 83 D5
MONK NE25 25 E6
WBAY NE26 40 A4
Holywell Cl ELS/FEN NE4 80 A2 6
MONK NE25 25 E6
Holywell Dene Rd MONK NE25 38 B1
Home Av LWF/SPW/WRK NE9 99 E6
Home Pk WLSD/HOW NE28 66 A3
Homestall Cl HAR/WTLS NE34 88 C3 3
Honeycomb Cl SUNDSW SR3 160 B3 7
Honeysuckle Av HAR/WTLS NE34 88 A4
Honeysuckle Cl SUNDSW SR3 160 C3
Honister Av JES NE2 64 A3
Honister Cl
BW/LEM/TK/HW NE15 76 C1 3
Honister Dr SWCK/CAS SR5 126 B1 3
Honister Pl BW/LEM/TK/HW NE15 76 C1
Honister Rd TYNE/NSHE NE30 55 D2
Honister Wy BLYTH NE24 16 B3
Honiton Cl HLS DH4 157 E4 4
Honiton Ct WD/WHPE/BLK NE5 45 D6 1
Honiton Wy NSHW NE29 53 D4
Hood Cl SWCK/CAS SR5 126 B3 5
Hood St CNUT NE1 2 D3
WICK/BNPF NE16 95 F1 3
Hooper Ter RDHAMSE DH6 206 B2
Hopedene FELL NE10 101 F5
Hope Shield WASHS NE38 137 E5
Hope St HAR/WTLS NE34 88 A3 2
JRW NE32 86 B1
RDHAMSE DH6 197 E5
SUND SR1 4 A3
Hopgarth Gdns CLS/BIR/GTL DH3 153 F4
Hopkins Ct MLFD/PNYW SR4 125 E5
Hopper Pl GATE NE8 81 E5 4
Hopper Rd FELL NE10 100 B3
Hopper St GATE NE8 81 E5
NSHW NE29 70 B1
WLSD/HOW NE28 67 D4 6
Horatio St CLDN/WHIT/ROK SR6 127 D3
CNUT NE1 81 F3
Hornbeam Pl ELS/FEN NE4 80 A5 6
Horncliffe Gdns
WICK/BNPF NE16 96 B2 3
Horncliffe Pl
BW/LEM/TK/HW NE15 57 D4
Hornsea Cl DIN/WO NE13 33 D5 3
Hornsey Ter HLH DH5 186 A3 1
Horse Crofts BLAY NE21 76 B5 3
Horsham Gdns SUNDSW SR3 143 F3 8
Horsham Gv NSHW NE29 70 A2
Horsley Av SMOOR NE27 52 B2
Horsley Ct GOS/KPK NE3 46 A6 1
Horsley Gdns DUN/TMV NE11 97 F2
MONK NE25 25 E6 2
Horsley Gv SUNDSW SR3 143 F3
Horsley Hill Rd SSH NE33 72 A5
Horsley Hill Sq HAR/WTLS NE34 90 A1 1
Horsley Rd LGB/HTN NE7 65 D5
WASHS NE38 121 F6
Horsley Ter BYK/HTN/WLK NE6 83 E3 1
Horsley V HAR/WTLS NE34 89 E1
Horton Av BDLGTN NE22 7 E4
HAR/WTLS NE34 88 C5
SMOOR NE27 52 B2
Horton Crs DIN/WO NE13 31 D3 3
Hortondale Gv BLYTH NE24 10 A5
Horton Dr CRAM NE23 13 F5
Horton Pl BLYTH NE24 16 A2 3
Horton Rd BLYTH NE24 8 B6
Horwood Av WD/WHPE/BLK NE5 59 F4
Hospital Dr HEBB NE31 84 C4 4
Hospital La BW/LEM/TK/HW NE15 76 A1
Hotch Pudding Pl
WD/WHPE/BLK NE5 60 B6
Hotspur Av BDLGTN NE22 7 E4
HAR/WTLS NE34 89 D1 3
MONK NE25 40 C6
Hotspur Rd WLSD/HOW NE28 66 C1
Hotspur St BYK/HTN/WLK NE6 81 F1
TYNE/NSHE NE30 55 F4
Houghton Av TYNE/NSHE NE30 55 D1
WD/WHPE/BLK NE5 61 F3
Houghton Cut HLH DH5 171 D1
Houghton Rd HLH DH5 171 E4
HLS DH4 157 F5
Houghton St MLFD/PNYW SR4 125 F6
Houlskye Cl SUNDSW SR3 161 E1 4
Houndelee Pl
WD/WHPE/BLK NE5 61 E5 4
Hounslow Gdns JRW NE32 86 C6 3
House Ter WASHN NE37 120 C4
Houston Ct ELS/FEN NE4 80 A4 5
Houxty Rd MONK NE25 39 D5
Hovingham Cl PLEE/EAS SR8 209 D3
Hovingham Gdns SUNDSW SR3 143 F3 9
Howardian Cl WASHS NE38 138 A3
Howard St CNUT NE1 3 H3
FELL NE10 100 B4
GATE NE8 100 A1 7
JRW NE32 86 B2
SWCK/CAS SR5 126 C3 4
TYNE/NSHE NE30 55 D6
Howarth St MLFD/PNYW SR4 125 F6
Howat Av WD/WHPE/BLK NE5 62 A5 1
Howdene Rd
BW/LEM/TK/HW NE15 77 E2
Howdon La WLSD/HOW NE28 68 C3
Howdon Rd NSHW NE29 70 C2
WLSD/HOW NE28 69 E4
Howe Sq MLFD/PNYW SR4 142 B1
Howe St GATE NE8 100 A1
HEBB NE31 85 F2 2
Howick Av GOS/KPK NE3 46 C5
Howletch La PLEE/EAS SR8 208 B2
Howlett Hall Rd
BW/LEM/TK/HW NE15 77 E2
Howley Av SWCK/CAS SR5 124 B2 2
Hownam Cl GOS/KPK NE3 62 C2 3
Hoy Crs SEA/MUR SR7 175 E1
Hoylake Av LGB/HTN NE7 65 E1
Hoyle Av ELS/FEN NE4 79 D2
Hoyle Fold SUNDSW SR3 160 C4
Hubert St BOLCOL NE35 105 E2
Huddlestone Ri
CLDN/WHIT/ROK SR6 127 D4 1
Huddleston Rd BYK/HTN/WLK NE6 82 C1
Hudson Av BDLGTN NE22 8 A3
Hudson Rd SUND SR1 5 E3
Hudson St GATE NE8 81 D5 3
HAR/WTLS NE34 88 A2
TYNE/NSHE NE30 55 E6
Hudspeth Crs DHAM DH1 179 F5
Hugh St CLDN/WHIT/ROK SR6 127 D1
WASHS NE38 139 E2 4
WLSD/HOW NE28 67 D5
Hull St ELS/FEN NE4 79 E4
Hulme Ct PLEE/EAS SR8 208 B3 1
Hulne Av TYNE/NSHE NE30 55 E5
Humber Gdns GATE NE8 100 A1
Humber Hl STLY/ANP DH9 148 C3
Humbert St JRW NE32 86 A2 3
Hume St BYK/HTN/WLK NE6 81 F3
MLFD/PNYW SR4 125 F5
Humford Gn BLYTH NE24 9 E5
Humford Wy BDLGTN NE22 7 F5
Humsford Gv CRAM NE23 14 B6
Humshaugh Cl LGB/KIL NE12 50 C4 1
Humshaugh Rd NSHW NE29 53 E6 1
Hunstanton Ct
LWF/SPW/WRK NE9 117 D1
Huntcliffe Av
CLDN/WHIT/ROK SR6 109 D4
Huntcliffe Gdns BYK/HTN/WLK NE6 65 E5
Hunter Av BLYTH NE24 11 E6
Hunter Cl BOL NE36 106 C4
Hunter Rd PLEE/EAS SR8 207 F3
Hunters Cl NSHW NE29 69 F3
Hunters Ct WLSD/HOW NE28 67 E4 4
Hunters Hall Rd
MLFD/PNYW SR4 144 A1 9
Hunters Ldg WLSD/HOW NE28 67 D4
Hunter's Moor Cl JES NE2 62 C6
Hunter's Pl JES NE2 63 D6 3
Hunter's Rd GOS/KPK NE3 64 B1
JES NE2 79 F1
Hunter St HLS DH4 156 C3
SSH NE33 71 F5
Hunter Ter ASHBK/HED/RY SR2 145 D3
Huntingdon Cl DIN/WO NE13 45 E4
Huntingdon Gdns
SUNDSW SR3 143 F3 10
Huntingdon Pl TYNE/NSHE NE30 55 F5
Huntingdon Rd PLEE/EAS SR8 200 B6
Huntingdonshire Dr DHAM DH1 196 C3 2
Huntington Dr CRAM NE23 22 B1
Hunt Lea WICK/BNPF NE16 95 D5 2
Huntley Av SEA/MUR SR7 188 A1 1
Huntley Crs BLAY NE21 93 F2
Huntley Sq MLFD/PNYW SR4 142 C1 1
Huntly Rd MONK NE25 39 E3
Hurst Ter BYK/HTN/WLK NE6 83 D2
Hurstwood Rd MLFD/PNYW SR4 143 F2
Hurworth Av HAR/WTLS NE34 89 F2
Hurworth Pl JRW NE32 86 A2
Hustledown Gdns
STLY/ANP DH9 148 B4 1
Hustledown Rd STLY/ANP DH9 148 A4
Hutton Cl HLS DH4 170 B2
WASHS NE38 137 E1
Hutton St BOLCOL NE35 105 D1
MLFD/PNYW SR4 144 A1
Hutton Ter JES NE2 81 E1
LWF/SPW/WRK NE9 99 E6
Huxley Crs GATE NE8 98 C3
Hyacinth Ct MLFD/PNYW SR4 126 A5 5
Hyde Pk WLSD/HOW NE28 66 B3
Hydepark St GATE NE8 98 C2
Hyde St ASHBK/HED/RY SR2 145 E2
SSH NE33 71 F4
Hyde Ter GOS/KPK NE3 63 F1
Hylton Av HAR/WTLS NE34 90 A2
Hylton Bank MLFD/PNYW SR4 124 A6
Hylton Castle Rd SWCK/CAS SR5 124 A3
Hylton Cl BDLGTN NE22 6 C3
Hylton Gra SWCK/CAS SR5 123 E5
Hylton La BOL NE36 105 F4
SWCK/CAS SR5 123 F1
Hylton Park Rd SWCK/CAS SR5 125 D3
Hylton Rd DHAM DH1 180 B6
JRW NE32 86 A4
MLFD/PNYW SR4 125 D6
MLFD/PNYW SR4 126 A5 6
Hylton St GATE NE8 100 A1
HLS DH4 157 F6 2
MLFD/PNYW SR4 125 F6
NSHW NE29 70 C2 4
Hylton Wk MLFD/PNYW SR4 141 F1 1
MLFD/PNYW SR4 142 A1 2
Hymers Av HAR/WTLS NE34 87 E4
Hyperion Av HAR/WTLS NE34 87 F3

I

Ilchester St SEA/MUR SR7 176 C4 4
Ilderton Pl WD/WHPE/BLK NE5 60 A6 3
Ilex St DUN/TMV NE11 98 B4
Ilford Av CRAM NE23 13 F5 4
Ilford Pl GATE NE8 99 F2
Ilford Rd JES NE2 63 F3
WLSD/HOW NE28 68 B3
Ilfracombe Av ELS/FEN NE4 79 D3
Ilminster Ct GOS/KPK NE3 45 E6 2
Imeary Gv SSH NE33 71 F5 5
Imeary St SSH NE33 71 F5
Inchberry Cl ELS/FEN NE4 79 D4
Inchbury Cl ELS/FEN NE4 79 D4 1
Inchcliffe Crs WD/WHPE/BLK NE5 61 E4
Indigo St DUN/TMV NE11 98 B4
Industrial Rd WASHN NE37 121 D5
Industrial St CLSW/PEL DH2 151 E2
Industry Rd BYK/HTN/WLK NE6 65 F4
Ingham Gra SSH NE33 72 A5 4
Ingham Gv CRAM NE23 13 F5 5
Ingleby Ter MLFD/PNYW SR4 143 F1 5

Ingleby Wy *BLYTH* NE24 **16** C3
Inglemere Pl
BW/LEM/TK/HW NE15 **77** F2 1
Ingleside *WICK/BNPF* NE16 **95** E4
Ingleside Rd *NSHW* NE29 **54** B5
Ingleton Dr *BW/LEM/TK/HW* NE15 **57** D4
Ingleton Gdns *BLYTH* NE24 **16** B3
Inglewood Cl *BLYTH* NE24 **9** E5
Inglewood Pl *GOS/KPK* NE3 **47** E3 2
Ingoe Av *GOS/KPK* NE3 **46** B5 2
Ingoe Cl *BLYTH* NE24 **10** B5
Ingoe St *BW/LEM/TK/HW* NE15 **76** B2
WLSD/HOW NE28 **69** E4
Ingoldsby Ct *MLFD/PNYW* SR4 **143** D2 3
Ingram Av *GOS/KPK* NE3 **46** B4 3
Ingram Cl *CLSW/PEL* DH2 **165** F1
WLSD/HOW NE28 **68** B1 1
Ingram Dr *BLYTH* NE24 **10** A5
WD/WHPE/BLK NE5 **59** F2
Ingram Ter *BYK/HTN/WLK* NE6 **83** F2 1
Inkerman Rd *WASHN* NE37 **120** C3
Inkerman St *SWCK/CAS* SR5 **125** F3
Inleborough Dr *RYTON* NE40 **74** C4
Innesmoor *HEBB* NE31 **84** C1
Inskip Ter *GATE* NE8 **99** E2
Institute Ter West *CLSW/PEL* DH2 **135** E6
Inverness Rd *JRW* NE32 **87** D5
Inverness St *CLDN/WHIT/ROK* SR6 **126** C2
Invincible Dr *ELS/FEN* NE4 **79** F5
Iolanthe Crs *BYK/HTN/WLK* NE6 **83** D1
Iolanthe Ter *SSH* NE33 **72** A4
Iona Pl *BYK/HTN/WLK* NE6 **83** F2 2
Iona Rd *FELL* NE10 **100** A3
JRW NE32 **87** D5
Irene Av *ASHBK/HED/RY* SR2 **145** E5
Iris Crs *CLSW/PEL* DH2 **135** E4
Iris Pl *ELS/FEN* NE4 **78** C1
Iris St *DUN/TMV* NE11 **98** B4
Iroko St *DUN/TMV* NE11 **98** B4
Ironside St *HLH* DH5 **171** D1
Irthing Av *BYK/HTN/WLK* NE6 **82** C4
Irton St *GOS/KPK* NE3 **63** E1
Irwin Av *WLSD/HOW* NE28 **67** D3
Isabella Cl *ELS/FEN* NE4 **79** D5 1
Isabella Rd *BLYTH* NE24 **10** B6
Isabella Wk
BW/LEM/TK/HW NE15 **57** F5 4
Isis Rd *PLEE/EAS* SR8 **208** B3
Ivanhoe *MONK* NE25 **40** A5
Ivanhoe Vw *LWF/SPW/WRK* NE9 **118** A2
Iveagh Cl *ELS/FEN* NE4 **78** C4
Iveson St *BDN/LAN/SAC* DH7 **178** A1
Iveston Ter *STLY/ANP* DH9 **148** B1
Ivor St *ASHBK/HED/RY* SR2 **145** F4
Ivy Av *RYTON* NE40 **74** B2 3
SEA/MUR SR7 **176** A3
Ivy Cl *ELS/FEN* NE4 **80** A5
Ivy La *LWF/SPW/WRK* NE9 **117** F1
Ivymount Rd *BYK/HTN/WLK* NE6 **65** D5
Ivy Rd *BYK/HTN/WLK* NE6 **66** B6
GOS/KPK NE3 **63** E2
LGB/KIL NE12 **50** A4
Ivy St *DUN/TMV* NE11 **98** B4
Ivyway *CLSW/PEL* DH2 **152** A1
Ixia St *DUN/TMV* NE11 **98** B4

J

Jackson Av *PONT/DH* NE20 **28** B3
Jackson St *BYK/HTN/WLK* NE6 **83** E2 4
GATE NE8 **81** E5
MLFD/PNYW SR4 **143** F1
TYNE/NSHE NE30 **55** D6
Jackson St West *TYNE/NSHE* NE30 **55** D6
Jack's Ter *HAR/WTLS* NE34 **88** B3
Jacques St *MLFD/PNYW* SR4 **125** E5 4
Jacques Ter *CLSW/PEL* DH2 **153** D5
Jade Cl *BW/LEM/TK/HW* NE15 **59** E6
James Armitage St
SWCK/CAS SR5 **126** A2 9
James Mather St *SSH* NE33 **71** F2
James St *ELS/FEN* NE4 **79** E4
PLEE/EAS SR8 **200** C1
SEA/MUR SR7 **176** C4
SWCK/CAS SR5 **125** F2 4
WD/WHPE/BLK NE5 **60** B4 4
WICK/BNPF NE16 **95** F3 7
James Ter *HLH* DH5 **186** A4
HLS DH4 **169** F2
SUNDSW SR3 **161** D1
WLSD/HOW NE28 **67** D5 9
James Williams St *SUND* SR1 **5** F1
Jane Eyre Ter *GATE* NE8 **100** A1 8
Jane St *BYK/HTN/WLK* NE6 **82** B2 5
Jane Ter *BYK/HTN/WLK* NE6 **83** F3
Janet St *BYK/HTN/WLK* NE6 **82** B3 1
Janus Cl *WD/WHPE/BLK* NE5 **59** E2 2
Jarrow Rd *HAR/WTLS* NE34 **87** F2
JRW NE32 **87** E2
Jarvis Rd *PLEE/EAS* SR8 **200** C6
Jasmin Av *WD/WHPE/BLK* NE5 **59** E2
Jasmine Cl *BYK/HTN/WLK* NE6 **66** A5
Jasmine Ct *MLFD/PNYW* SR4 **126** A5 7
Jasmine Crs *SEA/MUR* SR7 **176** B5
Jasper Av *RYTON* NE40 **92** A1
Jedburgh Cl *GATE* NE8 **99** E1 6
NSHW NE29 **54** A4
WD/WHPE/BLK NE5 **59** E2
Jedburgh Gdns
BW/LEM/TK/HW NE15 **78** A2
Jedburgh Rd *HLS* DH4 **157** D2 4
Jedmoor *HEBB* NE31 **84** C1
Jefferson Pl *ELS/FEN* NE4 **80** A2 7
Jellicoe Rd *BYK/HTN/WLK* NE6 **83** D5 1
Jenifer Gv *LGB/HTN* NE7 **64** C3
Jenison Av *BW/LEM/TK/HW* NE15 **78** B3
Jennifer Av *SWCK/CAS* SR5 **124** A3 5
Jervis St *HEBB* NE31 **85** E2
Jesmond Dene Rd *JES* NE2 **63** F4
Jesmond Gdns *JES* NE2 **64** B5 3
Jesmond Pk East *LGB/HTN* NE7 **65** D4
Jesmond Pk West *LGB/HTN* NE7 **65** D5 1
Jesmond Rd *JES* NE2 **64** C6 3
Jesmond Ter *WBAY* NE26 **40** C6
Jesmond V *BYK/HTN/WLK* NE6 **81** F1
Jesmond Vale La
BYK/HTN/WLK NE6 **65** D6
Jessel St *LWF/SPW/WRK* NE9 **99** E6
Joan Av *ASHBK/HED/RY* SR2 **145** E5
Joannah St *SWCK/CAS* SR5 **126** B1 4
Joan St *ELS/FEN* NE4 **78** C4
Jobling Av *BLAY* NE21 **75** F6
Joel Ter *FELL* NE10 **84** A6
John Av *RYTON* NE40 **92** A1
John Brown Ct *BDLGTN* NE22 **7** E3 3
John Candlish Rd
MLFD/PNYW SR4 **125** F5
John Clay St *SSH* NE33 **71** F5 6
John Dobson St *CNUT* NE1 **2** D1
John Reid Rd *HAR/WTLS* NE34 **87** E4
Johnson Cl *PLEE/EAS* SR8 **200** C6
Johnson St
BW/LEM/TK/HW NE15 **76** B2 2
DUN/TMV NE11 **97** E1
GATE NE8 **98** A1
SSH NE33 **88** B1
Johnston Av *HEBB* NE31 **84** C5
John St *BDN/LAN/SAC* DH7 **178** B1
BLYTH NE24 **10** A4
DHAM DH1 **194** A5
FELL NE10 **101** E1 3
GATE NE8 **100** A1
GOS/KPK NE3 **62** C1
HLH DH5 **171** E2
HLH DH5 **185** F1
HLH DH5 **186** A1 1
HLS DH4 **169** F2
MLFD/PNYW SR4 **123** F5 2
MONK NE25 **38** C5
PLEE/EAS SR8 **201** D1
STLY/ANP DH9 **147** F4
STLY/ANP DH9 **149** E6
STLY/ANP DH9 **149** F1
SUND SR1 **4** D2 1
TYNE/NSHE NE30 **41** E6
WLSD/HOW NE28 **67** D4
John Taylor Ct *SWCK/CAS* SR5 **125** F1 2
John Williamson St *SSH* NE33 **88** A1
John Wilson Ct *PLEE/EAS* SR8 **209** F1 3
Joicey Gdns *STLY/ANP* DH9 **148** B1 4
Joicey Rd *LWF/SPW/WRK* NE9 **99** E4
Joicey St *FELL* NE10 **101** F1
Jolliffe St *CLS/BIR/GTL* DH3 **166** C1
Jonadab Rd *FELL* NE10 **83** F6
Jonadab St *FELL* NE10 **101** F1
Jones St *CLS/BIR/GTL* DH3 **136** A2
Jonquil Cl *WD/WHPE/BLK* NE5 **59** E2 3
Joseph Cl *ELS/FEN* NE4 **79** D4
Joseph St *STLY/ANP* DH9 **148** A3 1
Jowett Sq *SWCK/CAS* SR5 **125** F2 5
Joyce Ter *SWCK/CAS* SR5 **124** A3 6
Jubilee Av *LWF/SPW/WRK* NE9 **118** B3
Jubilee Cl *BDN/LAN/SAC* DH7 **164** A3
Jubilee Crs *GOS/KPK* NE3 **46** C6
Jubilee Pl *RDHAMSE* DH6 **206** B1 1
Jubilee Rd *BLYTH* NE24 **11** D6
CNUT NE1 **3** G3
GOS/KPK NE3 **62** C1
Jubilee Sq *HLH* DH5 **186** B3 1
Jubilee Ter *WICK/BNPF* NE16 **95** F1 4
Jude Pl *PLEE/EAS* SR8 **200** B6 1
PLEE/EAS SR8 **200** C6 1
Julian Av *BYK/HTN/WLK* NE6 **66** A6
SSH NE33 **71** F2
Julian Rd *FELL* NE10 **102** C2
Julian St *SSH* NE33 **71** F2
Juliet Av *NSHW* NE29 **53** F6 3
Julius Caesar St *SWCK/CAS* SR5 **125** F2 6
June Av *BLAY* NE21 **94** B4
Juniper Cl *BLYTH* NE24 **16** B2
GOS/KPK NE3 **47** F3 4
Jupiter Ct *PLEE/EAS* SR8 **200** B2 2
Jutland Av *HEBB* NE31 **85** D2
Jutland Ter *STLY/ANP* DH9 **130** C6

K

Kalmia St *DUN/TMV* NE11 **98** B5
Kane Gdns *FELL* NE10 **100** B4
Katrine Cl *CLSW/PEL* DH2 **153** D6
Katrine Ct *SUNDSW* SR3 **160** C3 4
Kayll Rd *MLFD/PNYW* SR4 **125** E6
Kay St *STLY/ANP* DH9 **148** B1
Kearsley Cl *MONK* NE25 **24** C5 2
Kearton Av *WD/WHPE/BLK* NE5 **59** E3
Keats Av *BLYTH* NE24 **16** B1 4
BOLCOL NE35 **106** A2
SWCK/CAS SR5 **125** F2 7
Keats Cl *STLY/ANP* DH9 **148** C2
Keats Rd *BW/LEM/TK/HW* NE15 **75** F2
Keebledale Av
BYK/HTN/WLK NE6 **83** E1 1
Keelman's La *MLFD/PNYW* SR4 **124** A5
Keelman's Rd *MLFD/PNYW* SR4 **124** A5
Keir Hardie Av *FELL* NE10 **101** F2
STLY/ANP DH9 **148** B4
Keir Hardie St *HLS* DH4 **170** A2
Keir Hardie Wy *SWCK/CAS* SR5 **126** A3
Keith Cl *ELS/FEN* NE4 **79** D4
Keldane Gdns *ELS/FEN* NE4 **79** D3
Kelfield Gv *CRAM* NE23 **14** A4 3
Kellfield Av *LWF/SPW/WRK* NE9 **99** F4
Kellfield Rd *LWF/SPW/WRK* NE9 **99** F5
Kell Rd *PLEE/EAS* SR8 **209** E2 2
Kells La *LWF/SPW/WRK* NE9 **99** E6
Kellsway *FELL* NE10 **101** E5 3
Kell's Wy *ROWG* NE39 **111** D3
Kelly Rd *HEBB* NE31 **85** D5
Kelsey Wy *CRAM* NE23 **14** A4
Kelso Cl *WD/WHPE/BLK* NE5 **59** E2 4
Kelso Dr *NSHW* NE29 **54** A4
Kelso Gdns *BW/LEM/TK/HW* NE15 **78** A2
WLSD/HOW NE28 **68** C2
Kelso Gv *HLS* DH4 **156** C2 2
Kelson Wy *WD/WHPE/BLK* NE5 **59** E2 5
Kelso Pl *GATE* NE8 **98** A1
Kelston Wy *WD/WHPE/BLK* NE5 **61** E4
Kelvin Gv *CLDN/WHIT/ROK* SR6 **107** D1 2
CLDN/WHIT/ROK SR6 **127** D2
GATE NE8 **98** C2
HAR/WTLS NE34 **72** B5
JES NE2 **81** E1
NSHW NE29 **54** C4
Kemble Cl *CRAM* NE23 **14** A4 4
Kemp Rd *PLEE/EAS* SR8 **208** B1
Kempton Gdns *GATE* NE8 **98** B3 1
Kendal Av *BLYTH* NE24 **10** C6 4
TYNE/NSHE NE30 **55** D2
Kendal Cl *PLEE/EAS* SR8 **207** F5
Kendal Crs *LWF/SPW/WRK* NE9 **100** A6
Kendal Dr *BOL* NE36 **106** B3
CRAM NE23 **14** B6
Kendale Wk *WD/WHPE/BLK* NE5 **60** A3 4
Kendal Gdns *WLSD/HOW* NE28 **68** C1
Kenilworth *LGB/KIL* NE12 **35** F6
Kenilworth Rd *ELS/FEN* NE4 **79** F4 4
MONK NE25 **40** B6
Kenilworth Sq *SWCK/CAS* SR5 **106** B6
Kenilworth Vw
LWF/SPW/WRK NE9 **117** F2
Kenley Rd *WD/WHPE/BLK* NE5 **60** C6
Kenmoor Wy *WD/WHPE/BLK* NE5 **59** E3
Kenmore Crs *RYTON* NE40 **74** A6
Kennersdene *TYNE/NSHE* NE30 **55** E4
Kennet Av *JRW* NE32 **86** B5
Kennington Gv *BYK/HTN/WLK* NE6 **83** D3
Kenny Pl *DHAM* DH1 **195** E3
Kensington Av *GOS/KPK* NE3 **47** E5
Kensington Gdns
TYNE/NSHE NE30 **55** D6 2
WLSD/HOW NE28 **66** A3
Kensington Gv *TYNE/NSHE* NE30 **55** D5 1
Kensington Ter *JES* NE2 **80** C1
Kent Av *DUN/TMV* NE11 **97** F2 1
HEBB NE31 **84** C3
WLSD/HOW NE28 **68** B4
Kentchester Rd *SWCK/CAS* SR5 **106** A6
Kent Gdns *HLH* DH5 **171** E6
Kentmere Av *BYK/HTN/WLK* NE6 **83** E2
CLDN/WHIT/ROK SR6 **108** B5
Kentmere Cl *CRAM* NE23 **23** F6
Kentmere Pl *PLEE/EAS* SR8 **209** D2 6
Kenton Av *GOS/KPK* NE3 **62** C3
Kenton Ct *SSH* NE33 **71** F5
Kenton Crs *GOS/KPK* NE3 **62** B2
Kenton Gv *CLDN/WHIT/ROK* SR6 **126** C3
Kenton La *GOS/KPK* NE3 **61** F2
WD/WHPE/BLK NE5 **62** A2
Kenton Rd *GOS/KPK* NE3 **62** C1
NSHW NE29 **53** E5
Kent Pl *HAR/WTLS* NE34 **89** E2
Kent St *JRW* NE32 **85** F2
Kentucky Rd *SWCK/CAS* SR5 **105** F6
Kenya Rd *SWCK/CAS* SR5 **106** A6
Kepier Ct *DHAM* DH1 **194** C4

Kepier Gdns *MLFD/PNYW* SR4 123 F6 3
Keppel St *SSH* NE33 71 E3
Kerry Cl *BLYTH* NE24 11 D4 7
Kerryhill Dr *DHAM* DH1 180 B4 3
Keston Dr *CRAM* NE23 14 A4
Kestrel Cl *WASHS* NE38 137 F4
Kestrel Ms *WICK/BNPF* NE16 95 F3 8
Kestrel Pl *LGB/KIL* NE12 49 D5
Kestrel St *DUN/TMV* NE11 98 B4
Kestrel Wy *HAR/WTLS* NE34 88 A4
NSHW NE29 70 C3
Keswick Av *CLDN/WHIT/ROK* SR6 108 B6
Keswick Dr *TYNE/NSHE* NE30 55 D2
Keswick Gdns *WLSD/HOW* NE28 68 C3
Keswick Gv *WD/WHPE/BLK* NE5 60 C6
Keswick Rd *PLEE/EAS* SR8 209 D2
STLY/ANP DH9 147 F4
Keswick St *GATE* NE8 99 D1
Keswic Ter *RDHAMSE* DH6 187 D4
Kettering Pl *CRAM* NE23 14 B6 1
Kettlewell Ter *TYNE/NSHE* NE30 55 D6
Ketton Cl *LGB/KIL* NE12 49 D6 4
Kew Gdns *WBAY* NE26 40 B4
Keyes Gdns *JES* NE2 64 A3
Kibblesworth Bank
DUN/TMV NE11 116 A6
Kidd Av *RDHAMSE* DH6 197 E5
Kidderminster Dr
WD/WHPE/BLK NE5 59 E3 2
Kidderminster Rd *SWCK/CAS* SR5 124 A1
Kidlandlee Gn
WD/WHPE/BLK NE5 60 C2 3
Kidlandlee Pl *WD/WHPE/BLK* NE5 60 C2
Kielder Av *CRAM* NE23 20 C2
Kielder Cl *BLYTH* NE24 16 A1
LGB/KIL NE12 35 E6 3
WD/WHPE/BLK NE5 60 C2 4
Kielder Gdns *JRW* NE32 85 F5
Kielder Pl *MONK* NE25 39 D5
Kielder Rd *BW/LEM/TK/HW* NE15 76 A1
MONK NE25 39 D5
Kielder Ter *TYNE/NSHE* NE30 55 D6 3
Kielder Wy *GOS/KPK* NE3 47 D5 2
Kier Hardie Av *STLY/ANP* DH9 148 B3
Kilburn Dr *PLEE/EAS* SR8 201 E5
Kilburne Cl *LGB/HTN* NE7 66 A3 3
Kilburn Gdns *NSHW* NE29 69 F3
Kildale *HLS* DH4 139 D6 3
Killin Cl *WD/WHPE/BLK* NE5 59 E2 6
Killingworth Av *SMOOR* NE27 36 C6
Killingworth Dr *LGB/KIL* NE12 49 D2
SUNDSW SR3 142 C2
Killingworth La *LGB/KIL* NE12 50 C1
Killingworth Pl *CNUT* NE1 2 C2
Killingworth Rd *GOS/KPK* NE3 64 B1
LGB/KIL NE12 50 A3
Killingworth Wy *CRAM* NE23 36 A5
LGB/KIL NE12 34 C6
Kiln Ri *WICK/BNPF* NE16 95 F6
Kilnshaw Pl *GOS/KPK* NE3 47 F3 3
Kimberley *WASHS* NE38 139 F1
Kimberley Av *NSHW* NE29 54 A6
Kimberley Gdns *JES* NE2 64 C6 4
Kimberley St *BLYTH* NE24 10 C4
MLFD/PNYW SR4 125 E6 5
Kingarth Av *CLDN/WHIT/ROK* SR6 109 D5
Kingdom Pl *NSHW* NE29 70 C3 3
King Edward Pl *GATE* NE8 100 A1 9
King Edward Rd
BYK/HTN/WLK NE6 65 D5
MLFD/PNYW SR4 124 A6 2
RYTON NE40 75 D4
SEA/MUR SR7 176 C4
TYNE/NSHE NE30 55 E5
King Edward St *GATE* NE8 100 A1
Kingfisher Rd *LGB/KIL* NE12 48 C5
Kingfisher Wy *BLYTH* NE24 17 D2
WLSD/HOW NE28 52 C6
King George Av *DUN/TMV* NE11 97 E3
King George Rd *GOS/KPK* NE3 46 A6
HAR/WTLS NE34 89 D1
Kingham Ct *LGB/HTN* NE7 64 B2 2
King John St *BYK/HTN/WLK* NE6 65 D6
King John Ter *BYK/HTN/WLK* NE6 65 D6
Kings Av *CLDN/WHIT/ROK* SR6 109 D5
HEBB NE31 85 E3
Kingsbridge *LGB/KIL* NE12 48 B5 1
Kings Cl *GATE* NE8 100 A1 10
Kingsdale Av *BLYTH* NE24 9 F5
Kingsdale Rd *LGB/KIL* NE12 48 B5
King's Dr *WBAY* NE26 40 C5
King's Gdns *BLYTH* NE24 10 B4
Kings Gv *DHAM* DH1 204 C1
Kingsland *JES* NE2 64 A6 2
King's La *CLSW/PEL* DH2 151 F1
Kingsley Av *GOS/KPK* NE3 47 F3
HAR/WTLS NE34 87 F5
MONK NE25 40 B6
Kingsley Cl *SWCK/CAS* SR5 125 F3 4
Kingsley Pl *DUN/TMV* NE11 97 E1 2
WICK/BNPF NE16 96 A2
WLSD/HOW NE28 68 B3 4
Kingsley Ter *ELS/FEN* NE4 79 F3
Kingsmere *CLS/BIR/GTL* DH3 153 E1
Kingsmere Gdns
BYK/HTN/WLK NE6 83 F4 3
King's Pl *MLFD/PNYW* SR4 125 F5
King's Rd *BDLGTN* NE22 8 C2
CNUT NE1 2 C1
LGB/KIL NE12 49 E3
WBAY NE26 40 B4
Kings Rd North *WLSD/HOW* NE28 67 D2
Kings Rd South *WLSD/HOW* NE28 67 D3
The King's Rd *SWCK/CAS* SR5 125 F2
King's Ter *MLFD/PNYW* SR4 125 E5
Kingston Av *BYK/HTN/WLK* NE6 82 C3
Kingston Cl *WBAY* NE26 40 B2
Kingston Dr *WBAY* NE26 40 B3
Kingston Park Av *GOS/KPK* NE3 45 E6
Kingston Park Rd *DIN/WO* NE13 45 F4
GOS/KPK NE3 46 B5
Kingston Rd *GATE* NE8 99 F2
Kingston Ter *CLDN/WHIT/ROK* SR6 126 C2
King St *BLYTH* NE24 11 D4
CLDN/WHIT/ROK SR6 108 C6
CLS/BIR/GTL DH3 136 A2
CNUT NE1 3 F5
FELL NE10 101 F1
GATE NE8 98 B2
RDHAMSE DH6 197 E5
RDHAMSE DH6 206 C2
SSH NE33 71 E3
SUND SR1 4 C2
TYNE/NSHE NE30 55 D6
Kingsway *BLYTH* NE24 11 D6 5
ELS/FEN NE4 62 A6
HLH DH5 171 E2
PONT/DH NE20 28 A4
SSH NE33 72 B4
TYNE/NSHE NE30 55 E4
WICK/BNPF NE16 113 F1
Kingsway Av *GOS/KPK* NE3 47 E5
Kingsway North *DUN/TMV* NE11 98 B4
Kingsway Rd *SWCK/CAS* SR5 105 F6
Kingsway South *DUN/TMV* NE11 98 C6
Kingswood Av *JES* NE2 63 F3 2
Kingswood Cl *BOLCOL* NE35 105 D1
Kingswood Gv *MLFD/PNYW* SR4 141 E4
Kingswood Rd *CRAM* NE23 14 B6
King Ter *STLY/ANP* DH9 147 F3
Kinlett *WASHS* NE38 139 F1 2
Kinley Rd *DHAM* DH1 196 C1
Kinloch Ct *CLSW/PEL* DH2 166 A1
Kinloss Sq *CRAM* NE23 14 B6 2
Kinnaird Av *BW/LEM/TK/HW* NE15 77 F2
Kinross Ct *FELL* NE10 84 A6
Kinross Dr *GOS/KPK* NE3 62 A1
STLY/ANP DH9 149 D2
Kinver Dr *WD/WHPE/BLK* NE5 59 E3
Kiphill Ct *STLY/ANP* DH9 131 F6
Kipling Av *BOLCOL* NE35 106 A2
HEBB NE31 85 E2
WICK/BNPF NE16 96 A2
Kipling Cl *STLY/ANP* DH9 148 C2
Kipling Ct *WICK/BNPF* NE16 96 A2 3
Kipling St *SWCK/CAS* SR5 125 F3 3
Kira Dr *DHAM* DH1 180 B4
Kirby Av *DHAM* DH1 193 F1
Kirby Cl *HAR/WTLS* NE34 87 E4
Kirkbride Pl *CRAM* NE23 14 B6 3
Kirkdale Gn *ELS/FEN* NE4 80 A4 6
Kirkdale St *HLH* DH5 185 E2
Kirkham Av *GOS/KPK* NE3 45 E5 1
Kirkham Rd *DHAM* DH1 180 C6
Kirkheaton Pl *WD/WHPE/BLK* NE5 61 E6
Kirkland Hl *PLEE/EAS* SR8 208 C1
Kirklands *CRAM* NE23 35 E5
Kirkland Wk *SMOOR* NE27 52 A1
Kirklea Rd *HLH* DH5 171 E2
Kirkleatham Gdns
BYK/HTN/WLK NE6 65 F4 4
Kirkley Av *HAR/WTLS* NE34 89 F2
Kirkley Cl *GOS/KPK* NE3 47 D6
Kirkley Dr *PONT/DH* NE20 28 A3
Kirkley Rd *SMOOR* NE27 52 B2
Kirklinton Rd *TYNE/NSHE* NE30 54 C2
Kirknewton Cl *HLH* DH5 171 E2 5
Kirkside *HLS* DH4 158 A2
Kirkston Av *BW/LEM/TK/HW* NE15 76 C1
Kirkstone *CLS/BIR/GTL* DH3 136 C4
Kirkstone Av *JRW* NE32 86 C5
PLEE/EAS SR8 209 D2
SWCK/CAS SR5 126 B1
TYNE/NSHE NE30 54 C2
Kirkstone Cl *HLH* DH5 171 E2
Kirkstone Dr *DHAM* DH1 196 B1
Kirkstone Gdns *LGB/HTN* NE7 64 C3 2
Kirkstone Rd *FELL* NE10 101 E1
Kirk Vw *HLS* DH4 157 F5 6
Kirkwall Cl *SWCK/CAS* SR5 123 F3
Kirkwood *CRAM* NE23 35 E5
Kirkwood Av *MLFD/PNYW* SR4 141 F4
Kirkwood Cl *CRAM* NE23 23 F6
Kirkwood Dr *GOS/KPK* NE3 62 B1 6
Kirkwood Gdns *FELL* NE10 102 A2
Kirton Av *ELS/FEN* NE4 79 D2
Kirton Wy *CRAM* NE23 14 B6
Kismet St *SWCK/CAS* SR5 125 F2
Kitchener Rd *CLDN/WHIT/ROK* SR6 91 D4
Kitchener St *LWF/SPW/WRK* NE9 99 F2 5
MLFD/PNYW SR4 143 E2
Kitchener Ter *ASHBK/HED/RY* SR2 145 E4
JRW NE32 86 A3
TYNE/NSHE NE30 55 E5
Kitching Rd *PLEE/EAS* SR8 199 F5
Kittiwake Cl *BLYTH* NE24 17 D3
NSHW NE29 52 C5
Kittiwake Dr *WASHS* NE38 137 E3
Kittiwake St *DUN/TMV* NE11 98 B5
Kitty Brewster Rd *BLYTH* NE24 9 E4
Knaresborough Cl *BDLGTN* NE22 6 C2
Knaresborough Rd *SEA/MUR* SR7 188 B1
Knaresdale *CLS/BIR/GTL* DH3 136 C5
Knarsdale Av *NSHW* NE29 53 F6
Knarsdale Pl *WD/WHPE/BLK* NE5 60 A5 3
Kneller Cl *STLY/ANP* DH9 148 B2
Knightsbridge *GOS/KPK* NE3 47 E6
SUNDSW SR3 143 D6 2
Knightside Gdns *DUN/TMV* NE11 97 E4 4
Knivestone Ct *LGB/KIL* NE12 36 A6
Knobbyends La *BLAY* NE21 93 E2
Knoll Ri *DUN/TMV* NE11 97 E3
Knollside Cl *SUNDSW* SR3 160 B3
Knott Pl *BW/LEM/TK/HW* NE15 77 F3
Knoulberry *WASHN* NE37 119 F6
Knoulberry Rd *WASHN* NE37 119 F6
Knowledge Hl *BLAY* NE21 94 A1
Knowle Pl *LGB/KIL* NE12 65 D1
Knowsley Ct
WD/WHPE/BLK NE5 61 D1 1
Knox Cl *BDLGTN* NE22 8 C2 4
Knox Rd *BDLGTN* NE22 8 A4
Knox Sq *SWCK/CAS* SR5 125 F1
Kristin Av *JRW* NE32 86 B4
Kyffin Vw *HAR/WTLS* NE34 90 A3
Kyle Cl *ELS/FEN* NE4 80 A4
Kyle Rd *GATE* NE8 98 B2
Kyloe Av *MONK* NE25 24 C6
Kyloe Cl *GOS/KPK* NE3 46 A5
Kyloe Pl *WD/WHPE/BLK* NE5 60 C3
Kyloe Vls *WD/WHPE/BLK* NE5 60 C3 5
Kyo Heugh Rd *STLY/ANP* DH9 146 C2
Kyo La *STLY/ANP* DH9 147 D3
Kyo Rd *STLY/ANP* DH9 146 B3

L

Laburnam Pk
BDN/LAN/SAC DH7 202 C5 1
Laburnam Rd
CLDN/WHIT/ROK SR6 126 C1 5
Laburnum Av *BLYTH* NE24 10 C4
BYK/HTN/WLK NE6 66 B6
DHAM DH1 194 A5
FELL NE10 101 F3
WLSD/HOW NE28 67 D4
Laburnum Ct *LGB/KIL* NE12 35 E6 9
Laburnum Crs *DUN/TMV* NE11 116 B6
SEA/MUR SR7 176 B6 1
Laburnum Gdns *JRW* NE32 85 F4
Laburnum Gv
CLDN/WHIT/ROK SR6 107 F1
HAR/WTLS NE34 89 E3
SWCK/CAS SR5 123 F4
WICK/BNPF NE16 95 F3 9
WICK/BNPF NE16 114 A1
Laburnum Rd *BLAY* NE21 76 B6
CLDN/WHIT/ROK SR6 126 C1 6
Lacebark *SUNDSW* SR3 160 A4
Ladock Cl *ASHBK/HED/RY* SR2 145 F6 1
Lady Anne Rd *RDHAMSE* DH6 197 E4
Ladybank *WD/WHPE/BLK* NE5 59 D3
Ladyhaugh Dr *WICK/BNPF* NE16 95 F6 1
Ladykirk Rd *ELS/FEN* NE4 79 D3
Ladykirk Wy *CRAM* NE23 21 D2 1
Ladysmith Ct *STLY/ANP* DH9 148 C3
Ladysmith St *SSH* NE33 71 F4
Lady's Piece La *RDHAMSE* DH6 183 F6
Lady's Wk *SSH* NE33 71 E2
Ladywell Rd *BLAY* NE21 76 B6
Ladywood Pk *HLS* DH4 139 E6 2
Laet St *NSHW* NE29 71 D1
Laindon Av *CLDN/WHIT/ROK* SR6 108 C6
Laing Gv *WLSD/HOW* NE28 68 C3
Laith Rd *GOS/KPK* NE3 62 A1
Lake Ap *BLAY* NE21 95 E1 1
Lake Av *HAR/WTLS* NE34 90 B2
Lake Ct *SUNDSW* SR3 160 C2 4
Lakeland Dr *PLEE/EAS* SR8 209 D1
Lake Rd *HLH* DH5 171 D2
Lakeside *BLAY* NE21 95 E1
HAR/WTLS NE34 90 C2
Lake Vw *HEBB* NE31 84 C4
Lambden Cl *NSHW* NE29 70 A3
Lambert Rd *WASHN* NE37 119 E5
Lambeth Pl *GATE* NE8 99 F2 6
Lambley Av *TYNE/NSHE* NE30 55 D2
Lambley Cl *WICK/BNPF* NE16 113 F2
Lambley Crs *HEBB* NE31 84 C5
Lambourn Av *LGB/KIL* NE12 49 E5
NSHW NE29 69 F2
Lambourne Cl *HLS* DH4 156 A5

Lambourne Rd
ASHBK/HED/RY SR2 144 B3
Lamb St BYK/HTN/WLK NE6 83 F3 2
Lambton Av WICK/BNPF NE16 96 B2
Lambton Ct PLEE/EAS SR8 208 B5
SUNDSW SR3 159 E1 3
WASHS NE38 137 D6
Lambton Dr HLH DH5 185 F2
Lambton Rd HEBB NE31 85 E1 2
JES NE2 64 A6
Lambton St DHAM DH1 194 A4 2
GATE NE8 81 D5
SUND SR1 4 D1
Lambton Ter JRW NE32 86 A5
Lampeter Cl WD/WHPE/BLK NE5 61 D2 7
Lamport St HEBB NE31 84 B1 2
Lampton Ct BDLGTN NE22 8 B2 1
Lanark Cl NSHW NE29 53 E4
Lanark Dr JRW NE32 87 D5
Lancashire Dr DHAM DH1 196 C3
Lancaster Ct GOS/KPK NE3 45 F5 3
Lancaster Dr WLSD/HOW NE28 51 F5
Lancaster Rd DUN/TMV NE11 97 D1
Lancaster St ELS/FEN NE4 80 A3 12
Lancaster Ter CLS/BIR/GTL DH3 153 F6
Lancastrian Rd CRAM NE23 21 F3
Lancefield Av BYK/HTN/WLK NE6 83 E4
Lanchester Av
LWF/SPW/WRK NE9 118 C1
Lanchester Cl FELL NE10 102 B4 1
Lanchester Gn BDLGTN NE22 7 E2 1
Lanchester Pk WASHS NE38 139 D4 2
Lancing Ct GOS/KPK NE3 45 E5
Landseer Cl STLY/ANP DH9 148 B2
Landseer Gdns HAR/WTLS NE34 88 C6
LWF/SPW/WRK NE9 100 A2 4
Lane Cnr HAR/WTLS NE34 88 B3
Lanercost WASHS NE38 138 B1
Lanercost Av BLAY NE21 76 A6 1
Lanercost Dr WD/WHPE/BLK NE5 61 D6
Lanercost Gdns
BW/LEM/TK/HW NE15 57 F3
FELL NE10 100 B4 2
Lanercost Rd NSHW NE29 70 A1
Langdale MONK NE25 40 A5
Langdale Cl LGB/KIL NE12 48 C6
Langdale Crs DHAM DH1 196 B1
Langdale Dr CRAM NE23 21 D2
Langdale Gdns
BYK/HTN/WLK NE6 83 F2 3
WLSD/HOW NE28 68 C2
Langdale Pl PLEE/EAS SR8 209 D2 7
Langdale Rd HLS DH4 139 F6
LWF/SPW/WRK NE9 99 F5
Langdale St HLH DH5 185 E2
Langdale Wy BOL NE36 106 B2
Langdon Cl NSHW NE29 54 B3 1
Langdon Rd WD/WHPE/BLK NE5 59 F4
Langford Dr BOLCOL NE35 87 D6
Langham Av NSHW NE29 53 E4
Langham Rd
BW/LEM/TK/HW NE15 77 E3 1
Langholm Rd BOL NE36 106 C2
GOS/KPK NE3 47 E5 1
Langhurst ASHBK/HED/RY SR2 145 D6
Langleeford Rd
WD/WHPE/BLK NE5 60 C3
Langley Av BLYTH NE24 10 A4
FELL NE10 102 A4
MONK NE25 53 F1
SMOOR NE27 52 C2
Langley Cl WASHS NE38 138 A2
Langley Crs BDN/LAN/SAC DH7 203 F3
Langley Rd BYK/HTN/WLK NE6 83 E2
DHAM DH1 180 B6
NSHW NE29 53 F6
SUNDSW SR3 144 A4
WD/WHPE/BLK NE5 60 B6
Langley St HLS DH4 157 F2
Langley Ter JRW NE32 86 A5
Langport Rd
ASHBK/HED/RY SR2 144 C3 2
Langton Cl MLFD/PNYW SR4 126 A6 7
Langton Dr CRAM NE23 14 B4
Langton St GATE NE8 99 F1 2
Langton Ter LGB/HTN NE7 65 D4 1
Lanivet Cl ASHBK/HED/RY SR2 145 E6
Lansbury Cl CLS/BIR/GTL DH3 118 A6
Lansbury Dr CLS/BIR/GTL DH3 118 A6
SEA/MUR SR7 188 B1 4
Lansbury Gdns FELL NE10 101 F2
Lansbury Rd WICK/BNPF NE16 96 B4
Lansbury Wy SWCK/CAS SR5 124 A3
Lansdowne ASHBK/HED/RY SR2 162 A1
Lansdowne Gdns JES NE2 64 C6
Lansdowne Rd LGB/KIL NE12 49 F4
Lansdowne St MLFD/PNYW SR4 126 A5 8
Lansdowne Ter NSHW NE29 54 B6
Lansdowne Ter West NSHW NE29 54 A6
Lanthwaite Rd LWF/SPW/WRK NE9 99 F5
Lanton St HLS DH4 157 F2
Lapford Dr CRAM NE23 14 B5
Lapwing Cl BLYTH NE24 17 D2
WASHS NE38 137 E3
Lapwing Ct WICK/BNPF NE16 130 B1
L'arbre Crs WICK/BNPF NE16 95 E3
Larch Av CLDN/WHIT/ROK SR6 109 F1
HAR/WTLS NE34 89 F3
HLS DH4 170 C1
Larch Cl LWF/SPW/WRK NE9 118 C2
Larches Rd DHAM DH1 193 F3 1
The Larches WICK/BNPF NE16 112 A5 1
Larch Rd BLAY NE21 76 C5
Larch Ter STLY/ANP DH9 129 F5
Larchwood WASHS NE38 138 A5
Larchwood Av BYK/HTN/WLK NE6 66 A6
DIN/WO NE13 33 E5
GOS/KPK NE3 46 B5 3
Larchwood Gdns DUN/TMV NE11 98 A5
Larchwood Gv
ASHBK/HED/RY SR2 144 B4 4
Larkfield Crs HLS DH4 156 C3 1
Larkfield Rd ASHBK/HED/RY SR2 144 B3
Lark Rise Cl LGB/HTN NE7 65 F3 3
Larkspur Cl STLY/ANP DH9 130 C6
Larkspur Rd WICK/BNPF NE16 95 F4
Larkspur Ter JES NE2 64 A5
Larne Crs LWF/SPW/WRK NE9 99 F5
Larriston Pl CRAM NE23 21 E2 1
Lartington Cl CLS/BIR/GTL DH3 168 A4
Lartington Gdns GOS/KPK NE3 64 B1 4
Larwood Cl CLS/BIR/GTL DH3 167 D1
Larwood Ct STLY/ANP DH9 146 A5
Lascelles Av HAR/WTLS NE34 89 D3
Laski Gdns FELL NE10 102 A2
Latimer St TYNE/NSHE NE30 55 F4
Lauderdale Av WLSD/HOW NE28 67 D2
Launceston Cl DIN/WO NE13 45 F4
Launceston Dr SUNDSW SR3 159 E1
Laura St SUND SR1 4 D4
Laurel Av DHAM DH1 195 F4
GOS/KPK NE3 46 C6
LGB/KIL NE12 50 C3
SEA/MUR SR7 176 A3
Laurel Ct CLSW/PEL DH2 153 D3
Laurel Crs BYK/HTN/WLK NE6 66 B5
STLY/ANP DH9 151 D1
Laurel Gv ASHBK/HED/RY SR2 144 B4
Laurel Rd BLAY NE21 76 C6
Laurel St BW/LEM/TK/HW NE15 57 F3
WLSD/HOW NE28 67 E5
Laurelwood Gdns DUN/TMV NE11 98 A5
Lauren Ct PLEE/EAS SR8 200 B2
Laurens Ct WASHN NE37 120 C4 1
Lavender Gdns BDN/LAN/SAC DH7 178 C1
JES NE2 63 F5
Lavender Gv SWCK/CAS SR5 123 F3
Lavender La HAR/WTLS NE34 88 A3
Lavender Rd WICK/BNPF NE16 95 F4
Laverock Hall Rd BLYTH NE24 15 F3
Laverock Pl BLYTH NE24 16 A3 2
GOS/KPK NE3 61 F1 7
Lavington Rd HAR/WTLS NE34 72 A6
Lawe Rd SSH NE33 71 F2
Lawmill Wy WD/WHPE/BLK NE5 61 D4 7
Lawn Dr BOL NE36 105 E4
The Lawns HLH DH5 186 B3
Lawnswood HLH DH5 171 E3
Lawrence Av BLAY NE21 76 B5
HAR/WTLS NE34 88 C5
Lawrence Ct BLAY NE21 76 B5 4
Lawrence St SUND SR1 5 F3
Lawson Av JRW NE32 86 B4
Lawson Crs CLDN/WHIT/ROK SR6 108 C6
Lawson St NSHW NE29 70 C2
WLSD/HOW NE28 67 E5
Lawson Ter DHAM DH1 194 A5
ELS/FEN NE4 79 D4 2
HLH DH5 186 A3
Laws St CLDN/WHIT/ROK SR6 108 C6
Laxford Ct SUNDSW SR3 160 C3
Laybourn Gdns HAR/WTLS NE34 87 F4 3
Layburn Gdns
BW/LEM/TK/HW NE15 60 A6 4
Layburn Pl PLEE/EAS SR8 208 A1
Layfield Rd GOS/KPK NE3 47 E3
Laygate SSH NE33 71 E6 5
Laygate Pl SSH NE33 71 E5
Laygate St SSH NE33 71 D5
Lea Av JRW NE32 86 B6
Leabank BW/LEM/TK/HW NE15 59 F6
Leafield Crs HAR/WTLS NE34 72 C6
Lea Gn CLS/BIR/GTL DH3 137 D5
Leagreen Ct GOS/KPK NE3 62 C1 3
Leaholme Crs BLYTH NE24 10 B6
Lea La PLEE/EAS SR8 190 A6
Lealholm Rd LGB/HTN NE7 64 C1 2
Leam Gdns FELL NE10 102 B2
Leamington St MLFD/PNYW SR4 126 A6
Leam La FELL NE10 101 F5
JRW NE32 86 C4
JRW NE32 103 F1
LWF/SPW/WRK NE9 101 E6
Leamside FELL NE10 101 E4
JRW NE32 86 B4
Leander Av CLS/BIR/GTL DH3 153 F1
Leander Dr BOLCOL NE35 105 D2
Leaplish WASHS NE38 139 E4
Lea Riggs HLS DH4 183 F2 1
The Leas HLS DH4 157 F5
Leazes Ct DHAM DH1 194 C4
Leazes Crs CNUT NE1 2 B2
Leazes La CNUT NE1 2 C2
DHAM DH1 194 C4
Leazes Park Rd CNUT NE1 2 B2
Leazes Pkwy
BW/LEM/TK/HW NE15 57 E5
Leazes Pl DHAM DH1 194 C4
Leazes Ri PLEE/EAS SR8 209 E2
Leazes Rd DHAM DH1 194 C4
Leazes Ter CNUT NE1 2 B1
The Leazes HAR/WTLS NE34 89 E2
SUND SR1 126 A6 8
Leazes Vw ROWG NE39 110 C2
Lecondale FELL NE10 101 E5
Ledbury Rd ASHBK/HED/RY SR2 144 C3
Leechmere Rd
ASHBK/HED/RY SR2 144 B4
Leechmere Wy
ASHBK/HED/RY SR2 145 D6
Lee Cl WASHS NE38 140 A1
Leeds St CLDN/WHIT/ROK SR6 126 C2 4
Leeholme HLH DH5 171 E3
Leeholme Ct STLY/ANP DH9 146 C5 1
Leeming Gdns
LWF/SPW/WRK NE9 100 A4
Leesfield Dr BDN/LAN/SAC DH7 203 E5
Leesfield Gdns BDN/LAN/SAC DH7 203 D5
Leesfield Rd BDN/LAN/SAC DH7 203 E5 1
Lees St STLY/ANP DH9 148 B1
Lee St CLDN/WHIT/ROK SR6 108 C6
SWCK/CAS SR5 126 A3 3
Legg Av BDLGTN NE22 9 D1
Legges Dr DIN/WO NE13 18 C2
Legion Gv BW/LEM/TK/HW NE15 77 E1 4
Legion Rd BW/LEM/TK/HW NE15 77 E1 5
Leicester Cl WLSD/HOW NE28 66 C1
Leicestershire Dr DHAM DH1 196 C3 3
Leicester St BYK/HTN/WLK NE6 83 D3
Leighton Rd ASHBK/HED/RY SR2 144 C4
Leighton St BYK/HTN/WLK NE6 81 F2 7
SSH NE33 72 A4
Leith Ct HAR/WTLS NE34 88 B3
Leith Gdns STLY/ANP DH9 130 C5
Lemington Gdns
WD/WHPE/BLK NE5 78 B1
Lemington Rd
BW/LEM/TK/HW NE15 75 F1
Lemon St SSH NE33 88 A2
Lena Av MONK NE25 40 A6
Lenin Ter STLY/ANP DH9 148 C3
Leominster Rd
ASHBK/HED/RY SR2 144 C4
Leopold St JRW NE32 86 A2 4
Lesbury Av SMOOR NE27 52 A1
WLSD/HOW NE28 68 B3
Lesbury Cha GOS/KPK NE3 47 D6
Lesbury Cl CLSW/PEL DH2 165 E1
Lesbury Rd BYK/HTN/WLK NE6 65 D5
Lesbury St BW/LEM/TK/HW NE15 76 C2
WLSD/HOW NE28 69 E5 2
Leslie Av HEBB NE31 85 D3
Leslie Cl RYTON NE40 75 D4
Leslie Crs GOS/KPK NE3 63 E3 1
Letch Av SEA/MUR SR7 189 F4
Leven Av CLSW/PEL DH2 166 A1
Levisham Cl SUNDSW SR3 161 E1 5
Lewis Crs ASHBK/HED/RY SR2 5 G6
Lewis Dr ELS/FEN NE4 79 E2
Lexington Ct BDN/LAN/SAC DH7 202 C5
Leybourne Av LGB/KIL NE12 49 F3
Leyburn Cl CLSW/PEL DH2 134 C5
HLS DH4 170 B1
Leyburn Dr LGB/HTN NE7 64 C3
Leyburn Gv HLS DH4 170 B1
Leyburn Pl CLS/BIR/GTL DH3 118 A6
Leyfield Cl SUNDSW SR3 161 D3 1
Leyton Pl GATE NE8 100 A2 5
Liburn Cl BOL NE36 106 A2
Lichfield Av BYK/HTN/WLK NE6 83 D4
Lichfield Cl CLS/BIR/GTL DH3 167 F4 2
GOS/KPK NE3 45 F5
Lichfield Rd SWCK/CAS SR5 125 F1
Lidcombe Cl SUNDSW SR3 161 D1
Liddell St CLDN/WHIT/ROK SR6 126 C4 5
NSHW NE29 71 D1
Liddell Ter GATE NE8 98 C2
Liddle Av RDHAMSE DH6 197 E4 2
Liddle Cl PLEE/EAS SR8 200 A6
Liddle Rd ELS/FEN NE4 79 F3
Lieven St DIN/WO NE13 32 C6 3
Liffey Rd HEBB NE31 85 E5
Lightbourne Rd
BYK/HTN/WLK NE6 83 F2
Lightwood Av
BW/LEM/TK/HW NE15 77 F4 1
Lilac Av BDN/LAN/SAC DH7 178 B1
BLYTH NE24 10 C4
CLDN/WHIT/ROK SR6 91 E5
DHAM DH1 194 A1
HAR/WTLS NE34 89 E3
LGB/KIL NE12 50 B4
SUNDSW SR3 144 A6
Lilac Cl WD/WHPE/BLK NE5 59 D2 5
Lilac Gdns LWF/SPW/WRK NE9 99 E4

WICK/BNPF NE16 95 F4
Lilac Gv CLSW/PEL DH2 152 C3
Lilac Pk BDN/LAN/SAC DH7 192 A5
Lilac Rd BYK/HTN/WLK NE6 66 C5
Lilac Sq HLS DH4 156 A5
Lilac St MLFD/PNYW SR4 123 F6
Lilac Ter RDHAMSE DH6 206 B2
Lilburn Cl CLSW/PEL DH2 165 F2
Lilburn Gdns GOS/KPK NE3 64 B2
Lilburn Pl SWCK/CAS SR5 125 F3 6
Lilburn Rd SMOOR NE27 52 A2
Lilburn St NSHW NE29 70 B1
Lilian Av ASHBK/HED/RY SR2 145 D6
WLSD/HOW NE28 66 C5
Lilley Gv SWCK/CAS SR5 124 A3
Lily Av BDLGTN NE22 8 A4
JES NE2 64 A5
Lily Bank WLSD/HOW NE28 67 D4
Lily Crs CLDN/WHIT/ROK SR6 91 E5
JES NE2 64 A5
Lily Gdns STLY/ANP DH9 129 D6
Lily St MLFD/PNYW SR4 126 A5
Lily Ter WD/WHPE/BLK NE5 60 C3
Lilywhite Ter HLH DH5 186 A2
Lime Av HLS DH4 170 B2
Limecragg Av DHAM DH1 196 A3
Limecroft JRW NE32 104 B1
Lime Gv RYTON NE40 74 B3
Limekiln Rd WLSD/HOW NE28 67 F4
Lime Pk BDN/LAN/SAC DH7 203 D4
The Limes HLS DH4 140 A6
Lime St BLAY NE21 94 C1
CNUT NE1 81 F3 3
MLFD/PNYW SR4 126 A5
Limetrees Gdns
LWF/SPW/WRK NE9 99 E3
Limewood Ct JES NE2 63 D6 4
Limewood Gv DIN/WO NE13 33 D5
Linacre Cl DIN/WO NE13 45 D6
Linbridge Dr WD/WHPE/BLK NE5 60 A5 9
Linburn WASHS NE38 137 F5
Lincoln Av SUNDSW SR3 143 F6
WLSD/HOW NE28 66 C3
Lincoln Gn GOS/KPK NE3 47 D3
Lincoln Rd CRAM NE23 14 B5 1
DHAM DH1 180 C5 1
HAR/WTLS NE34 90 A1
Lincolnshire Cl DHAM DH1 196 B3
Lincoln St GATE NE8 99 D1 6
MLFD/PNYW SR4 125 E5 5
Lindale Av WICK/BNPF NE16 95 F5
Lindale Rd ELS/FEN NE4 62 A6
Lindean Pl CRAM NE23 21 E2 2
Linden Av ELS/FEN NE4 78 C1
GOS/KPK NE3 63 E2 2
Linden Gdns
ASHBK/HED/RY SR2 144 B3 6
Linden Gv DUN/TMV NE11 97 E2
HLS DH4 170 C2 1
Linden Pk BDN/LAN/SAC DH7 203 D4 3
Linden Rd ASHBK/HED/RY SR2 144 B3 7
BLAY NE21 76 C6
GOS/KPK NE3 63 E2
LGB/KIL NE12 49 F5
MONK NE25 24 A5
Lindfield Av WD/WHPE/BLK NE5 61 D5
Lindisfarne PLEE/EAS SR8 208 B4
WASHS NE38 138 B2
Lindisfarne Av CLS/BIR/GTL DH3 153 F5
Lindisfarne Cl HLS DH4 170 A1
JES NE2 64 B3
WD/WHPE/BLK NE5 60 B5 4
Lindisfarne Ct JRW NE32 87 E2
Lindisfarne Dr GATE NE8 81 E5
Lindisfarne Pl WLSD/HOW NE28 67 F3
Lindisfarne Recess JRW NE32 86 C4
Lindisfarne Rd DHAM DH1 194 C1
HEBB NE31 85 D5
JES NE2 64 B4
Lindisfarne Ter TYNE/NSHE NE30 54 C5
Lindom Av CLS/BIR/GTL DH3 153 F5
Lindon Rd STLY/ANP DH9 148 A3
Lindrick Ct FELL NE10 102 B3
Lindsay Av BLYTH NE24 10 B4
Lindsay Cl ASHBK/HED/RY SR2 5 E5
Lindsay Rd ASHBK/HED/RY SR2 5 F5 2
Lindsay St HLH DH5 172 A4
Lindsey Cl CRAM NE23 21 D2
Lindum Rd LWF/SPW/WRK NE9 99 E2
Lingdale DHAM DH1 196 C3
Lingdale Av CLDN/WHIT/ROK SR6 109 D4
Lingey Gdns FELL NE10 102 B2
Lingey La FELL NE10 102 A3
Lingholme CLSW/PEL DH2 152 C4
Lingmell WASHN NE37 120 A6
Lingshaw FELL NE10 102 A3
Linhope Av GOS/KPK NE3 46 B5
Linhope Rd WD/WHPE/BLK NE5 60 B4
Link Av BDLGTN NE22 6 C3
Link Rd WD/WHPE/BLK NE5 62 A4 1
Links Av TYNE/NSHE NE30 55 E2
WBAY NE26 40 B3
Links Gn GOS/KPK NE3 47 F6
Links Rd BLYTH NE24 17 E3
TYNE/NSHE NE30 55 E2
The Links DHAM DH1 196 C2 1
WBAY NE26 26 B2
Links Vw BLYTH NE24 16 B2
Linkway JRW NE32 104 C1
Linley Hl WICK/BNPF NE16 95 D6
Linnel Dr BW/LEM/TK/HW NE15 77 D1
Linnet Gv SWCK/CAS SR5 124 B3
Linskell ASHBK/HED/RY SR2 145 D6
Linskill Pl TYNE/NSHE NE30 55 D5
Linskill St TYNE/NSHE NE30 71 D1
Linskill Ter TYNE/NSHE NE30 55 D6
Lintfort CLS/BIR/GTL DH3 153 F1
Linthorpe Rd GOS/KPK NE3 47 E5
TYNE/NSHE NE30 55 D3
Linton Rd LWF/SPW/WRK NE9 117 E1
WBAY NE26 40 A1
Lintzford Gdns
BW/LEM/TK/HW NE15 77 D2 1
ROWG NE39 110 C4
Lintzford La ROWG NE39 110 A4
Lintz Green La ROWG NE39 110 A5
Lintz La WICK/BNPF NE16 128 C2
Linum Pl ELS/FEN NE4 62 A6
Linwood Pl GOS/KPK NE3 47 E3 3
Lisa Av MLFD/PNYW SR4 141 F1
Lisburn Ter MLFD/PNYW SR4 125 F5
Lisle Gv WLSD/HOW NE28 68 C3
Lisle Rd HAR/WTLS NE34 89 E1
Lisle St WLSD/HOW NE28 67 D4
Lismore Av SSH NE33 88 C1 1
Lismore Pl BW/LEM/TK/HW NE15 78 B2
Lister Av DUN/TMV NE11 97 E1
Lister Cl HLH DH5 170 C4
Lister Rd PLEE/EAS SR8 199 F6
Litchfield La BLAY NE21 94 A1
Litchfield Rd DHAM DH1 180 C4
Little Bedford St NSHW NE29 71 D1
Littlebridge Ct DHAM DH1 179 F5 1
Littleburn Cl HLS DH4 157 E6 2
Littleburn La BDN/LAN/SAC DH7 204 A3
Littleburn Rd BDN/LAN/SAC DH7 204 A4
Littledene LWF/SPW/WRK NE9 99 E3
Little Eden PLEE/EAS SR8 208 C1
Little Villiers St SUND SR1 4 D2 2
Little Wy BW/LEM/TK/HW NE15 78 A4
Littondale WLSD/HOW NE28 66 B2
Livingstone Rd SUND SR1 4 A2
Livingstone St SSH NE33 71 F2 3
Lizard La CLDN/WHIT/ROK SR6 91 D6
HAR/WTLS NE34 90 C2
Lloyd Av HLH DH5 170 B6
Lobban Av HEBB NE31 84 C5
Lobelia Av FELL NE10 82 A6
Lobelia Cl WD/WHPE/BLK NE5 59 E3 3
Lobley Gdns DUN/TMV NE11 97 F4
Lobley Hill Rd DUN/TMV NE11 97 F4
Lobleyhill Rd WICK/BNPF NE16 112 C4
Lochcraig Pl CRAM NE23 21 E2 3
Lochmaben Ter SWCK/CAS SR5 126 C2
Lockerbie Rd CRAM NE23 21 E2
Lockhaugh Rd ROWG NE39 111 E1
Locksley Cl NSHW NE29 53 D3
Locomotion Wy LGB/KIL NE12 35 D5
NSHW NE29 70 C3
Lodgeside Meadow SUNDSW SR3 161 D3
The Lodges Rd
LWF/SPW/WRK NE9 117 D1
Lodore Gv JRW NE32 86 C5
Lodore Rd JES NE2 63 F3
Logan Rd BYK/HTN/WLK NE6 66 B5
Logan St HLH DH5 185 F1
Lola St DIN/WO NE13 32 B5 1
Lombard Dr CLS/BIR/GTL DH3 153 E1
Lombard St SUND SR1 5 F2
Lomond Ct SUNDSW SR3 160 C2 5
Lomond Pl CLSW/PEL DH2 166 A1
London Av WASHN NE37 120 A3
Londonderry Av DHAM DH1 195 F5
Londonderry St SEA/MUR SR7 177 D5 1
SUNDSW SR3 160 C1
Londonderry Ter SUNDSW SR3 161 D1
Longacre HLS DH4 170 B2
WASHS NE38 139 D5 2
Long Acres DHAM DH1 195 D3
Long Bank CLS/BIR/GTL DH3 118 B5
LWF/SPW/WRK NE9 118 B4
Longborough Ct LGB/HTN NE7 64 C2 2
Long Burn Dr CLSW/PEL DH2 152 B6
Long Dl CLSW/PEL DH2 152 B6
Longdean Cl HEBB NE31 84 B3 1
Longdean Pk CLS/BIR/GTL DH3 153 E2
Longfield Rd CLDN/WHIT/ROK SR6 126 C1
Longfield Ter BYK/HTN/WLK NE6 83 E4
Long Gair BLAY NE21 93 F2
Long Garth DHAM DH1 193 E2
Longhirst FELL NE10 101 F3
LGB/KIL NE12 35 F6
WD/WHPE/BLK NE5 60 B4
Longhirst Dr DIN/WO NE13 33 D5
Longlands Dr HLH DH5 171 D3
Longley St ELS/FEN NE4 79 F2
Longmeadows SUNDSW SR3 159 E2
Longnewton St SEA/MUR SR7 176 C5
Longniddry WASHN NE37 120 B1
Longniddry Ct
LWF/SPW/WRK NE9 117 D1
Longridge Av LGB/HTN NE7 65 F3
WASHS NE38 137 F4
Longridge Dr WBAY NE26 40 A3
Long Ridge Rd RYTON NE40 74 B6
Longridge Sq
ASHBK/HED/RY SR2 144 C4 1
Longridge Wy CRAM NE23 21 E2
STKFD/GP NE62 7 F1
Longrigg FELL NE10 101 E3 2
Long Rigg WICK/BNPF NE16 95 F1 5
Longrigg Rd WICK/BNPF NE16 95 F1
Long Rw SSH NE33 71 D3
Longsdale Av BLYTH NE24 9 D4
Longshank La CLS/BIR/GTL DH3 117 F6
Longston Av TYNE/NSHE NE30 55 D1
Longstone Ct LGB/KIL NE12 36 A6
Longstone Sq WD/WHPE/BLK NE5 59 F5
Longwood Cl WICK/BNPF NE16 114 A1
Lonnen Av ELS/FEN NE4 78 C1
Lonnen Dr WICK/BNPF NE16 95 F2
The Lonnen HAR/WTLS NE34 90 A4
Lonsdale CLS/BIR/GTL DH3 137 D5
Lonsdale Av CLDN/WHIT/ROK SR6 109 D4
Lonsdale Gdns WLSD/HOW NE28 68 C2
Lonsdale Rd CLDN/WHIT/ROK SR6 127 D2
Lonsdale Ter JES NE2 64 A4
Loraine Ter
BW/LEM/TK/HW NE15 76 B2 3
Lord Byrons Wk SEA/MUR SR7 175 E1
Lordenshaw WD/WHPE/BLK NE5 60 B4 5
Lord Nelson St HAR/WTLS NE34 88 A2
Lord St SEA/MUR SR7 176 C4
SSH NE33 72 A5
SUNDSW SR3 161 D1
Lorimers Cl PLEE/EAS SR8 208 A4
Lorne St HLH DH5 186 A4
Lorne Ter ASHBK/HED/RY SR2 4 B6
Lorrain Rd HAR/WTLS NE34 88 C6
Lorton Av TYNE/NSHE NE30 54 C2
Lorton Rd LWF/SPW/WRK NE9 99 F6
Losh Ter BYK/HTN/WLK NE6 83 E3
Lossiemouth Rd NSHW NE29 69 D1
Lothian Ct WD/WHPE/BLK NE5 61 E3 5
Lotus Cl WD/WHPE/BLK NE5 59 D3
Lotus Pl ELS/FEN NE4 78 C1 2
Loudon St HAR/WTLS NE34 88 B3 11
Loughborough Av
ASHBK/HED/RY SR2 144 B3
Loughrigg Av CRAM NE23 21 D2
Louie Ter LWF/SPW/WRK NE9 99 F5
Louis Av CLDN/WHIT/ROK SR6 126 C1
Loup St BLAY NE21 76 B5 5
Lovaine Av MONK NE25 40 C6
NSHW NE29 70 C1 5
Lovaine Pl NSHW NE29 70 C1
Lovaine Pl West NSHW NE29 70 B1 4
Lovaine Rw TYNE/NSHE NE30 55 F4
Lovaine St BW/LEM/TK/HW NE15 58 A6
CLSW/PEL DH2 151 E2
Lovaine Ter NSHW NE29 54 C6 8
Love Av CRAM NE23 35 D3
Loveless Gdns FELL NE10 102 A3
Lowbiggin WD/WHPE/BLK NE5 44 A6
Low Chare CLS/BIR/GTL DH3 153 F5
Lowdham Av NSHW NE29 70 A2
Low Downs Rd HLH DH5 171 F4
Lower Dundas St
CLDN/WHIT/ROK SR6 126 C4 6
Lower Rudyerd St NSHW NE29 71 D1 4
Lowerson Av HLS DH4 156 C3
Lowery La STLY/ANP DH9 149 F6
Lowe's Barn Bank DHAM DH1 204 B1
Lowes Ct DHAM DH1 193 F6
Lowes Fall DHAM DH1 193 F6
Lowes Ri DHAM DH1 204 C1
Loweswater Av HLH DH5 186 B4
Loweswater Cl BLYTH NE24 9 E3
Loweswater Rd
WD/WHPE/BLK NE5 61 D5 6
Loweswood Cl LGB/HTN NE7 64 C5
Lowes Wynd DHAM DH1 193 F6
Lowfield Ter BYK/HTN/WLK NE6 83 E4
Low Flatts Rd CLSW/PEL DH2 153 D2
Low Friar St CNUT NE1 2 C4
Lowgate BW/LEM/TK/HW NE15 57 F5
Low Gosforth Ct GOS/KPK NE3 47 F3 6
Low Haugh PONT/DH NE20 28 B3
Low Heyworth La FELL NE10 101 E1
Lowhills Rd PLEE/EAS SR8 200 A6
Lowland Cl SUNDSW SR3 160 C3
Lowland Rd BDN/LAN/SAC DH7 203 D4
Low La HAR/WTLS NE34 88 B4
Low Meadow
CLDN/WHIT/ROK SR6 107 F1 1
Lownds Ter BYK/HTN/WLK NE6 83 D2
Low Quay BLYTH NE24 11 E5
Lowrey's La LWF/SPW/WRK NE9 99 E5 7
Low Rw PLEE/EAS SR8 200 A2
Lowry Gdns HAR/WTLS NE34 88 C6
Lowry Rd CLDN/WHIT/ROK SR6 109 D5
Low Station Rd HLS DH4 183 D2
Low St SUND SR1 5 F1
Lowther Cl PLEE/EAS SR8 208 C1 4

Lowther Ct *PLEE/EAS* SR8 **208** A6
Lowthian Crs *BYK/HTN/WLK* NE6 **83** D3
Low West Av *ROWG* NE39 **110** B3
Lucknow St *SUND* SR1 **5** G1
Lucock St *HAR/WTLS* NE34 **88** A3 3
Ludlow Av *NSHW* NE29 **54** A4
Ludlow Ct *GOS/KPK* NE3 **46** A5 6
Ludlow Dr *MONK* NE25 **39** D6
Ludlow Rd *ASHBK/HED/RY* SR2 **144** C4
Luffness Dr *HAR/WTLS* NE34 **89** E5
Luke Crs *SEA/MUR* SR7 **188** A1
Luke's La *HEBB* NE31 **85** E6
Lulsgate *SWCK/CAS* SR5 **123** F3
Lulworth Av *JRW* NE32 **86** C3
Lulworth Ct *SUNDSW* SR3 **159** E1 4
Lulworth Gdns
ASHBK/HED/RY SR2 **144** B3 8
Lumley Av *HAR/WTLS* NE34 **90** A2
WICK/BNPF NE16 **96** A1
Lumley Cl *WASHS* NE38 **138** A1
Lumley Ct *BDLGTN* NE22 **8** B2 2
SUNDSW SR3 **159** E1 5
Lumley Dr *PLEE/EAS* SR8 **208** C5
Lumley Gdns *GATE* NE8 **100** A1
Lumley New Rd *CLS/BIR/GTL* DH3 **154** B6
HLS DH4 **168** C1
Lumley Rd *DHAM* DH1 **180** B5
Lumley St *HLS* DH4 **157** F6
MLFD/PNYW SR4 **125** F6
Lumley Ter *CLS/BIR/GTL* DH3 **153** F6
JRW NE32 **86** A5
Lumsden Sq *SEA/MUR* SR7 **188** A1 2
Lund Av *DHAM* DH1 **179** F6
Lunedale Av *CLDN/WHIT/ROK* SR6 **108** B5
Lunedale Dr *CLS/BIR/GTL* DH3 **168** A4 1
Lunesdale St *HLH* DH5 **185** F2
Lupin Cl *WD/WHPE/BLK* NE5 **59** E2 7
Luss Av *JRW* NE32 **87** D5
Lutterworth Cl *LGB/KIL* NE12 **49** D6 5
Lutterworth Dr *LGB/KIL* NE12 **48** C6
Lutterworth Rd
ASHBK/HED/RY SR2 **144** B3
LGB/KIL NE12 **65** D1 3
Luxembourg Rd *MLFD/PNYW* SR4 **124** C5
Lydbury Cl *CRAM* NE23 **14** B5 2
Lydcott *WASHS* NE38 **140** A2
Lydford Ct *HLS* DH4 **157** E5 2
WD/WHPE/BLK NE5 **45** E6
Lydford Wy *CLS/BIR/GTL* DH3 **136** C3
Lyncroft Rd *NSHW* NE29 **54** A6
Lyndale *CRAM* NE23 **14** B5
Lyndhurst Av *CLS/BIR/GTL* DH3 **153** E2
JES NE2 **63** F4
LWF/SPW/WRK NE9 **99** E6
Lyndhurst Cl *BLAY* NE21 **93** F2 5
Lyndhurst Crs *LWF/SPW/WRK* NE9 **99** F6
Lyndhurst Dr *DHAM* DH1 **193** F5 2
LWF/SPW/WRK NE9 **99** F6
Lyndhurst Gdns *JES* NE2 **63** F4 2
Lyndhurst Gv *LWF/SPW/WRK* NE9 **99** F6
Lyndhurst Rd *LGB/KIL* NE12 **49** F5
STLY/ANP DH9 **147** F2 1
Lyndhurst St *SSH* NE33 **71** F4 9
Lyndhurst Ter *MLFD/PNYW* SR4 **125** D4 1
Lyndon Cl *BOL* NE36 **106** A3
Lyndon Dr *BOL* NE36 **106** A3
Lyndon Gv *BOL* NE36 **106** A3
Lyndon Wk *BLYTH* NE24 **9** E4
Lyne Cl *CLSW/PEL* DH2 **135** E6
Lyne's Dr *BDN/LAN/SAC* DH7 **203** F3
Lynfield *WBAY* NE26 **40** A2
Lynfield Ct *WD/WHPE/BLK* NE5 **61** D3 2
Lynfield Pl *WD/WHPE/BLK* NE5 **61** D3 3
Lynford Gdns
ASHBK/HED/RY SR2 **144** B3 9
Lynholm Gv *LGB/KIL* NE12 **49** F4 4
Lynmouth Pl *LGB/HTN* NE7 **65** D3 1
Lynmouth Rd *NSHW* NE29 **69** E1 3
Lynndale Av *BLYTH* NE24 **9** F5
Lynnholme Gdns
LWF/SPW/WRK NE9 **99** F2 7
Lynn Rd *NSHW* NE29 **53** F5 2
WLSD/HOW NE28 **66** C5
Lynn St *BLYTH* NE24 **10** C5
Lynnwood Av *ELS/FEN* NE4 **79** E3 2
Lynthorpe *ASHBK/HED/RY* SR2 **145** E6
Lyn-thorpe Gv
CLDN/WHIT/ROK SR6 **127** D1 2
Lynton Av *JRW* NE32 **87** D3
Lynton Ct *HLS* DH4 **157** E5
Lynton Pl *WD/WHPE/BLK* NE5 **61** D3
Lynton Wy *WD/WHPE/BLK* NE5 **61** D3
Lynwood Av *BLAY* NE21 **76** B5 6
MLFD/PNYW SR4 **141** F4
Lyons Av *HLH* DH5 **186** A2
Lyons La *HLH* DH5 **186** B3
Lyon St *HEBB* NE31 **84** C2
Lyric Cl *NSHW* NE29 **53** D4
Lysdon Av *MONK* NE25 **24** C2
Lyster Cl *SEA/MUR* SR7 **175** D1
Lytham Cl *CRAM* NE23 **21** D2 2
WASHN NE37 **120** B2 3
WLSD/HOW NE28 **52** A5
Lytham Dr *MONK* NE25 **39** F5
Lytham Gra *HLS* DH4 **156** C4
Lytham Pl *BYK/HTN/WLK* NE6 **83** D3
Lythe Wy *LGB/KIL* NE12 **49** E6

M

Mabel St *BLAY* NE21 **76** B5
Macadam St *GATE* NE8 **98** C3
Maclynn Cl *SUNDSW* SR3 **160** A2
Macmerry Cl *SWCK/CAS* SR5 **123** E4 1
Macmillan Gdns *FELL* NE10 **101** F2 2
Maddison St *BLYTH* NE24 **11** D4
Maddox Rd *LGB/KIL* NE12 **49** F6
Madeira Av *WBAY* NE26 **40** B3
Madeira Cl *WD/WHPE/BLK* NE5 **59** E2
Madeira Ter *SSH* NE33 **71** F5
Madras St *HAR/WTLS* NE34 **87** F4
Mafeking Pl *NSHW* NE29 **53** D3
Mafeking St *BYK/HTN/WLK* NE6 **83** E5 2
LWF/SPW/WRK NE9 **99** F2 8
MLFD/PNYW SR4 **125** E6
Magdalene Av *DHAM* DH1 **196** B2
Magdalene Hts *DHAM* DH1 **195** D4 2
Magdalene St *DHAM* DH1 **195** D4 3
Magdelene Pl *MLFD/PNYW* SR4 **125** E5
Magenta Crs *WD/WHPE/BLK* NE5 **59** E2
Maglona St *SEA/MUR* SR7 **176** C5
Maiden Law *HLS* DH4 **169** F3 1
Maiden St *ELS/FEN* NE4 **80** A5 7
Maidstone Cl *SUNDSW* SR3 **159** F2 1
Main Crs *WLSD/HOW* NE28 **66** B2
Main Rd *DIN/WO* NE13 **31** D3
DIN/WO NE13 **45** D5
RYTON NE40 **74** A3
Mainsforth Ter West
ASHBK/HED/RY SR2 **145** D2
Mains Park Rd *CLS/BIR/GTL* DH3 **153** F6
Mainstone Cl *CRAM* NE23 **21** F2 1
Main St *PONT/DH* NE20 **28** A4
Main St North *CRAM* NE23 **36** A2
Makendon St *HEBB* NE31 **85** D1
Malaburn Wy *SWCK/CAS* SR5 **125** F3 7
Malaga Cl *WD/WHPE/BLK* NE5 **59** D2
Malaya Dr *BYK/HTN/WLK* NE6 **83** F3
Malcolm St *BYK/HTN/WLK* NE6 **81** F2
SEA/MUR SR7 **176** C4 5
Malden Cl *CRAM* NE23 **21** E2
Maling Pk *MLFD/PNYW* SR4 **124** A5 2
Malings Cl *SUND* SR1 **5** G3
Maling St *BYK/HTN/WLK* NE6 **81** F3 4
Mallard Cl *WASHS* NE38 **137** E2
Mallard Wy *BLYTH* NE24 **17** E3
WLSD/HOW NE28 **52** C6
Mallowburn Crs *GOS/KPK* NE3 **61** E2
Malmo Cl *NSHW* NE29 **69** D1
Malone Gdns *CLS/BIR/GTL* DH3 **118** C6
Maltby Cl *WASHS* NE38 **138** C2
Malton Cl *BLYTH* NE24 **10** A5 3
BW/LEM/TK/HW NE15 **77** D2 2
Malton Crs *NSHW* NE29 **70** A2
Malton Gdns *WLSD/HOW* NE28 **67** D3
Malvern Ct *BW/LEM/TK/HW* NE15 **76** A1
Malvern Crs *SEA/MUR* SR7 **175** F3
Malvern Gdns
CLDN/WHIT/ROK SR6 **127** D1
DUN/TMV NE11 **97** F4 4
DUN/TMV NE11 **97** F3 2
Malvern Rd *NSHW* NE29 **54** A4
WBAY NE26 **26** C3
WLSD/HOW NE28 **68** B3
Malvern St *SSH* NE33 **88** B1
Malvern Ter *STLY/ANP* DH9 **148** C3
Malvins Close Rd *BLYTH* NE24 **10** B5
Malvins Rd *BLYTH* NE24 **10** A4
Mandale Crs *TYNE/NSHE* NE30 **54** C1
Mandarin Cl *WD/WHPE/BLK* NE5 **59** D2
Mandela Cl *STLY/ANP* DH9 **147** F3
Mandela Wy *DUN/TMV* NE11 **78** B5
Mandeville *WASHN* NE37 **121** D4
Manet Gdns *HAR/WTLS* NE34 **88** C4
Mangrove Cl *WD/WHPE/BLK* NE5 **59** D2
Manila St *ASHBK/HED/RY* SR2 **145** D2
Manisty Ter *PLEE/EAS* SR8 **200** B2
Mann Crs *SEA/MUR* SR7 **174** C6 1
Manningford Cl *CRAM* NE23 **21** F3 1
Manningford Dr *SUNDSW* SR3 **160** A3
Manor Av *LGB/HTN* NE7 **65** E1
Manor Chare *CNUT* NE1 **3** F4
Manor Cl *GOS/KPK* NE3 **63** F1 2
Manor Dr *LGB/HTN* NE7 **65** E1
STLY/ANP DH9 **146** B3
Manorfields *LGB/KIL* NE12 **49** F6
Manor Gdns *FELL* NE10 **102** B2
LGB/HTN NE7 **65** E1 4
Manor Gv *BW/LEM/TK/HW* NE15 **75** E1
HLS DH4 **158** B1
LGB/HTN NE7 **65** E1
Manor Hall Cl *SEA/MUR* SR7 **175** D2
Manor House Rd *JES* NE2 **64** B5
Manor Pl *LGB/HTN* NE7 **65** E1
Manor Rd *LGB/HTN* NE7 **65** E2
STLY/ANP DH9 **148** B1 5
TYNE/NSHE NE30 **55** F4
WASHN NE37 **120** C4
Manor Ter *BLAY* NE21 **94** B3
Manor Vw *WASHN* NE37 **120** C4
Manor Vw East *WASHN* NE37 **121** D4
Manor Wk *LGB/HTN* NE7 **65** E1 5
Manor Wy *PLEE/EAS* SR8 **209** D3
Manorway *TYNE/NSHE* NE30 **55** F4 4
Mansell Crs *PLEE/EAS* SR8 **209** D1
Mansell Pl *GOS/KPK* NE3 **62** A3
Mansfield Ct *BOL* NE36 **105** F3
Mansfield Crs
CLDN/WHIT/ROK SR6 **127** D1
Mansfield Pl *ELS/FEN* NE4 **80** A3 13
Mansfield St *ELS/FEN* NE4 **80** A3
Manston Cl *SUNDSW* SR3 **159** F3
Manx Sq *SWCK/CAS* SR5 **126** A1
Maple Av *DHAM* DH1 **195** F4
DUN/TMV NE11 **97** F3
MONK NE25 **54** B1
SUNDSW SR3 **144** A6
Maplebeck Cl *SUNDSW* SR3 **159** F3 1
Maple Cl *BW/LEM/TK/HW* NE15 **77** D2 3
Maple Ct *BDN/LAN/SAC* DH7 **202** B5
MONK NE25 **24** C2 1
Maple Crs *BLYTH* NE24 **9** E4
SEA/MUR SR7 **176** A6
Mapledene Rd *GOS/KPK* NE3 **46** B6
Maple Gv *CLDN/WHIT/ROK* SR6 **109** E1
FELL NE10 **101** D2 3
GATE NE8 **99** D3
HAR/WTLS NE34 **89** E3
Maple Pk *BDN/LAN/SAC* DH7 **192** A5
Maple Rd *BLAY* NE21 **76** B6
Maple Rw *WICK/BNPF* NE16 **78** A6
Maple St *ELS/FEN* NE4 **80** A4
JRW NE32 **85** F1
STLY/ANP DH9 **147** F4
Maple Ter *HLS* DH4 **156** C3
Maplewood *CLSW/PEL* DH2 **153** D4
Maplewood Av *SWCK/CAS* SR5 **125** E1
Maplewood St *HLS* DH4 **169** D1
Mapperley Dr
BW/LEM/TK/HW NE15 **77** D1
Marblet Ct *DUN/TMV* NE11 **98** A3 1
Marbury Cl *SUNDSW* SR3 **159** F2 2
March Rd *CRAM* NE23 **35** D3 1
Marcia Av *CLDN/WHIT/ROK* SR6 **126** C1 7
Marconi Wy *WICK/BNPF* NE16 **96** A1
Marcross Cl *WD/WHPE/BLK* NE5 **59** D4 2
Marcross Dr *SUNDSW* SR3 **159** F3
Mardale *WASHN* NE37 **120** A5
Mardale Gdns *LWF/SPW/WRK* NE9 **117** F1
Mardale Rd *WD/WHPE/BLK* NE5 **61** D5
Mardale St *HLH* DH5 **185** F2
Marden Av *TYNE/NSHE* NE30 **55** E1
Marden Ct *WBAY* NE26 **26** A1 2
Marden Crs *WBAY* NE26 **41** E6
Marden Rd South *MONK* NE25 **40** C6
Marden Ter *TYNE/NSHE* NE30 **55** E1
Mareburn Crs *FELL* NE10 **101** D2
Maree Cl *SUNDSW* SR3 **160** A3
Margaret Alice St
MLFD/PNYW SR4 **125** D5 1
Margaret Dr *LGB/KIL* NE12 **50** C4 2
Margaret Gv *HAR/WTLS* NE34 **87** F3 2
Margaret Rd *WBAY* NE26 **41** E6
Margaret St *ASHBK/HED/RY* SR2 **145** E4
SEA/MUR SR7 **176** C4
Margaret Ter *ROWG* NE39 **110** B3
Margery La *DHAM* DH1 **194** A6
Marguerite Ct *MLFD/PNYW* SR4 **126** A5 9
Marian Ct *GATE* NE8 **98** C1 5
Marian Dr *FELL* NE10 **84** A6
Marian Wy *HAR/WTLS* NE34 **89** E5
Maria St *ELS/FEN* NE4 **79** D4
SEA/MUR SR7 **176** C3
SUNDSW SR3 **160** C1
Marie Curie Dr *ELS/FEN* NE4 **79** E4 5
Marigold Av *FELL* NE10 **82** A6
Marigold Ct *MLFD/PNYW* SR4 **126** A5 10
Marigold Crs *HLS* DH4 **156** A5
Marigold Wk *HAR/WTLS* NE34 **88** A3
Marina Av *CLDN/WHIT/ROK* SR6 **108** B6
Marina Ct *CLDN/WHIT/ROK* SR6 **126** C1 8
Marina Dr *MONK* NE25 **39** E6
SSH NE33 **72** A3
Marina Gv *CLDN/WHIT/ROK* SR6 **126** C1 9
Marina Ter *CLDN/WHIT/ROK* SR6 **109** E1 2
Marina Veiw *WLSD/HOW* NE28 **68** B4
Marina Vw *HEBB* NE31 **84** C2
Marine Ap *SSH* NE33 **72** A4
Marine Av *WBAY* NE26 **40** C4 1
Marine Dr *ASHBK/HED/RY* SR2 **145** E6
HEBB NE31 **85** F5
JRW NE32 **85** F6
Marine Gdns *WBAY* NE26 **40** C5
Mariners' La *TYNE/NSHE* NE30 **55** E5
Marine Ter *BLYTH* NE24 **10** C5
Marine Wk *CLDN/WHIT/ROK* SR6 **127** E2
Marion St *ASHBK/HED/RY* SR2 **145** D2
Maritime Crs *PLEE/EAS* SR8 **201** E4
Maritime St *SUND* SR1 **4** C3 1
Marius Av *BW/LEM/TK/HW* NE15 **56** B4
Mariville East *ASHBK/HED/RY* SR2 **162** C3

Mariville West
ASHBK/HED/RY SR2 162 C3
Markby Cl *SUNDSW* SR3 160 A3 4
Market La *CNUT* NE1 2 D4
WICK/BNPF NE16 95 F1
WICK/BNPF NE16 96 C2
Market Pl *HLH* DH5 171 E2
Market Sq *JRW* NE32 86 A1 6
Market St *CNUT* NE1 2 D3
CRAM NE23 34 C2
HLH DH5 172 A6
Market Wy *DUN/TMV* NE11 98 C4
Markham Av *CLDN/WHIT/ROK* SR6 109 F2
Markham St
ASHBK/HED/RY SR2 145 E4 5
Markington Dr
ASHBK/HED/RY SR2 162 B2
Markle Gv *HLH* DH5 170 C5
Mark Ri *HLH* DH5 171 F5
Mark's La *HLS* DH4 169 E6
Marlboro Av *WICK/BNPF* NE16 96 A2
Marlborough Ap *GOS/KPK* NE3 47 E5 2
Marlborough Av *GOS/KPK* NE3 47 D6
Marlborough Ct *GOS/KPK* NE3 45 F5
HLH DH5 171 D4 1
Marlborough Rd
MLFD/PNYW SR4 141 E3
WASHN NE37 121 D3
Marlborough St North *SSH* NE33 71 F6 4
Marlborough St South *SSH* NE33 71 F6
Marleen Av *BYK/HTN/WLK* NE6 65 E6
Marleen Ct *BYK/HTN/WLK* NE6 65 E6 5
Marley Crs *SWCK/CAS* SR5 125 E1
Marlfield Ct *WD/WHPE/BLK* NE5 61 D3 4
Marlow Dr *SUNDSW* SR3 159 F3
Marlowe Gdns *GATE* NE8 99 E1 7
Marlowe Pl *HLH* DH5 171 D3
Marlow Pl *LGB/KIL* NE12 49 E6
Marlow St *BLYTH* NE24 10 C5
Marmion Rd *BYK/HTN/WLK* NE6 66 B6
Marmion Ter *MONK* NE25 40 B5
Marne St *HLS* DH4 157 D2
Marondale Av *BYK/HTN/WLK* NE6 83 E1
Marquis Av *WD/WHPE/BLK* NE5 59 E1
Marr Rd *HEBB* NE31 85 E3
Marsden Av *CLDN/WHIT/ROK* SR6 91 E6
Marsden Cl *HLS* DH4 170 B2
Marsden Gv
LWF/SPW/WRK NE9 118 C1 2
Marsden La *HAR/WTLS* NE34 90 A1
WD/WHPE/BLK NE5 60 C3
Marsden Rd *CLDN/WHIT/ROK* SR6 107 E2
HAR/WTLS NE34 89 E1
Marshall St *CLDN/WHIT/ROK* SR6 108 C6
Marshall Wallis Rd *SSH* NE33 71 E6
Marsham Cl *BW/LEM/TK/HW* NE15 77 D1
CLDN/WHIT/ROK SR6 89 F6
Marsham Rd
WD/WHPE/BLK NE5 60 A3 5
Marsh Ct *DUN/TMV* NE11 98 A3
Marske Ter *BYK/HTN/WLK* NE6 83 D2
Marston *LGB/KIL* NE12 35 F6 9
Martello Gdns *LGB/HTN* NE7 65 F4
Martin Ct *WASHS* NE38 137 E4
Martindale Av
CLDN/WHIT/ROK SR6 108 B5
Martindale Pk *HLH* DH5 171 D3
Martin Rd *WLSD/HOW* NE28 68 B4
Marwell Dr *WASHN* NE37 121 D2 1
Marwood Gv *PLEE/EAS* SR8 208 B5
Mary Agnes St *GOS/KPK* NE3 62 C1 4
Mary Av *CLS/BIR/GTL* DH3 118 A6
Maryhill Cl *ELS/FEN* NE4 79 D4 5
Mary's Pl *BYK/HTN/WLK* NE6 84 A2
Mary St *BLAY* NE21 75 F6
BLAY NE21 76 B5
SEA/MUR SR7 177 D3 2
SUND SR1 4 B4 1
SUNDSW SR3 143 F6
Mary Ter *WD/WHPE/BLK* NE5 60 C4
Masefield Av *WICK/BNPF* NE16 96 A1 5
Masefield Cl *STLY/ANP* DH9 149 D1
Masefield Dr *HAR/WTLS* NE34 87 F6
Mason Rd *WLSD/HOW* NE28 66 C2
Mason St *BYK/HTN/WLK* NE6 82 B3 2
Mast La *TYNE/NSHE* NE30 55 D1
Matamba Ter *MLFD/PNYW* SR4 126 A6
Matanzas St *ASHBK/HED/RY* SR2 145 D3
Matfen Av *SMOOR* NE27 52 B1
Matfen Cl *BLYTH* NE24 10 B5
BW/LEM/TK/HW NE15 77 D2 4
Matfen Dr *SUNDSW* SR3 159 F2 5
Matfen Gdns *WLSD/HOW* NE28 68 B1
Matfen Pl *ELS/FEN* NE4 79 E1
GOS/KPK NE3 46 C6 7
Mather Rd *ELS/FEN* NE4 80 A4 7
Matlock Gdns
WD/WHPE/BLK NE5 60 B3 6
Matlock Rd *JRW* NE32 86 B3 7
Matlock St *SUND* SR1 4 C1
Matterdale Rd *PLEE/EAS* SR8 209 E2
Matthew Bank *JES* NE2 64 A3
Matthew Rd *BLYTH* NE24 17 E1
Matthew St *BYK/HTN/WLK* NE6 82 A2 8
Maudlin Pl *WD/WHPE/BLK* NE5 61 F5 6
Maudlin St *HLH* DH5 172 A4
Mauds La *SUND* SR1 5 F2
Maud St *BW/LEM/TK/HW* NE15 76 B2 4
CLDN/WHIT/ROK SR6 109 D6
Maughan St *BLYTH* NE24 11 E5
Maureen Ter *SEA/MUR* SR7 176 B3
Maurice Rd *WLSD/HOW* NE28 67 D6 2
Mautland St *HLS* DH4 171 D1 1
Mavin St *DHAM* DH1 194 C6
Maxton Cl *SUNDSW* SR3 159 F3 2
Maxwell *SSH* NE33 71 E4
Maxwell St *GATE* NE8 98 C3
MLFD/PNYW SR4 125 E5 6
SSH NE33 71 E4
May Av *BLAY* NE21 94 B3
RYTON NE40 74 B2 4
Maydown Cl *SWCK/CAS* SR5 123 E4 2
Mayfair Gdns *GATE* NE8 99 F2 9
HAR/WTLS NE34 89 D1
PONT/DH NE20 28 B4
Mayfair Rd *JES* NE2 63 F4 5
Mayfield *WICK/BNPF* NE16 96 A5 4
Mayfield Av *BW/LEM/TK/HW* NE15 58 A5
CRAM NE23 22 B2
Mayfield Ct *CLDN/WHIT/ROK* SR6 126 C1
Mayfield Dr
CLDN/WHIT/ROK SR6 108 A2 1
Mayfield Gdns
BW/LEM/TK/HW NE15 58 A5 2
JRW NE32 85 F2
WLSD/HOW NE28 66 B3 1
Mayfield Gv *MLFD/PNYW* SR4 141 F4
Mayfield Pl *DIN/WO* NE13 32 C5
Mayfield Rd *GOS/KPK* NE3 63 D2
MLFD/PNYW SR4 123 E6
Mayfield Ter *WD/WHPE/BLK* NE5 62 A5 2
May Gv *CLDN/WHIT/ROK* SR6 91 E5
May Lea *BDN/LAN/SAC* DH7 178 A3
Maynard's Rw *DHAM* DH1 195 E4
Mayo Dr *SUNDSW* SR3 160 A3 5
Mayoral Wy *DUN/TMV* NE11 116 C2
Mayorswell Cl *DHAM* DH1 194 C4 2
Mayorswell Fld *DHAM* DH1 194 C4 3
Mayorswell St *DHAM* DH1 194 C4 4
Maypole Cl *SWCK/CAS* SR5 126 A3 4
May St *BLAY* NE21 94 A1
CLS/BIR/GTL DH3 136 B1
DHAM DH1 194 A5
MLFD/PNYW SR4 126 A5
SSH NE33 71 F5 7
Mayswood Rd
CLDN/WHIT/ROK SR6 126 C1
Maythorne Dr *RDHAMSE* DH6 188 A6
Maywood Cl *GOS/KPK* NE3 62 A2
Mcanany Av *HAR/WTLS* NE34 88 C3
Mcclaren Wy *HLS* DH4 158 B1
Mccracken Cl *GOS/KPK* NE3 47 E4
Mccracken Dr *DIN/WO* NE13 33 E3
Mcewan Gdns *ELS/FEN* NE4 79 E3 5
Mcintyre Rd *HEBB* NE31 85 E1 5
Mckendrick Vls
WD/WHPE/BLK NE5 61 F5
Mcnally Pl *DHAM* DH1 195 E4 1
Mcnamara Rd *WLSD/HOW* NE28 68 A3
Meacham Wy *WICK/BNPF* NE16 95 F5
Mead Av *LGB/KIL* NE12 50 A4
Mead Crs *LGB/KIL* NE12 50 A4
Meadowbrook Dr *FELL* NE10 102 B3 5
Meadow Cl *BLAY* NE21 93 E1
CRAM NE23 23 E6 1
HLH DH5 171 E3
LGB/KIL NE12 49 D6 6
RYTON NE40 74 C3
Meadow Ct *BDLGTN* NE22 7 D3
PONT/DH NE20 28 A5
Meadowdale Crs *BDLGTN* NE22 6 C3
WD/WHPE/BLK NE5 61 F3
Meadow Dr *CLSW/PEL* DH2 152 B6
DIN/WO NE13 33 E2
SUNDSW SR3 159 D3
Meadowfield *MONK* NE25 39 F5
PONT/DH NE20 28 A3
Meadowfield Av *GOS/KPK* NE3 46 C6
Meadowfield Dr
CLDN/WHIT/ROK SR6 107 F1
Meadowfield Gdns
BYK/HTN/WLK NE6 66 C5 4
Meadowfield Rd *GOS/KPK* NE3 63 D2 5
Meadowfield Wy *STLY/ANP* DH9 130 B6
Meadow Gdns *SUNDSW* SR3 144 A3 8
Meadow Gra *HLS* DH4 156 A6
Meadow Gv *MLFD/PNYW* SR4 141 F1
Meadow La *DUN/TMV* NE11 97 E1 5
Meadow Laws *HAR/WTLS* NE34 89 F4
Meadow Ri *WD/WHPE/BLK* NE5 61 D2
Meadow Rd *BW/LEM/TK/HW* NE15 76 C1
MONK NE25 39 F6
WBAY NE26 26 A2
WLSD/HOW NE28 68 B5 1
Meadowside *ASHBK/HED/RY* SR2 144 A2
Meadows La *HLS* DH4 170 A6
The Meadows *GOS/KPK* NE3 46 B6
HLS DH4 155 F5
HLS DH4 183 F1
RYTON NE40 74 C3
Meadow St *HLH* DH5 170 B6
Meadow V *ASHBK/HED/RY* SR2 144 B2
Meadow Vw *MONK* NE25 24 C2
STLY/ANP DH9 129 D5 1
SUNDSW SR3 159 D3
Meadow Well Wy *NSHW* NE29 70 A2 5
Mead Wk *BYK/HTN/WLK* NE6 83 E2
Mead Wy *LGB/KIL* NE12 50 B4
Meadway Dr *LGB/KIL* NE12 50 B5
Means Dr *CRAM* NE23 35 D5
Medburn Av *TYNE/NSHE* NE30 55 E2
Medburn Rd *BW/LEM/TK/HW* NE15 76 A1
MONK NE25 25 D6
Medham Cl *FELL* NE10 101 D4 2
Medina Cl *SUNDSW* SR3 160 A3 6
Medomsley Gdns
LWF/SPW/WRK NE9 101 D6 1
Medomsly St *MLFD/PNYW* SR4 125 F5
Medway *JRW* NE32 86 B6
Medway Av *HEBB* NE31 85 D5
Medway Cl *PLEE/EAS* SR8 208 B4
Medway Crs *GATE* NE8 100 A2
Medway Gdns *MLFD/PNYW* SR4 142 C2 5
TYNE/NSHE NE30 54 C5 1
Medway Pl *CRAM* NE23 14 B5
Megstone Av *CRAM* NE23 21 F3
Megstone Ct *LGB/KIL* NE12 36 A6
Melbeck Dr *CLSW/PEL* DH2 135 D4
Melbourne Crs *MONK* NE25 54 A1
Melbourne Gdns *HAR/WTLS* NE34 87 E5
Melbourne Pl *MLFD/PNYW* SR4 143 D2
Melbourne St *CNUT* NE1 3 F4
Melbury *MONK* NE25 39 E4
Melbury Ct
CLDN/WHIT/ROK SR6 126 C1 10
Melbury Rd *LGB/HTN* NE7 64 C5
Melbury St *SEA/MUR* SR7 176 C5
Meldon Av *GOS/KPK* NE3 46 B5 4
HAR/WTLS NE34 89 D2
RDHAMSE DH6 197 F5
Meldon Gdns *DUN/TMV* NE11 97 F5
Meldon Rd *MLFD/PNYW* SR4 125 E5 7
Meldon St *WLSD/HOW* NE28 69 E5
Meldon Ter *BYK/HTN/WLK* NE6 65 D6
Meldon Wy *BLAY* NE21 93 E2
STLY/ANP DH9 147 D4
Melgarve Dr *SUNDSW* SR3 160 A3
Melkington Ct
WD/WHPE/BLK NE5 61 D3 5
Melkridge Pl *CRAM* NE23 21 E3
Mellendean Cl
WD/WHPE/BLK NE5 61 D3 6
Melling Rd *CRAM* NE23 21 E2
Melmerby Cl *GOS/KPK* NE3 47 F5
Melness Rd *DIN/WO* NE13 32 C5
Melrose *WASHS* NE38 138 C3
Melrose Av *BDLGTN* NE22 8 C3
HEBB NE31 85 D5
SEA/MUR SR7 187 F2
SMOOR NE27 37 E5
TYNE/NSHE NE30 54 C2
Melrose Cl *BW/LEM/TK/HW* NE15 77 D2
GOS/KPK NE3 47 D2 5
Melrose Ct *BDLGTN* NE22 8 C2
Melrose Crs *SEA/MUR* SR7 175 E2
Melrose Gdns
CLDN/WHIT/ROK SR6 127 D1
WLSD/HOW NE28 68 C2
Melrose Gv *JRW* NE32 87 D4 1
Melsonby Cl *SUNDSW* SR3 159 F2 4
Meltham Ct *WD/WHPE/BLK* NE5 59 D4 5
Meltham Dr *SUNDSW* SR3 160 A3 7
Melton Av *BYK/HTN/WLK* NE6 83 E3 2
Melton Crs *WBAY* NE26 26 C4
Melton Dr *MONK* NE25 24 C2
Melvaig Cl *SUNDSW* SR3 160 A3
Melville Av *BLYTH* NE24 16 C1
Melville Gdns *MONK* NE25 39 E6
Melville Gv *LGB/HTN* NE7 64 C3
Melville St *CLS/BIR/GTL* DH3 153 E6
Melvin Pl *WD/WHPE/BLK* NE5 61 D4
Melvyn Gdns
CLDN/WHIT/ROK SR6 127 D1
Membury Cl *SUNDSW* SR3 160 A3 8
Memorial Av *PLEE/EAS* SR8 201 D1
Mendip Av *CLSW/PEL* DH2 153 D6
Mendip Cl *PLEE/EAS* SR8 208 A2
Mendip Dr *WASHS* NE38 138 A3
Mendip Gdns *DUN/TMV* NE11 98 A4 1
Mendip Ter *STLY/ANP* DH9 148 C3
Mendip Wy *LGB/KIL* NE12 48 B6 5
Menvill Pl *SUND* SR1 5 F3
Mercantile Rd *HLS* DH4 170 B3
Merchants Whf
BYK/HTN/WLK NE6 82 B4 2
Mercia Wy *BW/LEM/TK/HW* NE15 77 D3
Mere Dr *DHAM* DH1 180 A5
Mere Knolls Rd
CLDN/WHIT/ROK SR6 109 D6
Meresyde *FELL* NE10 101 F3
Merevale Cl *WASHN* NE37 121 D2
Meridan Wy *LGB/HTN* NE7 65 F3
Merlay Dr *DIN/WO* NE13 31 D4 2
Merle Ter *MLFD/PNYW* SR4 125 E4 1
Merlin Cl *SEA/MUR* SR7 176 B2

Merlin Crs *WLSD/HOW* NE28 .... 68 B3
Merlin Dr *CLS/BIR/GTL* DH3 .... 153 F1
Merlin Pl *LGB/KIL* NE12 .... 48 C5
Merlin Wy *SMOOR* NE27 .... 52 C3
Merrington Cl *SUNDSW* SR3 .... 159 F2 5
Merrion Cl *SUNDSW* SR3 .... 159 F2 6
Merryfield Gdns
CLDN/WHIT/ROK SR6 .... 127 D1 3
Mersey Pl *GATE* NE8 .... 100 A1
Mersey Rd *GATE* NE8 .... 100 A2
HEBB NE31 .... 85 D5
Merton Ct *ELS/FEN* NE4 .... 78 C4
Merton Rd *BYK/HTN/WLK* NE6 .... 83 E4
PONT/DH NE20 .... 28 A4 1
Merton Sq *BLYTH* NE24 .... 11 D4 8
Metcalfe Crs *SEA/MUR* SR7 .... 188 A1
Methuen St
LWF/SPW/WRK NE9 .... 99 F2 10
Methven Wy *CRAM* NE23 .... 14 B4
The Mews *BLAY* NE21 .... 77 D6
HLS DH4 .... 169 F3 2
SUNDSW SR3 .... 159 D1
TYNE/NSHE NE30 .... 54 C6
Michaelgate *BYK/HTN/WLK* NE6 .... 82 B2 6
Mickle Cl *WASHN* NE37 .... 119 F6
Mickleton Cl *CLS/BIR/GTL* DH3 .... 168 A3 3
Mickleton Gdns *SUNDSW* SR3 .... 144 A4 5
Middle Cl *WASHS* NE38 .... 138 A5
Middle Dr *DIN/WO* NE13 .... 44 B3
Middle Engine La *SMOOR* NE27 .... 52 C5
WLSD/HOW NE28 .... 68 B1
Middlefield *CLSW/PEL* DH2 .... 152 A1
Middlegarth *WD/WHPE/BLK* NE5 .. 61 F4 8
Middle Ga *WD/WHPE/BLK* NE5 .... 59 F5
Middle Gn *MONK* NE25 .... 39 E6
Middleham Cl *CLSW/PEL* DH2 .... 135 D5
Middleham Ct *SWCK/CAS* SR5 .... 125 D1
Middleham Rd *DHAM* DH1 .... 180 C5
Middles Rd *STLY/ANP* DH9 .... 148 C5
Middle St *BYK/HTN/WLK* NE6 .... 83 E2
SUND SR1 .... 4 B2 3
TYNE/NSHE NE30 .... 55 F5
Middle St East *BYK/HTN/WLK* NE6 .... 83 F2
Middleton Av *ELS/FEN* NE4 .... 79 D2
ROWG NE39 .... 111 E3 1
Middleton Cl *SEA/MUR* SR7 .... 175 D1
Middleton St *BLYTH* NE24 .... 11 D5
Middlewood Pk *ELS/FEN* NE4 .... 62 A6
Midfield Dr *CLDN/WHIT/ROK* SR6 .... 127 D2
Midgley Dr *SUNDSW* SR3 .... 160 A3
Midhill Cl *BDN/LAN/SAC* DH7 .... 203 D3
Midhurst Av *HAR/WTLS* NE34 .... 72 B6
Midhurst Cl *SUNDSW* SR3 .... 159 F2
Midhurst Rd *LGB/KIL* NE12 .... 49 F5
Midmoor Rd *MLFD/PNYW* SR4 .... 125 D5
Midsomer Cl *SUNDSW* SR3 .... 159 F3 3
Midway *BYK/HTN/WLK* NE6 .... 83 F2
Milbanke Cl *CLSW/PEL* DH2 .... 135 F5
Milbank Ter *RDHAMSE* DH6 .... 206 B2
Milburn Dr *BW/LEM/TK/HW* NE15 .... 78 A2
Mildmay Rd *JES* NE2 .... 63 F4 4
Milecastle Ct *WD/WHPE/BLK* NE5 .... 59 F4
Mile End Rd *SSH* NE33 .... 71 E2
Milfield Av *SMOOR* NE27 .... 52 B1
WLSD/HOW NE28 .... 67 E2
Milford Gdns *GOS/KPK* NE3 .... 47 D3
Milford Rd *BW/LEM/TK/HW* NE15 .... 78 B3
Military Rd *TYNE/NSHE* NE30 .... 55 D6
Milk Market *CNUT* NE1 .... 3 G4
Millais Gdns *HAR/WTLS* NE34 .... 88 B6
Mill Bank *SWCK/CAS* SR5 .... 108 B6
Millbank Pl *BDLGTN* NE22 .... 8 A4
Millbank Rd *BDLGTN* NE22 .... 8 A3
BYK/HTN/WLK NE6 .... 83 F4
Millbeck Gv *HLH* DH5 .... 170 C4 1
Millbrook *NSHW* NE29 .... 70 A1 1
Millbrook Rd *CRAM* NE23 .... 14 B5
Millburngate *DHAM* DH1 .... 194 B4 3
Millburn St *MLFD/PNYW* SR4 .... 126 A5 11
Mill Cl *NSHW* NE29 .... 70 A1 2
Mill Ct *HLS* DH4 .... 156 A6
Mill Crs *HEBB* NE31 .... 84 B6
Milldale *SEA/MUR* SR7 .... 175 E2
Milldale Av *BLYTH* NE24 .... 9 F5 3
Mill Dam *SSH* NE33 .... 71 D4
Milldene Av *TYNE/NSHE* NE30 .... 55 E4
Mill Dene Vw *JRW* NE32 .... 86 A3
Mill Dyke Cl *MONK* NE25 .... 39 E4
Millenium Wy *SWCK/CAS* SR5 .... 126 B4
Miller Gdns *CLSW/PEL* DH2 .... 151 F4
Miller's La *WICK/BNPF* NE16 .... 96 A1
Millers Rd *BYK/HTN/WLK* NE6 .... 82 B1
Miller St *GATE* NE8 .... 98 C2 4
Miller Ter *SUNDSW* SR3 .... 143 F6
Millfield *BDLGTN* NE22 .... 7 F5
WBAY NE26 .... 26 C3
Millfield Av *GOS/KPK* NE3 .... 62 A3
Millfield Cl
BW/LEM/TK/HW NE15 .... 58 B6 2
CLSW/PEL DH2 .... 165 F1
Millfield Ct *BDLGTN* NE22 .... 7 F4
Millfield East *BDLGTN* NE22 .... 7 F4
Millfield Gdns *BLYTH* NE24 .... 10 C3 2
FELL NE10 .... 100 B2 4
TYNE/NSHE NE30 .... 55 E4
Millfield Gv *TYNE/NSHE* NE30 .... 55 E4
Millfield La *BW/LEM/TK/HW* NE15 .... 58 B6
Millfield North *BDLGTN* NE22 .... 7 F4
Millfield Rd *WICK/BNPF* NE16 .... 96 A4
Millfield South *BDLGTN* NE22 .... 7 F5
Millfield West *BDLGTN* NE22 .... 7 F4
Millford *FELL* NE10 .... 101 F5
Mill Gv *HAR/WTLS* NE34 .... 90 A4
TYNE/NSHE NE30 .... 55 E4
Millgrove Vw *GOS/KPK* NE3 .... 62 B3 3
Mill Hl *HLH* DH5 .... 170 C4
PLEE/EAS SR8 .... 199 F6
Mill Hill Rd *SUNDSW* SR3 .... 160 B2
WD/WHPE/BLK NE5 .... 60 B6
Mill La *BLAY* NE21 .... 94 A3
BW/LEM/TK/HW NE15 .... 56 B3
CLDN/WHIT/ROK SR6 .... 91 E5
CLSW/PEL DH2 .... 166 A6
CRAM NE23 .... 35 E1
DHAM DH1 .... 195 F3
ELS/FEN NE4 .... 79 F4
HEBB NE31 .... 84 C6
NSHW NE29 .... 71 D2
RDHAMSE DH6 .... 197 E5
STLY/ANP DH9 .... 134 C4
Millne Ct *BDLGTN* NE22 .... 7 E3
Millom Ct *PLEE/EAS* SR8 .... 207 F5
Millom Pl *LWF/SPW/WRK* NE9 .... 100 A5
Mill Pit *HLS* DH4 .... 157 D2 5
Mill Ri *GOS/KPK* NE3 .... 64 A2
Mill Rd *BDN/LAN/SAC* DH7 .... 204 A3
GATE NE8 .... 3 H6
SEA/MUR SR7 .... 175 E2
Mills Gdns *WLSD/HOW* NE28 .... 67 D3
Mill St *MLFD/PNYW* SR4 .... 126 A5
Millthorp Cl *ASHBK/HED/RY* SR2 .. 145 F5 2
Mill Vw *BOL* NE36 .... 105 F3
FELL NE10 .... 100 B3
Mill View Av *CLDN/WHIT/ROK* SR6 .. 126 C1
Millview Dr *TYNE/NSHE* NE30 .... 55 E4
Millway *LWF/SPW/WRK* NE9 .... 99 F3
WBAY NE26 .... 26 C3
Milner Crs *BLAY* NE21 .... 93 F1 7
Milner St *SSH* NE33 .... 72 A4
Milne Wy *GOS/KPK* NE3 .... 46 B6 5
Milrig Cl *SUNDSW* SR3 .... 160 A3 9
Milsted Cl *SUNDSW* SR3 .... 159 F3 4
Milsted Ct *WD/WHPE/BLK* NE5 .... 59 D4 4
Milton Av *HEBB* NE31 .... 85 D2
HLH DH5 .... 171 E3
Milton Cl *JES* NE2 .... 81 E1
SEA/MUR SR7 .... 176 A3
STLY/ANP DH9 .... 149 D2
Milton Gv *NSHW* NE29 .... 54 B6 2
RDHAMSE DH6 .... 206 C2
Milton La *PLEE/EAS* SR8 .... 200 B2
Milton Pl *JES* NE2 .... 81 E1
LWF/SPW/WRK NE9 .... 119 D3
NSHW NE29 .... 54 B6 3
Milton Rd *WICK/BNPF* NE16 .... 96 A2
Milton St *JRW* NE32 .... 69 D6 1
MLFD/PNYW SR4 .... 125 F5
SSH NE33 .... 71 F5
Milton Ter *NSHW* NE29 .... 54 B6
Milvain Av *ELS/FEN* NE4 .... 79 D2
Milvain Cl *GATE* NE8 .... 99 E1 8
Milvain St *GATE* NE8 .... 99 E1 9
Milverton Ct *GOS/KPK* NE3 .... 45 E6
Mimosa Dr *HEBB* NE31 .... 85 D5
Mimosa Pl *ELS/FEN* NE4 .... 61 F6
Mindrum Ter *BYK/HTN/WLK* NE6 .... 83 E4
NSHW NE29 .... 69 F2
Mindrum Wy *MONK* NE25 .... 24 C5
Minehead Gdns *SUNDSW* SR3 .... 143 F6 3
Minerva Cl *WD/WHPE/BLK* NE5 .... 59 E2
Mingary Cl *HLH* DH5 .... 170 B6 1
Minorca Cl *SUND* SR1 .... 5 F3
Minorca Pl *GOS/KPK* NE3 .... 62 B3
Minskip Cl *SUNDSW* SR3 .... 159 F3 5
Minster Gv *WD/WHPE/BLK* NE5 .... 59 D3
Minster Pde *JRW* NE32 .... 86 B1 2
Minting Pl *CRAM* NE23 .... 21 E2
Minton Ct *NSHW* NE29 .... 70 B2
Minton La *NSHW* NE29 .... 70 B2
Minton Sq *MLFD/PNYW* SR4 .... 125 D5 2
Mirk La *GATE* NE8 .... 3 F6
Mirlaw Rd *CRAM* NE23 .... 21 E3 1
Mistletoe Rd *JES* NE2 .... 64 A5
Mistletoe St *DHAM* DH1 .... 194 A5
Mitcham Crs *LGB/HTN* NE7 .... 65 D3
Mitchell Av *JES* NE2 .... 64 A4
MONK NE25 .... 39 F6
Mitchell Cl *PLEE/EAS* SR8 .... 200 A6 2
Mitchell Gdns *HAR/WTLS* NE34 .... 89 E1
Mitchell St *BYK/HTN/WLK* NE6 .... 84 A3 1
DHAM DH1 .... 194 A4 3
STLY/ANP DH9 .... 147 F4
Mitford Av *BLYTH* NE24 .... 10 B6 7
MONK NE25 .... 24 B5
Mitford Cl *WASHS* NE38 .... 138 A2
Mitford Ct *PLEE/EAS* SR8 .... 208 C4 1
Mitford Dr *RDHAMSE* DH6 .... 197 F4
WD/WHPE/BLK NE5 .... 60 A3 6
Mitford Gdns *DUN/TMV* NE11 .... 97 F5
WLSD/HOW NE28 .... 68 B1
Mitford Pl *GOS/KPK* NE3 .... 46 C6 8
Mitford Rd *HAR/WTLS* NE34 .... 89 D2
Mitford St *CLDN/WHIT/ROK* SR6 .... 109 D6
WLSD/HOW NE28 .... 69 E4 1
Mitford Ter *JRW* NE32 .... 86 A6
Mitford Wy *DIN/WO* NE13 .... 31 D4
Mithras Gdns
BW/LEM/TK/HW NE15 .... 56 A4
Mitre Pl *SSH* NE33 .... 71 D6
Moat Gdns *FELL* NE10 .... 102 B2
Modder St *BYK/HTN/WLK* NE6 .... 83 E5
Moffat Av *JRW* NE32 .... 87 D4
Moffat Cl *NSHW* NE29 .... 53 E4
Moine Gdns *CLDN/WHIT/ROK* SR6 .. 127 D1
Molineux St *BYK/HTN/WLK* NE6 .... 82 A2 9
Monarch Rd *ELS/FEN* NE4 .... 79 F5
Monarch Wy *SUNDSW* SR3 .... 159 E3
Mona St *STLY/ANP* DH9 .... 148 B1 6
Moncreiff Ter *PLEE/EAS* SR8 .... 200 B2
Monday Crs *ELS/FEN* NE4 .... 80 A2 8
Monday Pl *ELS/FEN* NE4 .... 80 A2 9
Money Slack *DHAM* DH1 .... 205 D3
Monkchester Rd
BYK/HTN/WLK NE6 .... 83 D3
Monk Ct *PLEE/EAS* SR8 .... 208 A5
Monkdale Av *BLYTH* NE24 .... 9 F6
Monkhouse Av *TYNE/NSHE* NE30 .... 54 C3
Monkridge *WBAY* NE26 .... 40 A3
WD/WHPE/BLK NE5 .... 59 D4
Monkridge Gdns *DUN/TMV* NE11 .... 97 E3
Monks Av *MONK* NE25 .... 53 F1
Monks' Crs *DHAM* DH1 .... 195 E3
Monkseaton Dr *MONK* NE25 .... 39 E5
Monkseaton Rd *MONK* NE25 .... 39 D5
Monksfeld *FELL* NE10 .... 101 D3 4
Monksfield Cl *SUNDSW* SR3 .... 160 B3 8
Monkside Cl *WASHS* NE38 .... 137 F4
Monks Park Wy *LGB/KIL* NE12 .... 48 C6
Monks Rd *MONK* NE25 .... 53 E1
Monkstone Av *TYNE/NSHE* NE30 .. 55 E4 1
Monkstone Cl *TYNE/NSHE* NE30 .... 55 E4 2
Monkstone Crs *TYNE/NSHE* NE30 .... 55 E4
Monk St *CLDN/WHIT/ROK* SR6 .... 126 C3 5
Monksway *JRW* NE32 .... 87 D2
Monks Wy *TYNE/NSHE* NE30 .... 55 E3
Monks Wd *NSHW* NE29 .... 54 A4
Monkswood Sq *SUNDSW* SR3 .... 161 D2 4
Monkton *FELL* NE10 .... 101 E4
Monkton Av *HAR/WTLS* NE34 .... 87 E4
Monkton La *HEBB* NE31 .... 85 D6
JRW NE32 .... 85 E4
Monkton Rd *JRW* NE32 .... 86 A1 7
Monkton Ter *JRW* NE32 .... 86 A2
Monmouth Gdns *WLSD/HOW* NE28 .. 68 C2
Monroe Pl *WD/WHPE/BLK* NE5 .... 61 F4 9
Mons Av *HEBB* NE31 .... 85 D3
Montagu Av *GOS/KPK* NE3 .... 62 C4
Montagu Ct *GOS/KPK* NE3 .... 62 C4
Montague St
BW/LEM/TK/HW NE15 .... 76 C2
CLDN/WHIT/ROK SR6 .... 126 C1 11
Monterey *SUNDSW* SR3 .... 160 A3 10
WASHN NE37 .... 120 C3
Montfalcon Cl *PLEE/EAS* SR8 .... 208 B2 1
Montford Cl *SUNDSW* SR3 .... 159 F3 6
Montgomery Rd *DHAM* DH1 .... 195 E3
Montpellier Pl *GOS/KPK* NE3 .... 62 B3 4
Montpellier Ter
ASHBK/HED/RY SR2 .... 145 D2
Montrose Cl *MONK* NE25 .... 24 C2
Montrose Crs *LWF/SPW/WRK* NE9 .. 100 A3
Montrose Dr *FELL* NE10 .... 102 B3
Montrose Gdns *SUNDSW* SR3 .... 143 F3
Monument Vw *HLS* DH4 .... 139 F6
Moor Cl *NSHW* NE29 .... 53 E4
Moor Ct *CLDN/WHIT/ROK* SR6 .... 109 D2
Moor Crs *DHAM* DH1 .... 195 F3
GOS/KPK NE3 .... 63 E3
Moorcroft Cl
BW/LEM/TK/HW NE15 .... 76 C1
Moorcroft Rd
BW/LEM/TK/HW NE15 .... 77 D1
Moordale Av *BLYTH* NE24 .... 9 F6 1
Moore Av *HAR/WTLS* NE34 .... 89 D2
Moore Crs South *HLH* DH5 .... 171 D3
Moor Edge *BDN/LAN/SAC* DH7 .... 203 D5
Moor Edge Rd *SMOOR* NE27 .... 38 A6
Moore St *GATE* NE8 .... 99 F1
STLY/ANP DH9 .... 148 A4 2
Moorfield *JES* NE2 .... 63 F3
Moorfield Gdns
CLDN/WHIT/ROK SR6 .... 107 F3 1
Moorfoot Av *CLSW/PEL* DH2 .... 153 E6
Moorfoot Gdns *DUN/TMV* NE11 .... 97 F3
Moorhead *WD/WHPE/BLK* NE5 .... 62 A5
Moorhill *DUN/TMV* NE11 .... 116 B6
Moorhouse Cl *HAR/WTLS* NE34 .... 88 C3 4
Moorhouses Rd *NSHW* NE29 .... 53 E5 3
The Moorings
BYK/HTN/WLK NE6 .... 82 B4 3
Moorland Av *BDLGTN* NE22 .... 9 D1
Moorland Ct *BDLGTN* NE22 .... 9 D1 2
Moorland Crs *BDLGTN* NE22 .... 9 D1 3
BYK/HTN/WLK NE6 .... 83 D1
Moorland Dr *BDLGTN* NE22 .... 9 D2

Moorlands JRW NE32 104 C1
The Moorlands STLY/ANP DH9 129 D5 2
Moorland Vls BDLGTN NE22 9 D1
Moorland Wy CRAM NE23 13 D5
Moor La BOL NE36 107 D2
CLDN/WHIT/ROK SR6 108 B2
HAR/WTLS NE34 89 D2
WD/WHPE/BLK NE5 61 F2
Moor La East HAR/WTLS NE34 89 E2
Moormill La DUN/TMV NE11 117 D6
Moor Park Ct NSHW NE29 53 E5
Moor Park Rd NSHW NE29 53 D5
Moor Pl GOS/KPK NE3 63 E3
Moor Rd North GOS/KPK NE3 63 F2
Moor Rd South JES NE2 63 F3
Moorsburn Dr HLS DH4 170 B1
Moors Cl HLS DH4 170 A2
Moorsfield HLS DH4 170 A2
Moorside WASHN NE37 120 A5
Moorside North ELS/FEN NE4 62 A5
Moorside Rd SUNDSW SR3 159 F3
Moorside South ELS/FEN NE4 79 E1
Moorsley Rd HLH DH5 184 B4
HLH DH5 185 E2
Moor St SUND SR1 5 F2
Moor Ter SUND SR1 5 G3
Moorvale La WD/WHPE/BLK NE5 62 A4
Moor Vw CLDN/WHIT/ROK SR6 109 D2 1
LGB/KIL NE12 35 E6
Moorview Crs WD/WHPE/BLK NE5 62 A4
Moorway WASHN NE37 120 A6
Moorway Dr BW/LEM/TK/HW NE15 77 D1
Moralee Cl LGB/HTN NE7 65 F3
Moran St CLDN/WHIT/ROK SR6 108 C6 5
Moray Cl CLS/BIR/GTL DH3 136 C5
PLEE/EAS SR8 208 B3
Moray St CLDN/WHIT/ROK SR6 126 C2
Morcott Gdns NSHW NE29 70 B2 1
Morden St CNUT NE1 2 C2
Mordey Cl ASHBK/HED/RY SR2 5 F5
Moreland Rd HAR/WTLS NE34 88 C6
Moreland St
CLDN/WHIT/ROK SR6 126 C2 5
Morgan St SWCK/CAS SR5 126 A2
Morgans Wy BLAY NE21 75 F6
Morland Av WASHS NE38 139 D3
Morland Gdns
LWF/SPW/WRK NE9 100 A3 3
Morley Hill Rd
WD/WHPE/BLK NE5 60 B6 3
Morley Ter HLS DH4 169 F2
Morningside BDN/LAN/SAC DH7 164 B6
WASHS NE38 137 D6
Mornington Av GOS/KPK NE3 62 B3
Morpeth Av DIN/WO NE13 33 E3
HAR/WTLS NE34 89 D1
JRW NE32 86 A5 3
Morpeth Cl WASHS NE38 137 F2
Morpeth Dr SUNDSW SR3 159 F2
Morpeth St JES NE2 63 D6
PLEE/EAS SR8 201 E6
Morpeth Ter NSHW NE29 69 F2
Morris Av HAR/WTLS NE34 88 A5
Morris Crs BOLCOL NE35 105 F2
Morris Gdns FELL NE10 102 A2
Morrison St GATE NE8 80 B6
Morris Rd WICK/BNPF NE16 96 A2
Morris St CLS/BIR/GTL DH3 136 A2
Morston Dr BW/LEM/TK/HW NE15 77 D2
Mortimer Av NSHW NE29 53 F6 6
WD/WHPE/BLK NE5 60 C3
Mortimer Cha CRAM NE23 14 A3 1
Mortimer Rd HAR/WTLS NE34 89 D1
SSH NE33 71 F6
Mortimer St MLFD/PNYW SR4 125 E5
Morton Cl WASHS NE38 138 C2 2
Morton Sq PLEE/EAS SR8 208 B1
Morton St BYK/HTN/WLK NE6 82 C2
SSH NE33 71 E2 2
Morval Cl SUNDSW SR3 159 F3
Morven Dr FELL NE10 102 A1
Morwick Cl CRAM NE23 21 E3
Morwick Pl WD/WHPE/BLK NE5 61 F5 7
Morwick Rd NSHW NE29 53 F4
Mosley St CNUT NE1 2 D4
Moss Bank LWF/SPW/WRK NE9 118 A1
Moss Cl BW/LEM/TK/HW NE15 59 E6 4
Mossdale DHAM DH1 196 C2
Moss Side LWF/SPW/WRK NE9 118 A1
Mossway CLSW/PEL DH2 151 F1
Moulton Pl WD/WHPE/BLK NE5 61 E4
Mountbatten Av HEBB NE31 85 D4
Mount Cl LGB/KIL NE12 35 F6
MLFD/PNYW SR4 124 A6
MONK NE25 53 F1
Mountfield Gdns GOS/KPK NE3 62 B2
Mountford Rd MONK NE25 24 C1
Mount Gv DUN/TMV NE11 97 E3
MLFD/PNYW SR4 143 F2
Mount La LWF/SPW/WRK NE9 119 D4
Mount Pleasant BLAY NE21 94 A1 3
CLS/BIR/GTL DH3 136 B1
HLH DH5 171 E2
STLY/ANP DH9 129 D5 3
SWCK/CAS SR5 125 F3 8
Mount Pleasant Ct
BW/LEM/TK/HW NE15 57 F4 2
Mount Rd CLS/BIR/GTL DH3 136 C1
LWF/SPW/WRK NE9 119 D4
MLFD/PNYW SR4 143 E2
Mountside Gdns DUN/TMV NE11 97 E3
Mount Stewart St SEA/MUR SR7 176 C5
Mount Ter SSH NE33 71 E4 1
The Mount BW/LEM/TK/HW NE15 57 E4
RYTON NE40 74 B3
Mount Vw WICK/BNPF NE16 96 A2
Mourne Gdns DUN/TMV NE11 97 F4
Moutter Cl PLEE/EAS SR8 201 D6
Mowbray Cl ASHBK/HED/RY SR2 4 D6
Mowbray Rd ASHBK/HED/RY SR2 5 E6
LGB/KIL NE12 49 F4
NSHW NE29 53 F6
SSH NE33 72 A5
Mowbray St BYK/HTN/WLK NE6 81 F2
DHAM DH1 194 A4
Mozart St SSH NE33 71 F4
Muirfield MONK NE25 39 F5
SSH NE33 72 B5
Muirfield Dr FELL NE10 100 C4
WASHN NE37 120 B2
Muirfield Rd LGB/HTN NE7 65 E1
Mulben Cl ELS/FEN NE4 79 D4 4
Mulberry Pl ELS/FEN NE4 80 A5 8
Mulberry St FELL NE10 100 C1
Mulcaster Gdns
WLSD/HOW NE28 66 C3 4
Mulgrave Dr CLDN/WHIT/ROK SR6 127 D4
Mulgrave Ter GATE NE8 81 D5
Mullen Dr RYTON NE40 74 B4
Mullen Gdns WLSD/HOW NE28 66 C2
Mullen Rd WLSD/HOW NE28 66 C2
Mull Gv JRW NE32 87 D5 2
Muncaster Ms PLEE/EAS SR8 207 F5
Mundella Ter BYK/HTN/WLK NE6 82 A1
Mundell St STLY/ANP DH9 147 F4
Mundle Av BLAY NE21 94 B4
Mundles La BOL NE36 106 B3
Munslow Rd SUNDSW SR3 142 B6 1
Muriel St STLY/ANP DH9 148 A5
Murphy Gv ASHBK/HED/RY SR2 162 A1 1
Murray Av HLS DH4 169 F1 2
Murrayfield CRAM NE23 23 E6 2
Murrayfield Dr BDN/LAN/SAC DH7 202 C5
Murrayfield Rd
WD/WHPE/BLK NE5 61 F3 3
Murrayfields SMOOR NE27 51 F3
Murray Gdns DUN/TMV NE11 97 F3 3
Murray Rd CLSW/PEL DH2 153 D5
WLSD/HOW NE28 68 B3
Murray St BLAY NE21 76 B5
PLEE/EAS SR8 209 F2
Murton La HLH DH5 186 C3
NSHW NE29 52 C3
Murton St SUND SR1 5 E4
Muscott Gv
BW/LEM/TK/HW NE15 77 F2 2
Musgrave Rd LWF/SPW/WRK NE9 99 E4
Musgrave Ter
BYK/HTN/WLK NE6 83 D2 1
Muswell Hl BW/LEM/TK/HW NE15 77 F3
Mutual St WLSD/HOW NE28 67 D4
Mylord Crs LGB/KIL NE12 35 D5
Myrella Crs ASHBK/HED/RY SR2 144 B4
Myreside Pl LGB/KIL NE12 49 D5 3
Myrtle Av CLDN/WHIT/ROK SR6 109 E1
DUN/TMV NE11 97 E3
Myrtle Crs LGB/KIL NE12 49 F3
Myrtle Gv HAR/WTLS NE34 89 E4 1
JES NE2 64 A4
LWF/SPW/WRK NE9 99 E6
SUNDSW SR3 161 D1
WLSD/HOW NE28 67 F5
Myrtle Rd BLAY NE21 94 B1 3
Myrtles CLSW/PEL DH2 153 D3

N

Nafferton Pl WD/WHPE/BLK NE5 61 E6
Nailsworth Cl BOLCOL NE35 87 D6 7
Nairn Cl CLS/BIR/GTL DH3 136 C4
WASHN NE37 120 B2
Nairn Rd CRAM NE23 22 A1
Nairn St JRW NE32 87 D5
Naisbitt Av PLEE/EAS SR8 201 D6
Nansen Cl WD/WHPE/BLK NE5 60 B4 6
Napier Rd SEA/MUR SR7 175 F2
WICK/BNPF NE16 95 F1 6
Napier St HAR/WTLS NE34 88 A2
JES NE2 3 G1
JRW NE32 86 A1 8
Napier Wy BLAY NE21 77 D6 1
Narvik Wy NSHW NE29 69 D1
Nash Av HAR/WTLS NE34 88 C5
Naters St WBAY NE26 41 E6
Natley Av BOL NE36 107 D3
Navenby Cl GOS/KPK NE3 47 F4 3
Naworth Av TYNE/NSHE NE30 54 C3
Naworth Ct PLEE/EAS SR8 208 A5
Naworth Dr WD/WHPE/BLK NE5 60 A3
Naworth Ter JRW NE32 86 C4
Nawton Av SWCK/CAS SR5 126 B2
Nayland Rd CRAM NE23 21 F1
Naylor Av BLAY NE21 94 B4
Naylor Pl WBAY NE26 26 A1
Neale St CLDN/WHIT/ROK SR6 126 C1
Nearlane Cl DIN/WO NE13 33 E2 1
Neasdon Crs TYNE/NSHE NE30 55 D3
Neasham Rd SEA/MUR SR7 175 F1
Nedderton Cl
WD/WHPE/BLK NE5 59 D2 6
Needham Pl CRAM NE23 22 A1
Neill Dr WICK/BNPF NE16 114 A2
Neilson Rd FELL NE10 82 A6
Neil St HLH DH5 186 B3
Nelson Av CRAM NE23 13 D6
GOS/KPK NE3 62 C1 5
SSH NE33 72 A3
Nelson Cl PLEE/EAS SR8 209 F1 4
Nelson Crs NSHW NE29 69 F3 2
Nelson Dr CRAM NE23 13 D6
Nelson Rd BYK/HTN/WLK NE6 84 A4
CRAM NE23 13 D5
MONK NE25 39 D5
Nelson St ASHBK/HED/RY SR2 162 B1 1
CLS/BIR/GTL DH3 153 E6
CNUT NE1 2 C3
DUN/TMV NE11 97 E1 4
GATE NE8 81 E5 5
HLH DH5 185 F1 1
SEA/MUR SR7 176 A2
SSH NE33 71 E3 5
WASHS NE38 139 D2
Nelson Ter NSHW NE29 69 F3
Nelson Wy CRAM NE23 12 C4
Nenthead Cl CLS/BIR/GTL DH3 168 A3
Neptune Rd BW/LEM/TK/HW NE15 76 C2
WLSD/HOW NE28 67 D6
Nesbit Rd PLEE/EAS SR8 209 D3
Nesburn Rd MLFD/PNYW SR4 143 F2
Nesham Pl HLH DH5 171 D2
Ness Ct BLAY NE21 75 F6
Nest Rd FELL NE10 82 C6
Netherburn Rd SWCK/CAS SR5 126 B2
Netherby Dr WD/WHPE/BLK NE5 61 E6
Netherdale BDLGTN NE22 6 C3 3
Nether Farm Rd FELL NE10 101 E1
Nether Riggs BDLGTN NE22 7 E4 2
Netherton LGB/KIL NE12 35 E5 3
Netherton Av NSHW NE29 53 F5
Netherton Cl CLSW/PEL DH2 152 B6
Netherton Gdns DIN/WO NE13 33 D4 3
Netherton Gv NSHW NE29 53 F5 3
Netherton La BDLGTN NE22 6 B2
BDLGTN NE22 7 D3 4
Nettleham Rd SWCK/CAS SR5 126 B2
Nettles La SUNDSW SR3 161 D2
Neville Dene DHAM DH1 193 E5
Neville Rd BW/LEM/TK/HW NE15 76 C1
MLFD/PNYW SR4 125 E5
PLEE/EAS SR8 208 B1
Neville's Cross Bank DHAM DH1 193 F6 1
Neville's Cross Rd HEBB NE31 85 E3
Neville Sq DHAM DH1 204 C1 2
Neville St CNUT NE1 2 B5
DHAM DH1 194 B5
Nevinson Av HAR/WTLS NE34 88 C5
Nevis Cl WBAY NE26 39 F2
Nevis Gv BOL NE36 106 A3
Newacres Rd STLY/ANP DH9 148 A6
Newark Cl PLEE/EAS SR8 208 B1
Newark Crs SEA/MUR SR7 175 F2
Newark Dr CLDN/WHIT/ROK SR6 109 E2
Newarth Cl BW/LEM/TK/HW NE15 76 C1
Newbiggin La
WD/WHPE/BLK NE5 60 B3 7
Newbold Av SWCK/CAS SR5 126 B2
Newbold St BYK/HTN/WLK NE6 82 C3
Newbottle La HLS DH4 169 E3
Newbottle St HLS DH4 157 F6
Newbridge Av SWCK/CAS SR5 126 B2 3
Newbridge Bank
CLS/BIR/GTL DH3 154 A3
Newbridge Banks CLSW/PEL DH2 150 C4
New Bridge St CNUT NE1 3 F2
New Bridge St West CNUT NE1 3 E2 2
Newbrough Crs JES NE2 64 A4 2
Newburgh Av MONK NE25 24 B6
Newburn Av SWCK/CAS SR5 126 B2
Newburn Bridge Rd BLAY NE21 75 D2
Newburn Ct SSH NE33 71 F5 8
Newburn Crs HLS DH4 170 C1
Newburn Rd
BW/LEM/TK/HW NE15 58 A5
STLY/ANP DH9 131 F6
Newbury LGB/KIL NE12 35 F6
Newbury Av GATE NE8 98 C2
Newbury Cl BW/LEM/TK/HW NE15 76 C1
Newbury St SSH NE33 88 C1 2
SWCK/CAS SR5 126 B1
Newby Pl LWF/SPW/WRK NE9 100 A6
Newcastle Av PLEE/EAS SR8 201 E6
Newcastle Bank CLS/BIR/GTL DH3 118 A5
Newcastle Rd BLYTH NE24 16 B2

BOL NE36 103 F3
CLS/BIR/GTL DH3 118 B6 1
CLS/BIR/GTL DH3 153 E3
DHAM DH1 193 F6 2
HAR/WTLS NE34 87 E3
SWCK/CAS SR5 107 F5
Newcastle St NSHW NE29 70 C1 6
New Dr SEA/MUR SR7 176 A1
New Durham Rd
ASHBK/HED/RY SR2 126 A6
New Elvet DHAM DH1 194 C5
New Front STLY/ANP DH9 146 B4
New Front St STLY/ANP DH9 130 C5
New George St SSH NE33 71 E6
New Grange Ter CLSW/PEL DH2 151 F4
New Green St SSH NE33 71 E5 3
Newham Av DIN/WO NE13 32 C6
Newhaven Av SWCK/CAS SR5 126 B2
Newington Ct SWCK/CAS SR5 126 B2
Newington Rd BYK/HTN/WLK NE6 81 F2
JES NE2 81 E1
Newland Ct HAR/WTLS NE34 88 B3 12
Newlands Av BLYTH NE24 16 C1 3
GOS/KPK NE3 47 E3
MONK NE25 53 F1
SUNDSW SR3 144 A3
Newlands Pl BLYTH NE24 16 C1 4
Newlands Rd BLYTH NE24 16 C1
DHAM DH1 196 B2
JES NE2 63 F3
Newlands Rd East
SEA/MUR SR7 176 A2 3
Newlands Rd West SEA/MUR SR7 175 F1
Newlyn Crs NSHW NE29 70 A1
Newlyn Dr CRAM NE23 14 A6
JRW NE32 86 C2
Newlyn Rd GOS/KPK NE3 62 A1
Newman Ter GATE NE8 99 F2 11
Newmarch St JRW NE32 85 F1
New Mills ELS/FEN NE4 80 A2
Newminster Cl HLS DH4 157 D6
Newport Gv SUNDSW SR3 143 F6 4
New Quay NSHW NE29 71 D2
Newquay Gdns
LWF/SPW/WRK NE9 117 E2
Newriggs WASHS NE38 139 D4
New Rd BOLCOL NE35 105 F2
DUN/TMV NE11 98 A4
FELL NE10 102 B5
STLY/ANP DH9 150 B1
WICK/BNPF NE16 111 F5
Newsham Cl WD/WHPE/BLK NE5 59 D2 7
Newsham Rd BLYTH NE24 16 B1
Newstead Ct WASHS NE38 138 B1 2
Newstead Rd HLS DH4 157 E6
Newsteads Cl MONK NE25 39 F5 1
Newsteads Dr MONK NE25 39 E5
Newstead Sq SUNDSW SR3 160 C2 6
New Strangford Rd SEA/MUR SR7 176 B3
New St DHAM DH1 194 A5
MLFD/PNYW SR4 123 F6 4
Newton Av TYNE/NSHE NE30 55 D1
WLSD/HOW NE28 68 B3
Newton Cl BW/LEM/TK/HW NE15 77 D1
Newton Dr DHAM DH1 194 A1
Newton Gv HAR/WTLS NE34 87 F3 3
Newton Pl LGB/HTN NE7 65 D4
Newton Rd LGB/HTN NE7 64 C4
Newton St DUN/TMV NE11 97 E1 5
GATE NE8 98 C2 5
New York Rd NSHW NE29 53 D3
SMOOR NE27 52 A2
New York Wy SMOOR NE27 52 C4
Nicholas Av CLDN/WHIT/ROK SR6 109 E2
Nicholas St HLH DH5 172 A5
Nicholson Ter LGB/KIL NE12 50 A3
Nichol St ELS/FEN NE4 78 C3
Nickleby Chare DHAM DH1 205 D1
Nidderdale Av HLH DH5 185 E2
Nidderdale Cl BLYTH NE24 9 F4
Nidsdale Av BYK/HTN/WLK NE6 83 F1
Nightingale Cl MLFD/PNYW SR4 141 F2
Nightingale Pl STLY/ANP DH9 149 D3
Nile Cl BW/LEM/TK/HW NE15 59 E6
Nile St NSHW NE29 70 C1 2
SSH NE33 71 D4
SUND SR1 5 E2
Nilverton Av ASHBK/HED/RY SR2 144 C3
Nimbus Ct SUNDSW SR3 160 C2 2
Nine Lands HLS DH4 170 B2
Ninth Av BLYTH NE24 10 C6
BYK/HTN/WLK NE6 65 E6
CLSW/PEL DH2 153 D5
Ninth St PLEE/EAS SR8 209 F1 5
Nissan Wy WASHN NE37 122 A5
Nixon St GATE NE8 81 F4
Nixon Ter BLYTH NE24 11 E6 2
Noble's Bank Rd
ASHBK/HED/RY SR2 5 G5 2
Noble St ASHBK/HED/RY SR2 5 G6
ELS/FEN NE4 79 E5
FELL NE10 100 C1 5
PLEE/EAS SR8 200 C1
Noble Ter ASHBK/HED/RY SR2 5 G6 1
Noel Av BLAY NE21 94 B4
Noel St STLY/ANP DH9 148 C1
Noel Ter BLAY NE21 94 C3
Noirmont Wy SUNDSW SR3 160 A2
Nookside MLFD/PNYW SR4 142 C2
Nookside Ct MLFD/PNYW SR4 142 B2 4
The Nook NSHW NE29 70 B1
Nora St HAR/WTLS NE34 88 B3
MLFD/PNYW SR4 143 E2
Norbury Gv BYK/HTN/WLK NE6 82 C3
Nordale Wy BLYTH NE24 9 F4
Norfolk Av CLS/BIR/GTL DH3 136 B5
SUNDSW SR3 143 E6
Norfolk Cl SEA/MUR SR7 175 F1
Norfolk Dr WASHN NE37 120 C2
Norfolk Gdns WLSD/HOW NE28 68 A2
Norfolk Rd GATE NE8 81 F4
HAR/WTLS NE34 90 B1
Norfolk St SUND SR1 4 D2
TYNE/NSHE NE30 55 D6
Norfolk Wk PLEE/EAS SR8 200 B6 2
Norfolk Wy
BW/LEM/TK/HW NE15 77 D2 5
Norham Av HAR/WTLS NE34 72 C6
Norham Av North HAR/WTLS NE34 72 C6
Norham Av South HAR/WTLS NE34 72 C6
Norham Cl BLYTH NE24 10 B5
DIN/WO NE13 32 C5 5
Norham Dr PLEE/EAS SR8 208 B5 2
WD/WHPE/BLK NE5 60 A3 7
Norham Pl JES NE2 64 A5 3
Norham Rd DHAM DH1 180 B5
GOS/KPK NE3 47 D6
MONK NE25 40 B5
NSHW NE29 53 E6 2
NSHW NE29 69 E1 4
Norham Rd North NSHW NE29 53 D4
Norham Ter JRW NE32 86 A4
Norhurst WICK/BNPF NE16 95 D5
Norland Rd BW/LEM/TK/HW NE15 77 E3
Norley Av SWCK/CAS SR5 126 B2
Norma Crs WBAY NE26 41 F6
Norman Av SUNDSW SR3 161 D1
Normanby Cl SEA/MUR SR7 175 F1
Normandy Crs HLH DH5 171 E2
Norman Rd ROWG NE39 111 D3
Norman Ter WLSD/HOW NE28 69 D4
Normanton Ter ELS/FEN NE4 79 F3
Normount Rd ELS/FEN NE4 79 D3
Northampton Rd PLEE/EAS SR8 200 B6
Northamptonshire Dr
DHAM DH1 196 C3 4
North Ap CLSW/PEL DH2 153 D4
North Av GOS/KPK NE3 63 D2
HAR/WTLS NE34 89 D2
LGB/KIL NE12 49 F6
PLEE/EAS SR8 209 E1 4
WD/WHPE/BLK NE5 60 B4
North Bailey DHAM DH1 194 B5
Northbourne Rd HEBB NE31 85 F2
Northbourne St ELS/FEN NE4 79 E4
GATE NE8 99 E2
North Brancepeth Cl
BDN/LAN/SAC DH7 204 A2 1
North Bridge St
CLDN/WHIT/ROK SR6 126 C4 2
SWCK/CAS SR5 126 C4
North Burns CLS/BIR/GTL DH3 153 E4
North Cl BYK/HTN/WLK NE6 82 B1
HAR/WTLS NE34 89 E2
RYTON NE40 74 B3
Northcote WICK/BNPF NE16 95 F5
Northcote Av SUND SR1 5 E4
WD/WHPE/BLK NE5 59 E5
Northcote St ELS/FEN NE4 79 F3
SSH NE33 71 F6
North Crs PLEE/EAS SR8 200 B3
WASHS NE38 138 B5 1
North Cft LGB/KIL NE12 50 A5
North Cross St GOS/KPK NE3 63 E1
Northdene CLS/BIR/GTL DH3 118 B6
Northdene Av SEA/MUR SR7 176 C2
North Dr CLDN/WHIT/ROK SR6 107 D1
CLS/BIR/GTL DH3 153 F1
HEBB NE31 84 B3
North Durham St SUND SR1 5 F2
North End BDN/LAN/SAC DH7 202 C3
DHAM DH1 194 A3 1
Northern Wy SWCK/CAS SR5 125 F2
North Farm Av MLFD/PNYW SR4 142 A4
North Farm Rd HEBB NE31 84 C3
Northfield Cl WICK/BNPF NE16 95 E5
Northfield Dr LGB/KIL NE12 49 D2
MLFD/PNYW SR4 142 A4 8
Northfield Gdns HAR/WTLS NE34 72 B6
Northfield Rd GOS/KPK NE3 63 D2
SSH NE33 72 B5
Northgate LGB/KIL NE12 35 F6
North Gra PONT/DH NE20 28 A2
North Gv CLDN/WHIT/ROK SR6 127 D1
RYTON NE40 74 C3
North Guards
CLDN/WHIT/ROK SR6 109 D2
North Hall Rd MLFD/PNYW SR4 142 C2
North Hvn SEA/MUR SR7 176 A2
North Hylton Rd SWCK/CAS SR5 124 C2
North Jesmond Av JES NE2 64 A4 3
North King St TYNE/NSHE NE30 55 D6
Northlands BLAY NE21 94 A1 4
North La BOL NE36 106 B3
HLH DH5 172 C5
Northlea BW/LEM/TK/HW NE15 60 A6 5
Northlea Rd SEA/MUR SR7 175 F2
North Mason Ldg DIN/WO NE13 30 C2
North Milburn St
MLFD/PNYW SR4 126 A5
North Moor Ct SUNDSW SR3 143 D5
North Moor La SUNDSW SR3 143 D5
Northmoor Rd BYK/HTN/WLK NE6 66 A6
North Moor Rd SUNDSW SR3 143 D5
Northolt Av CRAM NE23 22 A1
North Pde WBAY NE26 41 D5
North Railway St SEA/MUR SR7 176 C3 9
North Ravensworth St
MLFD/PNYW SR4 126 A5 12
North Rdg BDLGTN NE22 6 C3
MONK NE25 39 E5
North Rd BOL NE36 106 B3
BOLCOL NE35 105 D1
CLS/BIR/GTL DH3 153 E1
DHAM DH1 194 B4
HLH DH5 171 D5
NSHW NE29 54 B4
PONT/DH NE20 28 A2
SEA/MUR SR7 176 C1
STLY/ANP DH9 129 D6
WLSD/HOW NE28 67 D4
Northside Pl MONK NE25 25 D6
North St BLAY NE21 75 F6
CLDN/WHIT/ROK SR6 107 F1
CNUT NE1 2 D2
HLH DH5 170 C5
HLS DH4 157 F4
JRW NE32 86 A1
SSH NE33 71 E3
SUNDSW SR3 143 F6
SWCK/CAS SR5 126 B3 6
North Ter SEA/MUR SR7 176 C2
SUNDSW SR3 143 F6 5
WLSD/HOW NE28 68 A4
Northumberland Av BDLGTN NE22 7 D3
GOS/KPK NE3 62 C2
LGB/KIL NE12 49 F5
Northumberland Dock Rd
WLSD/HOW NE28 69 E5
Northumberland Gdns JES NE2 64 C6 5
WD/WHPE/BLK NE5 59 D3
Northumberland Pl
PLEE/EAS SR8 200 A6 3
Northumberland Rd
BW/LEM/TK/HW NE15 76 B2 5
CNUT NE1 3 E1
RYTON NE40 74 B2
Northumberland Sq
TYNE/NSHE NE30 54 C6 9
Northumberland St CNUT NE1 2 D2
GATE NE8 98 B1 1
PLEE/EAS SR8 201 E6
TYNE/NSHE NE30 55 E6
WLSD/HOW NE28 67 E4
Northumberland Ter
TYNE/NSHE NE30 55 F5 1
Northumberland Vls
WLSD/HOW NE28 68 A4
Northumberland Wy
WASHN NE37 120 C2
WASHS NE38 139 D3
Northumbrian Rd CRAM NE23 14 B6
Northumbrian Wy LGB/KIL NE12 49 E2
NSHW NE29 70 C3
Northumbria Pl STLY/ANP DH9 148 C1
North Vw BYK/HTN/WLK NE6 82 A2
CLDN/WHIT/ROK SR6 126 C1
DIN/WO NE13 31 D3
HAR/WTLS NE34 72 B6 2
HLH DH5 186 C3
JRW NE32 85 F2
LGB/KIL NE12 49 F4 5
SWCK/CAS SR5 124 B3
WBAY NE26 41 E6
WICK/BNPF NE16 95 F3
WLSD/HOW NE28 67 E4
North Walbottle Rd
WD/WHPE/BLK NE5 58 C4
Northway BW/LEM/TK/HW NE15 57 F3
LWF/SPW/WRK NE9 100 A3
Northwood Ct SWCK/CAS SR5 126 B2 4
Northwood Rd SEA/MUR SR7 176 A2
Norton Av SEA/MUR SR7 175 F1
Norton Cl CLSW/PEL DH2 165 E1
Norton Rd SWCK/CAS SR5 125 F1
Norton Wy BW/LEM/TK/HW NE15 77 D2
Norway Av MLFD/PNYW SR4 143 D2
Norwich Av DIN/WO NE13 33 D5 4
Norwich Cl CLS/BIR/GTL DH3 167 F3
Norwich Rd DHAM DH1 180 C5
Norwood Av BYK/HTN/WLK NE6 65 D5
GOS/KPK NE3 47 E2
Norwood Rd
BW/LEM/TK/HW NE15 59 F6
DUN/TMV NE11 98 A3

Nottingham Pl *PLEE/EAS* SR8 **200** A6
Nottinghamshire Rd *DHAM* DH1 **196** B3
Nuneaton Wy *WD/WHPE/BLK* NE5 **59** D2
Nuns La *CNUT* NE1 **2** C4
GATE NE8 **81** E5 6
Nuns Moor Crs *ELS/FEN* NE4 **79** D1
Nuns Moor Rd *ELS/FEN* NE4 **79** D1
Nuns' Rw *DHAM* DH1 **195** E3
Nun St *CNUT* NE1 **2** C3
Nunwick Gdns *NSHW* NE29 **53** E6 3
Nunwick Wy *LGB/HTN* NE7 **65** F3
Nursery Cl *SUNDSW* SR3 **143** F4
Nursery Gdns *PLEE/EAS* SR8 **200** A3
Nursery La *CLDN/WHIT/ROK* SR6 **107** F1
FELL NE10 **100** B3
Nursery Rd *SUNDSW* SR3 **143** F4
Nutley Pl *BW/LEM/TK/HW* NE15 **77** F3
Nye Dene *SWCK/CAS* SR5 **124** A3

O

Oakapple Cl *BDLGTN* NE22 **7** E3
Oak Av *DHAM* DH1 **195** F5
DIN/WO NE13 **31** E3
DUN/TMV NE11 **97** E3
HAR/WTLS NE34 **89** F3
Oak Crs *CLDN/WHIT/ROK* SR6 **109** F1
CLSW/PEL DH2 **179** F1
Oakdale *BDLGTN* NE22 **6** A4
Oakdale Cl *BW/LEM/TK/HW* NE15 **76** C2
Oakenshaw *BW/LEM/TK/HW* NE15 **76** C2
Oakerside Dr *PLEE/EAS* SR8 **208** B4
Oakes Pl *ELS/FEN* NE4 **80** A3
Oakeys Rd *STLY/ANP* DH9 **131** E5
Oakfield Av *WICK/BNPF* NE16 **96** A4
Oakfield Cl *SUNDSW* SR3 **159** E2
WICK/BNPF NE16 **96** A4
Oakfield Dr *LGB/KIL* NE12 **50** B1
WICK/BNPF NE16 **96** A4 2
Oakfield Gdns
BW/LEM/TK/HW NE15 **78** C3
WLSD/HOW NE28 **66** B3 2
Oakfield Gra *DIN/WO* NE13 **31** D3
Oakfield North *RYTON* NE40 **74** A3 1
Oakfield Rd *DUN/TMV* NE11 **97** F4
GOS/KPK NE3 **63** D3
WICK/BNPF NE16 **95** E5
Oakfields *WICK/BNPF* NE16 **112** A5
Oakfield Ter *GOS/KPK* NE3 **63** D2
Oakfield Wy *CRAM* NE23 **36** B1
Oakgreen Flats
BDN/LAN/SAC DH7 **203** D4
Oak Gv *WLSD/HOW* NE28 **67** F4
Oakham Av *WICK/BNPF* NE16 **95** E4
Oakham Dr *DHAM* DH1 **196** C1
Oakham Gdns *NSHW* NE29 **70** A2
Oakhurst Dr *GOS/KPK* NE3 **62** C4
Oakhurst Ter *LGB/KIL* NE12 **49** F6 3
Oakland Rd *JES* NE2 **63** F4 5
MONK NE25 **39** F6
Oaklands *GOS/KPK* NE3 **63** E3
WICK/BNPF NE16 **96** A2
Oaklands Crs *SWCK/CAS* SR5 **125** F2
Oaklands Ter *MLFD/PNYW* SR4 **143** F1 6
Oak Lea *BDN/LAN/SAC* DH7 **178** A3
Oaklea *CLSW/PEL* DH2 **152** C4
Oakleigh Gdns
CLDN/WHIT/ROK SR6 **89** F6 2
Oakley Cl *CRAM* NE23 **35** D2
Oakley Dr *CRAM* NE23 **22** B1
Oakmere Cl *HLS* DH4 **157** D2 6
Oakridge *WICK/BNPF* NE16 **95** E4
Oak Rd *NSHW* NE29 **52** C5
PLEE/EAS SR8 **200** C3
The Oaks *RYTON* NE40 **92** A1 1
Oak St *HLS* DH4 **169** D1
JRW NE32 **85** F1
SUND SR1 **5** H3
Oak Ter *CLSW/PEL* DH2 **151** E1
SEA/MUR SR7 **188** B1
STLY/ANP DH9 **149** D5
Oaktree Av *WLSD/HOW* NE28 **66** C5
Oaktree Gdns *MONK* NE25 **54** A1
Oakwellgate *GATE* NE8 **3** G6
Oakwood *FELL* NE10 **101** D5
HEBB NE31 **84** B1
RDHAMSE DH6 **188** A6
Oakwood Av *DIN/WO* NE13 **33** E5
LWF/SPW/WRK NE9 **117** F1
Oakwood Gdns *DUN/TMV* NE11 **98** A5
Oakwood Pl *WD/WHPE/BLK* NE5 **61** E5 5
Oakwood St
ASHBK/HED/RY SR2 **144** A1 10
Oates St *MLFD/PNYW* SR4 **125** F6
Oatlands Rd *MLFD/PNYW* SR4 **143** D2
Oatlands Wy *DHAM* DH1 **180** B4
Oban Av *WLSD/HOW* NE28 **68** B2
Oban St *FELL* NE10 **100** B1
JRW NE32 **87** D5
Obelisk La *DHAM* DH1 **194** A4
Ocean Rd *ASHBK/HED/RY* SR2 **145** F4
SSH NE33 **71** E3
Ocean Vw *ASHBK/HED/RY* SR2 **162** B1
WBAY NE26 **41** D5 1
Ochiltree Ct *WBAY* NE26 **26** C2
Octavia Cl *BDLGTN* NE22 **7** D2
Octavia Ct *WLSD/HOW* NE28 **68** A2
Octavian Wy *DUN/TMV* NE11 **116** B1
Offerton Cl *MLFD/PNYW* SR4 **123** E6
Offerton La *MLFD/PNYW* SR4 **123** E6
MLFD/PNYW SR4 **141** E3
Offerton St *MLFD/PNYW* SR4 **125** F6
Office Pl *HLH* DH5 **185** F1
Office St *PLEE/EAS* SR8 **201** E2
Ogden St *MLFD/PNYW* SR4 **125** F6
Ogle Av *DIN/WO* NE13 **32** C6 4
Ogle Dr *BLYTH* NE24 **10** B6
Ogle Gv *JRW* NE32 **85** F5
O'hanlon Crs *WLSD/HOW* NE28 **66** C2
Oil Mill Rd *BYK/HTN/WLK* NE6 **84** A1
Okehampton Dr *HLS* DH4 **157** E4
Okehampton Sq *SWCK/CAS* SR5 **125** F1 3
Old Coronation St *SSH* NE33 **71** E4 2
Old Course Rd
CLDN/WHIT/ROK SR6 **107** F2 1
Old Durham Rd
LWF/SPW/WRK NE9 **100** A5
Old Elvet *DHAM* DH1 **194** C5
Old Farm Ct *WICK/BNPF* NE16 **114** A2 1
Oldfield Rd *BYK/HTN/WLK* NE6 **83** E5
Old Fold Rd *FELL* NE10 **82** A6
GATE NE8 **100** A1 11
Old Mill La *CLS/BIR/GTL* DH3 **167** E4
Old Mill Rd *ASHBK/HED/RY* SR2 **5** H5
SWCK/CAS SR5 **125** F1
Oldstead Gdns *MLFD/PNYW* SR4 **143** D2
Old Well La *BLAY* NE21 **94** A1
Olive Gdns *LWF/SPW/WRK* NE9 **99** F4
Olive Pl *ELS/FEN* NE4 **78** C1
Oliver Pl *DHAM* DH1 **204** C1
Oliver St *BW/LEM/TK/HW* NE15 **78** A3
SEA/MUR SR7 **176** A2
STLY/ANP DH9 **148** A4 3
Olive St *CLSW/PEL* DH2 **165** D1
SSH NE33 **88** A2
SUND SR1 **4** B4
Ollerton Dr *BW/LEM/TK/HW* NE15 **57** D4
Ollerton Gdns *FELL* NE10 **100** B3
Olney Cl *CRAM* NE23 **22** C1
O'neil Dr *PLEE/EAS* SR8 **208** C3
Ongar Wy *LGB/KIL* NE12 **49** D5
Onslow Gdns *LWF/SPW/WRK* NE9 **99** E5
Onslow St *MLFD/PNYW* SR4 **125** D5 3
Orange Gv *CRAM* NE23 **35** D1
WICK/BNPF NE16 **96** B3
Orb Ct *ELS/FEN* NE4 **78** C1
Orchard Av *ROWG* NE39 **110** C3
Orchard Cl *HAR/WTLS* NE34 **88** A3
LGB/KIL NE12 **50** B2
ROWG NE39 **110** C4
STLY/ANP DH9 **150** C2
Orchard Ct *RYTON* NE40 **74** B3
Orchard Dene *ROWG* NE39 **110** C3
Orchard Dr *DHAM* DH1 **195** D3
Orchard Gdns
CLDN/WHIT/ROK SR6 **109** D2
CLS/BIR/GTL DH3 **166** B1
LWF/SPW/WRK NE9 **99** F6
WLSD/HOW NE28 **66** C3
Orchard-leigh
BW/LEM/TK/HW NE15 **76** C2
Orchard Pk *CLS/BIR/GTL* DH3 **136** B2
Orchard Pl *JES* NE2 **64** B5
Orchard Priory *DHAM* DH1 **194** A5
Orchard Rd *ROWG* NE39 **110** C3
WICK/BNPF NE16 **96** B3
The Orchards *BLYTH* NE24 **10** A4
Orchard St *CLS/BIR/GTL* DH3 **136** B2
CLSW/PEL DH2 **152** A1
CNUT NE1 **2** D5
MLFD/PNYW SR4 **125** E5
Orchard Ter *CLS/BIR/GTL* DH3 **166** B1
The Orchard
BW/LEM/TK/HW NE15 **76** C2 1
DHAM DH1 **180** A4
WICK/BNPF NE16 **96** B3 3
Orde Av *WLSD/HOW* NE28 **68** A3
Ordley Cl *BW/LEM/TK/HW* NE15 **77** D2
Ord St *ELS/FEN* NE4 **80** B5 1
Oriel Cl *CLDN/WHIT/ROK* SR6 **126** C3 6
Orkney Dr *ASHBK/HED/RY* SR2 **144** C6
Orlando Rd *NSHW* NE29 **53** F6
Ormesby Rd
CLDN/WHIT/ROK SR6 **126** C1 12
Ormiscraig *BW/LEM/TK/HW* NE15 **77** D2
Ormiston *BW/LEM/TK/HW* NE15 **77** D2
Ormonde Av
BW/LEM/TK/HW NE15 **77** F2
Ormonde St *JRW* NE32 **86** A1
MLFD/PNYW SR4 **143** E1
Ormskirk Cl *BW/LEM/TK/HW* NE15 **76** C2
Ormskirk Gv *CRAM* NE23 **22** B1 1
Ormston St *CRAM* NE23 **14** A3
Orpen Av *HAR/WTLS* NE34 **88** B5
Orpington Av *BYK/HTN/WLK* NE6 **83** D1
Orpington Rd *CRAM* NE23 **22** B1
Orr Av *SUNDSW* SR3 **161** D2
Orton Cl *ELS/FEN* NE4 **79** D4 5
Orwell Cl *HAR/WTLS* NE34 **88** A6
PLEE/EAS SR8 **208** A4
Orwell Gdns *STLY/ANP* DH9 **148** A4
Osbaldeston Gdns *GOS/KPK* NE3 **63** D3
Osborne Av *JES* NE2 **64** A6
SSH NE33 **71** F5
Osborne Cl *BDLGTN* NE22 **8** B2
Osborne Gdns *NSHW* NE29 **54** C5 2
WBAY NE26 **40** B5
Osborne Rd *JES* NE2 **64** A6
SWCK/CAS SR5 **123** F5
Osborne St *CLDN/WHIT/ROK* SR6 **126** C2
SSH NE33 **72** A5
Osborne Ter *JES* NE2 **81** D1 6
Oslo Cl *NSHW* NE29 **69** D2
Osman Cl *ASHBK/HED/RY* SR2 **5** E5
Osprey Dr *BLYTH* NE24 **17** D2
NSHW NE29 **52** C6
Osprey Wy *HAR/WTLS* NE34 **87** F4
Oswald Cl *DHAM* DH1 **195** F5
Oswald Ct *DHAM* DH1 **194** C6
Oswald Rd *HLH* DH5 **171** F5
Oswald St *MLFD/PNYW* SR4 **125** F5 3
Oswald Ter *ASHBK/HED/RY* SR2 **145** E4
GATE NE8 **98** C1 6
PLEE/EAS SR8 **200** C1 2
Oswald Ter South *SWCK/CAS* SR5 **124** B3
Oswald Wk *GOS/KPK* NE3 **64** A1
Oswestry Pl *CRAM* NE23 **22** B1
Oswin Av *LGB/KIL* NE12 **50** A4
Oswin Ct *LGB/KIL* NE12 **50** A3
Oswin Ter *NSHW* NE29 **69** F1
Otley Cl *CRAM* NE23 **22** C1
Otterburn Av *MONK* NE25 **39** D6
Otterburn Cl *LGB/KIL* NE12 **50** B4
Otterburn Crs *HLS* DH4 **170** B1
Otterburn Gdns *DUN/TMV* NE11 **97** F3 4
HAR/WTLS NE34 **89** D2
LWF/SPW/WRK NE9 **99** D6
WICK/BNPF NE16 **96** A3
Otterburn Gv *BLYTH* NE24 **10** A6
Otterburn Rd *NSHW* NE29 **54** B5
Otterburn Ter *JES* NE2 **64** A5
Ottercap Cl *BW/LEM/TK/HW* NE15 **76** C2
Otterington *WASHS* NE38 **139** F2
Ottershaw *BW/LEM/TK/HW* NE15 **77** D2
Otto Ter *ASHBK/HED/RY* SR2 **144** A1
Ottovale Crs *BLAY* NE21 **93** F1
Ottringham Cl
BW/LEM/TK/HW NE15 **76** C2
Oulton Cl *CRAM* NE23 **22** C1
Ousby Ct *DIN/WO* NE13 **45** F5 4
Ouseburn Cl
ASHBK/HED/RY SR2 **145** E6 2
Ouseburn Rd *BYK/HTN/WLK* NE6 **65** D5
CNUT NE1 **81** F2 8
Ouselaw *DUN/TMV* NE11 **116** C6
Ouse St *CNUT* NE1 **81** F3
Ouslaw La *DUN/TMV* NE11 **116** A6
Ousterley Ter *STLY/ANP* DH9 **149** D6
Ouston Cl *FELL* NE10 **102** B3
Ouston La *CLSW/PEL* DH2 **152** B1
Ouston St *BW/LEM/TK/HW* NE15 **77** E3
Outram St *HLH* DH5 **171** D1
Oval Park Vw *FELL* NE10 **100** C3 2
The Oval *BDLGTN* NE22 **8** B3
BLYTH NE24 **16** A3
BYK/HTN/WLK NE6 **83** D5
CLSW/PEL DH2 **135** E4
CLSW/PEL DH2 **166** A3
DIN/WO NE13 **44** B4
HLS DH4 **170** B2
LGB/KIL NE12 **49** F6
Overdene *BW/LEM/TK/HW* NE15 **77** E1 6
SEA/MUR SR7 **175** E5 1
Overfield Rd *GOS/KPK* NE3 **62** B1
Overton Cl *BW/LEM/TK/HW* NE15 **76** C2
Overton Rd *NSHW* NE29 **54** A4 2
Ovingham Cl *WASHS* NE38 **139** E1
Ovingham Gdns *DIN/WO* NE13 **33** D4 4
Ovington Gv *WD/WHPE/BLK* NE5 **61** E6
Owen Brannigan Dr *CRAM* NE23 **35** D2 4
Owen Dr *BOL* NE36 **106** A2
Owengate *DHAM* DH1 **194** B5 3
Owen St *HAR/WTLS* NE34 **88** A3
Owlet Cl *BLAY* NE21 **93** F1 8
Oxbridge St *ASHBK/HED/RY* SR2 **145** E4
Oxclose Rd *WASHS* NE38 **139** D2
Oxford Av *CRAM* NE23 **22** B1
SSH NE33 **71** F6 5
WASHN NE37 **120** A4
WLSD/HOW NE28 **66** C3
Oxford Cl *SUNDSW* SR3 **143** E6
Oxford Crs *HEBB* NE31 **85** E2
Oxford Pl *CLS/BIR/GTL* DH3 **136** B5
Oxfordshire Dr *DHAM* DH1 **196** B3 2
Oxford Sq *MLFD/PNYW* SR4 **125** D5
Oxford St *BLYTH* NE24 **11** E5 5
CNUT NE1 **3** E2
MLFD/PNYW SR4 **125** D5
SEA/MUR SR7 **175** F3
SSH NE33 **71** F6
TYNE/NSHE NE30 **55** F5
WBAY NE26 **41** D5
Oxnam Crs *JES* NE2 **80** A1

Oxted Cl *CRAM* NE23 22 C1
Oxted Pl *BYK/HTN/WLK* NE6 83 D5
Oyston St *SSH* NE33 71 E4
Ozanan Cl *CRAM* NE23 35 D3

P

Pacific Hall *SEA/MUR* SR7 175 D2 1
Packham Rd *MLFD/PNYW* SR4 142 B1
Paddock Cl
CLDN/WHIT/ROK SR6 107 D1 3
HLS DH4 156 B3
Paddock Hl *PONT/DH* NE20 28 B3
Paddock La *SUNDSW* SR3 161 E1
The Paddock *BLYTH* NE24 10 B5
BW/LEM/TK/HW NE15 58 B5
CRAM NE23 22 C2
DIN/WO NE13 44 B4
FELL NE10 101 E4
HLS DH4 158 B1
STLY/ANP DH9 130 B6
Pader Cl *DIN/WO* NE13 33 D5 5
Padgate Rd *MLFD/PNYW* SR4 142 B1
Padstow Cl *ASHBK/HED/RY* SR2 145 E6 3
Padstow Rd *NSHW* NE29 70 A2
Page Av *HAR/WTLS* NE34 89 D1
Page St *HEBB* NE31 85 E1 4
Paignton Av *ELS/FEN* NE4 79 D3
MONK NE25 39 F6
Paignton Sq *SUNDSW* SR3 143 D4 2
Paisley Sq *SUNDSW* SR3 143 D4 3
Palace Rd *BDLGTN* NE22 8 C2
Palace St *ELS/FEN* NE4 80 A4 8
Palermo St *MLFD/PNYW* SR4 125 E4
Paley St *SUND* SR1 4 A2 2
Palgrove Rd *MLFD/PNYW* SR4 142 B1
Palgrove Sq *MLFD/PNYW* SR4 142 B1
Pallinsburn Ct
WD/WHPE/BLK NE5 61 D3 7
Pallion New Rd *MLFD/PNYW* SR4 125 E4
Pallion Pk *MLFD/PNYW* SR4 125 E4
Pallion Rd *MLFD/PNYW* SR4 125 E6
Pallion Subway
MLFD/PNYW SR4 125 E4 2
Palm Av *ELS/FEN* NE4 78 C1
HAR/WTLS NE34 89 F3
Palmer Crs *HEBB* NE31 85 E2
Palmer Rd *PLEE/EAS* SR8 207 F3
STLY/ANP DH9 129 D5
Palmers Garth *DHAM* DH1 194 C5
Palmers Gn *LGB/KIL* NE12 50 B3
Palmer's Hill Rd
CLDN/WHIT/ROK SR6 126 C4
Palmerston Av *BYK/HTN/WLK* NE6 83 D1
Palmerston Rd *MLFD/PNYW* SR4 142 A3
Palmer St *JRW* NE32 85 F1
STLY/ANP DH9 147 F3 1
Palm Lea *BDN/LAN/SAC* DH7 202 C4 2
Palmstead Rd *MLFD/PNYW* SR4 142 B1
Palmstead Sq *MLFD/PNYW* SR4 142 B1
Palm Ter *STLY/ANP* DH9 149 D5
Pancras Rd *SUNDSW* SR3 143 D4
Pandon *CNUT* NE1 3 F4
Pandon Bank *CNUT* NE1 3 F3
Pangbourne Cl
BW/LEM/TK/HW NE15 59 E6
Pankhurst Gdns *FELL* NE10 101 F2 3
Pankhurst Pl *STLY/ANP* DH9 149 D3 1
Pann La *SUND* SR1 4 C2
Panns Bank *SUND* SR1 4 D1
The Parade *ASHBK/HED/RY* SR2 5 H4
BYK/HTN/WLK NE6 83 F3
CLSW/PEL DH2 151 E2
Paradise Crs *PLEE/EAS* SR8 200 C2
Paradise La *PLEE/EAS* SR8 200 C2
Paradise Rw *CRAM* NE23 22 A2 4
Park Av *BDLGTN* NE22 9 D1
BLAY NE21 76 B6
CLDN/WHIT/ROK SR6 127 D1
GOS/KPK NE3 46 B5
HAR/WTLS NE34 89 E4
SMOOR NE27 52 B1
SUNDSW SR3 161 D1
TYNE/NSHE NE30 55 E5
WBAY NE26 40 C5
WLSD/HOW NE28 67 D4
Park Chare *WASHS* NE38 139 D1 1
Park Cl *ELS/FEN* NE4 79 F4 5
STLY/ANP DH9 146 C5
Park Crs *SMOOR* NE27 52 B1
TYNE/NSHE NE30 55 D6
Park Crs East *TYNE/NSHE* NE30 55 E5
Parkdale Ri *WICK/BNPF* NE16 95 E3
Park Dr *BLYTH* NE24 16 A2
GOS/KPK NE3 47 E3
LGB/KIL NE12 50 A4
WICK/BNPF NE16 96 B3
Parker Av *GOS/KPK* NE3 63 D3
Park Farm Vls *BLYTH* NE24 16 B4
Park Fld *RYTON* NE40 74 B3
Park Field Ter *WBAY* NE26 26 B2
Park Gdns *WBAY* NE26 40 C5
Park Ga *CLDN/WHIT/ROK* SR6 127 D1
Parkgate La *BLAY* NE21 94 A2
Park Gv *SMOOR* NE27 52 B1
WASHN NE37 120 C3
Parkham Cl *CRAM* NE23 14 A5 3
Parkhead *STLY/ANP* DH9 146 A6
Parkhead Gdns *BLAY* NE21 94 A2
Park Head Rd *LGB/HTN* NE7 64 C4
Parkhouse Av *SWCK/CAS* SR5 124 A4
Park House Cl *RDHAMSE* DH6 197 E4 3
Park House Rd *DHAM* DH1 204 C1
Parkhurst Rd *MLFD/PNYW* SR4 142 A2
Parkin Gdns *FELL* NE10 101 D3 5
Parkland *BLAY* NE21 75 F4
LGB/KIL NE12 49 F6 4
Parkland Av *BLAY* NE21 94 A2
Parkland Ct *SEA/MUR* SR7 176 A2
Parklands Ct *FELL* NE10 102 B1
Parklands Wy *FELL* NE10 102 B1
Parkland Ter *SEA/MUR* SR7 176 A2
Park La *BLAY* NE21 94 A2
GATE NE8 81 F5
PLEE/EAS SR8 209 F1
SEA/MUR SR7 188 A1
SMOOR NE27 52 B1
SUND SR1 4 C4
Park Lea *SUNDSW* SR3 159 D2
Park Lea Rd *CLDN/WHIT/ROK* SR6 127 D1
Parkmore Rd *MLFD/PNYW* SR4 141 F3 2
Park Pde *CLDN/WHIT/ROK* SR6 127 D2
WBAY NE26 40 C5
Park Pl *CLS/BIR/GTL* DH3 153 F3
Park Ri *BW/LEM/TK/HW* NE15 76 B1
Park Rd *ASHBK/HED/RY* SR2 4 C5
BDLGTN NE22 7 F3
BW/LEM/TK/HW NE15 58 B6
ELS/FEN NE4 79 F4
FELL NE10 82 B6
GATE NE8 82 A6
HEBB NE31 85 D3
JRW NE32 85 F2 3
MONK NE25 24 B5
PLEE/EAS SR8 201 E6
ROWG NE39 110 C2 3
SMOOR NE27 52 B1
STLY/ANP DH9 147 F3
WBAY NE26 40 C4
WLSD/HOW NE28 67 D4
Park Road Central
CLS/BIR/GTL DH3 153 F5
Park Rd North *CLS/BIR/GTL* DH3 153 E3
Park Rd South *CLS/BIR/GTL* DH3 153 F6
Park Rw *FELL* NE10 100 C2 5
SWCK/CAS SR5 125 F3 9
Parkshiel *HAR/WTLS* NE34 89 E4
Parkside *BDLGTN* NE22 9 D1
BDN/LAN/SAC DH7 178 B1
BW/LEM/TK/HW NE15 58 A5
DUN/TMV NE11 97 E2
HEBB NE31 84 B4
STLY/ANP DH9 130 B5
TYNE/NSHE NE30 55 F3
WLSD/HOW NE28 67 F3 2
Parkside Av *BLAY* NE21 94 A1
LGB/HTN NE7 65 D1
Parkside Crs *SEA/MUR* SR7 176 B5
TYNE/NSHE NE30 55 F4
The Parks *CLS/BIR/GTL* DH3 167 D1
Parkstone Cl *MLFD/PNYW* SR4 141 F4
Park St *SEA/MUR* SR7 176 C4
Park St South *SWCK/CAS* SR5 124 B3 5
Park Ter *BDLGTN* NE22 8 B1
DUN/TMV NE11 97 D2
JES NE2 80 C1
PLEE/EAS SR8 209 F2
SWCK/CAS SR5 125 E2
TYNE/NSHE NE30 55 E6
WICK/BNPF NE16 95 F1
WLSD/HOW NE28 67 D4
Park Vw *BLAY* NE21 94 B2
BLYTH NE24 11 E5
BYK/HTN/WLK NE6 83 F3 3
CLSW/PEL DH2 165 E6
HLH DH5 185 F1
JRW NE32 86 A4
LGB/KIL NE12 49 F4 6
MONK NE25 24 C5
WBAY NE26 40 C5
WLSD/HOW NE28 67 D4
Parkway *WASHS* NE38 138 C1
WICK/BNPF NE16 95 D5
Parmeter St *STLY/ANP* DH9 148 A4 4
Parmontley St
BW/LEM/TK/HW NE15 77 E3 2
Parnell St *HLS* DH4 170 A2
Parry Dr *CLDN/WHIT/ROK* SR6 109 D1
Parson's Av *BYK/HTN/WLK* NE6 83 E3
Parsons Rd *PLEE/EAS* SR8 200 C5
WASHN NE37 120 A5
Partick Rd *MLFD/PNYW* SR4 142 A2
Partick Sq *MLFD/PNYW* SR4 142 B2 5
Partridge Cl *WASHS* NE38 137 E3
Passfield Wy *PLEE/EAS* SR8 207 F4
Pasteur Rd *RDHAMSE* DH6 187 E5 1
Paston Rd *MONK* NE25 24 C6
The Pastures *BLYTH* NE24 16 C2
Pathside *JRW* NE32 86 A6
Patience Av *DIN/WO* NE13 33 E2
Patina Cl *BW/LEM/TK/HW* NE15 59 E6 5
Paton Rd *SUNDSW* SR3 143 E4
Paton Sq *SUNDSW* SR3 143 E4
Patrick Crs *RDHAMSE* DH6 187 D4
Patterdale Cl *BOL* NE36 106 B3 3
DHAM DH1 197 D2 3
Patterdale Gdns *LGB/HTN* NE7 65 D3
Patterdale Gv *SWCK/CAS* SR5 108 B6 3
Patterdale Rd *BLYTH* NE24 9 F4
Patterdale St *HLH* DH5 185 F2
Patterdale Ter *GATE* NE8 99 E2 1
Patterson St *BLAY* NE21 77 D4
Pattinson Gdns *FELL* NE10 82 B6
LWF/SPW/WRK NE9 100 A3
Pattinson Rd *WASHS* NE38 122 A6
Pauline Av
CLDN/WHIT/ROK SR6 126 C1 13
Pauline Gdns
BW/LEM/TK/HW NE15 77 F1
Pauls Gn *HLH* DH5 171 F4
Paulsway *JRW* NE32 87 D2
Paxford Cl *LGB/HTN* NE7 64 B1
Paxton Ter *MLFD/PNYW* SR4 125 F5 4
Peacock Ct *DUN/TMV* NE11 98 A3
Peacock St West
MLFD/PNYW SR4 125 E6
Pea Flatts La *CLS/BIR/GTL* DH3 168 B3
Peareth Gv *CLDN/WHIT/ROK* SR6 127 D1
Peareth Hall Rd
LWF/SPW/WRK NE9 119 E3
WASHN NE37 120 A2
Peareth Rd *CLDN/WHIT/ROK* SR6 109 D6
Pear Lea *BDN/LAN/SAC* DH7 202 C4
Pearl Rd *SUNDSW* SR3 143 E4
Pearson Pl *JRW* NE32 69 E6 2
TYNE/NSHE NE30 55 D6
Pearson St *SSH* NE33 71 F2
STLY/ANP DH9 131 E6 4
Peart Cl *RDHAMSE* DH6 197 F5 2
Peartree Gdns *BYK/HTN/WLK* NE6 66 B5
Peary Cl *WD/WHPE/BLK* NE5 60 B4
Pease Av *BW/LEM/TK/HW* NE15 78 B2
Peasemoor Rd *MLFD/PNYW* SR4 142 A1
Pease Rd *PLEE/EAS* SR8 199 E6
Pecket Cl *BLYTH* NE24 15 F1
Peebles Cl *NSHW* NE29 53 D4
Peebles Rd *SUNDSW* SR3 143 D4
Peel Av *DHAM* DH1 196 A3
Peel La *CNUT* NE1 2 B5
Peggy's Wicket *STLY/ANP* DH9 133 E6
Pegwood Rd *MLFD/PNYW* SR4 142 B1 1
Pelaw Av *CLSW/PEL* DH2 153 D3
STLY/ANP DH9 131 F6
Pelaw Bank *CLS/BIR/GTL* DH3 153 E4
Pelaw Crs *CLSW/PEL* DH2 153 D3
Pelaw Grange Ct
CLS/BIR/GTL DH3 136 B6
Pelaw Leazes La *DHAM* DH1 194 C4 5
Pelaw Pl *CLSW/PEL* DH2 153 E3
Pelaw Rd *CLSW/PEL* DH2 153 D3
Pelaw Sq *CLSW/PEL* DH2 153 D3
MLFD/PNYW SR4 124 B5 2
Pelaw Wy *FELL* NE10 101 F2
Peldon Cl *LGB/HTN* NE7 64 B1
Pelham Ct *GOS/KPK* NE3 46 A5 7
Peltondale Av *BLYTH* NE24 9 F6
Pelton Fell Rd *CLSW/PEL* DH2 152 C4
Pelton La *CLSW/PEL* DH2 151 E1
Pelton Ms *CLSW/PEL* DH2 151 E2
Pelton Rd *MLFD/PNYW* SR4 142 B2 6
Pemberton Bank *HLH* DH5 186 A3
Pemberton Cl *SWCK/CAS* SR5 126 A3 5
Pemberton Gdns *SUNDSW* SR3 144 A3 9
Pemberton St *HLH* DH5 171 F6 3
Pembroke Av *CLS/BIR/GTL* DH3 136 C5
SUNDSW SR3 160 C2
Pembroke Gdns *WLSD/HOW* NE28 68 C2
Pembroke Ter *SSH* NE33 88 B1 2
Pembrooke Av *BYK/HTN/WLK* NE6 66 A6
Pendeford *WASHS* NE38 139 F2
Pendle Cl *WASHS* NE38 138 A3
Pendleton Dr *CRAM* NE23 13 F5
Pendower Wy
BW/LEM/TK/HW NE15 78 B2
Penfold Cl *LGB/HTN* NE7 65 E2 6
Penhale Dr *ASHBK/HED/RY* SR2 162 B1
Penhill Cl *CLSW/PEL* DH2 135 D5
Penistone Rd *MLFD/PNYW* SR4 141 F2
Penman Pl *NSHW* NE29 70 C2 5
Penman Sq *MLFD/PNYW* SR4 142 A2 1
Penman St *NSHW* NE29 70 C2 6
Pennant Sq *MLFD/PNYW* SR4 124 B6 2
Pennine Dr *PLEE/EAS* SR8 208 A2
Pennine Gdns *DUN/TMV* NE11 97 F3
STLY/ANP DH9 148 C3
Pennine Gv *BOL* NE36 106 A3
Pennine Wy *LGB/KIL* NE12 48 C6
Penn Sq *MLFD/PNYW* SR4 124 B6
Penn St *ELS/FEN* NE4 80 A5
Pennycross Rd *MLFD/PNYW* SR4 141 F2
Pennycross Sq *MLFD/PNYW* SR4 141 F1 2
Pennyfine Cl *NSHW* NE29 54 C4 3

Pennyfine Rd WICK/BNPF NE16 114 B1
Pennygate Sq MLFD/PNYW SR4 141 F1 3
Pennygreen Sq
MLFD/PNYW SR4 141 F1 4
Pennymore Sq
MLFD/PNYW SR4 141 F2 2
Pennywell Rd MLFD/PNYW SR4 142 B2
Penrith Av TYNE/NSHE NE30 54 C2
Penrith Gdns LWF/SPW/WRK NE9 100 A6
Penrith Rd HEBB NE31 85 E4
SWCK/CAS SR5 108 B6
Penryn Av SEA/MUR SR7 188 C1
Penryn Wy BDN/LAN/SAC DH7 203 E4
Pensford Ct GOS/KPK NE3 61 E1 1
Penshaw Gn WD/WHPE/BLK NE5 61 F3
Penshaw La HLS DH4 140 A6
Penshaw Vw BDN/LAN/SAC DH7 178 C2
FELL NE10 102 B2
HEBB NE31 84 C4 5
JRW NE32 86 A4 1
Penshaw Wy CLS/BIR/GTL DH3 137 D2
Pensher St MLFD/PNYW SR4 125 F6
Pensher St East FELL NE10 100 B1
Pentland Cl CRAM NE23 14 A5 4
NSHW NE29 54 B3 2
PLEE/EAS SR8 207 F3
WASHS NE38 138 A3
Pentland Gdns DUN/TMV NE11 97 F3 5
Pentland Gv LGB/KIL NE12 49 D3
Pentlands Ter STLY/ANP DH9 148 C3
Pentridge Cl CRAM NE23 22 B1
Penwood Rd MLFD/PNYW SR4 142 B1
Penyghent Wy WASHN NE37 119 F6
Penzance Bungs SEA/MUR SR7 174 C6
Penzance Rd MLFD/PNYW SR4 142 A2
Percival St MLFD/PNYW SR4 125 E5 8
Percy Av WBAY NE26 40 B5
Percy Ct NSHW NE29 69 F3
Percy Crs NSHW NE29 69 F3
Percy Gdns DUN/TMV NE11 97 F3
LGB/KIL NE12 49 F4 7
MONK NE25 40 C6
Percy La DHAM DH1 193 F5
Percy Pk TYNE/NSHE NE30 55 F4
Percy Park Rd TYNE/NSHE NE30 55 F4
Percy Rd WBAY NE26 41 D5
Percy Scott St HAR/WTLS NE34 88 B5
Percy Sq DHAM DH1 204 C1 3
Percy St BLYTH NE24 11 E4
BW/LEM/TK/HW NE15 76 B2 6
CNUT NE1 2 C2
CRAM NE23 22 B3
HLH DH5 172 A6
JRW NE32 86 B1
LGB/KIL NE12 50 B3
SSH NE33 71 F4 10
TYNE/NSHE NE30 55 F5 2
WLSD/HOW NE28 67 E4
Percy St South BLYTH NE24 11 E5 6
Percy Ter ASHBK/HED/RY SR2 145 D2
DHAM DH1 193 F5
MONK NE25 40 A5
Percy Ter South
ASHBK/HED/RY SR2 145 D3
Percy Wy BW/LEM/TK/HW NE15 58 C5
Peregrine Pl LGB/KIL NE12 48 C5
Perivale Rd MLFD/PNYW SR4 142 A2
Perrycrofts SUNDSW SR3 160 C4 3
Perry St GATE NE8 99 E2 2
Perth Av JRW NE32 86 C5
Perth Cl NSHW NE29 53 E4 4
WLSD/HOW NE28 68 B2 2
Perth Ct SUNDSW SR3 143 D5
Perth Gdns WLSD/HOW NE28 68 B2
Perth Rd SUNDSW SR3 143 D5
Perth Sq SUNDSW SR3 143 E4 1
Pesspool La RDHAMSE DH6 198 A2
Peterborough Rd DHAM DH1 181 D6
Peter's Bank STLY/ANP DH9 146 C1
Petersfield Rd MLFD/PNYW SR4 142 A2
Petersham Rd MLFD/PNYW SR4 124 B6
Petherton Ct GOS/KPK NE3 45 E6
Peth Gn HLH DH5 186 A3 2
Peth La RYTON NE40 74 C2
Petrel Cl SSH NE33 71 E2 3
Petrel Wy BLYTH NE24 17 E2
Petteril WASHS NE38 137 F5
Petwell Crs PLEE/EAS SR8 200 B2
Petwell La PLEE/EAS SR8 200 C1
Pevensey Cl NSHW NE29 54 B3 3
Philadelphia La HLS DH4 157 E3
Philiphaugh WLSD/HOW NE28 67 D6 3
Philip Pl ELS/FEN NE4 79 F2 2
Philipson St BYK/HTN/WLK NE6 83 E2
Philip Sq SUNDSW SR3 143 D4
Phillips Av WICK/BNPF NE16 95 F2 4
Phoenix Cha NSHW NE29 53 D4
Phoenix Rd MLFD/PNYW SR4 124 B6
WASHS NE38 119 D6
Phoenix Wy HLS DH4 170 B3
Piccadilly SUNDSW SR3 143 D6 3
Picherwell FELL NE10 100 C3 3
Pickard Cl PLEE/EAS SR8 209 D1
Pickard St MLFD/PNYW SR4 125 F5 5
Pickering Rd MLFD/PNYW SR4 141 F3
Pickering Sq MLFD/PNYW SR4 142 A2
Pickhurst Rd MLFD/PNYW SR4 142 A3
Pickhurst Sq MLFD/PNYW SR4 142 A3 6
Picktree La CLS/BIR/GTL DH3 153 F4
WASHS NE38 137 D6
Picktree Ldg CLS/BIR/GTL DH3 136 C6
Pickwick Cl DHAM DH1 205 D1 1
Pier Pde SSH NE33 72 A2
Pier Vw CLDN/WHIT/ROK SR6 127 E2
Pikestone Cl WASHS NE38 137 F3
Pilgrim Cl SWCK/CAS SR5 126 B3
Pilgrim St CNUT NE1 3 F5 1
Pilgrims' Wy DHAM DH1 195 E3
Pilgrimsway JRW NE32 87 D2
LWF/SPW/WRK NE9 99 F3
Pilton Rd WD/WHPE/BLK NE5 60 B3
Pimlico DHAM DH1 194 B6
Pimlico Rd HLH DH5 186 A3
MLFD/PNYW SR4 142 A2
Pine Av DHAM DH1 195 F5
DIN/WO NE13 31 E3
GOS/KPK NE3 46 B5
HAR/WTLS NE34 89 F3
Pinedale Dr RDHAMSE DH6 187 E5
Pine Lea BDN/LAN/SAC DH7 202 C4
Pine Pk BDN/LAN/SAC DH7 192 A5
Pine Rd BLAY NE21 76 B6 4
The Pines RYTON NE40 92 A1
Pine St CLS/BIR/GTL DH3 136 B1
CLSW/PEL DH2 150 C3
JRW NE32 85 F2
MLFD/PNYW SR4 125 E5 9
STLY/ANP DH9 147 F4
Pinesway SUNDSW SR3 144 A3
Pinetree Gdns MONK NE25 54 A1
Pinetree Wy WICK/BNPF NE16 78 A6
Pinewood HEBB NE31 84 B1 3
Pinewood Av CRAM NE23 14 A5 5
DIN/WO NE13 33 E5
GOS/KPK NE3 33 E5
WASHS NE38 138 B5
Pinewood Cl BYK/HTN/WLK NE6 66 A5
DIN/WO NE13 45 D6
Pinewood Gdns DUN/TMV NE11 97 F5
Pinewood Rd SWCK/CAS SR5 125 E2
Pinewood Sq SWCK/CAS SR5 125 E2 1
Pinewood St HLS DH4 169 D1
Pinewood Vls HAR/WTLS NE34 89 F2 2
Pink La CNUT NE1 2 C5 1
Pinner Pl BYK/HTN/WLK NE6 83 D4
Pinner Rd MLFD/PNYW SR4 142 B1 2
Pipershaw WASHN NE37 119 E6
Pipe Track La ELS/FEN NE4 78 C4
Pipewellgate GATE NE8 80 C5
Pitcairn Rd MLFD/PNYW SR4 142 B1
Pithouse La HLS DH4 183 D1
Pit La DHAM DH1 180 B6
Pittington La DHAM DH1 197 D1
Pittington Rd HLH DH5 183 F4
Pitt St ELS/FEN NE4 80 A2
Plains Rd SUNDSW SR3 143 E4
Plaistow Sq MLFD/PNYW SR4 124 B6 3
Plaistow Wy CRAM NE23 14 A5 6
Planesway FELL NE10 101 D5 1
Planet Pl LGB/KIL NE12 49 E2
Planetree Av ELS/FEN NE4 61 F6
Plane Tree Ct SUNDSW SR3 160 A2 5
Plantation Av WICK/BNPF NE16 95 F2
Plantation Gv FELL NE10 84 A6
Plantation Rd MLFD/PNYW SR4 125 D5
Plantation Sq MLFD/PNYW SR4 125 D5 4
Plantation St WLSD/HOW NE28 67 D6 4
The Plantation LWF/SPW/WRK NE9 99 F5
Plantation Vw STLY/ANP DH9 150 B2
Plantation Wk RDHAMSE DH6 187 E5
Plawsworth Gdns
LWF/SPW/WRK NE9 118 B1
Plawsworth Rd
BDN/LAN/SAC DH7 178 B1
Plenmeller Pl WICK/BNPF NE16 113 F1
Plessey Av BLYTH NE24 11 D6
Plessey Crs MONK NE25 41 D6
Plessey Gdns NSHW NE29 69 F1 3
Plessey Rd BLYTH NE24 11 E4 3
BLYTH NE24 16 A2
Plessey Ter LGB/HTN NE7 65 D4
Plough Rd SUNDSW SR3 160 B3
Plover Cl BLYTH NE24 17 D2
Plover Dr WICK/BNPF NE16 130 B1
Plunkett Rd STLY/ANP DH9 129 D5
Plunkett Ter CLSW/PEL DH2 151 F4
Plymouth Cl SEA/MUR SR7 175 E4 3
Plymouth Sq SUNDSW SR3 143 D4 4
Point Pleasant Ter
WLSD/HOW NE28 68 A4
Polden Cl PLEE/EAS SR8 207 F3
Polden Crs NSHW NE29 54 A2
Polebrook Rd MLFD/PNYW SR4 124 B6 4
Pollard St SSH NE33 71 F2
Polmuir Rd SUNDSW SR3 143 D4
Polmuir Sq SUNDSW SR3 143 D4 5
Polpero Cl CLS/BIR/GTL DH3 136 C3
Polperro Cl ASHBK/HED/RY SR2 162 B1
Polton Sq MLFD/PNYW SR4 124 B6
Polwarth Crs GOS/KPK NE3 47 E4
Polwarth Dr GOS/KPK NE3 47 E3
Polwarth Rd GOS/KPK NE3 47 E3
Polworth Sq SUNDSW SR3 143 E4 2
Pontefract Rd
MLFD/PNYW SR4 142 A3 7
Ponteland Cl NSHW NE29 53 E5
WASHS NE38 137 E2
Ponteland Rd
BW/LEM/TK/HW NE15 57 F2
DIN/WO NE13 44 C5
ELS/FEN NE4 62 B5
PONT/DH NE20 28 C4
WD/WHPE/BLK NE5 45 D6
WD/WHPE/BLK NE5 62 A5
Ponthaugh ROWG NE39 111 E1
Pontop Sq MLFD/PNYW SR4 124 B6 5
Pontop St HLH DH5 170 B6
Pontop Vw ROWG NE39 110 C2
Pont Vw PONT/DH NE20 28 B3
Poole Cl CRAM NE23 22 B1
Poole Rd MLFD/PNYW SR4 124 B6 6
Pooley Cl WD/WHPE/BLK NE5 61 D5
Pooley Rd WD/WHPE/BLK NE5 61 D5
Poplar Av BLYTH NE24 10 C3
BYK/HTN/WLK NE6 66 B5 2
DIN/WO NE13 31 E3
Poplar Crs CLS/BIR/GTL DH3 136 A1
DUN/TMV NE11 97 E3
GATE NE8 81 D6 5
Poplar Dr CLDN/WHIT/ROK SR6 109 E1
DHAM DH1 195 F3
Poplar Gv ASHBK/HED/RY SR2 145 D6
BDLGTN NE22 8 A3
HAR/WTLS NE34 89 E3
Poplar Lea BDN/LAN/SAC DH7 202 C4
Poplar Rd BLAY NE21 94 B1 4
DHAM DH1 196 C2 2
The Poplars GOS/KPK NE3 63 E3
HLH DH5 186 B3
SWCK/CAS SR5 125 E2 2
Poplar St CLS/BIR/GTL DH3 153 E5
STLY/ANP DH9 147 F4
Popplewell Gdns
LWF/SPW/WRK NE9 99 F6
Popplewell Ter NSHW NE29 54 C4 4
The Populars HLS DH4 140 A6
Porchester Dr CRAM NE23 22 B1
Porlock Ct CRAM NE23 13 F5
Porlock Rd JRW NE32 86 C3
Portadown Rd
MLFD/PNYW SR4 142 A3 8
Portberry St SSH NE33 71 D6
Portberry Wy SSH NE33 71 D5
Portchester Gv BOLCOL NE35 105 D2
Portchester Rd MLFD/PNYW SR4 142 B1
Portchester Sq MLFD/PNYW SR4 142 B2
Porter Ter SEA/MUR SR7 188 B1
Porthcawl Dr WASHN NE37 120 B2
Portland Av SEA/MUR SR7 175 F3
Portland Gdns CRAM NE23 22 B1
LWF/SPW/WRK NE9 117 E2
TYNE/NSHE NE30 54 C5
Portland Ms JES NE2 81 E1 2
Portland Rd BW/LEM/TK/HW NE15 58 A4
JES NE2 81 E1
SUNDSW SR3 143 E4
Portland Sq SUNDSW SR3 143 E3 2
Portland St BLYTH NE24 10 C3
ELS/FEN NE4 79 E4 6
ELS/FEN NE4 79 F4 6
FELL NE10 101 F1 2
Portland Ter JES NE2 81 D1
Portman Pl BYK/HTN/WLK NE6 83 D5 2
Portman Sq MLFD/PNYW SR4 142 B1
Portmeads Rd CLS/BIR/GTL DH3 136 C2
Portobello La
CLDN/WHIT/ROK SR6 126 C3
Portree Sq SUNDSW SR3 143 D5
Portrush Cl WASHN NE37 120 B2 4
Portrush Rd MLFD/PNYW SR4 124 B6
Portrush Wy LGB/HTN NE7 65 E1
Portslade Rd MLFD/PNYW SR4 142 A2
Portsmouth Rd MLFD/PNYW SR4 142 A1
NSHW NE29 69 E1
Portsmouth Sq MLFD/PNYW SR4 142 A2
Portugal Pl WLSD/HOW NE28 67 D5 10
Post Office La NSHW NE29 54 C4 5
Post Office St BLYTH NE24 11 E4 4
Potterhouse La DHAM DH1 179 E4
Potter Pl STLY/ANP DH9 149 D3
Potters Bank DHAM DH1 205 D1
Potters Cl DHAM DH1 204 C1
Potter Sq SUNDSW SR3 143 D4
Potter St JRW NE32 85 F1
WLSD/HOW NE28 68 C5
Pottersway LWF/SPW/WRK NE9 99 F4
Pottery Bank BYK/HTN/WLK NE6 83 E5
Pottery La CNUT NE1 80 B5
MLFD/PNYW SR4 123 F5 3
Pottery Rd SWCK/CAS SR5 125 F3
Pottery Yd HLS DH4 171 D2 2
Potto St RDHAMSE DH6 206 C2 5
Potts St BYK/HTN/WLK NE6 82 B2
Powburn Cl CLSW/PEL DH2 165 F1
Powburn Gdns ELS/FEN NE4 62 A6

Powis Rd SUNDSW SR3 143 E4
Powis Sq SUNDSW SR3 143 E4 3
Poynings Cl WD/WHPE/BLK NE5 61 E1
Praetorian Dr WLSD/HOW NE28 67 D6 5
Prebends Fld DHAM DH1 195 E2
Prefect Pl LWF/SPW/WRK NE9 99 F3 2
Premier Rd SUNDSW SR3 143 D4
Prendwick Av HEBB NE31 84 C5
Prendwick Cl CLSW/PEL DH2 165 F2
Prengarth Av
CLDN/WHIT/ROK SR6 126 C1
Prensgarth Wy HAR/WTLS NE34 87 E5 2
Prescot Rd MLFD/PNYW SR4 124 B6
Press La SUND SR1 4 D2
Prestbury Av CRAM NE23 13 F5
Prestbury Rd MLFD/PNYW SR4 141 F2
Prestdale Av BLYTH NE24 9 F5
Presthope Rd MLFD/PNYW SR4 141 F2
Prestmede FELL NE10 101 D3 6
Preston Av TYNE/NSHE NE30 54 C5
Preston North Rd NSHW NE29 54 B3
Preston Pk NSHW NE29 54 C5
Preston Rd ASHBK/HED/RY SR2 145 E2
Preston Wd TYNE/NSHE NE30 54 C3
Prestwick FELL NE10 101 D5 2
Prestwick Av NSHW NE29 53 E5
Prestwick Cl WASHN NE37 120 B2 5
Prestwick Dr FELL NE10 102 B3
Prestwick Gdns GOS/KPK NE3 62 B2
Prestwick Rd MLFD/PNYW SR4 124 B6
Pretoria Sq SUNDSW SR3 143 D4 6
Pretoria St
BW/LEM/TK/HW NE15 77 F4 2
Price St HEBB NE31 84 B1 4
Priestfield Cl SUNDSW SR3 160 B3
Priestley Ct HAR/WTLS NE34 87 F5
Priestley Gdns FELL NE10 102 A2 5
Priestly Crs MLFD/PNYW SR4 126 A4 1
Priestman Ct MLFD/PNYW SR4 124 C6 8
Primate Rd SUNDSW SR3 143 D4
Primrose Av HAR/WTLS NE34 88 A3 4
Primrose Cl CRAM NE23 34 C2
Primrose Crs
CLDN/WHIT/ROK SR6 126 C1
HLS DH4 156 A5
Primrose Gdns WLSD/HOW NE28 66 C2 2
Primrose Hl LWF/SPW/WRK NE9 99 F5 3
Primrose Prec
CLDN/WHIT/ROK SR6 126 C1 14
Primrose St MLFD/PNYW SR4 123 F6 5
Primrose Ter CLS/BIR/GTL DH3 136 C2
JRW NE32 86 B4
Prince Albert Ter JES NE2 3 G2 2
Prince Consort La HEBB NE31 84 C2
Prince Consort Rd GATE NE8 81 D6
HEBB NE31 84 B2
JRW NE32 86 B2
Prince Consort Wy NSHW NE29 70 C3
Prince Edward Gv HAR/WTLS NE34 90 B2
Prince Edward Rd HAR/WTLS NE34 89 E3
Prince Edward Rd East
HAR/WTLS NE34 90 B2
Prince George Av
CLDN/WHIT/ROK SR6 108 C6 6
Prince of Wales Cl
HAR/WTLS NE34 89 D3 1
Prince Philip Cl
BW/LEM/TK/HW NE15 78 B3
Prince Rd WLSD/HOW NE28 67 D3
Princes Av CLDN/WHIT/ROK SR6 109 D5
GOS/KPK NE3 47 D6
Princes Cl GOS/KPK NE3 47 D4
Prince's Gdns BLYTH NE24 10 B4
CLDN/WHIT/ROK SR6 109 D5 2
Prince's Meadow GOS/KPK NE3 62 C1
Princes Pk DUN/TMV NE11 98 A5
Princes Rd GOS/KPK NE3 47 D3
Princess Dr GATE NE8 97 F2
Princess Louise Rd BLYTH NE24 10 C5
Princess Rd SEA/MUR SR7 176 B3
Princess St ASHBK/HED/RY SR2 4 B5
FELL NE10 101 F1 5
WICK/BNPF NE16 114 A2
Princes' St DHAM DH1 194 A4
HLS DH4 156 C3
TYNE/NSHE NE30 55 D5
Prince St SUND SR1 4 C2 2
Princesway DUN/TMV NE11 98 B4
Princetown Ter SUNDSW SR3 143 D4
Princeway TYNE/NSHE NE30 55 F4
Pringle Cl BDN/LAN/SAC DH7 202 A1
Pringle Gv BDN/LAN/SAC DH7 202 B1
Pringle Pl BDN/LAN/SAC DH7 202 B1
Prinn Pl WICK/BNPF NE16 114 A2
Priors Cl DHAM DH1 193 F4
Prior's Ter TYNE/NSHE NE30 55 F5
Priors Wy WLSD/HOW NE28 68 A4
Priory Av MONK NE25 40 B6
Priory Ct BDN/LAN/SAC DH7 178 B2
Priory Gra BLYTH NE24 10 B4
Priory Gv MLFD/PNYW SR4 143 E1
Priory Pl BYK/HTN/WLK NE6 82 B3 5
DIN/WO NE13 32 C5 6
Priory Rd DHAM DH1 194 A1
JRW NE32 69 E6 5
Priory Wy WD/WHPE/BLK NE5 60 B2
Proctor Sq SUNDSW SR3 143 E4 4
Proctor St BYK/HTN/WLK NE6 83 F3 4
Promenade ASHBK/HED/RY SR2 145 F3
SEA/MUR SR7 176 C2
SSH NE33 72 B3
WBAY NE26 40 C4
Prospect Av MONK NE25 24 B5
WLSD/HOW NE28 67 D3
Prospect Av North
WLSD/HOW NE28 67 D2
Prospect Crs HLH DH5 186 B4
Prospect Gdns BOL NE36 105 F3
Prospect Pl ELS/FEN NE4 79 F3
Prospect Rw SUND SR1 5 C1
Prospect Ter TYNE/NSHE NE30 55 E6
Prospect Vw HLS DH4 183 E2
Providence Pl FELL NE10 100 C1 6
Providence Rw DHAM DH1 194 C4
Provident St CLSW/PEL DH2 151 E2
Provost Gdns ELS/FEN NE4 78 C4 1
Prudhoe Gv JRW NE32 85 F5
Prudhoe St MLFD/PNYW SR4 125 E5 10
NSHW NE29 70 C2
Prudhoe Ter TYNE/NSHE NE30 55 F4 5
Pudding Chare CNUT NE1 2 D5
Purbeck Gdns CRAM NE23 22 B1
Purbeck Rd LGB/KIL NE12 49 D6
Purley WASHS NE38 139 F2 2
Purley Cl WLSD/HOW NE28 68 B2
Purley Gdns GOS/KPK NE3 62 B2
Purley Rd SUNDSW SR3 143 D4
Purley Sq SUNDSW SR3 143 D4
Putney Sq MLFD/PNYW SR4 142 A2
Pykerley Rd MONK NE25 40 A5

Q

The Quadrant NSHW NE29 70 A1
SUND SR1 5 C1
Quality Rw BYK/HTN/WLK NE6 82 A3
Quality Row Rd
WICK/BNPF NE16 95 F1 7
Quantock Cl LGB/KIL NE12 48 C6 5
NSHW NE29 54 B2 1
Quantock Pl PLEE/EAS SR8 207 F2
Quarry Bank ELS/FEN NE4 80 A3 14
Quarryfield Rd GATE NE8 3 H6
Quarryheads La DHAM DH1 194 A6
Quarry House La DHAM DH1 193 E5
HLH DH5 170 C6
Quarry La HAR/WTLS NE34 89 F3
HAR/WTLS NE34 90 C2 1
Quarry Rd BW/LEM/TK/HW NE15 76 B2 7
HEBB NE31 85 D3
STLY/ANP DH9 148 B1
SUNDSW SR3 161 D1 3
Quarry Rw FELL NE10 100 C1 7
Quarry St SUNDSW SR3 160 C1
Quay Rd BLYTH NE24 11 E4 5
Quayside BLYTH NE24 11 E4 6
BYK/HTN/WLK NE6 82 A4
CNUT NE1 3 F5
The Quay HLH DH5 185 F1
Quay Vw WLSD/HOW NE28 68 B4
Queen Alexandra Rd
ASHBK/HED/RY SR2 145 D4
NSHW NE29 54 B5
SEA/MUR SR7 176 C4
SUNDSW SR3 144 A3
Queen Alexandra Rd West
NSHW NE29 54 A5
Queen Elizabeth Av
LWF/SPW/WRK NE9 100 A5
Queen Elizabeth Dr HLH DH5 186 C4
Queens Av CLDN/WHIT/ROK SR6 109 D5
Queensberry St
MLFD/PNYW SR4 126 A5 13
Queensbridge LGB/KIL NE12 48 B5 2
Queensbury Dr
WD/WHPE/BLK NE5 59 D4
Queensbury Rd SEA/MUR SR7 175 F3
Queen's Ct BW/LEM/TK/HW NE15 58 C5
GATE NE8 98 B1 2
GOS/KPK NE3 47 E2 1
Queen's Crs HEBB NE31 84 C4
MLFD/PNYW SR4 143 F1
WLSD/HOW NE28 66 C3
Queen's Dr WBAY NE26 40 C5
WICK/BNPF NE16 96 A5
Queen's Gdns BLYTH NE24 10 B4
Queens Gv DHAM DH1 204 C1
Queensland Av HAR/WTLS NE34 87 D4
Queens La CNUT NE1 2 D5 2
Queensmere CLS/BIR/GTL DH3 153 E1
Queen's Rd BDLGTN NE22 8 C2
BW/LEM/TK/HW NE15 58 C5
CRAM NE23 35 D1
JES NE2 64 B5
SWCK/CAS SR5 126 A3 6
WBAY NE26 26 C2
WBAY NE26 40 B4
WD/WHPE/BLK NE5 60 C4
Queen's Ter JES NE2 64 B5
WLSD/HOW NE28 67 D4
Queen St ASHBK/HED/RY SR2 145 E6
CLSW/PEL DH2 150 C3
CNUT NE1 3 F5
GATE NE8 98 B2 2
HLH DH5 171 F5
SEA/MUR SR7 176 B3
SSH NE33 71 E3
SUND SR1 4 B1 1
TYNE/NSHE NE30 55 D6
Queen St East SUND SR1 5 F2 2
Queensway ELS/FEN NE4 61 F6
GOS/KPK NE3 47 D3
HLH DH5 171 E2 6
TYNE/NSHE NE30 55 F4
Queensway North DUN/TMV NE11 98 B3
Queen Victoria Rd CNUT NE1 2 C1
Queen Victoria St FELL NE10 101 E1
Quentin Av GOS/KPK NE3 61 F1
Quinn Cl PLEE/EAS SR8 208 C3
Qulton Cl WD/WHPE/BLK NE5 61 D2

R

Rabbit Banks Rd GATE NE8 80 C5
Raby Av PLEE/EAS SR8 201 D1
Raby Cl HLS DH4 169 F1 3
Raby Dr SUNDSW SR3 159 E1
Raby Gdns JRW NE32 86 A4
Raby Rd DHAM DH1 180 B5
WASHS NE38 137 E1
Raby St BYK/HTN/WLK NE6 82 B2
GATE NE8 99 E2
MLFD/PNYW SR4 126 A6
Raby Wy BYK/HTN/WLK NE6 82 B2
Rachel Cl ASHBK/HED/RY SR2 161 E1
Rackly Wy CLDN/WHIT/ROK SR6 109 E2
Radcliffe Pl WD/WHPE/BLK NE5 61 F4 10
Radcliffe Rd SWCK/CAS SR5 125 D2
Radcliffe St CLS/BIR/GTL DH3 136 B3
Radlett Rd SWCK/CAS SR5 124 C2
Radnor Gdns WLSD/HOW NE28 68 C3
Radnor St CNUT NE1 3 F1
Radstock Pl LGB/KIL NE12 49 E5 2
Rae Av WLSD/HOW NE28 67 D2
Raeburn Av WASHS NE38 139 D3
Raeburn Gdns
LWF/SPW/WRK NE9 100 A3
Raeburn Rd HAR/WTLS NE34 88 C6
SWCK/CAS SR5 124 B1 2
Raglan WASHS NE38 137 F1
Raglan Av ASHBK/HED/RY SR2 145 D3
Raglan Pl WICK/BNPF NE16 112 A6
Railway Cl DHAM DH1 197 D5
Railway Rw SUND SR1 126 A6
Railway St DUN/TMV NE11 79 E6
ELS/FEN NE4 80 A5
HEBB NE31 85 E1
HLH DH5 171 F6 4
HLS DH4 157 F6
JRW NE32 85 F1
STLY/ANP DH9 146 C5
STLY/ANP DH9 149 E6
SUND SR1 5 G3 1
Railway Ter ELS/FEN NE4 80 A5
NSHW NE29 70 C1 8
Raine Gv SUND SR1 5 F4
Rainford Av ASHBK/HED/RY SR2 145 D3
Rainhill Cl WASHN NE37 121 D3
Rainhill Rd WASHN NE37 121 D3
Rainton Cl FELL NE10 102 B4 2
Rainton Gv HLH DH5 171 D4 2
Rainton St HLS DH4 140 A6
MLFD/PNYW SR4 125 F6
SEA/MUR SR7 176 C4
Rainton Vw HLS DH4 183 E2
Rake La NSHW NE29 53 E3
Raleigh Cl SSH NE33 71 D6
Raleigh Rd SWCK/CAS SR5 124 C2
Raleigh Sq SWCK/CAS SR5 124 C2
Ralph Av ASHBK/HED/RY SR2 145 D6
Ralph St HEBB NE31 85 E1
Ramilies ASHBK/HED/RY SR2 161 F2
Ramillies Rd SWCK/CAS SR5 124 B1
The Ramparts
BW/LEM/TK/HW NE15 60 A6
Ramsay St BLAY NE21 94 A1 5
Ramsey Cl DHAM DH1 195 F4 1
PLEE/EAS SR8 200 C6
Ramsey St CLS/BIR/GTL DH3 153 E6
Ramsgate Rd SWCK/CAS SR5 125 D1
Ramside Vw DHAM DH1 196 C1 3
Randolph St JRW NE32 86 B1 3
Rangoon Rd SWCK/CAS SR5 124 B1 3
Ranmere Rd BW/LEM/TK/HW NE15 77 F3
Ranmore Cl CRAM NE23 22 A1
Rannoch Av CLSW/PEL DH2 166 A1
Rannoch Cl FELL NE10 102 B2
Rannoch Rd SWCK/CAS SR5 124 B1
Ranson Crs HAR/WTLS NE34 87 E3 1
Ranson St MLFD/PNYW SR4 143 F2

Raphael Av *HAR/WTLS* NE34 .... **88** B5
Rathmore Gdns *TYNE/NSHE* NE30 .... **54** C4
Ratho Ct *FELL* NE10 .... **101** D4
Ravenburn Gdns
BW/LEM/TK/HW NE15 .... **77** E2 1
Ravenna Rd *SWCK/CAS* SR5 .... **124** A1
Ravensbourne Av *BOL* NE36 .... **106** C2
Ravenscar Cl *WICK/BNPF* NE16 .... **95** D5 3
Ravenscourt Rd *SWCK/CAS* SR5 ...... **124** B2
Ravensdale Gv *BLYTH* NE24 .... **9** F5
Ravenshill Rd *WD/WHPE/BLK* NE5 .... **59** F5
Ravenside Rd *ELS/FEN* NE4 .... **62** A6
Ravenstone *WASHN* NE37 .... **120** A5
Ravenswood Cl *LGB/KIL* NE12 .... **50** A4
Ravenswood Gdns
LWF/SPW/WRK NE9 .... **117** E1
Ravenswood Rd
BYK/HTN/WLK NE6 .... **65** E5
SWCK/CAS SR5 .... **124** B1
Ravenswood Sq *SWCK/CAS* SR5 ...... **124** A1
Ravensworh St *MLFD/PNYW* SR4 .... **126** A5
Ravensworth *ASHBK/HED/RY* SR2 .. **161** F2
Ravensworth Av *HLS* DH4 .... **169** E1
LWF/SPW/WRK NE9 .... **118** B2
Ravensworth Cl *WLSD/HOW* NE28 .... **68** B4
Ravensworth Ct *DUN/TMV* NE11 .. **97** F1 3
RDHAMSE DH6 .... **187** E5
Ravensworth Rd
CLS/BIR/GTL DH3 .... **136** A1
DUN/TMV NE11 .... **97** F2
Ravensworth St *WLSD/HOW* NE28 .... **68** B4
Ravensworth Ter *DHAM* DH1 ...... **194** C4 6
DUN/TMV NE11 .... **97** F2
ELS/FEN NE4 .... **80** A3 15
JRW NE32 .... **86** A5 4
SSH NE33 .... **88** B1
Rawdon Rd *SWCK/CAS* SR5 .... **125** D1
Rawling Rd *GATE* NE8 .... **99** D3
Rawlston Wy *WD/WHPE/BLK* NE5 .... **61** E3
Rawmarsh Rd *SWCK/CAS* SR5 ...... **124** B1 4
Raydale *SWCK/CAS* SR5 .... **125** D1 1
Raydale Av *WASHN* NE37 .... **120** A4
Raylees Gdns *DUN/TMV* NE11 ...... **97** F3 6
Rayleigh Dr *DIN/WO* NE13 .... **33** D3
Rayleigh Gv *GATE* NE8 .... **98** C3
Raynham Cl *CRAM* NE23 .... **21** E5
Readhead Av *SSH* NE33 .... **72** A5
Readhead Dr *BYK/HTN/WLK* NE6 ...... **83** E4
Readhead Rd *HAR/WTLS* NE34 .... **72** A6
Reading Rd *HAR/WTLS* NE34 .... **88** C1
SWCK/CAS SR5 .... **124** B1
Reading Sq *SWCK/CAS* SR5 .... **124** B1
Rea Pl *GOS/KPK* NE3 .... **62** C1 6
Reasby Gdns *RYTON* NE40 .... **74** A3
Reavley Av *BDLGTN* NE22 .... **9** D1
Reay Crs *BOLCOL* NE35 .... **106** A2
Reay Gdns *WD/WHPE/BLK* NE5 ...... **60** C4
Reay St *FELL* NE10 .... **84** A6
Rectory Bank *BOL* NE36 .... **105** F3 5
Rectory Ct *WICK/BNPF* NE16 .... **96** A3
Rectory Dr *JES* NE2 .... **64** A2
Rectory Gn *BOL* NE36 .... **105** E3 1
Rectory Gv *GOS/KPK* NE3 .... **63** F1
Rectory La *BLAY* NE21 .... **94** A1
WICK/BNPF NE16 .... **96** A4
Rectory Pl *GATE* NE8 .... **98** C1
Rectory Rd *FELL* NE10 .... **100** B3
GATE NE8 .... **99** D1
GOS/KPK NE3 .... **63** F2
HLH DH5 .... **185** F1 2
Rectory Rd East *FELL* NE10 .... **100** C3
Red Admiral Ct *DUN/TMV* NE11 .... **98** A3 2
Red Barnes *CNUT* NE1 .... **3** H3
Red Berry Wy *HAR/WTLS* NE34 .... **88** A4
Redburn Cl *HLS* DH4 .... **170** B2 1
Redburn Rd *WD/WHPE/BLK* NE5 ...... **60** B2
Redcar Rd *BYK/HTN/WLK* NE6 .... **65** F5
SWCK/CAS SR5 .... **125** D2
WLSD/HOW NE28 .... **68** C3
Redcar Sq *SWCK/CAS* SR5 .... **125** D2 1
Redcliffe Wy *WD/WHPE/BLK* NE5 .... **61** D3
Redditch Sq *SWCK/CAS* SR5 .... **124** C1 1
Rede Av *HEBB* NE31 .... **85** D2 2
Redemarsh *FELL* NE10 .... **101** F4 2
Redesdale Av *BLAY* NE21 .... **93** E2
GOS/KPK NE3 .... **62** C1
Redesdale Cl *LGB/KIL* NE12 .... **49** E4 1
Redesdale Gdns *DUN/TMV* NE11 ...... **97** E3
Redesdale Gv *NSHW* NE29 .... **53** E6
Redesdale Pl *BLYTH* NE24 .... **10** A5 4
Redesdale Rd *CLSW/PEL* DH2 .... **165** F1
NSHW NE29 .... **53** E6
SWCK/CAS SR5 .... **124** B1
Rede St *DUN/TMV* NE11 .... **98** B5
JRW NE32 .... **85** F3 1
Redewater Gdns
WICK/BNPF NE16 .... **95** F4 1
Redewater Rd *ELS/FEN* NE4 .... **62** A6
Red Firs *BDN/LAN/SAC* DH7 .... **203** D4
Redford Pl *LGB/KIL* NE12 .... **35** E5 4
Red Hall Dr *LGB/HTN* NE7 .... **65** F3
Redheugh Bridge Rd
ELS/FEN NE4 .... **80** B5 2
Redheugh Rd *MONK* NE25 .... **39** D5
Redhill *CLDN/WHIT/ROK* SR6 .... **109** D2
Redhill Dr *WICK/BNPF* NE16 .... **95** D6 1
Redhill Rd *SWCK/CAS* SR5 .... **124** C1
Redhills La *DHAM* DH1 .... **193** F4
Redhills Wy *HLH* DH5 .... **185** F2
Redhouse Cl *BDN/LAN/SAC* DH7 ...... **178** C2
Red House Dr *MONK* NE25 .... **39** E4
Red House Farm *BDLGTN* NE22 .... **6** B4
Red House Rd *HEBB* NE31 .... **85** E2
Redland Av *GOS/KPK* NE3 .... **45** F6
Red Lion La *WASHN* NE37 .... **120** B2
Redmires Cl *CLSW/PEL* DH2 .... **135** D5
Redmond Rd *SWCK/CAS* SR5 .... **125** D1
Redmond Sq *SWCK/CAS* SR5 .... **125** D1
Rednam Pl *WD/WHPE/BLK* NE5 .... **61** D4
Redruth Gdns
LWF/SPW/WRK NE9 .... **117** E2
Redruth Sq *SWCK/CAS* SR5 .... **124** C1 2
Redshank Cl *WASHS* NE38 .... **137** E4
Redshank Dr *BLYTH* NE24 .... **17** D2 5
Red Wk *LGB/HTN* NE7 .... **64** C4
Redwell Ct *HAR/WTLS* NE34 .... **90** B1 2
Redwell La *HAR/WTLS* NE34 .... **90** C1
Redwing Cl *WASHS* NE38 .... **137** E3
Redwood *BDN/LAN/SAC* DH7 .... **203** D4
Redwood Cl *HLH* DH5 .... **185** E1
LGB/KIL NE12 .... **35** E6 10
Reed Av *LGB/KIL* NE12 .... **35** E5
Reedham Ct *WD/WHPE/BLK* NE5 .. **61** D2 8
Reedling Ct *SWCK/CAS* SR5 .... **106** B6 1
Reedside *RYTON* NE40 .... **74** C3
Reedsmouth Pl
WD/WHPE/BLK NE5 .... **61** D6
Reed St *SSH* NE33 .... **71** D6
TYNE/NSHE NE30 .... **55** D6
Reedswood Crs *CRAM* NE23 .... **22** C3
Reestones Pl *GOS/KPK* NE3 .... **61** F1
Reeth Rd *SWCK/CAS* SR5 .... **124** C2
Reeth Sq *SWCK/CAS* SR5 .... **124** C2
Reeth Wy *BW/LEM/TK/HW* NE15 ...... **57** E5
Regal Rd *MLFD/PNYW* SR4 .... **125** F5
Regency Ct *SEA/MUR* SR7 .... **176** C3
Regency Dr *SUNDSW* SR3 .... **144** A6
WICK/BNPF NE16 .... **95** E4
Regency Gdns *NSHW* NE29 .... **54** A6
Regent Av *GOS/KPK* NE3 .... **63** D1
Regent Dr *WICK/BNPF* NE16 .... **95** E6
Regent Farm Rd *GOS/KPK* NE3 .... **46** C6
Regent Rd *ASHBK/HED/RY* SR2 .... **162** C3
GOS/KPK NE3 .... **63** E1
JRW NE32 .... **86** B2
WLSD/HOW NE28 .... **66** C3 5
Regents Ct *WLSD/HOW* NE28 .... **66** A2
Regents Dr *TYNE/NSHE* NE30 .... **55** E4
Regents Pk *WLSD/HOW* NE28 .... **66** A3
Regent St *BLYTH* NE24 .... **11** D4
HLH DH5 .... **171** F5
Regent Ter *ASHBK/HED/RY* SR2 ...... **145** E4
NSHW NE29 .... **54** A5
Reginald St *BOLCOL* NE35 .... **105** E2
GATE NE8 .... **100** A1
MLFD/PNYW SR4 .... **125** E5 11
Regina Sq *SWCK/CAS* SR5 .... **124** C1 3
Reid Av *WLSD/HOW* NE28 .... **67** D3
Reid Park Cl *JES* NE2 .... **64** B4 4
Reid Park Rd *JES* NE2 .... **64** B4
Reid's La *CRAM* NE23 .... **36** A1
Reigate Sq *CRAM* NE23 .... **22** A1
Rekendyke La *SSH* NE33 .... **71** D5
Relley Cl *BDN/LAN/SAC* DH7 .... **192** A5 2
Relly Pth *DHAM* DH1 .... **193** F6
Relton Av *BYK/HTN/WLK* NE6 .... **82** C4
Relton Cl *HLS* DH4 .... **169** F3
Relton Ter *CLS/BIR/GTL* DH3 .... **153** E6
MONK NE25 .... **40** A5
Rembrandt Av *HAR/WTLS* NE34 .... **88** B6
Remus Cl *DIN/WO* NE13 .... **33** D5 6
Rendel St *DUN/TMV* NE11 .... **97** E1
Rendle Rd *BYK/HTN/WLK* NE6 .... **84** A4
Renforth St *DUN/TMV* NE11 .... **97** E2
Renfrew Cl *NSHW* NE29 .... **53** E4
Renfrew Rd *SWCK/CAS* SR5 .... **124** C1
Rennie Rd *SWCK/CAS* SR5 .... **124** A1
Rennie Sq *SWCK/CAS* SR5 .... **124** A1 1
Rennington *FELL* NE10 .... **101** E5
Rennington Av *TYNE/NSHE* NE30 ...... **55** E3
Rennington Pl
WD/WHPE/BLK NE5 .... **61** F5 8
Renny's La *DHAM* DH1 .... **195** F4
Renny St *DHAM* DH1 .... **195** D4 4
Renoir Gdns *HAR/WTLS* NE34 .... **88** C6
Renwick Av *GOS/KPK* NE3 .... **46** A6
Renwick Rd *BLYTH* NE24 .... **10** C5
Renwick St *BYK/HTN/WLK* NE6 .... **82** C2
Resida Cl *BW/LEM/TK/HW* NE15 .... **59** E6 6
Retford Rd *SWCK/CAS* SR5 .... **124** C1
Retford Sq *SWCK/CAS* SR5 .... **124** C1
The Retreat
ASHBK/HED/RY SR2 .... **126** A6 9
Revell Ter *WD/WHPE/BLK* NE5 ...... **62** A5 3
Revelstoke Rd *SWCK/CAS* SR5 .... **124** A1
Revesby St *SSH* NE33 .... **88** B2 3
Reynolds Av *HAR/WTLS* NE34 .... **88** C5
LGB/KIL NE12 .... **49** D2
WASHS NE38 .... **139** D2
Reynolds Cl *STLY/ANP* DH9 .... **148** B2
Rheims Ct *MLFD/PNYW* SR4 .... **124** C5
Rheydt Av *WLSD/HOW* NE28 .... **66** B4
Rhodesia Rd *SWCK/CAS* SR5 .... **124** C1
Rhodes St *BYK/HTN/WLK* NE6 .... **83** F3
Rhondda Rd *SWCK/CAS* SR5 .... **124** A1
Rhuddlan Ct *WD/WHPE/BLK* NE5 .. **61** D2 9
Rhyl Sq *SWCK/CAS* SR5 .... **125** D1
Ribbledale Gdns *LGB/HTN* NE7 ...... **65** D3 2
Ribble Rd *SWCK/CAS* SR5 .... **124** B2 3
Ribblesdale *HLS* DH4 .... **157** D1
WLSD/HOW NE28 .... **66** B2 1
Ribblesdale Av *BLYTH* NE24 .... **9** F4 4
Richard Av *MLFD/PNYW* SR4 .... **143** F2
Richard Browell Rd
BW/LEM/TK/HW NE15 .... **57** F5
Richardson Av *HAR/WTLS* NE34 .... **87** E4 1
Richardson Rd *JES* NE2 .... **80** A1
Richardson St
BYK/HTN/WLK NE6 .... **65** E6 4
WLSD/HOW NE28 .... **67** E4
Richardson Ter
ASHBK/HED/RY SR2 .... **162** C2
Richard St *BLYTH* NE24 .... **11** D5
HLH DH5 .... **185** F1
Richmond *ASHBK/HED/RY* SR2 .... **161** E1
Richmond Av *FELL* NE10 .... **102** B1
WASHS NE38 .... **120** C6
WICK/BNPF NE16 .... **96** A1
Richmond Cl *BDLGTN* NE22 .... **7** D2
Richmond Ct *GATE* NE8 .... **99** E1 10
Richmond Gdns *WLSD/HOW* NE28 .... **68** A3
Richmond Gv *NSHW* NE29 .... **70** A1
Richmond Ms *GOS/KPK* NE3 .... **63** D3 1
Richmond Pk *WLSD/HOW* NE28 .... **66** B3 3
Richmond Rd *DHAM* DH1 .... **180** C5
HAR/WTLS NE34 .... **88** B2
Richmond St *SWCK/CAS* SR5 .... **126** B4
Richmond Ter *WBAY* NE26 .... **40** B3
Richmond Wy *CRAM* NE23 .... **21** F5 5
Rickgarth *FELL* NE10 .... **101** E5
Rickleton Av *CLS/BIR/GTL* DH3 .... **153** F3
Rickleton Wy *WASHS* NE38 .... **137** E5
Riddell Av *BW/LEM/TK/HW* NE15 ...... **78** B3
Riddings Rd *SWCK/CAS* SR5 .... **124** C1
Riddings Sq *SWCK/CAS* SR5 .... **124** C1 4
Ridgely Dr *PONT/DH* NE20 .... **28** C4
Ridge Ter *BDLGTN* NE22 .... **7** D3
The Ridge *RYTON* NE40 .... **74** B4
Ridgeway *ASHBK/HED/RY* SR2 .... **161** E2
ELS/FEN NE4 .... **62** A6
FELL NE10 .... **102** A4
Ridge Wy *MONK* NE25 .... **38** A1
Ridgeway Crs *SUNDSW* SR3 .... **144** A3
The Ridge Wy *GOS/KPK* NE3 .... **62** B2
The Ridgeway *HAR/WTLS* NE34 .... **89** E5
Ridgewood Crs *GOS/KPK* NE3 .... **64** B1
Ridgewood Gdns *GOS/KPK* NE3 ...... **64** A1 6
Ridgewood Vls *GOS/KPK* NE3 .... **64** A1 7
Riding Hill Rd *STLY/ANP* DH9 .... **146** B3
Riding La *DUN/TMV* NE11 .... **134** A2
Riding Lea *BLAY* NE21 .... **93** F1
The Ridings *MONK* NE25 .... **39** E4
The Riding *GOS/KPK* NE3 .... **62** A3
Ridley Av *ASHBK/HED/RY* SR2 .... **162** B1
BLYTH NE24 .... **11** E5
WLSD/HOW NE28 .... **68** C2
Ridley Cl *GOS/KPK* NE3 .... **46** B4 4
Ridley Gdns *WICK/BNPF* NE16 .... **95** F1 8
Ridley Gv *HAR/WTLS* NE34 .... **89** F1
Ridley Pl *CNUT* NE1 .... **2** D1
Ridley St *BLYTH* NE24 .... **11** E4 7
GATE NE8 .... **98** C2 6
STLY/ANP DH9 .... **148** B1
SWCK/CAS SR5 .... **126** A2 10
Ridley Ter *ASHBK/HED/RY* SR2 .... **5** G6
Ridsdale Av *WD/WHPE/BLK* NE5 ...... **59** F5
Ridsdale Cl *MONK* NE25 .... **24** B5
WLSD/HOW NE28 .... **67** E2
Ridsdale Ct *GATE* NE8 .... **98** C1 7
Rievaulx *WASHS* NE38 .... **138** B3
Riga Sq *SWCK/CAS* SR5 .... **124** B1
The Riggs *HLH* DH5 .... **171** E2
Rignall *WASHS* NE38 .... **139** F1
Riley St *JRW* NE32 .... **85** F1
Ringmore Ct
ASHBK/HED/RY SR2 .... **144** B4 5
Ringway *SWCK/CAS* SR5 .... **123** F4
Ringwood Dr *CRAM* NE23 .... **22** A1 1
Ringwood Gn *LGB/KIL* NE12 .... **49** E5 3
Ringwood Rd *SWCK/CAS* SR5 .... **124** C1
Ringwood Sq *SWCK/CAS* SR5 ...... **124** C1 5
Rink St *BLYTH* NE24 .... **11** E4
Ripley Av *NSHW* NE29 .... **70** A2
Ripley Cl *BDLGTN* NE22 .... **6** C2
Ripley Dr *CRAM* NE23 .... **21** E5
Ripley Ter *BYK/HTN/WLK* NE6 .... **83** D2
Ripon Cl *CRAM* NE23 .... **21** E5
Ripon Ct *BDN/LAN/SAC* DH7 .... **178** A1
Ripon Gdns *JES* NE2 .... **64** C6
WLSD/HOW NE28 .... **68** A3
Ripon Rd *DHAM* DH1 .... **180** C4 3
Ripon St *CLDN/WHIT/ROK* SR6 .... **127** D3
GATE NE8 .... **99** D1
Ripon Ter *SEA/MUR* SR7 .... **188** B1
The Rise *BLAY* NE21 .... **75** F4

GOS/KPK NE3 .... 62 A2
WBAY NE26 .... 26 C4
Rishton Sq SWCK/CAS SR5 .... 124 B1 5
Ritson Cl NSHW NE29 .... 54 A5
Ritson St CLDN/WHIT/ROK SR6 .... 109 D6
STLY/ANP DH9 .... 148 A2 1
Riverbank Rd SWCK/CAS SR5 .... 124 C2
Riverdale SWCK/CAS SR5 .... 124 A4
River Dr SSH NE33 .... 71 E2
River La RYTON NE40 .... 74 B2
Rivermead Wy WASHS NE38 .... 139 D5 3
Riversdale Wy
BW/LEM/TK/HW NE15 .... 76 A2
Riverside PONT/DH NE20 .... 28 A4
Riverside Ct DUN/TMV NE11 .... 97 F1 4
SSH NE33 .... 71 D4 3
Riverside Pk MLFD/PNYW SR4 .... 124 A5
Riverside Rd SWCK/CAS SR5 .... 125 D2
Riverside Wy BLAY NE21 .... 77 F5
ROWG NE39 .... 110 C4
WICK/BNPF NE16 .... 77 F5
River Vw BLAY NE21 .... 76 A6
TYNE/NSHE NE30 .... 55 E6
River View Cl BDLGTN NE22 .... 8 C3
Roachburn Rd WD/WHPE/BLK NE5 .. 60 A4
Robert Owen Gdns FELL NE10 .... 100 B3
Robertson Rd SWCK/CAS SR5 .... 124 A1
Robertson Sq SWCK/CAS SR5 .... 124 A2 2
Robert Sq SEA/MUR SR7 .... 177 D4
Roberts St BW/LEM/TK/HW NE15 .... 77 F4
Roberts Ter JRW NE32 .... 86 A3
Robert St MLFD/PNYW SR4 .... 125 F5
SEA/MUR SR7 .... 177 D4 1
SSH NE33 .... 71 F5
SUNDSW SR3 .... 161 D1
Robert Ter STLY/ANP DH9 .... 131 E6 5
Robert Westall Wy NSHW NE29 .... 70 C3
Robin Ct HLH DH5 .... 184 B1
Robin Gv SWCK/CAS SR5 .... 124 B3 6
Robin La HLH DH5 .... 184 A2
Robinson Gdns
CLDN/WHIT/ROK SR6 .... 109 E1 3
WLSD/HOW NE28 .... 68 C3
Robinson St BYK/HTN/WLK NE6 .... 82 B2 7
SSH NE33 .... 71 F5 9
Robinson Ter ASHBK/HED/RY SR2 .. 145 E2
SUNDSW SR3 .... 161 D1
Robsheugh Pl WD/WHPE/BLK NE5 .. 61 E6
Robson Av PLEE/EAS SR8 .... 208 C1
Robson Pl ASHBK/HED/RY SR2 .... 162 C2
Robson St BYK/HTN/WLK NE6 .... 81 F2
LWF/SPW/WRK NE9 .... 99 E5
Rochdale Rd SWCK/CAS SR5 .... 124 C1
Rochdale St HLH DH5 .... 185 F2
WLSD/HOW NE28 .... 66 C5 5
Rochdale Wy SWCK/CAS SR5 .... 124 C1 6
Roche Ct WASHS NE38 .... 138 B2
Rochester Gdns DUN/TMV NE11 .... 97 F2
Rochester Rd DHAM DH1 .... 180 C5
Rochester St BYK/HTN/WLK NE6 .... 83 F3
Rochford Gv CRAM NE23 .... 21 E6
Rochford Rd SWCK/CAS SR5 .... 124 B1 6
Rockcliffe SSH NE33 .... 72 B5
Rockcliffe Gdns
BW/LEM/TK/HW NE15 .... 77 E1 7
Rockcliffe St WBAY NE26 .... 41 E5
Rockcliffe Wy
LWF/SPW/WRK NE9 .... 118 B2
Rocket Wy LGB/KIL NE12 .... 50 B4
Rock Gv LWF/SPW/WRK NE9 .... 99 E5 8
Rockhope WASHS NE38 .... 137 E6
Rockingham Rd SWCK/CAS SR5 .... 124 B1
Rockingham Sq SWCK/CAS SR5 .. 124 B1 7
Rock Lodge Rd
CLDN/WHIT/ROK SR6 .... 127 D1
Rockmore Rd BLAY NE21 .... 94 B1
Rock Ter JES NE2 .... 3 G1
Rockville CLDN/WHIT/ROK SR6 .... 109 D6 6
Rodin Av HAR/WTLS NE34 .... 88 C6
Rodney Cl ASHBK/HED/RY SR2 .... 161 E2 1
TYNE/NSHE NE30 .... 55 F5
Rodney St BYK/HTN/WLK NE6 .... 82 A3
Rodney Wy WBAY NE26 .... 39 F3
Rodsley Av GATE NE8 .... 99 D2
Roeburn Wy GOS/KPK NE3 .... 62 B3
Roedean Rd SWCK/CAS SR5 .... 125 D1
Roehedge FELL NE10 .... 102 A4 4
Rogers Cl PLEE/EAS SR8 .... 209 F2 2
Rogerson Ter WD/WHPE/BLK NE5 .... 60 A3
Roger St BYK/HTN/WLK NE6 .... 82 A2
Rokeby Av BW/LEM/TK/HW NE15 .... 76 C2
Rokeby Dr GOS/KPK NE3 .... 62 B2
Rokeby Sq DHAM DH1 .... 204 C1 4
Rokeby St BW/LEM/TK/HW NE15 .... 76 C2
MLFD/PNYW SR4 .... 126 A6
Rokeby Ter BYK/HTN/WLK NE6 .... 65 E5 3
Rokeby Vw LWF/SPW/WRK NE9 .... 117 F3
Roker Av CLDN/WHIT/ROK SR6 .... 126 C4
MONK NE25 .... 54 A1
Roker Baths Rd
CLDN/WHIT/ROK SR6 .... 127 D2
Rokerby Av WICK/BNPF NE16 .... 96 B4
Roker Park Rd
CLDN/WHIT/ROK SR6 .... 127 D2
Roker Park Ter
CLDN/WHIT/ROK SR6 .... 127 E2
Roker Ter CLDN/WHIT/ROK SR6 .... 127 E1
Roland Rd WLSD/HOW NE28 .... 68 A4
Rollesby Ct WD/WHPE/BLK NE5 .. 61 D2 10
Rolling Mill Rd JRW NE32 .... 68 C6
Romaldskirk Cl
MLFD/PNYW SR4 .... 142 A1 3
Roman Av BYK/HTN/WLK NE6 .... 83 D1
CLS/BIR/GTL DH3 .... 153 F5
Roman Rd SSH NE33 .... 71 F2
Roman Rd North SSH NE33 .... 71 E2 4
The Roman Wy
WD/WHPE/BLK NE5 .... 59 F5
Romford Cl CRAM NE23 .... 21 F5 6
Romford Pl LWF/SPW/WRK NE9 .... 99 F3
Romford St MLFD/PNYW SR4 .... 125 E6 6
Romilly St SSH NE33 .... 71 F4
Romley Gv FELL NE10 .... 102 C3 2
Romney Av ASHBK/HED/RY SR2 .. 145 D3 1
HAR/WTLS NE34 .... 88 C5 1
WASHS NE38 .... 139 D2
Romney Cl HLS DH4 .... 157 E3
Romney Dr DHAM DH1 .... 196 C1
Romney Gdns
LWF/SPW/WRK NE9 .... 100 A3
Romsey Cl CRAM NE23 .... 22 A1
Romsey Dr BOLCOL NE35 .... 105 D1 4
Romsey Gv BW/LEM/TK/HW NE15 .... 59 E6
Ronald Dr BW/LEM/TK/HW NE15 .... 77 F2
Ronald Gdns HEBB NE31 .... 84 C4
Ronaldsay Cl
ASHBK/HED/RY SR2 .... 145 D6 1
Ronald Sq
CLDN/WHIT/ROK SR6 .... 126 C1 15
Rookery Cl BLYTH NE24 .... 10 A5
Rookery La WICK/BNPF NE16 .... 95 D6 2
Rookswood Gdns ROWG NE39 .... 111 D1
Rookwood Dr DIN/WO NE13 .... 33 E2
Rookwood Rd WD/WHPE/BLK NE5 .. 60 C6
Roosevelt Rd DHAM DH1 .... 195 E3
Ropery La CLS/BIR/GTL DH3 .... 153 F6
CLS/BIR/GTL DH3 .... 154 C6
HEBB NE31 .... 84 C2 3
WLSD/HOW NE28 .... 68 A4
Ropery Rd GATE NE8 .... 98 A1
MLFD/PNYW SR4 .... 125 F4
The Ropery BYK/HTN/WLK NE6 .... 82 C4
Ropery Wk SEA/MUR SR7 .... 177 D4 2
Rosalie Ter ASHBK/HED/RY SR2 .... 145 D2
Rosalind Av BDLGTN NE22 .... 7 F4
Rosamond Pl BLYTH NE24 .... 11 E5 7
Rosa St SSH NE33 .... 71 F4
Rose Av HLS DH4 .... 169 E1
STLY/ANP DH9 .... 147 F3
WICK/BNPF NE16 .... 96 A3
Rosebank Cl
ASHBK/HED/RY SR2 .... 145 D6 2
Rosebay Rd BDN/LAN/SAC DH7 .... 204 A4
Roseberry Gra LGB/KIL NE12 .... 50 C3 1
Roseberry St STLY/ANP DH9 .... 149 F1
Roseberry Vls CLSW/PEL DH2 .... 151 E3
Rosebery Av BLYTH NE24 .... 10 C5 2
GATE NE8 .... 99 F2 12
NSHW NE29 .... 54 B4
SSH NE33 .... 72 A5
Rosebery Crs JES NE2 .... 64 C6
Rosebery Pl JES NE2 .... 64 C6
Rosebery St SWCK/CAS SR5 .... 126 C3 7
Roseby Rd PLEE/EAS SR8 .... 209 E1
Rose Ct PLEE/EAS SR8 .... 208 A5
Rose Crs BDN/LAN/SAC DH7 .... 178 C1
CLDN/WHIT/ROK SR6 .... 91 E6
Rosedale BDLGTN NE22 .... 7 D3
WLSD/HOW NE28 .... 66 B2
Rosedale Av CLDN/WHIT/ROK SR6 .. 109 D4
Rosedale Ct WD/WHPE/BLK NE5 .... 59 F5
Rosedale Crs HLS DH4 .... 157 E6 3
Rosedale Rd DHAM DH1 .... 196 C2
Rosedale St HLH DH5 .... 185 D3
SUND SR1 .... 126 A6
Rosedale Ter
CLDN/WHIT/ROK SR6 .... 109 D6
JES NE2 .... 81 E1
PLEE/EAS SR8 .... 209 E1
TYNE/NSHE NE30 .... 55 D5 2
Roseden Ct LGB/KIL NE12 .... 49 E5 4
Rosedene Vls CRAM NE23 .... 22 C2
Rose Gdns WLSD/HOW NE28 .... 67 D2
Rosegill WASHN NE37 .... 120 A6
Rosehill WLSD/HOW NE28 .... 68 A4
Rosehill Rd WLSD/HOW NE28 .... 68 B4
Rose Hill Wy WD/WHPE/BLK NE5 .... 61 E5
Rose Lea BDN/LAN/SAC DH7 .... 178 A3
Roselea Av ASHBK/HED/RY SR2 .... 162 B1
Rosemary La PLEE/EAS SR8 .... 200 A2
Rosemary Rd SWCK/CAS SR5 .... 124 C1
Rosemary Ter BLYTH NE24 .... 11 E6
Rosemount DHAM DH1 .... 180 C4
MLFD/PNYW SR4 .... 141 F1
WD/WHPE/BLK NE5 .... 60 B4
Rosemount Cl WASHN NE37 .... 120 B2 6
Rosemount Ct BOL NE36 .... 106 A3 3
Rosemount Wy LGB/HTN NE7 .... 65 E1 6
MONK NE25 .... 39 E5
Rose St GATE NE8 .... 80 B6
HEBB NE31 .... 84 C3
MLFD/PNYW SR4 .... 126 A5
Rose St West HLS DH4 .... 140 A6
Rose Ter WD/WHPE/BLK NE5 .... 62 A5
Roseville St MLFD/PNYW SR4 .... 144 A1 11
Rosewell Pl WICK/BNPF NE16 .... 95 F6
Rosewood LGB/KIL NE12 .... 50 B1 9
Rosewood Av GOS/KPK NE3 .... 47 F6
Rosewood Crs BYK/HTN/WLK NE6 .... 66 B5
WBAY NE26 .... 26 C4
Rosewood Gdns GOS/KPK NE3 .... 62 B2
LWF/SPW/WRK NE9 .... 100 A4
Rosewood Sq MLFD/PNYW SR4 .. 141 F4 1
Rosewood Ter WLSD/HOW NE28 .. 68 C4 2
Roseworth Av GOS/KPK NE3 .... 63 E2 3
Roseworth Crs GOS/KPK NE3 .... 63 E3
Roslin Pk BDLGTN NE22 .... 8 B3
Roslin Wy CRAM NE23 .... 21 F5 7
Ross CLSW/PEL DH2 .... 135 F4
Ross Av DUN/TMV NE11 .... 97 E1
Rosse Cl WASHN NE37 .... 120 A4
Rossendale Pl LGB/KIL NE12 .... 48 B5 3
Ross Gv CRAM NE23 .... 21 E1
Ross Lea HLS DH4 .... 156 C4
Rosslyn Av ASHBK/HED/RY SR2 .... 162 B1
GOS/KPK NE3 .... 62 A1
Rosslyn St MLFD/PNYW SR4 .... 125 F6
Ross St SWCK/CAS SR5 .... 126 B3 7
Ross Wy GOS/KPK NE3 .... 46 B4
WBAY NE26 .... 40 A3
Rosyth Rd SWCK/CAS SR5 .... 125 D1
Rosyth Sq SWCK/CAS SR5 .... 125 D1
Rotary Wy BLYTH NE24 .... 17 E2
NSHW NE29 .... 70 A3
Rothay Pl WD/WHPE/BLK NE5 .... 61 E4 2
Rothbury ASHBK/HED/RY SR2 .... 161 F2
Rothbury Av BLYTH NE24 .... 10 A6
FELL NE10 .... 101 F1
GOS/KPK NE3 .... 47 D6
JRW NE32 .... 85 E4
PLEE/EAS SR8 .... 201 E6
Rothbury Cl CLSW/PEL DH2 .... 165 F1
LGB/KIL NE12 .... 35 E6 11
Rothbury Gdns DUN/TMV NE11 .... 97 F5
WLSD/HOW NE28 .... 68 B3
Rothbury Rd DHAM DH1 .... 180 B5
SWCK/CAS SR5 .... 124 C1
Rothbury Ter BYK/HTN/WLK NE6 .... 65 D6
NSHW NE29 .... 69 E2
Rotherfield Cl CRAM NE23 .... 22 A1
Rotherfield Gdns
LWF/SPW/WRK NE9 .... 117 F2 1
Rotherfield Rd SWCK/CAS SR5 .... 124 B1
Rotherfield Sq SWCK/CAS SR5 .... 124 B1 8
Rotherham Cl HLH DH5 .... 170 C4 2
Rotherham Rd SWCK/CAS SR5 .... 124 B1
Rothley WASHS NE38 .... 139 E4
Rothley Av WD/WHPE/BLK NE5 .... 78 B1
Rothley Cl GOS/KPK NE3 .... 63 F1 3
Rothley Ct SWCK/CAS SR5 .... 107 E6 2
Rothley Gdns TYNE/NSHE NE30 .... 54 C2
Rothley Gv MONK NE25 .... 24 B5 2
Rothley Wy WBAY NE26 .... 40 A3
Rothsay CLSW/PEL DH2 .... 135 E5
Rothwell Rd GOS/KPK NE3 .... 63 E1
SWCK/CAS SR5 .... 124 B1
Roundhill Av WD/WHPE/BLK NE5 .. 61 E4 3
The Roundway LGB/KIL NE12 .... 49 D5 4
Rowan Av WASHS NE38 .... 138 B5
Rowanberry Rd LGB/KIL NE12 .... 49 D6
Rowan Cl BDLGTN NE22 .... 7 E2
MLFD/PNYW SR4 .... 142 A1
Rowan Ct BLYTH NE24 .... 10 C6 5
Rowan Dr DHAM DH1 .... 181 D4
GOS/KPK NE3 .... 46 A6
HLH DH5 .... 171 E6
PONT/DH NE20 .... 28 A3
Rowan Lea BDN/LAN/SAC DH7 .... 203 D4
Rowan Tree Av DHAM DH1 .... 195 F2
Rowantree Rd BYK/HTN/WLK NE6 .... 66 C5
Rowanwood Gdns DUN/TMV NE11 .. 97 F5
Rowell Cl SUNDSW SR3 .... 161 E2
Rowes Ms BYK/HTN/WLK NE6 .... 82 B4 4
Rowlandson Crs FELL NE10 .... 100 C2
Rowland Sq SEA/MUR SR7 .... 188 A1
Rowley Cl BDN/LAN/SAC DH7 .... 202 A1
Rowley Dr BDN/LAN/SAC DH7 .... 192 A5
Rowley St BLYTH NE24 .... 11 D5
Rowntree Wy NSHW NE29 .... 70 C3
Rowsley Rd JRW NE32 .... 86 B3 3
Roxburgh Cl BLAY NE21 .... 93 F2
Roxburgh Pl BYK/HTN/WLK NE6 .. 82 A1 3
Roxburgh St CLDN/WHIT/ROK SR6 .. 126 C2
Roxburgh Ter WBAY NE26 .... 40 C5
Roxby Gdns NSHW NE29 .... 70 A1
Royal Crs ELS/FEN NE4 .... 62 A6
Royal Rd STLY/ANP DH9 .... 148 A1
The Royalty
ASHBK/HED/RY SR2 .... 126 A6 10
Roydon Av ASHBK/HED/RY SR2 .. 145 D3 2
Royle St ASHBK/HED/RY SR2 .... 145 E4
Royston Ter BYK/HTN/WLK NE6 .... 83 F4 9
Ruabon Cl CRAM NE23 .... 21 F5
Rubens Av HAR/WTLS NE34 .... 88 C5

Ruby St HLS DH4 157 F6
Rudby Cl GOS/KPK NE3 47 F4
Rudchester Pl WD/WHPE/BLK NE5 61 E6
Rudyard Av
ASHBK/HED/RY SR2 145 D3 3
Rudyerd St NSHW NE29 70 C1 9
Rugby Gdns LWF/SPW/WRK NE9 118 C1
Ruislip Pl CRAM NE23 21 E5
Ruislip Rd MLFD/PNYW SR4 141 F1
Runcorn ASHBK/HED/RY SR2 161 E1
Runcorn Rd SWCK/CAS SR5 124 B1
Runhead Est RYTON NE40 74 C3
Runnymede
ASHBK/HED/RY SR2 161 F1 1
Runnymede Rd SWCK/CAS SR5 124 C1
WICK/BNPF NE16 95 F4
Runnymede Wy GOS/KPK NE3 62 A2 2
SWCK/CAS SR5 124 C1
Runswick Av LGB/KIL NE12 48 B6
Runswick Cl SUNDSW SR3 161 E1
Rupert Sq SWCK/CAS SR5 125 D1
Rupert St CLDN/WHIT/ROK SR6 109 E1
Rushall Pl LGB/KIL NE12 49 D6
Rushey Gill BDN/LAN/SAC DH7 202 C4 3
Rushford ASHBK/HED/RY SR2 161 F1
Rushie Av BW/LEM/TK/HW NE15 78 B3
Rushley Crs BLAY NE21 76 B5
Rushsyde Cl WICK/BNPF NE16 95 D5
Rushton Av
ASHBK/HED/RY SR2 145 D3 4
Rushyrig WASHN NE37 119 F6
Ruskin Av CLSW/PEL DH2 152 A5
DUN/TMV NE11 97 E1 6
HLH DH5 186 B4
LGB/KIL NE12 49 F3 1
Ruskin Cl STLY/ANP DH9 149 D2
Ruskin Crs HAR/WTLS NE34 88 A5
Ruskin Dr BOLCOL NE35 105 F2
LGB/HTN NE7 66 A4
Ruskin Rd CLS/BIR/GTL DH3 136 B2 3
LWF/SPW/WRK NE9 100 A3
WICK/BNPF NE16 95 F2
Russell Av HAR/WTLS NE34 89 F2
Russell Sq DIN/WO NE13 33 E2
Russell St JRW NE32 86 B1
NSHW NE29 70 C1
SSH NE33 71 E3 6
SUND SR1 5 E1
Russell Ter BDLGTN NE22 7 E4
JES NE2 3 G2 3
Ruswarp Dr SUNDSW SR3 161 D2
Rutherford Av SEA/MUR SR7 175 E2
Rutherford Rd SWCK/CAS SR5 124 A1
WASHN NE37 121 D3
Rutherford Sq SWCK/CAS SR5 124 A1
Rutherford St BLYTH NE24 11 D6 6
CNUT NE1 2 B4 2
WLSD/HOW NE28 69 D3
Rutherglen Rd SWCK/CAS SR5 125 D1
Rutland Av BYK/HTN/WLK NE6 83 F1
SUNDSW SR3 160 B1
Rutland Pl NSHW NE29 54 A6 1
WASHN NE37 120 C2 2
Rutland Rd HEBB NE31 85 E5
WLSD/HOW NE28 66 C5
Rutland Sq CLS/BIR/GTL DH3 136 A1
Rutland St HAR/WTLS NE34 88 A2 2
MLFD/PNYW SR4 125 E5
Ryal Cl BLYTH NE24 10 A5
MONK NE25 24 C5
Ryal Ter BYK/HTN/WLK NE6 83 E3
Rydal FELL NE10 101 F2 4
Rydal Av HLH DH5 186 B4
STLY/ANP DH9 147 F4
TYNE/NSHE NE30 54 C2
Rydal Cl BDN/LAN/SAC DH7 178 A1
BOL NE36 106 B2
LGB/KIL NE12 50 B1
Rydal Crs BLAY NE21 94 A2
PLEE/EAS SR8 209 D2
Rydal Gdns HAR/WTLS NE34 89 D2
Rydal Mt PLEE/EAS SR8 200 C2
SWCK/CAS SR5 123 F4
SWCK/CAS SR5 126 B1
Rydal Rd BW/LEM/TK/HW NE15 59 F6
CLSW/PEL DH2 166 A1
GOS/KPK NE3 63 F1
Rydal St GATE NE8 99 D1
Ryde Pl CRAM NE23 22 A1
Rye Cl BW/LEM/TK/HW NE15 58 A5 3
Ryedale CLDN/WHIT/ROK SR6 109 E3
DHAM DH1 196 C3
WLSD/HOW NE28 66 B1
Rye Hl ELS/FEN NE4 80 A4
Ryehill Vw HLH DH5 170 B6
Ryelands Wy DHAM DH1 180 B4
Ryemount Rd ASHBK/HED/RY SR2 161 F1
Rye View Rd ASHBK/HED/RY SR2 145 E6
Ryhope Gdns LWF/SPW/WRK NE9 118 C1
Ryhope Rd ASHBK/HED/RY SR2 145 E5
Ryhope St ASHBK/HED/RY SR2 162 A1
HLH DH5 171 E2
Rymers Cl PLEE/EAS SR8 199 F3
Ryton Ct SSH NE33 71 F5
Ryton Crs SEA/MUR SR7 175 F3
STLY/ANP DH9 131 E6 6
Ryton Hall Dr RYTON NE40 74 B2 5
Ryton Ter BYK/HTN/WLK NE6 83 E4

S

Sackville Rd BYK/HTN/WLK NE6 65 E5
SUNDSW SR3 143 D3
Sacriston Av SUNDSW SR3 143 E3 3
Saddleback WASHN NE37 120 A4
Saddler St DHAM DH1 194 B4
Saffron Pl BYK/HTN/WLK NE6 83 F3 5
Sage Cl BW/LEM/TK/HW NE15 59 E6 7
St Aidan's Av ASHBK/HED/RY SR2 145 E5
DHAM DH1 193 F1
LGB/KIL NE12 51 E3
St Aidan's Cl NSHW NE29 53 F4 1
St Aidan's Crs DHAM DH1 193 F4
STLY/ANP DH9 146 B5
St Aidan's Rd SSH NE33 71 F2
WLSD/HOW NE28 66 C5 6
St Aidan's St GATE NE8 98 C1 8
St Aidan's Ter HLS DH4 158 A2
St Alban's Cl CLS/BIR/GTL DH3 168 A3
St Alban's Crs BYK/HTN/WLK NE6 65 F4
St Alban's St ASHBK/HED/RY SR2 145 D3
St Alban's Ter GATE NE8 99 E1 11
St Albans Vw SMOOR NE27 52 A2
St Aldwyn Rd SEA/MUR SR7 176 A2
St Aloysius Vw HEBB NE31 84 C2
St Andrews HLS DH4 170 A2
St Andrews Av WASHN NE37 120 A4
St Andrew's Dr
LWF/SPW/WRK NE9 117 D1
St Andrew's Rd STLY/ANP DH9 131 E5
St Andrew's St CNUT NE1 2 B3
HEBB NE31 84 B1 5
St Andrew's Ter
CLDN/WHIT/ROK SR6 127 D2 3
St Ann's Cl CNUT NE1 81 F3
St Ann's St CNUT NE1 3 H4
St Anselm Crs NSHW NE29 53 E5
St Anselm Rd NSHW NE29 53 E5
St Anthony's Rd
BYK/HTN/WLK NE6 83 D4
St Asaph Cl LGB/HTN NE7 65 F2
St Aubyn's Wy STLY/ANP DH9 149 D1 1
St Austell Cl WD/WHPE/BLK NE5 61 E2 1
St Austell Gdns
LWF/SPW/WRK NE9 117 E2
St Barnabas HLS DH4 155 F5
St Barnabas Wy
ASHBK/HED/RY SR2 5 G6
St Bede's Cl DHAM DH1 193 F5
St Bede's Dr GATE NE8 81 E6 2
St Bedes Pl BLYTH NE24 16 A2
St Bedes Rd BLYTH NE24 16 A2 4
St Bedes Wy BDN/LAN/SAC DH7 204 A3 1
St Brandon's Gv
BDN/LAN/SAC DH7 202 C4
St Buryan Crs WD/WHPE/BLK NE5 61 E2
St Catherine's Ct SWCK/CAS SR5 124 C3
St Chad's Crs SUNDSW SR3 159 D1 1
St Chad's Rd SUNDSW SR3 159 D1
St Chad's Vls BOL NE36 106 C3 5
St Christopher's Rd SUNDSW SR3 143 F4
Saint Ct SUNDSW SR3 160 C3
St Cuthbert Av CLS/BIR/GTL DH3 153 F5
St Cuthberts Av DHAM DH1 193 F1
HAR/WTLS NE34 72 C6
St Cuthberts Ct BLYTH NE24 11 E5 3
St Cuthberts Dr
BDN/LAN/SAC DH7 178 A1
FELL NE10 101 E3
St Cuthberts Pk WICK/BNPF NE16 113 F4
St Cuthbert's Pl GATE NE8 98 C1 9
St Cuthbert's Rd GATE NE8 80 C6
HLS DH4 157 F5 7
PLEE/EAS SR8 208 C3 1
WD/WHPE/BLK NE5 78 A1
WICK/BNPF NE16 113 F5
WLSD/HOW NE28 67 F3
St Cuthbert's Ter
MLFD/PNYW SR4 126 A5 14
St Cuthberts Wk
BDN/LAN/SAC DH7 204 A3
St Cuthberts Wy BLAY NE21 76 C5
RDHAMSE DH6 197 E5
St David's Wy WBAY NE26 40 B2
St Edmund's Ct GATE NE8 99 F1 3
St Edmund's Dr FELL NE10 101 E3
St Edmund's Rd GATE NE8 99 E1 12
St Gabriel's Av BYK/HTN/WLK NE6 65 D5
MLFD/PNYW SR4 125 E6
St George's Av SSH NE33 72 A6
St George's Cl JES NE2 64 A4
St Georges Crs MONK NE25 40 B6
NSHW NE29 70 B1
St George's Est WASHS NE38 138 B6 1
St George's Pl
BW/LEM/TK/HW NE15 77 D3 1
St George's Rd
BW/LEM/TK/HW NE15 77 D3 2
TYNE/NSHE NE30 55 D1
St George's Ter BOL NE36 106 C3
BW/LEM/TK/HW NE15 77 D3 3
CLDN/WHIT/ROK SR6 127 E2
JES NE2 64 A4
St George's Wy
ASHBK/HED/RY SR2 4 C5 1
St Giles Cl DHAM DH1 195 E4
St Godric's Cl DHAM DH1 180 B5
St Godric's Dr HLS DH4 183 F2
St Helen's Crs
LWF/SPW/WRK NE9 99 D5 3
St Heliers Wy STLY/ANP DH9 149 D1
St Hilda's Av WLSD/HOW NE28 68 A3 2
St Hilda St SSH NE33 71 E4
St Hilds Ct DHAM DH1 195 F4
St Hild's La DHAM DH1 195 D4 3
St Ignatius Cl ASHBK/HED/RY SR2 5 F5 3
St Ives Wy WD/WHPE/BLK NE5 61 E2
St James Ct GATE NE8 100 A1 12
St James' Crs
BW/LEM/TK/HW NE15 78 C4 2
St James' Rd
BW/LEM/TK/HW NE15 78 C3
GATE NE8 81 F6
St James Sq GATE NE8 81 F6
St James' St CNUT NE1 2 B2
GOS/KPK NE3 63 F1
St James' Ter NSHW NE29 69 F3
St John's Av HEBB NE31 84 C3
St John's Cl WBAY NE26 40 B2 3
St John's Crs BDLGTN NE22 8 C1
St John's Gn NSHW NE29 69 F3
St John's Pl BDLGTN NE22 8 C1
CLS/BIR/GTL DH3 136 B2
FELL NE10 100 C2
WBAY NE26 40 B2 4
St John's Rd BDLGTN NE22 8 C2
BDN/LAN/SAC DH7 204 A4
DHAM DH1 193 F5
ELS/FEN NE4 79 D4
St John's St NSHW NE29 69 F3
St John's Ter BOL NE36 107 D3
JRW NE32 86 A1 9
NSHW NE29 69 F3
St John St CNUT NE1 2 C4
St Johns V MLFD/PNYW SR4 141 F2 3
St John's Wk NSHW NE29 69 F3 3
St Joseph's Cl DHAM DH1 195 F4
St Joseph's Ct HEBB NE31 84 C5 2
St Joseph's Wy JRW NE32 104 A1
St Jude's Ter SSH NE33 71 E5
St Julien Gdns LGB/HTN NE7 65 F3
WLSD/HOW NE28 69 D3 2
St Lawrence Rd BYK/HTN/WLK NE6 82 A4
St Lawrence Sq BYK/HTN/WLK NE6 82 A3
St Leonard St ASHBK/HED/RY SR2 145 D2
St Lucia Cl ASHBK/HED/RY SR2 5 E6 2
WBAY NE26 40 A2
St Luke's Rd MLFD/PNYW SR4 124 B5 3
St Luke's St NSHW NE29 69 F3
St Luke's Ter MLFD/PNYW SR4 125 E5
St Margaret's Av SWCK/CAS SR5 123 F3
St Margaret's Ct DHAM DH1 194 A5 3
St Margaret's Dr STLY/ANP DH9 130 B3
St Margaret's Rd
BW/LEM/TK/HW NE15 78 A4
St Margargets Av LGB/KIL NE12 49 F6 5
St Mark's Cl BYK/HTN/WLK NE6 82 B1
St Mark's Rd MLFD/PNYW SR4 126 A6
St Mark's Rd North
MLFD/PNYW SR4 125 F5
St Mark's St MLFD/PNYW SR4 126 A6 11
St Mark's Ter MLFD/PNYW SR4 126 A6 12
St Mark's Wy SSH NE33 71 E5
St Martin's Cl WBAY NE26 40 A3
St Mary's Av HAR/WTLS NE34 89 E2
WBAY NE26 40 B3
St Marys Cl CLSW/PEL DH2 153 D6
PLEE/EAS SR8 199 F3 1
St Mary's Dr BLYTH NE24 16 A1
HLS DH4 183 F2 2
RDHAMSE DH6 197 E5
St Mary's Pl
BW/LEM/TK/HW NE15 58 A4 4
CNUT NE1 2 D1
St Mary's Rd DHAM DH1 196 B2
St Mary's Ter BOL NE36 106 C3
St Mary's Wy SUND SR1 4 B2
St Mary's Wynd WBAY NE26 27 D4
St Matthews Vw SUNDSW SR3 160 C1 4
St Michaels HLS DH4 170 A2
St Michael's Av MONK NE25 25 D2
SSH NE33 71 F5
St Michael's Av North SSH NE33 71 F5
St Michael's Rd BYK/HTN/WLK NE6 82 A3
St Michaels Wy SUND SR1 4 A2
WICK/BNPF NE16 96 A1
St Monica Gv DHAM DH1 193 F5
St Nicholas Av GOS/KPK NE3 63 E2 4
SUNDSW SR3 144 A3
St Nicholas' Church Yd CNUT NE1 2 D4 1
St Nicholas Dr DHAM DH1 193 E2
St Nicholas Rd BOL NE36 105 F3 6
St Nicholas' St CNUT NE1 2 D4

St Nicholas Ter PLEE/EAS SR8 200 C2 1
St Omers Rd DUN/TMV NE11 79 E6
St Oswald Av BYK/HTN/WLK NE6 83 D1
St Oswald's Dr DHAM DH1 204 C3
St Oswald's Gn BYK/HTN/WLK NE6 83 D1
St Oswald's Rd HEBB NE31 85 E1
  WLSD/HOW NE28 67 F2
St Oswin's Pl TYNE/NSHE NE30 55 F5
St Oswin's St SSH NE33 88 C1
St Pauls Dr HLS DH4 139 D6
St Paul's Gdns MONK NE25 40 C6
St Paul's Rd JRW NE32 86 B1
St Peter's Av HAR/WTLS NE34 89 D2
St Peter's Quayside East
  BYK/HTN/WLK NE6 82 C4 3
St Peter's Quayside West
  BYK/HTN/WLK NE6 82 B5 1
St Peter's Rd BYK/HTN/WLK NE6 82 B4
  WLSD/HOW NE28 67 F2
St Peters' Wy
  CLDN/WHIT/ROK SR6 127 D4
St Peter's Whf
  BYK/HTN/WLK NE6 82 B4 5
St Philips Cl ELS/FEN NE4 80 A3 16
St Philips Wy ELS/FEN NE4 80 A3 17
St Ronan's Dr WBAY NE26 26 A1
St Ronan's Rd MONK NE25 40 B6
St Ronans Vw
  LWF/SPW/WRK NE9 117 F2
St Simon St HAR/WTLS NE34 87 F4
St Stephen's Cl MONK NE25 24 A5 1
St Stephen's Wy NSHW NE29 69 F4
St Stevens Cl HLS DH4 139 D6 4
St Thomas Cl PLEE/EAS SR8 199 F3 2
St Thomas' Crs CNUT NE1 2 C1
St Thomas' St CNUT NE1 2 C1
  LWF/SPW/WRK NE9 99 F5 4
  SUND SR1 4 D2
St Vincent Ct GATE NE8 99 F1 4
St Vincents Cl
  BW/LEM/TK/HW NE15 60 A6 6
St Vincent's Pl WBAY NE26 40 B2 5
St Vincent St ASHBK/HED/RY SR2 5 E5
  GATE NE8 99 F1
  SSH NE33 72 A5
St Vincent's Wy WBAY NE26 40 B2 6
Salcombe Av JRW NE32 86 C3
Salcombe Cl SEA/MUR SR7 175 F4 5
Salcombe Gdns
  LWF/SPW/WRK NE9 117 E2
Salem Hl ASHBK/HED/RY SR2 5 E6
Salem Rd ASHBK/HED/RY SR2 5 E5
Salem St ASHBK/HED/RY SR2 5 E5
  JRW NE32 86 B1
  SSH NE33 71 E3 7
Salem St South ASHBK/HED/RY SR2 5 E6
Salem Ter ASHBK/HED/RY SR2 5 E5 1
Salisbury Av NSHW NE29 54 B5
Salisbury Cl CLS/BIR/GTL DH3 167 F4
  CRAM NE23 21 D2
Salisbury Gdns JES NE2 64 C6
Salisbury Pl SSH NE33 72 A3
Salisbury Rd DHAM DH1 181 D5
Salisbury St ASHBK/HED/RY SR2 4 D4
  FELL NE10 101 F1 4
  SSH NE33 71 F4 11
  STLY/ANP DH9 147 F3
Salkeld Gdns LWF/SPW/WRK NE9 99 F2
Salkeld Rd LWF/SPW/WRK NE9 99 F4
Salmon St SSH NE33 71 F2
Saltburn Gdns WLSD/HOW NE28 69 D3 3
Saltburn Rd SUNDSW SR3 143 D3
Saltburn Sq SUNDSW SR3 143 D3
Salterfen La ASHBK/HED/RY SR2 145 F6
Salterfen Rd ASHBK/HED/RY SR2 145 F6
Salters Cl GOS/KPK NE3 48 A6
Salter's La HLH DH5 160 A6
  HLH DH5 187 D1
  LGB/KIL NE12 48 B6
  RDHAMSE DH6 187 D6
  RDHAMSE DH6 206 B5
  SEA/MUR SR7 173 E4
Salters' Rd GOS/KPK NE3 62 C2
Saltmeadows Rd GATE NE8 82 A5
Saltwell Rd GATE NE8 98 C3
Saltwell Rd South
  LWF/SPW/WRK NE9 99 D4
Saltwell St GATE NE8 98 C2
Saltwell Vw LWF/SPW/WRK NE9 99 D3
Samson Cl LGB/KIL NE12 49 D2
Sancroft Dr HLH DH5 171 D3
Sandalwood HAR/WTLS NE34 88 C5 2
Sandalwood Sq MLFD/PNYW SR4 141 F4
Sanderling Cl RYTON NE40 75 D4 4
Sanderson Rd JES NE2 64 A4 4
Sanderson St ELS/FEN NE4 79 E5
Sandfield Rd TYNE/NSHE NE30 55 D1
Sandford Av CRAM NE23 14 A5
Sandford Ms DIN/WO NE13 32 B5
Sandgate CNUT NE1 3 G4
  STLY/ANP DH9 147 D4
Sandgrove
  CLDN/WHIT/ROK SR6 107 F1 2
Sandholm Cl WLSD/HOW NE28 68 B1 2
Sandhurst Av TYNE/NSHE NE30 55 D2
Sandmere Pl
  BW/LEM/TK/HW NE15 77 F3 1
Sandmere Rd
  ASHBK/HED/RY SR2 145 D5 2
Sandoe Gdns
  BW/LEM/TK/HW NE15 78 A3
Sandon Cl SMOOR NE27 37 E5
Sandown MONK NE25 39 E5
Sandown Cl SMOOR NE27 37 F1
Sandown Gdns GATE NE8 98 B3
  SUNDSW SR3 143 E6 1
  WLSD/HOW NE28 68 B2
Sandpiper Cl BLYTH NE24 17 D2
  RYTON NE40 74 C4 2
Sand Point Rd
  CLDN/WHIT/ROK SR6 127 D3
Sandray Cl CLS/BIR/GTL DH3 136 C5
Sandringham Av LGB/KIL NE12 49 E6
Sandringham Dr BLYTH NE24 16 C3
  MONK NE25 39 D6
  STLY/ANP DH9 146 B3 1
  WICK/BNPF NE16 95 F3 10
Sandringham Gdns NSHW NE29 54 C5
Sandringham Rd
  CLDN/WHIT/ROK SR6 126 C2
  GOS/KPK NE3 64 A2
  WD/WHPE/BLK NE5 60 A6 7
Sandringham Ter
  CLDN/WHIT/ROK SR6 127 D2
Sandsay Cl ASHBK/HED/RY SR2 144 C6
Sands Rd WICK/BNPF NE16 95 F1
Sandstone Cl HAR/WTLS NE34 87 E5
Sandwell Dr HLS DH4 139 E6
Sandwich Rd NSHW NE29 54 B3
Sandwich St BYK/HTN/WLK NE6 83 E5 3
Sandy Chare CLDN/WHIT/ROK SR6 109 D2
Sandy Crs BYK/HTN/WLK NE6 83 D4
Sandyford CLSW/PEL DH2 151 F1
Sandyford Rd CNUT NE1 3 E1
  JES NE2 81 D1 7
Sandy La DIN/WO NE13 31 F4
  GOS/KPK NE3 34 A6
  LWF/SPW/WRK NE9 118 C3
Sandypath La WICK/BNPF NE16 111 F5 1
Sans St South SUND SR1 5 E3 1
Sargent Av HAR/WTLS NE34 88 C6
Satley Gdns SUNDSW SR3 144 A4
Saturn Cl PLEE/EAS SR8 200 B2 3
Saturn St SEA/MUR SR7 175 F3
Saunton Ct HLS DH4 157 E5 3
Saville St SSH NE33 71 F3 4
  TYNE/NSHE NE30 71 D1
Saville St West NSHW NE29 70 C1 10
Savory Rd WLSD/HOW NE28 68 B3
Sawmill La BDN/LAN/SAC DH7 202 C4
Saxilby Dr GOS/KPK NE3 47 F4
Saxon Cl CLDN/WHIT/ROK SR6 107 D1 4
Saxon Crs SUNDSW SR3 143 E3
Saxondale Rd GOS/KPK NE3 62 A1
Saxon Dr TYNE/NSHE NE30 55 E3
Saxon Wy JRW NE32 69 E6
Saxton Gv LGB/HTN NE7 64 C2
Scafell CLS/BIR/GTL DH3 136 C4
Scafell Cl PLEE/EAS SR8 209 D2
Scafell Dr WD/WHPE/BLK NE5 61 F3
Scafell Gdns DUN/TMV NE11 97 F4
Scalby Cl GOS/KPK NE3 47 F4 4
Scarborough Ct
  BYK/HTN/WLK NE6 82 C2 5
Scarborough Rd
  BYK/HTN/WLK NE6 82 C2
  SUNDSW SR3 143 E6
Scardale Wy DHAM DH1 197 D2
Sceptre Pl ELS/FEN NE4 79 F3 6
Sceptre St ELS/FEN NE4 79 F3
Schalksmuhle Rd BDLGTN NE22 7 E3
Schimel St SWCK/CAS SR5 126 A2 11
School Ap HAR/WTLS NE34 89 F2
School Av DUN/TMV NE11 97 E2
School Cl FELL NE10 100 C4
Schoolhouse La WICK/BNPF NE16 113 D5
School La STLY/ANP DH9 147 F3 2
  WICK/BNPF NE16 96 A3
School Loaning HAR/WTLS NE34 88 A3 5
School Rd BDLGTN NE22 8 C1
  HLH DH5 170 B6
School St CLS/BIR/GTL DH3 136 B2
  HEBB NE31 85 D1
  PLEE/EAS SR8 201 D2
  SEA/MUR SR7 176 C5 2
  WICK/BNPF NE16 95 F3
School Ter STLY/ANP DH9 147 F3
School Vw HLH DH5 186 C4
  HLS DH4 183 E3 1
Scorer's La CLS/BIR/GTL DH3 168 A2
Scorer St NSHW NE29 70 B1
Scotland Head BLAY NE21 93 F3
Scotland St ASHBK/HED/RY SR2 162 C2
Scotswood Rd
  BW/LEM/TK/HW NE15 76 C3
  CNUT NE1 2 A6
  ELS/FEN NE4 78 C5
Scotswood Vw WICK/BNPF NE16 78 B6
Scott Av CRAM NE23 13 E6
Scott Ct CLS/BIR/GTL DH3 167 F3
Scott's Ter HLH DH5 171 F6
Scott St CRAM NE23 14 A3
  STLY/ANP DH9 148 A2
Scripton Gill BDN/LAN/SAC DH7 202 C4
Scripton Gill Rd
  BDN/LAN/SAC DH7 202 B5
Scripton La BDN/LAN/SAC DH7 202 C6
Scrogg Rd BYK/HTN/WLK NE6 83 D1
Scruton Av SUNDSW SR3 143 E4
Seaburn Dr HLS DH4 170 B2
Seaburn Gdns
  CLDN/WHIT/ROK SR6 109 D6
  LWF/SPW/WRK NE9 118 C1
Seaburn Gv WBAY NE26 26 B2
Seaburn Hl
  CLDN/WHIT/ROK SR6 109 D6 7
Seaburn Ter
  CLDN/WHIT/ROK SR6 109 E6 1
Seaburn Vw MONK NE25 24 C2
Seacombe Av TYNE/NSHE NE30 55 D1
Seacrest Av TYNE/NSHE NE30 55 D2
Seafield Rd BLYTH NE24 17 D1 7
Seafields CLDN/WHIT/ROK SR6 109 D5
Seafield Ter SSH NE33 71 F3
Seafield Vw TYNE/NSHE NE30 55 F4
Seaforth Rd SUNDSW SR3 143 F3
Seaforth St BLYTH NE24 11 D4 9
Seaham Cl HAR/WTLS NE34 90 A2
Seaham Gdns LWF/SPW/WRK NE9 118 B2
Seaham Rd HLH DH5 171 E2
Seaham St SEA/MUR SR7 177 D5 2
  SUNDSW SR3 160 C1
Sea La CLDN/WHIT/ROK SR6 109 D6
Sea Rd CLDN/WHIT/ROK SR6 108 C6
  SSH NE33 71 F3
Seascale Pl LWF/SPW/WRK NE9 100 A6
Seaside La PLEE/EAS SR8 200 B2
Seaton Av BLYTH NE24 16 B2
  HLH DH5 171 F2
Seaton Cl FELL NE10 102 A4 5
Seaton Crs MONK NE25 25 E6
  MONK NE25 40 A5
  SEA/MUR SR7 175 D1
Seaton Cft CRAM NE23 35 E2 2
Seaton Gv SEA/MUR SR7 174 C2
Seaton La SEA/MUR SR7 175 D1
Seaton Pk SEA/MUR SR7 175 E2
Seaton Pl BYK/HTN/WLK NE6 83 D5
  DIN/WO NE13 32 C4
Seaton Rd SMOOR NE27 38 C6
  SUNDSW SR3 142 C3
Seatonville Crs MONK NE25 54 A1
Seatonville Rd MONK NE25 54 A1
Sea Vw ASHBK/HED/RY SR2 162 C2
  PLEE/EAS SR8 200 A3
Sea View Gdns
  CLDN/WHIT/ROK SR6 127 D1
  PLEE/EAS SR8 201 F6
Sea View Pk CLDN/WHIT/ROK SR6 108 C2
  CRAM NE23 22 C2
Sea View Rd ASHBK/HED/RY SR2 145 D4
Sea View Rd West
  ASHBK/HED/RY SR2 145 D4
Sea View St ASHBK/HED/RY SR2 145 E4
Sea View Wk SEA/MUR SR7 175 D6
Sea Wy SSH NE33 72 A3
Second Av BLYTH NE24 10 C6 6
  BYK/HTN/WLK NE6 82 B1
  CLSW/PEL DH2 136 A6
  CLSW/PEL DH2 153 D6
  DUN/TMV NE11 98 B4
  NSHW NE29 69 D2
Second St GATE NE8 98 C1
Sedgeletch Rd HLS DH4 169 F1
Sedgemoor LGB/KIL NE12 35 F6
Sedgemoor Av
  BW/LEM/TK/HW NE15 77 F4
Sedgewick Pl GATE NE8 99 D1 6
Sedley Rd WLSD/HOW NE28 67 D5
Sedling Rd WASHS NE38 138 A4
Sefton Av BYK/HTN/WLK NE6 65 D5
Sefton Ct CRAM NE23 14 B5
Sefton Sq SUNDSW SR3 143 D3
Selborne Gdns JES NE2 64 C6
Selbourne Cl CRAM NE23 21 D2 3
Selbourne St SSH NE33 71 F4 12
Selby Cl CRAM NE23 14 A5
Selby Gdns BYK/HTN/WLK NE6 66 B6
  WLSD/HOW NE28 67 D3
Selby Sq SUNDSW SR3 143 D3
Selkirk Crs CLS/BIR/GTL DH3 118 B6
Selkirk Gv CRAM NE23 14 B5
Selkirk Sq SUNDSW SR3 142 C3 1
Selkirk St JRW NE32 87 D5
Selkirk Wy NSHW NE29 53 E4
Selsdon Av MLFD/PNYW SR4 141 F4 2
Selsey Ct FELL NE10 101 D4
Selwood Ct HAR/WTLS NE34 89 E3 1
Selwyn Av MONK NE25 53 F1
Serlby Cl WASHN NE37 120 B3
Seton Av HAR/WTLS NE34 87 E4
Setting Stones WASHS NE38 137 F6
Sevenoaks Dr MLFD/PNYW SR4 141 F3
Seventh Av BLYTH NE24 10 C6
  BYK/HTN/WLK NE6 82 B1

CLSW/PEL DH2 153 D5
Seventh St PLEE/EAS SR8 209 F1
Severn Av HEBB NE31 85 D5
Severn Cl PLEE/EAS SR8 208 B4
Severn Dr JRW NE32 86 B6
Severn Gdns GATE NE8 100 A2
Severus Rd ELS/FEN NE4 79 D1
Seymour Ct DUN/TMV NE11 97 F1 5
Seymour Sq SUNDSW SR3 143 D3 1
Seymour St DUN/TMV NE11 97 F1
NSHW NE29 70 C2
Seymour Ter HLH DH5 186 A3
Shadforth Cl PLEE/EAS SR8 207 F4
Shadon Wy CLS/BIR/GTL DH3 137 D2
Shaftesbury Av
ASHBK/HED/RY SR2 162 A1
HAR/WTLS NE34 87 D3
JRW NE32 86 C2
WBAY NE26 40 B3
Shaftesbury Crs SUNDSW SR3 143 E3
TYNE/NSHE NE30 54 C1
Shaftesbury Gv BYK/HTN/WLK NE6 82 A1
Shaftoe Rd SUNDSW SR3 143 D4
Shaftoe Sq SUNDSW SR3 142 C4 1
Shaftoe Wy DIN/WO NE13 30 C3
Shafto St BW/LEM/TK/HW NE15 77 F3
WLSD/HOW NE28 68 A3
Shaftsbury Dr BDN/LAN/SAC DH7 202 C6
Shakespeare Av HEBB NE31 85 D2
Shakespeare St HLH DH5 171 D3
JRW NE32 69 D6 2
SEA/MUR SR7 176 C3 10
SSH NE33 71 F5 10
SWCK/CAS SR5 125 F1
WLSD/HOW NE28 68 B4
Shakespeare Ter
ASHBK/HED/RY SR2 4 A5
PLEE/EAS SR8 200 B2
Shakespere Ter CLSW/PEL DH2 152 A5
Shalcombe Cl SUNDSW SR3 160 C2
Shallcross ASHBK/HED/RY SR2 144 A2
Shalstone WASHN NE37 121 E3 1
Shamrock Cl
BW/LEM/TK/HW NE15 59 E6
Shandon Wy GOS/KPK NE3 62 A1 4
Shanklin Pl CRAM NE23 21 D2 4
Shannon Cl SWCK/CAS SR5 123 F3 2
Shap Cl WASHS NE38 138 C3
Shap La WD/WHPE/BLK NE5 60 C5
Shap Rd TYNE/NSHE NE30 54 C2
Sharnford Cl SMOOR NE27 37 F5
Sharon Cl LGB/KIL NE12 49 D2
Sharp Crs DHAM DH1 195 F3
Sharpendon St HEBB NE31 85 D1 1
Sharpley Dr SEA/MUR SR7 175 D2
Shaw Av HAR/WTLS NE34 88 A4
Shawdon Cl
WD/WHPE/BLK NE5 61 D2 11
Shaw Gdns FELL NE10 102 A2 6
Shaw St SEA/MUR SR7 176 C3 11
Shaw Wood Cl DHAM DH1 193 F3
Shearlegs Rd GATE NE8 81 F5
Shearwater CLDN/WHIT/ROK SR6 91 E5
Shearwater Av LGB/KIL NE12 48 C5
Shearwater Cl
WD/WHPE/BLK NE5 61 D2 12
Shearwater Wy BLYTH NE24 17 E2
Sheelin Av CLSW/PEL DH2 166 B1
Sheen Cl HLS DH4 183 F2 3
Sheen Ct WD/WHPE/BLK NE5 61 D1
Sheepfolds North
SWCK/CAS SR5 126 C4 8
Sheepfolds Rd SWCK/CAS SR5 126 C4 9
Sheep Hl WICK/BNPF NE16 112 A6
Sheldon Gv CRAM NE23 14 A5
GOS/KPK NE3 62 B4
Sheldon Rd HAR/WTLS NE34 72 B5
Sheldon St JRW NE32 86 A1
Shelford Gdns
BW/LEM/TK/HW NE15 77 D1 3
Shelley Av BOLCOL NE35 105 F2
HAR/WTLS NE34 90 A3
HLH DH5 186 C4 2
LWF/SPW/WRK NE9 119 D3
Shelley Ct CLSW/PEL DH2 152 A5
Shelley Dr GATE NE8 81 F6
Shelley Gdns CLSW/PEL DH2 152 B5
Shelley Rd BW/LEM/TK/HW NE15 75 E1
Shelley St SEA/MUR SR7 176 C3
Shepherd St MLFD/PNYW SR4 125 F5 6
Shepherds Wy BOL NE36 105 F3 7
Shepherd Wy WASHS NE38 139 D4
Sheppard Ter SWCK/CAS SR5 124 A3 7
Sheppey Ct SUNDSW SR3 160 C2 8
Shepton Cottages
WICK/BNPF NE16 114 B1
Sheraton FELL NE10 101 F5
Sheraton St JES NE2 63 D6
Sherborne Av NSHW NE29 53 F4 2
Sherburn Gra North JRW NE32 85 F3 2
Sherburn Gra South JRW NE32 85 F4 1
Sherburn Gn ROWG NE39 111 E1
Sherburn Gv HLS DH4 170 B1
Sherburn Park Dr ROWG NE39 111 E1
Sherburn Rd DHAM DH1 195 F4 2
Sherburn Wy FELL NE10 102 A4
Sherfield Dr LGB/HTN NE7 65 F4
Sheridan Gn WASHS NE38 137 F5
Sheridan Rd HAR/WTLS NE34 87 F5
Sheridan St MLFD/PNYW SR4 125 E5
Sheriffs Cl FELL NE10 100 A2
Sheriff's Moor Av HLH DH5 186 B4
Sheringham Av NSHW NE29 53 F5
Sheringham Cl SUNDSW SR3 160 C4 4
Sheringham Dr CRAM NE23 21 D2
Sheringham Gdns
BW/LEM/TK/HW NE15 57 D4
Sherringham Av GOS/KPK NE3 62 A1
Sherwood Cl SMOOR NE27 53 D2
WASHS NE38 138 C1 1
Sherwood Ct SUNDSW SR3 160 C2 9
Sherwood Pl GOS/KPK NE3 47 E2
Sherwood Vw WLSD/HOW NE28 66 C2
Shetland Ct SUNDSW SR3 160 C2 10
Shibdon Bank BLAY NE21 76 C6
Shibdon Crs BLAY NE21 76 C6 1
Shibdon Park Vw BLAY NE21 76 C6 2
Shibdon Rd BLAY NE21 76 B5
Shibdon Wy BLAY NE21 77 E6
Shield Av WICK/BNPF NE16 96 A1 4
Shieldfield La JES NE2 3 G2
Shield Rd CLDN/WHIT/ROK SR6 108 B5
Shieldrow La STLY/ANP DH9 146 C5
Shields Rd BDLGTN NE22 12 A1
BYK/HTN/WLK NE6 82 A2
CLDN/WHIT/ROK SR6 108 A4
CLS/BIR/GTL DH3 153 F3
FELL NE10 101 F1
HAR/WTLS NE34 89 F5
MONK NE25 54 B2
Shields Rd West
BYK/HTN/WLK NE6 81 F2 9
Shield St JES NE2 3 G1
Shiel Gdns CRAM NE23 21 D2
Shillaw Pl CRAM NE23 35 D5 3
Shilmore Rd GOS/KPK NE3 62 B1 7
Shilton Cl HAR/WTLS NE34 90 A3 4
Shincliffe Av SWCK/CAS SR5 124 B2 4
Shincliffe Gdns
LWF/SPW/WRK NE9 118 B1
Shinwell Ter SEA/MUR SR7 188 A1
Shipcote La GATE NE8 99 E2
Shipcote Ter GATE NE8 99 E2
Shipley Av ELS/FEN NE4 79 D2
Shipley Ct GATE NE8 99 E1 13
Shipley Rd TYNE/NSHE NE30 55 E5
Shipley St BW/LEM/TK/HW NE15 76 B2
Shipton Cl BOLCOL NE35 105 D1
Shire Cha DHAM DH1 180 C4 4
Shirley Gdns SUNDSW SR3 144 A3
Shirwood Av WICK/BNPF NE16 95 F5
Shop Spouts BLAY NE21 76 B5 7
Shoreham Sq SUNDSW SR3 143 D3 2
Shorestone Av TYNE/NSHE NE30 55 D1
Shore St CLDN/WHIT/ROK SR6 126 C3 8
Short Gv SEA/MUR SR7 187 F1
Shortridge St SSH NE33 71 F3 5
Shortridge Ter JES NE2 64 B5
Shot Factory La CNUT NE1 80 B5
Shotley Av SWCK/CAS SR5 126 A1
Shotley Gdns LWF/SPW/WRK NE9 99 F3
Shotton Av BLYTH NE24 11 D6
Shotton Bank PLEE/EAS SR8 207 E5
Shotton La CRAM NE23 12 B4
PLEE/EAS SR8 207 F4
RDHAMSE DH6 206 C2
RDHAMSE DH6 207 E3
Shotton Rd PLEE/EAS SR8 207 D1
PLEE/EAS SR8 209 E1
Shotton Wy FELL NE10 103 D4
Shrewsbury Cl LGB/KIL NE12 65 F2
PLEE/EAS SR8 208 A3
Shrewsbury Crs SUNDSW SR3 143 E3
Shrewsbury Dr SMOOR NE27 37 E5
Shrewsbury St DUN/TMV NE11 97 E2
SEA/MUR SR7 176 C5
Shrewsbury Ter SSH NE33 88 B1 3
Shrigley Gdns GOS/KPK NE3 62 B1
Shropshire Dr DHAM DH1 196 B4
Shunner Cl WASHN NE37 119 F6
Sibthorpe St NSHW NE29 71 D1 5
Side CNUT NE1 3 E5
Side Cliff Rd CLDN/WHIT/ROK SR6 126 C1
Sidegate DHAM DH1 194 B4
Sidlaw Av CLSW/PEL DH2 152 C6
NSHW NE29 54 B3
Sidmouth Cl HLS DH4 157 E4 5
SEA/MUR SR7 175 E4
Sidmouth Rd LWF/SPW/WRK NE9 117 E1
NSHW NE29 53 E6
Sidney Gv ELS/FEN NE4 79 F2
GATE NE8 98 C1 10
Sidney St BLYTH NE24 10 C5
BOLCOL NE35 105 E2
NSHW NE29 70 C1
Sidney Ter STLY/ANP DH9 130 C6
Silkey's La NSHW NE29 70 B1
Silksworth Cl SUNDSW SR3 143 E6 2
Silksworth Gdns
LWF/SPW/WRK NE9 118 B2
Silksworth Hall Dr SUNDSW SR3 160 B2
Silksworth La
ASHBK/HED/RY SR2 144 A2 2
SUNDSW SR3 143 E6
Silksworth Rd SUNDSW SR3 159 E1
Silksworth Rw SUND SR1 4 A2 3
Silksworth Ter SUNDSW SR3 160 C1 5
Silksworth Wy SUNDSW SR3 159 F2
Silkwood Cl CRAM NE23 14 A5
Silloth Av WD/WHPE/BLK NE5 60 C6
Silloth Dr WASHN NE37 120 B2
Silloth Pl TYNE/NSHE NE30 55 D2
Silloth Rd SUNDSW SR3 142 C4 2
Silver Cts BDN/LAN/SAC DH7 203 D4
Silverdale SUNDSW SR3 160 C4
Silverdale Av FELL NE10 102 C3
Silverdale Dr BLAY NE21 93 E1
Silverdale Rd CRAM NE23 14 A5
Silverdale Ter GATE NE8 99 E2 3
Silverdale Wy HAR/WTLS NE34 87 E5
WICK/BNPF NE16 95 E6
Silver Fox Wy SMOOR NE27 52 B4
Silverhill Dr WD/WHPE/BLK NE5 77 F1
The Silverlink North SMOOR NE27 52 A3
The Silverlink SMOOR NE27 52 C5
Silver Lonnen WD/WHPE/BLK NE5 61 D6
Silvermere Dr RYTON NE40 74 C4
Silverstone LGB/KIL NE12 50 A1
Silverstone Rd WASHN NE37 121 D4
Silver St DHAM DH1 194 B5
TYNE/NSHE NE30 55 F5 3
Silverwood Gdns DUN/TMV NE11 98 A5
Simonburn Av ELS/FEN NE4 62 A6
NSHW NE29 53 E6
Simon Pl DIN/WO NE13 32 C5 7
Simonside WBAY NE26 26 C4
Simonside Av WLSD/HOW NE28 68 B2
Simonside Rd BLAY NE21 94 B1 5
SUNDSW SR3 142 C3
Simonside Ter BYK/HTN/WLK NE6 65 D6
Simonside Vw JRW NE32 86 B4
Simonside Wy LGB/KIL NE12 36 B6
Simpson St BLYTH NE24 11 D4 10
MLFD/PNYW SR4 126 A4
NSHW NE29 70 A1
TYNE/NSHE NE30 41 E6 1
Simpson Ter JES NE2 3 G2
Sinclair Dr CLS/BIR/GTL DH3 136 C6
Sinclair Gdns MONK NE25 24 C5
Sinderby Cl GOS/KPK NE3 47 F4
Six-mile Br DIN/WO NE13 33 E2
Sixth Av BLYTH NE24 10 C6
BYK/HTN/WLK NE6 82 B1
Sixth St PLEE/EAS SR8 209 F1
Skaylock Dr WASHS NE38 137 F3
Skelder Av LGB/KIL NE12 49 D6
Skelton Ct GOS/KPK NE3 46 A4
Skerne Cl PLEE/EAS SR8 208 B4
Skiddaw Cl PLEE/EAS SR8 209 D2
Skiddaw Dr
CLDN/WHIT/ROK SR6 108 B5 5
Skiddaw Pl LWF/SPW/WRK NE9 100 A6
Skinnerburn Rd ELS/FEN NE4 80 A6
Skipton Cl BDLGTN NE22 6 C2
CRAM NE23 14 B5 3
Skirlaw Cl WASHS NE38 138 C2
Ski Vw SUNDSW SR3 143 E6
Skye Ct SUNDSW SR3 160 B2
Skye Gv JRW NE32 87 D6 8
Slaidburn Rd STLY/ANP DH9 148 B1 7
Slake Rd JRW NE32 69 F6
Slaley WASHS NE38 139 D5
Slaley Cl FELL NE10 102 B3
Slaley Ct BDLGTN NE22 7 F3
SUNDSW SR3 160 C2
Slatyford La WD/WHPE/BLK NE5 60 C6
Sledmere Cl PLEE/EAS SR8 200 C6 2
Sleekburn Av BDLGTN NE22 8 C1 2
Slingley Cl SEA/MUR SR7 175 D2 2
Slingsby Gdns LGB/HTN NE7 65 F3
Smailes La ROWG NE39 110 B2 1
Smailes St STLY/ANP DH9 148 A3
Smeaton Ct WLSD/HOW NE28 68 C5 5
Smeaton St WLSD/HOW NE28 68 C5 6
Smillie Cl PLEE/EAS SR8 208 C1
Smithburn Rd FELL NE10 100 C3
Smith Cl RDHAMSE DH6 197 D5
Smithfield DHAM DH1 180 A4
Smith Gv ASHBK/HED/RY SR2 162 A2
Smith St ASHBK/HED/RY SR2 162 B2
SSH NE33 71 D6
Smith Ter GATE NE8 98 A1
Smithyford LWF/SPW/WRK NE9 117 F3
Smithy La DUN/TMV NE11 117 D3
Smithy St SSH NE33 71 E3 8
Smyrna Pl SUND SR1 5 F3
Snipes Dene ROWG NE39 111 D1
Snowdon Gdns DUN/TMV NE11 97 F4 5
Snowdon Gv BOL NE36 106 A3 6
Soane Gdns HAR/WTLS NE34 88 C5
Softley Pl BW/LEM/TK/HW NE15 77 E1
Solingen Est BLYTH NE24 17 E1
Solway Av TYNE/NSHE NE30 54 C2
Solway Rd HEBB NE31 85 D4
Solway Sq SUNDSW SR3 143 D3

Somersby Dr GOS/KPK NE3 62 A1
Somerset Gdns
WLSD/HOW NE28 66 C3 6
Somerset Gv NSHW NE29 53 F4 3
Somerset Pl ELS/FEN NE4 79 F3
Somerset Rd HEBB NE31 85 E5 3
SUNDSW SR3 142 C3
Somerset Sq SUNDSW SR3 142 C3 2
Somerset St SUNDSW SR3 143 F5 1
Somerton Ct GOS/KPK NE3 45 E6
Sophia St SEA/MUR SR7 176 C3
Sophy St SWCK/CAS SR5 126 A2 12
Sorley St MLFD/PNYW SR4 125 F6
Sorrel Gdns HAR/WTLS NE34 89 D5
Soulby Ct DIN/WO NE13 45 F4
Sourmilk Hill La
LWF/SPW/WRK NE9 99 F4
Souter Rd GOS/KPK NE3 62 C1 7
South Ap CLSW/PEL DH2 153 E6
South Av HAR/WTLS NE34 89 E3
South Bailey DHAM DH1 194 B6
South Bend GOS/KPK NE3 47 D3
South Bents Av
CLDN/WHIT/ROK SR6 109 D4
South Benwell Rd
BW/LEM/TK/HW NE15 78 B4
Southburn Cl HLS DH4 170 B2 2
South Burns CLS/BIR/GTL DH3 153 E4
South Cl HAR/WTLS NE34 89 E3
HLH DH5 186 C4
RYTON NE40 74 B4
Southcote WICK/BNPF NE16 95 F5
South Crs BOLCOL NE35 105 E2
SEA/MUR SR7 177 D3
WASHS NE38 138 A6
South Cft LGB/KIL NE12 50 A5
Southcroft WASHS NE38 138 C5
South Dene HAR/WTLS NE34 88 A3
South Dr CLDN/WHIT/ROK SR6 107 E1 2
DIN/WO NE13 19 D2
DIN/WO NE13 44 B4
HEBB NE31 84 B4
South Eldon St SSH NE33 88 A1
Southend Av BLYTH NE24 10 B6
Southend Rd LWF/SPW/WRK NE9 100 A5
SUNDSW SR3 143 D4
Southern Rd BYK/HTN/WLK NE6 83 E4
Southern Wy RYTON NE40 74 B4 1
Southey St SSH NE33 71 F6 6
Southfield CLSW/PEL DH2 152 A1
Southfield Gdns WICK/BNPF NE16 96 B3
Southfield Rd HAR/WTLS NE34 72 B6
LGB/KIL NE12 49 E6
WICK/BNPF NE16 96 B4
Southfields CRAM NE23 34 C2 1
Southfield Ter
BYK/HTN/WLK NE6 83 F4 10
Southfield Wy DHAM DH1 193 F2
Southfork BW/LEM/TK/HW NE15 59 E6
South Frederick St SSH NE33 88 A1 3
Southgate LGB/KIL NE12 49 F2
South Grange Pk SEA/MUR SR7 162 B6
South Gv RYTON NE40 74 C4
South Hetton Rd HLH DH5 186 C4
South Hill Rd GATE NE8 98 B1
Southhill Rd HAR/WTLS NE34 89 F2
Southlands JRW NE32 104 C1
LGB/HTN NE7 64 C4
TYNE/NSHE NE30 55 D4
South La BOL NE36 106 B3
South Lea BDN/LAN/SAC DH7 178 A4
South Market St HLH DH5 172 A6
Southmayne Rd
MLFD/PNYW SR4 142 C2 4
Southmead Av WD/WHPE/BLK NE5 61 D5
South Mdw STLY/ANP DH9 128 C6
Southmoor Rd BYK/HTN/WLK NE6 83 D1
South Moor Rd STLY/ANP DH9 148 A4
South Nelson Rd CRAM NE23 13 D6
South Newsham Rd BLYTH NE24 16 B3
South Pde FELL NE10 84 A6
WBAY NE26 41 D5
South Preston Gv NSHW NE29 70 C1 11
South Railway St SEA/MUR SR7 176 C3
South Rdg GOS/KPK NE3 47 D4
South Riggs BDLGTN NE22 7 E4
South Rd DHAM DH1 205 E2
South Rw GATE NE8 82 A4 1
South Shore Rd GATE NE8 3 H5
South Side PLEE/EAS SR8 200 A3
South St CLSW/PEL DH2 153 D4
CNUT NE1 2 C6
DHAM DH1 194 B5
GATE NE8 99 E1 14
GOS/KPK NE3 62 C1 8
HLH DH5 170 B6 2
HLS DH4 157 F5
SMOOR NE27 38 B6
SUND SR1 4 C2
South Ter DHAM DH1 193 F1
PLEE/EAS SR8 209 E1
SEA/MUR SR7 177 D3 3
SWCK/CAS SR5 126 A3 7
WLSD/HOW NE28 68 A4
South Vw BDN/LAN/SAC DH7 203 E5
BLYTH NE24 16 B2
CLDN/WHIT/ROK SR6 126 C1
CLS/BIR/GTL DH3 136 C2
HLH DH5 186 C5
JRW NE32 85 F2
SEA/MUR SR7 175 E5
STLY/ANP DH9 130 A4
WASHS NE38 139 D5
WD/WHPE/BLK NE5 60 A6
South View Rd MLFD/PNYW SR4 141 F1
South View Ter HLS DH4 170 A2
WICK/BNPF NE16 96 A2
South Vw West BYK/HTN/WLK NE6 81 F2
Southward WBAY NE26 26 C3
Southward Cl WBAY NE26 26 C3 1
Southward Wy MONK NE25 38 A1
Southway BW/LEM/TK/HW NE15 77 D1
LWF/SPW/WRK NE9 100 A4
PLEE/EAS SR8 208 B3
Southwick Rd SWCK/CAS SR5 126 C4 10
SWCK/CAS SR5 126 C3 9
Southwold Gdns SUNDSW SR3 143 E6 3
Southwold Pl CRAM NE23 21 D2 5
South Woodbine St SSH NE33 71 F4
Southwood Gdns GOS/KPK NE3 62 B2
Sovereign Pl ELS/FEN NE4 79 F4
Spalding Cl LGB/HTN NE7 65 E2 7
Sparkwell Cl HLS DH4 157 F4 2
Spartylea WASHS NE38 139 E5 1
Spa Well Cl BLAY NE21 94 A2
Spa Well Dr SWCK/CAS SR5 124 B2
Spelter Works Rd
ASHBK/HED/RY SR2 145 E3
Spencer Cl STLY/ANP DH9 149 D2
Spencer Ct BLYTH NE24 10 A3
Spencer Gv WICK/BNPF NE16 96 A2 4
Spencer Rd BLYTH NE24 10 A3
Spencers Bank WICK/BNPF NE16 95 F1 9
Spencer St BYK/HTN/WLK NE6 65 E6
NSHW NE29 70 C1 12
Spence Ter NSHW NE29 70 B1
Spenfield Rd WD/WHPE/BLK NE5 61 F3 4
Spenser St JRW NE32 69 D6 3
Spen St STLY/ANP DH9 148 A3
Spinneyside Gdns DUN/TMV NE11 97 E3
The Spinney CRAM NE23 35 E2
PLEE/EAS SR8 199 F2
WASHS NE38 138 C4
Spire Hollin PLEE/EAS SR8 208 B2
Spire Rd WASHN NE37 121 E5
Spires La BYK/HTN/WLK NE6 82 B2
Spital Ter GOS/KPK NE3 63 E1
Split Crow Rd GATE NE8 99 F2
Spohr Ter SSH NE33 71 F5
Spoor St DUN/TMV NE11 97 E1
Spout La WASHN NE37 120 C5
WASHS NE38 120 C6
Springbank Rd
BYK/HTN/WLK NE6 81 F1 4
JES NE2 81 F1
SUNDSW SR3 142 C3
Springbank Sq SUNDSW SR3 142 C3 3
Springfield NSHW NE29 54 C6 10
Springfield Av
LWF/SPW/WRK NE9 118 B3
Springfield Crs SEA/MUR SR7 176 B4
Springfield Gdns
CLS/BIR/GTL DH3 153 E3
WLSD/HOW NE28 66 B3
Springfield Gv MONK NE25 54 A1
Springfield Pk DHAM DH1 193 F3
Springfield Pl LWF/SPW/WRK NE9 99 F4
Springfield Rd BLAY NE21 76 A6
HLS DH4 157 F5 8
WD/WHPE/BLK NE5 61 E5 6
Spring Garden Cl SUND SR1 5 F2 3
Spring Garden La ELS/FEN NE4 80 A2 10
Springhill Gdns
BW/LEM/TK/HW NE15 78 C2
Spring Pk BDLGTN NE22 7 F4
Springside BDN/LAN/SAC DH7 178 B1
The Springs CLS/BIR/GTL DH3 136 C3
Springsyde Cl WICK/BNPF NE16 95 D5 4
Spring Ter NSHW NE29 54 C6 11
Springwell Av BYK/HTN/WLK NE6 83 D4
DHAM DH1 193 F3
JRW NE32 86 B2
LWF/SPW/WRK NE9 118 B2 1
Springwell Rd DHAM DH1 193 F3
JRW NE32 86 A3
LWF/SPW/WRK NE9 118 C1
MLFD/PNYW SR4 142 C3
Springwood HEBB NE31 84 B1
Squires Gdns FELL NE10 100 C3
Stack Garth BDN/LAN/SAC DH7 203 E3
Stadium Wy SWCK/CAS SR5 126 B4 2
Stafford Gv ASHBK/HED/RY SR2 162 A2 1
SWCK/CAS SR5 126 A2
Stafford Pl PLEE/EAS SR8 208 A1
Staffordshire Dr DHAM DH1 196 C3
Staffords La
CLDN/WHIT/ROK SR6 109 E2 2
Stafford St SUND SR1 127 E4 1
Stagshaw LGB/KIL NE12 35 E5 5
Staindrop FELL NE10 101 F5
Staindrop Rd DHAM DH1 180 C6
Staines Rd BYK/HTN/WLK NE6 82 C4
Stainmore Dr CLS/BIR/GTL DH3 168 A4
Stainton Dr FELL NE10 100 C2 6
Stainton Gv CLDN/WHIT/ROK SR6 108 B5
Stainton St East SSH NE33 71 F5 11
Stainton Wy PLEE/EAS SR8 208 B2
Staithes Av LGB/KIL NE12 49 E6
Staithes Rd WASHS NE38 139 F3
Staithes St BYK/HTN/WLK NE6 84 A2
Staith La BLAY NE21 75 F4
Staiths Rd DUN/TMV NE11 79 F6 1
Stalks Rd DIN/WO NE13 33 D4
Stamford Av MONK NE25 25 D6
SUNDSW SR3 143 E3
Stamfordham Av NSHW NE29 69 F1
Stamfordham Cl
WLSD/HOW NE28 66 C4 3
Stamfordham Ms
WD/WHPE/BLK NE5 61 F5 9
Stamfordham Rd
WD/WHPE/BLK NE5 42 B6
Stampley Cl BLAY NE21 93 F2 6
Stamps La SUND SR1 5 G1
Standfield Gdns FELL NE10 102 B2 2
Standish St STLY/ANP DH9 147 F3
Stanelaw Wy STLY/ANP DH9 131 E5
Staneway FELL NE10 101 D6
Stanfield Ct LGB/HTN NE7 66 A3 4
Stanhope WASHS NE38 137 E1
Stanhope Cl BDN/LAN/SAC DH7 203 E4 5
DHAM DH1 180 C5
HLS DH4 170 C3
Stanhope Pde SSH NE33 71 F6 7
Stanhope Rd
CLDN/WHIT/ROK SR6 109 D6
HAR/WTLS NE34 88 A2
JRW NE32 86 C3
SSH NE33 88 C1
Stanhope St ELS/FEN NE4 79 F2
SSH NE33 71 E3
Stanley Cl RDHAMSE DH6 197 E5
Stanley Gdns LWF/SPW/WRK NE9 118 B2
Stanley Gv BDLGTN NE22 8 A3
LGB/HTN NE7 64 C3
Stanley St BLYTH NE24 11 E4
HAR/WTLS NE34 88 A3
JRW NE32 86 B1
NSHW NE29 70 C1 13
SEA/MUR SR7 176 A2
SWCK/CAS SR5 124 A3 8
WLSD/HOW NE28 68 B3
Stanley St West NSHW NE29 70 C1
Stanmore Rd BYK/HTN/WLK NE6 65 E5
Stannington Av BYK/HTN/WLK NE6 82 A1
Stannington Gdns
ASHBK/HED/RY SR2 144 B4 6
Stannington Gv
ASHBK/HED/RY SR2 144 B4
BYK/HTN/WLK NE6 82 A1 4
Stannington Pl
BYK/HTN/WLK NE6 82 A1 5
PONT/DH NE20 28 A2
Stannington Rd NSHW NE29 69 E1
Stannington St BLYTH NE24 11 E5
Stansfield St CLDN/WHIT/ROK SR6 107 D3
Stanstead Cl SWCK/CAS SR5 123 F4 2
Stanton Av BLYTH NE24 16 A1
HAR/WTLS NE34 89 D1
Stanton Cl FELL NE10 102 C3
Stanton Rd SMOOR NE27 52 A2
TYNE/NSHE NE30 54 B3
Stanton St ELS/FEN NE4 79 F2
Stanway Dr LGB/HTN NE7 64 C3
Stanwick St TYNE/NSHE NE30 55 F4 6
Stapeley Vw GOS/KPK NE3 61 F1
Staple Rd JRW NE32 69 D6
Stapylton Dr ASHBK/HED/RY SR2 144 A2
Starbeck Av JES NE2 81 E1 3
Starbeck Ms JES NE2 81 E1 4
Stardale Av BLYTH NE24 9 F6
Stargate La RYTON NE40 75 D4
Starlight Crs MONK NE25 24 B5 3
Startforth Cl CLS/BIR/GTL DH3 168 A3 4
Station Ap BOL NE36 107 D3
DHAM DH1 194 A4
LGB/KIL NE12 49 F6 6
SSH NE33 71 E3 9
Station Av BDN/LAN/SAC DH7 203 E4
HLH DH5 185 F1
Station Bank DHAM DH1 194 B4 4
RYTON NE40 74 B2
Station Crs SEA/MUR SR7 176 A2
Station Est East SEA/MUR SR7 187 F1
Station Est North SEA/MUR SR7 187 F1
Station Est South SEA/MUR SR7 187 F1
Station Field Rd STLY/ANP DH9 131 E5
Station La CLS/BIR/GTL DH3 136 A2
CLSW/PEL DH2 151 F2
DHAM DH1 195 D4
Station Rd ASHBK/HED/RY SR2 162 C2
BDLGTN NE22 8 B2
BDN/LAN/SAC DH7 203 E4
BOLCOL NE35 87 D6
BW/LEM/TK/HW NE15 56 B4

BW/LEM/TK/HW NE15 **75** E1
CLS/BIR/GTL DH3 **153** E5
CLSW/PEL DH2 **153** E5
CRAM NE23 **21** F1
CRAM NE23 **22** A1 2
CRAM NE23 **34** B2
CRAM NE23 **36** B1
DIN/WO NE13 **45** D6
FELL NE10 **84** A6
GOS/KPK NE3 **64** A1
HEBB NE31 **84** C2
HLH DH5 **185** F1
HLS DH4 **139** E6
HLS DH4 **156** C2 3
HLS DH4 **170** C1
HLS DH4 **183** E3
LGB/KIL NE12 **35** D6
LGB/KIL NE12 **49** F6
LGB/KIL NE12 **49** D1
LWF/SPW/WRK NE9 **99** D6
NSHW NE29 **69** F2
PLEE/EAS SR8 **201** E2
RDHAMSE DH6 **183** F5
RDHAMSE DH6 **206** A1
ROWG NE39 **111** E3
SEA/MUR SR7 **175** E2
SEA/MUR SR7 **187** F1
SMOOR NE27 **51** F1
SSH NE33 **71** E4
STLY/ANP DH9 **133** D6
STLY/ANP DH9 **146** B5
STLY/ANP DH9 **148** B1
SWCK/CAS SR5 **108** B6
TYNE/NSHE NE30 **55** E1
WASHS NE38 **139** D1
WASHS NE38 **139** D5
WBAY NE26 **41** D6
WLSD/HOW NE28 **66** C4
WLSD/HOW NE28 **66** B1
WLSD/HOW NE28 **67** E5
WLSD/HOW NE28 **68** C5
Station Rd North *LGB/KIL* NE12 **49** F4 8
Station St *BLYTH* NE24 **11** D4
SUND SR1 **4** C2
Station Ter *TYNE/NSHE* NE30 **55** F5
Station Vw *HLH* DH5 **185** F1
Staveley Rd *CLDN/WHIT/ROK* SR6 **108** B5
PLEE/EAS SR8 **209** D2
Stavordale St *SEA/MUR* SR7 **176** C4 6
Stavordale St West
SEA/MUR SR7 **176** C5 5
Stavordale Ter
LWF/SPW/WRK NE9 **99** F3 5
Staward Av *MONK* NE25 **24** C6
Staward Ter *BYK/HTN/WLK* NE6 **83** E4 2
Staynebrigg *FELL* NE10 **101** F4 3
Stead La *BDLGTN* NE22 **8** A3
Stead St *WLSD/HOW* NE28 **68** C3
Stedham Cl *WASHN* NE37 **121** D2
Steep Hl *SUNDSW* SR3 **142** A6
Stella Bank *BLAY* NE21 **75** E3
Stella Hall *BLAY* NE21 **75** F4
Stella La *BLAY* NE21 **75** E4
Stella Rd *BLAY* NE21 **75** F4
Stephenson Cl *HLH* DH5 **172** A6 2
Stephenson Rd *BYK/HTN/WLK* NE6 **65** D5
PLEE/EAS SR8 **200** B5
WASHN NE37 **121** D2
Stephenson St *GATE* NE8 **98** C2 7
SEA/MUR SR7 **188** B1 5
TYNE/NSHE NE30 **55** F5 4
WLSD/HOW NE28 **69** D5
Stephenson Ter *FELL* NE10 **100** C3
Stephenson Wy *BLAY* NE21 **94** A2
Stephens Rd *SEA/MUR* SR7 **188** A1
Stephen St *BLYTH* NE24 **11** D4
BYK/HTN/WLK NE6 **81** F2
Stepney La *CNUT* NE1 **3** G3
Stepney Rd *JES* NE2 **3** H1
Sterling St *MLFD/PNYW* SR4 **125** F6
Steward Crs *HAR/WTLS* NE34 **90** A1
Stewart Av *ASHBK/HED/RY* SR2 **162** A2
Stewart Dr *BOL* NE36 **106** A3 7
Stewart St *MLFD/PNYW* SR4 **125** F6
PLEE/EAS SR8 **200** C2
SEA/MUR SR7 **177** D4
SUNDSW SR3 **160** C1
Stileford *FELL* NE10 **101** F3
Stirling Av *JRW* NE32 **87** D4
ROWG NE39 **111** D3
Stirling Cl *WASHS* NE38 **139** E2
Stirling Dr *BDLGTN* NE22 **8** B2
NSHW NE29 **53** E4
Stirling La *ROWG* NE39 **111** D3
Stobart St *BDN/LAN/SAC* DH7 **164** A3 1
SWCK/CAS SR5 **126** B4
Stockholm Cl *NSHW* NE29 **69** D1
Stockley Av *SWCK/CAS* SR5 **124** B2 5
Stockley Ct *BDN/LAN/SAC* DH7 **192** B5
Stocksfield Av *WD/WHPE/BLK* NE5 **78** B1
Stockton Rd *ASHBK/HED/RY* SR2 **4** B5
ASHBK/HED/RY SR2 **162** B3
DHAM DH1 **194** C6
NSHW NE29 **70** B3 2
PLEE/EAS SR8 **199** F4
SEA/MUR SR7 **162** B6
SEA/MUR SR7 **189** F4
SUND SR1 **4** B4 2
Stockton St *SEA/MUR* SR7 **176** A2
Stockwell Gn *BYK/HTN/WLK* NE6 **66** B6
Stoddart St *HAR/WTLS* NE34 **88** B2 4
JES NE2 **3** H1
Stoker Av *HAR/WTLS* NE34 **87** E4
Stokesley Gv *LGB/HTN* NE7 **64** C3
Stone Cellar Rd *WASHN* NE37 **120** A2
Stonechat Pl *LGB/KIL* NE12 **48** C5
Stonecroft Gdns *LGB/HTN* NE7 **65** F3
Stonefold Cl *WD/WHPE/BLK* NE5 **61** D3 8
Stoneleigh Av *LGB/KIL* NE12 **48** C5
Stoneleigh Cl *HLS* DH4 **170** B1 1
Stone Rw *CLSW/PEL* DH2 **150** C3
Stonesdale *HLS* DH4 **139** D6
Stone St *FELL* NE10 **100** B4
Stoneygate La *FELL* NE10 **83** D6
Stoneyhurst Av
BW/LEM/TK/HW NE15 **78** A3 5
Stoneyhurst Rd *GOS/KPK* NE3 **64** A2
Stoney La *LWF/SPW/WRK* NE9 **119** E3
SWCK/CAS SR5 **125** F3 10
Stoneylea Rd *WD/WHPE/BLK* NE5 **60** B6
Stony La *STLY/ANP* DH9 **133** F6
Store St *BW/LEM/TK/HW* NE15 **76** B2 8
Storey La *BLAY* NE21 **75** F4 1
Stormont St *NSHW* NE29 **70** B1
Stotfold Cl *SEA/MUR* SR7 **175** D2
Stothard St *JRW* NE32 **86** B1
Stotts Rd *BYK/HTN/WLK* NE6 **66** C6
Stowell St *CNUT* NE1 **2** B4
The Stow *LGB/KIL* NE12 **64** C1
Straker St *JRW* NE32 **86** C2
Straker Ter *HAR/WTLS* NE34 **88** A3
The Strand *SUNDSW* SR3 **143** D6 4
Strangford Rd *SEA/MUR* SR7 **176** A3
Strangways St *SEA/MUR* SR7 **176** C4 7
Stranton Ter *CLDN/WHIT/ROK* SR6 **126** C2
Stratfield St *MLFD/PNYW* SR4 **125** D5 5
Stratford Av *ASHBK/HED/RY* SR2 **145** D3
Stratford Cl *CRAM* NE23 **21** D1
LGB/KIL NE12 **50** A1
Stratford Gdns
LWF/SPW/WRK NE9 **99** E4 5
Stratford Gv West
BYK/HTN/WLK NE6 **81** F1
Stratford Rd *BYK/HTN/WLK* NE6 **81** F1
Strathearn Wy *GOS/KPK* NE3 **46** B5
Strathmore Av *ROWG* NE39 **111** D3 1
Strathmore Cl *STLY/ANP* DH9 **149** D1
Strathmore Crs *ELS/FEN* NE4 **79** D3
Strathmore Rd *GOS/KPK* NE3 **47** E5
LWF/SPW/WRK NE9 **100** A3
ROWG NE39 **110** C3
SUNDSW SR3 **143** D4
Strathmore Sq *SUNDSW* SR3 **143** D4 7
Stratton Cl *ASHBK/HED/RY* SR2 **145** F6
Stratus Ct *SUNDSW* SR3 **160** C2
Strawberry Gdns *WLSD/HOW* NE28 **66** C2
Strawberry La *CNUT* NE1 **2** B2
Strawberry Pl *CNUT* NE1 **2** B3
Street Gate Pk *WICK/BNPF* NE16 **114** B1
Stretton Cl *HLS* DH4 **169** F3 5
Stretton Wy *SMOOR* NE27 **37** E5
Stridingedge *WASHN* NE37 **119** F6
Stuart Ct *GOS/KPK* NE3 **45** D6
Stuart Gdns *BW/LEM/TK/HW* NE15 **57** E4
Stubbs Av *WICK/BNPF* NE16 **95** F2 5
Studdon Wk *GOS/KPK* NE3 **61** F1
Studley Gdns
LWF/SPW/WRK NE9 **99** E5 9
MONK NE25 **40** C6
Studley Ter *ELS/FEN* NE4 **79** E1
Studley Vls *LGB/KIL* NE12 **50** A5 1
Sturdee Gdns *JES* NE2 **64** A3
Styford Gdns
BW/LEM/TK/HW NE15 **77** D1 4
Success Rd *HLS* DH4 **157** D3
Sudbury Wy *CRAM* NE23 **21** D1
Suddick St *SWCK/CAS* SR5 **126** A3 8
Suez St *TYNE/NSHE* NE30 **55** D6 4
Suffolk Gdns *HAR/WTLS* NE34 **90** B1
WLSD/HOW NE28 **68** A2
Suffolk Pl *CLS/BIR/GTL* DH3 **136** C5
GATE NE8 **81** F4
Suffolk Rd *HEBB* NE31 **85** E5
Suffolk St *ASHBK/HED/RY* SR2 **5** F6
JRW NE32 **86** A2
Suffolk Wk *PLEE/EAS* SR8 **200** B6 5
Suffolk Wy *DHAM* DH1 **180** C4 5
Sugley Dr *BW/LEM/TK/HW* NE15 **76** C2
Sugley St *BW/LEM/TK/HW* NE15 **76** C2
Sulgrave Rd *WASHN* NE37 **121** E3
Sullivan Wk *HEBB* NE31 **85** D3
Summerfield *STLY/ANP* DH9 **150** C2
Summerfield Rd
LWF/SPW/WRK NE9 **99** E3
Summerhill *BLAY* NE21 **76** A5
JRW NE32 **104** C1
SUNDSW SR3 **159** D1
Summerhill Av *GOS/KPK* NE3 **47** F3
Summerhill Rd *HAR/WTLS* NE34 **89** E1
Summerhill St *ELS/FEN* NE4 **80** A4
Summerhill Ter *CNUT* NE1 **2** A5
Summerhouse Farm *HLH* DH5 **170** C5 1
Summerson St *HLH* DH5 **172** A6
Summerson Wy *BDLGTN* NE22 **8** C2
Summer St *FELL* NE10 **100** C1
Summerville *DHAM* DH1 **194** A5
Sunbury Av *JES* NE2 **64** A4
Sunderland Av *PLEE/EAS* SR8 **201** E6
Sunderland Hwy *WASHS* NE38 **119** E6
Sunderland Rd *BOL* NE36 **107** D3
CLDN/WHIT/ROK SR6 **108** A2
DHAM DH1 **195** E4
FELL NE10 **101** E2
FELL NE10 **102** C2 1
GATE NE8 **81** E6
HAR/WTLS NE34 **89** D1
HLS DH4 **158** A5
PLEE/EAS SR8 **200** A2
SEA/MUR SR7 **190** A6
SSH NE33 **71** F6
SWCK/CAS SR5 **125** F2
Sunderland St *CNUT* NE1 **2** B5
HLH DH5 **171** D1
HLS DH4 **171** D2 3
Sundew Rd *LWF/SPW/WRK* NE9 **100** B5
Sundridge Dr *FELL* NE10 **102** B3
Sunholme Dr *WLSD/HOW* NE28 **66** C1
Sunlea Av *TYNE/NSHE* NE30 **55** E2
Sunnidale *WICK/BNPF* NE16 **95** D5
Sunnilaws *HAR/WTLS* NE34 **89** F4
Sunningdale *SSH* NE33 **72** A5 5
Sunningdale Av
BYK/HTN/WLK NE6 **83** F2 4
WLSD/HOW NE28 **67** E4 5
Sunningdale Cl *FELL* NE10 **100** C3
Sunningdale Dr *WASHN* NE37 **120** B2 7
Sunningdale Rd *SUNDSW* SR3 **142** C3
Sunnirise *HAR/WTLS* NE34 **89** F4
Sunniside *MLFD/PNYW* SR4 **123** F6
NSHW NE29 **69** F1
Sunniside Ct *WICK/BNPF* NE16 **114** A2
Sunniside Dr *HAR/WTLS* NE34 **89** F4
Sunniside Gdns
BW/LEM/TK/HW NE15 **78** A2 4
Sunniside La *CLDN/WHIT/ROK* SR6 **90** A6
Sunniside Rd *WICK/BNPF* NE16 **96** A5
Sunniside Ter *CLDN/WHIT/ROK* SR6 **89** F6
Sunnybank Av
BW/LEM/TK/HW NE15 **78** C3
Sunny Blunts *PLEE/EAS* SR8 **208** B4
Sunnybrow *SUNDSW* SR3 **143** E6
Sunnycrest Av *BYK/HTN/WLK* NE6 **83** E2
Sunny Ter *STLY/ANP* DH9 **148** A1
Sunnyway *WD/WHPE/BLK* NE5 **61** E4
Surrey Av *SUNDSW* SR3 **160** C2
Surrey Pl *ELS/FEN* NE4 **79** F3
Surrey Rd *HEBB* NE31 **85** E5
NSHW NE29 **53** F6 7
Surrey St *JRW* NE32 **85** F2
Surtees Dr *DHAM* DH1 **193** F4
Surtees Rd *PLEE/EAS* SR8 **209** D2
Sussex Gdns *WLSD/HOW* NE28 **68** A3
Sussex Pl *WASHN* NE37 **120** C3 5
Sussex St *BLYTH* NE24 **11** E4 8
JRW NE32 **85** F2 4
Sutherland Av *ELS/FEN* NE4 **79** D1
Sutherland Ct *HAR/WTLS* NE34 **88** C6 1
Sutherland Gra *HLS* DH4 **157** F2 1
Sutherland St
CLDN/WHIT/ROK SR6 **126** C2
GATE NE8 **99** E1 15
SEA/MUR SR7 **176** A2
Sutton Cl *HLS* DH4 **156** C2
Sutton Ct *WLSD/HOW* NE28 **66** B1
Sutton St *BYK/HTN/WLK* NE6 **66** A6
DHAM DH1 **194** A4 4
Sutton Wy *HAR/WTLS* NE34 **90** A3
Swainby Cl *GOS/KPK* NE3 **47** F4
Swaledale *CLDN/WHIT/ROK* SR6 **109** E3
WLSD/HOW NE28 **66** B1 5
Swaledale Av *BLYTH* NE24 **9** F5
Swaledale Cl *HLH* DH5 **185** D3
Swaledale Crs *HLS* DH4 **139** F6
Swaledale Gdns *LGB/HTN* NE7 **65** D3
MLFD/PNYW SR4 **143** E1 5
The Swallows *WLSD/HOW* NE28 **52** A5
Swallow Tail Ct *HAR/WTLS* NE34 **88** A4 1
Swallow Tail Dr *DUN/TMV* NE11 **98** A3
Swalwell Bank *WICK/BNPF* NE16 **95** F1
Swan Av *WLSD/HOW* NE28 **67** F3 5
Swan Dr *DUN/TMV* NE11 **97** F1 6
Swan Rd *BYK/HTN/WLK* NE6 **84** A4
PLEE/EAS SR8 **207** E3
WASHS NE38 **139** E3
Swan St *GATE* NE8 **81** E5 7
STLY/ANP DH9 **146** A3
SWCK/CAS SR5 **126** B3
Swanton Cl *WD/WHPE/BLK* NE5 **61** D2
Swards Rd *FELL* NE10 **101** D3
Swarland Av *LGB/HTN* NE7 **65** D1
Swarland Rd *MONK* NE25 **24** C6
Swarth Cl *WASHN* NE37 **119** F6
Sweetbriar Wy *BLYTH* NE24 **16** B2
Sweethope Av *BLYTH* NE24 **10** C4 5
Swiftden Dr *MLFD/PNYW* SR4 **141** F2

Swinbourne Gdns WBAY NE26 40 B4
Swinbourne Ter JRW NE32 86 A5
Swinburne Pl GATE NE8 81 D5 4
Swinburne St GATE NE8 81 D5
JRW NE32 87 D2
Swinburn Rd MONK NE25 24 C6
Swindale Dr LGB/KIL NE12 49 E1
Swindon Rd SUNDSW SR3 142 C3
Swindon Sq SUNDSW SR3 143 D3 3
Swindon St HEBB NE31 84 C2
Swindon Ter BYK/HTN/WLK NE6 65 D5 2
Swing Br CNUT NE1 3 E5
Swinhoe Gdns DIN/WO NE13 33 D3
Swinhope WASHS NE38 137 F6
Swinley Gdns
BW/LEM/TK/HW NE15 77 E2
Swinside Dr DHAM DH1 196 B2
The Swirle CNUT NE1 3 H4 1
Sycamore Av BLYTH NE24 10 C3
DIN/WO NE13 31 E3
HAR/WTLS NE34 89 E4
MONK NE25 40 B6
Sycamore Cl JES NE2 64 B4 5
Sycamore Dr SWCK/CAS SR5 126 A1
Sycamore Gv FELL NE10 101 D2
LWF/SPW/WRK NE9 119 E3
Sycamore Rd BLAY NE21 76 B6
CLDN/WHIT/ROK SR6 109 E1
CLSW/PEL DH2 179 E1
The Sycamores
ASHBK/HED/RY SR2 145 D3
WICK/BNPF NE16 130 B1
Sycamore St
BW/LEM/TK/HW NE15 57 F3
WLSD/HOW NE28 67 E5 2
Sydenham Ter MLFD/PNYW SR4 143 F1
SSH NE33 71 F3 6
Sydney Gdns HAR/WTLS NE34 87 E5
Sydney Gv WLSD/HOW NE28 66 C1
Sydney St HLS DH4 156 A6
STLY/ANP DH9 150 C1
Syke Rd WICK/BNPF NE16 111 E6
Sylvia Ter STLY/ANP DH9 131 E6
Symington Gdns SUNDSW SR3 143 E6 4
Syon St TYNE/NSHE NE30 55 F4
Syron WICK/BNPF NE16 95 E4
Syston Cl HLS DH4 169 F3

T

Taberna Cl BW/LEM/TK/HW NE15 56 A4
Tadcaster Rd SUNDSW SR3 142 B5
Tadema Rd SSH NE33 72 B4
Talbot Cl WASHS NE38 138 C2
Talbot Gn WD/WHPE/BLK NE5 60 B6
Talbot Pl SEA/MUR SR7 176 C3
Talbot Rd CLDN/WHIT/ROK SR6 127 D1
HAR/WTLS NE34 88 B2
Talgarth WASHS NE38 140 A1
Talisman Cl RDHAMSE DH6 197 E5
Talley Ct WASHS NE38 138 B1
Tamar Cl NSHW NE29 53 E4
PLEE/EAS SR8 208 B3
Tamar St HLH DH5 186 B4
Tamerton Dr CLS/BIR/GTL DH3 136 C4
Tamerton St MLFD/PNYW SR4 125 E6 7
Tamworth Rd ELS/FEN NE4 79 F2
Tamworth Sq SUNDSW SR3 142 B5 1
Tanfield Gdns HAR/WTLS NE34 90 A2
Tanfield Pl LWF/SPW/WRK NE9 118 B2
Tanfield Rd BW/LEM/TK/HW NE15 77 F2
LWF/SPW/WRK NE9 118 B2
SUNDSW SR3 142 C5
Tanfield St MLFD/PNYW SR4 125 D5 6
Tangmere Cl CRAM NE23 22 B1
Tankerville Pl JES NE2 64 A5 4
Tankerville Ter JES NE2 64 A6
Tanmeads CLSW/PEL DH2 165 E6
Tanners' Bank TYNE/NSHE NE30 55 E6
Tantobie Rd BW/LEM/TK/HW NE15 77 F2
Tarlton Crs FELL NE10 100 B2 5
Tarn Cl PLEE/EAS SR8 209 D2 8
Tarn Dr ASHBK/HED/RY SR2 145 E6
Tarragon Wy HAR/WTLS NE34 88 C5
Tarrington Cl WLSD/HOW NE28 68 B1 5
Tarset Rd MONK NE25 39 D5
Tarset St CNUT NE1 81 F3
Tasmania Rd HAR/WTLS NE34 87 E5
Tasman Rd SUNDSW SR3 142 B6
Tate St BLYTH NE24 11 E4 9
Tatham St SUND SR1 5 E3
Tatham Street Back SUND SR1 5 E3
Tattershall ASHBK/HED/RY SR2 144 A2
Taunton Av JRW NE32 87 D3
NSHW NE29 53 F4 4
Taunton Cl WLSD/HOW NE28 68 B1
Taunton Pl CRAM NE23 14 A6
Taunton Rd SUNDSW SR3 142 C5
Tavistock Ct HLS DH4 157 E5 4
Tavistock Pl JRW NE32 86 C3
SUND SR1 4 D3
Tavistock Rd JES NE2 64 A4
Tavistock Sq SUNDSW SR3 143 F6
Taylor Av BDN/LAN/SAC DH7 192 A3
DIN/WO NE13 33 E4
ROWG NE39 111 E3
Taylor Gdns WBAY NE26 26 C2
Taylor St BLYTH NE24 9 F4
SSH NE33 88 A1
STLY/ANP DH9 146 A3
Taynton Gv CRAM NE23 23 E6 3
Tay Rd SUNDSW SR3 142 B4
Tay St HLH DH5 186 B4
Teal Av BLYTH NE24 17 E2
Teal Cl WASHS NE38 137 E3
Team St GATE NE8 98 A1
Teasdale St ASHBK/HED/RY SR2 5 G6 2
Tebay Dr WD/WHPE/BLK NE5 60 B6
Teddington Cl DIN/WO NE13 45 D5
Teddington Sq SUNDSW SR3 142 B4 2
Tedham Rd BW/LEM/TK/HW NE15 76 B1
Tees Cl PLEE/EAS SR8 208 B4
Tees Ct HAR/WTLS NE34 88 B2
Tees Crs STLY/ANP DH9 148 B3
Teesdale Av HLS DH4 139 F6
Teesdale Gdns LGB/HTN NE7 65 D3
Teesdale Gv LGB/KIL NE12 49 F4 9
Teesdale Pl BLYTH NE24 9 E4
Tees Rd HEBB NE31 85 D5
Tees St HLH DH5 186 C4 3
PLEE/EAS SR8 209 F1
SEA/MUR SR7 176 C2
Teign Cl PLEE/EAS SR8 208 B3
Teindland Cl ELS/FEN NE4 79 D4
Tel-el-kebir Rd
ASHBK/HED/RY SR2 145 D2
Telford Cl SMOOR NE27 37 E5
Telford Ct WLSD/HOW NE28 69 E4
Telford Rd SUNDSW SR3 142 C4
Telford St GATE NE8 98 C3
WLSD/HOW NE28 68 E4
Tempest Rd SEA/MUR SR7 176 C3
Tempest St BLAY NE21 75 F4 2
SUNDSW SR3 160 C1 6
Temple Gn GATE NE8 98 B2 3
HAR/WTLS NE34 89 D3
Temple Park Rd HAR/WTLS NE34 88 C2
Temple St CNUT NE1 2 B5
FELL NE10 100 C1
SSH NE33 88 A1
Temple St West SSH NE33 71 D6 3
Temple Town SSH NE33 71 D6
Tenbury Crs LGB/KIL NE12 49 E5
NSHW NE29 54 A3
Tenby Rd SUNDSW SR3 142 B6 2
Tenby Sq CRAM NE23 14 B6 4
Ten Flds HLH DH5 185 E1
Tennant St HAR/WTLS NE34 87 F4
Tennyson Av BOLCOL NE35 106 A2
HEBB NE31 85 E2 1
Tennyson Crs WICK/BNPF NE16 95 F2 6
Tennyson Rd CLSW/PEL DH2 152 A5
PLEE/EAS SR8 200 C2 2
Tennyson St SWCK/CAS SR5 125 F2 8
Tennyson Ter NSHW NE29 71 D2 1
Tenter Ter DHAM DH1 194 B4
Tenth Av BLYTH NE24 16 C1
BYK/HTN/WLK NE6 65 E6
DUN/TMV NE11 116 C2
Tenth Av West DUN/TMV NE11 116 B2
Tenth St PLEE/EAS SR8 209 F1
Tern Cl BLYTH NE24 17 E2
Terrace Pl CNUT NE1 2 B2
Terrier Cl BDLGTN NE22 8 B3
Territorial La DHAM DH1 194 C5
Tetford Pl LGB/KIL NE12 49 E5
Teviot WASHS NE38 137 F5
Teviotdale Gdns LGB/HTN NE7 65 D3
Teviot St GATE NE8 99 F2 13
HLH DH5 186 B4 1
Teviot Wy JRW NE32 85 F3 3
Tewkesbury LGB/KIL NE12 35 F6 10
Tewkesbury Rd
BW/LEM/TK/HW NE15 76 B1
Thackeray Rd SUNDSW SR3 142 C4
Thames Av JRW NE32 86 B5
Thames Crs HLS DH4 169 F2
STLY/ANP DH9 148 B4
Thames Gdns WLSD/HOW NE28 67 D5 11
Thames Rd HEBB NE31 85 E4
PLEE/EAS SR8 208 B3
SUNDSW SR3 142 B6 3
Thames St GATE NE8 99 F2
HLH DH5 186 B4
Thanet Rd SUNDSW SR3 142 C5
Tharsis Rd HEBB NE31 84 C3
Thatcher Cl WICK/BNPF NE16 95 F5
Thelma St MLFD/PNYW SR4 126 A6
Theme Rd SUNDSW SR3 142 B6
Theresa St BLAY NE21 76 B5
Third Av BLYTH NE24 10 C6
BYK/HTN/WLK NE6 82 B1
CLSW/PEL DH2 153 D1
DUN/TMV NE11 98 B5
NSHW NE29 69 D1
Third St PLEE/EAS SR8 209 F1
Thirkeld Pl HLS DH4 157 D1 3
Thirlington Cl WD/WHPE/BLK NE5 61 D3
Thirlmere CLDN/WHIT/ROK SR6 107 F1
CLS/BIR/GTL DH3 137 D4
FELL NE10 101 F2 5
Thirlmere Av CLSW/PEL DH2 166 A1
HLH DH5 186 B4
TYNE/NSHE NE30 54 C2
Thirlmere Cl LGB/KIL NE12 50 B1
Thirlmere Ct HEBB NE31 85 E4 3
Thirlmere Crs BLAY NE21 94 A2 5
HLS DH4 157 D2
Thirlmere Rd PLEE/EAS SR8 209 D1
Thirlmere Wy BLYTH NE24 9 F3
WD/WHPE/BLK NE5 61 D5
Thirlmoor WASHN NE37 119 F6
Thirlwell Gv JRW NE32 85 F5
Thirlwell Rd GATE NE8 81 F5 1
Thirsk Rd SUNDSW SR3 142 C4 3
Thirston Dr CRAM NE23 22 B2
Thirston Pl NSHW NE29 53 F5 4
Thirston Wy GOS/KPK NE3 61 F1 8
Thistlecroft HLH DH5 171 D3
Thistledon Av WICK/BNPF NE16 95 E5
Thistle Rd BDN/LAN/SAC DH7 204 B4
SUNDSW SR3 142 B5
Thistley Cl BYK/HTN/WLK NE6 66 A6 1
Thomas Hawksley Pk
SUNDSW SR3 143 F3
Thomas St ASHBK/HED/RY SR2 162 B2
LWF/SPW/WRK NE9 118 C3
PLEE/EAS SR8 201 D1
SSH NE33 71 E3 10
STLY/ANP DH9 149 F5
WICK/BNPF NE16 95 F3 11
Thomas St North
CLDN/WHIT/ROK SR6 126 C4
Thomas St South
ASHBK/HED/RY SR2 162 B2
SWCK/CAS SR5 125 F3
Thompson Av LGB/KIL NE12 35 E6 12
Thompson Crs SWCK/CAS SR5 124 A3 9
Thompson Gdns
WLSD/HOW NE28 67 D4 7
Thompson Pl FELL NE10 100 C2 7
Thompson Rd SWCK/CAS SR5 126 B2
Thompson St BLYTH NE24 10 C4 4
BLYTH NE24 11 D4 11
BLYTH NE24 11 D3 2
HAR/WTLS NE34 88 A3 6
PLEE/EAS SR8 201 F6
Thorburn St
CLDN/WHIT/ROK SR6 108 C6 7
Thornbank Cl SUNDSW SR3 160 C4 5
Thornbridge WASHS NE38 139 F1
Thornbury Av CRAM NE23 23 E6
Thornbury Cl BOLCOL NE35 105 D1 5
DIN/WO NE13 45 D6
Thornbury Dr MONK NE25 39 E4
Thornbury St MLFD/PNYW SR4 125 F5
Thorncliffe Pl NSHW NE29 70 A1 3
Thorn Cl DIN/WO NE13 32 C5 8
Thorndale Pl BLYTH NE24 9 F4 5
Thorndale Rd
BW/LEM/TK/HW NE15 77 E3
DHAM DH1 196 C3
SUNDSW SR3 142 B5
Thorne Av FELL NE10 102 A2
Thorne Brake FELL NE10 101 F3 1
Thorne Rd SUNDSW SR3 142 B5 2
Thornes Cl PLEE/EAS SR8 209 E3 2
Thorne Sq SUNDSW SR3 142 B5
Thorne Ter BYK/HTN/WLK NE6 83 D1
Thorneyburn Cl HLS DH4 157 E6 4
Thorneyburn Wy BLYTH NE24 10 B5 2
Thorney Close Rd SUNDSW SR3 142 C5
Thorneyford Pl PONT/DH NE20 28 A3 1
Thorneyholme Ter STLY/ANP DH9 148 A2
Thornfield Gv
ASHBK/HED/RY SR2 145 D4 1
Thornfield Pl ROWG NE39 111 D1 4
Thornfield Rd GOS/KPK NE3 63 D2 4
Thorngill WASHN NE37 120 A6
Thornhaugh Av
WICK/BNPF NE16 95 E4 1
Thornhill Cl MONK NE25 24 C6
Thornhill Gdns
ASHBK/HED/RY SR2 144 B2
Thornhill Pk ASHBK/HED/RY SR2 4 A6
PONT/DH NE20 28 A3 2
Thornhill Rd LGB/KIL NE12 49 F6
PONT/DH NE20 28 A3
RDHAMSE DH6 206 B2
Thornhill St HLS DH4 170 C2
Thornhill Ter ASHBK/HED/RY SR2 4 A5
Thornholme Av HAR/WTLS NE34 90 A2
Thornholme Rd
ASHBK/HED/RY SR2 144 A1
Thornhope Cl WASHS NE38 121 E6 1
Thornlea Gdns LWF/SPW/WRK NE9 99 E4
Thornleigh Gdns
CLDN/WHIT/ROK SR6 89 F6
Thornleigh Rd JES NE2 64 A5 5
Thornley Av CRAM NE23 22 B2
FELL NE10 102 A4 6
Thornley Cl BDN/LAN/SAC DH7 192 A5

WICK/BNPF NE16 95 F6
Thornley La BLAY NE21 93 F4
ROWG NE39 93 F6
Thornley Rd WD/WHPE/BLK NE5 60 A5
Thornley Vw ROWG NE39 111 E2
Thornton Cl HLS DH4 156 C1
Thornton Ct WASHS NE38 138 B1
Thornton Crs BLAY NE21 76 B5
Thornton Lea CLSW/PEL DH2 151 F1
Thornton St CNUT NE1 2 B5
Thorntree Av DIN/WO NE13 33 D1
Thorn Tree Dr BDLGTN NE22 7 E2
Thorntree Dr
BW/LEM/TK/HW NE15 77 F1
MONK NE25 39 D6
Thorntree Ter STLY/ANP DH9 149 D1
Thorntree Wy BLYTH NE24 9 E5
Thornwood Gdns DUN/TMV NE11 98 A5
Thornygarth FELL NE10 101 D3 7
Thorp Cl BLYTH NE24 16 A1 1
Thorpe Cl ELS/FEN NE4 79 F2
Thorpe Dr RYTON NE40 74 C3
Thorpeness Rd SUNDSW SR3 142 B5 3
Thorpe Rd PLEE/EAS SR8 200 A3 4
Thorpe St PLEE/EAS SR8 201 D1
PLEE/EAS SR8 209 F1 6
Threap Gdns WLSD/HOW NE28 68 A2
Three Rivers Ct BOL NE36 105 F3 8
Threlkeld Gv
CLDN/WHIT/ROK SR6 108 B5 6
Thrift St NSHW NE29 70 C2 7
Thristley Gdns
ASHBK/HED/RY SR2 144 B3
Throckley Wy HAR/WTLS NE34 88 A2
Thropton Av BLYTH NE24 16 B1 5
LGB/HTN NE7 65 D1
Thropton Cl FELL NE10 102 B3
Thropton Ct BLYTH NE24 10 B6 8
Thropton Crs GOS/KPK NE3 47 D6
Thropton Pl NSHW NE29 53 F5
Thropton Ter LGB/HTN NE7 65 D4
Thrush Gv SWCK/CAS SR5 124 B3 7
Thursby Av TYNE/NSHE NE30 55 D2
Thurso Cl SUNDSW SR3 142 A5 1
Tiberius Cl WLSD/HOW NE28 67 D5
Tilbeck Sq SUNDSW SR3 160 C2 11
Tilbury Cl HLS DH4 157 E3
Tilbury Gdns SUNDSW SR3 142 B6 4
Tilbury Gv MONK NE25 54 C1
Tilbury Rd SUNDSW SR3 142 B6
Tileshed La BOL NE36 106 B1
Till Av BLAY NE21 76 A6
Tilley Rd WASHS NE38 137 E1
Tillmouth Av MONK NE25 24 C6
Tillmouth Gdns ELS/FEN NE4 78 B2
Tillmouth Park Rd
BW/LEM/TK/HW NE15 57 F5
Till St BYK/HTN/WLK NE6 82 B4
Tilson Wy GOS/KPK NE3 46 B6 6
Timber Beach Rd SWCK/CAS SR5 124 C3
Timber Rd PLEE/EAS SR8 201 F5
Timlin Gdns WLSD/HOW NE28 69 D3
Tindal Cl ELS/FEN NE4 80 A3 18
Tindale Av CRAM NE23 22 B2
Tindale Dr WICK/BNPF NE16 95 F4
Tindal St ELS/FEN NE4 80 A3 19
Tintagel Cl CRAM NE23 14 A6
SUNDSW SR3 142 A5 2
Tintagel Dr SEA/MUR SR7 176 B2
Tintern WASHS NE38 138 B3
Tintern Cl HLS DH4 157 E6
Tintern Crs BYK/HTN/WLK NE6 82 A1
NSHW NE29 53 F4
Tintern St MLFD/PNYW SR4 126 A6 13
Tiree Cl BDN/LAN/SAC DH7 203 E5
Tiree Ct SUNDSW SR3 160 C2 12
Tirril Pl WD/WHPE/BLK NE5 60 C5
Titan Rd BYK/HTN/WLK NE6 83 F2
Titchfield Rd WASHS NE38 138 B2
Titian Av HAR/WTLS NE34 88 B6
Titlington Gv HEBB NE31 84 C5
Tiverton Av ELS/FEN NE4 79 D3
NSHW NE29 53 E4
Tiverton Cl WLSD/HOW NE28 68 B1
Tiverton Gdns
LWF/SPW/WRK NE9 117 E1
Tiverton Pl CRAM NE23 14 A6
Tiverton Sq SUNDSW SR3 142 B5
Toberty Gdns FELL NE10 102 A2
Toft Crs SEA/MUR SR7 188 B1
Togstone Pl WD/WHPE/BLK NE5 61 E5 7
Toll WLSD/HOW NE28 69 D5
Toll Bar Rd ASHBK/HED/RY SR2 144 C5
Toll Bridge Rd BLAY NE21 77 E5
Tollerton Dr SWCK/CAS SR5 123 E3
Tollgate Flds HLS DH4 183 E3 2
Toll House Rd DHAM DH1 193 E4
Tolls Cl MONK NE25 39 E5
Toll Sq TYNE/NSHE NE30 55 E6
Tomlea Av BDLGTN NE22 8 C3
Tonbridge Av NSHW NE29 70 A1
Toner Av HEBB NE31 84 C5
Topaz St SEA/MUR SR7 175 F3
Topcliff CLDN/WHIT/ROK SR6 127 D4
Torcross Wy CRAM NE23 14 A6
Toronto Rd SUNDSW SR3 142 C4
Toronto Sq SUNDSW SR3 142 C4
Torquay Gdns LWF/SPW/WRK NE9 117 E1
Torquay Rd SUNDSW SR3 142 C4
Torrens Rd SUNDSW SR3 142 C4
Torrington Cl HLS DH4 157 E4 6
Torver Cl DIN/WO NE13 32 C5
Torver Crs CLDN/WHIT/ROK SR6 108 B5
Torver Pl LWF/SPW/WRK NE9 100 A6
Torver Wy TYNE/NSHE NE30 54 B2
Tosson Pl NSHW NE29 69 F1 4
Tosson Ter BYK/HTN/WLK NE6 65 E5 4
Totnes Dr CRAM NE23 14 A6
Toward Rd ASHBK/HED/RY SR2 5 E5
SUND SR1 4 D3
Toward St BYK/HTN/WLK NE6 82 A2 10
Tower Gdns RYTON NE40 74 B3
Tower Pl ASHBK/HED/RY SR2 5 F6 3
Tower Rd STLY/ANP DH9 146 A6
WASHN NE37 121 D5
Towers Av JES NE2 64 A3
Towers Cl BDLGTN NE22 7 F4
Towers Pl HAR/WTLS NE34 87 D3
Tower St ASHBK/HED/RY SR2 5 G6
CNUT NE1 3 F4
PLEE/EAS SR8 201 E1
Tower St West
ASHBK/HED/RY SR2 145 D2
The Towne Ga
BW/LEM/TK/HW NE15 56 A4
Townend Ct HAR/WTLS NE34 88 B3
Townfield Gdns
BW/LEM/TK/HW NE15 58 B6
Townley Flds ROWG NE39 111 E2
Townley Rd ROWG NE39 110 C2 4
Townsend Rd SUNDSW SR3 142 B6
Townsville Av MONK NE25 53 F1
Towton LGB/KIL NE12 35 F6 11
Toynbee WASHS NE38 139 F1
Tracey Av BOL NE36 106 A2
Trafalgar Rd WASHN NE37 121 E3 2
Trafalgar St CNUT NE1 3 F3 1
Trafford LWF/SPW/WRK NE9 117 F2
Trafford Rd SWCK/CAS SR5 125 F3
Trafford Wk WD/WHPE/BLK NE5 60 A3 8
Trajan Av SSH NE33 71 F2
Trajan St SSH NE33 71 F2
Tranwell Cl GOS/KPK NE3 46 B4 5
Tranwell Dr MONK NE25 25 D6
Treby St MLFD/PNYW SR4 125 F5
Tredegar Cl
WD/WHPE/BLK NE5 61 D2 13
Treecone Cl SUNDSW SR3 160 C3
Treen Crs SEA/MUR SR7 188 C1 1
Trefoil Rd STLY/ANP DH9 130 C6
Tregoney Av SEA/MUR SR7 188 C1
Treherne Rd JES NE2 63 F3 3
Trent Av HEBB NE31 85 D5
Trent Dr JRW NE32 86 B6
Trent Gdns GATE NE8 100 A2 6
Trentham Av LGB/HTN NE7 65 D1
Trenton Av WASHS NE38 120 C6 1
Trent Rd SUNDSW SR3 142 B5
Trent St HLH DH5 186 B4
Trevarren Dr ASHBK/HED/RY SR2 145 E6
Trevelyan Av BDLGTN NE22 8 A3
BLYTH NE24 10 B6
Trevelyan Cl SUNDSW SR3 142 A5 3
Trevelyan Dr WD/WHPE/BLK NE5 60 C3
Trevethick St GATE NE8 98 C2
Trevone Pl CRAM NE23 23 F6
Trevone Sq SEA/MUR SR7 188 C1
Trevor Gv CLDN/WHIT/ROK SR6 107 F2
Trevor Ter TYNE/NSHE NE30 54 C5
Trewhitt Rd BYK/HTN/WLK NE6 65 E6 5
Tribune Pl LWF/SPW/WRK NE9 100 A4
Trident Rd SUNDSW SR3 160 C1
Trimdon St MLFD/PNYW SR4 126 A5
Trinity Ctyd BYK/HTN/WLK NE6 82 C4 4
Trinity Gv CRAM NE23 23 F6
Trinity Pk HLS DH4 157 D3
Trinity Pl NSHW NE29 70 C2 8
Trinity St NSHW NE29 70 C2
SWCK/CAS SR5 125 E2
Trinity Wk SSH NE33 71 D5
Trojan Av BYK/HTN/WLK NE6 83 D1
Tromso Cl NSHW NE29 69 D1
Trool Ct SUNDSW SR3 160 C3
Troon Cl WASHN NE37 120 B2 8
Trotter Gv BDLGTN NE22 8 B3 3
Trotter Ter ASHBK/HED/RY SR2 162 B2
Troutbeck Av BYK/HTN/WLK NE6 83 E3 3
Troutbeck Rd
CLDN/WHIT/ROK SR6 108 B5 7
Troutbeck Wy HAR/WTLS NE34 87 E5
PLEE/EAS SR8 209 D1 4
Troutdale Pl LGB/KIL NE12 48 B6 4
Trout's La DHAM DH1 178 C5
Trowbridge Wy GOS/KPK NE3 62 B1
Truro Av SEA/MUR SR7 174 C6
Truro Gv NSHW NE29 53 F4
Truro Rd SUNDSW SR3 142 C5 1
Tuart St CLS/BIR/GTL DH3 153 E5
Tudor Av NSHW NE29 54 A6
Tudor Ct RDHAMSE DH6 206 C2
Tudor Dr STLY/ANP DH9 130 C3 1
Tudor Gra PLEE/EAS SR8 199 F3
Tudor Gv SUNDSW SR3 143 E3
Tudor Rd CLS/BIR/GTL DH3 153 F3
SSH NE33 71 E4
Tudor Wy GOS/KPK NE3 45 E6
WD/WHPE/BLK NE5 61 D1
Tudor Wynd BYK/HTN/WLK NE6 65 F5
Tulip St GATE NE8 100 A1
Tumulus Av BYK/HTN/WLK NE6 66 C6
Tunbridge Rd SUNDSW SR3 142 C4
Tundry Wy BLAY NE21 77 E4
Tuneside FELL NE10 102 A3
Tunis Rd SUNDSW SR3 143 D4 8
Tunstall Av BYK/HTN/WLK NE6 82 C2 6
HAR/WTLS NE34 90 A2
Tunstall Bank SUNDSW SR3 161 E1
Tunstall Hill Cl
ASHBK/HED/RY SR2 144 B4 7
Tunstall Pk ASHBK/HED/RY SR2 144 B2
Tunstall Rd ASHBK/HED/RY SR2 4 B4
ASHBK/HED/RY SR2 144 B4
SUNDSW SR3 144 A5
Tunstall Ter ASHBK/HED/RY SR2 4 B4
Tunstall Ter West
ASHBK/HED/RY SR2 4 A4
Tunstall V ASHBK/HED/RY SR2 144 B2
Tunstall Vw SUNDSW SR3 144 A6
Tunstall Village Gn SUNDSW SR3 161 D1
Tunstall Village Rd SUNDSW SR3 161 D1
Tunstall Vls SUNDSW SR3 161 D1 4
Turbinia Gdns LGB/HTN NE7 65 E4
Turnberry CLSW/PEL DH2 135 E4
MONK NE25 39 E5
SSH NE33 72 A5 6
Turnberry Cl WASHN NE37 120 B2 9
Turnberry Wy GOS/KPK NE3 48 A6 1
Turner Av HAR/WTLS NE34 88 C5
Turner Cl RYTON NE40 74 C4
Turner Crs GOS/KPK NE3 62 C1 9
Turner St SMOOR NE27 52 A3
Turnham Rd SUNDSW SR3 142 B5
Turnstone Dr WASHS NE38 137 E3
Turret Rd BW/LEM/TK/HW NE15 77 E1
Tuscan Cl BDN/LAN/SAC DH7 202 A1
Tuscan Rd SUNDSW SR3 142 B5
Tweed Cl ASHBK/HED/RY SR2 145 E6
CLSW/PEL DH2 135 E6
PLEE/EAS SR8 208 B3
Tweed Gv BW/LEM/TK/HW NE15 76 B1
Tweed St ELS/FEN NE4 79 E3
HEBB NE31 84 C2
HLH DH5 186 B4 2
JRW NE32 85 F3
WASHS NE38 139 D2
Tweed Ter STLY/ANP DH9 148 B3
Tweedy St BLYTH NE24 9 F4 6
Tweedy Ter BYK/HTN/WLK NE6 83 E3 4
Twelfth Av BLYTH NE24 10 C6
CLSW/PEL DH2 153 D4
Twelfth St PLEE/EAS SR8 209 E1
Twentieth Av BLYTH NE24 16 C1 5
Twentyfifth Av BLYTH NE24 16 C1 6
Twentysecond Av BLYTH NE24 16 B1 6
Twentysixth Av BLYTH NE24 16 B1
Twentythird Av BLYTH NE24 16 B1
Twickenham Ct CRAM NE23 23 E6
Twickenham Rd SUNDSW SR3 142 B4
Twizell La STLY/ANP DH9 150 A3
Twizell Pl PONT/DH NE20 28 A3
Twizell St BLYTH NE24 11 E6 3
Twyford Cl CRAM NE23 14 A6
Tyldesley Sq SUNDSW SR3 142 B5 4
Tyne Ap JRW NE32 68 C6
Tynebank BLAY NE21 76 A6
Tyne Br CNUT NE1 3 F5
Tynedale Av WBAY NE26 40 B4
WLSD/HOW NE28 67 D2
Tynedale Crs HLS DH4 157 D1
Tynedale Dr BLYTH NE24 9 F5
Tynedale Rd HAR/WTLS NE34 72 A6
Tynedale St HLH DH5 185 D3
Tynedale Ter LGB/KIL NE12 49 F6 7
Tyne Gdns WASHN NE37 120 C3
Tyne Main Rd FELL NE10 82 B5
Tynemouth Rd BYK/HTN/WLK NE6 82 A2
JRW NE32 85 F6
TYNE/NSHE NE30 55 E6
WLSD/HOW NE28 68 B4
WLSD/HOW NE28 69 D3 4
Tynemouth Sq SUNDSW SR3 142 C5 2
Tynemouth Ter
TYNE/NSHE NE30 55 F5 5
Tyne Rd STLY/ANP DH9 148 A3
Tyne Rd East GATE NE8 80 B6
STLY/ANP DH9 148 A3
Tyneside Rd ELS/FEN NE4 80 A5 9
Tyne St BLAY NE21 76 B4
CNUT NE1 81 F3
FELL NE10 83 E6
HLH DH5 186 B4
JRW NE32 69 D6
SEA/MUR SR7 176 C3 12
TYNE/NSHE NE30 71 D1
Tyne Ter HAR/WTLS NE34 88 A3

Tynevale Av *BLAY* NE21 94 A1
Tyne Vw *BW/LEM/TK/HW* NE15 76 B2
HEBB NE31 84 B2
Tyne View Av *WICK/BNPF* NE16 96 B2
Tyne View Ter *WLSD/HOW* NE28 69 D5
Tyne-Wear Trail *DUN/TMV* NE11 96 C1
WICK/BNPF NE16 96 C5

U

Ugly La *CLSW/PEL* DH2 165 E6
Uldale Ct *GOS/KPK* NE3 46 A5 8
Ullerdale Cl *DHAM* DH1 197 D2
Ullswater Av *HLH* DH5 186 B4
JRW NE32 86 C5
Ullswater Cl *BLYTH* NE24 9 D4
Ullswater Crs *BLAY* NE21 94 A2 6
Ullswater Dr *LGB/KIL* NE12 50 B1
Ullswater Gdns *HAR/WTLS* NE34 88 C1
Ullswater Gv *SWCK/CAS* SR5 108 B6 4
Ullswater Rd *CLSW/PEL* DH2 166 A1
Ullswater Wy *WD/WHPE/BLK* NE5 61 D5
Ulverstone Ter *BYK/HTN/WLK* NE6 83 D1
Ulverston Gdns
LWF/SPW/WRK NE9 118 A1
Underhill Rd *CLDN/WHIT/ROK* SR6 107 E2
Underwood Gv *CRAM* NE23 13 F5
Union Aly *SSH* NE33 71 E3
Union Hall Rd
BW/LEM/TK/HW NE15 59 E6
Union La *CLSW/PEL* DH2 166 A3
SUND SR1 5 F1 2
Union Quay *TYNE/NSHE* NE30 71 E1
Union Rd *BYK/HTN/WLK* NE6 82 B2
TYNE/NSHE NE30 55 E6
Union St *BLYTH* NE24 11 D4
HLH DH5 171 F6
JES NE2 3 H2
JRW NE32 69 D6
MLFD/PNYW SR4 123 F6 6
NSHW NE29 71 D1
SEA/MUR SR7 176 C4 8
SSH NE33 88 A2 3
SUND SR1 4 C2
WLSD/HOW NE28 67 D6
Unity Ter *STLY/ANP* DH9 130 A4
STLY/ANP DH9 146 A1
Uplands *MONK* NE25 39 F5
The Uplands *CLS/BIR/GTL* DH3 136 C1
GOS/KPK NE3 62 B2
Uplands Wy *LWF/SPW/WRK* NE9 119 E3
Upper Camden St
TYNE/NSHE NE30 54 C6 12
Upper Elsdon St *NSHW* NE29 70 C2 9
Upper Norfolk St
TYNE/NSHE NE30 55 D6 5
Upper Pearson St
TYNE/NSHE NE30 55 D6 6
Upper Queen St *TYNE/NSHE* NE30 55 D6
Upton St *GATE* NE8 98 B1 3
Urswick Ct *WD/WHPE/BLK* NE5 61 D1
Urwin St *HLH* DH5 186 A1
Ushaw Rd *HEBB* NE31 85 E2
Usher Av *RDHAMSE* DH6 197 E4
Usher St *SWCK/CAS* SR5 126 A3 9
Usk Av *JRW* NE32 86 B5
Usworth Station Rd
WASHN NE37 121 D4 3

V

Valebrooke Av
ASHBK/HED/RY SR2 144 B2
Valebrooke Gdns
ASHBK/HED/RY SR2 4 B6
Valehead *MONK* NE25 39 F5
Valentia Av *BYK/HTN/WLK* NE6 83 D1
Valeria Cl *WLSD/HOW* NE28 51 F6
Valerian Av *BW/LEM/TK/HW* NE15 56 B4
Valeside *BW/LEM/TK/HW* NE15 57 E4
Vale St *HLH* DH5 186 A4
MLFD/PNYW SR4 144 A1 12
Vale Wk *JES* NE2 81 F1
Valley Crs *BLAY* NE21 75 F6
Valley Dr *LWF/SPW/WRK* NE9 99 F3
WICK/BNPF NE16 95 F2
Valley Forge *WASHS* NE38 120 C6
Valley Gdns *LWF/SPW/WRK* NE9 99 F3
MONK NE25 39 F5
WLSD/HOW NE28 67 F3
Valley La *HAR/WTLS* NE34 90 B2
Valley Rd *CLSW/PEL* DH2 152 A4
MONK NE25 25 E6
Valley Vw *BDN/LAN/SAC* DH7 178 A2
BDN/LAN/SAC DH7 192 A5
BW/LEM/TK/HW NE15 76 B1
CLS/BIR/GTL DH3 118 A5
JES NE2 64 B5
JRW NE32 86 A4
ROWG NE39 110 C2
WASHS NE38 139 D5
WICK/BNPF NE16 111 E5
Vallum Rd *BW/LEM/TK/HW* NE15 58 A4
BYK/HTN/WLK NE6 83 D2
Vanborough Ct *MONK* NE25 24 C6 1
Vancouver Dr *LGB/HTN* NE7 65 F4
Vane St *PLEE/EAS* SR8 201 D2
SUNDSW SR3 160 C1 7
Vane Ter *ASHBK/HED/RY* SR2 5 H5
SEA/MUR SR7 176 C2 2
Van Mildert Cl *PLEE/EAS* SR8 208 A4 1
Vardy Ter *HLS* DH4 158 A1
Vauxhall Rd *BYK/HTN/WLK* NE6 66 C6
Vedra St *SWCK/CAS* SR5 126 A3 10
Velville Ct *WD/WHPE/BLK* NE5 45 D6
Ventnor Av *ELS/FEN* NE4 79 E3
Ventnor Crs *LWF/SPW/WRK* NE9 99 D4
Ventnor Gdns *LWF/SPW/WRK* NE9 99 D4
WBAY NE26 40 C4
Verdun Av *HEBB* NE31 85 D2
Vermont *WASHN* NE37 120 C4
Verne Rd *NSHW* NE29 69 F1
Vernon Cl *SSH* NE33 71 D6
Vernon Dr *MONK* NE25 40 A6
Vernon St *WASHN* NE37 120 C4
Veryan Gdns *SUNDSW* SR3 144 A3
Vespasian Av *SSH* NE33 71 F2
Viador *CLS/BIR/GTL* DH3 153 E4
Viaduct St *WLSD/HOW* NE28 68 A4
Vicarage Cl *CLSW/PEL* DH2 152 A1 1
SUNDSW SR3 160 B1
Vicarage Flats
BDN/LAN/SAC DH7 203 D4 4
Vicarage La *MLFD/PNYW* SR4 123 F6 7
Vicarage Rd *SUNDSW* SR3 160 C1
Vicarage St *NSHW* NE29 70 C1
Vicarsholme Cl *SUNDSW* SR3 160 A3
Vicars' La *LGB/HTN* NE7 64 C1
Vicars Wy *LGB/KIL* NE12 48 B6
Viceroy St *SEA/MUR* SR7 176 C3
Victoria Av *ASHBK/HED/RY* SR2 145 D4
BDN/LAN/SAC DH7 203 E4
FELL NE10 100 B2
LGB/KIL NE12 49 F5
MLFD/PNYW SR4 124 A6
WLSD/HOW NE28 67 D4 8
Victoria Av West
ASHBK/HED/RY SR2 145 D4
Victoria Crs *NSHW* NE29 70 B2
Victoria Ms *BLYTH* NE24 10 C6
Victoria Rd *GATE* NE8 98 B2
SSH NE33 71 E5
WASHN NE37 120 C4
Victoria Rd East *HEBB* NE31 85 E2
Victoria Rd West *FELL* NE10 84 B6
HEBB NE31 84 B6
Victoria St *DUN/TMV* NE11 97 F1
ELS/FEN NE4 80 A4 9
HLH DH5 171 F6 5
NSHW NE29 70 C2
RDHAMSE DH6 206 C2
SEA/MUR SR7 176 B3
Victoria Ter *JRW* NE32 85 F2
WBAY NE26 41 D5
Victor St *CLS/BIR/GTL* DH3 153 E5
Victory St *MLFD/PNYW* SR4 125 D5
Victory St East *HLH* DH5 172 A6 3
Victory St West *HLH* DH5 172 A6 4
Victory Wy *SUNDSW* SR3 159 E3
Viewforth Dr *SWCK/CAS* SR5 126 B1
Viewforth Rd *ASHBK/HED/RY* SR2 162 B3
Viewforth Ter *SWCK/CAS* SR5 126 A1
View La *STLY/ANP* DH9 148 B1
View Pk *MONK* NE25 24 C5
Vigo La *CLS/BIR/GTL* DH3 136 C5
CLS/BIR/GTL DH3 154 A2
WASHS NE38 137 E6
Village Centre *WASHS* NE38 138 C2 3
Village Ct *WBAY* NE26 40 B5
Village East *RYTON* NE40 74 B2
Village Farm
BW/LEM/TK/HW NE15 58 C5 1
Village La *WASHS* NE38 120 C6
Village Rd *CRAM* NE23 22 B2
The Village *ASHBK/HED/RY* SR2 162 C2
Villa Pl *GATE* NE8 99 D1 7
Villa Vw *LWF/SPW/WRK* NE9 99 F4 6
Villette Brook St
ASHBK/HED/RY SR2 145 D2 4
Villette Pth *ASHBK/HED/RY* SR2 145 D2
Villette Rd *ASHBK/HED/RY* SR2 145 D2
Villiers St *SUND* SR1 5 E2
Villiers St South *SUND* SR1 5 E3
Vimy Av *HEBB* NE31 85 D2
Vincent St *PLEE/EAS* SR8 201 D2 1
SEA/MUR SR7 176 C4 9
Vine La *CNUT* NE1 2 D1
Vine Pl *HLS* DH4 171 D2
SUND SR1 4 B4
Vine St *SSH* NE33 88 B2
WLSD/HOW NE28 67 E5
Viola Crs *BDN/LAN/SAC* DH7 178 B2
CLSW/PEL DH2 135 E4
Viola St *WASHN* NE37 120 C4
Violet Cl *ELS/FEN* NE4 78 C4 3
Violet St *HLS* DH4 170 C2
MLFD/PNYW SR4 123 F6
MLFD/PNYW SR4 126 A5
Viscount Rd *SUNDSW* SR3 160 C1 8
Vivian Crs *CLSW/PEL* DH2 153 E6
Vivian Sq *CLDN/WHIT/ROK* SR6 126 C1 16
Voltage Ter *HLS* DH4 157 F4 3
Vulcan Pl *BDLGTN* NE22 7 F4

W

Waddington St *DHAM* DH1 194 A4
Wadsley Sq *ASHBK/HED/RY* SR2 145 D3
Wagon Wy *WLSD/HOW* NE28 67 F4
Wagonway Rd *HEBB* NE31 84 C1
Wagtail La *STLY/ANP* DH9 149 E6
Wagtail Ter *STLY/ANP* DH9 149 E6
Wakefield Av *HAR/WTLS* NE34 90 A3
Wakenshaw Rd *DHAM* DH1 195 E3
Walbottle Rd
BW/LEM/TK/HW NE15 58 B5
Walden Cl *CLSW/PEL* DH2 134 C5
Waldo St *NSHW* NE29 70 C1
Waldridge La *CLSW/PEL* DH2 152 C6
Waldridge Rd *CLSW/PEL* DH2 153 D6
Waldron Sq *ASHBK/HED/RY* SR2 145 D3
Walkerburn *CRAM* NE23 22 A5
Walkergate *DHAM* DH1 194 B4 5
Walker Pl *TYNE/NSHE* NE30 55 E6 3
Walker Rd *BYK/HTN/WLK* NE6 82 A4
Wallace Av *WICK/BNPF* NE16 96 B2
Wallace Gdns *LWF/SPW/WRK* NE9 101 D6
Wallace St *DUN/TMV* NE11 97 F1 7
HLS DH4 170 C2
JES NE2 80 A1
SWCK/CAS SR5 126 B3
Wallingford Av
ASHBK/HED/RY SR2 145 D4
Wallington Av *DIN/WO* NE13 32 C4
TYNE/NSHE NE30 54 C3
Wallington Cl *BDLGTN* NE22 8 B2
Wallington Ct *MONK* NE25 24 C5 3
Wallington Dr
BW/LEM/TK/HW NE15 60 A6
Wallis St *HLS* DH4 140 A6 2
SSH NE33 71 E3 11
Wallridge Dr *MONK* NE25 38 A1
Wallsend Rd *NSHW* NE29 69 F2
WLSD/HOW NE28 69 E3
Wall St *GOS/KPK* NE3 62 C1
Wall Ter *BYK/HTN/WLK* NE6 83 D1
Walnut Gdns *GATE* NE8 98 B2 4
Walnut Pl *GOS/KPK* NE3 62 B3
Walpole Cl *SEA/MUR* SR7 175 E4
Walpole Ct *MLFD/PNYW* SR4 125 E6 8
Walpole St *BYK/HTN/WLK* NE6 66 A6 2
Walsham Cl *BLYTH* NE24 16 A1
Walsh Av *HEBB* NE31 85 D1
Walsingham *WASHS* NE38 138 B3
Walter St *JRW* NE32 69 D6
Walter Ter *ELS/FEN* NE4 79 F2
HLH DH5 186 A3
Walter Thomas St
SWCK/CAS SR5 125 E2 3
Waltham *WASHS* NE38 138 C2
Waltham Cl *WLSD/HOW* NE28 66 B3 4
Waltham Pl *WD/WHPE/BLK* NE5 61 D4 8
Walton Av *BLYTH* NE24 10 B4
NSHW NE29 54 B5
SEA/MUR SR7 175 E4
Walton Cl *STLY/ANP* DH9 148 C3
Walton La *SUND* SR1 5 F1
Walton Pk *NSHW* NE29 54 B4
Walton Rd *WASHS* NE38 140 A1
WD/WHPE/BLK NE5 60 C5
Walwick Av *NSHW* NE29 53 F6
Walwick Rd *MONK* NE25 39 D5
Walworth Av *HAR/WTLS* NE34 90 B2
Walworth Gv *JRW* NE32 86 A5
Wandsworth Rd
BYK/HTN/WLK NE6 82 A1
Wanebeck *WASHS* NE38 137 F5
Wanlass Ter *DHAM* DH1 194 C4
Wanley St *BLYTH* NE24 11 D4
Wanlock Cl *CRAM* NE23 22 A5
Wanny Rd *BDLGTN* NE22 8 A3 1
Wansbeck Av *BLYTH* NE24 11 D6
STLY/ANP DH9 148 B3
TYNE/NSHE NE30 55 E1
Wansbeck Cl *CLSW/PEL* DH2 135 E6
WICK/BNPF NE16 113 F1
Wansbeck Gv *MONK* NE25 24 C2 2
Wansbeck Rd *CRAM* NE23 34 B2
JRW NE32 85 F3
Wansbeck Rd North
GOS/KPK NE3 46 C5 4
Wansbeck Rd South
GOS/KPK NE3 46 C6 9
Wansfell Av *WD/WHPE/BLK* NE5 61 F3
Wansford Av *WD/WHPE/BLK* NE5 61 D5
Wantage Av *NSHW* NE29 69 F2
Wantage Rd *DHAM* DH1 196 C1
Wantage St *SSH* NE33 88 C1

Wapping St SSH NE33 71 D2
Warbeck Cl WD/WHPE/BLK NE5 45 D6
Warburton Crs
LWF/SPW/WRK NE9 99 F2 14
Warcop Ct GOS/KPK NE3 46 A5
Warden Law La SUNDSW SR3 160 A2
Wardill Gdns LWF/SPW/WRK NE9 100 A3
Wardle Av SSH NE33 72 A5
Wardle Dr CRAM NE23 35 D2
Wardle Gdns FELL NE10 101 D3
Wardle St GOS/KPK NE3 64 A1 8
STLY/ANP DH9 148 A5
Wardley Ct FELL NE10 102 C2
Wardley Dr FELL NE10 102 C2
Wardley La FELL NE10 102 B1
Warenford Cl CRAM NE23 22 B4 3
Warenford Pl
WD/WHPE/BLK NE5 78 B1 3
Warenmill Cl
BW/LEM/TK/HW NE15 76 A1
Warennes St MLFD/PNYW SR4 125 D5 7
Warenton Pl NSHW NE29 53 D3
Waring Av WBAY NE26 26 A1
Waring Ter SEA/MUR SR7 175 E4
Wark Av NSHW NE29 53 E6
SMOOR NE27 38 B6
Wark Crs JRW NE32 86 A6
Warkdale Av BLYTH NE24 9 F6 2
Warkworth Av BLYTH NE24 17 D1
HAR/WTLS NE34 90 A1
WLSD/HOW NE28 67 E2
Warkworth Cl WASHS NE38 138 A2
Warkworth Crs GOS/KPK NE3 47 D6
SEA/MUR SR7 175 D3
Warkworth Dr CLSW/PEL DH2 165 F2
DIN/WO NE13 33 E3
Warkworth Gdns FELL NE10 100 B2 6
Warkworth Rd DHAM DH1 180 B5
Warkworth St
BW/LEM/TK/HW NE15 76 B2
BYK/HTN/WLK NE6 82 B2 8
Warkworth Ter JRW NE32 86 A5
TYNE/NSHE NE30 55 F4 7
Warnham Av ASHBK/HED/RY SR2 145 D4
Warnhead Rd BDLGTN NE22 8 A3
Warren Av BYK/HTN/WLK NE6 66 C6
Warren Cl HLS DH4 157 E4 7
Warrenmor FELL NE10 101 F3
Warren St PLEE/EAS SR8 209 F2
Warrington Rd ELS/FEN NE4 79 F4
GOS/KPK NE3 46 A6
Warton Ter BYK/HTN/WLK NE6 65 E6 6
Warwick Av WICK/BNPF NE16 95 F5
Warwick Cl CRAM NE23 36 A1 3
WICK/BNPF NE16 95 F5 1
Warwick Ct DHAM DH1 204 C1 5
GOS/KPK NE3 45 F5
Warwick Dr HLH DH5 171 D4
SUNDSW SR3 159 E1
WASHN NE37 120 C2
WICK/BNPF NE16 96 A5
Warwick Gv BDLGTN NE22 6 C3
Warwick Hall Wk LGB/HTN NE7 65 F4
Warwick Pl PLEE/EAS SR8 200 A6
Warwick Rd HAR/WTLS NE34 88 C1
HEBB NE31 85 E5 4
WD/WHPE/BLK NE5 60 A6 8
WLSD/HOW NE28 67 D5
Warwickshire Dr DHAM DH1 196 C4 1
Warwick St BLYTH NE24 16 A2
GATE NE8 81 E6
JES NE2 81 E1
SWCK/CAS SR5 126 C3
Warwick Ter SUNDSW SR3 143 F6
Wasdale Cl CRAM NE23 22 A5
PLEE/EAS SR8 209 D2
Wasdale Ct CLDN/WHIT/ROK SR6 108 B5 8
Wasdale Rd WD/WHPE/BLK NE5 61 D6
Washington Hwy WASHN NE37 119 F4
WASHS NE38 138 B4
Washington Rd SWCK/CAS SR5 123 E1
Washington St
MLFD/PNYW SR4 125 E6 9
Washingwell La WICK/BNPF NE16 96 C3
Washingwell Pk WICK/BNPF NE16 96 B4
Waskdale Crs BLAY NE21 94 A2 7
Waskerley Cl WICK/BNPF NE16 113 F1
Waskerley Dr RDHAMSE DH6 206 A1
Waskerley Rd WASHS NE38 139 E1
Watch House Cl NSHW NE29 70 C3 4
Watcombe Cl WASHN NE37 121 E2 1
Waterbeach Pl WD/WHPE/BLK NE5 60 C4
Waterbeck Cl CRAM NE23 22 A5
Waterbury Rd GOS/KPK NE3 47 D3
Waterford Cl HLH DH5 170 C6 2
WBAY NE26 26 C2 2
Waterford Pk DIN/WO NE13 32 B4
Waterloo Pl NSHW NE29 54 C6
SUND SR1 4 C3
Waterloo Rd BLYTH NE24 11 D5
MONK NE25 38 C5
WASHN NE37 121 D3
Waterloo Sq SSH NE33 71 E3 12
Waterloo St BLAY NE21 93 F1 9
CNUT NE1 2 B5
Waterloo V SSH NE33 71 E3 13
Waterlow Cl SWCK/CAS SR5 107 E6 3
Watermill RYTON NE40 74 C3
Watermill La FELL NE10 101 D2
Water Rw BW/LEM/TK/HW NE15 75 D1
Waterside Dr DUN/TMV NE11 79 D6
Waterside Elvet DHAM DH1 194 C5
Waterson Crs BDN/LAN/SAC DH7 178 A3
Water St BDN/LAN/SAC DH7 178 B1
ELS/FEN NE4 80 A5
Waterville Rd NSHW NE29 69 F2
Waterworks Rd SUND SR1 126 A6 14
Watford Cl SWCK/CAS SR5 107 E6 4
Watkin Crs SEA/MUR SR7 188 B1
Watling Av SEA/MUR SR7 175 E4
Watling Pl LWF/SPW/WRK NE9 100 A4 6
Watling St HAR/WTLS NE34 88 A3 7
Watson Av HAR/WTLS NE34 90 A3
Watson Cl SEA/MUR SR7 175 E4
Watson Gdns WLSD/HOW NE28 68 C3 1
Watson Pl HAR/WTLS NE34 90 A3 5
Watson St JRW NE32 69 E6
STLY/ANP DH9 131 E6
WICK/BNPF NE16 112 A6 2
Watt's Rd WBAY NE26 40 C4
Watts St SEA/MUR SR7 188 B1 6
Watt St GATE NE8 98 C3
Wavendon Crs MLFD/PNYW SR4 142 C2
Waveney Gdns STLY/ANP DH9 148 A4
Waveney Rd PLEE/EAS SR8 208 A4
Waverdale Av BYK/HTN/WLK NE6 83 F1
Waverdale Wy SSH NE33 88 A2
Waverley Av BDLGTN NE22 8 B2 3
MONK NE25 40 B6
Waverley Cl BLAY NE21 93 E2 2
RDHAMSE DH6 206 A1
Waverley Crs
BW/LEM/TK/HW NE15 76 C1
Waverley Dr BDLGTN NE22 8 B2
Waverley Rd ELS/FEN NE4 80 A4 10
LWF/SPW/WRK NE9 117 F2
Waverley Ter MLFD/PNYW SR4 125 D5
Waverton Cl CRAM NE23 22 A5
Wawn St SSH NE33 71 F6 8
Wayfarer Rd SWCK/CAS SR5 125 F3
Wayland Sq ASHBK/HED/RY SR2 145 D5
Wayman St SWCK/CAS SR5 126 B3
Wayside ASHBK/HED/RY SR2 144 A2 3
BW/LEM/TK/HW NE15 78 A3
Wealcroft FELL NE10 101 E5 4
Wear Ct HAR/WTLS NE34 88 B3
Weardale Av BLYTH NE24 9 E4
BYK/HTN/WLK NE6 83 F1
CLDN/WHIT/ROK SR6 109 D3
LGB/KIL NE12 49 F4
WASHN NE37 120 B4
WLSD/HOW NE28 67 D2 4
Weardale Crs HLS DH4 157 D1
Weardale St HLH DH5 185 D3
Wearfield SWCK/CAS SR5 125 D3
Wear Ldg CLS/BIR/GTL DH3 153 E1
Wearmouth Av SWCK/CAS SR5 126 C2 6
Wearmouth Br SUND SR1 4 C1
Wearmouth Dr SWCK/CAS SR5 126 B2
Wearmouth St SWCK/CAS SR5 126 C3 10
Wear Rd HEBB NE31 85 D4
STLY/ANP DH9 148 B3
Wearside Dr DHAM DH1 194 C3
Wear St HLH DH5 185 F1
HLS DH4 169 F3
JRW NE32 86 A1 10
MLFD/PNYW SR4 123 F5
SEA/MUR SR7 176 C3 13
SUND SR1 5 G3
SWCK/CAS SR5 125 F3
Wear Vw DHAM DH1 194 C4
Weathercock La
LWF/SPW/WRK NE9 99 E5 10
Weatherside BLAY NE21 94 A1 6
Webb Av SEA/MUR SR7 174 B6
SEA/MUR SR7 175 D3
Webb Gdns FELL NE10 101 F2 6
Webb Sq PLEE/EAS SR8 201 D5
Wedgewood Cottages
BW/LEM/TK/HW NE15 76 C2 2
Wedgwood Rd SEA/MUR SR7 175 D4
Wedmore Rd WD/WHPE/BLK NE5 59 F4
Weetman St SSH NE33 71 D5 2
Weetslade Crs CRAM NE23 34 C3
Weetslade Rd CRAM NE23 34 C3
Weetwood Rd CRAM NE23 22 B4 4
Weidner Rd BW/LEM/TK/HW NE15 78 C3
Welbeck Rd BYK/HTN/WLK NE6 82 B3
Weldon Av ASHBK/HED/RY SR2 145 D4 2
Weldon Crs LGB/HTN NE7 65 D4
Weldon Pl NSHW NE29 53 F4
Weldon Rd CRAM NE23 23 D3 1
LGB/KIL NE12 49 D6
Weldon Ter CLS/BIR/GTL DH3 153 F6
Weldon Wy GOS/KPK NE3 47 D6
Welfare Cl PLEE/EAS SR8 201 D2
Welfare Rd HLH DH5 171 F6
Welford Av GOS/KPK NE3 62 C1
Welland Cl PLEE/EAS SR8 208 B4
Welland La CLDN/WHIT/ROK SR6 109 D1
Wellands Cl CLDN/WHIT/ROK SR6 109 D1
Wellands Ct CLDN/WHIT/ROK SR6 109 D1
Well Bank Rd WASHN NE37 120 A4
Wellburn Rd WASHN NE37 120 A3
Well Close Wk WICK/BNPF NE16 95 F4 2
Wellesley St JRW NE32 86 A3
Wellfield Cl BW/LEM/TK/HW NE15 57 E5
Wellfield La WD/WHPE/BLK NE5 61 D4 9
Wellfield Rd ELS/FEN NE4 78 C3
ROWG NE39 110 B2
SEA/MUR SR7 188 A1
Wellington Av MONK NE25 38 C5 2
Wellington Dr SSH NE33 71 E2
Wellington La MLFD/PNYW SR4 126 A4
Wellington Rd DUN/TMV NE11 96 C1
Wellington St BLYTH NE24 11 E5 9
ELS/FEN NE4 2 A2
FELL NE10 100 B2
HEBB NE31 84 C3
Well La SMOOR NE27 53 D2
Well Ridge Cl MONK NE25 39 E4
Well Ridge Pk MONK NE25 39 E3
Wells Cl LGB/KIL NE12 65 F2 1
Wells Crs SEA/MUR SR7 175 E3
Wells Gdns LWF/SPW/WRK NE9 117 E2
Wells Gv HAR/WTLS NE34 89 F1
Well St MLFD/PNYW SR4 125 E5
Welsh Ter STLY/ANP DH9 146 C5
Welwyn Cl SWCK/CAS SR5 123 F4
WLSD/HOW NE28 66 B2
Wembley Av MONK NE25 40 A6
Wembley Rd SWCK/CAS SR5 125 E1
Wendover Cl SWCK/CAS SR5 107 D6
Wendover Wy SWCK/CAS SR5 107 D6
Wenham Sq
ASHBK/HED/RY SR2 144 A2 4
Wenlock WASHS NE38 138 B2
Wenlock Dr NSHW NE29 54 A4
Wenlock Rd HAR/WTLS NE34 87 F3
Wensley Cl CLSW/PEL DH2 135 D5
Wensleydale WLSD/HOW NE28 66 B1 4
Wensleydale Av HLS DH4 156 C1
WASHN NE37 120 B4 2
Wens Leydale Dr LGB/KIL NE12 49 F4 10
Wensleydale Ter BLYTH NE24 11 E6
Wentworth SSH NE33 72 A5
Wentworth Cl FELL NE10 100 C3 4
Wentworth Dr WASHN NE37 120 B2
Wentworth Gdns MONK NE25 39 E5
Wentworth Pl ELS/FEN NE4 80 A4 11
Wentworth Ter MLFD/PNYW SR4 126 A5
Werhale Gn FELL NE10 100 C2 8
Wesley Dr LGB/KIL NE12 51 D3
Wesley St LWF/SPW/WRK NE9 99 E5 11
Wesley Wy BW/LEM/TK/HW NE15 57 F4
LGB/KIL NE12 51 D3
SEA/MUR SR7 175 E3
Wessex Cl SWCK/CAS SR5 107 E6
Wessington Wy SWCK/CAS SR5 123 E5
SWCK/CAS SR5 125 F3 11
SWCK/CAS SR5 125 D3
Westacre Gdns
WD/WHPE/BLK NE5 78 B1 4
West Acres DIN/WO NE13 31 D2 1
Westacres Av WICK/BNPF NE16 96 A6
Westacres Crs
BW/LEM/TK/HW NE15 78 B2 3
West Av CLDN/WHIT/ROK SR6 109 D1
GOS/KPK NE3 63 E2
HAR/WTLS NE34 89 D2
LGB/KIL NE12 49 F6
NSHW NE29 69 F1
PLEE/EAS SR8 201 D1
ROWG NE39 110 C3 2
SEA/MUR SR7 188 B1 7
WASHS NE38 138 A5
WD/WHPE/BLK NE5 60 B4
West Bailey LGB/KIL NE12 35 F6 12
LGB/KIL NE12 49 F1 3
Westbourne Av BYK/HTN/WLK NE6 66 B6
GATE NE8 99 D2
GOS/KPK NE3 47 E5
Westbourne Dr HLS DH4 156 C2
Westbourne Rd SUND SR1 126 A6
Westburn Gdns
WLSD/HOW NE28 66 B2 2
Westburn Ter
CLDN/WHIT/ROK SR6 127 D2
Westbury Av BYK/HTN/WLK NE6 66 B6
Westbury Rd NSHW NE29 54 B4 1
Westbury St MLFD/PNYW SR4 126 A5
Westcliff Cl PLEE/EAS SR8 199 F3 3
Westcliffe Rd
CLDN/WHIT/ROK SR6 109 E6 2
Westcliffe Wy HAR/WTLS NE34 87 E5
West Clifton LGB/KIL NE12 35 E6 13
West Copperas
BW/LEM/TK/HW NE15 77 D1 5
Westcott Av SSH NE33 72 A5
Westcott Dr DHAM DH1 193 F1
Westcott Rd HAR/WTLS NE34 88 B3
PLEE/EAS SR8 208 C1
West Crs FELL NE10 102 B2
Westcroft Rd LGB/KIL NE12 50 A4
West Dene Dr TYNE/NSHE NE30 54 C4

West Denton Cl
BW/LEM/TK/HW NE15 .... 59 F6
West Denton Rd
BW/LEM/TK/HW NE15 .... 59 F6
West Denton Wy
WD/WHPE/BLK NE5 .... 59 F4
WD/WHPE/BLK NE5 .... 60 C4
West Dr *BLYTH* NE24 .... 16 B2 6
CLDN/WHIT/ROK SR6 .... 107 D1
CLSW/PEL DH2 .... 152 B6
West End Front St *BDLGTN* NE22 .... 7 E4 3
Westerdale *HLS* DH4 .... 139 D6
WLSD/HOW NE28 .... 66 B2
Westerdale Pl *BYK/HTN/WLK* NE6 .... 84 A2
Westerham Cl *SWCK/CAS* SR5 .... 107 E6
Westerhope Gdns
WD/WHPE/BLK NE5 .... 61 F5 10
Westerhope Rd *WASHS* NE38 .... 139 E1
Westerkirk *CRAM* NE23 .... 22 A4
Western Ap *SSH* NE33 .... 71 E5
Western Av *ELS/FEN* NE4 .... 79 E3
MONK NE25 .... 24 B5
WD/WHPE/BLK NE5 .... 59 F5
Western Dr *ELS/FEN* NE4 .... 79 E3
Western Hwy *WASHS* NE38 .... 137 F4
Western Hl
ASHBK/HED/RY SR2 .... 144 A1 13
ASHBK/HED/RY SR2 .... 162 A1
MLFD/PNYW SR4 .... 126 A6 15
MLFD/PNYW SR4 .... 144 A1
Westernmoor *WASHN* NE37 .... 119 E6
Western Rd *JRW* NE32 .... 85 F1
WLSD/HOW NE28 .... 68 B4
Western Ter *BOL* NE36 .... 105 F3
CRAM NE23 .... 34 B2
Western Wy *BLAY* NE21 .... 77 D6
RYTON NE40 .... 74 B4
WBAY NE26 .... 40 B2
West Farm Av *LGB/KIL* NE12 .... 48 B6 5
West Farm Ct *CRAM* NE23 .... 22 A1 3
West Farm Rd *BYK/HTN/WLK* NE6 .... 83 D1
CLDN/WHIT/ROK SR6 .... 108 A2
WLSD/HOW NE28 .... 68 A3
West Farm Wynd *LGB/KIL* NE12 .... 64 B1
Westfield *GOS/KPK* NE3 .... 63 D4
Westfield Av *DIN/WO* NE13 .... 32 C4
GOS/KPK NE3 .... 63 E3
MONK NE25 .... 39 F6
Westfield Ct *MLFD/PNYW* SR4 .... 143 D2 4
WLSD/HOW NE28 .... 67 D6
Westfield Dr *GOS/KPK* NE3 .... 63 D3
Westfield Gv *GOS/KPK* NE3 .... 63 D3
MLFD/PNYW SR4 .... 143 D2
Westfield La *RYTON* NE40 .... 74 A2
Westfield Pk *WLSD/HOW* NE28 .... 66 C4
Westfield Rd
BW/LEM/TK/HW NE15 .... 78 B3
Westfield Ter *GATE* NE8 .... 99 D2 1
Westgarth *WD/WHPE/BLK* NE5 .... 60 A2
Westgarth Gv *RDHAMSE* DH6 .... 206 A1
Westgate Av *SUNDSW* SR3 .... 143 F6
Westgate Cl *MONK* NE25 .... 39 E4
Westgate Gv *SUNDSW* SR3 .... 143 F6
Westgate Hill Ter *CNUT* NE1 .... 2 A5
Westgate Rd *CNUT* NE1 .... 2 A4
ELS/FEN NE4 .... 79 D2
West George Potts St
SSH NE33 .... 71 F5 12
West Gra *SWCK/CAS* SR5 .... 126 B1
West Gv *MLFD/PNYW* SR4 .... 142 A1
Westheath Av
ASHBK/HED/RY SR2 .... 145 D5
West High Horse Cl *ROWG* NE39 .... 93 E6
West Hl *MLFD/PNYW* SR4 .... 143 D2
Westhills *STLY/ANP* DH9 .... 129 F4 1
Westhills Cl *BDN/LAN/SAC* DH7 .... 164 A5
West Holborn *SSH* NE33 .... 71 D5
Westholme Gdns
BW/LEM/TK/HW NE15 .... 78 C2
Westhope Cl *HAR/WTLS* NE34 .... 89 F1
Westhope Rd *HAR/WTLS* NE34 .... 89 F1
West Jesmond Av *JES* NE2 .... 64 A4 5
Westlands *BW/LEM/TK/HW* NE15 .... 59 E5
JRW NE32 .... 104 C1
LGB/HTN NE7 .... 64 C3
TYNE/NSHE NE30 .... 55 D3
WBAY NE26 .... 26 A2
West La *BLAY* NE21 .... 93 F2
CLS/BIR/GTL DH3 .... 153 E6
LGB/KIL NE12 .... 49 F3
RDHAMSE DH6 .... 188 C6
SEA/MUR SR7 .... 189 E5
WICK/BNPF NE16 .... 112 B3
West Lawn *ASHBK/HED/RY* SR2 .... 144 B2
West Lawson St *NSHW* NE29 .... 70 C2 10
West Lea *BLAY* NE21 .... 94 B2
Westleigh Ct *MLFD/PNYW* SR4 .... 125 E6 10
Westleigh Rd *HLS* DH4 .... 157 E4
Westley Av *WBAY* NE26 .... 40 A1
Westley Cl *WBAY* NE26 .... 40 A1
Westloch Rd *CRAM* NE23 .... 22 A5
Westmacott St
BW/LEM/TK/HW NE15 .... 58 A6 1
West Mdw *WD/WHPE/BLK* NE5 .... 59 F2 2
West Meadows Dr
CLDN/WHIT/ROK SR6 .... 107 F2
West Meadows Rd
CLDN/WHIT/ROK SR6 .... 107 F2
Westminster Av *NSHW* NE29 .... 53 D4
Westminster Crs *HEBB* NE31 .... 85 D6
Westminster Dr *DUN/TMV* NE11 .... 97 E4 5
Westminster St *GATE* NE8 .... 98 C2
Westminster Wy *LGB/HTN* NE7 .... 65 E2
West Moffett St *SSH* NE33 .... 71 F5 13
West Moor Dr
CLDN/WHIT/ROK SR6 .... 107 F3
Westmoor Dr *LGB/KIL* NE12 .... 49 D3
Westmoor Rd *MLFD/PNYW* SR4 .... 124 C5
Westmoreland St
WLSD/HOW NE28 .... 67 E4
Westmorland Av *BDLGTN* NE22 .... 7 D3
WASHN NE37 .... 120 C2
WLSD/HOW NE28 .... 69 D5 4
Westmorland Gdns
LWF/SPW/WRK NE9 .... 99 E5 12
Westmorland La *CNUT* NE1 .... 2 B5
Westmorland Rd *CNUT* NE1 .... 2 A5
ELS/FEN NE4 .... 79 E4
HAR/WTLS NE34 .... 90 B1
NSHW NE29 .... 53 D5
Westmorland Wy *CRAM* NE23 .... 21 E2
West Mt *MLFD/PNYW* SR4 .... 143 D1
Westoe Av *SSH* NE33 .... 72 A5
Westoe Dr *SSH* NE33 .... 72 A5
Westoe Rd *SSH* NE33 .... 71 F4
Westoe Village *SSH* NE33 .... 72 A6
Weston Av *WICK/BNPF* NE16 .... 95 E5
Weston Vw *PLEE/EAS* SR8 .... 208 B1
West Ousterley Rd *STLY/ANP* DH9 .... 148 C6
Westover Gdns
LWF/SPW/WRK NE9 .... 99 E3
West Pde *ELS/FEN* NE4 .... 80 A4
HEBB NE31 .... 84 C4
West Pk *SUNDSW* SR3 .... 159 D2
West Park Gdns *BLAY* NE21 .... 94 B1
West Park Rd
CLDN/WHIT/ROK SR6 .... 107 F1
LWF/SPW/WRK NE9 .... 99 D3
SSH NE33 .... 71 E6
West Park Vw *CRAM* NE23 .... 34 B2
West Pastures *BOL* NE36 .... 104 B5
West Percy Rd *NSHW* NE29 .... 70 B2
TYNE/NSHE NE30 .... 54 C6 13
West Percy St *NSHW* NE29 .... 70 C1 14
Westport Cl *SWCK/CAS* SR5 .... 107 E6 5
West Quay Rd *SWCK/CAS* SR5 .... 125 E3
West Riggs *BDLGTN* NE22 .... 7 E4
The West Rig *GOS/KPK* NE3 .... 62 A2
West Rd *BDLGTN* NE22 .... 8 C2
STLY/ANP DH9 .... 129 F5
STLY/ANP DH9 .... 146 B5
West Salisbury St *BLYTH* NE24 .... 10 C4
West Stainton St *SSH* NE33 .... 71 F5 14
West Stevenson St *SSH* NE33 .... 71 F5 15
West Stoneycroft *LGB/KIL* NE12 .... 50 A2 2
West St *CLS/BIR/GTL* DH3 .... 136 B2
CLSW/PEL DH2 .... 150 C3
GATE NE8 .... 81 D5
HEBB NE31 .... 85 D1
RDHAMSE DH6 .... 206 B2
SEA/MUR SR7 .... 176 C3
SMOOR NE27 .... 51 F3
STLY/ANP DH9 .... 130 C6
SUND SR1 .... 4 B2
SUNDSW SR3 .... 143 F6 6
WICK/BNPF NE16 .... 95 F3
WLSD/HOW NE28 .... 66 C4
West Sunniside *SUND* SR1 .... 4 D2
West Ter *WBAY* NE26 .... 26 C2
West Thorp *WD/WHPE/BLK* NE5 .... 60 B1
West Vallum
BW/LEM/TK/HW NE15 .... 77 E1 8
West Vw *BDLGTN* NE22 .... 8 B1
BDN/LAN/SAC DH7 .... 203 E5
BLAY NE21 .... 76 B5
BW/LEM/TK/HW NE15 .... 76 B2
CLDN/WHIT/ROK SR6 .... 126 C1
DHAM DH1 .... 195 D4
DUN/TMV NE11 .... 116 C6
ELS/FEN NE4 .... 79 E4
HLS DH4 .... 157 D4
LGB/KIL NE12 .... 49 F4 11
SWCK/CAS SR5 .... 124 A3 10
West Walls *CNUT* NE1 .... 2 B4
West Walpole St *SSH* NE33 .... 71 D5
Westward Ct
WD/WHPE/BLK NE5 .... 60 A3 9
Westward Pl *WASHS* NE38 .... 138 A5
West Wy *DUN/TMV* NE11 .... 97 F2
SSH NE33 .... 88 B1
Westway *BLAY* NE21 .... 76 A6 2
BW/LEM/TK/HW NE15 .... 57 F3
PLEE/EAS SR8 .... 208 B3 2
West Wear St *SUND* SR1 .... 4 C1
Westwell Ct *LGB/HTN* NE7 .... 64 B2 3
West Wellington St
NSHW NE29 .... 70 C1 15
Westwood Av
BYK/HTN/WLK NE6 .... 65 E5 5
Westwood Cl *WICK/BNPF* NE16 .... 112 A5
Westwood Gdns *GOS/KPK* NE3 .... 62 A2
Westwood Rd *GOS/KPK* NE3 .... 47 E3
Westwood St
MLFD/PNYW SR4 .... 125 E6 11
West Wynd *LGB/KIL* NE12 .... 49 F1
Wetheral Gdns
LWF/SPW/WRK NE9 .... 117 F1
Wetheral Ter *BYK/HTN/WLK* NE6 .... 83 E4 3
Wetherburn Av *SEA/MUR* SR7 .... 188 A1
Wetherby Gv *GATE* NE8 .... 98 C3 3
Wetherby Rd *ASHBK/HED/RY* SR2 .... 145 F5
Wettondale Av *BLYTH* NE24 .... 9 F5
Weybourne Sq
ASHBK/HED/RY SR2 .... 145 D4 3
Weyhill Av *NSHW* NE29 .... 69 F2
Weymouth Dr *SEA/MUR* SR7 .... 175 F4
Weymouth Gdns
LWF/SPW/WRK NE9 .... 117 E2
Whaggs La *WICK/BNPF* NE16 .... 96 A4
Whalton Av *GOS/KPK* NE3 .... 46 C6
Whalton Cl *FELL* NE10 .... 102 B3
RDHAMSE DH6 .... 197 F5
Whalton Ct *HAR/WTLS* NE34 .... 89 D2 3
Wharfdale Pl *BYK/HTN/WLK* NE6 .... 83 F2
Wharfedale *HLS* DH4 .... 139 F6 3
WLSD/HOW NE28 .... 66 B1
Wharfedale Av *WASHN* NE37 .... 120 A4
Wharfedale Dr *SSH* NE33 .... 88 B1 4
Wharfedale Gdns *BLYTH* NE24 .... 9 F4
Wharmlands Rd
BW/LEM/TK/HW NE15 .... 77 E1
Wharncliffe St *SUND* SR1 .... 126 A6
Wharrier St *BYK/HTN/WLK* NE6 .... 83 E4
Wharton St *BLYTH* NE24 .... 16 A2
SSH NE33 .... 71 F4
Wheatall Dr *CLDN/WHIT/ROK* SR6 .... 91 E6
Wheatfield Gv *LGB/KIL* NE12 .... 49 D5
Wheatfield Rd *WD/WHPE/BLK* NE5 .... 60 B3
Wheatley Gdns *BOL* NE36 .... 105 F3
Wheatleywell La
CLS/BIR/GTL DH3 .... 166 B5
Whernside Pl *CRAM* NE23 .... 22 A5 2
Whernside Wk *RYTON* NE40 .... 74 C4 3
Whickham Cl *HLS* DH4 .... 170 B2
Whickham Hwy *DUN/TMV* NE11 .... 97 D3
WICK/BNPF NE16 .... 96 C3
Whickham Ldg *WICK/BNPF* NE16 .... 96 B3
Whickham Pk *WICK/BNPF* NE16 .... 96 B3 4
Whickham Rd *HEBB* NE31 .... 84 C3
Whickham St
CLDN/WHIT/ROK SR6 .... 127 D3
PLEE/EAS SR8 .... 200 C2 3
Whickham St East
CLDN/WHIT/ROK SR6 .... 127 D3
Whickham Vw
BW/LEM/TK/HW NE15 .... 77 F2
LWF/SPW/WRK NE9 .... 99 F5
Whickhope *WASHS* NE38 .... 139 D4
Whinbrooke *FELL* NE10 .... 101 F4
Whinbush Pl
BW/LEM/TK/HW NE15 .... 77 F3
Whinfell Cl *CRAM* NE23 .... 22 B5
Whinfield Av *RDHAMSE* DH6 .... 206 B2
Whinfield Ter *ROWG* NE39 .... 110 C2
Whinfield Wy *ROWG* NE39 .... 110 B3
Whinlatter Gdns
LWF/SPW/WRK NE9 .... 99 F6
Whinmoor Pl *WD/WHPE/BLK* NE5 .... 62 A5
Whinney Cl *BLAY* NE21 .... 93 F2 7
Whinneyfield Rd
BYK/HTN/WLK NE6 .... 66 B6
BYK/HTN/WLK NE6 .... 83 E1
Whinney Hl *DHAM* DH1 .... 194 C6
Whinshaw *FELL* NE10 .... 101 E3
Whistler Gdns *HAR/WTLS* NE34 .... 88 C5
Whitbay Crs *LGB/KIL* NE12 .... 49 E6
Whitbeck Rd *WD/WHPE/BLK* NE5 .... 60 C6
Whitbourne Cl *WASHN* NE37 .... 121 D2 2
Whitburn Bents Rd
CLDN/WHIT/ROK SR6 .... 109 E3 1
Whitburn Gdns
LWF/SPW/WRK NE9 .... 118 C1
Whitburn Pl *CRAM* NE23 .... 22 A5
Whitburn Rd
CLDN/WHIT/ROK SR6 .... 107 E2
CLDN/WHIT/ROK SR6 .... 109 E6
Whitburn Rd East
CLDN/WHIT/ROK SR6 .... 108 A1
Whitburn St
CLDN/WHIT/ROK SR6 .... 126 C4 11
Whitburn Ter *BOL* NE36 .... 106 C3
CLDN/WHIT/ROK SR6 .... 108 C6 8
Whitby Av *CLDN/WHIT/ROK* SR6 .... 109 E4
Whitby Cl *GATE* NE8 .... 99 E1 16
Whitby Dr *WASHS* NE38 .... 138 C3
Whitby Gdns *WLSD/HOW* NE28 .... 68 A2
Whitby St *TYNE/NSHE* NE30 .... 55 D6
Whitchurch Cl *BOLCOL* NE35 .... 105 D1 6
SWCK/CAS SR5 .... 107 E6 6
Whitchurch Rd *SWCK/CAS* SR5 .... 107 E6
Whitebark *SUNDSW* SR3 .... 160 A4 1
Whitebeam Pl *ELS/FEN* NE4 .... 80 A5 10
Whitebridge Cl *GOS/KPK* NE3 .... 47 E4
Whitebridge Ct *GOS/KPK* NE3 .... 47 E5 3

Whitebridge Pk GOS/KPK NE3 47 F5
White Cedars BDN/LAN/SAC DH7 202 C5
Whitecliff Cl NSHW NE29 54 B4
Whitecroft Rd LGB/KIL NE12 48 C2
Whitefield Crs HLS DH4 156 C1
Whitefield Gv FELL NE10 100 C2
Whitefield Ter BYK/HTN/WLK NE6 65 F5
Whiteford Pl CRAM NE23 23 F6
Whitefriars Wy LGB/KIL NE12 64 C1
White Gates Dr HLH DH5 186 A2 2
Whitegates Rd RDHAMSE DH6 197 E3
Whitehall Rd
BW/LEM/TK/HW NE15 58 B4
GATE NE8 99 D2
Whitehall St SSH NE33 88 B2
Whitehead St SSH NE33 88 A1 4
Whitehill FELL NE10 101 E5
Whitehill Crs CLSW/PEL DH2 152 A4
Whitehill Dr FELL NE10 100 C4
Whitehill Hall Gdns
CLSW/PEL DH2 152 C4
Whitehill Rd CRAM NE23 13 F5 6
White Hill Rd HLH DH5 186 B4
Whitehorn Crs WD/WHPE/BLK NE5 61 F4
White Horse Vw
HAR/WTLS NE34 90 B2 1
Whitehouse Crs
LWF/SPW/WRK NE9 101 D6
Whitehouse La NSHW NE29 53 F4
White House Pl
ASHBK/HED/RY SR2 5 G4 1
White House Rd
ASHBK/HED/RY SR2 5 F5 2
Whitehouse Rd
BW/LEM/TK/HW NE15 78 A4
White House Wy FELL NE10 101 D5
Whitehouse Wy PLEE/EAS SR8 207 E2
RDHAMSE DH6 207 E4
Whitelaw Pl CRAM NE23 22 B4 5
White Lea Cl PLEE/EAS SR8 209 E3
Whiteleas Wy HAR/WTLS NE34 88 C6
Whitelees Ct GOS/KPK NE3 46 A5 9
White Le Head Gdns
STLY/ANP DH9 129 F4 2
Whiteley Rd BLAY NE21 77 D4
Whitemere Cl ASHBK/HED/RY SR2 145 D4
White Mere Gdns FELL NE10 102 B2
Whiteoak Av DHAM DH1 196 A3
White Oaks FELL NE10 101 D5
White Rocks Gv
CLDN/WHIT/ROK SR6 91 E5
Whites Gdns HEBB NE31 84 B2
Whitesmocks DHAM DH1 193 F2
Whitesmocks Av DHAM DH1 193 E3
White St BYK/HTN/WLK NE6 84 A3
Whitewell La RYTON NE40 74 B3
Whitewell Rd BLAY NE21 76 B6
Whitfield Dr LGB/KIL NE12 49 E6
Whitfield Rd BW/LEM/TK/HW NE15 77 E3
LGB/KIL NE12 49 F4 12
MONK NE25 24 C5
Whitgrave Rd WD/WHPE/BLK NE5 61 F3
Whithorn Ct BLYTH NE24 10 B5 3
Whitley Rd LGB/KIL NE12 50 A6
MONK NE25 38 C5
WBAY NE26 41 D6
Whitmore Rd BLAY NE21 76 B5
Whittingham Rd TYNE/NSHE NE30 55 E2
WD/WHPE/BLK NE5 60 B2 2
Whittington Gv
WD/WHPE/BLK NE5 78 B1
Whittleburn FELL NE10 101 E5
Whitton Av BLYTH NE24 16 A1
Whitton Gdns NSHW NE29 53 F5 3
Whitton Pl LGB/HTN NE7 64 C2
MONK NE25 24 C5
Whittonstall WASHS NE38 139 E5
Whitton Wy GOS/KPK NE3 47 D6
Whitworth Cl BYK/HTN/WLK NE6 83 F3 6
GATE NE8 98 C3 4
Whitworth Rd PLEE/EAS SR8 207 E2
WASHN NE37 119 E5
Whorlton Pl
WD/WHPE/BLK NE5 60 A3 10
Whyndyke FELL NE10 101 D5
Whytrigg Cl MONK NE25 24 A4
Widdrington Av HAR/WTLS NE34 73 D6
Widdrington Gdns DIN/WO NE13 33 E4 2
Widdrington Rd BLAY NE21 76 B6
Widnes Pl LGB/KIL NE12 49 E5
Wigeon Cl WASHS NE38 137 E4
Wigmore Av BYK/HTN/WLK NE6 83 D4
Wilber Ct MLFD/PNYW SR4 125 E6 12
Wilberforce St JRW NE32 86 B1
WLSD/HOW NE28 67 D6 6
Wilber St MLFD/PNYW SR4 125 E6 13
Wilbury Pl WD/WHPE/BLK NE5 61 E4 4
Wilden Ct SUNDSW SR3 144 A4 6
Wilden Rd WASHS NE38 139 E3
Wildshaw Cl CRAM NE23 22 B5
Wilfred St BOLCOL NE35 105 E3
BYK/HTN/WLK NE6 81 F2 10
CLS/BIR/GTL DH3 153 E6
MLFD/PNYW SR4 125 D5 8
Wilfrid St CLS/BIR/GTL DH3 136 B3
Wilkes Cl WD/WHPE/BLK NE5 60 B4 7
Wilkinson Av HEBB NE31 84 C5 3
Wilkinson Rd PLEE/EAS SR8 201 D5
Wilkwood Cl CRAM NE23 22 B4 6
Willerby Dr GOS/KPK NE3 47 F4
Willerby Gv PLEE/EAS SR8 208 B1 2
William Armstrong Dr
ELS/FEN NE4 79 D5
William Cl LGB/KIL NE12 50 C4 3
William Morris Av ROWG NE39 110 A2
William Pl DHAM DH1 195 E4
Williams Cl STLY/ANP DH9 148 C3
Williamson Ter
CLDN/WHIT/ROK SR6 126 C4 12
Williams Rd SEA/MUR SR7 188 B1
William St BLYTH NE24 11 D5
FELL NE10 100 C1
GOS/KPK NE3 64 A1
HEBB NE31 84 C1
NSHW NE29 70 C1 16
SUND SR1 4 D1
WICK/BNPF NE16 95 F3 12
William St West HEBB NE31 84 C2
NSHW NE29 70 C1
Willington Ter WLSD/HOW NE28 68 A3
Willis St HLH DH5 171 F5 3
Willmore St MLFD/PNYW SR4 125 F6
Willoughby Dr WBAY NE26 40 A3
Willoughby Rd NSHW NE29 53 F6
Willow Av BLYTH NE24 10 C3
DUN/TMV NE11 97 E2 3
ELS/FEN NE4 61 F6
Willowbank Gdns JES NE2 64 A2 6
Willow Bank Rd
ASHBK/HED/RY SR2 144 B3 10
Willow Cl BDN/LAN/SAC DH7 203 D4
Willow Ct RYTON NE40 74 C2
Willow Crs BLYTH NE24 16 B2
HLH DH5 186 C3
Willowdene LGB/KIL NE12 50 A3 4
Willowfield Av GOS/KPK NE3 46 B6
Willow Gdns LGB/KIL NE12 35 E6 14
Willow Gra JRW NE32 85 F1 2
Willow Gv HAR/WTLS NE34 89 E3
WLSD/HOW NE28 67 F4
Willow Pl PONT/DH NE20 28 A6
Willow Rd BLAY NE21 76 C6
HLS DH4 170 B2
Willows Cl DIN/WO NE13 32 C5 9
The Willows BW/LEM/TK/HW NE15 57 F5
WASHS NE38 139 E2
Willowtree Av DHAM DH1 195 F2
Willow Wy PONT/DH NE20 42 A2
Wilmington Cl WD/WHPE/BLK NE5 45 D6
Wilson Av CLS/BIR/GTL DH3 136 B1
Wilson Dr BOL NE36 106 A2 1
Wilson Gdns GOS/KPK NE3 63 D3
Wilson Pl PLEE/EAS SR8 200 C6
Wilson's La LWF/SPW/WRK NE9 99 E5
Wilson St DUN/TMV NE11 97 E2
MLFD/PNYW SR4 125 F5
SSH NE33 71 E5
WLSD/HOW NE28 67 D4
Wilson St North SWCK/CAS SR5 126 B4
Wilson Ter LGB/KIL NE12 49 F4 13
SUNDSW SR3 143 F6
Wilsway BW/LEM/TK/HW NE15 57 E4
Wilton Av BYK/HTN/WLK NE6 83 D3
Wilton Cl CRAM NE23 22 B5
MONK NE25 39 D5
Wilton Dr MONK NE25 39 D6
Wilton Gdns North BOLCOL NE35 87 D6 9
Wilton Gdns South BOLCOL NE35 105 D1
Wiltshire Cl DHAM DH1 196 B3 3
SWCK/CAS SR5 107 D6 1
Wiltshire Dr WLSD/HOW NE28 66 B1
Wiltshire Gdns WLSD/HOW NE28 66 B3
Wiltshire Pl WASHN NE37 120 C2
Wiltshire Rd SWCK/CAS SR5 107 E6 7
Wimbledon Cl SWCK/CAS SR5 125 E1 1
Wimborne Cl BOLCOL NE35 105 D2 2
Wimbourne Av
MLFD/PNYW SR4 143 D2 5
Wimbourne Gn
WD/WHPE/BLK NE5 60 B3 8
Wimpole Cl WASHN NE37 121 D2 3
Wimslow Cl WLSD/HOW NE28 66 B3
Winalot Av ASHBK/HED/RY SR2 145 D4
Wincanton Pl NSHW NE29 70 A2 4
Winchcombe Pl LGB/HTN NE7 64 C3 3
Winchester Av BLYTH NE24 11 D5
Winchester Cl CLS/BIR/GTL DH3 167 F3
Winchester Ct JRW NE32 104 A1
MLFD/PNYW SR4 125 E6 14
Winchester Dr BDN/LAN/SAC DH7 202 C6
PLEE/EAS SR8 207 E3 1
Winchester Rd DHAM DH1 181 D5
Winchester St SSH NE33 71 F3 7
Winchester Wk DIN/WO NE13 33 D5
Winchester Wy BDLGTN NE22 7 E2
Wincomblee Rd
BYK/HTN/WLK NE6 84 A5
Windburgh Dr CRAM NE23 22 A5
Windermere
CLDN/WHIT/ROK SR6 107 F1 3
Windermere Av CLSW/PEL DH2 166 B1
FELL NE10 101 E2
HLH DH5 186 B4
Windermere Cl CRAM NE23 22 A5
Windermere Crs BLAY NE21 94 A2 3
HAR/WTLS NE34 89 D2
HEBB NE31 85 E3
HLS DH4 157 D2
JRW NE32 86 C5
Windermere Gdns
WICK/BNPF NE16 96 B3
Windermere Rd RDHAMSE DH6 188 A4
SEA/MUR SR7 175 D3
WD/WHPE/BLK NE5 61 D6 4
Windermere St
ASHBK/HED/RY SR2 145 E4
Windermere Ter NSHW NE29 54 B6
Windhill Rd BYK/HTN/WLK NE6 83 E5
The Winding DIN/WO NE13 31 D3 4
Windlass Ct HAR/WTLS NE34 88 B3 13
Windlass La WASHN NE37 120 B5
Windmill Ct JES NE2 63 E6 1
JES NE2 80 B1 2
Windmill Gv BLYTH NE24 9 F4
Windmill Hl SSH NE33 71 D5 3
Windmill Sq SWCK/CAS SR5 108 B6 5
Windmill Wy HEBB NE31 68 A6
Winds La SEA/MUR SR7 188 A2
Winds Lonnen Est SEA/MUR SR7 187 F1
Windsor Av GATE NE8 99 D2
Windsor Cl WICK/BNPF NE16 95 E6
Windsor Cottages
WLSD/HOW NE28 68 C2 3
Windsor Ct BDLGTN NE22 7 E4
CRAM NE23 13 F5
GOS/KPK NE3 46 A5
Windsor Crs HEBB NE31 85 E2
HLH DH5 171 E2
WBAY NE26 41 E6
WD/WHPE/BLK NE5 60 C3
Windsor Dr CLDN/WHIT/ROK SR6 107 D1
HLH DH5 171 D4
RDHAMSE DH6 187 E4
STLY/ANP DH9 146 B3
SUNDSW SR3 160 C1
WLSD/HOW NE28 68 C3
Windsor Gdns BDLGTN NE22 7 E4
FELL NE10 100 B2 7
HAR/WTLS NE34 89 D1
NSHW NE29 54 C5
WBAY NE26 40 B4
Windsor Pk WLSD/HOW NE28 66 B3
Windsor Pl JES NE2 81 D1 8
RDHAMSE DH6 206 C1
SMOOR NE27 51 E3
Windsor Rd CLS/BIR/GTL DH3 118 A6
LWF/SPW/WRK NE9 119 D3
MONK NE25 40 A5
SEA/MUR SR7 175 E3
Windsor St WLSD/HOW NE28 67 D4
Windsor Ter GOS/KPK NE3 64 A2
JES NE2 80 C1
SEA/MUR SR7 188 C1 2
SEA/MUR SR7 188 C2 1
WBAY NE26 41 E6
Windsor Wy GOS/KPK NE3 45 E5
Windt St DIN/WO NE13 32 C5 10
Windy Nook Rd
LWF/SPW/WRK NE9 100 A4
Windy Ridge Vls FELL NE10 100 B3 4
Wingate Cl BW/LEM/TK/HW NE15 77 D2
HLS DH4 170 C2
Wingate Gdns
LWF/SPW/WRK NE9 100 C6
Wingrove ROWG NE39 110 C3 3
Wingrove Av
CLDN/WHIT/ROK SR6 109 D6
ELS/FEN NE4 79 E2
Wingrove Gdns ELS/FEN NE4 79 E2
Wingrove Rd ELS/FEN NE4 62 A5
Winifred St CLDN/WHIT/ROK SR6 127 D1
Winifred Ter SUND SR1 5 E4 1
Winshields CRAM NE23 22 B4
Winship Cl HAR/WTLS NE34 88 B6
Winship St BLYTH NE24 16 B1
Winskell Rd HAR/WTLS NE34 87 E4
Winslade Cl SUNDSW SR3 144 A6 2
Winslow Cl BOLCOL NE35 87 E6
BYK/HTN/WLK NE6 83 F2 5
SWCK/CAS SR5 107 E6
Winslow Crs SEA/MUR SR7 175 E3
Winslow Gdns
LWF/SPW/WRK NE9 99 D5 4
Winslow Pl BYK/HTN/WLK NE6 83 F2
Winsten WASHS NE38 137 F5
Winston Crs MLFD/PNYW SR4 143 D2 6
Winston Gn HLS DH4 139 E6
Winton Cl CRAM NE23 23 F6
Winton Wy GOS/KPK NE3 62 B1 8
Wishaw Cl CRAM NE23 22 B4
Wishaw Ri BW/LEM/TK/HW NE15 77 D1
Witham Rd HEBB NE31 85 E5
Witherington Cl LGB/HTN NE7 66 A3 5
Withernsea Gv
ASHBK/HED/RY SR2 161 F1

Witney Cl *SWCK/CAS* SR5 107 D6
Witney Wy *BOL* NE36 105 D3
Witton Av *BDN/LAN/SAC* DH7 178 B1
HAR/WTLS NE34 89 F2
Witton Ct *GOS/KPK* NE3 46 A6
SUNDSW SR3 144 A4
Witton Gdns *JRW* NE32 86 A5
Witton Garth *PLEE/EAS* SR8 208 B5
Witton Gv *DHAM* DH1 193 E2
HLS DH4 170 B3
Witton Rd *BDN/LAN/SAC* DH7 178 A2
HEBB NE31 68 B6
SMOOR NE27 52 B1
Witty Av *HEBB* NE31 85 E3
Woburn *WASHS* NE38 138 C2
Woburn Cl *CRAM* NE23 13 F5
WLSD/HOW NE28 66 B3 5
Woburn Dr *BDLGTN* NE22 8 B2
SUNDSW SR3 160 C2
Woburn Wy *WD/WHPE/BLK* NE5 60 C4
Wolmer Rd *BLYTH* NE24 17 E1
Wolseley Cl *GATE* NE8 98 B1
Wolseley Gdns *JES* NE2 64 C6 6
Wolseley Ter *MLFD/PNYW* SR4 143 F1 7
Wolsey Ct *HAR/WTLS* NE34 88 B2
Wolsey Rd *SEA/MUR* SR7 175 D4
Wolsingham Ct *CRAM* NE23 21 E1
Wolsingham Dr *DHAM* DH1 180 C6
Wolsingham Rd *GOS/KPK* NE3 63 D2
Wolsingham St *ELS/FEN* NE4 79 F5
Wolsley Rd *BLYTH* NE24 11 D4
Wolveleigh Ter *GOS/KPK* NE3 63 F1
Woodbine Av *WLSD/HOW* NE28 67 D4
Woodbine Rd *DHAM* DH1 179 F5
GOS/KPK NE3 63 E2
Woodbine St *GATE* NE8 99 D1
SSH NE33 71 F3 8
SUND SR1 5 G3
Woodbine Ter *BLYTH* NE24 11 E6
FELL NE10 100 A2
MLFD/PNYW SR4 125 E4
Woodbrook Av
WD/WHPE/BLK NE5 60 C6
Woodburn *FELL* NE10 101 D5
STLY/ANP DH9 130 B6
Woodburn Av *ELS/FEN* NE4 62 A5
Woodburn Cl *BLAY* NE21 93 F2 8
Woodburn Dr *HLS* DH4 170 B1
WBAY NE26 40 A3
Woodburn Gdns *DUN/TMV* NE11 97 F4
Woodburn Sq *WBAY* NE26 39 F3
Woodburn St
BW/LEM/TK/HW NE15 76 B1 5
Woodchurch Cl *LGB/KIL* NE12 65 F2
Woodcroft Cl *CRAM* NE23 34 C1
Woodend Wy *GOS/KPK* NE3 45 E4
Woodfield *PLEE/EAS* SR8 208 B2 2
Wood Flds *PONT/DH* NE20 28 B4
Woodford *LWF/SPW/WRK* NE9 117 E3
Woodford Cl *SWCK/CAS* SR5 107 E6 8
Woodgate Gdns *FELL* NE10 102 A1
Woodgate La *FELL* NE10 84 A6
Wood Gv *BW/LEM/TK/HW* NE15 77 E1
Woodhall Spa *HLS* DH4 156 C4
Woodhead Rd *BYK/HTN/WLK* NE6 66 A6
Woodhill Rd *CRAM* NE23 22 B4 7
Woodhorn Gdns *DIN/WO* NE13 33 D4
Woodhouses La
WICK/BNPF NE16 95 D6 3
Woodhurst Gv
MLFD/PNYW SR4 141 F4 3
Woodland Crs
BW/LEM/TK/HW NE15 78 A4
Woodland Dr *MLFD/PNYW* SR4 143 D2
Woodland Gra *HLS* DH4 169 E1
Woodland Ri *SUNDSW* SR3 160 A2
Woodlands *BW/LEM/TK/HW* NE15 57 E4
GOS/KPK NE3 63 E3
NSHW NE29 54 C4
WASHS NE38 137 D6
Woodlands Cl *MONK* NE25 38 C5
Woodlands Dr
CLDN/WHIT/ROK SR6 107 F2
Woodlands Gra *LGB/KIL* NE12 50 A3
Woodlands Park Dr *BLAY* NE21 76 C6
Woodlands Rd
BW/LEM/TK/HW NE15 76 C1 4
CLDN/WHIT/ROK SR6 107 E2
ROWG NE39 110 C2
Woodlands Ter *FELL* NE10 100 B2 8
Woodlands Vw
CLDN/WHIT/ROK SR6 107 F2
Wood La *BDLGTN* NE22 8 A3
Wood Lea *HLH* DH5 171 F3
Woodlea *LGB/KIL* NE12 49 F3
Woodlea Cl *HLH* DH5 171 F6
Woodlea Ct *NSHW* NE29 70 A3 1
Woodlea Gdns *GOS/KPK* NE3 48 A5
Woodlea Sq *NSHW* NE29 70 A3
Woodleigh Rd *MONK* NE25 40 A6
Woodleigh Vw
WD/WHPE/BLK NE5 62 A3 2
Woodman St *WLSD/HOW* NE28 69 D3
Woodmans Wy *WICK/BNPF* NE16 95 D6
Woodnansey Cl *PLEE/EAS* SR8 208 A1
Woodpack Av *WICK/BNPF* NE16 95 E4
Woodside *ASHBK/HED/RY* SR2 4 B6
BDLGTN NE22 8 B3
BLYTH NE24 11 E6 4
Woodside Av
BW/LEM/TK/HW NE15 58 A4
MONK NE25 24 C6
Woodside Cl *RYTON* NE40 74 A3
Woodside Crs *LGB/KIL* NE12 50 A4
Woodside Gdns *DUN/TMV* NE11 97 E3
STLY/ANP DH9 149 D5
Woodside La *HLS* DH4 183 D3
RYTON NE40 74 A4
Woodside Rd *RYTON* NE40 74 A3
Woodside Ter *SUNDSW* SR3 159 E2
Woodside Wk *ROWG* NE39 110 B3
Woodside Wy *RYTON* NE40 74 A3 2
SSH NE33 88 A1
Woods Ter *GATE* NE8 99 E1
SEA/MUR SR7 188 C1
Woodstock Rd
BW/LEM/TK/HW NE15 77 F3
LWF/SPW/WRK NE9 117 F2
Wood St *CLSW/PEL* DH2 152 A1
DUN/TMV NE11 97 E2
MLFD/PNYW SR4 125 F5 7
Wood Ter *FELL* NE10 84 A6 8
JRW NE32 85 F4
SSH NE33 71 F6
Woodthorne Rd *JES* NE2 64 A3 1
Woodvale Dr *HEBB* NE31 84 B4
Woodvale Gdns
LWF/SPW/WRK NE9 100 B4 3
Woodvale Rd *BLAY* NE21 94 C1
LGB/KIL NE12 35 E6
Woodville Ct *MLFD/PNYW* SR4 143 D2 7
Woodville Crs *MLFD/PNYW* SR4 143 D2 8
Woodville Rd
BW/LEM/TK/HW NE15 59 F6
Wooler Av *NSHW* NE29 69 F2
Wooler Crs *GATE* NE8 98 B2 5
Wooler Sq *ASHBK/HED/RY* SR2 145 D3
DIN/WO NE13 33 E3 2
Woolerton Dr
BW/LEM/TK/HW NE15 77 D1
LWF/SPW/WRK NE9 100 A4 7
Wooler Wk *JRW* NE32 85 F4
Wooley Dr *BDN/LAN/SAC* DH7 192 B5
Wooley St *WLSD/HOW* NE28 67 D5
Woolmer Ct *LGB/HTN* NE7 66 A3 6
Woolsington Ct
MLFD/PNYW SR4 125 E6 15
Woolsington Gdns *DIN/WO* NE13 44 B4
Woolsington Pk South
DIN/WO NE13 44 B4
Woolsington Rd *NSHW* NE29 53 E5
Woolwich Cl *SWCK/CAS* SR5 107 E6
Woolwich Rd *SWCK/CAS* SR5 107 E6
Wooperton Gdns
WD/WHPE/BLK NE5 78 B1
Worcester Cl *CLS/BIR/GTL* DH3 167 F3
Worcester Rd *DHAM* DH1 180 C5
Worcester St *ASHBK/HED/RY* SR2 4 B5 1
Worcester Ter
ASHBK/HED/RY SR2 4 B5 2
Worcester Wy *DIN/WO* NE13 33 D5
Wordsworth Av *BLYTH* NE24 16 B1
CLSW/PEL DH2 152 A6
HEBB NE31 85 D2
HLH DH5 186 C4 4
SEA/MUR SR7 175 D3
WICK/BNPF NE16 96 A2
Wordsworth Rd *PLEE/EAS* SR8 200 B2
Wordsworth St *GATE* NE8 99 F1
Worley Cl *ELS/FEN* NE4 80 A3 20
Worley St *ELS/FEN* NE4 80 A3 21
Worm Hill Ter *WASHS* NE38 139 D5
Worsdell St *BLYTH* NE24 11 D3 3
Worsley Cl *WLSD/HOW* NE28 66 B3
Worswick St *CNUT* NE1 3 E3
Worthing Cl *WLSD/HOW* NE28 66 B3 6
Worton Cl *RDHAMSE* DH6 206 B1
Wouldhave Ct *SSH* NE33 72 A3 1
Wraysbury Ct *GOS/KPK* NE3 45 F5 5
Wreigh St *HEBB* NE31 84 C2
Wreken Gdns *FELL* NE10 102 B2
Wrekenton Rw
LWF/SPW/WRK NE9 118 B2
Wren Cl *WASHS* NE38 137 F3
Wren Gv *SWCK/CAS* SR5 124 B3 8
Wretham Pl *JES* NE2 3 G1
Wright Dr *CRAM* NE23 34 C3
Wrightson St *CRAM* NE23 14 A3
Wright St *BLYTH* NE24 10 C4
Wright Ter *HLS* DH4 156 C3
Wroxham Ct *ASHBK/HED/RY* SR2 145 D4
WD/WHPE/BLK NE5 61 D2 14
Wroxton *WASHS* NE38 138 B3
Wuppertal Ct *JRW* NE32 86 A2
Wychcroft Wy
WD/WHPE/BLK NE5 61 E4 5
Wych Elm Crs *LGB/HTN* NE7 65 E3
Wycliffe Av *GOS/KPK* NE3 62 B3
Wycliffe Rd *MLFD/PNYW* SR4 143 E2
SEA/MUR SR7 175 D3
Wye Av *JRW* NE32 86 B5
Wye Rd *HEBB* NE31 85 D5
Wylam Av *MONK* NE25 25 E6
Wylam Cl *HAR/WTLS* NE34 89 D3 2
WASHN NE37 121 D3 1
Wylam Gdns *WLSD/HOW* NE28 68 B2
Wylam Gv *SUND* SR1 5 F4
Wylam Rd *NSHW* NE29 70 B3
STLY/ANP DH9 148 C1
Wylam St *JRW* NE32 86 A1
STLY/ANP DH9 149 E6
Wylam Ter *STLY/ANP* DH9 131 E6 7
Wylam Vw *BLAY* NE21 76 A6
Wynbury Rd *LWF/SPW/WRK* NE9 99 F5 5
Wyncote Ct *LGB/HTN* NE7 65 D4 2
The Wynde *HAR/WTLS* NE34 88 B3
Wyndfall Wy *GOS/KPK* NE3 62 C3
Wyndham Av *GOS/KPK* NE3 62 B3
Wyndham Wy *NSHW* NE29 53 D4
The Wynding *BDLGTN* NE22 7 D2
CRAM NE23 34 C1
Wyndley Cl *WICK/BNPF* NE16 95 E6
Wyndley Pl *GOS/KPK* NE3 62 B3
Wyndsail Pl *GOS/KPK* NE3 62 C3 3
The Wynd *BW/LEM/TK/HW* NE15 57 F5 5
CLSW/PEL DH2 152 A2
GOS/KPK NE3 62 C2
TYNE/NSHE NE30 54 C4
Wyndtop Pl *GOS/KPK* NE3 62 C3 4
Wyndways Dr *STLY/ANP* DH9 129 D5
Wynn Gdns *FELL* NE10 101 E1
Wynyard *CLSW/PEL* DH2 152 C5
Wynyard Dr *BDLGTN* NE22 8 B1
Wynyard Gdns
LWF/SPW/WRK NE9 118 B2
Wynyard Sq *ASHBK/HED/RY* SR2 145 D3
Wynyard St *DUN/TMV* NE11 97 E2
HLS DH4 169 F2
SEA/MUR SR7 176 C5
SUNDSW SR3 160 C1
Wyvern Sq *ASHBK/HED/RY* SR2 145 D4

Y

Yardley Cl *SUNDSW* SR3 160 C3
Yardley Gv *CRAM* NE23 13 F6 1
Yarmouth Cl *SEA/MUR* SR7 175 F4 6
Yarmouth Dr *CRAM* NE23 13 F6
Yatesbury Av *WD/WHPE/BLK* NE5 61 D4
Yelverton Ct *CRAM* NE23 13 F6
Yelverton Crs *BYK/HTN/WLK* NE6 83 E5
Yeoman St *NSHW* NE29 71 D2
Yeovil Cl *CRAM* NE23 13 F6 2
Yetholm Av *CLSW/PEL* DH2 153 D6
Yetholm Pl *WD/WHPE/BLK* NE5 60 C2 5
Yetholm Rd *GATE* NE8 98 A1
Yetlington Dr *GOS/KPK* NE3 62 C2
Yewbank Av *DHAM* DH1 196 A3
Yewburn Wy *LGB/KIL* NE12 49 D6
Yewcroft Av *BW/LEM/TK/HW* NE15 77 E2
Yewdale Gdns
LWF/SPW/WRK NE9 99 F6 1
Yewtree Av *SWCK/CAS* SR5 125 E2
Yew Tree Dr *BDLGTN* NE22 7 E2
Yewtree Gdns *BYK/HTN/WLK* NE6 66 C5
Yewtrees *FELL* NE10 101 D5 3
Yewvale Rd *WD/WHPE/BLK* NE5 61 F5
Yoden Av *PLEE/EAS* SR8 201 E6
Yoden Crs *PLEE/EAS* SR8 201 E6
Yoden Rd *PLEE/EAS* SR8 208 C1
Yoden Wy *PLEE/EAS* SR8 209 E2
York Av *JRW* NE32 86 A5 5
York Cl *CRAM* NE23 13 F6
York Crs *DHAM* DH1 180 C4
HLH DH5 171 E6
Yorkdale Pl *BYK/HTN/WLK* NE6 83 F2 6
York Dr *WLSD/HOW* NE28 66 C5
York Rd *CLS/BIR/GTL* DH3 136 B5
PLEE/EAS SR8 200 B6
WBAY NE26 41 D5
Yorkshire Dr *DHAM* DH1 196 C3
York St *ELS/FEN* NE4 80 A3
FELL NE10 101 F1
HLH DH5 185 D3
JRW NE32 85 F2
SUND SR1 4 C2
York Ter *CLS/BIR/GTL* DH3 153 F6
York Wy *HAR/WTLS* NE34 89 F2
Yorkwood *HEBB* NE31 84 B1
Young Rd *LGB/KIL* NE12 50 B3
Young St *DHAM* DH1 195 E4 2

Z

Zetland Dr *MONK* NE25 54 B2
Zetland St *CLDN/WHIT/ROK* SR6 127 D3
Zion St *SUND* SR1 5 F2 4
Zion Ter *SWCK/CAS* SR5 126 B1

Abbey Sports Centre
DHAM DH1 ... 180 B4
Acre Rigg Junior & Infant School
PLEE/EAS SR8 ... 200 A6
Adamsez West Industrial Estate
BLAY NE21 ... 77 E4
Adelaide Row Medical Centre
SEA/MUR SR7 ... 176 C3
Airport Church
WD/WHPE/BLK NE5 ... 61 E4
Akhurst Preparatory School
JES NE2 ... 64 B4
Albert Elliott County Junior Mixed School
HAR/WTLS NE34 ... 88 B6
Albert Road Surgery
JRW NE32 ... 86 A2
Alexandra Business Park
MLFD/PNYW SR4 ... 125 D4
Algernon Industrial Estate
SMOOR NE27 ... 52 B3
All Saints Junior Mixed School
HAR/WTLS NE34 ... 88 A4
Amberley First School
LGB/KIL NE12 ... 36 A6
AMF Bowling
ELS/FEN NE4 ... 79 F3
AMF Bowling
WASHS NE38 ... 138 B1
Amphitheatre
SSH NE33 ... 72 A3
Annfield Plain County Junior Mixed School
STLY/ANP DH9 ... 146 C5
Annfield Plain Cricket Club
STLY/ANP DH9 ... 146 A5
Annfield Plain Infants School
STLY/ANP DH9 ... 146 B5
Appletree Gardens First School
MONK NE25 ... 40 A6
Arbeia Roman Fort & Museum
SSH NE33 ... 71 E2
Archbishop Runcie C of E School
GOS/KPK NE3 ... 47 F6
Archibald First School
GOS/KPK NE3 ... 63 D1
Arena Business Park
HLS DH4 ... 170 C4
Argyle House School
ASHBK/HED/RY SR2 ... 4 A6
The Art Gallery
SUND SR1 ... 4 C3
Arthurs Hill Clinic
ELS/FEN NE4 ... 80 A2
Ascham House School
GOS/KPK NE3 ... 63 E2
Ashburne Medical Centre
ASHBK/HED/RY SR2 ... 145 D2
Ashleigh School
TYNE/NSHE NE30 ... 71 D1
Ashley Road County JMI School
HAR/WTLS NE34 ... 88 B2
Astley Community High School
MONK NE25 ... 24 B5
Atkinson House School
CRAM NE23 ... 23 E6
Atkinson Road Primary School
BW/LEM/TK/HW NE15 ... 78 B4
The Avenues Medical Practice
GOS/KPK NE3 ... 63 E3
Aykley Heads Business Centre
DHAM DH1 ... 194 A2
Ayton Primary School
WASHS NE38 ... 137 E3
Backworth County First School
SMOOR NE27 ... 37 E5
Bailey Green First School
LGB/KIL NE12 ... 35 E6
Balliol Business Park
LGB/KIL NE12 ... 48 C4
Balliol First School
LGB/KIL NE12 ... 49 D6
Barbara Priestman School
ASHBK/HED/RY SR2 ... 144 A2
Barley Mow Primary School
CLS/BIR/GTL DH3 ... 136 C4
Barmston Medical Centre
WASHS NE38 ... 121 E6
Barmston Village Primary School
WASHS NE38 ... 139 E1
Barnes Junior School
MLFD/PNYW SR4 ... 143 E2
Barnwell Primary School
HLS DH4 ... 140 A6
Battle Hill First School
WLSD/HOW NE28 ... 67 F1
BBC North & Radio Newcastle
ELS/FEN NE4 ... 79 F1
Beaconhill County First School
CRAM NE23 ... 21 D2
Beamish County School
STLY/ANP DH9 ... 149 F1
Beamish Park Golf Club
STLY/ANP DH9 ... 132 B4
Beaumont Park Surgery
MONK NE25 ... 39 F4
Bebside County Middle School
BLYTH NE24 ... 9 E4
Bebside Social Club House
BLYTH NE24 ... 8 C5
Bede Infant School
FELL NE10 ... 82 A6
Bedewell School
HEBB NE31 ... 85 D4
Bedlington Community High School
BDLGTN NE22 ... 8 C2
Bedlington Station County First School
BDLGTN NE22 ... 8 C1
Bedlington Stead County First School
BDLGTN NE22 ... 8 B3
Belford House Sports Club
ASHBK/HED/RY SR2 ... 144 C3
Bellway Industrial Estate
LGB/KIL NE12 ... 50 B5
Belmont C of E (Controlled) Junior School
DHAM DH1 ... 196 B3
Belmont Comprehensive School
DHAM DH1 ... 196 B3
Belmont County Infant School
DHAM DH1 ... 196 B3
Belmont Grange Clinic
DHAM DH1 ... 196 B2
Belvedere Retail Park
GOS/KPK NE3 ... 45 E6
Benedict Biscop C of E School
SUNDSW SR3 ... 159 F3
Benfield Comprehensive School
BYK/HTN/WLK NE6 ... 66 A5
Bensham District Clinic
GATE NE8 ... 98 C2
Bensham Family Practice
GATE NE8 ... 98 C1
Bensham Synagogue
GATE NE8 ... 98 C1
Benton Park Primary School
LGB/HTN NE7 ... 65 D2
Benwell Hill Cricket Club
BW/LEM/TK/HW NE15 ... 78 A1
Bernard Gilpin Primary School
HLH DH5 ... 171 D2
Bessie Surtees House
CNUT NE1 ... 3 E5
Bewicke Health Centre
WLSD/HOW NE28 ... 68 C4
Bewick Road Medical Centre
GATE NE8 ... 81 E6
Bexhill Primary School
SWCK/CAS SR5 ... 123 E1
Biddick Hall County Infant School
HAR/WTLS NE34 ... 87 F5
Biddick Hall County Junior School
HAR/WTLS NE34 ... 88 A4
Biddick School
WASHS NE38 ... 139 D3
Bill Quay Cricket Club
FELL NE10 ... 84 A6
Birtley East Primary School
CLS/BIR/GTL DH3 ... 118 B6
Birtley Lane Surgery
CLS/BIR/GTL DH3 ... 136 B2
Birtley Medical Group Practice
CLS/BIR/GTL DH3 ... 136 B3
Birtley St Josephs RC School
CLS/BIR/GTL DH3 ... 136 B2
Birtley Swimming Baths
CLS/BIR/GTL DH3 ... 136 B3
Blackfell Primary School
WASHN NE37 ... 119 F6
Blackfriars Craft Centre
CNUT NE1 ... 2 B3
Black Gate
CNUT NE1 ... 2 D5
Blakelaw Health Centre
WD/WHPE/BLK NE5 ... 61 E4
Blakelaw School
WD/WHPE/BLK NE5 ... 61 E4
Blaydon Business Centre
BLAY NE21 ... 77 D5
Blaydon Business Park
BLAY NE21 ... 77 E4
Blaydon Cricket Club
BLAY NE21 ... 76 B6
Blaydon Haugh Industrial Estate
BLAY NE21 ... 77 D5
Blaydon Industrial Park
BLAY NE21 ... 76 C5
Blaydon Rugby Football Club
WICK/BNPF NE16 ... 95 E1
Blaydon Swimming Pool
BLAY NE21 ... 77 D6
Blaydon West Primary School
BLAY NE21 ... 76 B5
Bloemfontein County Junior Mixed School
STLY/ANP DH9 ... 148 C5
Blyth Delaval County Middle School
BLYTH NE24 ... 16 C1
Blyth New Delaval County First School
BLYTH NE24 ... 16 A2
Blyth Newsham County First School
BLYTH NE24 ... 16 B1
Blyth Plessey Road County First School
BLYTH NE24 ... 11 E5
Blyth Spartans AFC
BLYTH NE24 ... 11 D6
Blyth Sports Centre
BLYTH NE24 ... 10 C5
Blyth Tynedale County High School
BLYTH NE24 ... 9 F5
Blyth Tynedale County Middle School
BLYTH NE24 ... 9 F5
Blyth Valley Borough Council
BLYTH NE24 ... 10 A3
Blyth Valley Borough Council
MONK NE25 ... 24 B5
Boker Lane Health Centre
BOLCOL NE35 ... 106 A2
Bolam Business Park
CRAM NE23 ... 12 C6
Boldon Comprehensive School
BOLCOL NE35 ... 105 F2
Boldon Lane Health Centre
HAR/WTLS NE34 ... 88 B4
Bow School
DHAM DH1 ... 205 E1
Brandling Primary School
FELL NE10 ... 100 C1
Brandon & Byshottles Parish Council
BDN/LAN/SAC DH7 ... 203 F3
Brandon Cricket Club
BDN/LAN/SAC DH7 ... 203 F3
Brandon Modern School
BDN/LAN/SAC DH7 ... 203 D4
Brandon United Football Club
BDN/LAN/SAC DH7 ... 203 E3
Brewery
ELS/FEN NE4 ... 2 A3
Brewery
SUND SR1 ... 4 B1
Bridges Shopping Centre
SUND SR1 ... 4 B3
Brighton Avenue Primary School
GATE NE8 ... 98 C1
Brinkburn School
HAR/WTLS NE34 ... 88 C3
Broadway East First School
GOS/KPK NE3 ... 47 F5
Broadway Junior School
MLFD/PNYW SR4 ... 142 C2
Broadwood Junior & Infant School
BW/LEM/TK/HW NE15 ... 77 E1
Brockwell Clinic
CRAM NE23 ... 14 A6
Brockwell County Middle School
CRAM NE23 ... 14 A6
Broomside Lane Surgery
DHAM DH1 ... 196 B2
Browney County Primary School
BDN/LAN/SAC DH7 ... 203 F5

Browns Gallery
JES NE2 .... 64 A4
Brunswick Beech Special School
DIN/WO NE13 .... 32 C4
Buddle Industrial Estate
WLSD/HOW NE28 .... 67 D6
Bugatti Industrial Park
NSHW NE29 .... 69 E1
Bullion Lane Primary School
CLSW/PEL DH2 .... 153 D6
Burnmoor Cricket Club
HLS DH4 .... 156 A4
Burnopfield Primary School
WICK/BNPF NE16 .... 111 E6
Burnside County First School
CRAM NE23 .... 14 B5
Burnside High School
WLSD/HOW NE28 .... 67 F4
Burnside JMI School
STLY/ANP DH9 .... 149 D3
Burnside Primary School
HLS DH4 .... 170 C1
Burradon First School
CRAM NE23 .... 35 E5
Byermoor RC Aided Junior & Infant School
WICK/BNPF NE16 .... 112 C5
Byker Primary School
BYK/HTN/WLK NE6 .... 82 A3
Caedman Primary School
GATE NE8 .... 99 D1
Camden Square Secondary School
SEA/MUR SR7 .... 176 B3
Carr Hill Infant & Junior School
LWF/SPW/WRK NE9 .... 100 A2
Cartmel Business Centre
FELL NE10 .... 101 F1
Carville First School
WLSD/HOW NE28 .... 67 D6
Castle
DHAM DH1 .... 194 B5
Castle Dene Special School
GOS/KPK NE3 .... 64 B2
Castle Keep
CNUT NE1 .... 3 E5
Castle Leazes Halls
JES NE2 .... 80 A1
Castle View School
SWCK/CAS SR5 .... 123 F3
Catchgate Primary School
STLY/ANP DH9 .... 146 A4
Cedars Special School
LWF/SPW/WRK NE9 .... 117 F1
Central First School
WLSD/HOW NE28 .... 67 F4
Central High School
GOS/KPK NE3 .... 63 E2
Central Newcastle High School
JES NE2 .... 64 A6
Central Surgery
SUND SR1 .... 4 D3
Cestria Health Centre
CLSW/PEL DH2 .... 152 B6
Cestria Primary School
CLS/BIR/GTL DH3 .... 153 F5
Chapel House Middle School
WD/WHPE/BLK NE5 .... 59 D4
Chapel Park Shopping Centre
WD/WHPE/BLK NE5 .... 59 F2
Chase School
WICK/BNPF NE16 .... 96 A3
Chastleton Surgery
DHAM DH1 .... 180 A6
Chester Le Street Leisure Centre
CLS/BIR/GTL DH3 .... 153 F5
Chester Le Street C of E Junior School
CLSW/PEL DH2 .... 153 D4
Chester Le Street Cricket Club
CLS/BIR/GTL DH3 .... 153 F6
Chester Le Street District Council
CLS/BIR/GTL DH3 .... 153 E4
Chester Le Street District Council
CLSW/PEL DH2 .... 152 C5
Chester Le Street Health Centre
CLS/BIR/GTL DH3 .... 153 F4
Chester Road Surgery
MLFD/PNYW SR4 .... 125 F6
Cheveley Park Medical Centre
DHAM DH1 .... 196 C3
Cheveley Park Primary School
DHAM DH1 .... 196 C2
Cheviot County Junior Mixed School
HAR/WTLS NE34 .... 72 C6
Cheviot First School
WD/WHPE/BLK NE5 .... 60 C2
Chevyside Middle School
WD/WHPE/BLK NE5 .... 60 C2
Childrens Hospital
SUNDSW SR3 .... 143 F2
Chillingham Industrial Estate
BYK/HTN/WLK NE6 .... 82 C1
Chillingham Road Primary School
BYK/HTN/WLK NE6 .... 65 E6
The Chorister School
DHAM DH1 .... 194 B6
Christ Church C of E Primary School
JES NE2 .... 3 F2
Church of England Primary School
WLSD/HOW NE28 .... 68 A4
Church View Medical Centre
SUNDSW SR3 .... 160 C1
Cinema
SUND SR1 .... 4 C4
City Hall
CNUT NE1 .... 3 E1
City of Sunderland College
ASHBK/HED/RY SR2 .... 145 D4
City of Sunderland College
HLS DH4 .... 157 D3
City of Sunderland College
SUND SR1 .... 4 C2
City of Sunderland College
SWCK/CAS SR5 .... 124 C2
City Pool
CNUT NE1 .... 2 D1
Civic Centre
CLS/BIR/GTL DH3 .... 153 F4
Civic Centre
CNUT NE1 .... 2 D1
Civic Centre
GATE NE8 .... 81 D6
Civic Centre
SUND SR1 .... 4 C4
Civic Hall
WLSD/HOW NE28 .... 67 D4
Civil Service Sports Club
LGB/KIL NE12 .... 66 A1
Claremont Footcare Surgery
WBAY NE26 .... 40 A3
Claypath Medical Practice
DHAM DH1 .... 194 C4
Clayton Street Indoor Mini Market
CNUT NE1 .... 2 C4
Cleadon Village C of E Infant School
CLDN/WHIT/ROK SR6 .... 108 A1
Cleadon Village County JM School
CLDN/WHIT/ROK SR6 .... 107 E1
Club House
DHAM DH1 .... 205 D2
Club House
HLH DH5 .... 172 A2
Collierley County Primary School
STLY/ANP DH9 .... 128 B6
Collingwood Primary School
NSHW NE29 .... 69 F1
Community College
SEA/MUR SR7 .... 176 B2
Coquet Park First School
WBAY NE26 .... 40 C4
Corpus Christi RC Primary School
GATE NE8 .... 99 D2
Corrymella Scott Gallery
JES NE2 .... 63 F6
County Durham Health Authority
PLEE/EAS SR8 .... 208 C2
County Hall Durham County Council
DHAM DH1 .... 194 A2
County Hospital
DHAM DH1 .... 194 A4
County Junior & Infant School
BDN/LAN/SAC DH7 .... 192 A3
County Junior Middle & Infant School
STLY/ANP DH9 .... 150 B2
Cowgate Leisure Centre
WD/WHPE/BLK NE5 .... 61 F3
Cowgate Primary School
ELS/FEN NE4 .... 62 A5
Cragside County First School
CRAM NE23 .... 22 A4
Cragside Primary School
LGB/HTN NE7 .... 64 C3
Craigievar School
CLDN/WHIT/ROK SR6 .... 127 D1
Cramlington Football Club
CRAM NE23 .... 22 C2
Crook Hall
DHAM DH1 .... 194 B3
Crookhill Junior School
RYTON NE40 .... 75 D3
Crown Court
CNUT NE1 .... 3 E5
Crowtree Leisure Centre
SUND SR1 .... 4 B3
Cruddas Park Health Centre
ELS/FEN NE4 .... 79 F4
Cruddas Park Surgery
ELS/FEN NE4 .... 80 A4
Cullercoats Primary School
TYNE/NSHE NE30 .... 55 E1
Custom House
CNUT NE1 .... 3 F5
Dame Allans Boys School
ELS/FEN NE4 .... 79 D1
Dame Dorothy Street School
CLDN/WHIT/ROK SR6 .... 127 D4
Davenport School
HLH DH5 .... 171 D4
Deerness Park Medical Centre
ASHBK/HED/RY SR2 .... 5 F5
Delaval Primary School
BW/LEM/TK/HW NE15 .... 78 A3
Denbigh Community First School
WLSD/HOW NE28 .... 68 C3
Dene House County Mixed Modern School
PLEE/EAS SR8 .... 209 F2
Deneside Junior & Infant School
SEA/MUR SR7 .... 175 F4
Deneside Medical Centre
SEA/MUR SR7 .... 176 A3
Denton Park Middle School
WD/WHPE/BLK NE5 .... 60 B4
Denton Road Primary School
BW/LEM/TK/HW NE15 .... 77 E3
Derwenthaugh Industrial Estate
BLAY NE21 .... 77 E5
Derwent Infant School
GATE NE8 .... 98 B1
Derwentside District Council
STLY/ANP DH9 .... 146 C6
Derwentside District Council
STLY/ANP DH9 .... 148 B2
Diamond Hall Junior & Infant School
MLFD/PNYW SR4 .... 125 E5
Dinnington Village First School
DIN/WO NE13 .... 31 E3
Dipton Surgery
STLY/ANP DH9 .... 128 B6
DLI Museum & Arts Centre
DHAM DH1 .... 194 B3
Donwell Primary School
WASHN NE37 .... 120 B3
Downhill Primary School
SWCK/CAS SR5 .... 106 A6
Dragonville Industrial Park
DHAM DH1 .... 196 A4
Dr Chandy's Surgery
PLEE/EAS SR8 .... 209 F1
Dr Dhuny's Surgery
STLY/ANP DH9 .... 149 D5
The Drive Primary School
FELL NE10 .... 101 D2
Dr Krishnans Surgery
GATE NE8 .... 98 C2
Dr Rannus Surgery
DUN/TMV NE11 .... 97 F2
Dr Reg Carrs Surgery
BLYTH NE24 .... 11 E5
Dryburn Hospital
DHAM DH1 .... 193 F2
DSS
SUND SR1 .... 4 A2
Dubmire County Junior & Infant School
HLS DH4 .... 169 F2
Dudley Surgery
CRAM NE23 .... 35 D2
Dunelm Medical Practice
BDN/LAN/SAC DH7 .... 192 A3

Dunelm Medical Practice
DHAM DH1 ... 195 E4
Dunholme School
DHAM DH1 ... 194 A1
Dunston Federation Football Club
DUN/TMV NE11 ... 97 D1
Dunston Health Centre
DUN/TMV NE11 ... 97 D2
Dunston Hill Hospital
WICK/BNPF NE16 ... 96 C3
Dunston Hill Junior & Infant School
DUN/TMV NE11 ... 97 D2
Dunston Industrial Estate
DUN/TMV NE11 ... 97 D1
Dunston Riverside Primary School
DUN/TMV NE11 ... 97 E1
Dunston Swimming Pool
DUN/TMV NE11 ... 97 D3
Durham Baths
DHAM DH1 ... 194 C5
Durham Blue Coat C of E (Aided) Junior School
DHAM DH1 ... 180 B6
Durham Business Centre
BDN/LAN/SAC DH7 ... 204 A3
Durham Cathedral
DHAM DH1 ... 194 B5
Durham City Amateur Football Club
DHAM DH1 ... 196 A2
Durham City Cricket Club
DHAM DH1 ... 195 D5
Durham City Rugby Club
DHAM DH1 ... 195 D5
Durham County Constabulary
PLEE/EAS SR8 ... 208 C2
Durham County Council
CLS/BIR/GTL DH3 ... 168 A3
Durham County Council
DHAM DH1 ... 194 A1
Durham County Council
DHAM DH1 ... 196 B4
Durham County Council
PLEE/EAS SR8 ... 200 B5
Durham County Council
SEA/MUR SR7 ... 188 B1
Durham County Council
STLY/ANP DH9 ... 148 A2
Durham County Cricket Club
CLS/BIR/GTL DH3 ... 154 A6
Durham County NHS Trust
DHAM DH1 ... 179 D5
Durham Crown Court
DHAM DH1 ... 194 C5
Durham Gilesgate Comprehensive School
DHAM DH1 ... 195 F3
Durham High School
DHAM DH1 ... 205 D3
Durham Johnston Comprehensive School
DHAM DH1 ... 193 F4
Durham Johnston Comprehensive School
DHAM DH1 ... 195 D6
Durham Markets Co
DHAM DH1 ... 194 B4
Durham Newton Hall County Infant School
DHAM DH1 ... 180 B6
Durham St Hilds C of E (Aided) Primary School
DHAM DH1 ... 195 F4
Durham School
DHAM DH1 ... 194 A6
Durham Sixth Form Centre
DHAM DH1 ... 194 B4
Earls House Hospital
DHAM DH1 ... 179 D6
Easington C of E School
PLEE/EAS SR8 ... 199 F3
Easington Colliery Primary School
PLEE/EAS SR8 ... 200 B2
Easington Comprehensive School
PLEE/EAS SR8 ... 199 F3
Easington District Council
PLEE/EAS SR8 ... 200 A2
Easington District Council
SEA/MUR SR7 ... 175 F3
Easington District Council
SEA/MUR SR7 ... 188 C1
Easington District Leisure Centre
SEA/MUR SR7 ... 176 A3
Easington Lane Primary School
HLH DH5 ... 186 C4
East Boldon Junior School
BOL NE36 ... 106 B3
Eastcliffe Grammar School
GOS/KPK NE3 ... 63 F2
East Durham Community College
PLEE/EAS SR8 ... 208 C2
East Herrington Primary School
SUNDSW SR3 ... 159 E1
Eastlea First School
CRAM NE23 ... 14 B6
East Rainton JMI School
HLH DH5 ... 170 B6
Eden Hall Infant School
PLEE/EAS SR8 ... 209 D1
Edmondsley JMI School
BDN/LAN/SAC DH7 ... 164 A3
Eldon Square Shopping Centre
CNUT NE1 ... 2 D2
Elemore Leisure Centre
HLH DH5 ... 186 B3
Ellison C of E JMI School
JRW NE32 ... 86 A2
Elswick Way Industrial Estate
HAR/WTLS NE34 ... 87 F2
Emmanuel College
DUN/TMV NE11 ... 97 E5
Empire Theatre
SUND SR1 ... 4 A2
English Martyrs RC Primary School
SWCK/CAS SR5 ... 125 D2
Epinay Special School
JRW NE32 ... 86 B2
Eppleton Cricket Club
HLH DH5 ... 171 F4
The Evergreen Gallery
CNUT NE1 ... 2 C5
Eye Clinic
CNUT NE1 ... 2 D1
Farne First School
WD/WHPE/BLK NE5 ... 60 C3
Farnham Medical Centre
HAR/WTLS NE34 ... 88 B2
Farringdon School
SUNDSW SR3 ... 159 F1
Farrington Infant School
SUNDSW SR3 ... 142 C6
Farrington Junior School
SUNDSW SR3 ... 142 C6
Fatfield Junior & Infant School
WASHS NE38 ... 138 C4
Felldyke Primary & Infant School
LWF/SPW/WRK NE9 ... 118 C1
Fellgate JMI School
JRW NE32 ... 104 A1
Felling Business Centre
FELL NE10 ... 82 C6
Fellrose Surgery
CLSW/PEL DH2 ... 152 A4
Fellside County Primary School
WICK/BNPF NE16 ... 95 F4
Fell Tower Medical Centre Whereis Building
LWF/SPW/WRK NE9 ... 99 E6
Felstead School
MLFD/PNYW SR4 ... 124 C6
Fence Houses Surgery
HLS DH4 ... 156 A6
Finchale County Infant School
DHAM DH1 ... 181 D5
Finchale Priory
DHAM DH1 ... 182 A1
Fire Station
CNUT NE1 ... 3 E3
Fire Station
SUND SR1 ... 126 A5
First School
MONK NE25 ... 24 A4
Fordley Clinic
CRAM NE23 ... 34 C2
Formica Social & Sports Club
NSHW NE29 ... 53 D5
Framwellgate Moor Comprehensive School
DHAM DH1 ... 180 A6
Framwellgate Moor Junior & Infant School
DHAM DH1 ... 180 A6
Freeman Hospital
LGB/HTN NE7 ... 64 C2
Front Street Industrial Estate
RDHAMSE DH6 ... 187 E5
Front Street Junior & Infant School
WICK/BNPF NE16 ... 95 F3
Front Street Surgery
BLAY NE21 ... 94 A1
Fulwell Grange Christian School
SWCK/CAS SR5 ... 126 B1
Fulwell Junior School
CLDN/WHIT/ROK SR6 ... 109 D6
Fulwell Medical Centre
CLDN/WHIT/ROK SR6 ... 108 C6
Fyndoune Community College
BDN/LAN/SAC DH7 ... 178 B2
The Gables Medical Group
BDLGTN NE22 ... 8 C2
Galactic Zoo
CNUT NE1 ... 2 B5
Gallery of Fine Art
CNUT NE1 ... 2 C2
The Gallery
CLSW/PEL DH2 ... 166 A3
The Gambling Man Gallery
TYNE/NSHE NE30 ... 71 D2
Garden Park Surgery
WLSD/HOW NE28 ... 68 C2
The Garrick Gallery
STLY/ANP DH9 ... 148 A2
Gateshead Area Health Authority
BLAY NE21 ... 77 E6
Gateshead Area Health Authority
DUN/TMV NE11 ... 97 F4
Gateshead Area Health Authority
GATE NE8 ... 81 D6
Gateshead Area Health Authority
GATE NE8 ... 98 B1
Gateshead Area Health Authority
LWF/SPW/WRK NE9 ... 100 A4
Gateshead Area Health Authority
WICK/BNPF NE16 ... 96 A3
Gateshead College
LWF/SPW/WRK NE9 ... 99 E3
Gateshead Complimentary Health Centre
GATE NE8 ... 99 D1
Gateshead Fell Cricket Club
LWF/SPW/WRK NE9 ... 99 F4
Gateshead Health Care
FELL NE10 ... 102 A4
Gateshead Health NHS Trust
LWF/SPW/WRK NE9 ... 99 E3
Gateshead Hospitals NHS Trust
GATE NE8 ... 98 C3
Gateshead International Stadium
FELL NE10 ... 82 B5
Gateshead Jewish Boys School
GATE NE8 ... 99 D1
Gateshead Leisure Centre
GATE NE8 ... 99 E2
Gateshead Little Theatre
LWF/SPW/WRK NE9 ... 99 E3
Gateshead Magistrates Court
GATE NE8 ... 81 E6
Gateshead Metropolitan Borough Council
BLAY NE21 ... 76 C5
Gateshead Metropolitan Borough Council
CLS/BIR/GTL DH3 ... 136 B1
Gateshead Metropolitan Borough Council
DUN/TMV NE11 ... 116 C1
Gateshead Metropolitan Borough Council
FELL NE10 ... 100 C2
Gateshead Metropolitan Borough Council
GATE NE8 ... 80 C6
Gateshead Metropolitan Borough Council
GATE NE8 ... 82 A5
Gateshead Metropolitan Borough Council
LWF/SPW/WRK NE9 ... 99 E5
Gateshead Metropolitan Borough Council
LWF/SPW/WRK NE9 ... 117 F1
Gateshead Metropolitan Borough Council
ROWG NE39 ... 110 B2

Gateshead Metropolitan Borough Council
WICK/BNPF NE16 ... 96 A3
Gateshead & South Tyneside Health Authority
SSH NE33 ... 71 F5
Gateshead Talmudical College
GATE NE8 ... 99 D1
George Stephenson High School
LGB/KIL NE12 ... 49 F2
Gibside School
WICK/BNPF NE16 ... 95 F5
Gilesgate County Infant School
DHAM DH1 ... 195 F3
Gilesgate County Junior School
DHAM DH1 ... 195 F3
Glebe School
WBAY NE26 ... 40 A2
Glebe Village Primary School
WASHS NE38 ... 138 C1
Glen Dene School
PLEE/EAS SR8 ... 199 F2
The Globe Gallery
TYNE/NSHE NE30 ... 71 D1
Glover Industrial Estate
WASHN NE37 ... 121 E5
Glynwood Primary School
LWF/SPW/WRK NE9 ... 99 F5
Goathland Primary School
LGB/KIL NE12 ... 49 E6
Gosforth Central Middle School
GOS/KPK NE3 ... 47 E6
Gosforth Cricket Club
GOS/KPK NE3 ... 63 E2
Gosforth High School
GOS/KPK NE3 ... 47 E6
Gosforth Industrial Estate
GOS/KPK NE3 ... 47 F6
Gosforth Memorial Health Centre
GOS/KPK NE3 ... 63 F1
Gosforth West Middle School
GOS/KPK NE3 ... 63 D1
Grainger Market
CNUT NE1 ... 2 C3
Grange First School
GOS/KPK NE3 ... 47 D6
Grange Park Primary School
SWCK/CAS SR5 ... 126 B2
Grange Terrace Surgery
ASHBK/HED/RY SR2 ... 4 B5
Grangetown Family Dental Health Centre
ASHBK/HED/RY SR2 ... 145 D4
Grangetown Junior & Infant School
ASHBK/HED/RY SR2 ... 145 E3
Grangewood Surgery
HLS DH4 ... 156 C2
Greencroft Comprehensive School
STLY/ANP DH9 ... 146 A4
Greenesfield Business Centre
GATE NE8 ... 81 D5
Greenfields Special School
HEBB NE31 ... 85 E1
Greenland County JMI School
STLY/ANP DH9 ... 147 F4
Grey College
DHAM DH1 ... 205 E1
Grindon Infants School
MLFD/PNYW SR4 ... 142 A3
Hadrian JMI School
SSH NE33 ... 71 E2
Hadrian Park First School
WLSD/HOW NE28 ... 52 A5
Hadrian Park Middle School
WLSD/HOW NE28 ... 52 A5
Hadrian School
BW/LEM/TK/HW NE15 ... 78 B2
Halls of Residence
MLFD/PNYW SR4 ... 126 A6
Hancock Museum
CNUT NE1 ... 80 C1
Harlow Green Infant School
LWF/SPW/WRK NE9 ... 117 F2
Harraton Primary School
WASHS NE38 ... 138 A5
Hartlepool Community Care NHS Trust
PLEE/EAS SR8 ... 208 C2
Harton School
HAR/WTLS NE34 ... 89 F2
Hatfield College
DHAM DH1 ... 194 B5
Havelock Primary School
MLFD/PNYW SR4 ... 124 C6
Hawthorn House Medical Centre
BYK/HTN/WLK NE6 ... 82 B2
Hawthorn Primary School
ELS/FEN NE4 ... 79 F4
Hawthorns Hospital
PLEE/EAS SR8 ... 209 D3
Hazlewood Community Primary School
DIN/WO NE13 ... 33 D5
Headway Theatre
BLYTH NE24 ... 11 E4
Heaton Manor Lower School
LGB/HTN NE7 ... 64 C4
Heaton Manor Upper School
LGB/HTN NE7 ... 65 E2
Hebrew Synagogue
WBAY NE26 ... 40 C5
Heddon on the Wall C of E Controlled First School
BW/LEM/TK/HW NE15 ... 56 A4
Hedworthfield Comprehensive School
JRW NE32 ... 104 A1
Heritage Centre
DHAM DH1 ... 194 C5
Herrington Medical Centre
HLS DH4 ... 157 E2
Hetton Health Centre
HLH DH5 ... 171 F6
Hetton Lyons School
HLH DH5 ... 185 F2
Hetton Primary School
HLH DH5 ... 185 E1
Hetton Secondary School
HLH DH5 ... 185 E1
Hetton UDC Swimming Baths
HLH DH5 ... 185 E1
Heworth Grange Comprehensive School
FELL NE10 ... 101 E2
High Farm Middle School
WLSD/HOW NE28 ... 67 D1
High Fell Special School
LWF/SPW/WRK NE9 ... 99 F3
Highfield County Infant School
HAR/WTLS NE34 ... 72 C5
Highfield Hospital
CLS/BIR/GTL DH3 ... 153 E3
Highfield Junior & Infant School
ROWG NE39 ... 110 A2
High Spen Industrial Estate
ROWG NE39 ... 111 E1
Hillcrest Day Special School
CRAM NE23 ... 22 A2
Hillsview Surgery
GOS/KPK NE3 ... 46 A6
Hill Top School
LWF/SPW/WRK NE9 ... 101 D6
Hillview Clinic
ASHBK/HED/RY SR2 ... 144 C4
Hill View Infant School
ASHBK/HED/RY SR2 ... 144 C4
Hill View Junior School
ASHBK/HED/RY SR2 ... 144 C4
Hilton Primary School
WD/WHPE/BLK NE5 ... 61 D4
Hindu Temple
ELS/FEN NE4 ... 78 C2
HM Prison
DHAM DH1 ... 194 C5
HMS Calliope Cadet Training Centre
GATE NE8 ... 3 G5
The Hobart Gallery
GOS/KPK NE3 ... 63 E2
Hollyhurst Medical Centre
BLAY NE21 ... 94 A1
Holly Park Primary School
WASHS NE38 ... 137 E3
Holmside & South Moor Hospital
STLY/ANP DH9 ... 148 C4
Holy Cross RC Primary School
WLSD/HOW NE28 ... 68 B2
Holystone First School
SMOOR NE27 ... 51 E2
Holywell County First School
MONK NE25 ... 25 E6
Hookergate Comprehensive School
ROWG NE39 ... 110 A1
Horden & Easington RC Primary School
PLEE/EAS SR8 ... 201 E5
Horton Grange First School
BLYTH NE24 ... 9 E4
Hotspur Primary School
BYK/HTN/WLK NE6 ... 81 F2
Houghton Colliery Welfare Cricket Club
HLS DH4 ... 170 B1
Houghton Health Centre
HLH DH5 ... 171 D2
Houghton Kepier School
HLS DH4 ... 170 C2
Howden Green Industrial Estate
WLSD/HOW NE28 ... 69 D4
Howletch Lane Junior & Infant School
PLEE/EAS SR8 ... 208 A2
Hudson Road Primary School
SUND SR1 ... 5 E4
Hylton Castle
SWCK/CAS SR5 ... 124 A2
Hylton Castle Health Centre
SWCK/CAS SR5 ... 124 A2
Hylton Castle Junior School
SWCK/CAS SR5 ... 123 E2
Imex Business Centre
DHAM DH1 ... 180 A4
Industrial Estate
BDN/LAN/SAC DH7 ... 178 B1
Ivy Road Primary School
LGB/KIL NE12 ... 50 A4
Jewish High School
GATE NE8 ... 99 D1
Jewish Infant School
GATE NE8 ... 99 E1
John Spence Community High School
TYNE/NSHE NE30 ... 54 C4
Joseph Swan School
LWF/SPW/WRK NE9 ... 117 D1
Jubilee Infant School
SEA/MUR SR7 ... 188 C1
Kenton Comprehensive School
GOS/KPK NE3 ... 61 F2
Kenton Lodge Residential School
ELS/FEN NE4 ... 63 D4
Kepier Clinic
DHAM DH1 ... 195 F3
Kibblesworth Primary School
DUN/TMV NE11 ... 116 C6
Killingworth Middle School
LGB/KIL NE12 ... 49 F2
King Edward Junior & Infant School
TYNE/NSHE NE30 ... 55 D5
Kingfisher Industrial Estate
SEA/MUR SR7 ... 175 F2
King George Comprehensive School
HAR/WTLS NE34 ... 89 E5
Kingsmeadow Comprehensive School
DUN/TMV NE11 ... 97 D2
Kings School
TYNE/NSHE NE30 ... 55 F5
Kingston Park Primary School
GOS/KPK NE3 ... 45 E6
Kingsway First School
BLYTH NE24 ... 11 D6
Knoplaw First School
WD/WHPE/BLK NE5 ... 59 E4
Laing Art Gallery
CNUT NE1 ... 3 E2
Lancaster University
CNUT NE1 ... 2 D5
Langley Moor Primary School
BDN/LAN/SAC DH7 ... 204 A2
Larkspur Primary School
LWF/SPW/WRK NE9 ... 100 B6
La Sagesse Convent High School
JES NE2 ... 64 A3
Laurel Avenue County Junior & Infant School
DHAM DH1 ... 195 E5
Law Courts
CNUT NE1 ... 3 F4
Laygate Lane County Infant School
SSH NE33 ... 71 E5
Laygate School
SSH NE33 ... 71 E5

Leafield House School
CLS/BIR/GTL DH3 .... 136 C3
Lemington Clinic
BW/LEM/TK/HW NE15........ 76 C2
Lemington First School
BW/LEM/TK/HW NE15........ 76 C2
Lemington Middle School
BW/LEM/TK/HW NE15........ 59 F6
Linden School
LGB/KIL NE12 .... 49 F4
Lindisfarne County
Primary School
GATE NE8........ 81 E6
Lingey House Primary School
FELL NE10 .... 102 A3
Linhope First School
WD/WHPE/BLK NE5........ 60 B4
Little Theatre
CLDN/WHIT/ROK SR6........ 107 F1
Live Theatre
CNUT NE1 .... 3 F5
Lobley Hill Junior & Infant School
DUN/TMV NE11 .... 97 F5
Longbenton Community College
LGB/KIL NE12 .... 49 E5
Longrigg Medical Centre
FELL NE10 .... 101 F3
Lord Chancellors Department
CNUT NE1 .... 2 C5
Lord Chancellors Department
GATE NE8........ 81 D5
Lord Lawson of Beamish
Secondary School
CLS/BIR/GTL DH3 .... 136 C3
Louisa Surgery
STLY/ANP DH9 .... 148 A2
Low Fell Clinic
LWF/SPW/WRK NE9........ 99 F6
Low Fell Junior & Infant School
LWF/SPW/WRK NE9........ 99 E5
Lumley County Infant School
CLS/BIR/GTL DH3 .... 167 F2
Lumley Junior Middle &
Infant School
CLS/BIR/GTL DH3 .... 168 A3
Lynnwood Business Centre
ELS/FEN NE4........ 79 E3
Malvins Close County First School
BLYTH NE24........ 10 B4
Maplewood School
SWCK/CAS SR5 .... 125 D1
Marden Bridge Middle School
MONK NE25........ 40 C6
Marden High School
TYNE/NSHE NE30........ 55 D3
Marine Avenue Medical Centre
WBAY NE26 .... 40 B5
Marine Park JMI School
SSH NE33........ 71 F3
Market Place Industrial Estate
HLH DH5 .... 171 E1
Marlborough Clinic
SEA/MUR SR7 .... 176 B3
Marley Hill Primary School
WICK/BNPF NE16 .... 113 F4
Mary Trevelyan Primary School
ELS/FEN NE4........ 79 F5
Masonic Temple
ASHBK/HED/RY SR2........ 4 C5
Mayfield Medical Centre
JRW NE32 .... 85 F2
Meadowfield Clinic
BDN/LAN/SAC DH7........ 203 F4
Meadowfield Sports Centre
BDN/LAN/SAC DH7........ 203 F4
Meadow Well Primary School
NSHW NE29........ 69 F2
Megabowl
LGB/KIL NE12 .... 50 C5
Metrocentre East Business Park
DUN/TMV NE11 .... 78 C6
The Metro Centre
WICK/BNPF NE16 .... 96 B1
Millburngate Shopping Precinct
DHAM DH1 .... 194 B4
Modern Mixed School
RDHAMSE DH6 .... 206 B1
Monkhouse Primary School
TYNE/NSHE NE30........ 55 D3
Monkseaton Clinic
MONK NE25........ 40 A6
Monkseaton High School
MONK NE25........ 54 A2
Monkseaton Medical Centre
MONK NE25........ 39 F6
Monkseaton Middle School
MONK NE25........ 40 A6
Monkton County Infant School
HAR/WTLS NE34 .... 87 F4
Monkton County Junior
Mixed School
HAR/WTLS NE34 .... 87 E4
Monkton Hall Hospital
HEBB NE31 .... 85 E4
Monkwearmouth Health Centre
SWCK/CAS SR5 .... 126 C4
Monkwearmouth Hospital
SWCK/CAS SR5 .... 126 B2
Monkwearmouth
Railway Station Museum
CLDN/WHIT/ROK SR6........ 126 C4
Montagu Junior & Infant School
WD/WHPE/BLK NE5........ 62 A3
Moor Edge First School
LGB/KIL NE12 .... 49 D1
Moorside Community
Primary School
ELS/FEN NE4........ 79 F2
Mortimer
Comprehensive School
HAR/WTLS NE34 .... 88 C1
Mosque
BYK/HTN/WLK NE6 .... 65 D6
Mosque
MLFD/PNYW SR4 .... 126 A6
Mosque
SSH NE33........ 71 D5
Mountbatten Medical Centre
HEBB NE31 .... 84 C3
Mountfield Primary School
GOS/KPK NE3 .... 62 A1
Murton Primary School
SEA/MUR SR7 .... 188 C1
Museum & Art Gallery
SSH NE33........ 71 E3
Museum of Science and Industry
ELS/FEN NE4........ 80 A4
Music School
DHAM DH1 .... 194 B5
The Natural Therapy Clinic
TYNE/NSHE NE30........ 54 C6
Nature Reserve
LGB/KIL NE12 .... 51 E5
Nelson Health Centre
NSHW NE29........ 54 C6
Nettlesworth Primary School
CLSW/PEL DH2 .... 165 E6
Nevilles Cross Primary School
DHAM DH1 .... 193 E5
Newbottle Primary School
HLS DH4........ 157 E5
New Brancepeth Primary School
BDN/LAN/SAC DH7........ 202 B1
Newburn Hall Motor Museum
BW/LEM/TK/HW NE15........ 58 B6
Newburn Industrial Estate
BW/LEM/TK/HW NE15........ 75 F2
Newburn Leisure Centre
BW/LEM/TK/HW NE15........ 58 A6
Newburn Manor First School
BW/LEM/TK/HW NE15........ 58 B6
Newcastle Antiques &
Independent Museum
CNUT NE1 .... 2 C4
Newcastle Area Health Authority
BW/LEM/TK/HW NE15........ 78 A3
Newcastle Area Health Authority
ELS/FEN NE4........ 79 F4
Newcastle Area Health Authority
JES NE2 .... 80 B1
Newcastle Arena
ELS/FEN NE4........ 80 B5
Newcastle City Council
BW/LEM/TK/HW NE15........ 57 F5
Newcastle City Council
BW/LEM/TK/HW NE15........ 58 B6
Newcastle City Council
BW/LEM/TK/HW NE15........ 78 A4
Newcastle City Council
BYK/HTN/WLK NE6 .... 82 B4
Newcastle City Council
BYK/HTN/WLK NE6 .... 83 E5
Newcastle City Council
CNUT NE1 .... 2 C2
Newcastle City Council
ELS/FEN NE4........ 78 C3
Newcastle City Council
ELS/FEN NE4........ 79 D4
Newcastle City Council
ELS/FEN NE4........ 79 E4
Newcastle City Council
GOS/KPK NE3 .... 62 B3
Newcastle City Council
JES NE2 .... 64 A3
Newcastle City Council
JES NE2 .... 64 A3
Newcastle City Council
JES NE2 .... 81 E1
Newcastle City Council
JES NE2 .... 81 F1
Newcastle City Council
JES NE2 .... 81 F2
Newcastle City Council
JES NE2 .... 81 D1
Newcastle City Council
WD/WHPE/BLK NE5........ 60 B3
Newcastle City Council
WD/WHPE/BLK NE5........ 61 D5
Newcastle City Council
WD/WHPE/BLK NE5........ 61 F4
Newcastle City Council
WD/WHPE/BLK NE5........ 61 F5
Newcastle Clinic
JES NE2 .... 64 A3
Newcastle College
ELS/FEN NE4........ 80 A4
Newcastle College Concert Hall
ELS/FEN NE4........ 80 A4
Newcastle Falcons Rugby
Football Club
DIN/WO NE13 .... 45 D5
Newcastle General Hospital
ELS/FEN NE4........ 79 E3
Newcastle Nuffield Hospital
JES NE2 .... 64 A6
Newcastle Playhouse &
Gulbenkian Studio Theatre
CNUT NE1 .... 80 C1
Newcastle Preparatory School
JES NE2 .... 81 D1
Newcastle Reform Synagogue
GOS/KPK NE3 .... 62 C2
The New City Medical Centre
SUND SR1 .... 5 E3
New College Durham
DHAM DH1 .... 193 F6
New College Durham
DHAM DH1 .... 193 F1
New College Durham
DHAM DH1 .... 194 A6
Newgate Shopping Mall
CNUT NE1 .... 2 C4
Newker Junior & Infant School
CLSW/PEL DH2 .... 153 D6
New Seaham Primary School
SEA/MUR SR7 .... 175 E1
Newsham Surgery
BLYTH NE24........ 16 B2
NHS Clinic
SEA/MUR SR7 .... 188 C1
Norfolk Clinic
SUND SR1 .... 4 D2
Norham Community High School
NSHW NE29........ 69 F1
North Biddick Club House
WASHS NE38........ 138 C6
North Blunts Primary School
PLEE/EAS SR8........ 208 C2
Northburn County First School
CRAM NE23........ 14 A5
North Durham NHS Trust
CLS/BIR/GTL DH3 .... 153 E6
North East Aircraft Museum
SWCK/CAS SR5 .... 122 C2
Northern Land & Leisure Centre
DHAM DH1 .... 194 A2
Northern Rugby Club
GOS/KPK NE3 .... 47 E4
North Fawdon Primary School
GOS/KPK NE3 .... 46 B5
North Heaton Sports Club
BYK/HTN/WLK NE6 .... 65 E6
North Sands Business Centre
CLDN/WHIT/ROK SR6........ 127 D4
North Shields Rugby Club
NSHW NE29........ 54 B4
North Tyne Industrial Estate
LGB/KIL NE12 .... 50 C4

North Tyneside Area Health Authority *LGB/KIL* NE12 .... 49 F1
North Tyneside Area Health Authority *NSHW* NE29.... 54 B6
North Tyneside Area Health Authority *WLSD/HOW* NE28.... 52 A5
North Tyneside Area Health Authority *WLSD/HOW* NE28.... 67 E3
North Tyneside Borough Council *NSHW* NE29.... 70 C1
North Tyneside College *WLSD/HOW* NE28.... 68 A1
North Tyneside Council *LGB/KIL* NE12 .... 48 C6
North Tyneside Council *LGB/KIL* NE12 .... 49 D1
North Tyneside Council *LGB/KIL* NE12 .... 49 F4
North Tyneside Council *TYNE/NSHE* NE30.... 55 D6
North Tyneside Council *WLSD/HOW* NE28.... 67 F5
North Tyneside Council *WLSD/HOW* NE28.... 69 D5
North Tyneside Council Offices *WBAY* NE26.... 41 D5
North Tyneside Metropolitan Borough Council *NSHW* NE29.... 70 B2
Northumberland Area Health Authority *BLYTH* NE24.... 10 A5
Northumberland County Council *BLYTH* NE24.... 9 E4
Northumberland County Council *BLYTH* NE24.... 11 E5
Northumberland County Council *BLYTH* NE24.... 16 B1
Northumberland County Council *CRAM* NE23.... 21 D1
Northumberland County Council *GOS/KPK* NE3.... 47 F3
Northumberland County Cricket Club *JES* NE2 .... 64 B6
Northumberland Mental Health NHS Trust *CRAM* NE23.... 22 A1
Northumbria Sports Centre *WASHN* NE37.... 121 D1
Novacastrians Rugby Football Club *LGB/HTN* NE7 .... 65 D2
Oakfield College *ELS/FEN* NE4.... 78 C2
Oakfield Junior School *LWF/SPW/WRK* NE9.... 117 E1
Oakleigh Gardens School *CLDN/WHIT/ROK* SR6.... 90 A6
The Old Forge Surgery *MLFD/PNYW* SR4 .... 125 E5
The Open University *GOS/KPK* NE3 .... 47 E6
The Osborne Clinic *JES* NE2 .... 64 B5
Our Lady of Peace RC School *HLS* DH4.... 156 C1
Our Lady & St Annes Primary School *ELS/FEN* NE4.... 80 A3
Ouston County Infant School *CLSW/PEL* DH2 .... 135 E5
Ouston Junior School *CLSW/PEL* DH2 .... 135 D5
Oxclose Community School *WASHS* NE38 .... 137 F2
Pallion Health Centre *MLFD/PNYW* SR4 .... 125 E6
Pallion Primary School *MLFD/PNYW* SR4 .... 125 D4
Palmer Community Hospital *JRW* NE32 .... 86 A1
Parkside Infant School *SEA/MUR* SR7 .... 176 A5
Parkside Middle School *CRAM* NE23.... 22 A1
Parkside School *WLSD/HOW* NE28.... 66 C1
The Parks Sports Centre *NSHW* NE29.... 70 B2
Park View Community School *CLS/BIR/GTL* DH3 .... 153 F5
Park View Comprehensive School *CLS/BIR/GTL* DH3 .... 153 E1
Parkway Medical Centre *WD/WHPE/BLK* NE5.... 59 E4
Parkway School *WD/WHPE/BLK* NE5.... 59 F4
Pelaw County Infant School *CLSW/PEL* DH2 .... 153 D3
Pelton County Junior & Infant School *CLSW/PEL* DH2 .... 152 B1
Pelton Fell Surgery Building *CLSW/PEL* DH2 .... 152 A4
Pelton Health Clinic *CLSW/PEL* DH2 .... 152 B1
Pendower Clinic *BW/LEM/TK/HW* NE15.... 78 A3
Pennywell Comprehensive School *MLFD/PNYW* SR4 .... 142 A1
Percy Main Cricket Club *NSHW* NE29.... 69 F3
Percy Main Primary School *NSHW* NE29.... 69 F4
Percy St Johns Primary School *NSHW* NE29.... 70 A3
Peterlee College *PLEE/EAS* SR8.... 208 B1
Peterlee Leisure Centre *PLEE/EAS* SR8.... 208 C3
Peterlee Town Council *PLEE/EAS* SR8.... 208 A4
Philadelphia Cricket Club *HLS* DH4.... 157 E3
Phoenix Theatre *BLYTH* NE24.... 11 E5
Plawsworth Road County Infant School *BDN/LAN/SAC* DH7.... 178 B1
Plessey Road County Junior School *BLYTH* NE24.... 11 E5
Police Headquarters and Magistrates Court *SUND* SR1 .... 4 B2
Ponteland County First School *PONT/DH* NE20.... 28 B3
Ponteland County High School *PONT/DH* NE20.... 28 A5
Ponteland County Middle School *PONT/DH* NE20.... 28 B5
Ponteland Health Centre *PONT/DH* NE20.... 28 A3
Ponteland Leisure Centre *PONT/DH* NE20.... 28 B4
Ponteland Parish Council *PONT/DH* NE20.... 28 A4
Portland School *SUNDSW* SR3.... 143 F4
Portobello County Junior Infant School *CLS/BIR/GTL* DH3 .... 136 C4
Primary School *NSHW* NE29.... 70 B1
Primrose Hill Hospital *JRW* NE32 .... 86 B4
Princess Louise First School *BLYTH* NE24.... 10 C5
Princess Road Junior School *SEA/MUR* SR7 .... 176 B3
Priory Primary School *TYNE/NSHE* NE30.... 55 F4
Priory Theatre *TYNE/NSHE* NE30.... 55 F4
Queen Elizabeth Hospital *LWF/SPW/WRK* NE9.... 100 A5
Raby Cross Medical Centre *BYK/HTN/WLK* NE6 .... 82 A2
Ramside Hall (Hotel) *DHAM* DH1 .... 183 D6
Ravenswood Infant & Primary School *BYK/HTN/WLK* NE6 .... 65 E5
Ravensworth Surgery *SSH* NE33.... 72 A5
Ravensworth Terrace Primary School *CLS/BIR/GTL* DH3 .... 136 B2
RC JMI School *BDN/LAN/SAC* DH7 .... 164 A6
Recreation Centre *CNUT* NE1 .... 2 D3
Redesdale First School *WLSD/HOW* NE28.... 66 B2
Red House Junior Mixed School *SWCK/CAS* SR5 .... 124 C2
Red Rose Primary School *CLS/BIR/GTL* DH3 .... 166 C1
Regent Farm First School *GOS/KPK* NE3 .... 46 C6
Regional National Blood Transfusion Centre *JES* NE2 .... 80 A1
Richard Avenue Primary School *MLFD/PNYW* SR4 .... 143 F2
Richard Coates Church of England Middle School *PONT/DH* NE20.... 28 A3
Richardson Dees First School *WLSD/HOW* NE28.... 67 F4
Rickleton Primary School *WASHS* NE38.... 137 E6
Riverview House Business Centre *SUND* SR1 .... 4 D1
Roman Road Primary School *FELL* NE10 .... 101 F5
Ronald Moore Gallery *TYNE/NSHE* NE30.... 55 D5
Ropery Walk Primary School *SEA/MUR* SR7 .... 177 D3
Roseberry Primary School *CLSW/PEL* DH2 .... 151 E3
Rowlands Gill Infant School *ROWG* NE39.... 111 E1
Rowlands Gill Junior School *ROWG* NE39.... 111 E1
Rowletch Burn Industrial Estate *CLS/BIR/GTL* DH3 .... 136 A2
Royal College of Nursing *CNUT* NE1 .... 2 D4
Royal Grammar School *JES* NE2 .... 81 D1
Royalty Theatre *MLFD/PNYW* SR4 .... 126 A6
Royal Victoria Infirmary *JES* NE2 .... 80 B1
Rye Hill Sports Centre *ELS/FEN* NE4.... 80 A4
Ryhope General Hospital *ASHBK/HED/RY* SR2.... 162 B3
Ryhope Health Centre *ASHBK/HED/RY* SR2.... 162 A1
Ryhope Junior & Infant School *ASHBK/HED/RY* SR2.... 162 A1
Ryhope Village C of E Primary School *ASHBK/HED/RY* SR2.... 162 B2
Ryton Industrial Estate *BLAY* NE21.... 75 F3
Sacred Heart Primary School *ELS/FEN* NE4.... 78 C1
Sacriston Cricket Club *BDN/LAN/SAC* DH7.... 178 A1
Sacriston Junior School *BDN/LAN/SAC* DH7.... 178 B2
Sacriston Swimming Baths *BDN/LAN/SAC* DH7.... 178 A1
St Aidans College *DHAM* DH1 .... 205 D1
St Aidans RC Comprehensive School *ASHBK/HED/RY* SR2.... 144 B2
St Albans Medical Group *FELL* NE10 .... 100 C2
St Aloysius RC Infants School *HEBB* NE31 .... 85 D1
St Aloysius RC Junior School *HEBB* NE31 .... 85 D1
St Andrews RC Aided First School *BLYTH* NE24.... 10 B5
St Annes Mixed High School *SSH* NE33.... 72 A6
St Annes RC Primary School *MLFD/PNYW* SR4 .... 142 A1
St Anthonys Health Centre *BYK/HTN/WLK* NE6 .... 83 E4
St Anthonys RC School *ASHBK/HED/RY* SR2.... 4 A5
St Augustines RC Infant School *FELL* NE10 .... 101 E4
St Bede Medical Centre *CLDN/WHIT/ROK* SR6.... 127 D4
St Bedes First School *BDLGTN* NE22 .... 7 D3

St Bedes RC Comprehensive School *PLEE/EAS* SR8 ..... 208 B2
St Bedes RC Infants School *JRW* NE32 ..... 86 B1
St Bedes RC Jmi School *JRW* NE32 ..... 86 B1
St Bedes RC Primary School *BW/LEM/TK/HW* NE15 ..... 77 E1
St Bedes RC Primary School *SSH* NE33 ..... 71 E4
St Bedes RC Primary School *WASHN* NE37 ..... 120 C3
St Benet Biscops RC High School *BDLGTN* NE22 ..... 7 D4
St Benets Primary RC School *CLSW/PEL* DH2 ..... 135 E5
St Benets RC Primary School *CLDN/WHIT/ROK* SR6 ..... 126 C2
St Bernadettes RC First School *WLSD/HOW* NE28 ..... 67 D1
St Catherines RC Primary School *JES* NE2 ..... 64 B6
St Chads College *DHAM* DH1 ..... 194 B5
St Charles RC Primary School *GOS/KPK* NE3 ..... 47 D6
St Columbas RC First School *WLSD/HOW* NE28 ..... 66 C4
St Cuthberts C of E Junior School *GATE* NE8 ..... 98 B1
St Cuthberts High School *BW/LEM/TK/HW* NE15 ..... 78 A2
St Cuthberts RC Lower School *BW/LEM/TK/HW* NE15 ..... 78 A2
St Cuthberts RC Primary School *BW/LEM/TK/HW* NE15 ..... 58 B4
St Cuthberts RC Primary School *CLS/BIR/GTL* DH3 ..... 153 F6
St Cuthberts RC Primary School *GOS/KPK* NE3 ..... 61 F2
St Cuthberts RC Primary School *NSHW* NE29 ..... 70 C1
St Cuthberts RC School *SEA/MUR* SR7 ..... 175 D2
St Edmunds RC Comprehensive School *LWF/SPW/WRK* NE9 ..... 100 C6
St Georges RC Primary School *BW/LEM/TK/HW* NE15 ..... 76 C3
St Godrics RC Junior & Infant School *DHAM* DH1 ..... 180 B6
St Hilda Industrial Estate *SSH* NE33 ..... 71 E4
St Hildas RC School *SWCK/CAS* SR5 ..... 125 F2
St Hild & St. Bede College *DHAM* DH1 ..... 195 D4
St James Park (Newcastle United FC) *CNUT* NE1 ..... 2 B2
St John Bosco RC Primary School *SWCK/CAS* SR5 ..... 105 F6
St John Boste RC Primary School *WASHS* NE38 ..... 137 F1
St John Vianney School *WD/WHPE/BLK* NE5 ..... 59 F5
St Joseph RC Junior Primary School *BW/LEM/TK/HW* NE15 ..... 78 B4
St Josephs Infant School *CLS/BIR/GTL* DH3 ..... 136 A1
St Josephs RC School *DHAM* DH1 ..... 195 F4
St Josephs RC School *MLFD/PNYW* SR4 ..... 125 E5
St Josephs RC School *SEA/MUR* SR7 ..... 188 B2
St Josephs School *NSHW* NE29 ..... 70 A2
St Josephs School *ROWG* NE39 ..... 110 A2
St Josephs School *WASHS* NE38 ..... 120 C6
St Lawrence RC Primary School *BYK/HTN/WLK* NE6 ..... 82 B2
St Leonards Junior & Infants School *SUNDSW* SR3 ..... 144 A6
St Leonards RC Comprehensive School *DHAM* DH1 ..... 194 A3
St Margarets C of E Infants School *DHAM* DH1 ..... 193 F6
St Margarets C of E Primary School *DHAM* DH1 ..... 194 A6
St Marks RC Primary School *WD/WHPE/BLK* NE5 ..... 60 B2
St Mary Magdalene RC Primary School *SEA/MUR* SR7 ..... 176 B2
St Marys College *ELS/FEN* NE4 ..... 78 C1
St Marys Junior & Infant School *STLY/ANP* DH9 ..... 148 B4
St Marys RC Comprehensive School *LGB/HTN* NE7 ..... 64 C1
St Marys RC Primary School *ASHBK/HED/RY* SR2 ..... 144 A2
St Marys RC Primary School *JRW* NE32 ..... 86 C5
St Marys RC Primary School *TYNE/NSHE* NE30 ..... 54 C2
St Marys RC Primary School *WICK/BNPF* NE16 ..... 96 B3
St Mary's Roman Catholic Cathedral *CNUT* NE1 ..... 2 B5
St Michaels Industrial Estate *BYK/HTN/WLK* NE6 ..... 82 A3
St Michaels RC Primary School *ELS/FEN* NE4 ..... 79 F5
St Nicholas Cathedral *CNUT* NE1 ..... 3 E5
St Oswalds CE Junior Mixed & Infant School *HEBB* NE31 ..... 85 E1
St Oswalds Clinic *FELL* NE10 ..... 100 C2
St Oswalds C of E Infants School *DHAM* DH1 ..... 194 C6
St Oswalds RC Infant & Junior School *LWF/SPW/WRK* NE9 ..... 118 B1
St Patricks RC School *ASHBK/HED/RY* SR2 ..... 162 B2
St Patricks RC School *BDN/LAN/SAC* DH7 ..... 204 A3
St Pauls RC First School *CRAM* NE23 ..... 22 A3
St Peter RC Junior & Infant School *LWF/SPW/WRK* NE9 ..... 99 F4
St Peters JMI School *JRW* NE32 ..... 69 E6
St Peters RC Middle School *CRAM* NE23 ..... 22 A4
St Robert of Newminster RC Comprehensive School *WASHS* NE38 ..... 138 C4
St Stephens RC Primary School *LGB/KIL* NE12 ..... 49 D5
St Teresas RC Primary School *BYK/HTN/WLK* NE6 ..... 65 D6
St Thomas More RC (Aided) Comprehensive School *BLAY* NE21 ..... 76 A5
St Thomas Mores RC School *DHAM* DH1 ..... 196 C3
St Thomas Street Business Centre *CNUT* NE1 ..... 2 C2
St Vincents RC Primary School *BYK/HTN/WLK* NE6 ..... 83 D4
St Wilfreds RC Junior & Infant School *FELL* NE10 ..... 82 A6
St Wilfrids Middle School *BLYTH* NE24 ..... 10 C5
St Wilfrids RC Comprehensive School *HAR/WTLS* NE34 ..... 88 C2
Sam Smiths Sports Ground *BYK/HTN/WLK* NE6 ..... 66 A5
Sanderson Hospital *GOS/KPK* NE3 ..... 63 D2
Saville Clinic *CNUT* NE1 ..... 2 D2
Seaburn Dene Primary School *CLDN/WHIT/ROK* SR6 ..... 108 C5
Seaham College *SEA/MUR* SR7 ..... 176 C3
Seaham Comprehensive School *SEA/MUR* SR7 ..... 175 E1
Seaham Town Council *SEA/MUR* SR7 ..... 176 C3
Seaton Delaval Whytrig County Middle School *MONK* NE25 ..... 24 A4
Seaton Sluice Middle School *WBAY* NE26 ..... 26 A1
Segedunum Business Centre *WLSD/HOW* NE28 ..... 67 E5
Seghill County First School *CRAM* NE23 ..... 36 B1
Shanklea First School *CRAM* NE23 ..... 22 A1
Sherburn Hospital *DHAM* DH1 ..... 196 C6
Shieldfield Health Centre *JES* NE2 ..... 3 G1
Shield Row Junior & Infants School *STLY/ANP* DH9 ..... 131 F6
Shiney Row Primary School *HLS* DH4 ..... 157 D2
Shipley Art Gallery *GATE* NE8 ..... 99 E2
Shiremoor First School *SMOOR* NE27 ..... 52 A1
Shiremoor Middle School *SMOOR* NE27 ..... 38 B6
The Shopping Centre *STLY/ANP* DH9 ..... 148 B3
Shotton Colliery Primary School *RDHAMSE* DH6 ..... 206 B1
Shotton Hall Comprehensive School *PLEE/EAS* SR8 ..... 208 A4
Shotton Hall Junior School *PLEE/EAS* SR8 ..... 208 A4
Shotton Parish Council *RDHAMSE* DH6 ..... 206 C2
Shotton RC JMI School *RDHAMSE* DH6 ..... 206 A1
The Side Gallery *CNUT* NE1 ..... 3 E5
Sidegate Gallery *WICK/BNPF* NE16 ..... 114 A1
Sikh Temple *ELS/FEN* NE4 ..... 80 A3
Silksworth Health Centre *SUNDSW* SR3 ..... 160 C1
Silverlink Business Park *WLSD/HOW* NE28 ..... 52 C6
Simonside First School *WD/WHPE/BLK* NE5 ..... 60 B1
Simonside Industrial Estate *HAR/WTLS* NE34 ..... 87 D3
Sir G B Hunter Memorial Hospital *WLSD/HOW* NE28 ..... 67 E4
Smiths Surgery *BOLCOL* NE35 ..... 105 D2
South Benwell Primary School *ELS/FEN* NE4 ..... 79 D4
Southdene Medical Centre *RDHAMSE* DH6 ..... 206 C1
South Gosforth First School *JES* NE2 ..... 64 A2
South Hetton Health Centre *RDHAMSE* DH6 ..... 187 E5
South Hetton Primary School *RDHAMSE* DH6 ..... 187 E5
South Hylton Primary School *MLFD/PNYW* SR4 ..... 123 F6
Southlands Middle School *CRAM* NE23 ..... 22 A5
Southlands School *TYNE/NSHE* NE30 ..... 54 C4
Southmoor School *ASHBK/HED/RY* SR2 ..... 145 D3
Southridge First School *MONK* NE25 ..... 39 F4
South Shields FC *JRW* NE32 ..... 87 D2
South Stanley Comprehensive School *STLY/ANP* DH9 ..... 148 A3
South Stanley County Junior Mixed School *STLY/ANP* DH9 ..... 148 A3
South Street County Primary School *GATE* NE8 ..... 99 E1
South Tyneside Area Health Authority *HAR/WTLS* NE34 ..... 89 F1
South Tyneside Borough Council *HEBB* NE31 ..... 84 C3

South Tyneside College
HEBB NE31 .... 84 C6
South Tyneside College
SSH NE33 .... 72 A6
South Tyneside Health Care Trust
HAR/WTLS NE34 .... 88 C3
South Tyneside Health Care Trust
HEBB NE31 .... 85 D3
South Tyneside Health Care Trust
SSH NE33 .... 71 F3
South Tyneside Magistrates Court
SSH NE33 .... 71 D4
South Tyneside
Metropolitan Borough Council
HAR/WTLS NE34 .... 90 A1
South Tyneside
Metropolitan Borough Council
SSH NE33 .... 71 F3
South Wellfield First School
MONK NE25 .... 39 D6
Southwick Health Centre
SWCK/CAS SR5 .... 125 F3
Sports Centre
RDHAMSE DH6 .... 197 E5
Springfield Clinic
GATE NE8 .... 99 E2
Springfield Comprehensive School
JRW NE32 .... 86 A3
Spring Terrace Health Centre
NSHW NE29 .... 54 C6
Springwell Health Centre
SUNDSW SR3 .... 143 D3
Springwell House Surgery
SUNDSW SR3 .... 143 D4
Springwell Village Primary School
LWF/SPW/WRK NE9 .... 119 E3
Stanhope County Infants School
SSH NE33 .... 88 B1
Stanhope County Junior
Mixed School
SSH NE33 .... 88 A2
Stanhope Parade Health Centre
SSH NE33 .... 71 E6
Stanley Health Centre
STLY/ANP DH9 .... 148 A2
Stanley RC Junior Mixed &
Infants School
STLY/ANP DH9 .... 148 B1
Star Clinic
DHAM DH1 .... 194 B4
Stephenson Railway Museum
SMOOR NE27 .... 52 C5
Stonelaw County Middle School
CRAM NE23 .... 21 F4
Studio Gallery
TYNE/NSHE NE30 .... 55 F5
Sunderland AFC Club Shop
SUND SR1 .... 4 C2
Sunderland Bowling Centre
SWCK/CAS SR5 .... 126 B3
Sunderland City Council
HLS DH4 .... 170 C2
Sunderland City Council
SUND SR1 .... 4 D3
Sunderland Counselling Services
MLFD/PNYW SR4 .... 142 B1
Sunderland County Court
SUND SR1 .... 4 D3
Sunderland Cricket &
Rugby Football Club
ASHBK/HED/RY SR2 .... 144 B2
Sunderland Cricket &
Rugby Football Club House
ASHBK/HED/RY SR2 .... 144 B2
Sunderland District General
Hospital
MLFD/PNYW SR4 .... 125 E6
Sunderland Eye Infirmary
ASHBK/HED/RY SR2 .... 144 C3
Sunderland Football Club
SWCK/CAS SR5 .... 126 B4
Sunderland High School
ASHBK/HED/RY SR2 .... 4 D6
Sunderland Museum & Art Gallery
SUND SR1 .... 4 D4
Sunderland Retail Park
CLDN/WHIT/ROK SR6 .... 126 C3
Sunderland Royal Hospital
MLFD/PNYW SR4 .... 125 E6
Sunderland Royal Infirmary
ASHBK/HED/RY SR2 .... 126 A6
Sunderland Talmudical College
GATE NE8 .... 99 E2
Sunderland University
SUND SR1 .... 4 D2
Swalwell Cricket Club
WICK/BNPF NE16 .... 95 E1
Talbot House Special School
BW/LEM/TK/HW NE15 .... 58 A4
Tanfield Lea County
Junior Mixed & Infant School
STLY/ANP DH9 .... 130 C6
Tanfield Lea County
Junior Mixed & Infantschool
STLY/ANP DH9 .... 130 B5
Tanfield View Surgery
STLY/ANP DH9 .... 148 A2
Tax Office
SUND SR1 .... 4 B2
Team Valley Business Centre
DUN/TMV NE11 .... 98 C4
Team Valley Trading Estate
Post Office
DUN/TMV NE11 .... 117 D2
Tedco Business Centre
HEBB NE31 .... 68 B6
Tedco Business Park
JRW NE32 .... 68 C6
Theatre Royal
CNUT NE1 .... 2 D3
Thockley First School
BW/LEM/TK/HW NE15 .... 57 E4
Thomas Bewick Special School
WD/WHPE/BLK NE5 .... 59 E4
Thomas Hepburn
Community School
FELL NE10 .... 101 D3
Thornhill
Comprehensive School
ASHBK/HED/RY SR2 .... 144 A2
Throckley Industrial Estate
BW/LEM/TK/HW NE15 .... 57 F3
Throckley Middle School
BW/LEM/TK/HW NE15 .... 57 E4
Throckley Surgery
BW/LEM/TK/HW NE15 .... 57 F4
The Toco Gallery
JES NE2 .... 64 A4
Toner Avenue County
Infant School
HEBB NE31 .... 84 C5
Townend Primary School
SWCK/CAS SR5 .... 105 E6
Town Hall & Civic Offices
SSH NE33 .... 71 F4
Trevelyan College
DHAM DH1 .... 205 E1
Trinity Maritime Museum
CNUT NE1 .... 3 F4
Trinity Medical Centre
SSH NE33 .... 71 E5
Trinity School
BLAY NE21 .... 95 D1
Trouts Lane School
DHAM DH1 .... 179 D5
Tynemouth Business Centre
TYNE/NSHE NE30 .... 55 D6
Tynemouth College
NSHW NE29 .... 54 B6
Tynemouth Cricket Club
TYNE/NSHE NE30 .... 55 D4
Tyne Point Industrial Estate
JRW NE32 .... 87 D2
Tyne Tees TV Studios
CNUT NE1 .... 3 H4
Tyne Theatre and Opera House
CNUT NE1 .... 2 A4
Tyneview Primary School
BYK/HTN/WLK NE6 .... 83 F3
Tyne View Primary School
GATE NE8 .... 80 B6
Tyne & Wear County Council
SSH NE33 .... 71 E3
Univeristy Halls of Residence
CLDN/WHIT/ROK SR6 .... 126 C4
Univeristy Halls of Residence
SUND SR1 .... 5 E1
University College
DHAM DH1 .... 194 B5
University for Industry
SUND SR1 .... 4 C2
University Library
DHAM DH1 .... 194 B5
University of Durham
DHAM DH1 .... 194 C4
University of Durham
DHAM DH1 .... 194 B5
University of Durham
DHAM DH1 .... 194 C5
University of Durham
DHAM DH1 .... 195 D5
University of Durham
DHAM DH1 .... 196 A1
University of Durham
DHAM DH1 .... 205 D1
University of Newcastle
Upon Tyne
JES NE2 .... 2 A1
University of Newcastle
Upon Tyne
JES NE2 .... 64 A6
University of Newcastle
Upon Tyne
JES NE2 .... 80 B1
University of Newcastle
Upon Tyne
LGB/HTN NE7 .... 65 E3
University of Northumbria
at Newcastle
CNUT NE1 .... 3 E1
University of Northumbria
at Newcastle
CNUT NE1 .... 81 D1
University of Northumbria
at Newcastle
LGB/HTN NE7 .... 65 E2
University of Sunderland
ASHBK/HED/RY SR2 .... 4 D6
University of Sunderland
ASHBK/HED/RY SR2 .... 4 C5
University of Sunderland
ASHBK/HED/RY SR2 .... 144 C2
University of Sunderland
CLDN/WHIT/ROK SR6 .... 127 D4
University of Sunderland
CLDN/WHIT/ROK SR6 .... 127 D3
University of Sunderland
MLFD/PNYW SR4 .... 125 D4
University of Sunderland
SUND SR1 .... 4 A3
University of Sunderland
SUND SR1 .... 126 A6
University of Sunderland
SWCK/CAS SR5 .... 124 A4
University of Sunderland
WASHN NE37 .... 119 F5
University of Sunderland (Library)
SUND SR1 .... 4 A4
University Technology Park
ASHBK/HED/RY SR2 .... 4 A4
Usworth Colliery Junior School
WASHN NE37 .... 121 D3
Usworth Grange Primary School
WASHN NE37 .... 121 E3
Usworth Secondary School
WASHN NE37 .... 120 C2
Valley Road Infant School
ASHBK/HED/RY SR2 .... 145 E2
Valley Road Junior School
ASHBK/HED/RY SR2 .... 145 E2
Valley View County Infant School
JRW NE32 .... 86 A4
Van Mildert College
DHAM DH1 .... 205 D2
Victoria Industrial Estate
FELL NE10 .... 84 B5
Victoria Medical Centre
HEBB NE31 .... 84 C2
Victoria Road Health Centre
WASHN NE37 .... 120 C4
Viking Gallery
JRW NE32 .... 86 A1
Village Gallery
WICK/BNPF NE16 .... 96 A3
Wagonway Industrial Estate
HEBB NE31 .... 68 A6
Walker Comprehensive School
BYK/HTN/WLK NE6 .... 83 E2
Walkerdene Special School
BYK/HTN/WLK NE6 .... 83 E2
Walkergate Hospital
BYK/HTN/WLK NE6 .... 66 A6
Walkergate Infant School
BYK/HTN/WLK NE6 .... 66 A6
Wallsend Business Centre
WLSD/HOW NE28 .... 67 E5
Wallsend Sports Centre
WLSD/HOW NE28 .... 66 B4
Wansbeck District Council
BDLGTN NE22 .... 7 E4

Wardley Primary School
FELL NE10 .... **101** F2
War Memorial
SUND SR1 .... **4** D4
Washington Albany Infants School
WASHN NE37 .... **120** A5
Washington Football Club
WASHN NE37 .... **120** C5
Washington F Pit Museum
WASHN NE37 .... **120** B5
Washington Hospital
WASHS NE38 .... **137** D6
Washington Secondary School
WASHN NE37 .... **120** C5
Washington Village Primary School
WASHS NE38 .... **121** D6
Washingwell Primary School
WICK/BNPF NE16 .... **96** B4
Waterloo Medical Group
BLYTH NE24 .... **10** C4
Waterville Primary School
NSHW NE29 .... **70** B2
Waverley First School
BW/LEM/TK/HW NE15 .... **77** D2
Waygood Gallery & Studios
CNUT NE1 .... **2** D4
Wearside College
SUNDSW SR3 .... **143** E3
Welbeck Primary School
BYK/HTN/WLK NE6 .... **82** C3
Wellbank Special School
WASHN NE37 .... **120** A3
West Boldon Junior Mixed School
BOL NE36 .... **105** F2
Westbourne Surgery
HLS DH4 .... **156** C2
West Denton First School
WD/WHPE/BLK NE5 .... **59** F5
West Denton High School
WD/WHPE/BLK NE5 .... **60** A4
Westerhope Clinic
WD/WHPE/BLK NE5 .... **60** B3
Westerhope First School
WD/WHPE/BLK NE5 .... **60** A3
Westerhope Small Business Park
WD/WHPE/BLK NE5 .... **60** A2
Western First School
WLSD/HOW NE28 .... **66** C4
Western Infant School
NSHW NE29 .... **70** B2
Western Middle School
WLSD/HOW NE28 .... **66** C5
Westfield School
GOS/KPK NE3 .... **63** D3
West Gate Community College
ELS/FEN NE4 .... **78** C2
Westgate Hill Primary School
ELS/FEN NE4 .... **79** F3
West Jesmond Junior School
JES NE2 .... **64** A5
West Lane Junior & Infant School
BLAY NE21 .... **93** F2
Westlea Junior School
SEA/MUR SR7 .... **175** D2
West Moor First School
LGB/KIL NE12 .... **49** E3
Westmoor Middle School
LGB/KIL NE12 .... **49** D3
Westmorland Business Centre
ELS/FEN NE4 .... **2** A5
Westmorland Business Centre
ELS/FEN NE4 .... **80** A4
Westoe Gallery
SSH NE33 .... **71** F4
Westovian Theatre Society
SSH NE33 .... **72** A2
West Rainton Primary School
HLS DH4 .... **183** E2
West Walker School
BYK/HTN/WLK NE6 .... **83** F4
Whickham Comprehensive School
WICK/BNPF NE16 .... **95** F4
Whickham Parochial C of E Junior & Infant School
WICK/BNPF NE16 .... **95** E5
Whinfield Industrial Estate
ROWG NE39 .... **110** B3
Whitburn Comprehensive School
CLDN/WHIT/ROK SR6 .... **109** F2
Whitburn Cricket Club
CLDN/WHIT/ROK SR6 .... **109** E2
Whitburn Junior Mixed School
CLDN/WHIT/ROK SR6 .... **109** D2
Whitburn Surgery
CLDN/WHIT/ROK SR6 .... **109** D2
Whitehouse Industrial Estate
BW/LEM/TK/HW NE15 .... **78** B4
Whitehouse Primary School
NSHW NE29 .... **53** E5
Whitley Bay Cricket Club
MONK NE25 .... **54** C1
Whitley Bay Football Club
MONK NE25 .... **54** C1
Whitley Bay High School
MONK NE25 .... **40** A4
Whitley Bay Ice Rink
MONK NE25 .... **54** B1
Whitley Bay Rockcliff RFC
MONK NE25 .... **54** C1
Whitley Lodge First School
WBAY NE26 .... **40** A2
Whitley Memorial School
BDLGTN NE22 .... **7** F4
Willington High School
WLSD/HOW NE28 .... **68** B1
Windy Nook Primary School
FELL NE10 .... **100** C4
Wingrove Primary School
ELS/FEN NE4 .... **79** D2
Winlaton Park Junior School
BLAY NE21 .... **94** B2
Winlaton Vulcans Rugby Club
BLAY NE21 .... **94** B1
Witherwack Primary School
SWCK/CAS SR5 .... **107** E6
Woodlands Park Health Centre
DIN/WO NE13 .... **33** D5
Woodlea County Primary School
HLS DH4 .... **169** D1
Wrekenton Health Centre
LWF/SPW/WRK NE9 .... **118** C1
Yates Jewish School for Girls
GATE NE8 .... **99** D1
The Yemeni School
SSH NE33 .... **71** D5

Page 5

E4
1 Winifred Ter

Page 35

F5
1 Algernon
2 Callerton
3 Hauxley
4 Havanna

F6
1 Agincourt
2 Alresford
3 Bannockburn
4 Blenheim
5 Cannock
6 Culloden Wk
7 East Bailey
8 Falkirk
9 Marston
10 Tewkesbury
11 Towton
12 West Bailey

Page 46

A5
1 Alnham Ct
2 Cartington Ct
3 Espley Ct
4 Fawdon Park Rd
5 Hesket Ct
6 Ludlow Ct
7 Pelham Ct
8 Uldale Ct
9 Whitelees Ct

Page 49

D5
1 Ashdown Cl
2 Aylesbury Pl
3 Myreside Pl
4 The Roundway

F4
1 Albany Av
2 Avondale Av
3 Cambridge Av
4 Lynholm Gv
5 North Vw
6 Park Vw
7 Percy Gdns
8 Station Rd North
9 Teesdale Gv
10 Wens Leydale Dr
11 West Vw
12 Whitfield Rd
13 Wilson Ter

F6
1 Belvedere Gdns
2 Eastfield Ter
3 Oakhurst Ter
4 Parkland
5 St Margarets Av
6 Station Ap
7 Tynedale Ter

Page 54

C5
1 Medway Gdns
2 Osborne Gdns

C6
1 Albion Ter
2 Ashfield Gv
3 Ayre's Ter
4 Church Wy
5 Cleveland Crs
6 Cleveland Ter
7 Frank Pl
8 Lovaine Ter
9 Northumberland Sq
10 Springfield
11 Spring Ter
12 Upper Camden St
13 West Percy Rd

Page 55

F5
1 Northumberland Ter
2 Percy St
3 Silver St
4 Stephenson St
5 Tynemouth Ter

Page 59

D2
1 Abbey Dr
2 Ashford Gv
3 Callerton Vw
4 Claverdon St
5 Lilac Cl
6 Nedderton Cl
7 Newsham Cl

Page 60

A3
1 Bamburgh Rd
2 Baybridge Rd
3 Counden Rd
4 Kendale Wk
5 Marsham Rd
6 Mitford Dr
7 Norham Dr
8 Trafford Wk
9 Westward Ct
10 Whorlton Pl

A6
1 The Close
2 Hedgeley Rd
3 Ilderton Pl
4 Layburn Gdns
5 Northlea
6 St Vincents Cl
7 Sandringham Rd
8 Warwick Rd

B4
1 Barents Cl
2 Bruce Cl
3 Frankham St
4 James St
5 Lordenshaw
6 Nansen Cl
7 Wilkes Cl

Page 61

D3
1 Hendersyde Cl
2 Lynfield Ct
3 Lynfield Pl
4 Marlfield Ct
5 Melkington Ct
6 Mellendean Cl
7 Pallinsburn Ct
8 Stonefold Cl

D5
1 Buttermere Cl
2 Cotehill Rd
3 Finsmere Av
4 Finsmere Pl
5 Fulwell Gn
6 Loweswater Rd

F4
1 Brieryside
2 Coldingham Gdns
3 Crossbrook Rd
4 Fallodon Gdns
5 Fuchsia Pl
6 Hauxley Gdns
7 Holden Pl
8 Middlegarth
9 Monroe Pl
10 Radcliffe Pl

F5
1 Bondicarr Pl
2 Broomhill Gdns
3 Chevington Gdns
4 Doxford Gdns
5 Embleton Gdns
6 Maudlin Pl
7 Morwick Pl
8 Rennington Pl
9 Stamfordham Ms
10 Westerhope Gdns

F6
1 Genister Pl

Page 62

C2
1 Delaval Ter
2 Dunmoor Cl
3 Hownam Cl

Page 64

A1
1 Bowes St
2 Bowsden Ct
3 Christon Cl
4 Commercial Rd
5 Donald St
6 Ridgewood Gdns
7 Ridgewood Vls
8 Wardle St

C6
1 Granville Gdns
2 Grosvenor Gdns
3 Jesmond Rd
4 Kimberley Gdns
5 Northumberland Gdns
6 Wolseley Gdns

Page 66

A3
1 Allingham Ct
2 Highworth Dr
3 Kilburne Cl
4 Stanfield Ct
5 Witherington Cl
6 Woolmer Ct

Page 67

D5
1 Atkinson St
2 Benton Wy
3 Border Rd
4 Chadwick St
5 Curzon Rd West
6 Eden St
7 Equitable St
8 Hedley Pl
9 James Ter
10 Portugal Pl
11 Thames Gdns

E2
1 Baildon Cl
2 Boscombe Dr
3 Bridgewater Cl

F2
1 Bellingham Cl
2 Blanchland Cl

Page 68

C5
1 Addison Ct
2 Carlyle Ct
3 Carlyle St
4 Douglas St
5 Smeaton Ct
6 Smeaton St

Page 71

E4
1 Mount Ter
2 Old Coronation St

F4
1 Beethoven St
2 Berkely St
3 Bolingbroke St
4 Burleigh St
5 Dunelm St
6 Elizabeth St
7 Graham St
8 Handel St
9 Lyndhurst St
10 Percy St
11 Salisbury St
12 Selbourne St

F5
1 Chichester Rd
2 East George Potts St
3 East Moffett St
4 East Stevenson St
5 Imeary Gv
6 John Clay St
7 May St
8 Newburn Ct
9 Robinson St
10 Shakespeare St
11 Stainton St East
12 West George Potts St
13 West Moffett St
14 West Stainton St
15 West Stevenson St

F6
1 Alansway Gdns
2 Albany St East
3 Albany St West
4 Marlborough St North
5 Oxford Av
6 Southey St
7 Stanhope Pde
8 Wawn St

Page 76

B4
1 Cochran St

Page 79

F4
1 Bristol Ter
2 Gloucester Ter
3 Hawthorn Ter
4 Kenilworth Rd
5 Park Cl
6 Portland St

Page 80

A2
1 Avison Pl
2 Avolon Pl
3 Bassington Cl
4 Frosterley Pl
5 Hamilton Crs
6 Holywell Cl
7 Jefferson Pl
8 Monday Crs
9 Monday Pl
10 Spring Garden La

A4
1 Belgrave Pde
2 Cambridge St
3 Cross Pde
4 Hawthorn Pl
5 Houston Ct
6 Kirkdale Gn
7 Mather Rd
8 Palace St
9 Victoria St
10 Waverley Rd
11 Wentworth Pl

A5
1 Back Mitford St
2 Blackthorn Pl
3 Charlotte Cl
4 Clasper St
5 Dobson Cl
6 Hornbeam Pl
7 Maiden St
8 Mulberry Pl
9 Tyneside Rd
10 Whitebeam Pl

B5
1 Ord St
2 Redheugh Bridge Rd

Page 81

D1
1 Archbold Ter
2 Eslington Rd
3 Gladstone Pl
4 Gladstone Ter
5 Harrison Pl
6 Osborne Ter
7 Sandyford Rd
8 Windsor Pl

D4
1 Akenside Hl
2 Bridge St
3 Cannon St
4 Castle Garth
5 Dog Bank
6 Hills St
7 King St
8 Lombard St
9 Mirk La
10 Pilgrim St
11 Pipewellgate
12 Quayside
13 Queen St
14 William Iv Yd

D5
1 Half Moon La
2 High West St
3 Hudson St
4 Swinburne Pl

E3
1 Blagdon St
2 Buxton St
3 Causey Bank
4 Forster St
5 Grenville Ter
6 Milk Market
7 The Swirle

F2
1 Back Stephen St
2 Byker Buildings
3 Claypath St
4 Coquet St
5 Foundry La
6 Hannington Pl
7 Leighton St
8 Ouseburn Rd
9 Shields Rd West
10 Wilfred St

F5
1 Thirlwell Rd

F6
1 Bede Ct

Page 82

A2
1 Albion Rw
2 Back Heaton Park Rd
3 Brinkburn St
4 Dalton St
5 Edwin St
6 Flora St
7 Grafton St
8 Matthew St
9 Molineux St
10 Toward St

Page 83

F5
1 Burwood Cl

Page 86

A1
1 Albert Rd
2 Burns St
3 Clayton St
4 Ellison St
5 Hibernian Rd
6 Market Sq
7 Monkton Rd
8 Napier St
9 St John's Ter
10 Wear St

Page 88

B4
1 Carnegie Cl
2 Douglas Cl

Page 95

F4
1 Redewater Gdns
2 Well Close Wk

Page 99

D1
1 Claremont St
2 Ely St
3 Grasmere St
4 Grasmere St West
5 Lincoln St
6 Sedgewick Pl
7 Villa Pl

E2
1 Patterdale Ter
2 Perry St
3 Silverdale Ter

E6
1 Albert Pl

F3
1 Baden Powell St
2 Prefect Pl
3 Stavordale Ter

Page 100

A1
1 Allhusen Ter
2 Beaufront Gdns
3 Bronte St
4 Elliot Rd
5 Emily St
6 Ford St
7 Howard St
8 Jane Eyre Ter
9 King Edward Pl
10 Kings Cl
11 Old Fold Rd
12 St James Ct

Page 120

B2
1 Blackheath Cl
2 Canton Cl
3 Lytham Cl
4 Portrush Cl
5 Prestwick Cl
6 Rosemount Cl
7 Sunningdale Dr
8 Troon Cl
9 Turnberry Cl

Page 123

E1
1 Barking Sq
2 Bathgate Sq
3 Batley St
4 Beeston Av
5 Belgrade Sq
6 Berwick Sq
7 Craigshaw Rd

F6
1 Cambria Gn
2 Frederick St
3 Kepier Gdns
4 New St
5 Primrose St
6 Union St
7 Vicarage La

Page 124

A5
1 Claxheugh Rd
2 Maling Pk

B2
1 Bowburn Av
2 Howley Av
3 Ribble Rd
4 Shincliffe Av
5 Stockley Av

B4
1 Defender Ct

Page 125

E6
1 Arlington St
2 Bell St
3 Brookland Rd
4 Hazledene Ter
5 Kimberley St
6 Romford St
7 Tamerton St
8 Walpole Ct
9 Washington St
10 Westleigh Ct
11 Westwood St
12 Wilber Ct
13 Wilber St
14 Winchester Ct
15 Woolsington Ct

F2
1 Cato St
2 Churchill Av
3 Clarence St
4 James St
5 Jowett Sq
6 Julius Caesar St
7 Keats Av
8 Tennyson St

F5
1 Gilsland St
2 Handel St
3 Oswald St
4 Paxton Ter
5 Pickard St
6 Shepherd St
7 Wood St

Page 126

A2
1 Amy St
2 Church St
3 Coldstream Av
4 Collingwood St
5 Columba St
6 Cornhill Rd
7 Edward Burdis St
8 Frank St
9 James Armitage St
10 Ridley St
11 Schimel St
12 Sophy St

A4
1 Priestly Crs

A6
1 Chepstow St
2 Chester St East
3 Chester Ter North
4 East Cleft Rd
5 Gilhurst Gra
6 Harlow St
7 Langton Cl
8 The Leazes
9 The Retreat
10 The Royalty
11 St Mark's St
12 St Mark's Ter
13 Tintern St
14 Waterworks Rd
15 Western Hl

C1
1 Alexander Ter
2 Folldon Av
3 Friarage Av
4 Hilda St
5 Laburnam Rd
6 Laburnum Rd
7 Marcia Av
8 Marina Ct
9 Marina Gv
10 Melbury Ct
11 Montague St
12 Ormesby Rd
13 Pauline Av
14 Primrose Prec
15 Ronald Sq
16 Vivian Sq

C3
1 Abbs St
2 Dixon's Sq
3 Fulwell Rd
4 Howard St
5 Monk St
6 Oriel Cl
7 Rosebery St
8 Shore St
9 Southwick Rd
10 Wearmouth St

C4
1 Barclay St
2 Causeway
3 Dundas St
4 George St North
5 Liddell St
6 Lower Dundas St
7 North Bridge St
8 Sheepfolds North
9 Sheepfolds Rd
10 Southwick Rd
11 Whitburn St
12 Williamson Ter

C5
1 Back Bridge St
2 Bedford St
3 Bridge Crs
4 Bridge St
5 Charman St
6 Cumberland St
7 Fawcett St
8 Frederick Rd
9 Green St
10 John St
11 Lambton St
12 Pann La
13 Press La
14 Prince St
15 Queen St
16 Sheepfolds South
17 Station St
18 Union St
19 West Sunniside
20 York St

C6
1 Athenaeum St
2 Cowan Ter
3 Fawcett St
4 Frederick St
5 King St
6 Maritime St
7 Park La
8 Tavistock Pl
9 Waterloo Pl

Page 142

A5
1 Thurso Cl
2 Tintagel Cl
3 Trevelyan Cl

C5
1 Truro Rd
2 Tynemouth Sq

C6
1 Alloa Rd
2 Archer Sq

Page 143

D2
1 Arncliffe Av
2 Corry Ct
3 Ingoldsby Ct
4 Westfield Ct
5 Wimbourne Av
6 Winston Crs
7 Woodville Ct
8 Woodville Crs

D6
1 Buckingham
2 Knightsbridge
3 Piccadilly
4 The Strand

F5
1 Somerset St

Page 144

A1
1 Beachcross Rd
2 Beachville St
3 Beresford Pk
4 Burnville Rd South
5 Elmwood St
6 Ewing Rd
7 Fernville St
8 Havelock Ter
9 Hunters Hall Rd
10 Oakwood St
11 Roseville St
12 Vale St
13 Western Hl

B4
1 Brackenwood Gv
2 Glenesk Gdns
3 Greybourne Gdns
4 Larchwood Gv
5 Ringmore Ct
6 Stannington Gdns
7 Tunstall Hill Cl

Page 160

C3
1 Fairgreen Cl
2 Fernwood Cl
3 Hightree Cl
4 Katrine Ct

Notes

Notes